America's Top-Rated Cities: A Statistical Handbook

Volume 3

2021
Twenty-Eighth Edition

America's
Top-Rated Cities:
A Statistical Handbook

Volume 3: Central Region

A UNIVERSAL REFERENCE BOOK

Grey House
Publishing

Cover image: Minneapolis, Minnesota

PRESIDENT: Richard Gottlieb
PUBLISHER: Leslie Mackenzie
EDITORIAL DIRECTOR: Laura Mars
SENIOR EDITOR: David Garoogian

RESEARCHER & WRITER: Jael Bridgemahon
PRODUCTION MANAGER: Kristen Hayes
MARKETING DIRECTOR: Jessica Moody

A Universal Reference Book
Grey House Publishing, Inc.
4919 Route 22
Amenia, NY 12501
518.789.8700 • Fax 845.373.6390
www.greyhouse.com
books@greyhouse.com

While every effort has been made to ensure the reliability of the information presented in this publication, Grey House Publishing neither guarantees the accuracy of the data contained herein nor assumes any responsibility for errors, omissions or discrepancies. Grey House accepts no payment for listing; inclusion in the publication of any organization, agency, institution, publication, service or individual does not imply endorsement of the editors or publisher.

Errors brought to the attention of the publisher and verified to the satisfaction of the publisher will be corrected in future editions.

Except by express prior written permission of the Copyright Proprietor no part of this work may be copied by any means of publication or communication now known or developed hereafter including, but not limited to, use in any directory or compilation or other print publication, in any information storage and retrieval system, in any other electronic device, or in any visual or audio-visual device or product.

This publication is an original and creative work, copyrighted by Grey House Publishing, Inc. and is fully protected by all applicable copyright laws, as well as by laws covering misappropriation, trade secrets and unfair competition.

Grey House has added value to the underlying factual material through one or more of the following efforts: unique and original selection; expression; arrangement; coordination; and classification.

Grey House Publishing, Inc. will defend its rights in this publication.

Copyright © 2021 Grey House Publishing, Inc.
All rights reserved

Twenty-eighth Edition
Printed in the USA

Publisher's Cataloging-in-Publication Data
(Prepared by The Donohue Group, Inc.)

America's top-rated cities. Vol. 3, Central region : a statistical handbook. — 1992-

   v. : ill. ; cm.
   Annual, 1995-
   Irregular, 1992-1993
   ISSN: 1082-7102

1. Cities and towns--Ratings--Central States--Statistics--Periodicals. 2. Cities and towns--Central States--Statistics--Periodicals. 3. Social indicators--Central States--Periodicals. 4. Quality of life--Central States--Statistics--Periodicals. 5. Central States--Social conditions--Statistics--Periodicals. I. Title: America's top rated cities. II. Title: Central region

HT123.5.S6 A44
307.76/0973/05   95644648

4-Volume Set	ISBN: 978-1-64265-821-7
Volume 1	ISBN: 978-1-64265-823-1
Volume 2	ISBN: 978-1-64265-824-8
Volume 3	**ISBN: 978-1-64265-825-5**
Volume 4	ISBN: 978-1-64265-826-2

Ann Arbor, Michigan

Background	1
Rankings	2
Business Environment	4
Demographics	4
Economy	5
Income	6
City Finances	7
Employment	8
Taxes	9
Transportation	10
Businesses	11
Living Environment	12
Cost of Living	12
Housing	12
Health	14
Education	16
Employers	17
Public Safety	17
Politics	18
Sports	18
Climate	18
Hazardous Waste	19
Air Quality	19

Cedar Rapids, Iowa

Background	21
Rankings	22
Business Environment	24
Demographics	24
Economy	25
Income	26
City Finances	27
Employment	28
Taxes	29
Transportation	30
Businesses	31
Living Environment	32
Cost of Living	32
Housing	32
Health	34
Education	36
Employers	37
Public Safety	37
Politics	38
Sports	38
Climate	38
Hazardous Waste	38
Air Quality	38

Chicago, Illinois

Background	41
Rankings	42
Business Environment	47
Demographics	47
Economy	48
Income	49
City Finances	50
Employment	51
Taxes	52
Transportation	53
Businesses	54
Living Environment	56
Cost of Living	56
Housing	56
Health	58
Education	60
Employers	62
Public Safety	63
Politics	63
Sports	63
Climate	63
Hazardous Waste	64
Air Quality	64

Columbia, Missouri

Background	67
Rankings	68
Business Environment	69
Demographics	69
Economy	70
Income	71
City Finances	72
Employment	73
Taxes	74
Transportation	75
Businesses	76
Living Environment	77
Cost of Living	77
Housing	77
Health	79
Education	81
Employers	82
Public Safety	82
Politics	83
Sports	83
Climate	83
Hazardous Waste	83
Air Quality	83

Davenport, Iowa

Background	85
Rankings	86
Business Environment	88
Demographics	88
Economy	89
Income	90
City Finances	91
Employment	92
Taxes	93
Transportation	94
Businesses	95
Living Environment	96
Cost of Living	96
Housing	96
Health	98
Education	100
Employers	101
Public Safety	101
Politics	101
Sports	101
Climate	102
Hazardous Waste	102
Air Quality	102

Des Moines, Iowa

Background	105
Rankings	106
Business Environment	109
Demographics	109
Economy	110
Income	111
City Finances	112
Employment	113
Taxes	114
Transportation	115
Businesses	116
Living Environment	117
Cost of Living	117
Housing	117
Health	119
Education	121
Employers	122
Public Safety	122
Politics	123
Sports	123
Climate	123
Hazardous Waste	123
Air Quality	124

Fargo, North Dakota

Background	127
Rankings	128
Business Environment	130
Demographics	130
Economy	131
Income	132
City Finances	133
Employment	134
Taxes	135
Transportation	136
Businesses	137
Living Environment	138
Cost of Living	138
Housing	138
Health	140
Education	142
Employers	143
Public Safety	143
Politics	143
Sports	144
Climate	144
Hazardous Waste	144
Air Quality	144

Fort Wayne, Indiana

Background	147
Rankings	148
Business Environment	150
Demographics	150
Economy	151
Income	152
City Finances	153
Employment	154
Taxes	155
Transportation	156
Businesses	157
Living Environment	158
Cost of Living	158
Housing	158
Health	160
Education	162
Employers	163
Public Safety	163
Politics	164
Sports	164
Climate	164
Hazardous Waste	164
Air Quality	164

Grand Rapids, Michigan

Background	167
Rankings	168
Business Environment	171
Demographics	171
Economy	172
Income	173
City Finances	174
Employment	175
Taxes	176
Transportation	177
Businesses	178
Living Environment	179
Cost of Living	179
Housing	179
Health	181
Education	183
Employers	184
Public Safety	184
Politics	185
Sports	185
Climate	185
Hazardous Waste	185
Air Quality	185

Green Bay, Wisconsin

Background	187
Rankings	188
Business Environment	189
Demographics	189
Economy	190
Income	191
City Finances	192
Employment	193
Taxes	194
Transportation	195
Businesses	196
Living Environment	198
Cost of Living	198
Housing	198
Health	200
Education	202
Employers	203
Public Safety	203
Politics	203
Sports	204
Climate	204
Hazardous Waste	204
Air Quality	204

Indianapolis, Indiana

Background	207
Rankings	208
Business Environment	212
Demographics	212
Economy	213
Income	214
City Finances	215
Employment	216
Taxes	217
Transportation	218
Businesses	219
Living Environment	220
Cost of Living	220
Housing	220
Health	222
Education	224
Employers	225
Public Safety	226
Politics	227
Sports	227
Climate	227
Hazardous Waste	227
Air Quality	228

Kansas City, Missouri

Background	231
Rankings	232
Business Environment	235
Demographics	235
Economy	236
Income	237
City Finances	238
Employment	239
Taxes	240
Transportation	241
Businesses	242
Living Environment	243
Cost of Living	243
Housing	243
Health	245
Education	247
Employers	248
Public Safety	248
Politics	249
Sports	249
Climate	249
Hazardous Waste	250
Air Quality	250

Lincoln, Nebraska

Background	253
Rankings	254
Business Environment	256
Demographics	256
Economy	257
Income	258
City Finances	259
Employment	260
Taxes	261
Transportation	262
Businesses	263
Living Environment	264
Cost of Living	264
Housing	264
Health	266
Education	268
Employers	269
Public Safety	269
Politics	270
Sports	270
Climate	270
Hazardous Waste	270
Air Quality	270

Madison, Wisconsin

Background	293
Rankings	294
Business Environment	297
Demographics	297
Economy	298
Income	299
City Finances	300
Employment	301
Taxes	302
Transportation	303
Businesses	304
Living Environment	305
Cost of Living	305
Housing	305
Health	307
Education	309
Employers	310
Public Safety	310
Politics	311
Sports	311
Climate	311
Hazardous Waste	311
Air Quality	312

Little Rock, Arkansas

Background	273
Rankings	274
Business Environment	276
Demographics	276
Economy	277
Income	278
City Finances	279
Employment	280
Taxes	281
Transportation	282
Businesses	283
Living Environment	284
Cost of Living	284
Housing	284
Health	286
Education	288
Employers	289
Public Safety	289
Politics	290
Sports	290
Climate	290
Hazardous Waste	290
Air Quality	290

Milwaukee, Wisconsin

Background	315
Rankings	316
Business Environment	320
Demographics	320
Economy	321
Income	322
City Finances	323
Employment	324
Taxes	325
Transportation	326
Businesses	327
Living Environment	328
Cost of Living	328
Housing	328
Health	330
Education	332
Employers	333
Public Safety	333
Politics	334
Sports	334
Climate	334
Hazardous Waste	334
Air Quality	335

Minneapolis, Minnesota

Background	337
Rankings	338
Business Environment	343
Demographics	343
Economy	344
Income	345
City Finances	346
Employment	347
Taxes	348
Transportation	349
Businesses	350
Living Environment	352
Cost of Living	352
Housing	352
Health	354
Education	356
Employers	357
Public Safety	358
Politics	359
Sports	359
Climate	359
Hazardous Waste	359
Air Quality	360

Omaha, Nebraska

Background	385
Rankings	386
Business Environment	389
Demographics	389
Economy	390
Income	391
City Finances	392
Employment	393
Taxes	394
Transportation	395
Businesses	396
Living Environment	397
Cost of Living	397
Housing	397
Health	399
Education	401
Employers	402
Public Safety	402
Politics	403
Sports	403
Climate	403
Hazardous Waste	404
Air Quality	404

Oklahoma City, Oklahoma

Background	363
Rankings	364
Business Environment	367
Demographics	367
Economy	368
Income	369
City Finances	370
Employment	371
Taxes	372
Transportation	373
Businesses	374
Living Environment	375
Cost of Living	375
Housing	375
Health	377
Education	379
Employers	380
Public Safety	381
Politics	381
Sports	381
Climate	381
Hazardous Waste	382
Air Quality	382

Peoria, Illinois

Background	407
Rankings	408
Business Environment	410
Demographics	410
Economy	411
Income	412
City Finances	413
Employment	414
Taxes	415
Transportation	416
Businesses	417
Living Environment	418
Cost of Living	418
Housing	418
Health	420
Education	422
Employers	423
Public Safety	423
Politics	424
Sports	424
Climate	424
Hazardous Waste	424
Air Quality	424

Rochester, Minnesota

Background	427
Rankings	428
Business Environment	430
Demographics	430
Economy	431
Income	432
City Finances	433
Employment	434
Taxes	435
Transportation	436
Businesses	437
Living Environment	438
Cost of Living	438
Housing	438
Health	440
Education	442
Employers	443
Public Safety	443
Politics	444
Sports	444
Climate	444
Hazardous Waste	444
Air Quality	444

Springfield, Illinois

Background	467
Rankings	468
Business Environment	469
Demographics	469
Economy	470
Income	471
City Finances	472
Employment	473
Taxes	474
Transportation	475
Businesses	476
Living Environment	477
Cost of Living	477
Housing	477
Health	479
Education	481
Employers	482
Public Safety	482
Politics	482
Sports	482
Climate	483
Hazardous Waste	483
Air Quality	483

Sioux Falls, South Dakota

Background	447
Rankings	448
Business Environment	450
Demographics	450
Economy	451
Income	452
City Finances	453
Employment	454
Taxes	455
Transportation	456
Businesses	457
Living Environment	458
Cost of Living	458
Housing	458
Health	460
Education	462
Employers	463
Public Safety	463
Politics	464
Sports	464
Climate	464
Hazardous Waste	464
Air Quality	464

Tulsa, Oklahoma

Background	485
Rankings	486
Business Environment	489
Demographics	489
Economy	490
Income	491
City Finances	492
Employment	493
Taxes	494
Transportation	495
Businesses	496
Living Environment	497
Cost of Living	497
Housing	497
Health	499
Education	501
Employers	502
Public Safety	502
Politics	502
Sports	503
Climate	503
Hazardous Waste	503
Air Quality	503

Wichita, Kansas

Background	505
Rankings	506
Business Environment	509
Demographics	509
Economy	510
Income	511
City Finances	512
Employment	513
Taxes	514
Transportation	515
Businesses	516
Living Environment	517
Cost of Living	517
Housing	517
Health	519
Education	521
Employers	522
Public Safety	522
Politics	523
Sports	523
Climate	523
Hazardous Waste	523
Air Quality	523

Appendixes

Appendix A: Comparative Statistics	A-3
Appendix B: Metropolitan Area Definitions	A-171
Appendix C: Government Type & Primary County	A-175
Appendix D: Chambers of Commerce	A-177
Appendix E: State Departments of Labor	A-183

Introduction

This twenty-eighth edition of *America's Top-Rated Cities* is a concise, statistical, 4-volume work identifying America's top-rated cities with estimated populations of approximately 100,000 or more. It profiles 100 cities that have received high marks for business and living from prominent sources such as *Forbes, Fortune, U.S. News & World Report, The Brookings Institution, U.S. Conference of Mayors, The Wall Street Journal,* and *CNNMoney.*

Each volume covers a different region of the country—Southern, Western, Central, Eastern—and includes a detailed Table of Contents, City Chapters, Appendices, and Maps. Each city chapter incorporates information from hundreds of resources to create the following major sections:

- **Background**—lively narrative of significant, up-to-date news for both businesses and residents. These combine historical facts with current developments, "known-for" annual events, and climate data.
- **Rankings**—fun-to-read, bulleted survey results from over 230 books, magazines, and online articles, ranging from general (Great Places to Live), to specific (Friendliest Cities), and everything in between.
- **Statistical Tables**—87 tables and detailed topics that offer an unparalleled view of each city's Business and Living Environments. They are carefully organized with data that is easy to read and understand.
- **Appendices**—five in all, appearing at the end of each volume. These range from listings of Metropolitan Statistical Areas to Comparative Statistics for all 100 cities.

This new edition of *America's Top-Rated Cities* includes cities that not only surveyed well, but ranked highest using our unique weighting system. We looked at violent crime, property crime, population growth, median household income, housing affordability, poverty, educational attainment, and unemployment. You'll find that we have included several American cities despite less-than-stellar numbers. New York, Los Angeles, and Miami remain world-class cities despite challenges faced by many large urban centers. Part of the criteria, in most cases, is that it be the "primary" city in a given metropolitan area. For example, if the metro area is Raleigh-Cary, NC, we would consider Raleigh, not Cary. This allows for a more equitable core city comparison. In general, the core city of a metro area is defined as having substantial influence on neighboring cities. A final consideration is location—we strive to include as many states in the country as possible.

New to this edition are:
Volume 1 - Memphis, TN
Volume 2 - Riverside, CA
Volume 4 - Cincnnati, OH

Praise for previous editions:

> *"...[ATRC] has...proven its worth to a wide audience...from businesspeople and corporations planning to launch, relocate, or expand their operations to market researchers, real estate professionals, urban planners, job-seekers, students...interested in...reliable, attractively presented statistical information about larger U.S. cities."*
> —ARBA

> *"...For individuals or businesses looking to relocate, this resource conveniently reports rankings from more than 300 sources for the top 100 US cities. Recommended..."*
> —Choice

> *"...While patrons are becoming increasingly comfortable locating statistical data online, there is still something to be said for the ease associated with such a compendium of otherwise scattered data. A well-organized and appropriate update...*
> —Library Journal

BACKGROUND

Each city begins with an informative Background that combines history with current events. These narratives often reflect changes that have occurred during the past year, and touch on the city's environment, politics, employment, cultural offerings, and climate, and include interesting trivia. For example: Peregrine Falcons were rehabilitated and released into the wild from Boise City's World Center for Birds of Prey; Grand Rapids was the first city to introduce fluoride into its drinking water in 1945; and Thomas Alva Edison discovered the phonograph and the light bulb in the city whose name was changed in 1954 from Raritan Township to Edison in his honor. This year, many backgrounds incluce an interesting fact about how the city is reacting to the COVID-19 pandemic.

xiv Introduction

RANKINGS

This section has rankings from a possible 233 books, articles, and reports. For easy reference, these Rankings are categorized into 16 topics including Business/Finance, Dating/Romance, and Health/Fitness.

The Rankings are presented in an easy-to-read, bulleted format and include results from both annual surveys and one-shot studies. **Fastest-Growing Economies . . . Best Drivers . . . Most Well-Read . . . Most Wired . . . Healthiest for Women . . . Best for Minority Entrepreneurs . . . Safest . . . Best to Retire . . . Most Polite . . . Best for Moviemakers . . . Most Frugal . . . Best for Bikes . . . Most Cultured . . . Least Stressful . . . Best for Families . . . Most Romantic . . . Most Charitable . . . Best for Telecommuters . . . Best for Singles . . . Nerdiest . . . Fittest . . . Best for Dogs . . . Most Tattooed . . . Best for Wheelchair Users**, and more. A number of these relate specifically to COVID-19.

Sources for these Rankings include both well-known magazines and other media, including *Forbes, Fortune, USA Today, Condé Nast Traveler, Gallup, Kiplinger's Personal Finance, Men's Journal,* and *Travel + Leisure,* as well as *Asthma & Allergy Foundation of America, American Lung Association, League of American Bicyclists, The Advocate, National Civic League, National Alliance to End Homelessness, MovieMaker Magazine, National Insurance Crime Bureau, Center for Digital Government, National Association of Home Builders,* and the *Milken Institute.*

Rankings cover a variety of geographic areas; see Appendix B for full geographic definitions.

STATISTICAL TABLES

Each city chapter includes a possible 87 tables and detailed topics—44 in Business and 43 in Living. Over 90% of statistical data has been updated.

Business Environment includes hard facts and figures on 8 major categories, including Demographics, Income, Economy, Employment, and Taxes. *Living Environment* includes 11 major categories, such as Cost of Living, Housing, Health, Education, Safety, and Climate.

To compile the Statistical Tables, editors have again turned to a wide range of sources, some well known, such as the *U.S. Census Bureau, U.S. Environmental Protection Agency, Bureau of Labor Statistics, Centers for Disease Control and Prevention,* and the *Federal Bureau of Investigation,* plus others like *The Council for Community and Economic Research, Texas A&M Transportation Institute,* and *Federation of Tax Administrators.*

APPENDICES: Data for all cities appear in all volumes.
- **Appendix A**—*Comparative Statistics*
- **Appendix B**—*Metropolitan Area Definitions*
- **Appendix C**—*Government Type and County*
- **Appendix D**—*Chambers of Commerce and Economic Development Organizations*
- **Appendix E**—*State Departments of Labor and Employment*

Material provided by public and private agencies and organizations was supplemented by original research, numerous library sources and Internet sites. *America's Top-Rated Cities, 2021,* is designed for a wide range of readers: private individuals considering relocating a residence or business; professionals considering expanding their businesses or changing careers; corporations considering relocating, opening up additional offices or creating new divisions; government agencies; general and market researchers; real estate consultants; human resource personnel; urban planners; investors; and urban government students.

Customers who purchase the four-volume set receive free online access to *America's Top-Rated Cities* allowing them to download city reports and sort and rank by 50-plus data points.

AMERICA'S TOP-RATED CITIES

CBSA: Core Based Statistical Area

STATE

○ Top Rated City

East Region

Central Region

West Region

South Region

©Larry Mandelin 2021

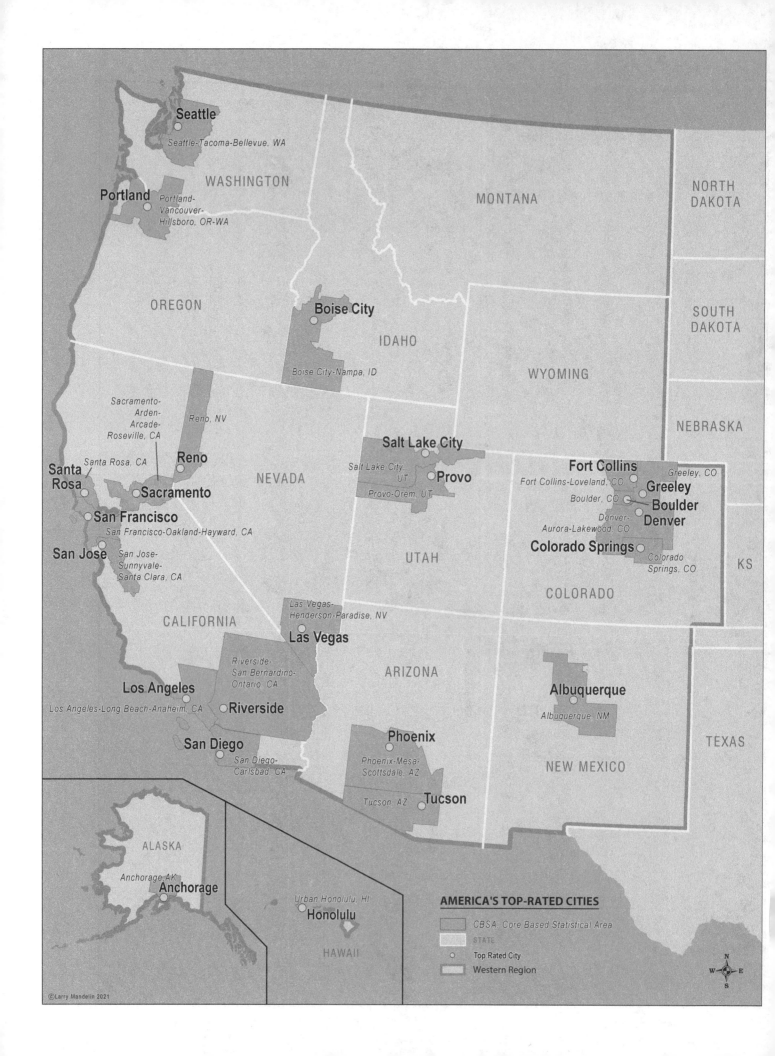

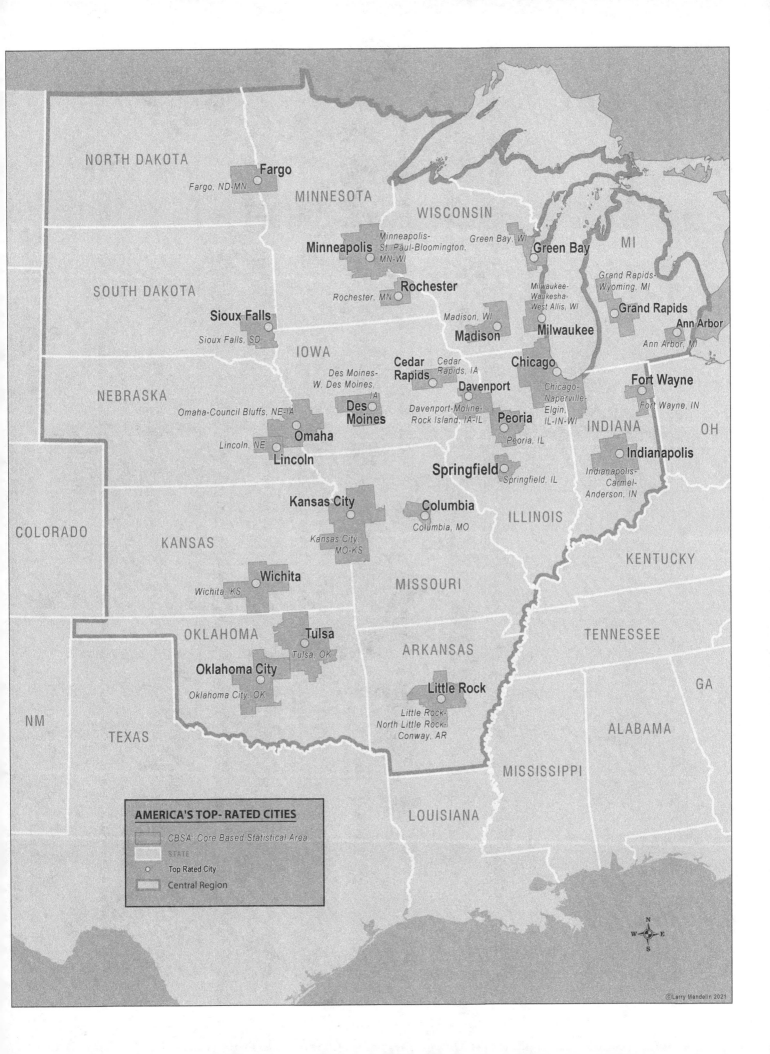

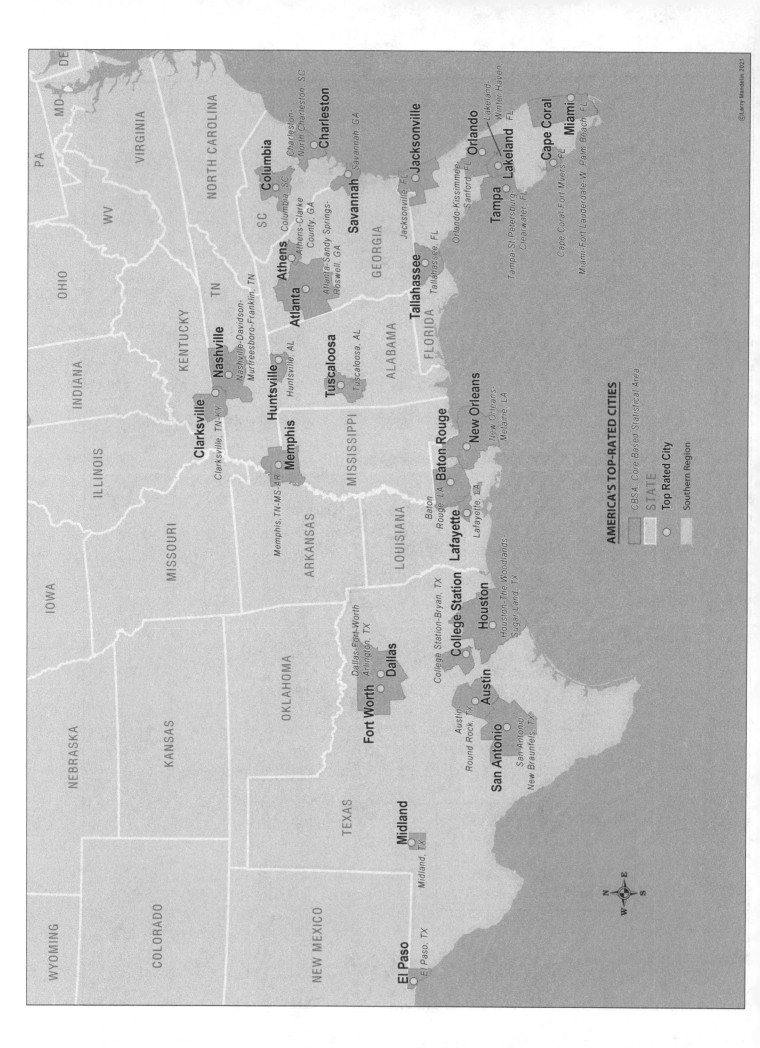

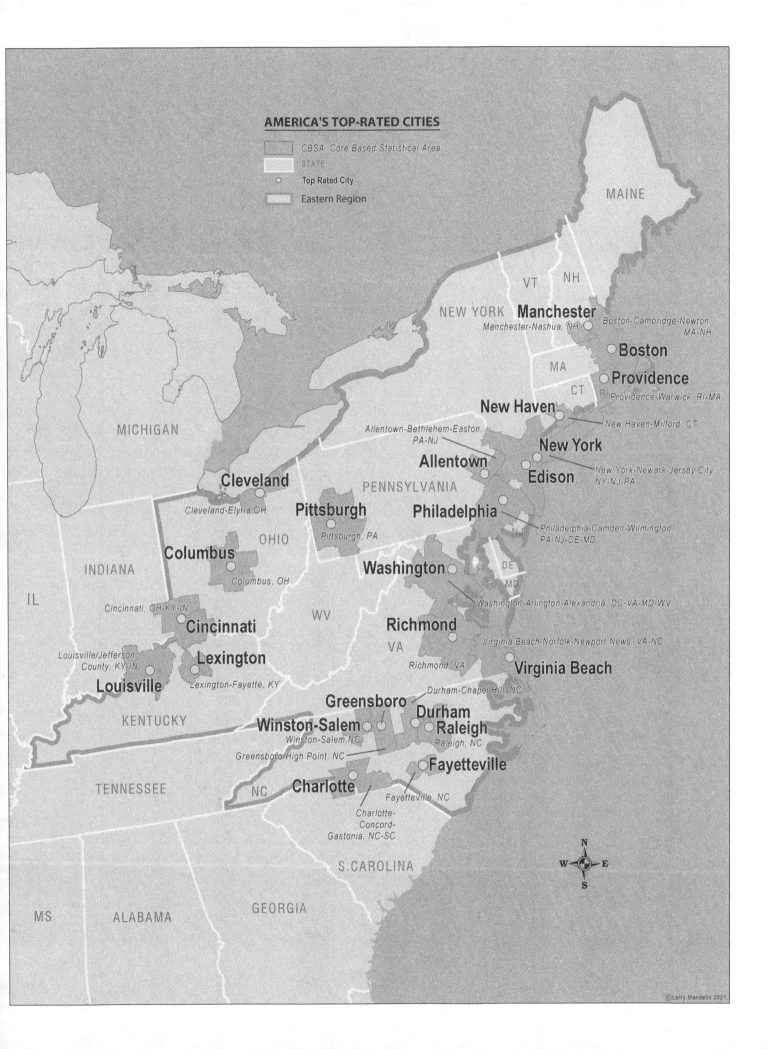

Ann Arbor, Michigan

Background

Ann Arbor is located on the Huron River, 36 miles west of Detroit. It was founded in 1824 by John Allen and Elisha W. Rumsey, two East Coast entrepreneurs who named the settlement for their wives—both Ann—and for the community's location within natural groves. In 1851, Ann Arbor was chartered as a city.

After the arrival of the Michigan Central Railroad in 1839, the settlement developed as an agricultural center, and it continues to be such for the rich agricultural area surrounding it.

Before the arrival of settlers, the Ojibwa tribe roamed the area, which they called Washtenaw—the land beyond—which now serves as the county for which Ann Arbor is the seat.

The city manufactures machinery, tools, steel ball bearings, scientific instruments, doors and blinds, cameras, and coil springs. Lasers, computers, hospital and laboratory equipment, automotive parts, and high-tech/software products are also vibrant industries. Major opportunities exist in health care, with the University of Michigan Medical Center and St. Joseph Mercy Hospital employing over 11,000. The region is also strong in book printing and manufacturing.

Ann Arbor's population is about one-third college or university students. The University of Michigan, the town's largest employer, played a prominent role in Ann Arbor's development as a major Midwest center for aeronautical, space, nuclear, chemical, and metallurgical research. The university also houses fascinating exhibits within its Museum of Natural History, known for an outstanding collection of dinosaur and mastodon skeletons and fossils, detailed dioramas of prehistoric life and Native American cultures, exhibits on Michigan wildlife, anthropology, and geology, and even its planetarium. Also located at the university is a 250-acre botanical garden with a conservatory featuring tropical, temperate, and arid houses, over six miles of nature trails, and a variety of outdoor display gardens. The University of Michigan Museum of Art (UMMA), with more than 18,000 works of art from all over the world, and the university's Detroit Observatory, a historic scientific laboratory built in 1854, make this a truly unique, world-class institution. UMMA expanded in 2009, more than doubling its space.

The university is also home to the Gerald R. Ford School of Policy, named in honor of the former President, who graduated from the university in 1935. The 85,000 square-foot Joan and Sanford Weill Hall, designed by the noted firm of Robert A. M. Stern Architects, opened in 2006. The University of Michigan is also the site of the Ford Presidential Library.

Other cultural attractions in the city include: the African-American Cultural and Historical Museum; the Ann Arbor Art Center, including two contemporary art galleries, and art classes for all ages; the Ann Arbor Hands-On Museum, offering interactive exhibits in physics, mathematics, biology, physiology, botany and geology; and Gallery Von Glahn, specializing in serigraphs, lithographs, and original bronze and porcelain art. The Detroit Institute of Arts displays Diego Rivera's spectacular "Detroit Industry" frescoes. In addition, Ann Arbor offers dozens more artists' guilds, museums, top-rated art fairs, music and film festivals, plus its share of fine restaurants with cuisine ranging from Italian to Ethiopian.

In nearby Dearborn are the Henry Ford Estate and Museum and the Automotive Hall of Fame. Historic Ypsilanti hosts the annual Orphan Car Show, which pays homage to elegant vehicles of a bygone era such as the Kaiser, Triumph and Packard.

With its high-tech industries and great university, Ann Arbor is an exceptionally livable city and full of cultural events, including an annual arts fair, and jazz, film, and summer festivals. The city boasts 157 city parks, seven golf courses and endless trails.

Located in the humid continental climate zone, Ann Arbor's summers are hot, winters are cold, and there is an above-average occurrence of snow and rain. Proximity to the Great Lakes causes extreme temperatures to be moderated, but also results in high humidity and cloud cover two-thirds of the year.

Rankings

General Rankings

- *US News & World Report* conducted a survey of more than 3,000 people and analyzed the 150 largest metropolitan areas to determine what matters most when selecting the next place to live. Ann Arbor ranked #12 out of the top 25 as having the best combination of desirable factors. Criteria: cost of living; quality of life; net migration; job market; desirability; and other factors. *realestate.usnews.com, "The 25 Best Places to Live in the U.S. in 2020-21," October 13, 2020*

- In their seventh annual survey, Livability.com looked at data for more than 1,000 small to mid-sized U.S. cities to determine the rankings for Livability's "Top 100 Best Places to Live" in 2020. Ann Arbor ranked #2. Criteria: housing and affordable living; vibrant economy; social and civic engagement; education; demographics; health care options; transportation & infrastructure; and abundant lifestyle amenities. *Livability.com, "Top 100 Best Places to Live 2020" October 2020*

Business/Finance Rankings

- According to *Business Insider*, the Ann Arbor metro area is a prime place to run a startup or move an existing business to. The area ranked #19. Nearly 190 metro areas were analyzed on overall economic health and investments. Data was based on the 2019 U.S. Census Bureau American Community Survey, the marketing company PitchBook, Bureau of Labor Statistics employment report, and Zillow. Criteria: percentage of change in typical home values and employment rates; quarterly venture capital investment activity; and median household income. *www.businessinsider.com, "The 25 Best Cities to Start a Business-Or Move Your Current One," January 12, 2021*

- 24/7 Wall Street used metro data from the Bureau of Labor Statistics' Occupational Employment database to identify the cities with the highest percentage of those employed in jobs requiring knowledge in the science, technology, engineering, and math (STEM) fields as well as average wages for STEM jobs. The Ann Arbor metro area was #13. *247wallst.com, "15 Cities with the Most High-Tech Jobs," January 11, 2020*

- The Ann Arbor metro area appeared on the Milken Institute "2021 Best Performing Cities" list. Rank: #68 out of 200 large metro areas (population over 250,000). Criteria: job growth; wage and salary growth; high-tech output growth; housing affordability; household broadband access. *Milken Institute, "Best-Performing Cities 2021," February 16, 2021*

- *Forbes* ranked the 200 most populous metro areas to determine the nation's "Best Places for Business and Careers." The Ann Arbor metro area was ranked #71. Criteria: costs (business and living); job growth (past and projected); income growth; quality of life; educational attainment (college and high school); projected economic growth; cultural and leisure opportunities; workplace tolerance laws; net migration patterns. *Forbes, "The Best Places for Business and Careers 2019: Seattle Still On Top," October 30, 2019*

Dating/Romance Rankings

- Ann Arbor was selected as one of America's best cities for singles by the readers of *Travel + Leisure* in their annual "America's Favorite Cities" survey. Criteria included good-looking locals, cool shopping, an active bar scene and hipster-magnet coffee bars. *Travel + Leisure, "Best Cities in America for Singles," July 21, 2017*

- Ann Arbor was selected as one of the nation's most romantic cities with 100,000 or more residents by Amazon.com. The city ranked #10 of 20. Criteria: per capita sales of romance novels, relationship books, romantic comedy movies, romantic music, and sexual wellness products. *Amazon.com, "Top 20 Most Romantic Cities in the U.S.," February 1, 2017*

Education Rankings

- Personal finance website *WalletHub* analyzed the 150 largest U.S. metropolitan statistical areas to determine where the most educated Americans are putting their degrees to work. Criteria: education levels; percentage of workers with degrees; education quality and attainment gap; public school quality rankings; quality and enrollment of each metro area's universities. Ann Arbor was ranked #1 (#1 = most educated city). *www.WalletHub.com, "Most and Least Educated Cities in America," July 20, 2020*

Environmental Rankings

- Niche compiled a list of the nation's snowiest cities, based on the National Oceanic and Atmospheric Administration's 30-year average snowfall data. Among cities with a population of at least 50,000, Ann Arbor ranked #19. *Niche.com, Top 25 Snowiest Cities in America, December 10, 2018*

Food/Drink Rankings

- Ann Arbor was selected as one of America's 10 most vegan-friendly areas. The city was ranked #8. Criteria now includes smaller urban areas, following the migration to smaller cities due to the pandemic. *People for the Ethical Treatment of Animals, "Top 10 Vegan-Friendly Towns and Small Cities of 2020," December 14, 2020*

Health/Fitness Rankings

- The Sharecare Community Well-Being Index evaluates 10 individual and social health factors in order to measure what matters to Americans in the communities in which they live. The Ann Arbor metro area ranked #2 in the top 10 across all 10 domains. Criteria: access to healthcare, food, and community resources; housng and transportation; economic security; feeling of purpose; physical, financial, social, and community well-being. *www.sharecare.com, "Community Well-Being Index: 2019 Metro Area & County Rankings Report," August 31, 2020*

Real Estate Rankings

- The Ann Arbor metro area was identified as one of the 20 worst housing markets in the U.S. in 2020. The area ranked #174 out of 180 markets. Criteria: year-over-year change of median sales price of existing single-family homes between the 4th quarter of 2019 and the 4th quarter of 2020. *National Association of Realtors®, Median Sales Price of Existing Single-Family Homes for Metropolitan Areas, 4th Quarter 2020*

Safety Rankings

- The National Insurance Crime Bureau ranked 384 metro areas in the U.S. in terms of per capita rates of vehicle theft. The Ann Arbor metro area ranked #282 (#1 = highest rate). Criteria: number of vehicle theft offenses per 100,000 inhabitants in 2019. *National Insurance Crime Bureau, "Hot Spots 2019," July 21, 2020*

Seniors/Retirement Rankings

- From its Best Cities for Successful Aging indexes, the Milken Institute generated rankings for metropolitan areas, weighing data in nine categories—health care, wellness, living arrangements, transportation and convenience, financial characteristics, education, employment, community engagement, and overall livability. The Ann Arbor metro area was ranked #6 overall in the small metro area category. *Milken Institute, "Best Cities for Successful Aging, 2017" March 14, 2017*

Women/Minorities Rankings

- NerdWallet examined data for 529 U.S. cities and ranked them based on the environment for working women. Ann Arbor ranked #7. Criteria: women's earnings; labor force participation rate; cost of living; unemployment rate. *www.nerdwallet.com, "Best Cities for Women in the Workforce 2016," April 4, 2016*

- *24/7 Wall St.* compared median annual earnings for men and women who worked full-time, year-round, female employment in management roles, bachelor's degree attainment among women, female life expectancy, uninsured rates, and preschool enrollment to identify the best cities for women. The U.S. metropolitan area, Ann Arbor was ranked #7 in pay disparity and other gender gaps. *24/7 Wall St., "The Easiest (and Toughest) Cities to Be a Woman," January 11, 2020*

4   Ann Arbor, Michigan

Business Environment

DEMOGRAPHICS

Population Growth

Area	1990 Census	2000 Census	2010 Census	2019* Estimate	Population Growth (%)	
					1990-2019	2010-2019
City	111,018	114,024	113,934	120,735	8.8	6.0
MSA[1]	282,937	322,895	344,791	367,000	29.7	6.4
U.S.	248,709,873	281,421,906	308,745,538	324,697,795	30.6	5.2

Note: (1) Figures cover the Ann Arbor, MI Metropolitan Statistical Area; (*) 2015-2019 5-year estimated population
Source: U.S. Census Bureau, 1990 Census, Census 2000, Census 2010, 2015-2019 American Community Survey 5-Year Estimates

Household Size

Area	Persons in Household (%)							Average Household Size
	One	Two	Three	Four	Five	Six	Seven or More	
City	34.7	37.8	11.7	10.4	3.0	1.5	0.8	2.30
MSA[1]	29.6	36.9	13.7	12.3	4.5	1.8	1.0	2.50
U.S.	27.9	33.9	15.6	12.9	6.0	2.3	1.4	2.60

Note: (1) Figures cover the Ann Arbor, MI Metropolitan Statistical Area
Source: U.S. Census Bureau, 2015-2019 American Community Survey 5-Year Estimates

Race

Area	White Alone[2] (%)	Black Alone[2] (%)	Asian Alone[2] (%)	AIAN[3] Alone[2] (%)	NHOPI[4] Alone[2] (%)	Other Race Alone[2] (%)	Two or More Races (%)
City	71.1	6.8	16.9	0.4	0.1	0.7	4.1
MSA[1]	73.6	11.9	9.1	0.4	0.0	0.8	4.2
U.S.	72.5	12.7	5.5	0.8	0.2	4.9	3.3

Note: (1) Figures cover the Ann Arbor, MI Metropolitan Statistical Area; (2) Alone is defined as not being in combination with one or more other races; (3) American Indian and Alaska Native; (4) Native Hawaiian and Other Pacific Islander
Source: U.S. Census Bureau, 2015-2019 American Community Survey 5-Year Estimates

Hispanic or Latino Origin

Area	Total (%)	Mexican (%)	Puerto Rican (%)	Cuban (%)	Other (%)
City	4.8	2.2	0.4	0.3	1.9
MSA[1]	4.7	2.6	0.3	0.2	1.6
U.S.	18.0	11.2	1.7	0.7	4.3

Note: Persons of Hispanic or Latino origin can be of any race; (1) Figures cover the Ann Arbor, MI Metropolitan Statistical Area
Source: U.S. Census Bureau, 2015-2019 American Community Survey 5-Year Estimates

Ancestry

Area	German	Irish	English	American	Italian	Polish	French[2]	Scottish	Dutch
City	17.1	9.9	9.5	3.8	4.9	6.0	3.0	2.7	2.3
MSA[1]	19.0	10.7	9.9	6.6	4.7	6.4	3.1	2.6	2.1
U.S.	13.3	9.7	7.2	6.2	5.1	2.8	2.3	1.7	1.2

Note: Figures are the percentage of the total population reporting a particular ancestry. The nine most commonly reported ancestries in the U.S. are shown. Figures include multiple ancestries (e.g. if a person reported being Irish and Italian, they were included in both columns); (1) Figures cover the Ann Arbor, MI Metropolitan Statistical Area; (2) Excludes Basque
Source: U.S. Census Bureau, 2015-2019 American Community Survey 5-Year Estimates

Foreign-born Population

Area	Percent of Population Born in								
	Any Foreign Country	Asia	Mexico	Europe	Caribbean	Central America[2]	South America	Africa	Canada
City	19.1	12.7	0.4	3.0	0.2	0.1	0.8	0.9	0.9
MSA[1]	12.5	7.4	0.4	2.1	0.2	0.3	0.5	0.9	0.6
U.S.	13.6	4.2	3.5	1.5	1.3	1.1	1.0	0.7	0.2

Note: (1) Figures cover the Ann Arbor, MI Metropolitan Statistical Area; (2) Excludes Mexico.
Source: U.S. Census Bureau, 2015-2019 American Community Survey 5-Year Estimates

Marital Status

Area	Never Married	Now Married[2]	Separated	Widowed	Divorced
City	56.5	33.8	0.4	2.6	6.6
MSA[1]	43.0	44.1	0.8	3.7	8.4
U.S.	33.4	48.1	1.9	5.8	10.9

Note: Figures are percentages and cover the population 15 years of age and older; (1) Figures cover the Ann Arbor, MI Metropolitan Statistical Area; (2) Excludes separated
Source: U.S. Census Bureau, 2015-2019 American Community Survey 5-Year Estimates

Disability by Age

Area	All Ages	Under 18 Years Old	18 to 64 Years Old	65 Years and Over
City	7.1	3.0	4.9	25.7
MSA[1]	9.4	3.7	7.3	27.9
U.S.	12.6	4.2	10.3	34.5

Note: Figures show percent of the civilian noninstitutionalized population that reported having a disability. Disability status is determined from six types of difficulty: vision, hearing, cognitive, ambulatory, self-care, and independent living. For children under 5 years old, hearing and vision difficulty are used to determine disability status. For children between the ages of 5 and 14, disability status is determined from hearing, vision, cognitive, ambulatory, and self-care difficulties. For people aged 15 years and older, they are considered to have a disability if they have difficulty with any one of the six difficulty types; Note: (1) Figures cover the Ann Arbor, MI Metropolitan Statistical Area
Source: U.S. Census Bureau, 2015-2019 American Community Survey 5-Year Estimates

Age

Area	Percent of Population									Median Age
	Under Age 5	Age 5–19	Age 20–34	Age 35–44	Age 45–54	Age 55–64	Age 65–74	Age 75–84	Age 85+	
City	3.7	18.5	40.1	9.5	8.3	8.2	6.8	3.4	1.5	27.5
MSA[1]	4.9	19.5	27.4	11.5	11.8	11.5	8.2	3.7	1.6	33.6
U.S.	6.1	19.1	20.7	12.6	13.0	12.9	9.1	4.6	1.9	38.1

Note: (1) Figures cover the Ann Arbor, MI Metropolitan Statistical Area
Source: U.S. Census Bureau, 2015-2019 American Community Survey 5-Year Estimates

Gender

Area	Males	Females	Males per 100 Females
City	60,089	60,646	99.1
MSA[1]	181,923	185,077	98.3
U.S.	159,886,919	164,810,876	97.0

Note: (1) Figures cover the Ann Arbor, MI Metropolitan Statistical Area
Source: U.S. Census Bureau, 2015-2019 American Community Survey 5-Year Estimates

Religious Groups by Family

Area	Catholic	Baptist	Non-Den.	Methodist[2]	Lutheran	LDS[3]	Pentecostal	Presbyterian[4]	Muslim[5]	Judaism
MSA[1]	12.4	2.2	1.6	3.1	2.9	0.9	1.9	3.0	1.3	0.9
U.S.	19.1	9.3	4.0	4.0	2.3	2.0	1.9	1.6	0.8	0.7

Note: Figures are the number of adherents as a percentage of the total population; (1) Figures cover the Ann Arbor, MI Metropolitan Statistical Area; (2) Methodist/Pietist; (3) Latter Day Saints; (4) Reformed; (5) Figures are estimates
Source: Association of Statisticians of American Religious Bodies, 2010 U.S. Religion Census: Religious Congregations & Membership Study

Religious Groups by Tradition

Area	Catholic	Evangelical Protestant	Mainline Protestant	Other Tradition	Black Protestant	Orthodox
MSA[1]	12.4	7.3	7.5	3.8	1.6	0.3
U.S.	19.1	16.2	7.3	4.3	1.6	0.3

Note: Figures are the number of adherents as a percentage of the total population; (1) Figures cover the Ann Arbor, MI Metropolitan Statistical Area
Source: Association of Statisticians of American Religious Bodies, 2010 U.S. Religion Census: Religious Congregations & Membership Study

ECONOMY

Gross Metropolitan Product

Area	2017	2018	2019	2020	Rank[2]
MSA[1]	23.5	24.6	25.5	26.4	112

Note: Figures are in billions of dollars; (1) Figures cover the Ann Arbor, MI Metropolitan Statistical Area; (2) Rank is based on 2018 data and ranges from 1 to 381
Source: U.S. Conference of Mayors, U.S. Metro Economies: GMP & Employment 2018-2020, September 2019

Economic Growth

Area	2015-17 (%)	2018 (%)	2019 (%)	2020 (%)	Rank[2]
MSA[1]	2.1	2.5	1.9	1.3	123
U.S.	1.9	2.9	2.3	2.1	—

Note: Figures are real gross metropolitan product (GMP) growth rates and represent average annual percent change; (1) Figures cover the Ann Arbor, MI Metropolitan Statistical Area; (2) Rank is based on 2017 2-year average annual percent change and ranges from 1 to 381
Source: U.S. Conference of Mayors, U.S. Metro Economies: GMP & Employment 2018-2020, September 2019

Metropolitan Area Exports

Area	2014	2015	2016	2017	2018	2019	Rank[2]
MSA[1]	1,213.6	1,053.0	1,207.9	1,447.4	1,538.7	1,432.7	128

Note: Figures are in millions of dollars; (1) Figures cover the Ann Arbor, MI Metropolitan Statistical Area; (2) Rank is based on 2019 data and ranges from 1 to 386
Source: U.S. Department of Commerce, International Trade Administration, Office of Trade and Economic Analysis, Industry and Analysis, Exports by Metropolitan Area, data extracted March 24, 2021

Building Permits

Area	Single-Family			Multi-Family			Total		
	2018	2019	Pct. Chg.	2018	2019	Pct. Chg.	2018	2019	Pct. Chg.
City	126	96	-23.8	0	0	0.0	126	96	-23.8
MSA[1]	652	608	-6.7	153	207	35.3	805	815	1.2
U.S.	855,300	862,100	0.7	473,500	523,900	10.6	1,328,800	1,386,000	4.3

Note: (1) Figures cover the Ann Arbor, MI Metropolitan Statistical Area; Figures represent new, privately-owned housing units authorized (unadjusted data); All permit data are based on estimates with imputation
Source: U.S. Census Bureau, Manufacturing, Mining, and Construction Statistics, Building Permits, 2018, 2019

Bankruptcy Filings

Area	Business Filings			Nonbusiness Filings		
	2019	2020	% Chg.	2019	2020	% Chg.
Washtenaw County	10	13	30.0	654	454	-30.6
U.S.	22,780	21,655	-4.9	752,160	522,808	-30.5

Note: Business filings include Chapter 7, Chapter 9, Chapter 11, Chapter 12, Chapter 13, Chapter 15, and Section 304; Nonbusiness filings include Chapter 7, Chapter 11, and Chapter 13
Source: Administrative Office of the U.S. Courts, Business and Nonbusiness Bankruptcy, County Cases Commenced by Chapter of the Bankruptcy Code, During the 12-Month Period Ending December 31, 2019 and Business and Nonbusiness Bankruptcy, County Cases Commenced by Chapter of the Bankruptcy Code, During the 12-Month Period Ending December 31, 2020

Housing Vacancy Rates

Area	Gross Vacancy Rate[2] (%)			Year-Round Vacancy Rate[3] (%)			Rental Vacancy Rate[4] (%)			Homeowner Vacancy Rate[5] (%)		
	2018	2019	2020	2018	2019	2020	2018	2019	2020	2018	2019	2020
MSA[1]	n/a	n/a	n/a	n/a	n/a	n/a	n/a	n/a	n/a	n/a	n/a	n/a
U.S.	12.3	12.0	10.6	9.7	9.5	8.2	6.9	6.7	6.3	1.5	1.4	1.0

Note: (1) Figures cover the Ann Arbor, MI Metropolitan Statistical Area; (2) The percentage of the total housing inventory that is vacant; (3) The percentage of the housing inventory (excluding seasonal units) that is year-round vacant; (4) The percentage of rental inventory that is vacant for rent; (5) The percentage of homeowner inventory that is vacant for sale; n/a not available
Source: U.S. Census Bureau, Housing Vacancies and Homeownership Annual Statistics: 2018, 2019, 2020

INCOME

Income

Area	Per Capita ($)	Median Household ($)	Average Household ($)
City	42,674	65,745	96,906
MSA[1]	41,399	72,586	101,787
U.S.	34,103	62,843	88,607

Note: (1) Figures cover the Ann Arbor, MI Metropolitan Statistical Area
Source: U.S. Census Bureau, 2015-2019 American Community Survey 5-Year Estimates

Household Income Distribution

Area	Percent of Households Earning							
	Under $15,000	$15,000 -$24,999	$25,000 -$34,999	$35,000 -$49,999	$50,000 -$74,999	$75,000 -$99,999	$100,000 -$149,999	$150,000 and up
City	14.5	7.3	7.6	9.3	15.8	11.4	14.5	19.7
MSA[1]	10.6	7.1	7.1	10.5	16.0	12.5	16.7	19.6
U.S.	10.3	8.9	8.9	12.3	17.2	12.7	15.1	14.5

Note: (1) Figures cover the Ann Arbor, MI Metropolitan Statistical Area
Source: U.S. Census Bureau, 2015-2019 American Community Survey 5-Year Estimates

Poverty Rate

Area	All Ages	Under 18 Years Old	18 to 64 Years Old	65 Years and Over
City	22.3	9.8	27.3	7.7
MSA[1]	14.0	12.0	16.1	6.7
U.S.	13.4	18.5	12.6	9.3

Note: Figures are percentage of people whose income during the past 12 months was below the poverty level;
(1) Figures cover the Ann Arbor, MI Metropolitan Statistical Area
Source: U.S. Census Bureau, 2015-2019 American Community Survey 5-Year Estimates

CITY FINANCES

City Government Finances

Component	2017 ($000)	2017 ($ per capita)
Total Revenues	349,154	2,982
Total Expenditures	312,269	2,667
Debt Outstanding	313,661	2,679
Cash and Securities[1]	728,499	6,223

Note: (1) Cash and security holdings of a government at the close of its fiscal year,
including those of its dependent agencies, utilities, and liquor stores.
Source: U.S. Census Bureau, State & Local Government Finances 2017

City Government Revenue by Source

Source	2017 ($000)	2017 ($ per capita)	2017 (%)
General Revenue			
From Federal Government	34,881	298	10.0
From State Government	22,652	193	6.5
From Local Governments	3,433	29	1.0
Taxes			
Property	94,880	810	27.2
Sales and Gross Receipts	2,232	19	0.6
Personal Income	0	0	0.0
Corporate Income	0	0	0.0
Motor Vehicle License	0	0	0.0
Other Taxes	5,479	47	1.6
Current Charges	76,476	653	21.9
Liquor Store	0	0	0.0
Utility	26,602	227	7.6
Employee Retirement	64,030	547	18.3

Source: U.S. Census Bureau, State & Local Government Finances 2017

City Government Expenditures by Function

Function	2017 ($000)	2017 ($ per capita)	2017 (%)
General Direct Expenditures			
Air Transportation	697	6	0.2
Corrections	0	0	0.0
Education	0	0	0.0
Employment Security Administration	0	0	0.0
Financial Administration	3,578	30	1.1
Fire Protection	16,415	140	5.3
General Public Buildings	0	0	0.0
Governmental Administration, Other	2,334	19	0.7
Health	0	0	0.0
Highways	33,301	284	10.7
Hospitals	0	0	0.0
Housing and Community Development	21,971	187	7.0
Interest on General Debt	6,675	57	2.1
Judicial and Legal	6,587	56	2.1
Libraries	0	0	0.0
Parking	21,971	187	7.0
Parks and Recreation	15,097	129	4.8
Police Protection	27,267	232	8.7
Public Welfare	0	0	0.0
Sewerage	34,277	292	11.0
Solid Waste Management	15,498	132	5.0
Veterans' Services	0	0	0.0
Liquor Store	0	0	0.0
Utility	21,035	179	6.7
Employee Retirement	35,437	302	11.3

Source: U.S. Census Bureau, State & Local Government Finances 2017

8 Ann Arbor, Michigan

EMPLOYMENT

Labor Force and Employment

Area	Civilian Labor Force			Workers Employed		
	Dec. 2019	Dec. 2020	% Chg.	Dec. 2019	Dec. 2020	% Chg.
City	66,802	63,917	-4.3	65,636	62,017	-5.5
MSA[1]	200,349	192,221	-4.1	196,082	185,271	-5.5
U.S.	164,007,000	160,017,000	-2.4	158,504,000	149,613,000	-5.6

Note: Data is not seasonally adjusted and covers workers 16 years of age and older; (1) Figures cover the Ann Arbor, MI Metropolitan Statistical Area
Source: Bureau of Labor Statistics, Local Area Unemployment Statistics

Unemployment Rate

Area	2020											
	Jan.	Feb.	Mar.	Apr.	May	Jun.	Jul.	Aug.	Sep.	Oct.	Nov.	Dec.
City	2.0	1.8	1.9	12.4	11.6	8.9	6.6	5.7	5.0	3.3	2.8	3.0
MSA[1]	2.5	2.2	2.3	14.8	13.9	10.7	8.0	6.9	6.1	4.0	3.4	3.6
U.S.	4.0	3.8	4.5	14.4	13.0	11.2	10.5	8.5	7.7	6.6	6.4	6.5

Note: Data is not seasonally adjusted and covers workers 16 years of age and older; (1) Figures cover the Ann Arbor, MI Metropolitan Statistical Area
Source: Bureau of Labor Statistics, Local Area Unemployment Statistics

Average Wages

Occupation	$/Hr.	Occupation	$/Hr.
Accountants and Auditors	36.70	Maintenance and Repair Workers	22.10
Automotive Mechanics	30.70	Marketing Managers	61.90
Bookkeepers	21.60	Network and Computer Systems Admin.	39.10
Carpenters	27.80	Nurses, Licensed Practical	25.80
Cashiers	12.10	Nurses, Registered	39.10
Computer Programmers	38.50	Nursing Assistants	17.60
Computer Systems Analysts	40.60	Office Clerks, General	16.80
Computer User Support Specialists	23.80	Physical Therapists	42.90
Construction Laborers	22.50	Physicians	92.80
Cooks, Restaurant	15.60	Plumbers, Pipefitters and Steamfitters	35.70
Customer Service Representatives	18.80	Police and Sheriff's Patrol Officers	33.40
Dentists	71.20	Postal Service Mail Carriers	25.60
Electricians	33.70	Real Estate Sales Agents	23.90
Engineers, Electrical	42.10	Retail Salespersons	15.20
Fast Food and Counter Workers	11.90	Sales Representatives, Technical/Scientific	50.30
Financial Managers	65.00	Secretaries, Exc. Legal/Medical/Executive	21.90
First-Line Supervisors of Office Workers	29.60	Security Guards	18.20
General and Operations Managers	68.80	Surgeons	n/a
Hairdressers/Cosmetologists	13.00	Teacher Assistants, Exc. Postsecondary*	14.30
Home Health and Personal Care Aides	12.30	Teachers, Secondary School, Exc. Sp. Ed.*	30.90
Janitors and Cleaners	16.00	Telemarketers	n/a
Landscaping/Groundskeeping Workers	16.80	Truck Drivers, Heavy/Tractor-Trailer	23.10
Lawyers	55.40	Truck Drivers, Light/Delivery Services	21.00
Maids and Housekeeping Cleaners	13.30	Waiters and Waitresses	12.40

Note: Wage data covers the Ann Arbor, MI Metropolitan Statistical Area; (*) Hourly wages were calculated from annual wage data based on a 40 hour work week; n/a not available.
Source: Bureau of Labor Statistics, Metro Area Occupational Employment & Wage Estimates, May 2020

Employment by Industry

Sector	MSA[1]		U.S.
	Number of Employees	Percent of Total	Percent of Total
Construction, Mining, and Logging	4,600	2.2	5.5
Education and Health Services	27,900	13.4	16.3
Financial Activities	6,400	3.1	6.1
Government	80,000	38.3	15.2
Information	6,000	2.9	1.9
Leisure and Hospitality	9,800	4.7	9.0
Manufacturing	13,200	6.3	8.5
Other Services	5,300	2.5	3.8
Professional and Business Services	29,400	14.1	14.4
Retail Trade	15,400	7.4	10.9
Transportation, Warehousing, and Utilities	4,600	2.2	4.6
Wholesale Trade	6,300	3.0	3.9

Note: Figures are non-farm employment as of December 2020. Figures are not seasonally adjusted and include workers 16 years of age and older; (1) Figures cover the Ann Arbor, MI Metropolitan Statistical Area
Source: Bureau of Labor Statistics, Current Employment Statistics, Employment, Hours, and Earnings

Employment by Occupation

Occupation Classification	City (%)	MSA[1] (%)	U.S. (%)
Management, Business, Science, and Arts	66.2	54.3	38.5
Natural Resources, Construction, and Maintenance	1.7	4.2	8.9
Production, Transportation, and Material Moving	5.5	9.6	13.2
Sales and Office	13.9	16.3	21.6
Service	12.7	15.6	17.8

Note: Figures cover employed civilians 16 years of age and older; (1) Figures cover the Ann Arbor, MI Metropolitan Statistical Area
Source: U.S. Census Bureau, 2015-2019 American Community Survey 5-Year Estimates

Occupations with Greatest Projected Employment Growth: 2020 – 2022

Occupation[1]	2020 Employment	2022 Projected Employment	Numeric Employment Change	Percent Employment Change
Registered Nurses	100,730	101,870	1,140	1.1
Laborers and Freight, Stock, and Material Movers, Hand	72,870	73,850	980	1.3
Heavy and Tractor-Trailer Truck Drivers	61,290	62,120	830	1.4
Construction Laborers	31,450	32,160	710	2.3
Light Truck or Delivery Services Drivers	27,780	28,390	610	2.2
Carpenters	25,160	25,610	450	1.8
Insurance Sales Agents	13,310	13,720	410	3.1
Market Research Analysts and Marketing Specialists	18,600	19,000	400	2.2
Stockers and Order Fillers	67,090	67,480	390	0.6
Industrial Truck and Tractor Operators	22,490	22,850	360	1.6

Note: Projections cover Michigan; (1) Sorted by numeric employment change
Source: www.projectionscentral.com, State Occupational Projections, 2020–2022 Short-Term Projections

Fastest-Growing Occupations: 2020 – 2022

Occupation[1]	2020 Employment	2022 Projected Employment	Numeric Employment Change	Percent Employment Change
Tank Car, Truck, and Ship Loaders	250	300	50	20.0
Conveyor Operators and Tenders	720	770	50	6.9
Operations Research Analysts	1,900	1,980	80	4.2
Veterinary Assistants and Laboratory Animal Caretakers	3,340	3,480	140	4.2
Veterinary Technologists and Technicians	2,430	2,530	100	4.1
Veterinarians	2,310	2,400	90	3.9
Dental Laboratory Technicians	1,660	1,720	60	3.6
Respiratory Therapists	4,700	4,860	160	3.4
Nursing Instructors and Teachers, Postsecondary	1,810	1,870	60	3.3
Insurance Sales Agents	13,310	13,720	410	3.1

Note: Projections cover Michigan; (1) Sorted by percent employment change and excludes occupations with numeric employment change less than 50
Source: www.projectionscentral.com, State Occupational Projections, 2020–2022 Short-Term Projections

TAXES

State Corporate Income Tax Rates

State	Tax Rate (%)	Income Brackets ($)	Num. of Brackets	Financial Institution Tax Rate (%)[a]	Federal Income Tax Ded.
Michigan	6.0	Flat rate	1	(a)	No

Note: Tax rates as of January 1, 2021; (a) Rates listed are the corporate income tax rate applied to financial institutions or excise taxes based on income. Some states have other taxes based upon the value of deposits or shares.
Source: Federation of Tax Administrators, State Corporate Income Tax Rates, January 1, 2021

State Individual Income Tax Rates

State	Tax Rate (%)	Income Brackets ($)	Personal Exemptions ($)			Standard Ded. ($)	
			Single	Married	Depend.	Single	Married
Michigan (a)	4.25	Flat rate	4,750	9,500	4,750	–	–

Note: Tax rates as of January 1, 2021; Local- and county-level taxes are not included; Federal income tax is not deductible on state income tax returns; (a) 19 states have statutory provision for automatically adjusting to the rate of inflation the dollar values of the income tax brackets, standard deductions, and/or personal exemptions. Michigan indexes the personal exemption only. Oregon does not index the income brackets for $125,000 and over.
Source: Federation of Tax Administrators, State Individual Income Tax Rates, January 1, 2021

Various State Sales and Excise Tax Rates

State	State Sales Tax (%)	Gasoline[1] (¢/gal.)	Cigarette[2] ($/pack)	Spirits[3] ($/gal.)	Wine[4] ($/gal.)	Beer[5] ($/gal.)	Recreational Marijuana (%)
Michigan	6	41.98	2	11.95	0.51	0.2	(h)

Note: All tax rates as of January 1, 2021; (1) The American Petroleum Institute has developed a methodology for determining the average tax rate on a gallon of fuel. Rates may include any of the following: excise taxes, environmental fees, storage tank fees, other fees or taxes, general sales tax, and local taxes; (2) The federal excise tax of $1.0066 per pack and local taxes are not included; (3) Rates are those applicable to off-premise sales of 40% alcohol by volume (a.b.v.) distilled spirits in 750ml containers. Local excise taxes are excluded; (4) Rates are those applicable to off-premise sales of 11% a.b.v. non-carbonated wine in 750ml containers; (5) Rates are those applicable to off-premise sales of 4.7% a.b.v. beer in 12 ounce containers; (h) 10% excise tax (retail price)
Source: Tax Foundation, 2021 Facts & Figures: How Does Your State Compare?

State Business Tax Climate Index Rankings

State	Overall Rank	Corporate Tax Rank	Individual Income Tax Rank	Sales Tax Rank	Property Tax Rank	Unemployment Insurance Tax Rank
Michigan	14	20	12	10	35	18

Note: The index is a measure of how each state's tax laws affect economic performance. The lower the rank, the more favorable a state's tax system is for business. States without a given tax are given a ranking of 1. The scores/rankings for the District of Columbia do not affect other states. The 2021 index represents the tax climate as of July 1, 2020.
Source: Tax Foundation, State Business Tax Climate Index 2021

TRANSPORTATION

Means of Transportation to Work

Area	Car/Truck/Van		Public Transportation			Bicycle	Walked	Other Means	Worked at Home
	Drove Alone	Car-pooled	Bus	Subway	Railroad				
City	54.0	6.4	10.3	0.2	0.0	3.9	16.5	0.7	8.0
MSA[1]	71.8	7.9	5.1	0.1	0.0	1.6	7.0	0.6	5.9
U.S.	76.3	9.0	2.4	1.9	0.6	0.5	2.7	1.4	5.2

Note: Figures are percentages and cover workers 16 years of age and older; (1) Figures cover the Ann Arbor, MI Metropolitan Statistical Area
Source: U.S. Census Bureau, 2015-2019 American Community Survey 5-Year Estimates

Travel Time to Work

Area	Less Than 10 Minutes	10 to 19 Minutes	20 to 29 Minutes	30 to 44 Minutes	45 to 59 Minutes	60 to 89 Minutes	90 Minutes or More
City	12.9	45.5	19.9	13.3	5.3	2.4	0.7
MSA[1]	10.6	32.7	24.5	19.3	7.6	4.1	1.3
U.S.	12.2	28.4	20.8	20.8	8.3	6.4	2.9

Note: Note: Figures are percentages and include workers 16 years old and over; (1) Figures cover the Ann Arbor, MI Metropolitan Statistical Area
Source: U.S. Census Bureau, 2015-2019 American Community Survey 5-Year Estimates

Key Congestion Measures

Measure	1982	1992	2002	2012	2017
Annual Hours of Delay, Total (000)	n/a	n/a	n/a	n/a	7,020
Annual Hours of Delay, Per Auto Commuter	n/a	n/a	n/a	n/a	22
Annual Congestion Cost, Total (million $)	n/a	n/a	n/a	n/a	146
Annual Congestion Cost, Per Auto Commuter ($)	n/a	n/a	n/a	n/a	466

Note: n/a not available
Source: Texas A&M Transportation Institute, 2019 Urban Mobility Report

Freeway Travel Time Index

Measure	1982	1987	1992	1997	2002	2007	2012	2017
Urban Area Index[1]	n/a	n/a	n/a	n/a	n/a	n/a	n/a	1.11
Urban Area Rank[1,2]	n/a	n/a	n/a	n/a	n/a	n/a	n/a	n/a

Note: Freeway Travel Time Index—the ratio of travel time in the peak period to the travel time at free-flow conditions. For example, a value of 1.30 indicates a 20-minute free-flow trip takes 26 minutes in the peak (20 minutes x 1.30 = 26 minutes); (1) Covers the Ann Arbor MI urban area; (2) Rank is based on 101 larger urban areas (#1 = highest travel time index); n/a not available
Source: Texas A&M Transportation Institute, 2019 Urban Mobility Report

Public Transportation

Agency Name / Mode of Transportation	Vehicles Operated in Maximum Service[1]	Annual Unlinked Passenger Trips[2] (in thous.)	Annual Passenger Miles[3] (in thous.)
Ann Arbor Transportation Authority (AATA)			
Bus (directly operated)	85	6,383.8	22,796.0
Commuter Bus (directly operated)	3	29.1	493.9
Commuter Bus (purchased transportation)	2	93.3	2,474.9
Demand Response (purchased transportation)	58	184.4	1,660.9
Demand Response Taxi (purchased transportation)	7	26.4	263.7
Vanpool (purchased transportation)	118	246.6	8,396.9

Note: (1) Number of revenue vehicles operated by the given mode and type of service to meet the annual maximum service requirement. This is the revenue vehicle count during the peak season of the year; on the week and day that maximum service is provided. Vehicles operated in maximum service (VOMS) exclude atypical days and one-time special events; (2) Number of passengers who boarded public transportation vehicles. Passengers are counted each time they board a vehicle no matter how many vehicles they use to travel from their origin to their destination. (3) Sum of the distances ridden by all passengers during the entire fiscal year.
Source: Federal Transit Administration, National Transit Database, 2019

Air Transportation

Airport Name and Code / Type of Service	Passenger Airlines[1]	Passenger Enplanements	Freight Carriers[2]	Freight (lbs)
Detroit Metro Wayne County (25 miles) (DTW)				
Domestic service (U.S. carriers - 2020)	27	6,394,435	18	123,337,411
International service (U.S. carriers - 2019)	9	1,560,141	3	34,371,209

Note: (1) Includes all U.S.-based major, minor and commuter airlines that carried at least one passenger during the year; (2) Includes all U.S.-based airlines and freight carriers that transported at least one pound of freight during the year.
Source: Bureau of Transportation Statistics, The Intermodal Transportation Database, Air Carriers: T-100 Domestic Market (U.S. Carriers), 2020; Bureau of Transportation Statistics, The Intermodal Transportation Database, Air Carriers: T-100 International Market (U.S. Carriers), 2019

BUSINESSES

Major Business Headquarters

Company Name	Industry	Rankings	
		Fortune[1]	Forbes[2]
No companies listed	-	-	-

Note: (1) Companies that produce a 10-K are ranked 1 to 500 based on 2019 revenue; (2) All private companies with at least $2 billion in annual revenue through the end of their most current fiscal year are ranked 1 to 219; companies listed are headquartered in the city; dashes indicate no ranking
Source: Fortune, "Fortune 500," June/July 2020; Forbes, "America's Largest Private Companies," 2020

Minority Business Opportunity

Ann Arbor is home to one company which is on the *Black Enterprise* Industrial/Service list (100 largest companies based on gross sales): **Arcade Travel** (#54). Criteria: operational in previous calendar year; at least 51% black-owned and manufactures/owns the product it sells or provides industrial or consumer services. Brokerages, real estate firms and firms that provide professional services are not eligible. *Black Enterprise, B.E. 100s, 2019*

Living Environment

COST OF LIVING

Cost of Living Index

Composite Index	Groceries	Housing	Utilities	Trans- portation	Health Care	Misc. Goods/ Services
n/a	n/a	n/a	n/a	n/a	n/a	n/a

Note: The Cost of Living Index measures regional differences in the cost of consumer goods and services, excluding taxes and non-consumer expenditures, for professional and managerial households in the top income quintile. It is based on more than 50,000 prices covering almost 60 different items for which prices are collected three times a year by chambers of commerce, economic development organizations or university applied economic centers in each participating urban area. The numbers shown should be read as a percentage above or below the national average of 100. For example, a value of 115.4 in the groceries column indicates that grocery prices are 15.4% higher than the national average. Small differences in the index numbers should not be interpreted as significant; n/a not available.
Source: The Council for Community and Economic Research, Cost of Living Index, 2020

Grocery Prices

Area[1]	T-Bone Steak ($/pound)	Frying Chicken ($/pound)	Whole Milk ($/half gal.)	Eggs ($/dozen)	Orange Juice ($/64 oz.)	Coffee ($/11.5 oz.)
City[2]	n/a	n/a	n/a	n/a	n/a	n/a
Avg.	11.78	1.39	2.05	1.47	3.57	4.34
Min.	8.03	0.94	1.03	0.74	2.94	3.02
Max.	15.86	2.65	4.31	3.77	5.44	8.69

*Note: (1) Values for the local area are compared with the average, minimum and maximum values for all 284 areas in the Cost of Living Index; (2) Figures cover the Ann Arbor MI urban area; n/a not available; **T-Bone Steak** (price per pound); **Frying Chicken** (price per pound, whole fryer); **Whole Milk** (half gallon carton); **Eggs** (price per dozen, Grade A, large); **Orange Juice** (64 oz. Tropicana or Florida Natural); **Coffee** (11.5 oz. can, vacuum-packed, Maxwell House, Hills Bros, or Folgers).*
Source: The Council for Community and Economic Research, Cost of Living Index, 2020

Housing and Utility Costs

Area[1]	New Home Price ($)	Apartment Rent ($/month)	All Electric ($/month)	Part Electric ($/month)	Other Energy ($/month)	Telephone ($/month)
City[2]	n/a	n/a	n/a	n/a	n/a	n/a
Avg.	368,594	1,168	170.86	100.47	65.28	184.30
Min.	190,567	502	91.58	31.42	26.08	169.60
Max.	2,227,806	4,738	470.38	280.31	280.06	206.50

*Note: (1) Values for the local area are compared with the average, minimum and maximum values for all 284 areas in the Cost of Living Index; (2) Figures cover the Ann Arbor MI urban area; n/a not available; **New Home Price** (2,400 sf living area, 8,000 sf lot, in urban area with full utilities); **Apartment Rent** (950 sf 2 bedroom/1.5 or 2 bath, unfurnished, excluding all utilities except water); **All Electric** (average monthly cost for an all-electric home); **Part Electric** (average monthly cost for a part-electric home); **Other Energy** (average monthly cost for natural gas, fuel oil, coal, wood, and any other forms of energy except electricity); **Telephone** (price includes the base monthly rate plus taxes and fees for three lines of mobile phone service).*
Source: The Council for Community and Economic Research, Cost of Living Index, 2020

Health Care, Transportation, and Other Costs

Area[1]	Doctor ($/visit)	Dentist ($/visit)	Optometrist ($/visit)	Gasoline ($/gallon)	Beauty Salon ($/visit)	Men's Shirt ($)
City[2]	n/a	n/a	n/a	n/a	n/a	n/a
Avg.	115.44	99.32	108.10	2.21	39.27	31.37
Min.	36.68	59.00	51.36	1.71	19.00	11.00
Max.	219.00	153.10	250.97	3.46	82.05	58.33

*Note: (1) Values for the local area are compared with the average, minimum and maximum values for all 284 areas in the Cost of Living Index; (2) Figures cover the Ann Arbor MI urban area; n/a not available; **Doctor** (general practitioners routine exam of an established patient); **Dentist** (adult teeth cleaning and periodic oral examination); **Optometrist** (full vision eye exam for established adult patient); **Gasoline** (one gallon regular unleaded, national brand, including all taxes, cash price at self-service pump if available); **Beauty Salon** (woman's shampoo, trim, and blow-dry); **Men's Shirt** (cotton/polyester dress shirt, pinpoint weave, long sleeves).*
Source: The Council for Community and Economic Research, Cost of Living Index, 2020

HOUSING

Homeownership Rate

Area	2012 (%)	2013 (%)	2014 (%)	2015 (%)	2016 (%)	2017 (%)	2018 (%)	2019 (%)	2020 (%)
MSA[1]	n/a	n/a	n/a	n/a	n/a	n/a	n/a	n/a	n/a
U.S.	65.4	65.1	64.5	63.7	63.4	63.9	64.4	64.6	66.6

Note: (1) Figures cover the Ann Arbor, MI Metropolitan Statistical Area; n/a not available
Source: U.S. Census Bureau, Housing Vacancies and Homeownership Annual Statistics: 2012-2020

House Price Index (HPI)

Area	National Ranking[2]	Quarterly Change (%)	One-Year Change (%)	Five-Year Change (%)	Since 1991Q1 (%)
MSA[1]	224	0.98	3.78	29.65	164.45
U.S.[3]	–	3.81	10.77	38.99	205.12

Note: The HPI is a weighted repeat sales index. It measures average price changes in repeat sales or refinancings on the same properties. This information is obtained by reviewing repeat mortgage transactions on single-family properties whose mortgages have been purchased or securitized by Fannie Mae or Freddie Mac since January 1975; (1) Figures cover the Ann Arbor, MI Metropolitan Statistical Area; (2) Rankings are based on annual percentage change for all metro areas containing at least 15,000 transactions over the last 10 years and ranges from 1 to 253; (3) figures based on a weighted average of Census Division estimates using a seasonally adjusted, purchase-only index; all figures are for the period ending December 31, 2020
Source: Federal Housing Finance Agency, Change in Metropolitan Area House Price Indexes, April 7, 2021

Median Single-Family Home Prices

Area	2018	2019	2020p	Percent Change 2019 to 2020
MSA[1]	281.0	294.7	312.4	6.0
U.S. Average	261.6	274.6	299.9	9.2

Note: Figures are median sales prices of existing single-family homes in thousands of dollars; (p) preliminary; (1) Figures cover the Ann Arbor, MI Metropolitan Statistical Area
Source: National Association of Realtors, Median Sales Price of Existing Single-Family Homes for Metropolitan Areas, 4th Quarter 2020

Qualifying Income Based on Median Sales Price of Existing Single-Family Homes

Area	With 5% Down ($)	With 10% Down ($)	With 20% Down ($)
MSA[1]	56,327	53,362	47,433
U.S. Average	59,266	56,147	49,908

Note: Figures are preliminary; Qualifying income is based on a mortgage rate of 2.81%. Monthly principal and interest payment is limited to 25% of income; (1) Figures cover the Ann Arbor, MI Metropolitan Statistical Area
Source: National Association of Realtors, Qualifying Income Based on Median Sales Price of Existing Single-Family Homes for Metropolitan Areas, 4th Quarter 2020

Home Value Distribution

Area	Under $50,000	$50,000 -$99,999	$100,000 -$149,999	$150,000 -$199,999	$200,000 -$299,999	$300,000 -$499,999	$500,000 -$999,999	$1,000,000 or more
City	1.3	3.6	6.0	8.2	25.2	37.6	15.7	2.4
MSA[1]	5.5	6.1	8.0	13.7	24.9	28.8	11.3	1.7
U.S.	6.9	12.0	13.3	14.0	19.6	19.3	11.4	3.4

Note: Figures are percentages and cover owner-occupied housing units; (1) Figures cover the Ann Arbor, MI Metropolitan Statistical Area
Source: U.S. Census Bureau, 2015-2019 American Community Survey 5-Year Estimates

Year Housing Structure Built

Area	2010 or Later	2000 -2009	1990 -1999	1980 -1989	1970 -1979	1960 -1969	1950 -1959	1940 -1949	Before 1940	Median Year
City	3.7	6.3	10.8	10.8	17.2	18.2	12.6	5.0	15.6	1969
MSA[1]	3.7	13.2	17.0	11.5	16.1	12.6	10.1	4.2	11.8	1977
U.S.	5.2	14.0	13.9	13.4	15.2	10.6	10.3	4.9	12.6	1978

Note: Figures are percentages except for Median Year; Note: (1) Figures cover the Ann Arbor, MI Metropolitan Statistical Area
Source: U.S. Census Bureau, 2015-2019 American Community Survey 5-Year Estimates

Gross Monthly Rent

Area	Under $500	$500 -$999	$1,000 -$1,499	$1,500 -$1,999	$2,000 -$2,499	$2,500 -$2,999	$3,000 and up	Median ($)
City	4.6	23.6	39.5	19.8	7.3	2.4	2.8	1,237
MSA[1]	5.5	33.9	37.6	14.7	4.5	1.6	2.2	1,114
U.S.	9.4	36.2	30.0	14.0	5.6	2.4	2.4	1,062

Note: Figures are percentages except for Median; Gross rent is the contract rent plus the estimated average monthly cost of utilities (electricity, gas, and water and sewer) and fuels (oil, coal, kerosene, wood, etc.) if these are paid by the renter (or paid for the renter by someone else); (1) Figures cover the Ann Arbor, MI Metropolitan Statistical Area
Source: U.S. Census Bureau, 2015-2019 American Community Survey 5-Year Estimates

HEALTH

Health Risk Factors

Category	MSA[1] (%)	U.S. (%)
Adults aged 18–64 who have any kind of health care coverage	n/a	87.3
Adults who reported being in good or better health	n/a	82.4
Adults who have been told they have high blood cholesterol	n/a	33.0
Adults who have been told they have high blood pressure	n/a	32.3
Adults who are current smokers	n/a	17.1
Adults who currently use E-cigarettes	n/a	4.6
Adults who currently use chewing tobacco, snuff, or snus	n/a	4.0
Adults who are heavy drinkers[2]	n/a	6.3
Adults who are binge drinkers[3]	n/a	17.4
Adults who are overweight (BMI 25.0 - 29.9)	n/a	35.3
Adults who are obese (BMI 30.0 - 99.8)	n/a	31.3
Adults who participated in any physical activities in the past month	n/a	74.4
Adults who always or nearly always wears a seat belt	n/a	94.3

Note: n/a not available; (1) Figures cover the Ann Arbor, MI Metropolitan Statistical Area; (2) Heavy drinkers are classified as adult men having more than 14 drinks per week and adult women having more than 7 drinks per week; (3) Binge drinkers are classified as males having five or more drinks on one occasion or females having four or more drinks on one occasion
Source: Centers for Disease Control and Prevention, Behaviorial Risk Factor Surveillance System, SMART: Selected Metropolitan Area Risk Trends, 2017

Acute and Chronic Health Conditions

Category	MSA[1] (%)	U.S. (%)
Adults who have ever been told they had a heart attack	n/a	4.2
Adults who have ever been told they have angina or coronary heart disease	n/a	3.9
Adults who have ever been told they had a stroke	n/a	3.0
Adults who have ever been told they have asthma	n/a	14.2
Adults who have ever been told they have arthritis	n/a	24.9
Adults who have ever been told they have diabetes[2]	n/a	10.5
Adults who have ever been told they had skin cancer	n/a	6.2
Adults who have ever been told they had any other types of cancer	n/a	7.1
Adults who have ever been told they have COPD	n/a	6.5
Adults who have ever been told they have kidney disease	n/a	3.0
Adults who have ever been told they have a form of depression	n/a	20.5

Note: n/a not available; (1) Figures cover the Ann Arbor, MI Metropolitan Statistical Area; (2) Figures do not include pregnancy-related, borderline, or pre-diabetes
Source: Centers for Disease Control and Prevention, Behaviorial Risk Factor Surveillance System, SMART: Selected Metropolitan Area Risk Trends, 2017

Health Screening and Vaccination Rates

Category	MSA[1] (%)	U.S. (%)
Adults aged 65+ who have had flu shot within the past year	n/a	60.7
Adults aged 65+ who have ever had a pneumonia vaccination	n/a	75.4
Adults who have ever been tested for HIV	n/a	36.1
Adults who have ever had the shingles or zoster vaccine?	n/a	28.9
Adults who have had their blood cholesterol checked within the last five years	n/a	85.9

Note: n/a not available; (1) Figures cover the Ann Arbor, MI Metropolitan Statistical Area.
Source: Centers for Disease Control and Prevention, Behaviorial Risk Factor Surveillance System, SMART: Selected Metropolitan Area Risk Trends, 2017

Disability Status

Category	MSA[1] (%)	U.S. (%)
Adults who reported being deaf	n/a	6.7
Are you blind or have serious difficulty seeing, even when wearing glasses?	n/a	4.5
Are you limited in any way in any of your usual activities due of arthritis?	n/a	12.9
Do you have difficulty doing errands alone?	n/a	6.8
Do you have difficulty dressing or bathing?	n/a	3.6
Do you have serious difficulty concentrating/remembering/making decisions?	n/a	10.7
Do you have serious difficulty walking or climbing stairs?	n/a	13.6

Note: n/a not available; (1) Figures cover the Ann Arbor, MI Metropolitan Statistical Area.
Source: Centers for Disease Control and Prevention, Behaviorial Risk Factor Surveillance System, SMART: Selected Metropolitan Area Risk Trends, 2017

Mortality Rates for the Top 10 Causes of Death in the U.S.

ICD-10[a] Sub-Chapter	ICD-10[a] Code	Age-Adjusted Mortality Rate[1] per 100,000 population	
		County[2]	U.S.
Malignant neoplasms	C00-C97	135.8	149.2
Ischaemic heart diseases	I20-I25	81.6	90.5
Other forms of heart disease	I30-I51	44.3	52.2
Chronic lower respiratory diseases	J40-J47	26.4	39.6
Other degenerative diseases of the nervous system	G30-G31	44.2	37.6
Cerebrovascular diseases	I60-I69	35.8	37.2
Other external causes of accidental injury	W00-X59	36.7	36.1
Organic, including symptomatic, mental disorders	F01-F09	21.3	29.4
Hypertensive diseases	I10-I15	32.3	24.1
Diabetes mellitus	E10-E14	11.5	21.5

Note: (a) ICD-10 = International Classification of Diseases 10th Revision; (1) Mortality rates are a three-year average covering 2017-2019; (2) Figures cover Washtenaw County.
Source: Centers for Disease Control and Prevention, National Center for Health Statistics. Underlying Cause of Death 1999-2019 on CDC WONDER Online Database

Mortality Rates for Selected Causes of Death

ICD-10[a] Sub-Chapter	ICD-10[a] Code	Age-Adjusted Mortality Rate[1] per 100,000 population	
		County[2]	U.S.
Assault	X85-Y09	3.3	6.0
Diseases of the liver	K70-K76	9.2	14.4
Human immunodeficiency virus (HIV) disease	B20-B24	Suppressed	1.5
Influenza and pneumonia	J09-J18	8.6	13.8
Intentional self-harm	X60-X84	11.2	14.1
Malnutrition	E40-E46	2.3	2.3
Obesity and other hyperalimentation	E65-E68	Suppressed	2.1
Renal failure	N17-N19	10.8	12.6
Transport accidents	V01-V99	7.0	12.3
Viral hepatitis	B15-B19	Unreliable	1.2

Note: (a) ICD-10 = International Classification of Diseases 10th Revision; (1) Mortality rates are a three-year average covering 2017-2019; (2) Figures cover Washtenaw County; Data are suppressed when the data meet the criteria for confidentiality constraints; Mortality rates are flagged as unreliable when the rate would be calculated with a numerator of 20 or less.
Source: Centers for Disease Control and Prevention, National Center for Health Statistics. Underlying Cause of Death 1999-2019 on CDC WONDER Online Database

Health Insurance Coverage

Area	With Health Insurance	With Private Health Insurance	With Public Health Insurance	Without Health Insurance	Population Under Age 19 Without Health Insurance
City	97.3	87.7	19.7	2.7	1.1
MSA[1]	96.5	83.3	25.9	3.5	1.8
U.S.	91.2	67.9	35.1	8.8	5.1

Note: Figures are percentages that cover the civilian noninstitutionalized population; (1) Figures cover the Ann Arbor, MI Metropolitan Statistical Area
Source: U.S. Census Bureau, 2015-2019 American Community Survey 5-Year Estimates

Number of Medical Professionals

Area	MDs[3]	DOs[3,4]	Dentists	Podiatrists	Chiropractors	Optometrists
County[1] (number)	4,701	153	674	27	98	63
County[1] (rate[2])	1,272.3	41.4	183.4	7.3	26.7	17.1
U.S. (rate[2])	282.9	22.7	71.2	6.2	28.1	16.9

26161
Note: Data as of 2019 unless noted; (1) Data covers Washtenaw County; (2) Rate per 100,000 population; (3) Data as of 2018 and includes all active, non-federal physicians; (4) Doctor of Osteopathic Medicine
Source: U.S. Department of Health and Human Services, Health Resources and Services Administration, Bureau of Health Professions, Area Resource File (ARF) 2019-2020

Best Hospitals

According to *U.S. News*, the Ann Arbor, MI metro area is home to one of the best hospitals in the U.S.: **University of Michigan Hospitals-Michigan Medicine** (Honor Roll/13 adult specialties and 10 pediatric specialties). The hospital listed was nationally ranked in at least one of 16 adult or 10 pediatric specialties. Only 134 hospitals nationwide were nationally ranked in one or more adult or pediatric specialty; this number increases to 178 counting specialized centers within hospitals. Twenty hospitals in the U.S. made the Honor Roll. The Best Hospitals Honor Roll takes both the national rankings and the procedure and condition ratings into account. Hospitals received points if they were nationally ranked in one of the 16 adult specialties—the higher they ranked, the more points they

16 Ann Arbor, Michigan

got—and how many ratings of "high performing" they earned in the 10 procedures and conditions. *U.S. News Online, "America's Best Hospitals 2020-21"*

According to *U.S. News,* the Ann Arbor, MI metro area is home to one of the best children's hospitals in the U.S.: **C.S. Mott Children's Hospital-Michigan Medicine** (10 pediatric specialties). The hospital listed was highly ranked in at least one of 10 pediatric specialties. Eighty-eight children's hospitals in the U.S. were nationally ranked in at least one specialty. Hospitals received points for being ranked in a specialty, and the 10 hospitals with the most points across the 10 specialties make up the Honor Roll. *U.S. News Online, "America's Best Children's Hospitals 2020-21"*

EDUCATION

Public School District Statistics

District Name	Schls	Pupils	Pupil/ Teacher Ratio	Minority Pupils[1] (%)	Free Lunch Eligible[2] (%)	IEP[3] (%)
Ann Arbor Public Schools	33	18,054	15.3	48.6	22.2	11.9

Note: Table includes school districts with 2,000 or more students; (1) Percentage of students that are not non-Hispanic white; (2) Percentage of students that are eligible for the free lunch program; (3) Percentage of students that have an Individualized Education Program.
Source: U.S. Department of Education, National Center for Education Statistics, Common Core of Data, Local Education Agency (School District) Universe Survey: School Year 2018-2019; U.S. Department of Education, National Center for Education Statistics, Common Core of Data, Public Elementary/Secondary School Universe Survey: School Year 2018-2019

Highest Level of Education

Area	Less than H.S.	H.S. Diploma	Some College, No Deg.	Associate Degree	Bachelor's Degree	Master's Degree	Prof. School Degree	Doctorate Degree
City	2.7	7.1	10.0	4.2	30.2	26.9	7.1	11.7
MSA[1]	4.7	14.6	17.6	7.1	26.3	18.8	4.7	6.0
U.S.	12.0	27.0	20.4	8.5	19.8	8.8	2.1	1.4

Note: Figures cover persons age 25 and over; (1) Figures cover the Ann Arbor, MI Metropolitan Statistical Area
Source: U.S. Census Bureau, 2015-2019 American Community Survey 5-Year Estimates

Educational Attainment by Race

Area	High School Graduate or Higher (%)					Bachelor's Degree or Higher (%)				
	Total	White	Black	Asian	Hisp.[2]	Total	White	Black	Asian	Hisp.[2]
City	97.3	98.1	90.6	97.8	92.0	76.0	78.4	38.2	86.4	68.6
MSA[1]	95.3	96.3	89.2	96.6	85.5	55.9	57.7	27.4	83.0	42.9
U.S.	88.0	89.9	86.0	87.1	68.7	32.1	33.5	21.6	54.3	16.4

Note: Figures shown cover persons 25 years old and over; (1) Figures cover the Ann Arbor, MI Metropolitan Statistical Area; (2) People of Hispanic origin can be of any race
Source: U.S. Census Bureau, 2015-2019 American Community Survey 5-Year Estimates

School Enrollment by Grade and Control

Area	Preschool (%)		Kindergarten (%)		Grades 1 - 4 (%)		Grades 5 - 8 (%)		Grades 9 - 12 (%)	
	Public	Private	Public	Private	Public	Private	Public	Private	Public	Private
City	25.7	74.3	94.1	5.9	91.8	8.2	87.6	12.4	94.2	5.8
MSA[1]	49.6	50.4	89.6	10.4	87.3	12.7	87.7	12.3	91.8	8.2
U.S.	59.1	40.9	87.6	12.4	89.5	10.5	89.4	10.6	90.1	9.9

Note: Figures shown cover persons 3 years old and over; (1) Figures cover the Ann Arbor, MI Metropolitan Statistical Area
Source: U.S. Census Bureau, 2015-2019 American Community Survey 5-Year Estimates

Higher Education

Four-Year Colleges			Two-Year Colleges			Medical Schools[1]	Law Schools[2]	Voc/ Tech[3]
Public	Private Non-profit	Private For-profit	Public	Private Non-profit	Private For-profit			
1	1	0	1	0	0	1	1	1

Note: Figures cover institutions located within the city limits and include main campuses only; (1) includes schools accredited by the Liaison Committee on Medical Education and the American Osteopathic Association's Commission on Osteopathic College Accreditation; (2) includes ABA-accredited schools, schools with provisional ABA accreditation, and state accredited schools; (3) includes all schools with programs that are less than 2 years.
Source: National Center for Education Statistics, Integrated Postsecondary Education System (IPEDS), 2019-20; Wikipedia, List of Medical Schools in the United States, accessed April 2, 2021; Wikipedia, List of Law Schools in the United States, accessed April 2, 2021

According to *U.S. News & World Report,* the Ann Arbor, MI metro area is home to one of the top 200 national universities in the U.S.: **University of Michigan—Ann Arbor** (#24 tie). The indicators used to capture academic quality fall into a number of categories: assessment by administrators at peer institutions; retention of students; faculty resources; student selectivity; financial resources;

alumni giving; high school counselor ratings of colleges; and graduation rate. *U.S. News & World Report, "America's Best Colleges 2021"*

According to *U.S. News & World Report,* the Ann Arbor, MI metro area is home to one of the top 100 law schools in the U.S.: **University of Michigan—Ann Arbor** (#10 tie). The rankings are based on a weighted average of 12 measures of quality: peer assessment score; assessment score by lawyers/judges; median LSAT scores; median undergrad GPA; acceptance rate; employment rates for graduates; placement success; bar passage rate; faculty resources; expenditures per student; student/faculty ratio; and library resources. *U.S. News & World Report, "America's Best Graduate Schools, Law, 2022"*

According to *U.S. News & World Report,* the Ann Arbor, MI metro area is home to one of the top 75 medical schools for research in the U.S.: **University of Michigan—Ann Arbor** (#15 tie). The rankings are based on a weighted average of 11 measures of quality: quality assessment; peer assessment score; assessment score by residency directors; research activity; total research activity; average research activity per faculty member; student selectivity; median MCAT total score; median undergraduate GPA; acceptance rate; and faculty resources. *U.S. News & World Report, "America's Best Graduate Schools, Medical, 2022"*

According to *U.S. News & World Report,* the Ann Arbor, MI metro area is home to one of the top 75 business schools in the U.S.: **University of Michigan—Ann Arbor (Ross)** (#13 tie). The rankings are based on a weighted average of the following nine measures: quality assessment; peer assessment; recruiter assessment; placement success; mean starting salary and bonus; student selectivity; mean GMAT and GRE scores; mean undergraduate GPA; and acceptance rate. *U.S. News & World Report, "America's Best Graduate Schools, Business, 2022"*

EMPLOYERS

Major Employers

Company Name	Industry
Ann Arbor Public Schools	Education
Citizens Insurance Company of America	FInance & insurance
City of Ann Arbor	Municipal government
Domino's Pizza	Food services
Eastern Michigan University	Education
Faurecia Interior Systems	Automotive component mfg.
Ford Motor Company	Automotive component mfg.
General Motors Milford Proving Grounds	OEM research
Grupo Antolin	Automotive component mfg.
Integrated Health Associates (IHA)	Medical center
JAC Products	Auto component mfg.
ProQuest	Data & information
Terumo Carviocascular Systems	Medical device manufacturer
Thai Summit America	Automotive component mfg.
Thomson Reuters	Software/IT
Toyota Technical Center	Automotive research & development
Trinity Health	Medical center
Truven Health Analytics	Data & information
University of Michigan	Education
University of Michigan Medical Center	Medical center
VA Ann Arbor Healthcare System	Medical center
Washtenaw Community College	Education
Washtenaw County Government	Government
Ypsilanti Public Schools	Education
Zingerman's	Food processing

Note: Companies shown are located within the Ann Arbor, MI Metropolitan Statistical Area.
Source: Hoovers.com; Wikipedia

PUBLIC SAFETY

Crime Rate

Area	All Crimes	Violent Crimes				Property Crimes		
		Murder	Rape[3]	Robbery	Aggrav. Assault	Burglary	Larceny -Theft	Motor Vehicle Theft
City	1,979.8	1.6	62.7	37.4	149.7	160.3	1,455.7	112.3
Suburbs[1]	2,017.9	2.4	69.1	38.7	296.3	218.0	1,258.3	135.0
Metro[2]	2,005.3	2.1	67.0	38.3	248.1	199.0	1,323.3	127.5
U.S.	2,489.3	5.0	42.6	81.6	250.2	340.5	1,549.5	219.9

Note: Figures are crimes per 100,000 population; (1) All areas within the metro area that are located outside the city limits; (2) Figures cover the Ann Arbor, MI Metropolitan Statistical Area; (3) All figures shown were reported using the revised Uniform Crime Reporting (UCR) definition of rape.
Source: FBI Uniform Crime Reports, 2019

Hate Crimes

Area	Number of Quarters Reported	Number of Incidents per Bias Motivation					
		Race/Ethnicity/Ancestry	Religion	Sexual Orientation	Disability	Gender	Gender Identity
City	4	3	0	0	0	0	0
U.S.	4	3,963	1,521	1,195	157	69	198

Source: Federal Bureau of Investigation, Hate Crime Statistics 2019

Identity Theft Consumer Reports

Area	Reports	Reports per 100,000 Population	Rank[2]
MSA[1]	1,215	331	103
U.S.	1,387,615	423	-

Note: (1) Figures cover the Ann Arbor, MI Metropolitan Statistical Area; (2) Rank ranges from 1 to 391 where 1 indicates greatest number of identity theft reports per 100,000 population
Source: Federal Trade Commission, Consumer Sentinel Network Data Book 2020

Fraud and Other Consumer Reports

Area	Reports	Reports per 100,000 Population	Rank[2]
MSA[1]	2,675	728	163
U.S.	3,385,133	1,031	-

Note: (1) Figures cover the Ann Arbor, MI Metropolitan Statistical Area; (2) Rank ranges from 1 to 391 where 1 indicates greatest number of fraud and other consumer reports per 100,000 population
Source: Federal Trade Commission, Consumer Sentinel Network Data Book 2020

POLITICS

2020 Presidential Election Results

Area	Biden	Trump	Jorgensen	Hawkins	Other
Washtenaw County	72.4	25.9	0.9	0.3	0.4
U.S.	51.3	46.8	1.2	0.3	0.5

Note: Results are percentages and may not add to 100% due to rounding
Source: Dave Leip's Atlas of U.S. Presidential Elections

SPORTS

Professional Sports Teams

Team Name	League	Year Established
No teams are located in the metro area		

Source: Wikipedia, Major Professional Sports Teams of the United States and Canada, April 6, 2021

CLIMATE

Average and Extreme Temperatures

Temperature	Jan	Feb	Mar	Apr	May	Jun	Jul	Aug	Sep	Oct	Nov	Dec	Yr.
Extreme High (°F)	62	65	81	89	93	104	102	100	98	91	77	68	104
Average High (°F)	30	33	44	58	70	79	83	81	74	61	48	35	58
Average Temp. (°F)	23	26	36	48	59	68	72	71	64	52	40	29	49
Average Low (°F)	16	18	27	37	47	56	61	60	53	41	32	21	39
Extreme Low (°F)	-21	-15	-4	10	25	36	41	38	29	17	9	-10	-21

Note: Figures cover the years 1958-1990
Source: National Climatic Data Center, International Station Meteorological Climate Summary, 9/96

Average Precipitation/Snowfall/Humidity

Precip./Humidity	Jan	Feb	Mar	Apr	May	Jun	Jul	Aug	Sep	Oct	Nov	Dec	Yr.
Avg. Precip. (in.)	1.8	1.8	2.5	3.0	2.9	3.6	3.1	3.4	2.8	2.2	2.6	2.7	32.4
Avg. Snowfall (in.)	10	9	7	2	Tr	0	0	0	0	Tr	3	11	41
Avg. Rel. Hum. 7am (%)	80	79	79	78	78	79	82	86	87	84	82	81	81
Avg. Rel. Hum. 4pm (%)	67	63	59	53	51	52	52	54	55	55	64	70	58

Note: Figures cover the years 1958-1990; Tr = Trace amounts (<0.05 in. of rain; <0.5 in. of snow)
Source: National Climatic Data Center, International Station Meteorological Climate Summary, 9/96

Weather Conditions

Temperature			Daytime Sky			Precipitation		
5°F & below	32°F & below	90°F & above	Clear	Partly cloudy	Cloudy	0.01 inch or more precip.	0.1 inch or more snow/ice	Thunderstorms
15	136	12	74	134	157	135	38	32

Note: Figures are average number of days per year and cover the years 1958-1990
Source: National Climatic Data Center, International Station Meteorological Climate Summary, 9/96

Ann Arbor, Michigan   **19**

HAZARDOUS WASTE   **Superfund Sites**

The Ann Arbor, MI metro area has no sites on the EPA's Superfund Final National Priorities List. There are a total of 1,375 Superfund sites with a status of proposed or final on the list in the U.S. *U.S. Environmental Protection Agency, National Priorities List, April 7, 2021*

AIR QUALITY   **Air Quality Trends: Ozone**

	1990	1995	2000	2005	2010	2015	2016	2017	2018	2019
MSA[1]	n/a	n/a	n/a	n/a	n/a	n/a	n/a	n/a	n/a	n/a
U.S.	0.088	0.089	0.082	0.080	0.073	0.068	0.069	0.068	0.069	0.065

Note: (1) Data covers the Ann Arbor, MI Metropolitan Statistical Area; n/a not available. The values shown are the composite ozone concentration averages among trend sites based on the highest fourth daily maximum 8-hour concentration in parts per million. These trends are based on sites having an adequate record of monitoring data during the trend period. Data from exceptional events are included.
Source: U.S. Environmental Protection Agency, Air Quality Monitoring Information, "Air Quality Trends by City, 1990-2019"

Air Quality Index

Area	Percent of Days when Air Quality was...[2]					AQI Statistics[2]	
	Good	Moderate	Unhealthy for Sensitive Groups	Unhealthy	Very Unhealthy	Maximum	Median
MSA[1]	80.5	19.5	0.0	0.0	0.0	88	39

Note: (1) Data covers the Ann Arbor, MI Metropolitan Statistical Area; (2) Based on 365 days with AQI data in 2019. Air Quality Index (AQI) is an index for reporting daily air quality. EPA calculates the AQI for five major air pollutants regulated by the Clean Air Act: ground-level ozone, particle pollution (aka particulate matter), carbon monoxide, sulfur dioxide, and nitrogen dioxide. The AQI runs from 0 to 500. The higher the AQI value, the greater the level of air pollution and the greater the health concern. There are six AQI categories: "Good" AQI is between 0 and 50. Air quality is considered satisfactory; "Moderate" AQI is between 51 and 100. Air quality is acceptable; "Unhealthy for Sensitive Groups" When AQI values are between 101 and 150, members of sensitive groups may experience health effects; "Unhealthy" When AQI values are between 151 and 200 everyone may begin to experience health effects; "Very Unhealthy" AQI values between 201 and 300 trigger a health alert; "Hazardous" AQI values over 300 trigger warnings of emergency conditions (not shown).
Source: U.S. Environmental Protection Agency, Air Quality Index Report, 2019

Air Quality Index Pollutants

Area	Percent of Days when AQI Pollutant was...[2]					
	Carbon Monoxide	Nitrogen Dioxide	Ozone	Sulfur Dioxide	Particulate Matter 2.5	Particulate Matter 10
MSA[1]	0.0	0.0	66.6	0.0	33.4	0.0

Note: (1) Data covers the Ann Arbor, MI Metropolitan Statistical Area; (2) Based on 365 days with AQI data in 2019. The Air Quality Index (AQI) is an index for reporting daily air quality. EPA calculates the AQI for five major air pollutants regulated by the Clean Air Act: ground-level ozone, particle pollution (also known as particulate matter), carbon monoxide, sulfur dioxide, and nitrogen dioxide. The AQI runs from 0 to 500. The higher the AQI value, the greater the level of air pollution and the greater the health concern.
Source: U.S. Environmental Protection Agency, Air Quality Index Report, 2019

Maximum Air Pollutant Concentrations: Particulate Matter, Ozone, CO and Lead

	Particulate Matter 10 (ug/m^3)	Particulate Matter 2.5 Wtd AM (ug/m^3)	Particulate Matter 2.5 24-Hr (ug/m^3)	Ozone (ppm)	Carbon Monoxide (ppm)	Lead (ug/m^3)
MSA[1] Level	n/a	8.5	22	0.060	n/a	n/a
NAAQS[2]	150	15	35	0.075	9	0.15
Met NAAQS[2]	n/a	Yes	Yes	Yes	n/a	n/a

Note: (1) Data covers the Ann Arbor, MI Metropolitan Statistical Area; Data from exceptional events are included; (2) National Ambient Air Quality Standards; ppm = parts per million; ug/m^3 = micrograms per cubic meter; n/a not available.
Concentrations: Particulate Matter 10 (coarse particulate)—highest second maximum 24-hour concentration; Particulate Matter 2.5 Wtd AM (fine particulate)—highest weighted annual mean concentration; Particulate Matter 2.5 24-Hour (fine particulate)—highest 98th percentile 24-hour concentration; Ozone—highest fourth daily maximum 8-hour concentration; Carbon Monoxide—highest second maximum non-overlapping 8-hour concentration; Lead—maximum running 3-month average
Source: U.S. Environmental Protection Agency, Air Quality Monitoring Information, "Air Quality Statistics by City, 2019"

Maximum Air Pollutant Concentrations: Nitrogen Dioxide and Sulfur Dioxide

	Nitrogen Dioxide AM (ppb)	Nitrogen Dioxide 1-Hr (ppb)	Sulfur Dioxide AM (ppb)	Sulfur Dioxide 1-Hr (ppb)	Sulfur Dioxide 24-Hr (ppb)
MSA[1] Level	n/a	n/a	n/a	n/a	n/a
NAAQS[2]	53	100	30	75	140
Met NAAQS[2]	n/a	n/a	n/a	n/a	n/a

Note: (1) Data covers the Ann Arbor, MI Metropolitan Statistical Area; Data from exceptional events are included; (2) National Ambient Air Quality Standards; ppm = parts per million; ug/m³ = micrograms per cubic meter; n/a not available.

Concentrations: Nitrogen Dioxide AM—highest arithmetic mean concentration; Nitrogen Dioxide 1-Hr—highest 98th percentile 1-hour daily maximum concentration; Sulfur Dioxide AM—highest annual mean concentration; Sulfur Dioxide 1-Hr—highest 99th percentile 1-hour daily maximum concentration; Sulfur Dioxide 24-Hr—highest second maximum 24-hour concentration

Source: U.S. Environmental Protection Agency, Air Quality Monitoring Information, "Air Quality Statistics by City, 2019"

Cedar Rapids, Iowa

Background

Cedar Rapids, on the Cedar River that gave it its name, is the principal city in eastern Iowa, located some 100 miles northeast of Des Moines. The Cedar Rapids of today is one of the Midwest's most diversified and modern cities.

Prior to European expansion, the site was intermittently home to nomadic bands of Fox, Meskwaki, and Winnebago Indians. Its first western settler was Osgood Shephard, a hunter, trapper, and horse trader who lived in a cabin on the river at the current corner of First Avenue and First Street SE. A stainless-steel sculpture, The Tree of Five Seasons, commemorates Shephard's first settlement, and is a common point of reference for the city's citizens.

Cedar Rapids, first called Rapids City, was incorporated as a town in 1849 and as a city in 1856. By 1858 the city boasted a population of 1,400. Both in the city itself and in the immediate environs, one is exposed to rich ethnic traditions and a pride in the preservation of local performing and visual arts.

Cedar Rapids, distinctively, was the first home of the North Star Oatmeal Mill, which eventually became Quaker Oats, long a giant in the cereal industry. The Cedar Rapids-based company still operates, under one roof, the largest cereal mill in the world.

The city has extensively diversified, however, from its original agricultural focus. Many industries, both locally and internationally owned, provide stability and dynamism to the local economy, which is increasingly tied into a larger global framework. Cedar Rapids also hosts industries specializing in food processing, construction machinery, pharmaceuticals, financial services, and biotechnology, and is one of the largest exporter per capita in the United States, with the nearby Eastern Iowa Airport designated as a foreign trade zone. The city has also become a major telecommunications hub.

Cedar Rapids is home to Coe College, founded in 1851, and Mount Mercy College, founded in 1928. The National Capital Language Resource Center (NCLRC) in Washington DC maintains 93 schools that teach Arabic, one of which is in Cedar Rapids. The town also benefits from the presence of the Cedar Rapids Museum of Art, the Cedar Rapids Symphony Orchestra, the Science Station, which boasts the first IMAX Theater in Iowa, the History Center, and the National Czech and Slovak Museum and Library. Other area attractions include Duffy's Collectible Cars, Brucemore Mansion, the Iowa Children's Museum, the Indian Creek Nature Center, and the Czech Village. Government buildings are located on Municipal Island in the main channel of the Cedar River. Within a half-hour's drive are 75 public parks and seven public golf courses.

Nearby are several points of historical interest, including the Herbert Hoover Birthplace and Library, and the Amana Colonies, founded in the 1850s as a utopian society by members of a German religious sect. At the Amana villages, visitors can still view the operations of working farms, wool mills, and bakeries. Cedar Rapids is also the home to a large number of American Muslims. The oldest exclusively Muslim cemetery in the United States is located in Cedar Rapids, along with the historic Mother Mosque of America.

Grant Wood—the famous painter of *American Gothic* and other icons of the Great Plains—was a resident of the city and taught there for many years. Many of his canvases are on display and others are owned by private citizens. The Cedar Rapids Museum houses 7,200 works of art, including the world's largest collections of works by Wood, Marvin D. Cone, and Mauricio Lasansky. The Museum also operates the Grant Wood Studio and Visitor Center.

In June 2008, the Cedar River flooded its banks, leaving 1,300 city blocks under water. The city was almost entirely evacuated and hundreds of homes were destroyed. Rebuilding efforts have been strong and a restored City Hall and Paramount Theater opened in 2012, with many other facilities opening in 2013, including fire stations, the library, and the ground transportation center.

In September 2016, when Hurricane Paine threatened to flood Cedar Rapids again, the residents were prepared as hundreds of thousands of volunteers, as well as over 400 National Guard troops, filled more than 250,000 sand bags which effectively prevented major flooding of the city. In 2020 an intense derecho (wind storm) caused major damage to the city.

There are four distinct seasons in Cedar Rapids. Winters are cold and dry, with winds out of the northwest. Some summer days bring rain from the Gulf of Mexico, but on other days hot dry air from the southwest can cause unusually high temperatures. Fall and spring can be mild, tempered by air from the Pacific. Precipitation throughout the year is moderate.

Rankings

General Rankings

- In their seventh annual survey, Livability.com looked at data for more than 1,000 small to mid-sized U.S. cities to determine the rankings for Livability's "Top 100 Best Places to Live" in 2020. Cedar Rapids ranked #94. Criteria: housing and affordable living; vibrant economy; social and civic engagement; education; demographics; health care options; transportation & infrastructure; and abundant lifestyle amenities. *Livability.com, "Top 100 Best Places to Live 2020" October 2020*

Business/Finance Rankings

- The Cedar Rapids metro area appeared on the Milken Institute "2021 Best Performing Cities" list. Rank: #141 out of 200 large metro areas (population over 250,000). Criteria: job growth; wage and salary growth; high-tech output growth; housing affordability; household broadband access. *Milken Institute, "Best-Performing Cities 2021," February 16, 2021*

- *Forbes* ranked the 200 most populous metro areas to determine the nation's "Best Places for Business and Careers." The Cedar Rapids metro area was ranked #154. Criteria: costs (business and living); job growth (past and projected); income growth; quality of life; educational attainment (college and high school); projected economic growth; cultural and leisure opportunities; workplace tolerance laws; net migration patterns. *Forbes, "The Best Places for Business and Careers 2019: Seattle Still On Top," October 30, 2019*

Health/Fitness Rankings

- The Cedar Rapids metro area was identified as one of the worst cities for bed bugs in America by pest control company Orkin. The area ranked #35 out of 50 based on the number of bed bug treatments Orkin performed from December 2019 to November 2020. *Orkin, "New Year, New Top City on Orkin's 2021 Bed Bug Cities List: Chicago," February 1, 2021*

Real Estate Rankings

- *WalletHub* compared the most populated U.S. cities to determine which had the best markets for real estate agents. Cedar Rapids ranked #141 where demand was high and pay was the best. Criteria: sales per agent; annual median wage for real-estate agents; monthly average starting salary for real estate agents; real estate job density and competition; unemployment rate; home turnover rate; housing-market health index; and other relevant metrics. *www.WalletHub.com, "2019's Best Places to Be a Real Estate Agent," April 24, 2019*

- The Cedar Rapids metro area was identified as one of the 20 worst housing markets in the U.S. in 2020. The area ranked #172 out of 180 markets. Criteria: year-over-year change of median sales price of existing single-family homes between the 4th quarter of 2019 and the 4th quarter of 2020. *National Association of Realtors®, Median Sales Price of Existing Single-Family Homes for Metropolitan Areas, 4th Quarter 2020*

Safety Rankings

- The National Insurance Crime Bureau ranked 384 metro areas in the U.S. in terms of per capita rates of vehicle theft. The Cedar Rapids metro area ranked #159 (#1 = highest rate). Criteria: number of vehicle theft offenses per 100,000 inhabitants in 2019. *National Insurance Crime Bureau, "Hot Spots 2019," July 21, 2020*

Seniors/Retirement Rankings

- From its Best Cities for Successful Aging indexes, the Milken Institute generated rankings for metropolitan areas, weighing data in nine categories—health care, wellness, living arrangements, transportation and convenience, financial characteristics, education, employment, community engagement, and overall livability. The Cedar Rapids metro area was ranked #82 overall in the small metro area category. *Milken Institute, "Best Cities for Successful Aging, 2017" March 14, 2017*

Women/Minorities Rankings

- Personal finance website *WalletHub* compared more than 180 U.S. cities across two key dimensions, "Hispanic Business-Friendliness" and "Hispanic Purchasing Power," to arrive at the most favorable conditions for Hispanic entrepreneurs. Cedar Rapids was ranked #89 out of 182. Criteria includes: share of Hispanic-Owned Businesses; Hispanic entrepreneurship rate to median annual income of Hispanics; Small Business-Friendliness score; cost of living; and number of Hispanics with at least a bachelor's degree. *WalletHub.com, "2019's Best Cities for Hispanic Entrepreneurs," May 1, 2019*

Miscellaneous Rankings

- *WalletHub* compared the 150 most populated U.S. cities to determine their operating efficiency. A "Quality of City Services" score was constructed for each city and then divided by the total budget per capita to reveal which were managed the best. Cedar Rapids ranked #14. Criteria: financial stability; economy; education; safety; health; infrastructure and pollution. *www.WalletHub.com, "2020's Best- & Worst-Run Cities in America," June 29, 2020*

Business Environment

DEMOGRAPHICS

Population Growth

Area	1990 Census	2000 Census	2010 Census	2019* Estimate	Population Growth (%)	
					1990-2019	2010-2019
City	110,829	120,758	126,326	132,301	19.4	4.7
MSA[1]	210,640	237,230	257,940	270,056	28.2	4.7
U.S.	248,709,873	281,421,906	308,745,538	324,697,795	30.6	5.2

Note: (1) Figures cover the Cedar Rapids, IA Metropolitan Statistical Area; (*) 2015-2019 5-year estimated population
Source: U.S. Census Bureau, 1990 Census, Census 2000, Census 2010, 2015-2019 American Community Survey 5-Year Estimates

Household Size

Area	Persons in Household (%)							Average Household Size
	One	Two	Three	Four	Five	Six	Seven or More	
City	34.2	33.9	14.0	10.6	4.5	2.2	0.6	2.30
MSA[1]	29.7	36.5	13.8	12.0	5.0	2.1	0.8	2.40
U.S.	27.9	33.9	15.6	12.9	6.0	2.3	1.4	2.60

Note: (1) Figures cover the Cedar Rapids, IA Metropolitan Statistical Area
Source: U.S. Census Bureau, 2015-2019 American Community Survey 5-Year Estimates

Race

Area	White Alone[2] (%)	Black Alone[2] (%)	Asian Alone[2] (%)	AIAN[3] Alone[2] (%)	NHOPI[4] Alone[2] (%)	Other Race Alone[2] (%)	Two or More Races (%)
City	83.9	7.8	2.9	0.3	0.2	1.1	3.8
MSA[1]	89.4	4.8	2.0	0.2	0.1	0.7	2.8
U.S.	72.5	12.7	5.5	0.8	0.2	4.9	3.3

Note: (1) Figures cover the Cedar Rapids, IA Metropolitan Statistical Area; (2) Alone is defined as not being in combination with one or more other races; (3) American Indian and Alaska Native; (4) Native Hawaiian and Other Pacific Islander
Source: U.S. Census Bureau, 2015-2019 American Community Survey 5-Year Estimates

Hispanic or Latino Origin

Area	Total (%)	Mexican (%)	Puerto Rican (%)	Cuban (%)	Other (%)
City	4.0	2.8	0.2	0.0	1.0
MSA[1]	3.0	2.1	0.1	0.0	0.8
U.S.	18.0	11.2	1.7	0.7	4.3

Note: Persons of Hispanic or Latino origin can be of any race; (1) Figures cover the Cedar Rapids, IA Metropolitan Statistical Area
Source: U.S. Census Bureau, 2015-2019 American Community Survey 5-Year Estimates

Ancestry

Area	German	Irish	English	American	Italian	Polish	French[2]	Scottish	Dutch
City	30.6	13.8	7.8	4.5	1.9	1.6	2.3	1.6	1.9
MSA[1]	34.2	14.5	8.0	4.7	1.9	1.2	2.4	1.5	2.0
U.S.	13.3	9.7	7.2	6.2	5.1	2.8	2.3	1.7	1.2

Note: Figures are the percentage of the total population reporting a particular ancestry. The nine most commonly reported ancestries in the U.S. are shown. Figures include multiple ancestries (e.g. if a person reported being Irish and Italian, they were included in both columns); (1) Figures cover the Cedar Rapids, IA Metropolitan Statistical Area; (2) Excludes Basque
Source: U.S. Census Bureau, 2015-2019 American Community Survey 5-Year Estimates

Foreign-born Population

Area	Percent of Population Born in								
	Any Foreign Country	Asia	Mexico	Europe	Caribbean	Central America[2]	South America	Africa	Canada
City	6.1	2.7	0.7	0.5	0.1	0.1	0.2	1.5	0.1
MSA[1]	3.8	1.8	0.5	0.4	0.1	0.1	0.1	0.8	0.1
U.S.	13.6	4.2	3.5	1.5	1.3	1.1	1.0	0.7	0.2

Note: (1) Figures cover the Cedar Rapids, IA Metropolitan Statistical Area; (2) Excludes Mexico.
Source: U.S. Census Bureau, 2015-2019 American Community Survey 5-Year Estimates

Cedar Rapids, Iowa   25

Marital Status

Area	Never Married	Now Married[2]	Separated	Widowed	Divorced
City	35.2	45.7	1.0	6.0	12.1
MSA[1]	30.0	52.0	0.9	5.8	11.2
U.S.	33.4	48.1	1.9	5.8	10.9

Note: Figures are percentages and cover the population 15 years of age and older; (1) Figures cover the Cedar Rapids, IA Metropolitan Statistical Area; (2) Excludes separated
Source: U.S. Census Bureau, 2015-2019 American Community Survey 5-Year Estimates

Disability by Age

Area	All Ages	Under 18 Years Old	18 to 64 Years Old	65 Years and Over
City	10.6	3.5	8.5	29.7
MSA[1]	10.4	3.6	8.1	29.8
U.S.	12.6	4.2	10.3	34.5

Note: Figures show percent of the civilian noninstitutionalized population that reported having a disability. Disability status is determined from six types of difficulty: vision, hearing, cognitive, ambulatory, self-care, and independent living. For children under 5 years old, hearing and vision difficulty are used to determine disability status. For children between the ages of 5 and 14, disability status is determined from hearing, vision, cognitive, ambulatory, and self-care difficulties. For people aged 15 years and older, they are considered to have a disability if they have difficulty with any one of the six difficulty types; Note: (1) Figures cover the Cedar Rapids, IA Metropolitan Statistical Area
Source: U.S. Census Bureau, 2015-2019 American Community Survey 5-Year Estimates

Age

Area	Percent of Population									Median Age
	Under Age 5	Age 5–19	Age 20–34	Age 35–44	Age 45–54	Age 55–64	Age 65–74	Age 75–84	Age 85+	
City	6.5	18.9	22.8	13.0	11.6	11.9	8.4	4.4	2.4	36.3
MSA[1]	6.2	19.5	19.6	12.7	12.9	12.9	9.0	4.8	2.3	38.4
U.S.	6.1	19.1	20.7	12.6	13.0	12.9	9.1	4.6	1.9	38.1

Note: (1) Figures cover the Cedar Rapids, IA Metropolitan Statistical Area
Source: U.S. Census Bureau, 2015-2019 American Community Survey 5-Year Estimates

Gender

Area	Males	Females	Males per 100 Females
City	64,863	67,438	96.2
MSA[1]	133,800	136,256	98.2
U.S.	159,886,919	164,810,876	97.0

Note: (1) Figures cover the Cedar Rapids, IA Metropolitan Statistical Area
Source: U.S. Census Bureau, 2015-2019 American Community Survey 5-Year Estimates

Religious Groups by Family

Area	Catholic	Baptist	Non-Den.	Methodist[2]	Lutheran	LDS[3]	Pente-costal	Presby-terian[4]	Muslim[5]	Judaism
MSA[1]	18.8	2.4	3.0	7.3	11.3	0.9	1.8	3.3	0.5	0.1
U.S.	19.1	9.3	4.0	4.0	2.3	2.0	1.9	1.6	0.8	0.7

Note: Figures are the number of adherents as a percentage of the total population; (1) Figures cover the Cedar Rapids, IA Metropolitan Statistical Area; (2) Methodist/Pietist; (3) Latter Day Saints; (4) Reformed; (5) Figures are estimates
Source: Association of Statisticians of American Religious Bodies, 2010 U.S. Religion Census: Religious Congregations & Membership Study

Religious Groups by Tradition

Area	Catholic	Evangelical Protestant	Mainline Protestant	Other Tradition	Black Protestant	Orthodox
MSA[1]	18.8	13.7	17.5	2.0	0.2	0.2
U.S.	19.1	16.2	7.3	4.3	1.6	0.3

Note: Figures are the number of adherents as a percentage of the total population; (1) Figures cover the Cedar Rapids, IA Metropolitan Statistical Area
Source: Association of Statisticians of American Religious Bodies, 2010 U.S. Religion Census: Religious Congregations & Membership Study

ECONOMY

Gross Metropolitan Product

Area	2017	2018	2019	2020	Rank[2]
MSA[1]	17.8	18.4	18.8	19.4	141

Note: Figures are in billions of dollars; (1) Figures cover the Cedar Rapids, IA Metropolitan Statistical Area; (2) Rank is based on 2018 data and ranges from 1 to 381
Source: U.S. Conference of Mayors, U.S. Metro Economies: GMP & Employment 2018-2020, September 2019

26   Cedar Rapids, Iowa

Economic Growth

Area	2015-17 (%)	2018 (%)	2019 (%)	2020 (%)	Rank[2]
MSA[1]	-1.6	0.9	0.8	1.0	354
U.S.	1.9	2.9	2.3	2.1	—

Note: Figures are real gross metropolitan product (GMP) growth rates and represent average annual percent change; (1) Figures cover the Cedar Rapids, IA Metropolitan Statistical Area; (2) Rank is based on 2017 2-year average annual percent change and ranges from 1 to 381
Source: U.S. Conference of Mayors, U.S. Metro Economies: GMP & Employment 2018-2020, September 2019

Metropolitan Area Exports

Area	2014	2015	2016	2017	2018	2019	Rank[2]
MSA[1]	879.0	873.5	945.0	1,071.6	1,025.0	1,028.4	157

Note: Figures are in millions of dollars; (1) Figures cover the Cedar Rapids, IA Metropolitan Statistical Area; (2) Rank is based on 2019 data and ranges from 1 to 386
Source: U.S. Department of Commerce, International Trade Administration, Office of Trade and Economic Analysis, Industry and Analysis, Exports by Metropolitan Area, data extracted March 24, 2021

Building Permits

Area	Single-Family			Multi-Family			Total		
	2018	2019	Pct. Chg.	2018	2019	Pct. Chg.	2018	2019	Pct. Chg.
City	147	173	17.7	325	197	-39.4	472	370	-21.6
MSA[1]	490	509	3.9	469	305	-35.0	959	814	-15.1
U.S.	855,300	862,100	0.7	473,500	523,900	10.6	1,328,800	1,386,000	4.3

Note: (1) Figures cover the Cedar Rapids, IA Metropolitan Statistical Area; Figures represent new, privately-owned housing units authorized (unadjusted data); All permit data are based on estimates with imputation
Source: U.S. Census Bureau, Manufacturing, Mining, and Construction Statistics, Building Permits, 2018, 2019

Bankruptcy Filings

Area	Business Filings			Nonbusiness Filings		
	2019	2020	% Chg.	2019	2020	% Chg.
Linn County	11	9	-18.2	365	285	-21.9
U.S.	22,780	21,655	-4.9	752,160	522,808	-30.5

Note: Business filings include Chapter 7, Chapter 9, Chapter 11, Chapter 12, Chapter 13, Chapter 15, and Section 304; Nonbusiness filings include Chapter 7, Chapter 11, and Chapter 13
Source: Administrative Office of the U.S. Courts, Business and Nonbusiness Bankruptcy, County Cases Commenced by Chapter of the Bankruptcy Code, During the 12-Month Period Ending December 31, 2019 and Business and Nonbusiness Bankruptcy, County Cases Commenced by Chapter of the Bankruptcy Code, During the 12-Month Period Ending December 31, 2020

Housing Vacancy Rates

Area	Gross Vacancy Rate[2] (%)			Year-Round Vacancy Rate[3] (%)			Rental Vacancy Rate[4] (%)			Homeowner Vacancy Rate[5] (%)		
	2018	2019	2020	2018	2019	2020	2018	2019	2020	2018	2019	2020
MSA[1]	n/a	n/a	n/a	n/a	n/a	n/a	n/a	n/a	n/a	n/a	n/a	n/a
U.S.	12.3	12.0	10.6	9.7	9.5	8.2	6.9	6.7	6.3	1.5	1.4	1.0

Note: (1) Figures cover the Cedar Rapids, IA Metropolitan Statistical Area; (2) The percentage of the total housing inventory that is vacant; (3) The percentage of the housing inventory (excluding seasonal units) that is year-round vacant; (4) The percentage of rental inventory that is vacant for rent; (5) The percentage of homeowner inventory that is vacant for sale; n/a not available
Source: U.S. Census Bureau, Housing Vacancies and Homeownership Annual Statistics: 2018, 2019, 2020

INCOME

Income

Area	Per Capita ($)	Median Household ($)	Average Household ($)
City	32,290	58,511	75,289
MSA[1]	34,039	64,687	82,498
U.S.	34,103	62,843	88,607

Note: (1) Figures cover the Cedar Rapids, IA Metropolitan Statistical Area
Source: U.S. Census Bureau, 2015-2019 American Community Survey 5-Year Estimates

Household Income Distribution

Area	Percent of Households Earning							
	Under $15,000	$15,000 -$24,999	$25,000 -$34,999	$35,000 -$49,999	$50,000 -$74,999	$75,000 -$99,999	$100,000 -$149,999	$150,000 and up
City	9.0	8.8	10.0	13.9	20.9	13.4	15.1	8.9
MSA[1]	7.7	7.9	9.1	13.3	19.3	14.4	16.9	11.4
U.S.	10.3	8.9	8.9	12.3	17.2	12.7	15.1	14.5

Note: (1) Figures cover the Cedar Rapids, IA Metropolitan Statistical Area
Source: U.S. Census Bureau, 2015-2019 American Community Survey 5-Year Estimates

Poverty Rate

Area	All Ages	Under 18 Years Old	18 to 64 Years Old	65 Years and Over
City	12.5	17.0	12.2	7.0
MSA[1]	10.0	12.8	9.8	6.6
U.S.	13.4	18.5	12.6	9.3

Note: Figures are percentage of people whose income during the past 12 months was below the poverty level; (1) Figures cover the Cedar Rapids, IA Metropolitan Statistical Area
Source: U.S. Census Bureau, 2015-2019 American Community Survey 5-Year Estimates

CITY FINANCES

City Government Finances

Component	2017 ($000)	2017 ($ per capita)
Total Revenues	415,539	3,187
Total Expenditures	435,280	3,338
Debt Outstanding	489,631	3,755
Cash and Securities[1]	462,724	3,548

Note: (1) Cash and security holdings of a government at the close of its fiscal year, including those of its dependent agencies, utilities, and liquor stores.
Source: U.S. Census Bureau, State & Local Government Finances 2017

City Government Revenue by Source

Source	2017 ($000)	2017 ($ per capita)	2017 (%)
General Revenue			
From Federal Government	60,539	464	14.6
From State Government	38,079	292	9.2
From Local Governments	772	6	0.2
Taxes			
Property	97,949	751	23.6
Sales and Gross Receipts	36,926	283	8.9
Personal Income	0	0	0.0
Corporate Income	0	0	0.0
Motor Vehicle License	0	0	0.0
Other Taxes	2,644	20	0.6
Current Charges	111,605	856	26.9
Liquor Store	0	0	0.0
Utility	34,360	263	8.3
Employee Retirement	0	0	0.0

Source: U.S. Census Bureau, State & Local Government Finances 2017

City Government Expenditures by Function

Function	2017 ($000)	2017 ($ per capita)	2017 (%)
General Direct Expenditures			
Air Transportation	26,109	200	6.0
Corrections	0	0	0.0
Education	0	0	0.0
Employment Security Administration	0	0	0.0
Financial Administration	5,150	39	1.2
Fire Protection	20,748	159	4.8
General Public Buildings	1,127	8	0.3
Governmental Administration, Other	2,826	21	0.6
Health	1,198	9	0.3
Highways	19,315	148	4.4
Hospitals	0	0	0.0
Housing and Community Development	7,739	59	1.8
Interest on General Debt	14,516	111	3.3
Judicial and Legal	876	6	0.2
Libraries	5,710	43	1.3
Parking	1,033	7	0.2
Parks and Recreation	11,072	84	2.5
Police Protection	45,215	346	10.4
Public Welfare	0	0	0.0
Sewerage	38,095	292	8.8
Solid Waste Management	23,139	177	5.3
Veterans' Services	0	0	0.0
Liquor Store	0	0	0.0
Utility	47,466	364	10.9
Employee Retirement	0	0	0.0

Source: U.S. Census Bureau, State & Local Government Finances 2017

EMPLOYMENT

Labor Force and Employment

Area	Civilian Labor Force			Workers Employed		
	Dec. 2019	Dec. 2020	% Chg.	Dec. 2019	Dec. 2020	% Chg.
City	73,629	67,681	-8.1	71,125	64,790	-8.9
MSA[1]	148,694	136,358	-8.3	143,975	131,243	-8.8
U.S.	164,007,000	160,017,000	-2.4	158,504,000	149,613,000	-5.6

Note: Data is not seasonally adjusted and covers workers 16 years of age and older; (1) Figures cover the Cedar Rapids, IA Metropolitan Statistical Area
Source: Bureau of Labor Statistics, Local Area Unemployment Statistics

Unemployment Rate

Area	2020											
	Jan.	Feb.	Mar.	Apr.	May	Jun.	Jul.	Aug.	Sep.	Oct.	Nov.	Dec.
City	4.0	3.5	4.1	14.2	12.9	11.3	9.3	10.1	6.8	4.7	4.9	4.3
MSA[1]	3.8	3.4	3.9	12.5	11.1	9.6	7.9	8.3	5.6	3.8	4.1	3.8
U.S.	4.0	3.8	4.5	14.4	13.0	11.2	10.5	8.5	7.7	6.6	6.4	6.5

Note: Data is not seasonally adjusted and covers workers 16 years of age and older; (1) Figures cover the Cedar Rapids, IA Metropolitan Statistical Area
Source: Bureau of Labor Statistics, Local Area Unemployment Statistics

Average Wages

Occupation	$/Hr.	Occupation	$/Hr.
Accountants and Auditors	35.30	Maintenance and Repair Workers	22.70
Automotive Mechanics	22.30	Marketing Managers	68.00
Bookkeepers	19.60	Network and Computer Systems Admin.	40.50
Carpenters	24.30	Nurses, Licensed Practical	21.30
Cashiers	11.60	Nurses, Registered	29.60
Computer Programmers	39.00	Nursing Assistants	14.90
Computer Systems Analysts	40.40	Office Clerks, General	18.10
Computer User Support Specialists	20.80	Physical Therapists	37.40
Construction Laborers	19.80	Physicians	120.60
Cooks, Restaurant	11.90	Plumbers, Pipefitters and Steamfitters	29.10
Customer Service Representatives	19.70	Police and Sheriff's Patrol Officers	31.20
Dentists	55.20	Postal Service Mail Carriers	25.60
Electricians	29.20	Real Estate Sales Agents	20.50
Engineers, Electrical	51.80	Retail Salespersons	13.30
Fast Food and Counter Workers	11.10	Sales Representatives, Technical/Scientific	55.20
Financial Managers	59.00	Secretaries, Exc. Legal/Medical/Executive	19.10
First-Line Supervisors of Office Workers	28.10	Security Guards	17.60
General and Operations Managers	53.30	Surgeons	n/a
Hairdressers/Cosmetologists	14.90	Teacher Assistants, Exc. Postsecondary*	12.80
Home Health and Personal Care Aides	14.10	Teachers, Secondary School, Exc. Sp. Ed.*	25.90
Janitors and Cleaners	15.20	Telemarketers	12.90
Landscaping/Groundskeeping Workers	16.20	Truck Drivers, Heavy/Tractor-Trailer	18.20
Lawyers	55.30	Truck Drivers, Light/Delivery Services	16.80
Maids and Housekeeping Cleaners	12.30	Waiters and Waitresses	10.60

Note: Wage data covers the Cedar Rapids, IA Metropolitan Statistical Area; (*) Hourly wages were calculated from annual wage data based on a 40 hour work week; n/a not available.
Source: Bureau of Labor Statistics, Metro Area Occupational Employment & Wage Estimates, May 2020

Employment by Industry

Sector	MSA[1]		U.S.
	Number of Employees	Percent of Total	Percent of Total
Construction, Mining, and Logging	8,300	6.0	5.5
Education and Health Services	20,400	14.8	16.3
Financial Activities	11,300	8.2	6.1
Government	15,700	11.4	15.2
Information	2,900	2.1	1.9
Leisure and Hospitality	9,400	6.8	9.0
Manufacturing	19,300	14.0	8.5
Other Services	4,800	3.5	3.8
Professional and Business Services	14,100	10.2	14.4
Retail Trade	15,200	11.0	10.9
Transportation, Warehousing, and Utilities	10,700	7.8	4.6
Wholesale Trade	5,700	4.1	3.9

Note: Figures are non-farm employment as of December 2020. Figures are not seasonally adjusted and include workers 16 years of age and older; (1) Figures cover the Cedar Rapids, IA Metropolitan Statistical Area
Source: Bureau of Labor Statistics, Current Employment Statistics, Employment, Hours, and Earnings

Employment by Occupation

Occupation Classification	City (%)	MSA[1] (%)	U.S. (%)
Management, Business, Science, and Arts	36.2	37.6	38.5
Natural Resources, Construction, and Maintenance	8.0	8.9	8.9
Production, Transportation, and Material Moving	16.7	16.2	13.2
Sales and Office	23.0	22.2	21.6
Service	16.1	15.2	17.8

Note: Figures cover employed civilians 16 years of age and older; (1) Figures cover the Cedar Rapids, IA Metropolitan Statistical Area
Source: U.S. Census Bureau, 2015-2019 American Community Survey 5-Year Estimates

Occupations with Greatest Projected Employment Growth: 2020 – 2022

Occupation[1]	2020 Employment	2022 Projected Employment	Numeric Employment Change	Percent Employment Change
Fast Food and Counter Workers	31,160	41,700	10,540	33.8
Waiters and Waitresses	16,720	24,050	7,330	43.8
Retail Salespersons	36,650	42,840	6,190	16.9
Cooks, Restaurant	9,170	13,630	4,460	48.6
Maids and Housekeeping Cleaners	9,970	13,650	3,680	36.9
Bartenders	7,430	10,480	3,050	41.0
First-Line Supervisors of Food Preparation and Serving Workers	8,150	11,090	2,940	36.1
Janitors and Cleaners, Except Maids and Housekeeping Cleaners	25,060	27,650	2,590	10.3
Laborers and Freight, Stock, and Material Movers, Hand	29,980	32,090	2,110	7.0
Childcare Workers	12,040	14,050	2,010	16.7

Note: Projections cover Iowa; (1) Sorted by numeric employment change
Source: www.projectionscentral.com, State Occupational Projections, 2020–2022 Short-Term Projections

Fastest-Growing Occupations: 2020 – 2022

Occupation[1]	2020 Employment	2022 Projected Employment	Numeric Employment Change	Percent Employment Change
Personal Care Aides	90	280	190	211.1
Actors	100	240	140	140.0
Motion Picture Projectionists	60	130	70	116.7
Ushers, Lobby Attendants, and Ticket Takers	670	1,420	750	111.9
Public Address System and Other Announcers	80	150	70	87.5
Gaming Cage Workers	180	330	150	83.3
Hotel, Motel, and Resort Desk Clerks	2,270	4,090	1,820	80.2
Gaming Change Persons and Booth Cashiers	250	450	200	80.0
Gaming Dealers	990	1,770	780	78.8
Gaming Surveillance Officers and Gaming Investigators	130	230	100	76.9

Note: Projections cover Iowa; (1) Sorted by percent employment change and excludes occupations with numeric employment change less than 50
Source: www.projectionscentral.com, State Occupational Projections, 2020–2022 Short-Term Projections

TAXES

State Corporate Income Tax Rates

State	Tax Rate (%)	Income Brackets ($)	Num. of Brackets	Financial Institution Tax Rate (%)[a]	Federal Income Tax Ded.
Iowa	5.5 - 9.8	100,000 - 250,001	3	5.0	Yes (j)

Note: Tax rates as of January 1, 2021; (a) Rates listed are the corporate income tax rate applied to financial institutions or excise taxes based on income. Some states have other taxes based upon the value of deposits or shares; (j) 50% of the federal income tax is deductible.
Source: Federation of Tax Administrators, State Corporate Income Tax Rates, January 1, 2021

State Individual Income Tax Rates

State	Tax Rate (%)	Income Brackets ($)	Personal Exemptions ($)			Standard Ded. ($)	
			Single	Married	Depend.	Single	Married
Iowa (a)	0.33 - 8.53	1,676 - 74,970	40 (c)	80 (c)	40 (c)	2,130	5,250 (a)

Note: Tax rates as of January 1, 2021; Local- and county-level taxes are not included; Federal income tax is deductible on state income tax returns; (a) 19 states have statutory provision for automatically adjusting to the rate of inflation the dollar values of the income tax brackets, standard deductions, and/or personal exemptions. Michigan indexes the personal exemption only. Oregon does not index the income brackets for $125,000 and over; (c) The personal exemption takes the form of a tax credit instead of a deduction
Source: Federation of Tax Administrators, State Individual Income Tax Rates, January 1, 2021

Various State Sales and Excise Tax Rates

State	State Sales Tax (%)	Gasoline[1] (¢/gal.)	Cigarette[2] ($/pack)	Spirits[3] ($/gal.)	Wine[4] ($/gal.)	Beer[5] ($/gal.)	Recreational Marijuana (%)
Iowa	6	30	1.36	13.03	1.75	0.19	Not legal

Note: All tax rates as of January 1, 2021; (1) The American Petroleum Institute has developed a methodology for determining the average tax rate on a gallon of fuel. Rates may include any of the following: excise taxes, environmental fees, storage tank fees, other fees or taxes, general sales tax, and local taxes; (2) The federal excise tax of $1.0066 per pack and local taxes are not included; (3) Rates are those applicable to off-premise sales of 40% alcohol by volume (a.b.v.) distilled spirits in 750ml containers. Local excise taxes are excluded; (4) Rates are those applicable to off-premise sales of 11% a.b.v. non-carbonated wine in 750ml containers; (5) Rates are those applicable to off-premise sales of 4.7% a.b.v. beer in 12 ounce containers.
Source: Tax Foundation, 2021 Facts & Figures: How Does Your State Compare?

State Business Tax Climate Index Rankings

State	Overall Rank	Corporate Tax Rank	Individual Income Tax Rank	Sales Tax Rank	Property Tax Rank	Unemployment Insurance Tax Rank
Iowa	40	46	40	14	38	37

Note: The index is a measure of how each state's tax laws affect economic performance. The lower the rank, the more favorable a state's tax system is for business. States without a given tax are given a ranking of 1. The scores/rankings for the District of Columbia do not affect other states. The 2021 index represents the tax climate as of July 1, 2020.
Source: Tax Foundation, State Business Tax Climate Index 2021

TRANSPORTATION

Means of Transportation to Work

Area	Car/Truck/Van		Public Transportation			Bicycle	Walked	Other Means	Worked at Home
	Drove Alone	Car-pooled	Bus	Subway	Railroad				
City	84.0	8.2	0.8	0.0	0.0	0.5	1.7	1.1	3.6
MSA[1]	84.7	7.5	0.5	0.0	0.0	0.3	2.0	0.7	4.2
U.S.	76.3	9.0	2.4	1.9	0.6	0.5	2.7	1.4	5.2

Note: Figures are percentages and cover workers 16 years of age and older; (1) Figures cover the Cedar Rapids, IA Metropolitan Statistical Area
Source: U.S. Census Bureau, 2015-2019 American Community Survey 5-Year Estimates

Travel Time to Work

Area	Less Than 10 Minutes	10 to 19 Minutes	20 to 29 Minutes	30 to 44 Minutes	45 to 59 Minutes	60 to 89 Minutes	90 Minutes or More
City	18.0	49.5	18.0	9.7	2.2	1.5	1.1
MSA[1]	17.4	40.6	21.6	13.1	3.9	2.0	1.3
U.S.	12.2	28.4	20.8	20.8	8.3	6.4	2.9

Note: Note: Figures are percentages and include workers 16 years old and over; (1) Figures cover the Cedar Rapids, IA Metropolitan Statistical Area
Source: U.S. Census Bureau, 2015-2019 American Community Survey 5-Year Estimates

Key Congestion Measures

Measure	1982	1992	2002	2012	2017
Annual Hours of Delay, Total (000)	n/a	n/a	n/a	n/a	3,369
Annual Hours of Delay, Per Auto Commuter	n/a	n/a	n/a	n/a	17
Annual Congestion Cost, Total (million $)	n/a	n/a	n/a	n/a	69
Annual Congestion Cost, Per Auto Commuter ($)	n/a	n/a	n/a	n/a	346

Note: n/a not available
Source: Texas A&M Transportation Institute, 2019 Urban Mobility Report

Freeway Travel Time Index

Measure	1982	1987	1992	1997	2002	2007	2012	2017
Urban Area Index[1]	n/a	n/a	n/a	n/a	n/a	n/a	n/a	1.08
Urban Area Rank[1,2]	n/a	n/a	n/a	n/a	n/a	n/a	n/a	n/a

Note: Freeway Travel Time Index—the ratio of travel time in the peak period to the travel time at free-flow conditions. For example, a value of 1.30 indicates a 20-minute free-flow trip takes 26 minutes in the peak (20 minutes x 1.30 = 26 minutes); (1) Covers the Cedar Rapids IA urban area; (2) Rank is based on 101 larger urban areas (#1 = highest travel time index); n/a not available
Source: Texas A&M Transportation Institute, 2019 Urban Mobility Report

Public Transportation

Agency Name / Mode of Transportation	Vehicles Operated in Maximum Service[1]	Annual Unlinked Passenger Trips[2] (in thous.)	Annual Passenger Miles[3] (in thous.)
Five Seasons Transportation and Parking (FSTP)			
Bus (directly operated)	21	1,246.4	5,858.0
Demand Response (purchased transportation)	15	87.3	509.0

Note: (1) Number of revenue vehicles operated by the given mode and type of service to meet the annual maximum service requirement. This is the revenue vehicle count during the peak season of the year; on the week and day that maximum service is provided. Vehicles operated in maximum service (VOMS) exclude atypical days and one-time special events; (2) Number of passengers who boarded public transportation vehicles. Passengers are counted each time they board a vehicle no matter how many vehicles they use to travel from their origin to their destination. (3) Sum of the distances ridden by all passengers during the entire fiscal year.
Source: Federal Transit Administration, National Transit Database, 2019

Air Transportation

Airport Name and Code / Type of Service	Passenger Airlines[1]	Passenger Enplanements	Freight Carriers[2]	Freight (lbs)
The Eastern Iowa (CID)				
Domestic service (U.S. carriers - 2020)	19	312,888	8	53,784,938
International service (U.S. carriers - 2019)	0	0	0	0

Note: (1) Includes all U.S.-based major, minor and commuter airlines that carried at least one passenger during the year; (2) Includes all U.S.-based airlines and freight carriers that transported at least one pound of freight during the year.
Source: Bureau of Transportation Statistics, The Intermodal Transportation Database, Air Carriers: T-100 Domestic Market (U.S. Carriers), 2020; Bureau of Transportation Statistics, The Intermodal Transportation Database, Air Carriers: T-100 International Market (U.S. Carriers), 2019

BUSINESSES

Major Business Headquarters

Company Name	Industry	Rankings	
		Fortune[1]	Forbes[2]
No companies listed	-	-	-

Note: (1) Companies that produce a 10-K are ranked 1 to 500 based on 2019 revenue; (2) All private companies with at least $2 billion in annual revenue through the end of their most current fiscal year are ranked 1 to 219; companies listed are headquartered in the city; dashes indicate no ranking
Source: Fortune, "Fortune 500," June/July 2020; Forbes, "America's Largest Private Companies," 2020

32 Cedar Rapids, Iowa

Living Environment

COST OF LIVING

Cost of Living Index

Composite Index	Groceries	Housing	Utilities	Trans-portation	Health Care	Misc. Goods/ Services
95.8	98.0	82.7	106.8	97.8	110.1	100.1

Note: The Cost of Living Index measures regional differences in the cost of consumer goods and services, excluding taxes and non-consumer expenditures, for professional and managerial households in the top income quintile. It is based on more than 50,000 prices covering almost 60 different items for which prices are collected three times a year by chambers of commerce, economic development organizations or university applied economic centers in each participating urban area. The numbers shown should be read as a percentage above or below the national average of 100. For example, a value of 115.4 in the groceries column indicates that grocery prices are 15.4% higher than the national average. Small differences in the index numbers should not be interpreted as significant; Figures cover the Cedar Rapids IA urban area.
Source: The Council for Community and Economic Research, Cost of Living Index, 2020

Grocery Prices

Area[1]	T-Bone Steak ($/pound)	Frying Chicken ($/pound)	Whole Milk ($/half gal.)	Eggs ($/dozen)	Orange Juice ($/64 oz.)	Coffee ($/11.5 oz.)
City[2]	10.99	1.68	2.49	1.24	3.31	4.86
Avg.	11.78	1.39	2.05	1.47	3.57	4.34
Min.	8.03	0.94	1.03	0.74	2.94	3.02
Max.	15.86	2.65	4.31	3.77	5.44	8.69

*Note: (1) Values for the local area are compared with the average, minimum and maximum values for all 284 areas in the Cost of Living Index; (2) Figures cover the Cedar Rapids IA urban area; **T-Bone Steak** (price per pound); **Frying Chicken** (price per pound, whole fryer); **Whole Milk** (half gallon carton); **Eggs** (price per dozen, Grade A, large); **Orange Juice** (64 oz. Tropicana or Florida Natural); **Coffee** (11.5 oz. can, vacuum-packed, Maxwell House, Hills Bros, or Folgers).*
Source: The Council for Community and Economic Research, Cost of Living Index, 2020

Housing and Utility Costs

Area[1]	New Home Price ($)	Apartment Rent ($/month)	All Electric ($/month)	Part Electric ($/month)	Other Energy ($/month)	Telephone ($/month)
City[2]	322,911	831	-	139.90	48.93	180.80
Avg.	368,594	1,168	170.86	100.47	65.28	184.30
Min.	190,567	502	91.58	31.42	26.08	169.60
Max.	2,227,806	4,738	470.38	280.31	280.06	206.50

*Note: (1) Values for the local area are compared with the average, minimum and maximum values for all 284 areas in the Cost of Living Index; (2) Figures cover the Cedar Rapids IA urban area; **New Home Price** (2,400 sf living area, 8,000 sf lot, in urban area with full utilities); **Apartment Rent** (950 sf 2 bedroom/1.5 or 2 bath, unfurnished, excluding all utilities except water); **All Electric** (average monthly cost for an all-electric home); **Part Electric** (average monthly cost for a part-electric home); **Other Energy** (average monthly cost for natural gas, fuel oil, coal, wood, and any other forms of energy except electricity); **Telephone** (price includes the base monthly rate plus taxes and fees for three lines of mobile phone service).*
Source: The Council for Community and Economic Research, Cost of Living Index, 2020

Health Care, Transportation, and Other Costs

Area[1]	Doctor ($/visit)	Dentist ($/visit)	Optometrist ($/visit)	Gasoline ($/gallon)	Beauty Salon ($/visit)	Men's Shirt ($)
City[2]	122.25	115.00	102.58	2.15	37.59	28.78
Avg.	115.44	99.32	108.10	2.21	39.27	31.37
Min.	36.68	59.00	51.36	1.71	19.00	11.00
Max.	219.00	153.10	250.97	3.46	82.05	58.33

*Note: (1) Values for the local area are compared with the average, minimum and maximum values for all 284 areas in the Cost of Living Index; (2) Figures cover the Cedar Rapids IA urban area; **Doctor** (general practitioners routine exam of an established patient); **Dentist** (adult teeth cleaning and periodic oral examination); **Optometrist** (full vision eye exam for established adult patient); **Gasoline** (one gallon regular unleaded, national brand, including all taxes, cash price at self-service pump if available); **Beauty Salon** (woman's shampoo, trim, and blow-dry); **Men's Shirt** (cotton/polyester dress shirt, pinpoint weave, long sleeves).*
Source: The Council for Community and Economic Research, Cost of Living Index, 2020

HOUSING

Homeownership Rate

Area	2012 (%)	2013 (%)	2014 (%)	2015 (%)	2016 (%)	2017 (%)	2018 (%)	2019 (%)	2020 (%)
MSA[1]	n/a	n/a	n/a	n/a	n/a	n/a	n/a	n/a	n/a
U.S.	65.4	65.1	64.5	63.7	63.4	63.9	64.4	64.6	66.6

Note: (1) Figures cover the Cedar Rapids, IA Metropolitan Statistical Area; n/a not available
Source: U.S. Census Bureau, Housing Vacancies and Homeownership Annual Statistics: 2012-2020

House Price Index (HPI)

Area	National Ranking[2]	Quarterly Change (%)	One-Year Change (%)	Five-Year Change (%)	Since 1991Q1 (%)
MSA[1]	218	1.99	4.00	17.00	130.16
U.S.[3]	–	3.81	10.77	38.99	205.12

Note: The HPI is a weighted repeat sales index. It measures average price changes in repeat sales or refinancings on the same properties. This information is obtained by reviewing repeat mortgage transactions on single-family properties whose mortgages have been purchased or securitized by Fannie Mae or Freddie Mac since January 1975; (1) Figures cover the Cedar Rapids, IA Metropolitan Statistical Area; (2) Rankings are based on annual percentage change for all metro areas containing at least 15,000 transactions over the last 10 years and ranges from 1 to 253; (3) figures based on a weighted average of Census Division estimates using a seasonally adjusted, purchase-only index; all figures are for the period ending December 31, 2020
Source: Federal Housing Finance Agency, Change in Metropolitan Area House Price Indexes, April 7, 2021

Median Single-Family Home Prices

Area	2018	2019	2020p	Percent Change 2019 to 2020
MSA[1]	159.2	165.6	173.1	4.5
U.S. Average	261.6	274.6	299.9	9.2

Note: Figures are median sales prices of existing single-family homes in thousands of dollars; (p) preliminary; (1) Figures cover the Cedar Rapids, IA Metropolitan Statistical Area
Source: National Association of Realtors, Median Sales Price of Existing Single-Family Homes for Metropolitan Areas, 4th Quarter 2020

Qualifying Income Based on Median Sales Price of Existing Single-Family Homes

Area	With 5% Down ($)	With 10% Down ($)	With 20% Down ($)
MSA[1]	32,854	31,125	27,667
U.S. Average	59,266	56,147	49,908

Note: Figures are preliminary; Qualifying income is based on a mortgage rate of 2.81%. Monthly principal and interest payment is limited to 25% of income; (1) Figures cover the Cedar Rapids, IA Metropolitan Statistical Area
Source: National Association of Realtors, Qualifying Income Based on Median Sales Price of Existing Single-Family Homes for Metropolitan Areas, 4th Quarter 2020

Home Value Distribution

Area	Under $50,000	$50,000 -$99,999	$100,000 -$149,999	$150,000 -$199,999	$200,000 -$299,999	$300,000 -$499,999	$500,000 -$999,999	$1,000,000 or more
City	5.5	16.3	34.2	20.9	16.3	5.1	1.4	0.2
MSA[1]	6.5	13.7	27.1	19.7	20.8	9.2	2.4	0.6
U.S.	6.9	12.0	13.3	14.0	19.6	19.3	11.4	3.4

Note: Figures are percentages and cover owner-occupied housing units; (1) Figures cover the Cedar Rapids, IA Metropolitan Statistical Area
Source: U.S. Census Bureau, 2015-2019 American Community Survey 5-Year Estimates

Year Housing Structure Built

Area	2010 or Later	2000 -2009	1990 -1999	1980 -1989	1970 -1979	1960 -1969	1950 -1959	1940 -1949	Before 1940	Median Year
City	6.9	11.1	13.0	8.2	14.4	13.9	12.3	4.2	16.0	1972
MSA[1]	6.8	14.2	14.6	7.5	13.4	12.3	9.9	3.6	17.7	1975
U.S.	5.2	14.0	13.9	13.4	15.2	10.6	10.3	4.9	12.6	1978

Note: Figures are percentages except for Median Year; Note: (1) Figures cover the Cedar Rapids, IA Metropolitan Statistical Area
Source: U.S. Census Bureau, 2015-2019 American Community Survey 5-Year Estimates

Gross Monthly Rent

Area	Under $500	$500 -$999	$1,000 -$1,499	$1,500 -$1,999	$2,000 -$2,499	$2,500 -$2,999	$3,000 and up	Median ($)
City	15.8	61.0	20.2	1.5	0.6	0.3	0.7	767
MSA[1]	16.9	60.9	18.9	1.9	0.5	0.3	0.7	753
U.S.	9.4	36.2	30.0	14.0	5.6	2.4	2.4	1,062

Note: Figures are percentages except for Median; Gross rent is the contract rent plus the estimated average monthly cost of utilities (electricity, gas, and water and sewer) and fuels (oil, coal, kerosene, wood, etc.) if these are paid by the renter (or paid for the renter by someone else); (1) Figures cover the Cedar Rapids, IA Metropolitan Statistical Area
Source: U.S. Census Bureau, 2015-2019 American Community Survey 5-Year Estimates

HEALTH

Health Risk Factors

Category	MSA[1] (%)	U.S. (%)
Adults aged 18–64 who have any kind of health care coverage	93.7	87.3
Adults who reported being in good or better health	86.4	82.4
Adults who have been told they have high blood cholesterol	36.1	33.0
Adults who have been told they have high blood pressure	28.4	32.3
Adults who are current smokers	18.1	17.1
Adults who currently use E-cigarettes	3.5	4.6
Adults who currently use chewing tobacco, snuff, or snus	6.7	4.0
Adults who are heavy drinkers[2]	5.9	6.3
Adults who are binge drinkers[3]	22.9	17.4
Adults who are overweight (BMI 25.0 - 29.9)	35.3	35.3
Adults who are obese (BMI 30.0 - 99.8)	34.2	31.3
Adults who participated in any physical activities in the past month	75.4	74.4
Adults who always or nearly always wears a seat belt	96.4	94.3

Note: (1) Figures cover the Cedar Rapids, IA Metropolitan Statistical Area; (2) Heavy drinkers are classified as adult men having more than 14 drinks per week and adult women having more than 7 drinks per week; (3) Binge drinkers are classified as males having five or more drinks on one occasion or females having four or more drinks on one occasion
Source: Centers for Disease Control and Prevention, Behaviorial Risk Factor Surveillance System, SMART: Selected Metropolitan Area Risk Trends, 2017

Acute and Chronic Health Conditions

Category	MSA[1] (%)	U.S. (%)
Adults who have ever been told they had a heart attack	3.4	4.2
Adults who have ever been told they have angina or coronary heart disease	3.7	3.9
Adults who have ever been told they had a stroke	2.8	3.0
Adults who have ever been told they have asthma	11.5	14.2
Adults who have ever been told they have arthritis	20.6	24.9
Adults who have ever been told they have diabetes[2]	8.4	10.5
Adults who have ever been told they had skin cancer	6.7	6.2
Adults who have ever been told they had any other types of cancer	9.3	7.1
Adults who have ever been told they have COPD	5.3	6.5
Adults who have ever been told they have kidney disease	2.3	3.0
Adults who have ever been told they have a form of depression	20.8	20.5

Note: (1) Figures cover the Cedar Rapids, IA Metropolitan Statistical Area; (2) Figures do not include pregnancy-related, borderline, or pre-diabetes
Source: Centers for Disease Control and Prevention, Behaviorial Risk Factor Surveillance System, SMART: Selected Metropolitan Area Risk Trends, 2017

Health Screening and Vaccination Rates

Category	MSA[1] (%)	U.S. (%)
Adults aged 65+ who have had flu shot within the past year	71.4	60.7
Adults aged 65+ who have ever had a pneumonia vaccination	86.7	75.4
Adults who have ever been tested for HIV	27.8	36.1
Adults who have ever had the shingles or zoster vaccine?	38.8	28.9
Adults who have had their blood cholesterol checked within the last five years	85.3	85.9

Note: n/a not available; (1) Figures cover the Cedar Rapids, IA Metropolitan Statistical Area.
Source: Centers for Disease Control and Prevention, Behaviorial Risk Factor Surveillance System, SMART: Selected Metropolitan Area Risk Trends, 2017

Disability Status

Category	MSA[1] (%)	U.S. (%)
Adults who reported being deaf	6.7	6.7
Are you blind or have serious difficulty seeing, even when wearing glasses?	4.2	4.5
Are you limited in any way in any of your usual activities due of arthritis?	9.8	12.9
Do you have difficulty doing errands alone?	5.2	6.8
Do you have difficulty dressing or bathing?	2.4	3.6
Do you have serious difficulty concentrating/remembering/making decisions?	8.6	10.7
Do you have serious difficulty walking or climbing stairs?	9.0	13.6

Note: (1) Figures cover the Cedar Rapids, IA Metropolitan Statistical Area.
Source: Centers for Disease Control and Prevention, Behaviorial Risk Factor Surveillance System, SMART: Selected Metropolitan Area Risk Trends, 2017

Mortality Rates for the Top 10 Causes of Death in the U.S.

ICD-10[a] Sub-Chapter	ICD-10[a] Code	Age-Adjusted Mortality Rate[1] per 100,000 population	
		County[2]	U.S.
Malignant neoplasms	C00-C97	156.2	149.2
Ischaemic heart diseases	I20-I25	98.4	90.5
Other forms of heart disease	I30-I51	37.7	52.2
Chronic lower respiratory diseases	J40-J47	38.1	39.6
Other degenerative diseases of the nervous system	G30-G31	47.2	37.6
Cerebrovascular diseases	I60-I69	24.3	37.2
Other external causes of accidental injury	W00-X59	28.6	36.1
Organic, including symptomatic, mental disorders	F01-F09	25.0	29.4
Hypertensive diseases	I10-I15	14.3	24.1
Diabetes mellitus	E10-E14	13.0	21.5

Note: (a) ICD-10 = International Classification of Diseases 10th Revision; (1) Mortality rates are a three-year average covering 2017-2019; (2) Figures cover Linn County.
Source: Centers for Disease Control and Prevention, National Center for Health Statistics. Underlying Cause of Death 1999-2019 on CDC WONDER Online Database

Mortality Rates for Selected Causes of Death

ICD-10[a] Sub-Chapter	ICD-10[a] Code	Age-Adjusted Mortality Rate[1] per 100,000 population	
		County[2]	U.S.
Assault	X85-Y09	3.4	6.0
Diseases of the liver	K70-K76	14.1	14.4
Human immunodeficiency virus (HIV) disease	B20-B24	Suppressed	1.5
Influenza and pneumonia	J09-J18	13.2	13.8
Intentional self-harm	X60-X84	18.2	14.1
Malnutrition	E40-E46	3.0	2.3
Obesity and other hyperalimentation	E65-E68	Suppressed	2.1
Renal failure	N17-N19	9.6	12.6
Transport accidents	V01-V99	9.9	12.3
Viral hepatitis	B15-B19	Suppressed	1.2

Note: (a) ICD-10 = International Classification of Diseases 10th Revision; (1) Mortality rates are a three-year average covering 2017-2019; (2) Figures cover Linn County; Data are suppressed when the data meet the criteria for confidentiality constraints; Mortality rates are flagged as unreliable when the rate would be calculated with a numerator of 20 or less.
Source: Centers for Disease Control and Prevention, National Center for Health Statistics. Underlying Cause of Death 1999-2019 on CDC WONDER Online Database

Health Insurance Coverage

Area	With Health Insurance	With Private Health Insurance	With Public Health Insurance	Without Health Insurance	Population Under Age 19 Without Health Insurance
City	95.5	74.3	34.3	4.5	2.7
MSA[1]	96.5	77.1	33.1	3.5	2.0
U.S.	91.2	67.9	35.1	8.8	5.1

Note: Figures are percentages that cover the civilian noninstitutionalized population; (1) Figures cover the Cedar Rapids, IA Metropolitan Statistical Area
Source: U.S. Census Bureau, 2015-2019 American Community Survey 5-Year Estimates

Number of Medical Professionals

Area	MDs[3]	DOs[3,4]	Dentists	Podiatrists	Chiropractors	Optometrists
County[1] (number)	418	50	167	19	135	41
County[1] (rate[2])	185.1	22.1	73.7	8.4	59.5	18.1
U.S. (rate[2])	282.9	22.7	71.2	6.2	28.1	16.9

19113
Note: Data as of 2019 unless noted; (1) Data covers Linn County; (2) Rate per 100,000 population; (3) Data as of 2018 and includes all active, non-federal physicians; (4) Doctor of Osteopathic Medicine
Source: U.S. Department of Health and Human Services, Health Resources and Services Administration, Bureau of Health Professions, Area Resource File (ARF) 2019-2020

36 Cedar Rapids, Iowa

EDUCATION

Public School District Statistics

District Name	Schls	Pupils	Pupil/ Teacher Ratio	Minority Pupils[1] (%)	Free Lunch Eligible[2] (%)	IEP[3] (%)
Cedar Rapids CSD	31	16,717	15.1	37.2	48.3	15.7
College Comm School District	9	5,761	15.8	22.3	26.5	10.6

Note: Table includes school districts with 2,000 or more students; (1) Percentage of students that are not non-Hispanic white; (2) Percentage of students that are eligible for the free lunch program; (3) Percentage of students that have an Individualized Education Program.
Source: U.S. Department of Education, National Center for Education Statistics, Common Core of Data, Local Education Agency (School District) Universe Survey: School Year 2018-2019; U.S. Department of Education, National Center for Education Statistics, Common Core of Data, Public Elementary/Secondary School Universe Survey: School Year 2018-2019

Highest Level of Education

Area	Less than H.S.	H.S. Diploma	Some College, No Deg.	Associate Degree	Bachelor's Degree	Master's Degree	Prof. School Degree	Doctorate Degree
City	6.7	26.6	22.2	12.4	22.9	6.6	1.5	1.0
MSA[1]	5.7	29.0	21.5	12.8	21.9	6.9	1.4	0.8
U.S.	12.0	27.0	20.4	8.5	19.8	8.8	2.1	1.4

Note: Figures cover persons age 25 and over; (1) Figures cover the Cedar Rapids, IA Metropolitan Statistical Area
Source: U.S. Census Bureau, 2015-2019 American Community Survey 5-Year Estimates

Educational Attainment by Race

Area	High School Graduate or Higher (%)					Bachelor's Degree or Higher (%)				
	Total	White	Black	Asian	Hisp.[2]	Total	White	Black	Asian	Hisp.[2]
City	93.3	94.7	83.4	83.8	75.8	32.1	32.7	15.0	51.2	21.0
MSA[1]	94.3	95.2	84.0	81.4	77.6	31.0	31.3	15.4	51.7	22.0
U.S.	88.0	89.9	86.0	87.1	68.7	32.1	33.5	21.6	54.3	16.4

Note: Figures shown cover persons 25 years old and over; (1) Figures cover the Cedar Rapids, IA Metropolitan Statistical Area; (2) People of Hispanic origin can be of any race
Source: U.S. Census Bureau, 2015-2019 American Community Survey 5-Year Estimates

School Enrollment by Grade and Control

Area	Preschool (%)		Kindergarten (%)		Grades 1 - 4 (%)		Grades 5 - 8 (%)		Grades 9 - 12 (%)	
	Public	Private	Public	Private	Public	Private	Public	Private	Public	Private
City	67.5	32.5	86.4	13.6	88.9	11.1	93.0	7.0	90.0	10.0
MSA[1]	69.1	30.9	87.8	12.2	89.0	11.0	92.3	7.7	92.3	7.7
U.S.	59.1	40.9	87.6	12.4	89.5	10.5	89.4	10.6	90.1	9.9

Note: Figures shown cover persons 3 years old and over; (1) Figures cover the Cedar Rapids, IA Metropolitan Statistical Area
Source: U.S. Census Bureau, 2015-2019 American Community Survey 5-Year Estimates

Higher Education

Four-Year Colleges			Two-Year Colleges			Medical Schools[1]	Law Schools[2]	Voc/ Tech[3]
Public	Private Non-profit	Private For-profit	Public	Private Non-profit	Private For-profit			
1	2	0	1	1	1	0	0	0

Note: Figures cover institutions located within the city limits and include main campuses only; (1) includes schools accredited by the Liaison Committee on Medical Education and the American Osteopathic Association's Commission on Osteopathic College Accreditation; (2) includes ABA-accredited schools, schools with provisional ABA accreditation, and state accredited schools; (3) includes all schools with programs that are less than 2 years.
Source: National Center for Education Statistics, Integrated Postsecondary Education System (IPEDS), 2019-20; Wikipedia, List of Medical Schools in the United States, accessed April 2, 2021; Wikipedia, List of Law Schools in the United States, accessed April 2, 2021

According to *U.S. News & World Report,* the Cedar Rapids, IA metro area is home to one of the top 100 liberal arts colleges in the U.S.: **Cornell College** (#76 tie). The indicators used to capture academic quality fall into a number of categories: assessment by administrators at peer institutions; retention of students; faculty resources; student selectivity; financial resources; alumni giving; high school counselor ratings of colleges; and graduation rate. *U.S. News & World Report, "America's Best Colleges 2021"*

Cedar Rapids, Iowa **37**

EMPLOYERS

Major Employers

Company Name	Industry
AEGON USA	Insurance
Alliant Energy	Energy
Amana Refrigeration Products	Appliances
Cedar Rapids Community School District	Education
City of Cedar Rapids	Municipal government
Gazette Communications	Publishing
General Mills	Food products
Hy-Vee Food Stores	Grocery stores
Kirkwood Community College	Education
Linn County Offices	Government
Linn-Mar Community Schools	Education
Maytag Appliances	Appliances
MCI	Communications
McLeodUSA Incorporated	Communications
Mercy Medical Center	Healthcare
Nash Finch Company	Retail
Rockwell Collins	Aerospace/defense
St. Luke's Hospital	Education
Wal-Mart Stores	Retail
Yellowbook USA	Publisher

Note: Companies shown are located within the Cedar Rapids, IA Metropolitan Statistical Area.
Source: Hoovers.com; Wikipedia

Best Companies to Work For

Transamerica, headquartered in Cedar Rapids, is among the "100 Best Companies for Working Mothers." Criteria: paid time off and leaves; workforce profile; benefits; women's issues and advancement; flexible work; company culture and work life programs. *Working Mother, "100 Best Companies for Working Mothers," 2020*

Transamerica, headquartered in Cedar Rapids, is among the "Best Companies for Dads." *Working Mother's* newest list recognizes the growing importance companies place on giving dads time off and support for their families. Rankings are determined by measuring gender-neutral or paternity leave offered, as well as actual time taken, phase-back policies, child- and dependent-care benefits, and corporate support groups for men and dads. *Working Mother, "Best Companies for Dads," 2020*

PUBLIC SAFETY

Crime Rate

Area	All Crimes	Violent Crimes				Property Crimes		
		Murder	Rape[3]	Robbery	Aggrav. Assault	Burglary	Larceny -Theft	Motor Vehicle Theft
City	3,593.1	1.5	20.1	61.9	173.9	624.6	2,438.7	272.4
Suburbs[1]	911.9	0.0	21.6	5.0	95.2	183.1	523.4	83.6
Metro[2]	2,229.3	0.7	20.9	33.0	133.8	400.0	1,464.5	176.4
U.S.	2,489.3	5.0	42.6	81.6	250.2	340.5	1,549.5	219.9

Note: Figures are crimes per 100,000 population; (1) All areas within the metro area that are located outside the city limits; (2) Figures cover the Cedar Rapids, IA Metropolitan Statistical Area; (3) All figures shown were reported using the revised Uniform Crime Reporting (UCR) definition of rape.
Source: FBI Uniform Crime Reports, 2019

Hate Crimes

Area	Number of Quarters Reported	Number of Incidents per Bias Motivation					
		Race/Ethnicity/ Ancestry	Religion	Sexual Orientation	Disability	Gender	Gender Identity
City	4	0	0	0	0	0	0
U.S.	4	3,963	1,521	1,195	157	69	198

Source: Federal Bureau of Investigation, Hate Crime Statistics 2019

Identity Theft Consumer Reports

Area	Reports	Reports per 100,000 Population	Rank[2]
MSA[1]	293	107	355
U.S.	1,387,615	423	-

Note: (1) Figures cover the Cedar Rapids, IA Metropolitan Statistical Area; (2) Rank ranges from 1 to 391 where 1 indicates greatest number of identity theft reports per 100,000 population
Source: Federal Trade Commission, Consumer Sentinel Network Data Book 2020

Fraud and Other Consumer Reports

Area	Reports	Reports per 100,000 Population	Rank[2]
MSA[1]	1,539	564	325
U.S.	3,385,133	1,031	-

Note: (1) Figures cover the Cedar Rapids, IA Metropolitan Statistical Area; (2) Rank ranges from 1 to 391 where 1 indicates greatest number of fraud and other consumer reports per 100,000 population
Source: Federal Trade Commission, Consumer Sentinel Network Data Book 2020

POLITICS

2020 Presidential Election Results

Area	Biden	Trump	Jorgensen	Hawkins	Other
Linn County	55.6	41.9	1.6	0.3	0.7
U.S.	51.3	46.8	1.2	0.3	0.5

Note: Results are percentages and may not add to 100% due to rounding
Source: Dave Leip's Atlas of U.S. Presidential Elections

SPORTS

Professional Sports Teams

Team Name	League	Year Established

No teams are located in the metro area
Source: Wikipedia, Major Professional Sports Teams of the United States and Canada, April 6, 2021

CLIMATE

Average and Extreme Temperatures

Temperature	Jan	Feb	Mar	Apr	May	Jun	Jul	Aug	Sep	Oct	Nov	Dec	Yr.
Extreme High (°F)	58	66	87	100	94	103	105	105	97	95	76	65	105
Average High (°F)	24	30	43	59	71	81	84	82	73	62	45	29	57
Average Temp. (°F)	15	21	34	48	60	69	73	71	62	50	36	21	47
Average Low (°F)	6	11	24	36	48	58	62	59	50	39	26	12	36
Extreme Low (°F)	-33	-29	-34	-4	25	38	42	38	22	11	-17	-27	-34

Note: Figures cover the years 1960-1995
Source: National Climatic Data Center, International Station Meteorological Climate Summary, 9/96

Average Precipitation/Snowfall/Humidity

Precip./Humidity	Jan	Feb	Mar	Apr	May	Jun	Jul	Aug	Sep	Oct	Nov	Dec	Yr.
Avg. Precip. (in.)	0.8	1.0	2.3	3.6	4.1	4.5	4.8	4.0	3.5	2.5	1.9	1.3	34.4
Avg. Snowfall (in.)	7	7	6	2	Tr	0	0	0	0	Tr	4	8	33
Avg. Rel. Hum. 6am (%)	77	80	82	81	81	83	87	90	89	84	83	82	83
Avg. Rel. Hum. 3pm (%)	68	66	62	52	51	51	55	55	55	52	62	70	58

Note: Figures cover the years 1960-1995; Tr = Trace amounts (<0.05 in. of rain; <0.5 in. of snow)
Source: National Climatic Data Center, International Station Meteorological Climate Summary, 9/96

Weather Conditions

Temperature			Daytime Sky			Precipitation		
5°F & below	32°F & below	90°F & above	Clear	Partly cloudy	Cloudy	0.01 inch or more precip.	0.1 inch or more snow/ice	Thunder-storms
38	156	16	89	132	144	109	28	42

Note: Figures are average number of days per year and cover the years 1960-1995
Source: National Climatic Data Center, International Station Meteorological Climate Summary, 9/96

HAZARDOUS WASTE

Superfund Sites

The Cedar Rapids, IA metro area has no sites on the EPA's Superfund Final National Priorities List. There are a total of 1,375 Superfund sites with a status of proposed or final on the list in the U.S. *U.S. Environmental Protection Agency, National Priorities List, April 7, 2021*

AIR QUALITY

Air Quality Trends: Ozone

	1990	1995	2000	2005	2010	2015	2016	2017	2018	2019
MSA[1]	n/a	n/a	n/a	n/a	n/a	n/a	n/a	n/a	n/a	n/a
U.S.	0.088	0.089	0.082	0.080	0.073	0.068	0.069	0.068	0.069	0.065

Note: (1) Data covers the Cedar Rapids, IA Metropolitan Statistical Area; n/a not available. The values shown are the composite ozone concentration averages among trend sites based on the highest fourth daily maximum 8-hour concentration in parts per million. These trends are based on sites having an adequate record of monitoring data during the trend period. Data from exceptional events are included.
Source: U.S. Environmental Protection Agency, Air Quality Monitoring Information, "Air Quality Trends by City, 1990-2019"

Air Quality Index

Area	Percent of Days when Air Quality was...[2]					AQI Statistics[2]	
	Good	Moderate	Unhealthy for Sensitive Groups	Unhealthy	Very Unhealthy	Maximum	Median
MSA[1]	78.6	21.4	0.0	0.0	0.0	84	39

Note: (1) Data covers the Cedar Rapids, IA Metropolitan Statistical Area; (2) Based on 365 days with AQI data in 2019. Air Quality Index (AQI) is an index for reporting daily air quality. EPA calculates the AQI for five major air pollutants regulated by the Clean Air Act: ground-level ozone, particle pollution (aka particulate matter), carbon monoxide, sulfur dioxide, and nitrogen dioxide. The AQI runs from 0 to 500. The higher the AQI value, the greater the level of air pollution and the greater the health concern. There are six AQI categories: "Good" AQI is between 0 and 50. Air quality is considered satisfactory; "Moderate" AQI is between 51 and 100. Air quality is acceptable; "Unhealthy for Sensitive Groups" When AQI values are between 101 and 150, members of sensitive groups may experience health effects; "Unhealthy" When AQI values are between 151 and 200 everyone may begin to experience health effects; "Very Unhealthy" AQI values between 201 and 300 trigger a health alert; "Hazardous" AQI values over 300 trigger warnings of emergency conditions (not shown).
Source: U.S. Environmental Protection Agency, Air Quality Index Report, 2019

Air Quality Index Pollutants

Area	Percent of Days when AQI Pollutant was...[2]					
	Carbon Monoxide	Nitrogen Dioxide	Ozone	Sulfur Dioxide	Particulate Matter 2.5	Particulate Matter 10
MSA[1]	0.0	0.0	47.9	1.1	51.0	0.0

Note: (1) Data covers the Cedar Rapids, IA Metropolitan Statistical Area; (2) Based on 365 days with AQI data in 2019. The Air Quality Index (AQI) is an index for reporting daily air quality. EPA calculates the AQI for five major air pollutants regulated by the Clean Air Act: ground-level ozone, particle pollution (also known as particulate matter), carbon monoxide, sulfur dioxide, and nitrogen dioxide. The AQI runs from 0 to 500. The higher the AQI value, the greater the level of air pollution and the greater the health concern.
Source: U.S. Environmental Protection Agency, Air Quality Index Report, 2019

Maximum Air Pollutant Concentrations: Particulate Matter, Ozone, CO and Lead

	Particulate Matter 10 (ug/m^3)	Particulate Matter 2.5 Wtd AM (ug/m^3)	Particulate Matter 2.5 24-Hr (ug/m^3)	Ozone (ppm)	Carbon Monoxide (ppm)	Lead (ug/m^3)
MSA[1] Level	38	7.9	20	0.060	n/a	n/a
NAAQS[2]	150	15	35	0.075	9	0.15
Met NAAQS[2]	Yes	Yes	Yes	Yes	n/a	n/a

Note: (1) Data covers the Cedar Rapids, IA Metropolitan Statistical Area; Data from exceptional events are included; (2) National Ambient Air Quality Standards; ppm = parts per million; ug/m^3 = micrograms per cubic meter; n/a not available.
Concentrations: Particulate Matter 10 (coarse particulate)—highest second maximum 24-hour concentration; Particulate Matter 2.5 Wtd AM (fine particulate)—highest weighted annual mean concentration; Particulate Matter 2.5 24-Hour (fine particulate)—highest 98th percentile 24-hour concentration; Ozone—highest fourth daily maximum 8-hour concentration; Carbon Monoxide—highest second maximum non-overlapping 8-hour concentration; Lead—maximum running 3-month average
Source: U.S. Environmental Protection Agency, Air Quality Monitoring Information, "Air Quality Statistics by City, 2019"

Maximum Air Pollutant Concentrations: Nitrogen Dioxide and Sulfur Dioxide

	Nitrogen Dioxide AM (ppb)	Nitrogen Dioxide 1-Hr (ppb)	Sulfur Dioxide AM (ppb)	Sulfur Dioxide 1-Hr (ppb)	Sulfur Dioxide 24-Hr (ppb)
MSA[1] Level	n/a	n/a	n/a	25	n/a
NAAQS[2]	53	100	30	75	140
Met NAAQS[2]	n/a	n/a	n/a	Yes	n/a

Note: (1) Data covers the Cedar Rapids, IA Metropolitan Statistical Area; Data from exceptional events are included; (2) National Ambient Air Quality Standards; ppm = parts per million; ug/m^3 = micrograms per cubic meter; n/a not available.
Concentrations: Nitrogen Dioxide AM—highest arithmetic mean concentration; Nitrogen Dioxide 1-Hr—highest 98th percentile 1-hour daily maximum concentration; Sulfur Dioxide AM—highest annual mean concentration; Sulfur Dioxide 1-Hr—highest 99th percentile 1-hour daily maximum concentration; Sulfur Dioxide 24-Hr—highest second maximum 24-hour concentration
Source: U.S. Environmental Protection Agency, Air Quality Monitoring Information, "Air Quality Statistics by City, 2019"

Chicago, Illinois

Background

City of Big Shoulders, The Windy City, That Toddling Town, and The Second City, are some of Chicago's nicknames. Whatever one calls Chicago, it has always exemplified a great American city, from a bustling downtown with towering skyscrapers to a quaint collection of closely packed urban neighborhoods stretching into the suburban landscape, then into the fields of the Illinois prairie.

Innovation has been part of Chicago's history from the very start. Cyrus McCormick invented his McCormick Reaper in 1831 and put Chicago on the map, revolutionizing harvesting across the world. The first mail-order business, Montgomery Ward, was established in Chicago in 1872. The world's first skyscraper was built in Chicago in 1885 for the Home Insurance Company. In 1907, University of Chicago's Albert Michelson, received the first American Nobel Prize for science. In 1931, Enrico Fermi split the atom underneath the University of Chicago football field. In 1983, Motorola set up the first modern portable cellular phone system in Chicago. All of this is part of the same history that has given Chicago 78 Nobel Prize Winners, more than any city in the world.

Present-day Chicago is "greener" than ever before. It has 300 square miles of protected lands and is home to 131 plant species of global importance. The city is the nation's largest municipal marina with over 5,000 boat slips. Bicycling, walking trails, beaches and golf are all abundant and top notch. The Oceanarium is the world's largest indoor marine mammal pavilion.

Chicago, with the third largest gross metropolitan product in the nation, has been rated the most balanced economy in the United States, due to its high level of diversification. The Boeing Company relocated its corporate headquarters from Seattle to Chicago in 2001. The city is also a major convention destination. Chicago is first in the country and third worldwide, in number of conventions hosted annually. In addition, Chicago and its metro area are home to dozens of Fortune 500 companies.

Chicago was the former home of former President Barack Obama and his family; the Barack Obama Presidential Center opened in 2020 at the University of Chicago.

When the Willis (formerly Sears) Tower was completed in 1973, it was the tallest building in North America. Chicago is also home to the tenth and twenty-second tallest buildings in the world, and the work of homegrown architects Frank Lloyd Wright, Louis Sullivan, and Helmut Jahn. In addition, Mies van der Rohe immigrated here and became one of the most influential architects of the post-World War II era.

In 2019, the city elected the first African American women and openly LBGTQ+ mayor. Chicago boasts the Art Institute of Chicago, the Adler Planetarium, the Chicago Architecture Foundation, and the Hellenic Museum and Cultural Center. Classical musical offerings include the Chicago Symphony Orchestra, its Chamber Music Series, the Chicago Opera Theater, and the Lyric Opera of Chicago. The city is famous for its eclectic nightlife. You can hear music at dozens of clubs, and comedy at Second City, where such comics as John Belushi, John Candy, Chris Farley, and Stephen Colbert had their start.

Chicago professional sports have long been in the national spotlight. Chicago is home to two major league baseball teams, the Chicago Cubs who play at Wrigley Field in the city's North Side and the Chicago White Sox who play in the city's South Side at U.S. Cellular Field. The Cubs won the 2016 World Series, ending a 108-year record World Series Champion drought. The Chicago Bears, the city's NFL team, won thirteen NFL championships, and Chicago's professional basketball team, the Chicago Bulls, is one of the world's most recognized teams. The NHL's Chicago Blackhawks, who share the United Center on the Near West Side with the Bulls, hosted the 2008-2009 Winter Classic.

The Chicago Marathon, one of five world marathon events, has been held every October since 1977. Chicago is also the starting point for the Chicago Yacht Club Race to Mackinac—the longest annual freshwater sailboat race in the world. Considering Chicago's athletic legacy, it's not surprising that the city was selected by the International Olympic Committee as one of four candidates for the 2016 games, but lost the bid to Rio de Janeiro.

Outstanding educational institutions in Chicago include the University of Chicago (1891); Northwestern University (1851); DePaul University; Loyola University; and the School of the Art Institute of Chicago.

Located along the southwest shore of Lake Michigan, Chicago has four true seasons, with a white Christmas, spring flowers, a steamy summer, and the beautiful colors of fall. Summers can be very hot and winters are often quite cold.

Rankings

General Rankings

- In its eighth annual survey, *Travel + Leisure* readers nominated their favorite small cities and towns in America—those with 100,000 or fewer residents—voting on numerous attractive features in categories including culture, food and drink, quality of life, style, and people. After 50,000 votes, Chicago was ranked #6 among the proposed favorites. *www.travelandleisure.com, "America's Favorite Cities," October 20, 2017*

- Chicago was selected as one of the best places to live in America by *Outside Magazine*. Criteria included population, park acreage, neighborhood and resident diversity, new and upcoming things of interest, and opportunities for outdoor adventure. *Outside Magazine, "The 12 Best Places to Live in 2019," July 11, 2019*

- The human resources consulting firm Mercer ranked 231 major cities worldwide in terms of overall quality of life. Chicago ranked #49. Criteria: political, social, economic, and socio-cultural factors; medical and health considerations; schools and education; public services and transportation; recreation; consumer goods; housing; and natural environment. *Mercer, "Mercer 2019 Quality of Living Survey," March 13, 2019*

- Chicago appeared on *Travel + Leisure's* list of the 15 best cities in the United States. The city was ranked #5. Criteria: sights/landmarks; culture; food; friendliness; shopping; and overall value. *Travel + Leisure, "The World's Best Awards 2020" July 8, 2020*

- For its 33rd annual "Readers' Choice Awards" survey, *Condé Nast Traveler* ranked its readers' favorite cities in the U.S. These places brought feelings of comfort in a time of limited travel. The list was broken into large cities and cities under 250,000. Chicago ranked #1 in the big city category. *Condé Nast Traveler, Readers' Choice Awards 2020, "Best Big Cities in the U.S." October 6, 2020*

Business/Finance Rankings

- Based on metro area social media reviews, the employment opinion group Glassdoor surveyed 50 of the most populous U.S. metro areas and equally weighed cost of living, hiring opportunity, and job satisfaction to compose a list of "25 Best Cities for Jobs." Median pay and home value, and number of active job openings were also factored in. The Chicago metro area was ranked #15 in overall job satisfaction. *www.glassdoor.com, "Best Cities for Jobs," February 25, 2020*

- The Brookings Institution ranked the nation's largest cities based on income inequality. Chicago was ranked #22 (#1 = greatest inequality). Criteria: the "95/20 ratio," a figure representing the income at which a household earns more than 95 percent of all other households, divided by the income at which a household earns more than only 20 percent of all other households. *Brookings Institution, "Household Income Inequality, Largest Cities of 97 Large U.S. Metro Areas, 2014-2016," February 5, 2018*

- The Brookings Institution ranked the 100 largest metro areas in the U.S. based on income inequality. Chicago was ranked #15 (#1 = greatest inequality). Criteria: the "95/20 ratio," a figure representing the income at which a household earns more than 95 percent of all other households, divided by the income at which a household earns more than only 20 percent of all other households. *Brookings Institution, "Household Income Inequality, 100 Largest U.S. Metro Areas, 2014-2016," February 5, 2018*

- Payscale.com ranked the 32 largest metro areas in terms of wage growth. The Chicago metro area ranked #21. Criteria: private-sector and education professional wage growth between the 4th quarter of 2019 and the 4th quarter of 2020. *PayScale, "Wage Trends by Metro Area-4th Quarter," January 11, 2021*

- The Chicago metro area was identified as one of the most debt-ridden places in America by the finance site Credit.com. The metro area was ranked #12. Criteria: residents' average credit card debt as well as median income. *Credit.com, "25 Cities With the Most Credit Card Debt," February 28, 2018*

- Chicago was cited as one of America's top metros for new and expanded facility projects in 2020. The area ranked #1 in the large metro area category (population over 1 million). *Site Selection, "Top Metros of 2020," March 2021*

- Chicago was identified as one of the happiest cities to work in by CareerBliss.com, an online community for career advancement. The city ranked #2 out of 10. Criteria: an employee's relationship with his or her boss and co-workers; daily tasks; general work environment; compensation; opportunities for advancement; company culture and job reputation; and resources. *Businesswire.com, "CareerBliss Happiest Cities to Work 2019," February 12, 2019*

- The Chicago metro area appeared on the Milken Institute "2021 Best Performing Cities" list. Rank: #152 out of 200 large metro areas (population over 250,000). Criteria: job growth; wage and salary growth; high-tech output growth; housing affordability; household broadband access. *Milken Institute, "Best-Performing Cities 2021," February 16, 2021*

- *Forbes* ranked the 200 most populous metro areas to determine the nation's "Best Places for Business and Careers." The Chicago metro area was ranked #75. Criteria: costs (business and living); job growth (past and projected); income growth; quality of life; educational attainment (college and high school); projected economic growth; cultural and leisure opportunities; workplace tolerance laws; net migration patterns. *Forbes, "The Best Places for Business and Careers 2019: Seattle Still On Top," October 30, 2019*

- Mercer Human Resources Consulting ranked 209 cities worldwide in terms of cost-of-living. Chicago ranked #30 (the lower the ranking, the higher the cost-of-living). The survey measured the comparative cost of over 200 items (such as housing, food, clothing, household goods, transportation, and entertainment) in each location. *Mercer, "2020 Cost of Living Survey," June 9, 2020*

Children/Family Rankings

- Chicago was selected as one of the most playful cities in the U.S. by KaBOOM! The organization's Playful City USA initiative honors cities and towns across the nation that have made their communities more playable. Criteria: pledging to integrate play as a solution to challenges in their communities; making it easy for children to get active and balanced play; creating more family-friendly and innovative communities as a result. *KaBOOM! National Campaign for Play, "2017 Playful City USA Communities"*

Culture/Performing Arts Rankings

- Chicago was selected as one of the 25 best cities for moviemakers in North America. COVID-19 has spurred a quest for great film cities that offer more creative space, lower costs, and more great outdoors. NYC & LA were intentionally excluded. Criteria: longstanding reputations as film-friendly communities; efforts to deal with pandemic-specific challenges; and establish appropriate COVID-19 guidelines. The city was ranked #4. *MovieMaker Magazine, "Best Places to Live and Work as a Moviemaker, 2021," January 26, 2021*

- Chicago was selected as one of "America's Favorite Cities." The city ranked #3 in the "Architecture" category. Respondents to an online survey were asked to rate their favorite place (population over 100,000) in over 65 categories. *Travelandleisure.com, "America's Favorite Cities for Architecture 2016," March 2, 2017*

Education Rankings

- Personal finance website *WalletHub* analyzed the 150 largest U.S. metropolitan statistical areas to determine where the most educated Americans are putting their degrees to work. Criteria: education levels; percentage of workers with degrees; education quality and attainment gap; public school quality rankings; quality and enrollment of each metro area's universities. Chicago was ranked #30 (#1 = most educated city). *www.WalletHub.com, "Most and Least Educated Cities in America," July 20, 2020*

- Chicago was selected as one of America's most literate cities. The city ranked #19 out of the 84 largest U.S. cities. Criteria: number of booksellers; library resources; Internet resources; educational attainment; periodical publishing resources; newspaper circulation. *Central Connecticut State University, "America's Most Literate Cities, 2018," February 2019*

Environmental Rankings

- The U.S. Environmental Protection Agency (EPA) released a list of U.S. metropolitan areas with the most ENERGY STAR certified buildings in 2019. The Chicago metro area was ranked #6 out of 25. *U.S. Environmental Protection Agency, "2020 Energy Star Top Cities," March 2020*

- Chicago was highlighted as one of the 25 most ozone-polluted metro areas in the U.S. during 2016 through 2018. The area ranked #16. *American Lung Association, "State of the Air 2020," April 21, 2020*

- Chicago was highlighted as one of the 25 metro areas most polluted by year-round particle pollution (Annual PM 2.5) in the U.S. during 2016 through 2018. The area ranked #20. *American Lung Association, "State of the Air 2020," April 21, 2020*

Food/Drink Rankings

- The U.S. Chamber of Commerce Foundation conducted an in-depth study on local food truck regulations, surveyed 288 food truck owners, and ranked 20 major American cities based on how friendly they are for operating a food truck. The compiled index assessed the following: procedures for obtaining permits and licenses; complying with restrictions; and financial obligations associated with operating a food truck. Chicago ranked #13 overall (1 being the best). *www.foodtrucknation.us, "Food Truck Nation," March 20, 2018*

Health/Fitness Rankings

- For each of the 100 largest cities in the United States, the American Fitness Index®, published by the American College of Sports Medicine and the Anthem Foundation, evaluated community infrastructure and 33 health behaviors including preventive health, levels of chronic disease conditions, pedestrian safety, air quality, and community resources that support physical activity. Chicago ranked #13 for "community fitness." *americanfitnessindex.org, "2020 ACSM American Fitness Index Summary Report," July 14, 2020*

- Chicago was identified as one of the 10 most walkable cities in the U.S. by Walk Score. The city ranked #6. Walk Score measures walkability by analyzing hundreds of walking routes to nearby amenities, and also measures pedestrian friendliness by analyzing population density and road metrics such as block length and intersection density. *WalkScore.com, April 13, 2021*

- The Chicago metro area was identified as one of the worst cities for bed bugs in America by pest control company Orkin. The area ranked #1 out of 50 based on the number of bed bug treatments Orkin performed from December 2019 to November 2020. *Orkin, "New Year, New Top City on Orkin's 2021 Bed Bug Cities List: Chicago," February 1, 2021*

- Chicago was identified as a "2021 Spring Allergy Capital." The area ranked #71 out of 100. Three groups of factors were used to identify the most challenging cities for people with allergies during the spring season: annual spring pollen levels; over the counter medicine use; number of board-certified allergy specialists. *Asthma and Allergy Foundation of America, "Spring Allergy Capitals 2021," February 23, 2021*

- Chicago was identified as a "2021 Fall Allergy Capital." The area ranked #54 out of 100. Three groups of factors were used to identify the most challenging cities for people with allergies during the fall season: annual fall pollen levels; over the counter medicine use; number of board-certified allergy specialists. *Asthma and Allergy Foundation of America, "Fall Allergy Capitals 2021," February 23, 2021*

- Chicago was identified as a "2019 Asthma Capital." The area ranked #36 out of the nation's 100 largest metropolitan areas. Criteria: estimated asthma prevalence; crude death rate from asthma; and ER visits due to asthma. Risk factors analyzed but not factored in the rankings: annual pollen score; annual air quality; public smoking laws; number of board-certified asthma specialists; rescue medication use; controller medication use; uninsured rate; poverty rate. *Asthma and Allergy Foundation of America, "Asthma Capitals 2019: The Most Challenging Places to Live With Asthma," May 7, 2019*

Pet Rankings

- Chicago appeared on *The Dogington Post* site as one of the top cities for dog lovers, ranking #2 out of 20. The real estate brokerage, Redfin and Rover, the largest pet sitter and dog walker network, compiled a list from over 14,000 U.S. cities to come up with a "Rover Rank." Criteria: highest count of dog walks, the city's Walk Score®, for-sale home listings that mention "dog," number of dog walkers and pet sitters and the hours spent and distance logged. *www.dogingtonpost.com, "The 20 Most Dog-Friendly Cities of 2019," April 4, 2019*

Real Estate Rankings

- FitSmallBusiness looked at 50 of the largest metropolitan areas in the U.S. to determine which metro was the best to start a real estate business. Data was compiled from such sources as: Zillow, Trulia, U.S. Census Bureau, and the Bureau of Labor Statistics. Criteria: location; inventory; annual wages; median sales price of homes; days on the market; median price cut percentage; and other factors that would influence real estate professional growth. The Chicago metro area ranked #4. *fitsmallbusiness.com, "The Best Cities to Become a Real Estate Agent in 2018," January 30, 2018*

- *WalletHub* compared the most populated U.S. cities to determine which had the best markets for real estate agents. Chicago ranked #85 where demand was high and pay was the best. Criteria: sales per agent; annual median wage for real-estate agents; monthly average starting salary for real estate agents; real estate job density and competition; unemployment rate; home turnover rate; housing-market health index; and other relevant metrics. *www.WalletHub.com, "2019's Best Places to Be a Real Estate Agent," April 24, 2019*

- Chicago was ranked #183 out of 268 metro areas in terms of housing affordability in 2020 by the National Association of Home Builders (#1 = most affordable). Criteria: the share of homes sold in that area affordable to a family earning the local median income, based on standard mortgage underwriting criteria. *National Association of Home Builders®, NAHB-Wells Fargo Housing Opportunity Index, 4th Quarter 2020*

- The nation's largest metro areas were analyzed in terms of the percentage of households entering some stage of foreclosure in 2020. The Chicago metro area ranked #7 out of 10 (#1 = highest foreclosure rate). *ATTOM Data Solutions, "2020 Year-End U.S. Foreclosure Market Report™," January 14, 2021*

Safety Rankings

- To identify the most dangerous cities in America, 24/7 Wall Street focused on violent crime categories—murder, non-negligent manslaughter, rape, robbery, and aggravated assault—and property crime as reported in the FBI's 2019 annual Uniform Crime Report. Criteria also included median income from American Community Survey and unemployment figures from Bureau of Labor Statistics. For cities with populations over 100,000, Chicago was ranked #33. *247wallst.com, "America's 50 Most Dangerous Cities" November 16, 2020*

- Allstate ranked the 200 largest cities in America in terms of driver safety. Chicago ranked #133. Criteria: internal property damage claims over a two-year period from January 2016 to December 2017. The report helps increase the importance of safety and awareness behind the wheel. *Allstate, "Allstate America's Best Drivers Report, 2019" June 24, 2019*

- Chicago was identified as one of the most dangerous cities in America by NeighborhoodScout. The city ranked #73 out of 100 (#1 = most dangerous). Criteria: number of violent crimes per 1,000 residents. The editors evaluated cities with 25,000 or more residents. *NeighborhoodScout.com, "2021 Top 100 Most Dangerous Cities in the U.S.," January 2, 2021*

- The National Insurance Crime Bureau ranked 384 metro areas in the U.S. in terms of per capita rates of vehicle theft. The Chicago metro area ranked #141 (#1 = highest rate). Criteria: number of vehicle theft offenses per 100,000 inhabitants in 2019. *National Insurance Crime Bureau, "Hot Spots 2019," July 21, 2020*

Seniors/Retirement Rankings

- From its Best Cities for Successful Aging indexes, the Milken Institute generated rankings for metropolitan areas, weighing data in nine categories—health care, wellness, living arrangements, transportation and convenience, financial characteristics, education, employment, community engagement, and overall livability. The Chicago metro area was ranked #52 overall in the large metro area category. *Milken Institute, "Best Cities for Successful Aging, 2017" March 14, 2017*

Sports/Recreation Rankings

- Chicago was chosen as one of America's best cities for bicycling. The city ranked #6 out of 50. Criteria: cycling infrastructure that is safe and friendly for all ages; energy and bike culture. The editors evaluated cities with populations of 100,000 or more. *Bicycling, "The 50 Best Bike Cities in America," October 10, 2018*

Transportation Rankings

- Business Insider presented an AllTransit Performance Score ranking of public transportation in major U.S. cities and towns, with populations over 250,000, in which Chicago earned the #6-ranked "Transit Score," awarded for frequency of service, access to jobs, quality and number of stops, and affordability. *www.businessinsider.com, "The 17 Major U.S. Cities with the Best Public Transportation," April 17, 2018*

- Chicago was identified as one of the most congested metro areas in the U.S. The area ranked #10 out of 10. Criteria: yearly delay per auto commuter in hours. *Texas A&M Transportation Institute, "2019 Urban Mobility Report," December 2019*

- According to the INRIX "2019 Global Traffic Scorecard," Chicago was identified as one of the most congested metro areas in the U.S. The area ranked #2 out of 10. Criteria: average annual time spent in traffic and average cost of congestion per motorist. *Inrix.com, "Congestion Costs Each American Nearly 100 hours, $1,400 A Year," March 9, 2020*

Women/Minorities Rankings

- *Travel + Leisure* listed the best cities in and around the US for a memorable and fun girls' trip, even on a budget. Whether it is for a special occasion or just to get away, Chicago is sure to have something for all the ladies in your tribe. *Travel + Leisure, "25 Girls' Weekend Getaways That Won't Break the Bank," June 8, 2020*

- The *Houston Chronicle* listed the Chicago metro area as #8 in top places for young Latinos to live in the U.S. Research was largely based on housing and occupational data from the largest metropolitan areas performed by *Forbes* and NBC Universo. Criteria: percentage of 18-34 year-olds; Latino college grad rates; and diversity. *blog.chron.com, "The 15 Best Big Cities for Latino Millenials," January 26, 2016*

- Personal finance website *WalletHub* compared more than 180 U.S. cities across two key dimensions, "Hispanic Business-Friendliness" and "Hispanic Purchasing Power," to arrive at the most favorable conditions for Hispanic entrepreneurs. Chicago was ranked #122 out of 182. Criteria includes: share of Hispanic-Owned Businesses; Hispanic entrepreneurship rate to median annual income of Hispanics; Small Business-Friendliness score; cost of living; and number of Hispanics with at least a bachelor's degree. *WalletHub.com, "2019's Best Cities for Hispanic Entrepreneurs," May 1, 2019*

Miscellaneous Rankings

- While the majority of travel ground to a halt in 2020, plugged-in travel influencers and experts were able to rediscover their local regions. Chicago appeared on a *Forbes* list of 15 U.S. cities that provided solace as well as local inspiration. Whether it be quirky things to see and do, delicious take out, outdoor exploring and daytrips, these places are must-see destinations. *Forbes, "Bucket List Travel: The 15 Best U.S. Destinations For 2021," January 1, 2021*

- Chicago was selected as a 2020 Digital Cities Survey winner. The city ranked #8 in the large city (500,000 or more population) category. The survey examined and assessed how city governments are utilizing technology to improve transparency, enhance cybersecurity, and respond to the pandemic. Survey questions focused on ten initiatives: cybersecurity, citizen experience, disaster recovery, business intelligence, IT personnel, data governance, collaboration, infrastructure modernization, cloud computing, and mobile applications. *Center for Digital Government, "2020 Digital Cities Survey," November 10, 2020*

- In its roundup of St. Patrick's Day parades "Gayot" listed the best festivals and parades of all things Irish. The festivities in Chicago as among the best. *www.gayot.com, "Best St. Patrick's Day Parades," March 2020*

- The watchdog site, Charity Navigator, conducted a study of charities in major markets both to analyze statistical differences in their financial, accountability, and transparency practices and to track year-to-year variations in individual philanthropic communities. The Chicago metro area was ranked #11 among the 30 metro markets in the rating category of Overall Score. *www.charitynavigator.org, "2017 Metro Market Study," May 1, 2017*

- *WalletHub* compared the 150 most populated U.S. cities to determine their operating efficiency. A "Quality of City Services" score was constructed for each city and then divided by the total budget per capita to reveal which were managed the best. Chicago ranked #142. Criteria: financial stability; economy; education; safety; health; infrastructure and pollution. *www.WalletHub.com, "2020's Best- & Worst-Run Cities in America," June 29, 2020*

- The National Alliance to End Homelessness listed the 25 most populous metro areas with the highest rate of homelessness. The Chicago metro area had a high rate of homelessness. Criteria: number of homeless people per 10,000 population in 2016. *National Alliance to End Homelessness, "Homelessness in the 25 Most Populous U.S. Metro Areas," September 1, 2017*

Business Environment

DEMOGRAPHICS

Population Growth

Area	1990 Census	2000 Census	2010 Census	2019* Estimate	Population Growth (%)	
					1990-2019	2010-2019
City	2,783,726	2,896,016	2,695,598	2,709,534	-2.7	0.5
MSA[1]	8,182,076	9,098,316	9,461,105	9,508,605	16.2	0.5
U.S.	248,709,873	281,421,906	308,745,538	324,697,795	30.6	5.2

Note: (1) Figures cover the Chicago-Naperville-Elgin, IL-IN-WI Metropolitan Statistical Area; (*) 2015-2019 5-year estimated population
Source: U.S. Census Bureau, 1990 Census, Census 2000, Census 2010, 2015-2019 American Community Survey 5-Year Estimates

Household Size

Area	Persons in Household (%)							Average Household Size
	One	Two	Three	Four	Five	Six	Seven or More	
City	37.2	29.7	13.8	10.2	5.2	2.3	1.6	2.50
MSA[1]	28.9	31.1	15.6	13.8	6.7	2.5	1.4	2.70
U.S.	27.9	33.9	15.6	12.9	6.0	2.3	1.4	2.60

Note: (1) Figures cover the Chicago-Naperville-Elgin, IL-IN-WI Metropolitan Statistical Area
Source: U.S. Census Bureau, 2015-2019 American Community Survey 5-Year Estimates

Race

Area	White Alone[2] (%)	Black Alone[2] (%)	Asian Alone[2] (%)	AIAN[3] Alone[2] (%)	NHOPI[4] Alone[2] (%)	Other Race Alone[2] (%)	Two or More Races (%)
City	50.0	29.6	6.6	0.3	0.0	10.6	2.8
MSA[1]	65.7	16.6	6.6	0.3	0.0	8.0	2.7
U.S.	72.5	12.7	5.5	0.8	0.2	4.9	3.3

Note: (1) Figures cover the Chicago-Naperville-Elgin, IL-IN-WI Metropolitan Statistical Area; (2) Alone is defined as not being in combination with one or more other races; (3) American Indian and Alaska Native; (4) Native Hawaiian and Other Pacific Islander
Source: U.S. Census Bureau, 2015-2019 American Community Survey 5-Year Estimates

Hispanic or Latino Origin

Area	Total (%)	Mexican (%)	Puerto Rican (%)	Cuban (%)	Other (%)
City	28.8	21.3	3.6	0.3	3.5
MSA[1]	22.1	17.3	2.2	0.2	2.4
U.S.	18.0	11.2	1.7	0.7	4.3

Note: Persons of Hispanic or Latino origin can be of any race; (1) Figures cover the Chicago-Naperville-Elgin, IL-IN-WI Metropolitan Statistical Area
Source: U.S. Census Bureau, 2015-2019 American Community Survey 5-Year Estimates

Ancestry

Area	German	Irish	English	American	Italian	Polish	French[2]	Scottish	Dutch
City	7.3	7.5	2.4	2.0	4.0	5.6	1.0	0.6	0.5
MSA[1]	14.3	10.8	4.2	2.6	6.6	8.8	1.4	0.9	1.2
U.S.	13.3	9.7	7.2	6.2	5.1	2.8	2.3	1.7	1.2

Note: Figures are the percentage of the total population reporting a particular ancestry. The nine most commonly reported ancestries in the U.S. are shown. Figures include multiple ancestries (e.g. if a person reported being Irish and Italian, they were included in both columns); (1) Figures cover the Chicago-Naperville-Elgin, IL-IN-WI Metropolitan Statistical Area; (2) Excludes Basque
Source: U.S. Census Bureau, 2015-2019 American Community Survey 5-Year Estimates

Foreign-born Population

Area	Percent of Population Born in								
	Any Foreign Country	Asia	Mexico	Europe	Caribbean	Central America[2]	South America	Africa	Canada
City	20.6	5.2	8.4	3.5	0.4	0.9	1.1	1.0	0.2
MSA[1]	17.7	5.2	6.5	3.7	0.3	0.6	0.6	0.6	0.2
U.S.	13.6	4.2	3.5	1.5	1.3	1.1	1.0	0.7	0.2

Note: (1) Figures cover the Chicago-Naperville-Elgin, IL-IN-WI Metropolitan Statistical Area; (2) Excludes Mexico.
Source: U.S. Census Bureau, 2015-2019 American Community Survey 5-Year Estimates

48 Chicago, Illinois

Marital Status

Area	Never Married	Now Married[2]	Separated	Widowed	Divorced
City	48.7	35.5	2.3	5.2	8.3
MSA[1]	37.0	46.9	1.6	5.5	8.9
U.S.	33.4	48.1	1.9	5.8	10.9

Note: Figures are percentages and cover the population 15 years of age and older; (1) Figures cover the Chicago-Naperville-Elgin, IL-IN-WI Metropolitan Statistical Area; (2) Excludes separated
Source: U.S. Census Bureau, 2015-2019 American Community Survey 5-Year Estimates

Disability by Age

Area	All Ages	Under 18 Years Old	18 to 64 Years Old	65 Years and Over
City	10.5	2.9	8.3	35.5
MSA[1]	9.9	3.0	7.7	31.8
U.S.	12.6	4.2	10.3	34.5

Note: Figures show percent of the civilian noninstitutionalized population that reported having a disability. Disability status is determined from six types of difficulty: vision, hearing, cognitive, ambulatory, self-care, and independent living. For children under 5 years old, hearing and vision difficulty are used to determine disability status. For children between the ages of 5 and 14, disability status is determined from hearing, vision, cognitive, ambulatory, and self-care difficulties. For people aged 15 years and older, they are considered to have a disability if they have difficulty with any one of the six difficulty types; Note: (1) Figures cover the Chicago-Naperville-Elgin, IL-IN-WI Metropolitan Statistical Area
Source: U.S. Census Bureau, 2015-2019 American Community Survey 5-Year Estimates

Age

Area	Percent of Population									Median Age
	Under Age 5	Age 5–19	Age 20–34	Age 35–44	Age 45–54	Age 55–64	Age 65–74	Age 75–84	Age 85+	
City	6.3	17.0	27.3	14.0	11.9	10.9	7.2	3.7	1.5	34.6
MSA[1]	6.1	19.4	21.0	13.3	13.3	12.7	8.2	4.1	1.8	37.5
U.S.	6.1	19.1	20.7	12.6	13.0	12.9	9.1	4.6	1.9	38.1

Note: (1) Figures cover the Chicago-Naperville-Elgin, IL-IN-WI Metropolitan Statistical Area
Source: U.S. Census Bureau, 2015-2019 American Community Survey 5-Year Estimates

Gender

Area	Males	Females	Males per 100 Females
City	1,317,791	1,391,743	94.7
MSA[1]	4,654,160	4,854,445	95.9
U.S.	159,886,919	164,810,876	97.0

Note: (1) Figures cover the Chicago-Naperville-Elgin, IL-IN-WI Metropolitan Statistical Area
Source: U.S. Census Bureau, 2015-2019 American Community Survey 5-Year Estimates

Religious Groups by Family

Area	Catholic	Baptist	Non-Den.	Methodist[2]	Lutheran	LDS[3]	Pentecostal	Presbyterian[4]	Muslim[5]	Judaism
MSA[1]	34.2	3.2	4.5	1.9	3.0	0.4	1.2	1.9	3.3	0.8
U.S.	19.1	9.3	4.0	4.0	2.3	2.0	1.9	1.6	0.8	0.7

Note: Figures are the number of adherents as a percentage of the total population; (1) Figures cover the Chicago-Naperville-Elgin, IL-IN-WI Metropolitan Statistical Area; (2) Methodist/Pietist; (3) Latter Day Saints; (4) Reformed; (5) Figures are estimates
Source: Association of Statisticians of American Religious Bodies, 2010 U.S. Religion Census: Religious Congregations & Membership Study

Religious Groups by Tradition

Area	Catholic	Evangelical Protestant	Mainline Protestant	Other Tradition	Black Protestant	Orthodox
MSA[1]	34.2	9.8	5.1	5.1	2.1	0.9
U.S.	19.1	16.2	7.3	4.3	1.6	0.3

Note: Figures are the number of adherents as a percentage of the total population; (1) Figures cover the Chicago-Naperville-Elgin, IL-IN-WI Metropolitan Statistical Area
Source: Association of Statisticians of American Religious Bodies, 2010 U.S. Religion Census: Religious Congregations & Membership Study

ECONOMY

Gross Metropolitan Product

Area	2017	2018	2019	2020	Rank[2]
MSA[1]	683.3	716.3	743.3	770.7	3

Note: Figures are in billions of dollars; (1) Figures cover the Chicago-Naperville-Elgin, IL-IN-WI Metropolitan Statistical Area; (2) Rank is based on 2018 data and ranges from 1 to 381
Source: U.S. Conference of Mayors, U.S. Metro Economies: GMP & Employment 2018-2020, September 2019

Economic Growth

Area	2015-17 (%)	2018 (%)	2019 (%)	2020 (%)	Rank[2]
MSA[1]	0.8	2.3	2.0	1.6	247
U.S.	1.9	2.9	2.3	2.1	–

Note: Figures are real gross metropolitan product (GMP) growth rates and represent average annual percent change; (1) Figures cover the Chicago-Naperville-Elgin, IL-IN-WI Metropolitan Statistical Area; (2) Rank is based on 2017 2-year average annual percent change and ranges from 1 to 381
Source: U.S. Conference of Mayors, U.S. Metro Economies: GMP & Employment 2018-2020, September 2019

Metropolitan Area Exports

Area	2014	2015	2016	2017	2018	2019	Rank[2]
MSA[1]	47,340.1	44,820.9	43,932.7	46,140.2	47,287.8	42,438.8	4

Note: Figures are in millions of dollars; (1) Figures cover the Chicago-Naperville-Elgin, IL-IN-WI Metropolitan Statistical Area; (2) Rank is based on 2019 data and ranges from 1 to 386
Source: U.S. Department of Commerce, International Trade Administration, Office of Trade and Economic Analysis, Industry and Analysis, Exports by Metropolitan Area, data extracted March 24, 2021

Building Permits

Area	Single-Family			Multi-Family			Total		
	2018	2019	Pct. Chg.	2018	2019	Pct. Chg.	2018	2019	Pct. Chg.
City	439	410	-6.6	6,010	7,504	24.9	6,449	7,914	22.7
MSA[1]	8,546	7,598	-11.1	9,135	10,487	14.8	17,681	18,085	2.3
U.S.	855,300	862,100	0.7	473,500	523,900	10.6	1,328,800	1,386,000	4.3

Note: (1) Figures cover the Chicago-Naperville-Elgin, IL-IN-WI Metropolitan Statistical Area; Figures represent new, privately-owned housing units authorized (unadjusted data); All permit data are based on estimates with imputation
Source: U.S. Census Bureau, Manufacturing, Mining, and Construction Statistics, Building Permits, 2018, 2019

Bankruptcy Filings

Area	Business Filings			Nonbusiness Filings		
	2019	2020	% Chg.	2019	2020	% Chg.
Cook County	413	335	-18.9	27,789	16,384	-41.0
U.S.	22,780	21,655	-4.9	752,160	522,808	-30.5

Note: Business filings include Chapter 7, Chapter 9, Chapter 11, Chapter 12, Chapter 13, Chapter 15, and Section 304; Nonbusiness filings include Chapter 7, Chapter 11, and Chapter 13
Source: Administrative Office of the U.S. Courts, Business and Nonbusiness Bankruptcy, County Cases Commenced by Chapter of the Bankruptcy Code, During the 12-Month Period Ending December 31, 2019 and Business and Nonbusiness Bankruptcy, County Cases Commenced by Chapter of the Bankruptcy Code, During the 12-Month Period Ending December 31, 2020

Housing Vacancy Rates

Area	Gross Vacancy Rate[2] (%)			Year-Round Vacancy Rate[3] (%)			Rental Vacancy Rate[4] (%)			Homeowner Vacancy Rate[5] (%)		
	2018	2019	2020	2018	2019	2020	2018	2019	2020	2018	2019	2020
MSA[1]	7.5	7.6	7.4	7.4	7.6	7.2	7.0	5.7	7.4	1.6	1.5	1.2
U.S.	12.3	12.0	10.6	9.7	9.5	8.2	6.9	6.7	6.3	1.5	1.4	1.0

Note: (1) Figures cover the Chicago-Naperville-Elgin, IL-IN-WI Metropolitan Statistical Area; (2) The percentage of the total housing inventory that is vacant; (3) The percentage of the housing inventory (excluding seasonal units) that is year-round vacant; (4) The percentage of rental inventory that is vacant for rent; (5) The percentage of homeowner inventory that is vacant for sale
Source: U.S. Census Bureau, Housing Vacancies and Homeownership Annual Statistics: 2018, 2019, 2020

INCOME

Income

Area	Per Capita ($)	Median Household ($)	Average Household ($)
City	37,103	58,247	90,713
MSA[1]	38,157	71,770	100,233
U.S.	34,103	62,843	88,607

Note: (1) Figures cover the Chicago-Naperville-Elgin, IL-IN-WI Metropolitan Statistical Area
Source: U.S. Census Bureau, 2015-2019 American Community Survey 5-Year Estimates

Household Income Distribution

Area	Percent of Households Earning							
	Under $15,000	$15,000 -$24,999	$25,000 -$34,999	$35,000 -$49,999	$50,000 -$74,999	$75,000 -$99,999	$100,000 -$149,999	$150,000 and up
City	14.0	10.3	8.9	11.0	15.1	11.2	13.8	15.7
MSA[1]	9.3	7.9	7.8	10.8	16.0	12.8	17.0	18.4
U.S.	10.3	8.9	8.9	12.3	17.2	12.7	15.1	14.5

Note: (1) Figures cover the Chicago-Naperville-Elgin, IL-IN-WI Metropolitan Statistical Area
Source: U.S. Census Bureau, 2015-2019 American Community Survey 5-Year Estimates

Poverty Rate

Area	All Ages	Under 18 Years Old	18 to 64 Years Old	65 Years and Over
City	18.4	26.8	16.2	15.5
MSA[1]	11.8	16.5	10.7	9.1
U.S.	13.4	18.5	12.6	9.3

Note: Figures are percentage of people whose income during the past 12 months was below the poverty level;
(1) Figures cover the Chicago-Naperville-Elgin, IL-IN-WI Metropolitan Statistical Area
Source: U.S. Census Bureau, 2015-2019 American Community Survey 5-Year Estimates

CITY FINANCES

City Government Finances

Component	2017 ($000)	2017 ($ per capita)
Total Revenues	9,903,182	3,640
Total Expenditures	10,401,108	3,823
Debt Outstanding	23,539,562	8,653
Cash and Securities[1]	16,038,297	5,895

Note: (1) Cash and security holdings of a government at the close of its fiscal year,
including those of its dependent agencies, utilities, and liquor stores.
Source: U.S. Census Bureau, State & Local Government Finances 2017

City Government Revenue by Source

Source	2017 ($000)	2017 ($ per capita)	2017 (%)
General Revenue			
From Federal Government	619,242	228	6.3
From State Government	1,084,923	399	11.0
From Local Governments	6,583	2	0.1
Taxes			
Property	1,294,063	476	13.1
Sales and Gross Receipts	1,807,606	664	18.3
Personal Income	0	0	0.0
Corporate Income	0	0	0.0
Motor Vehicle License	24,335	9	0.2
Other Taxes	435,393	160	4.4
Current Charges	1,914,278	704	19.3
Liquor Store	0	0	0.0
Utility	760,638	280	7.7
Employee Retirement	881,784	324	8.9

Source: U.S. Census Bureau, State & Local Government Finances 2017

City Government Expenditures by Function

Function	2017 ($000)	2017 ($ per capita)	2017 (%)
General Direct Expenditures			
Air Transportation	1,279,601	470	12.3
Corrections	0	0	0.0
Education	0	0	0.0
Employment Security Administration	0	0	0.0
Financial Administration	146,554	53	1.4
Fire Protection	585,010	215	5.6
General Public Buildings	217,731	80	2.1
Governmental Administration, Other	64,026	23	0.6
Health	131,616	48	1.3
Highways	669,770	246	6.4
Hospitals	0	0	0.0
Housing and Community Development	241,747	88	2.3
Interest on General Debt	931,275	342	9.0
Judicial and Legal	29,525	10	0.3
Libraries	95,327	35	0.9
Parking	7,476	2	0.1
Parks and Recreation	28,506	10	0.3
Police Protection	1,456,302	535	14.0
Public Welfare	304,839	112	2.9
Sewerage	283,217	104	2.7
Solid Waste Management	159,572	58	1.5
Veterans' Services	0	0	0.0
Liquor Store	0	0	0.0
Utility	610,909	224	5.9
Employee Retirement	2,021,004	742	19.4

Source: U.S. Census Bureau, State & Local Government Finances 2017

EMPLOYMENT

Labor Force and Employment

Area	Civilian Labor Force			Workers Employed		
	Dec. 2019	Dec. 2020	% Chg.	Dec. 2019	Dec. 2020	% Chg.
City	1,322,199	1,308,831	-1.0	1,281,869	1,177,846	-8.1
MD[1]	3,687,479	3,541,085	-4.0	3,574,836	3,232,803	-9.6
U.S.	164,007,000	160,017,000	-2.4	158,504,000	149,613,000	-5.6

Note: Data is not seasonally adjusted and covers workers 16 years of age and older; (1) Figures cover the Chicago-Naperville-Arlington Heights, IL Metropolitan Division
Source: Bureau of Labor Statistics, Local Area Unemployment Statistics

Unemployment Rate

Area	2020											
	Jan.	Feb.	Mar.	Apr.	May	Jun.	Jul.	Aug.	Sep.	Oct.	Nov.	Dec.
City	3.7	3.5	5.0	18.7	17.2	18.6	15.2	15.5	14.4	10.5	8.6	10.0
MD[1]	3.8	3.7	3.9	16.4	15.8	15.7	13.3	13.0	12.2	8.8	8.9	8.7
U.S.	4.0	3.8	4.5	14.4	13.0	11.2	10.5	8.5	7.7	6.6	6.4	6.5

Note: Data is not seasonally adjusted and covers workers 16 years of age and older; (1) Figures cover the Chicago-Naperville-Arlington Heights, IL Metropolitan Division
Source: Bureau of Labor Statistics, Local Area Unemployment Statistics

Average Wages

Occupation	$/Hr.	Occupation	$/Hr.
Accountants and Auditors	37.80	Maintenance and Repair Workers	23.40
Automotive Mechanics	24.90	Marketing Managers	68.70
Bookkeepers	22.40	Network and Computer Systems Admin.	43.70
Carpenters	34.70	Nurses, Licensed Practical	28.50
Cashiers	12.60	Nurses, Registered	37.50
Computer Programmers	49.80	Nursing Assistants	15.60
Computer Systems Analysts	45.00	Office Clerks, General	19.20
Computer User Support Specialists	26.70	Physical Therapists	47.80
Construction Laborers	32.10	Physicians	108.90
Cooks, Restaurant	14.70	Plumbers, Pipefitters and Steamfitters	44.20
Customer Service Representatives	20.10	Police and Sheriff's Patrol Officers	39.60
Dentists	92.30	Postal Service Mail Carriers	25.90
Electricians	40.50	Real Estate Sales Agents	21.40
Engineers, Electrical	46.50	Retail Salespersons	14.70
Fast Food and Counter Workers	11.90	Sales Representatives, Technical/Scientific	43.30
Financial Managers	75.20	Secretaries, Exc. Legal/Medical/Executive	20.80
First-Line Supervisors of Office Workers	33.00	Security Guards	16.70
General and Operations Managers	66.10	Surgeons	126.50
Hairdressers/Cosmetologists	15.60	Teacher Assistants, Exc. Postsecondary*	14.90
Home Health and Personal Care Aides	13.70	Teachers, Secondary School, Exc. Sp. Ed.*	39.70
Janitors and Cleaners	15.90	Telemarketers	15.20
Landscaping/Groundskeeping Workers	16.90	Truck Drivers, Heavy/Tractor-Trailer	26.10
Lawyers	76.50	Truck Drivers, Light/Delivery Services	23.90
Maids and Housekeeping Cleaners	14.10	Waiters and Waitresses	11.30

Note: Wage data covers the Chicago-Naperville-Elgin, IL-IN-WI Metropolitan Statistical Area; (*) Hourly wages were calculated from annual wage data based on a 40 hour work week; n/a not available.
Source: Bureau of Labor Statistics, Metro Area Occupational Employment & Wage Estimates, May 2020

Employment by Industry

Sector	MD[1]		U.S.
	Number of Employees	Percent of Total	Percent of Total
Construction	121,900	3.5	5.1
Education and Health Services	577,500	16.5	16.3
Financial Activities	275,500	7.9	6.1
Government	400,100	11.5	15.2
Information	64,600	1.9	1.9
Leisure and Hospitality	230,000	6.6	9.0
Manufacturing	266,000	7.6	8.5
Mining and Logging	1,200	<0.1	0.4
Other Services	143,600	4.1	3.8
Professional and Business Services	669,300	19.2	14.4
Retail Trade	337,700	9.7	10.9
Transportation, Warehousing, and Utilities	224,200	6.4	4.6
Wholesale Trade	179,300	5.1	3.9

Note: Figures are non-farm employment as of December 2020. Figures are not seasonally adjusted and include workers 16 years of age and older; (1) Figures cover the Chicago-Naperville-Arlington Heights, IL Metropolitan Division
Source: Bureau of Labor Statistics, Current Employment Statistics, Employment, Hours, and Earnings

Employment by Occupation

Occupation Classification	City (%)	MSA[1] (%)	U.S. (%)
Management, Business, Science, and Arts	42.3	40.0	38.5
Natural Resources, Construction, and Maintenance	5.1	6.7	8.9
Production, Transportation, and Material Moving	13.0	14.3	13.2
Sales and Office	20.4	22.2	21.6
Service	19.2	16.7	17.8

Note: Figures cover employed civilians 16 years of age and older; (1) Figures cover the Chicago-Naperville-Elgin, IL-IN-WI Metropolitan Statistical Area
Source: U.S. Census Bureau, 2015-2019 American Community Survey 5-Year Estimates

Occupations with Greatest Projected Employment Growth: 2019 – 2021

Occupation[1]	2019 Employment	2021 Projected Employment	Numeric Employment Change	Percent Employment Change
Total,, All Occupations	6,370,620	6,449,130	78,510	1.2
Combined Food Preparation and Serving Workers,, Including Fast Food	140,460	145,280	4,820	3.4
Registered Nurses	133,320	137,300	3,980	3.0
Personal Care Aides	56,160	59,830	3,670	6.5
Laborers and Freight,, Stock,, and Material Movers,, Hand	158,620	162,170	3,550	2.2
Insurance Sales Agents	49,730	52,420	2,690	5.4
Heavy and Tractor-Trailer Truck Drivers	73,100	75,610	2,510	3.4
General and Operations Managers	120,880	123,200	2,320	1.9
Cooks,, Restaurant	47,520	49,620	2,100	4.4
Janitors and Cleaners,, Except Maids and Housekeeping Cleaners	85,160	86,710	1,550	1.8

Note: Projections cover Illinois; Projections for 2020-2022 were not available at time of publication; (1) Sorted by numeric employment change
Source: www.projectionscentral.com, State Occupational Projections, 2019–2021 Short-Term Projections

Fastest-Growing Occupations: 2019 – 2021

Occupation[1]	2019 Employment	2021 Projected Employment	Numeric Employment Change	Percent Employment Change
Actuaries	1,940	2,070	130	6.7
Personal Care Aides	56,160	59,830	3,670	6.5
Statisticians	1,910	2,030	120	6.3
Nurse Practitioners	8,130	8,610	480	5.9
Physician Assistants	3,800	4,020	220	5.8
Insurance Sales Agents	49,730	52,420	2,690	5.4
Operations Research Analysts	5,080	5,350	270	5.3
Computer Numerically Controlled Machine Tool Programmers,, Metal and Plastic	1,150	1,210	60	5.2
Veterinary Technologists and Technicians	4,010	4,210	200	5.0
Massage Therapists	6,720	7,050	330	4.9

Note: Projections cover Illinois; Projections for 2020-2022 were not available at time of publication; (1) Sorted by percent employment change and excludes occupations with numeric employment change less than 50
Source: www.projectionscentral.com, State Occupational Projections, 2019–2021 Short-Term Projections

TAXES

State Corporate Income Tax Rates

State	Tax Rate (%)	Income Brackets ($)	Num. of Brackets	Financial Institution Tax Rate (%)[a]	Federal Income Tax Ded.
Illinois	9.5 (h)	Flat rate	1	9.5 (h)	No

Note: Tax rates as of January 1, 2021; (a) Rates listed are the corporate income tax rate applied to financial institutions or excise taxes based on income. Some states have other taxes based upon the value of deposits or shares; (h) The Illinois rate of 9.5% is the sum of a corporate income tax rate of 7.0% plus a replacement tax of 2.5%.
Source: Federation of Tax Administrators, State Corporate Income Tax Rates, January 1, 2021

State Individual Income Tax Rates

State	Tax Rate (%)	Income Brackets ($)	Personal Exemptions ($)			Standard Ded. ($)	
			Single	Married	Depend.	Single	Married
Illinois (a)	4.95	Flat rate	2,325	4,650	2,325	–	–

Note: Tax rates as of January 1, 2021; Local- and county-level taxes are not included; Federal income tax is not deductible on state income tax returns; (a) 19 states have statutory provision for automatically adjusting to the rate of inflation the dollar values of the income tax brackets, standard deductions, and/or personal exemptions. Michigan indexes the personal exemption only. Oregon does not index the income brackets for $125,000 and over.
Source: Federation of Tax Administrators, State Individual Income Tax Rates, January 1, 2021

Various State Sales and Excise Tax Rates

State	State Sales Tax (%)	Gasoline[1] (¢/gal.)	Cigarette[2] ($/pack)	Spirits[3] ($/gal.)	Wine[4] ($/gal.)	Beer[5] ($/gal.)	Recreational Marijuana (%)
Illinois	6.25	52.16	2.98	8.55	1.39	0.23	(e)

Note: All tax rates as of January 1, 2021; (1) The American Petroleum Institute has developed a methodology for determining the average tax rate on a gallon of fuel. Rates may include any of the following: excise taxes, environmental fees, storage tank fees, other fees or taxes, general sales tax, and local taxes; (2) The federal excise tax of $1.0066 per pack and local taxes are not included; (3) Rates are those applicable to off-premise sales of 40% alcohol by volume (a.b.v.) distilled spirits in 750ml containers. Local excise taxes are excluded; (4) Rates are those applicable to off-premise sales of 11% a.b.v. non-carbonated wine in 750ml containers; (5) Rates are those applicable to off-premise sales of 4.7% a.b.v. beer in 12 ounce containers; (e) 7% excise tax of value at wholesale level; 10% tax on cannabis flower or products with less than 35% THC; 20% tax on products infused with cannabis, such as edible products; 25% tax on any product with a THC concentration higher than 35%
Source: Tax Foundation, 2021 Facts & Figures: How Does Your State Compare?

State Business Tax Climate Index Rankings

State	Overall Rank	Corporate Tax Rank	Individual Income Tax Rank	Sales Tax Rank	Property Tax Rank	Unemployment Insurance Tax Rank
Illinois	36	36	13	38	48	43

Note: The index is a measure of how each state's tax laws affect economic performance. The lower the rank, the more favorable a state's tax system is for business. States without a given tax are given a ranking of 1. The scores/rankings for the District of Columbia do not affect other states. The 2021 index represents the tax climate as of July 1, 2020.
Source: Tax Foundation, State Business Tax Climate Index 2021

TRANSPORTATION

Means of Transportation to Work

Area	Car/Truck/Van		Public Transportation			Bicycle	Walked	Other Means	Worked at Home
	Drove Alone	Car-pooled	Bus	Subway	Railroad				
City	48.8	7.7	13.3	13.0	1.8	1.7	6.5	2.0	5.2
MSA[1]	70.0	7.7	4.4	4.4	3.3	0.7	3.0	1.4	5.2
U.S.	76.3	9.0	2.4	1.9	0.6	0.5	2.7	1.4	5.2

Note: Figures are percentages and cover workers 16 years of age and older; (1) Figures cover the Chicago-Naperville-Elgin, IL-IN-WI Metropolitan Statistical Area
Source: U.S. Census Bureau, 2015-2019 American Community Survey 5-Year Estimates

Travel Time to Work

Area	Less Than 10 Minutes	10 to 19 Minutes	20 to 29 Minutes	30 to 44 Minutes	45 to 59 Minutes	60 to 89 Minutes	90 Minutes or More
City	4.5	16.0	17.4	30.6	15.3	12.8	3.5
MSA[1]	8.2	21.5	18.4	25.2	12.4	10.8	3.5
U.S.	12.2	28.4	20.8	20.8	8.3	6.4	2.9

Note: Note: Figures are percentages and include workers 16 years old and over; (1) Figures cover the Chicago-Naperville-Elgin, IL-IN-WI Metropolitan Statistical Area
Source: U.S. Census Bureau, 2015-2019 American Community Survey 5-Year Estimates

Key Congestion Measures

Measure	1982	1992	2002	2012	2017
Annual Hours of Delay, Total (000)	99,294	160,710	254,740	319,661	352,759
Annual Hours of Delay, Per Auto Commuter	31	43	54	63	73
Annual Congestion Cost, Total (million $)	754	1,706	3,458	5,777	6,530
Annual Congestion Cost, Per Auto Commuter ($)	902	1,004	1,241	1,221	1,307

Note: Covers the Chicago IL-IN urban area
Source: Texas A&M Transportation Institute, 2019 Urban Mobility Report

54 Chicago, Illinois

Freeway Travel Time Index

Measure	1982	1987	1992	1997	2002	2007	2012	2017
Urban Area Index[1]	1.16	1.19	1.22	1.25	1.27	1.30	1.29	1.32
Urban Area Rank[1,2]	7	8	6	9	14	13	17	16

Note: Freeway Travel Time Index—the ratio of travel time in the peak period to the travel time at free-flow conditions. For example, a value of 1.30 indicates a 20-minute free-flow trip takes 26 minutes in the peak (20 minutes x 1.30 = 26 minutes); (1) Covers the Chicago IL-IN urban area; (2) Rank is based on 101 larger urban areas (#1 = highest travel time index)
Source: Texas A&M Transportation Institute, 2019 Urban Mobility Report

Public Transportation

Agency Name / Mode of Transportation	Vehicles Operated in Maximum Service[1]	Annual Unlinked Passenger Trips[2] (in thous.)	Annual Passenger Miles[3] (in thous.)
Chicago Transit Authority (CTA)			
Bus (directly operated)	1,566	237,276.4	581,742.0
Heavy Rail (directly operated)	1,164	218,467.1	1,378,128.4
Northeast Illinois Regional Commuter Railroad (Metra)			
Commuter Rail (directly operated)	1,066	61,456.7	1,365,137.9

Note: (1) Number of revenue vehicles operated by the given mode and type of service to meet the annual maximum service requirement. This is the revenue vehicle count during the peak season of the year; on the week and day that maximum service is provided. Vehicles operated in maximum service (VOMS) exclude atypical days and one-time special events; (2) Number of passengers who boarded public transportation vehicles. Passengers are counted each time they board a vehicle no matter how many vehicles they use to travel from their origin to their destination. (3) Sum of the distances ridden by all passengers during the entire fiscal year.
Source: Federal Transit Administration, National Transit Database, 2019

Air Transportation

Airport Name and Code / Type of Service	Passenger Airlines[1]	Passenger Enplanements	Freight Carriers[2]	Freight (lbs)
O'Hare International (ORD)				
Domestic service (U.S. carriers - 2020)	27	12,866,803	21	519,549,576
International service (U.S. carriers - 2019)	16	3,178,297	12	119,099,611
Midway International (MDW)				
Domestic service (U.S. carriers - 2020)	16	4,102,511	3	21,152,783
International service (U.S. carriers - 2019)	3	151,156	1	6,543

Note: (1) Includes all U.S.-based major, minor and commuter airlines that carried at least one passenger during the year; (2) Includes all U.S.-based airlines and freight carriers that transported at least one pound of freight during the year.
Source: Bureau of Transportation Statistics, The Intermodal Transportation Database, Air Carriers: T-100 Domestic Market (U.S. Carriers), 2020; Bureau of Transportation Statistics, The Intermodal Transportation Database, Air Carriers: T-100 International Market (U.S. Carriers), 2019

BUSINESSES

Major Business Headquarters

Company Name	Industry	Rankings	
		Fortune[1]	Forbes[2]
Amsted Industries	Capital Goods	-	108
Archer Daniels Midland	Food Production	54	-
Boeing	Aerospace and Defense	40	-
Conagra Brands	Food Consumer Products	334	-
Exelon	Utilities, Gas and Electric	95	-
Heico Cos	Capital Goods	-	165
Jones Lang LaSalle	Real Estate	179	-
Kirkland & Ellis	Services	-	106
LKQ	Wholesalers, Diversified	257	-
Northern Trust	Commercial Banks	440	-
Old Republic International	Insurance, Property and Casualty (Stock)	427	-
R.R. Donnelley & Sons	Publishing, Printing	471	-
Sidley Austin	Services	-	199
United Airlines Holdings	Airlines	76	-
Walsh Group	Construction	-	89

Note: (1) Companies that produce a 10-K are ranked 1 to 500 based on 2019 revenue; (2) All private companies with at least $2 billion in annual revenue through the end of their most current fiscal year are ranked 1 to 219; companies listed are headquartered in the city; dashes indicate no ranking
Source: Fortune, "Fortune 500," June/July 2020; Forbes, "America's Largest Private Companies," 2020

Fastest-Growing Businesses

According to *Inc.*, Chicago is home to 14 of America's 500 fastest-growing private companies:
Inspire11 (#10); **Mugsy Jeans** (#69); **Supernova Companies** (#101); **FarmLogix** (#165); **Eligo En-**

ergy (#222); **Booksy** (#299); **Fitness Cubed** (#300); **Setna iO** (#321); **Packback** (#352); **Arcalea** (#354); **Wavicle Data Solutions** (#401); **ShipBob** (#441); **All Metal Solutions** (#464); **Key Tower** (#493). Criteria: must be an independent, privately-held, for-profit, U.S. corporation, proprietorship or partnership as of December 31, 2019; revenues must be at least $100,000 in 2016 and $2 million in 2019; must have four-year operating/sales history. *Inc., "America's 500 Fastest-Growing Private Companies," 2020*

According to *Fortune*, Chicago is home to four of the 100 fastest-growing companies in the world: **Kemper** (#11); **Byline Bancorp** (#32); **Cboe Global Markets** (#60); **TransUnion** (#93). Companies were ranked by their revenue growth rate; their EPS growth rate; and their three-year annualized total return to investors for the period ending June 30, 2020. Criteria for inclusion: a company, foreign or domestic, must trade on a major U.S. stock exchange; must file quarterly reports with the SEC; must have a minimum market capitalization of $250 million; must have a stock price of at least $5 on June 30, 2020; must have been trading continuously since June 30, 2017; must have revenue and net income for the four quarters ended on or before April 30, 2020, of at least $50 million and $10 million, respectively; and must have posted a compound annual growth in revenue and earnings per share of at least 15% annually over the three years ending on or before April 30, 2020. Real estate investment trusts, limited-liability companies, limited parterships, business development companies, closed-end investment firms, companies about to be acquired, and companies that lost money in the quarter ending April 30, 2020 were excluded. *Fortune, "100 Fastest-Growing Companies," 2020*

According to *Initiative for a Competitive Inner City (ICIC)*, Chicago is home to five of America's 100 fastest-growing "inner city" companies: **Cloudbakers** (#10); **Trice Construction Company** (#30); **Supply Logistics & Procurement Services** (#43); **Lasalle Staffing** (#58); **Original Soul Vegetarian** (#94). Criteria for inclusion: company must be headquartered in or have 51 percent or more of its physical operations in an economically distressed urban area; must be an independent, for-profit corporation, partnership or proprietorship; must have 10 or more employees and have a five-year sales history that includes sales of at least $200,000 in the base year and at least $1 million in the current year with no decrease in sales over the two most recent years. Companies were ranked overall by revenue growth over the five-year period between 2015 and 2019. *Initiative for a Competitive Inner City (ICIC), "Inner City 100 Companies," 2020*

According to Deloitte, Chicago is home to eight of North America's 500 fastest-growing high-technology companies: **Cubii** (#77); **ShipBob** (#116); **OppLoans** (#138); **Built In** (#244); **Braviant Holdings** (#377); **Hireology** (#401); **NowSecure** (#419); **Topstep** (#487). Companies are ranked by percentage growth in revenue over a four-year period. Criteria for inclusion: company must be headquartered within North America; must own proprietary intellectual property or technology that is sold to customers in products that contributes to a significant portion of the company's operating revenue; must have been in business for a minumum of four years with 2016 operating revenues of at least $50,000 USD/CD and 2019 operating revenues of at least $5 million USD/CD. *Deloitte, 2020 Technology Fast 500*[TM]

Minority Business Opportunity

Chicago is home to two companies which are on the *Black Enterprise* Industrial/Service list (100 largest companies based on gross sales): **Harpo** (#52); **UJAMAA Construction** (#58). Criteria: operational in previous calendar year; at least 51% black-owned and manufactures/owns the product it sells or provides industrial or consumer services. Brokerages, real estate firms and firms that provide professional services are not eligible. *Black Enterprise, B.E. 100s, 2019*

Chicago is home to one company which is on the *Black Enterprise* Bank list (15 largest banks based on total assets, capital, deposits and loans, including mortgage-backed securities for the calendar year): **GN Bank** (#11). Only commercial banks or savings and loans that are classified by the Federal Reserve as black institutions and have been fully operational for the previous calendar year were considered. *Black Enterprise, B.E. 100s, 2019*

Chicago is home to three companies which are on the *Black Enterprise* Asset Manager list (10 largest asset management firms based on assets under management): **Ariel Investments** (#1); **Capri Capital Partners** (#7); **Channing Capital Management** (#10). Criteria: company must have been operational in previous calendar year and be at least 51% black-owned. *Black Enterprise, B.E. 100s, 2019*

Chicago is home to one company which is on the *Black Enterprise* Private Equity list (10 largest private equity firms based on capital under management): **Muller & Monroe Asset Management** (#7). Criteria: company must be operational in previous calendar year and be at least 51% black-owned. *Black Enterprise, B.E. 100s, 2019*

56 Chicago, Illinois

Living Environment

COST OF LIVING

Cost of Living Index

Composite Index	Groceries	Housing	Utilities	Transportation	Health Care	Misc. Goods/ Services
124.1	107.2	163.7	92.6	113.7	99.1	113.9

Note: The Cost of Living Index measures regional differences in the cost of consumer goods and services, excluding taxes and non-consumer expenditures, for professional and managerial households in the top income quintile. It is based on more than 50,000 prices covering almost 60 different items for which prices are collected three times a year by chambers of commerce, economic development organizations or university applied economic centers in each participating urban area. The numbers shown should be read as a percentage above or below the national average of 100. For example, a value of 115.4 in the groceries column indicates that grocery prices are 15.4% higher than the national average. Small differences in the index numbers should not be interpreted as significant; Figures cover the Chicago IL urban area.
Source: The Council for Community and Economic Research, Cost of Living Index, 2020

Grocery Prices

Area[1]	T-Bone Steak ($/pound)	Frying Chicken ($/pound)	Whole Milk ($/half gal.)	Eggs ($/dozen)	Orange Juice ($/64 oz.)	Coffee ($/11.5 oz.)
City[2]	12.67	1.99	2.42	1.47	3.96	4.48
Avg.	11.78	1.39	2.05	1.47	3.57	4.34
Min.	8.03	0.94	1.03	0.74	2.94	3.02
Max.	15.86	2.65	4.31	3.77	5.44	8.69

Note: (1) Values for the local area are compared with the average, minimum and maximum values for all 284 areas in the Cost of Living Index; (2) Figures cover the Chicago IL urban area; T-Bone Steak (price per pound); Frying Chicken (price per pound, whole fryer); Whole Milk (half gallon carton); Eggs (price per dozen, Grade A, large); Orange Juice (64 oz. Tropicana or Florida Natural); Coffee (11.5 oz. can, vacuum-packed, Maxwell House, Hills Bros, or Folgers).
Source: The Council for Community and Economic Research, Cost of Living Index, 2020

Housing and Utility Costs

Area[1]	New Home Price ($)	Apartment Rent ($/month)	All Electric ($/month)	Part Electric ($/month)	Other Energy ($/month)	Telephone ($/month)
City[2]	537,912	2,334	-	80.80	51.09	203.20
Avg.	368,594	1,168	170.86	100.47	65.28	184.30
Min.	190,567	502	91.58	31.42	26.08	169.60
Max.	2,227,806	4,738	470.38	280.31	280.06	206.50

Note: (1) Values for the local area are compared with the average, minimum and maximum values for all 284 areas in the Cost of Living Index; (2) Figures cover the Chicago IL urban area; New Home Price (2,400 sf living area, 8,000 sf lot, in urban area with full utilities); Apartment Rent (950 sf 2 bedroom/1.5 or 2 bath, unfurnished, excluding all utilities except water); All Electric (average monthly cost for an all-electric home); Part Electric (average monthly cost for a part-electric home); Other Energy (average monthly cost for natural gas, fuel oil, coal, wood, and any other forms of energy except electricity); Telephone (price includes the base monthly rate plus taxes and fees for three lines of mobile phone service).
Source: The Council for Community and Economic Research, Cost of Living Index, 2020

Health Care, Transportation, and Other Costs

Area[1]	Doctor ($/visit)	Dentist ($/visit)	Optometrist ($/visit)	Gasoline ($/gallon)	Beauty Salon ($/visit)	Men's Shirt ($)
City[2]	104.96	101.82	96.76	2.51	65.57	32.92
Avg.	115.44	99.32	108.10	2.21	39.27	31.37
Min.	36.68	59.00	51.36	1.71	19.00	11.00
Max.	219.00	153.10	250.97	3.46	82.05	58.33

Note: (1) Values for the local area are compared with the average, minimum and maximum values for all 284 areas in the Cost of Living Index; (2) Figures cover the Chicago IL urban area; Doctor (general practitioners routine exam of an established patient); Dentist (adult teeth cleaning and periodic oral examination); Optometrist (full vision eye exam for established adult patient); Gasoline (one gallon regular unleaded, national brand, including all taxes, cash price at self-service pump if available); Beauty Salon (woman's shampoo, trim, and blow-dry); Men's Shirt (cotton/polyester dress shirt, pinpoint weave, long sleeves).
Source: The Council for Community and Economic Research, Cost of Living Index, 2020

HOUSING

Homeownership Rate

Area	2012 (%)	2013 (%)	2014 (%)	2015 (%)	2016 (%)	2017 (%)	2018 (%)	2019 (%)	2020 (%)
MSA[1]	67.1	68.2	66.3	64.3	64.5	64.1	64.6	63.4	66.0
U.S.	65.4	65.1	64.5	63.7	63.4	63.9	64.4	64.6	66.6

Note: (1) Figures cover the Chicago-Naperville-Elgin, IL-IN-WI Metropolitan Statistical Area
Source: U.S. Census Bureau, Housing Vacancies and Homeownership Annual Statistics: 2012-2020

House Price Index (HPI)

Area	National Ranking[2]	Quarterly Change (%)	One-Year Change (%)	Five-Year Change (%)	Since 1991Q1 (%)
MD[1]	239	1.11	2.98	16.74	122.65
U.S.[3]	–	3.81	10.77	38.99	205.12

Note: The HPI is a weighted repeat sales index. It measures average price changes in repeat sales or refinancings on the same properties. This information is obtained by reviewing repeat mortgage transactions on single-family properties whose mortgages have been purchased or securitized by Fannie Mae or Freddie Mac since January 1975; (1) Figures cover the Chicago-Naperville-Arlington Heights, IL Metropolitan Division; (2) Rankings are based on annual percentage change for all metro areas containing at least 15,000 transactions over the last 10 years and ranges from 1 to 253; (3) figures based on a weighted average of Census Division estimates using a seasonally adjusted, purchase-only index; all figures are for the period ending December 31, 2020
Source: Federal Housing Finance Agency, Change in Metropolitan Area House Price Indexes, April 7, 2021

Median Single-Family Home Prices

Area	2018	2019	2020p	Percent Change 2019 to 2020
MSA[1]	259.4	265.1	287.6	8.5
U.S. Average	261.6	274.6	299.9	9.2

Note: Figures are median sales prices of existing single-family homes in thousands of dollars; (p) preliminary; (1) Figures cover the Chicago-Naperville-Elgin, IL-IN-WI Metropolitan Statistical Area
Source: National Association of Realtors, Median Sales Price of Existing Single-Family Homes for Metropolitan Areas, 4th Quarter 2020

Qualifying Income Based on Median Sales Price of Existing Single-Family Homes

Area	With 5% Down ($)	With 10% Down ($)	With 20% Down ($)
MSA[1]	55,248	52,341	46,525
U.S. Average	59,266	56,147	49,908

Note: Figures are preliminary; Qualifying income is based on a mortgage rate of 2.81%. Monthly principal and interest payment is limited to 25% of income; (1) Figures cover the Chicago-Naperville-Elgin, IL-IN-WI Metropolitan Statistical Area
Source: National Association of Realtors, Qualifying Income Based on Median Sales Price of Existing Single-Family Homes for Metropolitan Areas, 4th Quarter 2020

Home Value Distribution

Area	Under $50,000	$50,000 -$99,999	$100,000 -$149,999	$150,000 -$199,999	$200,000 -$299,999	$300,000 -$499,999	$500,000 -$999,999	$1,000,000 or more
City	2.7	7.0	11.1	15.0	23.8	24.1	12.5	3.9
MSA[1]	3.2	7.2	12.4	16.4	25.5	23.1	9.9	2.4
U.S.	6.9	12.0	13.3	14.0	19.6	19.3	11.4	3.4

Note: Figures are percentages and cover owner-occupied housing units; (1) Figures cover the Chicago-Naperville-Elgin, IL-IN-WI Metropolitan Statistical Area
Source: U.S. Census Bureau, 2015-2019 American Community Survey 5-Year Estimates

Year Housing Structure Built

Area	2010 or Later	2000 -2009	1990 -1999	1980 -1989	1970 -1979	1960 -1969	1950 -1959	1940 -1949	Before 1940	Median Year
City	2.6	8.0	4.9	4.3	7.5	9.7	11.9	9.3	41.8	1949
MSA[1]	2.4	11.5	11.1	9.0	14.2	11.6	13.0	6.1	21.0	1968
U.S.	5.2	14.0	13.9	13.4	15.2	10.6	10.3	4.9	12.6	1978

Note: Figures are percentages except for Median Year; Note: (1) Figures cover the Chicago-Naperville-Elgin, IL-IN-WI Metropolitan Statistical Area
Source: U.S. Census Bureau, 2015-2019 American Community Survey 5-Year Estimates

Gross Monthly Rent

Area	Under $500	$500 -$999	$1,000 -$1,499	$1,500 -$1,999	$2,000 -$2,499	$2,500 -$2,999	$3,000 and up	Median ($)
City	9.6	31.9	31.5	15.2	6.7	3.0	2.1	1,112
MSA[1]	7.7	32.0	34.9	15.8	5.8	2.2	1.7	1,122
U.S.	9.4	36.2	30.0	14.0	5.6	2.4	2.4	1,062

Note: Figures are percentages except for Median; Gross rent is the contract rent plus the estimated average monthly cost of utilities (electricity, gas, and water and sewer) and fuels (oil, coal, kerosene, wood, etc.) if these are paid by the renter (or paid for the renter by someone else); (1) Figures cover the Chicago-Naperville-Elgin, IL-IN-WI Metropolitan Statistical Area
Source: U.S. Census Bureau, 2015-2019 American Community Survey 5-Year Estimates

HEALTH

Health Risk Factors

Category	MSA[1] (%)	U.S. (%)
Adults aged 18–64 who have any kind of health care coverage	86.1	87.3
Adults who reported being in good or better health	82.6	82.4
Adults who have been told they have high blood cholesterol	31.6	33.0
Adults who have been told they have high blood pressure	31.5	32.3
Adults who are current smokers	13.6	17.1
Adults who currently use E-cigarettes	3.9	4.6
Adults who currently use chewing tobacco, snuff, or snus	2.1	4.0
Adults who are heavy drinkers[2]	6.3	6.3
Adults who are binge drinkers[3]	19.9	17.4
Adults who are overweight (BMI 25.0 - 29.9)	34.4	35.3
Adults who are obese (BMI 30.0 - 99.8)	30.1	31.3
Adults who participated in any physical activities in the past month	77.3	74.4
Adults who always or nearly always wears a seat belt	95.7	94.3

Note: (1) Figures cover the Chicago-Naperville-Elgin, IL-IN-WI Metropolitan Statistical Area; (2) Heavy drinkers are classified as adult men having more than 14 drinks per week and adult women having more than 7 drinks per week; (3) Binge drinkers are classified as males having five or more drinks on one occasion or females having four or more drinks on one occasion
Source: Centers for Disease Control and Prevention, Behaviorial Risk Factor Surveillance System, SMART: Selected Metropolitan Area Risk Trends, 2017

Acute and Chronic Health Conditions

Category	MSA[1] (%)	U.S. (%)
Adults who have ever been told they had a heart attack	3.3	4.2
Adults who have ever been told they have angina or coronary heart disease	3.5	3.9
Adults who have ever been told they had a stroke	2.8	3.0
Adults who have ever been told they have asthma	13.1	14.2
Adults who have ever been told they have arthritis	22.5	24.9
Adults who have ever been told they have diabetes[2]	10.3	10.5
Adults who have ever been told they had skin cancer	3.9	6.2
Adults who have ever been told they had any other types of cancer	5.6	7.1
Adults who have ever been told they have COPD	6.1	6.5
Adults who have ever been told they have kidney disease	2.9	3.0
Adults who have ever been told they have a form of depression	16.3	20.5

Note: (1) Figures cover the Chicago-Naperville-Elgin, IL-IN-WI Metropolitan Statistical Area; (2) Figures do not include pregnancy-related, borderline, or pre-diabetes
Source: Centers for Disease Control and Prevention, Behaviorial Risk Factor Surveillance System, SMART: Selected Metropolitan Area Risk Trends, 2017

Health Screening and Vaccination Rates

Category	MSA[1] (%)	U.S. (%)
Adults aged 65+ who have had flu shot within the past year	55.4	60.7
Adults aged 65+ who have ever had a pneumonia vaccination	71.8	75.4
Adults who have ever been tested for HIV	37.8	36.1
Adults who have ever had the shingles or zoster vaccine?	25.3	28.9
Adults who have had their blood cholesterol checked within the last five years	88.4	85.9

Note: n/a not available; (1) Figures cover the Chicago-Naperville-Elgin, IL-IN-WI Metropolitan Statistical Area.
Source: Centers for Disease Control and Prevention, Behaviorial Risk Factor Surveillance System, SMART: Selected Metropolitan Area Risk Trends, 2017

Disability Status

Category	MSA[1] (%)	U.S. (%)
Adults who reported being deaf	3.2	6.7
Are you blind or have serious difficulty seeing, even when wearing glasses?	4.0	4.5
Are you limited in any way in any of your usual activities due of arthritis?	10.8	12.9
Do you have difficulty doing errands alone?	6.0	6.8
Do you have difficulty dressing or bathing?	3.2	3.6
Do you have serious difficulty concentrating/remembering/making decisions?	8.1	10.7
Do you have serious difficulty walking or climbing stairs?	11.8	13.6

Note: (1) Figures cover the Chicago-Naperville-Elgin, IL-IN-WI Metropolitan Statistical Area.
Source: Centers for Disease Control and Prevention, Behaviorial Risk Factor Surveillance System, SMART: Selected Metropolitan Area Risk Trends, 2017

Mortality Rates for the Top 10 Causes of Death in the U.S.

ICD-10[a] Sub-Chapter	ICD-10[a] Code	Age-Adjusted Mortality Rate[1] per 100,000 population	
		County[2]	U.S.
Malignant neoplasms	C00-C97	151.3	149.2
Ischaemic heart diseases	I20-I25	79.1	90.5
Other forms of heart disease	I30-I51	60.6	52.2
Chronic lower respiratory diseases	J40-J47	26.9	39.6
Other degenerative diseases of the nervous system	G30-G31	25.9	37.6
Cerebrovascular diseases	I60-I69	40.9	37.2
Other external causes of accidental injury	W00-X59	34.2	36.1
Organic, including symptomatic, mental disorders	F01-F09	30.7	29.4
Hypertensive diseases	I10-I15	29.5	24.1
Diabetes mellitus	E10-E14	19.1	21.5

Note: (a) ICD-10 = International Classification of Diseases 10th Revision; (1) Mortality rates are a three-year average covering 2017-2019; (2) Figures cover Cook County.
Source: Centers for Disease Control and Prevention, National Center for Health Statistics. Underlying Cause of Death 1999-2019 on CDC WONDER Online Database

Mortality Rates for Selected Causes of Death

ICD-10[a] Sub-Chapter	ICD-10[a] Code	Age-Adjusted Mortality Rate[1] per 100,000 population	
		County[2]	U.S.
Assault	X85-Y09	13.7	6.0
Diseases of the liver	K70-K76	11.2	14.4
Human immunodeficiency virus (HIV) disease	B20-B24	1.7	1.5
Influenza and pneumonia	J09-J18	15.1	13.8
Intentional self-harm	X60-X84	8.6	14.1
Malnutrition	E40-E46	2.2	2.3
Obesity and other hyperalimentation	E65-E68	2.1	2.1
Renal failure	N17-N19	16.7	12.6
Transport accidents	V01-V99	7.1	12.3
Viral hepatitis	B15-B19	0.7	1.2

Note: (a) ICD-10 = International Classification of Diseases 10th Revision; (1) Mortality rates are a three-year average covering 2017-2019; (2) Figures cover Cook County; Data are suppressed when the data meet the criteria for confidentiality constraints; Mortality rates are flagged as unreliable when the rate would be calculated with a numerator of 20 or less.
Source: Centers for Disease Control and Prevention, National Center for Health Statistics. Underlying Cause of Death 1999-2019 on CDC WONDER Online Database

Health Insurance Coverage

Area	With Health Insurance	With Private Health Insurance	With Public Health Insurance	Without Health Insurance	Population Under Age 19 Without Health Insurance
City	90.4	60.3	36.9	9.6	3.4
MSA[1]	92.4	70.2	31.7	7.6	3.2
U.S.	91.2	67.9	35.1	8.8	5.1

Note: Figures are percentages that cover the civilian noninstitutionalized population; (1) Figures cover the Chicago-Naperville-Elgin, IL-IN-WI Metropolitan Statistical Area
Source: U.S. Census Bureau, 2015-2019 American Community Survey 5-Year Estimates

Number of Medical Professionals

Area	MDs[3]	DOs[3,4]	Dentists	Podiatrists	Chiropractors	Optometrists
County[1] (number)	22,385	1,210	4,868	640	1,476	1,070
County[1] (rate[2])	432.8	23.4	94.5	12.4	28.7	20.8
U.S. (rate[2])	282.9	22.7	71.2	6.2	28.1	16.9

17031
Note: Data as of 2019 unless noted; (1) Data covers Cook County; (2) Rate per 100,000 population; (3) Data as of 2018 and includes all active, non-federal physicians; (4) Doctor of Osteopathic Medicine
Source: U.S. Department of Health and Human Services, Health Resources and Services Administration, Bureau of Health Professions, Area Resource File (ARF) 2019-2020

Best Hospitals

According to *U.S. News,* the Chicago-Naperville-Arlington Heights, IL metro area is home to eight of the best hospitals in the U.S.: **Advocate Christ Medical Center** (1 adult specialty and 1 pediatric specialty); **Advocate Lutheran General Hospital** (1 adult specialty); **Loyola University Medical Center** (5 adult specialties); **Northwestern Medicine Lake Forest Hospital** (2 adult specialties); **Northwestern Memorial Hospital** (Honor Roll/11 adult specialties); **Rush University Medical Center** (Honor Roll/11 adult specialties); **Shirley Ryan AbilityLab (formerly Rehabilitation Institute of Chicago)** (1 adult specialty); **University of Chicago Medical Center** (9 adult specialties and 2 pediatric specialties). The hospitals listed were nationally ranked in at least one of 16 adult or 10 pediatric specialties. Only 134 hospitals nationwide were nationally ranked in one or more adult or

60   Chicago, Illinois

pediatric specialty; this number increases to 178 counting specialized centers within hospitals. Twenty hospitals in the U.S. made the Honor Roll. The Best Hospitals Honor Roll takes both the national rankings and the procedure and condition ratings into account. Hospitals received points if they were nationally ranked in one of the 16 adult specialties—the higher they ranked, the more points they got—and how many ratings of "high performing" they earned in the 10 procedures and conditions. *U.S. News Online, "America's Best Hospitals 2020-21"*

According to *U.S. News,* the Chicago-Naperville-Arlington Heights, IL metro area is home to three of the best children's hospitals in the U.S.: **Advocate Children's Hospital** (1 pediatric specialty); **Ann and Robert H. Lurie Children's Hospital of Chicago** (10 pediatric specialties); **University of Chicago Comer Children's Hospital** (2 pediatric specialties). The hospitals listed were highly ranked in at least one of 10 pediatric specialties. Eighty-eight children's hospitals in the U.S. were nationally ranked in at least one specialty. Hospitals received points for being ranked in a specialty, and the 10 hospitals with the most points across the 10 specialties make up the Honor Roll. *U.S. News Online, "America's Best Children's Hospitals 2020-21"*

EDUCATION

Public School District Statistics

District Name	Schls	Pupils	Pupil/ Teacher Ratio	Minority Pupils[1] (%)	Free Lunch Eligible[2] (%)	IEP[3] (%)
City of Chicago SD 299	658	359,476	16.5	89.4	78.4	14.2

Note: Table includes school districts with 2,000 or more students; (1) Percentage of students that are not non-Hispanic white; (2) Percentage of students that are eligible for the free lunch program; (3) Percentage of students that have an Individualized Education Program.
Source: U.S. Department of Education, National Center for Education Statistics, Common Core of Data, Local Education Agency (School District) Universe Survey: School Year 2018-2019; U.S. Department of Education, National Center for Education Statistics, Common Core of Data, Public Elementary/Secondary School Universe Survey: School Year 2018-2019

Best High Schools

According to *U.S. News,* Chicago is home to eight of the top 500 high schools in the U.S.: **Payton College Preparatory High School** (#9); **Northside College Preparatory High School** (#38); **Jones College Prep High School** (#66); **Young Magnet High School** (#77); **Lane Technical High School** (#81); **Lindblom Math and Science Academy** (#296); **Brooks College Prep Academy High School** (#304); **Lincoln Park High School** (#432). Nearly 18,000 public, magnet and charter schools were ranked based on their performance on state assessments and how well they prepare students for college. *U.S. News & World Report, "Best High Schools 2020"*

Highest Level of Education

Area	Less than H.S.	H.S. Diploma	Some College, No Deg.	Associate Degree	Bachelor's Degree	Master's Degree	Prof. School Degree	Doctorate Degree
City	14.9	22.5	17.3	5.8	23.3	11.3	3.3	1.6
MSA[1]	11.3	23.9	19.5	7.2	23.0	10.9	2.6	1.4
U.S.	12.0	27.0	20.4	8.5	19.8	8.8	2.1	1.4

Note: Figures cover persons age 25 and over; (1) Figures cover the Chicago-Naperville-Elgin, IL-IN-WI Metropolitan Statistical Area
Source: U.S. Census Bureau, 2015-2019 American Community Survey 5-Year Estimates

Educational Attainment by Race

Area	High School Graduate or Higher (%)					Bachelor's Degree or Higher (%)				
	Total	White	Black	Asian	Hisp.[2]	Total	White	Black	Asian	Hisp.[2]
City	85.1	88.7	85.2	87.1	68.4	39.5	50.9	21.4	60.5	16.5
MSA[1]	88.7	91.4	87.8	90.7	68.0	38.0	41.6	22.7	64.7	14.8
U.S.	88.0	89.9	86.0	87.1	68.7	32.1	33.5	21.6	54.3	16.4

Note: Figures shown cover persons 25 years old and over; (1) Figures cover the Chicago-Naperville-Elgin, IL-IN-WI Metropolitan Statistical Area; (2) People of Hispanic origin can be of any race
Source: U.S. Census Bureau, 2015-2019 American Community Survey 5-Year Estimates

School Enrollment by Grade and Control

Area	Preschool (%)		Kindergarten (%)		Grades 1 - 4 (%)		Grades 5 - 8 (%)		Grades 9 - 12 (%)	
	Public	Private	Public	Private	Public	Private	Public	Private	Public	Private
City	58.4	41.6	79.9	20.1	85.9	14.1	85.4	14.6	87.4	12.6
MSA[1]	58.0	42.0	84.8	15.2	89.3	10.7	89.0	11.0	90.6	9.4
U.S.	59.1	40.9	87.6	12.4	89.5	10.5	89.4	10.6	90.1	9.9

Note: Figures shown cover persons 3 years old and over; (1) Figures cover the Chicago-Naperville-Elgin, IL-IN-WI Metropolitan Statistical Area
Source: U.S. Census Bureau, 2015-2019 American Community Survey 5-Year Estimates

Higher Education

Four-Year Colleges			Two-Year Colleges			Medical Schools[1]	Law Schools[2]	Voc/ Tech[3]
Public	Private Non-profit	Private For-profit	Public	Private Non-profit	Private For-profit			
3	34	3	7	1	4	4	6	14

Note: Figures cover institutions located within the city limits and include main campuses only; (1) includes schools accredited by the Liaison Committee on Medical Education and the American Osteopathic Association's Commission on Osteopathic College Accreditation; (2) includes ABA-accredited schools, schools with provisional ABA accreditation, and state accredited schools; (3) includes all schools with programs that are less than 2 years.
Source: National Center for Education Statistics, Integrated Postsecondary Education System (IPEDS), 2019-20; Wikipedia, List of Medical Schools in the United States, accessed April 2, 2021; Wikipedia, List of Law Schools in the United States, accessed April 2, 2021

According to *U.S. News & World Report,* the Chicago-Naperville-Arlington Heights, IL metro division is home to six of the top 200 national universities in the U.S.: **University of Chicago** (#6 tie); **Northwestern University** (#9 tie); **Loyola University Chicago** (#112 tie); **University of Illinois—Chicago** (#112 tie); **DePaul University** (#124 tie); **Illinois Institute of Technology** (#124 tie). The indicators used to capture academic quality fall into a number of categories: assessment by administrators at peer institutions; retention of students; faculty resources; student selectivity; financial resources; alumni giving; high school counselor ratings of colleges; and graduation rate. *U.S. News & World Report, "America's Best Colleges 2021"*

According to *U.S. News & World Report,* the Chicago-Naperville-Arlington Heights, IL metro division is home to one of the top 100 liberal arts colleges in the U.S.: **Wheaton College (IL)** (#61 tie). The indicators used to capture academic quality fall into a number of categories: assessment by administrators at peer institutions; retention of students; faculty resources; student selectivity; financial resources; alumni giving; high school counselor ratings of colleges; and graduation rate. *U.S. News & World Report, "America's Best Colleges 2021"*

According to *U.S. News & World Report,* the Chicago-Naperville-Arlington Heights, IL metro division is home to four of the top 100 law schools in the U.S.: **University of Chicago** (#4 tie); **Northwestern University (Pritzker)** (#12); **Loyola University Chicago** (#78 tie); **Illinois Institute of Technology (Chicago-Kent)** (#91 tie). The rankings are based on a weighted average of 12 measures of quality: peer assessment score; assessment score by lawyers/judges; median LSAT scores; median undergrad GPA; acceptance rate; employment rates for graduates; placement success; bar passage rate; faculty resources; expenditures per student; student/faculty ratio; and library resources. *U.S. News & World Report, "America's Best Graduate Schools, Law, 2022"*

According to *U.S. News & World Report,* the Chicago-Naperville-Arlington Heights, IL metro division is home to four of the top 75 medical schools for research in the U.S.: **Northwestern University (Feinberg)** (#15 tie); **University of Chicago (Pritzker)** (#17 tie); **University of Illinois** (#55 tie); **Rush University** (#64 tie). The rankings are based on a weighted average of 11 measures of quality: quality assessment; peer assessment score; assessment score by residency directors; research activity; total research activity; average research activity per faculty member; student selectivity; median MCAT total score; median undergraduate GPA; acceptance rate; and faculty resources. *U.S. News & World Report, "America's Best Graduate Schools, Medical, 2022"*

According to *U.S. News & World Report,* the Chicago-Naperville-Arlington Heights, IL metro division is home to two of the top 75 business schools in the U.S.: **University of Chicago (Booth)** (#3); **Northwestern University (Kellogg)** (#4). The rankings are based on a weighted average of the following nine measures: quality assessment; peer assessment; recruiter assessment; placement success; mean starting salary and bonus; student selectivity; mean GMAT and GRE scores; mean undergraduate GPA; and acceptance rate. *U.S. News & World Report, "America's Best Graduate Schools, Business, 2022"*

EMPLOYERS

Major Employers

Company Name	Industry
Abbott Laboratories	Pharmaceutical preparations
Addus HomeCare Corporation	Home health care services
Advocate Lutheran General Hospital	General medical & surgical hospitals
BMO Bankcorp	National commercial banks
City of Chicago	Municipal government
Cook County Bureau of Health Services	Administration of public health programs
Graphic Packaging International	Folding boxboard
Loyola University Health System	General medical & surgical hospitals
Northshore University Healthsystem	General medical & surgical hospitals
Northwestern Memorial Hospital	General medical & surgical hospitals
SCC Holding Co.	Cups, plastics, except foam
Schneider Electric Holdings	Air transportation, scheduled
SOLO Cup Company	Cups, plastics, except foam
The Allstate Corporation	Fire, marine, & casualty insurance
The University of Chicago Medical Center	General medical & surgical hospitals
United Parcel Service	Package delivery services
United States Steel Corporation	Steel foundries
WM Recycle America	Material recovery

Note: Companies shown are located within the Chicago-Naperville-Elgin, IL-IN-WI Metropolitan Statistical Area.
Source: Hoovers.com; Wikipedia

Best Companies to Work For

Crowe; Hyatt Hotels; West Monroe Partners, headquartered in Chicago, are among "The 100 Best Companies to Work For." To pick the best companies, *Fortune* partnered with the Great Place to Work Institute. Two-thirds of a company's score is based on the results of the Institute's Trust Index survey, which is sent to a random sample of employees from each company. The questions related to attitudes about management's credibility, job satisfaction, and camaraderie. The other third of the scoring is based on the company's responses to the Institute's Culture Audit, which includes detailed questions about pay and benefit programs, and a series of open-ended questions about hiring practices, internal communication, training, recognition programs, and diversity efforts. Any company that is at least five years old with more than 1,000 U.S. employees is eligible. *Fortune, "The 100 Best Companies to Work For," 2020*

Aon; BDO; Federal Reserve Bank of Chicago; Grant Thornton; Katten; Kearney; Leo Burnett Group USA; RSM, headquartered in Chicago, are among the "100 Best Companies for Working Mothers." Criteria: paid time off and leaves; workforce profile; benefits; women's issues and advancement; flexible work; company culture and work life programs. *Working Mother, "100 Best Companies for Working Mothers," 2020*

CME Group; Enova International; Motorola Solutions; Nitel; RSM US, headquartered in Chicago, are among the "100 Best Places to Work in IT." To qualify, companies had to be U.S.-based organizations or be non-U.S.-based employers that met the following criteria: have a minimum of 300 total employees at a U.S. headquarters and a minimum of 30 IT employees in the U.S., with at least 50% of their IT employees based in the U.S. The best places to work were selected based on compensation, benefits, work/life balance, employee morale, and satisfaction with training and development programs. In addition, *InsiderPro* and *Computerworld* looked at retention efforts, programs for recognizing and rewarding outstanding performances, and benefits such as flextime, elder care and child care, and reimbursement for college tuition and the cost of pursuing technology certifications. *InsiderPro and Computerworld, "100 Best Places to Work in IT," 2020*

BDO; Grant Thornton; JLL; Katten; Leo Burnett Group USA, headquartered in Chicago, are among the "Top Companies for Executive Women." This list is determined by organizations filling out an in-depth survey that measures female demographics at every level, but with an emphasis on women in senior corporate roles, with profit & loss (P&L) responsibility, and those earning in the top 20 percent of the organization. *Working Mother* defines P&L as having responsibility that involves monitoring the net income after expenses for a department or entire organization, with direct influence on how company resources are allocated. *Working Mother, "Top Companies for Executive Women," 2020+*

BDO; BP; Federal Reserve Bank of Chicago; Grant Thornton; JLL; Kearney; Leo Burnett Group USA; Northern Trust; RSM, headquartered in Chicago, are among the "Best Companies for Dads." *Working Mother's* newest list recognizes the growing importance companies place on giving dads time off and support for their families. Rankings are determined by measuring gender-neutral or paternity leave offered, as well as actual time taken, phase-back policies, child- and dependent-care benefits, and corporate support groups for men and dads. *Working Mother, "Best Companies for Dads," 2020*

Chicago, Illinois 63

PUBLIC SAFETY

Crime Rate

| Area | All Crimes | Violent Crimes | | | | Property Crimes | | |
		Murder	Rape[3]	Robbery	Aggrav. Assault	Burglary	Larceny -Theft	Motor Vehicle Theft
City	3,925.8	18.2	65.1	294.9	565.0	353.8	2,293.4	335.5
Suburbs[1]	n/a	n/a	n/a	n/a	n/a	n/a	n/a	n/a
Metro[2]	n/a	n/a	n/a	n/a	n/a	n/a	n/a	n/a
U.S.	2,489.3	5.0	42.6	81.6	250.2	340.5	1,549.5	219.9

Note: Figures are crimes per 100,000 population; (1) All areas within the metro area that are located outside the city limits; (2) Figures cover the Chicago-Naperville-Arlington Heights, IL Metropolitan Division; n/a not available; (3) All figures shown were reported using the revised Uniform Crime Reporting (UCR) definition of rape.
Source: FBI Uniform Crime Reports, 2019

Hate Crimes

| Area | Number of Quarters Reported | Number of Incidents per Bias Motivation | | | | | |
		Race/Ethnicity/ Ancestry	Religion	Sexual Orientation	Disability	Gender	Gender Identity
City[1]	4	18	5	11	0	0	6
U.S.	4	3,963	1,521	1,195	157	69	198

Note: (1) Figures include one incident reported with more than one bias motivation.
Source: Federal Bureau of Investigation, Hate Crime Statistics 2019

Identity Theft Consumer Reports

Area	Reports	Reports per 100,000 Population	Rank[2]
MSA[1]	108,287	1,145	7
U.S.	1,387,615	423	-

Note: (1) Figures cover the Chicago-Naperville-Elgin, IL-IN-WI Metropolitan Statistical Area; (2) Rank ranges from 1 to 391 where 1 indicates greatest number of identity theft reports per 100,000 population
Source: Federal Trade Commission, Consumer Sentinel Network Data Book 2020

Fraud and Other Consumer Reports

Area	Reports	Reports per 100,000 Population	Rank[2]
MSA[1]	80,359	850	73
U.S.	3,385,133	1,031	-

Note: (1) Figures cover the Chicago-Naperville-Elgin, IL-IN-WI Metropolitan Statistical Area; (2) Rank ranges from 1 to 391 where 1 indicates greatest number of fraud and other consumer reports per 100,000 population
Source: Federal Trade Commission, Consumer Sentinel Network Data Book 2020

POLITICS

2020 Presidential Election Results

Area	Biden	Trump	Jorgensen	Hawkins	Other
Cook County	74.2	24.0	0.8	0.5	0.5
U.S.	51.3	46.8	1.2	0.3	0.5

Note: Results are percentages and may not add to 100% due to rounding
Source: Dave Leip's Atlas of U.S. Presidential Elections

SPORTS

Professional Sports Teams

Team Name	League	Year Established
Chicago Bears	National Football League (NFL)	1921
Chicago Blackhawks	National Hockey League (NHL)	1926
Chicago Bulls	National Basketball Association (NBA)	1966
Chicago Cubs	Major League Baseball (MLB)	1874
Chicago Fire	Major League Soccer (MLS)	1997
Chicago White Sox	Major League Baseball (MLB)	1900

Note: Includes teams located in the Chicago-Naperville-Elgin, IL-IN-WI Metropolitan Statistical Area.
Source: Wikipedia, Major Professional Sports Teams of the United States and Canada, April 6, 2021

CLIMATE

Average and Extreme Temperatures

Temperature	Jan	Feb	Mar	Apr	May	Jun	Jul	Aug	Sep	Oct	Nov	Dec	Yr.
Extreme High (°F)	65	71	88	91	93	104	102	100	99	91	78	71	104
Average High (°F)	29	33	45	59	70	79	84	82	75	63	48	34	59
Average Temp. (°F)	21	26	37	49	59	69	73	72	65	53	40	27	49
Average Low (°F)	13	17	28	39	48	57	63	62	54	42	32	19	40
Extreme Low (°F)	-27	-17	-8	7	24	36	40	41	28	17	1	-25	-27

Note: Figures cover the years 1958-1990
Source: National Climatic Data Center, International Station Meteorological Climate Summary, 9/96

Average Precipitation/Snowfall/Humidity

Precip./Humidity	Jan	Feb	Mar	Apr	May	Jun	Jul	Aug	Sep	Oct	Nov	Dec	Yr.
Avg. Precip. (in.)	1.6	1.4	2.7	3.6	3.3	3.7	3.7	4.1	3.7	2.4	2.8	2.3	35.4
Avg. Snowfall (in.)	11	8	7	2	Tr	0	0	0	0	1	2	9	39
Avg. Rel. Hum. 6am (%)	76	77	79	77	77	78	82	85	85	82	80	80	80
Avg. Rel. Hum. 3pm (%)	65	63	59	53	51	52	54	55	55	53	61	68	57

Note: Figures cover the years 1958-1990; Tr = Trace amounts (<0.05 in. of rain; <0.5 in. of snow)
Source: National Climatic Data Center, International Station Meteorological Climate Summary, 9/96

Weather Conditions

Temperature			Daytime Sky			Precipitation		
5°F & below	32°F & below	90°F & above	Clear	Partly cloudy	Cloudy	0.01 inch or more precip.	0.1 inch or more snow/ice	Thunder-storms
21	132	17	84	135	146	125	31	38

Note: Figures are average number of days per year and cover the years 1958-1990
Source: National Climatic Data Center, International Station Meteorological Climate Summary, 9/96

HAZARDOUS WASTE

Superfund Sites

The Chicago-Naperville-Arlington Heights, IL metro division is home to 10 sites on the EPA's Superfund National Priorities List: **Amoco Chemicals (Joliet Landfill)** (final); **Estech General Chemical Company** (final); **Joliet Army Ammunition Plant (Load-Assembly-Packing Area)** (final); **Joliet Army Ammunition Plant (Manufacturing Area)** (final); **Kerr-Mcgee (Kress Creek/West Branch Of Dupage River)** (final); **Kerr-Mcgee (Residential Areas)** (final); **Lake Calumet Cluster** (final); **Lenz Oil Service, Inc.** (final); **Schroud Property** (final); **Woodstock Municipal Landfill** (final). There are a total of 1,375 Superfund sites with a status of proposed or final on the list in the U.S. *U.S. Environmental Protection Agency, National Priorities List, April 7, 2021*

AIR QUALITY

Air Quality Trends: Ozone

	1990	1995	2000	2005	2010	2015	2016	2017	2018	2019
MSA[1]	0.074	0.094	0.073	0.084	0.070	0.066	0.074	0.071	0.073	0.069
U.S.	0.088	0.089	0.082	0.080	0.073	0.068	0.069	0.068	0.069	0.065

Note: (1) Data covers the Chicago-Naperville-Elgin, IL-IN-WI Metropolitan Statistical Area. The values shown are the composite ozone concentration averages among trend sites based on the highest fourth daily maximum 8-hour concentration in parts per million. These trends are based on sites having an adequate record of monitoring data during the trend period. Data from exceptional events are included.
Source: U.S. Environmental Protection Agency, Air Quality Monitoring Information, "Air Quality Trends by City, 1990-2019"

Air Quality Index

Area	Percent of Days when Air Quality was...[2]					AQI Statistics[2]	
	Good	Moderate	Unhealthy for Sensitive Groups	Unhealthy	Very Unhealthy	Maximum	Median
MSA[1]	33.2	62.2	4.4	0.3	0.0	174	55

Note: (1) Data covers the Chicago-Naperville-Elgin, IL-IN-WI Metropolitan Statistical Area; (2) Based on 365 days with AQI data in 2019. Air Quality Index (AQI) is an index for reporting daily air quality. EPA calculates the AQI for five major air pollutants regulated by the Clean Air Act: ground-level ozone, particle pollution (aka particulate matter), carbon monoxide, sulfur dioxide, and nitrogen dioxide. The AQI runs from 0 to 500. The higher the AQI value, the greater the level of air pollution and the greater the health concern. There are six AQI categories: "Good" AQI is between 0 and 50. Air quality is considered satisfactory; "Moderate" AQI is between 51 and 100. Air quality is acceptable; "Unhealthy for Sensitive Groups" When AQI values are between 101 and 150, members of sensitive groups may experience health effects; "Unhealthy" When AQI values are between 151 and 200 everyone may begin to experience health effects; "Very Unhealthy" AQI values between 201 and 300 trigger a health alert; "Hazardous" AQI values over 300 trigger warnings of emergency conditions (not shown).
Source: U.S. Environmental Protection Agency, Air Quality Index Report, 2019

Air Quality Index Pollutants

Area	Percent of Days when AQI Pollutant was...[2]					
	Carbon Monoxide	Nitrogen Dioxide	Ozone	Sulfur Dioxide	Particulate Matter 2.5	Particulate Matter 10
MSA[1]	0.0	5.5	24.1	4.9	62.5	3.0

Note: (1) Data covers the Chicago-Naperville-Elgin, IL-IN-WI Metropolitan Statistical Area; (2) Based on 365 days with AQI data in 2019. The Air Quality Index (AQI) is an index for reporting daily air quality. EPA calculates the AQI for five major air pollutants regulated by the Clean Air Act: ground-level ozone, particle pollution (also known as particulate matter), carbon monoxide, sulfur dioxide, and nitrogen dioxide. The AQI runs from 0 to 500. The higher the AQI value, the greater the level of air pollution and the greater the health concern.
Source: U.S. Environmental Protection Agency, Air Quality Index Report, 2019

Maximum Air Pollutant Concentrations: Particulate Matter, Ozone, CO and Lead

	Particulate Matter 10 (ug/m^3)	Particulate Matter 2.5 Wtd AM (ug/m^3)	Particulate Matter 2.5 24-Hr (ug/m^3)	Ozone (ppm)	Carbon Monoxide (ppm)	Lead (ug/m^3)
MSA[1] Level	73	10.8	26	0.071	2	0.19
NAAQS[2]	150	15	35	0.075	9	0.15
Met NAAQS[2]	Yes	Yes	Yes	Yes	Yes	No

Note: (1) Data covers the Chicago-Naperville-Elgin, IL-IN-WI Metropolitan Statistical Area; Data from exceptional events are included; (2) National Ambient Air Quality Standards; ppm = parts per million; ug/m^3 = micrograms per cubic meter; n/a not available.
Concentrations: Particulate Matter 10 (coarse particulate)—highest second maximum 24-hour concentration; Particulate Matter 2.5 Wtd AM (fine particulate)—highest weighted annual mean concentration; Particulate Matter 2.5 24-Hour (fine particulate)—highest 98th percentile 24-hour concentration; Ozone—highest fourth daily maximum 8-hour concentration; Carbon Monoxide—highest second maximum non-overlapping 8-hour concentration; Lead—maximum running 3-month average
Source: U.S. Environmental Protection Agency, Air Quality Monitoring Information, "Air Quality Statistics by City, 2019"

Maximum Air Pollutant Concentrations: Nitrogen Dioxide and Sulfur Dioxide

	Nitrogen Dioxide AM (ppb)	Nitrogen Dioxide 1-Hr (ppb)	Sulfur Dioxide AM (ppb)	Sulfur Dioxide 1-Hr (ppb)	Sulfur Dioxide 24-Hr (ppb)
MSA[1] Level	17	56	n/a	79	n/a
NAAQS[2]	53	100	30	75	140
Met NAAQS[2]	Yes	Yes	n/a	No	n/a

Note: (1) Data covers the Chicago-Naperville-Elgin, IL-IN-WI Metropolitan Statistical Area; Data from exceptional events are included; (2) National Ambient Air Quality Standards; ppm = parts per million; ug/m^3 = micrograms per cubic meter; n/a not available.
Concentrations: Nitrogen Dioxide AM—highest arithmetic mean concentration; Nitrogen Dioxide 1-Hr—highest 98th percentile 1-hour daily maximum concentration; Sulfur Dioxide AM—highest annual mean concentration; Sulfur Dioxide 1-Hr—highest 99th percentile 1-hour daily maximum concentration; Sulfur Dioxide 24-Hr—highest second maximum 24-hour concentration
Source: U.S. Environmental Protection Agency, Air Quality Monitoring Information, "Air Quality Statistics by City, 2019"

Columbia, Missouri

Background

In the middle of the state, along its namesake river, Columbia is a college town teeming with the bright young minds and technological breakthroughs.

The city, located in Boone County, has ridden out the economic downturn with less trauma than the rest of Missouri. Recent surveys give the city high marks in general and for retirees.

The founding of its colleges and university dovetails with the growth and founding of the city itself. A settlement called Smithton grew from the Smithton Land Company's 2,000-acre land purchase on the other side of Flat Branch, not far from where Lewis and Clark passed by during their 1803 explorations. In 1821 the settlement moved across the river and Columbia was established. Daniel Boone and sons ran a salt lick about forty miles away.

Six counties competed for the right to host Missouri's university when it was founded in 1838, the first public university west of the Mississippi River. Boone County responded by raising more than $118,000 in land, cash and buildings. It was forced to repeat its largess decades later, when the academic hall burned down and talked turned to moving the university. The city responded by raising $50,000 to build Jesse Hall, now a local landmark.

Two other institutions of higher learning contributed to Columbia's focus on education. Stephens College, a private women's college, was founded in 1833, and Columbia College, now grown to 30,000 students, was founded as the Christian Female College in 1851. This school arrived as the first women's college west of the Mississippi chartered by a state legislature, and it went co-ed in 1970.

Although these three institutions help to define the historic downtown area, it is the state's massive flagship university—with a rare combination of law school, medical school, and veterinary school all on the same campus—that is Boone County's largest employer. As a major research institution, "Mizzou" conducts $435 million in research and even has a nuclear research reactor on campus. It is the nation's largest supplier of radioisotopes for diagnosing and treating cancer, and hosts interdisciplinary research in a range of scientific enterprises: biofuels, energy logistics, energy policy, wind, biomass and solar. The licensing of products invented by MU products by various companies is a huge market.

The MU Life Science Business Incubator, which opened in 2008, encourages and supports business based on these technologies. For instance, the Indian pharma company Shasun collaborated to create Shasun-NBI based in the incubator and to develop a cancer treatment. Another research park, Discovery Ridge, recently opened. Columbia is also home to several more state-certified sites under development.

> Columbia's annual Restaurant Week looked slightly different because of COVID-19, with establishments participating through deliveries and curbside pickups along with limited dine-ins.

The campus also houses a well-regarded journalism school and IRE, Investigative Reporters and Editors, Inc. The 1,250-acre campus is also home to a botanic garden and a number of cultural opportunities enjoyed by the community at large including the Missouri Theatre Center for the Arts, the Jesse Auditorium, and the university's Museum of Art and Architecture. The State Historical Society of Missouri also operates a research center at the university.

The county's other large employers include University Hospital and Clinics, Columbia Public Schools, Boone Hospital Center, the City of Columbia, and the U.S. Dept. of Veterans Affairs.

The city operates a regional airport, a short line railroad, and utilities for both water and electricity. It also has its own Office of Cultural Affairs, which distributes art guides and a cultural newsletter, funds local arts organizations, and underwrites advertising for local arts opportunities. Columbia offers a "percent for art" program that allows one percent of the cost of new city construction or renovation to be used for site-specific public art. The town is also full of galleries and various arts organizations.

Columbia has four distinct seasons, with highs in the upper 80s in July and August, lows below 20 degrees in January, and rainfall peaking in May.

Rankings

General Rankings

- In their seventh annual survey, Livability.com looked at data for more than 1,000 small to mid-sized U.S. cities to determine the rankings for Livability's "Top 100 Best Places to Live" in 2020. Columbia ranked #30. Criteria: housing and affordable living; vibrant economy; social and civic engagement; education; demographics; health care options; transportation & infrastructure; and abundant lifestyle amenities. *Livability.com, "Top 100 Best Places to Live 2020" October 2020*

Business/Finance Rankings

- The Columbia metro area appeared on the Milken Institute "2021 Best Performing Cities" list. Rank: #51 out of 201 small metro areas (population over 60,000). Criteria: job growth; wage and salary growth; high-tech output growth; housing affordability; household broadband access. *Milken Institute, "Best-Performing Cities 2021," February 16, 2021*

- *Forbes* ranked 203 smaller metro areas (population under 268,000) to determine the nation's "Best Small Places for Business and Careers." The Columbia metro area was ranked #43. Criteria: costs (business and living); job growth (past and projected); income growth; quality of life; educational attainment (college and high school); projected economic growth; cultural and leisure opportunities; workplace tolerance laws; net migration patterns. *Forbes, "The Best Small Places for Business and Careers 2019," October 30, 2019*

Dating/Romance Rankings

- Columbia was selected as one of the most romantic cities in the U.S. by video-rental kiosk company Redbox. The city ranked #6 out of 20. Criteria: number of romance-related rentals in 2016. *Redbox, "20 Most Romantic Cities," February 6, 2017*

Environmental Rankings

- The U.S. Environmental Protection Agency (EPA) released a list of small U.S. metropolitan areas with the most ENERGY STAR certified buildings in 2019. The Columbia metro area was ranked #10 out of 10. *U.S. Environmental Protection Agency, "2020 Energy Star Top Cities," March 2020*

Safety Rankings

- The National Insurance Crime Bureau ranked 384 metro areas in the U.S. in terms of per capita rates of vehicle theft. The Columbia metro area ranked #140 (#1 = highest rate). Criteria: number of vehicle theft offenses per 100,000 inhabitants in 2019. *National Insurance Crime Bureau, "Hot Spots 2019," July 21, 2020*

Seniors/Retirement Rankings

- From its Best Cities for Successful Aging indexes, the Milken Institute generated rankings for metropolitan areas, weighing data in nine categories—health care, wellness, living arrangements, transportation and convenience, financial characteristics, education, employment, community engagement, and overall livability. The Columbia metro area was ranked #4 overall in the small metro area category. *Milken Institute, "Best Cities for Successful Aging, 2017" March 14, 2017*

Sports/Recreation Rankings

- Columbia was chosen as one of America's best cities for bicycling. The city ranked #46 out of 50. Criteria: cycling infrastructure that is safe and friendly for all ages; energy and bike culture. The editors evaluated cities with populations of 100,000 or more. *Bicycling, "The 50 Best Bike Cities in America," October 10, 2018*

Miscellaneous Rankings

- Columbia was selected as a 2020 Digital Cities Survey winner. The city ranked #3 in the small city (75,000 to 124,999 population) category. The survey examined and assessed how city governments are utilizing technology to improve transparency, enhance cybersecurity, and respond to the pandemic. Survey questions focused on ten initiatives: cybersecurity, citizen experience, disaster recovery, business intelligence, IT personnel, data governance, collaboration, infrastructure modernization, cloud computing, and mobile applications. *Center for Digital Government, "2020 Digital Cities Survey," November 10, 2020*

Business Environment

DEMOGRAPHICS

Population Growth

Area	1990 Census	2000 Census	2010 Census	2019* Estimate	Population Growth (%)	
					1990-2019	2010-2019
City	71,069	84,531	108,500	121,230	70.6	11.7
MSA[1]	122,010	145,666	172,786	205,369	68.3	18.9
U.S.	248,709,873	281,421,906	308,745,538	324,697,795	30.6	5.2

Note: (1) Figures cover the Columbia, MO Metropolitan Statistical Area; (*) 2015-2019 5-year estimated population
Source: U.S. Census Bureau, 1990 Census, Census 2000, Census 2010, 2015-2019 American Community Survey 5-Year Estimates

Household Size

Area	Persons in Household (%)							Average Household Size
	One	Two	Three	Four	Five	Six	Seven or More	
City	32.8	32.9	15.1	12.9	4.7	1.1	0.5	2.30
MSA[1]	30.2	34.5	15.1	13.2	4.9	1.3	0.8	2.40
U.S.	27.9	33.9	15.6	12.9	6.0	2.3	1.4	2.60

Note: (1) Figures cover the Columbia, MO Metropolitan Statistical Area
Source: U.S. Census Bureau, 2015-2019 American Community Survey 5-Year Estimates

Race

Area	White Alone[2] (%)	Black Alone[2] (%)	Asian Alone[2] (%)	AIAN[3] Alone[2] (%)	NHOPI[4] Alone[2] (%)	Other Race Alone[2] (%)	Two or More Races (%)
City	77.1	10.9	6.2	0.4	0.1	0.9	4.4
MSA[1]	82.3	8.6	3.9	0.4	0.1	0.9	3.8
U.S.	72.5	12.7	5.5	0.8	0.2	4.9	3.3

Note: (1) Figures cover the Columbia, MO Metropolitan Statistical Area; (2) Alone is defined as not being in combination with one or more other races; (3) American Indian and Alaska Native; (4) Native Hawaiian and Other Pacific Islander
Source: U.S. Census Bureau, 2015-2019 American Community Survey 5-Year Estimates

Hispanic or Latino Origin

Area	Total (%)	Mexican (%)	Puerto Rican (%)	Cuban (%)	Other (%)
City	3.6	2.2	0.3	0.1	1.1
MSA[1]	3.2	2.1	0.2	0.1	0.8
U.S.	18.0	11.2	1.7	0.7	4.3

Note: Persons of Hispanic or Latino origin can be of any race; (1) Figures cover the Columbia, MO Metropolitan Statistical Area
Source: U.S. Census Bureau, 2015-2019 American Community Survey 5-Year Estimates

Ancestry

Area	German	Irish	English	American	Italian	Polish	French[2]	Scottish	Dutch
City	23.9	12.3	8.8	5.6	3.7	2.4	2.5	1.9	1.5
MSA[1]	25.0	11.9	9.0	6.8	3.0	1.7	2.4	2.0	1.5
U.S.	13.3	9.7	7.2	6.2	5.1	2.8	2.3	1.7	1.2

Note: Figures are the percentage of the total population reporting a particular ancestry. The nine most commonly reported ancestries in the U.S. are shown. Figures include multiple ancestries (e.g. if a person reported being Irish and Italian, they were included in both columns); (1) Figures cover the Columbia, MO Metropolitan Statistical Area; (2) Excludes Basque
Source: U.S. Census Bureau, 2015-2019 American Community Survey 5-Year Estimates

Foreign-born Population

Area	Percent of Population Born in								
	Any Foreign Country	Asia	Mexico	Europe	Caribbean	Central America[2]	South America	Africa	Canada
City	9.1	5.3	0.5	1.3	0.1	0.3	0.3	1.0	0.2
MSA[1]	6.1	3.3	0.4	1.0	0.1	0.2	0.2	0.6	0.2
U.S.	13.6	4.2	3.5	1.5	1.3	1.1	1.0	0.7	0.2

Note: (1) Figures cover the Columbia, MO Metropolitan Statistical Area; (2) Excludes Mexico.
Source: U.S. Census Bureau, 2015-2019 American Community Survey 5-Year Estimates

Marital Status

Area	Never Married	Now Married[2]	Separated	Widowed	Divorced
City	48.0	39.0	1.2	3.4	8.4
MSA[1]	40.0	44.6	1.2	4.4	9.7
U.S.	33.4	48.1	1.9	5.8	10.9

Note: Figures are percentages and cover the population 15 years of age and older; (1) Figures cover the Columbia, MO Metropolitan Statistical Area; (2) Excludes separated
Source: U.S. Census Bureau, 2015-2019 American Community Survey 5-Year Estimates

Disability by Age

Area	All Ages	Under 18 Years Old	18 to 64 Years Old	65 Years and Over
City	10.1	2.9	8.0	38.2
MSA[1]	12.1	4.0	10.0	37.2
U.S.	12.6	4.2	10.3	34.5

Note: Figures show percent of the civilian noninstitutionalized population that reported having a disability. Disability status is determined from six types of difficulty: vision, hearing, cognitive, ambulatory, self-care, and independent living. For children under 5 years old, hearing and vision difficulty are used to determine disability status. For children between the ages of 5 and 14, disability status is determined from hearing, vision, cognitive, ambulatory, and self-care difficulties. For people aged 15 years and older, they are considered to have a disability if they have difficulty with any one of the six difficulty types; Note: (1) Figures cover the Columbia, MO Metropolitan Statistical Area
Source: U.S. Census Bureau, 2015-2019 American Community Survey 5-Year Estimates

Age

Area	Percent of Population									Median Age
	Under Age 5	Age 5–19	Age 20–34	Age 35–44	Age 45–54	Age 55–64	Age 65–74	Age 75–84	Age 85+	
City	5.9	19.0	34.6	11.0	9.5	9.4	6.0	3.2	1.3	28.5
MSA[1]	5.8	19.4	28.5	11.6	10.7	11.3	7.5	3.7	1.4	32.1
U.S.	6.1	19.1	20.7	12.6	13.0	12.9	9.1	4.6	1.9	38.1

Note: (1) Figures cover the Columbia, MO Metropolitan Statistical Area
Source: U.S. Census Bureau, 2015-2019 American Community Survey 5-Year Estimates

Gender

Area	Males	Females	Males per 100 Females
City	58,250	62,980	92.5
MSA[1]	100,711	104,658	96.2
U.S.	159,886,919	164,810,876	97.0

Note: (1) Figures cover the Columbia, MO Metropolitan Statistical Area
Source: U.S. Census Bureau, 2015-2019 American Community Survey 5-Year Estimates

Religious Groups by Family

Area	Catholic	Baptist	Non-Den.	Methodist[2]	Lutheran	LDS[3]	Pente-costal	Presby-terian[4]	Muslim[5]	Judaism
MSA[1]	6.6	14.7	5.4	4.3	1.7	1.4	1.1	2.3	0.3	0.3
U.S.	19.1	9.3	4.0	4.0	2.3	2.0	1.9	1.6	0.8	0.7

Note: Figures are the number of adherents as a percentage of the total population; (1) Figures cover the Columbia, MO Metropolitan Statistical Area; (2) Methodist/Pietist; (3) Latter Day Saints; (4) Reformed; (5) Figures are estimates
Source: Association of Statisticians of American Religious Bodies, 2010 U.S. Religion Census: Religious Congregations & Membership Study

Religious Groups by Tradition

Area	Catholic	Evangelical Protestant	Mainline Protestant	Other Tradition	Black Protestant	Orthodox
MSA[1]	6.6	19.9	10.5	2.3	0.5	0.1
U.S.	19.1	16.2	7.3	4.3	1.6	0.3

Note: Figures are the number of adherents as a percentage of the total population; (1) Figures cover the Columbia, MO Metropolitan Statistical Area
Source: Association of Statisticians of American Religious Bodies, 2010 U.S. Religion Census: Religious Congregations & Membership Study

ECONOMY

Gross Metropolitan Product

Area	2017	2018	2019	2020	Rank[2]
MSA[1]	9.2	9.6	9.9	10.3	220

Note: Figures are in billions of dollars; (1) Figures cover the Columbia, MO Metropolitan Statistical Area; (2) Rank is based on 2018 data and ranges from 1 to 381
Source: U.S. Conference of Mayors, U.S. Metro Economies: GMP & Employment 2018-2020, September 2019

Economic Growth

Area	2015-17 (%)	2018 (%)	2019 (%)	2020 (%)	Rank[2]
MSA[1]	0.9	1.6	1.5	1.8	242
U.S.	1.9	2.9	2.3	2.1	–

Note: Figures are real gross metropolitan product (GMP) growth rates and represent average annual percent change; (1) Figures cover the Columbia, MO Metropolitan Statistical Area; (2) Rank is based on 2017 2-year average annual percent change and ranges from 1 to 381
Source: U.S. Conference of Mayors, U.S. Metro Economies: GMP & Employment 2018-2020, September 2019

Metropolitan Area Exports

Area	2014	2015	2016	2017	2018	2019	Rank[2]
MSA[1]	237.7	214.0	213.7	224.0	238.6	291.4	260

Note: Figures are in millions of dollars; (1) Figures cover the Columbia, MO Metropolitan Statistical Area; (2) Rank is based on 2019 data and ranges from 1 to 386
Source: U.S. Department of Commerce, International Trade Administration, Office of Trade and Economic Analysis, Industry and Analysis, Exports by Metropolitan Area, data extracted March 24, 2021

Building Permits

Area	Single-Family			Multi-Family			Total		
	2018	2019	Pct. Chg.	2018	2019	Pct. Chg.	2018	2019	Pct. Chg.
City	261	338	29.5	2	166	8,200.0	263	504	91.6
MSA[1]	555	633	14.1	2	166	8,200.0	557	799	43.4
U.S.	855,300	862,100	0.7	473,500	523,900	10.6	1,328,800	1,386,000	4.3

Note: (1) Figures cover the Columbia, MO Metropolitan Statistical Area; Figures represent new, privately-owned housing units authorized (unadjusted data); All permit data are based on estimates with imputation
Source: U.S. Census Bureau, Manufacturing, Mining, and Construction Statistics, Building Permits, 2018, 2019

Bankruptcy Filings

Area	Business Filings			Nonbusiness Filings		
	2019	2020	% Chg.	2019	2020	% Chg.
Boone County	6	8	33.3	375	263	-29.9
U.S.	22,780	21,655	-4.9	752,160	522,808	-30.5

Note: Business filings include Chapter 7, Chapter 9, Chapter 11, Chapter 12, Chapter 13, Chapter 15, and Section 304; Nonbusiness filings include Chapter 7, Chapter 11, and Chapter 13
Source: Administrative Office of the U.S. Courts, Business and Nonbusiness Bankruptcy, County Cases Commenced by Chapter of the Bankruptcy Code, During the 12-Month Period Ending December 31, 2019 and Business and Nonbusiness Bankruptcy, County Cases Commenced by Chapter of the Bankruptcy Code, During the 12-Month Period Ending December 31, 2020

Housing Vacancy Rates

Area	Gross Vacancy Rate[2] (%)			Year-Round Vacancy Rate[3] (%)			Rental Vacancy Rate[4] (%)			Homeowner Vacancy Rate[5] (%)		
	2018	2019	2020	2018	2019	2020	2018	2019	2020	2018	2019	2020
MSA[1]	n/a	n/a	n/a	n/a	n/a	n/a	n/a	n/a	n/a	n/a	n/a	n/a
U.S.	12.3	12.0	10.6	9.7	9.5	8.2	6.9	6.7	6.3	1.5	1.4	1.0

Note: (1) Figures cover the Columbia, MO Metropolitan Statistical Area; (2) The percentage of the total housing inventory that is vacant; (3) The percentage of the housing inventory (excluding seasonal units) that is year-round vacant; (4) The percentage of rental inventory that is vacant for rent; (5) The percentage of homeowner inventory that is vacant for sale; n/a not available
Source: U.S. Census Bureau, Housing Vacancies and Homeownership Annual Statistics: 2018, 2019, 2020

INCOME

Income

Area	Per Capita ($)	Median Household ($)	Average Household ($)
City	30,244	51,276	74,727
MSA[1]	29,534	54,808	74,042
U.S.	34,103	62,843	88,607

Note: (1) Figures cover the Columbia, MO Metropolitan Statistical Area
Source: U.S. Census Bureau, 2015-2019 American Community Survey 5-Year Estimates

Household Income Distribution

Area	Percent of Households Earning							
	Under $15,000	$15,000 -$24,999	$25,000 -$34,999	$35,000 -$49,999	$50,000 -$74,999	$75,000 -$99,999	$100,000 -$149,999	$150,000 and up
City	14.8	10.6	9.8	13.8	15.2	11.2	13.6	11.0
MSA[1]	12.0	10.0	10.1	13.9	17.4	12.8	14.2	9.5
U.S.	10.3	8.9	8.9	12.3	17.2	12.7	15.1	14.5

Note: (1) Figures cover the Columbia, MO Metropolitan Statistical Area
Source: U.S. Census Bureau, 2015-2019 American Community Survey 5-Year Estimates

Poverty Rate

Area	All Ages	Under 18 Years Old	18 to 64 Years Old	65 Years and Over
City	21.8	15.1	26.2	5.0
MSA[1]	17.2	15.0	20.1	6.5
U.S.	13.4	18.5	12.6	9.3

Note: Figures are percentage of people whose income during the past 12 months was below the poverty level;
(1) Figures cover the Columbia, MO Metropolitan Statistical Area
Source: U.S. Census Bureau, 2015-2019 American Community Survey 5-Year Estimates

CITY FINANCES

City Government Finances

Component	2017 ($000)	2017 ($ per capita)
Total Revenues	355,513	2,985
Total Expenditures	340,473	2,859
Debt Outstanding	365,171	3,066
Cash and Securities[1]	628,618	5,278

Note: (1) Cash and security holdings of a government at the close of its fiscal year,
including those of its dependent agencies, utilities, and liquor stores.
Source: U.S. Census Bureau, State & Local Government Finances 2017

City Government Revenue by Source

Source	2017 ($000)	2017 ($ per capita)	2017 (%)
General Revenue			
From Federal Government	13,139	110	3.7
From State Government	4,995	42	1.4
From Local Governments	20,637	173	5.8
Taxes			
Property	12,015	101	3.4
Sales and Gross Receipts	58,981	495	16.6
Personal Income	0	0	0.0
Corporate Income	0	0	0.0
Motor Vehicle License	0	0	0.0
Other Taxes	2,496	21	0.7
Current Charges	54,879	461	15.4
Liquor Store	0	0	0.0
Utility	157,243	1,320	44.2
Employee Retirement	16,175	136	4.5

Source: U.S. Census Bureau, State & Local Government Finances 2017

City Government Expenditures by Function

Function	2017 ($000)	2017 ($ per capita)	2017 (%)
General Direct Expenditures			
Air Transportation	8,412	70	2.5
Corrections	0	0	0.0
Education	0	0	0.0
Employment Security Administration	0	0	0.0
Financial Administration	4,256	35	1.3
Fire Protection	13,013	109	3.8
General Public Buildings	1,962	16	0.6
Governmental Administration, Other	7,312	61	2.1
Health	5,388	45	1.6
Highways	20,767	174	6.1
Hospitals	0	0	0.0
Housing and Community Development	1,408	11	0.4
Interest on General Debt	4,990	41	1.5
Judicial and Legal	2,608	21	0.8
Libraries	0	0	0.0
Parking	2,714	22	0.8
Parks and Recreation	19,297	162	5.7
Police Protection	17,633	148	5.2
Public Welfare	875	7	0.3
Sewerage	17,027	143	5.0
Solid Waste Management	22,993	193	6.8
Veterans' Services	0	0	0.0
Liquor Store	0	0	0.0
Utility	172,488	1,448	50.7
Employee Retirement	11,264	94	3.3

Source: U.S. Census Bureau, State & Local Government Finances 2017

EMPLOYMENT

Labor Force and Employment

Area	Civilian Labor Force			Workers Employed		
	Dec. 2019	Dec. 2020	% Chg.	Dec. 2019	Dec. 2020	% Chg.
City	68,108	67,049	-1.6	66,459	64,199	-3.4
MSA[1]	99,481	97,891	-1.6	97,069	93,768	-3.4
U.S.	164,007,000	160,017,000	-2.4	158,504,000	149,613,000	-5.6

Note: Data is not seasonally adjusted and covers workers 16 years of age and older; (1) Figures cover the Columbia, MO Metropolitan Statistical Area
Source: Bureau of Labor Statistics, Local Area Unemployment Statistics

Unemployment Rate

Area	2020											
	Jan.	Feb.	Mar.	Apr.	May	Jun.	Jul.	Aug.	Sep.	Oct.	Nov.	Dec.
City	3.1	2.4	2.5	6.6	6.7	5.8	5.2	5.2	3.0	2.7	2.9	4.3
MSA[1]	3.2	2.5	2.6	6.5	6.5	5.7	5.1	5.1	2.9	2.6	2.8	4.2
U.S.	4.0	3.8	4.5	14.4	13.0	11.2	10.5	8.5	7.7	6.6	6.4	6.5

Note: Data is not seasonally adjusted and covers workers 16 years of age and older; (1) Figures cover the Columbia, MO Metropolitan Statistical Area
Source: Bureau of Labor Statistics, Local Area Unemployment Statistics

Average Wages

Occupation	$/Hr.	Occupation	$/Hr.
Accountants and Auditors	29.00	Maintenance and Repair Workers	15.90
Automotive Mechanics	20.90	Marketing Managers	54.40
Bookkeepers	17.90	Network and Computer Systems Admin.	34.20
Carpenters	24.10	Nurses, Licensed Practical	21.50
Cashiers	11.10	Nurses, Registered	31.40
Computer Programmers	30.70	Nursing Assistants	14.30
Computer Systems Analysts	38.60	Office Clerks, General	16.40
Computer User Support Specialists	22.00	Physical Therapists	37.20
Construction Laborers	20.00	Physicians	123.10
Cooks, Restaurant	12.30	Plumbers, Pipefitters and Steamfitters	31.70
Customer Service Representatives	15.30	Police and Sheriff's Patrol Officers	24.60
Dentists	95.90	Postal Service Mail Carriers	24.80
Electricians	22.20	Real Estate Sales Agents	15.70
Engineers, Electrical	n/a	Retail Salespersons	16.40
Fast Food and Counter Workers	12.40	Sales Representatives, Technical/Scientific	37.50
Financial Managers	57.40	Secretaries, Exc. Legal/Medical/Executive	17.90
First-Line Supervisors of Office Workers	26.60	Security Guards	15.10
General and Operations Managers	41.30	Surgeons	n/a
Hairdressers/Cosmetologists	15.90	Teacher Assistants, Exc. Postsecondary*	13.50
Home Health and Personal Care Aides	12.20	Teachers, Secondary School, Exc. Sp. Ed.*	25.90
Janitors and Cleaners	14.70	Telemarketers	n/a
Landscaping/Groundskeeping Workers	14.70	Truck Drivers, Heavy/Tractor-Trailer	21.50
Lawyers	43.60	Truck Drivers, Light/Delivery Services	19.90
Maids and Housekeeping Cleaners	11.40	Waiters and Waitresses	11.40

Note: Wage data covers the Columbia, MO Metropolitan Statistical Area; (*) Hourly wages were calculated from annual wage data based on a 40 hour work week; n/a not available.
Source: Bureau of Labor Statistics, Metro Area Occupational Employment & Wage Estimates, May 2020

Employment by Industry

Sector	MSA[1]		U.S.
	Number of Employees	Percent of Total	Percent of Total
Construction, Mining, and Logging	n/a	n/a	5.5
Education and Health Services	n/a	n/a	16.3
Financial Activities	n/a	n/a	6.1
Government	28,600	29.3	15.2
Information	n/a	n/a	1.9
Leisure and Hospitality	n/a	n/a	9.0
Manufacturing	n/a	n/a	8.5
Other Services	n/a	n/a	3.8
Professional and Business Services	n/a	n/a	14.4
Retail Trade	10,700	11.0	10.9
Transportation, Warehousing, and Utilities	n/a	n/a	4.6
Wholesale Trade	n/a	n/a	3.9

Note: Figures are non-farm employment as of December 2020. Figures are not seasonally adjusted and include workers 16 years of age and older; (1) Figures cover the Columbia, MO Metropolitan Statistical Area; n/a not available
Source: Bureau of Labor Statistics, Current Employment Statistics, Employment, Hours, and Earnings

Employment by Occupation

Occupation Classification	City (%)	MSA[1] (%)	U.S. (%)
Management, Business, Science, and Arts	47.5	44.4	38.5
Natural Resources, Construction, and Maintenance	4.9	7.4	8.9
Production, Transportation, and Material Moving	7.8	9.4	13.2
Sales and Office	21.1	21.2	21.6
Service	18.7	17.5	17.8

Note: Figures cover employed civilians 16 years of age and older; (1) Figures cover the Columbia, MO Metropolitan Statistical Area
Source: U.S. Census Bureau, 2015-2019 American Community Survey 5-Year Estimates

Occupations with Greatest Projected Employment Growth: 2020 – 2022

Occupation[1]	2020 Employment	2022 Projected Employment	Numeric Employment Change	Percent Employment Change
Fast Food and Counter Workers	58,510	76,310	17,800	30.4
Waiters and Waitresses	34,100	45,340	11,240	33.0
Cooks, Restaurant	22,920	31,610	8,690	37.9
Retail Salespersons	69,100	75,980	6,880	10.0
Home Health and Personal Care Aides	74,240	79,340	5,100	6.9
First-Line Supervisors of Food Preparation and Serving Workers	14,100	18,230	4,130	29.3
General and Operations Managers	51,050	54,590	3,540	6.9
Registered Nurses	72,020	75,320	3,300	4.6
Cashiers	67,360	70,390	3,030	4.5
Maids and Housekeeping Cleaners	20,070	23,020	2,950	14.7

Note: Projections cover Missouri; (1) Sorted by numeric employment change
Source: www.projectionscentral.com, State Occupational Projections, 2020–2022 Short-Term Projections

Fastest-Growing Occupations: 2020 – 2022

Occupation[1]	2020 Employment	2022 Projected Employment	Numeric Employment Change	Percent Employment Change
Athletes and Sports Competitors	100	150	50	50.0
Ushers, Lobby Attendants, and Ticket Takers	2,170	3,240	1,070	49.3
Baggage Porters and Bellhops	160	230	70	43.8
Gaming Dealers	910	1,300	390	42.9
Film and Video Editors	220	310	90	40.9
Gaming Change Persons and Booth Cashiers	280	390	110	39.3
Hotel, Motel, and Resort Desk Clerks	2,810	3,910	1,100	39.1
Cooks, Restaurant	22,920	31,610	8,690	37.9
Hosts and Hostesses, Restaurant, Lounge, and Coffee Shop	5,350	7,140	1,790	33.5
Dancers	180	240	60	33.3

Note: Projections cover Missouri; (1) Sorted by percent employment change and excludes occupations with numeric employment change less than 50
Source: www.projectionscentral.com, State Occupational Projections, 2020–2022 Short-Term Projections

TAXES

State Corporate Income Tax Rates

State	Tax Rate (%)	Income Brackets ($)	Num. of Brackets	Financial Institution Tax Rate (%)[a]	Federal Income Tax Ded.
Missouri	4.0	Flat rate	1	7.0	Yes (j)

Note: Tax rates as of January 1, 2021; (a) Rates listed are the corporate income tax rate applied to financial institutions or excise taxes based on income. Some states have other taxes based upon the value of deposits or shares; (j) 50% of the federal income tax is deductible.
Source: Federation of Tax Administrators, State Corporate Income Tax Rates, January 1, 2021

State Individual Income Tax Rates

State	Tax Rate (%)	Income Brackets ($)	Personal Exemptions ($)			Standard Ded. ($)	
			Single	Married	Depend.	Single	Married
Missouri (a)	1.5 - 5.4	1,088 - 8,704	(d)	(d)	(d)	12,550	25,100 (d)

Note: Tax rates as of January 1, 2021; Local- and county-level taxes are not included; The deduction for federal income tax is limited to $5,000 for individuals and $10,000 for joint returns in Missouri and Montana, and to $6,500 for all filers in Oregon; (a) 19 states have statutory provision for automatically adjusting to the rate of inflation the dollar values of the income tax brackets, standard deductions, and/or personal exemptions. Michigan indexes the personal exemption only. Oregon does not index the income brackets for $125,000 and over; (d) These states use the personal exemption/standard deduction amounts provided in the federal Internal Revenue Code.
Source: Federation of Tax Administrators, State Individual Income Tax Rates, January 1, 2021

Various State Sales and Excise Tax Rates

State	State Sales Tax (%)	Gasoline[1] (¢/gal.)	Cigarette[2] ($/pack)	Spirits[3] ($/gal.)	Wine[4] ($/gal.)	Beer[5] ($/gal.)	Recreational Marijuana (%)
Missouri	4.225	17.42	0.17	2	0.42	0.06	Not legal

Note: All tax rates as of January 1, 2021; (1) The American Petroleum Institute has developed a methodology for determining the average tax rate on a gallon of fuel. Rates may include any of the following: excise taxes, environmental fees, storage tank fees, other fees or taxes, general sales tax, and local taxes; (2) The federal excise tax of $1.0066 per pack and local taxes are not included; (3) Rates are those applicable to off-premise sales of 40% alcohol by volume (a.b.v.) distilled spirits in 750ml containers. Local excise taxes are excluded; (4) Rates are those applicable to off-premise sales of 11% a.b.v. non-carbonated wine in 750ml containers; (5) Rates are those applicable to off-premise sales of 4.7% a.b.v. beer in 12 ounce containers.
Source: Tax Foundation, 2021 Facts & Figures: How Does Your State Compare?

State Business Tax Climate Index Rankings

State	Overall Rank	Corporate Tax Rank	Individual Income Tax Rank	Sales Tax Rank	Property Tax Rank	Unemployment Insurance Tax Rank
Missouri	12	3	23	24	8	7

Note: The index is a measure of how each state's tax laws affect economic performance. The lower the rank, the more favorable a state's tax system is for business. States without a given tax are given a ranking of 1. The scores/rankings for the District of Columbia do not affect other states. The 2021 index represents the tax climate as of July 1, 2020.
Source: Tax Foundation, State Business Tax Climate Index 2021

TRANSPORTATION

Means of Transportation to Work

Area	Car/Truck/Van		Public Transportation			Bicycle	Walked	Other Means	Worked at Home
	Drove Alone	Car-pooled	Bus	Subway	Railroad				
City	77.1	10.5	1.3	0.0	0.0	1.3	4.8	0.9	4.2
MSA[1]	78.9	10.7	0.8	0.0	0.0	0.8	3.3	0.9	4.5
U.S.	76.3	9.0	2.4	1.9	0.6	0.5	2.7	1.4	5.2

Note: Figures are percentages and cover workers 16 years of age and older; (1) Figures cover the Columbia, MO Metropolitan Statistical Area
Source: U.S. Census Bureau, 2015-2019 American Community Survey 5-Year Estimates

Travel Time to Work

Area	Less Than 10 Minutes	10 to 19 Minutes	20 to 29 Minutes	30 to 44 Minutes	45 to 59 Minutes	60 to 89 Minutes	90 Minutes or More
City	20.2	55.0	11.8	8.2	2.8	0.8	1.2
MSA[1]	17.5	45.5	17.3	12.4	4.3	1.5	1.4
U.S.	12.2	28.4	20.8	20.8	8.3	6.4	2.9

Note: Note: Figures are percentages and include workers 16 years old and over; (1) Figures cover the Columbia, MO Metropolitan Statistical Area
Source: U.S. Census Bureau, 2015-2019 American Community Survey 5-Year Estimates

Key Congestion Measures

Measure	1982	1992	2002	2012	2017
Annual Hours of Delay, Total (000)	n/a	n/a	n/a	n/a	2,692
Annual Hours of Delay, Per Auto Commuter	n/a	n/a	n/a	n/a	19
Annual Congestion Cost, Total (million $)	n/a	n/a	n/a	n/a	56
Annual Congestion Cost, Per Auto Commuter ($)	n/a	n/a	n/a	n/a	404

Note: n/a not available
Source: Texas A&M Transportation Institute, 2019 Urban Mobility Report

Freeway Travel Time Index

Measure	1982	1987	1992	1997	2002	2007	2012	2017
Urban Area Index[1]	n/a	n/a	n/a	n/a	n/a	n/a	n/a	1.10
Urban Area Rank[1,2]	n/a	n/a	n/a	n/a	n/a	n/a	n/a	n/a

Note: Freeway Travel Time Index—the ratio of travel time in the peak period to the travel time at free-flow conditions. For example, a value of 1.30 indicates a 20-minute free-flow trip takes 26 minutes in the peak (20 minutes x 1.30 = 26 minutes); (1) Covers the Columbia MO urban area; (2) Rank is based on 101 larger urban areas (#1 = highest travel time index); n/a not available
Source: Texas A&M Transportation Institute, 2019 Urban Mobility Report

Public Transportation

Agency Name / Mode of Transportation	Vehicles Operated in Maximum Service[1]	Annual Unlinked Passenger Trips[2] (in thous.)	Annual Passenger Miles[3] (in thous.)
Columbia Transit (CT)			
Bus (directly operated)	27	1,055.7	2,907.1
Demand Response (directly operated)	9	52.9	295.0

Note: (1) Number of revenue vehicles operated by the given mode and type of service to meet the annual maximum service requirement. This is the revenue vehicle count during the peak season of the year; on the week and day that maximum service is provided. Vehicles operated in maximum service (VOMS) exclude atypical days and one-time special events; (2) Number of passengers who boarded public transportation vehicles. Passengers are counted each time they board a vehicle no matter how many vehicles they use to travel from their origin to their destination. (3) Sum of the distances ridden by all passengers during the entire fiscal year.
Source: Federal Transit Administration, National Transit Database, 2019

Air Transportation

Airport Name and Code / Type of Service	Passenger Airlines[1]	Passenger Enplanements	Freight Carriers[2]	Freight (lbs)
Columbia Regional (COU)				
Domestic service (U.S. carriers - 2020)	10	51,169	3	17,490
International service (U.S. carriers - 2019)	2	141	0	0

Note: (1) Includes all U.S.-based major, minor and commuter airlines that carried at least one passenger during the year; (2) Includes all U.S.-based airlines and freight carriers that transported at least one pound of freight during the year.
Source: Bureau of Transportation Statistics, The Intermodal Transportation Database, Air Carriers: T-100 Domestic Market (U.S. Carriers), 2020; Bureau of Transportation Statistics, The Intermodal Transportation Database, Air Carriers: T-100 International Market (U.S. Carriers), 2019

BUSINESSES

Major Business Headquarters

Company Name	Industry	Rankings	
		Fortune[1]	Forbes[2]
No companies listed	-	-	-

Note: (1) Companies that produce a 10-K are ranked 1 to 500 based on 2019 revenue; (2) All private companies with at least $2 billion in annual revenue through the end of their most current fiscal year are ranked 1 to 219; companies listed are headquartered in the city; dashes indicate no ranking
Source: Fortune, "Fortune 500," June/July 2020; Forbes, "America's Largest Private Companies," 2020

Living Environment

COST OF LIVING

Cost of Living Index

Composite Index	Groceries	Housing	Utilities	Trans-portation	Health Care	Misc. Goods/Services
92.5	98.9	78.5	98.2	89.3	98.8	99.6

Note: The Cost of Living Index measures regional differences in the cost of consumer goods and services, excluding taxes and non-consumer expenditures, for professional and managerial households in the top income quintile. It is based on more than 50,000 prices covering almost 60 different items for which prices are collected three times a year by chambers of commerce, economic development organizations or university applied economic centers in each participating urban area. The numbers shown should be read as a percentage above or below the national average of 100. For example, a value of 115.4 in the groceries column indicates that grocery prices are 15.4% higher than the national average. Small differences in the index numbers should not be interpreted as significant; Figures cover the Columbia MO urban area.
Source: The Council for Community and Economic Research, Cost of Living Index, 2020

Grocery Prices

Area[1]	T-Bone Steak ($/pound)	Frying Chicken ($/pound)	Whole Milk ($/half gal.)	Eggs ($/dozen)	Orange Juice ($/64 oz.)	Coffee ($/11.5 oz.)
City[2]	11.89	1.53	2.18	1.08	3.56	4.44
Avg.	11.78	1.39	2.05	1.47	3.57	4.34
Min.	8.03	0.94	1.03	0.74	2.94	3.02
Max.	15.86	2.65	4.31	3.77	5.44	8.69

Note: (1) Values for the local area are compared with the average, minimum and maximum values for all 284 areas in the Cost of Living Index; (2) Figures cover the Columbia MO urban area; **T-Bone Steak** (price per pound); **Frying Chicken** (price per pound, whole fryer); **Whole Milk** (half gallon carton); **Eggs** (price per dozen, Grade A, large); **Orange Juice** (64 oz. Tropicana or Florida Natural); **Coffee** (11.5 oz. can, vacuum-packed, Maxwell House, Hills Bros, or Folgers).
Source: The Council for Community and Economic Research, Cost of Living Index, 2020

Housing and Utility Costs

Area[1]	New Home Price ($)	Apartment Rent ($/month)	All Electric ($/month)	Part Electric ($/month)	Other Energy ($/month)	Telephone ($/month)
City[2]	313,945	808	-	96.59	60.50	190.50
Avg.	368,594	1,168	170.86	100.47	65.28	184.30
Min.	190,567	502	91.58	31.42	26.08	169.60
Max.	2,227,806	4,738	470.38	280.31	280.06	206.50

Note: (1) Values for the local area are compared with the average, minimum and maximum values for all 284 areas in the Cost of Living Index; (2) Figures cover the Columbia MO urban area; **New Home Price** (2,400 sf living area, 8,000 sf lot, in urban area with full utilities); **Apartment Rent** (950 sf 2 bedroom/1.5 or 2 bath, unfurnished, excluding all utilities except water); **All Electric** (average monthly cost for an all-electric home); **Part Electric** (average monthly cost for a part-electric home); **Other Energy** (average monthly cost for natural gas, fuel oil, coal, wood, and any other forms of energy except electricity); **Telephone** (price includes the base monthly rate plus taxes and fees for three lines of mobile phone service).
Source: The Council for Community and Economic Research, Cost of Living Index, 2020

Health Care, Transportation, and Other Costs

Area[1]	Doctor ($/visit)	Dentist ($/visit)	Optometrist ($/visit)	Gasoline ($/gallon)	Beauty Salon ($/visit)	Men's Shirt ($)
City[2]	126.58	89.08	104.24	1.99	39.17	33.37
Avg.	115.44	99.32	108.10	2.21	39.27	31.37
Min.	36.68	59.00	51.36	1.71	19.00	11.00
Max.	219.00	153.10	250.97	3.46	82.05	58.33

Note: (1) Values for the local area are compared with the average, minimum and maximum values for all 284 areas in the Cost of Living Index; (2) Figures cover the Columbia MO urban area; **Doctor** (general practitioners routine exam of an established patient); **Dentist** (adult teeth cleaning and periodic oral examination); **Optometrist** (full vision eye exam for established adult patient); **Gasoline** (one gallon regular unleaded, national brand, including all taxes, cash price at self-service pump if available); **Beauty Salon** (woman's shampoo, trim, and blow-dry); **Men's Shirt** (cotton/polyester dress shirt, pinpoint weave, long sleeves).
Source: The Council for Community and Economic Research, Cost of Living Index, 2020

HOUSING

Homeownership Rate

Area	2012 (%)	2013 (%)	2014 (%)	2015 (%)	2016 (%)	2017 (%)	2018 (%)	2019 (%)	2020 (%)
MSA[1]	n/a	n/a	n/a	n/a	n/a	n/a	n/a	n/a	n/a
U.S.	65.4	65.1	64.5	63.7	63.4	63.9	64.4	64.6	66.6

Note: (1) Figures cover the Columbia, MO Metropolitan Statistical Area; n/a not available
Source: U.S. Census Bureau, Housing Vacancies and Homeownership Annual Statistics: 2012-2020

House Price Index (HPI)

Area	National Ranking[2]	Quarterly Change (%)	One-Year Change (%)	Five-Year Change (%)	Since 1991Q1 (%)
MSA[1]	212	1.63	4.42	20.40	150.92
U.S.[3]	–	3.81	10.77	38.99	205.12

Note: The HPI is a weighted repeat sales index. It measures average price changes in repeat sales or refinancings on the same properties. This information is obtained by reviewing repeat mortgage transactions on single-family properties whose mortgages have been purchased or securitized by Fannie Mae or Freddie Mac since January 1975; (1) Figures cover the Columbia, MO Metropolitan Statistical Area; (2) Rankings are based on annual percentage change for all metro areas containing at least 15,000 transactions over the last 10 years and ranges from 1 to 253; (3) figures based on a weighted average of Census Division estimates using a seasonally adjusted, purchase-only index; all figures are for the period ending December 31, 2020
Source: Federal Housing Finance Agency, Change in Metropolitan Area House Price Indexes, April 7, 2021

Median Single-Family Home Prices

Area	2018	2019	2020p	Percent Change 2019 to 2020
MSA[1]	189.3	206.4	225.4	9.2
U.S. Average	261.6	274.6	299.9	9.2

Note: Figures are median sales prices of existing single-family homes in thousands of dollars; (p) preliminary; (1) Figures cover the Columbia, MO Metropolitan Statistical Area
Source: National Association of Realtors, Median Sales Price of Existing Single-Family Homes for Metropolitan Areas, 4th Quarter 2020

Qualifying Income Based on Median Sales Price of Existing Single-Family Homes

Area	With 5% Down ($)	With 10% Down ($)	With 20% Down ($)
MSA[1]	43,314	41,034	36,475
U.S. Average	59,266	56,147	49,908

Note: Figures are preliminary; Qualifying income is based on a mortgage rate of 2.81%. Monthly principal and interest payment is limited to 25% of income; (1) Figures cover the Columbia, MO Metropolitan Statistical Area
Source: National Association of Realtors, Qualifying Income Based on Median Sales Price of Existing Single-Family Homes for Metropolitan Areas, 4th Quarter 2020

Home Value Distribution

Area	Under $50,000	$50,000 -$99,999	$100,000 -$149,999	$150,000 -$199,999	$200,000 -$299,999	$300,000 -$499,999	$500,000 -$999,999	$1,000,000 or more
City	3.4	7.4	19.0	22.8	25.7	17.2	4.2	0.3
MSA[1]	5.4	11.2	19.9	20.9	22.9	14.8	4.3	0.7
U.S.	6.9	12.0	13.3	14.0	19.6	19.3	11.4	3.4

Note: Figures are percentages and cover owner-occupied housing units; (1) Figures cover the Columbia, MO Metropolitan Statistical Area
Source: U.S. Census Bureau, 2015-2019 American Community Survey 5-Year Estimates

Year Housing Structure Built

Area	2010 or Later	2000 -2009	1990 -1999	1980 -1989	1970 -1979	1960 -1969	1950 -1959	1940 -1949	Before 1940	Median Year
City	12.6	21.5	17.9	12.0	12.5	10.7	5.1	2.2	5.5	1991
MSA[1]	9.5	19.4	18.0	12.8	15.4	10.1	5.3	2.5	7.2	1988
U.S.	5.2	14.0	13.9	13.4	15.2	10.6	10.3	4.9	12.6	1978

Note: Figures are percentages except for Median Year; Note: (1) Figures cover the Columbia, MO Metropolitan Statistical Area
Source: U.S. Census Bureau, 2015-2019 American Community Survey 5-Year Estimates

Gross Monthly Rent

Area	Under $500	$500 -$999	$1,000 -$1,499	$1,500 -$1,999	$2,000 -$2,499	$2,500 -$2,999	$3,000 and up	Median ($)
City	6.1	58.0	26.4	5.7	3.3	0.3	0.2	887
MSA[1]	7.9	59.1	25.3	4.5	2.8	0.3	0.2	862
U.S.	9.4	36.2	30.0	14.0	5.6	2.4	2.4	1,062

Note: Figures are percentages except for Median; Gross rent is the contract rent plus the estimated average monthly cost of utilities (electricity, gas, and water and sewer) and fuels (oil, coal, kerosene, wood, etc.) if these are paid by the renter (or paid for the renter by someone else); (1) Figures cover the Columbia, MO Metropolitan Statistical Area
Source: U.S. Census Bureau, 2015-2019 American Community Survey 5-Year Estimates

HEALTH

Health Risk Factors

Category	MSA[1] (%)	U.S. (%)
Adults aged 18–64 who have any kind of health care coverage	n/a	87.3
Adults who reported being in good or better health	n/a	82.4
Adults who have been told they have high blood cholesterol	n/a	33.0
Adults who have been told they have high blood pressure	n/a	32.3
Adults who are current smokers	n/a	17.1
Adults who currently use E-cigarettes	n/a	4.6
Adults who currently use chewing tobacco, snuff, or snus	n/a	4.0
Adults who are heavy drinkers[2]	n/a	6.3
Adults who are binge drinkers[3]	n/a	17.4
Adults who are overweight (BMI 25.0 - 29.9)	n/a	35.3
Adults who are obese (BMI 30.0 - 99.8)	n/a	31.3
Adults who participated in any physical activities in the past month	n/a	74.4
Adults who always or nearly always wears a seat belt	n/a	94.3

Note: n/a not available; (1) Figures cover the Columbia, MO Metropolitan Statistical Area; (2) Heavy drinkers are classified as adult men having more than 14 drinks per week and adult women having more than 7 drinks per week; (3) Binge drinkers are classified as males having five or more drinks on one occasion or females having four or more drinks on one occasion
Source: Centers for Disease Control and Prevention, Behaviorial Risk Factor Surveillance System, SMART: Selected Metropolitan Area Risk Trends, 2017

Acute and Chronic Health Conditions

Category	MSA[1] (%)	U.S. (%)
Adults who have ever been told they had a heart attack	n/a	4.2
Adults who have ever been told they have angina or coronary heart disease	n/a	3.9
Adults who have ever been told they had a stroke	n/a	3.0
Adults who have ever been told they have asthma	n/a	14.2
Adults who have ever been told they have arthritis	n/a	24.9
Adults who have ever been told they have diabetes[2]	n/a	10.5
Adults who have ever been told they had skin cancer	n/a	6.2
Adults who have ever been told they had any other types of cancer	n/a	7.1
Adults who have ever been told they have COPD	n/a	6.5
Adults who have ever been told they have kidney disease	n/a	3.0
Adults who have ever been told they have a form of depression	n/a	20.5

Note: n/a not available; (1) Figures cover the Columbia, MO Metropolitan Statistical Area; (2) Figures do not include pregnancy-related, borderline, or pre-diabetes
Source: Centers for Disease Control and Prevention, Behaviorial Risk Factor Surveillance System, SMART: Selected Metropolitan Area Risk Trends, 2017

Health Screening and Vaccination Rates

Category	MSA[1] (%)	U.S. (%)
Adults aged 65+ who have had flu shot within the past year	n/a	60.7
Adults aged 65+ who have ever had a pneumonia vaccination	n/a	75.4
Adults who have ever been tested for HIV	n/a	36.1
Adults who have ever had the shingles or zoster vaccine?	n/a	28.9
Adults who have had their blood cholesterol checked within the last five years	n/a	85.9

Note: n/a not available; (1) Figures cover the Columbia, MO Metropolitan Statistical Area.
Source: Centers for Disease Control and Prevention, Behaviorial Risk Factor Surveillance System, SMART: Selected Metropolitan Area Risk Trends, 2017

Disability Status

Category	MSA[1] (%)	U.S. (%)
Adults who reported being deaf	n/a	6.7
Are you blind or have serious difficulty seeing, even when wearing glasses?	n/a	4.5
Are you limited in any way in any of your usual activities due of arthritis?	n/a	12.9
Do you have difficulty doing errands alone?	n/a	6.8
Do you have difficulty dressing or bathing?	n/a	3.6
Do you have serious difficulty concentrating/remembering/making decisions?	n/a	10.7
Do you have serious difficulty walking or climbing stairs?	n/a	13.6

Note: n/a not available; (1) Figures cover the Columbia, MO Metropolitan Statistical Area.
Source: Centers for Disease Control and Prevention, Behaviorial Risk Factor Surveillance System, SMART: Selected Metropolitan Area Risk Trends, 2017

Mortality Rates for the Top 10 Causes of Death in the U.S.

ICD-10[a] Sub-Chapter	ICD-10[a] Code	Age-Adjusted Mortality Rate[1] per 100,000 population	
		County[2]	U.S.
Malignant neoplasms	C00-C97	141.8	149.2
Ischaemic heart diseases	I20-I25	61.3	90.5
Other forms of heart disease	I30-I51	62.6	52.2
Chronic lower respiratory diseases	J40-J47	40.1	39.6
Other degenerative diseases of the nervous system	G30-G31	36.2	37.6
Cerebrovascular diseases	I60-I69	43.2	37.2
Other external causes of accidental injury	W00-X59	29.1	36.1
Organic, including symptomatic, mental disorders	F01-F09	37.3	29.4
Hypertensive diseases	I10-I15	23.1	24.1
Diabetes mellitus	E10-E14	25.7	21.5

Note: (a) ICD-10 = International Classification of Diseases 10th Revision; (1) Mortality rates are a three-year average covering 2017-2019; (2) Figures cover Boone County.
Source: Centers for Disease Control and Prevention, National Center for Health Statistics. Underlying Cause of Death 1999-2019 on CDC WONDER Online Database

Mortality Rates for Selected Causes of Death

ICD-10[a] Sub-Chapter	ICD-10[a] Code	Age-Adjusted Mortality Rate[1] per 100,000 population	
		County[2]	U.S.
Assault	X85-Y09	7.2	6.0
Diseases of the liver	K70-K76	11.1	14.4
Human immunodeficiency virus (HIV) disease	B20-B24	Suppressed	1.5
Influenza and pneumonia	J09-J18	13.1	13.8
Intentional self-harm	X60-X84	13.5	14.1
Malnutrition	E40-E46	Suppressed	2.3
Obesity and other hyperalimentation	E65-E68	Suppressed	2.1
Renal failure	N17-N19	12.5	12.6
Transport accidents	V01-V99	9.3	12.3
Viral hepatitis	B15-B19	Suppressed	1.2

Note: (a) ICD-10 = International Classification of Diseases 10th Revision; (1) Mortality rates are a three-year average covering 2017-2019; (2) Figures cover Boone County; Data are suppressed when the data meet the criteria for confidentiality constraints; Mortality rates are flagged as unreliable when the rate would be calculated with a numerator of 20 or less.
Source: Centers for Disease Control and Prevention, National Center for Health Statistics. Underlying Cause of Death 1999-2019 on CDC WONDER Online Database

Health Insurance Coverage

Area	With Health Insurance	With Private Health Insurance	With Public Health Insurance	Without Health Insurance	Population Under Age 19 Without Health Insurance
City	93.2	81.9	20.6	6.8	3.6
MSA[1]	92.8	79.5	24.1	7.2	4.6
U.S.	91.2	67.9	35.1	8.8	5.1

Note: Figures are percentages that cover the civilian noninstitutionalized population; (1) Figures cover the Columbia, MO Metropolitan Statistical Area
Source: U.S. Census Bureau, 2015-2019 American Community Survey 5-Year Estimates

Number of Medical Professionals

Area	MDs[3]	DOs[3,4]	Dentists	Podiatrists	Chiropractors	Optometrists
County[1] (number)	1,461	107	126	10	64	49
County[1] (rate[2])	815.9	59.8	69.8	5.5	35.5	27.2
U.S. (rate[2])	282.9	22.7	71.2	6.2	28.1	16.9

29019

Note: Data as of 2019 unless noted; (1) Data covers Boone County; (2) Rate per 100,000 population; (3) Data as of 2018 and includes all active, non-federal physicians; (4) Doctor of Osteopathic Medicine
Source: U.S. Department of Health and Human Services, Health Resources and Services Administration, Bureau of Health Professions, Area Resource File (ARF) 2019-2020

EDUCATION

Public School District Statistics

District Name	Schls	Pupils	Pupil/ Teacher Ratio	Minority Pupils[1] (%)	Free Lunch Eligible[2] (%)	IEP[3] (%)
Columbia 93	35	18,499	13.3	40.9	39.7	10.8

Note: Table includes school districts with 2,000 or more students; (1) Percentage of students that are not non-Hispanic white; (2) Percentage of students that are eligible for the free lunch program; (3) Percentage of students that have an Individualized Education Program.
Source: U.S. Department of Education, National Center for Education Statistics, Common Core of Data, Local Education Agency (School District) Universe Survey: School Year 2018-2019; U.S. Department of Education, National Center for Education Statistics, Common Core of Data, Public Elementary/Secondary School Universe Survey: School Year 2018-2019

Highest Level of Education

Area	Less than H.S.	H.S. Diploma	Some College, No Deg.	Associate Degree	Bachelor's Degree	Master's Degree	Prof. School Degree	Doctorate Degree
City	4.8	18.1	18.7	6.2	27.4	14.9	4.6	5.3
MSA[1]	6.4	23.7	19.8	7.4	24.5	11.3	3.2	3.7
U.S.	12.0	27.0	20.4	8.5	19.8	8.8	2.1	1.4

Note: Figures cover persons age 25 and over; (1) Figures cover the Columbia, MO Metropolitan Statistical Area
Source: U.S. Census Bureau, 2015-2019 American Community Survey 5-Year Estimates

Educational Attainment by Race

Area	High School Graduate or Higher (%)					Bachelor's Degree or Higher (%)				
	Total	White	Black	Asian	Hisp.[2]	Total	White	Black	Asian	Hisp.[2]
City	95.2	96.3	90.0	94.6	91.4	52.2	54.8	21.2	73.9	36.0
MSA[1]	93.6	94.3	89.3	93.9	86.8	42.7	43.8	18.8	71.2	34.4
U.S.	88.0	89.9	86.0	87.1	68.7	32.1	33.5	21.6	54.3	16.4

Note: Figures shown cover persons 25 years old and over; (1) Figures cover the Columbia, MO Metropolitan Statistical Area; (2) People of Hispanic origin can be of any race
Source: U.S. Census Bureau, 2015-2019 American Community Survey 5-Year Estimates

School Enrollment by Grade and Control

Area	Preschool (%)		Kindergarten (%)		Grades 1 - 4 (%)		Grades 5 - 8 (%)		Grades 9 - 12 (%)	
	Public	Private	Public	Private	Public	Private	Public	Private	Public	Private
City	36.1	63.9	76.7	23.3	87.5	12.5	88.1	11.9	88.8	11.2
MSA[1]	47.1	52.9	84.2	15.8	88.0	12.0	89.0	11.0	90.3	9.7
U.S.	59.1	40.9	87.6	12.4	89.5	10.5	89.4	10.6	90.1	9.9

Note: Figures shown cover persons 3 years old and over; (1) Figures cover the Columbia, MO Metropolitan Statistical Area
Source: U.S. Census Bureau, 2015-2019 American Community Survey 5-Year Estimates

Higher Education

Four-Year Colleges			Two-Year Colleges			Medical Schools[1]	Law Schools[2]	Voc/ Tech[3]
Public	Private Non-profit	Private For-profit	Public	Private Non-profit	Private For-profit			
1	2	0	0	0	0	1	1	2

Note: Figures cover institutions located within the city limits and include main campuses only; (1) includes schools accredited by the Liaison Committee on Medical Education and the American Osteopathic Association's Commission on Osteopathic College Accreditation; (2) includes ABA-accredited schools, schools with provisional ABA accreditation, and state accredited schools; (3) includes all schools with programs that are less than 2 years.
Source: National Center for Education Statistics, Integrated Postsecondary Education System (IPEDS), 2019-20; Wikipedia, List of Medical Schools in the United States, accessed April 2, 2021; Wikipedia, List of Law Schools in the United States, accessed April 2, 2021

According to *U.S. News & World Report,* the Columbia, MO metro area is home to one of the top 200 national universities in the U.S.: **University of Missouri** (#124 tie). The indicators used to capture academic quality fall into a number of categories: assessment by administrators at peer institutions; retention of students; faculty resources; student selectivity; financial resources; alumni giving; high school counselor ratings of colleges; and graduation rate. *U.S. News & World Report, "America's Best Colleges 2021"*

According to *U.S. News & World Report,* the Columbia, MO metro area is home to one of the top 100 law schools in the U.S.: **University of Missouri** (#60 tie). The rankings are based on a weighted average of 12 measures of quality: peer assessment score; assessment score by lawyers/judges; median LSAT scores; median undergrad GPA; acceptance rate; employment rates for graduates; placement success; bar passage rate; faculty resources; expenditures per student; student/faculty ratio; and library resources. *U.S. News & World Report, "America's Best Graduate Schools, Law, 2022"*

Columbia, Missouri

According to *U.S. News & World Report,* the Columbia, MO metro area is home to one of the top 75 medical schools for research in the U.S.: **University of Missouri** (#75 tie). The rankings are based on a weighted average of 11 measures of quality: quality assessment; peer assessment score; assessment score by residency directors; research activity; total research activity; average research activity per faculty member; student selectivity; median MCAT total score; median undergraduate GPA; acceptance rate; and faculty resources. *U.S. News & World Report, "America's Best Graduate Schools, Medical, 2022"*

EMPLOYERS

Major Employers

Company Name	Industry
BJC Health System	Hospital management
City of Columbia	Courts
Columbia College	Colleges & universities
Kraft Foods Global	Frankfurters, from purchased meat
MBS Textbook Exchange	Books, periodicals, & newspapers
MCI Worldcom Communications	Telephone communication, except radio
Regional Medical Pharmacy	Home health care services
Schneider Electric USA	Switchgear & switchboard apparatus
Shelter Insurance Companies	Fire, marine, & casualty insurance
State Farm Mutual Automobile Insurance	Insurance agents & brokers
University of Missouri Hospital	General medical & surgical hospitals
University of Missouri System	Colleges & universities
University Physicians Hospital	Gynecologist
Veterans Health Administration	Administration of veterans' affairs

Note: Companies shown are located within the Columbia, MO Metropolitan Statistical Area.
Source: Hoovers.com; Wikipedia

Best Companies to Work For

Veterans United Home Loans, headquartered in Columbia, is among "The 100 Best Companies to Work For." To pick the best companies, *Fortune* partnered with the Great Place to Work Institute. Two-thirds of a company's score is based on the results of the Institute's Trust Index survey, which is sent to a random sample of employees from each company. The questions related to attitudes about management's credibility, job satisfaction, and camaraderie. The other third of the scoring is based on the company's responses to the Institute's Culture Audit, which includes detailed questions about pay and benefit programs, and a series of open-ended questions about hiring practices, internal communication, training, recognition programs, and diversity efforts. Any company that is at least five years old with more than 1,000 U.S. employees is eligible. *Fortune, "The 100 Best Companies to Work For," 2020*

PUBLIC SAFETY

Crime Rate

Area	All Crimes	Violent Crimes				Property Crimes		
		Murder	Rape[3]	Robbery	Aggrav. Assault	Burglary	Larceny -Theft	Motor Vehicle Theft
City	2,914.8	8.8	55.2	59.2	197.6	399.1	1,944.5	250.4
Suburbs[1]	1,774.1	3.5	37.8	13.0	145.2	253.8	1,150.8	170.0
Metro[2]	2,454.0	6.7	48.2	40.5	176.4	340.4	1,623.9	217.9
U.S.	2,489.3	5.0	42.6	81.6	250.2	340.5	1,549.5	219.9

Note: Figures are crimes per 100,000 population; (1) All areas within the metro area that are located outside the city limits; (2) Figures cover the Columbia, MO Metropolitan Statistical Area; (3) All figures shown were reported using the revised Uniform Crime Reporting (UCR) definition of rape.
Source: FBI Uniform Crime Reports, 2019

Hate Crimes

Area	Number of Quarters Reported	Number of Incidents per Bias Motivation					
		Race/Ethnicity/ Ancestry	Religion	Sexual Orientation	Disability	Gender	Gender Identity
City	3	0	0	0	0	0	0
U.S.	4	3,963	1,521	1,195	157	69	198

Source: Federal Bureau of Investigation, Hate Crime Statistics 2019

Identity Theft Consumer Reports

Area	Reports	Reports per 100,000 Population	Rank[2]
MSA[1]	292	140	308
U.S.	1,387,615	423	-

Note: (1) Figures cover the Columbia, MO Metropolitan Statistical Area; (2) Rank ranges from 1 to 391 where 1 indicates greatest number of identity theft reports per 100,000 population
Source: Federal Trade Commission, Consumer Sentinel Network Data Book 2020

Fraud and Other Consumer Reports

Area	Reports	Reports per 100,000 Population	Rank[2]
MSA[1]	1,401	673	211
U.S.	3,385,133	1,031	-

Note: (1) Figures cover the Columbia, MO Metropolitan Statistical Area; (2) Rank ranges from 1 to 391 where 1 indicates greatest number of fraud and other consumer reports per 100,000 population
Source: Federal Trade Commission, Consumer Sentinel Network Data Book 2020

POLITICS

2020 Presidential Election Results

Area	Biden	Trump	Jorgensen	Hawkins	Other
Boone County	54.8	42.3	2.2	0.3	0.4
U.S.	51.3	46.8	1.2	0.3	0.5

Note: Results are percentages and may not add to 100% due to rounding
Source: Dave Leip's Atlas of U.S. Presidential Elections

SPORTS

Professional Sports Teams

Team Name	League	Year Established
No teams are located in the metro area		

Source: Wikipedia, Major Professional Sports Teams of the United States and Canada, April 6, 2021

CLIMATE

Average and Extreme Temperatures

Temperature	Jan	Feb	Mar	Apr	May	Jun	Jul	Aug	Sep	Oct	Nov	Dec	Yr.
Extreme High (°F)	74	76	85	90	90	103	111	110	101	93	83	76	111
Average High (°F)	36	42	54	66	74	83	89	87	79	67	53	41	64
Average Temp. (°F)	28	33	44	55	64	73	78	76	68	56	44	33	54
Average Low (°F)	19	23	34	44	53	62	67	65	57	45	34	24	44
Extreme Low (°F)	-19	-15	-5	19	29	40	48	42	32	22	0	-20	-20

Note: Figures cover the years 1969-1995
Source: National Climatic Data Center, International Station Meteorological Climate Summary, 9/96

Average Precipitation/Snowfall/Humidity

Precip./Humidity	Jan	Feb	Mar	Apr	May	Jun	Jul	Aug	Sep	Oct	Nov	Dec	Yr.
Avg. Precip. (in.)	1.6	2.0	3.2	4.3	5.1	3.9	3.9	3.8	3.7	3.1	3.5	2.6	40.6
Avg. Snowfall (in.)	7	7	4	1	0	0	0	0	0	Tr	2	5	25
Avg. Rel. Hum. 6am (%)	80	80	79	79	85	86	87	89	88	84	82	81	83
Avg. Rel. Hum. 3pm (%)	62	59	53	52	57	56	53	52	54	53	59	64	56

Note: Figures cover the years 1969-1995; Tr = Trace amounts (<0.05 in. of rain; <0.5 in. of snow)
Source: National Climatic Data Center, International Station Meteorological Climate Summary, 9/96

Weather Conditions

Temperature			Daytime Sky			Precipitation		
10°F & below	32°F & below	90°F & above	Clear	Partly cloudy	Cloudy	0.01 inch or more precip.	0.1 inch or more snow/ice	Thunder-storms
17	108	36	99	127	139	110	17	52

Note: Figures are average number of days per year and cover the years 1969-1995
Source: National Climatic Data Center, International Station Meteorological Climate Summary, 9/96

HAZARDOUS WASTE

Superfund Sites

The Columbia, MO metro area has no sites on the EPA's Superfund Final National Priorities List. There are a total of 1,375 Superfund sites with a status of proposed or final on the list in the U.S. *U.S. Environmental Protection Agency, National Priorities List, April 7, 2021*

AIR QUALITY

Air Quality Trends: Ozone

	1990	1995	2000	2005	2010	2015	2016	2017	2018	2019
MSA[1]	n/a	n/a	n/a	n/a	n/a	n/a	n/a	n/a	n/a	n/a
U.S.	0.088	0.089	0.082	0.080	0.073	0.068	0.069	0.068	0.069	0.065

Note: (1) Data covers the Columbia, MO Metropolitan Statistical Area; n/a not available. The values shown are the composite ozone concentration averages among trend sites based on the highest fourth daily maximum 8-hour concentration in parts per million. These trends are based on sites having an adequate record of monitoring data during the trend period. Data from exceptional events are included.
Source: U.S. Environmental Protection Agency, Air Quality Monitoring Information, "Air Quality Trends by City, 1990-2019"

Air Quality Index

Area	Percent of Days when Air Quality was...[2]					AQI Statistics[2]	
	Good	Moderate	Unhealthy for Sensitive Groups	Unhealthy	Very Unhealthy	Maximum	Median
MSA[1]	97.6	2.4	0.0	0.0	0.0	71	38

Note: (1) Data covers the Columbia, MO Metropolitan Statistical Area; (2) Based on 245 days with AQI data in 2019. Air Quality Index (AQI) is an index for reporting daily air quality. EPA calculates the AQI for five major air pollutants regulated by the Clean Air Act: ground-level ozone, particle pollution (aka particulate matter), carbon monoxide, sulfur dioxide, and nitrogen dioxide. The AQI runs from 0 to 500. The higher the AQI value, the greater the level of air pollution and the greater the health concern. There are six AQI categories: "Good" AQI is between 0 and 50. Air quality is considered satisfactory; "Moderate" AQI is between 51 and 100. Air quality is acceptable; "Unhealthy for Sensitive Groups" When AQI values are between 101 and 150, members of sensitive groups may experience health effects; "Unhealthy" When AQI values are between 151 and 200 everyone may begin to experience health effects; "Very Unhealthy" AQI values between 201 and 300 trigger a health alert; "Hazardous" AQI values over 300 trigger warnings of emergency conditions (not shown).
Source: U.S. Environmental Protection Agency, Air Quality Index Report, 2019

Air Quality Index Pollutants

Area	Percent of Days when AQI Pollutant was...[2]					
	Carbon Monoxide	Nitrogen Dioxide	Ozone	Sulfur Dioxide	Particulate Matter 2.5	Particulate Matter 10
MSA[1]	0.0	0.0	100.0	0.0	0.0	0.0

Note: (1) Data covers the Columbia, MO Metropolitan Statistical Area; (2) Based on 245 days with AQI data in 2019. The Air Quality Index (AQI) is an index for reporting daily air quality. EPA calculates the AQI for five major air pollutants regulated by the Clean Air Act: ground-level ozone, particle pollution (also known as particulate matter), carbon monoxide, sulfur dioxide, and nitrogen dioxide. The AQI runs from 0 to 500. The higher the AQI value, the greater the level of air pollution and the greater the health concern.
Source: U.S. Environmental Protection Agency, Air Quality Index Report, 2019

Maximum Air Pollutant Concentrations: Particulate Matter, Ozone, CO and Lead

	Particulate Matter 10 (ug/m^3)	Particulate Matter 2.5 Wtd AM (ug/m^3)	Particulate Matter 2.5 24-Hr (ug/m^3)	Ozone (ppm)	Carbon Monoxide (ppm)	Lead (ug/m^3)
MSA[1] Level	n/a	n/a	n/a	0.058	n/a	n/a
NAAQS[2]	150	15	35	0.075	9	0.15
Met NAAQS[2]	n/a	n/a	n/a	Yes	n/a	n/a

Note: (1) Data covers the Columbia, MO Metropolitan Statistical Area; Data from exceptional events are included; (2) National Ambient Air Quality Standards; ppm = parts per million; ug/m^3 = micrograms per cubic meter; n/a not available.
Concentrations: Particulate Matter 10 (coarse particulate)—highest second maximum 24-hour concentration; Particulate Matter 2.5 Wtd AM (fine particulate)—highest weighted annual mean concentration; Particulate Matter 2.5 24-Hour (fine particulate)—highest 98th percentile 24-hour concentration; Ozone—highest fourth daily maximum 8-hour concentration; Carbon Monoxide—highest second maximum non-overlapping 8-hour concentration; Lead—maximum running 3-month average
Source: U.S. Environmental Protection Agency, Air Quality Monitoring Information, "Air Quality Statistics by City, 2019"

Maximum Air Pollutant Concentrations: Nitrogen Dioxide and Sulfur Dioxide

	Nitrogen Dioxide AM (ppb)	Nitrogen Dioxide 1-Hr (ppb)	Sulfur Dioxide AM (ppb)	Sulfur Dioxide 1-Hr (ppb)	Sulfur Dioxide 24-Hr (ppb)
MSA[1] Level	n/a	n/a	n/a	n/a	n/a
NAAQS[2]	53	100	30	75	140
Met NAAQS[2]	n/a	n/a	n/a	n/a	n/a

Note: (1) Data covers the Columbia, MO Metropolitan Statistical Area; Data from exceptional events are included; (2) National Ambient Air Quality Standards; ppm = parts per million; ug/m^3 = micrograms per cubic meter; n/a not available.
Concentrations: Nitrogen Dioxide AM—highest arithmetic mean concentration; Nitrogen Dioxide 1-Hr—highest 98th percentile 1-hour daily maximum concentration; Sulfur Dioxide AM—highest annual mean concentration; Sulfur Dioxide 1-Hr—highest 99th percentile 1-hour daily maximum concentration; Sulfur Dioxide 24-Hr—highest second maximum 24-hour concentration
Source: U.S. Environmental Protection Agency, Air Quality Monitoring Information, "Air Quality Statistics by City, 2019"

Davenport, Iowa

Background

The city of Davenport was first incorporated in 1836 on the site of the bloody "Black Hawk War," between the Native American Sac tribe and eastern settlers, intent on westward expansion. In 1828, John Quincy Adams had declared that all land east of the Mississippi would be sold to settlers. When Chief Black Hawk and his warriors refused to leave their land, the Black Hawk War ensued, resulting in a treaty now known as the Black Hawk Purchase. Credit Island, which had originally been a fur trading post, hosted the treaty signing between the Sac chief and Colonel George Davenport, from whom Davenport derives its name.

In 1856, a new bridge was constructed between Davenport and Rock Island, Illinois—the first railroad bridge to span the Mississippi. Only months later, a riverboat, the Effie Afton, struck and damaged the bridge. The ensuing court case, *Hurd v. Rock Island Railroad Company*, would remain the most notable court case in the law career of Abraham Lincoln.

The decade preceding the Civil War saw a major influx of German immigrants to Davenport, increasing the population fivefold; it is estimated that about 50% of today's Davenport citizenry are of German descent. Many of these immigrants were fleeing political persecution, and were instrumental in the creation of the Republican Party, which, within a decade, would provide the country with one of its most influential presidents. The culture and work ethic of these immigrants remains a key factor in the Davenport ethos of hard work and industry. At the turn of the 19th century, Davenport earned the rather amusing moniker of "Washing Machine Capital of the World."

In 1861, Rock Island had opened a munitions arsenal to help the Union war efforts. It is now home to the largest, government-owned weapons manufacturing facility in the United States, and is a designated national historic landmark. Today, Davenport supports a diverse base of manufacturing industries that include everything from farm and military machinery to publishing products and food processing. Its central, mid-continent location makes Davenport an important, inland U.S. Customs Port of Entry for freight distribution. It is also designated a Foreign Trade Zone.

> String musicians from the local Quad City Symphony Orchestra performed to lineups at the local vaccination clinic, masked and socially distanced.

The largest employers in the area comprise a veritable who's who of American manufacturing, including John Deere & Co., Aluminum Co. of America (ALCOA), Oscar Meyer Food Corp. and Eagle Food Center. Davenport is also home to the regional headquarters of the United Parcel Service, and serves as the headquarters of the Von Maur department stores.

Davenport is home to four institutes of higher learning, including the Catholic liberal arts school St. Ambrose University, the city's oldest college. The Palmer College of Chiropractic, the first college of its kind, was established by the inventor of chiropractic practice—Daniel David Palmer, a Davenport resident. Within commuting distance of Davenport are Augustana College (Rock Island), the University of Iowa (Iowa City), and Knox College (Galesburg).

Iowa's first municipal art museum, the Figge Museum, is home to the *Grant Wood Archive.* The collection features Wood's wire-rimmed glasses, his easel and painting tools, and the iconic cameo broach in both the portrait of his mother, *Woman with Plants*, 1929, and his most famous painting, *American Gothic*, 1930.

Given Davenport's central location in the heart of America's Midwest, the climate is relatively temperate. Temperatures can fluctuate considerably; summers are hot and winters severe, with an average snowfall just over 30 inches.

Rankings

Business/Finance Rankings

- The Davenport metro area appeared on the Milken Institute "2021 Best Performing Cities" list. Rank: #179 out of 200 large metro areas (population over 250,000). Criteria: job growth; wage and salary growth; high-tech output growth; housing affordability; household broadband access. *Milken Institute, "Best-Performing Cities 2021," February 16, 2021*

- *Forbes* ranked the 200 most populous metro areas to determine the nation's "Best Places for Business and Careers." The Davenport metro area was ranked #175. Criteria: costs (business and living); job growth (past and projected); income growth; quality of life; educational attainment (college and high school); projected economic growth; cultural and leisure opportunities; workplace tolerance laws; net migration patterns. *Forbes, "The Best Places for Business and Careers 2019: Seattle Still On Top," October 30, 2019*

Children/Family Rankings

- Davenport was selected as one of the most playful cities in the U.S. by KaBOOM! The organization's Playful City USA initiative honors cities and towns across the nation that have made their communities more playable. Criteria: pledging to integrate play as a solution to challenges in their communities; making it easy for children to get active and balanced play; creating more family-friendly and innovative communities as a result. *KaBOOM! National Campaign for Play, "2017 Playful City USA Communities"*

Education Rankings

- Personal finance website *WalletHub* analyzed the 150 largest U.S. metropolitan statistical areas to determine where the most educated Americans are putting their degrees to work. Criteria: education levels; percentage of workers with degrees; education quality and attainment gap; public school quality rankings; quality and enrollment of each metro area's universities. Davenport was ranked #114 (#1 = most educated city). *www.WalletHub.com, "Most and Least Educated Cities in America," July 20, 2020*

Environmental Rankings

- Davenport was highlighted as one of the top 98 cleanest metro areas for short-term particle pollution (24-hour PM 2.5) in the U.S. during 2016 through 2018. Monitors in these cities reported no days with unhealthful PM 2.5 levels. *American Lung Association, "State of the Air 2020," April 21, 2020*

Health/Fitness Rankings

- The Davenport metro area was identified as one of the worst cities for bed bugs in America by pest control company Orkin. The area ranked #38 out of 50 based on the number of bed bug treatments Orkin performed from December 2019 to November 2020. *Orkin, "New Year, New Top City on Orkin's 2021 Bed Bug Cities List: Chicago," February 1, 2021*

Real Estate Rankings

- The Davenport metro area was identified as one of the 20 most affordable housing markets in the U.S. in 2020. The area ranked #12 out of 183 markets. Criteria: qualification for a mortgage loan with a 10 percent down payment on a typical home. *National Association of Realtors®, Qualifying Income Based on Sales Price of Existing Single-Family Homes for Metropolitan Areas, 2020*

- Davenport was ranked #7 out of 268 metro areas in terms of housing affordability in 2020 by the National Association of Home Builders (#1 = most affordable). Criteria: the share of homes sold in that area affordable to a family earning the local median income, based on standard mortgage underwriting criteria. *National Association of Home Builders®, NAHB-Wells Fargo Housing Opportunity Index, 4th Quarter 2020*

Safety Rankings

- The National Insurance Crime Bureau ranked 384 metro areas in the U.S. in terms of per capita rates of vehicle theft. The Davenport metro area ranked #119 (#1 = highest rate). Criteria: number of vehicle theft offenses per 100,000 inhabitants in 2019. *National Insurance Crime Bureau, "Hot Spots 2019," July 21, 2020*

Seniors/Retirement Rankings

- From its Best Cities for Successful Aging indexes, the Milken Institute generated rankings for metropolitan areas, weighing data in nine categories—health care, wellness, living arrangements, transportation and convenience, financial characteristics, education, employment, community engagement, and overall livability. The Davenport metro area was ranked #153 overall in the small metro area category. *Milken Institute, "Best Cities for Successful Aging, 2017" March 14, 2017*

Business Environment

DEMOGRAPHICS

Population Growth

Area	1990 Census	2000 Census	2010 Census	2019* Estimate	Population Growth (%)	
					1990-2019	2010-2019
City	95,705	98,359	99,685	102,169	6.8	2.5
MSA[1]	368,151	376,019	379,690	381,175	3.5	0.4
U.S.	248,709,873	281,421,906	308,745,538	324,697,795	30.6	5.2

Note: (1) Figures cover the Davenport-Moline-Rock Island, IA-IL Metropolitan Statistical Area; (*) 2015-2019 5-year estimated population
Source: U.S. Census Bureau, 1990 Census, Census 2000, Census 2010, 2015-2019 American Community Survey 5-Year Estimates

Household Size

Area	Persons in Household (%)							Average Household Size
	One	Two	Three	Four	Five	Six	Seven or More	
City	35.4	33.6	13.2	9.7	5.2	1.9	1.0	2.50
MSA[1]	31.2	35.7	13.2	11.9	5.3	1.8	0.8	2.40
U.S.	27.9	33.9	15.6	12.9	6.0	2.3	1.4	2.60

Note: (1) Figures cover the Davenport-Moline-Rock Island, IA-IL Metropolitan Statistical Area
Source: U.S. Census Bureau, 2015-2019 American Community Survey 5-Year Estimates

Race

Area	White Alone[2] (%)	Black Alone[2] (%)	Asian Alone[2] (%)	AIAN[3] Alone[2] (%)	NHOPI[4] Alone[2] (%)	Other Race Alone[2] (%)	Two or More Races (%)
City	81.4	11.3	2.3	0.5	0.0	1.0	3.5
MSA[1]	85.1	7.6	2.3	0.3	0.0	1.7	3.0
U.S.	72.5	12.7	5.5	0.8	0.2	4.9	3.3

Note: (1) Figures cover the Davenport-Moline-Rock Island, IA-IL Metropolitan Statistical Area; (2) Alone is defined as not being in combination with one or more other races; (3) American Indian and Alaska Native; (4) Native Hawaiian and Other Pacific Islander
Source: U.S. Census Bureau, 2015-2019 American Community Survey 5-Year Estimates

Hispanic or Latino Origin

Area	Total (%)	Mexican (%)	Puerto Rican (%)	Cuban (%)	Other (%)
City	8.7	7.8	0.3	0.0	0.5
MSA[1]	8.7	7.7	0.4	0.1	0.6
U.S.	18.0	11.2	1.7	0.7	4.3

Note: Persons of Hispanic or Latino origin can be of any race; (1) Figures cover the Davenport-Moline-Rock Island, IA-IL Metropolitan Statistical Area
Source: U.S. Census Bureau, 2015-2019 American Community Survey 5-Year Estimates

Ancestry

Area	German	Irish	English	American	Italian	Polish	French[2]	Scottish	Dutch
City	28.8	15.3	6.3	4.0	2.3	2.1	1.5	1.5	1.8
MSA[1]	27.7	14.7	7.6	4.2	2.4	2.1	1.8	1.5	2.0
U.S.	13.3	9.7	7.2	6.2	5.1	2.8	2.3	1.7	1.2

Note: Figures are the percentage of the total population reporting a particular ancestry. The nine most commonly reported ancestries in the U.S. are shown. Figures include multiple ancestries (e.g. if a person reported being Irish and Italian, they were included in both columns); (1) Figures cover the Davenport-Moline-Rock Island, IA-IL Metropolitan Statistical Area; (2) Excludes Basque
Source: U.S. Census Bureau, 2015-2019 American Community Survey 5-Year Estimates

Foreign-born Population

Area	Percent of Population Born in								
	Any Foreign Country	Asia	Mexico	Europe	Caribbean	Central America[2]	South America	Africa	Canada
City	4.5	1.6	1.9	0.4	0.3	0.0	0.0	0.2	0.1
MSA[1]	5.2	1.7	1.9	0.5	0.1	0.1	0.1	0.8	0.1
U.S.	13.6	4.2	3.5	1.5	1.3	1.1	1.0	0.7	0.2

Note: (1) Figures cover the Davenport-Moline-Rock Island, IA-IL Metropolitan Statistical Area; (2) Excludes Mexico.
Source: U.S. Census Bureau, 2015-2019 American Community Survey 5-Year Estimates

Marital Status

Area	Never Married	Now Married[2]	Separated	Widowed	Divorced
City	36.7	42.6	1.5	6.3	12.9
MSA[1]	29.9	50.2	1.3	6.6	12.0
U.S.	33.4	48.1	1.9	5.8	10.9

Note: Figures are percentages and cover the population 15 years of age and older; (1) Figures cover the Davenport-Moline-Rock Island, IA-IL Metropolitan Statistical Area; (2) Excludes separated
Source: U.S. Census Bureau, 2015-2019 American Community Survey 5-Year Estimates

Disability by Age

Area	All Ages	Under 18 Years Old	18 to 64 Years Old	65 Years and Over
City	12.4	4.8	10.3	33.5
MSA[1]	12.3	4.4	9.6	31.8
U.S.	12.6	4.2	10.3	34.5

Note: Figures show percent of the civilian noninstitutionalized population that reported having a disability. Disability status is determined from six types of difficulty: vision, hearing, cognitive, ambulatory, self-care, and independent living. For children under 5 years old, hearing and vision difficulty are used to determine disability status. For children between the ages of 5 and 14, disability status is determined from hearing, vision, cognitive, ambulatory, and self-care difficulties. For people aged 15 years and older, they are considered to have a disability if they have difficulty with any one of the six difficulty types; Note: (1) Figures cover the Davenport-Moline-Rock Island, IA-IL Metropolitan Statistical Area
Source: U.S. Census Bureau, 2015-2019 American Community Survey 5-Year Estimates

Age

Area	Percent of Population									Median Age
	Under Age 5	Age 5–19	Age 20–34	Age 35–44	Age 45–54	Age 55–64	Age 65–74	Age 75–84	Age 85+	
City	6.4	19.2	21.8	12.3	12.3	12.7	8.6	4.1	2.5	36.7
MSA[1]	6.2	19.3	18.3	12.3	12.5	13.8	10.0	5.3	2.4	39.7
U.S.	6.1	19.1	20.7	12.6	13.0	12.9	9.1	4.6	1.9	38.1

Note: (1) Figures cover the Davenport-Moline-Rock Island, IA-IL Metropolitan Statistical Area
Source: U.S. Census Bureau, 2015-2019 American Community Survey 5-Year Estimates

Gender

Area	Males	Females	Males per 100 Females
City	50,216	51,953	96.7
MSA[1]	187,831	193,344	97.1
U.S.	159,886,919	164,810,876	97.0

Note: (1) Figures cover the Davenport-Moline-Rock Island, IA-IL Metropolitan Statistical Area
Source: U.S. Census Bureau, 2015-2019 American Community Survey 5-Year Estimates

Religious Groups by Family

Area	Catholic	Baptist	Non-Den.	Methodist[2]	Lutheran	LDS[3]	Pentecostal	Presbyterian[4]	Muslim[5]	Judaism
MSA[1]	14.9	5.0	2.7	5.3	8.7	0.8	1.4	3.0	0.9	0.1
U.S.	19.1	9.3	4.0	4.0	2.3	2.0	1.9	1.6	0.8	0.7

Note: Figures are the number of adherents as a percentage of the total population; (1) Figures cover the Davenport-Moline-Rock Island, IA-IL Metropolitan Statistical Area; (2) Methodist/Pietist; (3) Latter Day Saints; (4) Reformed; (5) Figures are estimates
Source: Association of Statisticians of American Religious Bodies, 2010 U.S. Religion Census: Religious Congregations & Membership Study

Religious Groups by Tradition

Area	Catholic	Evangelical Protestant	Mainline Protestant	Other Tradition	Black Protestant	Orthodox
MSA[1]	14.9	11.4	15.1	2.4	1.6	0.1
U.S.	19.1	16.2	7.3	4.3	1.6	0.3

Note: Figures are the number of adherents as a percentage of the total population; (1) Figures cover the Davenport-Moline-Rock Island, IA-IL Metropolitan Statistical Area
Source: Association of Statisticians of American Religious Bodies, 2010 U.S. Religion Census: Religious Congregations & Membership Study

ECONOMY

Gross Metropolitan Product

Area	2017	2018	2019	2020	Rank[2]
MSA[1]	19.8	20.7	21.6	22.3	124

Note: Figures are in billions of dollars; (1) Figures cover the Davenport-Moline-Rock Island, IA-IL Metropolitan Statistical Area; (2) Rank is based on 2018 data and ranges from 1 to 381
Source: U.S. Conference of Mayors, U.S. Metro Economies: GMP & Employment 2018-2020, September 2019

Economic Growth

Area	2015-17 (%)	2018 (%)	2019 (%)	2020 (%)	Rank[2]
MSA[1]	-0.2	2.4	2.4	1.2	311
U.S.	1.9	2.9	2.3	2.1	—

Note: Figures are real gross metropolitan product (GMP) growth rates and represent average annual percent change; (1) Figures cover the Davenport-Moline-Rock Island, IA-IL Metropolitan Statistical Area; (2) Rank is based on 2017 2-year average annual percent change and ranges from 1 to 381
Source: U.S. Conference of Mayors, U.S. Metro Economies: GMP & Employment 2018-2020, September 2019

Metropolitan Area Exports

Area	2014	2015	2016	2017	2018	2019	Rank[2]
MSA[1]	6,563.2	5,711.8	4,497.6	5,442.7	6,761.9	6,066.3	51

Note: Figures are in millions of dollars; (1) Figures cover the Davenport-Moline-Rock Island, IA-IL Metropolitan Statistical Area; (2) Rank is based on 2019 data and ranges from 1 to 386
Source: U.S. Department of Commerce, International Trade Administration, Office of Trade and Economic Analysis, Industry and Analysis, Exports by Metropolitan Area, data extracted March 24, 2021

Building Permits

Area	Single-Family			Multi-Family			Total		
	2018	2019	Pct. Chg.	2018	2019	Pct. Chg.	2018	2019	Pct. Chg.
City	68	122	79.4	0	196	–	68	318	367.6
MSA[1]	490	533	8.8	69	268	288.4	559	801	43.3
U.S.	855,300	862,100	0.7	473,500	523,900	10.6	1,328,800	1,386,000	4.3

Note: (1) Figures cover the Davenport-Moline-Rock Island, IA-IL Metropolitan Statistical Area; Figures represent new, privately-owned housing units authorized (unadjusted data); All permit data are based on estimates with imputation
Source: U.S. Census Bureau, Manufacturing, Mining, and Construction Statistics, Building Permits, 2018, 2019

Bankruptcy Filings

Area	Business Filings			Nonbusiness Filings		
	2019	2020	% Chg.	2019	2020	% Chg.
Scott County	10	7	-30.0	329	246	-25.2
U.S.	22,780	21,655	-4.9	752,160	522,808	-30.5

Note: Business filings include Chapter 7, Chapter 9, Chapter 11, Chapter 12, Chapter 13, Chapter 15, and Section 304; Nonbusiness filings include Chapter 7, Chapter 11, and Chapter 13
Source: Administrative Office of the U.S. Courts, Business and Nonbusiness Bankruptcy, County Cases Commenced by Chapter of the Bankruptcy Code, During the 12-Month Period Ending December 31, 2019 and Business and Nonbusiness Bankruptcy, County Cases Commenced by Chapter of the Bankruptcy Code, During the 12-Month Period Ending December 31, 2020

Housing Vacancy Rates

Area	Gross Vacancy Rate[2] (%)			Year-Round Vacancy Rate[3] (%)			Rental Vacancy Rate[4] (%)			Homeowner Vacancy Rate[5] (%)		
	2018	2019	2020	2018	2019	2020	2018	2019	2020	2018	2019	2020
MSA[1]	n/a	n/a	n/a	n/a	n/a	n/a	n/a	n/a	n/a	n/a	n/a	n/a
U.S.	12.3	12.0	10.6	9.7	9.5	8.2	6.9	6.7	6.3	1.5	1.4	1.0

Note: (1) Figures cover the Davenport-Moline-Rock Island, IA-IL Metropolitan Statistical Area; (2) The percentage of the total housing inventory that is vacant; (3) The percentage of the housing inventory (excluding seasonal units) that is year-round vacant; (4) The percentage of rental inventory that is vacant for rent; (5) The percentage of homeowner inventory that is vacant for sale; n/a not available
Source: U.S. Census Bureau, Housing Vacancies and Homeownership Annual Statistics: 2018, 2019, 2020

INCOME

Income

Area	Per Capita ($)	Median Household ($)	Average Household ($)
City	28,645	51,029	68,559
MSA[1]	31,571	58,531	76,075
U.S.	34,103	62,843	88,607

Note: (1) Figures cover the Davenport-Moline-Rock Island, IA-IL Metropolitan Statistical Area
Source: U.S. Census Bureau, 2015-2019 American Community Survey 5-Year Estimates

Household Income Distribution

Area	Percent of Households Earning							
	Under $15,000	$15,000 -$24,999	$25,000 -$34,999	$35,000 -$49,999	$50,000 -$74,999	$75,000 -$99,999	$100,000 -$149,999	$150,000 and up
City	12.5	11.4	10.6	14.6	19.1	12.3	12.1	7.4
MSA[1]	10.2	9.4	9.5	13.4	19.0	13.8	15.4	9.3
U.S.	10.3	8.9	8.9	12.3	17.2	12.7	15.1	14.5

Note: (1) Figures cover the Davenport-Moline-Rock Island, IA-IL Metropolitan Statistical Area
Source: U.S. Census Bureau, 2015-2019 American Community Survey 5-Year Estimates

Davenport, Iowa   91

Poverty Rate

Area	All Ages	Under 18 Years Old	18 to 64 Years Old	65 Years and Over
City	16.6	24.3	15.5	9.0
MSA[1]	12.5	18.8	11.5	7.5
U.S.	13.4	18.5	12.6	9.3

Note: Figures are percentage of people whose income during the past 12 months was below the poverty level;
(1) Figures cover the Davenport-Moline-Rock Island, IA-IL Metropolitan Statistical Area
Source: U.S. Census Bureau, 2015-2019 American Community Survey 5-Year Estimates

CITY FINANCES

City Government Finances

Component	2017 ($000)	2017 ($ per capita)
Total Revenues	188,622	1,839
Total Expenditures	173,421	1,691
Debt Outstanding	317,307	3,093
Cash and Securities[1]	183,087	1,785

Note: (1) Cash and security holdings of a government at the close of its fiscal year,
including those of its dependent agencies, utilities, and liquor stores.
Source: U.S. Census Bureau, State & Local Government Finances 2017

City Government Revenue by Source

Source	2017 ($000)	2017 ($ per capita)	2017 (%)
General Revenue			
From Federal Government	18,345	179	9.7
From State Government	22,413	218	11.9
From Local Governments	657	6	0.3
Taxes			
Property	73,111	713	38.8
Sales and Gross Receipts	22,798	222	12.1
Personal Income	0	0	0.0
Corporate Income	0	0	0.0
Motor Vehicle License	0	0	0.0
Other Taxes	2,461	24	1.3
Current Charges	40,522	395	21.5
Liquor Store	0	0	0.0
Utility	410	4	0.2
Employee Retirement	0	0	0.0

Source: U.S. Census Bureau, State & Local Government Finances 2017

City Government Expenditures by Function

Function	2017 ($000)	2017 ($ per capita)	2017 (%)
General Direct Expenditures			
Air Transportation	272	2	0.2
Corrections	0	0	0.0
Education	0	0	0.0
Employment Security Administration	0	0	0.0
Financial Administration	1,895	18	1.1
Fire Protection	18,360	179	10.6
General Public Buildings	944	9	0.5
Governmental Administration, Other	2,445	23	1.4
Health	0	0	0.0
Highways	17,356	169	10.0
Hospitals	0	0	0.0
Housing and Community Development	7,333	71	4.2
Interest on General Debt	9,038	88	5.2
Judicial and Legal	0	0	0.0
Libraries	4,779	46	2.8
Parking	977	9	0.6
Parks and Recreation	7,368	71	4.2
Police Protection	25,100	244	14.5
Public Welfare	0	0	0.0
Sewerage	15,588	152	9.0
Solid Waste Management	5,059	49	2.9
Veterans' Services	0	0	0.0
Liquor Store	0	0	0.0
Utility	6,319	61	3.6
Employee Retirement	0	0	0.0

Source: U.S. Census Bureau, State & Local Government Finances 2017

EMPLOYMENT

Labor Force and Employment

Area	Civilian Labor Force			Workers Employed		
	Dec. 2019	Dec. 2020	% Chg.	Dec. 2019	Dec. 2020	% Chg.
City	51,918	47,841	-7.9	49,753	45,379	-8.8
MSA[1]	194,473	181,630	-6.6	185,909	172,320	-7.3
U.S.	164,007,000	160,017,000	-2.4	158,504,000	149,613,000	-5.6

Note: Data is not seasonally adjusted and covers workers 16 years of age and older; (1) Figures cover the Davenport-Moline-Rock Island, IA-IL Metropolitan Statistical Area
Source: Bureau of Labor Statistics, Local Area Unemployment Statistics

Unemployment Rate

Area	2020											
	Jan.	Feb.	Mar.	Apr.	May	Jun.	Jul.	Aug.	Sep.	Oct.	Nov.	Dec.
City	4.9	4.2	4.7	15.4	15.0	12.1	10.3	9.6	7.0	5.2	5.3	5.1
MSA[1]	4.7	4.0	4.0	15.3	14.4	11.5	9.4	8.5	7.1	5.0	5.0	5.1
U.S.	4.0	3.8	4.5	14.4	13.0	11.2	10.5	8.5	7.7	6.6	6.4	6.5

Note: Data is not seasonally adjusted and covers workers 16 years of age and older; (1) Figures cover the Davenport-Moline-Rock Island, IA-IL Metropolitan Statistical Area
Source: Bureau of Labor Statistics, Local Area Unemployment Statistics

Average Wages

Occupation	$/Hr.	Occupation	$/Hr.
Accountants and Auditors	32.30	Maintenance and Repair Workers	20.80
Automotive Mechanics	20.90	Marketing Managers	61.20
Bookkeepers	19.50	Network and Computer Systems Admin.	37.00
Carpenters	25.20	Nurses, Licensed Practical	21.80
Cashiers	11.10	Nurses, Registered	28.80
Computer Programmers	42.60	Nursing Assistants	14.30
Computer Systems Analysts	44.10	Office Clerks, General	16.00
Computer User Support Specialists	23.80	Physical Therapists	38.70
Construction Laborers	20.60	Physicians	125.50
Cooks, Restaurant	12.00	Plumbers, Pipefitters and Steamfitters	28.20
Customer Service Representatives	17.00	Police and Sheriff's Patrol Officers	29.70
Dentists	77.60	Postal Service Mail Carriers	25.10
Electricians	28.50	Real Estate Sales Agents	35.10
Engineers, Electrical	47.10	Retail Salespersons	16.00
Fast Food and Counter Workers	10.60	Sales Representatives, Technical/Scientific	41.20
Financial Managers	53.80	Secretaries, Exc. Legal/Medical/Executive	17.40
First-Line Supervisors of Office Workers	26.30	Security Guards	16.60
General and Operations Managers	48.10	Surgeons	n/a
Hairdressers/Cosmetologists	13.60	Teacher Assistants, Exc. Postsecondary*	13.60
Home Health and Personal Care Aides	13.30	Teachers, Secondary School, Exc. Sp. Ed.*	27.90
Janitors and Cleaners	14.90	Telemarketers	14.30
Landscaping/Groundskeeping Workers	16.10	Truck Drivers, Heavy/Tractor-Trailer	23.90
Lawyers	70.60	Truck Drivers, Light/Delivery Services	17.00
Maids and Housekeeping Cleaners	11.70	Waiters and Waitresses	11.60

Note: Wage data covers the Davenport-Moline-Rock Island, IA-IL Metropolitan Statistical Area; (*) Hourly wages were calculated from annual wage data based on a 40 hour work week; n/a not available.
Source: Bureau of Labor Statistics, Metro Area Occupational Employment & Wage Estimates, May 2020

Employment by Industry

Sector	MSA[1]		U.S.
	Number of Employees	Percent of Total	Percent of Total
Construction, Mining, and Logging	n/a	n/a	5.5
Education and Health Services	n/a	n/a	16.3
Financial Activities	n/a	n/a	6.1
Government	n/a	n/a	15.2
Information	n/a	n/a	1.9
Leisure and Hospitality	n/a	n/a	9.0
Manufacturing	n/a	n/a	8.5
Other Services	n/a	n/a	3.8
Professional and Business Services	n/a	n/a	14.4
Retail Trade	n/a	n/a	10.9
Transportation, Warehousing, and Utilities	n/a	n/a	4.6
Wholesale Trade	n/a	n/a	3.9

Note: Figures are non-farm employment as of December 2020. Figures are not seasonally adjusted and include workers 16 years of age and older; (1) Figures cover the Davenport-Moline-Rock Island, IA-IL Metropolitan Statistical Area; n/a not available
Source: Bureau of Labor Statistics, Current Employment Statistics, Employment, Hours, and Earnings

Employment by Occupation

Occupation Classification	City (%)	MSA[1] (%)	U.S. (%)
Management, Business, Science, and Arts	31.9	33.8	38.5
Natural Resources, Construction, and Maintenance	7.5	8.7	8.9
Production, Transportation, and Material Moving	19.1	18.7	13.2
Sales and Office	22.0	21.1	21.6
Service	19.6	17.7	17.8

Note: Figures cover employed civilians 16 years of age and older; (1) Figures cover the Davenport-Moline-Rock Island, IA-IL Metropolitan Statistical Area
Source: U.S. Census Bureau, 2015-2019 American Community Survey 5-Year Estimates

Occupations with Greatest Projected Employment Growth: 2020 – 2022

Occupation[1]	2020 Employment	2022 Projected Employment	Numeric Employment Change	Percent Employment Change
Fast Food and Counter Workers	31,160	41,700	10,540	33.8
Waiters and Waitresses	16,720	24,050	7,330	43.8
Retail Salespersons	36,650	42,840	6,190	16.9
Cooks, Restaurant	9,170	13,630	4,460	48.6
Maids and Housekeeping Cleaners	9,970	13,650	3,680	36.9
Bartenders	7,430	10,480	3,050	41.0
First-Line Supervisors of Food Preparation and Serving Workers	8,150	11,090	2,940	36.1
Janitors and Cleaners, Except Maids and Housekeeping Cleaners	25,060	27,650	2,590	10.3
Laborers and Freight, Stock, and Material Movers, Hand	29,980	32,090	2,110	7.0
Childcare Workers	12,040	14,050	2,010	16.7

Note: Projections cover Iowa; (1) Sorted by numeric employment change
Source: www.projectionscentral.com, State Occupational Projections, 2020–2022 Short-Term Projections

Fastest-Growing Occupations: 2020 – 2022

Occupation[1]	2020 Employment	2022 Projected Employment	Numeric Employment Change	Percent Employment Change
Personal Care Aides	90	280	190	211.1
Actors	100	240	140	140.0
Motion Picture Projectionists	60	130	70	116.7
Ushers, Lobby Attendants, and Ticket Takers	670	1,420	750	111.9
Public Address System and Other Announcers	80	150	70	87.5
Gaming Cage Workers	180	330	150	83.3
Hotel, Motel, and Resort Desk Clerks	2,270	4,090	1,820	80.2
Gaming Change Persons and Booth Cashiers	250	450	200	80.0
Gaming Dealers	990	1,770	780	78.8
Gaming Surveillance Officers and Gaming Investigators	130	230	100	76.9

Note: Projections cover Iowa; (1) Sorted by percent employment change and excludes occupations with numeric employment change less than 50
Source: www.projectionscentral.com, State Occupational Projections, 2020–2022 Short-Term Projections

TAXES

State Corporate Income Tax Rates

State	Tax Rate (%)	Income Brackets ($)	Num. of Brackets	Financial Institution Tax Rate (%)[a]	Federal Income Tax Ded.
Iowa	5.5 - 9.8	100,000 - 250,001	3	5.0	Yes (j)

Note: Tax rates as of January 1, 2021; (a) Rates listed are the corporate income tax rate applied to financial institutions or excise taxes based on income. Some states have other taxes based upon the value of deposits or shares; (j) 50% of the federal income tax is deductible.
Source: Federation of Tax Administrators, State Corporate Income Tax Rates, January 1, 2021

State Individual Income Tax Rates

State	Tax Rate (%)	Income Brackets ($)	Personal Exemptions ($)			Standard Ded. ($)	
			Single	Married	Depend.	Single	Married
Iowa (a)	0.33 - 8.53	1,676 - 74,970	40 (c)	80 (c)	40 (c)	2,130	5,250 (a)

Note: Tax rates as of January 1, 2021; Local- and county-level taxes are not included; Federal income tax is deductible on state income tax returns; (a) 19 states have statutory provision for automatically adjusting to the rate of inflation the dollar values of the income tax brackets, standard deductions, and/or personal exemptions. Michigan indexes the personal exemption only. Oregon does not index the income brackets for $125,000 and over; (c) The personal exemption takes the form of a tax credit instead of a deduction
Source: Federation of Tax Administrators, State Individual Income Tax Rates, January 1, 2021

Various State Sales and Excise Tax Rates

State	State Sales Tax (%)	Gasoline[1] (¢/gal.)	Cigarette[2] ($/pack)	Spirits[3] ($/gal.)	Wine[4] ($/gal.)	Beer[5] ($/gal.)	Recreational Marijuana (%)
Iowa	6	30	1.36	13.03	1.75	0.19	Not legal

Note: All tax rates as of January 1, 2021; (1) The American Petroleum Institute has developed a methodology for determining the average tax rate on a gallon of fuel. Rates may include any of the following: excise taxes, environmental fees, storage tank fees, other fees or taxes, general sales tax, and local taxes; (2) The federal excise tax of $1.0066 per pack and local taxes are not included; (3) Rates are those applicable to off-premise sales of 40% alcohol by volume (a.b.v.) distilled spirits in 750ml containers. Local excise taxes are excluded; (4) Rates are those applicable to off-premise sales of 11% a.b.v. non-carbonated wine in 750ml containers; (5) Rates are those applicable to off-premise sales of 4.7% a.b.v. beer in 12 ounce containers.
Source: Tax Foundation, 2021 Facts & Figures: How Does Your State Compare?

State Business Tax Climate Index Rankings

State	Overall Rank	Corporate Tax Rank	Individual Income Tax Rank	Sales Tax Rank	Property Tax Rank	Unemployment Insurance Tax Rank
Iowa	40	46	40	14	38	37

Note: The index is a measure of how each state's tax laws affect economic performance. The lower the rank, the more favorable a state's tax system is for business. States without a given tax are given a ranking of 1. The scores/rankings for the District of Columbia do not affect other states. The 2021 index represents the tax climate as of July 1, 2020.
Source: Tax Foundation, State Business Tax Climate Index 2021

TRANSPORTATION

Means of Transportation to Work

Area	Car/Truck/Van		Public Transportation			Bicycle	Walked	Other Means	Worked at Home
	Drove Alone	Car-pooled	Bus	Subway	Railroad				
City	85.6	6.6	0.9	0.0	0.0	0.4	2.3	0.5	3.7
MSA[1]	85.6	6.8	0.9	0.0	0.0	0.2	2.0	0.9	3.6
U.S.	76.3	9.0	2.4	1.9	0.6	0.5	2.7	1.4	5.2

Note: Figures are percentages and cover workers 16 years of age and older; (1) Figures cover the Davenport-Moline-Rock Island, IA-IL Metropolitan Statistical Area
Source: U.S. Census Bureau, 2015-2019 American Community Survey 5-Year Estimates

Travel Time to Work

Area	Less Than 10 Minutes	10 to 19 Minutes	20 to 29 Minutes	30 to 44 Minutes	45 to 59 Minutes	60 to 89 Minutes	90 Minutes or More
City	17.0	47.8	20.8	9.0	3.1	1.2	1.0
MSA[1]	17.9	37.4	24.3	13.6	3.7	1.9	1.3
U.S.	12.2	28.4	20.8	20.8	8.3	6.4	2.9

Note: Note: Figures are percentages and include workers 16 years old and over; (1) Figures cover the Davenport-Moline-Rock Island, IA-IL Metropolitan Statistical Area
Source: U.S. Census Bureau, 2015-2019 American Community Survey 5-Year Estimates

Key Congestion Measures

Measure	1982	1992	2002	2012	2017
Annual Hours of Delay, Total (000)	n/a	n/a	n/a	n/a	4,102
Annual Hours of Delay, Per Auto Commuter	n/a	n/a	n/a	n/a	14
Annual Congestion Cost, Total (million $)	n/a	n/a	n/a	n/a	85
Annual Congestion Cost, Per Auto Commuter ($)	n/a	n/a	n/a	n/a	284

Note: n/a not available
Source: Texas A&M Transportation Institute, 2019 Urban Mobility Report

Davenport, Iowa   95

Freeway Travel Time Index

Measure	1982	1987	1992	1997	2002	2007	2012	2017
Urban Area Index[1]	n/a	n/a	n/a	n/a	n/a	n/a	n/a	1.05
Urban Area Rank[1,2]	n/a	n/a	n/a	n/a	n/a	n/a	n/a	n/a

Note: Freeway Travel Time Index—the ratio of travel time in the peak period to the travel time at free-flow conditions. For example, a value of 1.30 indicates a 20-minute free-flow trip takes 26 minutes in the peak (20 minutes x 1.30 = 26 minutes); (1) Covers the Davenport IA-IL urban area; (2) Rank is based on 101 larger urban areas (#1 = highest travel time index); n/a not available
Source: Texas A&M Transportation Institute, 2019 Urban Mobility Report

Public Transportation

Agency Name / Mode of Transportation	Vehicles Operated in Maximum Service[1]	Annual Unlinked Passenger Trips[2] (in thous.)	Annual Passenger Miles[3] (in thous.)
Davenport Public Transit			
Bus (directly operated)	18	584.3	n/a

Note: (1) Number of revenue vehicles operated by the given mode and type of service to meet the annual maximum service requirement. This is the revenue vehicle count during the peak season of the year; on the week and day that maximum service is provided. Vehicles operated in maximum service (VOMS) exclude atypical days and one-time special events; (2) Number of passengers who boarded public transportation vehicles. Passengers are counted each time they board a vehicle no matter how many vehicles they use to travel from their origin to their destination. (3) Sum of the distances ridden by all passengers during the entire fiscal year.
Source: Federal Transit Administration, National Transit Database, 2019

Air Transportation

Airport Name and Code / Type of Service	Passenger Airlines[1]	Passenger Enplanements	Freight Carriers[2]	Freight (lbs)
Quad City International Airport (MLI)				
Domestic service (U.S. carriers - 2020)	11	150,548	3	5,000
International service (U.S. carriers - 2019)	0	0	1	21,731

Note: (1) Includes all U.S.-based major, minor and commuter airlines that carried at least one passenger during the year; (2) Includes all U.S.-based airlines and freight carriers that transported at least one pound of freight during the year.
Source: Bureau of Transportation Statistics, The Intermodal Transportation Database, Air Carriers: T-100 Domestic Market (U.S. Carriers), 2020; Bureau of Transportation Statistics, The Intermodal Transportation Database, Air Carriers: T-100 International Market (U.S. Carriers), 2019

BUSINESSES

Major Business Headquarters

Company Name	Industry	Rankings	
		Fortune[1]	Forbes[2]
No companies listed	-	-	-

Note: (1) Companies that produce a 10-K are ranked 1 to 500 based on 2019 revenue; (2) All private companies with at least $2 billion in annual revenue through the end of their most current fiscal year are ranked 1 to 219; companies listed are headquartered in the city; dashes indicate no ranking
Source: Fortune, "Fortune 500," June/July 2020; Forbes, "America's Largest Private Companies," 2020

Living Environment

COST OF LIVING

Cost of Living Index

Composite Index	Groceries	Housing	Utilities	Trans-portation	Health Care	Misc. Goods/ Services
90.5	102.9	69.8	91.9	105.3	106.6	95.7

Note: The Cost of Living Index measures regional differences in the cost of consumer goods and services, excluding taxes and non-consumer expenditures, for professional and managerial households in the top income quintile. It is based on more than 50,000 prices covering almost 60 different items for which prices are collected three times a year by chambers of commerce, economic development organizations or university applied economic centers in each participating urban area. The numbers shown should be read as a percentage above or below the national average of 100. For example, a value of 115.4 in the groceries column indicates that grocery prices are 15.4% higher than the national average. Small differences in the index numbers should not be interpreted as significant; Figures cover the Davenport-Moline-Rock Is IA-IL urban area.
Source: The Council for Community and Economic Research, Cost of Living Index, 2020

Grocery Prices

Area[1]	T-Bone Steak ($/pound)	Frying Chicken ($/pound)	Whole Milk ($/half gal.)	Eggs ($/dozen)	Orange Juice ($/64 oz.)	Coffee ($/11.5 oz.)
City[2]	11.56	1.53	2.60	1.32	3.44	4.60
Avg.	11.78	1.39	2.05	1.47	3.57	4.34
Min.	8.03	0.94	1.03	0.74	2.94	3.02
Max.	15.86	2.65	4.31	3.77	5.44	8.69

*Note: (1) Values for the local area are compared with the average, minimum and maximum values for all 284 areas in the Cost of Living Index; (2) Figures cover the Davenport-Moline-Rock Is IA-IL urban area; **T-Bone Steak** (price per pound); **Frying Chicken** (price per pound, whole fryer); **Whole Milk** (half gallon carton); **Eggs** (price per dozen, Grade A, large); **Orange Juice** (64 oz. Tropicana or Florida Natural); **Coffee** (11.5 oz. can, vacuum-packed, Maxwell House, Hills Bros, or Folgers).*
Source: The Council for Community and Economic Research, Cost of Living Index, 2020

Housing and Utility Costs

Area[1]	New Home Price ($)	Apartment Rent ($/month)	All Electric ($/month)	Part Electric ($/month)	Other Energy ($/month)	Telephone ($/month)
City[2]	248,085	880	-	85.19	52.80	191.30
Avg.	368,594	1,168	170.86	100.47	65.28	184.30
Min.	190,567	502	91.58	31.42	26.08	169.60
Max.	2,227,806	4,738	470.38	280.31	280.06	206.50

*Note: (1) Values for the local area are compared with the average, minimum and maximum values for all 284 areas in the Cost of Living Index; (2) Figures cover the Davenport-Moline-Rock Is IA-IL urban area; **New Home Price** (2,400 sf living area, 8,000 sf lot, in urban area with full utilities); **Apartment Rent** (950 sf 2 bedroom/1.5 or 2 bath, unfurnished, excluding all utilities except water); **All Electric** (average monthly cost for an all-electric home); **Part Electric** (average monthly cost for a part-electric home); **Other Energy** (average monthly cost for natural gas, fuel oil, coal, wood, and any other forms of energy except electricity); **Telephone** (price includes the base monthly rate plus taxes and fees for three lines of mobile phone service).*
Source: The Council for Community and Economic Research, Cost of Living Index, 2020

Health Care, Transportation, and Other Costs

Area[1]	Doctor ($/visit)	Dentist ($/visit)	Optometrist ($/visit)	Gasoline ($/gallon)	Beauty Salon ($/visit)	Men's Shirt ($)
City[2]	142.33	96.83	93.08	2.16	34.50	43.03
Avg.	115.44	99.32	108.10	2.21	39.27	31.37
Min.	36.68	59.00	51.36	1.71	19.00	11.00
Max.	219.00	153.10	250.97	3.46	82.05	58.33

*Note: (1) Values for the local area are compared with the average, minimum and maximum values for all 284 areas in the Cost of Living Index; (2) Figures cover the Davenport-Moline-Rock Is IA-IL urban area; **Doctor** (general practitioners routine exam of an established patient); **Dentist** (adult teeth cleaning and periodic oral examination); **Optometrist** (full vision eye exam for established adult patient); **Gasoline** (one gallon regular unleaded, national brand, including all taxes, cash price at self-service pump if available); **Beauty Salon** (woman's shampoo, trim, and blow-dry); **Men's Shirt** (cotton/polyester dress shirt, pinpoint weave, long sleeves).*
Source: The Council for Community and Economic Research, Cost of Living Index, 2020

HOUSING

Homeownership Rate

Area	2012 (%)	2013 (%)	2014 (%)	2015 (%)	2016 (%)	2017 (%)	2018 (%)	2019 (%)	2020 (%)
MSA[1]	n/a	n/a	n/a	n/a	n/a	n/a	n/a	n/a	n/a
U.S.	65.4	65.1	64.5	63.7	63.4	63.9	64.4	64.6	66.6

Note: (1) Figures cover the Davenport-Moline-Rock Island, IA-IL Metropolitan Statistical Area; n/a not available
Source: U.S. Census Bureau, Housing Vacancies and Homeownership Annual Statistics: 2012-2020

House Price Index (HPI)

Area	National Ranking[2]	Quarterly Change (%)	One-Year Change (%)	Five-Year Change (%)	Since 1991Q1 (%)
MSA[1]	225	0.97	3.73	15.46	153.27
U.S.[3]	—	3.81	10.77	38.99	205.12

Note: The HPI is a weighted repeat sales index. It measures average price changes in repeat sales or refinancings on the same properties. This information is obtained by reviewing repeat mortgage transactions on single-family properties whose mortgages have been purchased or securitized by Fannie Mae or Freddie Mac since January 1975; (1) Figures cover the Davenport-Moline-Rock Island, IA-IL Metropolitan Statistical Area; (2) Rankings are based on annual percentage change for all metro areas containing at least 15,000 transactions over the last 10 years and ranges from 1 to 253; (3) figures based on a weighted average of Census Division estimates using a seasonally adjusted, purchase-only index; all figures are for the period ending December 31, 2020
Source: Federal Housing Finance Agency, Change in Metropolitan Area House Price Indexes, April 7, 2021

Median Single-Family Home Prices

Area	2018	2019	2020p	Percent Change 2019 to 2020
MSA[1]	131.0	135.4	142.8	5.5
U.S. Average	261.6	274.6	299.9	9.2

Note: Figures are median sales prices of existing single-family homes in thousands of dollars; (p) preliminary; (1) Figures cover the Davenport-Moline-Rock Island, IA-IL Metropolitan Statistical Area
Source: National Association of Realtors, Median Sales Price of Existing Single-Family Homes for Metropolitan Areas, 4th Quarter 2020

Qualifying Income Based on Median Sales Price of Existing Single-Family Homes

Area	With 5% Down ($)	With 10% Down ($)	With 20% Down ($)
MSA[1]	28,220	26,735	23,764
U.S. Average	59,266	56,147	49,908

Note: Figures are preliminary; Qualifying income is based on a mortgage rate of 2.81%. Monthly principal and interest payment is limited to 25% of income; (1) Figures cover the Davenport-Moline-Rock Island, IA-IL Metropolitan Statistical Area
Source: National Association of Realtors, Qualifying Income Based on Median Sales Price of Existing Single-Family Homes for Metropolitan Areas, 4th Quarter 2020

Home Value Distribution

Area	Under $50,000	$50,000 -$99,999	$100,000 -$149,999	$150,000 -$199,999	$200,000 -$299,999	$300,000 -$499,999	$500,000 -$999,999	$1,000,000 or more
City	6.3	24.6	28.4	16.1	15.6	7.4	1.1	0.4
MSA[1]	7.3	23.5	24.9	17.5	15.3	9.1	2.0	0.4
U.S.	6.9	12.0	13.3	14.0	19.6	19.3	11.4	3.4

Note: Figures are percentages and cover owner-occupied housing units; (1) Figures cover the Davenport-Moline-Rock Island, IA-IL Metropolitan Statistical Area
Source: U.S. Census Bureau, 2015-2019 American Community Survey 5-Year Estimates

Year Housing Structure Built

Area	2010 or Later	2000 -2009	1990 -1999	1980 -1989	1970 -1979	1960 -1969	1950 -1959	1940 -1949	Before 1940	Median Year
City	3.4	8.6	7.9	5.9	15.7	13.3	11.2	5.6	28.5	1964
MSA[1]	3.6	7.5	8.3	6.4	16.6	13.4	11.9	7.1	25.2	1964
U.S.	5.2	14.0	13.9	13.4	15.2	10.6	10.3	4.9	12.6	1978

Note: Figures are percentages except for Median Year; Note: (1) Figures cover the Davenport-Moline-Rock Island, IA-IL Metropolitan Statistical Area
Source: U.S. Census Bureau, 2015-2019 American Community Survey 5-Year Estimates

Gross Monthly Rent

Area	Under $500	$500 -$999	$1,000 -$1,499	$1,500 -$1,999	$2,000 -$2,499	$2,500 -$2,999	$3,000 and up	Median ($)
City	9.2	68.6	16.4	3.2	0.8	0.7	1.1	771
MSA[1]	15.1	61.8	17.1	3.9	0.9	0.4	0.8	765
U.S.	9.4	36.2	30.0	14.0	5.6	2.4	2.4	1,062

Note: Figures are percentages except for Median; Gross rent is the contract rent plus the estimated average monthly cost of utilities (electricity, gas, and water and sewer) and fuels (oil, coal, kerosene, wood, etc.) if these are paid by the renter (or paid for the renter by someone else); (1) Figures cover the Davenport-Moline-Rock Island, IA-IL Metropolitan Statistical Area
Source: U.S. Census Bureau, 2015-2019 American Community Survey 5-Year Estimates

HEALTH

Health Risk Factors

Category	MSA[1] (%)	U.S. (%)
Adults aged 18–64 who have any kind of health care coverage	n/a	87.3
Adults who reported being in good or better health	n/a	82.4
Adults who have been told they have high blood cholesterol	n/a	33.0
Adults who have been told they have high blood pressure	n/a	32.3
Adults who are current smokers	n/a	17.1
Adults who currently use E-cigarettes	n/a	4.6
Adults who currently use chewing tobacco, snuff, or snus	n/a	4.0
Adults who are heavy drinkers[2]	n/a	6.3
Adults who are binge drinkers[3]	n/a	17.4
Adults who are overweight (BMI 25.0 - 29.9)	n/a	35.3
Adults who are obese (BMI 30.0 - 99.8)	n/a	31.3
Adults who participated in any physical activities in the past month	n/a	74.4
Adults who always or nearly always wears a seat belt	n/a	94.3

Note: n/a not available; (1) Figures cover the Davenport-Moline-Rock Island, IA-IL Metropolitan Statistical Area; (2) Heavy drinkers are classified as adult men having more than 14 drinks per week and adult women having more than 7 drinks per week; (3) Binge drinkers are classified as males having five or more drinks on one occasion or females having four or more drinks on one occasion
Source: Centers for Disease Control and Prevention, Behaviorial Risk Factor Surveillance System, SMART: Selected Metropolitan Area Risk Trends, 2017

Acute and Chronic Health Conditions

Category	MSA[1] (%)	U.S. (%)
Adults who have ever been told they had a heart attack	n/a	4.2
Adults who have ever been told they have angina or coronary heart disease	n/a	3.9
Adults who have ever been told they had a stroke	n/a	3.0
Adults who have ever been told they have asthma	n/a	14.2
Adults who have ever been told they have arthritis	n/a	24.9
Adults who have ever been told they have diabetes[2]	n/a	10.5
Adults who have ever been told they had skin cancer	n/a	6.2
Adults who have ever been told they had any other types of cancer	n/a	7.1
Adults who have ever been told they have COPD	n/a	6.5
Adults who have ever been told they have kidney disease	n/a	3.0
Adults who have ever been told they have a form of depression	n/a	20.5

Note: n/a not available; (1) Figures cover the Davenport-Moline-Rock Island, IA-IL Metropolitan Statistical Area; (2) Figures do not include pregnancy-related, borderline, or pre-diabetes
Source: Centers for Disease Control and Prevention, Behaviorial Risk Factor Surveillance System, SMART: Selected Metropolitan Area Risk Trends, 2017

Health Screening and Vaccination Rates

Category	MSA[1] (%)	U.S. (%)
Adults aged 65+ who have had flu shot within the past year	n/a	60.7
Adults aged 65+ who have ever had a pneumonia vaccination	n/a	75.4
Adults who have ever been tested for HIV	n/a	36.1
Adults who have ever had the shingles or zoster vaccine?	n/a	28.9
Adults who have had their blood cholesterol checked within the last five years	n/a	85.9

Note: n/a not available; (1) Figures cover the Davenport-Moline-Rock Island, IA-IL Metropolitan Statistical Area.
Source: Centers for Disease Control and Prevention, Behaviorial Risk Factor Surveillance System, SMART: Selected Metropolitan Area Risk Trends, 2017

Disability Status

Category	MSA[1] (%)	U.S. (%)
Adults who reported being deaf	n/a	6.7
Are you blind or have serious difficulty seeing, even when wearing glasses?	n/a	4.5
Are you limited in any way in any of your usual activities due of arthritis?	n/a	12.9
Do you have difficulty doing errands alone?	n/a	6.8
Do you have difficulty dressing or bathing?	n/a	3.6
Do you have serious difficulty concentrating/remembering/making decisions?	n/a	10.7
Do you have serious difficulty walking or climbing stairs?	n/a	13.6

Note: n/a not available; (1) Figures cover the Davenport-Moline-Rock Island, IA-IL Metropolitan Statistical Area.
Source: Centers for Disease Control and Prevention, Behaviorial Risk Factor Surveillance System, SMART: Selected Metropolitan Area Risk Trends, 2017

Mortality Rates for the Top 10 Causes of Death in the U.S.

ICD-10[a] Sub-Chapter	ICD-10[a] Code	Age-Adjusted Mortality Rate[1] per 100,000 population	
		County[2]	U.S.
Malignant neoplasms	C00-C97	158.9	149.2
Ischaemic heart diseases	I20-I25	85.8	90.5
Other forms of heart disease	I30-I51	48.8	52.2
Chronic lower respiratory diseases	J40-J47	49.4	39.6
Other degenerative diseases of the nervous system	G30-G31	31.9	37.6
Cerebrovascular diseases	I60-I69	37.7	37.2
Other external causes of accidental injury	W00-X59	34.8	36.1
Organic, including symptomatic, mental disorders	F01-F09	34.2	29.4
Hypertensive diseases	I10-I15	27.8	24.1
Diabetes mellitus	E10-E14	18.1	21.5

Note: (a) ICD-10 = International Classification of Diseases 10th Revision; (1) Mortality rates are a three-year average covering 2017-2019; (2) Figures cover Scott County.
Source: Centers for Disease Control and Prevention, National Center for Health Statistics. Underlying Cause of Death 1999-2019 on CDC WONDER Online Database

Mortality Rates for Selected Causes of Death

ICD-10[a] Sub-Chapter	ICD-10[a] Code	Age-Adjusted Mortality Rate[1] per 100,000 population	
		County[2]	U.S.
Assault	X85-Y09	4.3	6.0
Diseases of the liver	K70-K76	14.1	14.4
Human immunodeficiency virus (HIV) disease	B20-B24	Suppressed	1.5
Influenza and pneumonia	J09-J18	10.6	13.8
Intentional self-harm	X60-X84	16.3	14.1
Malnutrition	E40-E46	3.4	2.3
Obesity and other hyperalimentation	E65-E68	4.0	2.1
Renal failure	N17-N19	12.0	12.6
Transport accidents	V01-V99	7.8	12.3
Viral hepatitis	B15-B19	Suppressed	1.2

Note: (a) ICD-10 = International Classification of Diseases 10th Revision; (1) Mortality rates are a three-year average covering 2017-2019; (2) Figures cover Scott County; Data are suppressed when the data meet the criteria for confidentiality constraints; Mortality rates are flagged as unreliable when the rate would be calculated with a numerator of 20 or less.
Source: Centers for Disease Control and Prevention, National Center for Health Statistics. Underlying Cause of Death 1999-2019 on CDC WONDER Online Database

Health Insurance Coverage

Area	With Health Insurance	With Private Health Insurance	With Public Health Insurance	Without Health Insurance	Population Under Age 19 Without Health Insurance
City	94.4	66.2	40.2	5.6	3.3
MSA[1]	95.3	72.9	37.3	4.7	2.7
U.S.	91.2	67.9	35.1	8.8	5.1

Note: Figures are percentages that cover the civilian noninstitutionalized population; (1) Figures cover the Davenport-Moline-Rock Island, IA-IL Metropolitan Statistical Area
Source: U.S. Census Bureau, 2015-2019 American Community Survey 5-Year Estimates

Number of Medical Professionals

Area	MDs[3]	DOs[3,4]	Dentists	Podiatrists	Chiropractors	Optometrists
County[1] (number)	403	90	137	8	316	29
County[1] (rate[2])	233.2	52.1	79.2	4.6	182.7	16.8
U.S. (rate[2])	282.9	22.7	71.2	6.2	28.1	16.9

19163
Note: Data as of 2019 unless noted; (1) Data covers Scott County; (2) Rate per 100,000 population; (3) Data as of 2018 and includes all active, non-federal physicians; (4) Doctor of Osteopathic Medicine
Source: U.S. Department of Health and Human Services, Health Resources and Services Administration, Bureau of Health Professions, Area Resource File (ARF) 2019-2020

EDUCATION

Public School District Statistics

District Name	Schls	Pupils	Pupil/ Teacher Ratio	Minority Pupils[1] (%)	Free Lunch Eligible[2] (%)	IEP[3] (%)
Davenport Comm School District	30	15,519	13.2	45.4	57.6	19.1

Note: Table includes school districts with 2,000 or more students; (1) Percentage of students that are not non-Hispanic white; (2) Percentage of students that are eligible for the free lunch program; (3) Percentage of students that have an Individualized Education Program.
Source: U.S. Department of Education, National Center for Education Statistics, Common Core of Data, Local Education Agency (School District) Universe Survey: School Year 2018-2019; U.S. Department of Education, National Center for Education Statistics, Common Core of Data, Public Elementary/Secondary School Universe Survey: School Year 2018-2019

Highest Level of Education

Area	Less than H.S.	H.S. Diploma	Some College, No Deg.	Associate Degree	Bachelor's Degree	Master's Degree	Prof. School Degree	Doctorate Degree
City	9.5	32.5	21.8	10.7	17.0	6.3	1.5	0.8
MSA[1]	9.0	30.5	23.0	10.5	17.2	7.3	1.5	0.8
U.S.	12.0	27.0	20.4	8.5	19.8	8.8	2.1	1.4

Note: Figures cover persons age 25 and over; (1) Figures cover the Davenport-Moline-Rock Island, IA-IL Metropolitan Statistical Area
Source: U.S. Census Bureau, 2015-2019 American Community Survey 5-Year Estimates

Educational Attainment by Race

Area	High School Graduate or Higher (%)					Bachelor's Degree or Higher (%)				
	Total	White	Black	Asian	Hisp.[2]	Total	White	Black	Asian	Hisp.[2]
City	90.5	92.2	83.6	69.2	72.8	25.6	27.4	10.5	28.0	15.5
MSA[1]	91.0	92.6	79.5	80.4	72.9	26.9	27.6	13.8	46.8	15.6
U.S.	88.0	89.9	86.0	87.1	68.7	32.1	33.5	21.6	54.3	16.4

Note: Figures shown cover persons 25 years old and over; (1) Figures cover the Davenport-Moline-Rock Island, IA-IL Metropolitan Statistical Area; (2) People of Hispanic origin can be of any race
Source: U.S. Census Bureau, 2015-2019 American Community Survey 5-Year Estimates

School Enrollment by Grade and Control

Area	Preschool (%)		Kindergarten (%)		Grades 1 - 4 (%)		Grades 5 - 8 (%)		Grades 9 - 12 (%)	
	Public	Private	Public	Private	Public	Private	Public	Private	Public	Private
City	57.0	43.0	86.1	13.9	89.3	10.7	84.3	15.7	92.8	7.2
MSA[1]	69.0	31.0	89.9	10.1	91.6	8.4	91.6	8.4	93.2	6.8
U.S.	59.1	40.9	87.6	12.4	89.5	10.5	89.4	10.6	90.1	9.9

Note: Figures shown cover persons 3 years old and over; (1) Figures cover the Davenport-Moline-Rock Island, IA-IL Metropolitan Statistical Area
Source: U.S. Census Bureau, 2015-2019 American Community Survey 5-Year Estimates

Higher Education

Four-Year Colleges			Two-Year Colleges			Medical Schools[1]	Law Schools[2]	Voc/ Tech[3]
Public	Private Non-profit	Private For-profit	Public	Private Non-profit	Private For-profit			
1	2	1	1	0	2	0	0	0

Note: Figures cover institutions located within the city limits and include main campuses only; (1) includes schools accredited by the Liaison Committee on Medical Education and the American Osteopathic Association's Commission on Osteopathic College Accreditation; (2) includes ABA-accredited schools, schools with provisional ABA accreditation, and state accredited schools; (3) includes all schools with programs that are less than 2 years.
Source: National Center for Education Statistics, Integrated Postsecondary Education System (IPEDS), 2019-20; Wikipedia, List of Medical Schools in the United States, accessed April 2, 2021; Wikipedia, List of Law Schools in the United States, accessed April 2, 2021

According to *U.S. News & World Report,* the Davenport-Moline-Rock Island, IA-IL metro area is home to one of the top 100 liberal arts colleges in the U.S.: **Augustana College** (#96 tie). The indicators used to capture academic quality fall into a number of categories: assessment by administrators at peer institutions; retention of students; faculty resources; student selectivity; financial resources; alumni giving; high school counselor ratings of colleges; and graduation rate. *U.S. News & World Report, "America's Best Colleges 2021"*

Davenport, Iowa | **101**

EMPLOYERS

Major Employers

Company Name	Industry
Alcoa	Manufacturer
Deere and Company	Manufacturer
Genesis Health System	Healthcare
HNI Corporation/The Hon Company/Allsteel	Manufacturer
Hy-Vee Food Stores	Grocery stores
Kraft Foods/Oscar Mayer	Food processing
Rock Island Arsenal	U.S. military
Trinity Regional Health System	Healthcare
Tyson Fresh Meats	Food processing
XPAC	Service, parts, packaging

Note: Companies shown are located within the Davenport-Moline-Rock Island, IA-IL Metropolitan Statistical Area.
Source: Hoovers.com; Wikipedia

PUBLIC SAFETY

Crime Rate

Area	All Crimes	Violent Crimes				Property Crimes		
		Murder	Rape[3]	Robbery	Aggrav. Assault	Burglary	Larceny -Theft	Motor Vehicle Theft
City	4,421.2	2.0	82.0	121.1	389.7	727.6	2,763.9	335.0
Suburbs[1]	1,880.3	2.2	46.1	31.4	202.5	306.7	1,169.0	122.5
Metro[2]	2,565.2	2.1	55.8	55.5	253.0	420.1	1,598.8	179.8
U.S.	2,489.3	5.0	42.6	81.6	250.2	340.5	1,549.5	219.9

Note: Figures are crimes per 100,000 population; (1) All areas within the metro area that are located outside the city limits; (2) Figures cover the Davenport-Moline-Rock Island, IA-IL Metropolitan Statistical Area; (3) All figures shown were reported using the revised Uniform Crime Reporting (UCR) definition of rape.
Source: FBI Uniform Crime Reports, 2019

Hate Crimes

Area	Number of Quarters Reported	Number of Incidents per Bias Motivation					
		Race/Ethnicity/ Ancestry	Religion	Sexual Orientation	Disability	Gender	Gender Identity
City	4	1	0	0	0	0	0
U.S.	4	3,963	1,521	1,195	157	69	198

Source: Federal Bureau of Investigation, Hate Crime Statistics 2019

Identity Theft Consumer Reports

Area	Reports	Reports per 100,000 Population	Rank[2]
MSA[1]	1,387	366	86
U.S.	1,387,615	423	-

Note: (1) Figures cover the Davenport-Moline-Rock Island, IA-IL Metropolitan Statistical Area; (2) Rank ranges from 1 to 391 where 1 indicates greatest number of identity theft reports per 100,000 population
Source: Federal Trade Commission, Consumer Sentinel Network Data Book 2020

Fraud and Other Consumer Reports

Area	Reports	Reports per 100,000 Population	Rank[2]
MSA[1]	2,155	568	319
U.S.	3,385,133	1,031	-

Note: (1) Figures cover the Davenport-Moline-Rock Island, IA-IL Metropolitan Statistical Area; (2) Rank ranges from 1 to 391 where 1 indicates greatest number of fraud and other consumer reports per 100,000 population
Source: Federal Trade Commission, Consumer Sentinel Network Data Book 2020

POLITICS

2020 Presidential Election Results

Area	Biden	Trump	Jorgensen	Hawkins	Other
Scott County	50.7	47.2	1.2	0.2	0.7
U.S.	51.3	46.8	1.2	0.3	0.5

Note: Results are percentages and may not add to 100% due to rounding
Source: Dave Leip's Atlas of U.S. Presidential Elections

SPORTS

Professional Sports Teams

Team Name	League	Year Established

No teams are located in the metro area
Source: Wikipedia, Major Professional Sports Teams of the United States and Canada, April 6, 2021

102 Davenport, Iowa

CLIMATE

Average and Extreme Temperatures

Temperature	Jan	Feb	Mar	Apr	May	Jun	Jul	Aug	Sep	Oct	Nov	Dec	Yr.
Extreme High (°F)	65	70	91	93	98	103	105	108	99	95	76	69	108
Average High (°F)	29	34	45	61	72	82	86	84	76	65	48	33	60
Average Temp. (°F)	20	25	36	51	62	72	76	74	65	54	39	25	50
Average Low (°F)	11	16	27	40	51	61	66	64	54	43	29	17	40
Extreme Low (°F)	-24	-20	-22	9	28	42	47	40	28	14	-3	-22	-24

Note: Figures cover the years 1945-1990
Source: National Climatic Data Center, International Station Meteorological Climate Summary, 9/96

Average Precipitation/Snowfall/Humidity

Precip./Humidity	Jan	Feb	Mar	Apr	May	Jun	Jul	Aug	Sep	Oct	Nov	Dec	Yr.
Avg. Precip. (in.)	1.1	1.1	2.3	3.1	3.8	4.4	3.5	3.9	3.1	2.4	1.7	1.2	31.8
Avg. Snowfall (in.)	8	7	7	2	Tr	0	0	0	Tr	Tr	3	7	33
Avg. Rel. Hum. 6am (%)	77	79	79	78	78	81	83	86	85	80	79	80	80
Avg. Rel. Hum. 3pm (%)	65	63	57	50	51	52	52	54	52	50	58	66	56

Note: Figures cover the years 1945-1990; Tr = Trace amounts (<0.05 in. of rain; <0.5 in. of snow)
Source: National Climatic Data Center, International Station Meteorological Climate Summary, 9/96

Weather Conditions

Temperature			Daytime Sky			Precipitation		
5°F & below	32°F & below	90°F & above	Clear	Partly cloudy	Cloudy	0.01 inch or more precip.	0.1 inch or more snow/ice	Thunder-storms
25	137	26	99	128	138	106	25	46

Note: Figures are average number of days per year and cover the years 1945-1990
Source: National Climatic Data Center, International Station Meteorological Climate Summary, 9/96

HAZARDOUS WASTE

Superfund Sites

The Davenport-Moline-Rock Island, IA-IL metro area has no sites on the EPA's Superfund Final National Priorities List. There are a total of 1,375 Superfund sites with a status of proposed or final on the list in the U.S. *U.S. Environmental Protection Agency, National Priorities List, April 7, 2021*

AIR QUALITY

Air Quality Trends: Ozone

	1990	1995	2000	2005	2010	2015	2016	2017	2018	2019
MSA[1]	n/a	n/a	n/a	n/a	n/a	n/a	n/a	n/a	n/a	n/a
U.S.	0.088	0.089	0.082	0.080	0.073	0.068	0.069	0.068	0.069	0.065

Note: (1) Data covers the Davenport-Moline-Rock Island, IA-IL Metropolitan Statistical Area; n/a not available. The values shown are the composite ozone concentration averages among trend sites based on the highest fourth daily maximum 8-hour concentration in parts per million. These trends are based on sites having an adequate record of monitoring data during the trend period. Data from exceptional events are included.
Source: U.S. Environmental Protection Agency, Air Quality Monitoring Information, "Air Quality Trends by City, 1990-2019"

Air Quality Index

Area	Percent of Days when Air Quality was...[2]					AQI Statistics[2]	
	Good	Moderate	Unhealthy for Sensitive Groups	Unhealthy	Very Unhealthy	Maximum	Median
MSA[1]	59.5	39.7	0.8	0.0	0.0	115	46

Note: (1) Data covers the Davenport-Moline-Rock Island, IA-IL Metropolitan Statistical Area; (2) Based on 365 days with AQI data in 2019. Air Quality Index (AQI) is an index for reporting daily air quality. EPA calculates the AQI for five major air pollutants regulated by the Clean Air Act: ground-level ozone, particle pollution (aka particulate matter), carbon monoxide, sulfur dioxide, and nitrogen dioxide. The AQI runs from 0 to 500. The higher the AQI value, the greater the level of air pollution and the greater the health concern. There are six AQI categories: "Good" AQI is between 0 and 50. Air quality is considered satisfactory; "Moderate" AQI is between 51 and 100. Air quality is acceptable; "Unhealthy for Sensitive Groups" When AQI values are between 101 and 150, members of sensitive groups may experience health effects; "Unhealthy" When AQI values are between 151 and 200 everyone may begin to experience health effects; "Very Unhealthy" AQI values between 201 and 300 trigger a health alert; "Hazardous" AQI values over 300 trigger warnings of emergency conditions (not shown).
Source: U.S. Environmental Protection Agency, Air Quality Index Report, 2019

Davenport, Iowa 103

Air Quality Index Pollutants

Area	Percent of Days when AQI Pollutant was...[2]					
	Carbon Monoxide	Nitrogen Dioxide	Ozone	Sulfur Dioxide	Particulate Matter 2.5	Particulate Matter 10
MSA[1]	0.0	0.0	37.8	0.0	41.9	20.3

Note: (1) Data covers the Davenport-Moline-Rock Island, IA-IL Metropolitan Statistical Area; (2) Based on 365 days with AQI data in 2019. The Air Quality Index (AQI) is an index for reporting daily air quality. EPA calculates the AQI for five major air pollutants regulated by the Clean Air Act: ground-level ozone, particle pollution (also known as particulate matter), carbon monoxide, sulfur dioxide, and nitrogen dioxide. The AQI runs from 0 to 500. The higher the AQI value, the greater the level of air pollution and the greater the health concern.
Source: U.S. Environmental Protection Agency, Air Quality Index Report, 2019

Maximum Air Pollutant Concentrations: Particulate Matter, Ozone, CO and Lead

	Particulate Matter 10 (ug/m^3)	Particulate Matter 2.5 Wtd AM (ug/m^3)	Particulate Matter 2.5 24-Hr (ug/m^3)	Ozone (ppm)	Carbon Monoxide (ppm)	Lead (ug/m^3)
MSA[1] Level	129	8.6	22	0.066	1	n/a
NAAQS[2]	150	15	35	0.075	9	0.15
Met NAAQS[2]	Yes	Yes	Yes	Yes	Yes	n/a

Note: (1) Data covers the Davenport-Moline-Rock Island, IA-IL Metropolitan Statistical Area; Data from exceptional events are included; (2) National Ambient Air Quality Standards; ppm = parts per million; ug/m^3 = micrograms per cubic meter; n/a not available.
Concentrations: Particulate Matter 10 (coarse particulate)—highest second maximum 24-hour concentration; Particulate Matter 2.5 Wtd AM (fine particulate)—highest weighted annual mean concentration; Particulate Matter 2.5 24-Hour (fine particulate)—highest 98th percentile 24-hour concentration; Ozone—highest fourth daily maximum 8-hour concentration; Carbon Monoxide—highest second maximum non-overlapping 8-hour concentration; Lead—maximum running 3-month average
Source: U.S. Environmental Protection Agency, Air Quality Monitoring Information, "Air Quality Statistics by City, 2019"

Maximum Air Pollutant Concentrations: Nitrogen Dioxide and Sulfur Dioxide

	Nitrogen Dioxide AM (ppb)	Nitrogen Dioxide 1-Hr (ppb)	Sulfur Dioxide AM (ppb)	Sulfur Dioxide 1-Hr (ppb)	Sulfur Dioxide 24-Hr (ppb)
MSA[1] Level	n/a	n/a	n/a	5	n/a
NAAQS[2]	53	100	30	75	140
Met NAAQS[2]	n/a	n/a	n/a	Yes	n/a

Note: (1) Data covers the Davenport-Moline-Rock Island, IA-IL Metropolitan Statistical Area; Data from exceptional events are included; (2) National Ambient Air Quality Standards; ppm = parts per million; ug/m^3 = micrograms per cubic meter; n/a not available.
Concentrations: Nitrogen Dioxide AM—highest arithmetic mean concentration; Nitrogen Dioxide 1-Hr—highest 98th percentile 1-hour daily maximum concentration; Sulfur Dioxide AM—highest annual mean concentration; Sulfur Dioxide 1-Hr—highest 99th percentile 1-hour daily maximum concentration; Sulfur Dioxide 24-Hr—highest second maximum 24-hour concentration
Source: U.S. Environmental Protection Agency, Air Quality Monitoring Information, "Air Quality Statistics by City, 2019"

Des Moines, Iowa

Background

In 1843, Fort Des Moines was founded at the confluence of the Des Moines and Raccoon rivers. Though the fort was initially established to protect local Native American populations, within two years the area was opened to white settlers. By 1857, the state capital was moved from Iowa City to Des Moines. Today, Des Moines remains the capital of Iowa and is its largest city.

The city frequently finds itself near the top of best-of lists extolling its reasonable cost of living, quality of life, or job opportunities. It has taken an active role in acquiring properties in its downtown for redevelopment, and also takes a progressive approach to planning, having joined with other counties and regional partners to plan for transportation and other future needs. The Capital Corridor encourages the development of creative high-value growth and development for industry, including animal science.

Des Moines's significant industries include the financial services industry; Greater Des Moines has the nation's highest concentration of employment in this sector. Additionally, logistics, bioscience, and data centers are significant economic sectors.

Greater Des Moines is home to the first statewide fiber optics network in the country. The city proper also boasts world-class architecture. The Des Moines Art Center was designed in 1944 by Eliel Saarinen, a Finnish architect and then-president of the renowned Cranbrook Academy of Art in Detroit. In 1968, I.M. Pei, architect of the Pyramid du Louvre and the East Wing of the National Gallery of Art in Washington, D.C., designed a gallery addition to the main Art Center structure. In 1985, Richard Meier, who had designed the Museum of Modern Art in Florence, Italy, designed an addition to the Art Center's north wing and went on to design the famed Getty Center in Los Angeles. The city's Home Federal Savings and Loan Building was designed by Mies van der Rohe, of the famous German Bauhaus School of Design, and a sculpture called The Crusoe Umbrella, designed by pop artist Claes Oldenberg, stands in the middle of Nollen Plaza, a wooded park and popular gathering place.

The Greater Des Moines Botanical Center has been renovated to include Iowa's first "living wall," a new office suite and lobby, and improvements to the center's gardens.

Des Moines Civic Center offers ballet, symphony and other performances. The Science Center of Iowa features hands-on science and technology exhibits, an IMAX theater, and a planetarium with an interactive program and laser light show.

Every four years, Des Moines becomes the center of national attention as correspondents from all over the U.S. and abroad arrive to cover the Iowa political caucuses, which has become a financial boon for the state.

Located in the heart of North America, Des Moines has a continental climate, resulting in a seasonal contrast in both temperature and precipitation. Exceptionally high summer rains have caused the nearby Des Moines River and Raccoon River to breach the city's levees on two occasions, in 1993 and again in 2008. The winter is a season of cold, dry air, interrupted by occasional storms of short duration. The autumn is characteristically sunny with diminishing precipitation.

Rankings

General Rankings

- *US News & World Report* conducted a survey of more than 3,000 people and analyzed the 150 largest metropolitan areas to determine what matters most when selecting the next place to live. Des Moines ranked #7 out of the top 25 as having the best combination of desirable factors. Criteria: cost of living; quality of life; net migration; job market; desirability; and other factors. *realestate.usnews.com, "The 25 Best Places to Live in the U.S. in 2020-21," October 13, 2020*

- The Des Moines metro area was identified as one of America's fastest-growing areas in terms of population and business growth by *MagnifyMoney*. The area ranked #15 out of 35. The 100 most populous metro areas in the U.S. were evaluated on their change from 2011-2016 in the following categories: people and housing; workforce and employment opportunities; growing industry. *www.businessinsider.com, "The 35 Cities in the US with the Biggest Influx of People, the Most Work Opportunities, and the Hottest Business Growth," August 12, 2018*

- In their seventh annual survey, Livability.com looked at data for more than 1,000 small to mid-sized U.S. cities to determine the rankings for Livability's "Top 100 Best Places to Live" in 2020. Des Moines ranked #83. Criteria: housing and affordable living; vibrant economy; social and civic engagement; education; demographics; health care options; transportation & infrastructure; and abundant lifestyle amenities. *Livability.com, "Top 100 Best Places to Live 2020" October 2020*

Business/Finance Rankings

- Des Moines was the #10-ranked city for savers, according to a study by the finance site GOBankingRates, which considered the prospects for people trying to save money. Criteria: average monthly cost of grocery items; median home listing price; median rent; median income; transportation costs; gas prices; and the cost of eating out for an inexpensive and mid-range meal in 100 U.S. cities. *www.gobankingrates.com, "The 20 Best (and Worst) Places to Live If You're Trying to Save Money," August 27, 2019*

- Des Moines was ranked #10 among 100 U.S. cities for most difficult conditions for savers, according to a study by the finance site GOBankingRates. Criteria: average monthly cost of grocery items; median home listing price; median rent; median income; transportation costs; gas prices; and the cost of eating out for an inexpensive and mid-range meal. *www.gobankingrates.com, "The 20 Best (and Worst) Places to Live If You're Trying to Save Money," August 27, 2019*

- The Brookings Institution ranked the nation's largest cities based on income inequality. Des Moines was ranked #88 (#1 = greatest inequality). Criteria: the "95/20 ratio," a figure representing the income at which a household earns more than 95 percent of all other households, divided by the income at which a household earns more than only 20 percent of all other households. *Brookings Institution, "Household Income Inequality, Largest Cities of 97 Large U.S. Metro Areas, 2014-2016," February 5, 2018*

- The Brookings Institution ranked the 100 largest metro areas in the U.S. based on income inequality. Des Moines was ranked #93 (#1 = greatest inequality). Criteria: the "95/20 ratio," a figure representing the income at which a household earns more than 95 percent of all other households, divided by the income at which a household earns more than only 20 percent of all other households. *Brookings Institution, "Household Income Inequality, 100 Largest U.S. Metro Areas, 2014-2016," February 5, 2018*

- The Des Moines metro area appeared on the Milken Institute "2021 Best Performing Cities" list. Rank: #133 out of 200 large metro areas (population over 250,000). Criteria: job growth; wage and salary growth; high-tech output growth; housing affordability; household broadband access. *Milken Institute, "Best-Performing Cities 2021," February 16, 2021*

- *Forbes* ranked the 200 most populous metro areas to determine the nation's "Best Places for Business and Careers." The Des Moines metro area was ranked #10. Criteria: costs (business and living); job growth (past and projected); income growth; quality of life; educational attainment (college and high school); projected economic growth; cultural and leisure opportunities; workplace tolerance laws; net migration patterns. *Forbes, "The Best Places for Business and Careers 2019: Seattle Still On Top," October 30, 2019*

Dating/Romance Rankings

- Des Moines was ranked #6 out of 25 cities that stood out for inspiring romance and attracting diners on the website OpenTable.com. Criteria: percentage of people who dined out on Valentine's Day in 2018; percentage of romantic restaurants as rated by OpenTable diner reviews; and percentage of tables seated for two. *OpenTable, "25 Most Romantic Cities in America for 2019," February 7, 2019*

Education Rankings

- Personal finance website *WalletHub* analyzed the 150 largest U.S. metropolitan statistical areas to determine where the most educated Americans are putting their degrees to work. Criteria: education levels; percentage of workers with degrees; education quality and attainment gap; public school quality rankings; quality and enrollment of each metro area's universities. Des Moines was ranked #47 (#1 = most educated city). *www.WalletHub.com, "Most and Least Educated Cities in America," July 20, 2020*

Environmental Rankings

- The U.S. Environmental Protection Agency (EPA) released a list of U.S. metropolitan areas with the most ENERGY STAR certified buildings in 2019. The Des Moines metro area was ranked #24 out of 25. *U.S. Environmental Protection Agency, "2020 Energy Star Top Cities," March 2020*

- The U.S. Environmental Protection Agency (EPA) released a list of mid-size U.S. metropolitan areas with the most ENERGY STAR certified buildings in 2019. The Des Moines metro area was ranked #3 out of 10. *U.S. Environmental Protection Agency, "2020 Energy Star Top Cities," March 2020*

Health/Fitness Rankings

- Des Moines was identified as a "2021 Spring Allergy Capital." The area ranked #75 out of 100. Three groups of factors were used to identify the most challenging cities for people with allergies during the spring season: annual spring pollen levels; over the counter medicine use; number of board-certified allergy specialists. *Asthma and Allergy Foundation of America, "Spring Allergy Capitals 2021," February 23, 2021*

- Des Moines was identified as a "2021 Fall Allergy Capital." The area ranked #45 out of 100. Three groups of factors were used to identify the most challenging cities for people with allergies during the fall season: annual fall pollen levels; over the counter medicine use; number of board-certified allergy specialists. *Asthma and Allergy Foundation of America, "Fall Allergy Capitals 2021," February 23, 2021*

- Des Moines was identified as a "2019 Asthma Capital." The area ranked #60 out of the nation's 100 largest metropolitan areas. Criteria: estimated asthma prevalence; crude death rate from asthma; and ER visits due to asthma. Risk factors analyzed but not factored in the rankings: annual pollen score; annual air quality; public smoking laws; number of board-certified asthma specialists; rescue medication use; controller medication use; uninsured rate; poverty rate. *Asthma and Allergy Foundation of America, "Asthma Capitals 2019: The Most Challenging Places to Live With Asthma," May 7, 2019*

Real Estate Rankings

- *WalletHub* compared the most populated U.S. cities to determine which had the best markets for real estate agents. Des Moines ranked #117 where demand was high and pay was the best. Criteria: sales per agent; annual median wage for real-estate agents; monthly average starting salary for real estate agents; real estate job density and competition; unemployment rate; home turnover rate; housing-market health index; and other relevant metrics. *www.WalletHub.com, "2019's Best Places to Be a Real Estate Agent," April 24, 2019*

- Des Moines was ranked #33 out of 268 metro areas in terms of housing affordability in 2020 by the National Association of Home Builders (#1 = most affordable). Criteria: the share of homes sold in that area affordable to a family earning the local median income, based on standard mortgage underwriting criteria. *National Association of Home Builders®, NAHB-Wells Fargo Housing Opportunity Index, 4th Quarter 2020*

Safety Rankings

- Allstate ranked the 200 largest cities in America in terms of driver safety. Des Moines ranked #38. Criteria: internal property damage claims over a two-year period from January 2016 to December 2017. The report helps increase the importance of safety and awareness behind the wheel. *Allstate, "Allstate America's Best Drivers Report, 2019" June 24, 2019*

- The National Insurance Crime Bureau ranked 384 metro areas in the U.S. in terms of per capita rates of vehicle theft. The Des Moines metro area ranked #112 (#1 = highest rate). Criteria: number of vehicle theft offenses per 100,000 inhabitants in 2019. *National Insurance Crime Bureau, "Hot Spots 2019," July 21, 2020*

Seniors/Retirement Rankings

- From its Best Cities for Successful Aging indexes, the Milken Institute generated rankings for metropolitan areas, weighing data in nine categories—health care, wellness, living arrangements, transportation and convenience, financial characteristics, education, employment, community engagement, and overall livability. The Des Moines metro area was ranked #5 overall in the large metro area category. *Milken Institute, "Best Cities for Successful Aging, 2017" March 14, 2017*

- Des Moines made the 2020 *Forbes* list of "25 Best Places to Retire." Criteria, focused on high-quality retirement living at an affordable price, include: housing/living costs compared to the national average and state taxes; air quality; crime rates; good economic outlook; home price appreciation; risk associated with climate-change; availability of medical care; bikeability; walkability; healthy living. *Forbes.com, "The Best Places to Retire in 2020," August 14, 2020*

Sports/Recreation Rankings

- Des Moines was chosen as one of America's best cities for bicycling. The city ranked #38 out of 50. Criteria: cycling infrastructure that is safe and friendly for all ages; energy and bike culture. The editors evaluated cities with populations of 100,000 or more. *Bicycling, "The 50 Best Bike Cities in America," October 10, 2018*

Women/Minorities Rankings

- Personal finance website *WalletHub* compared more than 180 U.S. cities across two key dimensions, "Hispanic Business-Friendliness" and "Hispanic Purchasing Power," to arrive at the most favorable conditions for Hispanic entrepreneurs. Des Moines was ranked #158 out of 182. Criteria includes: share of Hispanic-Owned Businesses; Hispanic entrepreneurship rate to median annual income of Hispanics; Small Business-Friendliness score; cost of living; and number of Hispanics with at least a bachelor's degree. *WalletHub.com, "2019's Best Cities for Hispanic Entrepreneurs," May 1, 2019*

Miscellaneous Rankings

- *WalletHub* compared the 150 most populated U.S. cities to determine their operating efficiency. A "Quality of City Services" score was constructed for each city and then divided by the total budget per capita to reveal which were managed the best. Des Moines ranked #58. Criteria: financial stability; economy; education; safety; health; infrastructure and pollution. *www.WalletHub.com, "2020's Best- & Worst-Run Cities in America," June 29, 2020*

Business Environment

DEMOGRAPHICS

Population Growth

Area	1990 Census	2000 Census	2010 Census	2019* Estimate	Population Growth (%)	
					1990-2019	2010-2019
City	193,569	198,682	203,433	215,636	11.4	6.0
MSA[1]	416,346	481,394	569,633	680,439	63.4	19.5
U.S.	248,709,873	281,421,906	308,745,538	324,697,795	30.6	5.2

Note: (1) Figures cover the Des Moines-West Des Moines, IA Metropolitan Statistical Area; (*) 2015-2019 5-year estimated population
Source: U.S. Census Bureau, 1990 Census, Census 2000, Census 2010, 2015-2019 American Community Survey 5-Year Estimates

Household Size

Area	Persons in Household (%)							Average Household Size
	One	Two	Three	Four	Five	Six	Seven or More	
City	34.2	30.6	14.7	11.5	5.3	2.2	1.5	2.50
MSA[1]	28.0	34.2	14.7	13.9	6.2	2.2	0.9	2.50
U.S.	27.9	33.9	15.6	12.9	6.0	2.3	1.4	2.60

Note: (1) Figures cover the Des Moines-West Des Moines, IA Metropolitan Statistical Area
Source: U.S. Census Bureau, 2015-2019 American Community Survey 5-Year Estimates

Race

Area	White Alone[2] (%)	Black Alone[2] (%)	Asian Alone[2] (%)	AIAN[3] Alone[2] (%)	NHOPI[4] Alone[2] (%)	Other Race Alone[2] (%)	Two or More Races (%)
City	75.8	11.4	6.2	0.4	0.1	2.3	3.9
MSA[1]	86.9	5.2	3.9	0.3	0.1	1.1	2.5
U.S.	72.5	12.7	5.5	0.8	0.2	4.9	3.3

Note: (1) Figures cover the Des Moines-West Des Moines, IA Metropolitan Statistical Area; (2) Alone is defined as not being in combination with one or more other races; (3) American Indian and Alaska Native; (4) Native Hawaiian and Other Pacific Islander
Source: U.S. Census Bureau, 2015-2019 American Community Survey 5-Year Estimates

Hispanic or Latino Origin

Area	Total (%)	Mexican (%)	Puerto Rican (%)	Cuban (%)	Other (%)
City	13.6	10.6	0.4	0.1	2.4
MSA[1]	7.1	5.4	0.2	0.1	1.4
U.S.	18.0	11.2	1.7	0.7	4.3

Note: Persons of Hispanic or Latino origin can be of any race; (1) Figures cover the Des Moines-West Des Moines, IA Metropolitan Statistical Area
Source: U.S. Census Bureau, 2015-2019 American Community Survey 5-Year Estimates

Ancestry

Area	German	Irish	English	American	Italian	Polish	French[2]	Scottish	Dutch
City	20.3	11.6	6.6	3.6	3.9	1.0	1.8	1.3	2.6
MSA[1]	27.1	13.0	8.4	4.3	3.2	1.3	1.9	1.7	3.8
U.S.	13.3	9.7	7.2	6.2	5.1	2.8	2.3	1.7	1.2

Note: Figures are the percentage of the total population reporting a particular ancestry. The nine most commonly reported ancestries in the U.S. are shown. Figures include multiple ancestries (e.g. if a person reported being Irish and Italian, they were included in both columns); (1) Figures cover the Des Moines-West Des Moines, IA Metropolitan Statistical Area; (2) Excludes Basque
Source: U.S. Census Bureau, 2015-2019 American Community Survey 5-Year Estimates

Foreign-born Population

Area	Percent of Population Born in								
	Any Foreign Country	Asia	Mexico	Europe	Caribbean	Central America[2]	South America	Africa	Canada
City	12.5	4.5	3.3	0.9	0.1	1.1	0.2	2.3	0.1
MSA[1]	7.7	3.0	1.5	1.1	0.1	0.5	0.2	1.2	0.1
U.S.	13.6	4.2	3.5	1.5	1.3	1.1	1.0	0.7	0.2

Note: (1) Figures cover the Des Moines-West Des Moines, IA Metropolitan Statistical Area; (2) Excludes Mexico.
Source: U.S. Census Bureau, 2015-2019 American Community Survey 5-Year Estimates

Marital Status

Area	Never Married	Now Married[2]	Separated	Widowed	Divorced
City	39.0	40.0	2.0	5.3	13.7
MSA[1]	29.9	52.1	1.3	5.0	11.8
U.S.	33.4	48.1	1.9	5.8	10.9

Note: Figures are percentages and cover the population 15 years of age and older; (1) Figures cover the Des Moines-West Des Moines, IA Metropolitan Statistical Area; (2) Excludes separated
Source: U.S. Census Bureau, 2015-2019 American Community Survey 5-Year Estimates

Disability by Age

Area	All Ages	Under 18 Years Old	18 to 64 Years Old	65 Years and Over
City	14.0	5.8	12.7	38.2
MSA[1]	10.6	4.0	8.9	31.4
U.S.	12.6	4.2	10.3	34.5

Note: Figures show percent of the civilian noninstitutionalized population that reported having a disability. Disability status is determined from six types of difficulty: vision, hearing, cognitive, ambulatory, self-care, and independent living. For children under 5 years old, hearing and vision difficulty are used to determine disability status. For children between the ages of 5 and 14, disability status is determined from hearing, vision, cognitive, ambulatory, and self-care difficulties. For people aged 15 years and older, they are considered to have a disability if they have difficulty with any one of the six difficulty types; Note: (1) Figures cover the Des Moines-West Des Moines, IA Metropolitan Statistical Area
Source: U.S. Census Bureau, 2015-2019 American Community Survey 5-Year Estimates

Age

Area	Percent of Population									Median Age
	Under Age 5	Age 5–19	Age 20–34	Age 35–44	Age 45–54	Age 55–64	Age 65–74	Age 75–84	Age 85+	
City	6.9	19.7	24.5	13.0	12.0	11.8	7.1	3.3	1.6	34.2
MSA[1]	7.0	20.5	20.7	13.7	12.8	11.9	7.9	3.9	1.6	36.2
U.S.	6.1	19.1	20.7	12.6	13.0	12.9	9.1	4.6	1.9	38.1

Note: (1) Figures cover the Des Moines-West Des Moines, IA Metropolitan Statistical Area
Source: U.S. Census Bureau, 2015-2019 American Community Survey 5-Year Estimates

Gender

Area	Males	Females	Males per 100 Females
City	106,316	109,320	97.3
MSA[1]	336,082	344,357	97.6
U.S.	159,886,919	164,810,876	97.0

Note: (1) Figures cover the Des Moines-West Des Moines, IA Metropolitan Statistical Area
Source: U.S. Census Bureau, 2015-2019 American Community Survey 5-Year Estimates

Religious Groups by Family

Area	Catholic	Baptist	Non-Den.	Methodist[2]	Lutheran	LDS[3]	Pentecostal	Presbyterian[4]	Muslim[5]	Judaism
MSA[1]	13.6	4.8	3.3	7.0	8.2	1.0	2.4	3.0	0.3	0.3
U.S.	19.1	9.3	4.0	4.0	2.3	2.0	1.9	1.6	0.8	0.7

Note: Figures are the number of adherents as a percentage of the total population; (1) Figures cover the Des Moines-West Des Moines, IA Metropolitan Statistical Area; (2) Methodist/Pietist; (3) Latter Day Saints; (4) Reformed; (5) Figures are estimates
Source: Association of Statisticians of American Religious Bodies, 2010 U.S. Religion Census: Religious Congregations & Membership Study

Religious Groups by Tradition

Area	Catholic	Evangelical Protestant	Mainline Protestant	Other Tradition	Black Protestant	Orthodox
MSA[1]	13.6	12.4	16.8	1.9	0.9	0.1
U.S.	19.1	16.2	7.3	4.3	1.6	0.3

Note: Figures are the number of adherents as a percentage of the total population; (1) Figures cover the Des Moines-West Des Moines, IA Metropolitan Statistical Area
Source: Association of Statisticians of American Religious Bodies, 2010 U.S. Religion Census: Religious Congregations & Membership Study

ECONOMY

Gross Metropolitan Product

Area	2017	2018	2019	2020	Rank[2]
MSA[1]	55.0	57.7	60.3	62.8	58

Note: Figures are in billions of dollars; (1) Figures cover the Des Moines-West Des Moines, IA Metropolitan Statistical Area; (2) Rank is based on 2018 data and ranges from 1 to 381
Source: U.S. Conference of Mayors, U.S. Metro Economies: GMP & Employment 2018-2020, September 2019

Economic Growth

Area	2015-17 (%)	2018 (%)	2019 (%)	2020 (%)	Rank[2]
MSA[1]	2.8	1.8	2.7	1.9	78
U.S.	1.9	2.9	2.3	2.1	—

Note: Figures are real gross metropolitan product (GMP) growth rates and represent average annual percent change; (1) Figures cover the Des Moines-West Des Moines, IA Metropolitan Statistical Area; (2) Rank is based on 2017 2-year average annual percent change and ranges from 1 to 381
Source: U.S. Conference of Mayors, U.S. Metro Economies: GMP & Employment 2018-2020, September 2019

Metropolitan Area Exports

Area	2014	2015	2016	2017	2018	2019	Rank[2]
MSA[1]	1,361.8	1,047.8	1,052.2	1,141.2	1,293.7	1,437.8	126

Note: Figures are in millions of dollars; (1) Figures cover the Des Moines-West Des Moines, IA Metropolitan Statistical Area; (2) Rank is based on 2019 data and ranges from 1 to 386
Source: U.S. Department of Commerce, International Trade Administration, Office of Trade and Economic Analysis, Industry and Analysis, Exports by Metropolitan Area, data extracted March 24, 2021

Building Permits

Area	Single-Family			Multi-Family			Total		
	2018	2019	Pct. Chg.	2018	2019	Pct. Chg.	2018	2019	Pct. Chg.
City	180	391	117.2	391	279	-28.6	571	670	17.3
MSA[1]	3,233	3,915	21.1	1,690	1,354	-19.9	4,923	5,269	7.0
U.S.	855,300	862,100	0.7	473,500	523,900	10.6	1,328,800	1,386,000	4.3

Note: (1) Figures cover the Des Moines-West Des Moines, IA Metropolitan Statistical Area; Figures represent new, privately-owned housing units authorized (unadjusted data); All permit data are based on estimates with imputation
Source: U.S. Census Bureau, Manufacturing, Mining, and Construction Statistics, Building Permits, 2018, 2019

Bankruptcy Filings

Area	Business Filings			Nonbusiness Filings		
	2019	2020	% Chg.	2019	2020	% Chg.
Polk County	28	12	-57.1	962	782	-18.7
U.S.	22,780	21,655	-4.9	752,160	522,808	-30.5

Note: Business filings include Chapter 7, Chapter 9, Chapter 11, Chapter 12, Chapter 13, Chapter 15, and Section 304; Nonbusiness filings include Chapter 7, Chapter 11, and Chapter 13
Source: Administrative Office of the U.S. Courts, Business and Nonbusiness Bankruptcy, County Cases Commenced by Chapter of the Bankruptcy Code, During the 12-Month Period Ending December 31, 2019 and Business and Nonbusiness Bankruptcy, County Cases Commenced by Chapter of the Bankruptcy Code, During the 12-Month Period Ending December 31, 2020

Housing Vacancy Rates

Area	Gross Vacancy Rate[2] (%)			Year-Round Vacancy Rate[3] (%)			Rental Vacancy Rate[4] (%)			Homeowner Vacancy Rate[5] (%)		
	2018	2019	2020	2018	2019	2020	2018	2019	2020	2018	2019	2020
MSA[1]	n/a	n/a	n/a	n/a	n/a	n/a	n/a	n/a	n/a	n/a	n/a	n/a
U.S.	12.3	12.0	10.6	9.7	9.5	8.2	6.9	6.7	6.3	1.5	1.4	1.0

Note: (1) Figures cover the Des Moines-West Des Moines, IA Metropolitan Statistical Area; (2) The percentage of the total housing inventory that is vacant; (3) The percentage of the housing inventory (excluding seasonal units) that is year-round vacant; (4) The percentage of rental inventory that is vacant for rent; (5) The percentage of homeowner inventory that is vacant for sale; n/a not available
Source: U.S. Census Bureau, Housing Vacancies and Homeownership Annual Statistics: 2018, 2019, 2020

INCOME

Income

Area	Per Capita ($)	Median Household ($)	Average Household ($)
City	28,554	53,525	69,074
MSA[1]	36,310	70,126	90,791
U.S.	34,103	62,843	88,607

Note: (1) Figures cover the Des Moines-West Des Moines, IA Metropolitan Statistical Area
Source: U.S. Census Bureau, 2015-2019 American Community Survey 5-Year Estimates

Household Income Distribution

Area	Percent of Households Earning							
	Under $15,000	$15,000 -$24,999	$25,000 -$34,999	$35,000 -$49,999	$50,000 -$74,999	$75,000 -$99,999	$100,000 -$149,999	$150,000 and up
City	12.0	10.6	10.2	14.2	19.9	13.7	12.4	7.1
MSA[1]	7.2	7.5	8.1	12.0	18.8	14.4	17.6	14.3
U.S.	10.3	8.9	8.9	12.3	17.2	12.7	15.1	14.5

Note: (1) Figures cover the Des Moines-West Des Moines, IA Metropolitan Statistical Area
Source: U.S. Census Bureau, 2015-2019 American Community Survey 5-Year Estimates

Des Moines, Iowa

Poverty Rate

Area	All Ages	Under 18 Years Old	18 to 64 Years Old	65 Years and Over
City	16.1	23.2	14.7	9.3
MSA[1]	9.3	11.6	9.0	6.3
U.S.	13.4	18.5	12.6	9.3

Note: Figures are percentage of people whose income during the past 12 months was below the poverty level;
(1) Figures cover the Des Moines-West Des Moines, IA Metropolitan Statistical Area
Source: U.S. Census Bureau, 2015-2019 American Community Survey 5-Year Estimates

CITY FINANCES

City Government Finances

Component	2017 ($000)	2017 ($ per capita)
Total Revenues	528,256	2,512
Total Expenditures	483,529	2,299
Debt Outstanding	561,365	2,669
Cash and Securities[1]	350,621	1,667

Note: (1) Cash and security holdings of a government at the close of its fiscal year,
including those of its dependent agencies, utilities, and liquor stores.
Source: U.S. Census Bureau, State & Local Government Finances 2017

City Government Revenue by Source

Source	2017 ($000)	2017 ($ per capita)	2017 (%)
General Revenue			
From Federal Government	46,747	222	8.8
From State Government	37,771	180	7.2
From Local Governments	11,529	55	2.2
Taxes			
Property	143,562	683	27.2
Sales and Gross Receipts	34,489	164	6.5
Personal Income	0	0	0.0
Corporate Income	0	0	0.0
Motor Vehicle License	0	0	0.0
Other Taxes	5,268	25	1.0
Current Charges	144,447	687	27.3
Liquor Store	0	0	0.0
Utility	59,915	285	11.3
Employee Retirement	4,666	22	0.9

Source: U.S. Census Bureau, State & Local Government Finances 2017

City Government Expenditures by Function

Function	2017 ($000)	2017 ($ per capita)	2017 (%)
General Direct Expenditures			
Air Transportation	35,144	167	7.3
Corrections	0	0	0.0
Education	0	0	0.0
Employment Security Administration	0	0	0.0
Financial Administration	3,428	16	0.7
Fire Protection	38,164	181	7.9
General Public Buildings	4,647	22	1.0
Governmental Administration, Other	3,223	15	0.7
Health	1,028	4	0.2
Highways	29,025	138	6.0
Hospitals	0	0	0.0
Housing and Community Development	19,989	95	4.1
Interest on General Debt	22,584	107	4.7
Judicial and Legal	1,821	8	0.4
Libraries	8,645	41	1.8
Parking	8,471	40	1.8
Parks and Recreation	10,271	48	2.1
Police Protection	64,042	304	13.2
Public Welfare	9,089	43	1.9
Sewerage	45,739	217	9.5
Solid Waste Management	11,691	55	2.4
Veterans' Services	0	0	0.0
Liquor Store	0	0	0.0
Utility	68,905	327	14.3
Employee Retirement	3,322	15	0.7

Source: U.S. Census Bureau, State & Local Government Finances 2017

Des Moines, Iowa 113

EMPLOYMENT

Labor Force and Employment

Area	Civilian Labor Force			Workers Employed		
	Dec. 2019	Dec. 2020	% Chg.	Dec. 2019	Dec. 2020	% Chg.
City	115,631	106,451	-7.9	111,652	101,736	-8.9
MSA[1]	366,728	336,296	-8.3	356,630	324,997	-8.9
U.S.	164,007,000	160,017,000	-2.4	158,504,000	149,613,000	-5.6

Note: Data is not seasonally adjusted and covers workers 16 years of age and older; (1) Figures cover the Des Moines-West Des Moines, IA Metropolitan Statistical Area
Source: Bureau of Labor Statistics, Local Area Unemployment Statistics

Unemployment Rate

Area	2020											
	Jan.	Feb.	Mar.	Apr.	May	Jun.	Jul.	Aug.	Sep.	Oct.	Nov.	Dec.
City	4.6	4.0	4.4	14.6	14.0	12.2	9.5	9.1	6.6	4.6	4.5	4.4
MSA[1]	3.5	3.0	3.4	11.8	10.9	9.2	7.2	6.7	4.8	3.3	3.5	3.4
U.S.	4.0	3.8	4.5	14.4	13.0	11.2	10.5	8.5	7.7	6.6	6.4	6.5

Note: Data is not seasonally adjusted and covers workers 16 years of age and older; (1) Figures cover the Des Moines-West Des Moines, IA Metropolitan Statistical Area
Source: Bureau of Labor Statistics, Local Area Unemployment Statistics

Average Wages

Occupation	$/Hr.	Occupation	$/Hr.
Accountants and Auditors	37.00	Maintenance and Repair Workers	21.30
Automotive Mechanics	24.10	Marketing Managers	64.30
Bookkeepers	22.00	Network and Computer Systems Admin.	41.00
Carpenters	22.20	Nurses, Licensed Practical	23.40
Cashiers	11.90	Nurses, Registered	30.80
Computer Programmers	35.50	Nursing Assistants	15.70
Computer Systems Analysts	42.70	Office Clerks, General	19.90
Computer User Support Specialists	26.50	Physical Therapists	42.00
Construction Laborers	18.80	Physicians	118.90
Cooks, Restaurant	14.40	Plumbers, Pipefitters and Steamfitters	25.90
Customer Service Representatives	21.10	Police and Sheriff's Patrol Officers	33.60
Dentists	90.70	Postal Service Mail Carriers	25.40
Electricians	24.80	Real Estate Sales Agents	24.90
Engineers, Electrical	40.40	Retail Salespersons	13.90
Fast Food and Counter Workers	11.00	Sales Representatives, Technical/Scientific	48.50
Financial Managers	66.80	Secretaries, Exc. Legal/Medical/Executive	21.70
First-Line Supervisors of Office Workers	31.30	Security Guards	16.80
General and Operations Managers	53.20	Surgeons	n/a
Hairdressers/Cosmetologists	15.30	Teacher Assistants, Exc. Postsecondary*	13.70
Home Health and Personal Care Aides	14.10	Teachers, Secondary School, Exc. Sp. Ed.*	29.70
Janitors and Cleaners	13.40	Telemarketers	14.90
Landscaping/Groundskeeping Workers	17.10	Truck Drivers, Heavy/Tractor-Trailer	24.10
Lawyers	63.10	Truck Drivers, Light/Delivery Services	16.90
Maids and Housekeeping Cleaners	12.50	Waiters and Waitresses	10.60

Note: Wage data covers the Des Moines-West Des Moines, IA Metropolitan Statistical Area; (*) Hourly wages were calculated from annual wage data based on a 40 hour work week; n/a not available.
Source: Bureau of Labor Statistics, Metro Area Occupational Employment & Wage Estimates, May 2020

Employment by Industry

Sector	MSA[1]		U.S.
	Number of Employees	Percent of Total	Percent of Total
Construction, Mining, and Logging	21,100	5.8	5.5
Education and Health Services	50,500	14.0	16.3
Financial Activities	57,500	15.9	6.1
Government	45,800	12.7	15.2
Information	6,100	1.7	1.9
Leisure and Hospitality	28,300	7.8	9.0
Manufacturing	20,600	5.7	8.5
Other Services	12,700	3.5	3.8
Professional and Business Services	49,600	13.7	14.4
Retail Trade	39,600	10.9	10.9
Transportation, Warehousing, and Utilities	12,400	3.4	4.6
Wholesale Trade	17,800	4.9	3.9

Note: Figures are non-farm employment as of December 2020. Figures are not seasonally adjusted and include workers 16 years of age and older; (1) Figures cover the Des Moines-West Des Moines, IA Metropolitan Statistical Area
Source: Bureau of Labor Statistics, Current Employment Statistics, Employment, Hours, and Earnings

Employment by Occupation

Occupation Classification	City (%)	MSA[1] (%)	U.S. (%)
Management, Business, Science, and Arts	32.5	41.9	38.5
Natural Resources, Construction, and Maintenance	8.5	8.0	8.9
Production, Transportation, and Material Moving	15.6	12.1	13.2
Sales and Office	23.2	22.5	21.6
Service	20.2	15.5	17.8

Note: Figures cover employed civilians 16 years of age and older; (1) Figures cover the Des Moines-West Des Moines, IA Metropolitan Statistical Area
Source: U.S. Census Bureau, 2015-2019 American Community Survey 5-Year Estimates

Occupations with Greatest Projected Employment Growth: 2020 – 2022

Occupation[1]	2020 Employment	2022 Projected Employment	Numeric Employment Change	Percent Employment Change
Fast Food and Counter Workers	31,160	41,700	10,540	33.8
Waiters and Waitresses	16,720	24,050	7,330	43.8
Retail Salespersons	36,650	42,840	6,190	16.9
Cooks, Restaurant	9,170	13,630	4,460	48.6
Maids and Housekeeping Cleaners	9,970	13,650	3,680	36.9
Bartenders	7,430	10,480	3,050	41.0
First-Line Supervisors of Food Preparation and Serving Workers	8,150	11,090	2,940	36.1
Janitors and Cleaners, Except Maids and Housekeeping Cleaners	25,060	27,650	2,590	10.3
Laborers and Freight, Stock, and Material Movers, Hand	29,980	32,090	2,110	7.0
Childcare Workers	12,040	14,050	2,010	16.7

Note: Projections cover Iowa; (1) Sorted by numeric employment change
Source: www.projectionscentral.com, State Occupational Projections, 2020–2022 Short-Term Projections

Fastest-Growing Occupations: 2020 – 2022

Occupation[1]	2020 Employment	2022 Projected Employment	Numeric Employment Change	Percent Employment Change
Personal Care Aides	90	280	190	211.1
Actors	100	240	140	140.0
Motion Picture Projectionists	60	130	70	116.7
Ushers, Lobby Attendants, and Ticket Takers	670	1,420	750	111.9
Public Address System and Other Announcers	80	150	70	87.5
Gaming Cage Workers	180	330	150	83.3
Hotel, Motel, and Resort Desk Clerks	2,270	4,090	1,820	80.2
Gaming Change Persons and Booth Cashiers	250	450	200	80.0
Gaming Dealers	990	1,770	780	78.8
Gaming Surveillance Officers and Gaming Investigators	130	230	100	76.9

Note: Projections cover Iowa; (1) Sorted by percent employment change and excludes occupations with numeric employment change less than 50
Source: www.projectionscentral.com, State Occupational Projections, 2020–2022 Short-Term Projections

TAXES

State Corporate Income Tax Rates

State	Tax Rate (%)	Income Brackets ($)	Num. of Brackets	Financial Institution Tax Rate (%)[a]	Federal Income Tax Ded.
Iowa	5.5 - 9.8	100,000 - 250,001	3	5.0	Yes (j)

Note: Tax rates as of January 1, 2021; (a) Rates listed are the corporate income tax rate applied to financial institutions or excise taxes based on income. Some states have other taxes based upon the value of deposits or shares; (j) 50% of the federal income tax is deductible.
Source: Federation of Tax Administrators, State Corporate Income Tax Rates, January 1, 2021

State Individual Income Tax Rates

State	Tax Rate (%)	Income Brackets ($)	Personal Exemptions ($)			Standard Ded. ($)	
			Single	Married	Depend.	Single	Married
Iowa (a)	0.33 - 8.53	1,676 - 74,970	40 (c)	80 (c)	40 (c)	2,130	5,250 (a)

Note: Tax rates as of January 1, 2021; Local- and county-level taxes are not included; Federal income tax is deductible on state income tax returns; (a) 19 states have statutory provision for automatically adjusting to the rate of inflation the dollar values of the income tax brackets, standard deductions, and/or personal exemptions. Michigan indexes the personal exemption only. Oregon does not index the income brackets for $125,000 and over; (c) The personal exemption takes the form of a tax credit instead of a deduction
Source: Federation of Tax Administrators, State Individual Income Tax Rates, January 1, 2021

Various State Sales and Excise Tax Rates

State	State Sales Tax (%)	Gasoline[1] (¢/gal.)	Cigarette[2] ($/pack)	Spirits[3] ($/gal.)	Wine[4] ($/gal.)	Beer[5] ($/gal.)	Recreational Marijuana (%)
Iowa	6	30	1.36	13.03	1.75	0.19	Not legal

Note: All tax rates as of January 1, 2021; (1) The American Petroleum Institute has developed a methodology for determining the average tax rate on a gallon of fuel. Rates may include any of the following: excise taxes, environmental fees, storage tank fees, other fees or taxes, general sales tax, and local taxes; (2) The federal excise tax of $1.0066 per pack and local taxes are not included; (3) Rates are those applicable to off-premise sales of 40% alcohol by volume (a.b.v.) distilled spirits in 750ml containers. Local excise taxes are excluded; (4) Rates are those applicable to off-premise sales of 11% a.b.v. non-carbonated wine in 750ml containers; (5) Rates are those applicable to off-premise sales of 4.7% a.b.v. beer in 12 ounce containers.
Source: Tax Foundation, 2021 Facts & Figures: How Does Your State Compare?

State Business Tax Climate Index Rankings

State	Overall Rank	Corporate Tax Rank	Individual Income Tax Rank	Sales Tax Rank	Property Tax Rank	Unemployment Insurance Tax Rank
Iowa	40	46	40	14	38	37

Note: The index is a measure of how each state's tax laws affect economic performance. The lower the rank, the more favorable a state's tax system is for business. States without a given tax are given a ranking of 1. The scores/rankings for the District of Columbia do not affect other states. The 2021 index represents the tax climate as of July 1, 2020.
Source: Tax Foundation, State Business Tax Climate Index 2021

TRANSPORTATION

Means of Transportation to Work

Area	Car/Truck/Van		Public Transportation			Bicycle	Walked	Other Means	Worked at Home
	Drove Alone	Car-pooled	Bus	Subway	Railroad				
City	80.1	9.7	2.2	0.1	0.0	0.4	2.9	1.2	3.5
MSA[1]	83.6	7.8	1.1	0.0	0.0	0.2	1.8	0.8	4.6
U.S.	76.3	9.0	2.4	1.9	0.6	0.5	2.7	1.4	5.2

Note: Figures are percentages and cover workers 16 years of age and older; (1) Figures cover the Des Moines-West Des Moines, IA Metropolitan Statistical Area
Source: U.S. Census Bureau, 2015-2019 American Community Survey 5-Year Estimates

Travel Time to Work

Area	Less Than 10 Minutes	10 to 19 Minutes	20 to 29 Minutes	30 to 44 Minutes	45 to 59 Minutes	60 to 89 Minutes	90 Minutes or More
City	13.0	43.8	27.2	11.9	1.9	1.1	1.0
MSA[1]	15.2	35.2	27.3	16.3	3.4	1.5	1.1
U.S.	12.2	28.4	20.8	20.8	8.3	6.4	2.9

Note: Note: Figures are percentages and include workers 16 years old and over; (1) Figures cover the Des Moines-West Des Moines, IA Metropolitan Statistical Area
Source: U.S. Census Bureau, 2015-2019 American Community Survey 5-Year Estimates

Key Congestion Measures

Measure	1982	1992	2002	2012	2017
Annual Hours of Delay, Total (000)	n/a	n/a	n/a	n/a	8,998
Annual Hours of Delay, Per Auto Commuter	n/a	n/a	n/a	n/a	18
Annual Congestion Cost, Total (million $)	n/a	n/a	n/a	n/a	184
Annual Congestion Cost, Per Auto Commuter ($)	n/a	n/a	n/a	n/a	371

Note: n/a not available
Source: Texas A&M Transportation Institute, 2019 Urban Mobility Report

Freeway Travel Time Index

Measure	1982	1987	1992	1997	2002	2007	2012	2017
Urban Area Index[1]	n/a	n/a	n/a	n/a	n/a	n/a	n/a	1.08
Urban Area Rank[1,2]	n/a	n/a	n/a	n/a	n/a	n/a	n/a	n/a

Note: Freeway Travel Time Index—the ratio of travel time in the peak period to the travel time at free-flow conditions. For example, a value of 1.30 indicates a 20-minute free-flow trip takes 26 minutes in the peak (20 minutes x 1.30 = 26 minutes); (1) Covers the Des Moines IA urban area; (2) Rank is based on 101 larger urban areas (#1 = highest travel time index); n/a not available
Source: Texas A&M Transportation Institute, 2019 Urban Mobility Report

Public Transportation

Agency Name / Mode of Transportation	Vehicles Operated in Maximum Service[1]	Annual Unlinked Passenger Trips[2] (in thous.)	Annual Passenger Miles[3] (in thous.)
Des Moines Metropolitan Transit Authority (MTA)			
Bus (directly operated)	110	4,065.6	17,040.7
Demand Response (directly operated)	21	97.9	823.2
Demand Response Taxi (purchased transportation)	2	7.9	70.8
Vanpool (directly operated)	97	223.9	8,467.3

Note: (1) Number of revenue vehicles operated by the given mode and type of service to meet the annual maximum service requirement. This is the revenue vehicle count during the peak season of the year; on the week and day that maximum service is provided. Vehicles operated in maximum service (VOMS) exclude atypical days and one-time special events; (2) Number of passengers who boarded public transportation vehicles. Passengers are counted each time they board a vehicle no matter how many vehicles they use to travel from their origin to their destination. (3) Sum of the distances ridden by all passengers during the entire fiscal year.
Source: Federal Transit Administration, National Transit Database, 2019

Air Transportation

Airport Name and Code / Type of Service	Passenger Airlines[1]	Passenger Enplanements	Freight Carriers[2]	Freight (lbs)
Des Moines International (DSM)				
Domestic service (U.S. carriers - 2020)	21	635,075	8	34,914,091
International service (U.S. carriers - 2019)	3	373	0	0

Note: (1) Includes all U.S.-based major, minor and commuter airlines that carried at least one passenger during the year; (2) Includes all U.S.-based airlines and freight carriers that transported at least one pound of freight during the year.
Source: Bureau of Transportation Statistics, The Intermodal Transportation Database, Air Carriers: T-100 Domestic Market (U.S. Carriers), 2020; Bureau of Transportation Statistics, The Intermodal Transportation Database, Air Carriers: T-100 International Market (U.S. Carriers), 2019

BUSINESSES

Major Business Headquarters

Company Name	Industry	Rankings	
		Fortune[1]	Forbes[2]
Principal Financial	Insurance, Life, Health (Stock)	201	-

Note: (1) Companies that produce a 10-K are ranked 1 to 500 based on 2019 revenue; (2) All private companies with at least $2 billion in annual revenue through the end of their most current fiscal year are ranked 1 to 219; companies listed are headquartered in the city; dashes indicate no ranking
Source: Fortune, "Fortune 500," June/July 2020; Forbes, "America's Largest Private Companies," 2020

Minority Business Opportunity

Des Moines is home to one company which is on the *Black Enterprise* Industrial/Service list (100 largest companies based on gross sales): **Keystone Electrical Manufacturing Co.** (#73). Criteria: operational in previous calendar year; at least 51% black-owned and manufactures/owns the product it sells or provides industrial or consumer services. Brokerages, real estate firms and firms that provide professional services are not eligible. *Black Enterprise, B.E. 100s, 2019*

Living Environment

COST OF LIVING

Cost of Living Index

Composite Index	Groceries	Housing	Utilities	Trans-portation	Health Care	Misc. Goods/ Services
88.1	93.5	73.7	88.5	98.4	92.1	94.1

Note: The Cost of Living Index measures regional differences in the cost of consumer goods and services, excluding taxes and non-consumer expenditures, for professional and managerial households in the top income quintile. It is based on more than 50,000 prices covering almost 60 different items for which prices are collected three times a year by chambers of commerce, economic development organizations or university applied economic centers in each participating urban area. The numbers shown should be read as a percentage above or below the national average of 100. For example, a value of 115.4 in the groceries column indicates that grocery prices are 15.4% higher than the national average. Small differences in the index numbers should not be interpreted as significant; Figures cover the Des Moines IA urban area.
Source: The Council for Community and Economic Research, Cost of Living Index, 2020

Grocery Prices

Area[1]	T-Bone Steak ($/pound)	Frying Chicken ($/pound)	Whole Milk ($/half gal.)	Eggs ($/dozen)	Orange Juice ($/64 oz.)	Coffee ($/11.5 oz.)
City[2]	12.05	1.51	2.18	1.34	3.05	4.24
Avg.	11.78	1.39	2.05	1.47	3.57	4.34
Min.	8.03	0.94	1.03	0.74	2.94	3.02
Max.	15.86	2.65	4.31	3.77	5.44	8.69

Note: (1) Values for the local area are compared with the average, minimum and maximum values for all 284 areas in the Cost of Living Index; (2) Figures cover the Des Moines IA urban area; T-Bone Steak (price per pound); Frying Chicken (price per pound, whole fryer); Whole Milk (half gallon carton); Eggs (price per dozen, Grade A, large); Orange Juice (64 oz. Tropicana or Florida Natural); Coffee (11.5 oz. can, vacuum-packed, Maxwell House, Hills Bros, or Folgers).
Source: The Council for Community and Economic Research, Cost of Living Index, 2020

Housing and Utility Costs

Area[1]	New Home Price ($)	Apartment Rent ($/month)	All Electric ($/month)	Part Electric ($/month)	Other Energy ($/month)	Telephone ($/month)
City[2]	300,464	712	-	79.70	55.44	180.80
Avg.	368,594	1,168	170.86	100.47	65.28	184.30
Min.	190,567	502	91.58	31.42	26.08	169.60
Max.	2,227,806	4,738	470.38	280.31	280.06	206.50

Note: (1) Values for the local area are compared with the average, minimum and maximum values for all 284 areas in the Cost of Living Index; (2) Figures cover the Des Moines IA urban area; New Home Price (2,400 sf living area, 8,000 sf lot, in urban area with full utilities); Apartment Rent (950 sf 2 bedroom/1.5 or 2 bath, unfurnished, excluding all utilities except water); All Electric (average monthly cost for an all-electric home); Part Electric (average monthly cost for a part-electric home); Other Energy (average monthly cost for natural gas, fuel oil, coal, wood, and any other forms of energy except electricity); Telephone (price includes the base monthly rate plus taxes and fees for three lines of mobile phone service).
Source: The Council for Community and Economic Research, Cost of Living Index, 2020

Health Care, Transportation, and Other Costs

Area[1]	Doctor ($/visit)	Dentist ($/visit)	Optometrist ($/visit)	Gasoline ($/gallon)	Beauty Salon ($/visit)	Men's Shirt ($)
City[2]	110.85	82.19	108.45	2.17	32.13	15.16
Avg.	115.44	99.32	108.10	2.21	39.27	31.37
Min.	36.68	59.00	51.36	1.71	19.00	11.00
Max.	219.00	153.10	250.97	3.46	82.05	58.33

Note: (1) Values for the local area are compared with the average, minimum and maximum values for all 284 areas in the Cost of Living Index; (2) Figures cover the Des Moines IA urban area; Doctor (general practitioners routine exam of an established patient); Dentist (adult teeth cleaning and periodic oral examination); Optometrist (full vision eye exam for established adult patient); Gasoline (one gallon regular unleaded, national brand, including all taxes, cash price at self-service pump if available); Beauty Salon (woman's shampoo, trim, and blow-dry); Men's Shirt (cotton/polyester dress shirt, pinpoint weave, long sleeves).
Source: The Council for Community and Economic Research, Cost of Living Index, 2020

HOUSING

Homeownership Rate

Area	2012 (%)	2013 (%)	2014 (%)	2015 (%)	2016 (%)	2017 (%)	2018 (%)	2019 (%)	2020 (%)
MSA[1]	n/a	n/a	n/a	n/a	n/a	n/a	n/a	n/a	n/a
U.S.	65.4	65.1	64.5	63.7	63.4	63.9	64.4	64.6	66.6

Note: (1) Figures cover the Des Moines-West Des Moines, IA Metropolitan Statistical Area; n/a not available
Source: U.S. Census Bureau, Housing Vacancies and Homeownership Annual Statistics: 2012-2020

Des Moines, Iowa

House Price Index (HPI)

Area	National Ranking[2]	Quarterly Change (%)	One-Year Change (%)	Five-Year Change (%)	Since 1991Q1 (%)
MSA[1]	237	1.39	3.15	20.11	154.39
U.S.[3]	–	3.81	10.77	38.99	205.12

Note: The HPI is a weighted repeat sales index. It measures average price changes in repeat sales or refinancings on the same properties. This information is obtained by reviewing repeat mortgage transactions on single-family properties whose mortgages have been purchased or securitized by Fannie Mae or Freddie Mac since January 1975; (1) Figures cover the Des Moines-West Des Moines, IA Metropolitan Statistical Area; (2) Rankings are based on annual percentage change for all metro areas containing at least 15,000 transactions over the last 10 years and ranges from 1 to 253; (3) figures based on a weighted average of Census Division estimates using a seasonally adjusted, purchase-only index; all figures are for the period ending December 31, 2020
Source: Federal Housing Finance Agency, Change in Metropolitan Area House Price Indexes, April 7, 2021

Median Single-Family Home Prices

Area	2018	2019	2020[p]	Percent Change 2019 to 2020
MSA[1]	204.8	214.5	229.6	7.0
U.S. Average	261.6	274.6	299.9	9.2

Note: Figures are median sales prices of existing single-family homes in thousands of dollars; (p) preliminary; (1) Figures cover the Des Moines-West Des Moines, IA Metropolitan Statistical Area
Source: National Association of Realtors, Median Sales Price of Existing Single-Family Homes for Metropolitan Areas, 4th Quarter 2020

Qualifying Income Based on Median Sales Price of Existing Single-Family Homes

Area	With 5% Down ($)	With 10% Down ($)	With 20% Down ($)
MSA[1]	44,770	42,414	37,701
U.S. Average	59,266	56,147	49,908

Note: Figures are preliminary; Qualifying income is based on a mortgage rate of 2.81%. Monthly principal and interest payment is limited to 25% of income; (1) Figures cover the Des Moines-West Des Moines, IA Metropolitan Statistical Area
Source: National Association of Realtors, Qualifying Income Based on Median Sales Price of Existing Single-Family Homes for Metropolitan Areas, 4th Quarter 2020

Home Value Distribution

Area	Under $50,000	$50,000 -$99,999	$100,000 -$149,999	$150,000 -$199,999	$200,000 -$299,999	$300,000 -$499,999	$500,000 -$999,999	$1,000,000 or more
City	5.9	21.6	33.1	20.5	12.1	4.8	1.8	0.2
MSA[1]	4.5	11.9	19.7	19.9	24.4	14.9	4.2	0.5
U.S.	6.9	12.0	13.3	14.0	19.6	19.3	11.4	3.4

Note: Figures are percentages and cover owner-occupied housing units; (1) Figures cover the Des Moines-West Des Moines, IA Metropolitan Statistical Area
Source: U.S. Census Bureau, 2015-2019 American Community Survey 5-Year Estimates

Year Housing Structure Built

Area	2010 or Later	2000 -2009	1990 -1999	1980 -1989	1970 -1979	1960 -1969	1950 -1959	1940 -1949	Before 1940	Median Year
City	3.2	7.3	6.5	6.4	13.4	10.5	15.2	8.2	29.3	1958
MSA[1]	10.4	16.7	12.6	8.7	13.6	8.6	9.1	4.2	16.1	1979
U.S.	5.2	14.0	13.9	13.4	15.2	10.6	10.3	4.9	12.6	1978

Note: Figures are percentages except for Median Year; Note: (1) Figures cover the Des Moines-West Des Moines, IA Metropolitan Statistical Area
Source: U.S. Census Bureau, 2015-2019 American Community Survey 5-Year Estimates

Gross Monthly Rent

Area	Under $500	$500 -$999	$1,000 -$1,499	$1,500 -$1,999	$2,000 -$2,499	$2,500 -$2,999	$3,000 and up	Median ($)
City	8.6	61.1	25.1	4.1	0.9	0.2	0.1	855
MSA[1]	7.3	54.0	30.1	6.2	1.3	0.2	0.7	904
U.S.	9.4	36.2	30.0	14.0	5.6	2.4	2.4	1,062

Note: Figures are percentages except for Median; Gross rent is the contract rent plus the estimated average monthly cost of utilities (electricity, gas, and water and sewer) and fuels (oil, coal, kerosene, wood, etc.) if these are paid by the renter (or paid for the renter by someone else); (1) Figures cover the Des Moines-West Des Moines, IA Metropolitan Statistical Area
Source: U.S. Census Bureau, 2015-2019 American Community Survey 5-Year Estimates

HEALTH

Health Risk Factors

Category	MSA[1] (%)	U.S. (%)
Adults aged 18–64 who have any kind of health care coverage	91.6	87.3
Adults who reported being in good or better health	86.3	82.4
Adults who have been told they have high blood cholesterol	33.4	33.0
Adults who have been told they have high blood pressure	29.4	32.3
Adults who are current smokers	14.4	17.1
Adults who currently use E-cigarettes	5.5	4.6
Adults who currently use chewing tobacco, snuff, or snus	4.0	4.0
Adults who are heavy drinkers[2]	7.2	6.3
Adults who are binge drinkers[3]	21.5	17.4
Adults who are overweight (BMI 25.0 - 29.9)	34.4	35.3
Adults who are obese (BMI 30.0 - 99.8)	34.4	31.3
Adults who participated in any physical activities in the past month	79.4	74.4
Adults who always or nearly always wears a seat belt	95.6	94.3

Note: (1) Figures cover the Des Moines-West Des Moines, IA Metropolitan Statistical Area; (2) Heavy drinkers are classified as adult men having more than 14 drinks per week and adult women having more than 7 drinks per week; (3) Binge drinkers are classified as males having five or more drinks on one occasion or females having four or more drinks on one occasion
Source: Centers for Disease Control and Prevention, Behaviorial Risk Factor Surveillance System, SMART: Selected Metropolitan Area Risk Trends, 2017

Acute and Chronic Health Conditions

Category	MSA[1] (%)	U.S. (%)
Adults who have ever been told they had a heart attack	3.4	4.2
Adults who have ever been told they have angina or coronary heart disease	2.9	3.9
Adults who have ever been told they had a stroke	2.9	3.0
Adults who have ever been told they have asthma	12.9	14.2
Adults who have ever been told they have arthritis	22.8	24.9
Adults who have ever been told they have diabetes[2]	8.4	10.5
Adults who have ever been told they had skin cancer	6.3	6.2
Adults who have ever been told they had any other types of cancer	5.0	7.1
Adults who have ever been told they have COPD	5.6	6.5
Adults who have ever been told they have kidney disease	1.9	3.0
Adults who have ever been told they have a form of depression	20.1	20.5

Note: (1) Figures cover the Des Moines-West Des Moines, IA Metropolitan Statistical Area; (2) Figures do not include pregnancy-related, borderline, or pre-diabetes
Source: Centers for Disease Control and Prevention, Behaviorial Risk Factor Surveillance System, SMART: Selected Metropolitan Area Risk Trends, 2017

Health Screening and Vaccination Rates

Category	MSA[1] (%)	U.S. (%)
Adults aged 65+ who have had flu shot within the past year	70.6	60.7
Adults aged 65+ who have ever had a pneumonia vaccination	83.0	75.4
Adults who have ever been tested for HIV	34.1	36.1
Adults who have ever had the shingles or zoster vaccine?	38.4	28.9
Adults who have had their blood cholesterol checked within the last five years	85.6	85.9

Note: n/a not available; (1) Figures cover the Des Moines-West Des Moines, IA Metropolitan Statistical Area.
Source: Centers for Disease Control and Prevention, Behaviorial Risk Factor Surveillance System, SMART: Selected Metropolitan Area Risk Trends, 2017

Disability Status

Category	MSA[1] (%)	U.S. (%)
Adults who reported being deaf	5.4	6.7
Are you blind or have serious difficulty seeing, even when wearing glasses?	3.7	4.5
Are you limited in any way in any of your usual activities due of arthritis?	10.5	12.9
Do you have difficulty doing errands alone?	6.2	6.8
Do you have difficulty dressing or bathing?	2.5	3.6
Do you have serious difficulty concentrating/remembering/making decisions?	9.1	10.7
Do you have serious difficulty walking or climbing stairs?	10.1	13.6

Note: (1) Figures cover the Des Moines-West Des Moines, IA Metropolitan Statistical Area.
Source: Centers for Disease Control and Prevention, Behaviorial Risk Factor Surveillance System, SMART: Selected Metropolitan Area Risk Trends, 2017

Mortality Rates for the Top 10 Causes of Death in the U.S.

ICD-10[a] Sub-Chapter	ICD-10[a] Code	Age-Adjusted Mortality Rate[1] per 100,000 population	
		County[2]	U.S.
Malignant neoplasms	C00-C97	158.6	149.2
Ischaemic heart diseases	I20-I25	93.8	90.5
Other forms of heart disease	I30-I51	46.0	52.2
Chronic lower respiratory diseases	J40-J47	46.4	39.6
Other degenerative diseases of the nervous system	G30-G31	42.5	37.6
Cerebrovascular diseases	I60-I69	31.6	37.2
Other external causes of accidental injury	W00-X59	42.1	36.1
Organic, including symptomatic, mental disorders	F01-F09	34.3	29.4
Hypertensive diseases	I10-I15	21.9	24.1
Diabetes mellitus	E10-E14	20.4	21.5

Note: (a) ICD-10 = International Classification of Diseases 10th Revision; (1) Mortality rates are a three-year average covering 2017-2019; (2) Figures cover Polk County.
Source: Centers for Disease Control and Prevention, National Center for Health Statistics. Underlying Cause of Death 1999-2019 on CDC WONDER Online Database

Mortality Rates for Selected Causes of Death

ICD-10[a] Sub-Chapter	ICD-10[a] Code	Age-Adjusted Mortality Rate[1] per 100,000 population	
		County[2]	U.S.
Assault	X85-Y09	4.2	6.0
Diseases of the liver	K70-K76	14.2	14.4
Human immunodeficiency virus (HIV) disease	B20-B24	Unreliable	1.5
Influenza and pneumonia	J09-J18	12.2	13.8
Intentional self-harm	X60-X84	15.0	14.1
Malnutrition	E40-E46	4.2	2.3
Obesity and other hyperalimentation	E65-E68	1.6	2.1
Renal failure	N17-N19	7.0	12.6
Transport accidents	V01-V99	7.1	12.3
Viral hepatitis	B15-B19	Unreliable	1.2

Note: (a) ICD-10 = International Classification of Diseases 10th Revision; (1) Mortality rates are a three-year average covering 2017-2019; (2) Figures cover Polk County; Data are suppressed when the data meet the criteria for confidentiality constraints; Mortality rates are flagged as unreliable when the rate would be calculated with a numerator of 20 or less.
Source: Centers for Disease Control and Prevention, National Center for Health Statistics. Underlying Cause of Death 1999-2019 on CDC WONDER Online Database

Health Insurance Coverage

Area	With Health Insurance	With Private Health Insurance	With Public Health Insurance	Without Health Insurance	Population Under Age 19 Without Health Insurance
City	93.1	64.7	41.0	6.9	3.5
MSA[1]	95.6	77.4	31.2	4.4	2.2
U.S.	91.2	67.9	35.1	8.8	5.1

Note: Figures are percentages that cover the civilian noninstitutionalized population; (1) Figures cover the Des Moines-West Des Moines, IA Metropolitan Statistical Area
Source: U.S. Census Bureau, 2015-2019 American Community Survey 5-Year Estimates

Number of Medical Professionals

Area	MDs[3]	DOs[3,4]	Dentists	Podiatrists	Chiropractors	Optometrists
County[1] (number)	1,036	470	362	53	271	103
County[1] (rate[2])	213.2	96.7	73.9	10.8	55.3	21.0
U.S. (rate[2])	282.9	22.7	71.2	6.2	28.1	16.9

19153
Note: Data as of 2019 unless noted; (1) Data covers Polk County; (2) Rate per 100,000 population; (3) Data as of 2018 and includes all active, non-federal physicians; (4) Doctor of Osteopathic Medicine
Source: U.S. Department of Health and Human Services, Health Resources and Services Administration, Bureau of Health Professions, Area Resource File (ARF) 2019-2020

EDUCATION

Public School District Statistics

District Name	Schls	Pupils	Pupil/ Teacher Ratio	Minority Pupils[1] (%)	Free Lunch Eligible[2] (%)	IEP[3] (%)
Des Moines Independent CSD	60	33,623	14.6	62.2	67.9	16.8

Note: Table includes school districts with 2,000 or more students; (1) Percentage of students that are not non-Hispanic white; (2) Percentage of students that are eligible for the free lunch program; (3) Percentage of students that have an Individualized Education Program.
Source: U.S. Department of Education, National Center for Education Statistics, Common Core of Data, Local Education Agency (School District) Universe Survey: School Year 2018-2019; U.S. Department of Education, National Center for Education Statistics, Common Core of Data, Public Elementary/Secondary School Universe Survey: School Year 2018-2019

Highest Level of Education

Area	Less than H.S.	H.S. Diploma	Some College, No Deg.	Associate Degree	Bachelor's Degree	Master's Degree	Prof. School Degree	Doctorate Degree
City	13.7	29.5	21.2	8.9	18.6	5.5	1.7	0.9
MSA[1]	7.5	25.6	20.2	10.3	25.4	7.7	2.2	1.1
U.S.	12.0	27.0	20.4	8.5	19.8	8.8	2.1	1.4

Note: Figures cover persons age 25 and over; (1) Figures cover the Des Moines-West Des Moines, IA Metropolitan Statistical Area
Source: U.S. Census Bureau, 2015-2019 American Community Survey 5-Year Estimates

Educational Attainment by Race

Area	High School Graduate or Higher (%)					Bachelor's Degree or Higher (%)				
	Total	White	Black	Asian	Hisp.[2]	Total	White	Black	Asian	Hisp.[2]
City	86.3	89.7	81.3	60.8	57.2	26.7	29.2	13.6	20.3	9.0
MSA[1]	92.5	94.2	84.6	74.1	62.8	36.5	37.6	19.8	38.7	13.6
U.S.	88.0	89.9	86.0	87.1	68.7	32.1	33.5	21.6	54.3	16.4

Note: Figures shown cover persons 25 years old and over; (1) Figures cover the Des Moines-West Des Moines, IA Metropolitan Statistical Area; (2) People of Hispanic origin can be of any race
Source: U.S. Census Bureau, 2015-2019 American Community Survey 5-Year Estimates

School Enrollment by Grade and Control

Area	Preschool (%)		Kindergarten (%)		Grades 1 - 4 (%)		Grades 5 - 8 (%)		Grades 9 - 12 (%)	
	Public	Private	Public	Private	Public	Private	Public	Private	Public	Private
City	73.0	27.0	90.0	10.0	89.0	11.0	91.7	8.3	92.3	7.7
MSA[1]	65.6	34.4	87.6	12.4	91.6	8.4	91.3	8.7	92.1	7.9
U.S.	59.1	40.9	87.6	12.4	89.5	10.5	89.4	10.6	90.1	9.9

Note: Figures shown cover persons 3 years old and over; (1) Figures cover the Des Moines-West Des Moines, IA Metropolitan Statistical Area
Source: U.S. Census Bureau, 2015-2019 American Community Survey 5-Year Estimates

Higher Education

Four-Year Colleges			Two-Year Colleges			Medical Schools[1]	Law Schools[2]	Voc/ Tech[3]
Public	Private Non-profit	Private For-profit	Public	Private Non-profit	Private For-profit			
0	4	0	0	1	2	1	1	0

Note: Figures cover institutions located within the city limits and include main campuses only; (1) includes schools accredited by the Liaison Committee on Medical Education and the American Osteopathic Association's Commission on Osteopathic College Accreditation; (2) includes ABA-accredited schools, schools with provisional ABA accreditation, and state accredited schools; (3) includes all schools with programs that are less than 2 years.
Source: National Center for Education Statistics, Integrated Postsecondary Education System (IPEDS), 2019-20; Wikipedia, List of Medical Schools in the United States, accessed April 2, 2021; Wikipedia, List of Law Schools in the United States, accessed April 2, 2021

According to *U.S. News & World Report,* the Des Moines-West Des Moines, IA metro area is home to one of the top 200 national universities in the U.S.: **Drake University** (#124 tie). The indicators used to capture academic quality fall into a number of categories: assessment by administrators at peer institutions; retention of students; faculty resources; student selectivity; financial resources; alumni giving; high school counselor ratings of colleges; and graduation rate. *U.S. News & World Report, "America's Best Colleges 2021"*

122   Des Moines, Iowa

EMPLOYERS

Major Employers

Company Name	Industry
Bridgestone Americas Tire Operations	Global distribution center for tires
DuPont Pioneer	Crop inputs for worldwide agribusiness
Emerson Process Management Fisher Div	Control valves & systems, divisional headquarters
Grinnell Mutual Reinsurance Company	Reinsurance
Hy-Vee Food Stores	Retail grocery & drugstore chain
JBS USA	Pork processing & packaging
John Deere companies	Agricultural machinery, consumer financial services
Lennox Manufacturing	Heating & air conditioners
Mercer	Insurance
Mercy Medical Center	Healthcare
Meredith Corporation	Magazine, book publishing, tv, integrated marketing
Nationwide	Insurance
Principal Financial Group	Financial services
United Parcel Service	Package delivery services
UnityPoint Health	Healthcare
Vermeer Manufacturing Company	Manufacturing
Wellmark	Health insurance
Wells Fargo	Financial services & home mortgage

Note: Companies shown are located within the Des Moines-West Des Moines, IA Metropolitan Statistical Area.
Source: Hoovers.com; Wikipedia

Best Companies to Work For

Principal, headquartered in Des Moines, is among the "100 Best Companies for Working Mothers." Criteria: paid time off and leaves; workforce profile; benefits; women's issues and advancement; flexible work; company culture and work life programs. *Working Mother, "100 Best Companies for Working Mothers," 2020*

Principal Financial Group, headquartered in Des Moines, is among the "100 Best Places to Work in IT." To qualify, companies had to be U.S.-based organizations or be non-U.S.-based employers that met the following criteria: have a minimum of 300 total employees at a U.S. headquarters and a minimum of 30 IT employees in the U.S., with at least 50% of their IT employees based in the U.S. The best places to work were selected based on compensation, benefits, work/life balance, employee morale, and satisfaction with training and development programs. In addition, *InsiderPro* and *Computerworld* looked at retention efforts, programs for recognizing and rewarding outstanding performances, and benefits such as flextime, elder care and child care, and reimbursement for college tuition and the cost of pursuing technology certifications. *InsiderPro and Computerworld, "100 Best Places to Work in IT," 2020*

Principal Financial, headquartered in Des Moines, is among the "Top Companies for Executive Women." This list is determined by organizations filling out an in-depth survey that measures female demographics at every level, but with an emphasis on women in senior corporate roles, with profit & loss (P&L) responsibility, and those earning in the top 20 percent of the organization. *Working Mother* defines P&L as having responsibility that involves monitoring the net income after expenses for a department or entire organization, with direct influence on how company resources are allocated. *Working Mother, "Top Companies for Executive Women," 2020+*

PUBLIC SAFETY

Crime Rate

Area	All Crimes	Violent Crimes				Property Crimes		
		Murder	Rape[3]	Robbery	Aggrav. Assault	Burglary	Larceny -Theft	Motor Vehicle Theft
City	4,802.5	6.4	53.6	129.6	522.5	1,045.9	2,443.4	601.2
Suburbs[1]	n/a	n/a	n/a	n/a	n/a	n/a	n/a	n/a
Metro[2]	n/a	n/a	n/a	n/a	n/a	n/a	n/a	n/a
U.S.	2,489.3	5.0	42.6	81.6	250.2	340.5	1,549.5	219.9

Note: Figures are crimes per 100,000 population; (1) All areas within the metro area that are located outside the city limits; (2) Figures cover the Des Moines-West Des Moines, IA Metropolitan Statistical Area; n/a not available; (3) All figures shown were reported using the revised Uniform Crime Reporting (UCR) definition of rape.
Source: FBI Uniform Crime Reports, 2019

Hate Crimes

Area	Number of Quarters Reported	Number of Incidents per Bias Motivation					
		Race/Ethnicity/ Ancestry	Religion	Sexual Orientation	Disability	Gender	Gender Identity
City	4	0	0	0	0	0	0
U.S.	4	3,963	1,521	1,195	157	69	198

Source: Federal Bureau of Investigation, Hate Crime Statistics 2019

Identity Theft Consumer Reports

Area	Reports	Reports per 100,000 Population	Rank[2]
MSA[1]	805	115	345
U.S.	1,387,615	423	-

Note: (1) Figures cover the Des Moines-West Des Moines, IA Metropolitan Statistical Area; (2) Rank ranges from 1 to 391 where 1 indicates greatest number of identity theft reports per 100,000 population
Source: Federal Trade Commission, Consumer Sentinel Network Data Book 2020

Fraud and Other Consumer Reports

Area	Reports	Reports per 100,000 Population	Rank[2]
MSA[1]	4,113	588	298
U.S.	3,385,133	1,031	-

Note: (1) Figures cover the Des Moines-West Des Moines, IA Metropolitan Statistical Area; (2) Rank ranges from 1 to 391 where 1 indicates greatest number of fraud and other consumer reports per 100,000 population
Source: Federal Trade Commission, Consumer Sentinel Network Data Book 2020

POLITICS

2020 Presidential Election Results

Area	Biden	Trump	Jorgensen	Hawkins	Other
Polk County	56.5	41.3	1.3	0.2	0.7
U.S.	51.3	46.8	1.2	0.3	0.5

Note: Results are percentages and may not add to 100% due to rounding
Source: Dave Leip's Atlas of U.S. Presidential Elections

SPORTS

Professional Sports Teams

Team Name	League	Year Established
No teams are located in the metro area		

Source: Wikipedia, Major Professional Sports Teams of the United States and Canada, April 6, 2021

CLIMATE

Average and Extreme Temperatures

Temperature	Jan	Feb	Mar	Apr	May	Jun	Jul	Aug	Sep	Oct	Nov	Dec	Yr.
Extreme High (°F)	65	70	91	93	98	103	105	108	99	95	76	69	108
Average High (°F)	29	34	45	61	72	82	86	84	76	65	48	33	60
Average Temp. (°F)	20	25	36	51	62	72	76	74	65	54	39	25	50
Average Low (°F)	11	16	27	40	51	61	66	64	54	43	29	17	40
Extreme Low (°F)	-24	-20	-22	9	28	42	47	40	28	14	-3	-22	-24

Note: Figures cover the years 1945-1990
Source: National Climatic Data Center, International Station Meteorological Climate Summary, 9/96

Average Precipitation/Snowfall/Humidity

Precip./Humidity	Jan	Feb	Mar	Apr	May	Jun	Jul	Aug	Sep	Oct	Nov	Dec	Yr.
Avg. Precip. (in.)	1.1	1.1	2.3	3.1	3.8	4.4	3.5	3.9	3.1	2.4	1.7	1.2	31.8
Avg. Snowfall (in.)	8	7	7	2	Tr	0	0	0	Tr	Tr	3	7	33
Avg. Rel. Hum. 6am (%)	77	79	79	78	78	81	83	86	85	80	79	80	80
Avg. Rel. Hum. 3pm (%)	65	63	57	50	51	52	52	54	52	50	58	66	56

Note: Figures cover the years 1945-1990; Tr = Trace amounts (<0.05 in. of rain; <0.5 in. of snow)
Source: National Climatic Data Center, International Station Meteorological Climate Summary, 9/96

Weather Conditions

Temperature			Daytime Sky			Precipitation		
5°F & below	32°F & below	90°F & above	Clear	Partly cloudy	Cloudy	0.01 inch or more precip.	0.1 inch or more snow/ice	Thunder-storms
25	137	26	99	128	138	106	25	46

Note: Figures are average number of days per year and cover the years 1945-1990
Source: National Climatic Data Center, International Station Meteorological Climate Summary, 9/96

HAZARDOUS WASTE

Superfund Sites

The Des Moines-West Des Moines, IA metro area is home to two sites on the EPA's Superfund National Priorities List: **Des Moines TCE** (final); **Railroad Avenue Groundwater Contamination** (final). There are a total of 1,375 Superfund sites with a status of proposed or final on the list in the U.S.
U.S. Environmental Protection Agency, National Priorities List, April 7, 2021

124 Des Moines, Iowa

AIR QUALITY

Air Quality Trends: Ozone

	1990	1995	2000	2005	2010	2015	2016	2017	2018	2019
MSA[1]	n/a	n/a	n/a	n/a	n/a	n/a	n/a	n/a	n/a	n/a
U.S.	0.088	0.089	0.082	0.080	0.073	0.068	0.069	0.068	0.069	0.065

Note: (1) Data covers the Des Moines-West Des Moines, IA Metropolitan Statistical Area; n/a not available. The values shown are the composite ozone concentration averages among trend sites based on the highest fourth daily maximum 8-hour concentration in parts per million. These trends are based on sites having an adequate record of monitoring data during the trend period. Data from exceptional events are included.
Source: U.S. Environmental Protection Agency, Air Quality Monitoring Information, "Air Quality Trends by City, 1990-2019"

Air Quality Index

Area	Percent of Days when Air Quality was...[2]					AQI Statistics[2]	
	Good	Moderate	Unhealthy for Sensitive Groups	Unhealthy	Very Unhealthy	Maximum	Median
MSA[1]	83.8	16.2	0.0	0.0	0.0	100	39

Note: (1) Data covers the Des Moines-West Des Moines, IA Metropolitan Statistical Area; (2) Based on 365 days with AQI data in 2019. Air Quality Index (AQI) is an index for reporting daily air quality. EPA calculates the AQI for five major air pollutants regulated by the Clean Air Act: ground-level ozone, particle pollution (aka particulate matter), carbon monoxide, sulfur dioxide, and nitrogen dioxide. The AQI runs from 0 to 500. The higher the AQI value, the greater the level of air pollution and the greater the health concern. There are six AQI categories: "Good" AQI is between 0 and 50. Air quality is considered satisfactory; "Moderate" AQI is between 51 and 100. Air quality is acceptable; "Unhealthy for Sensitive Groups" When AQI values are between 101 and 150, members of sensitive groups may experience health effects; "Unhealthy" When AQI values are between 151 and 200 everyone may begin to experience health effects; "Very Unhealthy" AQI values between 201 and 300 trigger a health alert; "Hazardous" AQI values over 300 trigger warnings of emergency conditions (not shown).
Source: U.S. Environmental Protection Agency, Air Quality Index Report, 2019

Air Quality Index Pollutants

Area	Percent of Days when AQI Pollutant was...[2]					
	Carbon Monoxide	Nitrogen Dioxide	Ozone	Sulfur Dioxide	Particulate Matter 2.5	Particulate Matter 10
MSA[1]	0.0	0.8	67.4	0.0	31.8	0.0

Note: (1) Data covers the Des Moines-West Des Moines, IA Metropolitan Statistical Area; (2) Based on 365 days with AQI data in 2019. The Air Quality Index (AQI) is an index for reporting daily air quality. EPA calculates the AQI for five major air pollutants regulated by the Clean Air Act: ground-level ozone, particle pollution (also known as particulate matter), carbon monoxide, sulfur dioxide, and nitrogen dioxide. The AQI runs from 0 to 500. The higher the AQI value, the greater the level of air pollution and the greater the health concern.
Source: U.S. Environmental Protection Agency, Air Quality Index Report, 2019

Maximum Air Pollutant Concentrations: Particulate Matter, Ozone, CO and Lead

	Particulate Matter 10 (ug/m^3)	Particulate Matter 2.5 Wtd AM (ug/m^3)	Particulate Matter 2.5 24-Hr (ug/m^3)	Ozone (ppm)	Carbon Monoxide (ppm)	Lead (ug/m^3)
MSA[1] Level	39	7.0	19	0.064	1	n/a
NAAQS[2]	150	15	35	0.075	9	0.15
Met NAAQS[2]	Yes	Yes	Yes	Yes	Yes	n/a

Note: (1) Data covers the Des Moines-West Des Moines, IA Metropolitan Statistical Area; Data from exceptional events are included; (2) National Ambient Air Quality Standards; ppm = parts per million; ug/m^3 = micrograms per cubic meter; n/a not available.
Concentrations: Particulate Matter 10 (coarse particulate)—highest second maximum 24-hour concentration; Particulate Matter 2.5 Wtd AM (fine particulate)—highest weighted annual mean concentration; Particulate Matter 2.5 24-Hour (fine particulate)—highest 98th percentile 24-hour concentration; Ozone—highest fourth daily maximum 8-hour concentration; Carbon Monoxide—highest second maximum non-overlapping 8-hour concentration; Lead—maximum running 3-month average
Source: U.S. Environmental Protection Agency, Air Quality Monitoring Information, "Air Quality Statistics by City, 2019"

Maximum Air Pollutant Concentrations: Nitrogen Dioxide and Sulfur Dioxide

	Nitrogen Dioxide AM (ppb)	Nitrogen Dioxide 1-Hr (ppb)	Sulfur Dioxide AM (ppb)	Sulfur Dioxide 1-Hr (ppb)	Sulfur Dioxide 24-Hr (ppb)
MSA[1] Level	6	37	n/a	n/a	n/a
NAAQS[2]	53	100	30	75	140
Met NAAQS[2]	Yes	Yes	n/a	n/a	n/a

Note: (1) Data covers the Des Moines-West Des Moines, IA Metropolitan Statistical Area; Data from exceptional events are included; (2) National Ambient Air Quality Standards; ppm = parts per million; ug/m³ = micrograms per cubic meter; n/a not available.
Concentrations: Nitrogen Dioxide AM—highest arithmetic mean concentration; Nitrogen Dioxide 1-Hr—highest 98th percentile 1-hour daily maximum concentration; Sulfur Dioxide AM—highest annual mean concentration; Sulfur Dioxide 1-Hr—highest 99th percentile 1-hour daily maximum concentration; Sulfur Dioxide 24-Hr—highest second maximum 24-hour concentration
Source: U.S. Environmental Protection Agency, Air Quality Monitoring Information, "Air Quality Statistics by City, 2019"

Fargo, North Dakota

Background

Fargo sits on the western bank of the Red River in the Red River Valley in the southeastern part of the state. The city is in Cass County and about 300 miles northwest of Minneapolis.

Fargo was originally a stopping point for steamboats on the Red River in the later part of the 19th century. Founded in 1871, the city was first named Centralia, but renamed Fargo in honor of the Northern Pacific Railway director Wells Fargo. It began to flourish after the arrival of the railroad and became known as the Gateway to the West. During the 1880s, Fargo was also known for its lenient divorce laws.

A major fire in 1893 destroyed hundreds of homes and businesses but the city was quickly rebuilt with new brick buildings, new streets and a water system. The North Dakota State Agricultural College was founded in 1890 as the state's land-grant university, and was accredited by the North Central Association in 1915. The school eventually became known as North Dakota State University during the 1960s.

Fargo grew rapidly after World War II as the connection of two interstates, I-29 and I-94, revolutionized travel in the region and allowed for further expansion in the southern and western parts of the city. In 1972, the West Acres Shopping Center was constructed near the intersection of the two interstates and served as a catalyst for retail growth in the area.

> White House coronavirus task force member Dr. Birx came to Fargo to get an on-the-ground understanding of how the virus is spreading and how communities respond.

Fargo is the crossroads and economic center of eastern North Dakota and western Minnesota. Though the economy of the region was historically dependent on agriculture, other sectors have become increasingly prevalent in recent years. Today, the city's growing economy is based on food processing, manufacturing, technology, retail trade, higher education, and healthcare. The University is the city's largest public sector employer.

A significant landmark in Fargo is the main campus of North Dakota State University, which has a full-time enrollment of nearly 9,000. The city also features a large number of public parks including Percy Godwin Park, Lindenwood Park, Mickelson Field, Island Park, Roosevelt Playground, and Oak Grove Park.

As the city continues to energize the downtown area, the Renaissance Zone and Storefront Rehab programs encourage new business, renovate deteriorating buildings, and increase the availability of housing in the downtown area. The renovated Fargo Public Library's main downtown branch is popular with the city's residents.

Fargo ,an Academy Award-winning 1996 film named after the city, shows the city briefly at the film's opening scene set in a bar, and is mentioned twice in the film. *Fargo* the TV series based on the film, debuted on FX in 2014. The city was featured in its seventh episode of season 1, "Who Shaves the Barber?" and more prominently in season 2. The series was filmed in Calgary, Alberta, Canada.

Fargo has a moderate northern climate. Summer temperatures average 65 degrees, while winter averages fall to 10 degrees during of December and January. The city averages 2.5 inches of rainfall per month from April to October and 8 inches of snowfall per month from December to March. Natural disaster struck in 2009, when heavy snowfall caused the Red River to flood the area, followed by extended periods of freezing temperatures.

Rankings

General Rankings

- In their seventh annual survey, Livability.com looked at data for more than 1,000 small to mid-sized U.S. cities to determine the rankings for Livability's "Top 100 Best Places to Live" in 2020. Fargo ranked #8. Criteria: housing and affordable living; vibrant economy; social and civic engagement; education; demographics; health care options; transportation & infrastructure; and abundant lifestyle amenities. *Livability.com, "Top 100 Best Places to Live 2020" October 2020*

Business/Finance Rankings

- The Fargo metro area appeared on the Milken Institute "2021 Best Performing Cities" list. Rank: #23 out of 201 small metro areas (population over 60,000). Criteria: job growth; wage and salary growth; high-tech output growth; housing affordability; household broadband access. *Milken Institute, "Best-Performing Cities 2021," February 16, 2021*

- *Forbes* ranked 203 smaller metro areas (population under 268,000) to determine the nation's "Best Small Places for Business and Careers." The Fargo metro area was ranked #23. Criteria: costs (business and living); job growth (past and projected); income growth; quality of life; educational attainment (college and high school); projected economic growth; cultural and leisure opportunities; workplace tolerance laws; net migration patterns. *Forbes, "The Best Small Places for Business and Careers 2019," October 30, 2019*

Dating/Romance Rankings

- Fargo was selected as one of the most romantic cities in the U.S. by video-rental kiosk company Redbox. The city ranked #10 out of 20. Criteria: number of romance-related rentals in 2016. *Redbox, "20 Most Romantic Cities," February 6, 2017*

Environmental Rankings

- Niche compiled a list of the nation's snowiest cities, based on the National Oceanic and Atmospheric Administration's 30-year average snowfall data. Among cities with a population of at least 50,000, Fargo ranked #18. *Niche.com, Top 25 Snowiest Cities in America, December 10, 2018*

- Fargo was highlighted as one of the cleanest metro areas for ozone air pollution in the U.S. during 2016 through 2018. The list represents cities with no monitored ozone air pollution in unhealthful ranges. *American Lung Association, "State of the Air 2020," April 21, 2020*

Real Estate Rankings

- *WalletHub* compared the most populated U.S. cities to determine which had the best markets for real estate agents. Fargo ranked #13 where demand was high and pay was the best. Criteria: sales per agent; annual median wage for real-estate agents; monthly average starting salary for real estate agents; real estate job density and competition; unemployment rate; home turnover rate; housing-market health index; and other relevant metrics. *www.WalletHub.com, "2019's Best Places to Be a Real Estate Agent," April 24, 2019*

- The Fargo metro area was identified as one of the 20 worst housing markets in the U.S. in 2020. The area ranked #170 out of 180 markets. Criteria: year-over-year change of median sales price of existing single-family homes between the 4th quarter of 2019 and the 4th quarter of 2020. *National Association of Realtors®, Median Sales Price of Existing Single-Family Homes for Metropolitan Areas, 4th Quarter 2020*

- Fargo was ranked #41 out of 268 metro areas in terms of housing affordability in 2020 by the National Association of Home Builders (#1 = most affordable). Criteria: the share of homes sold in that area affordable to a family earning the local median income, based on standard mortgage underwriting criteria. *National Association of Home Builders®, NAHB-Wells Fargo Housing Opportunity Index, 4th Quarter 2020*

Safety Rankings

- The National Insurance Crime Bureau ranked 384 metro areas in the U.S. in terms of per capita rates of vehicle theft. The Fargo metro area ranked #144 (#1 = highest rate). Criteria: number of vehicle theft offenses per 100,000 inhabitants in 2019. *National Insurance Crime Bureau, "Hot Spots 2019," July 21, 2020*

Seniors/Retirement Rankings

- From its Best Cities for Successful Aging indexes, the Milken Institute generated rankings for metropolitan areas, weighing data in nine categories—health care, wellness, living arrangements, transportation and convenience, financial characteristics, education, employment, community engagement, and overall livability. The Fargo metro area was ranked #14 overall in the small metro area category. *Milken Institute, "Best Cities for Successful Aging, 2017" March 14, 2017*

- Fargo made the 2020 *Forbes* list of "25 Best Places to Retire." Criteria, focused on high-quality retirement living at an affordable price, include: housing/living costs compared to the national average and state taxes; air quality; crime rates; good economic outlook; home price appreciation; risk associated with climate-change; availability of medical care; bikeability; walkability; healthy living. *Forbes.com, "The Best Places to Retire in 2020," August 14, 2020*

Women/Minorities Rankings

- Personal finance website *WalletHub* compared more than 180 U.S. cities across two key dimensions, "Hispanic Business-Friendliness" and "Hispanic Purchasing Power," to arrive at the most favorable conditions for Hispanic entrepreneurs. Fargo was ranked #111 out of 182. Criteria includes: share of Hispanic-Owned Businesses; Hispanic entrepreneurship rate to median annual income of Hispanics; Small Business-Friendliness score; cost of living; and number of Hispanics with at least a bachelor's degree. *WalletHub.com, "2019's Best Cities for Hispanic Entrepreneurs," May 1, 2019*

Miscellaneous Rankings

- *WalletHub* compared the 150 most populated U.S. cities to determine their operating efficiency. A "Quality of City Services" score was constructed for each city and then divided by the total budget per capita to reveal which were managed the best. Fargo ranked #23. Criteria: financial stability; economy; education; safety; health; infrastructure and pollution. *www.WalletHub.com, "2020's Best- & Worst-Run Cities in America," June 29, 2020*

130 Fargo, North Dakota

Business Environment

DEMOGRAPHICS

Population Growth

Area	1990 Census	2000 Census	2010 Census	2019* Estimate	Population Growth (%)	
					1990-2019	2010-2019
City	74,372	90,599	105,549	121,889	63.9	15.5
MSA[1]	153,296	174,367	208,777	240,421	56.8	15.2
U.S.	248,709,873	281,421,906	308,745,538	324,697,795	30.6	5.2

Note: (1) Figures cover the Fargo, ND-MN Metropolitan Statistical Area; (*) 2015-2019 5-year estimated population
Source: U.S. Census Bureau, 1990 Census, Census 2000, Census 2010, 2015-2019 American Community Survey 5-Year Estimates

Household Size

Area	Persons in Household (%)							Average Household Size
	One	Two	Three	Four	Five	Six	Seven or More	
City	36.5	34.0	14.4	9.0	4.2	1.4	0.5	2.10
MSA[1]	31.2	35.0	14.6	11.6	5.1	1.6	0.9	2.30
U.S.	27.9	33.9	15.6	12.9	6.0	2.3	1.4	2.60

Note: (1) Figures cover the Fargo, ND-MN Metropolitan Statistical Area
Source: U.S. Census Bureau, 2015-2019 American Community Survey 5-Year Estimates

Race

Area	White Alone[2] (%)	Black Alone[2] (%)	Asian Alone[2] (%)	AIAN[3] Alone[2] (%)	NHOPI[4] Alone[2] (%)	Other Race Alone[2] (%)	Two or More Races (%)
City	84.6	7.0	3.5	1.2	0.0	0.5	3.1
MSA[1]	88.0	5.1	2.5	1.2	0.1	0.6	2.7
U.S.	72.5	12.7	5.5	0.8	0.2	4.9	3.3

Note: (1) Figures cover the Fargo, ND-MN Metropolitan Statistical Area; (2) Alone is defined as not being in combination with one or more other races; (3) American Indian and Alaska Native; (4) Native Hawaiian and Other Pacific Islander
Source: U.S. Census Bureau, 2015-2019 American Community Survey 5-Year Estimates

Hispanic or Latino Origin

Area	Total (%)	Mexican (%)	Puerto Rican (%)	Cuban (%)	Other (%)
City	3.0	1.9	0.4	0.0	0.6
MSA[1]	3.2	2.2	0.3	0.0	0.7
U.S.	18.0	11.2	1.7	0.7	4.3

Note: Persons of Hispanic or Latino origin can be of any race; (1) Figures cover the Fargo, ND-MN Metropolitan Statistical Area
Source: U.S. Census Bureau, 2015-2019 American Community Survey 5-Year Estimates

Ancestry

Area	German	Irish	English	American	Italian	Polish	French[2]	Scottish	Dutch
City	37.1	8.8	3.9	2.2	1.1	3.1	3.6	1.2	1.1
MSA[1]	37.4	8.2	4.3	2.0	1.1	2.8	3.1	1.2	1.2
U.S.	13.3	9.7	7.2	6.2	5.1	2.8	2.3	1.7	1.2

Note: Figures are the percentage of the total population reporting a particular ancestry. The nine most commonly reported ancestries in the U.S. are shown. Figures include multiple ancestries (e.g. if a person reported being Irish and Italian, they were included in both columns); (1) Figures cover the Fargo, ND-MN Metropolitan Statistical Area; (2) Excludes Basque
Source: U.S. Census Bureau, 2015-2019 American Community Survey 5-Year Estimates

Foreign-born Population

Area	Percent of Population Born in								
	Any Foreign Country	Asia	Mexico	Europe	Caribbean	Central America[2]	South America	Africa	Canada
City	9.0	3.5	0.1	1.0	0.2	0.1	0.2	3.7	0.2
MSA[1]	6.7	2.7	0.2	0.8	0.1	0.1	0.2	2.4	0.3
U.S.	13.6	4.2	3.5	1.5	1.3	1.1	1.0	0.7	0.2

Note: (1) Figures cover the Fargo, ND-MN Metropolitan Statistical Area; (2) Excludes Mexico.
Source: U.S. Census Bureau, 2015-2019 American Community Survey 5-Year Estimates

Marital Status

Area	Never Married	Now Married[2]	Separated	Widowed	Divorced
City	42.8	42.9	1.1	4.5	8.7
MSA[1]	36.8	49.6	0.9	4.3	8.3
U.S.	33.4	48.1	1.9	5.8	10.9

Note: Figures are percentages and cover the population 15 years of age and older; (1) Figures cover the Fargo, ND-MN Metropolitan Statistical Area; (2) Excludes separated
Source: U.S. Census Bureau, 2015-2019 American Community Survey 5-Year Estimates

Disability by Age

Area	All Ages	Under 18 Years Old	18 to 64 Years Old	65 Years and Over
City	10.0	2.8	7.7	36.5
MSA[1]	9.5	3.1	7.4	33.9
U.S.	12.6	4.2	10.3	34.5

Note: Figures show percent of the civilian noninstitutionalized population that reported having a disability. Disability status is determined from six types of difficulty: vision, hearing, cognitive, ambulatory, self-care, and independent living. For children under 5 years old, hearing and vision difficulty are used to determine disability status. For children between the ages of 5 and 14, disability status is determined from hearing, vision, cognitive, ambulatory, and self-care difficulties. For people aged 15 years and older, they are considered to have a disability if they have difficulty with any one of the six difficulty types; Note: (1) Figures cover the Fargo, ND-MN Metropolitan Statistical Area
Source: U.S. Census Bureau, 2015-2019 American Community Survey 5-Year Estimates

Age

Area	Percent of Population									Median Age
	Under Age 5	Age 5–19	Age 20–34	Age 35–44	Age 45–54	Age 55–64	Age 65–74	Age 75–84	Age 85+	
City	6.7	17.4	32.0	12.3	9.5	10.1	6.6	3.3	2.0	31.0
MSA[1]	7.1	19.5	27.4	12.8	10.5	10.7	6.6	3.4	1.9	32.5
U.S.	6.1	19.1	20.7	12.6	13.0	12.9	9.1	4.6	1.9	38.1

Note: (1) Figures cover the Fargo, ND-MN Metropolitan Statistical Area
Source: U.S. Census Bureau, 2015-2019 American Community Survey 5-Year Estimates

Gender

Area	Males	Females	Males per 100 Females
City	61,988	59,901	103.5
MSA[1]	120,992	119,429	101.3
U.S.	159,886,919	164,810,876	97.0

Note: (1) Figures cover the Fargo, ND-MN Metropolitan Statistical Area
Source: U.S. Census Bureau, 2015-2019 American Community Survey 5-Year Estimates

Religious Groups by Family

Area	Catholic	Baptist	Non-Den.	Methodist[2]	Lutheran	LDS[3]	Pente-costal	Presby-terian[4]	Muslim[5]	Judaism
MSA[1]	17.4	0.4	0.5	3.3	32.5	0.6	1.5	1.9	0.1	<0.1
U.S.	19.1	9.3	4.0	4.0	2.3	2.0	1.9	1.6	0.8	0.7

Note: Figures are the number of adherents as a percentage of the total population; (1) Figures cover the Fargo, ND-MN Metropolitan Statistical Area; (2) Methodist/Pietist; (3) Latter Day Saints; (4) Reformed; (5) Figures are estimates
Source: Association of Statisticians of American Religious Bodies, 2010 U.S. Religion Census: Religious Congregations & Membership Study

Religious Groups by Tradition

Area	Catholic	Evangelical Protestant	Mainline Protestant	Other Tradition	Black Protestant	Orthodox
MSA[1]	17.4	10.7	30.8	0.9	<0.1	<0.1
U.S.	19.1	16.2	7.3	4.3	1.6	0.3

Note: Figures are the number of adherents as a percentage of the total population; (1) Figures cover the Fargo, ND-MN Metropolitan Statistical Area
Source: Association of Statisticians of American Religious Bodies, 2010 U.S. Religion Census: Religious Congregations & Membership Study

ECONOMY

Gross Metropolitan Product

Area	2017	2018	2019	2020	Rank[2]
MSA[1]	15.3	16.1	16.8	17.5	156

Note: Figures are in billions of dollars; (1) Figures cover the Fargo, ND-MN Metropolitan Statistical Area; (2) Rank is based on 2018 data and ranges from 1 to 381
Source: U.S. Conference of Mayors, U.S. Metro Economies: GMP & Employment 2018-2020, September 2019

Economic Growth

Area	2015-17 (%)	2018 (%)	2019 (%)	2020 (%)	Rank[2]
MSA[1]	0.4	2.1	2.6	2.0	283
U.S.	1.9	2.9	2.3	2.1	–

Note: Figures are real gross metropolitan product (GMP) growth rates and represent average annual percent change; (1) Figures cover the Fargo, ND-MN Metropolitan Statistical Area; (2) Rank is based on 2017 2-year average annual percent change and ranges from 1 to 381
Source: U.S. Conference of Mayors, U.S. Metro Economies: GMP & Employment 2018-2020, September 2019

Metropolitan Area Exports

Area	2014	2015	2016	2017	2018	2019	Rank[2]
MSA[1]	782.8	543.2	474.5	519.5	553.5	515.0	207

Note: Figures are in millions of dollars; (1) Figures cover the Fargo, ND-MN Metropolitan Statistical Area; (2) Rank is based on 2019 data and ranges from 1 to 386
Source: U.S. Department of Commerce, International Trade Administration, Office of Trade and Economic Analysis, Industry and Analysis, Exports by Metropolitan Area, data extracted March 24, 2021

Building Permits

Area	Single-Family			Multi-Family			Total		
	2018	2019	Pct. Chg.	2018	2019	Pct. Chg.	2018	2019	Pct. Chg.
City	313	311	-0.6	897	172	-80.8	1,210	483	-60.1
MSA[1]	1,080	939	-13.1	1,233	486	-60.6	2,313	1,425	-38.4
U.S.	855,300	862,100	0.7	473,500	523,900	10.6	1,328,800	1,386,000	4.3

Note: (1) Figures cover the Fargo, ND-MN Metropolitan Statistical Area; Figures represent new, privately-owned housing units authorized (unadjusted data); All permit data are based on estimates with imputation
Source: U.S. Census Bureau, Manufacturing, Mining, and Construction Statistics, Building Permits, 2018, 2019

Bankruptcy Filings

Area	Business Filings			Nonbusiness Filings		
	2019	2020	% Chg.	2019	2020	% Chg.
Cass County	4	5	25.0	198	183	-7.6
U.S.	22,780	21,655	-4.9	752,160	522,808	-30.5

Note: Business filings include Chapter 7, Chapter 9, Chapter 11, Chapter 12, Chapter 13, Chapter 15, and Section 304; Nonbusiness filings include Chapter 7, Chapter 11, and Chapter 13
Source: Administrative Office of the U.S. Courts, Business and Nonbusiness Bankruptcy, County Cases Commenced by Chapter of the Bankruptcy Code, During the 12-Month Period Ending December 31, 2019 and Business and Nonbusiness Bankruptcy, County Cases Commenced by Chapter of the Bankruptcy Code, During the 12-Month Period Ending December 31, 2020

Housing Vacancy Rates

Area	Gross Vacancy Rate[2] (%)			Year-Round Vacancy Rate[3] (%)			Rental Vacancy Rate[4] (%)			Homeowner Vacancy Rate[5] (%)		
	2018	2019	2020	2018	2019	2020	2018	2019	2020	2018	2019	2020
MSA[1]	n/a	n/a	n/a	n/a	n/a	n/a	n/a	n/a	n/a	n/a	n/a	n/a
U.S.	12.3	12.0	10.6	9.7	9.5	8.2	6.9	6.7	6.3	1.5	1.4	1.0

Note: (1) Figures cover the Fargo, ND-MN Metropolitan Statistical Area; (2) The percentage of the total housing inventory that is vacant; (3) The percentage of the housing inventory (excluding seasonal units) that is year-round vacant; (4) The percentage of rental inventory that is vacant for rent; (5) The percentage of homeowner inventory that is vacant for sale; n/a not available
Source: U.S. Census Bureau, Housing Vacancies and Homeownership Annual Statistics: 2018, 2019, 2020

INCOME

Income

Area	Per Capita ($)	Median Household ($)	Average Household ($)
City	35,205	55,551	78,237
MSA[1]	35,812	64,666	85,794
U.S.	34,103	62,843	88,607

Note: (1) Figures cover the Fargo, ND-MN Metropolitan Statistical Area
Source: U.S. Census Bureau, 2015-2019 American Community Survey 5-Year Estimates

Household Income Distribution

Area	Percent of Households Earning							
	Under $15,000	$15,000 -$24,999	$25,000 -$34,999	$35,000 -$49,999	$50,000 -$74,999	$75,000 -$99,999	$100,000 -$149,999	$150,000 and up
City	11.1	10.1	9.7	13.8	18.2	14.0	12.6	10.4
MSA[1]	9.4	8.6	8.2	12.1	18.3	15.3	15.7	12.4
U.S.	10.3	8.9	8.9	12.3	17.2	12.7	15.1	14.5

Note: (1) Figures cover the Fargo, ND-MN Metropolitan Statistical Area
Source: U.S. Census Bureau, 2015-2019 American Community Survey 5-Year Estimates

Poverty Rate

Area	All Ages	Under 18 Years Old	18 to 64 Years Old	65 Years and Over
City	13.2	12.8	14.3	7.6
MSA[1]	11.1	11.1	11.9	6.3
U.S.	13.4	18.5	12.6	9.3

Note: Figures are percentage of people whose income during the past 12 months was below the poverty level;
(1) Figures cover the Fargo, ND-MN Metropolitan Statistical Area
Source: U.S. Census Bureau, 2015-2019 American Community Survey 5-Year Estimates

CITY FINANCES

City Government Finances

Component	2017 ($000)	2017 ($ per capita)
Total Revenues	318,925	2,691
Total Expenditures	400,707	3,381
Debt Outstanding	795,379	6,711
Cash and Securities[1]	499,475	4,214

Note: (1) Cash and security holdings of a government at the close of its fiscal year,
including those of its dependent agencies, utilities, and liquor stores.
Source: U.S. Census Bureau, State & Local Government Finances 2017

City Government Revenue by Source

Source	2017 ($000)	2017 ($ per capita)	2017 (%)
General Revenue			
From Federal Government	5,653	48	1.8
From State Government	71,530	604	22.4
From Local Governments	0	0	0.0
Taxes			
Property	26,914	227	8.4
Sales and Gross Receipts	58,288	492	18.3
Personal Income	0	0	0.0
Corporate Income	0	0	0.0
Motor Vehicle License	0	0	0.0
Other Taxes	6,596	56	2.1
Current Charges	59,221	500	18.6
Liquor Store	0	0	0.0
Utility	24,166	204	7.6
Employee Retirement	15,870	134	5.0

Source: U.S. Census Bureau, State & Local Government Finances 2017

City Government Expenditures by Function

Function	2017 ($000)	2017 ($ per capita)	2017 (%)
General Direct Expenditures			
Air Transportation	0	0	0.0
Corrections	805	6	0.2
Education	0	0	0.0
Employment Security Administration	0	0	0.0
Financial Administration	3,724	31	0.9
Fire Protection	12,355	104	3.1
General Public Buildings	1,838	15	0.5
Governmental Administration, Other	3,641	30	0.9
Health	10,971	92	2.7
Highways	110,683	933	27.6
Hospitals	0	0	0.0
Housing and Community Development	1,382	11	0.3
Interest on General Debt	23,414	197	5.8
Judicial and Legal	1,763	14	0.4
Libraries	4,154	35	1.0
Parking	1,796	15	0.4
Parks and Recreation	15,839	133	4.0
Police Protection	18,779	158	4.7
Public Welfare	328	2	0.1
Sewerage	7,188	60	1.8
Solid Waste Management	11,966	101	3.0
Veterans' Services	0	0	0.0
Liquor Store	0	0	0.0
Utility	18,457	155	4.6
Employee Retirement	9,106	76	2.3

Source: U.S. Census Bureau, State & Local Government Finances 2017

134 Fargo, North Dakota

EMPLOYMENT

Labor Force and Employment

Area	Civilian Labor Force			Workers Employed		
	Dec. 2019	Dec. 2020	% Chg.	Dec. 2019	Dec. 2020	% Chg.
City	69,702	73,397	5.3	68,423	71,067	3.9
MSA[1]	138,402	143,685	3.8	135,435	139,201	2.8
U.S.	164,007,000	160,017,000	-2.4	158,504,000	149,613,000	-5.6

Note: Data is not seasonally adjusted and covers workers 16 years of age and older; (1) Figures cover the Fargo, ND-MN Metropolitan Statistical Area
Source: Bureau of Labor Statistics, Local Area Unemployment Statistics

Unemployment Rate

Area	2020											
	Jan.	Feb.	Mar.	Apr.	May	Jun.	Jul.	Aug.	Sep.	Oct.	Nov.	Dec.
City	2.5	2.3	2.3	9.6	8.5	7.0	5.5	4.0	3.0	3.1	3.1	3.2
MSA[1]	2.8	2.6	2.5	7.7	7.2	6.4	5.1	3.9	3.0	2.9	3.0	3.1
U.S.	4.0	3.8	4.5	14.4	13.0	11.2	10.5	8.5	7.7	6.6	6.4	6.5

Note: Data is not seasonally adjusted and covers workers 16 years of age and older; (1) Figures cover the Fargo, ND-MN Metropolitan Statistical Area
Source: Bureau of Labor Statistics, Local Area Unemployment Statistics

Average Wages

Occupation	$/Hr.	Occupation	$/Hr.
Accountants and Auditors	32.70	Maintenance and Repair Workers	21.00
Automotive Mechanics	24.60	Marketing Managers	61.60
Bookkeepers	20.00	Network and Computer Systems Admin.	36.80
Carpenters	23.10	Nurses, Licensed Practical	22.20
Cashiers	12.30	Nurses, Registered	35.70
Computer Programmers	36.00	Nursing Assistants	16.60
Computer Systems Analysts	42.30	Office Clerks, General	20.50
Computer User Support Specialists	22.60	Physical Therapists	39.50
Construction Laborers	21.50	Physicians	n/a
Cooks, Restaurant	15.50	Plumbers, Pipefitters and Steamfitters	26.30
Customer Service Representatives	18.70	Police and Sheriff's Patrol Officers	32.50
Dentists	83.80	Postal Service Mail Carriers	25.40
Electricians	28.90	Real Estate Sales Agents	30.10
Engineers, Electrical	47.70	Retail Salespersons	15.60
Fast Food and Counter Workers	12.70	Sales Representatives, Technical/Scientific	41.70
Financial Managers	70.20	Secretaries, Exc. Legal/Medical/Executive	19.40
First-Line Supervisors of Office Workers	27.10	Security Guards	15.00
General and Operations Managers	55.50	Surgeons	n/a
Hairdressers/Cosmetologists	16.90	Teacher Assistants, Exc. Postsecondary*	16.30
Home Health and Personal Care Aides	15.10	Teachers, Secondary School, Exc. Sp. Ed.*	31.20
Janitors and Cleaners	14.70	Telemarketers	n/a
Landscaping/Groundskeeping Workers	18.30	Truck Drivers, Heavy/Tractor-Trailer	24.50
Lawyers	54.10	Truck Drivers, Light/Delivery Services	20.00
Maids and Housekeeping Cleaners	13.60	Waiters and Waitresses	12.90

Note: Wage data covers the Fargo, ND-MN Metropolitan Statistical Area; (*) Hourly wages were calculated from annual wage data based on a 40 hour work week; n/a not available.
Source: Bureau of Labor Statistics, Metro Area Occupational Employment & Wage Estimates, May 2020

Employment by Industry

Sector	MSA[1]		U.S.
	Number of Employees	Percent of Total	Percent of Total
Construction, Mining, and Logging	9,100	6.5	5.5
Education and Health Services	27,300	19.4	16.3
Financial Activities	11,800	8.4	6.1
Government	18,800	13.4	15.2
Information	3,000	2.1	1.9
Leisure and Hospitality	11,500	8.2	9.0
Manufacturing	10,000	7.1	8.5
Other Services	4,800	3.4	3.8
Professional and Business Services	13,400	9.5	14.4
Retail Trade	15,400	10.9	10.9
Transportation, Warehousing, and Utilities	6,600	4.7	4.6
Wholesale Trade	9,100	6.5	3.9

Note: Figures are non-farm employment as of December 2020. Figures are not seasonally adjusted and include workers 16 years of age and older; (1) Figures cover the Fargo, ND-MN Metropolitan Statistical Area
Source: Bureau of Labor Statistics, Current Employment Statistics, Employment, Hours, and Earnings

Employment by Occupation

Occupation Classification	City (%)	MSA[1] (%)	U.S. (%)
Management, Business, Science, and Arts	39.5	40.3	38.5
Natural Resources, Construction, and Maintenance	7.9	8.9	8.9
Production, Transportation, and Material Moving	12.8	12.3	13.2
Sales and Office	21.2	22.2	21.6
Service	18.7	16.4	17.8

Note: Figures cover employed civilians 16 years of age and older; (1) Figures cover the Fargo, ND-MN Metropolitan Statistical Area
Source: U.S. Census Bureau, 2015-2019 American Community Survey 5-Year Estimates

Occupations with Greatest Projected Employment Growth: 2020 – 2022

Occupation[1]	2020 Employment	2022 Projected Employment	Numeric Employment Change	Percent Employment Change
Fast Food and Counter Workers	10,110	10,470	360	3.6
Cooks, Restaurant	3,060	3,280	220	7.2
Home Health and Personal Care Aides	6,530	6,740	210	3.2
Registered Nurses	10,320	10,500	180	1.7
Waiters and Waitresses	5,250	5,420	170	3.2
Maids and Housekeeping Cleaners	5,140	5,290	150	2.9
Bartenders	4,010	4,150	140	3.5
Industrial Truck and Tractor Operators	1,400	1,520	120	8.6
Hotel, Motel, and Resort Desk Clerks	1,310	1,400	90	6.9
Elementary School Teachers, Except Special Education	4,120	4,200	80	1.9

Note: Projections cover North Dakota; (1) Sorted by numeric employment change
Source: www.projectionscentral.com, State Occupational Projections, 2020–2022 Short-Term Projections

Fastest-Growing Occupations: 2020 – 2022

Occupation[1]	2020 Employment	2022 Projected Employment	Numeric Employment Change	Percent Employment Change
Nurse Practitioners	520	570	50	9.6
Industrial Truck and Tractor Operators	1,400	1,520	120	8.6
Cooks, Restaurant	3,060	3,280	220	7.2
Hotel, Motel, and Resort Desk Clerks	1,310	1,400	90	6.9
Medical and Health Services Managers	820	870	50	6.1
Dining Room and Cafeteria Attendants and Bartender Helpers	950	1,000	50	5.3
Fitness Trainers and Aerobics Instructors	1,580	1,650	70	4.4
Amusement and Recreation Attendants	1,470	1,530	60	4.1
Fast Food and Counter Workers	10,110	10,470	360	3.6
Bartenders	4,010	4,150	140	3.5

Note: Projections cover North Dakota; (1) Sorted by percent employment change and excludes occupations with numeric employment change less than 50
Source: www.projectionscentral.com, State Occupational Projections, 2020–2022 Short-Term Projections

TAXES

State Corporate Income Tax Rates

State	Tax Rate (%)	Income Brackets ($)	Num. of Brackets	Financial Institution Tax Rate (%)[a]	Federal Income Tax Ded.
North Dakota	1.41 - 4.31 (s)	25,000 - 50,001	3	1.41 - 4.31 (s)	No

Note: Tax rates as of January 1, 2021; (a) Rates listed are the corporate income tax rate applied to financial institutions or excise taxes based on income. Some states have other taxes based upon the value of deposits or shares; (s) North Dakota imposes a 3.5% surtax for filers electing to use the water's edge method to apportion income.
Source: Federation of Tax Administrators, State Corporate Income Tax Rates, January 1, 2021

State Individual Income Tax Rates

State	Tax Rate (%)	Income Brackets ($)	Personal Exemptions ($)			Standard Ded. ($)	
			Single	Married	Depend.	Single	Married
North Dakota (a)	1.1 - 2.9	40,525 - 445,600 (r)	(d)	(d)	(d)	12,550	25,100 (d)

Note: Tax rates as of January 1, 2021; Local- and county-level taxes are not included; Federal income tax is not deductible on state income tax returns; (a) 19 states have statutory provision for automatically adjusting to the rate of inflation the dollar values of the income tax brackets, standard deductions, and/or personal exemptions. Michigan indexes the personal exemption only. Oregon does not index the income brackets for $125,000 and over; (d) These states use the personal exemption/standard deduction amounts provided in the federal Internal Revenue Code; (r) The income brackets reported for North Dakota are for single individuals. For married couples filing jointly, the same tax rates apply to income brackets ranging from $67,700 to $445,000.
Source: Federation of Tax Administrators, State Individual Income Tax Rates, January 1, 2021

136 Fargo, North Dakota

Various State Sales and Excise Tax Rates

State	State Sales Tax (%)	Gasoline[1] (¢/gal.)	Cigarette[2] ($/pack)	Spirits[3] ($/gal.)	Wine[4] ($/gal.)	Beer[5] ($/gal.)	Recreational Marijuana (%)
North Dakota	5	23	0.44	5.12	1.22	0.45	Not legal

Note: All tax rates as of January 1, 2021; (1) The American Petroleum Institute has developed a methodology for determining the average tax rate on a gallon of fuel. Rates may include any of the following: excise taxes, environmental fees, storage tank fees, other fees or taxes, general sales tax, and local taxes; (2) The federal excise tax of $1.0066 per pack and local taxes are not included; (3) Rates are those applicable to off-premise sales of 40% alcohol by volume (a.b.v.) distilled spirits in 750ml containers. Local excise taxes are excluded; (4) Rates are those applicable to off-premise sales of 11% a.b.v. non-carbonated wine in 750ml containers; (5) Rates are those applicable to off-premise sales of 4.7% a.b.v. beer in 12 ounce containers.
Source: Tax Foundation, 2021 Facts & Figures: How Does Your State Compare?

State Business Tax Climate Index Rankings

State	Overall Rank	Corporate Tax Rank	Individual Income Tax Rank	Sales Tax Rank	Property Tax Rank	Unemployment Insurance Tax Rank
North Dakota	17	8	20	29	12	12

Note: The index is a measure of how each state's tax laws affect economic performance. The lower the rank, the more favorable a state's tax system is for business. States without a given tax are given a ranking of 1. The scores/rankings for the District of Columbia do not affect other states. The 2021 index represents the tax climate as of July 1, 2020.
Source: Tax Foundation, State Business Tax Climate Index 2021

TRANSPORTATION

Means of Transportation to Work

Area	Car/Truck/Van		Public Transportation			Bicycle	Walked	Other Means	Worked at Home
	Drove Alone	Car-pooled	Bus	Subway	Railroad				
City	82.8	8.3	0.9	0.0	0.0	0.6	3.7	0.8	2.9
MSA[1]	82.2	8.6	0.7	0.0	0.0	0.5	2.8	0.8	4.4
U.S.	76.3	9.0	2.4	1.9	0.6	0.5	2.7	1.4	5.2

Note: Figures are percentages and cover workers 16 years of age and older; (1) Figures cover the Fargo, ND-MN Metropolitan Statistical Area
Source: U.S. Census Bureau, 2015-2019 American Community Survey 5-Year Estimates

Travel Time to Work

Area	Less Than 10 Minutes	10 to 19 Minutes	20 to 29 Minutes	30 to 44 Minutes	45 to 59 Minutes	60 to 89 Minutes	90 Minutes or More
City	20.9	54.9	17.6	3.3	1.0	1.4	0.8
MSA[1]	18.5	50.6	19.3	7.0	2.0	1.6	1.1
U.S.	12.2	28.4	20.8	20.8	8.3	6.4	2.9

Note: Note: Figures are percentages and include workers 16 years old and over; (1) Figures cover the Fargo, ND-MN Metropolitan Statistical Area
Source: U.S. Census Bureau, 2015-2019 American Community Survey 5-Year Estimates

Key Congestion Measures

Measure	1982	1992	2002	2012	2017
Annual Hours of Delay, Total (000)	n/a	n/a	n/a	n/a	n/a
Annual Hours of Delay, Per Auto Commuter	n/a	n/a	n/a	n/a	n/a
Annual Congestion Cost, Total (million $)	n/a	n/a	n/a	n/a	n/a
Annual Congestion Cost, Per Auto Commuter ($)	n/a	n/a	n/a	n/a	n/a

Note: n/a not available
Source: Texas A&M Transportation Institute, 2019 Urban Mobility Report

Freeway Travel Time Index

Measure	1982	1987	1992	1997	2002	2007	2012	2017
Urban Area Index[1]	n/a	n/a	n/a	n/a	n/a	n/a	n/a	n/a
Urban Area Rank[1,2]	n/a	n/a	n/a	n/a	n/a	n/a	n/a	n/a

Note: Freeway Travel Time Index—the ratio of travel time in the peak period to the travel time at free-flow conditions. For example, a value of 1.30 indicates a 20-minute free-flow trip takes 26 minutes in the peak (20 minutes x 1.30 = 26 minutes); (1) Data for the Fargo, ND-MN urban area was not available; (2) Rank is based on 101 larger urban areas (#1 = highest travel time index)
Source: Texas A&M Transportation Institute, 2019 Urban Mobility Report

Public Transportation

Agency Name / Mode of Transportation	Vehicles Operated in Maximum Service[1]	Annual Unlinked Passenger Trips[2] (in thous.)	Annual Passenger Miles[3] (in thous.)
Fargo Metropolitan Area Transit (MAT)			
Bus (purchased transportation)	24	1,343.5	5,676.9
Demand Response (purchased transportation)	13	53.4	305.4

Note: (1) Number of revenue vehicles operated by the given mode and type of service to meet the annual maximum service requirement. This is the revenue vehicle count during the peak season of the year; on the week and day that maximum service is provided. Vehicles operated in maximum service (VOMS) exclude atypical days and one-time special events; (2) Number of passengers who boarded public transportation vehicles. Passengers are counted each time they board a vehicle no matter how many vehicles they use to travel from their origin to their destination. (3) Sum of the distances ridden by all passengers during the entire fiscal year. Source: Federal Transit Administration, National Transit Database, 2019

Air Transportation

Airport Name and Code / Type of Service	Passenger Airlines[1]	Passenger Enplanements	Freight Carriers[2]	Freight (lbs)
Hector International (FAR)				
Domestic service (U.S. carriers - 2020)	15	242,976	7	36,353,749
International service (U.S. carriers - 2019)	1	1	2	646,471

Note: (1) Includes all U.S.-based major, minor and commuter airlines that carried at least one passenger during the year; (2) Includes all U.S.-based airlines and freight carriers that transported at least one pound of freight during the year. Source: Bureau of Transportation Statistics, The Intermodal Transportation Database, Air Carriers: T-100 Domestic Market (U.S. Carriers), 2020; Bureau of Transportation Statistics, The Intermodal Transportation Database, Air Carriers: T-100 International Market (U.S. Carriers), 2019

BUSINESSES

Major Business Headquarters

Company Name	Industry	Rankings	
		Fortune[1]	Forbes[2]
No companies listed	-	-	-

Note: (1) Companies that produce a 10-K are ranked 1 to 500 based on 2019 revenue; (2) All private companies with at least $2 billion in annual revenue through the end of their most current fiscal year are ranked 1 to 219; companies listed are headquartered in the city; dashes indicate no ranking Source: Fortune, "Fortune 500," June/July 2020; Forbes, "America's Largest Private Companies," 2020

Fastest-Growing Businesses

According to Deloitte, Fargo is home to one of North America's 500 fastest-growing high-technology companies: **Aldevron** (#287). Companies are ranked by percentage growth in revenue over a four-year period. Criteria for inclusion: company must be headquartered within North America; must own proprietary intellectual property or technology that is sold to customers in products that contributes to a significant portion of the company's operating revenue; must have been in business for a minumum of four years with 2016 operating revenues of at least $50,000 USD/CD and 2019 operating revenues of at least $5 million USD/CD. Deloitte, 2020 Technology Fast 500™

Living Environment

COST OF LIVING

Cost of Living Index

Composite Index	Groceries	Housing	Utilities	Trans-portation	Health Care	Misc. Goods/ Services
n/a	n/a	n/a	n/a	n/a	n/a	n/a

Note: The Cost of Living Index measures regional differences in the cost of consumer goods and services, excluding taxes and non-consumer expenditures, for professional and managerial households in the top income quintile. It is based on more than 50,000 prices covering almost 60 different items for which prices are collected three times a year by chambers of commerce, economic development organizations or university applied economic centers in each participating urban area. The numbers shown should be read as a percentage above or below the national average of 100. For example, a value of 115.4 in the groceries column indicates that grocery prices are 15.4% higher than the national average. Small differences in the index numbers should not be interpreted as significant; n/a not available.
Source: The Council for Community and Economic Research, Cost of Living Index, 2020

Grocery Prices

Area[1]	T-Bone Steak ($/pound)	Frying Chicken ($/pound)	Whole Milk ($/half gal.)	Eggs ($/dozen)	Orange Juice ($/64 oz.)	Coffee ($/11.5 oz.)
City[2]	n/a	n/a	n/a	n/a	n/a	n/a
Avg.	11.78	1.39	2.05	1.47	3.57	4.34
Min.	8.03	0.94	1.03	0.74	2.94	3.02
Max.	15.86	2.65	4.31	3.77	5.44	8.69

*Note: (1) Values for the local area are compared with the average, minimum and maximum values for all 284 areas in the Cost of Living Index; (2) Figures cover the Fargo ND urban area; n/a not available; **T-Bone Steak** (price per pound); **Frying Chicken** (price per pound, whole fryer); **Whole Milk** (half gallon carton); **Eggs** (price per dozen, Grade A, large); **Orange Juice** (64 oz. Tropicana or Florida Natural); **Coffee** (11.5 oz. can, vacuum-packed, Maxwell House, Hills Bros, or Folgers).*
Source: The Council for Community and Economic Research, Cost of Living Index, 2020

Housing and Utility Costs

Area[1]	New Home Price ($)	Apartment Rent ($/month)	All Electric ($/month)	Part Electric ($/month)	Other Energy ($/month)	Telephone ($/month)
City[2]	n/a	n/a	n/a	n/a	n/a	n/a
Avg.	368,594	1,168	170.86	100.47	65.28	184.30
Min.	190,567	502	91.58	31.42	26.08	169.60
Max.	2,227,806	4,738	470.38	280.31	280.06	206.50

*Note: (1) Values for the local area are compared with the average, minimum and maximum values for all 284 areas in the Cost of Living Index; (2) Figures cover the Fargo ND urban area; n/a not available; **New Home Price** (2,400 sf living area, 8,000 sf lot, in urban area with full utilities); **Apartment Rent** (950 sf 2 bedroom/1.5 or 2 bath, unfurnished, excluding all utilities except water); **All Electric** (average monthly cost for an all-electric home); **Part Electric** (average monthly cost for a part-electric home); **Other Energy** (average monthly cost for natural gas, fuel oil, coal, wood, and any other forms of energy except electricity); **Telephone** (price includes the base monthly rate plus taxes and fees for three lines of mobile phone service).*
Source: The Council for Community and Economic Research, Cost of Living Index, 2020

Health Care, Transportation, and Other Costs

Area[1]	Doctor ($/visit)	Dentist ($/visit)	Optometrist ($/visit)	Gasoline ($/gallon)	Beauty Salon ($/visit)	Men's Shirt ($)
City[2]	n/a	n/a	n/a	n/a	n/a	n/a
Avg.	115.44	99.32	108.10	2.21	39.27	31.37
Min.	36.68	59.00	51.36	1.71	19.00	11.00
Max.	219.00	153.10	250.97	3.46	82.05	58.33

*Note: (1) Values for the local area are compared with the average, minimum and maximum values for all 284 areas in the Cost of Living Index; (2) Figures cover the Fargo ND urban area; n/a not available; **Doctor** (general practitioners routine exam of an established patient); **Dentist** (adult teeth cleaning and periodic oral examination); **Optometrist** (full vision eye exam for established adult patient); **Gasoline** (one gallon regular unleaded, national brand, including all taxes, cash price at self-service pump if available); **Beauty Salon** (woman's shampoo, trim, and blow-dry); **Men's Shirt** (cotton/polyester dress shirt, pinpoint weave, long sleeves).*
Source: The Council for Community and Economic Research, Cost of Living Index, 2020

HOUSING

Homeownership Rate

Area	2012 (%)	2013 (%)	2014 (%)	2015 (%)	2016 (%)	2017 (%)	2018 (%)	2019 (%)	2020 (%)
MSA[1]	n/a	n/a	n/a	n/a	n/a	n/a	n/a	n/a	n/a
U.S.	65.4	65.1	64.5	63.7	63.4	63.9	64.4	64.6	66.6

Note: (1) Figures cover the Fargo, ND-MN Metropolitan Statistical Area; n/a not available
Source: U.S. Census Bureau, Housing Vacancies and Homeownership Annual Statistics: 2012-2020

House Price Index (HPI)

Area	National Ranking[2]	Quarterly Change (%)	One-Year Change (%)	Five-Year Change (%)	Since 1991Q1 (%)
MSA[1]	240	0.70	2.82	16.07	201.82
U.S.[3]	–	3.81	10.77	38.99	205.12

Note: The HPI is a weighted repeat sales index. It measures average price changes in repeat sales or refinancings on the same properties. This information is obtained by reviewing repeat mortgage transactions on single-family properties whose mortgages have been purchased or securitized by Fannie Mae or Freddie Mac since January 1975; (1) Figures cover the Fargo, ND-MN Metropolitan Statistical Area; (2) Rankings are based on annual percentage change for all metro areas containing at least 15,000 transactions over the last 10 years and ranges from 1 to 253; (3) figures based on a weighted average of Census Division estimates using a seasonally adjusted, purchase-only index; all figures are for the period ending December 31, 2020
Source: Federal Housing Finance Agency, Change in Metropolitan Area House Price Indexes, April 7, 2021

Median Single-Family Home Prices

Area	2018	2019	2020p	Percent Change 2019 to 2020
MSA[1]	217.5	221.0	233.5	5.7
U.S. Average	261.6	274.6	299.9	9.2

Note: Figures are median sales prices of existing single-family homes in thousands of dollars; (p) preliminary; (1) Figures cover the Fargo, ND-MN Metropolitan Statistical Area
Source: National Association of Realtors, Median Sales Price of Existing Single-Family Homes for Metropolitan Areas, 4th Quarter 2020

Qualifying Income Based on Median Sales Price of Existing Single-Family Homes

Area	With 5% Down ($)	With 10% Down ($)	With 20% Down ($)
MSA[1]	46,207	43,775	38,912
U.S. Average	59,266	56,147	49,908

Note: Figures are preliminary; Qualifying income is based on a mortgage rate of 2.81%. Monthly principal and interest payment is limited to 25% of income; (1) Figures cover the Fargo, ND-MN Metropolitan Statistical Area
Source: National Association of Realtors, Qualifying Income Based on Median Sales Price of Existing Single-Family Homes for Metropolitan Areas, 4th Quarter 2020

Home Value Distribution

Area	Under $50,000	$50,000 -$99,999	$100,000 -$149,999	$150,000 -$199,999	$200,000 -$299,999	$300,000 -$499,999	$500,000 -$999,999	$1,000,000 or more
City	4.0	4.3	12.6	25.0	30.8	18.6	4.0	0.6
MSA[1]	3.7	5.3	13.1	23.0	30.1	19.4	4.8	0.7
U.S.	6.9	12.0	13.3	14.0	19.6	19.3	11.4	3.4

Note: Figures are percentages and cover owner-occupied housing units; (1) Figures cover the Fargo, ND-MN Metropolitan Statistical Area
Source: U.S. Census Bureau, 2015-2019 American Community Survey 5-Year Estimates

Year Housing Structure Built

Area	2010 or Later	2000 -2009	1990 -1999	1980 -1989	1970 -1979	1960 -1969	1950 -1959	1940 -1949	Before 1940	Median Year
City	16.1	15.8	16.5	13.8	14.0	6.0	6.9	2.6	8.2	1989
MSA[1]	15.1	18.4	14.2	11.2	14.9	6.9	7.4	2.7	9.1	1988
U.S.	5.2	14.0	13.9	13.4	15.2	10.6	10.3	4.9	12.6	1978

Note: Figures are percentages except for Median Year; Note: (1) Figures cover the Fargo, ND-MN Metropolitan Statistical Area
Source: U.S. Census Bureau, 2015-2019 American Community Survey 5-Year Estimates

Gross Monthly Rent

Area	Under $500	$500 -$999	$1,000 -$1,499	$1,500 -$1,999	$2,000 -$2,499	$2,500 -$2,999	$3,000 and up	Median ($)
City	7.0	65.6	20.7	5.3	1.1	0.2	0.1	823
MSA[1]	8.0	62.0	21.3	6.7	1.4	0.4	0.3	837
U.S.	9.4	36.2	30.0	14.0	5.6	2.4	2.4	1,062

Note: Figures are percentages except for Median; Gross rent is the contract rent plus the estimated average monthly cost of utilities (electricity, gas, and water and sewer) and fuels (oil, coal, kerosene, wood, etc.) if these are paid by the renter (or paid for the renter by someone else); (1) Figures cover the Fargo, ND-MN Metropolitan Statistical Area
Source: U.S. Census Bureau, 2015-2019 American Community Survey 5-Year Estimates

HEALTH

Health Risk Factors

Category	MSA[1] (%)	U.S. (%)
Adults aged 18–64 who have any kind of health care coverage	90.5	87.3
Adults who reported being in good or better health	86.1	82.4
Adults who have been told they have high blood cholesterol	29.8	33.0
Adults who have been told they have high blood pressure	25.4	32.3
Adults who are current smokers	16.7	17.1
Adults who currently use E-cigarettes	3.8	4.6
Adults who currently use chewing tobacco, snuff, or snus	5.9	4.0
Adults who are heavy drinkers[2]	8.4	6.3
Adults who are binge drinkers[3]	26.2	17.4
Adults who are overweight (BMI 25.0 - 29.9)	39.6	35.3
Adults who are obese (BMI 30.0 - 99.8)	29.0	31.3
Adults who participated in any physical activities in the past month	76.3	74.4
Adults who always or nearly always wears a seat belt	94.0	94.3

Note: (1) Figures cover the Fargo, ND-MN Metropolitan Statistical Area; (2) Heavy drinkers are classified as adult men having more than 14 drinks per week and adult women having more than 7 drinks per week; (3) Binge drinkers are classified as males having five or more drinks on one occasion or females having four or more drinks on one occasion
Source: Centers for Disease Control and Prevention, Behaviorial Risk Factor Surveillance System, SMART: Selected Metropolitan Area Risk Trends, 2017

Acute and Chronic Health Conditions

Category	MSA[1] (%)	U.S. (%)
Adults who have ever been told they had a heart attack	2.8	4.2
Adults who have ever been told they have angina or coronary heart disease	3.2	3.9
Adults who have ever been told they had a stroke	1.6	3.0
Adults who have ever been told they have asthma	11.1	14.2
Adults who have ever been told they have arthritis	20.7	24.9
Adults who have ever been told they have diabetes[2]	7.4	10.5
Adults who have ever been told they had skin cancer	4.9	6.2
Adults who have ever been told they had any other types of cancer	5.7	7.1
Adults who have ever been told they have COPD	4.4	6.5
Adults who have ever been told they have kidney disease	2.4	3.0
Adults who have ever been told they have a form of depression	22.4	20.5

Note: (1) Figures cover the Fargo, ND-MN Metropolitan Statistical Area; (2) Figures do not include pregnancy-related, borderline, or pre-diabetes
Source: Centers for Disease Control and Prevention, Behaviorial Risk Factor Surveillance System, SMART: Selected Metropolitan Area Risk Trends, 2017

Health Screening and Vaccination Rates

Category	MSA[1] (%)	U.S. (%)
Adults aged 65+ who have had flu shot within the past year	62.8	60.7
Adults aged 65+ who have ever had a pneumonia vaccination	78.5	75.4
Adults who have ever been tested for HIV	27.5	36.1
Adults who have ever had the shingles or zoster vaccine?	38.5	28.9
Adults who have had their blood cholesterol checked within the last five years	81.0	85.9

Note: n/a not available; (1) Figures cover the Fargo, ND-MN Metropolitan Statistical Area.
Source: Centers for Disease Control and Prevention, Behaviorial Risk Factor Surveillance System, SMART: Selected Metropolitan Area Risk Trends, 2017

Disability Status

Category	MSA[1] (%)	U.S. (%)
Adults who reported being deaf	5.0	6.7
Are you blind or have serious difficulty seeing, even when wearing glasses?	2.1	4.5
Are you limited in any way in any of your usual activities due of arthritis?	9.6	12.9
Do you have difficulty doing errands alone?	4.3	6.8
Do you have difficulty dressing or bathing?	n/a	3.6
Do you have serious difficulty concentrating/remembering/making decisions?	8.1	10.7
Do you have serious difficulty walking or climbing stairs?	8.6	13.6

Note: n/a not available; (1) Figures cover the Fargo, ND-MN Metropolitan Statistical Area.
Source: Centers for Disease Control and Prevention, Behaviorial Risk Factor Surveillance System, SMART: Selected Metropolitan Area Risk Trends, 2017

Mortality Rates for the Top 10 Causes of Death in the U.S.

ICD-10[a] Sub-Chapter	ICD-10[a] Code	Age-Adjusted Mortality Rate[1] per 100,000 population	
		County[2]	U.S.
Malignant neoplasms	C00-C97	135.6	149.2
Ischaemic heart diseases	I20-I25	58.5	90.5
Other forms of heart disease	I30-I51	46.3	52.2
Chronic lower respiratory diseases	J40-J47	31.2	39.6
Other degenerative diseases of the nervous system	G30-G31	41.5	37.6
Cerebrovascular diseases	I60-I69	25.4	37.2
Other external causes of accidental injury	W00-X59	25.7	36.1
Organic, including symptomatic, mental disorders	F01-F09	32.2	29.4
Hypertensive diseases	I10-I15	25.2	24.1
Diabetes mellitus	E10-E14	17.0	21.5

Note: (a) ICD-10 = International Classification of Diseases 10th Revision; (1) Mortality rates are a three-year average covering 2017-2019; (2) Figures cover Cass County.
Source: Centers for Disease Control and Prevention, National Center for Health Statistics. Underlying Cause of Death 1999-2019 on CDC WONDER Online Database

Mortality Rates for Selected Causes of Death

ICD-10[a] Sub-Chapter	ICD-10[a] Code	Age-Adjusted Mortality Rate[1] per 100,000 population	
		County[2]	U.S.
Assault	X85-Y09	Unreliable	6.0
Diseases of the liver	K70-K76	16.2	14.4
Human immunodeficiency virus (HIV) disease	B20-B24	Suppressed	1.5
Influenza and pneumonia	J09-J18	9.9	13.8
Intentional self-harm	X60-X84	17.2	14.1
Malnutrition	E40-E46	Suppressed	2.3
Obesity and other hyperalimentation	E65-E68	6.9	2.1
Renal failure	N17-N19	8.5	12.6
Transport accidents	V01-V99	7.0	12.3
Viral hepatitis	B15-B19	Suppressed	1.2

Note: (a) ICD-10 = International Classification of Diseases 10th Revision; (1) Mortality rates are a three-year average covering 2017-2019; (2) Figures cover Cass County; Data are suppressed when the data meet the criteria for confidentiality constraints; Mortality rates are flagged as unreliable when the rate would be calculated with a numerator of 20 or less.
Source: Centers for Disease Control and Prevention, National Center for Health Statistics. Underlying Cause of Death 1999-2019 on CDC WONDER Online Database

Health Insurance Coverage

Area	With Health Insurance	With Private Health Insurance	With Public Health Insurance	Without Health Insurance	Population Under Age 19 Without Health Insurance
City	93.5	80.6	24.3	6.5	4.1
MSA[1]	94.6	82.1	24.4	5.4	4.2
U.S.	91.2	67.9	35.1	8.8	5.1

Note: Figures are percentages that cover the civilian noninstitutionalized population; (1) Figures cover the Fargo, ND-MN Metropolitan Statistical Area
Source: U.S. Census Bureau, 2015-2019 American Community Survey 5-Year Estimates

Number of Medical Professionals

Area	MDs[3]	DOs[3,4]	Dentists	Podiatrists	Chiropractors	Optometrists
County[1] (number)	708	35	145	8	133	57
County[1] (rate[2])	392.7	19.4	79.7	4.4	73.1	31.3
U.S. (rate[2])	282.9	22.7	71.2	6.2	28.1	16.9

38017
Note: Data as of 2019 unless noted; (1) Data covers Cass County; (2) Rate per 100,000 population; (3) Data as of 2018 and includes all active, non-federal physicians; (4) Doctor of Osteopathic Medicine
Source: U.S. Department of Health and Human Services, Health Resources and Services Administration, Bureau of Health Professions, Area Resource File (ARF) 2019-2020

142   Fargo, North Dakota

EDUCATION

Public School District Statistics

District Name	Schls	Pupils	Pupil/ Teacher Ratio	Minority Pupils[1] (%)	Free Lunch Eligible[2] (%)	IEP[3] (%)
Fargo 1	22	11,514	13.4	28.1	25.5	14.2

Note: Table includes school districts with 2,000 or more students; (1) Percentage of students that are not non-Hispanic white; (2) Percentage of students that are eligible for the free lunch program; (3) Percentage of students that have an Individualized Education Program.
Source: U.S. Department of Education, National Center for Education Statistics, Common Core of Data, Local Education Agency (School District) Universe Survey: School Year 2018-2019; U.S. Department of Education, National Center for Education Statistics, Common Core of Data, Public Elementary/Secondary School Universe Survey: School Year 2018-2019

Highest Level of Education

Area	Less than H.S.	H.S. Diploma	Some College, No Deg.	Associate Degree	Bachelor's Degree	Master's Degree	Prof. School Degree	Doctorate Degree
City	5.7	20.9	19.6	13.8	28.0	8.0	2.1	1.8
MSA[1]	5.2	21.0	21.0	14.2	27.4	7.9	1.8	1.5
U.S.	12.0	27.0	20.4	8.5	19.8	8.8	2.1	1.4

Note: Figures cover persons age 25 and over; (1) Figures cover the Fargo, ND-MN Metropolitan Statistical Area
Source: U.S. Census Bureau, 2015-2019 American Community Survey 5-Year Estimates

Educational Attainment by Race

Area	High School Graduate or Higher (%)					Bachelor's Degree or Higher (%)				
	Total	White	Black	Asian	Hisp.[2]	Total	White	Black	Asian	Hisp.[2]
City	94.3	96.1	81.9	71.8	92.0	40.0	41.7	20.2	46.6	21.2
MSA[1]	94.8	96.1	81.7	78.4	83.4	38.6	39.8	22.2	46.8	19.5
U.S.	88.0	89.9	86.0	87.1	68.7	32.1	33.5	21.6	54.3	16.4

Note: Figures shown cover persons 25 years old and over; (1) Figures cover the Fargo, ND-MN Metropolitan Statistical Area; (2) People of Hispanic origin can be of any race
Source: U.S. Census Bureau, 2015-2019 American Community Survey 5-Year Estimates

School Enrollment by Grade and Control

Area	Preschool (%)		Kindergarten (%)		Grades 1 - 4 (%)		Grades 5 - 8 (%)		Grades 9 - 12 (%)	
	Public	Private	Public	Private	Public	Private	Public	Private	Public	Private
City	53.4	46.6	94.7	5.3	90.4	9.6	89.3	10.7	93.7	6.3
MSA[1]	58.8	41.2	93.6	6.4	89.5	10.5	89.3	10.7	93.8	6.2
U.S.	59.1	40.9	87.6	12.4	89.5	10.5	89.4	10.6	90.1	9.9

Note: Figures shown cover persons 3 years old and over; (1) Figures cover the Fargo, ND-MN Metropolitan Statistical Area
Source: U.S. Census Bureau, 2015-2019 American Community Survey 5-Year Estimates

Higher Education

Four-Year Colleges			Two-Year Colleges			Medical Schools[1]	Law Schools[2]	Voc/ Tech[3]
Public	Private Non-profit	Private For-profit	Public	Private Non-profit	Private For-profit			
1	0	1	0	0	2	0	0	2

Note: Figures cover institutions located within the city limits and include main campuses only; (1) includes schools accredited by the Liaison Committee on Medical Education and the American Osteopathic Association's Commission on Osteopathic College Accreditation; (2) includes ABA-accredited schools, schools with provisional ABA accreditation, and state accredited schools; (3) includes all schools with programs that are less than 2 years.
Source: National Center for Education Statistics, Integrated Postsecondary Education System (IPEDS), 2019-20; Wikipedia, List of Medical Schools in the United States, accessed April 2, 2021; Wikipedia, List of Law Schools in the United States, accessed April 2, 2021

Fargo, North Dakota   143

EMPLOYERS

Major Employers

Company Name	Industry
BlueCross BlueShield of North Dakota	Insurance
City of Fargo	Municipal government
CNH Industrial America	Agriculture equipment
Concordia College	Education
Essentia Health	General medical & surgical hospitals
Fargo Public School District	Education
John Deere Electronic Solutions	Manufacturers
Microsoft	Computer software
Minnesota State University Moorhead	Education
Moorhead Area Public Schools	Education
Noridian Heathcare Solutions	Insurance
North Dakota State University	Education
Sanford Fargo Medical Center	Healthcare services
U.S. Bank	Financial services
Veterans Affairs	General medical & surgical hospitals
West Fargo Public School	Education

Note: Companies shown are located within the Fargo, ND-MN Metropolitan Statistical Area.
Source: Hoovers.com; Wikipedia

PUBLIC SAFETY

Crime Rate

Area	All Crimes	Violent Crimes				Property Crimes		
		Murder	Rape[3]	Robbery	Aggrav. Assault	Burglary	Larceny -Theft	Motor Vehicle Theft
City	3,572.4	3.9	87.1	61.2	298.2	651.4	2,163.7	306.9
Suburbs[1]	1,642.9	0.0	34.9	22.4	76.5	277.5	1,087.8	143.8
Metro[2]	2,635.2	2.0	61.8	42.4	190.5	469.8	1,641.1	227.6
U.S.	2,489.3	5.0	42.6	81.6	250.2	340.5	1,549.5	219.9

Note: Figures are crimes per 100,000 population; (1) All areas within the metro area that are located outside the city limits; (2) Figures cover the Fargo, ND-MN Metropolitan Statistical Area; (3) All figures shown were reported using the revised Uniform Crime Reporting (UCR) definition of rape.
Source: FBI Uniform Crime Reports, 2019

Hate Crimes

Area	Number of Quarters Reported	Number of Incidents per Bias Motivation					
		Race/Ethnicity/ Ancestry	Religion	Sexual Orientation	Disability	Gender	Gender Identity
City	4	1	1	0	0	0	0
U.S.	4	3,963	1,521	1,195	157	69	198

Source: Federal Bureau of Investigation, Hate Crime Statistics 2019

Identity Theft Consumer Reports

Area	Reports	Reports per 100,000 Population	Rank[2]
MSA[1]	386	157	281
U.S.	1,387,615	423	-

Note: (1) Figures cover the Fargo, ND-MN Metropolitan Statistical Area; (2) Rank ranges from 1 to 391 where 1 indicates greatest number of identity theft reports per 100,000 population
Source: Federal Trade Commission, Consumer Sentinel Network Data Book 2020

Fraud and Other Consumer Reports

Area	Reports	Reports per 100,000 Population	Rank[2]
MSA[1]	1,271	516	353
U.S.	3,385,133	1,031	-

Note: (1) Figures cover the Fargo, ND-MN Metropolitan Statistical Area; (2) Rank ranges from 1 to 391 where 1 indicates greatest number of fraud and other consumer reports per 100,000 population
Source: Federal Trade Commission, Consumer Sentinel Network Data Book 2020

POLITICS

2020 Presidential Election Results

Area	Biden	Trump	Jorgensen	Hawkins	Other
Cass County	46.8	49.5	2.9	0.0	0.7
U.S.	51.3	46.8	1.2	0.3	0.5

Note: Results are percentages and may not add to 100% due to rounding
Source: Dave Leip's Atlas of U.S. Presidential Elections

144   Fargo, North Dakota

SPORTS

Professional Sports Teams

Team Name	League	Year Established
No teams are located in the metro area		

Source: Wikipedia, Major Professional Sports Teams of the United States and Canada, April 6, 2021

CLIMATE

Average and Extreme Temperatures

Temperature	Jan	Feb	Mar	Apr	May	Jun	Jul	Aug	Sep	Oct	Nov	Dec	Yr.
Extreme High (°F)	52	66	78	100	98	100	106	106	102	93	74	57	106
Average High (°F)	15	21	34	54	69	77	83	81	70	57	36	21	52
Average Temp. (°F)	6	12	26	43	56	66	71	69	58	46	28	13	41
Average Low (°F)	-3	3	17	32	44	54	59	57	46	35	19	4	31
Extreme Low (°F)	-36	-34	-34	-7	20	30	36	33	19	5	-24	-32	-36

Note: Figures cover the years 1948-1995
Source: National Climatic Data Center, International Station Meteorological Climate Summary, 9/96

Average Precipitation/Snowfall/Humidity

Precip./Humidity	Jan	Feb	Mar	Apr	May	Jun	Jul	Aug	Sep	Oct	Nov	Dec	Yr.
Avg. Precip. (in.)	0.6	0.5	1.0	1.7	2.3	3.1	3.2	2.4	1.8	1.5	0.8	0.6	19.6
Avg. Snowfall (in.)	9	6	7	3	Tr	0	0	0	Tr	1	6	7	40
Avg. Rel. Hum. 6am (%)	75	77	82	79	77	82	86	86	85	80	81	78	81
Avg. Rel. Hum. 3pm (%)	70	71	67	51	45	50	50	47	49	51	65	73	57

Note: Figures cover the years 1948-1995; Tr = Trace amounts (<0.05 in. of rain; <0.5 in. of snow)
Source: National Climatic Data Center, International Station Meteorological Climate Summary, 9/96

Weather Conditions

Temperature			Daytime Sky			Precipitation		
5°F & below	32°F & below	90°F & above	Clear	Partly cloudy	Cloudy	0.01 inch or more precip.	0.1 inch or more snow/ice	Thunder-storms
65	180	15	81	145	139	100	38	31

Note: Figures are average number of days per year and cover the years 1948-1995
Source: National Climatic Data Center, International Station Meteorological Climate Summary, 9/96

HAZARDOUS WASTE

Superfund Sites

The Fargo, ND-MN metro area has no sites on the EPA's Superfund Final National Priorities List. There are a total of 1,375 Superfund sites with a status of proposed or final on the list in the U.S. *U.S. Environmental Protection Agency, National Priorities List, April 7, 2021*

AIR QUALITY

Air Quality Trends: Ozone

	1990	1995	2000	2005	2010	2015	2016	2017	2018	2019
MSA[1]	n/a	n/a	n/a	n/a	n/a	n/a	n/a	n/a	n/a	n/a
U.S.	0.088	0.089	0.082	0.080	0.073	0.068	0.069	0.068	0.069	0.065

Note: (1) Data covers the Fargo, ND-MN Metropolitan Statistical Area; n/a not available. The values shown are the composite ozone concentration averages among trend sites based on the highest fourth daily maximum 8-hour concentration in parts per million. These trends are based on sites having an adequate record of monitoring data during the trend period. Data from exceptional events are included.
Source: U.S. Environmental Protection Agency, Air Quality Monitoring Information, "Air Quality Trends by City, 1990-2019"

Air Quality Index

Area	Percent of Days when Air Quality was...[2]					AQI Statistics[2]	
	Good	Moderate	Unhealthy for Sensitive Groups	Unhealthy	Very Unhealthy	Maximum	Median
MSA[1]	90.1	9.4	0.3	0.3	0.0	156	33

Note: (1) Data covers the Fargo, ND-MN Metropolitan Statistical Area; (2) Based on 363 days with AQI data in 2019. Air Quality Index (AQI) is an index for reporting daily air quality. EPA calculates the AQI for five major air pollutants regulated by the Clean Air Act: ground-level ozone, particle pollution (aka particulate matter), carbon monoxide, sulfur dioxide, and nitrogen dioxide. The AQI runs from 0 to 500. The higher the AQI value, the greater the level of air pollution and the greater the health concern. There are six AQI categories: "Good" AQI is between 0 and 50. Air quality is considered satisfactory; "Moderate" AQI is between 51 and 100. Air quality is acceptable; "Unhealthy for Sensitive Groups" When AQI values are between 101 and 150, members of sensitive groups may experience health effects; "Unhealthy" When AQI values are between 151 and 200 everyone may begin to experience health effects; "Very Unhealthy" AQI values between 201 and 300 trigger a health alert; "Hazardous" AQI values over 300 trigger warnings of emergency conditions (not shown).
Source: U.S. Environmental Protection Agency, Air Quality Index Report, 2019

Air Quality Index Pollutants

Area	Percent of Days when AQI Pollutant was...[2]					
	Carbon Monoxide	Nitrogen Dioxide	Ozone	Sulfur Dioxide	Particulate Matter 2.5	Particulate Matter 10
MSA[1]	0.0	2.5	72.7	0.0	24.2	0.6

Note: (1) Data covers the Fargo, ND-MN Metropolitan Statistical Area; (2) Based on 363 days with AQI data in 2019. The Air Quality Index (AQI) is an index for reporting daily air quality. EPA calculates the AQI for five major air pollutants regulated by the Clean Air Act: ground-level ozone, particle pollution (also known as particulate matter), carbon monoxide, sulfur dioxide, and nitrogen dioxide. The AQI runs from 0 to 500. The higher the AQI value, the greater the level of air pollution and the greater the health concern.
Source: U.S. Environmental Protection Agency, Air Quality Index Report, 2019

Maximum Air Pollutant Concentrations: Particulate Matter, Ozone, CO and Lead

	Particulate Matter 10 (ug/m^3)	Particulate Matter 2.5 Wtd AM (ug/m^3)	Particulate Matter 2.5 24-Hr (ug/m^3)	Ozone (ppm)	Carbon Monoxide (ppm)	Lead (ug/m^3)
MSA[1] Level	78	6.5	18	0.062	n/a	n/a
NAAQS[2]	150	15	35	0.075	9	0.15
Met NAAQS[2]	Yes	Yes	Yes	Yes	n/a	n/a

Note: (1) Data covers the Fargo, ND-MN Metropolitan Statistical Area; Data from exceptional events are included; (2) National Ambient Air Quality Standards; ppm = parts per million; ug/m^3 = micrograms per cubic meter; n/a not available.
Concentrations: Particulate Matter 10 (coarse particulate)—highest second maximum 24-hour concentration; Particulate Matter 2.5 Wtd AM (fine particulate)—highest weighted annual mean concentration; Particulate Matter 2.5 24-Hour (fine particulate)—highest 98th percentile 24-hour concentration; Ozone—highest fourth daily maximum 8-hour concentration; Carbon Monoxide—highest second maximum non-overlapping 8-hour concentration; Lead—maximum running 3-month average
Source: U.S. Environmental Protection Agency, Air Quality Monitoring Information, "Air Quality Statistics by City, 2019"

Maximum Air Pollutant Concentrations: Nitrogen Dioxide and Sulfur Dioxide

	Nitrogen Dioxide AM (ppb)	Nitrogen Dioxide 1-Hr (ppb)	Sulfur Dioxide AM (ppb)	Sulfur Dioxide 1-Hr (ppb)	Sulfur Dioxide 24-Hr (ppb)
MSA[1] Level	4	39	n/a	3	n/a
NAAQS[2]	53	100	30	75	140
Met NAAQS[2]	Yes	Yes	n/a	Yes	n/a

Note: (1) Data covers the Fargo, ND-MN Metropolitan Statistical Area; Data from exceptional events are included; (2) National Ambient Air Quality Standards; ppm = parts per million; ug/m^3 = micrograms per cubic meter; n/a not available.
Concentrations: Nitrogen Dioxide AM—highest arithmetic mean concentration; Nitrogen Dioxide 1-Hr—highest 98th percentile 1-hour daily maximum concentration; Sulfur Dioxide AM—highest annual mean concentration; Sulfur Dioxide 1-Hr—highest 99th percentile 1-hour daily maximum concentration; Sulfur Dioxide 24-Hr—highest second maximum 24-hour concentration
Source: U.S. Environmental Protection Agency, Air Quality Monitoring Information, "Air Quality Statistics by City, 2019"

Fort Wayne, Indiana

Background

Fort Wayne lies 100 miles northeast of Indianapolis, at the confluence of the St. Mary and St. Joseph rivers, which form the Maumee River. The waters, spanned by 21 bridges, divide the town into three parts.

Once the stronghold of the Miami tribe, the area was prominent in frontier history. The Miami Native Americans ruled the lower peninsula region, fighting against the Iroquois who had been armed by the English colonists. Later, the Miami tribe established itself in the Wabash Valley and built a village at the Lakeside district in Fort Wayne. They continued to side with the British during the American Revolution, after which President Washington ordered armies into the center of the Miami Territory to stop the Miami war parties, which had been encouraged to attack the new nation by the British. After Chief Little Turtle, one of the most feared and respected tribal leaders, defeated the army of General Arthur St. Clair, Washington sought the help of General "Mad" Anthony Wayne, who succeeded in defeating the rebellious tribes. Wayne marched on Miamitown and built the first American fort there. When the fort was turned over to Colonel John Hamtramck on October 21, 1794, the colonel immediately changed the name to Fort Wayne.

Fort Wayne's industrial growth began with the building of the Wabash and Erie Canal in the 1830s and was further stimulated in the 1850s when the railway came.

Nearly equidistant from Chicago, Cincinnati, and Detroit, the city is a regional transportation and communications center. Although the city is in an area rich in dairy, livestock, and vegetable farming, it is primarily a diversified industrial center, with several strong clusters of industry including advanced manufacturing, defense engineering, automotive-related development and production (home to the world's first full-size hybrid pickup truck), life science, higher education, aerospace/avionics-related, logistics and finance. Fort Wayne also enjoys additional prosperity due to its proximity to Warsaw, Indiana, termed the Orthopedic Capitol of the World due to its many orthopedic-implant manufacturers.

Institutions of higher education in the city include Indiana's Institute of Technology, Indiana University-Purdue University at Fort Wayne, and University of St. Francis. The city is also home to the Northeast Indiana Innovation Center, designed to attract high-tech businesses and to provide community outreach to local entrepreneurs and schools. Ongoing projects include the Core Incubation System, which specializes in biomedical, information systems, and advanced manufacturing plans, and the Digital Kids Initiative, which promotes early mastery of digital skills. The city has developed a blueprint for preservation and restoration of various downtown districts, including the Landing District, the Old Canal District, and the Barr Street District, which features an "International Marketplace," a cluster of businesses owned and operated by ethnic groups and supplemented by cultural centers serving them.

Fort Wayne is sometimes referred to as the "City of Churches," an unofficial moniker dating to the late-19th century when the city was the regional hub of Catholic, Lutheran, and Episcopal faiths. Today, there are nearly 400 churches in the city.

Parkview Field is home to the TinCaps, baseball's minor league team affiliated with the San Diego Padres. Not far from Parkview Field are condominiums, shops and a centrally located Courtyard Marriott hotel. Fort Wayne's renovated Grand Wayne Convention Center encompasses 225,000 square feet.

Fort Wayne's varied cultural and educational attractions combined with a low cost of living have earned Fort Wayne awards over the years, such as All-American City, Best Place to Live, and City Livability Outstanding Achievement. Arts events are held at the Allen County War Memorial Coliseum, Foellinger Outdoor Theater, and IPFW Performing Arts Center. Additional attractions include: the Foellinger-Freimann Botanical Conservatory with a Tropical House and cascading waterfall, Sonoran Desert House, Woody the talking tree, and hands-on exhibits; the Fort Wayne Museum of Art; the nationally acclaimed Fort Wayne Children's Zoo; and the Lincoln Museum with its award-winning permanent exhibit honoring the life and legacy of our 16th president.

The land surrounding the city is generally level to the south and east, rolling to the west and southwest, and quite hilly to the north and northwest. The climate is influenced by the Great Lakes, with rain fairly constant throughout the warmer months. Damaging hailstorms occur approximately twice a year, and severe flooding is possible. While snow generally covers the ground for about a month during the winter, heavy snowstorms are infrequent. With the exception of considerable cloudiness during the winter, Fort Wayne enjoys a good Midwestern average for sunshine.

Rankings

Business/Finance Rankings

- Fort Wayne was the #18-ranked city for savers, according to a study by the finance site GOBankingRates, which considered the prospects for people trying to save money. Criteria: average monthly cost of grocery items; median home listing price; median rent; median income; transportation costs; gas prices; and the cost of eating out for an inexpensive and mid-range meal in 100 U.S. cities. *www.gobankingrates.com, "The 20 Best (and Worst) Places to Live If You're Trying to Save Money," August 27, 2019*

- Fort Wayne was ranked #18 among 100 U.S. cities for most difficult conditions for savers, according to a study by the finance site GOBankingRates. Criteria: average monthly cost of grocery items; median home listing price; median rent; median income; transportation costs; gas prices; and the cost of eating out for an inexpensive and mid-range meal. *www.gobankingrates.com, "The 20 Best (and Worst) Places to Live If You're Trying to Save Money," August 27, 2019*

- The Fort Wayne metro area appeared on the Milken Institute "2021 Best Performing Cities" list. Rank: #82 out of 200 large metro areas (population over 250,000). Criteria: job growth; wage and salary growth; high-tech output growth; housing affordability; household broadband access. *Milken Institute, "Best-Performing Cities 2021," February 16, 2021*

- *Forbes* ranked the 200 most populous metro areas to determine the nation's "Best Places for Business and Careers." The Fort Wayne metro area was ranked #122. Criteria: costs (business and living); job growth (past and projected); income growth; quality of life; educational attainment (college and high school); projected economic growth; cultural and leisure opportunities; workplace tolerance laws; net migration patterns. *Forbes, "The Best Places for Business and Careers 2019: Seattle Still On Top," October 30, 2019*

Children/Family Rankings

- Fort Wayne was selected as one of the most playful cities in the U.S. by KaBOOM! The organization's Playful City USA initiative honors cities and towns across the nation that have made their communities more playable. Criteria: pledging to integrate play as a solution to challenges in their communities; making it easy for children to get active and balanced play; creating more family-friendly and innovative communities as a result. *KaBOOM! National Campaign for Play, "2017 Playful City USA Communities"*

Education Rankings

- Personal finance website *WalletHub* analyzed the 150 largest U.S. metropolitan statistical areas to determine where the most educated Americans are putting their degrees to work. Criteria: education levels; percentage of workers with degrees; education quality and attainment gap; public school quality rankings; quality and enrollment of each metro area's universities. Fort Wayne was ranked #105 (#1 = most educated city). *www.WalletHub.com, "Most and Least Educated Cities in America," July 20, 2020*

- Fort Wayne was selected as one of America's most literate cities. The city ranked #53 out of the 84 largest U.S. cities. Criteria: number of booksellers; library resources; Internet resources; educational attainment; periodical publishing resources; newspaper circulation. *Central Connecticut State University, "America's Most Literate Cities, 2018," February 2019*

Environmental Rankings

- Fort Wayne was highlighted as one of the top 98 cleanest metro areas for short-term particle pollution (24-hour PM 2.5) in the U.S. during 2016 through 2018. Monitors in these cities reported no days with unhealthful PM 2.5 levels. *American Lung Association, "State of the Air 2020," April 21, 2020*

Health/Fitness Rankings

- For each of the 100 largest cities in the United States, the American Fitness Index®, published by the American College of Sports Medicine and the Anthem Foundation, evaluated community infrastructure and 33 health behaviors including preventive health, levels of chronic disease conditions, pedestrian safety, air quality, and community resources that support physical activity. Fort Wayne ranked #92 for "community fitness." *americanfitnessindex.org, "2020 ACSM American Fitness Index Summary Report," July 14, 2020*

Real Estate Rankings

- *WalletHub* compared the most populated U.S. cities to determine which had the best markets for real estate agents. Fort Wayne ranked #108 where demand was high and pay was the best. Criteria: sales per agent; annual median wage for real-estate agents; monthly average starting salary for real estate agents; real estate job density and competition; unemployment rate; home turnover rate; housing-market health index; and other relevant metrics. *www.WalletHub.com, "2019's Best Places to Be a Real Estate Agent," April 24, 2019*

- The Fort Wayne metro area was identified as one of the nations's 20 hottest housing markets in 2021. Criteria: listing views as an indicator of demand and median days on the market as an indicator of supply. The area ranked #5. *Realtor.com, "January 2021 Top 20 Hottest Housing Markets," February 25, 2021*

Safety Rankings

- Allstate ranked the 200 largest cities in America in terms of driver safety. Fort Wayne ranked #36. Criteria: internal property damage claims over a two-year period from January 2016 to December 2017. The report helps increase the importance of safety and awareness behind the wheel. *Allstate, "Allstate America's Best Drivers Report, 2019" June 24, 2019*

- The National Insurance Crime Bureau ranked 384 metro areas in the U.S. in terms of per capita rates of vehicle theft. The Fort Wayne metro area ranked #198 (#1 = highest rate). Criteria: number of vehicle theft offenses per 100,000 inhabitants in 2019. *National Insurance Crime Bureau, "Hot Spots 2019," July 21, 2020*

Seniors/Retirement Rankings

- From its Best Cities for Successful Aging indexes, the Milken Institute generated rankings for metropolitan areas, weighing data in nine categories—health care, wellness, living arrangements, transportation and convenience, financial characteristics, education, employment, community engagement, and overall livability. The Fort Wayne metro area was ranked #115 overall in the small metro area category. *Milken Institute, "Best Cities for Successful Aging, 2017" March 14, 2017*

Sports/Recreation Rankings

- Fort Wayne was chosen as a bicycle friendly community by the League of American Bicyclists. A "Bicycle Friendly Community" welcomes cyclists by providing safe and supportive accommodation for cycling and encouraging people to bike for transportation and recreation. There are five award levels: Diamond; Platinum; Gold; Silver; and Bronze. The community achieved an award level of Bronze. *League of American Bicyclists, "Fall 2020 Awards-New & Renewing Bicycle Friendly Communities List," December 16, 2020*

Women/Minorities Rankings

- Personal finance website *WalletHub* compared more than 180 U.S. cities across two key dimensions, "Hispanic Business-Friendliness" and "Hispanic Purchasing Power," to arrive at the most favorable conditions for Hispanic entrepreneurs. Fort Wayne was ranked #118 out of 182. Criteria includes: share of Hispanic-Owned Businesses; Hispanic entrepreneurship rate to median annual income of Hispanics; Small Business-Friendliness score; cost of living; and number of Hispanics with at least a bachelor's degree. *WalletHub.com, "2019's Best Cities for Hispanic Entrepreneurs," May 1, 2019*

Miscellaneous Rankings

- *WalletHub* compared the 150 most populated U.S. cities to determine their operating efficiency. A "Quality of City Services" score was constructed for each city and then divided by the total budget per capita to reveal which were managed the best. Fort Wayne ranked #8. Criteria: financial stability; economy; education; safety; health; infrastructure and pollution. *www.WalletHub.com, "2020's Best- & Worst-Run Cities in America," June 29, 2020*

150   Fort Wayne, Indiana

Business Environment

DEMOGRAPHICS

Population Growth

Area	1990 Census	2000 Census	2010 Census	2019* Estimate	Population Growth (%) 1990-2019	2010-2019
City	205,671	205,727	253,691	265,752	29.2	4.8
MSA[1]	354,435	390,156	416,257	406,305	14.6	-2.4
U.S.	248,709,873	281,421,906	308,745,538	324,697,795	30.6	5.2

Note: (1) Figures cover the Fort Wayne, IN Metropolitan Statistical Area; (*) 2015-2019 5-year estimated population
Source: U.S. Census Bureau, 1990 Census, Census 2000, Census 2010, 2015-2019 American Community Survey 5-Year Estimates

Household Size

Area	Persons in Household (%)							Average Household Size
	One	Two	Three	Four	Five	Six	Seven or More	
City	32.1	33.0	14.4	11.2	5.9	2.2	1.1	2.50
MSA[1]	28.9	34.4	14.5	12.3	6.3	2.4	1.3	2.50
U.S.	27.9	33.9	15.6	12.9	6.0	2.3	1.4	2.60

Note: (1) Figures cover the Fort Wayne, IN Metropolitan Statistical Area
Source: U.S. Census Bureau, 2015-2019 American Community Survey 5-Year Estimates

Race

Area	White Alone[2] (%)	Black Alone[2] (%)	Asian Alone[2] (%)	AIAN[3] Alone[2] (%)	NHOPI[4] Alone[2] (%)	Other Race Alone[2] (%)	Two or More Races (%)
City	73.4	15.1	4.7	0.2	0.1	2.1	4.5
MSA[1]	80.4	10.6	3.5	0.2	0.0	1.7	3.6
U.S.	72.5	12.7	5.5	0.8	0.2	4.9	3.3

Note: (1) Figures cover the Fort Wayne, IN Metropolitan Statistical Area; (2) Alone is defined as not being in combination with one or more other races; (3) American Indian and Alaska Native; (4) Native Hawaiian and Other Pacific Islander
Source: U.S. Census Bureau, 2015-2019 American Community Survey 5-Year Estimates

Hispanic or Latino Origin

Area	Total (%)	Mexican (%)	Puerto Rican (%)	Cuban (%)	Other (%)
City	9.2	6.8	0.5	0.1	1.7
MSA[1]	7.0	5.2	0.4	0.1	1.3
U.S.	18.0	11.2	1.7	0.7	4.3

Note: Persons of Hispanic or Latino origin can be of any race; (1) Figures cover the Fort Wayne, IN Metropolitan Statistical Area
Source: U.S. Census Bureau, 2015-2019 American Community Survey 5-Year Estimates

Ancestry

Area	German	Irish	English	American	Italian	Polish	French[2]	Scottish	Dutch
City	24.3	9.5	6.9	5.7	2.4	2.1	3.0	1.5	1.3
MSA[1]	27.0	9.3	7.2	6.9	2.6	2.1	3.3	1.6	1.4
U.S.	13.3	9.7	7.2	6.2	5.1	2.8	2.3	1.7	1.2

Note: Figures are the percentage of the total population reporting a particular ancestry. The nine most commonly reported ancestries in the U.S. are shown. Figures include multiple ancestries (e.g. if a person reported being Irish and Italian, they were included in both columns); (1) Figures cover the Fort Wayne, IN Metropolitan Statistical Area; (2) Excludes Basque
Source: U.S. Census Bureau, 2015-2019 American Community Survey 5-Year Estimates

Foreign-born Population

Area	Percent of Population Born in								
	Any Foreign Country	Asia	Mexico	Europe	Caribbean	Central America[2]	South America	Africa	Canada
City	8.2	3.9	1.9	0.8	0.1	0.7	0.3	0.4	0.1
MSA[1]	6.3	3.0	1.4	0.7	0.1	0.5	0.2	0.3	0.1
U.S.	13.6	4.2	3.5	1.5	1.3	1.1	1.0	0.7	0.2

Note: (1) Figures cover the Fort Wayne, IN Metropolitan Statistical Area; (2) Excludes Mexico.
Source: U.S. Census Bureau, 2015-2019 American Community Survey 5-Year Estimates

Marital Status

Area	Never Married	Now Married[2]	Separated	Widowed	Divorced
City	35.3	44.4	1.5	5.8	13.0
MSA[1]	31.5	49.6	1.3	5.7	11.9
U.S.	33.4	48.1	1.9	5.8	10.9

Note: Figures are percentages and cover the population 15 years of age and older; (1) Figures cover the Fort Wayne, IN Metropolitan Statistical Area; (2) Excludes separated
Source: U.S. Census Bureau, 2015-2019 American Community Survey 5-Year Estimates

Disability by Age

Area	All Ages	Under 18 Years Old	18 to 64 Years Old	65 Years and Over
City	13.6	5.2	12.6	34.0
MSA[1]	12.6	4.5	11.3	32.8
U.S.	12.6	4.2	10.3	34.5

Note: Figures show percent of the civilian noninstitutionalized population that reported having a disability. Disability status is determined from six types of difficulty: vision, hearing, cognitive, ambulatory, self-care, and independent living. For children under 5 years old, hearing and vision difficulty are used to determine disability status. For children between the ages of 5 and 14, disability status is determined from hearing, vision, cognitive, ambulatory, and self-care difficulties. For people aged 15 years and older, they are considered to have a disability if they have difficulty with any one of the six difficulty types; Note: (1) Figures cover the Fort Wayne, IN Metropolitan Statistical Area
Source: U.S. Census Bureau, 2015-2019 American Community Survey 5-Year Estimates

Age

Area	Percent of Population									Median Age
	Under Age 5	Age 5–19	Age 20–34	Age 35–44	Age 45–54	Age 55–64	Age 65–74	Age 75–84	Age 85+	
City	7.1	20.6	22.2	12.1	11.7	12.1	8.3	3.8	1.8	35.0
MSA[1]	7.0	21.1	20.1	12.3	12.4	12.6	8.6	4.1	1.8	36.4
U.S.	6.1	19.1	20.7	12.6	13.0	12.9	9.1	4.6	1.9	38.1

Note: (1) Figures cover the Fort Wayne, IN Metropolitan Statistical Area
Source: U.S. Census Bureau, 2015-2019 American Community Survey 5-Year Estimates

Gender

Area	Males	Females	Males per 100 Females
City	128,483	137,269	93.6
MSA[1]	198,843	207,462	95.8
U.S.	159,886,919	164,810,876	97.0

Note: (1) Figures cover the Fort Wayne, IN Metropolitan Statistical Area
Source: U.S. Census Bureau, 2015-2019 American Community Survey 5-Year Estimates

Religious Groups by Family

Area	Catholic	Baptist	Non-Den.	Methodist[2]	Lutheran	LDS[3]	Pentecostal	Presbyterian[4]	Muslim[5]	Judaism
MSA[1]	14.2	6.1	6.8	5.1	8.5	0.4	1.5	1.7	0.3	0.1
U.S.	19.1	9.3	4.0	4.0	2.3	2.0	1.9	1.6	0.8	0.7

Note: Figures are the number of adherents as a percentage of the total population; (1) Figures cover the Fort Wayne, IN Metropolitan Statistical Area; (2) Methodist/Pietist; (3) Latter Day Saints; (4) Reformed; (5) Figures are estimates
Source: Association of Statisticians of American Religious Bodies, 2010 U.S. Religion Census: Religious Congregations & Membership Study

Religious Groups by Tradition

Area	Catholic	Evangelical Protestant	Mainline Protestant	Other Tradition	Black Protestant	Orthodox
MSA[1]	14.2	24.6	9.2	1.0	2.4	0.2
U.S.	19.1	16.2	7.3	4.3	1.6	0.3

Note: Figures are the number of adherents as a percentage of the total population; (1) Figures cover the Fort Wayne, IN Metropolitan Statistical Area
Source: Association of Statisticians of American Religious Bodies, 2010 U.S. Religion Census: Religious Congregations & Membership Study

ECONOMY

Gross Metropolitan Product

Area	2017	2018	2019	2020	Rank[2]
MSA[1]	21.9	22.9	23.9	24.8	117

Note: Figures are in billions of dollars; (1) Figures cover the Fort Wayne, IN Metropolitan Statistical Area; (2) Rank is based on 2018 data and ranges from 1 to 381
Source: U.S. Conference of Mayors, U.S. Metro Economies: GMP & Employment 2018-2020, September 2019

152 Fort Wayne, Indiana

Economic Growth

Area	2015-17 (%)	2018 (%)	2019 (%)	2020 (%)	Rank[2]
MSA[1]	1.9	2.5	2.5	1.3	149
U.S.	1.9	2.9	2.3	2.1	—

Note: Figures are real gross metropolitan product (GMP) growth rates and represent average annual percent change; (1) Figures cover the Fort Wayne, IN Metropolitan Statistical Area; (2) Rank is based on 2017 2-year average annual percent change and ranges from 1 to 381
Source: U.S. Conference of Mayors, U.S. Metro Economies: GMP & Employment 2018-2020, September 2019

Metropolitan Area Exports

Area	2014	2015	2016	2017	2018	2019	Rank[2]
MSA[1]	1,581.1	1,529.0	1,322.2	1,422.8	1,593.3	1,438.5	125

Note: Figures are in millions of dollars; (1) Figures cover the Fort Wayne, IN Metropolitan Statistical Area; (2) Rank is based on 2019 data and ranges from 1 to 386
Source: U.S. Department of Commerce, International Trade Administration, Office of Trade and Economic Analysis, Industry and Analysis, Exports by Metropolitan Area, data extracted March 24, 2021

Building Permits

Area	Single-Family			Multi-Family			Total		
	2018	2019	Pct. Chg.	2018	2019	Pct. Chg.	2018	2019	Pct. Chg.
City	n/a	n/a	n/a	n/a	n/a	n/a	n/a	n/a	n/a
MSA[1]	1,343	1,330	-1.0	541	626	15.7	1,884	1,956	3.8
U.S.	855,300	862,100	0.7	473,500	523,900	10.6	1,328,800	1,386,000	4.3

Note: (1) Figures cover the Fort Wayne, IN Metropolitan Statistical Area; Figures represent new, privately-owned housing units authorized (unadjusted data); All permit data are based on estimates with imputation
Source: U.S. Census Bureau, Manufacturing, Mining, and Construction Statistics, Building Permits, 2018, 2019

Bankruptcy Filings

Area	Business Filings			Nonbusiness Filings		
	2019	2020	% Chg.	2019	2020	% Chg.
Allen County	15	15	0.0	1,294	1,057	-18.3
U.S.	22,780	21,655	-4.9	752,160	522,808	-30.5

Note: Business filings include Chapter 7, Chapter 9, Chapter 11, Chapter 12, Chapter 13, Chapter 15, and Section 304; Nonbusiness filings include Chapter 7, Chapter 11, and Chapter 13
Source: Administrative Office of the U.S. Courts, Business and Nonbusiness Bankruptcy, County Cases Commenced by Chapter of the Bankruptcy Code, During the 12-Month Period Ending December 31, 2019 and Business and Nonbusiness Bankruptcy, County Cases Commenced by Chapter of the Bankruptcy Code, During the 12-Month Period Ending December 31, 2020

Housing Vacancy Rates

Area	Gross Vacancy Rate[2] (%)			Year-Round Vacancy Rate[3] (%)			Rental Vacancy Rate[4] (%)			Homeowner Vacancy Rate[5] (%)		
	2018	2019	2020	2018	2019	2020	2018	2019	2020	2018	2019	2020
MSA[1]	n/a	n/a	n/a	n/a	n/a	n/a	n/a	n/a	n/a	n/a	n/a	n/a
U.S.	12.3	12.0	10.6	9.7	9.5	8.2	6.9	6.7	6.3	1.5	1.4	1.0

Note: (1) Figures cover the Fort Wayne, IN Metropolitan Statistical Area; (2) The percentage of the total housing inventory that is vacant; (3) The percentage of the housing inventory (excluding seasonal units) that is year-round vacant; (4) The percentage of rental inventory that is vacant for rent; (5) The percentage of homeowner inventory that is vacant for sale; n/a not available
Source: U.S. Census Bureau, Housing Vacancies and Homeownership Annual Statistics: 2018, 2019, 2020

INCOME

Income

Area	Per Capita ($)	Median Household ($)	Average Household ($)
City	26,970	49,411	65,377
MSA[1]	29,383	55,341	73,578
U.S.	34,103	62,843	88,607

Note: (1) Figures cover the Fort Wayne, IN Metropolitan Statistical Area
Source: U.S. Census Bureau, 2015-2019 American Community Survey 5-Year Estimates

Household Income Distribution

Area	Percent of Households Earning							
	Under $15,000	$15,000 -$24,999	$25,000 -$34,999	$35,000 -$49,999	$50,000 -$74,999	$75,000 -$99,999	$100,000 -$149,999	$150,000 and up
City	11.5	11.3	11.9	15.8	19.4	12.6	10.8	6.6
MSA[1]	9.4	9.8	10.9	14.8	19.8	13.7	13.3	8.3
U.S.	10.3	8.9	8.9	12.3	17.2	12.7	15.1	14.5

Note: (1) Figures cover the Fort Wayne, IN Metropolitan Statistical Area
Source: U.S. Census Bureau, 2015-2019 American Community Survey 5-Year Estimates

Fort Wayne, Indiana 153

Poverty Rate

Area	All Ages	Under 18 Years Old	18 to 64 Years Old	65 Years and Over
City	16.0	24.1	14.5	7.5
MSA[1]	13.0	19.4	11.7	6.5
U.S.	13.4	18.5	12.6	9.3

Note: Figures are percentage of people whose income during the past 12 months was below the poverty level;
(1) Figures cover the Fort Wayne, IN Metropolitan Statistical Area
Source: U.S. Census Bureau, 2015-2019 American Community Survey 5-Year Estimates

CITY FINANCES

City Government Finances

Component	2017 ($000)	2017 ($ per capita)
Total Revenues	285,215	1,096
Total Expenditures	183,365	704
Debt Outstanding	497,681	1,912
Cash and Securities[1]	168,604	648

Note: (1) Cash and security holdings of a government at the close of its fiscal year,
including those of its dependent agencies, utilities, and liquor stores.
Source: U.S. Census Bureau, State & Local Government Finances 2017

City Government Revenue by Source

Source	2017 ($000)	2017 ($ per capita)	2017 (%)
General Revenue			
From Federal Government	0	0	0.0
From State Government	46,180	177	16.2
From Local Governments	0	0	0.0
Taxes			
Property	123,765	475	43.4
Sales and Gross Receipts	0	0	0.0
Personal Income	55,569	213	19.5
Corporate Income	0	0	0.0
Motor Vehicle License	4,558	18	1.6
Other Taxes	0	0	0.0
Current Charges	10,480	40	3.7
Liquor Store	0	0	0.0
Utility	44,642	171	15.7
Employee Retirement	0	0	0.0

Source: U.S. Census Bureau, State & Local Government Finances 2017

City Government Expenditures by Function

Function	2017 ($000)	2017 ($ per capita)	2017 (%)
General Direct Expenditures			
Air Transportation	0	0	0.0
Corrections	0	0	0.0
Education	0	0	0.0
Employment Security Administration	0	0	0.0
Financial Administration	7,070	27	3.9
Fire Protection	34,639	133	18.9
General Public Buildings	1,521	5	0.8
Governmental Administration, Other	974	3	0.5
Health	2,534	9	1.4
Highways	40,338	155	22.0
Hospitals	0	0	0.0
Housing and Community Development	10,089	38	5.5
Interest on General Debt	0	0	0.0
Judicial and Legal	533	2	0.3
Libraries	0	0	0.0
Parking	507	1	0.3
Parks and Recreation	13,320	51	7.3
Police Protection	62,459	239	34.1
Public Welfare	0	0	0.0
Sewerage	0	0	0.0
Solid Waste Management	9,255	35	5.0
Veterans' Services	0	0	0.0
Liquor Store	0	0	0.0
Utility	0	0	0.0
Employee Retirement	0	0	0.0

Source: U.S. Census Bureau, State & Local Government Finances 2017

154 Fort Wayne, Indiana

EMPLOYMENT

Labor Force and Employment

Area	Civilian Labor Force			Workers Employed		
	Dec. 2019	Dec. 2020	% Chg.	Dec. 2019	Dec. 2020	% Chg.
City	128,470	131,139	2.1	124,594	125,226	0.5
MSA[1]	216,998	220,641	1.7	210,942	212,055	0.5
U.S.	164,007,000	160,017,000	-2.4	158,504,000	149,613,000	-5.6

Note: Data is not seasonally adjusted and covers workers 16 years of age and older; (1) Figures cover the Fort Wayne, IN Metropolitan Statistical Area
Source: Bureau of Labor Statistics, Local Area Unemployment Statistics

Unemployment Rate

Area	2020											
	Jan.	Feb.	Mar.	Apr.	May	Jun.	Jul.	Aug.	Sep.	Oct.	Nov.	Dec.
City	3.6	3.5	3.2	20.6	14.9	12.9	9.6	7.7	6.8	6.0	5.6	4.5
MSA[1]	3.4	3.3	3.0	19.4	13.5	11.2	8.2	6.5	5.7	5.1	4.8	3.9
U.S.	4.0	3.8	4.5	14.4	13.0	11.2	10.5	8.5	7.7	6.6	6.4	6.5

Note: Data is not seasonally adjusted and covers workers 16 years of age and older; (1) Figures cover the Fort Wayne, IN Metropolitan Statistical Area
Source: Bureau of Labor Statistics, Local Area Unemployment Statistics

Average Wages

Occupation	$/Hr.	Occupation	$/Hr.
Accountants and Auditors	34.40	Maintenance and Repair Workers	21.50
Automotive Mechanics	18.80	Marketing Managers	60.10
Bookkeepers	19.70	Network and Computer Systems Admin.	32.60
Carpenters	20.20	Nurses, Licensed Practical	22.80
Cashiers	11.30	Nurses, Registered	30.10
Computer Programmers	25.60	Nursing Assistants	14.30
Computer Systems Analysts	37.10	Office Clerks, General	16.90
Computer User Support Specialists	23.10	Physical Therapists	42.50
Construction Laborers	20.00	Physicians	122.90
Cooks, Restaurant	13.20	Plumbers, Pipefitters and Steamfitters	27.80
Customer Service Representatives	18.80	Police and Sheriff's Patrol Officers	29.00
Dentists	80.10	Postal Service Mail Carriers	25.00
Electricians	26.10	Real Estate Sales Agents	23.90
Engineers, Electrical	48.50	Retail Salespersons	13.60
Fast Food and Counter Workers	10.90	Sales Representatives, Technical/Scientific	39.20
Financial Managers	57.60	Secretaries, Exc. Legal/Medical/Executive	18.00
First-Line Supervisors of Office Workers	28.50	Security Guards	17.30
General and Operations Managers	55.30	Surgeons	102.80
Hairdressers/Cosmetologists	13.00	Teacher Assistants, Exc. Postsecondary*	12.40
Home Health and Personal Care Aides	12.20	Teachers, Secondary School, Exc. Sp. Ed.*	26.60
Janitors and Cleaners	11.90	Telemarketers	n/a
Landscaping/Groundskeeping Workers	14.30	Truck Drivers, Heavy/Tractor-Trailer	21.80
Lawyers	59.10	Truck Drivers, Light/Delivery Services	19.40
Maids and Housekeeping Cleaners	11.30	Waiters and Waitresses	13.50

Note: Wage data covers the Fort Wayne, IN Metropolitan Statistical Area; (*) Hourly wages were calculated from annual wage data based on a 40 hour work week; n/a not available.
Source: Bureau of Labor Statistics, Metro Area Occupational Employment & Wage Estimates, May 2020

Employment by Industry

Sector	MSA[1]		U.S.
	Number of Employees	Percent of Total	Percent of Total
Construction, Mining, and Logging	11,700	5.3	5.5
Education and Health Services	42,200	19.2	16.3
Financial Activities	12,100	5.5	6.1
Government	19,400	8.8	15.2
Information	2,000	0.9	1.9
Leisure and Hospitality	18,500	8.4	9.0
Manufacturing	36,300	16.5	8.5
Other Services	10,400	4.7	3.8
Professional and Business Services	21,800	9.9	14.4
Retail Trade	25,000	11.4	10.9
Transportation, Warehousing, and Utilities	10,200	4.6	4.6
Wholesale Trade	10,300	4.7	3.9

Note: Figures are non-farm employment as of December 2020. Figures are not seasonally adjusted and include workers 16 years of age and older; (1) Figures cover the Fort Wayne, IN Metropolitan Statistical Area
Source: Bureau of Labor Statistics, Current Employment Statistics, Employment, Hours, and Earnings

Employment by Occupation

Occupation Classification	City (%)	MSA[1] (%)	U.S. (%)
Management, Business, Science, and Arts	32.8	34.0	38.5
Natural Resources, Construction, and Maintenance	6.7	7.9	8.9
Production, Transportation, and Material Moving	20.4	20.1	13.2
Sales and Office	23.0	22.0	21.6
Service	17.1	16.0	17.8

Note: Figures cover employed civilians 16 years of age and older; (1) Figures cover the Fort Wayne, IN Metropolitan Statistical Area
Source: U.S. Census Bureau, 2015-2019 American Community Survey 5-Year Estimates

Occupations with Greatest Projected Employment Growth: 2020 – 2022

Occupation[1]	2020 Employment	2022 Projected Employment	Numeric Employment Change	Percent Employment Change
Home Health and Personal Care Aides	43,510	45,760	2,250	5.2
Laborers and Freight, Stock, and Material Movers, Hand	92,910	94,760	1,850	2.0
Fast Food and Counter Workers	98,250	100,080	1,830	1.9
Registered Nurses	68,990	70,280	1,290	1.9
Cooks, Restaurant	28,220	29,360	1,140	4.0
Janitors and Cleaners, Except Maids and Housekeeping Cleaners	46,630	47,420	790	1.7
Software Developers and Software Quality Assurance Analysts and Testers	16,610	17,390	780	4.7
General and Operations Managers	51,930	52,600	670	1.3
Medical Assistants	16,740	17,390	650	3.9
Landscaping and Groundskeeping Workers	22,160	22,790	630	2.8

Note: Projections cover Indiana; (1) Sorted by numeric employment change
Source: www.projectionscentral.com, State Occupational Projections, 2020–2022 Short-Term Projections

Fastest-Growing Occupations: 2020 – 2022

Occupation[1]	2020 Employment	2022 Projected Employment	Numeric Employment Change	Percent Employment Change
Nurse Practitioners	5,630	6,210	580	10.3
Occupational Therapy Assistants	1,260	1,350	90	7.1
Physician Assistants	1,630	1,740	110	6.7
Physical Therapist Assistants	2,510	2,670	160	6.4
Medical and Health Services Managers	8,430	8,940	510	6.0
Information Security Analysts (SOC 2018)	1,240	1,310	70	5.6
Speech-Language Pathologists	2,700	2,850	150	5.6
Nonfarm Animal Caretakers	5,940	6,260	320	5.4
Veterinary Technologists and Technicians	2,070	2,180	110	5.3
Home Health and Personal Care Aides	43,510	45,760	2,250	5.2

Note: Projections cover Indiana; (1) Sorted by percent employment change and excludes occupations with numeric employment change less than 50
Source: www.projectionscentral.com, State Occupational Projections, 2020–2022 Short-Term Projections

TAXES

State Corporate Income Tax Rates

State	Tax Rate (%)	Income Brackets ($)	Num. of Brackets	Financial Institution Tax Rate (%)[a]	Federal Income Tax Ded.
Indiana	5.25 (i)	Flat rate	1	5.5	No

Note: Tax rates as of January 1, 2021; (a) Rates listed are the corporate income tax rate applied to financial institutions or excise taxes based on income. Some states have other taxes based upon the value of deposits or shares; (i) The Indiana Corporate tax rate is scheduled to decrease to 4.9% on July 1, 2021. Bank tax rate is scheduled to decrease to 5.0% on 1/1/22.
Source: Federation of Tax Administrators, State Corporate Income Tax Rates, January 1, 2021

State Individual Income Tax Rates

State	Tax Rate (%)	Income Brackets ($)	Personal Exemptions ($)			Standard Ded. ($)	
			Single	Married	Depend.	Single	Married
Indiana	3.23	Flat rate	1,000	2,000	2,500 (j)	–	–

Note: Tax rates as of January 1, 2021; Local- and county-level taxes are not included; Federal income tax is not deductible on state income tax returns; (j) In Indiana, includes an additional exemption of $1,500 for each dependent child.
Source: Federation of Tax Administrators, State Individual Income Tax Rates, January 1, 2021

Various State Sales and Excise Tax Rates

State	State Sales Tax (%)	Gasoline[1] (¢/gal.)	Cigarette[2] ($/pack)	Spirits[3] ($/gal.)	Wine[4] ($/gal.)	Beer[5] ($/gal.)	Recreational Marijuana (%)
Indiana	7	42.16	0.995	2.68	0.47	0.12	Not legal

Note: All tax rates as of January 1, 2021; (1) The American Petroleum Institute has developed a methodology for determining the average tax rate on a gallon of fuel. Rates may include any of the following: excise taxes, environmental fees, storage tank fees, other fees or taxes, general sales tax, and local taxes; (2) The federal excise tax of $1.0066 per pack and local taxes are not included; (3) Rates are those applicable to off-premise sales of 40% alcohol by volume (a.b.v.) distilled spirits in 750ml containers. Local excise taxes are excluded; (4) Rates are those applicable to off-premise sales of 11% a.b.v. non-carbonated wine in 750ml containers; (5) Rates are those applicable to off-premise sales of 4.7% a.b.v. beer in 12 ounce containers.
Source: Tax Foundation, 2021 Facts & Figures: How Does Your State Compare?

State Business Tax Climate Index Rankings

State	Overall Rank	Corporate Tax Rank	Individual Income Tax Rank	Sales Tax Rank	Property Tax Rank	Unemployment Insurance Tax Rank
Indiana	9	12	15	20	2	27

Note: The index is a measure of how each state's tax laws affect economic performance. The lower the rank, the more favorable a state's tax system is for business. States without a given tax are given a ranking of 1. The scores/rankings for the District of Columbia do not affect other states. The 2021 index represents the tax climate as of July 1, 2020.
Source: Tax Foundation, State Business Tax Climate Index 2021

TRANSPORTATION

Means of Transportation to Work

Area	Car/Truck/Van		Public Transportation			Bicycle	Walked	Other Means	Worked at Home
	Drove Alone	Car-pooled	Bus	Subway	Railroad				
City	83.4	9.6	0.8	0.0	0.0	0.3	1.6	0.7	3.7
MSA[1]	83.9	9.0	0.6	0.0	0.0	0.3	1.4	0.7	4.2
U.S.	76.3	9.0	2.4	1.9	0.6	0.5	2.7	1.4	5.2

Note: Figures are percentages and cover workers 16 years of age and older; (1) Figures cover the Fort Wayne, IN Metropolitan Statistical Area
Source: U.S. Census Bureau, 2015-2019 American Community Survey 5-Year Estimates

Travel Time to Work

Area	Less Than 10 Minutes	10 to 19 Minutes	20 to 29 Minutes	30 to 44 Minutes	45 to 59 Minutes	60 to 89 Minutes	90 Minutes or More
City	12.2	40.5	27.4	12.5	3.1	2.4	1.9
MSA[1]	12.7	36.5	28.2	15.0	3.5	2.3	1.8
U.S.	12.2	28.4	20.8	20.8	8.3	6.4	2.9

Note: Note: Figures are percentages and include workers 16 years old and over; (1) Figures cover the Fort Wayne, IN Metropolitan Statistical Area
Source: U.S. Census Bureau, 2015-2019 American Community Survey 5-Year Estimates

Key Congestion Measures

Measure	1982	1992	2002	2012	2017
Annual Hours of Delay, Total (000)	n/a	n/a	n/a	n/a	5,892
Annual Hours of Delay, Per Auto Commuter	n/a	n/a	n/a	n/a	18
Annual Congestion Cost, Total (million $)	n/a	n/a	n/a	n/a	124
Annual Congestion Cost, Per Auto Commuter ($)	n/a	n/a	n/a	n/a	376

Note: n/a not available
Source: Texas A&M Transportation Institute, 2019 Urban Mobility Report

Freeway Travel Time Index

Measure	1982	1987	1992	1997	2002	2007	2012	2017
Urban Area Index[1]	n/a	n/a	n/a	n/a	n/a	n/a	n/a	1.09
Urban Area Rank[1,2]	n/a	n/a	n/a	n/a	n/a	n/a	n/a	n/a

Note: Freeway Travel Time Index—the ratio of travel time in the peak period to the travel time at free-flow conditions. For example, a value of 1.30 indicates a 20-minute free-flow trip takes 26 minutes in the peak (20 minutes x 1.30 = 26 minutes); (1) Covers the Fort Wayne IN urban area; (2) Rank is based on 101 larger urban areas (#1 = highest travel time index); n/a not available
Source: Texas A&M Transportation Institute, 2019 Urban Mobility Report

Public Transportation

Agency Name / Mode of Transportation	Vehicles Operated in Maximum Service[1]	Annual Unlinked Passenger Trips[2] (in thous.)	Annual Passenger Miles[3] (in thous.)
Fort Wayne Public Transportation Corp. (Citilink)			
Bus (directly operated)	29	1,601.0	4,851.0
Demand Response (directly operated)	17	75.8	644.3

Note: (1) Number of revenue vehicles operated by the given mode and type of service to meet the annual maximum service requirement. This is the revenue vehicle count during the peak season of the year; on the week and day that maximum service is provided. Vehicles operated in maximum service (VOMS) exclude atypical days and one-time special events; (2) Number of passengers who boarded public transportation vehicles. Passengers are counted each time they board a vehicle no matter how many vehicles they use to travel from their origin to their destination. (3) Sum of the distances ridden by all passengers during the entire fiscal year.
Source: Federal Transit Administration, National Transit Database, 2019

Air Transportation

Airport Name and Code / Type of Service	Passenger Airlines[1]	Passenger Enplanements	Freight Carriers[2]	Freight (lbs)
Fort Wayne International (FWA)				
Domestic service (U.S. carriers - 2020)	9	216,606	7	23,800,303
International service (U.S. carriers - 2019)	0	0	2	31,084

Note: (1) Includes all U.S.-based major, minor and commuter airlines that carried at least one passenger during the year; (2) Includes all U.S.-based airlines and freight carriers that transported at least one pound of freight during the year.
Source: Bureau of Transportation Statistics, The Intermodal Transportation Database, Air Carriers: T-100 Domestic Market (U.S. Carriers), 2020; Bureau of Transportation Statistics, The Intermodal Transportation Database, Air Carriers: T-100 International Market (U.S. Carriers), 2019

BUSINESSES

Major Business Headquarters

Company Name	Industry	Rankings	
		Fortune[1]	Forbes[2]
Steel Dynamics	Metals	299	-

Note: (1) Companies that produce a 10-K are ranked 1 to 500 based on 2019 revenue; (2) All private companies with at least $2 billion in annual revenue through the end of their most current fiscal year are ranked 1 to 219; companies listed are headquartered in the city; dashes indicate no ranking
Source: Fortune, "Fortune 500," June/July 2020; Forbes, "America's Largest Private Companies," 2020

Living Environment

COST OF LIVING

Cost of Living Index

Composite Index	Groceries	Housing	Utilities	Trans-portation	Health Care	Misc. Goods/ Services
86.9	86.1	62.0	92.4	106.1	98.8	99.0

Note: The Cost of Living Index measures regional differences in the cost of consumer goods and services, excluding taxes and non-consumer expenditures, for professional and managerial households in the top income quintile. It is based on more than 50,000 prices covering almost 60 different items for which prices are collected three times a year by chambers of commerce, economic development organizations or university applied economic centers in each participating urban area. The numbers shown should be read as a percentage above or below the national average of 100. For example, a value of 115.4 in the groceries column indicates that grocery prices are 15.4% higher than the national average. Small differences in the index numbers should not be interpreted as significant; Figures cover the Fort Wayne-Allen County IN urban area.
Source: The Council for Community and Economic Research, Cost of Living Index, 2020

Grocery Prices

Area[1]	T-Bone Steak ($/pound)	Frying Chicken ($/pound)	Whole Milk ($/half gal.)	Eggs ($/dozen)	Orange Juice ($/64 oz.)	Coffee ($/11.5 oz.)
City[2]	11.87	1.07	1.31	0.74	3.13	3.47
Avg.	11.78	1.39	2.05	1.47	3.57	4.34
Min.	8.03	0.94	1.03	0.74	2.94	3.02
Max.	15.86	2.65	4.31	3.77	5.44	8.69

*Note: (1) Values for the local area are compared with the average, minimum and maximum values for all 284 areas in the Cost of Living Index; (2) Figures cover the Fort Wayne-Allen County IN urban area; **T-Bone Steak** (price per pound); **Frying Chicken** (price per pound, whole fryer); **Whole Milk** (half gallon carton); **Eggs** (price per dozen, Grade A, large); **Orange Juice** (64 oz. Tropicana or Florida Natural); **Coffee** (11.5 oz. can, vacuum-packed, Maxwell House, Hills Bros, or Folgers).*
Source: The Council for Community and Economic Research, Cost of Living Index, 2020

Housing and Utility Costs

Area[1]	New Home Price ($)	Apartment Rent ($/month)	All Electric ($/month)	Part Electric ($/month)	Other Energy ($/month)	Telephone ($/month)
City[2]	204,729	859	-	93.81	50.38	184.30
Avg.	368,594	1,168	170.86	100.47	65.28	184.30
Min.	190,567	502	91.58	31.42	26.08	169.60
Max.	2,227,806	4,738	470.38	280.31	280.06	206.50

*Note: (1) Values for the local area are compared with the average, minimum and maximum values for all 284 areas in the Cost of Living Index; (2) Figures cover the Fort Wayne-Allen County IN urban area; **New Home Price** (2,400 sf living area, 8,000 sf lot, in urban area with full utilities); **Apartment Rent** (950 sf 2 bedroom/1.5 or 2 bath, unfurnished, excluding all utilities except water); **All Electric** (average monthly cost for an all-electric home); **Part Electric** (average monthly cost for a part-electric home); **Other Energy** (average monthly cost for natural gas, fuel oil, coal, wood, and any other forms of energy except electricity); **Telephone** (price includes the base monthly rate plus taxes and fees for three lines of mobile phone service).*
Source: The Council for Community and Economic Research, Cost of Living Index, 2020

Health Care, Transportation, and Other Costs

Area[1]	Doctor ($/visit)	Dentist ($/visit)	Optometrist ($/visit)	Gasoline ($/gallon)	Beauty Salon ($/visit)	Men's Shirt ($)
City[2]	129.50	94.17	89.56	2.30	33.00	33.48
Avg.	115.44	99.32	108.10	2.21	39.27	31.37
Min.	36.68	59.00	51.36	1.71	19.00	11.00
Max.	219.00	153.10	250.97	3.46	82.05	58.33

*Note: (1) Values for the local area are compared with the average, minimum and maximum values for all 284 areas in the Cost of Living Index; (2) Figures cover the Fort Wayne-Allen County IN urban area; **Doctor** (general practitioners routine exam of an established patient); **Dentist** (adult teeth cleaning and periodic oral examination); **Optometrist** (full vision eye exam for established adult patient); **Gasoline** (one gallon regular unleaded, national brand, including all taxes, cash price at self-service pump if available); **Beauty Salon** (woman's shampoo, trim, and blow-dry); **Men's Shirt** (cotton/polyester dress shirt, pinpoint weave, long sleeves).*
Source: The Council for Community and Economic Research, Cost of Living Index, 2020

HOUSING

Homeownership Rate

Area	2012 (%)	2013 (%)	2014 (%)	2015 (%)	2016 (%)	2017 (%)	2018 (%)	2019 (%)	2020 (%)
MSA[1]	n/a	n/a	n/a	n/a	n/a	n/a	n/a	n/a	n/a
U.S.	65.4	65.1	64.5	63.7	63.4	63.9	64.4	64.6	66.6

Note: (1) Figures cover the Fort Wayne, IN Metropolitan Statistical Area; n/a not available
Source: U.S. Census Bureau, Housing Vacancies and Homeownership Annual Statistics: 2012-2020

House Price Index (HPI)

Area	National Ranking[2]	Quarterly Change (%)	One-Year Change (%)	Five-Year Change (%)	Since 1991Q1 (%)
MSA[1]	53	1.29	7.55	35.84	111.44
U.S.[3]	–	3.81	10.77	38.99	205.12

Note: The HPI is a weighted repeat sales index. It measures average price changes in repeat sales or refinancings on the same properties. This information is obtained by reviewing repeat mortgage transactions on single-family properties whose mortgages have been purchased or securitized by Fannie Mae or Freddie Mac since January 1975; (1) Figures cover the Fort Wayne, IN Metropolitan Statistical Area; (2) Rankings are based on annual percentage change for all metro areas containing at least 15,000 transactions over the last 10 years and ranges from 1 to 253; (3) figures based on a weighted average of Census Division estimates using a seasonally adjusted, purchase-only index; all figures are for the period ending December 31, 2020
Source: Federal Housing Finance Agency, Change in Metropolitan Area House Price Indexes, April 7, 2021

Median Single-Family Home Prices

Area	2018	2019	2020p	Percent Change 2019 to 2020
MSA[1]	143.3	155.3	169.3	9.0
U.S. Average	261.6	274.6	299.9	9.2

Note: Figures are median sales prices of existing single-family homes in thousands of dollars; (p) preliminary; (1) Figures cover the Fort Wayne, IN Metropolitan Statistical Area
Source: National Association of Realtors, Median Sales Price of Existing Single-Family Homes for Metropolitan Areas, 4th Quarter 2020

Qualifying Income Based on Median Sales Price of Existing Single-Family Homes

Area	With 5% Down ($)	With 10% Down ($)	With 20% Down ($)
MSA[1]	32,835	31,107	27,651
U.S. Average	59,266	56,147	49,908

Note: Figures are preliminary; Qualifying income is based on a mortgage rate of 2.81%. Monthly principal and interest payment is limited to 25% of income; (1) Figures cover the Fort Wayne, IN Metropolitan Statistical Area
Source: National Association of Realtors, Qualifying Income Based on Median Sales Price of Existing Single-Family Homes for Metropolitan Areas, 4th Quarter 2020

Home Value Distribution

Area	Under $50,000	$50,000 -$99,999	$100,000 -$149,999	$150,000 -$199,999	$200,000 -$299,999	$300,000 -$499,999	$500,000 -$999,999	$1,000,000 or more
City	10.6	30.1	28.9	16.1	9.6	3.7	0.9	0.1
MSA[1]	8.4	24.8	26.3	17.2	13.7	7.2	2.0	0.4
U.S.	6.9	12.0	13.3	14.0	19.6	19.3	11.4	3.4

Note: Figures are percentages and cover owner-occupied housing units; (1) Figures cover the Fort Wayne, IN Metropolitan Statistical Area
Source: U.S. Census Bureau, 2015-2019 American Community Survey 5-Year Estimates

Year Housing Structure Built

Area	2010 or Later	2000 -2009	1990 -1999	1980 -1989	1970 -1979	1960 -1969	1950 -1959	1940 -1949	Before 1940	Median Year
City	1.5	6.6	14.3	11.7	16.7	15.0	12.2	6.6	15.3	1970
MSA[1]	3.8	11.0	15.2	10.9	15.2	13.0	10.8	5.4	14.7	1974
U.S.	5.2	14.0	13.9	13.4	15.2	10.6	10.3	4.9	12.6	1978

Note: Figures are percentages except for Median Year; Note: (1) Figures cover the Fort Wayne, IN Metropolitan Statistical Area
Source: U.S. Census Bureau, 2015-2019 American Community Survey 5-Year Estimates

Gross Monthly Rent

Area	Under $500	$500 -$999	$1,000 -$1,499	$1,500 -$1,999	$2,000 -$2,499	$2,500 -$2,999	$3,000 and up	Median ($)
City	11.5	71.0	15.0	1.5	0.7	0.2	0.1	764
MSA[1]	11.5	69.3	16.1	2.0	0.8	0.2	0.1	771
U.S.	9.4	36.2	30.0	14.0	5.6	2.4	2.4	1,062

Note: Figures are percentages except for Median; Gross rent is the contract rent plus the estimated average monthly cost of utilities (electricity, gas, and water and sewer) and fuels (oil, coal, kerosene, wood, etc.) if these are paid by the renter (or paid for the renter by someone else); (1) Figures cover the Fort Wayne, IN Metropolitan Statistical Area
Source: U.S. Census Bureau, 2015-2019 American Community Survey 5-Year Estimates

HEALTH

Health Risk Factors

Category	MSA[1] (%)	U.S. (%)
Adults aged 18–64 who have any kind of health care coverage	85.9	87.3
Adults who reported being in good or better health	78.3	82.4
Adults who have been told they have high blood cholesterol	32.3	33.0
Adults who have been told they have high blood pressure	35.0	32.3
Adults who are current smokers	21.1	17.1
Adults who currently use E-cigarettes	3.9	4.6
Adults who currently use chewing tobacco, snuff, or snus	3.9	4.0
Adults who are heavy drinkers[2]	4.3	6.3
Adults who are binge drinkers[3]	15.5	17.4
Adults who are overweight (BMI 25.0 - 29.9)	30.4	35.3
Adults who are obese (BMI 30.0 - 99.8)	33.9	31.3
Adults who participated in any physical activities in the past month	72.6	74.4
Adults who always or nearly always wears a seat belt	94.7	94.3

Note: (1) Figures cover the Fort Wayne, IN Metropolitan Statistical Area; (2) Heavy drinkers are classified as adult men having more than 14 drinks per week and adult women having more than 7 drinks per week; (3) Binge drinkers are classified as males having five or more drinks on one occasion or females having four or more drinks on one occasion
Source: Centers for Disease Control and Prevention, Behaviorial Risk Factor Surveillance System, SMART: Selected Metropolitan Area Risk Trends, 2017

Acute and Chronic Health Conditions

Category	MSA[1] (%)	U.S. (%)
Adults who have ever been told they had a heart attack	5.3	4.2
Adults who have ever been told they have angina or coronary heart disease	5.8	3.9
Adults who have ever been told they had a stroke	3.3	3.0
Adults who have ever been told they have asthma	14.7	14.2
Adults who have ever been told they have arthritis	29.3	24.9
Adults who have ever been told they have diabetes[2]	10.9	10.5
Adults who have ever been told they had skin cancer	3.9	6.2
Adults who have ever been told they had any other types of cancer	6.5	7.1
Adults who have ever been told they have COPD	7.8	6.5
Adults who have ever been told they have kidney disease	2.2	3.0
Adults who have ever been told they have a form of depression	24.7	20.5

Note: (1) Figures cover the Fort Wayne, IN Metropolitan Statistical Area; (2) Figures do not include pregnancy-related, borderline, or pre-diabetes
Source: Centers for Disease Control and Prevention, Behaviorial Risk Factor Surveillance System, SMART: Selected Metropolitan Area Risk Trends, 2017

Health Screening and Vaccination Rates

Category	MSA[1] (%)	U.S. (%)
Adults aged 65+ who have had flu shot within the past year	46.3	60.7
Adults aged 65+ who have ever had a pneumonia vaccination	69.2	75.4
Adults who have ever been tested for HIV	31.9	36.1
Adults who have ever had the shingles or zoster vaccine?	22.5	28.9
Adults who have had their blood cholesterol checked within the last five years	83.5	85.9

Note: n/a not available; (1) Figures cover the Fort Wayne, IN Metropolitan Statistical Area.
Source: Centers for Disease Control and Prevention, Behaviorial Risk Factor Surveillance System, SMART: Selected Metropolitan Area Risk Trends, 2017

Disability Status

Category	MSA[1] (%)	U.S. (%)
Adults who reported being deaf	4.4	6.7
Are you blind or have serious difficulty seeing, even when wearing glasses?	3.2	4.5
Are you limited in any way in any of your usual activities due of arthritis?	16.0	12.9
Do you have difficulty doing errands alone?	7.5	6.8
Do you have difficulty dressing or bathing?	3.8	3.6
Do you have serious difficulty concentrating/remembering/making decisions?	11.1	10.7
Do you have serious difficulty walking or climbing stairs?	14.7	13.6

Note: (1) Figures cover the Fort Wayne, IN Metropolitan Statistical Area.
Source: Centers for Disease Control and Prevention, Behaviorial Risk Factor Surveillance System, SMART: Selected Metropolitan Area Risk Trends, 2017

Mortality Rates for the Top 10 Causes of Death in the U.S.

ICD-10[a] Sub-Chapter	ICD-10[a] Code	Age-Adjusted Mortality Rate[1] per 100,000 population	
		County[2]	U.S.
Malignant neoplasms	C00-C97	160.3	149.2
Ischaemic heart diseases	I20-I25	82.8	90.5
Other forms of heart disease	I30-I51	56.4	52.2
Chronic lower respiratory diseases	J40-J47	51.4	39.6
Other degenerative diseases of the nervous system	G30-G31	40.6	37.6
Cerebrovascular diseases	I60-I69	41.8	37.2
Other external causes of accidental injury	W00-X59	45.6	36.1
Organic, including symptomatic, mental disorders	F01-F09	44.5	29.4
Hypertensive diseases	I10-I15	42.6	24.1
Diabetes mellitus	E10-E14	29.4	21.5

Note: (a) ICD-10 = International Classification of Diseases 10th Revision; (1) Mortality rates are a three-year average covering 2017-2019; (2) Figures cover Allen County.
Source: Centers for Disease Control and Prevention, National Center for Health Statistics. Underlying Cause of Death 1999-2019 on CDC WONDER Online Database

Mortality Rates for Selected Causes of Death

ICD-10[a] Sub-Chapter	ICD-10[a] Code	Age-Adjusted Mortality Rate[1] per 100,000 population	
		County[2]	U.S.
Assault	X85-Y09	10.3	6.0
Diseases of the liver	K70-K76	13.7	14.4
Human immunodeficiency virus (HIV) disease	B20-B24	Unreliable	1.5
Influenza and pneumonia	J09-J18	11.6	13.8
Intentional self-harm	X60-X84	14.1	14.1
Malnutrition	E40-E46	3.9	2.3
Obesity and other hyperalimentation	E65-E68	2.1	2.1
Renal failure	N17-N19	17.6	12.6
Transport accidents	V01-V99	10.8	12.3
Viral hepatitis	B15-B19	Unreliable	1.2

Note: (a) ICD-10 = International Classification of Diseases 10th Revision; (1) Mortality rates are a three-year average covering 2017-2019; (2) Figures cover Allen County; Data are suppressed when the data meet the criteria for confidentiality constraints; Mortality rates are flagged as unreliable when the rate would be calculated with a numerator of 20 or less.
Source: Centers for Disease Control and Prevention, National Center for Health Statistics. Underlying Cause of Death 1999-2019 on CDC WONDER Online Database

Health Insurance Coverage

Area	With Health Insurance	With Private Health Insurance	With Public Health Insurance	Without Health Insurance	Population Under Age 19 Without Health Insurance
City	91.0	65.0	36.5	9.0	5.6
MSA[1]	91.5	69.2	33.1	8.5	6.4
U.S.	91.2	67.9	35.1	8.8	5.1

Note: Figures are percentages that cover the civilian noninstitutionalized population; (1) Figures cover the Fort Wayne, IN Metropolitan Statistical Area
Source: U.S. Census Bureau, 2015-2019 American Community Survey 5-Year Estimates

Number of Medical Professionals

Area	MDs[3]	DOs[3,4]	Dentists	Podiatrists	Chiropractors	Optometrists
County[1] (number)	992	103	252	21	83	98
County[1] (rate[2])	264.5	27.5	66.4	5.5	21.9	25.8
U.S. (rate[2])	282.9	22.7	71.2	6.2	28.1	16.9

18003
Note: Data as of 2019 unless noted; (1) Data covers Allen County; (2) Rate per 100,000 population; (3) Data as of 2018 and includes all active, non-federal physicians; (4) Doctor of Osteopathic Medicine
Source: U.S. Department of Health and Human Services, Health Resources and Services Administration, Bureau of Health Professions, Area Resource File (ARF) 2019-2020

EDUCATION

Public School District Statistics

District Name	Schls	Pupils	Pupil/ Teacher Ratio	Minority Pupils[1] (%)	Free Lunch Eligible[2] (%)	IEP[3] (%)
Fort Wayne Community Schools	49	29,404	19.0	59.2	51.5	19.0
M S D Southwest Allen Co. Schls	9	7,471	17.7	20.6	13.3	10.1
Northwest Allen County Schools	11	7,722	17.6	15.9	13.2	14.6

Note: Table includes school districts with 2,000 or more students; (1) Percentage of students that are not non-Hispanic white; (2) Percentage of students that are eligible for the free lunch program; (3) Percentage of students that have an Individualized Education Program.
Source: U.S. Department of Education, National Center for Education Statistics, Common Core of Data, Local Education Agency (School District) Universe Survey: School Year 2018-2019; U.S. Department of Education, National Center for Education Statistics, Common Core of Data, Public Elementary/Secondary School Universe Survey: School Year 2018-2019

Highest Level of Education

Area	Less than H.S.	H.S. Diploma	Some College, No Deg.	Associate Degree	Bachelor's Degree	Master's Degree	Prof. School Degree	Doctorate Degree
City	11.5	28.2	22.1	10.3	18.3	7.1	1.4	1.0
MSA[1]	10.4	29.2	21.7	10.9	18.4	6.9	1.5	0.9
U.S.	12.0	27.0	20.4	8.5	19.8	8.8	2.1	1.4

Note: Figures cover persons age 25 and over; (1) Figures cover the Fort Wayne, IN Metropolitan Statistical Area
Source: U.S. Census Bureau, 2015-2019 American Community Survey 5-Year Estimates

Educational Attainment by Race

Area	High School Graduate or Higher (%)					Bachelor's Degree or Higher (%)				
	Total	White	Black	Asian	Hisp.[2]	Total	White	Black	Asian	Hisp.[2]
City	88.5	91.9	84.4	52.6	61.8	27.8	30.7	15.6	28.3	9.8
MSA[1]	89.6	91.9	85.2	57.5	63.5	27.8	29.4	15.8	33.7	10.4
U.S.	88.0	89.9	86.0	87.1	68.7	32.1	33.5	21.6	54.3	16.4

Note: Figures shown cover persons 25 years old and over; (1) Figures cover the Fort Wayne, IN Metropolitan Statistical Area; (2) People of Hispanic origin can be of any race
Source: U.S. Census Bureau, 2015-2019 American Community Survey 5-Year Estimates

School Enrollment by Grade and Control

Area	Preschool (%)		Kindergarten (%)		Grades 1 - 4 (%)		Grades 5 - 8 (%)		Grades 9 - 12 (%)	
	Public	Private	Public	Private	Public	Private	Public	Private	Public	Private
City	45.5	54.5	83.5	16.5	79.5	20.5	82.2	17.8	81.3	18.7
MSA[1]	42.6	57.4	78.5	21.5	77.9	22.1	79.3	20.7	81.7	18.3
U.S.	59.1	40.9	87.6	12.4	89.5	10.5	89.4	10.6	90.1	9.9

Note: Figures shown cover persons 3 years old and over; (1) Figures cover the Fort Wayne, IN Metropolitan Statistical Area
Source: U.S. Census Bureau, 2015-2019 American Community Survey 5-Year Estimates

Higher Education

Four-Year Colleges			Two-Year Colleges			Medical Schools[1]	Law Schools[2]	Voc/ Tech[3]
Public	Private Non-profit	Private For-profit	Public	Private Non-profit	Private For-profit			
1	5	0	0	0	2	0	1	2

Note: Figures cover institutions located within the city limits and include main campuses only; (1) includes schools accredited by the Liaison Committee on Medical Education and the American Osteopathic Association's Commission on Osteopathic College Accreditation; (2) includes ABA-accredited schools, schools with provisional ABA accreditation, and state accredited schools; (3) includes all schools with programs that are less than 2 years.
Source: National Center for Education Statistics, Integrated Postsecondary Education System (IPEDS), 2019-20; Wikipedia, List of Medical Schools in the United States, accessed April 2, 2021; Wikipedia, List of Law Schools in the United States, accessed April 2, 2021

EMPLOYERS

Major Employers

Company Name	Industry
Allen County Government	Government
BAE Systems Platform Solutions	Aircraft electronics
Benchmark Human Services	Services for people with disabilities
BFGoodrich	Rubber tire manufacturing
City of Fort Wayne	Municipal government
Dana Corp.	Motor vehicle parts manufacturing
Edy's Grand Ice Cream	Ice cream & other frozen treats
Fort Wayne Community Schools	Elementary & secondary schools
Fort Wayne Metals Research Products Corp.	Wire for medical devices
Frontier Communications Corp.	Wired telecommunications carriers
General Motors	Motor vehicle manufacturing
Harris Corporation	Wireless networking systems & satellite imaging systems
IPFW	University
Ivy Tech Community College- Northeast	Community college
Lincoln Financial Group	Insurance carriers
Lutheran Health Network	General medical & surgical hospitals
Norfolk Southern Corp2	Rail transportation
Northwest Allen County Schools	Elementary & secondary schools
Parker Hannifin Corporation	Metal product manufacturing for a/c systems
Parkview Health Systems	General medical & surgical hospitals
Raytheon Systems Co.	Mission solutions for aerospace industry
Shambaugh & Son	Commercial building construction
Steel Dynamics1	Corporate headquarters & scrap metal processing
Sweetwater Sound	Sound recording studio & equipment distribution
Vera Bradley	Handbags, luggage, & accessories

Note: Companies shown are located within the Fort Wayne, IN Metropolitan Statistical Area.
Source: Hoovers.com; Wikipedia

PUBLIC SAFETY

Crime Rate

Area	All Crimes	Violent Crimes				Property Crimes		
		Murder	Rape[3]	Robbery	Aggrav. Assault	Burglary	Larceny -Theft	Motor Vehicle Theft
City	3,122.5	9.7	53.8	132.5	165.6	367.5	2,182.5	210.9
Suburbs[1]	1,097.2	2.8	35.5	32.1	128.3	146.4	649.7	102.5
Metro[2]	2,418.7	7.3	47.5	97.6	152.6	290.7	1,649.8	173.2
U.S.	2,489.3	5.0	42.6	81.6	250.2	340.5	1,549.5	219.9

Note: Figures are crimes per 100,000 population; (1) All areas within the metro area that are located outside the city limits; (2) Figures cover the Fort Wayne, IN Metropolitan Statistical Area; (3) All figures shown were reported using the revised Uniform Crime Reporting (UCR) definition of rape.
Source: FBI Uniform Crime Reports, 2019

Hate Crimes

Area	Number of Quarters Reported	Number of Incidents per Bias Motivation					
		Race/Ethnicity/ Ancestry	Religion	Sexual Orientation	Disability	Gender	Gender Identity
City	4	1	1	1	0	0	0
U.S.	4	3,963	1,521	1,195	157	69	198

Source: Federal Bureau of Investigation, Hate Crime Statistics 2019

Identity Theft Consumer Reports

Area	Reports	Reports per 100,000 Population	Rank[2]
MSA[1]	1,193	289	128
U.S.	1,387,615	423	-

Note: (1) Figures cover the Fort Wayne, IN Metropolitan Statistical Area; (2) Rank ranges from 1 to 391 where 1 indicates greatest number of identity theft reports per 100,000 population
Source: Federal Trade Commission, Consumer Sentinel Network Data Book 2020

Fraud and Other Consumer Reports

Area	Reports	Reports per 100,000 Population	Rank[2]
MSA[1]	2,721	658	229
U.S.	3,385,133	1,031	-

Note: (1) Figures cover the Fort Wayne, IN Metropolitan Statistical Area; (2) Rank ranges from 1 to 391 where 1 indicates greatest number of fraud and other consumer reports per 100,000 population
Source: Federal Trade Commission, Consumer Sentinel Network Data Book 2020

164 Fort Wayne, Indiana

POLITICS

2020 Presidential Election Results

Area	Biden	Trump	Jorgensen	Hawkins	Other
Allen County	43.2	54.3	2.2	0.0	0.3
U.S.	51.3	46.8	1.2	0.3	0.5

Note: Results are percentages and may not add to 100% due to rounding
Source: Dave Leip's Atlas of U.S. Presidential Elections

SPORTS

Professional Sports Teams

Team Name	League	Year Established
No teams are located in the metro area		

Source: Wikipedia, Major Professional Sports Teams of the United States and Canada, April 6, 2021

CLIMATE

Average and Extreme Temperatures

Temperature	Jan	Feb	Mar	Apr	May	Jun	Jul	Aug	Sep	Oct	Nov	Dec	Yr.
Extreme High (°F)	69	69	82	88	94	106	103	101	100	90	79	71	106
Average High (°F)	31	35	46	60	71	81	84	82	76	64	49	36	60
Average Temp. (°F)	24	27	37	49	60	70	74	72	65	53	41	29	50
Average Low (°F)	16	19	28	39	49	59	63	61	53	42	32	22	40
Extreme Low (°F)	-22	-18	-10	7	27	38	44	38	29	19	-1	-18	-22

Note: Figures cover the years 1948-1990
Source: National Climatic Data Center, International Station Meteorological Climate Summary, 9/96

Average Precipitation/Snowfall/Humidity

Precip./Humidity	Jan	Feb	Mar	Apr	May	Jun	Jul	Aug	Sep	Oct	Nov	Dec	Yr.
Avg. Precip. (in.)	2.3	2.1	2.9	3.4	3.6	3.8	3.6	3.4	2.6	2.7	2.8	2.7	35.9
Avg. Snowfall (in.)	8	8	5	2	Tr	0	0	0	0	Tr	3	7	33
Avg. Rel. Hum. 7am (%)	81	81	80	77	76	78	81	86	86	84	83	83	81
Avg. Rel. Hum. 4pm (%)	71	68	62	54	52	52	53	55	53	55	67	74	59

Note: Figures cover the years 1948-1990; Tr = Trace amounts (<0.05 in. of rain; <0.5 in. of snow)
Source: National Climatic Data Center, International Station Meteorological Climate Summary, 9/96

Weather Conditions

Temperature			Daytime Sky			Precipitation		
5°F & below	32°F & below	90°F & above	Clear	Partly cloudy	Cloudy	0.01 inch or more precip.	0.1 inch or more snow/ice	Thunder-storms
16	131	16	75	140	150	131	31	39

Note: Figures are average number of days per year and cover the years 1948-1990
Source: National Climatic Data Center, International Station Meteorological Climate Summary, 9/96

HAZARDOUS WASTE

Superfund Sites

The Fort Wayne, IN metro area is home to two sites on the EPA's Superfund National Priorities List: **Fort Wayne Reduction Dump** (final); **Wayne Waste Oil** (final). There are a total of 1,375 Superfund sites with a status of proposed or final on the list in the U.S. *U.S. Environmental Protection Agency, National Priorities List, April 7, 2021*

AIR QUALITY

Air Quality Trends: Ozone

	1990	1995	2000	2005	2010	2015	2016	2017	2018	2019
MSA[1]	0.086	0.094	0.086	0.081	0.067	0.061	0.068	0.063	0.071	0.063
U.S.	0.088	0.089	0.082	0.080	0.073	0.068	0.069	0.068	0.069	0.065

Note: (1) Data covers the Fort Wayne, IN Metropolitan Statistical Area. The values shown are the composite ozone concentration averages among trend sites based on the highest fourth daily maximum 8-hour concentration in parts per million. These trends are based on sites having an adequate record of monitoring data during the trend period. Data from exceptional events are included.
Source: U.S. Environmental Protection Agency, Air Quality Monitoring Information, "Air Quality Trends by City, 1990-2019"

Air Quality Index

Area	Percent of Days when Air Quality was...[2]					AQI Statistics[2]	
	Good	Moderate	Unhealthy for Sensitive Groups	Unhealthy	Very Unhealthy	Maximum	Median
MSA[1]	64.7	35.1	0.3	0.0	0.0	101	45

Note: (1) Data covers the Fort Wayne, IN Metropolitan Statistical Area; (2) Based on 365 days with AQI data in 2019. Air Quality Index (AQI) is an index for reporting daily air quality. EPA calculates the AQI for five major air pollutants regulated by the Clean Air Act: ground-level ozone, particle pollution (aka particulate matter), carbon monoxide, sulfur dioxide, and nitrogen dioxide. The AQI runs from 0 to 500. The higher the AQI value, the greater the level of air pollution and the greater the health concern. There are six AQI categories: "Good" AQI is between 0 and 50. Air quality is considered satisfactory; "Moderate" AQI is between 51 and 100. Air quality is acceptable; "Unhealthy for Sensitive Groups" When AQI values are between 101 and 150, members of sensitive groups may experience health effects; "Unhealthy" When AQI values are between 151 and 200 everyone may begin to experience health effects; "Very Unhealthy" AQI values between 201 and 300 trigger a health alert; "Hazardous" AQI values over 300 trigger warnings of emergency conditions (not shown).
Source: U.S. Environmental Protection Agency, Air Quality Index Report, 2019

Air Quality Index Pollutants

Area	Percent of Days when AQI Pollutant was...[2]					
	Carbon Monoxide	Nitrogen Dioxide	Ozone	Sulfur Dioxide	Particulate Matter 2.5	Particulate Matter 10
MSA[1]	0.0	0.0	48.5	0.0	51.5	0.0

Note: (1) Data covers the Fort Wayne, IN Metropolitan Statistical Area; (2) Based on 365 days with AQI data in 2019. The Air Quality Index (AQI) is an index for reporting daily air quality. EPA calculates the AQI for five major air pollutants regulated by the Clean Air Act: ground-level ozone, particle pollution (also known as particulate matter), carbon monoxide, sulfur dioxide, and nitrogen dioxide. The AQI runs from 0 to 500. The higher the AQI value, the greater the level of air pollution and the greater the health concern.
Source: U.S. Environmental Protection Agency, Air Quality Index Report, 2019

Maximum Air Pollutant Concentrations: Particulate Matter, Ozone, CO and Lead

	Particulate Matter 10 (ug/m^3)	Particulate Matter 2.5 Wtd AM (ug/m^3)	Particulate Matter 2.5 24-Hr (ug/m^3)	Ozone (ppm)	Carbon Monoxide (ppm)	Lead (ug/m^3)
MSA[1] Level	n/a	9.0	22	0.063	n/a	n/a
NAAQS[2]	150	15	35	0.075	9	0.15
Met NAAQS[2]	n/a	Yes	Yes	Yes	n/a	n/a

Note: (1) Data covers the Fort Wayne, IN Metropolitan Statistical Area; Data from exceptional events are included; (2) National Ambient Air Quality Standards; ppm = parts per million; ug/m^3 = micrograms per cubic meter; n/a not available.
Concentrations: Particulate Matter 10 (coarse particulate)—highest second maximum 24-hour concentration; Particulate Matter 2.5 Wtd AM (fine particulate)—highest weighted annual mean concentration; Particulate Matter 2.5 24-Hour (fine particulate)—highest 98th percentile 24-hour concentration; Ozone—highest fourth daily maximum 8-hour concentration; Carbon Monoxide—highest second maximum non-overlapping 8-hour concentration; Lead—maximum running 3-month average
Source: U.S. Environmental Protection Agency, Air Quality Monitoring Information, "Air Quality Statistics by City, 2019"

Maximum Air Pollutant Concentrations: Nitrogen Dioxide and Sulfur Dioxide

	Nitrogen Dioxide AM (ppb)	Nitrogen Dioxide 1-Hr (ppb)	Sulfur Dioxide AM (ppb)	Sulfur Dioxide 1-Hr (ppb)	Sulfur Dioxide 24-Hr (ppb)
MSA[1] Level	n/a	n/a	n/a	n/a	n/a
NAAQS[2]	53	100	30	75	140
Met NAAQS[2]	n/a	n/a	n/a	n/a	n/a

Note: (1) Data covers the Fort Wayne, IN Metropolitan Statistical Area; Data from exceptional events are included; (2) National Ambient Air Quality Standards; ppm = parts per million; ug/m^3 = micrograms per cubic meter; n/a not available.
Concentrations: Nitrogen Dioxide AM—highest arithmetic mean concentration; Nitrogen Dioxide 1-Hr—highest 98th percentile 1-hour daily maximum concentration; Sulfur Dioxide AM—highest annual mean concentration; Sulfur Dioxide 1-Hr—highest 99th percentile 1-hour daily maximum concentration; Sulfur Dioxide 24-Hr—highest second maximum 24-hour concentration
Source: U.S. Environmental Protection Agency, Air Quality Monitoring Information, "Air Quality Statistics by City, 2019"

Grand Rapids, Michigan

Background

The city of Grand Rapids is located in the west-central part of Kent County in the picturesque Grand River Valley, about 30 miles east of Lake Michigan. It is known for its fine furniture making.

The presence of an abundant forest, as well as the hydropower and trade afforded by a powerful river, contributed to the reputation of a manufacturing industry that is known worldwide, producing not only furniture, but industrial machinery, metal, paper, plastics, and printing products. Food and information technology industries are also important to the economy of the city. There are 14 universities and colleges in Grand Rapids.

Before Grand Rapids became involved in making seating for churches, buses, and schools, among other furniture, the site was a Native American settlement of the Ottawa, Chippewa, and Potawatomi tribes. The earliest white settlers in the area were fur traders who bought pelts from the Native American tribes in the early nineteenth century. One by one, more white settlers found their way into the area on the rapids of the Grand River. A Baptist mission was established in 1825, and a year after that, Louis Campau erected a trading post. In 1833, the area's first permanent white settlement appeared, led by Samuel Dexter of Herkimer County, New York. In 1945, Grand Rapids became the first city in the United States to add fluoride to its drinking water.

Revitalization efforts have resulted in a thriving downtown district that includes restaurants, hotels, clubs, museums, and the 12,000-square foot Van Andel Arena. Also here is the DeVos Place Convention Center, with its 162,000-square foot, column-free exhibit hall, 40,000-square foot ballroom, 26 individual meeting rooms, and a 2,404-seat performing arts theater that is home to the Grand Rapids Symphony, the Grand Rapids Ballet Company, Opera Grand Rapids, and Broadway Grand Rapids.

> Restauranteur Davide Uccello turned to the increasingly lucrative cannabis industry, celebrating the opening of his Grand Rapids dispensary with a ribbon cutting.

The city's other attractions include a yearly Festival of the Arts held in June and featuring visual, performing and culinary arts, and annual jazz festival. Celebration on the Grand salutes summer with free concerts, West Michigan's largest fire works display and food booths. The annual Fulton Street Farmers Market has been held since 1922, and offers locally grown produce and handmade items.

The Frederik Meijer Gardens and Sculpture Park blends art and nature, maintaining outdoor (on 125 acres) and indoor exhibits. Each spring, visitors marvel at the thousands of butterflies, brought from all over the world and released into the Park's tropical conservatory.

Children enjoy the John Ball Zoo as well as the Grand Rapids Children's Museum, which offers a wide range of entertainment and educational programs.

Fall is a very colorful time of year in western Michigan, perhaps compensating for the late spring. During the winter, excessive cloudiness and numerous snow flurries occur with strong westerly winds. Lake Michigan has a tempering effect on cold waves coming in from the west in the winter. Prolonged, severe cold waves are infrequent. The snowfall season extends from mid-November to mid-March and some winters have had continuous snow cover throughout this period.

Rankings

General Rankings

- *US News & World Report* conducted a survey of more than 3,000 people and analyzed the 150 largest metropolitan areas to determine what matters most when selecting the next place to live. Grand Rapids ranked #23 out of the top 25 as having the best combination of desirable factors. Criteria: cost of living; quality of life; net migration; job market; desirability; and other factors. *realestate.usnews.com, "The 25 Best Places to Live in the U.S. in 2020-21," October 13, 2020*

- The Grand Rapids metro area was identified as one of America's fastest-growing areas in terms of population and business growth by *MagnifyMoney*. The area ranked #27 out of 35. The 100 most populous metro areas in the U.S. were evaluated on their change from 2011-2016 in the following categories: people and housing; workforce and employment opportunities; growing industry. *www.businessinsider.com, "The 35 Cities in the US with the Biggest Influx of People, the Most Work Opportunities, and the Hottest Business Growth," August 12, 2018*

- The Grand Rapids metro area was identified as one of America's fastest-growing areas in terms of population and economy by *Forbes*. The area ranked #25 out of 25. The 100 most populous metro areas in the U.S. were evaluated on the following criteria: estimated population growth; employment; economic output; wages; home values. *Forbes, "America's Fastest-Growing Cities 2018," February 28, 2018*

- In their seventh annual survey, Livability.com looked at data for more than 1,000 small to mid-sized U.S. cities to determine the rankings for Livability's "Top 100 Best Places to Live" in 2020. Grand Rapids ranked #21. Criteria: housing and affordable living; vibrant economy; social and civic engagement; education; demographics; health care options; transportation & infrastructure; and abundant lifestyle amenities. *Livability.com, "Top 100 Best Places to Live 2020" October 2020*

Business/Finance Rankings

- The Brookings Institution ranked the nation's largest cities based on income inequality. Grand Rapids was ranked #85 (#1 = greatest inequality). Criteria: the "95/20 ratio," a figure representing the income at which a household earns more than 95 percent of all other households, divided by the income at which a household earns more than only 20 percent of all other households. *Brookings Institution, "Household Income Inequality, Largest Cities of 97 Large U.S. Metro Areas, 2014-2016," February 5, 2018*

- The Brookings Institution ranked the 100 largest metro areas in the U.S. based on income inequality. Grand Rapids was ranked #97 (#1 = greatest inequality). Criteria: the "95/20 ratio," a figure representing the income at which a household earns more than 95 percent of all other households, divided by the income at which a household earns more than only 20 percent of all other households. *Brookings Institution, "Household Income Inequality, 100 Largest U.S. Metro Areas, 2014-2016," February 5, 2018*

- The Grand Rapids metro area appeared on the Milken Institute "2021 Best Performing Cities" list. Rank: #92 out of 200 large metro areas (population over 250,000). Criteria: job growth; wage and salary growth; high-tech output growth; housing affordability; household broadband access. *Milken Institute, "Best-Performing Cities 2021," February 16, 2021*

- *Forbes* ranked the 200 most populous metro areas to determine the nation's "Best Places for Business and Careers." The Grand Rapids metro area was ranked #68. Criteria: costs (business and living); job growth (past and projected); income growth; quality of life; educational attainment (college and high school); projected economic growth; cultural and leisure opportunities; workplace tolerance laws; net migration patterns. *Forbes, "The Best Places for Business and Careers 2019: Seattle Still On Top," October 30, 2019*

Dating/Romance Rankings

- *Apartment List* conducted its annual survey of renters for cities that have the best opportunities for dating. More than 11,000 single respondents rated their current city or neighborhood for opportunities to date. Grand Rapids ranked #10 out of 86 where single residents were very satisfied or somewhat satisfied, making it among the ten best areas for dating opportunities. Other criteria analyzed included gender and education levels of renters. *Apartment List, "The Best & Worst Metros for Dating 2020," February 4, 2020*

- Grand Rapids was ranked #7 out of 25 cities that stood out for inspiring romance and attracting diners on the website OpenTable.com. Criteria: percentage of people who dined out on Valentine's Day in 2018; percentage of romantic restaurants as rated by OpenTable diner reviews; and percentage of tables seated for two. *OpenTable, "25 Most Romantic Cities in America for 2019," February 7, 2019*

Education Rankings

- Personal finance website *WalletHub* analyzed the 150 largest U.S. metropolitan statistical areas to determine where the most educated Americans are putting their degrees to work. Criteria: education levels; percentage of workers with degrees; education quality and attainment gap; public school quality rankings; quality and enrollment of each metro area's universities. Grand Rapids was ranked #64 (#1 = most educated city). *www.WalletHub.com, "Most and Least Educated Cities in America," July 20, 2020*

Environmental Rankings

- Niche compiled a list of the nation's snowiest cities, based on the National Oceanic and Atmospheric Administration's 30-year average snowfall data. Among cities with a population of at least 50,000, Grand Rapids ranked #8. *Niche.com, Top 25 Snowiest Cities in America, December 10, 2018*

- Grand Rapids was highlighted as one of the top 98 cleanest metro areas for short-term particle pollution (24-hour PM 2.5) in the U.S. during 2016 through 2018. Monitors in these cities reported no days with unhealthful PM 2.5 levels. *American Lung Association, "State of the Air 2020," April 21, 2020*

Health/Fitness Rankings

- The Grand Rapids metro area was identified as one of the worst cities for bed bugs in America by pest control company Orkin. The area ranked #10 out of 50 based on the number of bed bug treatments Orkin performed from December 2019 to November 2020. *Orkin, "New Year, New Top City on Orkin's 2021 Bed Bug Cities List: Chicago," February 1, 2021*

- Grand Rapids was identified as a "2021 Spring Allergy Capital." The area ranked #34 out of 100. Three groups of factors were used to identify the most challenging cities for people with allergies during the spring season: annual spring pollen levels; over the counter medicine use; number of board-certified allergy specialists. *Asthma and Allergy Foundation of America, "Spring Allergy Capitals 2021," February 23, 2021*

- Grand Rapids was identified as a "2021 Fall Allergy Capital." The area ranked #19 out of 100. Three groups of factors were used to identify the most challenging cities for people with allergies during the fall season: annual fall pollen levels; over the counter medicine use; number of board-certified allergy specialists. *Asthma and Allergy Foundation of America, "Fall Allergy Capitals 2021," February 23, 2021*

- Grand Rapids was identified as a "2019 Asthma Capital." The area ranked #62 out of the nation's 100 largest metropolitan areas. Criteria: estimated asthma prevalence; crude death rate from asthma; and ER visits due to asthma. Risk factors analyzed but not factored in the rankings: annual pollen score; annual air quality; public smoking laws; number of board-certified asthma specialists; rescue medication use; controller medication use; uninsured rate; poverty rate. *Asthma and Allergy Foundation of America, "Asthma Capitals 2019: The Most Challenging Places to Live With Asthma," May 7, 2019*

Real Estate Rankings

- *WalletHub* compared the most populated U.S. cities to determine which had the best markets for real estate agents. Grand Rapids ranked #49 where demand was high and pay was the best. Criteria: sales per agent; annual median wage for real-estate agents; monthly average starting salary for real estate agents; real estate job density and competition; unemployment rate; home turnover rate; housing-market health index; and other relevant metrics. *www.WalletHub.com, "2019's Best Places to Be a Real Estate Agent," April 24, 2019*

- The Grand Rapids metro area was identified as one of the top 15 housing markets to invest in for 2021 by *Forbes*. Criteria: home price appreciation; percentage of home sales within a 2-week time frame; available inventory; number of home sales; and other factors. *Forbes.com, "Top Housing Markets To Watch In 2021," December 15, 2020*

- Grand Rapids was ranked #53 out of 268 metro areas in terms of housing affordability in 2020 by the National Association of Home Builders (#1 = most affordable). Criteria: the share of homes sold in that area affordable to a family earning the local median income, based on standard mortgage underwriting criteria. *National Association of Home Builders®, NAHB-Wells Fargo Housing Opportunity Index, 4th Quarter 2020*

Safety Rankings

- Allstate ranked the 200 largest cities in America in terms of driver safety. Grand Rapids ranked #131. Criteria: internal property damage claims over a two-year period from January 2016 to December 2017. The report helps increase the importance of safety and awareness behind the wheel. *Allstate, "Allstate America's Best Drivers Report, 2019" June 24, 2019*

- The National Insurance Crime Bureau ranked 384 metro areas in the U.S. in terms of per capita rates of vehicle theft. The Grand Rapids metro area ranked #290 (#1 = highest rate). Criteria: number of vehicle theft offenses per 100,000 inhabitants in 2019. *National Insurance Crime Bureau, "Hot Spots 2019," July 21, 2020*

Women/Minorities Rankings

- Personal finance website *WalletHub* compared more than 180 U.S. cities across two key dimensions, "Hispanic Business-Friendliness" and "Hispanic Purchasing Power," to arrive at the most favorable conditions for Hispanic entrepreneurs. Grand Rapids was ranked #101 out of 182. Criteria includes: share of Hispanic-Owned Businesses; Hispanic entrepreneurship rate to median annual income of Hispanics; Small Business-Friendliness score; cost of living; and number of Hispanics with at least a bachelor's degree. *WalletHub.com, "2019's Best Cities for Hispanic Entrepreneurs," May 1, 2019*

Miscellaneous Rankings

- *MoveHub* ranked 446 hipster cities across 20 countries, using its *alternative* Hipster Index and Grand Rapids came out as #28 among the top 50. Criteria: population over 150,000; number of vintage boutiques; density of tattoo parlors; vegan places to eat; coffee shops; and density of vinyl record stores. *www.movehub.com, "The Hipster Index: Brighton Pips Portland to Global Top Spot," February 20, 2020*

- *WalletHub* compared the 150 most populated U.S. cities to determine their operating efficiency. A "Quality of City Services" score was constructed for each city and then divided by the total budget per capita to reveal which were managed the best. Grand Rapids ranked #36. Criteria: financial stability; economy; education; safety; health; infrastructure and pollution. *www.WalletHub.com, "2020's Best- & Worst-Run Cities in America," June 29, 2020*

- Grand Rapids was selected as one of "America's Friendliest Cities." The city ranked #13 in the "Friendliest" category. Respondents to an online survey were asked to rate 38 top urban destinations in the United States as to general friendliness, as well as manners, politeness and warm disposition. *Travel + Leisure, "America's Friendliest Cities," October 20, 2017*

Business Environment

DEMOGRAPHICS

Population Growth

Area	1990 Census	2000 Census	2010 Census	2019* Estimate	Population Growth (%)	
					1990-2019	2010-2019
City	189,145	197,800	188,040	198,401	4.9	5.5
MSA[1]	645,914	740,482	774,160	1,062,392	64.5	37.2
U.S.	248,709,873	281,421,906	308,745,538	324,697,795	30.6	5.2

Note: (1) Figures cover the Grand Rapids-Wyoming, MI Metropolitan Statistical Area; (*) 2015-2019 5-year estimated population
Source: U.S. Census Bureau, 1990 Census, Census 2000, Census 2010, 2015-2019 American Community Survey 5-Year Estimates

Household Size

Area	Persons in Household (%)							Average Household Size
	One	Two	Three	Four	Five	Six	Seven or More	
City	33.1	31.4	13.8	11.1	5.9	2.6	2.0	2.50
MSA[1]	24.8	34.6	15.0	14.4	7.0	2.7	1.5	2.70
U.S.	27.9	33.9	15.6	12.9	6.0	2.3	1.4	2.60

Note: (1) Figures cover the Grand Rapids-Wyoming, MI Metropolitan Statistical Area
Source: U.S. Census Bureau, 2015-2019 American Community Survey 5-Year Estimates

Race

Area	White Alone[2] (%)	Black Alone[2] (%)	Asian Alone[2] (%)	AIAN[3] Alone[2] (%)	NHOPI[4] Alone[2] (%)	Other Race Alone[2] (%)	Two or More Races (%)
City	67.2	18.6	2.4	0.4	0.0	5.7	5.6
MSA[1]	83.9	6.7	2.6	0.3	0.0	2.9	3.5
U.S.	72.5	12.7	5.5	0.8	0.2	4.9	3.3

Note: (1) Figures cover the Grand Rapids-Wyoming, MI Metropolitan Statistical Area; (2) Alone is defined as not being in combination with one or more other races; (3) American Indian and Alaska Native; (4) Native Hawaiian and Other Pacific Islander
Source: U.S. Census Bureau, 2015-2019 American Community Survey 5-Year Estimates

Hispanic or Latino Origin

Area	Total (%)	Mexican (%)	Puerto Rican (%)	Cuban (%)	Other (%)
City	16.1	9.5	1.5	0.2	4.8
MSA[1]	9.6	6.7	0.8	0.3	1.8
U.S.	18.0	11.2	1.7	0.7	4.3

Note: Persons of Hispanic or Latino origin can be of any race; (1) Figures cover the Grand Rapids-Wyoming, MI Metropolitan Statistical Area
Source: U.S. Census Bureau, 2015-2019 American Community Survey 5-Year Estimates

Ancestry

Area	German	Irish	English	American	Italian	Polish	French[2]	Scottish	Dutch
City	15.0	8.7	7.0	2.3	3.0	6.8	2.2	1.6	13.9
MSA[1]	20.0	10.1	8.8	3.7	3.1	6.6	2.9	1.8	18.9
U.S.	13.3	9.7	7.2	6.2	5.1	2.8	2.3	1.7	1.2

Note: Figures are the percentage of the total population reporting a particular ancestry. The nine most commonly reported ancestries in the U.S. are shown. Figures include multiple ancestries (e.g. if a person reported being Irish and Italian, they were included in both columns); (1) Figures cover the Grand Rapids-Wyoming, MI Metropolitan Statistical Area; (2) Excludes Basque
Source: U.S. Census Bureau, 2015-2019 American Community Survey 5-Year Estimates

Foreign-born Population

Area	Percent of Population Born in								
	Any Foreign Country	Asia	Mexico	Europe	Caribbean	Central America[2]	South America	Africa	Canada
City	10.9	2.3	3.3	1.2	0.6	1.8	0.2	1.3	0.3
MSA[1]	6.8	2.1	1.8	1.0	0.4	0.6	0.1	0.5	0.2
U.S.	13.6	4.2	3.5	1.3	1.1	1.0	1.0	0.7	0.2

Note: (1) Figures cover the Grand Rapids-Wyoming, MI Metropolitan Statistical Area; (2) Excludes Mexico.
Source: U.S. Census Bureau, 2015-2019 American Community Survey 5-Year Estimates

Marital Status

Area	Never Married	Now Married[2]	Separated	Widowed	Divorced
City	46.2	36.9	1.3	5.1	10.4
MSA[1]	32.7	51.3	1.0	4.9	10.2
U.S.	33.4	48.1	1.9	5.8	10.9

Note: Figures are percentages and cover the population 15 years of age and older; (1) Figures cover the Grand Rapids-Wyoming, MI Metropolitan Statistical Area; (2) Excludes separated
Source: U.S. Census Bureau, 2015-2019 American Community Survey 5-Year Estimates

Disability by Age

Area	All Ages	Under 18 Years Old	18 to 64 Years Old	65 Years and Over
City	13.2	5.4	12.0	35.8
MSA[1]	11.4	4.0	9.8	31.7
U.S.	12.6	4.2	10.3	34.5

Note: Figures show percent of the civilian noninstitutionalized population that reported having a disability. Disability status is determined from six types of difficulty: vision, hearing, cognitive, ambulatory, self-care, and independent living. For children under 5 years old, hearing and vision difficulty are used to determine disability status. For children between the ages of 5 and 14, disability status is determined from hearing, vision, cognitive, ambulatory, and self-care difficulties. For people aged 15 years and older, they are considered to have a disability if they have difficulty with any one of the six difficulty types; Note: (1) Figures cover the Grand Rapids-Wyoming, MI Metropolitan Statistical Area
Source: U.S. Census Bureau, 2015-2019 American Community Survey 5-Year Estimates

Age

Area	Percent of Population									Median Age
	Under Age 5	Age 5–19	Age 20–34	Age 35–44	Age 45–54	Age 55–64	Age 65–74	Age 75–84	Age 85+	
City	6.9	18.6	30.3	11.2	10.1	10.8	6.6	3.4	2.1	31.4
MSA[1]	6.5	20.6	21.8	12.3	12.4	12.5	8.1	4.0	1.9	35.8
U.S.	6.1	19.1	20.7	12.6	13.0	12.9	9.1	4.6	1.9	38.1

Note: (1) Figures cover the Grand Rapids-Wyoming, MI Metropolitan Statistical Area
Source: U.S. Census Bureau, 2015-2019 American Community Survey 5-Year Estimates

Gender

Area	Males	Females	Males per 100 Females
City	97,940	100,461	97.5
MSA[1]	527,777	534,615	98.7
U.S.	159,886,919	164,810,876	97.0

Note: (1) Figures cover the Grand Rapids-Wyoming, MI Metropolitan Statistical Area
Source: U.S. Census Bureau, 2015-2019 American Community Survey 5-Year Estimates

Religious Groups by Family

Area	Catholic	Baptist	Non-Den.	Methodist[2]	Lutheran	LDS[3]	Pentecostal	Presbyterian[4]	Muslim[5]	Judaism
MSA[1]	17.2	1.7	8.4	3.1	2.1	0.6	1.1	10.0	1.1	0.1
U.S.	19.1	9.3	4.0	4.0	2.3	2.0	1.9	1.6	0.8	0.7

Note: Figures are the number of adherents as a percentage of the total population; (1) Figures cover the Grand Rapids-Wyoming, MI Metropolitan Statistical Area; (2) Methodist/Pietist; (3) Latter Day Saints; (4) Reformed; (5) Figures are estimates
Source: Association of Statisticians of American Religious Bodies, 2010 U.S. Religion Census: Religious Congregations & Membership Study

Religious Groups by Tradition

Area	Catholic	Evangelical Protestant	Mainline Protestant	Other Tradition	Black Protestant	Orthodox
MSA[1]	17.2	20.7	7.6	2.2	1.1	0.2
U.S.	19.1	16.2	7.3	4.3	1.6	0.3

Note: Figures are the number of adherents as a percentage of the total population; (1) Figures cover the Grand Rapids-Wyoming, MI Metropolitan Statistical Area
Source: Association of Statisticians of American Religious Bodies, 2010 U.S. Religion Census: Religious Congregations & Membership Study

ECONOMY

Gross Metropolitan Product

Area	2017	2018	2019	2020	Rank[2]
MSA[1]	60.6	63.6	66.2	68.3	54

Note: Figures are in billions of dollars; (1) Figures cover the Grand Rapids-Wyoming, MI Metropolitan Statistical Area; (2) Rank is based on 2018 data and ranges from 1 to 381
Source: U.S. Conference of Mayors, U.S. Metro Economies: GMP & Employment 2018-2020, September 2019

Economic Growth

Area	2015-17 (%)	2018 (%)	2019 (%)	2020 (%)	Rank[2]
MSA[1]	1.9	3.4	2.3	1.2	139
U.S.	1.9	2.9	2.3	2.1	–

Note: Figures are real gross metropolitan product (GMP) growth rates and represent average annual percent change; (1) Figures cover the Grand Rapids-Wyoming, MI Metropolitan Statistical Area; (2) Rank is based on 2017 2-year average annual percent change and ranges from 1 to 381
Source: U.S. Conference of Mayors, U.S. Metro Economies: GMP & Employment 2018-2020, September 2019

Metropolitan Area Exports

Area	2014	2015	2016	2017	2018	2019	Rank[2]
MSA[1]	5,244.5	5,143.0	5,168.5	5,385.8	5,420.9	5,214.1	55

Note: Figures are in millions of dollars; (1) Figures cover the Grand Rapids-Wyoming, MI Metropolitan Statistical Area; (2) Rank is based on 2019 data and ranges from 1 to 386
Source: U.S. Department of Commerce, International Trade Administration, Office of Trade and Economic Analysis, Industry and Analysis, Exports by Metropolitan Area, data extracted March 24, 2021

Building Permits

Area	Single-Family			Multi-Family			Total		
	2018	2019	Pct. Chg.	2018	2019	Pct. Chg.	2018	2019	Pct. Chg.
City	124	153	23.4	690	183	-73.5	814	336	-58.7
MSA[1]	2,749	2,531	-7.9	1,105	1,624	47.0	3,854	4,155	7.8
U.S.	855,300	862,100	0.7	473,500	523,900	10.6	1,328,800	1,386,000	4.3

Note: (1) Figures cover the Grand Rapids-Wyoming, MI Metropolitan Statistical Area; Figures represent new, privately-owned housing units authorized (unadjusted data); All permit data are based on estimates with imputation
Source: U.S. Census Bureau, Manufacturing, Mining, and Construction Statistics, Building Permits, 2018, 2019

Bankruptcy Filings

Area	Business Filings			Nonbusiness Filings		
	2019	2020	% Chg.	2019	2020	% Chg.
Kent County	35	47	34.3	935	613	-34.4
U.S.	22,780	21,655	-4.9	752,160	522,808	-30.5

Note: Business filings include Chapter 7, Chapter 9, Chapter 11, Chapter 12, Chapter 13, Chapter 15, and Section 304; Nonbusiness filings include Chapter 7, Chapter 11, and Chapter 13
Source: Administrative Office of the U.S. Courts, Business and Nonbusiness Bankruptcy, County Cases Commenced by Chapter of the Bankruptcy Code, During the 12-Month Period Ending December 31, 2019 and Business and Nonbusiness Bankruptcy, County Cases Commenced by Chapter of the Bankruptcy Code, During the 12-Month Period Ending December 31, 2020

Housing Vacancy Rates

Area	Gross Vacancy Rate[2] (%)			Year-Round Vacancy Rate[3] (%)			Rental Vacancy Rate[4] (%)			Homeowner Vacancy Rate[5] (%)		
	2018	2019	2020	2018	2019	2020	2018	2019	2020	2018	2019	2020
MSA[1]	8.9	7.4	7.1	6.8	5.1	4.7	6.8	4.5	4.6	0.3	0.5	1.1
U.S.	12.3	12.0	10.6	9.7	9.5	8.2	6.9	6.7	6.3	1.5	1.4	1.0

Note: (1) Figures cover the Grand Rapids-Wyoming, MI Metropolitan Statistical Area; (2) The percentage of the total housing inventory that is vacant; (3) The percentage of the housing inventory (excluding seasonal units) that is year-round vacant; (4) The percentage of rental inventory that is vacant for rent; (5) The percentage of homeowner inventory that is vacant for sale
Source: U.S. Census Bureau, Housing Vacancies and Homeownership Annual Statistics: 2018, 2019, 2020

INCOME

Income

Area	Per Capita ($)	Median Household ($)	Average Household ($)
City	26,120	50,103	65,615
MSA[1]	31,388	63,302	83,235
U.S.	34,103	62,843	88,607

Note: (1) Figures cover the Grand Rapids-Wyoming, MI Metropolitan Statistical Area
Source: U.S. Census Bureau, 2015-2019 American Community Survey 5-Year Estimates

Household Income Distribution

Area	Percent of Households Earning							
	Under $15,000	$15,000 -$24,999	$25,000 -$34,999	$35,000 -$49,999	$50,000 -$74,999	$75,000 -$99,999	$100,000 -$149,999	$150,000 and up
City	13.0	11.8	10.0	15.2	19.4	12.7	11.7	6.4
MSA[1]	7.6	9.0	8.8	13.5	19.8	14.4	15.9	11.0
U.S.	10.3	8.9	8.9	12.3	17.2	12.7	15.1	14.5

Note: (1) Figures cover the Grand Rapids-Wyoming, MI Metropolitan Statistical Area
Source: U.S. Census Bureau, 2015-2019 American Community Survey 5-Year Estimates

174 Grand Rapids, Michigan

Poverty Rate

Area	All Ages	Under 18 Years Old	18 to 64 Years Old	65 Years and Over
City	20.4	28.9	19.4	10.1
MSA[1]	11.0	13.7	10.9	6.9
U.S.	13.4	18.5	12.6	9.3

Note: Figures are percentage of people whose income during the past 12 months was below the poverty level;
(1) Figures cover the Grand Rapids-Wyoming, MI Metropolitan Statistical Area
Source: U.S. Census Bureau, 2015-2019 American Community Survey 5-Year Estimates

CITY FINANCES

City Government Finances

Component	2017 ($000)	2017 ($ per capita)
Total Revenues	478,920	2,455
Total Expenditures	478,803	2,454
Debt Outstanding	676,126	3,466
Cash and Securities[1]	1,296,027	6,643

Note: (1) Cash and security holdings of a government at the close of its fiscal year,
including those of its dependent agencies, utilities, and liquor stores.
Source: U.S. Census Bureau, State & Local Government Finances 2017

City Government Revenue by Source

Source	2017 ($000)	2017 ($ per capita)	2017 (%)
General Revenue			
From Federal Government	34,323	176	7.2
From State Government	39,306	201	8.2
From Local Governments	8,304	43	1.7
Taxes			
Property	55,540	285	11.6
Sales and Gross Receipts	0	0	0.0
Personal Income	93,951	482	19.6
Corporate Income	0	0	0.0
Motor Vehicle License	0	0	0.0
Other Taxes	5,110	26	1.1
Current Charges	108,871	558	22.7
Liquor Store	0	0	0.0
Utility	43,537	223	9.1
Employee Retirement	74,027	379	15.5

Source: U.S. Census Bureau, State & Local Government Finances 2017

City Government Expenditures by Function

Function	2017 ($000)	2017 ($ per capita)	2017 (%)
General Direct Expenditures			
Air Transportation	0	0	0.0
Corrections	0	0	0.0
Education	0	0	0.0
Employment Security Administration	0	0	0.0
Financial Administration	11,382	58	2.4
Fire Protection	28,775	147	6.0
General Public Buildings	0	0	0.0
Governmental Administration, Other	9,675	49	2.0
Health	578	3	0.1
Highways	20,547	105	4.3
Hospitals	0	0	0.0
Housing and Community Development	36,484	187	7.6
Interest on General Debt	20,409	104	4.3
Judicial and Legal	19,654	100	4.1
Libraries	9,036	46	1.9
Parking	15,311	78	3.2
Parks and Recreation	11,839	60	2.5
Police Protection	51,814	265	10.8
Public Welfare	0	0	0.0
Sewerage	38,566	197	8.1
Solid Waste Management	10,387	53	2.2
Veterans' Services	0	0	0.0
Liquor Store	0	0	0.0
Utility	44,804	229	9.4
Employee Retirement	62,328	319	13.0

Source: U.S. Census Bureau, State & Local Government Finances 2017

EMPLOYMENT

Labor Force and Employment

Area	Civilian Labor Force			Workers Employed		
	Dec. 2019	Dec. 2020	% Chg.	Dec. 2019	Dec. 2020	% Chg.
City	103,987	101,472	-2.4	100,701	95,669	-5.0
MSA[1]	575,885	557,316	-3.2	561,939	534,032	-5.0
U.S.	164,007,000	160,017,000	-2.4	158,504,000	149,613,000	-5.6

Note: Data is not seasonally adjusted and covers workers 16 years of age and older; (1) Figures cover the Grand Rapids-Wyoming, MI Metropolitan Statistical Area
Source: Bureau of Labor Statistics, Local Area Unemployment Statistics

Unemployment Rate

Area	2020											
	Jan.	Feb.	Mar.	Apr.	May	Jun.	Jul.	Aug.	Sep.	Oct.	Nov.	Dec.
City	3.8	3.2	3.3	26.7	22.0	16.0	11.5	10.0	8.7	5.9	5.2	5.7
MSA[1]	2.9	2.5	2.6	21.5	17.1	12.0	8.4	7.2	6.3	4.2	3.7	4.2
U.S.	4.0	3.8	4.5	14.4	13.0	11.2	10.5	8.5	7.7	6.6	6.4	6.5

Note: Data is not seasonally adjusted and covers workers 16 years of age and older; (1) Figures cover the Grand Rapids-Wyoming, MI Metropolitan Statistical Area
Source: Bureau of Labor Statistics, Local Area Unemployment Statistics

Average Wages

Occupation	$/Hr.	Occupation	$/Hr.
Accountants and Auditors	33.80	Maintenance and Repair Workers	19.50
Automotive Mechanics	21.20	Marketing Managers	60.10
Bookkeepers	19.60	Network and Computer Systems Admin.	34.60
Carpenters	23.40	Nurses, Licensed Practical	23.50
Cashiers	12.00	Nurses, Registered	33.50
Computer Programmers	34.10	Nursing Assistants	14.50
Computer Systems Analysts	37.60	Office Clerks, General	18.50
Computer User Support Specialists	25.00	Physical Therapists	40.20
Construction Laborers	18.00	Physicians	103.70
Cooks, Restaurant	13.50	Plumbers, Pipefitters and Steamfitters	25.20
Customer Service Representatives	18.80	Police and Sheriff's Patrol Officers	31.00
Dentists	115.40	Postal Service Mail Carriers	25.60
Electricians	23.50	Real Estate Sales Agents	26.80
Engineers, Electrical	40.00	Retail Salespersons	14.70
Fast Food and Counter Workers	11.70	Sales Representatives, Technical/Scientific	36.80
Financial Managers	58.00	Secretaries, Exc. Legal/Medical/Executive	18.90
First-Line Supervisors of Office Workers	27.80	Security Guards	14.20
General and Operations Managers	58.10	Surgeons	n/a
Hairdressers/Cosmetologists	16.60	Teacher Assistants, Exc. Postsecondary*	14.30
Home Health and Personal Care Aides	13.00	Teachers, Secondary School, Exc. Sp. Ed.*	29.10
Janitors and Cleaners	14.20	Telemarketers	12.10
Landscaping/Groundskeeping Workers	16.70	Truck Drivers, Heavy/Tractor-Trailer	22.40
Lawyers	57.10	Truck Drivers, Light/Delivery Services	20.40
Maids and Housekeeping Cleaners	13.10	Waiters and Waitresses	14.50

Note: Wage data covers the Grand Rapids-Wyoming, MI Metropolitan Statistical Area; (*) Hourly wages were calculated from annual wage data based on a 40 hour work week; n/a not available.
Source: Bureau of Labor Statistics, Metro Area Occupational Employment & Wage Estimates, May 2020

Employment by Industry

Sector	MSA[1]		U.S.
	Number of Employees	Percent of Total	Percent of Total
Construction, Mining, and Logging	24,900	4.8	5.5
Education and Health Services	92,300	17.6	16.3
Financial Activities	26,500	5.1	6.1
Government	47,100	9.0	15.2
Information	5,400	1.0	1.9
Leisure and Hospitality	30,700	5.9	9.0
Manufacturing	107,300	20.5	8.5
Other Services	19,800	3.8	3.8
Professional and Business Services	71,300	13.6	14.4
Retail Trade	48,500	9.3	10.9
Transportation, Warehousing, and Utilities	18,800	3.6	4.6
Wholesale Trade	31,000	5.9	3.9

Note: Figures are non-farm employment as of December 2020. Figures are not seasonally adjusted and include workers 16 years of age and older; (1) Figures cover the Grand Rapids-Wyoming, MI Metropolitan Statistical Area
Source: Bureau of Labor Statistics, Current Employment Statistics, Employment, Hours, and Earnings

176   Grand Rapids, Michigan

Employment by Occupation

Occupation Classification	City (%)	MSA[1] (%)	U.S. (%)
Management, Business, Science, and Arts	35.1	35.4	38.5
Natural Resources, Construction, and Maintenance	7.1	8.2	8.9
Production, Transportation, and Material Moving	17.7	19.0	13.2
Sales and Office	20.6	21.4	21.6
Service	19.5	16.0	17.8

Note: Figures cover employed civilians 16 years of age and older; (1) Figures cover the Grand Rapids-Wyoming, MI Metropolitan Statistical Area
Source: U.S. Census Bureau, 2015-2019 American Community Survey 5-Year Estimates

Occupations with Greatest Projected Employment Growth: 2020 – 2022

Occupation[1]	2020 Employment	2022 Projected Employment	Numeric Employment Change	Percent Employment Change
Registered Nurses	100,730	101,870	1,140	1.1
Laborers and Freight, Stock, and Material Movers, Hand	72,870	73,850	980	1.3
Heavy and Tractor-Trailer Truck Drivers	61,290	62,120	830	1.4
Construction Laborers	31,450	32,160	710	2.3
Light Truck or Delivery Services Drivers	27,780	28,390	610	2.2
Carpenters	25,160	25,610	450	1.8
Insurance Sales Agents	13,310	13,720	410	3.1
Market Research Analysts and Marketing Specialists	18,600	19,000	400	2.2
Stockers and Order Fillers	67,090	67,480	390	0.6
Industrial Truck and Tractor Operators	22,490	22,850	360	1.6

Note: Projections cover Michigan; (1) Sorted by numeric employment change
Source: www.projectionscentral.com, State Occupational Projections, 2020–2022 Short-Term Projections

Fastest-Growing Occupations: 2020 – 2022

Occupation[1]	2020 Employment	2022 Projected Employment	Numeric Employment Change	Percent Employment Change
Tank Car, Truck, and Ship Loaders	250	300	50	20.0
Conveyor Operators and Tenders	720	770	50	6.9
Operations Research Analysts	1,900	1,980	80	4.2
Veterinary Assistants and Laboratory Animal Caretakers	3,340	3,480	140	4.2
Veterinary Technologists and Technicians	2,430	2,530	100	4.1
Veterinarians	2,310	2,400	90	3.9
Dental Laboratory Technicians	1,660	1,720	60	3.6
Respiratory Therapists	4,700	4,860	160	3.4
Nursing Instructors and Teachers, Postsecondary	1,810	1,870	60	3.3
Insurance Sales Agents	13,310	13,720	410	3.1

Note: Projections cover Michigan; (1) Sorted by percent employment change and excludes occupations with numeric employment change less than 50
Source: www.projectionscentral.com, State Occupational Projections, 2020–2022 Short-Term Projections

TAXES

State Corporate Income Tax Rates

State	Tax Rate (%)	Income Brackets ($)	Num. of Brackets	Financial Institution Tax Rate (%)[a]	Federal Income Tax Ded.
Michigan	6.0	Flat rate	1	(a)	No

Note: Tax rates as of January 1, 2021; (a) Rates listed are the corporate income tax rate applied to financial institutions or excise taxes based on income. Some states have other taxes based upon the value of deposits or shares.
Source: Federation of Tax Administrators, State Corporate Income Tax Rates, January 1, 2021

State Individual Income Tax Rates

State	Tax Rate (%)	Income Brackets ($)	Personal Exemptions ($) Single	Personal Exemptions ($) Married	Personal Exemptions ($) Depend.	Standard Ded. ($) Single	Standard Ded. ($) Married
Michigan (a)	4.25	Flat rate	4,750	9,500	4,750	–	–

Note: Tax rates as of January 1, 2021; Local- and county-level taxes are not included; Federal income tax is not deductible on state income tax returns; (a) 19 states have statutory provision for automatically adjusting to the rate of inflation the dollar values of the income tax brackets, standard deductions, and/or personal exemptions. Michigan indexes the personal exemption only. Oregon does not index the income brackets for $125,000 and over.
Source: Federation of Tax Administrators, State Individual Income Tax Rates, January 1, 2021

Various State Sales and Excise Tax Rates

State	State Sales Tax (%)	Gasoline[1] (¢/gal.)	Cigarette[2] ($/pack)	Spirits[3] ($/gal.)	Wine[4] ($/gal.)	Beer[5] ($/gal.)	Recreational Marijuana (%)
Michigan	6	41.98	2	11.95	0.51	0.2	(h)

Note: All tax rates as of January 1, 2021; (1) The American Petroleum Institute has developed a methodology for determining the average tax rate on a gallon of fuel. Rates may include any of the following: excise taxes, environmental fees, storage tank fees, other fees or taxes, general sales tax, and local taxes; (2) The federal excise tax of $1.0066 per pack and local taxes are not included; (3) Rates are those applicable to off-premise sales of 40% alcohol by volume (a.b.v.) distilled spirits in 750ml containers. Local excise taxes are excluded; (4) Rates are those applicable to off-premise sales of 11% a.b.v. non-carbonated wine in 750ml containers; (5) Rates are those applicable to off-premise sales of 4.7% a.b.v. beer in 12 ounce containers; (h) 10% excise tax (retail price)
Source: Tax Foundation, 2021 Facts & Figures: How Does Your State Compare?

State Business Tax Climate Index Rankings

State	Overall Rank	Corporate Tax Rank	Individual Income Tax Rank	Sales Tax Rank	Property Tax Rank	Unemployment Insurance Tax Rank
Michigan	14	20	12	10	35	18

Note: The index is a measure of how each state's tax laws affect economic performance. The lower the rank, the more favorable a state's tax system is for business. States without a given tax are given a ranking of 1. The scores/rankings for the District of Columbia do not affect other states. The 2021 index represents the tax climate as of July 1, 2020.
Source: Tax Foundation, State Business Tax Climate Index 2021

TRANSPORTATION

Means of Transportation to Work

Area	Car/Truck/Van		Public Transportation			Bicycle	Walked	Other Means	Worked at Home
	Drove Alone	Car-pooled	Bus	Subway	Railroad				
City	75.3	11.1	3.6	0.1	0.0	1.1	4.1	1.0	3.8
MSA[1]	81.9	9.1	1.4	0.0	0.0	0.5	2.2	0.8	4.2
U.S.	76.3	9.0	2.4	1.9	0.6	0.5	2.7	1.4	5.2

Note: Figures are percentages and cover workers 16 years of age and older; (1) Figures cover the Grand Rapids-Wyoming, MI Metropolitan Statistical Area
Source: U.S. Census Bureau, 2015-2019 American Community Survey 5-Year Estimates

Travel Time to Work

Area	Less Than 10 Minutes	10 to 19 Minutes	20 to 29 Minutes	30 to 44 Minutes	45 to 59 Minutes	60 to 89 Minutes	90 Minutes or More
City	15.0	42.9	24.4	11.6	3.3	2.0	0.9
MSA[1]	14.8	35.3	24.9	16.1	5.0	2.5	1.5
U.S.	12.2	28.4	20.8	20.8	8.3	6.4	2.9

Note: Note: Figures are percentages and include workers 16 years old and over; (1) Figures cover the Grand Rapids-Wyoming, MI Metropolitan Statistical Area
Source: U.S. Census Bureau, 2015-2019 American Community Survey 5-Year Estimates

Key Congestion Measures

Measure	1982	1992	2002	2012	2017
Annual Hours of Delay, Total (000)	1,467	6,052	11,749	16,557	19,417
Annual Hours of Delay, Per Auto Commuter	8	24	34	40	41
Annual Congestion Cost, Total (million $)	11	64	159	299	360
Annual Congestion Cost, Per Auto Commuter ($)	121	344	521	575	654

Note: Covers the Grand Rapids MI urban area
Source: Texas A&M Transportation Institute, 2019 Urban Mobility Report

Freeway Travel Time Index

Measure	1982	1987	1992	1997	2002	2007	2012	2017
Urban Area Index[1]	1.03	1.07	1.11	1.14	1.14	1.15	1.14	1.13
Urban Area Rank[1,2]	76	55	49	47	69	72	79	83

Note: Freeway Travel Time Index—the ratio of travel time in the peak period to the travel time at free-flow conditions. For example, a value of 1.30 indicates a 20-minute free-flow trip takes 26 minutes in the peak (20 minutes x 1.30 = 26 minutes); (1) Covers the Grand Rapids MI urban area; (2) Rank is based on 101 larger urban areas (#1 = highest travel time index)
Source: Texas A&M Transportation Institute, 2019 Urban Mobility Report

Public Transportation

Agency Name / Mode of Transportation	Vehicles Operated in Maximum Service[1]	Annual Unlinked Passenger Trips[2] (in thous.)	Annual Passenger Miles[3] (in thous.)
Interurban Transit Partnership (The Rapid)			
Bus (directly operated)	124	9,242.4	31,339.5
Bus Rapid Transit (directly operated)	8	850.7	2,501.0
Demand Response (purchased transportation)	90	347.4	4,749.4
Vanpool (directly operated)	20	31.6	1,390.6

Note: (1) Number of revenue vehicles operated by the given mode and type of service to meet the annual maximum service requirement. This is the revenue vehicle count during the peak season of the year; on the week and day that maximum service is provided. Vehicles operated in maximum service (VOMS) exclude atypical days and one-time special events; (2) Number of passengers who boarded public transportation vehicles. Passengers are counted each time they board a vehicle no matter how many vehicles they use to travel from their origin to their destination. (3) Sum of the distances ridden by all passengers during the entire fiscal year.
Source: Federal Transit Administration, National Transit Database, 2019

Air Transportation

Airport Name and Code / Type of Service	Passenger Airlines[1]	Passenger Enplanements	Freight Carriers[2]	Freight (lbs)
Gerald R. Ford International (GRR)				
Domestic service (U.S. carriers - 2020)	24	864,553	11	44,696,973
International service (U.S. carriers - 2019)	1	11	2	90,029

Note: (1) Includes all U.S.-based major, minor and commuter airlines that carried at least one passenger during the year; (2) Includes all U.S.-based airlines and freight carriers that transported at least one pound of freight during the year.
Source: Bureau of Transportation Statistics, The Intermodal Transportation Database, Air Carriers: T-100 Domestic Market (U.S. Carriers), 2020; Bureau of Transportation Statistics, The Intermodal Transportation Database, Air Carriers: T-100 International Market (U.S. Carriers), 2019

BUSINESSES

Major Business Headquarters

Company Name	Industry	Rankings	
		Fortune[1]	Forbes[2]
Gordon Food Service	Food, Drink & Tobacco	-	20
Meijer	Food Markets	-	18
SpartanNash	Wholesalers, Food and Grocery	370	-

Note: (1) Companies that produce a 10-K are ranked 1 to 500 based on 2019 revenue; (2) All private companies with at least $2 billion in annual revenue through the end of their most current fiscal year are ranked 1 to 219; companies listed are headquartered in the city; dashes indicate no ranking
Source: Fortune, "Fortune 500," June/July 2020; Forbes, "America's Largest Private Companies," 2020

Fastest-Growing Businesses

According to *Inc.*, Grand Rapids is home to three of America's 500 fastest-growing private companies: **Ally Logistics** (#139); **ITPartners** (#214); **Sherpack** (#231). Criteria: must be an independent, privately-held, for-profit, U.S. corporation, proprietorship or partnership as of December 31, 2019; revenues must be at least $100,000 in 2016 and $2 million in 2019; must have four-year operating/sales history. *Inc., "America's 500 Fastest-Growing Private Companies," 2020*

According to Deloitte, Grand Rapids is home to one of North America's 500 fastest-growing high-technology companies: **Tech Defenders** (#166). Companies are ranked by percentage growth in revenue over a four-year period. Criteria for inclusion: company must be headquartered within North America; must own proprietary intellectual property or technology that is sold to customers in products that contributes to a significant portion of the company's operating revenue; must have been in business for a minumum of four years with 2016 operating revenues of at least $50,000 USD/CD and 2019 operating revenues of at least $5 million USD/CD. *Deloitte, 2020 Technology Fast 500*[TM]

Living Environment

COST OF LIVING

Cost of Living Index

Composite Index	Groceries	Housing	Utilities	Trans-portation	Health Care	Misc. Goods/Services
94.7	89.1	89.1	100.5	107.0	94.9	96.7

Note: The Cost of Living Index measures regional differences in the cost of consumer goods and services, excluding taxes and non-consumer expenditures, for professional and managerial households in the top income quintile. It is based on more than 50,000 prices covering almost 60 different items for which prices are collected three times a year by chambers of commerce, economic development organizations or university applied economic centers in each participating urban area. The numbers shown should be read as a percentage above or below the national average of 100. For example, a value of 115.4 in the groceries column indicates that grocery prices are 15.4% higher than the national average. Small differences in the index numbers should not be interpreted as significant; Figures cover the Grand Rapids MI urban area.
Source: The Council for Community and Economic Research, Cost of Living Index, 2020

Grocery Prices

Area[1]	T-Bone Steak ($/pound)	Frying Chicken ($/pound)	Whole Milk ($/half gal.)	Eggs ($/dozen)	Orange Juice ($/64 oz.)	Coffee ($/11.5 oz.)
City[2]	12.68	1.12	1.59	1.25	3.34	3.25
Avg.	11.78	1.39	2.05	1.47	3.57	4.34
Min.	8.03	0.94	1.03	0.74	2.94	3.02
Max.	15.86	2.65	4.31	3.77	5.44	8.69

*Note: (1) Values for the local area are compared with the average, minimum and maximum values for all 284 areas in the Cost of Living Index; (2) Figures cover the Grand Rapids MI urban area; **T-Bone Steak** (price per pound); **Frying Chicken** (price per pound, whole fryer); **Whole Milk** (half gallon carton); **Eggs** (price per dozen, Grade A, large); **Orange Juice** (64 oz. Tropicana or Florida Natural); **Coffee** (11.5 oz. can, vacuum-packed, Maxwell House, Hills Bros, or Folgers).*
Source: The Council for Community and Economic Research, Cost of Living Index, 2020

Housing and Utility Costs

Area[1]	New Home Price ($)	Apartment Rent ($/month)	All Electric ($/month)	Part Electric ($/month)	Other Energy ($/month)	Telephone ($/month)
City[2]	299,711	1,144	-	102.23	68.00	181.00
Avg.	368,594	1,168	170.86	100.47	65.28	184.30
Min.	190,567	502	91.58	31.42	26.08	169.60
Max.	2,227,806	4,738	470.38	280.31	280.06	206.50

*Note: (1) Values for the local area are compared with the average, minimum and maximum values for all 284 areas in the Cost of Living Index; (2) Figures cover the Grand Rapids MI urban area; **New Home Price** (2,400 sf living area, 8,000 sf lot, in urban area with full utilities); **Apartment Rent** (950 sf 2 bedroom/1.5 or 2 bath, unfurnished, excluding all utilities except water); **All Electric** (average monthly cost for an all-electric home); **Part Electric** (average monthly cost for a part-electric home); **Other Energy** (average monthly cost for natural gas, fuel oil, coal, wood, and any other forms of energy except electricity); **Telephone** (price includes the base monthly rate plus taxes and fees for three lines of mobile phone service).*
Source: The Council for Community and Economic Research, Cost of Living Index, 2020

Health Care, Transportation, and Other Costs

Area[1]	Doctor ($/visit)	Dentist ($/visit)	Optometrist ($/visit)	Gasoline ($/gallon)	Beauty Salon ($/visit)	Men's Shirt ($)
City[2]	98.00	94.78	105.11	2.23	32.55	17.24
Avg.	115.44	99.32	108.10	2.21	39.27	31.37
Min.	36.68	59.00	51.36	1.71	19.00	11.00
Max.	219.00	153.10	250.97	3.46	82.05	58.33

*Note: (1) Values for the local area are compared with the average, minimum and maximum values for all 284 areas in the Cost of Living Index; (2) Figures cover the Grand Rapids MI urban area; **Doctor** (general practitioners routine exam of an established patient); **Dentist** (adult teeth cleaning and periodic oral examination); **Optometrist** (full vision eye exam for established adult patient); **Gasoline** (one gallon regular unleaded, national brand, including all taxes, cash price at self-service pump if available); **Beauty Salon** (woman's shampoo, trim, and blow-dry); **Men's Shirt** (cotton/polyester dress shirt, pinpoint weave, long sleeves).*
Source: The Council for Community and Economic Research, Cost of Living Index, 2020

HOUSING

Homeownership Rate

Area	2012 (%)	2013 (%)	2014 (%)	2015 (%)	2016 (%)	2017 (%)	2018 (%)	2019 (%)	2020 (%)
MSA[1]	76.9	73.7	71.6	75.8	76.2	71.7	73.0	75.2	71.8
U.S.	65.4	65.1	64.5	63.7	63.4	63.9	64.4	64.6	66.6

Note: (1) Figures cover the Grand Rapids-Wyoming, MI Metropolitan Statistical Area
Source: U.S. Census Bureau, Housing Vacancies and Homeownership Annual Statistics: 2012-2020

180 Grand Rapids, Michigan

House Price Index (HPI)

Area	National Ranking[2]	Quarterly Change (%)	One-Year Change (%)	Five-Year Change (%)	Since 1991Q1 (%)
MSA[1]	71	2.11	7.32	44.57	175.35
U.S.[3]	–	3.81	10.77	38.99	205.12

Note: The HPI is a weighted repeat sales index. It measures average price changes in repeat sales or refinancings on the same properties. This information is obtained by reviewing repeat mortgage transactions on single-family properties whose mortgages have been purchased or securitized by Fannie Mae or Freddie Mac since January 1975; (1) Figures cover the Grand Rapids-Wyoming, MI Metropolitan Statistical Area; (2) Rankings are based on annual percentage change for all metro areas containing at least 15,000 transactions over the last 10 years and ranges from 1 to 253; (3) figures based on a weighted average of Census Division estimates using a seasonally adjusted, purchase-only index; all figures are for the period ending December 31, 2020
Source: Federal Housing Finance Agency, Change in Metropolitan Area House Price Indexes, April 7, 2021

Median Single-Family Home Prices

Area	2018	2019	2020[p]	Percent Change 2019 to 2020
MSA[1]	194.6	210.5	230.1	9.3
U.S. Average	261.6	274.6	299.9	9.2

Note: Figures are median sales prices of existing single-family homes in thousands of dollars; (p) preliminary; (1) Figures cover the Grand Rapids-Wyoming, MI Metropolitan Statistical Area
Source: National Association of Realtors, Median Sales Price of Existing Single-Family Homes for Metropolitan Areas, 4th Quarter 2020

Qualifying Income Based on Median Sales Price of Existing Single-Family Homes

Area	With 5% Down ($)	With 10% Down ($)	With 20% Down ($)
MSA[1]	44,032	41,715	37,080
U.S. Average	59,266	56,147	49,908

Note: Figures are preliminary; Qualifying income is based on a mortgage rate of 2.81%. Monthly principal and interest payment is limited to 25% of income; (1) Figures cover the Grand Rapids-Wyoming, MI Metropolitan Statistical Area
Source: National Association of Realtors, Qualifying Income Based on Median Sales Price of Existing Single-Family Homes for Metropolitan Areas, 4th Quarter 2020

Home Value Distribution

Area	Under $50,000	$50,000 -$99,999	$100,000 -$149,999	$150,000 -$199,999	$200,000 -$299,999	$300,000 -$499,999	$500,000 -$999,999	$1,000,000 or more
City	4.7	19.6	30.0	24.3	15.0	5.0	1.3	0.2
MSA[1]	6.7	11.6	20.2	21.8	22.4	13.0	3.6	0.7
U.S.	6.9	12.0	13.3	14.0	19.6	19.3	11.4	3.4

Note: Figures are percentages and cover owner-occupied housing units; (1) Figures cover the Grand Rapids-Wyoming, MI Metropolitan Statistical Area
Source: U.S. Census Bureau, 2015-2019 American Community Survey 5-Year Estimates

Year Housing Structure Built

Area	2010 or Later	2000 -2009	1990 -1999	1980 -1989	1970 -1979	1960 -1969	1950 -1959	1940 -1949	Before 1940	Median Year
City	2.5	4.2	6.1	7.0	8.5	10.3	15.7	8.9	36.8	1953
MSA[1]	4.7	12.4	16.3	12.1	14.0	9.5	10.4	5.0	15.7	1977
U.S.	5.2	14.0	13.9	13.4	15.2	10.6	10.3	4.9	12.6	1978

Note: Figures are percentages except for Median Year; Note: (1) Figures cover the Grand Rapids-Wyoming, MI Metropolitan Statistical Area
Source: U.S. Census Bureau, 2015-2019 American Community Survey 5-Year Estimates

Gross Monthly Rent

Area	Under $500	$500 -$999	$1,000 -$1,499	$1,500 -$1,999	$2,000 -$2,499	$2,500 -$2,999	$3,000 and up	Median ($)
City	10.2	48.9	31.0	6.5	2.8	0.5	0.1	925
MSA[1]	8.8	56.1	26.7	5.7	1.9	0.3	0.3	884
U.S.	9.4	36.2	30.0	14.0	5.6	2.4	2.4	1,062

Note: Figures are percentages except for Median; Gross rent is the contract rent plus the estimated average monthly cost of utilities (electricity, gas, and water and sewer) and fuels (oil, coal, kerosene, wood, etc.) if these are paid by the renter (or paid for the renter by someone else); (1) Figures cover the Grand Rapids-Wyoming, MI Metropolitan Statistical Area
Source: U.S. Census Bureau, 2015-2019 American Community Survey 5-Year Estimates

HEALTH

Health Risk Factors

Category	MSA[1] (%)	U.S. (%)
Adults aged 18–64 who have any kind of health care coverage	90.2	87.3
Adults who reported being in good or better health	86.0	82.4
Adults who have been told they have high blood cholesterol	31.5	33.0
Adults who have been told they have high blood pressure	32.8	32.3
Adults who are current smokers	14.5	17.1
Adults who currently use E-cigarettes	5.0	4.6
Adults who currently use chewing tobacco, snuff, or snus	3.9	4.0
Adults who are heavy drinkers[2]	8.0	6.3
Adults who are binge drinkers[3]	19.9	17.4
Adults who are overweight (BMI 25.0 - 29.9)	32.2	35.3
Adults who are obese (BMI 30.0 - 99.8)	32.3	31.3
Adults who participated in any physical activities in the past month	75.2	74.4
Adults who always or nearly always wears a seat belt	94.5	94.3

Note: (1) Figures cover the Grand Rapids-Wyoming, MI Metropolitan Statistical Area; (2) Heavy drinkers are classified as adult men having more than 14 drinks per week and adult women having more than 7 drinks per week; (3) Binge drinkers are classified as males having five or more drinks on one occasion or females having four or more drinks on one occasion
Source: Centers for Disease Control and Prevention, Behaviorial Risk Factor Surveillance System, SMART: Selected Metropolitan Area Risk Trends, 2017

Acute and Chronic Health Conditions

Category	MSA[1] (%)	U.S. (%)
Adults who have ever been told they had a heart attack	2.7	4.2
Adults who have ever been told they have angina or coronary heart disease	2.7	3.9
Adults who have ever been told they had a stroke	3.7	3.0
Adults who have ever been told they have asthma	14.5	14.2
Adults who have ever been told they have arthritis	25.6	24.9
Adults who have ever been told they have diabetes[2]	10.0	10.5
Adults who have ever been told they had skin cancer	6.4	6.2
Adults who have ever been told they had any other types of cancer	5.5	7.1
Adults who have ever been told they have COPD	6.8	6.5
Adults who have ever been told they have kidney disease	3.2	3.0
Adults who have ever been told they have a form of depression	25.0	20.5

Note: (1) Figures cover the Grand Rapids-Wyoming, MI Metropolitan Statistical Area; (2) Figures do not include pregnancy-related, borderline, or pre-diabetes
Source: Centers for Disease Control and Prevention, Behaviorial Risk Factor Surveillance System, SMART: Selected Metropolitan Area Risk Trends, 2017

Health Screening and Vaccination Rates

Category	MSA[1] (%)	U.S. (%)
Adults aged 65+ who have had flu shot within the past year	58.8	60.7
Adults aged 65+ who have ever had a pneumonia vaccination	79.1	75.4
Adults who have ever been tested for HIV	37.3	36.1
Adults who have ever had the shingles or zoster vaccine?	32.2	28.9
Adults who have had their blood cholesterol checked within the last five years	92.5	85.9

Note: n/a not available; (1) Figures cover the Grand Rapids-Wyoming, MI Metropolitan Statistical Area.
Source: Centers for Disease Control and Prevention, Behaviorial Risk Factor Surveillance System, SMART: Selected Metropolitan Area Risk Trends, 2017

Disability Status

Category	MSA[1] (%)	U.S. (%)
Adults who reported being deaf	6.8	6.7
Are you blind or have serious difficulty seeing, even when wearing glasses?	3.4	4.5
Are you limited in any way in any of your usual activities due of arthritis?	13.1	12.9
Do you have difficulty doing errands alone?	7.2	6.8
Do you have difficulty dressing or bathing?	4.3	3.6
Do you have serious difficulty concentrating/remembering/making decisions?	12.1	10.7
Do you have serious difficulty walking or climbing stairs?	14.4	13.6

Note: (1) Figures cover the Grand Rapids-Wyoming, MI Metropolitan Statistical Area.
Source: Centers for Disease Control and Prevention, Behaviorial Risk Factor Surveillance System, SMART: Selected Metropolitan Area Risk Trends, 2017

Mortality Rates for the Top 10 Causes of Death in the U.S.

ICD-10[a] Sub-Chapter	ICD-10[a] Code	Age-Adjusted Mortality Rate[1] per 100,000 population	
		County[2]	U.S.
Malignant neoplasms	C00-C97	144.1	149.2
Ischaemic heart diseases	I20-I25	102.1	90.5
Other forms of heart disease	I30-I51	39.5	52.2
Chronic lower respiratory diseases	J40-J47	35.7	39.6
Other degenerative diseases of the nervous system	G30-G31	50.9	37.6
Cerebrovascular diseases	I60-I69	31.6	37.2
Other external causes of accidental injury	W00-X59	37.0	36.1
Organic, including symptomatic, mental disorders	F01-F09	29.6	29.4
Hypertensive diseases	I10-I15	27.4	24.1
Diabetes mellitus	E10-E14	12.0	21.5

Note: (a) ICD-10 = International Classification of Diseases 10th Revision; (1) Mortality rates are a three-year average covering 2017-2019; (2) Figures cover Kent County.
Source: Centers for Disease Control and Prevention, National Center for Health Statistics. Underlying Cause of Death 1999-2019 on CDC WONDER Online Database

Mortality Rates for Selected Causes of Death

ICD-10[a] Sub-Chapter	ICD-10[a] Code	Age-Adjusted Mortality Rate[1] per 100,000 population	
		County[2]	U.S.
Assault	X85-Y09	3.7	6.0
Diseases of the liver	K70-K76	13.1	14.4
Human immunodeficiency virus (HIV) disease	B20-B24	Unreliable	1.5
Influenza and pneumonia	J09-J18	10.4	13.8
Intentional self-harm	X60-X84	12.2	14.1
Malnutrition	E40-E46	1.8	2.3
Obesity and other hyperalimentation	E65-E68	3.2	2.1
Renal failure	N17-N19	6.0	12.6
Transport accidents	V01-V99	9.5	12.3
Viral hepatitis	B15-B19	0.8	1.2

Note: (a) ICD-10 = International Classification of Diseases 10th Revision; (1) Mortality rates are a three-year average covering 2017-2019; (2) Figures cover Kent County; Data are suppressed when the data meet the criteria for confidentiality constraints; Mortality rates are flagged as unreliable when the rate would be calculated with a numerator of 20 or less.
Source: Centers for Disease Control and Prevention, National Center for Health Statistics. Underlying Cause of Death 1999-2019 on CDC WONDER Online Database

Health Insurance Coverage

Area	With Health Insurance	With Private Health Insurance	With Public Health Insurance	Without Health Insurance	Population Under Age 19 Without Health Insurance
City	91.4	62.1	39.6	8.6	3.9
MSA[1]	94.6	75.5	31.5	5.4	3.1
U.S.	91.2	67.9	35.1	8.8	5.1

Note: Figures are percentages that cover the civilian noninstitutionalized population; (1) Figures cover the Grand Rapids-Wyoming, MI Metropolitan Statistical Area
Source: U.S. Census Bureau, 2015-2019 American Community Survey 5-Year Estimates

Number of Medical Professionals

Area	MDs[3]	DOs[3,4]	Dentists	Podiatrists	Chiropractors	Optometrists
County[1] (number)	2,246	454	490	31	243	165
County[1] (rate[2])	343.8	69.5	74.6	4.7	37.0	25.1
U.S. (rate[2])	282.9	22.7	71.2	6.2	28.1	16.9

26081
Note: Data as of 2019 unless noted; (1) Data covers Kent County; (2) Rate per 100,000 population; (3) Data as of 2018 and includes all active, non-federal physicians; (4) Doctor of Osteopathic Medicine
Source: U.S. Department of Health and Human Services, Health Resources and Services Administration, Bureau of Health Professions, Area Resource File (ARF) 2019-2020

Best Hospitals

According to *U.S. News,* the Grand Rapids-Wyoming, MI metro area is home to one of the best children's hospitals in the U.S.: **Spectrum Health Helen DeVos Children's Hospital** (8 pediatric specialties). The hospital listed was highly ranked in at least one of 10 pediatric specialties. Eighty-eight children's hospitals in the U.S. were nationally ranked in at least one specialty. Hospitals received points for being ranked in a specialty, and the 10 hospitals with the most points across the 10 specialties make up the Honor Roll. *U.S. News Online, "America's Best Children's Hospitals 2020-21"*

EDUCATION

Public School District Statistics

District Name	Schls	Pupils	Pupil/ Teacher Ratio	Minority Pupils[1] (%)	Free Lunch Eligible[2] (%)	IEP[3] (%)
East Grand Rapids Public Schools	6	2,886	16.9	14.3	5.6	5.7
Forest Hills Public Schools	18	9,772	19.3	21.2	10.2	8.9
Godwin Heights Public Schools	5	2,076	18.7	83.6	80.3	15.6
Grand Rapids Public Schools	59	15,803	15.2	77.8	70.7	19.6
Kelloggsville Public Schools	7	2,418	17.3	74.0	80.9	11.7
Kenowa Hills Public Schools	7	3,137	18.6	29.9	41.3	14.5
Kentwood Public Schools	18	9,276	18.3	69.2	62.0	13.6
Michigan Virtual Charter Academy	1	2,916	23.1	38.5	73.7	16.3
Northview Public Schools	7	3,327	18.4	24.8	34.7	13.2

Note: Table includes school districts with 2,000 or more students; (1) Percentage of students that are not non-Hispanic white; (2) Percentage of students that are eligible for the free lunch program; (3) Percentage of students that have an Individualized Education Program.
Source: U.S. Department of Education, National Center for Education Statistics, Common Core of Data, Local Education Agency (School District) Universe Survey: School Year 2018-2019; U.S. Department of Education, National Center for Education Statistics, Common Core of Data, Public Elementary/Secondary School Universe Survey: School Year 2018-2019

Best High Schools

According to *U.S. News,* Grand Rapids is home to one of the top 500 high schools in the U.S.: **City High Middle School** (#21). Nearly 18,000 public, magnet and charter schools were ranked based on their performance on state assessments and how well they prepare students for college. *U.S. News & World Report, "Best High Schools 2020"*

Highest Level of Education

Area	Less than H.S.	H.S. Diploma	Some College, No Deg.	Associate Degree	Bachelor's Degree	Master's Degree	Prof. School Degree	Doctorate Degree
City	13.3	21.9	20.5	7.9	24.4	8.7	2.0	1.4
MSA[1]	8.8	27.2	22.0	9.3	21.8	8.1	1.7	1.1
U.S.	12.0	27.0	20.4	8.5	19.8	8.8	2.1	1.4

Note: Figures cover persons age 25 and over; (1) Figures cover the Grand Rapids-Wyoming, MI Metropolitan Statistical Area
Source: U.S. Census Bureau, 2015-2019 American Community Survey 5-Year Estimates

Educational Attainment by Race

Area	High School Graduate or Higher (%)					Bachelor's Degree or Higher (%)				
	Total	White	Black	Asian	Hisp.[2]	Total	White	Black	Asian	Hisp.[2]
City	86.7	90.8	83.2	72.3	50.3	36.4	43.1	17.4	43.9	11.9
MSA[1]	91.2	93.1	85.7	75.2	63.7	32.7	34.3	18.3	37.3	14.2
U.S.	88.0	89.9	86.0	87.1	68.7	32.1	33.5	21.6	54.3	16.4

Note: Figures shown cover persons 25 years old and over; (1) Figures cover the Grand Rapids-Wyoming, MI Metropolitan Statistical Area; (2) People of Hispanic origin can be of any race
Source: U.S. Census Bureau, 2015-2019 American Community Survey 5-Year Estimates

School Enrollment by Grade and Control

Area	Preschool (%)		Kindergarten (%)		Grades 1 - 4 (%)		Grades 5 - 8 (%)		Grades 9 - 12 (%)	
	Public	Private	Public	Private	Public	Private	Public	Private	Public	Private
City	60.4	39.6	74.5	25.5	83.4	16.6	83.4	16.6	84.9	15.1
MSA[1]	62.5	37.5	82.2	17.8	84.8	15.2	86.2	13.8	86.1	13.9
U.S.	59.1	40.9	87.6	12.4	89.5	10.5	89.4	10.6	90.1	9.9

Note: Figures shown cover persons 3 years old and over; (1) Figures cover the Grand Rapids-Wyoming, MI Metropolitan Statistical Area
Source: U.S. Census Bureau, 2015-2019 American Community Survey 5-Year Estimates

Higher Education

Four-Year Colleges			Two-Year Colleges			Medical Schools[1]	Law Schools[2]	Voc/ Tech[3]
Public	Private Non-profit	Private For-profit	Public	Private Non-profit	Private For-profit			
0	7	0	1	0	1	0	0	2

Note: Figures cover institutions located within the city limits and include main campuses only; (1) includes schools accredited by the Liaison Committee on Medical Education and the American Osteopathic Association's Commission on Osteopathic College Accreditation; (2) includes ABA-accredited schools, schools with provisional ABA accreditation, and state accredited schools; (3) includes all schools with programs that are less than 2 years.
Source: National Center for Education Statistics, Integrated Postsecondary Education System (IPEDS), 2019-20; Wikipedia, List of Medical Schools in the United States, accessed April 2, 2021; Wikipedia, List of Law Schools in the United States, accessed April 2, 2021

Grand Rapids, Michigan

EMPLOYERS

Major Employers

Company Name	Industry
Alticor	Consumer products, multi-level marketing
Farmers Insurance Group	Insurance
Grand Rapids Public Schools	Public elementary & secondary schools
Herman Miller	Manufacturing & industrial supply
Johnson Controls	Automotive interiors, HVAC equipment
Meijer	Retail, grocery & discount
Spectrum Health	Healthcare
Steelcase	Furniture

Note: Companies shown are located within the Grand Rapids-Wyoming, MI Metropolitan Statistical Area.
Source: Hoovers.com; Wikipedia

Best Companies to Work For

Spectrum Health, headquartered in Grand Rapids, is among the "100 Best Places to Work in IT." To qualify, companies had to be U.S.-based organizations or be non-U.S.-based employers that met the following criteria: have a minimum of 300 total employees at a U.S. headquarters and a minimum of 30 IT employees in the U.S., with at least 50% of their IT employees based in the U.S. The best places to work were selected based on compensation, benefits, work/life balance, employee morale, and satisfaction with training and development programs. In addition, *InsiderPro* and *Computerworld* looked at retention efforts, programs for recognizing and rewarding outstanding performances, and benefits such as flextime, elder care and child care, and reimbursement for college tuition and the cost of pursuing technology certifications. *InsiderPro and Computerworld, "100 Best Places to Work in IT," 2020*

PUBLIC SAFETY

Crime Rate

Area	All Crimes	Violent Crimes				Property Crimes		
		Murder	Rape[3]	Robbery	Aggrav. Assault	Burglary	Larceny -Theft	Motor Vehicle Theft
City	2,545.1	4.0	71.4	135.8	426.2	294.8	1,364.7	248.3
Suburbs[1]	n/a	1.8	81.2	19.6	146.3	n/a	933.5	85.2
Metro[2]	n/a	2.2	79.4	41.3	198.6	n/a	1,014.1	115.7
U.S.	2,489.3	5.0	42.6	81.6	250.2	340.5	1,549.5	219.9

Note: Figures are crimes per 100,000 population; (1) All areas within the metro area that are located outside the city limits; (2) Figures cover the Grand Rapids-Wyoming, MI Metropolitan Statistical Area; (3) All figures shown were reported using the revised Uniform Crime Reporting (UCR) definition of rape.
Source: FBI Uniform Crime Reports, 2019

Hate Crimes

Area	Number of Quarters Reported	Number of Incidents per Bias Motivation					
		Race/Ethnicity/ Ancestry	Religion	Sexual Orientation	Disability	Gender	Gender Identity
City	4	5	0	0	0	0	0
U.S.	4	3,963	1,521	1,195	157	69	198

Source: Federal Bureau of Investigation, Hate Crime Statistics 2019

Identity Theft Consumer Reports

Area	Reports	Reports per 100,000 Population	Rank[2]
MSA[1]	2,029	188	232
U.S.	1,387,615	423	-

Note: (1) Figures cover the Grand Rapids-Wyoming, MI Metropolitan Statistical Area; (2) Rank ranges from 1 to 391 where 1 indicates greatest number of identity theft reports per 100,000 population
Source: Federal Trade Commission, Consumer Sentinel Network Data Book 2020

Fraud and Other Consumer Reports

Area	Reports	Reports per 100,000 Population	Rank[2]
MSA[1]	6,699	622	259
U.S.	3,385,133	1,031	-

Note: (1) Figures cover the Grand Rapids-Wyoming, MI Metropolitan Statistical Area; (2) Rank ranges from 1 to 391 where 1 indicates greatest number of fraud and other consumer reports per 100,000 population
Source: Federal Trade Commission, Consumer Sentinel Network Data Book 2020

POLITICS

2020 Presidential Election Results

Area	Biden	Trump	Jorgensen	Hawkins	Other
Kent County	51.9	45.8	1.5	0.3	0.5
U.S.	51.3	46.8	1.2	0.3	0.5

Note: Results are percentages and may not add to 100% due to rounding
Source: Dave Leip's Atlas of U.S. Presidential Elections

SPORTS

Professional Sports Teams

Team Name	League	Year Established
No teams are located in the metro area		

Source: Wikipedia, Major Professional Sports Teams of the United States and Canada, April 6, 2021

CLIMATE

Average and Extreme Temperatures

Temperature	Jan	Feb	Mar	Apr	May	Jun	Jul	Aug	Sep	Oct	Nov	Dec	Yr.
Extreme High (°F)	66	67	80	88	92	102	100	100	97	87	81	67	102
Average High (°F)	30	32	42	57	69	79	83	81	73	61	46	34	57
Average Temp. (°F)	23	25	34	47	58	67	72	70	62	51	39	28	48
Average Low (°F)	15	16	25	36	46	56	60	59	51	41	31	21	38
Extreme Low (°F)	-22	-19	-8	3	22	33	41	39	28	18	-10	-18	-22

Note: Figures cover the years 1948-1990
Source: National Climatic Data Center, International Station Meteorological Climate Summary, 9/96

Average Precipitation/Snowfall/Humidity

Precip./Humidity	Jan	Feb	Mar	Apr	May	Jun	Jul	Aug	Sep	Oct	Nov	Dec	Yr.
Avg. Precip. (in.)	1.9	1.6	2.6	3.5	3.0	3.5	3.2	3.2	3.7	2.7	3.1	2.7	34.7
Avg. Snowfall (in.)	21	12	11	3	Tr	0	0	0	Tr	1	8	18	73
Avg. Rel. Hum. 7am (%)	81	80	80	79	79	81	84	88	89	85	83	83	83
Avg. Rel. Hum. 4pm (%)	71	66	61	54	50	52	52	55	58	60	68	74	60

Note: Figures cover the years 1948-1990; Tr = Trace amounts (<0.05 in. of rain; <0.5 in. of snow)
Source: National Climatic Data Center, International Station Meteorological Climate Summary, 9/96

Weather Conditions

Temperature			Daytime Sky			Precipitation		
5°F & below	32°F & below	90°F & above	Clear	Partly cloudy	Cloudy	0.01 inch or more precip.	0.1 inch or more snow/ice	Thunder-storms
15	146	11	67	119	179	142	57	34

Note: Figures are average number of days per year and cover the years 1948-1990
Source: National Climatic Data Center, International Station Meteorological Climate Summary, 9/96

HAZARDOUS WASTE

Superfund Sites

The Grand Rapids-Wyoming, MI metro area is home to nine sites on the EPA's Superfund National Priorities List: **Butterworth #2 Landfill** (final); **Chem Central** (final); **H. Brown Co., Inc.** (final); **Kentwood Landfill** (final); **Organic Chemicals, Inc.** (final); **Southwest Ottawa County Landfill** (final); **Sparta Landfill** (final); **Spartan Chemical Co.** (final); **State Disposal Landfill, Inc.** (final). There are a total of 1,375 Superfund sites with a status of proposed or final on the list in the U.S. *U.S. Environmental Protection Agency, National Priorities List, April 7, 2021*

AIR QUALITY

Air Quality Trends: Ozone

	1990	1995	2000	2005	2010	2015	2016	2017	2018	2019
MSA[1]	0.102	0.089	0.073	0.085	0.071	0.066	0.075	0.065	0.072	0.065
U.S.	0.088	0.089	0.082	0.080	0.073	0.068	0.069	0.068	0.069	0.065

Note: (1) Data covers the Grand Rapids-Wyoming, MI Metropolitan Statistical Area. The values shown are the composite ozone concentration averages among trend sites based on the highest fourth daily maximum 8-hour concentration in parts per million. These trends are based on sites having an adequate record of monitoring data during the trend period. Data from exceptional events are included.
Source: U.S. Environmental Protection Agency, Air Quality Monitoring Information, "Air Quality Trends by City, 1990-2019"

Air Quality Index

Area	Percent of Days when Air Quality was...[2]					AQI Statistics[2]	
	Good	Moderate	Unhealthy for Sensitive Groups	Unhealthy	Very Unhealthy	Maximum	Median
MSA[1]	81.6	18.4	0.0	0.0	0.0	100	38

Note: (1) Data covers the Grand Rapids-Wyoming, MI Metropolitan Statistical Area; (2) Based on 365 days with AQI data in 2019. Air Quality Index (AQI) is an index for reporting daily air quality. EPA calculates the AQI for five major air pollutants regulated by the Clean Air Act: ground-level ozone, particle pollution (aka particulate matter), carbon monoxide, sulfur dioxide, and nitrogen dioxide. The AQI runs from 0 to 500. The higher the AQI value, the greater the level of air pollution and the greater the health concern. There are six AQI categories: "Good" AQI is between 0 and 50. Air quality is considered satisfactory; "Moderate" AQI is between 51 and 100. Air quality is acceptable; "Unhealthy for Sensitive Groups" When AQI values are between 101 and 150, members of sensitive groups may experience health effects; "Unhealthy" When AQI values are between 151 and 200 everyone may begin to experience health effects; "Very Unhealthy" AQI values between 201 and 300 trigger a health alert; "Hazardous" AQI values over 300 trigger warnings of emergency conditions (not shown).
Source: U.S. Environmental Protection Agency, Air Quality Index Report, 2019

Air Quality Index Pollutants

Area	Percent of Days when AQI Pollutant was...[2]					
	Carbon Monoxide	Nitrogen Dioxide	Ozone	Sulfur Dioxide	Particulate Matter 2.5	Particulate Matter 10
MSA[1]	0.0	2.5	69.9	0.0	26.3	1.4

Note: (1) Data covers the Grand Rapids-Wyoming, MI Metropolitan Statistical Area; (2) Based on 365 days with AQI data in 2019. The Air Quality Index (AQI) is an index for reporting daily air quality. EPA calculates the AQI for five major air pollutants regulated by the Clean Air Act: ground-level ozone, particle pollution (also known as particulate matter), carbon monoxide, sulfur dioxide, and nitrogen dioxide. The AQI runs from 0 to 500. The higher the AQI value, the greater the level of air pollution and the greater the health concern.
Source: U.S. Environmental Protection Agency, Air Quality Index Report, 2019

Maximum Air Pollutant Concentrations: Particulate Matter, Ozone, CO and Lead

	Particulate Matter 10 (ug/m^3)	Particulate Matter 2.5 Wtd AM (ug/m^3)	Particulate Matter 2.5 24-Hr (ug/m^3)	Ozone (ppm)	Carbon Monoxide (ppm)	Lead (ug/m^3)
MSA[1] Level	104	8.3	24	0.065	1	0.01
NAAQS[2]	150	15	35	0.075	9	0.15
Met NAAQS[2]	Yes	Yes	Yes	Yes	Yes	Yes

Note: (1) Data covers the Grand Rapids-Wyoming, MI Metropolitan Statistical Area; Data from exceptional events are included; (2) National Ambient Air Quality Standards; ppm = parts per million; ug/m^3 = micrograms per cubic meter; n/a not available.
Concentrations: Particulate Matter 10 (coarse particulate)—highest second maximum 24-hour concentration; Particulate Matter 2.5 Wtd AM (fine particulate)—highest weighted annual mean concentration; Particulate Matter 2.5 24-Hour (fine particulate)—highest 98th percentile 24-hour concentration; Ozone—highest fourth daily maximum 8-hour concentration; Carbon Monoxide—highest second maximum non-overlapping 8-hour concentration; Lead—maximum running 3-month average
Source: U.S. Environmental Protection Agency, Air Quality Monitoring Information, "Air Quality Statistics by City, 2019"

Maximum Air Pollutant Concentrations: Nitrogen Dioxide and Sulfur Dioxide

	Nitrogen Dioxide AM (ppb)	Nitrogen Dioxide 1-Hr (ppb)	Sulfur Dioxide AM (ppb)	Sulfur Dioxide 1-Hr (ppb)	Sulfur Dioxide 24-Hr (ppb)
MSA[1] Level	6	36	n/a	14	n/a
NAAQS[2]	53	100	30	75	140
Met NAAQS[2]	Yes	Yes	n/a	Yes	n/a

Note: (1) Data covers the Grand Rapids-Wyoming, MI Metropolitan Statistical Area; Data from exceptional events are included; (2) National Ambient Air Quality Standards; ppm = parts per million; ug/m^3 = micrograms per cubic meter; n/a not available.
Concentrations: Nitrogen Dioxide AM—highest arithmetic mean concentration; Nitrogen Dioxide 1-Hr—highest 98th percentile 1-hour daily maximum concentration; Sulfur Dioxide AM—highest annual mean concentration; Sulfur Dioxide 1-Hr—highest 99th percentile 1-hour daily maximum concentration; Sulfur Dioxide 24-Hr—highest second maximum 24-hour concentration
Source: U.S. Environmental Protection Agency, Air Quality Monitoring Information, "Air Quality Statistics by City, 2019"

Green Bay, Wisconsin

Background

The city of Green Bay takes its name from an inlet at the mouth of the Fox River, off Lake Michigan. Green Bay is the oldest city in Wisconsin, and the seat of Brown County. The city, laid out on high ground on either side of the river, has always been an important port and, in recent decades, is known to Americans as the home of the nation's oldest professional football team, the Green Bay Packers, who play in Lambeau Field, the longest continuously-occupied stadium in the NFL.

Prior to European settlement, the area had been home to Winnebago and other settled, horticultural tribes. The French explorer Jean Nicolet, who was seeking a route to the Pacific and thence to Asia, was the first recorded European visitor. He landed his canoe in 1634 about 10 miles south of the present city, finding there a community of friendly Winnebago or Oneida, who at first he thought to be Chinese.

Later explorers and traders, mostly French, established a trading post at the site, and in 1720, Fort St. Francis was completed at the mouth of the river. In 1745, the first permanent settlement was begun at "Le Baye" in what are the boundaries of the present city. The so-called "Tank House," built by the voyageur Joseph Roy in 1766, is thought to be the oldest house in the state. Green Bay is also home to the oldest Roman Catholic bishopric in the area. Although the French influence was paramount, many of the fur traders who came into the area were associated with the American fur baron John Jacob Astor, who constructed warehouses and other buildings on the site.

Settlers regarded themselves as French citizens until the fort was occupied by the British in 1763. From 1763 until the War of 1812, they were under British control. When the Americans garrisoned Fort Howard, the city was brought firmly under rule of the new republic. The first newspaper in the state, the *Green Bay Intelligencer,* was established in 1833. In 1854, the city of Green Bay was chartered, and in 1893, the adjoining Fort Howard was incorporated into it. In the late nineteenth century, Green Bay was a major port for the thriving lumber trade.

> Green Bay Packers quarterback Aaron Rodgers guest hosted the TV quiz show *Jeopardy!* earning almost $150,000 for his small-business COVID-19 relief fund.

Forest products, particularly paper, are still a mainstay of the local economy, as are health care, finance, insurance and logistics. The Oneida Tribe of Indians of Wisconsin is headquartered in the region. Tourism is increasingly important, with visitors drawn to the city both for Green Bay Packers football, and for its proximity to some of the most attractive vacation spots in the state.

The city's downtown renaissance include office space and dwelling units in place along the Fox River, and a walking/biking trail along the river's east side. The CityDeck faces the water for four blocks. Similarly, the Broadway corridor has been revived. The KI Convention Center was expanded by 35,000 square feet and the 15,000-square foot Children's Museum of Green Bay is a popular attraction in the city's downtown.

Other attractions include the National Railroad Museum, which includes the world's largest steam locomotive, and the NEW Zoo, with more than 200 animals of nearly 90 species.

Green Bay is home to a local campus (1965) of the University of Wisconsin and Bellin College (1909), which specializes in nursing and radiologic sciences.

The weather in Green Bay is a mild version of the general northern plains complex, with four seasons, warm summers, and considerable winter snowfall. High and low temperatures are modified by the city's location on Green Bay, as well as its proximity to Lake Superior and Lake Michigan.

Rankings

General Rankings

- *US News & World Report* conducted a survey of more than 3,000 people and analyzed the 150 largest metropolitan areas to determine what matters most when selecting the next place to live. Green Bay ranked #25 out of the top 25 as having the best combination of desirable factors. Criteria: cost of living; quality of life; net migration; job market; desirability; and other factors. *realestate.usnews.com, "The 25 Best Places to Live in the U.S. in 2020-21," October 13, 2020*

- In their seventh annual survey, Livability.com looked at data for more than 1,000 small to mid-sized U.S. cities to determine the rankings for Livability's "Top 100 Best Places to Live" in 2020. Green Bay ranked #40. Criteria: housing and affordable living; vibrant economy; social and civic engagement; education; demographics; health care options; transportation & infrastructure; and abundant lifestyle amenities. *Livability.com, "Top 100 Best Places to Live 2020" October 2020*

Business/Finance Rankings

- The Green Bay metro area appeared on the Milken Institute "2021 Best Performing Cities" list. Rank: #139 out of 200 large metro areas (population over 250,000). Criteria: job growth; wage and salary growth; high-tech output growth; housing affordability; household broadband access. *Milken Institute, "Best-Performing Cities 2021," February 16, 2021*

- *Forbes* ranked the 200 most populous metro areas to determine the nation's "Best Places for Business and Careers." The Green Bay metro area was ranked #100. Criteria: costs (business and living); job growth (past and projected); income growth; quality of life; educational attainment (college and high school); projected economic growth; cultural and leisure opportunities; workplace tolerance laws; net migration patterns. *Forbes, "The Best Places for Business and Careers 2019: Seattle Still On Top," October 30, 2019*

Environmental Rankings

- Green Bay was highlighted as one of the top 98 cleanest metro areas for short-term particle pollution (24-hour PM 2.5) in the U.S. during 2016 through 2018. Monitors in these cities reported no days with unhealthful PM 2.5 levels. *American Lung Association, "State of the Air 2020," April 21, 2020*

Real Estate Rankings

- Green Bay was ranked #58 out of 268 metro areas in terms of housing affordability in 2020 by the National Association of Home Builders (#1 = most affordable). Criteria: the share of homes sold in that area affordable to a family earning the local median income, based on standard mortgage underwriting criteria. *National Association of Home Builders®, NAHB-Wells Fargo Housing Opportunity Index, 4th Quarter 2020*

Safety Rankings

- The National Insurance Crime Bureau ranked 384 metro areas in the U.S. in terms of per capita rates of vehicle theft. The Green Bay metro area ranked #349 (#1 = highest rate). Criteria: number of vehicle theft offenses per 100,000 inhabitants in 2019. *National Insurance Crime Bureau, "Hot Spots 2019," July 21, 2020*

Seniors/Retirement Rankings

- From its Best Cities for Successful Aging indexes, the Milken Institute generated rankings for metropolitan areas, weighing data in nine categories—health care, wellness, living arrangements, transportation and convenience, financial characteristics, education, employment, community engagement, and overall livability. The Green Bay metro area was ranked #162 overall in the small metro area category. *Milken Institute, "Best Cities for Successful Aging, 2017" March 14, 2017*

Business Environment

DEMOGRAPHICS

Population Growth

Area	1990 Census	2000 Census	2010 Census	2019* Estimate	Population Growth (%)	
					1990-2019	2010-2019
City	96,466	102,313	104,057	104,777	8.6	0.7
MSA[1]	243,698	282,599	306,241	319,401	31.1	4.3
U.S.	248,709,873	281,421,906	308,745,538	324,697,795	30.6	5.2

Note: (1) Figures cover the Green Bay, WI Metropolitan Statistical Area; (*) 2015-2019 5-year estimated population
Source: U.S. Census Bureau, 1990 Census, Census 2000, Census 2010, 2015-2019 American Community Survey 5-Year Estimates

Household Size

Area	Persons in Household (%)							Average Household Size
	One	Two	Three	Four	Five	Six	Seven or More	
City	34.1	32.1	12.7	11.4	6.6	1.6	1.5	2.40
MSA[1]	28.3	37.0	14.1	12.3	5.8	1.5	1.0	2.40
U.S.	27.9	33.9	15.6	12.9	6.0	2.3	1.4	2.60

Note: (1) Figures cover the Green Bay, WI Metropolitan Statistical Area
Source: U.S. Census Bureau, 2015-2019 American Community Survey 5-Year Estimates

Race

Area	White Alone[2] (%)	Black Alone[2] (%)	Asian Alone[2] (%)	AIAN[3] Alone[2] (%)	NHOPI[4] Alone[2] (%)	Other Race Alone[2] (%)	Two or More Races (%)
City	76.7	4.2	4.2	3.5	0.0	6.0	5.4
MSA[1]	87.1	2.1	2.7	2.2	0.0	2.9	3.0
U.S.	72.5	12.7	5.5	0.8	0.2	4.9	3.3

Note: (1) Figures cover the Green Bay, WI Metropolitan Statistical Area; (2) Alone is defined as not being in combination with one or more other races; (3) American Indian and Alaska Native; (4) Native Hawaiian and Other Pacific Islander
Source: U.S. Census Bureau, 2015-2019 American Community Survey 5-Year Estimates

Hispanic or Latino Origin

Area	Total (%)	Mexican (%)	Puerto Rican (%)	Cuban (%)	Other (%)
City	15.8	12.5	1.4	0.1	1.8
MSA[1]	7.4	5.8	0.7	0.0	0.9
U.S.	18.0	11.2	1.7	0.7	4.3

Note: Persons of Hispanic or Latino origin can be of any race; (1) Figures cover the Green Bay, WI Metropolitan Statistical Area
Source: U.S. Census Bureau, 2015-2019 American Community Survey 5-Year Estimates

Ancestry

Area	German	Irish	English	American	Italian	Polish	French[2]	Scottish	Dutch
City	29.5	9.3	3.8	3.4	2.3	7.9	4.2	0.6	3.0
MSA[1]	36.3	9.7	4.1	3.6	2.2	9.8	4.3	0.7	4.4
U.S.	13.3	9.7	7.2	6.2	5.1	2.8	2.3	1.7	1.2

Note: Figures are the percentage of the total population reporting a particular ancestry. The nine most commonly reported ancestries in the U.S. are shown. Figures include multiple ancestries (e.g. if a person reported being Irish and Italian, they were included in both columns); (1) Figures cover the Green Bay, WI Metropolitan Statistical Area; (2) Excludes Basque
Source: U.S. Census Bureau, 2015-2019 American Community Survey 5-Year Estimates

Foreign-born Population

Area	Percent of Population Born in								
	Any Foreign Country	Asia	Mexico	Europe	Caribbean	Central America[2]	South America	Africa	Canada
City	9.9	2.0	5.9	0.5	0.1	0.6	0.2	0.5	0.0
MSA[1]	5.1	1.5	2.4	0.5	0.0	0.4	0.1	0.2	0.1
U.S.	13.6	4.2	3.5	1.5	1.3	1.1	1.0	0.7	0.2

Note: (1) Figures cover the Green Bay, WI Metropolitan Statistical Area; (2) Excludes Mexico.
Source: U.S. Census Bureau, 2015-2019 American Community Survey 5-Year Estimates

Marital Status

Area	Never Married	Now Married[2]	Separated	Widowed	Divorced
City	37.9	43.2	1.5	5.1	12.3
MSA[1]	30.2	53.2	0.9	5.2	10.5
U.S.	33.4	48.1	1.9	5.8	10.9

Note: Figures are percentages and cover the population 15 years of age and older; (1) Figures cover the Green Bay, WI Metropolitan Statistical Area; (2) Excludes separated
Source: U.S. Census Bureau, 2015-2019 American Community Survey 5-Year Estimates

Disability by Age

Area	All Ages	Under 18 Years Old	18 to 64 Years Old	65 Years and Over
City	13.0	6.6	11.6	32.5
MSA[1]	11.2	4.7	9.1	29.4
U.S.	12.6	4.2	10.3	34.5

Note: Figures show percent of the civilian noninstitutionalized population that reported having a disability. Disability status is determined from six types of difficulty: vision, hearing, cognitive, ambulatory, self-care, and independent living. For children under 5 years old, hearing and vision difficulty are used to determine disability status. For children between the ages of 5 and 14, disability status is determined from hearing, vision, cognitive, ambulatory, and self-care difficulties. For people aged 15 years and older, they are considered to have a disability if they have difficulty with any one of the six difficulty types; Note: (1) Figures cover the Green Bay, WI Metropolitan Statistical Area
Source: U.S. Census Bureau, 2015-2019 American Community Survey 5-Year Estimates

Age

Area	Percent of Population									Median Age
	Under Age 5	Age 5–19	Age 20–34	Age 35–44	Age 45–54	Age 55–64	Age 65–74	Age 75–84	Age 85+	
City	7.6	20.3	22.8	12.4	12.3	11.8	7.2	3.7	1.9	34.5
MSA[1]	6.2	19.7	19.2	12.4	13.4	13.7	9.0	4.6	1.8	38.8
U.S.	6.1	19.1	20.7	12.6	13.0	12.9	9.1	4.6	1.9	38.1

Note: (1) Figures cover the Green Bay, WI Metropolitan Statistical Area
Source: U.S. Census Bureau, 2015-2019 American Community Survey 5-Year Estimates

Gender

Area	Males	Females	Males per 100 Females
City	51,929	52,848	98.3
MSA[1]	159,123	160,278	99.3
U.S.	159,886,919	164,810,876	97.0

Note: (1) Figures cover the Green Bay, WI Metropolitan Statistical Area
Source: U.S. Census Bureau, 2015-2019 American Community Survey 5-Year Estimates

Religious Groups by Family

Area	Catholic	Baptist	Non-Den.	Methodist[2]	Lutheran	LDS[3]	Pentecostal	Presbyterian[4]	Muslim[5]	Judaism
MSA[1]	42.0	0.7	3.4	2.2	12.7	0.4	0.6	1.0	0.1	0.1
U.S.	19.1	9.3	4.0	4.0	2.3	2.0	1.9	1.6	0.8	0.7

Note: Figures are the number of adherents as a percentage of the total population; (1) Figures cover the Green Bay, WI Metropolitan Statistical Area; (2) Methodist/Pietist; (3) Latter Day Saints; (4) Reformed; (5) Figures are estimates
Source: Association of Statisticians of American Religious Bodies, 2010 U.S. Religion Census: Religious Congregations & Membership Study

Religious Groups by Tradition

Area	Catholic	Evangelical Protestant	Mainline Protestant	Other Tradition	Black Protestant	Orthodox
MSA[1]	42.0	14.1	8.1	0.6	<0.1	<0.1
U.S.	19.1	16.2	7.3	4.3	1.6	0.3

Note: Figures are the number of adherents as a percentage of the total population; (1) Figures cover the Green Bay, WI Metropolitan Statistical Area
Source: Association of Statisticians of American Religious Bodies, 2010 U.S. Religion Census: Religious Congregations & Membership Study

ECONOMY

Gross Metropolitan Product

Area	2017	2018	2019	2020	Rank[2]
MSA[1]	19.4	20.4	21.3	22.1	128

Note: Figures are in billions of dollars; (1) Figures cover the Green Bay, WI Metropolitan Statistical Area; (2) Rank is based on 2018 data and ranges from 1 to 381
Source: U.S. Conference of Mayors, U.S. Metro Economies: GMP & Employment 2018-2020, September 2019

Economic Growth

Area	2015-17 (%)	2018 (%)	2019 (%)	2020 (%)	Rank[2]
MSA[1]	1.2	3.2	2.6	1.2	203
U.S.	1.9	2.9	2.3	2.1	–

Note: Figures are real gross metropolitan product (GMP) growth rates and represent average annual percent change; (1) Figures cover the Green Bay, WI Metropolitan Statistical Area; (2) Rank is based on 2017 2-year average annual percent change and ranges from 1 to 381
Source: U.S. Conference of Mayors, U.S. Metro Economies: GMP & Employment 2018-2020, September 2019

Metropolitan Area Exports

Area	2014	2015	2016	2017	2018	2019	Rank[2]
MSA[1]	988.7	968.1	1,044.0	1,054.8	1,044.3	928.2	167

Note: Figures are in millions of dollars; (1) Figures cover the Green Bay, WI Metropolitan Statistical Area; (2) Rank is based on 2019 data and ranges from 1 to 386
Source: U.S. Department of Commerce, International Trade Administration, Office of Trade and Economic Analysis, Industry and Analysis, Exports by Metropolitan Area, data extracted March 24, 2021

Building Permits

Area	Single-Family			Multi-Family			Total		
	2018	2019	Pct. Chg.	2018	2019	Pct. Chg.	2018	2019	Pct. Chg.
City	101	63	-37.6	0	0	0.0	101	63	-37.6
MSA[1]	766	723	-5.6	435	407	-6.4	1,201	1,130	-5.9
U.S.	855,300	862,100	0.7	473,500	523,900	10.6	1,328,800	1,386,000	4.3

Note: (1) Figures cover the Green Bay, WI Metropolitan Statistical Area; Figures represent new, privately-owned housing units authorized (unadjusted data); All permit data are based on estimates with imputation
Source: U.S. Census Bureau, Manufacturing, Mining, and Construction Statistics, Building Permits, 2018, 2019

Bankruptcy Filings

Area	Business Filings			Nonbusiness Filings		
	2019	2020	% Chg.	2019	2020	% Chg.
Brown County	25	9	-64.0	599	418	-30.2
U.S.	22,780	21,655	-4.9	752,160	522,808	-30.5

Note: Business filings include Chapter 7, Chapter 9, Chapter 11, Chapter 12, Chapter 13, Chapter 15, and Section 304; Nonbusiness filings include Chapter 7, Chapter 11, and Chapter 13
Source: Administrative Office of the U.S. Courts, Business and Nonbusiness Bankruptcy, County Cases Commenced by Chapter of the Bankruptcy Code, During the 12-Month Period Ending December 31, 2019 and Business and Nonbusiness Bankruptcy, County Cases Commenced by Chapter of the Bankruptcy Code, During the 12-Month Period Ending December 31, 2020

Housing Vacancy Rates

Area	Gross Vacancy Rate[2] (%)			Year-Round Vacancy Rate[3] (%)			Rental Vacancy Rate[4] (%)			Homeowner Vacancy Rate[5] (%)		
	2018	2019	2020	2018	2019	2020	2018	2019	2020	2018	2019	2020
MSA[1]	n/a	n/a	n/a	n/a	n/a	n/a	n/a	n/a	n/a	n/a	n/a	n/a
U.S.	12.3	12.0	10.6	9.7	9.5	8.2	6.9	6.7	6.3	1.5	1.4	1.0

Note: (1) Figures cover the Green Bay, WI Metropolitan Statistical Area; (2) The percentage of the total housing inventory that is vacant; (3) The percentage of the housing inventory (excluding seasonal units) that is year-round vacant; (4) The percentage of rental inventory that is vacant for rent; (5) The percentage of homeowner inventory that is vacant for sale; n/a not available
Source: U.S. Census Bureau, Housing Vacancies and Homeownership Annual Statistics: 2018, 2019, 2020

INCOME

Income

Area	Per Capita ($)	Median Household ($)	Average Household ($)
City	26,618	49,251	64,595
MSA[1]	32,520	62,405	79,316
U.S.	34,103	62,843	88,607

Note: (1) Figures cover the Green Bay, WI Metropolitan Statistical Area
Source: U.S. Census Bureau, 2015-2019 American Community Survey 5-Year Estimates

Household Income Distribution

Area	Percent of Households Earning							
	Under $15,000	$15,000 -$24,999	$25,000 -$34,999	$35,000 -$49,999	$50,000 -$74,999	$75,000 -$99,999	$100,000 -$149,999	$150,000 and up
City	11.9	10.9	11.8	16.2	19.6	12.6	11.4	5.5
MSA[1]	8.2	8.5	9.5	13.5	19.2	14.6	16.4	10.0
U.S.	10.3	8.9	8.9	12.3	17.2	12.7	15.1	14.5

Note: (1) Figures cover the Green Bay, WI Metropolitan Statistical Area
Source: U.S. Census Bureau, 2015-2019 American Community Survey 5-Year Estimates

Poverty Rate

Area	All Ages	Under 18 Years Old	18 to 64 Years Old	65 Years and Over
City	14.9	19.7	13.9	9.7
MSA[1]	9.6	12.5	9.0	7.3
U.S.	13.4	18.5	12.6	9.3

Note: Figures are percentage of people whose income during the past 12 months was below the poverty level;
(1) Figures cover the Green Bay, WI Metropolitan Statistical Area
Source: U.S. Census Bureau, 2015-2019 American Community Survey 5-Year Estimates

CITY FINANCES

City Government Finances

Component	2017 ($000)	2017 ($ per capita)
Total Revenues	185,002	1,758
Total Expenditures	185,784	1,766
Debt Outstanding	262,542	2,495
Cash and Securities[1]	12,017	114

Note: (1) Cash and security holdings of a government at the close of its fiscal year,
including those of its dependent agencies, utilities, and liquor stores.
Source: U.S. Census Bureau, State & Local Government Finances 2017

City Government Revenue by Source

Source	2017 ($000)	2017 ($ per capita)	2017 (%)
General Revenue			
From Federal Government	3,493	33	1.9
From State Government	30,728	292	16.6
From Local Governments	7,983	76	4.3
Taxes			
Property	56,174	534	30.4
Sales and Gross Receipts	397	4	0.2
Personal Income	0	0	0.0
Corporate Income	0	0	0.0
Motor Vehicle License	0	0	0.0
Other Taxes	2,710	26	1.5
Current Charges	36,429	346	19.7
Liquor Store	0	0	0.0
Utility	37,336	355	20.2
Employee Retirement	0	0	0.0

Source: U.S. Census Bureau, State & Local Government Finances 2017

City Government Expenditures by Function

Function	2017 ($000)	2017 ($ per capita)	2017 (%)
General Direct Expenditures			
Air Transportation	0	0	0.0
Corrections	0	0	0.0
Education	0	0	0.0
Employment Security Administration	0	0	0.0
Financial Administration	1,841	17	1.0
Fire Protection	22,999	218	12.4
General Public Buildings	598	5	0.3
Governmental Administration, Other	3,786	36	2.0
Health	283	2	0.2
Highways	19,057	181	10.3
Hospitals	0	0	0.0
Housing and Community Development	863	8	0.5
Interest on General Debt	7,617	72	4.1
Judicial and Legal	1,083	10	0.6
Libraries	0	0	0.0
Parking	3,287	31	1.8
Parks and Recreation	11,664	110	6.3
Police Protection	26,764	254	14.4
Public Welfare	0	0	0.0
Sewerage	19,720	187	10.6
Solid Waste Management	8,131	77	4.4
Veterans' Services	0	0	0.0
Liquor Store	0	0	0.0
Utility	41,671	396	22.4
Employee Retirement	0	0	0.0

Source: U.S. Census Bureau, State & Local Government Finances 2017

Green Bay, Wisconsin 193

EMPLOYMENT

Labor Force and Employment

Area	Civilian Labor Force			Workers Employed		
	Dec. 2019	Dec. 2020	% Chg.	Dec. 2019	Dec. 2020	% Chg.
City	53,859	54,419	1.0	52,110	51,623	-0.9
MSA[1]	172,794	173,847	0.6	167,575	165,813	-1.1
U.S.	164,007,000	160,017,000	-2.4	158,504,000	149,613,000	-5.6

Note: Data is not seasonally adjusted and covers workers 16 years of age and older; (1) Figures cover the Green Bay, WI Metropolitan Statistical Area
Source: Bureau of Labor Statistics, Local Area Unemployment Statistics

Unemployment Rate

Area	2020											
	Jan.	Feb.	Mar.	Apr.	May	Jun.	Jul.	Aug.	Sep.	Oct.	Nov.	Dec.
City	4.2	3.8	3.2	14.6	14.4	10.2	8.1	7.0	5.1	5.7	4.9	5.1
MSA[1]	4.0	3.7	3.1	12.9	12.1	8.6	6.7	5.6	4.1	4.8	4.2	4.6
U.S.	4.0	3.8	4.5	14.4	13.0	11.2	10.5	8.5	7.7	6.6	6.4	6.5

Note: Data is not seasonally adjusted and covers workers 16 years of age and older; (1) Figures cover the Green Bay, WI Metropolitan Statistical Area
Source: Bureau of Labor Statistics, Local Area Unemployment Statistics

Average Wages

Occupation	$/Hr.	Occupation	$/Hr.
Accountants and Auditors	33.60	Maintenance and Repair Workers	22.70
Automotive Mechanics	20.10	Marketing Managers	60.60
Bookkeepers	20.70	Network and Computer Systems Admin.	33.40
Carpenters	26.00	Nurses, Licensed Practical	20.80
Cashiers	11.30	Nurses, Registered	33.10
Computer Programmers	37.60	Nursing Assistants	15.40
Computer Systems Analysts	39.10	Office Clerks, General	17.60
Computer User Support Specialists	26.00	Physical Therapists	43.40
Construction Laborers	20.80	Physicians	134.70
Cooks, Restaurant	13.60	Plumbers, Pipefitters and Steamfitters	32.90
Customer Service Representatives	18.80	Police and Sheriff's Patrol Officers	34.70
Dentists	105.00	Postal Service Mail Carriers	25.10
Electricians	27.60	Real Estate Sales Agents	27.20
Engineers, Electrical	40.40	Retail Salespersons	15.80
Fast Food and Counter Workers	10.40	Sales Representatives, Technical/Scientific	45.70
Financial Managers	60.20	Secretaries, Exc. Legal/Medical/Executive	18.20
First-Line Supervisors of Office Workers	30.00	Security Guards	14.00
General and Operations Managers	66.80	Surgeons	n/a
Hairdressers/Cosmetologists	14.50	Teacher Assistants, Exc. Postsecondary*	16.00
Home Health and Personal Care Aides	12.80	Teachers, Secondary School, Exc. Sp. Ed.*	28.90
Janitors and Cleaners	14.60	Telemarketers	n/a
Landscaping/Groundskeeping Workers	16.00	Truck Drivers, Heavy/Tractor-Trailer	22.80
Lawyers	51.60	Truck Drivers, Light/Delivery Services	19.80
Maids and Housekeeping Cleaners	12.10	Waiters and Waitresses	9.90

Note: Wage data covers the Green Bay, WI Metropolitan Statistical Area; (*) Hourly wages were calculated from annual wage data based on a 40 hour work week; n/a not available.
Source: Bureau of Labor Statistics, Metro Area Occupational Employment & Wage Estimates, May 2020

Employment by Industry

Sector	MSA[1]		U.S.
	Number of Employees	Percent of Total	Percent of Total
Construction, Mining, and Logging	8,300	4.8	5.5
Education and Health Services	26,700	15.5	16.3
Financial Activities	11,800	6.9	6.1
Government	19,100	11.1	15.2
Information	1,400	0.8	1.9
Leisure and Hospitality	13,000	7.6	9.0
Manufacturing	30,800	17.9	8.5
Other Services	8,100	4.7	3.8
Professional and Business Services	19,200	11.2	14.4
Retail Trade	16,600	9.6	10.9
Transportation, Warehousing, and Utilities	8,900	5.2	4.6
Wholesale Trade	8,200	4.8	3.9

Note: Figures are non-farm employment as of December 2020. Figures are not seasonally adjusted and include workers 16 years of age and older; (1) Figures cover the Green Bay, WI Metropolitan Statistical Area
Source: Bureau of Labor Statistics, Current Employment Statistics, Employment, Hours, and Earnings

Employment by Occupation

Occupation Classification	City (%)	MSA[1] (%)	U.S. (%)
Management, Business, Science, and Arts	28.1	34.4	38.5
Natural Resources, Construction, and Maintenance	7.9	9.4	8.9
Production, Transportation, and Material Moving	22.9	19.1	13.2
Sales and Office	22.0	21.6	21.6
Service	19.2	15.4	17.8

Note: Figures cover employed civilians 16 years of age and older; (1) Figures cover the Green Bay, WI Metropolitan Statistical Area
Source: U.S. Census Bureau, 2015-2019 American Community Survey 5-Year Estimates

Occupations with Greatest Projected Employment Growth: 2020 – 2022

Occupation[1]	2020 Employment	2022 Projected Employment	Numeric Employment Change	Percent Employment Change
Combined Food Preparation and Serving Workers, Including Fast Food	54,410	72,710	18,300	33.6
Waiters and Waitresses	29,420	41,470	12,050	41.0
Retail Salespersons	64,040	75,960	11,920	18.6
Bartenders	17,450	26,690	9,240	53.0
Cooks, Restaurant	16,530	24,010	7,480	45.3
Personal Care Aides	64,090	70,310	6,220	9.7
Cashiers	58,470	63,910	5,440	9.3
Hairdressers, Hairstylists, and Cosmetologists	9,870	15,130	5,260	53.3
First-Line Supervisors of Food Preparation and Serving Workers	12,710	17,300	4,590	36.1
Laborers and Freight, Stock, and Material Movers, Hand	51,400	55,990	4,590	8.9

Note: Projections cover Wisconsin; (1) Sorted by numeric employment change
Source: www.projectionscentral.com, State Occupational Projections, 2020–2022 Short-Term Projections

Fastest-Growing Occupations: 2020 – 2022

Occupation[1]	2020 Employment	2022 Projected Employment	Numeric Employment Change	Percent Employment Change
Film and Video Editors	70	140	70	100.0
Ushers, Lobby Attendants, and Ticket Takers	1,280	2,490	1,210	94.5
Athletes and Sports Competitors	110	190	80	72.7
Manicurists and Pedicurists	1,470	2,450	980	66.7
Hotel, Motel, and Resort Desk Clerks	2,700	4,430	1,730	64.1
Lodging Managers	250	400	150	60.0
Gaming Cage Workers	100	160	60	60.0
Amusement and Recreation Attendants	2,720	4,340	1,620	59.6
Baggage Porters and Bellhops	110	170	60	54.5
Cooks, Short Order	1,580	2,440	860	54.4

Note: Projections cover Wisconsin; (1) Sorted by percent employment change and excludes occupations with numeric employment change less than 50
Source: www.projectionscentral.com, State Occupational Projections, 2020–2022 Short-Term Projections

TAXES

State Corporate Income Tax Rates

State	Tax Rate (%)	Income Brackets ($)	Num. of Brackets	Financial Institution Tax Rate (%)[a]	Federal Income Tax Ded.
Wisconsin	7.9	Flat rate	1	7.9	No

Note: Tax rates as of January 1, 2021; (a) Rates listed are the corporate income tax rate applied to financial institutions or excise taxes based on income. Some states have other taxes based upon the value of deposits or shares.
Source: Federation of Tax Administrators, State Corporate Income Tax Rates, January 1, 2021

State Individual Income Tax Rates

State	Tax Rate (%)	Income Brackets ($)	Personal Exemptions ($)			Standard Ded. ($)	
			Single	Married	Depend.	Single	Married
Wisconsin (a)	3.54 - 7.65	12,120 - 266,930 (w)	700	1,400	700	11,200	20,730 (y)

Note: Tax rates as of January 1, 2021; Local- and county-level taxes are not included; Federal income tax is not deductible on state income tax returns; (a) 19 states have statutory provision for automatically adjusting to the rate of inflation the dollar values of the income tax brackets, standard deductions, and/or personal exemptions. Michigan indexes the personal exemption only. Oregon does not index the income brackets for $125,000 and over; (w) The Wisconsin income brackets reported are for single individuals. For married taxpayers filing jointly, the same tax rates apply income brackets ranging from $16,160, to $355,910; (y) Alabama standard deduction is phased out for incomes over $23,000. Rhode Island exemptions & standard deductions phased out for incomes over $207,700; Wisconsin standard deduciton phases out for income over $16,149.
Source: Federation of Tax Administrators, State Individual Income Tax Rates, January 1, 2021

Various State Sales and Excise Tax Rates

State	State Sales Tax (%)	Gasoline[1] (¢/gal.)	Cigarette[2] ($/pack)	Spirits[3] ($/gal.)	Wine[4] ($/gal.)	Beer[5] ($/gal.)	Recreational Marijuana (%)
Wisconsin	5	32.9	2.52	3.25	0.25	0.06	Not legal

Note: All tax rates as of January 1, 2021; (1) The American Petroleum Institute has developed a methodology for determining the average tax rate on a gallon of fuel. Rates may include any of the following: excise taxes, environmental fees, storage tank fees, other fees or taxes, general sales tax, and local taxes; (2) The federal excise tax of $1.0066 per pack and local taxes are not included; (3) Rates are those applicable to off-premise sales of 40% alcohol by volume (a.b.v.) distilled spirits in 750ml containers. Local excise taxes are excluded; (4) Rates are those applicable to off-premise sales of 11% a.b.v. non-carbonated wine in 750ml containers; (5) Rates are those applicable to off-premise sales of 4.7% a.b.v. beer in 12 ounce containers.
Source: Tax Foundation, 2021 Facts & Figures: How Does Your State Compare?

State Business Tax Climate Index Rankings

State	Overall Rank	Corporate Tax Rank	Individual Income Tax Rank	Sales Tax Rank	Property Tax Rank	Unemployment Insurance Tax Rank
Wisconsin	25	30	37	7	17	35

Note: The index is a measure of how each state's tax laws affect economic performance. The lower the rank, the more favorable a state's tax system is for business. States without a given tax are given a ranking of 1. The scores/rankings for the District of Columbia do not affect other states. The 2021 index represents the tax climate as of July 1, 2020.
Source: Tax Foundation, State Business Tax Climate Index 2021

TRANSPORTATION

Means of Transportation to Work

Area	Car/Truck/Van		Public Transportation			Bicycle	Walked	Other Means	Worked at Home
	Drove Alone	Car-pooled	Bus	Subway	Railroad				
City	79.7	10.2	1.4	0.0	0.0	0.5	2.3	1.9	3.9
MSA[1]	83.8	7.9	0.7	0.0	0.0	0.2	1.8	0.9	4.7
U.S.	76.3	9.0	2.4	1.9	0.6	0.5	2.7	1.4	5.2

Note: Figures are percentages and cover workers 16 years of age and older; (1) Figures cover the Green Bay, WI Metropolitan Statistical Area
Source: U.S. Census Bureau, 2015-2019 American Community Survey 5-Year Estimates

Travel Time to Work

Area	Less Than 10 Minutes	10 to 19 Minutes	20 to 29 Minutes	30 to 44 Minutes	45 to 59 Minutes	60 to 89 Minutes	90 Minutes or More
City	18.1	48.8	19.4	7.7	3.1	1.8	1.1
MSA[1]	18.1	40.0	21.7	12.9	3.8	2.0	1.5
U.S.	12.2	28.4	20.8	20.8	8.3	6.4	2.9

Note: Note: Figures are percentages and include workers 16 years old and over; (1) Figures cover the Green Bay, WI Metropolitan Statistical Area
Source: U.S. Census Bureau, 2015-2019 American Community Survey 5-Year Estimates

Key Congestion Measures

Measure	1982	1992	2002	2012	2017
Annual Hours of Delay, Total (000)	n/a	n/a	n/a	n/a	3,421
Annual Hours of Delay, Per Auto Commuter	n/a	n/a	n/a	n/a	15
Annual Congestion Cost, Total (million $)	n/a	n/a	n/a	n/a	72
Annual Congestion Cost, Per Auto Commuter ($)	n/a	n/a	n/a	n/a	316

Note: n/a not available
Source: Texas A&M Transportation Institute, 2019 Urban Mobility Report

196 Green Bay, Wisconsin

Freeway Travel Time Index

Measure	1982	1987	1992	1997	2002	2007	2012	2017
Urban Area Index[1]	n/a	n/a	n/a	n/a	n/a	n/a	n/a	1.05
Urban Area Rank[1,2]	n/a	n/a	n/a	n/a	n/a	n/a	n/a	n/a

Note: Freeway Travel Time Index—the ratio of travel time in the peak period to the travel time at free-flow conditions. For example, a value of 1.30 indicates a 20-minute free-flow trip takes 26 minutes in the peak (20 minutes x 1.30 = 26 minutes); (1) Covers the Green Bay WI urban area; (2) Rank is based on 101 larger urban areas (#1 = highest travel time index); n/a not available
Source: Texas A&M Transportation Institute, 2019 Urban Mobility Report

Public Transportation

Agency Name / Mode of Transportation	Vehicles Operated in Maximum Service[1]	Annual Unlinked Passenger Trips[2] (in thous.)	Annual Passenger Miles[3] (in thous.)
Green Bay Metro			
Bus (directly operated)	22	1,292.7	3,820.9
Demand Response (purchased transportation)	10	31.9	246.2

Note: (1) Number of revenue vehicles operated by the given mode and type of service to meet the annual maximum service requirement. This is the revenue vehicle count during the peak season of the year; on the week and day that maximum service is provided. Vehicles operated in maximum service (VOMS) exclude atypical days and one-time special events; (2) Number of passengers who boarded public transportation vehicles. Passengers are counted each time they board a vehicle no matter how many vehicles they use to travel from their origin to their destination. (3) Sum of the distances ridden by all passengers during the entire fiscal year.
Source: Federal Transit Administration, National Transit Database, 2019

Air Transportation

Airport Name and Code / Type of Service	Passenger Airlines[1]	Passenger Enplanements	Freight Carriers[2]	Freight (lbs)
Austin-Bergstrom International (GRB)				
Domestic service (U.S. carriers - 2020)	18	141,463	6	125,692
International service (U.S. carriers - 2019)	1	173	0	0

Note: (1) Includes all U.S.-based major, minor and commuter airlines that carried at least one passenger during the year; (2) Includes all U.S.-based airlines and freight carriers that transported at least one pound of freight during the year.
Source: Bureau of Transportation Statistics, The Intermodal Transportation Database, Air Carriers: T-100 Domestic Market (U.S. Carriers), 2020; Bureau of Transportation Statistics, The Intermodal Transportation Database, Air Carriers: T-100 International Market (U.S. Carriers), 2019

BUSINESSES

Major Business Headquarters

Company Name	Industry	Rankings	
		Fortune[1]	Forbes[2]
Schreiber Foods	Food, Drink & Tobacco	-	86

Note: (1) Companies that produce a 10-K are ranked 1 to 500 based on 2019 revenue; (2) All private companies with at least $2 billion in annual revenue through the end of their most current fiscal year are ranked 1 to 219; companies listed are headquartered in the city; dashes indicate no ranking
Source: Fortune, "Fortune 500," June/July 2020; Forbes, "America's Largest Private Companies," 2020

Fastest-Growing Businesses

According to *Fortune*, Green Bay is home to one of the 100 fastest-growing companies in the world: **Nicolet Bankshares** (#95). Companies were ranked by their revenue growth rate; their EPS growth rate; and their three-year annualized total return to investors for the period ending June 30, 2020. Criteria for inclusion: a company, foreign or domestic, must trade on a major U.S. stock exchange; must file quarterly reports with the SEC; must have a minimum market capitalization of $250 million; must have a stock price of at least $5 on June 30, 2020; must have been trading continuously since June 30, 2017; must have revenue and net income for the four quarters ended on or before April 30, 2020, of at least $50 million and $10 million, respectively; and must have posted a compound annual growth in revenue and earnings per share of at least 15% annually over the three years ending on or before April 30, 2020. Real estate investment trusts, limited-liability companies, limited parterships, business development companies, closed-end investment firms, companies about to be acquired, and companies that lost money in the quarter ending April 30, 2020 were excluded. *Fortune, "100 Fastest-Growing Companies," 2020*

According to *Initiative for a Competitive Inner City (ICIC)*, Green Bay is home to one of America's 100 fastest-growing "inner city" companies: **American Tent** (#21). Criteria for inclusion: company must be headquartered in or have 51 percent or more of its physical operations in an economically distressed urban area; must be an independent, for-profit corporation, partnership or proprietorship; must have 10 or more employees and have a five-year sales history that includes sales of at least $200,000 in the base year and at least $1 million in the current year with no decrease in sales over the two most recent years. Companies were ranked overall by revenue growth over the five-year period between 2015 and 2019. *Initiative for a Competitive Inner City (ICIC), "Inner City 100 Companies," 2020*

198   Green Bay, Wisconsin

Living Environment

COST OF LIVING

Cost of Living Index

Composite Index	Groceries	Housing	Utilities	Transportation	Health Care	Misc. Goods/ Services
88.8	93.1	78.3	96.8	88.3	101.0	91.8

Note: The Cost of Living Index measures regional differences in the cost of consumer goods and services, excluding taxes and non-consumer expenditures, for professional and managerial households in the top income quintile. It is based on more than 50,000 prices covering almost 60 different items for which prices are collected three times a year by chambers of commerce, economic development organizations or university applied economic centers in each participating urban area. The numbers shown should be read as a percentage above or below the national average of 100. For example, a value of 115.4 in the groceries column indicates that grocery prices are 15.4% higher than the national average. Small differences in the index numbers should not be interpreted as significant; Figures cover the Green Bay WI urban area.
Source: The Council for Community and Economic Research, Cost of Living Index, 2020

Grocery Prices

Area[1]	T-Bone Steak ($/pound)	Frying Chicken ($/pound)	Whole Milk ($/half gal.)	Eggs ($/dozen)	Orange Juice ($/64 oz.)	Coffee ($/11.5 oz.)
City[2]	11.37	1.10	1.93	1.51	3.64	4.47
Avg.	11.78	1.39	2.05	1.47	3.57	4.34
Min.	8.03	0.94	1.03	0.74	2.94	3.02
Max.	15.86	2.65	4.31	3.77	5.44	8.69

Note: (1) Values for the local area are compared with the average, minimum and maximum values for all 284 areas in the Cost of Living Index; (2) Figures cover the Green Bay WI urban area; **T-Bone Steak** (price per pound); **Frying Chicken** (price per pound, whole fryer); **Whole Milk** (half gallon carton); **Eggs** (price per dozen, Grade A, large); **Orange Juice** (64 oz. Tropicana or Florida Natural); **Coffee** (11.5 oz. can, vacuum-packed, Maxwell House, Hills Bros, or Folgers).
Source: The Council for Community and Economic Research, Cost of Living Index, 2020

Housing and Utility Costs

Area[1]	New Home Price ($)	Apartment Rent ($/month)	All Electric ($/month)	Part Electric ($/month)	Other Energy ($/month)	Telephone ($/month)
City[2]	304,129	813	-	82.41	78.05	179.40
Avg.	368,594	1,168	170.86	100.47	65.28	184.30
Min.	190,567	502	91.58	31.42	26.08	169.60
Max.	2,227,806	4,738	470.38	280.31	280.06	206.50

Note: (1) Values for the local area are compared with the average, minimum and maximum values for all 284 areas in the Cost of Living Index; (2) Figures cover the Green Bay WI urban area; **New Home Price** (2,400 sf living area, 8,000 sf lot, in urban area with full utilities); **Apartment Rent** (950 sf 2 bedroom/1.5 or 2 bath, unfurnished, excluding all utilities except water); **All Electric** (average monthly cost for an all-electric home); **Part Electric** (average monthly cost for a part-electric home); **Other Energy** (average monthly cost for natural gas, fuel oil, coal, wood, and any other forms of energy except electricity); **Telephone** (price includes the base monthly rate plus taxes and fees for three lines of mobile phone service).
Source: The Council for Community and Economic Research, Cost of Living Index, 2020

Health Care, Transportation, and Other Costs

Area[1]	Doctor ($/visit)	Dentist ($/visit)	Optometrist ($/visit)	Gasoline ($/gallon)	Beauty Salon ($/visit)	Men's Shirt ($)
City[2]	176.50	81.33	74.00	1.71	22.70	30.51
Avg.	115.44	99.32	108.10	2.21	39.27	31.37
Min.	36.68	59.00	51.36	1.71	19.00	11.00
Max.	219.00	153.10	250.97	3.46	82.05	58.33

Note: (1) Values for the local area are compared with the average, minimum and maximum values for all 284 areas in the Cost of Living Index; (2) Figures cover the Green Bay WI urban area; **Doctor** (general practitioners routine exam of an established patient); **Dentist** (adult teeth cleaning and periodic oral examination); **Optometrist** (full vision eye exam for established adult patient); **Gasoline** (one gallon regular unleaded, national brand, including all taxes, cash price at self-service pump if available); **Beauty Salon** (woman's shampoo, trim, and blow-dry); **Men's Shirt** (cotton/polyester dress shirt, pinpoint weave, long sleeves).
Source: The Council for Community and Economic Research, Cost of Living Index, 2020

HOUSING

Homeownership Rate

Area	2012 (%)	2013 (%)	2014 (%)	2015 (%)	2016 (%)	2017 (%)	2018 (%)	2019 (%)	2020 (%)
MSA[1]	n/a	n/a	n/a	n/a	n/a	n/a	n/a	n/a	n/a
U.S.	65.4	65.1	64.5	63.7	63.4	63.9	64.4	64.6	66.6

Note: (1) Figures cover the Green Bay, WI Metropolitan Statistical Area; n/a not available
Source: U.S. Census Bureau, Housing Vacancies and Homeownership Annual Statistics: 2012-2020

House Price Index (HPI)

Area	National Ranking[2]	Quarterly Change (%)	One-Year Change (%)	Five-Year Change (%)	Since 1991Q1 (%)
MSA[1]	169	2.46	5.48	28.92	157.42
U.S.[3]	–	3.81	10.77	38.99	205.12

Note: The HPI is a weighted repeat sales index. It measures average price changes in repeat sales or refinancings on the same properties. This information is obtained by reviewing repeat mortgage transactions on single-family properties whose mortgages have been purchased or securitized by Fannie Mae or Freddie Mac since January 1975; (1) Figures cover the Green Bay, WI Metropolitan Statistical Area; (2) Rankings are based on annual percentage change for all metro areas containing at least 15,000 transactions over the last 10 years and ranges from 1 to 253; (3) figures based on a weighted average of Census Division estimates using a seasonally adjusted, purchase-only index; all figures are for the period ending December 31, 2020
Source: Federal Housing Finance Agency, Change in Metropolitan Area House Price Indexes, April 7, 2021

Median Single-Family Home Prices

Area	2018	2019	2020p	Percent Change 2019 to 2020
MSA[1]	177.3	189.4	204.2	7.8
U.S. Average	261.6	274.6	299.9	9.2

Note: Figures are median sales prices of existing single-family homes in thousands of dollars; (p) preliminary; (1) Figures cover the Green Bay, WI Metropolitan Statistical Area
Source: National Association of Realtors, Median Sales Price of Existing Single-Family Homes for Metropolitan Areas, 4th Quarter 2020

Qualifying Income Based on Median Sales Price of Existing Single-Family Homes

Area	With 5% Down ($)	With 10% Down ($)	With 20% Down ($)
MSA[1]	39,266	37,199	33,066
U.S. Average	59,266	56,147	49,908

Note: Figures are preliminary; Qualifying income is based on a mortgage rate of 2.81%. Monthly principal and interest payment is limited to 25% of income; (1) Figures cover the Green Bay, WI Metropolitan Statistical Area
Source: National Association of Realtors, Qualifying Income Based on Median Sales Price of Existing Single-Family Homes for Metropolitan Areas, 4th Quarter 2020

Home Value Distribution

Area	Under $50,000	$50,000 -$99,999	$100,000 -$149,999	$150,000 -$199,999	$200,000 -$299,999	$300,000 -$499,999	$500,000 -$999,999	$1,000,000 or more
City	3.3	20.8	35.3	20.4	12.8	5.7	1.5	0.3
MSA[1]	4.0	11.9	22.8	22.2	24.5	11.3	2.6	0.6
U.S.	6.9	12.0	13.3	14.0	19.6	19.3	11.4	3.4

Note: Figures are percentages and cover owner-occupied housing units; (1) Figures cover the Green Bay, WI Metropolitan Statistical Area
Source: U.S. Census Bureau, 2015-2019 American Community Survey 5-Year Estimates

Year Housing Structure Built

Area	2010 or Later	2000 -2009	1990 -1999	1980 -1989	1970 -1979	1960 -1969	1950 -1959	1940 -1949	Before 1940	Median Year
City	1.6	7.6	10.3	12.9	17.8	13.1	15.0	5.7	16.0	1970
MSA[1]	5.2	15.0	16.4	12.4	15.4	9.6	9.3	4.2	12.4	1979
U.S.	5.2	14.0	13.9	13.4	15.2	10.6	10.3	4.9	12.6	1978

Note: Figures are percentages except for Median Year; Note: (1) Figures cover the Green Bay, WI Metropolitan Statistical Area
Source: U.S. Census Bureau, 2015-2019 American Community Survey 5-Year Estimates

Gross Monthly Rent

Area	Under $500	$500 -$999	$1,000 -$1,499	$1,500 -$1,999	$2,000 -$2,499	$2,500 -$2,999	$3,000 and up	Median ($)
City	12.0	71.3	15.4	1.0	0.1	0.1	0.2	730
MSA[1]	9.9	69.3	18.6	1.4	0.3	0.2	0.3	784
U.S.	9.4	36.2	30.0	14.0	5.6	2.4	2.4	1,062

Note: Figures are percentages except for Median; Gross rent is the contract rent plus the estimated average monthly cost of utilities (electricity, gas, and water and sewer) and fuels (oil, coal, kerosene, wood, etc.) if these are paid by the renter (or paid for the renter by someone else); (1) Figures cover the Green Bay, WI Metropolitan Statistical Area
Source: U.S. Census Bureau, 2015-2019 American Community Survey 5-Year Estimates

HEALTH

Health Risk Factors

Category	MSA[1] (%)	U.S. (%)
Adults aged 18–64 who have any kind of health care coverage	n/a	87.3
Adults who reported being in good or better health	n/a	82.4
Adults who have been told they have high blood cholesterol	n/a	33.0
Adults who have been told they have high blood pressure	n/a	32.3
Adults who are current smokers	n/a	17.1
Adults who currently use E-cigarettes	n/a	4.6
Adults who currently use chewing tobacco, snuff, or snus	n/a	4.0
Adults who are heavy drinkers[2]	n/a	6.3
Adults who are binge drinkers[3]	n/a	17.4
Adults who are overweight (BMI 25.0 - 29.9)	n/a	35.3
Adults who are obese (BMI 30.0 - 99.8)	n/a	31.3
Adults who participated in any physical activities in the past month	n/a	74.4
Adults who always or nearly always wears a seat belt	n/a	94.3

Note: n/a not available; (1) Figures cover the Green Bay, WI Metropolitan Statistical Area; (2) Heavy drinkers are classified as adult men having more than 14 drinks per week and adult women having more than 7 drinks per week; (3) Binge drinkers are classified as males having five or more drinks on one occasion or females having four or more drinks on one occasion
Source: Centers for Disease Control and Prevention, Behaviorial Risk Factor Surveillance System, SMART: Selected Metropolitan Area Risk Trends, 2017

Acute and Chronic Health Conditions

Category	MSA[1] (%)	U.S. (%)
Adults who have ever been told they had a heart attack	n/a	4.2
Adults who have ever been told they have angina or coronary heart disease	n/a	3.9
Adults who have ever been told they had a stroke	n/a	3.0
Adults who have ever been told they have asthma	n/a	14.2
Adults who have ever been told they have arthritis	n/a	24.9
Adults who have ever been told they have diabetes[2]	n/a	10.5
Adults who have ever been told they had skin cancer	n/a	6.2
Adults who have ever been told they had any other types of cancer	n/a	7.1
Adults who have ever been told they have COPD	n/a	6.5
Adults who have ever been told they have kidney disease	n/a	3.0
Adults who have ever been told they have a form of depression	n/a	20.5

Note: n/a not available; (1) Figures cover the Green Bay, WI Metropolitan Statistical Area; (2) Figures do not include pregnancy-related, borderline, or pre-diabetes
Source: Centers for Disease Control and Prevention, Behaviorial Risk Factor Surveillance System, SMART: Selected Metropolitan Area Risk Trends, 2017

Health Screening and Vaccination Rates

Category	MSA[1] (%)	U.S. (%)
Adults aged 65+ who have had flu shot within the past year	n/a	60.7
Adults aged 65+ who have ever had a pneumonia vaccination	n/a	75.4
Adults who have ever been tested for HIV	n/a	36.1
Adults who have ever had the shingles or zoster vaccine?	n/a	28.9
Adults who have had their blood cholesterol checked within the last five years	n/a	85.9

Note: n/a not available; (1) Figures cover the Green Bay, WI Metropolitan Statistical Area.
Source: Centers for Disease Control and Prevention, Behaviorial Risk Factor Surveillance System, SMART: Selected Metropolitan Area Risk Trends, 2017

Disability Status

Category	MSA[1] (%)	U.S. (%)
Adults who reported being deaf	n/a	6.7
Are you blind or have serious difficulty seeing, even when wearing glasses?	n/a	4.5
Are you limited in any way in any of your usual activities due of arthritis?	n/a	12.9
Do you have difficulty doing errands alone?	n/a	6.8
Do you have difficulty dressing or bathing?	n/a	3.6
Do you have serious difficulty concentrating/remembering/making decisions?	n/a	10.7
Do you have serious difficulty walking or climbing stairs?	n/a	13.6

Note: n/a not available; (1) Figures cover the Green Bay, WI Metropolitan Statistical Area.
Source: Centers for Disease Control and Prevention, Behaviorial Risk Factor Surveillance System, SMART: Selected Metropolitan Area Risk Trends, 2017

Mortality Rates for the Top 10 Causes of Death in the U.S.

ICD-10[a] Sub-Chapter	ICD-10[a] Code	Age-Adjusted Mortality Rate[1] per 100,000 population	
		County[2]	U.S.
Malignant neoplasms	C00-C97	141.7	149.2
Ischaemic heart diseases	I20-I25	111.3	90.5
Other forms of heart disease	I30-I51	45.4	52.2
Chronic lower respiratory diseases	J40-J47	32.2	39.6
Other degenerative diseases of the nervous system	G30-G31	37.7	37.6
Cerebrovascular diseases	I60-I69	28.8	37.2
Other external causes of accidental injury	W00-X59	44.2	36.1
Organic, including symptomatic, mental disorders	F01-F09	50.2	29.4
Hypertensive diseases	I10-I15	16.6	24.1
Diabetes mellitus	E10-E14	16.9	21.5

Note: (a) ICD-10 = International Classification of Diseases 10th Revision; (1) Mortality rates are a three-year average covering 2017-2019; (2) Figures cover Brown County.
Source: Centers for Disease Control and Prevention, National Center for Health Statistics. Underlying Cause of Death 1999-2019 on CDC WONDER Online Database

Mortality Rates for Selected Causes of Death

ICD-10[a] Sub-Chapter	ICD-10[a] Code	Age-Adjusted Mortality Rate[1] per 100,000 population	
		County[2]	U.S.
Assault	X85-Y09	Unreliable	6.0
Diseases of the liver	K70-K76	12.1	14.4
Human immunodeficiency virus (HIV) disease	B20-B24	Suppressed	1.5
Influenza and pneumonia	J09-J18	11.7	13.8
Intentional self-harm	X60-X84	13.9	14.1
Malnutrition	E40-E46	Unreliable	2.3
Obesity and other hyperalimentation	E65-E68	Unreliable	2.1
Renal failure	N17-N19	10.8	12.6
Transport accidents	V01-V99	7.6	12.3
Viral hepatitis	B15-B19	Suppressed	1.2

Note: (a) ICD-10 = International Classification of Diseases 10th Revision; (1) Mortality rates are a three-year average covering 2017-2019; (2) Figures cover Brown County; Data are suppressed when the data meet the criteria for confidentiality constraints; Mortality rates are flagged as unreliable when the rate would be calculated with a numerator of 20 or less.
Source: Centers for Disease Control and Prevention, National Center for Health Statistics. Underlying Cause of Death 1999-2019 on CDC WONDER Online Database

Health Insurance Coverage

Area	With Health Insurance	With Private Health Insurance	With Public Health Insurance	Without Health Insurance	Population Under Age 19 Without Health Insurance
City	92.1	66.1	35.9	7.9	3.7
MSA[1]	94.8	75.7	30.4	5.2	3.6
U.S.	91.2	67.9	35.1	8.8	5.1

Note: Figures are percentages that cover the civilian noninstitutionalized population; (1) Figures cover the Green Bay, WI Metropolitan Statistical Area
Source: U.S. Census Bureau, 2015-2019 American Community Survey 5-Year Estimates

Number of Medical Professionals

Area	MDs[3]	DOs[3,4]	Dentists	Podiatrists	Chiropractors	Optometrists
County[1] (number)	644	64	213	9	124	48
County[1] (rate[2])	244.7	24.3	80.5	3.4	46.9	18.1
U.S. (rate[2])	282.9	22.7	71.2	6.2	28.1	16.9

55009
Note: Data as of 2019 unless noted; (1) Data covers Brown County; (2) Rate per 100,000 population; (3) Data as of 2018 and includes all active, non-federal physicians; (4) Doctor of Osteopathic Medicine
Source: U.S. Department of Health and Human Services, Health Resources and Services Administration, Bureau of Health Professions, Area Resource File (ARF) 2019-2020

EDUCATION

Public School District Statistics

District Name	Schls	Pupils	Pupil/ Teacher Ratio	Minority Pupils[1] (%)	Free Lunch Eligible[2] (%)	IEP[3] (%)
Ashwaubenon School District	5	3,313	15.4	23.6	26.9	12.3
Green Bay Area PSD	42	20,391	13.6	55.5	54.9	14.7
Howard-Suamico School District	9	6,103	15.7	11.3	15.8	11.8

Note: Table includes school districts with 2,000 or more students; (1) Percentage of students that are not non-Hispanic white; (2) Percentage of students that are eligible for the free lunch program; (3) Percentage of students that have an Individualized Education Program.
Source: U.S. Department of Education, National Center for Education Statistics, Common Core of Data, Local Education Agency (School District) Universe Survey: School Year 2018-2019; U.S. Department of Education, National Center for Education Statistics, Common Core of Data, Public Elementary/Secondary School Universe Survey: School Year 2018-2019

Highest Level of Education

Area	Less than H.S.	H.S. Diploma	Some College, No Deg.	Associate Degree	Bachelor's Degree	Master's Degree	Prof. School Degree	Doctorate Degree
City	12.5	31.4	20.1	11.2	17.9	5.1	1.1	0.7
MSA[1]	8.0	32.1	19.7	12.4	19.6	6.0	1.5	0.7
U.S.	12.0	27.0	20.4	8.5	19.8	8.8	2.1	1.4

Note: Figures cover persons age 25 and over; (1) Figures cover the Green Bay, WI Metropolitan Statistical Area
Source: U.S. Census Bureau, 2015-2019 American Community Survey 5-Year Estimates

Educational Attainment by Race

Area	High School Graduate or Higher (%)					Bachelor's Degree or Higher (%)				
	Total	White	Black	Asian	Hisp.[2]	Total	White	Black	Asian	Hisp.[2]
City	87.5	90.4	83.1	74.3	53.5	24.8	27.0	15.3	20.0	6.5
MSA[1]	92.0	93.5	83.2	83.1	57.0	27.8	28.5	17.3	44.2	9.2
U.S.	88.0	89.9	86.0	87.1	68.7	32.1	33.5	21.6	54.3	16.4

Note: Figures shown cover persons 25 years old and over; (1) Figures cover the Green Bay, WI Metropolitan Statistical Area; (2) People of Hispanic origin can be of any race
Source: U.S. Census Bureau, 2015-2019 American Community Survey 5-Year Estimates

School Enrollment by Grade and Control

Area	Preschool (%)		Kindergarten (%)		Grades 1 - 4 (%)		Grades 5 - 8 (%)		Grades 9 - 12 (%)	
	Public	Private	Public	Private	Public	Private	Public	Private	Public	Private
City	71.8	28.2	85.7	14.3	90.6	9.4	84.6	15.4	91.1	8.9
MSA[1]	69.2	30.8	85.4	14.6	88.9	11.1	88.4	11.6	93.2	6.8
U.S.	59.1	40.9	87.6	12.4	89.5	10.5	89.4	10.6	90.1	9.9

Note: Figures shown cover persons 3 years old and over; (1) Figures cover the Green Bay, WI Metropolitan Statistical Area
Source: U.S. Census Bureau, 2015-2019 American Community Survey 5-Year Estimates

Higher Education

Four-Year Colleges			Two-Year Colleges			Medical Schools[1]	Law Schools[2]	Voc/ Tech[3]
Public	Private Non-profit	Private For-profit	Public	Private Non-profit	Private For-profit			
1	1	1	1	0	0	0	0	1

Note: Figures cover institutions located within the city limits and include main campuses only; (1) includes schools accredited by the Liaison Committee on Medical Education and the American Osteopathic Association's Commission on Osteopathic College Accreditation; (2) includes ABA-accredited schools, schools with provisional ABA accreditation, and state accredited schools; (3) includes all schools with programs that are less than 2 years.
Source: National Center for Education Statistics, Integrated Postsecondary Education System (IPEDS), 2019-20; Wikipedia, List of Medical Schools in the United States, accessed April 2, 2021; Wikipedia, List of Law Schools in the United States, accessed April 2, 2021

Green Bay, Wisconsin   203

EMPLOYERS

Major Employers

Company Name	Industry
American Foods Group	Food manufacturing
APAC Customer Services	Business management
Associated Bank	Financial services
Aurora Health Care	Healthcare
Bellin Health	Healthcare
Georgia-Pacific	Paper manufacturing
Green Bay Packaging	Paper manufacturing
Green Bay Packers	NFL franchise
H.J. Martin and Son	Interior design
JBS	Food manufacturing
Nicolet National Bank	Financial services
Procter & Gamble Paper Products	Paper manufacturing
Schreiber Foods	Food manufacturing
Schwabe North America	Health products
St. Mary's Hospital Medical Center	Healthcare
St. Vincent Hospital	Healthcare
Wal-Mart Stores	Retail
Wisconsin Public Service	Utilities

Note: Companies shown are located within the Green Bay, WI Metropolitan Statistical Area.
Source: Hoovers.com; Wikipedia

PUBLIC SAFETY

Crime Rate

Area	All Crimes	Violent Crimes				Property Crimes		
		Murder	Rape[3]	Robbery	Aggrav. Assault	Burglary	Larceny -Theft	Motor Vehicle Theft
City	2,145.9	2.9	74.3	46.7	380.0	233.4	1,290.6	118.1
Suburbs[1]	928.9	0.9	26.1	3.2	61.9	81.6	725.8	29.3
Metro[2]	1,324.3	1.5	41.8	17.3	165.3	130.9	909.3	58.2
U.S.	2,489.3	5.0	42.6	81.6	250.2	340.5	1,549.5	219.9

Note: Figures are crimes per 100,000 population; (1) All areas within the metro area that are located outside the city limits; (2) Figures cover the Green Bay, WI Metropolitan Statistical Area; (3) All figures shown were reported using the revised Uniform Crime Reporting (UCR) definition of rape.
Source: FBI Uniform Crime Reports, 2019

Hate Crimes

Area	Number of Quarters Reported	Number of Incidents per Bias Motivation					
		Race/Ethnicity/ Ancestry	Religion	Sexual Orientation	Disability	Gender	Gender Identity
City	4	1	1	0	0	0	0
U.S.	4	3,963	1,521	1,195	157	69	198

Source: Federal Bureau of Investigation, Hate Crime Statistics 2019

Identity Theft Consumer Reports

Area	Reports	Reports per 100,000 Population	Rank[2]
MSA[1]	352	109	353
U.S.	1,387,615	423	-

Note: (1) Figures cover the Green Bay, WI Metropolitan Statistical Area; (2) Rank ranges from 1 to 391 where 1 indicates greatest number of identity theft reports per 100,000 population
Source: Federal Trade Commission, Consumer Sentinel Network Data Book 2020

Fraud and Other Consumer Reports

Area	Reports	Reports per 100,000 Population	Rank[2]
MSA[1]	1,882	583	305
U.S.	3,385,133	1,031	-

Note: (1) Figures cover the Green Bay, WI Metropolitan Statistical Area; (2) Rank ranges from 1 to 391 where 1 indicates greatest number of fraud and other consumer reports per 100,000 population
Source: Federal Trade Commission, Consumer Sentinel Network Data Book 2020

POLITICS

2020 Presidential Election Results

Area	Biden	Trump	Jorgensen	Hawkins	Other
Brown County	45.5	52.7	1.3	0.0	0.5
U.S.	51.3	46.8	1.2	0.3	0.5

Note: Results are percentages and may not add to 100% due to rounding
Source: Dave Leip's Atlas of U.S. Presidential Elections

204 Green Bay, Wisconsin

SPORTS

Professional Sports Teams

Team Name	League	Year Established
Green Bay Packers	National Football League (NFL)	1921

Note: Includes teams located in the Green Bay, WI Metropolitan Statistical Area.
Source: Wikipedia, Major Professional Sports Teams of the United States and Canada, April 6, 2021

CLIMATE

Average and Extreme Temperatures

Temperature	Jan	Feb	Mar	Apr	May	Jun	Jul	Aug	Sep	Oct	Nov	Dec	Yr.
Extreme High (°F)	50	55	77	89	91	98	99	99	95	88	72	62	99
Average High (°F)	23	27	38	54	67	76	81	78	70	58	42	28	54
Average Temp. (°F)	15	19	29	44	55	65	70	68	59	48	34	21	44
Average Low (°F)	6	10	21	34	44	53	58	56	48	38	26	13	34
Extreme Low (°F)	-31	-26	-29	7	21	32	40	38	24	15	-9	-27	-31

Note: Figures cover the years 1949-1990
Source: National Climatic Data Center, International Station Meteorological Climate Summary, 9/96

Average Precipitation/Snowfall/Humidity

Precip./Humidity	Jan	Feb	Mar	Apr	May	Jun	Jul	Aug	Sep	Oct	Nov	Dec	Yr.
Avg. Precip. (in.)	1.1	1.1	1.9	2.6	2.9	3.2	3.3	3.3	3.2	2.2	2.0	1.4	28.3
Avg. Snowfall (in.)	11	8	9	2	Tr	0	0	0	Tr	Tr	5	11	46
Avg. Rel. Hum. 6am (%)	77	79	81	79	79	82	86	90	89	85	82	80	83
Avg. Rel. Hum. 3pm (%)	68	65	63	54	52	55	55	58	59	59	67	71	60

Note: Figures cover the years 1949-1990; Tr = Trace amounts (<0.05 in. of rain; <0.5 in. of snow)
Source: National Climatic Data Center, International Station Meteorological Climate Summary, 9/96

Weather Conditions

Temperature			Daytime Sky			Precipitation		
5°F & below	32°F & below	90°F & above	Clear	Partly cloudy	Cloudy	0.01 inch or more precip.	0.1 inch or more snow/ice	Thunder-storms
39	163	7	86	125	154	120	40	33

Note: Figures are average number of days per year and cover the years 1949-1990
Source: National Climatic Data Center, International Station Meteorological Climate Summary, 9/96

HAZARDOUS WASTE

Superfund Sites

The Green Bay, WI metro area is home to three sites on the EPA's Superfund National Priorities List: **Algoma Municipal Landfill** (final); **Better Brite Plating Co. Chrome and Zinc Shops** (final); **Fox River Nrda/Pcb Releases** (proposed). There are a total of 1,375 Superfund sites with a status of proposed or final on the list in the U.S. *U.S. Environmental Protection Agency, National Priorities List, April 7, 2021*

AIR QUALITY

Air Quality Trends: Ozone

	1990	1995	2000	2005	2010	2015	2016	2017	2018	2019
MSA[1]	n/a	n/a	n/a	n/a	n/a	n/a	n/a	n/a	n/a	n/a
U.S.	0.088	0.089	0.082	0.080	0.073	0.068	0.069	0.068	0.069	0.065

Note: (1) Data covers the Green Bay, WI Metropolitan Statistical Area; n/a not available. The values shown are the composite ozone concentration averages among trend sites based on the highest fourth daily maximum 8-hour concentration in parts per million. These trends are based on sites having an adequate record of monitoring data during the trend period. Data from exceptional events are included.
Source: U.S. Environmental Protection Agency, Air Quality Monitoring Information, "Air Quality Trends by City, 1990-2019"

Air Quality Index

Area	Percent of Days when Air Quality was...[2]					AQI Statistics[2]	
	Good	Moderate	Unhealthy for Sensitive Groups	Unhealthy	Very Unhealthy	Maximum	Median
MSA[1]	85.2	14.8	0.0	0.0	0.0	97	36

Note: (1) Data covers the Green Bay, WI Metropolitan Statistical Area; (2) Based on 365 days with AQI data in 2019. Air Quality Index (AQI) is an index for reporting daily air quality. EPA calculates the AQI for five major air pollutants regulated by the Clean Air Act: ground-level ozone, particle pollution (aka particulate matter), carbon monoxide, sulfur dioxide, and nitrogen dioxide. The AQI runs from 0 to 500. The higher the AQI value, the greater the level of air pollution and the greater the health concern. There are six AQI categories: "Good" AQI is between 0 and 50. Air quality is considered satisfactory; "Moderate" AQI is between 51 and 100. Air quality is acceptable; "Unhealthy for Sensitive Groups" When AQI values are between 101 and 150, members of sensitive groups may experience health effects; "Unhealthy" When AQI values are between 151 and 200 everyone may begin to experience health effects; "Very Unhealthy" AQI values between 201 and 300 trigger a health alert; "Hazardous" AQI values over 300 trigger warnings of emergency conditions (not shown).
Source: U.S. Environmental Protection Agency, Air Quality Index Report, 2019

Air Quality Index Pollutants

Area	Percent of Days when AQI Pollutant was...[2]					
	Carbon Monoxide	Nitrogen Dioxide	Ozone	Sulfur Dioxide	Particulate Matter 2.5	Particulate Matter 10
MSA[1]	0.0	0.0	51.0	1.1	47.9	0.0

Note: (1) Data covers the Green Bay, WI Metropolitan Statistical Area; (2) Based on 365 days with AQI data in 2019. The Air Quality Index (AQI) is an index for reporting daily air quality. EPA calculates the AQI for five major air pollutants regulated by the Clean Air Act: ground-level ozone, particle pollution (also known as particulate matter), carbon monoxide, sulfur dioxide, and nitrogen dioxide. The AQI runs from 0 to 500. The higher the AQI value, the greater the level of air pollution and the greater the health concern.
Source: U.S. Environmental Protection Agency, Air Quality Index Report, 2019

Maximum Air Pollutant Concentrations: Particulate Matter, Ozone, CO and Lead

	Particulate Matter 10 (ug/m^3)	Particulate Matter 2.5 Wtd AM (ug/m^3)	Particulate Matter 2.5 24-Hr (ug/m^3)	Ozone (ppm)	Carbon Monoxide (ppm)	Lead (ug/m^3)
MSA[1] Level	n/a	7.3	19	0.061	n/a	n/a
NAAQS[2]	150	15	35	0.075	9	0.15
Met NAAQS[2]	n/a	Yes	Yes	Yes	n/a	n/a

Note: (1) Data covers the Green Bay, WI Metropolitan Statistical Area; Data from exceptional events are included; (2) National Ambient Air Quality Standards; ppm = parts per million; ug/m^3 = micrograms per cubic meter; n/a not available.
Concentrations: Particulate Matter 10 (coarse particulate)—highest second maximum 24-hour concentration; Particulate Matter 2.5 Wtd AM (fine particulate)—highest weighted annual mean concentration; Particulate Matter 2.5 24-Hour (fine particulate)—highest 98th percentile 24-hour concentration; Ozone—highest fourth daily maximum 8-hour concentration; Carbon Monoxide—highest second maximum non-overlapping 8-hour concentration; Lead—maximum running 3-month average
Source: U.S. Environmental Protection Agency, Air Quality Monitoring Information, "Air Quality Statistics by City, 2019"

Maximum Air Pollutant Concentrations: Nitrogen Dioxide and Sulfur Dioxide

	Nitrogen Dioxide AM (ppb)	Nitrogen Dioxide 1-Hr (ppb)	Sulfur Dioxide AM (ppb)	Sulfur Dioxide 1-Hr (ppb)	Sulfur Dioxide 24-Hr (ppb)
MSA[1] Level	n/a	n/a	n/a	5	n/a
NAAQS[2]	53	100	30	75	140
Met NAAQS[2]	n/a	n/a	n/a	Yes	n/a

Note: (1) Data covers the Green Bay, WI Metropolitan Statistical Area; Data from exceptional events are included; (2) National Ambient Air Quality Standards; ppm = parts per million; ug/m^3 = micrograms per cubic meter; n/a not available.
Concentrations: Nitrogen Dioxide AM—highest arithmetic mean concentration; Nitrogen Dioxide 1-Hr—highest 98th percentile 1-hour daily maximum concentration; Sulfur Dioxide AM—highest annual mean concentration; Sulfur Dioxide 1-Hr—highest 99th percentile 1-hour daily maximum concentration; Sulfur Dioxide 24-Hr—highest second maximum 24-hour concentration
Source: U.S. Environmental Protection Agency, Air Quality Monitoring Information, "Air Quality Statistics by City, 2019"

Indianapolis, Indiana

Background

Indianapolis sits within the boundaries of the Northern manufacturing belt and the midwestern Corn Belt, and its economy reflects both influences. On one side lies the Indianapolis industrial sector, including transportation, airplane and truck parts, paper and rubber products, and computer software. On the other side lies agriculture. Indianapolis is a leading grain market, as well as the largest meat-processing center outside of Chicago.

Despite pollution and other problems of urban decay in the late twentieth century, Indianapolis has made significant strides in this area, completing dozens of major downtown projects, including Dolphin Adventure at the Indianapolis Zoo, Eiteljorg Museum of American Indians and Western Art expansion, Eli Lilly and Company Insulin Finishing Building, the Indianapolis Museum of Art expansion, and Circle Centre, a retail and entertainment complex that draws one million visitors a month.

Known as the "Crossroads of America," Indianapolis is bisected by more interstate highways than any other city in the nation, making it accessible from many locations and within a day's drive of half the country's population. As a result, the city is a popular choice for conventions and offers excellent facilities at the Indiana Convention Center & RCA Dome. The Indianapolis Artsgarden, offering more than 300 free performances and exhibits each year, is linked to the Convention Center by a skywalk, and is a world-class venue for the arts.

The city is home to one of the finest children's museums in the United States, and its 85 parks offer many outdoor activities.

Indianapolis has been called by many the rising food star of the Midwest, with top-notch restaurants in the Fletcher Place neighborhood and a number of city chefs and restaurateurs recent semifinalists in the James Beard Foundation Awards. Microbreweries are a staple in the city, with more than 50 craft brewers.

Known as the "Racing Capital of the World," Indianapolis hosts the world's three biggest single-day sporting events at the world-famous Indianapolis Motor Speedway: Indy 500; Brickyard 400; and SAP United States Grand Prix. The National Collegiate Athletic Association is also in Indianapolis, as is the NCAA Hall of Champions. Housing divisions of both Indiana and Purdue Universities make for a lively learning center.

Indianapolis's Conseco Fieldhouse hosted the Big Ten college basketball tournament from 2008 through 2012. The city hosted the Women's NCAA basketball tournament Final Fours in 2011 and 2016, and the 2012 Super Bowl.

The Indianapolis Art Museum is one of the largest general museums in the United States. Collections include works of Gaugin, Seurat, and Turner. The museum has integrated its galleries with other properties on its campus, including the Virginia B. Fairbanks Art & Nature Park and the Oldfields-Lilly House.

Indianapolis was initially planned by Alexander Ralston, the American engineer who assisted French architect Pierre L'Enfant in planning Washington, D.C. Thus, like the nation's capital, Indianapolis is laid out on a mile-square grid and is easily navigable. Its centerpiece is Monument Circle, home of the 284-foot Soldiers and Sailors Monument, with a 32-story panoramic view of the Indianapolis skyline.

Indianapolis has a temperate climate, with very warm summers and no dry season. Very cold winter weather sometime occurs with the invasion of continental polar air from northern latitudes. In the summer, tropical air from the Gulf of Mexico brings warm temperatures and moderate humidity.

Rankings

General Rankings

- In its eighth annual survey, *Travel + Leisure* readers nominated their favorite small cities and towns in America—those with 100,000 or fewer residents—voting on numerous attractive features in categories including culture, food and drink, quality of life, style, and people. After 50,000 votes, Indianapolis was ranked #7 among the proposed favorites. *www.travelandleisure.com, "America's Favorite Cities," October 20, 2017*

Business/Finance Rankings

- According to *Business Insider*, the Indianapolis metro area is a prime place to run a startup or move an existing business to. The area ranked #23. Nearly 190 metro areas were analyzed on overall economic health and investments. Data was based on the 2019 U.S. Census Bureau American Community Survey, the marketing company PitchBook, Bureau of Labor Statistics employment report, and Zillow. Criteria: percentage of change in typical home values and employment rates; quarterly venture capital investment activity; and median household income. *www.businessinsider.com, "The 25 Best Cities to Start a Business-Or Move Your Current One," January 12, 2021*

- Based on metro area social media reviews, the employment opinion group Glassdoor surveyed 50 of the most populous U.S. metro areas and equally weighed cost of living, hiring opportunity, and job satisfaction to compose a list of "25 Best Cities for Jobs." Median pay and home value, and number of active job openings were also factored in. The Indianapolis metro area was ranked #3 in overall job satisfaction. *www.glassdoor.com, "Best Cities for Jobs," February 25, 2020*

- The Brookings Institution ranked the nation's largest cities based on income inequality. Indianapolis was ranked #72 (#1 = greatest inequality). Criteria: the "95/20 ratio," a figure representing the income at which a household earns more than 95 percent of all other households, divided by the income at which a household earns more than only 20 percent of all other households. *Brookings Institution, "Household Income Inequality, Largest Cities of 97 Large U.S. Metro Areas, 2014-2016," February 5, 2018*

- The Brookings Institution ranked the 100 largest metro areas in the U.S. based on income inequality. Indianapolis was ranked #58 (#1 = greatest inequality). Criteria: the "95/20 ratio," a figure representing the income at which a household earns more than 95 percent of all other households, divided by the income at which a household earns more than only 20 percent of all other households. *Brookings Institution, "Household Income Inequality, 100 Largest U.S. Metro Areas, 2014-2016," February 5, 2018*

- *Forbes* ranked the 100 largest metro areas in the U.S. in terms of the "Best Cities for Young Professionals." The Indianapolis metro area ranked #11 out of 25. Criteria: median rent of a two-bedroom apartment; job growth and unemployment rate; median salary of college graduates with 5 or less years of work experience; networking opportunities; social outlook; percentage of population 25 years of age and older with college degrees. *Forbes.com, "America's 25 Best Cities for Young Professionals in 2017," May 22, 2017*

- Indianapolis was identified as one of America's most frugal metro areas by *Coupons.com*. The city ranked #17 out of 25. Criteria: digital coupon usage. *Coupons.com, "America's Most Frugal Cities of 2017," March 22, 2018*

- Indianapolis was cited as one of America's top metros for new and expanded facility projects in 2020. The area ranked #5 in the large metro area category (population over 1 million). *Site Selection, "Top Metros of 2020," March 2021*

- Indianapolis was identified as one of the happiest cities to work in by CareerBliss.com, an online community for career advancement. The city ranked #7 out of 10. Criteria: an employee's relationship with his or her boss and co-workers; daily tasks; general work environment; compensation; opportunities for advancement; company culture and job reputation; and resources. *Businesswire.com, "CareerBliss Happiest Cities to Work 2019," February 12, 2019*

- The Indianapolis metro area appeared on the Milken Institute "2021 Best Performing Cities" list. Rank: #56 out of 200 large metro areas (population over 250,000). Criteria: job growth; wage and salary growth; high-tech output growth; housing affordability; household broadband access. *Milken Institute, "Best-Performing Cities 2021," February 16, 2021*

- *Forbes* ranked the 200 most populous metro areas to determine the nation's "Best Places for Business and Careers." The Indianapolis metro area was ranked #58. Criteria: costs (business and living); job growth (past and projected); income growth; quality of life; educational attainment (college and high school); projected economic growth; cultural and leisure opportunities; workplace tolerance laws; net migration patterns. *Forbes, "The Best Places for Business and Careers 2019: Seattle Still On Top," October 30, 2019*

Education Rankings

- Personal finance website *WalletHub* analyzed the 150 largest U.S. metropolitan statistical areas to determine where the most educated Americans are putting their degrees to work. Criteria: education levels; percentage of workers with degrees; education quality and attainment gap; public school quality rankings; quality and enrollment of each metro area's universities. Indianapolis was ranked #70 (#1 = most educated city). *www.WalletHub.com, "Most and Least Educated Cities in America," July 20, 2020*

- Indianapolis was selected as one of America's most literate cities. The city ranked #43 out of the 84 largest U.S. cities. Criteria: number of booksellers; library resources; Internet resources; educational attainment; periodical publishing resources; newspaper circulation. *Central Connecticut State University, "America's Most Literate Cities, 2018," February 2019*

Environmental Rankings

- Indianapolis was highlighted as one of the 25 metro areas most polluted by year-round particle pollution (Annual PM 2.5) in the U.S. during 2016 through 2018. The area ranked #16. *American Lung Association, "State of the Air 2020," April 21, 2020*

Food/Drink Rankings

- The U.S. Chamber of Commerce Foundation conducted an in-depth study on local food truck regulations, surveyed 288 food truck owners, and ranked 20 major American cities based on how friendly they are for operating a food truck. The compiled index assessed the following: procedures for obtaining permits and licenses; complying with restrictions; and financial obligations associated with operating a food truck. Indianapolis ranked #5 overall (1 being the best). *www.foodtrucknation.us, "Food Truck Nation," March 20, 2018*

Health/Fitness Rankings

- For each of the 100 largest cities in the United States, the American Fitness Index®, published by the American College of Sports Medicine and the Anthem Foundation, evaluated community infrastructure and 33 health behaviors including preventive health, levels of chronic disease conditions, pedestrian safety, air quality, and community resources that support physical activity. Indianapolis ranked #94 for "community fitness." *americanfitnessindex.org, "2020 ACSM American Fitness Index Summary Report," July 14, 2020*

- The Indianapolis metro area was identified as one of the worst cities for bed bugs in America by pest control company Orkin. The area ranked #7 out of 50 based on the number of bed bug treatments Orkin performed from December 2019 to November 2020. *Orkin, "New Year, New Top City on Orkin's 2021 Bed Bug Cities List: Chicago," February 1, 2021*

- Indianapolis was identified as a "2021 Spring Allergy Capital." The area ranked #76 out of 100. Three groups of factors were used to identify the most challenging cities for people with allergies during the spring season: annual spring pollen levels; over the counter medicine use; number of board-certified allergy specialists. *Asthma and Allergy Foundation of America, "Spring Allergy Capitals 2021," February 23, 2021*

- Indianapolis was identified as a "2021 Fall Allergy Capital." The area ranked #58 out of 100. Three groups of factors were used to identify the most challenging cities for people with allergies during the fall season: annual fall pollen levels; over the counter medicine use; number of board-certified allergy specialists. *Asthma and Allergy Foundation of America, "Fall Allergy Capitals 2021," February 23, 2021*

- Indianapolis was identified as a "2019 Asthma Capital." The area ranked #48 out of the nation's 100 largest metropolitan areas. Criteria: estimated asthma prevalence; crude death rate from asthma; and ER visits due to asthma. Risk factors analyzed but not factored in the rankings: annual pollen score; annual air quality; public smoking laws; number of board-certified asthma specialists; rescue medication use; controller medication use; uninsured rate; poverty rate. *Asthma and Allergy Foundation of America, "Asthma Capitals 2019: The Most Challenging Places to Live With Asthma," May 7, 2019*

Real Estate Rankings

- *WalletHub* compared the most populated U.S. cities to determine which had the best markets for real estate agents. Indianapolis ranked #142 where demand was high and pay was the best. Criteria: sales per agent; annual median wage for real-estate agents; monthly average starting salary for real estate agents; real estate job density and competition; unemployment rate; home turnover rate; housing-market health index; and other relevant metrics. *www.WalletHub.com, "2019's Best Places to Be a Real Estate Agent," April 24, 2019*

- The Indianapolis metro area was identified as one of the top 15 housing markets to invest in for 2021 by *Forbes*. Criteria: home price appreciation; percentage of home sales within a 2-week time frame; available inventory; number of home sales; and other factors. *Forbes.com, "Top Housing Markets To Watch In 2021," December 15, 2020*

- The Indianapolis metro area was identified as one of the 10 worst condo markets in the U.S. in 2020. The area ranked #54 out of 63 markets. Criteria: year-over-year change of median sales price of existing apartment condo-coop homes between the 4th quarter of 2019 and the 4th quarter of 2020. *National Association of Realtors®, Median Sales Price of Existing Apartment Condo-Coops Homes for Metropolitan Areas, 4th Quarter 2020*

- Indianapolis was ranked #37 out of 268 metro areas in terms of housing affordability in 2020 by the National Association of Home Builders (#1 = most affordable). Criteria: the share of homes sold in that area affordable to a family earning the local median income, based on standard mortgage underwriting criteria. *National Association of Home Builders®, NAHB-Wells Fargo Housing Opportunity Index, 4th Quarter 2020*

Safety Rankings

- Allstate ranked the 200 largest cities in America in terms of driver safety. Indianapolis ranked #75. Criteria: internal property damage claims over a two-year period from January 2016 to December 2017. The report helps increase the importance of safety and awareness behind the wheel. *Allstate, "Allstate America's Best Drivers Report, 2019" June 24, 2019*

- The National Insurance Crime Bureau ranked 384 metro areas in the U.S. in terms of per capita rates of vehicle theft. The Indianapolis metro area ranked #53 (#1 = highest rate). Criteria: number of vehicle theft offenses per 100,000 inhabitants in 2019. *National Insurance Crime Bureau, "Hot Spots 2019," July 21, 2020*

Seniors/Retirement Rankings

- From its Best Cities for Successful Aging indexes, the Milken Institute generated rankings for metropolitan areas, weighing data in nine categories—health care, wellness, living arrangements, transportation and convenience, financial characteristics, education, employment, community engagement, and overall livability. The Indianapolis metro area was ranked #44 overall in the large metro area category. *Milken Institute, "Best Cities for Successful Aging, 2017" March 14, 2017*

Sports/Recreation Rankings

- Indianapolis was chosen as one of America's best cities for bicycling. The city ranked #30 out of 50. Criteria: cycling infrastructure that is safe and friendly for all ages; energy and bike culture. The editors evaluated cities with populations of 100,000 or more. *Bicycling, "The 50 Best Bike Cities in America," October 10, 2018*

Women/Minorities Rankings

- Personal finance website *WalletHub* compared more than 180 U.S. cities across two key dimensions, "Hispanic Business-Friendliness" and "Hispanic Purchasing Power," to arrive at the most favorable conditions for Hispanic entrepreneurs. Indianapolis was ranked #121 out of 182. Criteria includes: share of Hispanic-Owned Businesses; Hispanic entrepreneurship rate to median annual income of Hispanics; Small Business-Friendliness score; cost of living; and number of Hispanics with at least a bachelor's degree. *WalletHub.com, "2019's Best Cities for Hispanic Entrepreneurs," May 1, 2019*

Miscellaneous Rankings

- While the majority of travel ground to a halt in 2020, plugged-in travel influencers and experts were able to rediscover their local regions. Indianapolis appeared on a *Forbes* list of 15 U.S. cities that provided solace as well as local inspiration. Whether it be quirky things to see and do, delicious take out, outdoor exploring and daytrips, these places are must-see destinations. *Forbes, "Bucket List Travel: The 15 Best U.S. Destinations For 2021," January 1, 2021*

- The watchdog site, Charity Navigator, conducted a study of charities in major markets both to analyze statistical differences in their financial, accountability, and transparency practices and to track year-to-year variations in individual philanthropic communities. The Indianapolis metro area was ranked #29 among the 30 metro markets in the rating category of Overall Score. *www.charitynavigator.org, "2017 Metro Market Study," May 1, 2017*

- *WalletHub* compared the 150 most populated U.S. cities to determine their operating efficiency. A "Quality of City Services" score was constructed for each city and then divided by the total budget per capita to reveal which were managed the best. Indianapolis ranked #101. Criteria: financial stability; economy; education; safety; health; infrastructure and pollution. *www.WalletHub.com, "2020's Best- & Worst-Run Cities in America," June 29, 2020*

- Indianapolis was selected as one of "America's Friendliest Cities." The city ranked #6 in the "Friendliest" category. Respondents to an online survey were asked to rate 38 top urban destinations in the United States as to general friendliness, as well as manners, politeness and warm disposition. *Travel + Leisure, "America's Friendliest Cities," October 20, 2017*

Business Environment

DEMOGRAPHICS

Population Growth

Area	1990 Census	2000 Census	2010 Census	2019* Estimate	Population Growth (%)	
					1990-2019	2010-2019
City	730,993	781,870	820,445	864,447	18.3	5.4
MSA[1]	1,294,217	1,525,104	1,756,241	2,029,472	56.8	15.6
U.S.	248,709,873	281,421,906	308,745,538	324,697,795	30.6	5.2

Note: (1) Figures cover the Indianapolis-Carmel-Anderson, IN Metropolitan Statistical Area; (*) 2015-2019 5-year estimated population
Source: U.S. Census Bureau, 1990 Census, Census 2000, Census 2010, 2015-2019 American Community Survey 5-Year Estimates

Household Size

Area	Persons in Household (%)							Average Household Size
	One	Two	Three	Four	Five	Six	Seven or More	
City	37.8	31.4	13.2	9.7	4.9	1.9	1.1	2.50
MSA[1]	30.2	33.5	14.8	12.9	5.7	1.9	1.0	2.60
U.S.	27.9	33.9	15.6	12.9	6.0	2.3	1.4	2.60

Note: (1) Figures cover the Indianapolis-Carmel-Anderson, IN Metropolitan Statistical Area
Source: U.S. Census Bureau, 2015-2019 American Community Survey 5-Year Estimates

Race

Area	White Alone[2] (%)	Black Alone[2] (%)	Asian Alone[2] (%)	AIAN[3] Alone[2] (%)	NHOPI[4] Alone[2] (%)	Other Race Alone[2] (%)	Two or More Races (%)
City	60.9	28.6	3.4	0.3	0.0	3.5	3.3
MSA[1]	76.6	15.2	3.2	0.2	0.0	2.0	2.7
U.S.	72.5	12.7	5.5	0.8	0.2	4.9	3.3

Note: (1) Figures cover the Indianapolis-Carmel-Anderson, IN Metropolitan Statistical Area; (2) Alone is defined as not being in combination with one or more other races; (3) American Indian and Alaska Native; (4) Native Hawaiian and Other Pacific Islander
Source: U.S. Census Bureau, 2015-2019 American Community Survey 5-Year Estimates

Hispanic or Latino Origin

Area	Total (%)	Mexican (%)	Puerto Rican (%)	Cuban (%)	Other (%)
City	10.5	7.1	0.6	0.2	2.6
MSA[1]	6.7	4.4	0.5	0.1	1.7
U.S.	18.0	11.2	1.7	0.7	4.3

Note: Persons of Hispanic or Latino origin can be of any race; (1) Figures cover the Indianapolis-Carmel-Anderson, IN Metropolitan Statistical Area
Source: U.S. Census Bureau, 2015-2019 American Community Survey 5-Year Estimates

Ancestry

Area	German	Irish	English	American	Italian	Polish	French[2]	Scottish	Dutch
City	13.5	8.6	5.9	5.9	2.2	1.6	1.5	1.5	1.0
MSA[1]	17.3	10.0	8.0	9.3	2.7	1.9	1.8	1.8	1.4
U.S.	13.3	9.7	7.2	6.2	5.1	2.8	2.3	1.7	1.2

Note: Figures are the percentage of the total population reporting a particular ancestry. The nine most commonly reported ancestries in the U.S. are shown. Figures include multiple ancestries (e.g. if a person reported being Irish and Italian, they were included in both columns); (1) Figures cover the Indianapolis-Carmel-Anderson, IN Metropolitan Statistical Area; (2) Excludes Basque
Source: U.S. Census Bureau, 2015-2019 American Community Survey 5-Year Estimates

Foreign-born Population

Area	Percent of Population Born in								
	Any Foreign Country	Asia	Mexico	Europe	Caribbean	Central America[2]	South America	Africa	Canada
City	9.7	2.8	3.0	0.5	0.4	0.9	0.3	1.6	0.1
MSA[1]	7.0	2.6	1.7	0.6	0.2	0.5	0.3	0.9	0.1
U.S.	13.6	4.2	3.5	1.5	1.3	1.1	1.0	0.7	0.2

Note: (1) Figures cover the Indianapolis-Carmel-Anderson, IN Metropolitan Statistical Area; (2) Excludes Mexico.
Source: U.S. Census Bureau, 2015-2019 American Community Survey 5-Year Estimates

Marital Status

Area	Never Married	Now Married[2]	Separated	Widowed	Divorced
City	42.9	37.7	1.8	5.1	12.5
MSA[1]	33.5	47.9	1.4	5.3	11.9
U.S.	33.4	48.1	1.9	5.8	10.9

Note: Figures are percentages and cover the population 15 years of age and older; (1) Figures cover the Indianapolis-Carmel-Anderson, IN Metropolitan Statistical Area; (2) Excludes separated
Source: U.S. Census Bureau, 2015-2019 American Community Survey 5-Year Estimates

Disability by Age

Area	All Ages	Under 18 Years Old	18 to 64 Years Old	65 Years and Over
City	13.3	5.1	12.0	37.5
MSA[1]	12.2	4.5	10.5	35.0
U.S.	12.6	4.2	10.3	34.5

Note: Figures show percent of the civilian noninstitutionalized population that reported having a disability. Disability status is determined from six types of difficulty: vision, hearing, cognitive, ambulatory, self-care, and independent living. For children under 5 years old, hearing and vision difficulty are used to determine disability status. For children between the ages of 5 and 14, disability status is determined from hearing, vision, cognitive, ambulatory, and self-care difficulties. For people aged 15 years and older, they are considered to have a disability if they have difficulty with any one of the six difficulty types; Note: (1) Figures cover the Indianapolis-Carmel-Anderson, IN Metropolitan Statistical Area
Source: U.S. Census Bureau, 2015-2019 American Community Survey 5-Year Estimates

Age

Area	Percent of Population									Median Age
	Under Age 5	Age 5–19	Age 20–34	Age 35–44	Age 45–54	Age 55–64	Age 65–74	Age 75–84	Age 85+	
City	7.3	19.8	24.1	12.8	11.9	11.9	7.2	3.4	1.5	34.2
MSA[1]	6.7	20.5	20.7	13.2	13.1	12.3	8.0	3.8	1.6	36.5
U.S.	6.1	19.1	20.7	12.6	13.0	12.9	9.1	4.6	1.9	38.1

Note: (1) Figures cover the Indianapolis-Carmel-Anderson, IN Metropolitan Statistical Area
Source: U.S. Census Bureau, 2015-2019 American Community Survey 5-Year Estimates

Gender

Area	Males	Females	Males per 100 Females
City	416,893	447,554	93.1
MSA[1]	991,392	1,038,080	95.5
U.S.	159,886,919	164,810,876	97.0

Note: (1) Figures cover the Indianapolis-Carmel-Anderson, IN Metropolitan Statistical Area
Source: U.S. Census Bureau, 2015-2019 American Community Survey 5-Year Estimates

Religious Groups by Family

Area	Catholic	Baptist	Non-Den.	Methodist[2]	Lutheran	LDS[3]	Pente-costal	Presby-terian[4]	Muslim[5]	Judaism
MSA[1]	10.5	10.3	7.2	5.0	1.7	0.7	1.6	1.7	0.2	0.4
U.S.	19.1	9.3	4.0	4.0	2.3	2.0	1.9	1.6	0.8	0.7

Note: Figures are the number of adherents as a percentage of the total population; (1) Figures cover the Indianapolis-Carmel-Anderson, IN Metropolitan Statistical Area; (2) Methodist/Pietist; (3) Latter Day Saints; (4) Reformed; (5) Figures are estimates
Source: Association of Statisticians of American Religious Bodies, 2010 U.S. Religion Census: Religious Congregations & Membership Study

Religious Groups by Tradition

Area	Catholic	Evangelical Protestant	Mainline Protestant	Other Tradition	Black Protestant	Orthodox
MSA[1]	10.5	18.3	9.6	1.7	1.9	0.3
U.S.	19.1	16.2	7.3	4.3	1.6	0.3

Note: Figures are the number of adherents as a percentage of the total population; (1) Figures cover the Indianapolis-Carmel-Anderson, IN Metropolitan Statistical Area
Source: Association of Statisticians of American Religious Bodies, 2010 U.S. Religion Census: Religious Congregations & Membership Study

ECONOMY

Gross Metropolitan Product

Area	2017	2018	2019	2020	Rank[2]
MSA[1]	140.6	147.0	152.8	159.1	27

Note: Figures are in billions of dollars; (1) Figures cover the Indianapolis-Carmel-Anderson, IN Metropolitan Statistical Area; (2) Rank is based on 2018 data and ranges from 1 to 381
Source: U.S. Conference of Mayors, U.S. Metro Economies: GMP & Employment 2018-2020, September 2019

214   Indianapolis, Indiana

Economic Growth

Area	2015-17 (%)	2018 (%)	2019 (%)	2020 (%)	Rank[2]
MSA[1]	2.5	1.9	2.1	2.0	101
U.S.	1.9	2.9	2.3	2.1	—

Note: Figures are real gross metropolitan product (GMP) growth rates and represent average annual percent change; (1) Figures cover the Indianapolis-Carmel-Anderson, IN Metropolitan Statistical Area; (2) Rank is based on 2017 2-year average annual percent change and ranges from 1 to 381
Source: U.S. Conference of Mayors, U.S. Metro Economies: GMP & Employment 2018-2020, September 2019

Metropolitan Area Exports

Area	2014	2015	2016	2017	2018	2019	Rank[2]
MSA[1]	9,539.4	9,809.4	9,655.4	10,544.2	11,069.9	11,148.7	33

Note: Figures are in millions of dollars; (1) Figures cover the Indianapolis-Carmel-Anderson, IN Metropolitan Statistical Area; (2) Rank is based on 2019 data and ranges from 1 to 386
Source: U.S. Department of Commerce, International Trade Administration, Office of Trade and Economic Analysis, Industry and Analysis, Exports by Metropolitan Area, data extracted March 24, 2021

Building Permits

Area	Single-Family			Multi-Family			Total		
	2018	2019	Pct. Chg.	2018	2019	Pct. Chg.	2018	2019	Pct. Chg.
City	1,090	1,153	5.8	1,196	1,229	2.8	2,286	2,382	4.2
MSA[1]	7,291	7,120	-2.3	1,603	2,601	62.3	8,894	9,721	9.3
U.S.	855,300	862,100	0.7	473,500	523,900	10.6	1,328,800	1,386,000	4.3

Note: (1) Figures cover the Indianapolis-Carmel-Anderson, IN Metropolitan Statistical Area; Figures represent new, privately-owned housing units authorized (unadjusted data); All permit data are based on estimates with imputation
Source: U.S. Census Bureau, Manufacturing, Mining, and Construction Statistics, Building Permits, 2018, 2019

Bankruptcy Filings

Area	Business Filings			Nonbusiness Filings		
	2019	2020	% Chg.	2019	2020	% Chg.
Marion County	100	39	-61.0	4,465	3,319	-25.7
U.S.	22,780	21,655	-4.9	752,160	522,808	-30.5

Note: Business filings include Chapter 7, Chapter 9, Chapter 11, Chapter 12, Chapter 13, Chapter 15, and Section 304; Nonbusiness filings include Chapter 7, Chapter 11, and Chapter 13
Source: Administrative Office of the U.S. Courts, Business and Nonbusiness Bankruptcy, County Cases Commenced by Chapter of the Bankruptcy Code, During the 12-Month Period Ending December 31, 2019 and Business and Nonbusiness Bankruptcy, County Cases Commenced by Chapter of the Bankruptcy Code, During the 12-Month Period Ending December 31, 2020

Housing Vacancy Rates

Area	Gross Vacancy Rate[2] (%)			Year-Round Vacancy Rate[3] (%)			Rental Vacancy Rate[4] (%)			Homeowner Vacancy Rate[5] (%)		
	2018	2019	2020	2018	2019	2020	2018	2019	2020	2018	2019	2020
MSA[1]	8.7	7.2	7.3	8.6	6.7	7.0	9.9	7.0	10.4	1.5	1.5	0.8
U.S.	12.3	12.0	10.6	9.7	9.5	8.2	6.9	6.7	6.3	1.5	1.4	1.0

Note: (1) Figures cover the Indianapolis-Carmel-Anderson, IN Metropolitan Statistical Area; (2) The percentage of the total housing inventory that is vacant; (3) The percentage of the housing inventory (excluding seasonal units) that is year-round vacant; (4) The percentage of rental inventory that is vacant for rent; (5) The percentage of homeowner inventory that is vacant for sale
Source: U.S. Census Bureau, Housing Vacancies and Homeownership Annual Statistics: 2018, 2019, 2020

INCOME

Income

Area	Per Capita ($)	Median Household ($)	Average Household ($)
City	28,363	47,873	68,367
MSA[1]	33,699	61,552	85,193
U.S.	34,103	62,843	88,607

Note: (1) Figures cover the Indianapolis-Carmel-Anderson, IN Metropolitan Statistical Area
Source: U.S. Census Bureau, 2015-2019 American Community Survey 5-Year Estimates

Household Income Distribution

Area	Percent of Households Earning							
	Under $15,000	$15,000 -$24,999	$25,000 -$34,999	$35,000 -$49,999	$50,000 -$74,999	$75,000 -$99,999	$100,000 -$149,999	$150,000 and up
City	13.5	11.1	11.8	15.3	17.9	11.3	11.0	8.0
MSA[1]	9.6	8.7	9.4	13.2	17.9	13.3	15.1	12.8
U.S.	10.3	8.9	8.9	12.3	17.2	12.7	15.1	14.5

Note: (1) Figures cover the Indianapolis-Carmel-Anderson, IN Metropolitan Statistical Area
Source: U.S. Census Bureau, 2015-2019 American Community Survey 5-Year Estimates

Poverty Rate

Area	All Ages	Under 18 Years Old	18 to 64 Years Old	65 Years and Over
City	18.0	26.8	16.1	10.2
MSA[1]	12.4	17.5	11.4	7.4
U.S.	13.4	18.5	12.6	9.3

Note: Figures are percentage of people whose income during the past 12 months was below the poverty level;
(1) Figures cover the Indianapolis-Carmel-Anderson, IN Metropolitan Statistical Area
Source: U.S. Census Bureau, 2015-2019 American Community Survey 5-Year Estimates

CITY FINANCES

City Government Finances

Component	2017 ($000)	2017 ($ per capita)
Total Revenues	3,565,593	4,179
Total Expenditures	3,331,544	3,905
Debt Outstanding	3,572,605	4,187
Cash and Securities[1]	2,775,016	3,253

Note: (1) Cash and security holdings of a government at the close of its fiscal year,
including those of its dependent agencies, utilities, and liquor stores.
Source: U.S. Census Bureau, State & Local Government Finances 2017

City Government Revenue by Source

Source	2017 ($000)	2017 ($ per capita)	2017 (%)
General Revenue			
From Federal Government	116,677	137	3.3
From State Government	569,241	667	16.0
From Local Governments	233,296	273	6.5
Taxes			
Property	280,887	329	7.9
Sales and Gross Receipts	0	0	0.0
Personal Income	138,814	163	3.9
Corporate Income	0	0	0.0
Motor Vehicle License	0	0	0.0
Other Taxes	4,944	6	0.1
Current Charges	1,539,093	1,804	43.2
Liquor Store	0	0	0.0
Utility	528,130	619	14.8
Employee Retirement	28,968	34	0.8

Source: U.S. Census Bureau, State & Local Government Finances 2017

City Government Expenditures by Function

Function	2017 ($000)	2017 ($ per capita)	2017 (%)
General Direct Expenditures			
Air Transportation	107,339	125	3.2
Corrections	142,805	167	4.3
Education	0	0	0.0
Employment Security Administration	0	0	0.0
Financial Administration	18,767	22	0.6
Fire Protection	158,006	185	4.7
General Public Buildings	0	0	0.0
Governmental Administration, Other	19,952	23	0.6
Health	105,846	124	3.2
Highways	0	0	0.0
Hospitals	1,217,062	1,426	36.5
Housing and Community Development	0	0	0.0
Interest on General Debt	203,833	238	6.1
Judicial and Legal	103,854	121	3.1
Libraries	0	0	0.0
Parking	0	0	0.0
Parks and Recreation	83,254	97	2.5
Police Protection	220,425	258	6.6
Public Welfare	0	0	0.0
Sewerage	0	0	0.0
Solid Waste Management	44,390	52	1.3
Veterans' Services	0	0	0.0
Liquor Store	0	0	0.0
Utility	857,838	1,005	25.7
Employee Retirement	11,648	13	0.3

Source: U.S. Census Bureau, State & Local Government Finances 2017

216   Indianapolis, Indiana

EMPLOYMENT

Labor Force and Employment

Area	Civilian Labor Force			Workers Employed		
	Dec. 2019	Dec. 2020	% Chg.	Dec. 2019	Dec. 2020	% Chg.
City	446,151	467,925	4.9	433,373	443,878	2.4
MSA[1]	1,060,176	1,101,669	3.9	1,032,445	1,057,751	2.5
U.S.	164,007,000	160,017,000	-2.4	158,504,000	149,613,000	-5.6

Note: Data is not seasonally adjusted and covers workers 16 years of age and older; (1) Figures cover the
Indianapolis-Carmel-Anderson, IN Metropolitan Statistical Area
Source: Bureau of Labor Statistics, Local Area Unemployment Statistics

Unemployment Rate

Area	2020											
	Jan.	Feb.	Mar.	Apr.	May	Jun.	Jul.	Aug.	Sep.	Oct.	Nov.	Dec.
City	3.4	3.2	3.1	14.0	11.3	12.6	9.9	8.4	7.7	7.0	6.4	5.1
MSA[1]	3.2	2.9	2.8	13.3	10.2	10.6	7.8	6.6	6.0	5.4	5.0	4.0
U.S.	4.0	3.8	4.5	14.4	13.0	11.2	10.5	8.5	7.7	6.6	6.4	6.5

Note: Data is not seasonally adjusted and covers workers 16 years of age and older; (1) Figures cover the
Indianapolis-Carmel-Anderson, IN Metropolitan Statistical Area
Source: Bureau of Labor Statistics, Local Area Unemployment Statistics

Average Wages

Occupation	$/Hr.	Occupation	$/Hr.
Accountants and Auditors	37.20	Maintenance and Repair Workers	20.40
Automotive Mechanics	21.50	Marketing Managers	61.80
Bookkeepers	20.90	Network and Computer Systems Admin.	41.00
Carpenters	24.10	Nurses, Licensed Practical	23.40
Cashiers	11.30	Nurses, Registered	34.00
Computer Programmers	46.00	Nursing Assistants	14.70
Computer Systems Analysts	40.10	Office Clerks, General	18.00
Computer User Support Specialists	24.30	Physical Therapists	42.90
Construction Laborers	19.50	Physicians	125.00
Cooks, Restaurant	13.40	Plumbers, Pipefitters and Steamfitters	26.00
Customer Service Representatives	19.00	Police and Sheriff's Patrol Officers	31.20
Dentists	69.40	Postal Service Mail Carriers	25.50
Electricians	28.20	Real Estate Sales Agents	24.10
Engineers, Electrical	45.00	Retail Salespersons	15.10
Fast Food and Counter Workers	11.00	Sales Representatives, Technical/Scientific	58.60
Financial Managers	68.20	Secretaries, Exc. Legal/Medical/Executive	18.10
First-Line Supervisors of Office Workers	30.70	Security Guards	15.10
General and Operations Managers	59.90	Surgeons	83.70
Hairdressers/Cosmetologists	15.30	Teacher Assistants, Exc. Postsecondary*	13.10
Home Health and Personal Care Aides	12.20	Teachers, Secondary School, Exc. Sp. Ed.*	27.40
Janitors and Cleaners	13.90	Telemarketers	16.60
Landscaping/Groundskeeping Workers	16.30	Truck Drivers, Heavy/Tractor-Trailer	23.30
Lawyers	60.40	Truck Drivers, Light/Delivery Services	20.80
Maids and Housekeeping Cleaners	12.10	Waiters and Waitresses	12.60

Note: Wage data covers the Indianapolis-Carmel-Anderson, IN Metropolitan Statistical Area; (*) Hourly wages
were calculated from annual wage data based on a 40 hour work week; n/a not available.
Source: Bureau of Labor Statistics, Metro Area Occupational Employment & Wage Estimates, May 2020

Employment by Industry

Sector	MSA[1]		U.S.
	Number of Employees	Percent of Total	Percent of Total
Construction	58,600	5.5	5.1
Education and Health Services	162,200	15.2	16.3
Financial Activities	71,800	6.7	6.1
Government	136,300	12.7	15.2
Information	11,600	1.1	1.9
Leisure and Hospitality	91,600	8.6	9.0
Manufacturing	90,600	8.5	8.5
Mining and Logging	700	0.1	0.4
Other Services	38,300	3.6	3.8
Professional and Business Services	170,700	16.0	14.4
Retail Trade	104,800	9.8	10.9
Transportation, Warehousing, and Utilities	84,500	7.9	4.6
Wholesale Trade	47,900	4.5	3.9

Note: Figures are non-farm employment as of December 2020. Figures are not seasonally adjusted and include
workers 16 years of age and older; (1) Figures cover the Indianapolis-Carmel-Anderson, IN Metropolitan
Statistical Area
Source: Bureau of Labor Statistics, Current Employment Statistics, Employment, Hours, and Earnings

Employment by Occupation

Occupation Classification	City (%)	MSA[1] (%)	U.S. (%)
Management, Business, Science, and Arts	35.6	39.8	38.5
Natural Resources, Construction, and Maintenance	7.1	7.5	8.9
Production, Transportation, and Material Moving	17.6	14.8	13.2
Sales and Office	22.6	22.6	21.6
Service	17.0	15.4	17.8

Note: Figures cover employed civilians 16 years of age and older; (1) Figures cover the Indianapolis-Carmel-Anderson, IN Metropolitan Statistical Area
Source: U.S. Census Bureau, 2015-2019 American Community Survey 5-Year Estimates

Occupations with Greatest Projected Employment Growth: 2020 – 2022

Occupation[1]	2020 Employment	2022 Projected Employment	Numeric Employment Change	Percent Employment Change
Home Health and Personal Care Aides	43,510	45,760	2,250	5.2
Laborers and Freight, Stock, and Material Movers, Hand	92,910	94,760	1,850	2.0
Fast Food and Counter Workers	98,250	100,080	1,830	1.9
Registered Nurses	68,990	70,280	1,290	1.9
Cooks, Restaurant	28,220	29,360	1,140	4.0
Janitors and Cleaners, Except Maids and Housekeeping Cleaners	46,630	47,420	790	1.7
Software Developers and Software Quality Assurance Analysts and Testers	16,610	17,390	780	4.7
General and Operations Managers	51,930	52,600	670	1.3
Medical Assistants	16,740	17,390	650	3.9
Landscaping and Groundskeeping Workers	22,160	22,790	630	2.8

Note: Projections cover Indiana; (1) Sorted by numeric employment change
Source: www.projectionscentral.com, State Occupational Projections, 2020–2022 Short-Term Projections

Fastest-Growing Occupations: 2020 – 2022

Occupation[1]	2020 Employment	2022 Projected Employment	Numeric Employment Change	Percent Employment Change
Nurse Practitioners	5,630	6,210	580	10.3
Occupational Therapy Assistants	1,260	1,350	90	7.1
Physician Assistants	1,630	1,740	110	6.7
Physical Therapist Assistants	2,510	2,670	160	6.4
Medical and Health Services Managers	8,430	8,940	510	6.0
Information Security Analysts (SOC 2018)	1,240	1,310	70	5.6
Speech-Language Pathologists	2,700	2,850	150	5.6
Nonfarm Animal Caretakers	5,940	6,260	320	5.4
Veterinary Technologists and Technicians	2,070	2,180	110	5.3
Home Health and Personal Care Aides	43,510	45,760	2,250	5.2

Note: Projections cover Indiana; (1) Sorted by percent employment change and excludes occupations with numeric employment change less than 50
Source: www.projectionscentral.com, State Occupational Projections, 2020–2022 Short-Term Projections

TAXES

State Corporate Income Tax Rates

State	Tax Rate (%)	Income Brackets ($)	Num. of Brackets	Financial Institution Tax Rate (%)[a]	Federal Income Tax Ded.
Indiana	5.25 (i)	Flat rate	1	5.5	No

Note: Tax rates as of January 1, 2021; (a) Rates listed are the corporate income tax rate applied to financial institutions or excise taxes based on income. Some states have other taxes based upon the value of deposits or shares; (i) The Indiana Corporate tax rate is scheduled to decrease to 4.9% on July 1, 2021. Bank tax rate is scheduled to decrease to 5.0% on 1/1/22.
Source: Federation of Tax Administrators, State Corporate Income Tax Rates, January 1, 2021

State Individual Income Tax Rates

State	Tax Rate (%)	Income Brackets ($)	Personal Exemptions ($)			Standard Ded. ($)	
			Single	Married	Depend.	Single	Married
Indiana	3.23	Flat rate	1,000	2,000	2,500 (j)	–	–

Note: Tax rates as of January 1, 2021; Local- and county-level taxes are not included; Federal income tax is not deductible on state income tax returns; (j) In Indiana, includes an additional exemption of $1,500 for each dependent child.
Source: Federation of Tax Administrators, State Individual Income Tax Rates, January 1, 2021

218 Indianapolis, Indiana

Various State Sales and Excise Tax Rates

State	State Sales Tax (%)	Gasoline[1] (¢/gal.)	Cigarette[2] ($/pack)	Spirits[3] ($/gal.)	Wine[4] ($/gal.)	Beer[5] ($/gal.)	Recreational Marijuana (%)
Indiana	7	42.16	0.995	2.68	0.47	0.12	Not legal

Note: All tax rates as of January 1, 2021; (1) The American Petroleum Institute has developed a methodology for determining the average tax rate on a gallon of fuel. Rates may include any of the following: excise taxes, environmental fees, storage tank fees, other fees or taxes, general sales tax, and local taxes; (2) The federal excise tax of $1.0066 per pack and local taxes are not included; (3) Rates are those applicable to off-premise sales of 40% alcohol by volume (a.b.v.) distilled spirits in 750ml containers. Local excise taxes are excluded; (4) Rates are those applicable to off-premise sales of 11% a.b.v. non-carbonated wine in 750ml containers; (5) Rates are those applicable to off-premise sales of 4.7% a.b.v. beer in 12 ounce containers.
Source: Tax Foundation, 2021 Facts & Figures: How Does Your State Compare?

State Business Tax Climate Index Rankings

State	Overall Rank	Corporate Tax Rank	Individual Income Tax Rank	Sales Tax Rank	Property Tax Rank	Unemployment Insurance Tax Rank
Indiana	9	12	15	20	2	27

Note: The index is a measure of how each state's tax laws affect economic performance. The lower the rank, the more favorable a state's tax system is for business. States without a given tax are given a ranking of 1. The scores/rankings for the District of Columbia do not affect other states. The 2021 index represents the tax climate as of July 1, 2020.
Source: Tax Foundation, State Business Tax Climate Index 2021

TRANSPORTATION

Means of Transportation to Work

Area	Car/Truck/Van		Public Transportation			Bicycle	Walked	Other Means	Worked at Home
	Drove Alone	Car-pooled	Bus	Subway	Railroad				
City	82.0	9.2	1.8	0.0	0.0	0.5	1.9	1.1	3.5
MSA[1]	83.2	8.3	0.8	0.0	0.0	0.3	1.5	0.9	4.9
U.S.	76.3	9.0	2.4	1.9	0.6	0.5	2.7	1.4	5.2

Note: Figures are percentages and cover workers 16 years of age and older; (1) Figures cover the Indianapolis-Carmel-Anderson, IN Metropolitan Statistical Area
Source: U.S. Census Bureau, 2015-2019 American Community Survey 5-Year Estimates

Travel Time to Work

Area	Less Than 10 Minutes	10 to 19 Minutes	20 to 29 Minutes	30 to 44 Minutes	45 to 59 Minutes	60 to 89 Minutes	90 Minutes or More
City	9.7	30.0	29.9	22.1	4.3	2.5	1.5
MSA[1]	11.4	27.5	24.4	24.1	7.6	3.5	1.5
U.S.	12.2	28.4	20.8	20.8	8.3	6.4	2.9

Note: Note: Figures are percentages and include workers 16 years old and over; (1) Figures cover the Indianapolis-Carmel-Anderson, IN Metropolitan Statistical Area
Source: U.S. Census Bureau, 2015-2019 American Community Survey 5-Year Estimates

Key Congestion Measures

Measure	1982	1992	2002	2012	2017
Annual Hours of Delay, Total (000)	6,965	13,196	23,514	37,744	43,003
Annual Hours of Delay, Per Auto Commuter	18	29	40	43	48
Annual Congestion Cost, Total (million $)	53	140	319	687	801
Annual Congestion Cost, Per Auto Commuter ($)	295	385	535	673	743

Note: Covers the Indianapolis IN urban area
Source: Texas A&M Transportation Institute, 2019 Urban Mobility Report

Freeway Travel Time Index

Measure	1982	1987	1992	1997	2002	2007	2012	2017
Urban Area Index[1]	1.08	1.10	1.12	1.15	1.17	1.18	1.18	1.18
Urban Area Rank[1,2]	28	36	40	41	41	44	40	45

Note: Freeway Travel Time Index—the ratio of travel time in the peak period to the travel time at free-flow conditions. For example, a value of 1.30 indicates a 20-minute free-flow trip takes 26 minutes in the peak (20 minutes x 1.30 = 26 minutes); (1) Covers the Indianapolis IN urban area; (2) Rank is based on 101 larger urban areas (#1 = highest travel time index)
Source: Texas A&M Transportation Institute, 2019 Urban Mobility Report

Public Transportation

Agency Name / Mode of Transportation	Vehicles Operated in Maximum Service[1]	Annual Unlinked Passenger Trips[2] (in thous.)	Annual Passenger Miles[3] (in thous.)
Indianapolis and Marion County Public Transportation (IndyGo)			
Bus (directly operated)	138	8,531.0	38,897.4
Bus Rapid Transit (directly operated)	18	704.7	2,550.2
Demand Response (purchased transportation)	74	282.3	3,565.1

Note: (1) Number of revenue vehicles operated by the given mode and type of service to meet the annual maximum service requirement. This is the revenue vehicle count during the peak season of the year; on the week and day that maximum service is provided. Vehicles operated in maximum service (VOMS) exclude atypical days and one-time special events; (2) Number of passengers who boarded public transportation vehicles. Passengers are counted each time they board a vehicle no matter how many vehicles they use to travel from their origin to their destination. (3) Sum of the distances ridden by all passengers during the entire fiscal year.
Source: Federal Transit Administration, National Transit Database, 2019

Air Transportation

Airport Name and Code / Type of Service	Passenger Airlines[1]	Passenger Enplanements	Freight Carriers[2]	Freight (lbs)
Indianapolis International (IND)				
Domestic service (U.S. carriers - 2020)	30	1,983,924	15	1,046,329,932
International service (U.S. carriers - 2019)	8	59,080	3	64,677,223

Note: (1) Includes all U.S.-based major, minor and commuter airlines that carried at least one passenger during the year; (2) Includes all U.S.-based airlines and freight carriers that transported at least one pound of freight during the year.
Source: Bureau of Transportation Statistics, The Intermodal Transportation Database, Air Carriers: T-100 Domestic Market (U.S. Carriers), 2020; Bureau of Transportation Statistics, The Intermodal Transportation Database, Air Carriers: T-100 International Market (U.S. Carriers), 2019

BUSINESSES

Major Business Headquarters

Company Name	Industry	Rankings	
		Fortune[1]	Forbes[2]
Anthem	Health Care, Insurance and Managed Care	29	-
Eli Lilly	Pharmaceuticals	145	-
Simon Property Group	Real Estate	497	-

Note: (1) Companies that produce a 10-K are ranked 1 to 500 based on 2019 revenue; (2) All private companies with at least $2 billion in annual revenue through the end of their most current fiscal year are ranked 1 to 219; companies listed are headquartered in the city; dashes indicate no ranking
Source: Fortune, "Fortune 500," June/July 2020; Forbes, "America's Largest Private Companies," 2020

Fastest-Growing Businesses

According to *Inc.*, Indianapolis is home to two of America's 500 fastest-growing private companies: **DemandJump** (#219); **GenTech Associates** (#393). Criteria: must be an independent, privately-held, for-profit, U.S. corporation, proprietorship or partnership as of December 31, 2019; revenues must be at least $100,000 in 2016 and $2 million in 2019; must have four-year operating/sales history. *Inc., "America's 500 Fastest-Growing Private Companies," 2020*

Minority Business Opportunity

Indianapolis is home to two companies which are on the *Black Enterprise* Industrial/Service list (100 largest companies based on gross sales): **Harris & Ford** (#21); **Mays Chemical Co.** (#43). Criteria: operational in previous calendar year; at least 51% black-owned and manufactures/owns the product it sells or provides industrial or consumer services. Brokerages, real estate firms and firms that provide professional services are not eligible. *Black Enterprise, B.E. 100s, 2019*

Living Environment

COST OF LIVING

Cost of Living Index

Composite Index	Groceries	Housing	Utilities	Trans-portation	Health Care	Misc. Goods/ Services
91.2	93.3	79.6	101.8	91.6	87.2	97.3

Note: The Cost of Living Index measures regional differences in the cost of consumer goods and services, excluding taxes and non-consumer expenditures, for professional and managerial households in the top income quintile. It is based on more than 50,000 prices covering almost 60 different items for which prices are collected three times a year by chambers of commerce, economic development organizations or university applied economic centers in each participating urban area. The numbers shown should be read as a percentage above or below the national average of 100. For example, a value of 115.4 in the groceries column indicates that grocery prices are 15.4% higher than the national average. Small differences in the index numbers should not be interpreted as significant; Figures cover the Indianapolis IN urban area.
Source: The Council for Community and Economic Research, Cost of Living Index, 2020

Grocery Prices

Area[1]	T-Bone Steak ($/pound)	Frying Chicken ($/pound)	Whole Milk ($/half gal.)	Eggs ($/dozen)	Orange Juice ($/64 oz.)	Coffee ($/11.5 oz.)
City[2]	11.98	1.37	1.68	1.13	3.34	4.17
Avg.	11.78	1.39	2.05	1.47	3.57	4.34
Min.	8.03	0.94	1.03	0.74	2.94	3.02
Max.	15.86	2.65	4.31	3.77	5.44	8.69

*Note: (1) Values for the local area are compared with the average, minimum and maximum values for all 284 areas in the Cost of Living Index; (2) Figures cover the Indianapolis IN urban area; **T-Bone Steak** (price per pound); **Frying Chicken** (price per pound, whole fryer); **Whole Milk** (half gallon carton); **Eggs** (price per dozen, Grade A, large); **Orange Juice** (64 oz. Tropicana or Florida Natural); **Coffee** (11.5 oz. can, vacuum-packed, Maxwell House, Hills Bros, or Folgers).*
Source: The Council for Community and Economic Research, Cost of Living Index, 2020

Housing and Utility Costs

Area[1]	New Home Price ($)	Apartment Rent ($/month)	All Electric ($/month)	Part Electric ($/month)	Other Energy ($/month)	Telephone ($/month)
City[2]	278,798	1,039	-	104.81	67.00	184.30
Avg.	368,594	1,168	170.86	100.47	65.28	184.30
Min.	190,567	502	91.58	31.42	26.08	169.60
Max.	2,227,806	4,738	470.38	280.31	280.06	206.50

*Note: (1) Values for the local area are compared with the average, minimum and maximum values for all 284 areas in the Cost of Living Index; (2) Figures cover the Indianapolis IN urban area; **New Home Price** (2,400 sf living area, 8,000 sf lot, in urban area with full utilities); **Apartment Rent** (950 sf 2 bedroom/1.5 or 2 bath, unfurnished, excluding all utilities except water); **All Electric** (average monthly cost for an all-electric home); **Part Electric** (average monthly cost for a part-electric home); **Other Energy** (average monthly cost for natural gas, fuel oil, coal, wood, and any other forms of energy except electricity); **Telephone** (price includes the base monthly rate plus taxes and fees for three lines of mobile phone service).*
Source: The Council for Community and Economic Research, Cost of Living Index, 2020

Health Care, Transportation, and Other Costs

Area[1]	Doctor ($/visit)	Dentist ($/visit)	Optometrist ($/visit)	Gasoline ($/gallon)	Beauty Salon ($/visit)	Men's Shirt ($)
City[2]	88.25	92.92	65.90	2.12	37.63	42.14
Avg.	115.44	99.32	108.10	2.21	39.27	31.37
Min.	36.68	59.00	51.36	1.71	19.00	11.00
Max.	219.00	153.10	250.97	3.46	82.05	58.33

*Note: (1) Values for the local area are compared with the average, minimum and maximum values for all 284 areas in the Cost of Living Index; (2) Figures cover the Indianapolis IN urban area; **Doctor** (general practitioners routine exam of an established patient); **Dentist** (adult teeth cleaning and periodic oral examination); **Optometrist** (full vision eye exam for established adult patient); **Gasoline** (one gallon regular unleaded, national brand, including all taxes, cash price at self-service pump if available); **Beauty Salon** (woman's shampoo, trim, and blow-dry); **Men's Shirt** (cotton/polyester dress shirt, pinpoint weave, long sleeves).*
Source: The Council for Community and Economic Research, Cost of Living Index, 2020

HOUSING

Homeownership Rate

Area	2012 (%)	2013 (%)	2014 (%)	2015 (%)	2016 (%)	2017 (%)	2018 (%)	2019 (%)	2020 (%)
MSA[1]	67.1	67.5	66.9	64.6	63.9	63.9	64.3	66.2	70.0
U.S.	65.4	65.1	64.5	63.7	63.4	63.9	64.4	64.6	66.6

Note: (1) Figures cover the Indianapolis-Carmel-Anderson, IN Metropolitan Statistical Area
Source: U.S. Census Bureau, Housing Vacancies and Homeownership Annual Statistics: 2012-2020

House Price Index (HPI)

Area	National Ranking[2]	Quarterly Change (%)	One-Year Change (%)	Five-Year Change (%)	Since 1991Q1 (%)
MSA[1]	46	2.17	7.74	36.43	135.15
U.S.[3]	–	3.81	10.77	38.99	205.12

Note: The HPI is a weighted repeat sales index. It measures average price changes in repeat sales or refinancings on the same properties. This information is obtained by reviewing repeat mortgage transactions on single-family properties whose mortgages have been purchased or securitized by Fannie Mae or Freddie Mac since January 1975; (1) Figures cover the Indianapolis-Carmel-Anderson, IN Metropolitan Statistical Area; (2) Rankings are based on annual percentage change for all metro areas containing at least 15,000 transactions over the last 10 years and ranges from 1 to 253; (3) figures based on a weighted average of Census Division estimates using a seasonally adjusted, purchase-only index; all figures are for the period ending December 31, 2020
Source: Federal Housing Finance Agency, Change in Metropolitan Area House Price Indexes, April 7, 2021

Median Single-Family Home Prices

Area	2018	2019	2020p	Percent Change 2019 to 2020
MSA[1]	187.1	200.1	227.6	13.7
U.S. Average	261.6	274.6	299.9	9.2

Note: Figures are median sales prices of existing single-family homes in thousands of dollars; (p) preliminary; (1) Figures cover the Indianapolis-Carmel-Anderson, IN Metropolitan Statistical Area
Source: National Association of Realtors, Median Sales Price of Existing Single-Family Homes for Metropolitan Areas, 4th Quarter 2020

Qualifying Income Based on Median Sales Price of Existing Single-Family Homes

Area	With 5% Down ($)	With 10% Down ($)	With 20% Down ($)
MSA[1]	43,957	41,643	37,016
U.S. Average	59,266	56,147	49,908

Note: Figures are preliminary; Qualifying income is based on a mortgage rate of 2.81%. Monthly principal and interest payment is limited to 25% of income; (1) Figures cover the Indianapolis-Carmel-Anderson, IN Metropolitan Statistical Area
Source: National Association of Realtors, Qualifying Income Based on Median Sales Price of Existing Single-Family Homes for Metropolitan Areas, 4th Quarter 2020

Home Value Distribution

Area	Under $50,000	$50,000 -$99,999	$100,000 -$149,999	$150,000 -$199,999	$200,000 -$299,999	$300,000 -$499,999	$500,000 -$999,999	$1,000,000 or more
City	7.1	22.9	27.0	18.8	12.5	8.0	3.1	0.7
MSA[1]	5.6	16.1	22.3	19.0	18.5	13.4	4.4	0.8
U.S.	6.9	12.0	13.3	14.0	19.6	19.3	11.4	3.4

Note: Figures are percentages and cover owner-occupied housing units; (1) Figures cover the Indianapolis-Carmel-Anderson, IN Metropolitan Statistical Area
Source: U.S. Census Bureau, 2015-2019 American Community Survey 5-Year Estimates

Year Housing Structure Built

Area	2010 or Later	2000 -2009	1990 -1999	1980 -1989	1970 -1979	1960 -1969	1950 -1959	1940 -1949	Before 1940	Median Year
City	3.4	9.2	13.2	12.1	13.5	13.1	12.7	6.1	16.8	1971
MSA[1]	6.5	15.5	16.7	10.6	12.5	10.6	10.3	4.4	12.8	1979
U.S.	5.2	14.0	13.9	13.4	15.2	10.6	10.3	4.9	12.6	1978

Note: Figures are percentages except for Median Year; Note: (1) Figures cover the Indianapolis-Carmel-Anderson, IN Metropolitan Statistical Area
Source: U.S. Census Bureau, 2015-2019 American Community Survey 5-Year Estimates

Gross Monthly Rent

Area	Under $500	$500 -$999	$1,000 -$1,499	$1,500 -$1,999	$2,000 -$2,499	$2,500 -$2,999	$3,000 and up	Median ($)
City	6.2	58.7	28.2	5.3	1.0	0.2	0.3	892
MSA[1]	6.3	54.7	30.5	6.4	1.4	0.3	0.5	916
U.S.	9.4	36.2	30.0	14.0	5.6	2.4	2.4	1,062

Note: Figures are percentages except for Median; Gross rent is the contract rent plus the estimated average monthly cost of utilities (electricity, gas, and water and sewer) and fuels (oil, coal, kerosene, wood, etc.) if these are paid by the renter (or paid for the renter by someone else); (1) Figures cover the Indianapolis-Carmel-Anderson, IN Metropolitan Statistical Area
Source: U.S. Census Bureau, 2015-2019 American Community Survey 5-Year Estimates

HEALTH

Health Risk Factors

Category	MSA[1] (%)	U.S. (%)
Adults aged 18–64 who have any kind of health care coverage	88.5	87.3
Adults who reported being in good or better health	81.9	82.4
Adults who have been told they have high blood cholesterol	33.0	33.0
Adults who have been told they have high blood pressure	34.6	32.3
Adults who are current smokers	19.4	17.1
Adults who currently use E-cigarettes	6.3	4.6
Adults who currently use chewing tobacco, snuff, or snus	3.8	4.0
Adults who are heavy drinkers[2]	6.4	6.3
Adults who are binge drinkers[3]	17.1	17.4
Adults who are overweight (BMI 25.0 - 29.9)	34.3	35.3
Adults who are obese (BMI 30.0 - 99.8)	32.0	31.3
Adults who participated in any physical activities in the past month	71.6	74.4
Adults who always or nearly always wears a seat belt	93.8	94.3

Note: (1) Figures cover the Indianapolis-Carmel-Anderson, IN Metropolitan Statistical Area; (2) Heavy drinkers are classified as adult men having more than 14 drinks per week and adult women having more than 7 drinks per week; (3) Binge drinkers are classified as males having five or more drinks on one occasion or females having four or more drinks on one occasion
Source: Centers for Disease Control and Prevention, Behaviorial Risk Factor Surveillance System, SMART: Selected Metropolitan Area Risk Trends, 2017

Acute and Chronic Health Conditions

Category	MSA[1] (%)	U.S. (%)
Adults who have ever been told they had a heart attack	4.3	4.2
Adults who have ever been told they have angina or coronary heart disease	4.2	3.9
Adults who have ever been told they had a stroke	3.4	3.0
Adults who have ever been told they have asthma	14.8	14.2
Adults who have ever been told they have arthritis	25.6	24.9
Adults who have ever been told they have diabetes[2]	11.8	10.5
Adults who have ever been told they had skin cancer	6.6	6.2
Adults who have ever been told they had any other types of cancer	6.9	7.1
Adults who have ever been told they have COPD	7.2	6.5
Adults who have ever been told they have kidney disease	3.4	3.0
Adults who have ever been told they have a form of depression	22.6	20.5

Note: (1) Figures cover the Indianapolis-Carmel-Anderson, IN Metropolitan Statistical Area; (2) Figures do not include pregnancy-related, borderline, or pre-diabetes
Source: Centers for Disease Control and Prevention, Behaviorial Risk Factor Surveillance System, SMART: Selected Metropolitan Area Risk Trends, 2017

Health Screening and Vaccination Rates

Category	MSA[1] (%)	U.S. (%)
Adults aged 65+ who have had flu shot within the past year	59.1	60.7
Adults aged 65+ who have ever had a pneumonia vaccination	81.2	75.4
Adults who have ever been tested for HIV	39.3	36.1
Adults who have ever had the shingles or zoster vaccine?	28.3	28.9
Adults who have had their blood cholesterol checked within the last five years	85.3	85.9

Note: n/a not available; (1) Figures cover the Indianapolis-Carmel-Anderson, IN Metropolitan Statistical Area.
Source: Centers for Disease Control and Prevention, Behaviorial Risk Factor Surveillance System, SMART: Selected Metropolitan Area Risk Trends, 2017

Disability Status

Category	MSA[1] (%)	U.S. (%)
Adults who reported being deaf	5.1	6.7
Are you blind or have serious difficulty seeing, even when wearing glasses?	4.5	4.5
Are you limited in any way in any of your usual activities due of arthritis?	13.1	12.9
Do you have difficulty doing errands alone?	7.6	6.8
Do you have difficulty dressing or bathing?	3.7	3.6
Do you have serious difficulty concentrating/remembering/making decisions?	10.9	10.7
Do you have serious difficulty walking or climbing stairs?	12.6	13.6

Note: (1) Figures cover the Indianapolis-Carmel-Anderson, IN Metropolitan Statistical Area.
Source: Centers for Disease Control and Prevention, Behaviorial Risk Factor Surveillance System, SMART: Selected Metropolitan Area Risk Trends, 2017

Mortality Rates for the Top 10 Causes of Death in the U.S.

ICD-10[a] Sub-Chapter	ICD-10[a] Code	Age-Adjusted Mortality Rate[1] per 100,000 population	
		County[2]	U.S.
Malignant neoplasms	C00-C97	170.4	149.2
Ischaemic heart diseases	I20-I25	92.6	90.5
Other forms of heart disease	I30-I51	62.4	52.2
Chronic lower respiratory diseases	J40-J47	58.0	39.6
Other degenerative diseases of the nervous system	G30-G31	33.6	37.6
Cerebrovascular diseases	I60-I69	39.9	37.2
Other external causes of accidental injury	W00-X59	54.5	36.1
Organic, including symptomatic, mental disorders	F01-F09	36.4	29.4
Hypertensive diseases	I10-I15	29.4	24.1
Diabetes mellitus	E10-E14	26.0	21.5

Note: (a) ICD-10 = International Classification of Diseases 10th Revision; (1) Mortality rates are a three-year average covering 2017-2019; (2) Figures cover Marion County.
Source: Centers for Disease Control and Prevention, National Center for Health Statistics. Underlying Cause of Death 1999-2019 on CDC WONDER Online Database

Mortality Rates for Selected Causes of Death

ICD-10[a] Sub-Chapter	ICD-10[a] Code	Age-Adjusted Mortality Rate[1] per 100,000 population	
		County[2]	U.S.
Assault	X85-Y09	17.8	6.0
Diseases of the liver	K70-K76	17.8	14.4
Human immunodeficiency virus (HIV) disease	B20-B24	1.7	1.5
Influenza and pneumonia	J09-J18	10.8	13.8
Intentional self-harm	X60-X84	14.5	14.1
Malnutrition	E40-E46	4.2	2.3
Obesity and other hyperalimentation	E65-E68	1.8	2.1
Renal failure	N17-N19	19.0	12.6
Transport accidents	V01-V99	12.8	12.3
Viral hepatitis	B15-B19	1.6	1.2

Note: (a) ICD-10 = International Classification of Diseases 10th Revision; (1) Mortality rates are a three-year average covering 2017-2019; (2) Figures cover Marion County; Data are suppressed when the data meet the criteria for confidentiality constraints; Mortality rates are flagged as unreliable when the rate would be calculated with a numerator of 20 or less.
Source: Centers for Disease Control and Prevention, National Center for Health Statistics. Underlying Cause of Death 1999-2019 on CDC WONDER Online Database

Health Insurance Coverage

Area	With Health Insurance	With Private Health Insurance	With Public Health Insurance	Without Health Insurance	Population Under Age 19 Without Health Insurance
City	89.5	62.3	36.7	10.5	6.0
MSA[1]	91.9	71.6	31.0	8.1	5.3
U.S.	91.2	67.9	35.1	8.8	5.1

Note: Figures are percentages that cover the civilian noninstitutionalized population; (1) Figures cover the Indianapolis-Carmel-Anderson, IN Metropolitan Statistical Area
Source: U.S. Census Bureau, 2015-2019 American Community Survey 5-Year Estimates

Number of Medical Professionals

Area	MDs[3]	DOs[3,4]	Dentists	Podiatrists	Chiropractors	Optometrists
County[1] (number)	4,203	205	871	59	152	191
County[1] (rate[2])	438.4	21.4	90.3	6.1	15.8	19.8
U.S. (rate[2])	282.9	22.7	71.2	6.2	28.1	16.9

18097
Note: Data as of 2019 unless noted; (1) Data covers Marion County; (2) Rate per 100,000 population; (3) Data as of 2018 and includes all active, non-federal physicians; (4) Doctor of Osteopathic Medicine
Source: U.S. Department of Health and Human Services, Health Resources and Services Administration, Bureau of Health Professions, Area Resource File (ARF) 2019-2020

Best Hospitals

According to *U.S. News,* the Indianapolis-Carmel-Anderson, IN metro area is home to one of the best hospitals in the U.S.: **Indiana University Health Medical Center** (3 adult specialties and 10 pediatric specialties). The hospital listed was nationally ranked in at least one of 16 adult or 10 pediatric specialties. Only 134 hospitals nationwide were nationally ranked in one or more adult or pediatric specialty; this number increases to 178 counting specialized centers within hospitals. Twenty hospitals in the U.S. made the Honor Roll. The Best Hospitals Honor Roll takes both the national rankings and the procedure and condition ratings into account. Hospitals received points if they were nationally ranked in one of the 16 adult specialties—the higher they ranked, the more points they got—and how many ratings of "high performing" they earned in the 10 procedures and conditions. *U.S. News Online, "America's Best Hospitals 2020-21"*

According to *U.S. News,* the Indianapolis-Carmel-Anderson, IN metro area is home to one of the best children's hospitals in the U.S.: **Riley Hospital for Children at IU Health** (10 pediatric specialties). The hospital listed was highly ranked in at least one of 10 pediatric specialties. Eighty-eight children's hospitals in the U.S. were nationally ranked in at least one specialty. Hospitals received points for being ranked in a specialty, and the 10 hospitals with the most points across the 10 specialties make up the Honor Roll. *U.S. News Online, "America's Best Children's Hospitals 2020-21"*

EDUCATION

Public School District Statistics

District Name	Schls	Pupils	Pupil/ Teacher Ratio	Minority Pupils[1] (%)	Free Lunch Eligible[2] (%)	IEP[3] (%)
Franklin Township Com Sch Corp	10	9,654	20.1	29.7	30.4	19.1
Indiana Connections Academy	1	4,852	41.4	20.4	31.8	17.2
Indiana Virtual Pathways Academy	1	6,266	120.1	34.0	73.9	4.5
Indianapolis Public Schools	59	26,410	14.0	79.0	63.9	22.0
M S D Decatur Township	9	6,810	18.2	34.0	56.5	16.7
M S D Lawrence Township	17	16,035	20.1	77.9	54.8	13.8
M S D Pike Township	13	11,150	17.1	91.6	60.9	15.2
M S D Warren Township	18	12,188	22.7	77.8	65.7	16.8
M S D Washington Township	13	11,140	18.1	70.3	49.9	17.8
M S D Wayne Township	18	16,484	15.8	71.2	62.6	14.6
Perry Township Schools	17	16,610	19.3	55.9	57.3	15.8

Note: Table includes school districts with 2,000 or more students; (1) Percentage of students that are not non-Hispanic white; (2) Percentage of students that are eligible for the free lunch program; (3) Percentage of students that have an Individualized Education Program.
Source: U.S. Department of Education, National Center for Education Statistics, Common Core of Data, Local Education Agency (School District) Universe Survey: School Year 2018-2019; U.S. Department of Education, National Center for Education Statistics, Common Core of Data, Public Elementary/Secondary School Universe Survey: School Year 2018-2019

Best High Schools

According to *U.S. News,* Indianapolis is home to one of the top 500 high schools in the U.S.: **Herron High School** (#218). Nearly 18,000 public, magnet and charter schools were ranked based on their performance on state assessments and how well they prepare students for college. *U.S. News & World Report, "Best High Schools 2020"*

Highest Level of Education

Area	Less than H.S.	H.S. Diploma	Some College, No Deg.	Associate Degree	Bachelor's Degree	Master's Degree	Prof. School Degree	Doctorate Degree
City	14.2	27.9	19.4	7.6	20.0	7.6	2.1	1.1
MSA[1]	10.3	27.9	19.3	7.9	22.4	8.8	2.2	1.3
U.S.	12.0	27.0	20.4	8.5	19.8	8.8	2.1	1.4

Note: Figures cover persons age 25 and over; (1) Figures cover the Indianapolis-Carmel-Anderson, IN Metropolitan Statistical Area
Source: U.S. Census Bureau, 2015-2019 American Community Survey 5-Year Estimates

Educational Attainment by Race

Area	High School Graduate or Higher (%)					Bachelor's Degree or Higher (%)				
	Total	White	Black	Asian	Hisp.[2]	Total	White	Black	Asian	Hisp.[2]
City	85.8	88.0	84.6	76.2	57.3	30.9	36.0	18.2	47.1	12.5
MSA[1]	89.7	91.3	85.9	82.6	63.7	34.7	36.7	20.7	56.2	17.6
U.S.	88.0	89.9	86.0	87.1	68.7	32.1	33.5	21.6	54.3	16.4

Note: Figures shown cover persons 25 years old and over; (1) Figures cover the Indianapolis-Carmel-Anderson, IN Metropolitan Statistical Area; (2) People of Hispanic origin can be of any race
Source: U.S. Census Bureau, 2015-2019 American Community Survey 5-Year Estimates

School Enrollment by Grade and Control

Area	Preschool (%)		Kindergarten (%)		Grades 1 - 4 (%)		Grades 5 - 8 (%)		Grades 9 - 12 (%)	
	Public	Private	Public	Private	Public	Private	Public	Private	Public	Private
City	61.8	38.2	85.6	14.4	88.5	11.5	87.1	12.9	89.2	10.8
MSA[1]	53.8	46.2	87.2	12.8	89.5	10.5	89.2	10.8	89.2	10.8
U.S.	59.1	40.9	87.6	12.4	89.5	10.5	89.4	10.6	90.1	9.9

Note: Figures shown cover persons 3 years old and over; (1) Figures cover the Indianapolis-Carmel-Anderson, IN Metropolitan Statistical Area
Source: U.S. Census Bureau, 2015-2019 American Community Survey 5-Year Estimates

Higher Education

Four-Year Colleges			Two-Year Colleges			Medical Schools[1]	Law Schools[2]	Voc/ Tech[3]
Public	Private Non-profit	Private For-profit	Public	Private Non-profit	Private For-profit			
2	6	3	1	0	4	2	1	8

Note: Figures cover institutions located within the city limits and include main campuses only; (1) includes schools accredited by the Liaison Committee on Medical Education and the American Osteopathic Association's Commission on Osteopathic College Accreditation; (2) includes ABA-accredited schools, schools with provisional ABA accreditation, and state accredited schools; (3) includes all schools with programs that are less than 2 years.
Source: National Center for Education Statistics, Integrated Postsecondary Education System (IPEDS), 2019-20; Wikipedia, List of Medical Schools in the United States, accessed April 2, 2021; Wikipedia, List of Law Schools in the United States, accessed April 2, 2021

According to *U.S. News & World Report,* the Indianapolis-Carmel-Anderson, IN metro area is home to one of the top 200 national universities in the U.S.: **Indiana University-Purdue University—Indianapolis** (#196 tie). The indicators used to capture academic quality fall into a number of categories: assessment by administrators at peer institutions; retention of students; faculty resources; student selectivity; financial resources; alumni giving; high school counselor ratings of colleges; and graduation rate. *U.S. News & World Report, "America's Best Colleges 2021"*

According to *U.S. News & World Report,* the Indianapolis-Carmel-Anderson, IN metro area is home to one of the top 100 liberal arts colleges in the U.S.: **DePauw University** (#47 tie). The indicators used to capture academic quality fall into a number of categories: assessment by administrators at peer institutions; retention of students; faculty resources; student selectivity; financial resources; alumni giving; high school counselor ratings of colleges; and graduation rate. *U.S. News & World Report, "America's Best Colleges 2021"*

According to *U.S. News & World Report,* the Indianapolis-Carmel-Anderson, IN metro area is home to one of the top 75 medical schools for research in the U.S.: **Indiana University—Indianapolis** (#42 tie). The rankings are based on a weighted average of 11 measures of quality: quality assessment; peer assessment score; assessment score by residency directors; research activity; total research activity; average research activity per faculty member; student selectivity; median MCAT total score; median undergraduate GPA; acceptance rate; and faculty resources. *U.S. News & World Report, "America's Best Graduate Schools, Medical, 2022"*

EMPLOYERS

Major Employers

Company Name	Industry
Allison Transmission	Motor vehicle parts & accessories
Ameritech	Local and long distance telephone
Apple American Indiana	Restaurant/family chain
Automotive Components Holdings	Steering mechanisms, motor vehicle
Celadon Trucking Service	Trucking, except local
CNO Financial Group	Insurance services
Communikty Hospitals of Indiana	General medical & surgical hospitals
Conseco Variable Ins Company	Life insurance
Defense Finance and Accounting Services	Accounting, auditing, & bookkeeping
Eli Lilly and Company	Pharmaceutical preparations
Family & Social Svcs Admin	Administration of social and human resources
Federal Express Corporation	Air cargo carrier
GEICO	Auto insurance
Hewlett-Packard Co.	Computer terminals
Indiana Department of Transportation	Regulation administration of transportation
Indiana Police State	General government, state government
Liberty Mutual	Insurance services
Meridian Citizens Mutual Ins Company	Fire, marine & casualty insurance
Methodist Hospital	General medical & surgical hospitals
Navient	Financial services
Rolls Royce Corporation	Aircraft engines & engine parts
St. Vincent Hospital and Healthcare Ctr	General medical & surgical hospitals
The Health Hospital of Marion County	General medical & surgical hospitals
Trustees of indiana University	University
United States Postal Service	U.S. postal service

Note: Companies shown are located within the Indianapolis-Carmel-Anderson, IN Metropolitan Statistical Area.
Source: Hoovers.com; Wikipedia

Best Companies to Work For

Eli Lilly; Roche Diagnotics, headquartered in Indianapolis, are among the "100 Best Companies for Working Mothers." Criteria: paid time off and leaves; workforce profile; benefits; women's issues and advancement; flexible work; company culture and work life programs. *Working Mother, "100 Best Companies for Working Mothers," 2020*

Anthem; Eli Lilly, headquartered in Indianapolis, are among the "Best Companies for Multicultural Women." *Working Mother* selected 50 companies based on a detailed application completed by public and private firms based in the United States, excluding government agencies, companies in the human resources field and non-autonomous divisions. Companies supplied data about the hiring, pay, and promotion of multicultural employees. Applications focused on representation of multicultural women, recruitment, retention and advancement programs, and company culture. *Working Mother, "Best Companies for Multicultural Women," 2020*

NCAA, headquartered in Indianapolis, is among the "100 Best Places to Work in IT." To qualify, companies had to be U.S.-based organizations or be non-U.S.-based employers that met the following criteria: have a minimum of 300 total employees at a U.S. headquarters and a minimum of 30 IT employees in the U.S., with at least 50% of their IT employees based in the U.S. The best places to work were selected based on compensation, benefits, work/life balance, employee morale, and satisfaction with training and development programs. In addition, *InsiderPro* and *Computerworld* looked at retention efforts, programs for recognizing and rewarding outstanding performances, and benefits such as flextime, elder care and child care, and reimbursement for college tuition and the cost of pursuing technology certifications. *InsiderPro and Computerworld, "100 Best Places to Work in IT," 2020*

Anthem; Eli Lilly; Roche, headquartered in Indianapolis, are among the "Top Companies for Executive Women." This list is determined by organizations filling out an in-depth survey that measures female demographics at every level, but with an emphasis on women in senior corporate roles, with profit & loss (P&L) responsibility, and those earning in the top 20 percent of the organization. *Working Mother* defines P&L as having responsibility that involves monitoring the net income after expenses for a department or entire organization, with direct influence on how company resources are allocated. *Working Mother, "Top Companies for Executive Women," 2020+*

Eli Lilly; Roche Diagnostics, headquartered in Indianapolis, are among the "Best Companies for Dads." *Working Mother's* newest list recognizes the growing importance companies place on giving dads time off and support for their families. Rankings are determined by measuring gender-neutral or paternity leave offered, as well as actual time taken, phase-back policies, child- and dependent-care benefits, and corporate support groups for men and dads. *Working Mother, "Best Companies for Dads," 2020*

PUBLIC SAFETY

Crime Rate

Area	All Crimes	Violent Crimes				Property Crimes		
		Murder	Rape[3]	Robbery	Aggrav. Assault	Burglary	Larceny -Theft	Motor Vehicle Theft
City	5,402.0	18.5	77.1	351.1	826.1	893.6	2,671.9	563.7
Suburbs[1]	1,699.1	2.5	23.1	28.7	114.1	199.2	1,200.7	130.7
Metro[2]	3,285.3	9.3	46.3	166.8	419.1	496.7	1,830.9	316.2
U.S.	2,593.1	5.0	44.0	86.1	248.2	378.0	1,601.6	230.2

Note: Figures are crimes per 100,000 population; (1) All areas within the metro area that are located outside the city limits; (2) Figures cover the Indianapolis-Carmel-Anderson, IN Metropolitan Statistical Area; (3) All figures shown were reported using the revised Uniform Crime Reporting (UCR) definition of rape.
Source: FBI Uniform Crime Reports, 2018 (data for 2019 was not available)

Hate Crimes

Area	Number of Quarters Reported	Number of Incidents per Bias Motivation					
		Race/Ethnicity/ Ancestry	Religion	Sexual Orientation	Disability	Gender	Gender Identity
City	4	13	5	3	0	0	1
U.S.	4	3,963	1,521	1,195	157	69	198

Source: Federal Bureau of Investigation, Hate Crime Statistics 2019

Identity Theft Consumer Reports

Area	Reports	Reports per 100,000 Population	Rank[2]
MSA[1]	7,412	357	93
U.S.	1,387,615	423	-

Note: (1) Figures cover the Indianapolis-Carmel-Anderson, IN Metropolitan Statistical Area; (2) Rank ranges from 1 to 391 where 1 indicates greatest number of identity theft reports per 100,000 population
Source: Federal Trade Commission, Consumer Sentinel Network Data Book 2020

Fraud and Other Consumer Reports

Area	Reports	Reports per 100,000 Population	Rank[2]
MSA[1]	15,510	748	146
U.S.	3,385,133	1,031	-

Note: (1) Figures cover the Indianapolis-Carmel-Anderson, IN Metropolitan Statistical Area; (2) Rank ranges from 1 to 391 where 1 indicates greatest number of fraud and other consumer reports per 100,000 population
Source: Federal Trade Commission, Consumer Sentinel Network Data Book 2020

POLITICS

2020 Presidential Election Results

Area	Biden	Trump	Jorgensen	Hawkins	Other
Marion County	63.3	34.3	1.8	0.1	0.4
U.S.	51.3	46.8	1.2	0.3	0.5

Note: Results are percentages and may not add to 100% due to rounding
Source: Dave Leip's Atlas of U.S. Presidential Elections

SPORTS

Professional Sports Teams

Team Name	League	Year Established
Indiana Pacers	National Basketball Association (NBA)	1967
Indianapolis Colts	National Football League (NFL)	1984

Note: Includes teams located in the Indianapolis-Carmel-Anderson, IN Metropolitan Statistical Area.
Source: Wikipedia, Major Professional Sports Teams of the United States and Canada, April 6, 2021

CLIMATE

Average and Extreme Temperatures

Temperature	Jan	Feb	Mar	Apr	May	Jun	Jul	Aug	Sep	Oct	Nov	Dec	Yr.
Extreme High (°F)	71	72	85	89	93	102	104	102	100	90	81	74	104
Average High (°F)	35	39	50	63	73	82	85	84	78	66	51	39	62
Average Temp. (°F)	27	31	41	52	63	72	76	73	67	55	43	31	53
Average Low (°F)	18	22	31	41	52	61	65	63	55	44	33	23	42
Extreme Low (°F)	-22	-21	-7	18	28	39	48	41	34	20	-2	-23	-23

Note: Figures cover the years 1948-1990
Source: National Climatic Data Center, International Station Meteorological Climate Summary, 9/96

Average Precipitation/Snowfall/Humidity

Precip./Humidity	Jan	Feb	Mar	Apr	May	Jun	Jul	Aug	Sep	Oct	Nov	Dec	Yr.
Avg. Precip. (in.)	2.8	2.5	3.6	3.6	4.0	3.9	4.3	3.4	2.9	2.6	3.3	3.3	40.2
Avg. Snowfall (in.)	7	6	4	1	Tr	0	0	0	0	Tr	2	5	25
Avg. Rel. Hum. 7am (%)	81	81	79	77	79	80	84	87	87	85	83	83	82
Avg. Rel. Hum. 4pm (%)	68	64	59	53	53	53	56	56	53	53	63	70	59

Note: Figures cover the years 1948-1990; Tr = Trace amounts (<0.05 in. of rain; <0.5 in. of snow)
Source: National Climatic Data Center, International Station Meteorological Climate Summary, 9/96

Weather Conditions

Temperature			Daytime Sky			Precipitation		
10°F & below	32°F & below	90°F & above	Clear	Partly cloudy	Cloudy	0.01 inch or more precip.	0.1 inch or more snow/ice	Thunder-storms
19	119	19	83	128	154	127	24	43

Note: Figures are average number of days per year and cover the years 1948-1990
Source: National Climatic Data Center, International Station Meteorological Climate Summary, 9/96

HAZARDOUS WASTE

Superfund Sites

The Indianapolis-Carmel-Anderson, IN metro area is home to seven sites on the EPA's Superfund National Priorities List: **Broadway Street Corridor Groundwater Contamination** (final); **Envirochem Corp.** (final); **Keystone Corridor Ground Water Contamination** (final); **Northside Sanitary Landfill, Inc** (final); **Pike and Mulberry Streets PCE Plume** (final); **Reilly Tar & Chemical Corp. (Indianapolis Plant)** (final); **Riverside Ground Water Contamination** (proposed).
There are a total of 1,375 Superfund sites with a status of proposed or final on the list in the U.S. *U.S. Environmental Protection Agency, National Priorities List, April 7, 2021*

AIR QUALITY

Air Quality Trends: Ozone

	1990	1995	2000	2005	2010	2015	2016	2017	2018	2019
MSA[1]	0.084	0.094	0.081	0.080	0.069	0.064	0.070	0.067	0.073	0.067
U.S.	0.088	0.089	0.082	0.080	0.073	0.068	0.069	0.068	0.069	0.065

Note: (1) Data covers the Indianapolis-Carmel-Anderson, IN Metropolitan Statistical Area. The values shown are the composite ozone concentration averages among trend sites based on the highest fourth daily maximum 8-hour concentration in parts per million. These trends are based on sites having an adequate record of monitoring data during the trend period. Data from exceptional events are included.
Source: U.S. Environmental Protection Agency, Air Quality Monitoring Information, "Air Quality Trends by City, 1990-2019"

Air Quality Index

Area	Percent of Days when Air Quality was...[2]					AQI Statistics[2]	
	Good	Moderate	Unhealthy for Sensitive Groups	Unhealthy	Very Unhealthy	Maximum	Median
MSA[1]	40.5	58.1	1.4	0.0	0.0	119	54

Note: (1) Data covers the Indianapolis-Carmel-Anderson, IN Metropolitan Statistical Area; (2) Based on 365 days with AQI data in 2019. Air Quality Index (AQI) is an index for reporting daily air quality. EPA calculates the AQI for five major air pollutants regulated by the Clean Air Act: ground-level ozone, particle pollution (aka particulate matter), carbon monoxide, sulfur dioxide, and nitrogen dioxide. The AQI runs from 0 to 500. The higher the AQI value, the greater the level of air pollution and the greater the health concern. There are six AQI categories: "Good" AQI is between 0 and 50. Air quality is considered satisfactory; "Moderate" AQI is between 51 and 100. Air quality is acceptable; "Unhealthy for Sensitive Groups" When AQI values are between 101 and 150, members of sensitive groups may experience health effects; "Unhealthy" When AQI values are between 151 and 200 everyone may begin to experience health effects; "Very Unhealthy" AQI values between 201 and 300 trigger a health alert; "Hazardous" AQI values over 300 trigger warnings of emergency conditions (not shown).
Source: U.S. Environmental Protection Agency, Air Quality Index Report, 2019

Air Quality Index Pollutants

Area	Percent of Days when AQI Pollutant was...[2]					
	Carbon Monoxide	Nitrogen Dioxide	Ozone	Sulfur Dioxide	Particulate Matter 2.5	Particulate Matter 10
MSA[1]	0.0	0.0	34.2	1.1	64.7	0.0

Note: (1) Data covers the Indianapolis-Carmel-Anderson, IN Metropolitan Statistical Area; (2) Based on 365 days with AQI data in 2019. The Air Quality Index (AQI) is an index for reporting daily air quality. EPA calculates the AQI for five major air pollutants regulated by the Clean Air Act: ground-level ozone, particle pollution (also known as particulate matter), carbon monoxide, sulfur dioxide, and nitrogen dioxide. The AQI runs from 0 to 500. The higher the AQI value, the greater the level of air pollution and the greater the health concern.
Source: U.S. Environmental Protection Agency, Air Quality Index Report, 2019

Maximum Air Pollutant Concentrations: Particulate Matter, Ozone, CO and Lead

	Particulate Matter 10 (ug/m^3)	Particulate Matter 2.5 Wtd AM (ug/m^3)	Particulate Matter 2.5 24-Hr (ug/m^3)	Ozone (ppm)	Carbon Monoxide (ppm)	Lead (ug/m^3)
MSA[1] Level	57	12.6	27	0.067	2	n/a
NAAQS[2]	150	15	35	0.075	9	0.15
Met NAAQS[2]	Yes	Yes	Yes	Yes	Yes	n/a

Note: (1) Data covers the Indianapolis-Carmel-Anderson, IN Metropolitan Statistical Area; Data from exceptional events are included; (2) National Ambient Air Quality Standards; ppm = parts per million; ug/m^3 = micrograms per cubic meter; n/a not available.
Concentrations: Particulate Matter 10 (coarse particulate)—highest second maximum 24-hour concentration; Particulate Matter 2.5 Wtd AM (fine particulate)—highest weighted annual mean concentration; Particulate Matter 2.5 24-Hour (fine particulate)—highest 98th percentile 24-hour concentration; Ozone—highest fourth daily maximum 8-hour concentration; Carbon Monoxide—highest second maximum non-overlapping 8-hour concentration; Lead—maximum running 3-month average
Source: U.S. Environmental Protection Agency, Air Quality Monitoring Information, "Air Quality Statistics by City, 2019"

Maximum Air Pollutant Concentrations: Nitrogen Dioxide and Sulfur Dioxide

	Nitrogen Dioxide AM (ppb)	Nitrogen Dioxide 1-Hr (ppb)	Sulfur Dioxide AM (ppb)	Sulfur Dioxide 1-Hr (ppb)	Sulfur Dioxide 24-Hr (ppb)
MSA[1] Level	9	37	n/a	n/a	n/a
NAAQS[2]	53	100	30	75	140
Met NAAQS[2]	Yes	Yes	n/a	n/a	n/a

Note: (1) Data covers the Indianapolis-Carmel-Anderson, IN Metropolitan Statistical Area; Data from exceptional events are included; (2) National Ambient Air Quality Standards; ppm = parts per million; ug/m³ = micrograms per cubic meter; n/a not available.
Concentrations: Nitrogen Dioxide AM—highest arithmetic mean concentration; Nitrogen Dioxide 1-Hr—highest 98th percentile 1-hour daily maximum concentration; Sulfur Dioxide AM—highest annual mean concentration; Sulfur Dioxide 1-Hr—highest 99th percentile 1-hour daily maximum concentration; Sulfur Dioxide 24-Hr—highest second maximum 24-hour concentration
Source: U.S. Environmental Protection Agency, Air Quality Monitoring Information, "Air Quality Statistics by City, 2019"

Kansas City, Missouri

Background

Kansas City lies on the western boundary of the state. With its sister city of the same name on the other side of the Kansas/Missouri border, both Kansas Cities make up the greater Kansas City metropolitan area.

The territory of the Kansa (or Kaw) tribe received intermittent visits from white settlers during the eighteenth and nineteenth centuries. In 1724, a fort was built in the general vicinity, and in 1804, Meriwether Lewis and William Clark explored the area on behalf of President Jefferson for the Louisiana Purchase. In 1821, the site was a trading post established by François Chouteau, who established the American Fur Company.

A combination of gold prospectors passing through on their way to California, via steamboat, rail, and coach, and the migration of would-be settlers to California and the Southwest stimulated economic activity in Kansas City during the 1800s. Three major trails—Santa Fe, California, and Oregon—all originated in Jackson County.

It was in this solid Midwestern city that the jazz clubs on 18th Street and Vine gave birth to the careers of Charlie Parker and Count Basie. Today a new generation of artists upholds Kansas City's reputation for great jazz, performing in dozens of clubs featuring live jazz nightly.

Kansas City is also home to more than 100 barbecue restaurants in the metropolitan area and each fall hosts what it claims is the world's biggest barbecue contest.

As one might expect from the heartland of America, Kansas City's major industries are hard wheat and cattle. This is not how to picture all of Kansas City. Downtown Kansas City continues to transform its skyline by incorporating modern skyscrapers among the more traditional nineteenth-century buildings. The city boasts over 100 parks and playgrounds, suburban areas with an above-average living standard, European statues that line wide stretching boulevards, and a foreign trade zone where foreign countries can store their goods free of import duties. It offers something for everyone, from cultural and sporting events

> The Up-Down arcade bar has launched a rewards program to say "Thank You" for receiving the COVID-19 vaccine, offering 20 free game tokens to customers with a completed vaccine card.

to casinos and gaming, from hot barbecue to even hotter jazz. The Sprint Center arena is a world class home for major league sports, concerts, and events.

In 2019, the USDA relocated two federal research labs to the downtown area. The Stowers Institute for Medical Research is home to genetic studies that help explain the relationship between cellular and molecular changes and disease.

The Kansas City International Airport is a modern and growing transportation hub. A new airport terminal is scheduled to open in 2022. The historic Union Station's restored grand hall, with its 95-foot ceilings, shares space with the Science City Museum, theaters, restaurants, and shops.

The city maintains its own symphony, lyric opera and ballet. It boasts dozens of museums and art galleries, many with free admission. The Kansas City Zoo offers over 200 acres of exhibits, including the Orangutan Primadome and a penguin exhibit. Visitors to the Harley-Davidson plant can see how a "Hog" is built; other attractions include the Children's Peace Pavilion, the Kansas City Renaissance Festival, and Fiesta Hispana, a yearly celebration of Hispanic heritage.

The NFL's Kansas City Chiefs won Super Bowl LIV in 2020. Also in 2020, the Sprint Center was renamed T-Mobile Center, poised to host future NBA and NHL franchises.

The National Weather Service office at Kansas City is very near the geographical center of the United States. The gently rolling terrain with no topographic impediments allows a free sweep of air from all directions, often with conflict between warm, moist air from the Gulf of Mexico and cold polar air from the north. The summer season is characterized by warm days, mild nights, and moderate humidity. Winters are not severely cold, and sizeable snowfalls are rare.

Rankings

General Rankings

- In their seventh annual survey, Livability.com looked at data for more than 1,000 small to mid-sized U.S. cities to determine the rankings for Livability's "Top 100 Best Places to Live" in 2020. Kansas City ranked #90. Criteria: housing and affordable living; vibrant economy; social and civic engagement; education; demographics; health care options; transportation & infrastructure; and abundant lifestyle amenities. *Livability.com, "Top 100 Best Places to Live 2020" October 2020*

Business/Finance Rankings

- Based on metro area social media reviews, the employment opinion group Glassdoor surveyed 50 of the most populous U.S. metro areas and equally weighed cost of living, hiring opportunity, and job satisfaction to compose a list of "25 Best Cities for Jobs." Median pay and home value, and number of active job openings were also factored in. The Kansas City metro area was ranked #11 in overall job satisfaction. *www.glassdoor.com, "Best Cities for Jobs," February 25, 2020*

- The Brookings Institution ranked the nation's largest cities based on income inequality. Kansas City was ranked #77 (#1 = greatest inequality). Criteria: the "95/20 ratio," a figure representing the income at which a household earns more than 95 percent of all other households, divided by the income at which a household earns more than only 20 percent of all other households. *Brookings Institution, "Household Income Inequality, Largest Cities of 97 Large U.S. Metro Areas, 2014-2016," February 5, 2018*

- The Brookings Institution ranked the 100 largest metro areas in the U.S. based on income inequality. Kansas City was ranked #81 (#1 = greatest inequality). Criteria: the "95/20 ratio," a figure representing the income at which a household earns more than 95 percent of all other households, divided by the income at which a household earns more than only 20 percent of all other households. *Brookings Institution, "Household Income Inequality, 100 Largest U.S. Metro Areas, 2014-2016," February 5, 2018*

- Payscale.com ranked the 32 largest metro areas in terms of wage growth. The Kansas City metro area ranked #32. Criteria: private-sector and education professional wage growth between the 4th quarter of 2019 and the 4th quarter of 2020. *PayScale, "Wage Trends by Metro Area-4th Quarter," January 11, 2021*

- Kansas City was identified as one of America's most frugal metro areas by *Coupons.com.* The city ranked #18 out of 25. Criteria: digital coupon usage. *Coupons.com, "America's Most Frugal Cities of 2017," March 22, 2018*

- The Kansas City metro area appeared on the Milken Institute "2021 Best Performing Cities" list. Rank: #95 out of 200 large metro areas (population over 250,000). Criteria: job growth; wage and salary growth; high-tech output growth; housing affordability; household broadband access. *Milken Institute, "Best-Performing Cities 2021," February 16, 2021*

- *Forbes* ranked the 200 most populous metro areas to determine the nation's "Best Places for Business and Careers." The Kansas City metro area was ranked #51. Criteria: costs (business and living); job growth (past and projected); income growth; quality of life; educational attainment (college and high school); projected economic growth; cultural and leisure opportunities; workplace tolerance laws; net migration patterns. *Forbes, "The Best Places for Business and Careers 2019: Seattle Still On Top," October 30, 2019*

Culture/Performing Arts Rankings

- Kansas City was selected as one of the 25 best cities for moviemakers in North America. COVID-19 has spurred a quest for great film cities that offer more creative space, lower costs, and more great outdoors. NYC & LA were intentionally excluded. Criteria: longstanding reputations as film-friendly communities; efforts to deal with pandemic-specific challenges; and establish appropriate COVID-19 guidelines. The city was ranked #21. *MovieMaker Magazine, "Best Places to Live and Work as a Moviemaker, 2021," January 26, 2021*

Dating/Romance Rankings

- Kansas City was selected as one of the best cities for post grads by *Rent.com.* The city ranked among the top 10. Criteria: jobs per capita; unemployment rate; mean annual income; cost of living; rental inventory. *Rent.com, "Best Cities for College Grads," December 11, 2018*

Education Rankings

- Personal finance website *WalletHub* analyzed the 150 largest U.S. metropolitan statistical areas to determine where the most educated Americans are putting their degrees to work. Criteria: education levels; percentage of workers with degrees; education quality and attainment gap; public school quality rankings; quality and enrollment of each metro area's universities. Kansas City was ranked #33 (#1 = most educated city). *www.WalletHub.com, "Most and Least Educated Cities in America, " July 20, 2020*

- Kansas City was selected as one of America's most literate cities. The city ranked #20 out of the 84 largest U.S. cities. Criteria: number of booksellers; library resources; Internet resources; educational attainment; periodical publishing resources; newspaper circulation. *Central Connecticut State University, "America's Most Literate Cities, 2018," February 2019*

Food/Drink Rankings

- Kauffman Stadium was selected as one of PETA's "Top 10 Vegan-Friendly Ballparks" for 2019. The park ranked #9. *People for the Ethical Treatment of Animals, "Top 10 Vegan-Friendly Ballparks, " May 23, 2019*

Health/Fitness Rankings

- For each of the 100 largest cities in the United States, the American Fitness Index®, published by the American College of Sports Medicine and the Anthem Foundation, evaluated community infrastructure and 33 health behaviors including preventive health, levels of chronic disease conditions, pedestrian safety, air quality, and community resources that support physical activity. Kansas City ranked #79 for "community fitness." *americanfitnessindex.org, "2020 ACSM American Fitness Index Summary Report," July 14, 2020*

- Kansas City was identified as a "2021 Spring Allergy Capital." The area ranked #77 out of 100. Three groups of factors were used to identify the most challenging cities for people with allergies during the spring season: annual spring pollen levels; over the counter medicine use; number of board-certified allergy specialists. *Asthma and Allergy Foundation of America, "Spring Allergy Capitals 2021," February 23, 2021*

- Kansas City was identified as a "2021 Fall Allergy Capital." The area ranked #65 out of 100. Three groups of factors were used to identify the most challenging cities for people with allergies during the fall season: annual fall pollen levels; over the counter medicine use; number of board-certified allergy specialists. *Asthma and Allergy Foundation of America, "Fall Allergy Capitals 2021," February 23, 2021*

- Kansas City was identified as a "2019 Asthma Capital." The area ranked #41 out of the nation's 100 largest metropolitan areas. Criteria: estimated asthma prevalence; crude death rate from asthma; and ER visits due to asthma. Risk factors analyzed but not factored in the rankings: annual pollen score; annual air quality; public smoking laws; number of board-certified asthma specialists; rescue medication use; controller medication use; uninsured rate; poverty rate. *Asthma and Allergy Foundation of America, "Asthma Capitals 2019: The Most Challenging Places to Live With Asthma," May 7, 2019*

Real Estate Rankings

- FitSmallBusiness looked at 50 of the largest metropolitan areas in the U.S. to determine which metro was the best to start a real estate business. Data was compiled from such sources as: Zillow, Trulia, U.S. Census Bureau, and the Bureau of Labor Statistics. Criteria: location; inventory; annual wages; median sales price of homes; days on the market; median price cut percentage; and other factors that would influence real estate professional growth. The Kansas City metro area ranked #41. *fitsmallbusiness.com, "The Best Cities to Become a Real Estate Agent in 2018," January 30, 2018*

- *WalletHub* compared the most populated U.S. cities to determine which had the best markets for real estate agents. Kansas City ranked #118 where demand was high and pay was the best. Criteria: sales per agent; annual median wage for real-estate agents; monthly average starting salary for real estate agents; real estate job density and competition; unemployment rate; home turnover rate; housing-market health index; and other relevant metrics. *www.WalletHub.com, "2019's Best Places to Be a Real Estate Agent," April 24, 2019*

- Kansas City was ranked #121 out of 268 metro areas in terms of housing affordability in 2020 by the National Association of Home Builders (#1 = most affordable). Criteria: the share of homes sold in that area affordable to a family earning the local median income, based on standard mortgage underwriting criteria. *National Association of Home Builders®, NAHB-Wells Fargo Housing Opportunity Index, 4th Quarter 2020*

Safety Rankings

- To identify the most dangerous cities in America, 24/7 Wall Street focused on violent crime categories—murder, non-negligent manslaughter, rape, robbery, and aggravated assault—and property crime as reported in the FBI's 2019 annual Uniform Crime Report. Criteria also included median income from American Community Survey and unemployment figures from Bureau of Labor Statistics. For cities with populations over 100,000, Kansas City was ranked #8. *247wallst.com, "America's 50 Most Dangerous Cities" November 16, 2020*

- Allstate ranked the 200 largest cities in America in terms of driver safety. Kansas City ranked #37. Criteria: internal property damage claims over a two-year period from January 2016 to December 2017. The report helps increase the importance of safety and awareness behind the wheel. *Allstate, "Allstate America's Best Drivers Report, 2019" June 24, 2019*

- Kansas City was identified as one of the most dangerous cities in America by NeighborhoodScout. The city ranked #17 out of 100 (#1 = most dangerous). Criteria: number of violent crimes per 1,000 residents. The editors evaluated cities with 25,000 or more residents. *NeighborhoodScout.com, "2021 Top 100 Most Dangerous Cities in the U.S.," January 2, 2021*

- The National Insurance Crime Bureau ranked 384 metro areas in the U.S. in terms of per capita rates of vehicle theft. The Kansas City metro area ranked #25 (#1 = highest rate). Criteria: number of vehicle theft offenses per 100,000 inhabitants in 2019. *National Insurance Crime Bureau, "Hot Spots 2019," July 21, 2020*

Seniors/Retirement Rankings

- From its Best Cities for Successful Aging indexes, the Milken Institute generated rankings for metropolitan areas, weighing data in nine categories—health care, wellness, living arrangements, transportation and convenience, financial characteristics, education, employment, community engagement, and overall livability. The Kansas City metro area was ranked #26 overall in the large metro area category. *Milken Institute, "Best Cities for Successful Aging, 2017" March 14, 2017*

Women/Minorities Rankings

- Personal finance website *WalletHub* compared more than 180 U.S. cities across two key dimensions, "Hispanic Business-Friendliness" and "Hispanic Purchasing Power," to arrive at the most favorable conditions for Hispanic entrepreneurs. Kansas City was ranked #84 out of 182. Criteria includes: share of Hispanic-Owned Businesses; Hispanic entrepreneurship rate to median annual income of Hispanics; Small Business-Friendliness score; cost of living; and number of Hispanics with at least a bachelor's degree. *WalletHub.com, "2019's Best Cities for Hispanic Entrepreneurs," May 1, 2019*

Miscellaneous Rankings

- Kansas City was selected as a 2020 Digital Cities Survey winner. The city ranked #8 in the large city (250,000 to 499,999 population) category. The survey examined and assessed how city governments are utilizing technology to improve transparency, enhance cybersecurity, and respond to the pandemic. Survey questions focused on ten initiatives: cybersecurity, citizen experience, disaster recovery, business intelligence, IT personnel, data governance, collaboration, infrastructure modernization, cloud computing, and mobile applications. *Center for Digital Government, "2020 Digital Cities Survey," November 10, 2020*

- The watchdog site, Charity Navigator, conducted a study of charities in major markets both to analyze statistical differences in their financial, accountability, and transparency practices and to track year-to-year variations in individual philanthropic communities. The Kansas City metro area was ranked #9 among the 30 metro markets in the rating category of Overall Score. *www.charitynavigator.org, "2017 Metro Market Study," May 1, 2017*

- *WalletHub* compared the 150 most populated U.S. cities to determine their operating efficiency. A "Quality of City Services" score was constructed for each city and then divided by the total budget per capita to reveal which were managed the best. Kansas City ranked #110. Criteria: financial stability; economy; education; safety; health; infrastructure and pollution. *www.WalletHub.com, "2020's Best- & Worst-Run Cities in America," June 29, 2020*

- Kansas City was selected as one of "America's Friendliest Cities." The city ranked #16 in the "Friendliest" category. Respondents to an online survey were asked to rate 38 top urban destinations in the United States as to general friendliness, as well as manners, politeness and warm disposition. *Travel + Leisure, "America's Friendliest Cities," October 20, 2017*

Business Environment

DEMOGRAPHICS

Population Growth

Area	1990 Census	2000 Census	2010 Census	2019* Estimate	Population Growth (%)	
					1990-2019	2010-2019
City	434,967	441,545	459,787	486,404	11.8	5.8
MSA[1]	1,636,528	1,836,038	2,035,334	2,124,518	29.8	4.4
U.S.	248,709,873	281,421,906	308,745,538	324,697,795	30.6	5.2

Note: (1) Figures cover the Kansas City, MO-KS Metropolitan Statistical Area; (*) 2015-2019 5-year estimated population
Source: U.S. Census Bureau, 1990 Census, Census 2000, Census 2010, 2015-2019 American Community Survey 5-Year Estimates

Household Size

Area	Persons in Household (%)							Average Household Size
	One	Two	Three	Four	Five	Six	Seven or More	
City	37.0	31.9	13.0	10.1	5.0	1.9	1.2	2.40
MSA[1]	29.0	34.1	14.9	12.9	5.9	2.1	1.1	2.50
U.S.	27.9	33.9	15.6	12.9	6.0	2.3	1.4	2.60

Note: (1) Figures cover the Kansas City, MO-KS Metropolitan Statistical Area
Source: U.S. Census Bureau, 2015-2019 American Community Survey 5-Year Estimates

Race

Area	White Alone[2] (%)	Black Alone[2] (%)	Asian Alone[2] (%)	AIAN[3] Alone[2] (%)	NHOPI[4] Alone[2] (%)	Other Race Alone[2] (%)	Two or More Races (%)
City	60.9	28.2	2.7	0.4	0.2	4.0	3.6
MSA[1]	78.3	12.3	2.9	0.4	0.2	2.7	3.3
U.S.	72.5	12.7	5.5	0.8	0.2	4.9	3.3

Note: (1) Figures cover the Kansas City, MO-KS Metropolitan Statistical Area; (2) Alone is defined as not being in combination with one or more other races; (3) American Indian and Alaska Native; (4) Native Hawaiian and Other Pacific Islander
Source: U.S. Census Bureau, 2015-2019 American Community Survey 5-Year Estimates

Hispanic or Latino Origin

Area	Total (%)	Mexican (%)	Puerto Rican (%)	Cuban (%)	Other (%)
City	10.6	8.0	0.4	0.3	1.9
MSA[1]	9.0	6.9	0.4	0.2	1.6
U.S.	18.0	11.2	1.7	0.7	4.3

Note: Persons of Hispanic or Latino origin can be of any race; (1) Figures cover the Kansas City, MO-KS Metropolitan Statistical Area
Source: U.S. Census Bureau, 2015-2019 American Community Survey 5-Year Estimates

Ancestry

Area	German	Irish	English	American	Italian	Polish	French[2]	Scottish	Dutch
City	15.4	10.5	7.0	3.9	3.5	1.4	2.0	1.6	1.1
MSA[1]	20.7	12.3	9.7	5.4	3.3	1.5	2.3	1.9	1.4
U.S.	13.3	9.7	7.2	6.2	5.1	2.8	2.3	1.7	1.2

Note: Figures are the percentage of the total population reporting a particular ancestry. The nine most commonly reported ancestries in the U.S. are shown. Figures include multiple ancestries (e.g. if a person reported being Irish and Italian, they were included in both columns); (1) Figures cover the Kansas City, MO-KS Metropolitan Statistical Area; (2) Excludes Basque
Source: U.S. Census Bureau, 2015-2019 American Community Survey 5-Year Estimates

Foreign-born Population

Area	Percent of Population Born in								
	Any Foreign Country	Asia	Mexico	Europe	Caribbean	Central America[2]	South America	Africa	Canada
City	8.2	2.5	2.3	0.6	0.5	0.6	0.3	1.2	0.1
MSA[1]	6.9	2.3	2.0	0.6	0.2	0.6	0.3	0.7	0.1
U.S.	13.6	4.2	3.5	1.5	1.3	1.1	1.0	0.7	0.2

Note: (1) Figures cover the Kansas City, MO-KS Metropolitan Statistical Area; (2) Excludes Mexico.
Source: U.S. Census Bureau, 2015-2019 American Community Survey 5-Year Estimates

Marital Status

Area	Never Married	Now Married[2]	Separated	Widowed	Divorced
City	39.7	39.9	2.1	5.4	12.9
MSA[1]	30.5	50.4	1.6	5.4	12.0
U.S.	33.4	48.1	1.9	5.8	10.9

Note: Figures are percentages and cover the population 15 years of age and older; (1) Figures cover the Kansas City, MO-KS Metropolitan Statistical Area; (2) Excludes separated
Source: U.S. Census Bureau, 2015-2019 American Community Survey 5-Year Estimates

Disability by Age

Area	All Ages	Under 18 Years Old	18 to 64 Years Old	65 Years and Over
City	12.7	3.9	11.2	36.2
MSA[1]	12.1	3.9	10.2	34.2
U.S.	12.6	4.2	10.3	34.5

Note: Figures show percent of the civilian noninstitutionalized population that reported having a disability. Disability status is determined from six types of difficulty: vision, hearing, cognitive, ambulatory, self-care, and independent living. For children under 5 years old, hearing and vision difficulty are used to determine disability status. For children between the ages of 5 and 14, disability status is determined from hearing, vision, cognitive, ambulatory, and self-care difficulties. For people aged 15 years and older, they are considered to have a disability if they have difficulty with any one of the six difficulty types; Note: (1) Figures cover the Kansas City, MO-KS Metropolitan Statistical Area
Source: U.S. Census Bureau, 2015-2019 American Community Survey 5-Year Estimates

Age

Area	Percent of Population									Median Age
	Under Age 5	Age 5–19	Age 20–34	Age 35–44	Age 45–54	Age 55–64	Age 65–74	Age 75–84	Age 85+	
City	6.8	18.4	24.6	13.2	12.0	12.2	7.5	3.6	1.7	35.1
MSA[1]	6.5	20.0	20.0	13.2	12.9	12.8	8.5	4.2	1.8	37.4
U.S.	6.1	19.1	20.7	12.6	13.0	12.9	9.1	4.6	1.9	38.1

Note: (1) Figures cover the Kansas City, MO-KS Metropolitan Statistical Area
Source: U.S. Census Bureau, 2015-2019 American Community Survey 5-Year Estimates

Gender

Area	Males	Females	Males per 100 Females
City	235,974	250,430	94.2
MSA[1]	1,042,927	1,081,591	96.4
U.S.	159,886,919	164,810,876	97.0

Note: (1) Figures cover the Kansas City, MO-KS Metropolitan Statistical Area
Source: U.S. Census Bureau, 2015-2019 American Community Survey 5-Year Estimates

Religious Groups by Family

Area	Catholic	Baptist	Non-Den.	Methodist[2]	Lutheran	LDS[3]	Pentecostal	Presbyterian[4]	Muslim[5]	Judaism
MSA[1]	12.7	13.2	5.2	5.9	2.3	2.5	2.6	1.6	0.3	0.4
U.S.	19.1	9.3	4.0	4.0	2.3	2.0	1.9	1.6	0.8	0.7

Note: Figures are the number of adherents as a percentage of the total population; (1) Figures cover the Kansas City, MO-KS Metropolitan Statistical Area; (2) Methodist/Pietist; (3) Latter Day Saints; (4) Reformed; (5) Figures are estimates
Source: Association of Statisticians of American Religious Bodies, 2010 U.S. Religion Census: Religious Congregations & Membership Study

Religious Groups by Tradition

Area	Catholic	Evangelical Protestant	Mainline Protestant	Other Tradition	Black Protestant	Orthodox
MSA[1]	12.7	20.6	10.0	3.7	2.6	0.1
U.S.	19.1	16.2	7.3	4.3	1.6	0.3

Note: Figures are the number of adherents as a percentage of the total population; (1) Figures cover the Kansas City, MO-KS Metropolitan Statistical Area
Source: Association of Statisticians of American Religious Bodies, 2010 U.S. Religion Census: Religious Congregations & Membership Study

ECONOMY

Gross Metropolitan Product

Area	2017	2018	2019	2020	Rank[2]
MSA[1]	131.8	138.2	144.1	149.7	33

Note: Figures are in billions of dollars; (1) Figures cover the Kansas City, MO-KS Metropolitan Statistical Area; (2) Rank is based on 2018 data and ranges from 1 to 381
Source: U.S. Conference of Mayors, U.S. Metro Economies: GMP & Employment 2018-2020, September 2019

Economic Growth

Area	2015-17 (%)	2018 (%)	2019 (%)	2020 (%)	Rank[2]
MSA[1]	0.6	2.6	2.4	1.7	263
U.S.	1.9	2.9	2.3	2.1	—

Note: Figures are real gross metropolitan product (GMP) growth rates and represent average annual percent change; (1) Figures cover the Kansas City, MO-KS Metropolitan Statistical Area; (2) Rank is based on 2017 2-year average annual percent change and ranges from 1 to 381
Source: U.S. Conference of Mayors, U.S. Metro Economies: GMP & Employment 2018-2020, September 2019

Metropolitan Area Exports

Area	2014	2015	2016	2017	2018	2019	Rank[2]
MSA[1]	8,262.9	6,723.2	6,709.8	7,015.0	7,316.9	7,652.6	45

Note: Figures are in millions of dollars; (1) Figures cover the Kansas City, MO-KS Metropolitan Statistical Area; (2) Rank is based on 2019 data and ranges from 1 to 386
Source: U.S. Department of Commerce, International Trade Administration, Office of Trade and Economic Analysis, Industry and Analysis, Exports by Metropolitan Area, data extracted March 24, 2021

Building Permits

Area	Single-Family			Multi-Family			Total		
	2018	2019	Pct. Chg.	2018	2019	Pct. Chg.	2018	2019	Pct. Chg.
City	813	619	-23.9	1,341	879	-34.5	2,154	1,498	-30.5
MSA[1]	5,608	4,811	-14.2	4,660	4,536	-2.7	10,268	9,347	-9.0
U.S.	855,300	862,100	0.7	473,500	523,900	10.6	1,328,800	1,386,000	4.3

Note: (1) Figures cover the Kansas City, MO-KS Metropolitan Statistical Area; Figures represent new, privately-owned housing units authorized (unadjusted data); All permit data are based on estimates with imputation
Source: U.S. Census Bureau, Manufacturing, Mining, and Construction Statistics, Building Permits, 2018, 2019

Bankruptcy Filings

Area	Business Filings			Nonbusiness Filings		
	2019	2020	% Chg.	2019	2020	% Chg.
Jackson County	36	26	-27.8	2,080	1,394	-33.0
U.S.	22,780	21,655	-4.9	752,160	522,808	-30.5

Note: Business filings include Chapter 7, Chapter 9, Chapter 11, Chapter 12, Chapter 13, Chapter 15, and Section 304; Nonbusiness filings include Chapter 7, Chapter 11, and Chapter 13
Source: Administrative Office of the U.S. Courts, Business and Nonbusiness Bankruptcy, County Cases Commenced by Chapter of the Bankruptcy Code, During the 12-Month Period Ending December 31, 2019 and Business and Nonbusiness Bankruptcy, County Cases Commenced by Chapter of the Bankruptcy Code, During the 12-Month Period Ending December 31, 2020

Housing Vacancy Rates

Area	Gross Vacancy Rate[2] (%)			Year-Round Vacancy Rate[3] (%)			Rental Vacancy Rate[4] (%)			Homeowner Vacancy Rate[5] (%)		
	2018	2019	2020	2018	2019	2020	2018	2019	2020	2018	2019	2020
MSA[1]	7.8	8.9	9.1	7.7	8.7	9.1	7.9	10.0	9.4	1.2	1.4	0.7
U.S.	12.3	12.0	10.6	9.7	9.5	8.2	6.9	6.7	6.3	1.5	1.4	1.0

Note: (1) Figures cover the Kansas City, MO-KS Metropolitan Statistical Area; (2) The percentage of the total housing inventory that is vacant; (3) The percentage of the housing inventory (excluding seasonal units) that is year-round vacant; (4) The percentage of rental inventory that is vacant for rent; (5) The percentage of homeowner inventory that is vacant for sale
Source: U.S. Census Bureau, Housing Vacancies and Homeownership Annual Statistics: 2018, 2019, 2020

INCOME

Income

Area	Per Capita ($)	Median Household ($)	Average Household ($)
City	32,348	54,194	75,137
MSA[1]	35,761	66,632	89,308
U.S.	34,103	62,843	88,607

Note: (1) Figures cover the Kansas City, MO-KS Metropolitan Statistical Area
Source: U.S. Census Bureau, 2015-2019 American Community Survey 5-Year Estimates

Household Income Distribution

Area	Percent of Households Earning							
	Under $15,000	$15,000 -$24,999	$25,000 -$34,999	$35,000 -$49,999	$50,000 -$74,999	$75,000 -$99,999	$100,000 -$149,999	$150,000 and up
City	12.1	10.1	10.4	14.0	17.6	12.2	13.5	10.1
MSA[1]	8.4	7.8	8.7	12.6	17.8	13.9	16.8	14.1
U.S.	10.3	8.9	8.9	12.3	17.2	12.7	15.1	14.5

Note: (1) Figures cover the Kansas City, MO-KS Metropolitan Statistical Area
Source: U.S. Census Bureau, 2015-2019 American Community Survey 5-Year Estimates

Kansas City, Missouri

Poverty Rate

Area	All Ages	Under 18 Years Old	18 to 64 Years Old	65 Years and Over
City	16.1	24.3	14.5	9.6
MSA[1]	10.5	15.0	9.6	6.8
U.S.	13.4	18.5	12.6	9.3

Note: Figures are percentage of people whose income during the past 12 months was below the poverty level;
(1) Figures cover the Kansas City, MO-KS Metropolitan Statistical Area
Source: U.S. Census Bureau, 2015-2019 American Community Survey 5-Year Estimates

CITY FINANCES

City Government Finances

Component	2017 ($000)	2017 ($ per capita)
Total Revenues	2,092,987	4,403
Total Expenditures	1,985,767	4,177
Debt Outstanding	3,583,786	7,539
Cash and Securities[1]	4,926,544	10,363

Note: (1) Cash and security holdings of a government at the close of its fiscal year,
including those of its dependent agencies, utilities, and liquor stores.
Source: U.S. Census Bureau, State & Local Government Finances 2017

City Government Revenue by Source

Source	2017 ($000)	2017 ($ per capita)	2017 (%)
General Revenue			
From Federal Government	51,758	109	2.5
From State Government	40,071	84	1.9
From Local Governments	9,166	19	0.4
Taxes			
Property	123,811	260	5.9
Sales and Gross Receipts	325,898	686	15.6
Personal Income	236,637	498	11.3
Corporate Income	37,856	80	1.8
Motor Vehicle License	5,682	12	0.3
Other Taxes	9,145	19	0.4
Current Charges	433,529	912	20.7
Liquor Store	0	0	0.0
Utility	165,358	348	7.9
Employee Retirement	310,088	652	14.8

Source: U.S. Census Bureau, State & Local Government Finances 2017

City Government Expenditures by Function

Function	2017 ($000)	2017 ($ per capita)	2017 (%)
General Direct Expenditures			
Air Transportation	135,206	284	6.8
Corrections	0	0	0.0
Education	0	0	0.0
Employment Security Administration	0	0	0.0
Financial Administration	20,750	43	1.0
Fire Protection	154,793	325	7.8
General Public Buildings	0	0	0.0
Governmental Administration, Other	54,193	114	2.7
Health	54,541	114	2.7
Highways	73,823	155	3.7
Hospitals	0	0	0.0
Housing and Community Development	56,358	118	2.8
Interest on General Debt	77,995	164	3.9
Judicial and Legal	19,204	40	1.0
Libraries	0	0	0.0
Parking	4,067	8	0.2
Parks and Recreation	71,517	150	3.6
Police Protection	224,426	472	11.3
Public Welfare	11,749	24	0.6
Sewerage	221,655	466	11.2
Solid Waste Management	0	0	0.0
Veterans' Services	0	0	0.0
Liquor Store	0	0	0.0
Utility	99,477	209	5.0
Employee Retirement	175,405	369	8.8

Source: U.S. Census Bureau, State & Local Government Finances 2017

EMPLOYMENT

Labor Force and Employment

Area	Civilian Labor Force			Workers Employed		
	Dec. 2019	Dec. 2020	% Chg.	Dec. 2019	Dec. 2020	% Chg.
City	262,205	262,873	0.3	252,990	245,170	-3.1
MSA[1]	1,145,405	1,145,812	0.0	1,109,920	1,089,310	-1.9
U.S.	164,007,000	160,017,000	-2.4	158,504,000	149,613,000	-5.6

Note: Data is not seasonally adjusted and covers workers 16 years of age and older; (1) Figures cover the Kansas City, MO-KS Metropolitan Statistical Area
Source: Bureau of Labor Statistics, Local Area Unemployment Statistics

Unemployment Rate

Area	2020											
	Jan.	Feb.	Mar.	Apr.	May	Jun.	Jul.	Aug.	Sep.	Oct.	Nov.	Dec.
City	4.1	3.7	4.1	11.7	12.3	9.2	9.0	9.0	5.7	4.9	5.0	6.7
MSA[1]	3.7	3.4	3.5	11.3	10.8	7.8	7.6	7.3	5.0	4.4	4.4	4.9
U.S.	4.0	3.8	4.5	14.4	13.0	11.2	10.5	8.5	7.7	6.6	6.4	6.5

Note: Data is not seasonally adjusted and covers workers 16 years of age and older; (1) Figures cover the Kansas City, MO-KS Metropolitan Statistical Area
Source: Bureau of Labor Statistics, Local Area Unemployment Statistics

Average Wages

Occupation	$/Hr.	Occupation	$/Hr.
Accountants and Auditors	35.60	Maintenance and Repair Workers	21.10
Automotive Mechanics	23.50	Marketing Managers	69.30
Bookkeepers	20.60	Network and Computer Systems Admin.	41.40
Carpenters	28.50	Nurses, Licensed Practical	23.00
Cashiers	12.00	Nurses, Registered	33.80
Computer Programmers	42.00	Nursing Assistants	14.40
Computer Systems Analysts	37.00	Office Clerks, General	17.70
Computer User Support Specialists	26.40	Physical Therapists	42.60
Construction Laborers	22.20	Physicians	77.70
Cooks, Restaurant	13.90	Plumbers, Pipefitters and Steamfitters	32.50
Customer Service Representatives	18.70	Police and Sheriff's Patrol Officers	27.90
Dentists	82.20	Postal Service Mail Carriers	25.60
Electricians	29.30	Real Estate Sales Agents	25.20
Engineers, Electrical	44.00	Retail Salespersons	14.30
Fast Food and Counter Workers	11.80	Sales Representatives, Technical/Scientific	42.30
Financial Managers	72.10	Secretaries, Exc. Legal/Medical/Executive	18.80
First-Line Supervisors of Office Workers	30.60	Security Guards	19.80
General and Operations Managers	53.60	Surgeons	134.80
Hairdressers/Cosmetologists	15.00	Teacher Assistants, Exc. Postsecondary*	13.30
Home Health and Personal Care Aides	12.10	Teachers, Secondary School, Exc. Sp. Ed.*	26.10
Janitors and Cleaners	14.80	Telemarketers	15.90
Landscaping/Groundskeeping Workers	19.60	Truck Drivers, Heavy/Tractor-Trailer	24.20
Lawyers	62.20	Truck Drivers, Light/Delivery Services	18.50
Maids and Housekeeping Cleaners	12.00	Waiters and Waitresses	11.20

Note: Wage data covers the Kansas City, MO-KS Metropolitan Statistical Area; (*) Hourly wages were calculated from annual wage data based on a 40 hour work week; n/a not available.
Source: Bureau of Labor Statistics, Metro Area Occupational Employment & Wage Estimates, May 2020

Employment by Industry

Sector	MSA[1]		U.S.
	Number of Employees	Percent of Total	Percent of Total
Construction, Mining, and Logging	52,900	5.0	5.5
Education and Health Services	156,000	14.6	16.3
Financial Activities	79,700	7.5	6.1
Government	146,500	13.7	15.2
Information	14,500	1.4	1.9
Leisure and Hospitality	87,500	8.2	9.0
Manufacturing	79,500	7.4	8.5
Other Services	40,800	3.8	3.8
Professional and Business Services	189,200	17.7	14.4
Retail Trade	110,100	10.3	10.9
Transportation, Warehousing, and Utilities	61,400	5.8	4.6
Wholesale Trade	49,700	4.7	3.9

Note: Figures are non-farm employment as of December 2020. Figures are not seasonally adjusted and include workers 16 years of age and older; (1) Figures cover the Kansas City, MO-KS Metropolitan Statistical Area
Source: Bureau of Labor Statistics, Current Employment Statistics, Employment, Hours, and Earnings

Kansas City, Missouri

Employment by Occupation

Occupation Classification	City (%)	MSA[1] (%)	U.S. (%)
Management, Business, Science, and Arts	40.0	40.9	38.5
Natural Resources, Construction, and Maintenance	6.5	7.9	8.9
Production, Transportation, and Material Moving	13.6	13.2	13.2
Sales and Office	22.0	22.2	21.6
Service	17.9	15.8	17.8

Note: Figures cover employed civilians 16 years of age and older; (1) Figures cover the Kansas City, MO-KS Metropolitan Statistical Area
Source: U.S. Census Bureau, 2015-2019 American Community Survey 5-Year Estimates

Occupations with Greatest Projected Employment Growth: 2020 – 2022

Occupation[1]	2020 Employment	2022 Projected Employment	Numeric Employment Change	Percent Employment Change
Fast Food and Counter Workers	58,510	76,310	17,800	30.4
Waiters and Waitresses	34,100	45,340	11,240	33.0
Cooks, Restaurant	22,920	31,610	8,690	37.9
Retail Salespersons	69,100	75,980	6,880	10.0
Home Health and Personal Care Aides	74,240	79,340	5,100	6.9
First-Line Supervisors of Food Preparation and Serving Workers	14,100	18,230	4,130	29.3
General and Operations Managers	51,050	54,590	3,540	6.9
Registered Nurses	72,020	75,320	3,300	4.6
Cashiers	67,360	70,390	3,030	4.5
Maids and Housekeeping Cleaners	20,070	23,020	2,950	14.7

Note: Projections cover Missouri; (1) Sorted by numeric employment change
Source: www.projectionscentral.com, State Occupational Projections, 2020–2022 Short-Term Projections

Fastest-Growing Occupations: 2020 – 2022

Occupation[1]	2020 Employment	2022 Projected Employment	Numeric Employment Change	Percent Employment Change
Athletes and Sports Competitors	100	150	50	50.0
Ushers, Lobby Attendants, and Ticket Takers	2,170	3,240	1,070	49.3
Baggage Porters and Bellhops	160	230	70	43.8
Gaming Dealers	910	1,300	390	42.9
Film and Video Editors	220	310	90	40.9
Gaming Change Persons and Booth Cashiers	280	390	110	39.3
Hotel, Motel, and Resort Desk Clerks	2,810	3,910	1,100	39.1
Cooks, Restaurant	22,920	31,610	8,690	37.9
Hosts and Hostesses, Restaurant, Lounge, and Coffee Shop	5,350	7,140	1,790	33.5
Dancers	180	240	60	33.3

Note: Projections cover Missouri; (1) Sorted by percent employment change and excludes occupations with numeric employment change less than 50
Source: www.projectionscentral.com, State Occupational Projections, 2020–2022 Short-Term Projections

TAXES

State Corporate Income Tax Rates

State	Tax Rate (%)	Income Brackets ($)	Num. of Brackets	Financial Institution Tax Rate (%)[a]	Federal Income Tax Ded.
Missouri	4.0	Flat rate	1	7.0	Yes (j)

Note: Tax rates as of January 1, 2021; (a) Rates listed are the corporate income tax rate applied to financial institutions or excise taxes based on income. Some states have other taxes based upon the value of deposits or shares; (j) 50% of the federal income tax is deductible.
Source: Federation of Tax Administrators, State Corporate Income Tax Rates, January 1, 2021

State Individual Income Tax Rates

State	Tax Rate (%)	Income Brackets ($)	Personal Exemptions ($)			Standard Ded. ($)	
			Single	Married	Depend.	Single	Married
Missouri (a)	1.5 - 5.4	1,088 - 8,704	(d)	(d)	(d)	12,550	25,100 (d)

Note: Tax rates as of January 1, 2021; Local- and county-level taxes are not included; The deduction for federal income tax is limited to $5,000 for individuals and $10,000 for joint returns in Missouri and Montana, and to $6,500 for all filers in Oregon; (a) 19 states have statutory provision for automatically adjusting to the rate of inflation the dollar values of the income tax brackets, standard deductions, and/or personal exemptions. Michigan indexes the personal exemption only. Oregon does not index the income brackets for $125,000 and over; (d) These states use the personal exemption/standard deduction amounts provided in the federal Internal Revenue Code.
Source: Federation of Tax Administrators, State Individual Income Tax Rates, January 1, 2021

Various State Sales and Excise Tax Rates

State	State Sales Tax (%)	Gasoline[1] (¢/gal.)	Cigarette[2] ($/pack)	Spirits[3] ($/gal.)	Wine[4] ($/gal.)	Beer[5] ($/gal.)	Recreational Marijuana (%)
Missouri	4.225	17.42	0.17	2	0.42	0.06	Not legal

Note: All tax rates as of January 1, 2021; (1) The American Petroleum Institute has developed a methodology for determining the average tax rate on a gallon of fuel. Rates may include any of the following: excise taxes, environmental fees, storage tank fees, other fees or taxes, general sales tax, and local taxes; (2) The federal excise tax of $1.0066 per pack and local taxes are not included; (3) Rates are those applicable to off-premise sales of 40% alcohol by volume (a.b.v.) distilled spirits in 750ml containers. Local excise taxes are excluded; (4) Rates are those applicable to off-premise sales of 11% a.b.v. non-carbonated wine in 750ml containers; (5) Rates are those applicable to off-premise sales of 4.7% a.b.v. beer in 12 ounce containers.
Source: Tax Foundation, 2021 Facts & Figures: How Does Your State Compare?

State Business Tax Climate Index Rankings

State	Overall Rank	Corporate Tax Rank	Individual Income Tax Rank	Sales Tax Rank	Property Tax Rank	Unemployment Insurance Tax Rank
Missouri	12	3	23	24	8	7

Note: The index is a measure of how each state's tax laws affect economic performance. The lower the rank, the more favorable a state's tax system is for business. States without a given tax are given a ranking of 1. The scores/rankings for the District of Columbia do not affect other states. The 2021 index represents the tax climate as of July 1, 2020.
Source: Tax Foundation, State Business Tax Climate Index 2021

TRANSPORTATION

Means of Transportation to Work

Area	Car/Truck/Van		Public Transportation			Bicycle	Walked	Other Means	Worked at Home
	Drove Alone	Car-pooled	Bus	Subway	Railroad				
City	81.5	7.8	2.5	0.0	0.0	0.2	2.0	1.2	4.9
MSA[1]	83.7	7.8	0.8	0.0	0.0	0.1	1.2	0.9	5.4
U.S.	76.3	9.0	2.4	1.9	0.6	0.5	2.7	1.4	5.2

Note: Figures are percentages and cover workers 16 years of age and older; (1) Figures cover the Kansas City, MO-KS Metropolitan Statistical Area
Source: U.S. Census Bureau, 2015-2019 American Community Survey 5-Year Estimates

Travel Time to Work

Area	Less Than 10 Minutes	10 to 19 Minutes	20 to 29 Minutes	30 to 44 Minutes	45 to 59 Minutes	60 to 89 Minutes	90 Minutes or More
City	11.4	33.4	28.1	20.0	4.5	1.6	1.1
MSA[1]	12.2	30.7	25.2	21.7	6.6	2.6	1.1
U.S.	12.2	28.4	20.8	20.8	8.3	6.4	2.9

Note: Note: Figures are percentages and include workers 16 years old and over; (1) Figures cover the Kansas City, MO-KS Metropolitan Statistical Area
Source: U.S. Census Bureau, 2015-2019 American Community Survey 5-Year Estimates

Key Congestion Measures

Measure	1982	1992	2002	2012	2017
Annual Hours of Delay, Total (000)	6,319	18,760	32,336	43,434	48,328
Annual Hours of Delay, Per Auto Commuter	11	28	35	42	47
Annual Congestion Cost, Total (million $)	48	197	436	775	889
Annual Congestion Cost, Per Auto Commuter ($)	245	501	673	709	764

Note: Covers the Kansas City MO-KS urban area
Source: Texas A&M Transportation Institute, 2019 Urban Mobility Report

Freeway Travel Time Index

Measure	1982	1987	1992	1997	2002	2007	2012	2017
Urban Area Index[1]	1.04	1.08	1.11	1.12	1.14	1.14	1.15	1.15
Urban Area Rank[1,2]	61	44	49	69	69	80	71	71

Note: Freeway Travel Time Index—the ratio of travel time in the peak period to the travel time at free-flow conditions. For example, a value of 1.30 indicates a 20-minute free-flow trip takes 26 minutes in the peak (20 minutes x 1.30 = 26 minutes); (1) Covers the Kansas City MO-KS urban area; (2) Rank is based on 101 larger urban areas (#1 = highest travel time index)
Source: Texas A&M Transportation Institute, 2019 Urban Mobility Report

Public Transportation

Agency Name / Mode of Transportation	Vehicles Operated in Maximum Service[1]	Annual Unlinked Passenger Trips[2] (in thous.)	Annual Passenger Miles[3] (in thous.)
Kansas City Area Transportation Authority (KCATA)			
Bus (directly operated)	160	10,867.9	40,427.6
Bus Rapid Transit (directly operated)	11	1,109.6	2,903.9
Demand Response (directly operated)	9	66.7	270.5
Demand Response (purchased transportation)	56	204.2	1,566.2
Demand Response Taxi (purchased transportation)	45	103.1	587.6
Vanpool (purchased transportation)	36	57.8	1,987.7

*Note: (1) Number of revenue vehicles operated by the given mode and type of service to meet the annual maximum service requirement. This is the revenue vehicle count during the peak season of the year; on the week and day that maximum service is provided. Vehicles operated in maximum service (VOMS) exclude atypical days and one-time special events; (2) Number of passengers who boarded public transportation vehicles. Passengers are counted each time they board a vehicle no matter how many vehicles they use to travel from their origin to their destination. (3) Sum of the distances ridden by all passengers during the entire fiscal year.
Source: Federal Transit Administration, National Transit Database, 2019*

Air Transportation

Airport Name and Code / Type of Service	Passenger Airlines[1]	Passenger Enplanements	Freight Carriers[2]	Freight (lbs)
Kansas City International (MCI)				
Domestic service (U.S. carriers - 2020)	22	2,161,397	16	106,285,929
International service (U.S. carriers - 2019)	6	15,838	4	1,099,354

*Note: (1) Includes all U.S.-based major, minor and commuter airlines that carried at least one passenger during the year; (2) Includes all U.S.-based airlines and freight carriers that transported at least one pound of freight during the year.
Source: Bureau of Transportation Statistics, The Intermodal Transportation Database, Air Carriers: T-100 Domestic Market (U.S. Carriers), 2020; Bureau of Transportation Statistics, The Intermodal Transportation Database, Air Carriers: T-100 International Market (U.S. Carriers), 2019*

BUSINESSES

Major Business Headquarters

Company Name	Industry	Rankings	
		Fortune[1]	Forbes[2]
Hallmark Cards	Media	-	110
JE Dunn Construction Group	Construction	-	105

*Note: (1) Companies that produce a 10-K are ranked 1 to 500 based on 2019 revenue; (2) All private companies with at least $2 billion in annual revenue through the end of their most current fiscal year are ranked 1 to 219; companies listed are headquartered in the city; dashes indicate no ranking
Source: Fortune, "Fortune 500," June/July 2020; Forbes, "America's Largest Private Companies," 2020*

Fastest-Growing Businesses

According to *Inc.*, Kansas City is home to three of America's 500 fastest-growing private companies: **Amply Media** (#59); **RisingSun EPC** (#169); **Conexon** (#325). Criteria: must be an independent, privately-held, for-profit, U.S. corporation, proprietorship or partnership as of December 31, 2019; revenues must be at least $100,000 in 2016 and $2 million in 2019; must have four-year operating/sales history. *Inc., "America's 500 Fastest-Growing Private Companies," 2020*

Living Environment

COST OF LIVING

Cost of Living Index

Composite Index	Groceries	Housing	Utilities	Trans-portation	Health Care	Misc. Goods/Services
95.3	93.8	88.0	98.1	92.9	100.9	100.8

Note: The Cost of Living Index measures regional differences in the cost of consumer goods and services, excluding taxes and non-consumer expenditures, for professional and managerial households in the top income quintile. It is based on more than 50,000 prices covering almost 60 different items for which prices are collected three times a year by chambers of commerce, economic development organizations or university applied economic centers in each participating urban area. The numbers shown should be read as a percentage above or below the national average of 100. For example, a value of 115.4 in the groceries column indicates that grocery prices are 15.4% higher than the national average. Small differences in the index numbers should not be interpreted as significant; Figures cover the Kansas City MO-KS urban area.
Source: The Council for Community and Economic Research, Cost of Living Index, 2020

Grocery Prices

Area[1]	T-Bone Steak ($/pound)	Frying Chicken ($/pound)	Whole Milk ($/half gal.)	Eggs ($/dozen)	Orange Juice ($/64 oz.)	Coffee ($/11.5 oz.)
City[2]	11.83	1.92	1.87	1.17	3.22	3.44
Avg.	11.78	1.39	2.05	1.47	3.57	4.34
Min.	8.03	0.94	1.03	0.74	2.94	3.02
Max.	15.86	2.65	4.31	3.77	5.44	8.69

Note: (1) Values for the local area are compared with the average, minimum and maximum values for all 284 areas in the Cost of Living Index; (2) Figures cover the Kansas City MO-KS urban area; T-Bone Steak (price per pound); Frying Chicken (price per pound, whole fryer); Whole Milk (half gallon carton); Eggs (price per dozen, Grade A, large); Orange Juice (64 oz. Tropicana or Florida Natural); Coffee (11.5 oz. can, vacuum-packed, Maxwell House, Hills Bros, or Folgers).
Source: The Council for Community and Economic Research, Cost of Living Index, 2020

Housing and Utility Costs

Area[1]	New Home Price ($)	Apartment Rent ($/month)	All Electric ($/month)	Part Electric ($/month)	Other Energy ($/month)	Telephone ($/month)
City[2]	299,164	1,207	-	96.98	60.15	189.70
Avg.	368,594	1,168	170.86	100.47	65.28	184.30
Min.	190,567	502	91.58	31.42	26.08	169.60
Max.	2,227,806	4,738	470.38	280.31	280.06	206.50

Note: (1) Values for the local area are compared with the average, minimum and maximum values for all 284 areas in the Cost of Living Index; (2) Figures cover the Kansas City MO-KS urban area; New Home Price (2,400 sf living area, 8,000 sf lot, in urban area with full utilities); Apartment Rent (950 sf 2 bedroom/1.5 or 2 bath, unfurnished, excluding all utilities except water); All Electric (average monthly cost for an all-electric home); Part Electric (average monthly cost for a part-electric home); Other Energy (average monthly cost for natural gas, fuel oil, coal, wood, and any other forms of energy except electricity); Telephone (price includes the base monthly rate plus taxes and fees for three lines of mobile phone service).
Source: The Council for Community and Economic Research, Cost of Living Index, 2020

Health Care, Transportation, and Other Costs

Area[1]	Doctor ($/visit)	Dentist ($/visit)	Optometrist ($/visit)	Gasoline ($/gallon)	Beauty Salon ($/visit)	Men's Shirt ($)
City[2]	108.18	107.03	106.75	2.02	38.27	33.28
Avg.	115.44	99.32	108.10	2.21	39.27	31.37
Min.	36.68	59.00	51.36	1.71	19.00	11.00
Max.	219.00	153.10	250.97	3.46	82.05	58.33

Note: (1) Values for the local area are compared with the average, minimum and maximum values for all 284 areas in the Cost of Living Index; (2) Figures cover the Kansas City MO-KS urban area; Doctor (general practitioners routine exam of an established patient); Dentist (adult teeth cleaning and periodic oral examination); Optometrist (full vision eye exam for established adult patient); Gasoline (one gallon regular unleaded, national brand, including all taxes, cash price at self-service pump if available); Beauty Salon (woman's shampoo, trim, and blow-dry); Men's Shirt (cotton/polyester dress shirt, pinpoint weave, long sleeves).
Source: The Council for Community and Economic Research, Cost of Living Index, 2020

HOUSING

Homeownership Rate

Area	2012 (%)	2013 (%)	2014 (%)	2015 (%)	2016 (%)	2017 (%)	2018 (%)	2019 (%)	2020 (%)
MSA[1]	65.1	65.6	66.1	65.0	62.4	62.4	64.3	65.0	66.7
U.S.	65.4	65.1	64.5	63.7	63.4	63.9	64.4	64.6	66.6

Note: (1) Figures cover the Kansas City, MO-KS Metropolitan Statistical Area
Source: U.S. Census Bureau, Housing Vacancies and Homeownership Annual Statistics: 2012-2020

House Price Index (HPI)

Area	National Ranking[2]	Quarterly Change (%)	One-Year Change (%)	Five-Year Change (%)	Since 1991Q1 (%)
MSA[1]	75	2.00	7.29	37.81	175.77
U.S.[3]	–	3.81	10.77	38.99	205.12

Note: The HPI is a weighted repeat sales index. It measures average price changes in repeat sales or refinancings on the same properties. This information is obtained by reviewing repeat mortgage transactions on single-family properties whose mortgages have been purchased or securitized by Fannie Mae or Freddie Mac since January 1975; (1) Figures cover the Kansas City, MO-KS Metropolitan Statistical Area; (2) Rankings are based on annual percentage change for all metro areas containing at least 15,000 transactions over the last 10 years and ranges from 1 to 253; (3) figures based on a weighted average of Census Division estimates using a seasonally adjusted, purchase-only index; all figures are for the period ending December 31, 2020
Source: Federal Housing Finance Agency, Change in Metropolitan Area House Price Indexes, April 7, 2021

Median Single-Family Home Prices

Area	2018	2019	2020p	Percent Change 2019 to 2020
MSA[1]	206.5	219.4	237.4	8.2
U.S. Average	261.6	274.6	299.9	9.2

Note: Figures are median sales prices of existing single-family homes in thousands of dollars; (p) preliminary; (1) Figures cover the Kansas City, MO-KS Metropolitan Statistical Area
Source: National Association of Realtors, Median Sales Price of Existing Single-Family Homes for Metropolitan Areas, 4th Quarter 2020

Qualifying Income Based on Median Sales Price of Existing Single-Family Homes

Area	With 5% Down ($)	With 10% Down ($)	With 20% Down ($)
MSA[1]	47,002	44,528	39,580
U.S. Average	59,266	56,147	49,908

Note: Figures are preliminary; Qualifying income is based on a mortgage rate of 2.81%. Monthly principal and interest payment is limited to 25% of income; (1) Figures cover the Kansas City, MO-KS Metropolitan Statistical Area
Source: National Association of Realtors, Qualifying Income Based on Median Sales Price of Existing Single-Family Homes for Metropolitan Areas, 4th Quarter 2020

Home Value Distribution

Area	Under $50,000	$50,000 -$99,999	$100,000 -$149,999	$150,000 -$199,999	$200,000 -$299,999	$300,000 -$499,999	$500,000 -$999,999	$1,000,000 or more
City	11.2	17.4	19.4	18.4	18.5	10.8	3.6	0.7
MSA[1]	6.2	12.8	17.6	18.7	22.7	16.1	5.0	0.9
U.S.	6.9	12.0	13.3	14.0	19.6	19.3	11.4	3.4

Note: Figures are percentages and cover owner-occupied housing units; (1) Figures cover the Kansas City, MO-KS Metropolitan Statistical Area
Source: U.S. Census Bureau, 2015-2019 American Community Survey 5-Year Estimates

Year Housing Structure Built

Area	2010 or Later	2000 -2009	1990 -1999	1980 -1989	1970 -1979	1960 -1969	1950 -1959	1940 -1949	Before 1940	Median Year
City	4.6	9.9	9.3	8.6	12.0	12.7	14.3	6.3	22.1	1966
MSA[1]	4.8	13.7	14.5	12.3	15.4	11.6	11.4	4.4	11.8	1977
U.S.	5.2	14.0	13.9	13.4	15.2	10.6	10.3	4.9	12.6	1978

Note: Figures are percentages except for Median Year; Note: (1) Figures cover the Kansas City, MO-KS Metropolitan Statistical Area
Source: U.S. Census Bureau, 2015-2019 American Community Survey 5-Year Estimates

Gross Monthly Rent

Area	Under $500	$500 -$999	$1,000 -$1,499	$1,500 -$1,999	$2,000 -$2,499	$2,500 -$2,999	$3,000 and up	Median ($)
City	8.7	48.0	33.8	7.2	1.5	0.5	0.4	941
MSA[1]	8.2	46.4	34.4	8.0	2.0	0.5	0.6	961
U.S.	9.4	36.2	30.0	14.0	5.6	2.4	2.4	1,062

Note: Figures are percentages except for Median; Gross rent is the contract rent plus the estimated average monthly cost of utilities (electricity, gas, and water and sewer) and fuels (oil, coal, kerosene, wood, etc.) if these are paid by the renter (or paid for the renter by someone else); (1) Figures cover the Kansas City, MO-KS Metropolitan Statistical Area
Source: U.S. Census Bureau, 2015-2019 American Community Survey 5-Year Estimates

HEALTH

Health Risk Factors

Category	MSA[1] (%)	U.S. (%)
Adults aged 18–64 who have any kind of health care coverage	85.0	87.3
Adults who reported being in good or better health	85.8	82.4
Adults who have been told they have high blood cholesterol	34.1	33.0
Adults who have been told they have high blood pressure	29.6	32.3
Adults who are current smokers	17.1	17.1
Adults who currently use E-cigarettes	4.5	4.6
Adults who currently use chewing tobacco, snuff, or snus	4.0	4.0
Adults who are heavy drinkers[2]	6.0	6.3
Adults who are binge drinkers[3]	20.7	17.4
Adults who are overweight (BMI 25.0 - 29.9)	36.1	35.3
Adults who are obese (BMI 30.0 - 99.8)	31.2	31.3
Adults who participated in any physical activities in the past month	73.7	74.4
Adults who always or nearly always wears a seat belt	94.9	94.3

Note: (1) Figures cover the Kansas City, MO-KS Metropolitan Statistical Area; (2) Heavy drinkers are classified as adult men having more than 14 drinks per week and adult women having more than 7 drinks per week; (3) Binge drinkers are classified as males having five or more drinks on one occasion or females having four or more drinks on one occasion
Source: Centers for Disease Control and Prevention, Behaviorial Risk Factor Surveillance System, SMART: Selected Metropolitan Area Risk Trends, 2017

Acute and Chronic Health Conditions

Category	MSA[1] (%)	U.S. (%)
Adults who have ever been told they had a heart attack	3.9	4.2
Adults who have ever been told they have angina or coronary heart disease	3.8	3.9
Adults who have ever been told they had a stroke	3.4	3.0
Adults who have ever been told they have asthma	13.2	14.2
Adults who have ever been told they have arthritis	23.7	24.9
Adults who have ever been told they have diabetes[2]	9.7	10.5
Adults who have ever been told they had skin cancer	7.0	6.2
Adults who have ever been told they had any other types of cancer	6.4	7.1
Adults who have ever been told they have COPD	6.0	6.5
Adults who have ever been told they have kidney disease	2.5	3.0
Adults who have ever been told they have a form of depression	20.5	20.5

Note: (1) Figures cover the Kansas City, MO-KS Metropolitan Statistical Area; (2) Figures do not include pregnancy-related, borderline, or pre-diabetes
Source: Centers for Disease Control and Prevention, Behaviorial Risk Factor Surveillance System, SMART: Selected Metropolitan Area Risk Trends, 2017

Health Screening and Vaccination Rates

Category	MSA[1] (%)	U.S. (%)
Adults aged 65+ who have had flu shot within the past year	60.6	60.7
Adults aged 65+ who have ever had a pneumonia vaccination	78.2	75.4
Adults who have ever been tested for HIV	36.9	36.1
Adults who have ever had the shingles or zoster vaccine?	27.7	28.9
Adults who have had their blood cholesterol checked within the last five years	87.4	85.9

Note: n/a not available; (1) Figures cover the Kansas City, MO-KS Metropolitan Statistical Area.
Source: Centers for Disease Control and Prevention, Behaviorial Risk Factor Surveillance System, SMART: Selected Metropolitan Area Risk Trends, 2017

Disability Status

Category	MSA[1] (%)	U.S. (%)
Adults who reported being deaf	5.6	6.7
Are you blind or have serious difficulty seeing, even when wearing glasses?	3.7	4.5
Are you limited in any way in any of your usual activities due of arthritis?	11.2	12.9
Do you have difficulty doing errands alone?	6.5	6.8
Do you have difficulty dressing or bathing?	3.1	3.6
Do you have serious difficulty concentrating/remembering/making decisions?	9.4	10.7
Do you have serious difficulty walking or climbing stairs?	13.0	13.6

Note: (1) Figures cover the Kansas City, MO-KS Metropolitan Statistical Area.
Source: Centers for Disease Control and Prevention, Behaviorial Risk Factor Surveillance System, SMART: Selected Metropolitan Area Risk Trends, 2017

Mortality Rates for the Top 10 Causes of Death in the U.S.

ICD-10[a] Sub-Chapter	ICD-10[a] Code	Age-Adjusted Mortality Rate[1] per 100,000 population	
		County[2]	U.S.
Malignant neoplasms	C00-C97	161.2	149.2
Ischaemic heart diseases	I20-I25	74.0	90.5
Other forms of heart disease	I30-I51	67.7	52.2
Chronic lower respiratory diseases	J40-J47	45.5	39.6
Other degenerative diseases of the nervous system	G30-G31	28.1	37.6
Cerebrovascular diseases	I60-I69	38.2	37.2
Other external causes of accidental injury	W00-X59	37.9	36.1
Organic, including symptomatic, mental disorders	F01-F09	47.3	29.4
Hypertensive diseases	I10-I15	27.0	24.1
Diabetes mellitus	E10-E14	17.8	21.5

Note: (a) ICD-10 = International Classification of Diseases 10th Revision; (1) Mortality rates are a three-year average covering 2017-2019; (2) Figures cover Jackson County.
Source: Centers for Disease Control and Prevention, National Center for Health Statistics. Underlying Cause of Death 1999-2019 on CDC WONDER Online Database

Mortality Rates for Selected Causes of Death

ICD-10[a] Sub-Chapter	ICD-10[a] Code	Age-Adjusted Mortality Rate[1] per 100,000 population	
		County[2]	U.S.
Assault	X85-Y09	23.6	6.0
Diseases of the liver	K70-K76	13.8	14.4
Human immunodeficiency virus (HIV) disease	B20-B24	1.9	1.5
Influenza and pneumonia	J09-J18	14.3	13.8
Intentional self-harm	X60-X84	20.7	14.1
Malnutrition	E40-E46	3.0	2.3
Obesity and other hyperalimentation	E65-E68	1.3	2.1
Renal failure	N17-N19	22.0	12.6
Transport accidents	V01-V99	15.7	12.3
Viral hepatitis	B15-B19	1.2	1.2

Note: (a) ICD-10 = International Classification of Diseases 10th Revision; (1) Mortality rates are a three-year average covering 2017-2019; (2) Figures cover Jackson County; Data are suppressed when the data meet the criteria for confidentiality constraints; Mortality rates are flagged as unreliable when the rate would be calculated with a numerator of 20 or less.
Source: Centers for Disease Control and Prevention, National Center for Health Statistics. Underlying Cause of Death 1999-2019 on CDC WONDER Online Database

Health Insurance Coverage

Area	With Health Insurance	With Private Health Insurance	With Public Health Insurance	Without Health Insurance	Population Under Age 19 Without Health Insurance
City	88.2	68.6	29.1	11.8	6.6
MSA[1]	91.1	75.3	27.2	8.9	5.2
U.S.	91.2	67.9	35.1	8.8	5.1

Note: Figures are percentages that cover the civilian noninstitutionalized population; (1) Figures cover the Kansas City, MO-KS Metropolitan Statistical Area
Source: U.S. Census Bureau, 2015-2019 American Community Survey 5-Year Estimates

Number of Medical Professionals

Area	MDs[3]	DOs[3,4]	Dentists	Podiatrists	Chiropractors	Optometrists
County[1] (number)	2,153	420	634	45	318	142
County[1] (rate[2])	307.2	59.9	90.2	6.4	45.2	20.2
U.S. (rate[2])	282.9	22.7	71.2	6.2	28.1	16.9

29095
Note: Data as of 2019 unless noted; (1) Data covers Jackson County; (2) Rate per 100,000 population; (3) Data as of 2018 and includes all active, non-federal physicians; (4) Doctor of Osteopathic Medicine
Source: U.S. Department of Health and Human Services, Health Resources and Services Administration, Bureau of Health Professions, Area Resource File (ARF) 2019-2020

Best Hospitals

According to *U.S. News,* the Kansas City, MO-KS metro area is home to two of the best hospitals in the U.S.: **St. Luke's Hospital of Kansas City** (1 adult specialty); **University of Kansas Hospital** (6 adult specialties). The hospitals listed were nationally ranked in at least one of 16 adult or 10 pediatric specialties. Only 134 hospitals nationwide were nationally ranked in one or more adult or pediatric specialty; this number increases to 178 counting specialized centers within hospitals. Twenty hospitals in the U.S. made the Honor Roll. The Best Hospitals Honor Roll takes both the national rankings and the procedure and condition ratings into account. Hospitals received points if they were nationally ranked in one of the 16 adult specialties—the higher they ranked, the more points they got—and how many ratings of "high performing" they earned in the 10 procedures and conditions. *U.S. News Online, "America's Best Hospitals 2020-21"*

According to *U.S. News,* the Kansas City, MO-KS metro area is home to one of the best children's hospitals in the U.S.: **Children's Mercy Kansas City** (10 pediatric specialties). The hospital listed was highly ranked in at least one of 10 pediatric specialties. Eighty-eight children's hospitals in the U.S. were nationally ranked in at least one specialty. Hospitals received points for being ranked in a specialty, and the 10 hospitals with the most points across the 10 specialties make up the Honor Roll. *U.S. News Online, "America's Best Children's Hospitals 2020-21"*

EDUCATION

Public School District Statistics

District Name	Schls	Pupils	Pupil/ Teacher Ratio	Minority Pupils[1] (%)	Free Lunch Eligible[2] (%)	IEP[3] (%)
Center 58	8	2,639	11.8	80.1	67.9	15.3
Hickman Mills C-1	14	5,830	13.2	90.8	99.3	14.2
Kansas City 33	35	15,345	14.1	90.3	99.5	12.6
North Kansas City 74	32	20,763	15.1	43.6	40.5	11.8
Park Hill	18	12,038	15.0	32.6	22.8	11.0

Note: Table includes school districts with 2,000 or more students; (1) Percentage of students that are not non-Hispanic white; (2) Percentage of students that are eligible for the free lunch program; (3) Percentage of students that have an Individualized Education Program.
Source: U.S. Department of Education, National Center for Education Statistics, Common Core of Data, Local Education Agency (School District) Universe Survey: School Year 2018-2019; U.S. Department of Education, National Center for Education Statistics, Common Core of Data, Public Elementary/Secondary School Universe Survey: School Year 2018-2019

Best High Schools

According to *U.S. News,* Kansas City is home to one of the top 500 high schools in the U.S.: **Lincoln College Prep.** (#294). Nearly 18,000 public, magnet and charter schools were ranked based on their performance on state assessments and how well they prepare students for college. *U.S. News & World Report, "Best High Schools 2020"*

Highest Level of Education

Area	Less than H.S.	H.S. Diploma	Some College, No Deg.	Associate Degree	Bachelor's Degree	Master's Degree	Prof. School Degree	Doctorate Degree
City	10.0	25.3	22.0	7.4	22.2	9.3	2.5	1.2
MSA[1]	8.0	25.5	21.6	7.7	23.5	10.2	2.3	1.2
U.S.	12.0	27.0	20.4	8.5	19.8	8.8	2.1	1.4

Note: Figures cover persons age 25 and over; (1) Figures cover the Kansas City, MO-KS Metropolitan Statistical Area
Source: U.S. Census Bureau, 2015-2019 American Community Survey 5-Year Estimates

Educational Attainment by Race

Area	High School Graduate or Higher (%)					Bachelor's Degree or Higher (%)				
	Total	White	Black	Asian	Hisp.[2]	Total	White	Black	Asian	Hisp.[2]
City	90.0	93.2	86.5	80.3	70.2	35.2	43.5	16.6	47.2	18.6
MSA[1]	92.0	93.6	88.5	85.5	69.0	37.1	39.7	20.7	54.8	17.8
U.S.	88.0	89.9	86.0	87.1	68.7	32.1	33.5	21.6	54.3	16.4

Note: Figures shown cover persons 25 years old and over; (1) Figures cover the Kansas City, MO-KS Metropolitan Statistical Area; (2) People of Hispanic origin can be of any race
Source: U.S. Census Bureau, 2015-2019 American Community Survey 5-Year Estimates

School Enrollment by Grade and Control

Area	Preschool (%)		Kindergarten (%)		Grades 1 - 4 (%)		Grades 5 - 8 (%)		Grades 9 - 12 (%)	
	Public	Private	Public	Private	Public	Private	Public	Private	Public	Private
City	57.7	42.3	85.3	14.7	90.1	9.9	88.3	11.7	85.4	14.6
MSA[1]	58.1	41.9	88.5	11.5	89.6	10.4	89.2	10.8	89.4	10.6
U.S.	59.1	40.9	87.6	12.4	89.5	10.5	89.4	10.6	90.1	9.9

Note: Figures shown cover persons 3 years old and over; (1) Figures cover the Kansas City, MO-KS Metropolitan Statistical Area
Source: U.S. Census Bureau, 2015-2019 American Community Survey 5-Year Estimates

Higher Education

Four-Year Colleges			Two-Year Colleges			Medical Schools[1]	Law Schools[2]	Voc/ Tech[3]
Public	Private Non-profit	Private For-profit	Public	Private Non-profit	Private For-profit			
1	9	3	1	0	4	2	1	3

Note: Figures cover institutions located within the city limits and include main campuses only; (1) includes schools accredited by the Liaison Committee on Medical Education and the American Osteopathic Association's Commission on Osteopathic College Accreditation; (2) includes ABA-accredited schools, schools with provisional ABA accreditation, and state accredited schools; (3) includes all schools with programs that are less than 2 years.
Source: National Center for Education Statistics, Integrated Postsecondary Education System (IPEDS), 2019-20; Wikipedia, List of Medical Schools in the United States, accessed April 2, 2021; Wikipedia, List of Law Schools in the United States, accessed April 2, 2021

According to *U.S. News & World Report,* the Kansas City, MO-KS metro area is home to one of the top 75 medical schools for research in the U.S.: **University of Kansas Medical Center** (#75 tie). The rankings are based on a weighted average of 11 measures of quality: quality assessment; peer assessment score; assessment score by residency directors; research activity; total research activity; average research activity per faculty member; student selectivity; median MCAT total score; median undergraduate GPA; acceptance rate; and faculty resources. *U.S. News & World Report, "America's Best Graduate Schools, Medical, 2022"*

EMPLOYERS

Major Employers

Company Name	Industry
B&V Baker Guam JV	Engineering services
Black and Veatch Corp	Engineering services
DST Systems	Data processing
Embarq Corporation	Telephone communications
Ford Motor Company	Automobile assembly
Hallmark Cards	Greeting cards
HCA Midwest Division	Hospital management
Honeywell International	Search & navigation equipment
Internal Revenue Service	Taxation department, government
North Kansas City Hospital	General medical & surgical hospitals
Park University	Colleges & universities
Performance Contracting	Drywall
St. Lukes Hospital of Kansas	General medical & surgical hospitals
United Auto Workers	Labor union
University of Kansas	Medical centers
University of Missouri System	General medical & surgical hospitals

Note: Companies shown are located within the Kansas City, MO-KS Metropolitan Statistical Area.
Source: Hoovers.com; Wikipedia

Best Companies to Work For

Burns & McDonnell, headquartered in Kansas City, is among "The 100 Best Companies to Work For." To pick the best companies, *Fortune* partnered with the Great Place to Work Institute. Two-thirds of a company's score is based on the results of the Institute's Trust Index survey, which is sent to a random sample of employees from each company. The questions related to attitudes about management's credibility, job satisfaction, and camaraderie. The other third of the scoring is based on the company's responses to the Institute's Culture Audit, which includes detailed questions about pay and benefit programs, and a series of open-ended questions about hiring practices, internal communication, training, recognition programs, and diversity efforts. Any company that is at least five years old with more than 1,000 U.S. employees is eligible. *Fortune, "The 100 Best Companies to Work For," 2020*

PUBLIC SAFETY

Crime Rate

Area	All Crimes	Violent Crimes				Property Crimes		
		Murder	Rape[3]	Robbery	Aggrav. Assault	Burglary	Larceny -Theft	Motor Vehicle Theft
City	5,287.3	30.2	70.0	290.9	1,040.2	619.0	2,470.5	766.4
Suburbs[1]	n/a	n/a	n/a	n/a	n/a	n/a	n/a	n/a
Metro[2]	n/a	n/a	n/a	n/a	n/a	n/a	n/a	n/a
U.S.	2,489.3	5.0	42.6	81.6	250.2	340.5	1,549.5	219.9

Note: Figures are crimes per 100,000 population; (1) All areas within the metro area that are located outside the city limits; (2) Figures cover the Kansas City, MO-KS Metropolitan Statistical Area; n/a not available; (3) All figures shown were reported using the revised Uniform Crime Reporting (UCR) definition of rape.
Source: FBI Uniform Crime Reports, 2019

Hate Crimes

Area	Number of Quarters Reported	Number of Incidents per Bias Motivation					
		Race/Ethnicity/Ancestry	Religion	Sexual Orientation	Disability	Gender	Gender Identity
City	4	25	6	2	1	0	0
U.S.	4	3,963	1,521	1,195	157	69	198

Source: Federal Bureau of Investigation, Hate Crime Statistics 2019

Identity Theft Consumer Reports

Area	Reports	Reports per 100,000 Population	Rank[2]
MSA[1]	17,400	806	20
U.S.	1,387,615	423	-

Note: (1) Figures cover the Kansas City, MO-KS Metropolitan Statistical Area; (2) Rank ranges from 1 to 391 where 1 indicates greatest number of identity theft reports per 100,000 population
Source: Federal Trade Commission, Consumer Sentinel Network Data Book 2020

Fraud and Other Consumer Reports

Area	Reports	Reports per 100,000 Population	Rank[2]
MSA[1]	17,338	803	95
U.S.	3,385,133	1,031	-

Note: (1) Figures cover the Kansas City, MO-KS Metropolitan Statistical Area; (2) Rank ranges from 1 to 391 where 1 indicates greatest number of fraud and other consumer reports per 100,000 population
Source: Federal Trade Commission, Consumer Sentinel Network Data Book 2020

POLITICS

2020 Presidential Election Results

Area	Biden	Trump	Jorgensen	Hawkins	Other
Jackson County	59.8	37.9	1.4	0.4	0.5
U.S.	51.3	46.8	1.2	0.3	0.5

Note: Results are percentages and may not add to 100% due to rounding
Source: Dave Leip's Atlas of U.S. Presidential Elections

SPORTS

Professional Sports Teams

Team Name	League	Year Established
Kansas City Chiefs	National Football League (NFL)	1963
Kansas City Royals	Major League Baseball (MLB)	1969
Sporting Kansas City	Major League Soccer (MLS)	1996

Note: Includes teams located in the Kansas City, MO-KS Metropolitan Statistical Area.
Source: Wikipedia, Major Professional Sports Teams of the United States and Canada, April 6, 2021

CLIMATE

Average and Extreme Temperatures

Temperature	Jan	Feb	Mar	Apr	May	Jun	Jul	Aug	Sep	Oct	Nov	Dec	Yr.
Extreme High (°F)	69	76	86	93	92	105	107	109	102	92	82	70	109
Average High (°F)	35	40	54	65	74	84	90	87	79	66	52	39	64
Average Temp. (°F)	26	31	44	55	64	74	79	77	68	56	43	30	54
Average Low (°F)	17	22	34	44	54	63	69	66	58	45	34	21	44
Extreme Low (°F)	-17	-19	-10	12	30	42	54	43	33	21	1	-23	-23

Note: Figures cover the years 1972-1990
Source: National Climatic Data Center, International Station Meteorological Climate Summary, 9/96

Average Precipitation/Snowfall/Humidity

Precip./Humidity	Jan	Feb	Mar	Apr	May	Jun	Jul	Aug	Sep	Oct	Nov	Dec	Yr.
Avg. Precip. (in.)	1.1	1.2	2.8	3.0	5.5	4.1	3.8	4.1	4.9	3.6	2.1	1.6	38.1
Avg. Snowfall (in.)	6	5	3	1	0	0	0	0	0	Tr	1	5	21
Avg. Rel. Hum. 6am (%)	76	77	78	77	82	84	84	86	86	80	79	78	80
Avg. Rel. Hum. 3pm (%)	58	59	54	50	54	54	51	53	53	51	57	60	54

Note: Figures cover the years 1972-1990; Tr = Trace amounts (<0.05 in. of rain; <0.5 in. of snow)
Source: National Climatic Data Center, International Station Meteorological Climate Summary, 9/96

Weather Conditions

Temperature			Daytime Sky			Precipitation		
10°F & below	32°F & below	90°F & above	Clear	Partly cloudy	Cloudy	0.01 inch or more precip.	0.1 inch or more snow/ice	Thunder-storms
22	110	39	112	134	119	103	17	51

Note: Figures are average number of days per year and cover the years 1972-1990
Source: National Climatic Data Center, International Station Meteorological Climate Summary, 9/96

250 **Kansas City, Missouri**

HAZARDOUS WASTE

Superfund Sites

The Kansas City, MO-KS metro area is home to six sites on the EPA's Superfund National Priorities List: **Armour Road** (final); **Chemical Commodities, Inc.** (final); **Conservation Chemical Co.** (final); **Doepke Disposal (Holliday)** (final); **Lake City Army Ammunition Plant (Northwest Lagoon)** (final); **Lee Chemical** (final). There are a total of 1,375 Superfund sites with a status of proposed or final on the list in the U.S. *U.S. Environmental Protection Agency, National Priorities List, April 7, 2021*

AIR QUALITY

Air Quality Trends: Ozone

	1990	1995	2000	2005	2010	2015	2016	2017	2018	2019
MSA[1]	0.075	0.098	0.088	0.084	0.072	0.063	0.066	0.069	0.073	0.063
U.S.	0.088	0.089	0.082	0.080	0.073	0.068	0.069	0.068	0.069	0.065

Note: (1) Data covers the Kansas City, MO-KS Metropolitan Statistical Area. The values shown are the composite ozone concentration averages among trend sites based on the highest fourth daily maximum 8-hour concentration in parts per million. These trends are based on sites having an adequate record of monitoring data during the trend period. Data from exceptional events are included.
Source: U.S. Environmental Protection Agency, Air Quality Monitoring Information, "Air Quality Trends by City, 1990-2019"

Air Quality Index

Area	Percent of Days when Air Quality was...[2]					AQI Statistics[2]	
	Good	Moderate	Unhealthy for Sensitive Groups	Unhealthy	Very Unhealthy	Maximum	Median
MSA[1]	57.5	42.2	0.3	0.0	0.0	137	47

Note: (1) Data covers the Kansas City, MO-KS Metropolitan Statistical Area; (2) Based on 365 days with AQI data in 2019. Air Quality Index (AQI) is an index for reporting daily air quality. EPA calculates the AQI for five major air pollutants regulated by the Clean Air Act: ground-level ozone, particle pollution (aka particulate matter), carbon monoxide, sulfur dioxide, and nitrogen dioxide. The AQI runs from 0 to 500. The higher the AQI value, the greater the level of air pollution and the greater the health concern. There are six AQI categories: "Good" AQI is between 0 and 50. Air quality is considered satisfactory; "Moderate" AQI is between 51 and 100. Air quality is acceptable; "Unhealthy for Sensitive Groups" When AQI values are between 101 and 150, members of sensitive groups may experience health effects; "Unhealthy" When AQI values are between 151 and 200 everyone may begin to experience health effects; "Very Unhealthy" AQI values between 201 and 300 trigger a health alert; "Hazardous" AQI values over 300 trigger warnings of emergency conditions (not shown).
Source: U.S. Environmental Protection Agency, Air Quality Index Report, 2019

Air Quality Index Pollutants

Area	Percent of Days when AQI Pollutant was...[2]					
	Carbon Monoxide	Nitrogen Dioxide	Ozone	Sulfur Dioxide	Particulate Matter 2.5	Particulate Matter 10
MSA[1]	0.0	2.5	48.2	0.0	45.5	3.8

Note: (1) Data covers the Kansas City, MO-KS Metropolitan Statistical Area; (2) Based on 365 days with AQI data in 2019. The Air Quality Index (AQI) is an index for reporting daily air quality. EPA calculates the AQI for five major air pollutants regulated by the Clean Air Act: ground-level ozone, particle pollution (also known as particulate matter), carbon monoxide, sulfur dioxide, and nitrogen dioxide. The AQI runs from 0 to 500. The higher the AQI value, the greater the level of air pollution and the greater the health concern.
Source: U.S. Environmental Protection Agency, Air Quality Index Report, 2019

Maximum Air Pollutant Concentrations: Particulate Matter, Ozone, CO and Lead

	Particulate Matter 10 (ug/m^3)	Particulate Matter 2.5 Wtd AM (ug/m^3)	Particulate Matter 2.5 24-Hr (ug/m^3)	Ozone (ppm)	Carbon Monoxide (ppm)	Lead (ug/m^3)
MSA[1] Level	71	7.6	17	0.064	1	n/a
NAAQS[2]	150	15	35	0.075	9	0.15
Met NAAQS[2]	Yes	Yes	Yes	Yes	Yes	n/a

Note: (1) Data covers the Kansas City, MO-KS Metropolitan Statistical Area; Data from exceptional events are included; (2) National Ambient Air Quality Standards; ppm = parts per million; ug/m^3 = micrograms per cubic meter; n/a not available.
Concentrations: Particulate Matter 10 (coarse particulate)—highest second maximum 24-hour concentration; Particulate Matter 2.5 Wtd AM (fine particulate)—highest weighted annual mean concentration; Particulate Matter 2.5 24-Hour (fine particulate)—highest 98th percentile 24-hour concentration; Ozone—highest fourth daily maximum 8-hour concentration; Carbon Monoxide—highest second maximum non-overlapping 8-hour concentration; Lead—maximum running 3-month average
Source: U.S. Environmental Protection Agency, Air Quality Monitoring Information, "Air Quality Statistics by City, 2019"

Maximum Air Pollutant Concentrations: Nitrogen Dioxide and Sulfur Dioxide

	Nitrogen Dioxide AM (ppb)	Nitrogen Dioxide 1-Hr (ppb)	Sulfur Dioxide AM (ppb)	Sulfur Dioxide 1-Hr (ppb)	Sulfur Dioxide 24-Hr (ppb)
MSA[1] Level	11	47	n/a	7	n/a
NAAQS[2]	53	100	30	75	140
Met NAAQS[2]	Yes	Yes	n/a	Yes	n/a

Note: (1) Data covers the Kansas City, MO-KS Metropolitan Statistical Area; Data from exceptional events are included; (2) National Ambient Air Quality Standards; ppm = parts per million; ug/m^3 = micrograms per cubic meter; n/a not available.
Concentrations: Nitrogen Dioxide AM—highest arithmetic mean concentration; Nitrogen Dioxide 1-Hr—highest 98th percentile 1-hour daily maximum concentration; Sulfur Dioxide AM—highest annual mean concentration; Sulfur Dioxide 1-Hr—highest 99th percentile 1-hour daily maximum concentration; Sulfur Dioxide 24-Hr—highest second maximum 24-hour concentration
Source: U.S. Environmental Protection Agency, Air Quality Monitoring Information, "Air Quality Statistics by City, 2019"

Lincoln, Nebraska

Background

Lincoln, the capital of Nebraska and the seat of Lancaster County is located in the southeastern part of the state. It is a thriving and multifaceted city with a fascinating history and a dynamic and expanding contemporary economy and cultural life. Lincoln today is the second-largest city in Nebraska.

The site first attracted the attention of settlers in 1856 when commercial explorers found saline deposits on the banks of the Salt Creek, and what is today known as Capitol Beach Lake. Salt, in fact, constituted the first major commercial activity in the city, with two large salt "boilers," Cox and Peckham, supplying this vital resource to farmers and townspeople in a wide stretch of the Plains region. Captain W.T. Donovan came to the area as a salt company representative, settling there permanently in 1867. He named his claim Lancaster after his home in Pennsylvania, which became the county name.

Omaha had been the capital of Nebraska, but with statehood, a drive began to move the capital south of the Platte River. The new capital, originally to be called simply Capitol City, was sited at Lancaster. State Senator J.H.N. Patrick proposed changing the name to Lincoln, largely because he thought it would discourage Democratic support.

In the 1880s—a dynamic period of Lincoln's early economic growth—William Jennings Bryan came to town as a lawyer and budding politician, and two years later was elected to the U.S. Congress. Another Lincoln luminary from this period was General John J. Pershing, who was an instructor in military science at the recently established University of Nebraska.

Designated as a "refugee-friendly" city by the U.S. Department of State in the 1970s, the city was the twelfth-largest resettlement site per capita in the United States by 2000. Refugee Vietnamese, Karen (Burmese ethnic minority), Sudanese and Yazidi (Iraqi ethnic minority) people, as well as refugees from the Middle East, have been resettled in the city. The public school systems has taken in nearly 5,000 students speaking 50 languages in recent years.

The city's downtown is a modern entertainment, commercial, and office center, and on its west edge is the historic Haymarket District. The state capitol building, designed by Bertram Grosvenor Goodhue in 1919, is an architectural attraction of international repute, and its modernist central white stone column, visible from surrounding prairie hilltops for miles, still uniquely defines the Lincoln skyline. Lincoln is also a city of parks, with 100 parks covering more than 6,000 acres, including a children's zoo and, in cooperation with Lancaster County, a wilderness park. Recent years saw restoration and enhancement to the downtown and improved flood control measures.

The University of Nebraska is city's largest institution of higher learning and its football team attracts crowds of 78,000 to Memorial Stadium. The University of Nebraska is a major hub of cultural activity in the city, and is the site of the State Museum of Natural History. Nebraska Wesleyan University and Union College are also located in Lincoln.

> Local scientists conducted a study to see if the virus was present in wastewater, hoping to predict COVID-19 outbreaks before they showed up through individual swab tests.

The city offers rich cultural resources that draw on its increasingly cosmopolitan character, as well as on the rural traditions of the state as a whole. The Lied Center for Performing Arts, on the University of Nebraska's downtown campus, features a full range of musical and dramatic performances, and the city also hosts the Nebraska State Fair in early September. In 2010, Lincoln hosted the Special Olympics USA National Games.

Government is the largest employer in Lincoln, with health services the largest non-industrial private sector employer. The city hosts operations of many major employers, and Bryan Medical Center is one of the largest.

The joint County-City Building houses the mayor's office, the city council, Lancaster County commissioner's office, and county, district, and juvenile courts, and the judicial center is connected to the County-City Building by elevated walkways.

The climate in Lincoln is characterized by the robust and dramatic range of the Great Plains area as a whole. Most precipitation falls during April through September, and thunderstorms are predominant in the summer months. Lincoln lies in a valley that affords considerable protection against tornadoes, although more than 25 Federal Signal warning sirens throughout the city are still tested every Wednesday morning, except in the winter months.

Rankings

General Rankings

- For its "Best for Vets: Places to Live 2019" rankings, *Military Times* evaluated 599 cities (83 large, 234 medium, 282 small) and compared the locations across three broad categories: veteran and military culture/services; economic indicators; and livability factors such as health, crime, traffic, and school quality. Lincoln ranked #12 out of the top 25, in the large city category (population of more than 250,000). Data points more specific to veterans and the military weighed more heavily than others. *rebootcamp.militarytimes.com, "Military Times Best Places to Live 2019," September 10, 2018*

- In their seventh annual survey, Livability.com looked at data for more than 1,000 small to mid-sized U.S. cities to determine the rankings for Livability's "Top 100 Best Places to Live" in 2020. Lincoln ranked #12. Criteria: housing and affordable living; vibrant economy; social and civic engagement; education; demographics; health care options; transportation & infrastructure; and abundant lifestyle amenities. *Livability.com, "Top 100 Best Places to Live 2020" October 2020*

Business/Finance Rankings

- Lincoln was the #11-ranked city for savers, according to a study by the finance site GOBankingRates, which considered the prospects for people trying to save money. Criteria: average monthly cost of grocery items; median home listing price; median rent; median income; transportation costs; gas prices; and the cost of eating out for an inexpensive and mid-range meal in 100 U.S. cities. *www.gobankingrates.com, "The 20 Best (and Worst) Places to Live If You're Trying to Save Money," August 27, 2019*

- Lincoln was ranked #11 among 100 U.S. cities for most difficult conditions for savers, according to a study by the finance site GOBankingRates. Criteria: average monthly cost of grocery items; median home listing price; median rent; median income; transportation costs; gas prices; and the cost of eating out for an inexpensive and mid-range meal. *www.gobankingrates.com, "The 20 Best (and Worst) Places to Live If You're Trying to Save Money," August 27, 2019*

- The Lincoln metro area appeared on the Milken Institute "2021 Best Performing Cities" list. Rank: #80 out of 200 large metro areas (population over 250,000). Criteria: job growth; wage and salary growth; high-tech output growth; housing affordability; household broadband access. *Milken Institute, "Best-Performing Cities 2021," February 16, 2021*

- *Forbes* ranked the 200 most populous metro areas to determine the nation's "Best Places for Business and Careers." The Lincoln metro area was ranked #36. Criteria: costs (business and living); job growth (past and projected); income growth; quality of life; educational attainment (college and high school); projected economic growth; cultural and leisure opportunities; workplace tolerance laws; net migration patterns. *Forbes, "The Best Places for Business and Careers 2019: Seattle Still On Top," October 30, 2019*

Children/Family Rankings

- Lincoln was selected as one of the most playful cities in the U.S. by KaBOOM! The organization's Playful City USA initiative honors cities and towns across the nation that have made their communities more playable. Criteria: pledging to integrate play as a solution to challenges in their communities; making it easy for children to get active and balanced play; creating more family-friendly and innovative communities as a result. *KaBOOM! National Campaign for Play, "2017 Playful City USA Communities"*

- Lincoln was selected as one of the best cities for newlyweds by *Rent.com*. The city ranked #8 of 15. Criteria: cost of living; availability of affordable rental inventory; annual household income; activities and restaurant options; percentage of married couples; concentration of millennials; safety. *Rent.com, "The 15 Best Cities for Newlyweds," December 11, 2018*

Dating/Romance Rankings

- Lincoln was selected as one of the most romantic cities in the U.S. by video-rental kiosk company Redbox. The city ranked #8 out of 20. Criteria: number of romance-related rentals in 2016. *Redbox, "20 Most Romantic Cities," February 6, 2017*

Education Rankings

- Lincoln was selected as one of America's most literate cities. The city ranked #18 out of the 84 largest U.S. cities. Criteria: number of booksellers; library resources; Internet resources; educational attainment; periodical publishing resources; newspaper circulation. *Central Connecticut State University, "America's Most Literate Cities, 2018," February 2019*

Environmental Rankings

- Lincoln was highlighted as one of the cleanest metro areas for ozone air pollution in the U.S. during 2016 through 2018. The list represents cities with no monitored ozone air pollution in unhealthful ranges. *American Lung Association, "State of the Air 2020," April 21, 2020*

- Lincoln was highlighted as one of the top 98 cleanest metro areas for short-term particle pollution (24-hour PM 2.5) in the U.S. during 2016 through 2018. Monitors in these cities reported no days with unhealthful PM 2.5 levels. *American Lung Association, "State of the Air 2020," April 21, 2020*

Health/Fitness Rankings

- For each of the 100 largest cities in the United States, the American Fitness Index®, published by the American College of Sports Medicine and the Anthem Foundation, evaluated community infrastructure and 33 health behaviors including preventive health, levels of chronic disease conditions, pedestrian safety, air quality, and community resources that support physical activity. Lincoln ranked #19 for "community fitness." *americanfitnessindex.org, "2020 ACSM American Fitness Index Summary Report," July 14, 2020*

Real Estate Rankings

- *WalletHub* compared the most populated U.S. cities to determine which had the best markets for real estate agents. Lincoln ranked #126 where demand was high and pay was the best. Criteria: sales per agent; annual median wage for real-estate agents; monthly average starting salary for real estate agents; real estate job density and competition; unemployment rate; home turnover rate; housing-market health index; and other relevant metrics. *www.WalletHub.com, "2019's Best Places to Be a Real Estate Agent," April 24, 2019*

Safety Rankings

- Allstate ranked the 200 largest cities in America in terms of driver safety. Lincoln ranked #21. Criteria: internal property damage claims over a two-year period from January 2016 to December 2017. The report helps increase the importance of safety and awareness behind the wheel. *Allstate, "Allstate America's Best Drivers Report, 2019" June 24, 2019*

- The National Insurance Crime Bureau ranked 384 metro areas in the U.S. in terms of per capita rates of vehicle theft. The Lincoln metro area ranked #245 (#1 = highest rate). Criteria: number of vehicle theft offenses per 100,000 inhabitants in 2019. *National Insurance Crime Bureau, "Hot Spots 2019," July 21, 2020*

Seniors/Retirement Rankings

- From its Best Cities for Successful Aging indexes, the Milken Institute generated rankings for metropolitan areas, weighing data in nine categories—health care, wellness, living arrangements, transportation and convenience, financial characteristics, education, employment, community engagement, and overall livability. The Lincoln metro area was ranked #35 overall in the small metro area category. *Milken Institute, "Best Cities for Successful Aging, 2017" March 14, 2017*

Sports/Recreation Rankings

- Lincoln was chosen as one of America's best cities for bicycling. The city ranked #35 out of 50. Criteria: cycling infrastructure that is safe and friendly for all ages; energy and bike culture. The editors evaluated cities with populations of 100,000 or more. *Bicycling, "The 50 Best Bike Cities in America," October 10, 2018*

Women/Minorities Rankings

- Personal finance website *WalletHub* compared more than 180 U.S. cities across two key dimensions, "Hispanic Business-Friendliness" and "Hispanic Purchasing Power," to arrive at the most favorable conditions for Hispanic entrepreneurs. Lincoln was ranked #106 out of 182. Criteria includes: share of Hispanic-Owned Businesses; Hispanic entrepreneurship rate to median annual income of Hispanics; Small Business-Friendliness score; cost of living; and number of Hispanics with at least a bachelor's degree. *WalletHub.com, "2019's Best Cities for Hispanic Entrepreneurs," May 1, 2019*

Miscellaneous Rankings

- *WalletHub* compared the 150 most populated U.S. cities to determine their operating efficiency. A "Quality of City Services" score was constructed for each city and then divided by the total budget per capita to reveal which were managed the best. Lincoln ranked #26. Criteria: financial stability; economy; education; safety; health; infrastructure and pollution. *www.WalletHub.com, "2020's Best- & Worst-Run Cities in America," June 29, 2020*

Business Environment

DEMOGRAPHICS

Population Growth

Area	1990 Census	2000 Census	2010 Census	2019* Estimate	Population Growth (%)	
					1990-2019	2010-2019
City	193,629	225,581	258,379	283,839	46.6	9.9
MSA[1]	229,091	266,787	302,157	330,329	44.2	9.3
U.S.	248,709,873	281,421,906	308,745,538	324,697,795	30.6	5.2

Note: (1) Figures cover the Lincoln, NE Metropolitan Statistical Area; (*) 2015-2019 5-year estimated population
Source: U.S. Census Bureau, 1990 Census, Census 2000, Census 2010, 2015-2019 American Community Survey 5-Year Estimates

Household Size

Area	Persons in Household (%)							Average Household Size
	One	Two	Three	Four	Five	Six	Seven or More	
City	31.6	34.8	13.9	11.6	5.2	2.0	0.9	2.40
MSA[1]	30.1	35.8	13.7	11.9	5.4	2.1	1.0	2.40
U.S.	27.9	33.9	15.6	12.9	6.0	2.3	1.4	2.60

Note: (1) Figures cover the Lincoln, NE Metropolitan Statistical Area
Source: U.S. Census Bureau, 2015-2019 American Community Survey 5-Year Estimates

Race

Area	White Alone[2] (%)	Black Alone[2] (%)	Asian Alone[2] (%)	AIAN[3] Alone[2] (%)	NHOPI[4] Alone[2] (%)	Other Race Alone[2] (%)	Two or More Races (%)
City	84.9	4.4	4.6	0.7	0.1	1.5	3.9
MSA[1]	86.6	3.8	4.0	0.7	0.1	1.3	3.5
U.S.	72.5	12.7	5.5	0.8	0.2	4.9	3.3

Note: (1) Figures cover the Lincoln, NE Metropolitan Statistical Area; (2) Alone is defined as not being in combination with one or more other races; (3) American Indian and Alaska Native; (4) Native Hawaiian and Other Pacific Islander
Source: U.S. Census Bureau, 2015-2019 American Community Survey 5-Year Estimates

Hispanic or Latino Origin

Area	Total (%)	Mexican (%)	Puerto Rican (%)	Cuban (%)	Other (%)
City	7.6	5.5	0.3	0.2	1.6
MSA[1]	6.8	4.9	0.3	0.2	1.5
U.S.	18.0	11.2	1.7	0.7	4.3

Note: Persons of Hispanic or Latino origin can be of any race; (1) Figures cover the Lincoln, NE Metropolitan Statistical Area
Source: U.S. Census Bureau, 2015-2019 American Community Survey 5-Year Estimates

Ancestry

Area	German	Irish	English	American	Italian	Polish	French[2]	Scottish	Dutch
City	33.2	11.3	8.0	3.6	2.3	2.5	2.1	1.5	2.0
MSA[1]	34.6	11.1	8.0	3.7	2.2	2.5	2.1	1.4	2.2
U.S.	13.3	9.7	7.2	6.2	5.1	2.8	2.3	1.7	1.2

Note: Figures are the percentage of the total population reporting a particular ancestry. The nine most commonly reported ancestries in the U.S. are shown. Figures include multiple ancestries (e.g. if a person reported being Irish and Italian, they were included in both columns); (1) Figures cover the Lincoln, NE Metropolitan Statistical Area; (2) Excludes Basque
Source: U.S. Census Bureau, 2015-2019 American Community Survey 5-Year Estimates

Foreign-born Population

Area	Percent of Population Born in								
	Any Foreign Country	Asia	Mexico	Europe	Caribbean	Central America[2]	South America	Africa	Canada
City	8.5	4.5	1.3	0.9	0.2	0.4	0.3	0.8	0.1
MSA[1]	7.5	4.0	1.1	0.8	0.2	0.3	0.3	0.7	0.1
U.S.	13.6	4.2	3.5	1.5	1.3	1.1	1.0	0.7	0.2

Note: (1) Figures cover the Lincoln, NE Metropolitan Statistical Area; (2) Excludes Mexico.
Source: U.S. Census Bureau, 2015-2019 American Community Survey 5-Year Estimates

Marital Status

Area	Never Married	Now Married[2]	Separated	Widowed	Divorced
City	39.0	45.6	1.0	4.4	10.0
MSA[1]	36.7	48.2	0.9	4.4	9.7
U.S.	33.4	48.1	1.9	5.8	10.9

Note: Figures are percentages and cover the population 15 years of age and older; (1) Figures cover the Lincoln, NE Metropolitan Statistical Area; (2) Excludes separated
Source: U.S. Census Bureau, 2015-2019 American Community Survey 5-Year Estimates

Disability by Age

Area	All Ages	Under 18 Years Old	18 to 64 Years Old	65 Years and Over
City	10.8	4.4	8.6	32.7
MSA[1]	10.7	4.1	8.4	32.5
U.S.	12.6	4.2	10.3	34.5

Note: Figures show percent of the civilian noninstitutionalized population that reported having a disability. Disability status is determined from six types of difficulty: vision, hearing, cognitive, ambulatory, self-care, and independent living. For children under 5 years old, hearing and vision difficulty are used to determine disability status. For children between the ages of 5 and 14, disability status is determined from hearing, vision, cognitive, ambulatory, and self-care difficulties. For people aged 15 years and older, they are considered to have a disability if they have difficulty with any one of the six difficulty types; Note: (1) Figures cover the Lincoln, NE Metropolitan Statistical Area
Source: U.S. Census Bureau, 2015-2019 American Community Survey 5-Year Estimates

Age

Area	Percent of Population									Median Age
	Under Age 5	Age 5–19	Age 20–34	Age 35–44	Age 45–54	Age 55–64	Age 65–74	Age 75–84	Age 85+	
City	6.5	19.9	26.7	12.4	10.5	10.9	7.7	3.6	1.7	32.7
MSA[1]	6.4	20.4	25.0	12.3	10.9	11.4	8.1	3.8	1.8	33.7
U.S.	6.1	19.1	20.7	12.6	13.0	12.9	9.1	4.6	1.9	38.1

Note: (1) Figures cover the Lincoln, NE Metropolitan Statistical Area
Source: U.S. Census Bureau, 2015-2019 American Community Survey 5-Year Estimates

Gender

Area	Males	Females	Males per 100 Females
City	142,589	141,250	100.9
MSA[1]	165,977	164,352	101.0
U.S.	159,886,919	164,810,876	97.0

Note: (1) Figures cover the Lincoln, NE Metropolitan Statistical Area
Source: U.S. Census Bureau, 2015-2019 American Community Survey 5-Year Estimates

Religious Groups by Family

Area	Catholic	Baptist	Non-Den.	Methodist[2]	Lutheran	LDS[3]	Pente-costal	Presby-terian[4]	Muslim[5]	Judaism
MSA[1]	14.8	2.4	1.9	7.2	11.3	1.2	1.4	3.9	0.2	0.2
U.S.	19.1	9.3	4.0	4.0	2.3	2.0	1.9	1.6	0.8	0.7

Note: Figures are the number of adherents as a percentage of the total population; (1) Figures cover the Lincoln, NE Metropolitan Statistical Area; (2) Methodist/Pietist; (3) Latter Day Saints; (4) Reformed; (5) Figures are estimates
Source: Association of Statisticians of American Religious Bodies, 2010 U.S. Religion Census: Religious Congregations & Membership Study

Religious Groups by Tradition

Area	Catholic	Evangelical Protestant	Mainline Protestant	Other Tradition	Black Protestant	Orthodox
MSA[1]	14.8	14.8	16.2	2.0	0.1	0.1
U.S.	19.1	16.2	7.3	4.3	1.6	0.3

Note: Figures are the number of adherents as a percentage of the total population; (1) Figures cover the Lincoln, NE Metropolitan Statistical Area
Source: Association of Statisticians of American Religious Bodies, 2010 U.S. Religion Census: Religious Congregations & Membership Study

ECONOMY

Gross Metropolitan Product

Area	2017	2018	2019	2020	Rank[2]
MSA[1]	19.7	20.6	21.2	22.0	125

Note: Figures are in billions of dollars; (1) Figures cover the Lincoln, NE Metropolitan Statistical Area; (2) Rank is based on 2018 data and ranges from 1 to 381
Source: U.S. Conference of Mayors, U.S. Metro Economies: GMP & Employment 2018-2020, September 2019

Economic Growth

Area	2015-17 (%)	2018 (%)	2019 (%)	2020 (%)	Rank[2]
MSA[1]	0.3	2.1	1.3	1.5	287
U.S.	1.9	2.9	2.3	2.1	—

Note: Figures are real gross metropolitan product (GMP) growth rates and represent average annual percent change; (1) Figures cover the Lincoln, NE Metropolitan Statistical Area; (2) Rank is based on 2017 2-year average annual percent change and ranges from 1 to 381
Source: U.S. Conference of Mayors, U.S. Metro Economies: GMP & Employment 2018-2020, September 2019

Metropolitan Area Exports

Area	2014	2015	2016	2017	2018	2019	Rank[2]
MSA[1]	1,173.9	1,189.3	796.9	860.9	885.6	807.0	177

Note: Figures are in millions of dollars; (1) Figures cover the Lincoln, NE Metropolitan Statistical Area; (2) Rank is based on 2019 data and ranges from 1 to 386
Source: U.S. Department of Commerce, International Trade Administration, Office of Trade and Economic Analysis, Industry and Analysis, Exports by Metropolitan Area, data extracted March 24, 2021

Building Permits

Area	Single-Family			Multi-Family			Total		
	2018	2019	Pct. Chg.	2018	2019	Pct. Chg.	2018	2019	Pct. Chg.
City	859	863	0.5	673	864	28.4	1,532	1,727	12.7
MSA[1]	1,117	1,088	-2.6	687	1,010	47.0	1,804	2,098	16.3
U.S.	855,300	862,100	0.7	473,500	523,900	10.6	1,328,800	1,386,000	4.3

Note: (1) Figures cover the Lincoln, NE Metropolitan Statistical Area; Figures represent new, privately-owned housing units authorized (unadjusted data); All permit data are based on estimates with imputation
Source: U.S. Census Bureau, Manufacturing, Mining, and Construction Statistics, Building Permits, 2018, 2019

Bankruptcy Filings

Area	Business Filings			Nonbusiness Filings		
	2019	2020	% Chg.	2019	2020	% Chg.
Lancaster County	16	11	-31.3	653	485	-25.7
U.S.	22,780	21,655	-4.9	752,160	522,808	-30.5

Note: Business filings include Chapter 7, Chapter 9, Chapter 11, Chapter 12, Chapter 13, Chapter 15, and Section 304; Nonbusiness filings include Chapter 7, Chapter 11, and Chapter 13
Source: Administrative Office of the U.S. Courts, Business and Nonbusiness Bankruptcy, County Cases Commenced by Chapter of the Bankruptcy Code, During the 12-Month Period Ending December 31, 2019 and Business and Nonbusiness Bankruptcy, County Cases Commenced by Chapter of the Bankruptcy Code, During the 12-Month Period Ending December 31, 2020

Housing Vacancy Rates

Area	Gross Vacancy Rate[2] (%)			Year-Round Vacancy Rate[3] (%)			Rental Vacancy Rate[4] (%)			Homeowner Vacancy Rate[5] (%)		
	2018	2019	2020	2018	2019	2020	2018	2019	2020	2018	2019	2020
MSA[1]	n/a	n/a	n/a	n/a	n/a	n/a	n/a	n/a	n/a	n/a	n/a	n/a
U.S.	12.3	12.0	10.6	9.7	9.5	8.2	6.9	6.7	6.3	1.5	1.4	1.0

Note: (1) Figures cover the Lincoln, NE Metropolitan Statistical Area; (2) The percentage of the total housing inventory that is vacant; (3) The percentage of the housing inventory (excluding seasonal units) that is year-round vacant; (4) The percentage of rental inventory that is vacant for rent; (5) The percentage of homeowner inventory that is vacant for sale; n/a not available
Source: U.S. Census Bureau, Housing Vacancies and Homeownership Annual Statistics: 2018, 2019, 2020

INCOME

Income

Area	Per Capita ($)	Median Household ($)	Average Household ($)
City	31,301	57,746	76,763
MSA[1]	32,360	61,031	80,274
U.S.	34,103	62,843	88,607

Note: (1) Figures cover the Lincoln, NE Metropolitan Statistical Area
Source: U.S. Census Bureau, 2015-2019 American Community Survey 5-Year Estimates

Household Income Distribution

Area	Percent of Households Earning							
	Under $15,000	$15,000 -$24,999	$25,000 -$34,999	$35,000 -$49,999	$50,000 -$74,999	$75,000 -$99,999	$100,000 -$149,999	$150,000 and up
City	9.6	9.2	10.5	13.9	19.3	13.0	14.7	9.9
MSA[1]	8.9	8.8	9.9	13.4	19.0	13.3	15.9	10.8
U.S.	10.3	8.9	8.9	12.3	17.2	12.7	15.1	14.5

Note: (1) Figures cover the Lincoln, NE Metropolitan Statistical Area
Source: U.S. Census Bureau, 2015-2019 American Community Survey 5-Year Estimates

Poverty Rate

Area	All Ages	Under 18 Years Old	18 to 64 Years Old	65 Years and Over
City	13.5	14.2	14.8	6.4
MSA[1]	12.2	12.5	13.5	5.8
U.S.	13.4	18.5	12.6	9.3

Note: Figures are percentage of people whose income during the past 12 months was below the poverty level;
(1) Figures cover the Lincoln, NE Metropolitan Statistical Area
Source: U.S. Census Bureau, 2015-2019 American Community Survey 5-Year Estimates

CITY FINANCES

City Government Finances

Component	2017 ($000)	2017 ($ per capita)
Total Revenues	424,642	1,531
Total Expenditures	477,060	1,720
Debt Outstanding	1,368,810	4,935
Cash and Securities[1]	739,649	2,667

Note: (1) Cash and security holdings of a government at the close of its fiscal year, including those of its dependent agencies, utilities, and liquor stores.
Source: U.S. Census Bureau, State & Local Government Finances 2017

City Government Revenue by Source

Source	2017 ($000)	2017 ($ per capita)	2017 (%)
General Revenue			
From Federal Government	43,639	157	10.3
From State Government	24,735	89	5.8
From Local Governments	2,212	8	0.5
Taxes			
Property	71,254	257	16.8
Sales and Gross Receipts	74,546	269	17.6
Personal Income	0	0	0.0
Corporate Income	0	0	0.0
Motor Vehicle License	0	0	0.0
Other Taxes	25,052	90	5.9
Current Charges	76,816	277	18.1
Liquor Store	0	0	0.0
Utility	58,176	210	13.7
Employee Retirement	16,168	58	3.8

Source: U.S. Census Bureau, State & Local Government Finances 2017

City Government Expenditures by Function

Function	2017 ($000)	2017 ($ per capita)	2017 (%)
General Direct Expenditures			
Air Transportation	0	0	0.0
Corrections	0	0	0.0
Education	0	0	0.0
Employment Security Administration	0	0	0.0
Financial Administration	5,321	19	1.1
Fire Protection	26,166	94	5.5
General Public Buildings	1,064	3	0.2
Governmental Administration, Other	6,918	24	1.5
Health	28,979	104	6.1
Highways	62,909	226	13.2
Hospitals	0	0	0.0
Housing and Community Development	4,849	17	1.0
Interest on General Debt	50,005	180	10.5
Judicial and Legal	0	0	0.0
Libraries	5,756	20	1.2
Parking	6,204	22	1.3
Parks and Recreation	17,265	62	3.6
Police Protection	40,927	147	8.6
Public Welfare	8,279	29	1.7
Sewerage	28,450	102	6.0
Solid Waste Management	12,370	44	2.6
Veterans' Services	0	0	0.0
Liquor Store	0	0	0.0
Utility	91,315	329	19.1
Employee Retirement	12,134	43	2.5

Source: U.S. Census Bureau, State & Local Government Finances 2017

260   Lincoln, Nebraska

EMPLOYMENT

Labor Force and Employment

Area	Civilian Labor Force			Workers Employed		
	Dec. 2019	Dec. 2020	% Chg.	Dec. 2019	Dec. 2020	% Chg.
City	160,552	162,129	1.0	156,783	157,418	0.4
MSA[1]	186,998	188,745	0.9	182,613	183,294	0.4
U.S.	164,007,000	160,017,000	-2.4	158,504,000	149,613,000	-5.6

Note: Data is not seasonally adjusted and covers workers 16 years of age and older; (1) Figures cover the Lincoln, NE Metropolitan Statistical Area
Source: Bureau of Labor Statistics, Local Area Unemployment Statistics

Unemployment Rate

Area	2020											
	Jan.	Feb.	Mar.	Apr.	May	Jun.	Jul.	Aug.	Sep.	Oct.	Nov.	Dec.
City	2.8	2.7	3.7	9.6	5.3	5.9	5.2	3.9	3.3	2.7	2.7	2.9
MSA[1]	2.7	2.6	3.7	9.3	5.2	5.7	5.0	3.8	3.2	2.7	2.7	2.9
U.S.	4.0	3.8	4.5	14.4	13.0	11.2	10.5	8.5	7.7	6.6	6.4	6.5

Note: Data is not seasonally adjusted and covers workers 16 years of age and older; (1) Figures cover the Lincoln, NE Metropolitan Statistical Area
Source: Bureau of Labor Statistics, Local Area Unemployment Statistics

Average Wages

Occupation	$/Hr.	Occupation	$/Hr.
Accountants and Auditors	33.40	Maintenance and Repair Workers	21.20
Automotive Mechanics	22.30	Marketing Managers	43.50
Bookkeepers	19.40	Network and Computer Systems Admin.	35.90
Carpenters	19.80	Nurses, Licensed Practical	22.20
Cashiers	11.90	Nurses, Registered	32.80
Computer Programmers	36.00	Nursing Assistants	14.80
Computer Systems Analysts	36.80	Office Clerks, General	15.30
Computer User Support Specialists	22.50	Physical Therapists	41.90
Construction Laborers	17.20	Physicians	114.20
Cooks, Restaurant	14.40	Plumbers, Pipefitters and Steamfitters	26.80
Customer Service Representatives	16.30	Police and Sheriff's Patrol Officers	31.80
Dentists	60.40	Postal Service Mail Carriers	25.30
Electricians	24.60	Real Estate Sales Agents	26.20
Engineers, Electrical	47.40	Retail Salespersons	13.70
Fast Food and Counter Workers	11.40	Sales Representatives, Technical/Scientific	39.80
Financial Managers	58.70	Secretaries, Exc. Legal/Medical/Executive	18.50
First-Line Supervisors of Office Workers	26.70	Security Guards	17.90
General and Operations Managers	50.20	Surgeons	142.40
Hairdressers/Cosmetologists	13.40	Teacher Assistants, Exc. Postsecondary*	14.90
Home Health and Personal Care Aides	13.60	Teachers, Secondary School, Exc. Sp. Ed.*	30.70
Janitors and Cleaners	13.40	Telemarketers	11.10
Landscaping/Groundskeeping Workers	14.30	Truck Drivers, Heavy/Tractor-Trailer	26.00
Lawyers	56.00	Truck Drivers, Light/Delivery Services	19.70
Maids and Housekeeping Cleaners	13.50	Waiters and Waitresses	10.60

Note: Wage data covers the Lincoln, NE Metropolitan Statistical Area; (*) Hourly wages were calculated from annual wage data based on a 40 hour work week; n/a not available.
Source: Bureau of Labor Statistics, Metro Area Occupational Employment & Wage Estimates, May 2020

Employment by Industry

Sector	MSA[1]		U.S.
	Number of Employees	Percent of Total	Percent of Total
Construction, Mining, and Logging	9,600	5.1	5.5
Education and Health Services	31,000	16.6	16.3
Financial Activities	12,700	6.8	6.1
Government	40,900	21.9	15.2
Information	3,200	1.7	1.9
Leisure and Hospitality	14,300	7.7	9.0
Manufacturing	13,100	7.0	8.5
Other Services	6,800	3.6	3.8
Professional and Business Services	21,300	11.4	14.4
Retail Trade	18,300	9.8	10.9
Transportation, Warehousing, and Utilities	11,100	5.9	4.6
Wholesale Trade	4,300	2.3	3.9

Note: Figures are non-farm employment as of December 2020. Figures are not seasonally adjusted and include workers 16 years of age and older; (1) Figures cover the Lincoln, NE Metropolitan Statistical Area
Source: Bureau of Labor Statistics, Current Employment Statistics, Employment, Hours, and Earnings

Employment by Occupation

Occupation Classification	City (%)	MSA[1] (%)	U.S. (%)
Management, Business, Science, and Arts	40.4	40.8	38.5
Natural Resources, Construction, and Maintenance	7.5	8.1	8.9
Production, Transportation, and Material Moving	11.6	11.6	13.2
Sales and Office	22.5	22.0	21.6
Service	18.1	17.5	17.8

Note: Figures cover employed civilians 16 years of age and older; (1) Figures cover the Lincoln, NE Metropolitan Statistical Area
Source: U.S. Census Bureau, 2015-2019 American Community Survey 5-Year Estimates

Occupations with Greatest Projected Employment Growth: 2020 – 2022

Occupation[1]	2020 Employment	2022 Projected Employment	Numeric Employment Change	Percent Employment Change
Combined Food Preparation and Serving Workers, Including Fast Food	19,330	25,690	6,360	32.9
Waiters and Waitresses	11,920	16,420	4,500	37.8
Retail Salespersons	23,300	27,380	4,080	17.5
Cashiers	22,540	24,750	2,210	9.8
Cooks, Restaurant	4,630	6,640	2,010	43.4
First-Line Supervisors of Food Preparation and Serving Workers	5,390	7,200	1,810	33.6
Childcare Workers	10,750	12,540	1,790	16.7
General and Operations Managers	16,050	17,690	1,640	10.2
Bartenders	4,140	5,770	1,630	39.4
Janitors and Cleaners, Except Maids and Housekeeping Cleaners	15,050	16,620	1,570	10.4

Note: Projections cover Nebraska; (1) Sorted by numeric employment change
Source: www.projectionscentral.com, State Occupational Projections, 2020–2022 Short-Term Projections

Fastest-Growing Occupations: 2020 – 2022

Occupation[1]	2020 Employment	2022 Projected Employment	Numeric Employment Change	Percent Employment Change
Ushers, Lobby Attendants, and Ticket Takers	290	680	390	134.5
Actors	40	90	50	125.0
Craft Artists	50	110	60	120.0
Lodging Managers	90	160	70	77.8
Baggage Porters and Bellhops	90	160	70	77.8
Hotel, Motel, and Resort Desk Clerks	1,190	2,030	840	70.6
Gaming and Sports Book Writers and Runners	270	440	170	63.0
Amusement and Recreation Attendants	650	1,030	380	58.5
Fitness Trainers and Aerobics Instructors	2,180	3,200	1,020	46.8
Concierges	110	160	50	45.5

Note: Projections cover Nebraska; (1) Sorted by percent employment change and excludes occupations with numeric employment change less than 50
Source: www.projectionscentral.com, State Occupational Projections, 2020–2022 Short-Term Projections

TAXES

State Corporate Income Tax Rates

State	Tax Rate (%)	Income Brackets ($)	Num. of Brackets	Financial Institution Tax Rate (%)[a]	Federal Income Tax Ded.
Nebraska	5.58 - 7.81	100,000	2	(a)	No

Note: Tax rates as of January 1, 2021; (a) Rates listed are the corporate income tax rate applied to financial institutions or excise taxes based on income. Some states have other taxes based upon the value of deposits or shares.
Source: Federation of Tax Administrators, State Corporate Income Tax Rates, January 1, 2021

State Individual Income Tax Rates

State	Tax Rate (%)	Income Brackets ($)	Personal Exemptions ($)			Standard Ded. ($)	
			Single	Married	Depend.	Single	Married
Nebraska (a)	2.46 - 6.84	3,340 - 32,210 (b)	142	284 (c)	142 (c)	7,100	14,200

Note: Tax rates as of January 1, 2021; Local- and county-level taxes are not included; Federal income tax is not deductible on state income tax returns; (a) 19 states have statutory provision for automatically adjusting to the rate of inflation the dollar values of the income tax brackets, standard deductions, and/or personal exemptions. Michigan indexes the personal exemption only. Oregon does not index the income brackets for $125,000 and over; (b) For joint returns, taxes are twice the tax on half the couple's income; (c) The personal exemption takes the form of a tax credit instead of a deduction
Source: Federation of Tax Administrators, State Individual Income Tax Rates, January 1, 2021

Various State Sales and Excise Tax Rates

State	State Sales Tax (%)	Gasoline[1] (¢/gal.)	Cigarette[2] ($/pack)	Spirits[3] ($/gal.)	Wine[4] ($/gal.)	Beer[5] ($/gal.)	Recreational Marijuana (%)
Nebraska	5.5	29.6	0.64	3.75	0.95	0.31	Not legal

Note: All tax rates as of January 1, 2021; (1) The American Petroleum Institute has developed a methodology for determining the average tax rate on a gallon of fuel. Rates may include any of the following: excise taxes, environmental fees, storage tank fees, other fees or taxes, general sales tax, and local taxes; (2) The federal excise tax of $1.0066 per pack and local taxes are not included; (3) Rates are those applicable to off-premise sales of 40% alcohol by volume (a.b.v.) distilled spirits in 750ml containers. Local excise taxes are excluded; (4) Rates are those applicable to off-premise sales of 11% a.b.v. non-carbonated wine in 750ml containers; (5) Rates are those applicable to off-premise sales of 4.7% a.b.v. beer in 12 ounce containers.
Source: Tax Foundation, 2021 Facts & Figures: How Does Your State Compare?

State Business Tax Climate Index Rankings

State	Overall Rank	Corporate Tax Rank	Individual Income Tax Rank	Sales Tax Rank	Property Tax Rank	Unemployment Insurance Tax Rank
Nebraska	28	32	21	15	41	11

Note: The index is a measure of how each state's tax laws affect economic performance. The lower the rank, the more favorable a state's tax system is for business. States without a given tax are given a ranking of 1. The scores/rankings for the District of Columbia do not affect other states. The 2021 index represents the tax climate as of July 1, 2020.
Source: Tax Foundation, State Business Tax Climate Index 2021

TRANSPORTATION

Means of Transportation to Work

Area	Car/Truck/Van		Public Transportation			Bicycle	Walked	Other Means	Worked at Home
	Drove Alone	Car-pooled	Bus	Subway	Railroad				
City	81.0	9.0	1.3	0.0	0.0	1.2	3.4	0.6	3.4
MSA[1]	81.3	8.9	1.1	0.0	0.0	1.1	3.3	0.6	3.7
U.S.	76.3	9.0	2.4	1.9	0.6	0.5	2.7	1.4	5.2

Note: Figures are percentages and cover workers 16 years of age and older; (1) Figures cover the Lincoln, NE Metropolitan Statistical Area
Source: U.S. Census Bureau, 2015-2019 American Community Survey 5-Year Estimates

Travel Time to Work

Area	Less Than 10 Minutes	10 to 19 Minutes	20 to 29 Minutes	30 to 44 Minutes	45 to 59 Minutes	60 to 89 Minutes	90 Minutes or More
City	17.2	44.8	23.1	9.3	2.5	2.1	1.1
MSA[1]	17.1	41.8	23.8	11.2	2.9	2.0	1.2
U.S.	12.2	28.4	20.8	20.8	8.3	6.4	2.9

Note: Note: Figures are percentages and include workers 16 years old and over; (1) Figures cover the Lincoln, NE Metropolitan Statistical Area
Source: U.S. Census Bureau, 2015-2019 American Community Survey 5-Year Estimates

Key Congestion Measures

Measure	1982	1992	2002	2012	2017
Annual Hours of Delay, Total (000)	n/a	n/a	n/a	n/a	4,733
Annual Hours of Delay, Per Auto Commuter	n/a	n/a	n/a	n/a	16
Annual Congestion Cost, Total (million $)	n/a	n/a	n/a	n/a	97
Annual Congestion Cost, Per Auto Commuter ($)	n/a	n/a	n/a	n/a	334

Note: n/a not available
Source: Texas A&M Transportation Institute, 2019 Urban Mobility Report

Freeway Travel Time Index

Measure	1982	1987	1992	1997	2002	2007	2012	2017
Urban Area Index[1]	n/a	n/a	n/a	n/a	n/a	n/a	n/a	1.09
Urban Area Rank[1,2]	n/a	n/a	n/a	n/a	n/a	n/a	n/a	n/a

Note: Freeway Travel Time Index—the ratio of travel time in the peak period to the travel time at free-flow conditions. For example, a value of 1.30 indicates a 20-minute free-flow trip takes 26 minutes in the peak (20 minutes x 1.30 = 26 minutes); (1) Covers the Lincoln NE urban area; (2) Rank is based on 101 larger urban areas (#1 = highest travel time index); n/a not available
Source: Texas A&M Transportation Institute, 2019 Urban Mobility Report

Public Transportation

Agency Name / Mode of Transportation	Vehicles Operated in Maximum Service[1]	Annual Unlinked Passenger Trips[2] (in thous.)	Annual Passenger Miles[3] (in thous.)
StarTran			
Bus (directly operated)	56	2,369.7	7,078.9
Demand Response (directly operated)	9	43.5	227.1
Demand Response Taxi (purchased transportation)	13	28.3	185.6

Note: (1) Number of revenue vehicles operated by the given mode and type of service to meet the annual maximum service requirement. This is the revenue vehicle count during the peak season of the year; on the week and day that maximum service is provided. Vehicles operated in maximum service (VOMS) exclude atypical days and one-time special events; (2) Number of passengers who boarded public transportation vehicles. Passengers are counted each time they board a vehicle no matter how many vehicles they use to travel from their origin to their destination. (3) Sum of the distances ridden by all passengers during the entire fiscal year. Source: Federal Transit Administration, National Transit Database, 2019

Air Transportation

Airport Name and Code / Type of Service	Passenger Airlines[1]	Passenger Enplanements	Freight Carriers[2]	Freight (lbs)
Lincoln Municipal (LNK)				
Domestic service (U.S. carriers - 2020)	14	52,679	1	13,450
International service (U.S. carriers - 2019)	3	156	1	29,892

Note: (1) Includes all U.S.-based major, minor and commuter airlines that carried at least one passenger during the year; (2) Includes all U.S.-based airlines and freight carriers that transported at least one pound of freight during the year. Source: Bureau of Transportation Statistics, The Intermodal Transportation Database, Air Carriers: T-100 Domestic Market (U.S. Carriers), 2020; Bureau of Transportation Statistics, The Intermodal Transportation Database, Air Carriers: T-100 International Market (U.S. Carriers), 2019

BUSINESSES

Major Business Headquarters

Company Name	Industry	Rankings	
		Fortune[1]	Forbes[2]
No companies listed	-	-	-

Note: (1) Companies that produce a 10-K are ranked 1 to 500 based on 2019 revenue; (2) All private companies with at least $2 billion in annual revenue through the end of their most current fiscal year are ranked 1 to 219; companies listed are headquartered in the city; dashes indicate no ranking Source: Fortune, "Fortune 500," June/July 2020; Forbes, "America's Largest Private Companies," 2020

Fastest-Growing Businesses

According to *Inc.*, Lincoln is home to one of America's 500 fastest-growing private companies: **CompanyCam** (#273). Criteria: must be an independent, privately-held, for-profit, U.S. corporation, proprietorship or partnership as of December 31, 2019; revenues must be at least $100,000 in 2016 and $2 million in 2019; must have four-year operating/sales history. *Inc., "America's 500 Fastest-Growing Private Companies," 2020*

Living Environment

COST OF LIVING

Cost of Living Index

Composite Index	Groceries	Housing	Utilities	Trans-portation	Health Care	Misc. Goods/ Services
92.5	97.2	77.3	87.9	100.7	106.8	99.9

Note: The Cost of Living Index measures regional differences in the cost of consumer goods and services, excluding taxes and non-consumer expenditures, for professional and managerial households in the top income quintile. It is based on more than 50,000 prices covering almost 60 different items for which prices are collected three times a year by chambers of commerce, economic development organizations or university applied economic centers in each participating urban area. The numbers shown should be read as a percentage above or below the national average of 100. For example, a value of 115.4 in the groceries column indicates that grocery prices are 15.4% higher than the national average. Small differences in the index numbers should not be interpreted as significant; Figures cover the Lincoln NE urban area.
Source: The Council for Community and Economic Research, Cost of Living Index, 2020

Grocery Prices

Area[1]	T-Bone Steak ($/pound)	Frying Chicken ($/pound)	Whole Milk ($/half gal.)	Eggs ($/dozen)	Orange Juice ($/64 oz.)	Coffee ($/11.5 oz.)
City[2]	11.88	1.46	2.21	1.42	3.03	4.13
Avg.	11.78	1.39	2.05	1.47	3.57	4.34
Min.	8.03	0.94	1.03	0.74	2.94	3.02
Max.	15.86	2.65	4.31	3.77	5.44	8.69

Note: (1) Values for the local area are compared with the average, minimum and maximum values for all 284 areas in the Cost of Living Index; (2) Figures cover the Lincoln NE urban area; T-Bone Steak (price per pound); Frying Chicken (price per pound, whole fryer); Whole Milk (half gallon carton); Eggs (price per dozen, Grade A, large); Orange Juice (64 oz. Tropicana or Florida Natural); Coffee (11.5 oz. can, vacuum-packed, Maxwell House, Hills Bros, or Folgers).
Source: The Council for Community and Economic Research, Cost of Living Index, 2020

Housing and Utility Costs

Area[1]	New Home Price ($)	Apartment Rent ($/month)	All Electric ($/month)	Part Electric ($/month)	Other Energy ($/month)	Telephone ($/month)
City[2]	296,778	867	-	70.14	53.85	194.40
Avg.	368,594	1,168	170.86	100.47	65.28	184.30
Min.	190,567	502	91.58	31.42	26.08	169.60
Max.	2,227,806	4,738	470.38	280.31	280.06	206.50

Note: (1) Values for the local area are compared with the average, minimum and maximum values for all 284 areas in the Cost of Living Index; (2) Figures cover the Lincoln NE urban area; New Home Price (2,400 sf living area, 8,000 sf lot, in urban area with full utilities); Apartment Rent (950 sf 2 bedroom/1.5 or 2 bath, unfurnished, excluding all utilities except water); All Electric (average monthly cost for an all-electric home); Part Electric (average monthly cost for a part-electric home); Other Energy (average monthly cost for natural gas, fuel oil, coal, wood, and any other forms of energy except electricity); Telephone (price includes the base monthly rate plus taxes and fees for three lines of mobile phone service).
Source: The Council for Community and Economic Research, Cost of Living Index, 2020

Health Care, Transportation, and Other Costs

Area[1]	Doctor ($/visit)	Dentist ($/visit)	Optometrist ($/visit)	Gasoline ($/gallon)	Beauty Salon ($/visit)	Men's Shirt ($)
City[2]	148.06	94.73	104.48	2.20	40.62	43.69
Avg.	115.44	99.32	108.10	2.21	39.27	31.37
Min.	36.68	59.00	51.36	1.71	19.00	11.00
Max.	219.00	153.10	250.97	3.46	82.05	58.33

Note: (1) Values for the local area are compared with the average, minimum and maximum values for all 284 areas in the Cost of Living Index; (2) Figures cover the Lincoln NE urban area; Doctor (general practitioners routine exam of an established patient); Dentist (adult teeth cleaning and periodic oral examination); Optometrist (full vision eye exam for established adult patient); Gasoline (one gallon regular unleaded, national brand, including all taxes, cash price at self-service pump if available); Beauty Salon (woman's shampoo, trim, and blow-dry); Men's Shirt (cotton/polyester dress shirt, pinpoint weave, long sleeves).
Source: The Council for Community and Economic Research, Cost of Living Index, 2020

HOUSING

Homeownership Rate

Area	2012 (%)	2013 (%)	2014 (%)	2015 (%)	2016 (%)	2017 (%)	2018 (%)	2019 (%)	2020 (%)
MSA[1]	n/a	n/a	n/a	n/a	n/a	n/a	n/a	n/a	n/a
U.S.	65.4	65.1	64.5	63.7	63.4	63.9	64.4	64.6	66.6

Note: (1) Figures cover the Lincoln, NE Metropolitan Statistical Area; n/a not available
Source: U.S. Census Bureau, Housing Vacancies and Homeownership Annual Statistics: 2012-2020

House Price Index (HPI)

Area	National Ranking[2]	Quarterly Change (%)	One-Year Change (%)	Five-Year Change (%)	Since 1991Q1 (%)
MSA[1]	198	2.22	5.09	30.00	177.71
U.S.[3]	–	3.81	10.77	38.99	205.12

Note: The HPI is a weighted repeat sales index. It measures average price changes in repeat sales or refinancings on the same properties. This information is obtained by reviewing repeat mortgage transactions on single-family properties whose mortgages have been purchased or securitized by Fannie Mae or Freddie Mac since January 1975; (1) Figures cover the Lincoln, NE Metropolitan Statistical Area; (2) Rankings are based on annual percentage change for all metro areas containing at least 15,000 transactions over the last 10 years and ranges from 1 to 253; (3) figures based on a weighted average of Census Division estimates using a seasonally adjusted, purchase-only index; all figures are for the period ending December 31, 2020
Source: Federal Housing Finance Agency, Change in Metropolitan Area House Price Indexes, April 7, 2021

Median Single-Family Home Prices

Area	2018	2019	2020[p]	Percent Change 2019 to 2020
MSA[1]	189.0	198.4	219.8	10.8
U.S. Average	261.6	274.6	299.9	9.2

Note: Figures are median sales prices of existing single-family homes in thousands of dollars; (p) preliminary; (1) Figures cover the Lincoln, NE Metropolitan Statistical Area
Source: National Association of Realtors, Median Sales Price of Existing Single-Family Homes for Metropolitan Areas, 4th Quarter 2020

Qualifying Income Based on Median Sales Price of Existing Single-Family Homes

Area	With 5% Down ($)	With 10% Down ($)	With 20% Down ($)
MSA[1]	43,049	40,783	36,252
U.S. Average	59,266	56,147	49,908

Note: Figures are preliminary; Qualifying income is based on a mortgage rate of 2.81%. Monthly principal and interest payment is limited to 25% of income; (1) Figures cover the Lincoln, NE Metropolitan Statistical Area
Source: National Association of Realtors, Qualifying Income Based on Median Sales Price of Existing Single-Family Homes for Metropolitan Areas, 4th Quarter 2020

Home Value Distribution

Area	Under $50,000	$50,000 -$99,999	$100,000 -$149,999	$150,000 -$199,999	$200,000 -$299,999	$300,000 -$499,999	$500,000 -$999,999	$1,000,000 or more
City	3.5	9.8	25.5	23.9	23.3	11.2	2.4	0.5
MSA[1]	3.2	9.4	23.4	22.6	23.4	13.8	3.7	0.5
U.S.	6.9	12.0	13.3	14.0	19.6	19.3	11.4	3.4

Note: Figures are percentages and cover owner-occupied housing units; (1) Figures cover the Lincoln, NE Metropolitan Statistical Area
Source: U.S. Census Bureau, 2015-2019 American Community Survey 5-Year Estimates

Year Housing Structure Built

Area	2010 or Later	2000 -2009	1990 -1999	1980 -1989	1970 -1979	1960 -1969	1950 -1959	1940 -1949	Before 1940	Median Year
City	7.3	13.7	15.0	10.4	15.3	10.0	11.2	3.0	14.0	1978
MSA[1]	7.3	14.1	15.1	10.1	15.6	10.0	10.3	2.8	14.7	1978
U.S.	5.2	14.0	13.9	13.4	15.2	10.6	10.3	4.9	12.6	1978

Note: Figures are percentages except for Median Year; Note: (1) Figures cover the Lincoln, NE Metropolitan Statistical Area
Source: U.S. Census Bureau, 2015-2019 American Community Survey 5-Year Estimates

Gross Monthly Rent

Area	Under $500	$500 -$999	$1,000 -$1,499	$1,500 -$1,999	$2,000 -$2,499	$2,500 -$2,999	$3,000 and up	Median ($)
City	9.5	58.4	25.0	4.9	0.8	0.3	1.0	852
MSA[1]	9.9	58.2	24.9	4.8	0.8	0.4	1.0	848
U.S.	9.4	36.2	30.0	14.0	5.6	2.4	2.4	1,062

Note: Figures are percentages except for Median; Gross rent is the contract rent plus the estimated average monthly cost of utilities (electricity, gas, and water and sewer) and fuels (oil, coal, kerosene, wood, etc.) if these are paid by the renter (or paid for the renter by someone else); (1) Figures cover the Lincoln, NE Metropolitan Statistical Area
Source: U.S. Census Bureau, 2015-2019 American Community Survey 5-Year Estimates

HEALTH

Health Risk Factors

Category	MSA[1] (%)	U.S. (%)
Adults aged 18–64 who have any kind of health care coverage	87.5	87.3
Adults who reported being in good or better health	86.9	82.4
Adults who have been told they have high blood cholesterol	29.3	33.0
Adults who have been told they have high blood pressure	26.5	32.3
Adults who are current smokers	12.2	17.1
Adults who currently use E-cigarettes	3.4	4.6
Adults who currently use chewing tobacco, snuff, or snus	3.3	4.0
Adults who are heavy drinkers[2]	7.5	6.3
Adults who are binge drinkers[3]	24.2	17.4
Adults who are overweight (BMI 25.0 - 29.9)	38.1	35.3
Adults who are obese (BMI 30.0 - 99.8)	28.9	31.3
Adults who participated in any physical activities in the past month	80.1	74.4
Adults who always or nearly always wears a seat belt	92.3	94.3

Note: (1) Figures cover the Lincoln, NE Metropolitan Statistical Area; (2) Heavy drinkers are classified as adult men having more than 14 drinks per week and adult women having more than 7 drinks per week; (3) Binge drinkers are classified as males having five or more drinks on one occasion or females having four or more drinks on one occasion
Source: Centers for Disease Control and Prevention, Behaviorial Risk Factor Surveillance System, SMART: Selected Metropolitan Area Risk Trends, 2017

Acute and Chronic Health Conditions

Category	MSA[1] (%)	U.S. (%)
Adults who have ever been told they had a heart attack	3.7	4.2
Adults who have ever been told they have angina or coronary heart disease	3.5	3.9
Adults who have ever been told they had a stroke	2.3	3.0
Adults who have ever been told they have asthma	13.2	14.2
Adults who have ever been told they have arthritis	21.0	24.9
Adults who have ever been told they have diabetes[2]	8.3	10.5
Adults who have ever been told they had skin cancer	5.8	6.2
Adults who have ever been told they had any other types of cancer	6.4	7.1
Adults who have ever been told they have COPD	5.5	6.5
Adults who have ever been told they have kidney disease	2.9	3.0
Adults who have ever been told they have a form of depression	20.7	20.5

Note: (1) Figures cover the Lincoln, NE Metropolitan Statistical Area; (2) Figures do not include pregnancy-related, borderline, or pre-diabetes
Source: Centers for Disease Control and Prevention, Behaviorial Risk Factor Surveillance System, SMART: Selected Metropolitan Area Risk Trends, 2017

Health Screening and Vaccination Rates

Category	MSA[1] (%)	U.S. (%)
Adults aged 65+ who have had flu shot within the past year	68.4	60.7
Adults aged 65+ who have ever had a pneumonia vaccination	82.1	75.4
Adults who have ever been tested for HIV	27.1	36.1
Adults who have ever had the shingles or zoster vaccine?	37.7	28.9
Adults who have had their blood cholesterol checked within the last five years	86.2	85.9

Note: n/a not available; (1) Figures cover the Lincoln, NE Metropolitan Statistical Area.
Source: Centers for Disease Control and Prevention, Behaviorial Risk Factor Surveillance System, SMART: Selected Metropolitan Area Risk Trends, 2017

Disability Status

Category	MSA[1] (%)	U.S. (%)
Adults who reported being deaf	5.7	6.7
Are you blind or have serious difficulty seeing, even when wearing glasses?	2.5	4.5
Are you limited in any way in any of your usual activities due of arthritis?	9.5	12.9
Do you have difficulty doing errands alone?	3.7	6.8
Do you have difficulty dressing or bathing?	2.4	3.6
Do you have serious difficulty concentrating/remembering/making decisions?	8.0	10.7
Do you have serious difficulty walking or climbing stairs?	8.9	13.6

Note: (1) Figures cover the Lincoln, NE Metropolitan Statistical Area.
Source: Centers for Disease Control and Prevention, Behaviorial Risk Factor Surveillance System, SMART: Selected Metropolitan Area Risk Trends, 2017

Mortality Rates for the Top 10 Causes of Death in the U.S.

ICD-10[a] Sub-Chapter	ICD-10[a] Code	Age-Adjusted Mortality Rate[1] per 100,000 population	
		County[2]	U.S.
Malignant neoplasms	C00-C97	141.1	149.2
Ischaemic heart diseases	I20-I25	63.9	90.5
Other forms of heart disease	I30-I51	53.1	52.2
Chronic lower respiratory diseases	J40-J47	48.0	39.6
Other degenerative diseases of the nervous system	G30-G31	46.6	37.6
Cerebrovascular diseases	I60-I69	34.6	37.2
Other external causes of accidental injury	W00-X59	24.7	36.1
Organic, including symptomatic, mental disorders	F01-F09	30.0	29.4
Hypertensive diseases	I10-I15	20.5	24.1
Diabetes mellitus	E10-E14	19.8	21.5

Note: (a) ICD-10 = International Classification of Diseases 10th Revision; (1) Mortality rates are a three-year average covering 2017-2019; (2) Figures cover Lancaster County.
Source: Centers for Disease Control and Prevention, National Center for Health Statistics. Underlying Cause of Death 1999-2019 on CDC WONDER Online Database

Mortality Rates for Selected Causes of Death

ICD-10[a] Sub-Chapter	ICD-10[a] Code	Age-Adjusted Mortality Rate[1] per 100,000 population	
		County[2]	U.S.
Assault	X85-Y09	Unreliable	6.0
Diseases of the liver	K70-K76	13.0	14.4
Human immunodeficiency virus (HIV) disease	B20-B24	Suppressed	1.5
Influenza and pneumonia	J09-J18	12.4	13.8
Intentional self-harm	X60-X84	13.4	14.1
Malnutrition	E40-E46	4.7	2.3
Obesity and other hyperalimentation	E65-E68	3.2	2.1
Renal failure	N17-N19	8.4	12.6
Transport accidents	V01-V99	8.3	12.3
Viral hepatitis	B15-B19	Unreliable	1.2

Note: (a) ICD-10 = International Classification of Diseases 10th Revision; (1) Mortality rates are a three-year average covering 2017-2019; (2) Figures cover Lancaster County; Data are suppressed when the data meet the criteria for confidentiality constraints; Mortality rates are flagged as unreliable when the rate would be calculated with a numerator of 20 or less.
Source: Centers for Disease Control and Prevention, National Center for Health Statistics. Underlying Cause of Death 1999-2019 on CDC WONDER Online Database

Health Insurance Coverage

Area	With Health Insurance	With Private Health Insurance	With Public Health Insurance	Without Health Insurance	Population Under Age 19 Without Health Insurance
City	92.3	78.5	25.2	7.7	5.2
MSA[1]	92.9	79.5	24.9	7.1	4.8
U.S.	91.2	67.9	35.1	8.8	5.1

Note: Figures are percentages that cover the civilian noninstitutionalized population; (1) Figures cover the Lincoln, NE Metropolitan Statistical Area
Source: U.S. Census Bureau, 2015-2019 American Community Survey 5-Year Estimates

Number of Medical Professionals

Area	MDs[3]	DOs[3,4]	Dentists	Podiatrists	Chiropractors	Optometrists
County[1] (number)	691	40	324	17	144	69
County[1] (rate[2])	218.3	12.6	101.5	5.3	45.1	21.6
U.S. (rate[2])	282.9	22.7	71.2	6.2	28.1	16.9

31109
Note: Data as of 2019 unless noted; (1) Data covers Lancaster County; (2) Rate per 100,000 population; (3) Data as of 2018 and includes all active, non-federal physicians; (4) Doctor of Osteopathic Medicine
Source: U.S. Department of Health and Human Services, Health Resources and Services Administration, Bureau of Health Professions, Area Resource File (ARF) 2019-2020

268   Lincoln, Nebraska

EDUCATION

Public School District Statistics

District Name	Schls	Pupils	Pupil/ Teacher Ratio	Minority Pupils[1] (%)	Free Lunch Eligible[2] (%)	IEP[3] (%)
Lincoln Public Schools	74	42,020	13.5	33.8	37.8	17.5

Note: Table includes school districts with 2,000 or more students; (1) Percentage of students that are not non-Hispanic white; (2) Percentage of students that are eligible for the free lunch program; (3) Percentage of students that have an Individualized Education Program.
Source: U.S. Department of Education, National Center for Education Statistics, Common Core of Data, Local Education Agency (School District) Universe Survey: School Year 2018-2019; U.S. Department of Education, National Center for Education Statistics, Common Core of Data, Public Elementary/Secondary School Universe Survey: School Year 2018-2019

Highest Level of Education

Area	Less than H.S.	H.S. Diploma	Some College, No Deg.	Associate Degree	Bachelor's Degree	Master's Degree	Prof. School Degree	Doctorate Degree
City	6.7	21.3	21.2	11.2	24.8	9.8	2.2	2.8
MSA[1]	6.3	21.9	21.2	11.7	24.5	9.7	2.2	2.6
U.S.	12.0	27.0	20.4	8.5	19.8	8.8	2.1	1.4

Note: Figures cover persons age 25 and over; (1) Figures cover the Lincoln, NE Metropolitan Statistical Area
Source: U.S. Census Bureau, 2015-2019 American Community Survey 5-Year Estimates

Educational Attainment by Race

Area	High School Graduate or Higher (%)					Bachelor's Degree or Higher (%)				
	Total	White	Black	Asian	Hisp.[2]	Total	White	Black	Asian	Hisp.[2]
City	93.3	95.0	86.1	79.2	70.1	39.6	40.7	23.8	46.7	19.3
MSA[1]	93.7	95.2	86.1	78.9	70.4	39.0	39.8	23.9	46.3	19.7
U.S.	88.0	89.9	86.0	87.1	68.7	32.1	33.5	21.6	54.3	16.4

Note: Figures shown cover persons 25 years old and over; (1) Figures cover the Lincoln, NE Metropolitan Statistical Area; (2) People of Hispanic origin can be of any race
Source: U.S. Census Bureau, 2015-2019 American Community Survey 5-Year Estimates

School Enrollment by Grade and Control

Area	Preschool (%)		Kindergarten (%)		Grades 1 - 4 (%)		Grades 5 - 8 (%)		Grades 9 - 12 (%)	
	Public	Private	Public	Private	Public	Private	Public	Private	Public	Private
City	44.8	55.2	73.8	26.2	84.9	15.1	86.5	13.5	86.4	13.6
MSA[1]	44.3	55.7	75.3	24.7	84.3	15.7	86.7	13.3	86.9	13.1
U.S.	59.1	40.9	87.6	12.4	89.5	10.5	89.4	10.6	90.1	9.9

Note: Figures shown cover persons 3 years old and over; (1) Figures cover the Lincoln, NE Metropolitan Statistical Area
Source: U.S. Census Bureau, 2015-2019 American Community Survey 5-Year Estimates

Higher Education

Four-Year Colleges			Two-Year Colleges			Medical Schools[1]	Law Schools[2]	Voc/ Tech[3]
Public	Private Non-profit	Private For-profit	Public	Private Non-profit	Private For-profit			
2	4	0	1	0	5	0	1	0

Note: Figures cover institutions located within the city limits and include main campuses only; (1) includes schools accredited by the Liaison Committee on Medical Education and the American Osteopathic Association's Commission on Osteopathic College Accreditation; (2) includes ABA-accredited schools, schools with provisional ABA accreditation, and state accredited schools; (3) includes all schools with programs that are less than 2 years.
Source: National Center for Education Statistics, Integrated Postsecondary Education System (IPEDS), 2019-20; Wikipedia, List of Medical Schools in the United States, accessed April 2, 2021; Wikipedia, List of Law Schools in the United States, accessed April 2, 2021

According to *U.S. News & World Report,* the Lincoln, NE metro area is home to one of the top 200 national universities in the U.S.: **University of Nebraska—Lincoln** (#133 tie). The indicators used to capture academic quality fall into a number of categories: assessment by administrators at peer institutions; retention of students; faculty resources; student selectivity; financial resources; alumni giving; high school counselor ratings of colleges; and graduation rate. *U.S. News & World Report, "America's Best Colleges 2021"*

According to *U.S. News & World Report,* the Lincoln, NE metro area is home to one of the top 100 law schools in the U.S.: **University of Nebraska—Lincoln** (#87). The rankings are based on a weighted average of 12 measures of quality: peer assessment score; assessment score by lawyers/judges; median LSAT scores; median undergrad GPA; acceptance rate; employment rates for graduates; placement success; bar passage rate; faculty resources; expenditures per student; student/faculty ratio; and library resources. *U.S. News & World Report, "America's Best Graduate Schools, Law, 2022"*

EMPLOYERS

Major Employers

Company Name	Industry
Bank of the West	Financial services
Cargill Meat Solutions	Food processing
CHI Health Bergan Mercy	Healthcare
CHI Health Saint Elizabeth	Healthcare
Con Agra Foods Inc	Food manufacturing
Creighton University	Education
First Data	Commerce
Health & Human Svc Dept	Government
JBS USA	Food processing
Methodist Hospital	Healthcare
Mutual of Omaha Insurance Co	Insurance
Nebraska Medical Center	Healthcare
Nebraska Medicine	Healthcare
Offutt AFB	U.S. military
Pay Pal	Payment services
Smithfield Farmland	Agriculture
Tyson Fresh Meats	Food processing
Union Pacific Railroad Co	Railroad
University of NE Medical Ctr	Healthcare
University of Nebraska	Education
West Corp	Communications

Note: Companies shown are located within the Lincoln, NE Metropolitan Statistical Area.
Source: Hoovers.com; Wikipedia

PUBLIC SAFETY

Crime Rate

Area	All Crimes	Violent Crimes				Property Crimes		
		Murder	Rape[3]	Robbery	Aggrav. Assault	Burglary	Larceny -Theft	Motor Vehicle Theft
City	3,133.7	1.7	110.9	57.0	213.3	339.4	2,255.4	155.9
Suburbs[1]	1,017.1	0.0	77.9	0.0	41.1	119.0	705.4	73.6
Metro[2]	2,843.7	1.5	106.4	49.2	189.7	309.2	2,043.0	144.7
U.S.	2,489.3	5.0	42.6	81.6	250.2	340.5	1,549.5	219.9

Note: Figures are crimes per 100,000 population; (1) All areas within the metro area that are located outside the city limits; (2) Figures cover the Lincoln, NE Metropolitan Statistical Area; (3) All figures shown were reported using the revised Uniform Crime Reporting (UCR) definition of rape.
Source: FBI Uniform Crime Reports, 2019

Hate Crimes

Area	Number of Quarters Reported	Number of Incidents per Bias Motivation					
		Race/Ethnicity/ Ancestry	Religion	Sexual Orientation	Disability	Gender	Gender Identity
City	4	5	2	2	0	0	0
U.S.	4	3,963	1,521	1,195	157	69	198

Source: Federal Bureau of Investigation, Hate Crime Statistics 2019

Identity Theft Consumer Reports

Area	Reports	Reports per 100,000 Population	Rank[2]
MSA[1]	389	116	344
U.S.	1,387,615	423	-

Note: (1) Figures cover the Lincoln, NE Metropolitan Statistical Area; (2) Rank ranges from 1 to 391 where 1 indicates greatest number of identity theft reports per 100,000 population
Source: Federal Trade Commission, Consumer Sentinel Network Data Book 2020

Fraud and Other Consumer Reports

Area	Reports	Reports per 100,000 Population	Rank[2]
MSA[1]	2,008	597	286
U.S.	3,385,133	1,031	-

Note: (1) Figures cover the Lincoln, NE Metropolitan Statistical Area; (2) Rank ranges from 1 to 391 where 1 indicates greatest number of fraud and other consumer reports per 100,000 population
Source: Federal Trade Commission, Consumer Sentinel Network Data Book 2020

POLITICS

2020 Presidential Election Results

Area	Biden	Trump	Jorgensen	Hawkins	Other
Lancaster County	52.3	44.6	2.4	0.0	0.7
U.S.	51.3	46.8	1.2	0.3	0.5

Note: Results are percentages and may not add to 100% due to rounding
Source: Dave Leip's Atlas of U.S. Presidential Elections

SPORTS

Professional Sports Teams

Team Name	League	Year Established
No teams are located in the metro area		

Source: Wikipedia, Major Professional Sports Teams of the United States and Canada, April 6, 2021

CLIMATE

Average and Extreme Temperatures

Temperature	Jan	Feb	Mar	Apr	May	Jun	Jul	Aug	Sep	Oct	Nov	Dec	Yr.
Extreme High (°F)	73	77	89	97	99	107	108	107	101	93	82	69	108
Average High (°F)	33	38	50	64	74	85	89	86	78	66	49	36	62
Average Temp. (°F)	22	28	39	52	62	73	78	75	66	53	38	26	51
Average Low (°F)	11	16	27	39	50	60	66	64	53	40	27	16	39
Extreme Low (°F)	-33	-24	-19	3	24	39	45	39	26	11	-5	-27	-33

Note: Figures cover the years 1948-1995
Source: National Climatic Data Center, International Station Meteorological Climate Summary, 9/96

Average Precipitation/Snowfall/Humidity

Precip./Humidity	Jan	Feb	Mar	Apr	May	Jun	Jul	Aug	Sep	Oct	Nov	Dec	Yr.
Avg. Precip. (in.)	0.8	0.8	2.4	2.9	4.1	3.7	3.7	3.4	3.1	1.9	1.4	0.9	29.1
Avg. Snowfall (in.)	6	5	6	1	Tr	0	0	0	Tr	Tr	3	6	27
Avg. Rel. Hum. 6am (%)	78	81	81	80	83	83	83	86	84	80	80	80	82
Avg. Rel. Hum. 3pm (%)	61	60	55	47	51	49	48	51	49	46	54	60	53

Note: Figures cover the years 1948-1995; Tr = Trace amounts (<0.05 in. of rain; <0.5 in. of snow)
Source: National Climatic Data Center, International Station Meteorological Climate Summary, 9/96

Weather Conditions

Temperature			Daytime Sky			Precipitation		
5°F & below	32°F & below	90°F & above	Clear	Partly cloudy	Cloudy	0.01 inch or more precip.	0.1 inch or more snow/ice	Thunder-storms
25	145	40	108	135	122	94	19	46

Note: Figures are average number of days per year and cover the years 1948-1995
Source: National Climatic Data Center, International Station Meteorological Climate Summary, 9/96

HAZARDOUS WASTE

Superfund Sites

The Lincoln, NE metro area has no sites on the EPA's Superfund Final National Priorities List. There are a total of 1,375 Superfund sites with a status of proposed or final on the list in the U.S. *U.S. Environmental Protection Agency, National Priorities List, April 7, 2021*

AIR QUALITY

Air Quality Trends: Ozone

	1990	1995	2000	2005	2010	2015	2016	2017	2018	2019
MSA[1]	0.057	0.060	0.057	0.056	0.050	0.061	0.058	0.062	0.062	0.056
U.S.	0.088	0.089	0.082	0.080	0.073	0.068	0.069	0.068	0.069	0.065

Note: (1) Data covers the Lincoln, NE Metropolitan Statistical Area. The values shown are the composite ozone concentration averages among trend sites based on the highest fourth daily maximum 8-hour concentration in parts per million. These trends are based on sites having an adequate record of monitoring data during the trend period. Data from exceptional events are included.
Source: U.S. Environmental Protection Agency, Air Quality Monitoring Information, "Air Quality Trends by City, 1990-2019"

Air Quality Index

Area	Percent of Days when Air Quality was...[2]					AQI Statistics[2]	
	Good	Moderate	Unhealthy for Sensitive Groups	Unhealthy	Very Unhealthy	Maximum	Median
MSA[1]	93.9	6.1	0.0	0.0	0.0	66	31

Note: (1) Data covers the Lincoln, NE Metropolitan Statistical Area; (2) Based on 360 days with AQI data in 2019. Air Quality Index (AQI) is an index for reporting daily air quality. EPA calculates the AQI for five major air pollutants regulated by the Clean Air Act: ground-level ozone, particle pollution (aka particulate matter), carbon monoxide, sulfur dioxide, and nitrogen dioxide. The AQI runs from 0 to 500. The higher the AQI value, the greater the level of air pollution and the greater the health concern. There are six AQI categories: "Good" AQI is between 0 and 50. Air quality is considered satisfactory; "Moderate" AQI is between 51 and 100. Air quality is acceptable; "Unhealthy for Sensitive Groups" When AQI values are between 101 and 150, members of sensitive groups may experience health effects; "Unhealthy" When AQI values are between 151 and 200 everyone may begin to experience health effects; "Very Unhealthy" AQI values between 201 and 300 trigger a health alert; "Hazardous" AQI values over 300 trigger warnings of emergency conditions (not shown).
Source: U.S. Environmental Protection Agency, Air Quality Index Report, 2019

Air Quality Index Pollutants

Area	Percent of Days when AQI Pollutant was...[2]					
	Carbon Monoxide	Nitrogen Dioxide	Ozone	Sulfur Dioxide	Particulate Matter 2.5	Particulate Matter 10
MSA[1]	0.0	0.0	63.6	21.1	15.3	0.0

Note: (1) Data covers the Lincoln, NE Metropolitan Statistical Area; (2) Based on 360 days with AQI data in 2019. The Air Quality Index (AQI) is an index for reporting daily air quality. EPA calculates the AQI for five major air pollutants regulated by the Clean Air Act: ground-level ozone, particle pollution (also known as particulate matter), carbon monoxide, sulfur dioxide, and nitrogen dioxide. The AQI runs from 0 to 500. The higher the AQI value, the greater the level of air pollution and the greater the health concern.
Source: U.S. Environmental Protection Agency, Air Quality Index Report, 2019

Maximum Air Pollutant Concentrations: Particulate Matter, Ozone, CO and Lead

	Particulate Matter 10 (ug/m^3)	Particulate Matter 2.5 Wtd AM (ug/m^3)	Particulate Matter 2.5 24-Hr (ug/m^3)	Ozone (ppm)	Carbon Monoxide (ppm)	Lead (ug/m^3)
MSA[1] Level	n/a	6.5	17	0.056	n/a	n/a
NAAQS[2]	150	15	35	0.075	9	0.15
Met NAAQS[2]	n/a	Yes	Yes	Yes	n/a	n/a

Note: (1) Data covers the Lincoln, NE Metropolitan Statistical Area; Data from exceptional events are included; (2) National Ambient Air Quality Standards; ppm = parts per million; ug/m³ = micrograms per cubic meter; n/a not available.
Concentrations: Particulate Matter 10 (coarse particulate)—highest second maximum 24-hour concentration; Particulate Matter 2.5 Wtd AM (fine particulate)—highest weighted annual mean concentration; Particulate Matter 2.5 24-Hour (fine particulate)—highest 98th percentile 24-hour concentration; Ozone—highest fourth daily maximum 8-hour concentration; Carbon Monoxide—highest second maximum non-overlapping 8-hour concentration; Lead—maximum running 3-month average
Source: U.S. Environmental Protection Agency, Air Quality Monitoring Information, "Air Quality Statistics by City, 2019"

Maximum Air Pollutant Concentrations: Nitrogen Dioxide and Sulfur Dioxide

	Nitrogen Dioxide AM (ppb)	Nitrogen Dioxide 1-Hr (ppb)	Sulfur Dioxide AM (ppb)	Sulfur Dioxide 1-Hr (ppb)	Sulfur Dioxide 24-Hr (ppb)
MSA[1] Level	n/a	n/a	n/a	33	n/a
NAAQS[2]	53	100	30	75	140
Met NAAQS[2]	n/a	n/a	n/a	Yes	n/a

Note: (1) Data covers the Lincoln, NE Metropolitan Statistical Area; Data from exceptional events are included; (2) National Ambient Air Quality Standards; ppm = parts per million; ug/m³ = micrograms per cubic meter; n/a not available.
Concentrations: Nitrogen Dioxide AM—highest arithmetic mean concentration; Nitrogen Dioxide 1-Hr—highest 98th percentile 1-hour daily maximum concentration; Sulfur Dioxide AM—highest annual mean concentration; Sulfur Dioxide 1-Hr—highest 99th percentile 1-hour daily maximum concentration; Sulfur Dioxide 24-Hr—highest second maximum 24-hour concentration
Source: U.S. Environmental Protection Agency, Air Quality Monitoring Information, "Air Quality Statistics by City, 2019"

Little Rock, Arkansas

Background

Little Rock is the capital of Arkansas and the most populous city in the state. It is located along the banks of the Arkansas River and marks the point where the flat Mississippi Delta ends and the foothills of the Quachita Mountains begin. The city is best known for its place in the history of the United States Civil Rights Movement and for its connection to former President William Jefferson Clinton, who served as the Governor of Arkansas before being elected our forty-second President.

The area that is now Little Rock was originally inhabited by Native American tribes including the Quapaw, Choctaw and Cherokee, but the first Europeans in the area were the Spanish, who passed through in the mid-sixteenth century. The city got its name from a rock formation on the southern side of the Arkansas River that was a landmark for river crossings. When French explorer Jean-Baptiste Benard de la Harpe arrived in the area in 1722, he called the area *Le petite roche*, or "the little rock," and the nickname stuck. La Harpe built a trading post on the site, but it would be more than 100 years before the city is officially incorporated in 1831. When Arkansas became the 25th American State in 1836, Little Rock was chosen as its capital. Initially the city grew quickly, but many projects, including the railroad between Little Rock and Memphis, were put on hold when the Civil War broke out. Post-war reconstruction, however, brought a wealth of new development so that by the turn of the century, its transformation from a small, sleepy frontier town to a thriving, modern city was complete. After the Great Depression ended in the early 1930s, many residents began to move out to the suburbs and many new roads were built to accommodate the city's changing layout.

In 1957 the city was thrown into the national spotlight with Little Rock Nine—nine African-American students who enrolled in the all-white Central High School, claiming it was their right, based on the U.S. Supreme Court's ruling on *Brown v. Board of Education*. Governor Orval Faubus sent the National Guard to prevent the students from entering the school, but they were eventually admitted under the protection of the U.S. Army sent by President Eisenhower.

Little Rock was again brought to national prominence when then-Governor Bill Clinton started his presidential election campaign in 1992, and gave his election-night acceptance speech from the steps of the Old State House in downtown Little Rock. Clinton has since solidified his link to the city through the William J. Clinton Presidential Center and Park.

Today, the city has a diverse economy built upon manufacturing, education, healthcare and commercial trade. Many major corporations have headquarters in the city. The Little Rock Port is part of a comprehensive industrial business zone on the Arkansas River. In 2016, Little Rock was chosen to join "What Works Cities," a national initiative to help American cities enhance their use of data, improve services, and engage residents.

The Pulaski County Pedestrian and Bicycle Bridge, at 3,463 feet, is the world's longest bridge for pedestrians and bicyclists only. Prominent charitable organization Heifer International has its world headquarters in Little Rock. Dickey-Stephens Park, a 7,000-seat baseball park, is home to minor league team Arkansas Travelers.

Attractions in the city include the MacArthur Museum of Arkansas Military History, the Arkansas Museum of Discovery, and the Old State House Museum. In addition, the William J. Clinton Presidential Center and Park houses the Clinton Presidential Library and the headquarters of the Clinton Foundation. A section of downtown's Main Street, called Creative Corridor, combines the arts, entertainment, business and culture, and is home to the Arkansas Repertory Theatre, Arkansas Symphony Orchestra, and Ballet Arkansas. Other cultural attractions in Little Rock include the Arkansas Arts Center, the Robinson Center Music Hall, and Wildwood Center for the Performing Arts. The city's major institutions of higher learning are the University of Arkansas at Little Rock and the University of Arkansas for Medical Sciences.

Little Rock has a humid subtropical climate, typical of the southern United States. Summers are generally hot, while winters are cooler, but high humidity persists all year round. Rainfall can be heavy at times during the spring and fall but the city rarely receives any snow. In April of 2017, a deadly flood devastated the city. The highest temperature recorded is 114 degrees. A deadly tornado touched down 10 miles west of the city in 2014, when powerful storms killed 16 people in three states.

Rankings

Business/Finance Rankings

- The Brookings Institution ranked the nation's largest cities based on income inequality. Little Rock was ranked #19 (#1 = greatest inequality). Criteria: the "95/20 ratio," a figure representing the income at which a household earns more than 95 percent of all other households, divided by the income at which a household earns more than only 20 percent of all other households. *Brookings Institution, "Household Income Inequality, Largest Cities of 97 Large U.S. Metro Areas, 2014-2016," February 5, 2018*

- The Brookings Institution ranked the 100 largest metro areas in the U.S. based on income inequality. Little Rock was ranked #48 (#1 = greatest inequality). Criteria: the "95/20 ratio," a figure representing the income at which a household earns more than 95 percent of all other households, divided by the income at which a household earns more than only 20 percent of all other households. *Brookings Institution, "Household Income Inequality, 100 Largest U.S. Metro Areas, 2014-2016," February 5, 2018*

- The Little Rock metro area appeared on the Milken Institute "2021 Best Performing Cities" list. Rank: #150 out of 200 large metro areas (population over 250,000). Criteria: job growth; wage and salary growth; high-tech output growth; housing affordability; household broadband access. *Milken Institute, "Best-Performing Cities 2021," February 16, 2021*

- *Forbes* ranked the 200 most populous metro areas to determine the nation's "Best Places for Business and Careers." The Little Rock metro area was ranked #132. Criteria: costs (business and living); job growth (past and projected); income growth; quality of life; educational attainment (college and high school); projected economic growth; cultural and leisure opportunities; workplace tolerance laws; net migration patterns. *Forbes, "The Best Places for Business and Careers 2019: Seattle Still On Top," October 30, 2019*

Education Rankings

- Personal finance website *WalletHub* analyzed the 150 largest U.S. metropolitan statistical areas to determine where the most educated Americans are putting their degrees to work. Criteria: education levels; percentage of workers with degrees; education quality and attainment gap; public school quality rankings; quality and enrollment of each metro area's universities. Little Rock was ranked #75 (#1 = most educated city). *www.WalletHub.com, "Most and Least Educated Cities in America," July 20, 2020*

Environmental Rankings

- Little Rock was highlighted as one of the top 98 cleanest metro areas for short-term particle pollution (24-hour PM 2.5) in the U.S. during 2016 through 2018. Monitors in these cities reported no days with unhealthful PM 2.5 levels. *American Lung Association, "State of the Air 2020," April 21, 2020*

Health/Fitness Rankings

- Little Rock was identified as a "2021 Spring Allergy Capital." The area ranked #44 out of 100. Three groups of factors were used to identify the most challenging cities for people with allergies during the spring season: annual spring pollen levels; over the counter medicine use; number of board-certified allergy specialists. *Asthma and Allergy Foundation of America, "Spring Allergy Capitals 2021," February 23, 2021*

- Little Rock was identified as a "2021 Fall Allergy Capital." The area ranked #43 out of 100. Three groups of factors were used to identify the most challenging cities for people with allergies during the fall season: annual fall pollen levels; over the counter medicine use; number of board-certified allergy specialists. *Asthma and Allergy Foundation of America, "Fall Allergy Capitals 2021," February 23, 2021*

- Little Rock was identified as a "2019 Asthma Capital." The area ranked #56 out of the nation's 100 largest metropolitan areas. Criteria: estimated asthma prevalence; crude death rate from asthma; and ER visits due to asthma. Risk factors analyzed but not factored in the rankings: annual pollen score; annual air quality; public smoking laws; number of board-certified asthma specialists; rescue medication use; controller medication use; uninsured rate; poverty rate. *Asthma and Allergy Foundation of America, "Asthma Capitals 2019: The Most Challenging Places to Live With Asthma," May 7, 2019*

Real Estate Rankings

- *WalletHub* compared the most populated U.S. cities to determine which had the best markets for real estate agents. Little Rock ranked #157 where demand was high and pay was the best. Criteria: sales per agent; annual median wage for real-estate agents; monthly average starting salary for real estate agents; real estate job density and competition; unemployment rate; home turnover rate; housing-market health index; and other relevant metrics. *www.WalletHub.com, "2019's Best Places to Be a Real Estate Agent," April 24, 2019*

- Little Rock was ranked #50 out of 268 metro areas in terms of housing affordability in 2020 by the National Association of Home Builders (#1 = most affordable). Criteria: the share of homes sold in that area affordable to a family earning the local median income, based on standard mortgage underwriting criteria. *National Association of Home Builders®, NAHB-Wells Fargo Housing Opportunity Index, 4th Quarter 2020*

Safety Rankings

- To identify the most dangerous cities in America, 24/7 Wall Street focused on violent crime categories—murder, non-negligent manslaughter, rape, robbery, and aggravated assault—and property crime as reported in the FBI's 2019 annual Uniform Crime Report. Criteria also included median income from American Community Survey and unemployment figures from Bureau of Labor Statistics. For cities with populations over 100,000, Little Rock was ranked #6. *247wallst.com, "America's 50 Most Dangerous Cities" November 16, 2020*

- Allstate ranked the 200 largest cities in America in terms of driver safety. Little Rock ranked #112. Criteria: internal property damage claims over a two-year period from January 2016 to December 2017. The report helps increase the importance of safety and awareness behind the wheel. *Allstate, "Allstate America's Best Drivers Report, 2019" June 24, 2019*

- Little Rock was identified as one of the most dangerous cities in America by NeighborhoodScout. The city ranked #13 out of 100 (#1 = most dangerous). Criteria: number of violent crimes per 1,000 residents. The editors evaluated cities with 25,000 or more residents. *NeighborhoodScout.com, "2021 Top 100 Most Dangerous Cities in the U.S.," January 2, 2021*

- The National Insurance Crime Bureau ranked 384 metro areas in the U.S. in terms of per capita rates of vehicle theft. The Little Rock metro area ranked #37 (#1 = highest rate). Criteria: number of vehicle theft offenses per 100,000 inhabitants in 2019. *National Insurance Crime Bureau, "Hot Spots 2019," July 21, 2020*

Seniors/Retirement Rankings

- From its Best Cities for Successful Aging indexes, the Milken Institute generated rankings for metropolitan areas, weighing data in nine categories—health care, wellness, living arrangements, transportation and convenience, financial characteristics, education, employment, community engagement, and overall livability. The Little Rock metro area was ranked #47 overall in the large metro area category. *Milken Institute, "Best Cities for Successful Aging, 2017" March 14, 2017*

Women/Minorities Rankings

- Personal finance website *WalletHub* compared more than 180 U.S. cities across two key dimensions, "Hispanic Business-Friendliness" and "Hispanic Purchasing Power," to arrive at the most favorable conditions for Hispanic entrepreneurs. Little Rock was ranked #135 out of 182. Criteria includes: share of Hispanic-Owned Businesses; Hispanic entrepreneurship rate to median annual income of Hispanics; Small Business-Friendliness score; cost of living; and number of Hispanics with at least a bachelor's degree. *WalletHub.com, "2019's Best Cities for Hispanic Entrepreneurs," May 1, 2019*

Miscellaneous Rankings

- *WalletHub* compared the 150 most populated U.S. cities to determine their operating efficiency. A "Quality of City Services" score was constructed for each city and then divided by the total budget per capita to reveal which were managed the best. Little Rock ranked #71. Criteria: financial stability; economy; education; safety; health; infrastructure and pollution. *www.WalletHub.com, "2020's Best-& Worst-Run Cities in America," June 29, 2020*

Business Environment

DEMOGRAPHICS

Population Growth

Area	1990 Census	2000 Census	2010 Census	2019* Estimate	Population Growth (%)	
					1990-2019	2010-2019
City	177,519	183,133	193,524	197,958	11.5	2.3
MSA[1]	535,034	610,518	699,757	737,015	37.8	5.3
U.S.	248,709,873	281,421,906	308,745,538	324,697,795	30.6	5.2

Note: (1) Figures cover the Little Rock-North Little Rock-Conway, AR Metropolitan Statistical Area;
(*) 2015-2019 5-year estimated population
Source: U.S. Census Bureau, 1990 Census, Census 2000, Census 2010, 2015-2019 American Community
Survey 5-Year Estimates

Household Size

Area	Persons in Household (%)							Average Household Size
	One	Two	Three	Four	Five	Six	Seven or More	
City	36.7	32.1	14.0	10.1	4.6	1.8	0.7	2.40
MSA[1]	29.9	34.3	16.0	11.8	5.3	1.9	0.9	2.60
U.S.	27.9	33.9	15.6	12.9	6.0	2.3	1.4	2.60

Note: (1) Figures cover the Little Rock-North Little Rock-Conway, AR Metropolitan Statistical Area
Source: U.S. Census Bureau, 2015-2019 American Community Survey 5-Year Estimates

Race

Area	White Alone[2] (%)	Black Alone[2] (%)	Asian Alone[2] (%)	AIAN[3] Alone[2] (%)	NHOPI[4] Alone[2] (%)	Other Race Alone[2] (%)	Two or More Races (%)
City	50.3	42.0	3.3	0.3	0.1	1.8	2.3
MSA[1]	70.3	23.3	1.7	0.4	0.1	1.6	2.5
U.S.	72.5	12.7	5.5	0.8	0.2	4.9	3.3

Note: (1) Figures cover the Little Rock-North Little Rock-Conway, AR Metropolitan Statistical Area; (2) Alone
is defined as not being in combination with one or more other races; (3) American Indian and Alaska Native;
(4) Native Hawaiian and Other Pacific Islander
Source: U.S. Census Bureau, 2015-2019 American Community Survey 5-Year Estimates

Hispanic or Latino Origin

Area	Total (%)	Mexican (%)	Puerto Rican (%)	Cuban (%)	Other (%)
City	7.4	4.8	0.3	0.3	2.1
MSA[1]	5.3	3.7	0.2	0.1	1.3
U.S.	18.0	11.2	1.7	0.7	4.3

Note: Persons of Hispanic or Latino origin can be of any race; (1) Figures cover the Little Rock-North Little
Rock-Conway, AR Metropolitan Statistical Area
Source: U.S. Census Bureau, 2015-2019 American Community Survey 5-Year Estimates

Ancestry

Area	German	Irish	English	American	Italian	Polish	French[2]	Scottish	Dutch
City	7.1	6.8	7.5	5.5	1.6	0.9	1.8	1.6	0.5
MSA[1]	9.3	8.8	7.9	7.9	1.5	1.0	1.7	1.9	1.0
U.S.	13.3	9.7	7.2	6.2	5.1	2.8	2.3	1.7	1.2

Note: Figures are the percentage of the total population reporting a particular ancestry. The nine most
commonly reported ancestries in the U.S. are shown. Figures include multiple ancestries (e.g. if a person
reported being Irish and Italian, they were included in both columns); (1) Figures cover the Little Rock-North
Little Rock-Conway, AR Metropolitan Statistical Area; (2) Excludes Basque
Source: U.S. Census Bureau, 2015-2019 American Community Survey 5-Year Estimates

Foreign-born Population

Area	Percent of Population Born in								
	Any Foreign Country	Asia	Mexico	Europe	Caribbean	Central America[2]	South America	Africa	Canada
City	7.7	2.7	2.3	0.7	0.1	1.0	0.3	0.5	0.1
MSA[1]	4.3	1.4	1.3	0.5	0.1	0.6	0.2	0.2	0.1
U.S.	13.6	4.2	3.5	1.5	1.3	1.1	1.0	0.7	0.2

Note: (1) Figures cover the Little Rock-North Little Rock-Conway, AR Metropolitan Statistical Area; (2)
Excludes Mexico.
Source: U.S. Census Bureau, 2015-2019 American Community Survey 5-Year Estimates

Marital Status

Area	Never Married	Now Married[2]	Separated	Widowed	Divorced
City	37.7	39.9	2.5	6.2	13.7
MSA[1]	30.7	47.4	2.1	6.3	13.6
U.S.	33.4	48.1	1.9	5.8	10.9

Note: Figures are percentages and cover the population 15 years of age and older; (1) Figures cover the Little Rock-North Little Rock-Conway, AR Metropolitan Statistical Area; (2) Excludes separated
Source: U.S. Census Bureau, 2015-2019 American Community Survey 5-Year Estimates

Disability by Age

Area	All Ages	Under 18 Years Old	18 to 64 Years Old	65 Years and Over
City	13.4	5.8	11.5	35.4
MSA[1]	15.7	5.9	13.8	39.5
U.S.	12.6	4.2	10.3	34.5

Note: Figures show percent of the civilian noninstitutionalized population that reported having a disability. Disability status is determined from six types of difficulty: vision, hearing, cognitive, ambulatory, self-care, and independent living. For children under 5 years old, hearing and vision difficulty are used to determine disability status. For children between the ages of 5 and 14, disability status is determined from hearing, vision, cognitive, ambulatory, and self-care difficulties. For people aged 15 years and older, they are considered to have a disability if they have difficulty with any one of the six difficulty types; Note: (1) Figures cover the Little Rock-North Little Rock-Conway, AR Metropolitan Statistical Area
Source: U.S. Census Bureau, 2015-2019 American Community Survey 5-Year Estimates

Age

Area	Percent of Population									Median Age
	Under Age 5	Age 5–19	Age 20–34	Age 35–44	Age 45–54	Age 55–64	Age 65–74	Age 75–84	Age 85+	
City	6.7	18.8	22.1	13.5	11.9	12.8	8.4	3.6	2.2	36.7
MSA[1]	6.4	19.6	21.3	12.9	12.4	12.5	8.9	4.2	1.8	36.9
U.S.	6.1	19.1	20.7	12.6	13.0	12.9	9.1	4.6	1.9	38.1

Note: (1) Figures cover the Little Rock-North Little Rock-Conway, AR Metropolitan Statistical Area
Source: U.S. Census Bureau, 2015-2019 American Community Survey 5-Year Estimates

Gender

Area	Males	Females	Males per 100 Females
City	94,939	103,019	92.2
MSA[1]	356,611	380,404	93.7
U.S.	159,886,919	164,810,876	97.0

Note: (1) Figures cover the Little Rock-North Little Rock-Conway, AR Metropolitan Statistical Area
Source: U.S. Census Bureau, 2015-2019 American Community Survey 5-Year Estimates

Religious Groups by Family

Area	Catholic	Baptist	Non-Den.	Methodist[2]	Lutheran	LDS[3]	Pente-costal	Presby-terian[4]	Muslim[5]	Judaism
MSA[1]	4.5	25.9	6.1	7.3	0.5	0.9	2.9	0.9	0.1	0.1
U.S.	19.1	9.3	4.0	4.0	2.3	2.0	1.9	1.6	0.8	0.7

Note: Figures are the number of adherents as a percentage of the total population; (1) Figures cover the Little Rock-North Little Rock-Conway, AR Metropolitan Statistical Area; (2) Methodist/Pietist; (3) Latter Day Saints; (4) Reformed; (5) Figures are estimates
Source: Association of Statisticians of American Religious Bodies, 2010 U.S. Religion Census: Religious Congregations & Membership Study

Religious Groups by Tradition

Area	Catholic	Evangelical Protestant	Mainline Protestant	Other Tradition	Black Protestant	Orthodox
MSA[1]	4.5	33.9	8.2	1.7	3.5	0.1
U.S.	19.1	16.2	7.3	4.3	1.6	0.3

Note: Figures are the number of adherents as a percentage of the total population; (1) Figures cover the Little Rock-North Little Rock-Conway, AR Metropolitan Statistical Area
Source: Association of Statisticians of American Religious Bodies, 2010 U.S. Religion Census: Religious Congregations & Membership Study

ECONOMY

Gross Metropolitan Product

Area	2017	2018	2019	2020	Rank[2]
MSA[1]	38.5	39.8	41.1	42.7	76

Note: Figures are in billions of dollars; (1) Figures cover the Little Rock-North Little Rock-Conway, AR Metropolitan Statistical Area; (2) Rank is based on 2018 data and ranges from 1 to 381
Source: U.S. Conference of Mayors, U.S. Metro Economies: GMP & Employment 2018-2020, September 2019

Economic Growth

Area	2015-17 (%)	2018 (%)	2019 (%)	2020 (%)	Rank[2]
MSA[1]	0.4	0.9	1.6	1.5	286
U.S.	1.9	2.9	2.3	2.1	—

Note: Figures are real gross metropolitan product (GMP) growth rates and represent average annual percent change; (1) Figures cover the Little Rock-North Little Rock-Conway, AR Metropolitan Statistical Area; (2) Rank is based on 2017 2-year average annual percent change and ranges from 1 to 381
Source: U.S. Conference of Mayors, U.S. Metro Economies: GMP & Employment 2018-2020, September 2019

Metropolitan Area Exports

Area	2014	2015	2016	2017	2018	2019	Rank[2]
MSA[1]	2,463.5	1,777.5	1,871.0	2,146.1	1,607.4	1,642.5	113

Note: Figures are in millions of dollars; (1) Figures cover the Little Rock-North Little Rock-Conway, AR Metropolitan Statistical Area; (2) Rank is based on 2019 data and ranges from 1 to 386
Source: U.S. Department of Commerce, International Trade Administration, Office of Trade and Economic Analysis, Industry and Analysis, Exports by Metropolitan Area, data extracted March 24, 2021

Building Permits

Area	Single-Family			Multi-Family			Total		
	2018	2019	Pct. Chg.	2018	2019	Pct. Chg.	2018	2019	Pct. Chg.
City	325	480	47.7	145	539	271.7	470	1,019	116.8
MSA[1]	1,819	1,921	5.6	355	1,084	205.4	2,174	3,005	38.2
U.S.	855,300	862,100	0.7	473,500	523,900	10.6	1,328,800	1,386,000	4.3

Note: (1) Figures cover the Little Rock-North Little Rock-Conway, AR Metropolitan Statistical Area; Figures represent new, privately-owned housing units authorized (unadjusted data); All permit data are based on estimates with imputation
Source: U.S. Census Bureau, Manufacturing, Mining, and Construction Statistics, Building Permits, 2018, 2019

Bankruptcy Filings

Area	Business Filings			Nonbusiness Filings		
	2019	2020	% Chg.	2019	2020	% Chg.
Pulaski County	233	30	-87.1	2,318	1,519	-34.5
U.S.	22,780	21,655	-4.9	752,160	522,808	-30.5

Note: Business filings include Chapter 7, Chapter 9, Chapter 11, Chapter 12, Chapter 13, Chapter 15, and Section 304; Nonbusiness filings include Chapter 7, Chapter 11, and Chapter 13
Source: Administrative Office of the U.S. Courts, Business and Nonbusiness Bankruptcy, County Cases Commenced by Chapter of the Bankruptcy Code, During the 12-Month Period Ending December 31, 2019 and Business and Nonbusiness Bankruptcy, County Cases Commenced by Chapter of the Bankruptcy Code, During the 12-Month Period Ending December 31, 2020

Housing Vacancy Rates

Area	Gross Vacancy Rate[2] (%)			Year-Round Vacancy Rate[3] (%)			Rental Vacancy Rate[4] (%)			Homeowner Vacancy Rate[5] (%)		
	2018	2019	2020	2018	2019	2020	2018	2019	2020	2018	2019	2020
MSA[1]	10.5	9.9	9.4	10.2	9.6	9.1	10.9	11.4	9.1	1.8	1.7	1.3
U.S.	12.3	12.0	10.6	9.7	9.5	8.2	6.9	6.7	6.3	1.5	1.4	1.0

Note: (1) Figures cover the Little Rock-North Little Rock-Conway, AR Metropolitan Statistical Area; (2) The percentage of the total housing inventory that is vacant; (3) The percentage of the housing inventory (excluding seasonal units) that is year-round vacant; (4) The percentage of rental inventory that is vacant for rent; (5) The percentage of homeowner inventory that is vacant for sale
Source: U.S. Census Bureau, Housing Vacancies and Homeownership Annual Statistics: 2018, 2019, 2020

INCOME

Income

Area	Per Capita ($)	Median Household ($)	Average Household ($)
City	35,966	51,485	83,730
MSA[1]	30,599	54,746	76,145
U.S.	34,103	62,843	88,607

Note: (1) Figures cover the Little Rock-North Little Rock-Conway, AR Metropolitan Statistical Area
Source: U.S. Census Bureau, 2015-2019 American Community Survey 5-Year Estimates

Household Income Distribution

Area	Percent of Households Earning							
	Under $15,000	$15,000 -$24,999	$25,000 -$34,999	$35,000 -$49,999	$50,000 -$74,999	$75,000 -$99,999	$100,000 -$149,999	$150,000 and up
City	12.7	11.0	10.4	14.7	16.5	10.4	11.2	13.0
MSA[1]	12.0	10.0	10.4	13.7	18.1	11.9	14.1	9.8
U.S.	10.3	8.9	8.9	12.3	17.2	12.7	15.1	14.5

Note: (1) Figures cover the Little Rock-North Little Rock-Conway, AR Metropolitan Statistical Area
Source: U.S. Census Bureau, 2015-2019 American Community Survey 5-Year Estimates

Poverty Rate

Area	All Ages	Under 18 Years Old	18 to 64 Years Old	65 Years and Over
City	16.6	23.8	15.2	10.9
MSA[1]	15.1	20.5	14.2	9.7
U.S.	13.4	18.5	12.6	9.3

Note: Figures are percentage of people whose income during the past 12 months was below the poverty level;
(1) Figures cover the Little Rock-North Little Rock-Conway, AR Metropolitan Statistical Area
Source: U.S. Census Bureau, 2015-2019 American Community Survey 5-Year Estimates

CITY FINANCES

City Government Finances

Component	2017 ($000)	2017 ($ per capita)
Total Revenues	470,624	2,377
Total Expenditures	526,047	2,657
Debt Outstanding	592,815	2,994
Cash and Securities[1]	451,118	2,278

Note: (1) Cash and security holdings of a government at the close of its fiscal year,
including those of its dependent agencies, utilities, and liquor stores.
Source: U.S. Census Bureau, State & Local Government Finances 2017

City Government Revenue by Source

Source	2017 ($000)	2017 ($ per capita)	2017 (%)
General Revenue			
From Federal Government	14,181	72	3.0
From State Government	22,046	111	4.7
From Local Governments	54,161	274	11.5
Taxes			
Property	54,738	276	11.6
Sales and Gross Receipts	122,173	617	26.0
Personal Income	0	0	0.0
Corporate Income	0	0	0.0
Motor Vehicle License	0	0	0.0
Other Taxes	9,277	47	2.0
Current Charges	167,720	847	35.6
Liquor Store	0	0	0.0
Utility	0	0	0.0
Employee Retirement	9,255	47	2.0

Source: U.S. Census Bureau, State & Local Government Finances 2017

City Government Expenditures by Function

Function	2017 ($000)	2017 ($ per capita)	2017 (%)
General Direct Expenditures			
Air Transportation	42,799	216	8.1
Corrections	0	0	0.0
Education	0	0	0.0
Employment Security Administration	0	0	0.0
Financial Administration	8,744	44	1.7
Fire Protection	50,120	253	9.5
General Public Buildings	983	5	0.2
Governmental Administration, Other	5,635	28	1.1
Health	37,819	191	7.2
Highways	42,142	212	8.0
Hospitals	0	0	0.0
Housing and Community Development	7,106	35	1.4
Interest on General Debt	21,316	107	4.1
Judicial and Legal	5,036	25	1.0
Libraries	9,990	50	1.9
Parking	1,344	6	0.3
Parks and Recreation	42,911	216	8.2
Police Protection	71,608	361	13.6
Public Welfare	0	0	0.0
Sewerage	50,250	253	9.6
Solid Waste Management	16,095	81	3.1
Veterans' Services	0	0	0.0
Liquor Store	0	0	0.0
Utility	0	0	0.0
Employee Retirement	12,706	64	2.4

Source: U.S. Census Bureau, State & Local Government Finances 2017

280 Little Rock, Arkansas

EMPLOYMENT

Labor Force and Employment

Area	Civilian Labor Force			Workers Employed		
	Dec. 2019	Dec. 2020	% Chg.	Dec. 2019	Dec. 2020	% Chg.
City	96,600	95,461	-1.2	93,594	90,677	-3.1
MSA[1]	354,854	348,009	-1.9	343,794	333,024	-3.1
U.S.	164,007,000	160,017,000	-2.4	158,504,000	149,613,000	-5.6

Note: Data is not seasonally adjusted and covers workers 16 years of age and older; (1) Figures cover the Little Rock-North Little Rock-Conway, AR Metropolitan Statistical Area
Source: Bureau of Labor Statistics, Local Area Unemployment Statistics

Unemployment Rate

Area	2020											
	Jan.	Feb.	Mar.	Apr.	May	Jun.	Jul.	Aug.	Sep.	Oct.	Nov.	Dec.
City	3.7	3.6	4.6	12.0	11.7	10.4	10.1	10.4	9.8	7.9	7.7	5.0
MSA[1]	3.7	3.6	4.6	10.9	10.2	9.0	8.3	8.4	7.8	6.4	6.4	4.3
U.S.	4.0	3.8	4.5	14.4	13.0	11.2	10.5	8.5	7.7	6.6	6.4	6.5

Note: Data is not seasonally adjusted and covers workers 16 years of age and older; (1) Figures cover the Little Rock-North Little Rock-Conway, AR Metropolitan Statistical Area
Source: Bureau of Labor Statistics, Local Area Unemployment Statistics

Average Wages

Occupation	$/Hr.	Occupation	$/Hr.
Accountants and Auditors	32.30	Maintenance and Repair Workers	16.70
Automotive Mechanics	20.30	Marketing Managers	55.10
Bookkeepers	18.70	Network and Computer Systems Admin.	35.20
Carpenters	20.70	Nurses, Licensed Practical	21.70
Cashiers	11.80	Nurses, Registered	33.20
Computer Programmers	37.10	Nursing Assistants	13.40
Computer Systems Analysts	35.10	Office Clerks, General	17.00
Computer User Support Specialists	23.60	Physical Therapists	38.00
Construction Laborers	14.20	Physicians	90.20
Cooks, Restaurant	12.00	Plumbers, Pipefitters and Steamfitters	22.80
Customer Service Representatives	17.50	Police and Sheriff's Patrol Officers	24.30
Dentists	95.90	Postal Service Mail Carriers	25.60
Electricians	19.90	Real Estate Sales Agents	n/a
Engineers, Electrical	44.70	Retail Salespersons	13.80
Fast Food and Counter Workers	10.80	Sales Representatives, Technical/Scientific	31.80
Financial Managers	54.40	Secretaries, Exc. Legal/Medical/Executive	16.10
First-Line Supervisors of Office Workers	25.90	Security Guards	14.70
General and Operations Managers	49.20	Surgeons	n/a
Hairdressers/Cosmetologists	12.60	Teacher Assistants, Exc. Postsecondary*	11.40
Home Health and Personal Care Aides	11.50	Teachers, Secondary School, Exc. Sp. Ed.*	26.80
Janitors and Cleaners	12.20	Telemarketers	12.40
Landscaping/Groundskeeping Workers	13.90	Truck Drivers, Heavy/Tractor-Trailer	24.40
Lawyers	42.90	Truck Drivers, Light/Delivery Services	14.90
Maids and Housekeeping Cleaners	11.00	Waiters and Waitresses	10.90

Note: Wage data covers the Little Rock-North Little Rock-Conway, AR Metropolitan Statistical Area; (*) Hourly wages were calculated from annual wage data based on a 40 hour work week; n/a not available.
Source: Bureau of Labor Statistics, Metro Area Occupational Employment & Wage Estimates, May 2020

Employment by Industry

Sector	MSA[1]		U.S.
	Number of Employees	Percent of Total	Percent of Total
Construction, Mining, and Logging	17,500	5.0	5.5
Education and Health Services	58,900	16.7	16.3
Financial Activities	22,300	6.3	6.1
Government	67,900	19.3	15.2
Information	5,100	1.4	1.9
Leisure and Hospitality	28,300	8.0	9.0
Manufacturing	18,900	5.4	8.5
Other Services	17,600	5.0	3.8
Professional and Business Services	44,100	12.5	14.4
Retail Trade	39,700	11.3	10.9
Transportation, Warehousing, and Utilities	16,500	4.7	4.6
Wholesale Trade	15,100	4.3	3.9

Note: Figures are non-farm employment as of December 2020. Figures are not seasonally adjusted and include workers 16 years of age and older; (1) Figures cover the Little Rock-North Little Rock-Conway, AR Metropolitan Statistical Area
Source: Bureau of Labor Statistics, Current Employment Statistics, Employment, Hours, and Earnings

Employment by Occupation

Occupation Classification	City (%)	MSA[1] (%)	U.S. (%)
Management, Business, Science, and Arts	44.8	39.1	38.5
Natural Resources, Construction, and Maintenance	4.9	8.1	8.9
Production, Transportation, and Material Moving	12.0	13.4	13.2
Sales and Office	22.5	23.3	21.6
Service	15.8	16.0	17.8

Note: Figures cover employed civilians 16 years of age and older; (1) Figures cover the Little Rock-North Little Rock-Conway, AR Metropolitan Statistical Area
Source: U.S. Census Bureau, 2015-2019 American Community Survey 5-Year Estimates

Occupations with Greatest Projected Employment Growth: 2020 – 2022

Occupation[1]	2020 Employment	2022 Projected Employment	Numeric Employment Change	Percent Employment Change
Clergy	11,960	12,270	310	2.6
Insurance Sales Agents	10,480	10,780	300	2.9
Medical and Health Services Managers	6,050	6,340	290	4.8
Electricians	6,160	6,440	280	4.5
Nurse Practitioners	2,710	2,980	270	10.0
General and Operations Managers	21,960	22,220	260	1.2
Financial Managers	5,520	5,770	250	4.5
Software Developers and Software Quality Assurance Analysts and Testers	5,780	6,020	240	4.2
Janitors and Cleaners, Except Maids and Housekeeping Cleaners	20,030	20,260	230	1.1
Sales Representatives, Wholesale and Manufacturing, Except Technical and Scientific Products	12,630	12,850	220	1.7

Note: Projections cover Arkansas; (1) Sorted by numeric employment change
Source: www.projectionscentral.com, State Occupational Projections, 2020–2022 Short-Term Projections

Fastest-Growing Occupations: 2020 – 2022

Occupation[1]	2020 Employment	2022 Projected Employment	Numeric Employment Change	Percent Employment Change
Fundraisers	1,090	1,220	130	11.9
Nurse Practitioners	2,710	2,980	270	10.0
Farm Equipment Mechanics and Service Technicians	830	890	60	7.2
Information Security Analysts (SOC 2018)	820	870	50	6.1
Pest Control Workers	1,160	1,220	60	5.2
Heating, Air Conditioning, and Refrigeration Mechanics and Installers	3,090	3,250	160	5.2
Plumbers, Pipefitters, and Steamfitters	3,290	3,450	160	4.9
Medical and Health Services Managers	6,050	6,340	290	4.8
Loan Interviewers and Clerks	2,130	2,230	100	4.7
Financial Managers	5,520	5,770	250	4.5

Note: Projections cover Arkansas; (1) Sorted by percent employment change and excludes occupations with numeric employment change less than 50
Source: www.projectionscentral.com, State Occupational Projections, 2020–2022 Short-Term Projections

TAXES

State Corporate Income Tax Rates

State	Tax Rate (%)	Income Brackets ($)	Num. of Brackets	Financial Institution Tax Rate (%)[a]	Federal Income Tax Ded.
Arkansas	1.0 - 6.2	3,000 - 100,001	6	1.0 - 6.2	No

Note: Tax rates as of January 1, 2021; (a) Rates listed are the corporate income tax rate applied to financial institutions or excise taxes based on income. Some states have other taxes based upon the value of deposits or shares.
Source: Federation of Tax Administrators, State Corporate Income Tax Rates, January 1, 2021

State Individual Income Tax Rates

State	Tax Rate (%)	Income Brackets ($)	Personal Exemptions ($)			Standard Ded. ($)	
			Single	Married	Depend.	Single	Married
Arkansas (a)	2.0 - 5.9 (f)	4,000 - 79,300	29	58 (c)	29 (c)	2,200	4,400

Note: Tax rates as of January 1, 2021; Local- and county-level taxes are not included; Federal income tax is not deductible on state income tax returns; (a) 19 states have statutory provision for automatically adjusting to the rate of inflation the dollar values of the income tax brackets, standard deductions, and/or personal exemptions. Michigan indexes the personal exemption only. Oregon does not index the income brackets for $125,000 and over; (c) The personal exemption takes the form of a tax credit instead of a deduction; (f) Arkansas has separate brackets for taxpayers with income under $75,000 and $21,000.
Source: Federation of Tax Administrators, State Individual Income Tax Rates, January 1, 2021

Various State Sales and Excise Tax Rates

State	State Sales Tax (%)	Gasoline[1] (¢/gal.)	Cigarette[2] ($/pack)	Spirits[3] ($/gal.)	Wine[4] ($/gal.)	Beer[5] ($/gal.)	Recreational Marijuana (%)
Arkansas	6.5	24.8	1.15	8.33	1.47	0.34	Not legal

Note: All tax rates as of January 1, 2021; (1) The American Petroleum Institute has developed a methodology for determining the average tax rate on a gallon of fuel. Rates may include any of the following: excise taxes, environmental fees, storage tank fees, other fees or taxes, general sales tax, and local taxes; (2) The federal excise tax of $1.0066 per pack and local taxes are not included; (3) Rates are those applicable to off-premise sales of 40% alcohol by volume (a.b.v.) distilled spirits in 750ml containers. Local excise taxes are excluded; (4) Rates are those applicable to off-premise sales of 11% a.b.v. non-carbonated wine in 750ml containers; (5) Rates are those applicable to off-premise sales of 4.7% a.b.v. beer in 12 ounce containers.
Source: Tax Foundation, 2021 Facts & Figures: How Does Your State Compare?

State Business Tax Climate Index Rankings

State	Overall Rank	Corporate Tax Rank	Individual Income Tax Rank	Sales Tax Rank	Property Tax Rank	Unemployment Insurance Tax Rank
Arkansas	45	34	41	46	25	23

Note: The index is a measure of how each state's tax laws affect economic performance. The lower the rank, the more favorable a state's tax system is for business. States without a given tax are given a ranking of 1. The scores/rankings for the District of Columbia do not affect other states. The 2021 index represents the tax climate as of July 1, 2020.
Source: Tax Foundation, State Business Tax Climate Index 2021

TRANSPORTATION

Means of Transportation to Work

Area	Car/Truck/Van		Public Transportation			Bicycle	Walked	Other Means	Worked at Home
	Drove Alone	Car-pooled	Bus	Subway	Railroad				
City	81.6	9.8	0.9	0.0	0.0	0.1	1.8	1.5	4.2
MSA[1]	83.9	9.5	0.5	0.0	0.0	0.2	1.3	1.1	3.5
U.S.	76.3	9.0	2.4	1.9	0.6	0.5	2.7	1.4	5.2

Note: Figures are percentages and cover workers 16 years of age and older; (1) Figures cover the Little Rock-North Little Rock-Conway, AR Metropolitan Statistical Area
Source: U.S. Census Bureau, 2015-2019 American Community Survey 5-Year Estimates

Travel Time to Work

Area	Less Than 10 Minutes	10 to 19 Minutes	20 to 29 Minutes	30 to 44 Minutes	45 to 59 Minutes	60 to 89 Minutes	90 Minutes or More
City	14.0	44.4	26.5	10.8	2.0	1.3	1.1
MSA[1]	12.6	33.0	23.4	19.9	7.0	2.8	1.3
U.S.	12.2	28.4	20.8	20.8	8.3	6.4	2.9

Note: Note: Figures are percentages and include workers 16 years old and over; (1) Figures cover the Little Rock-North Little Rock-Conway, AR Metropolitan Statistical Area
Source: U.S. Census Bureau, 2015-2019 American Community Survey 5-Year Estimates

Key Congestion Measures

Measure	1982	1992	2002	2012	2017
Annual Hours of Delay, Total (000)	964	2,401	7,468	13,278	14,823
Annual Hours of Delay, Per Auto Commuter	6	12	31	36	43
Annual Congestion Cost, Total (million $)	7	25	100	233	269
Annual Congestion Cost, Per Auto Commuter ($)	109	187	454	632	684

Note: Covers the Little Rock AR urban area
Source: Texas A&M Transportation Institute, 2019 Urban Mobility Report

Little Rock, Arkansas 283

Freeway Travel Time Index

Measure	1982	1987	1992	1997	2002	2007	2012	2017
Urban Area Index[1]	1.02	1.03	1.04	1.07	1.11	1.13	1.13	1.13
Urban Area Rank[1,2]	90	93	97	94	84	85	85	83

Note: Freeway Travel Time Index—the ratio of travel time in the peak period to the travel time at free-flow conditions. For example, a value of 1.30 indicates a 20-minute free-flow trip takes 26 minutes in the peak (20 minutes x 1.30 = 26 minutes); (1) Covers the Little Rock AR urban area; (2) Rank is based on 101 larger urban areas (#1 = highest travel time index)
Source: Texas A&M Transportation Institute, 2019 Urban Mobility Report

Public Transportation

Agency Name / Mode of Transportation	Vehicles Operated in Maximum Service[1]	Annual Unlinked Passenger Trips[2] (in thous.)	Annual Passenger Miles[3] (in thous.)
Central Arkansas Transit Authority (CATA)			
Bus (directly operated)	49	2,340.2	11,247.5
Demand Response (directly operated)	20	93.6	751.9
Demand Response (purchased transportation)	4	4.1	29.5
Streetcar Rail (directly operated)	3	126.9	325.9

Note: (1) Number of revenue vehicles operated by the given mode and type of service to meet the annual maximum service requirement. This is the revenue vehicle count during the peak season of the year; on the week and day that maximum service is provided. Vehicles operated in maximum service (VOMS) exclude atypical days and one-time special events; (2) Number of passengers who boarded public transportation vehicles. Passengers are counted each time they board a vehicle no matter how many vehicles they use to travel from their origin to their destination. (3) Sum of the distances ridden by all passengers during the entire fiscal year.
Source: Federal Transit Administration, National Transit Database, 2019

Air Transportation

Airport Name and Code / Type of Service	Passenger Airlines[1]	Passenger Enplanements	Freight Carriers[2]	Freight (lbs)
Little Rock National Airport (LIT)				
Domestic service (U.S. carriers - 2020)	20	470,002	11	14,861,815
International service (U.S. carriers - 2019)	0	0	1	851

Note: (1) Includes all U.S.-based major, minor and commuter airlines that carried at least one passenger during the year; (2) Includes all U.S.-based airlines and freight carriers that transported at least one pound of freight during the year.
Source: Bureau of Transportation Statistics, The Intermodal Transportation Database, Air Carriers: T-100 Domestic Market (U.S. Carriers), 2020; Bureau of Transportation Statistics, The Intermodal Transportation Database, Air Carriers: T-100 International Market (U.S. Carriers), 2019

BUSINESSES

Major Business Headquarters

Company Name	Industry	Rankings	
		Fortune[1]	Forbes[2]
Dillard's	General Merchandisers	468	-

Note: (1) Companies that produce a 10-K are ranked 1 to 500 based on 2019 revenue; (2) All private companies with at least $2 billion in annual revenue through the end of their most current fiscal year are ranked 1 to 219; companies listed are headquartered in the city; dashes indicate no ranking
Source: Fortune, "Fortune 500," June/July 2020; Forbes, "America's Largest Private Companies," 2020

Fastest-Growing Businesses

According to *Inc.*, Little Rock is home to one of America's 500 fastest-growing private companies: **Integrity Construction of Arkansas** (#365). Criteria: must be an independent, privately-held, for-profit, U.S. corporation, proprietorship or partnership as of December 31, 2019; revenues must be at least $100,000 in 2016 and $2 million in 2019; must have four-year operating/sales history. *Inc., "America's 500 Fastest-Growing Private Companies," 2020*

According to *Initiative for a Competitive Inner City (ICIC)*, Little Rock is home to one of America's 100 fastest-growing "inner city" companies: **Team SI** (#20). Criteria for inclusion: company must be headquartered in or have 51 percent or more of its physical operations in an economically distressed urban area; must be an independent, for-profit corporation, partnership or proprietorship; must have 10 or more employees and have a five-year sales history that includes sales of at least $200,000 in the base year and at least $1 million in the current year with no decrease in sales over the two most recent years. Companies were ranked overall by revenue growth over the five-year period between 2015 and 2019. *Initiative for a Competitive Inner City (ICIC), "Inner City 100 Companies," 2020*

Living Environment

COST OF LIVING

Cost of Living Index

Composite Index	Groceries	Housing	Utilities	Trans- portation	Health Care	Misc. Goods/ Services
95.5	91.9	87.8	95.0	91.9	91.4	104.6

Note: The Cost of Living Index measures regional differences in the cost of consumer goods and services, excluding taxes and non-consumer expenditures, for professional and managerial households in the top income quintile. It is based on more than 50,000 prices covering almost 60 different items for which prices are collected three times a year by chambers of commerce, economic development organizations or university applied economic centers in each participating urban area. The numbers shown should be read as a percentage above or below the national average of 100. For example, a value of 115.4 in the groceries column indicates that grocery prices are 15.4% higher than the national average. Small differences in the index numbers should not be interpreted as significant; Figures cover the Little Rock-North Little Rock AR urban area.
Source: The Council for Community and Economic Research, Cost of Living Index, 2020

Grocery Prices

Area[1]	T-Bone Steak ($/pound)	Frying Chicken ($/pound)	Whole Milk ($/half gal.)	Eggs ($/dozen)	Orange Juice ($/64 oz.)	Coffee ($/11.5 oz.)
City[2]	10.99	1.16	1.78	1.43	3.23	3.89
Avg.	11.78	1.39	2.05	1.47	3.57	4.34
Min.	8.03	0.94	1.03	0.74	2.94	3.02
Max.	15.86	2.65	4.31	3.77	5.44	8.69

*Note: (1) Values for the local area are compared with the average, minimum and maximum values for all 284 areas in the Cost of Living Index; (2) Figures cover the Little Rock-North Little Rock AR urban area; **T-Bone Steak** (price per pound); **Frying Chicken** (price per pound, whole fryer); **Whole Milk** (half gallon carton); **Eggs** (price per dozen, Grade A, large); **Orange Juice** (64 oz. Tropicana or Florida Natural); **Coffee** (11.5 oz. can, vacuum-packed, Maxwell House, Hills Bros, or Folgers).*
Source: The Council for Community and Economic Research, Cost of Living Index, 2020

Housing and Utility Costs

Area[1]	New Home Price ($)	Apartment Rent ($/month)	All Electric ($/month)	Part Electric ($/month)	Other Energy ($/month)	Telephone ($/month)
City[2]	371,333	740	-	85.47	57.54	197.30
Avg.	368,594	1,168	170.86	100.47	65.28	184.30
Min.	190,567	502	91.58	31.42	26.08	169.60
Max.	2,227,806	4,738	470.38	280.31	280.06	206.50

*Note: (1) Values for the local area are compared with the average, minimum and maximum values for all 284 areas in the Cost of Living Index; (2) Figures cover the Little Rock-North Little Rock AR urban area; **New Home Price** (2,400 sf living area, 8,000 sf lot, in urban area with full utilities); **Apartment Rent** (950 sf 2 bedroom/1.5 or 2 bath, unfurnished, excluding all utilities except water); **All Electric** (average monthly cost for an all-electric home); **Part Electric** (average monthly cost for a part-electric home); **Other Energy** (average monthly cost for natural gas, fuel oil, coal, wood, and any other forms of energy except electricity); **Telephone** (price includes the base monthly rate plus taxes and fees for three lines of mobile phone service).*
Source: The Council for Community and Economic Research, Cost of Living Index, 2020

Health Care, Transportation, and Other Costs

Area[1]	Doctor ($/visit)	Dentist ($/visit)	Optometrist ($/visit)	Gasoline ($/gallon)	Beauty Salon ($/visit)	Men's Shirt ($)
City[2]	125.22	69.23	101.50	1.89	42.83	35.86
Avg.	115.44	99.32	108.10	2.21	39.27	31.37
Min.	36.68	59.00	51.36	1.71	19.00	11.00
Max.	219.00	153.10	250.97	3.46	82.05	58.33

*Note: (1) Values for the local area are compared with the average, minimum and maximum values for all 284 areas in the Cost of Living Index; (2) Figures cover the Little Rock-North Little Rock AR urban area; **Doctor** (general practitioners routine exam of an established patient); **Dentist** (adult teeth cleaning and periodic oral examination); **Optometrist** (full vision eye exam for established adult patient); **Gasoline** (one gallon regular unleaded, national brand, including all taxes, cash price at self-service pump if available); **Beauty Salon** (woman's shampoo, trim, and blow-dry); **Men's Shirt** (cotton/polyester dress shirt, pinpoint weave, long sleeves).*
Source: The Council for Community and Economic Research, Cost of Living Index, 2020

HOUSING

Homeownership Rate

Area	2012 (%)	2013 (%)	2014 (%)	2015 (%)	2016 (%)	2017 (%)	2018 (%)	2019 (%)	2020 (%)
MSA[1]	n/a	n/a	n/a	65.8	64.9	61.0	62.2	65.0	67.7
U.S.	65.4	65.1	64.5	63.7	63.4	63.9	64.4	64.6	66.6

Note: (1) Figures cover the Little Rock-North Little Rock-Conway, AR Metropolitan Statistical Area
Source: U.S. Census Bureau, Housing Vacancies and Homeownership Annual Statistics: 2012-2020

House Price Index (HPI)

Area	National Ranking[2]	Quarterly Change (%)	One-Year Change (%)	Five-Year Change (%)	Since 1991Q1 (%)
MSA[1]	196	1.79	5.10	16.24	131.58
U.S.[3]	–	3.81	10.77	38.99	205.12

Note: The HPI is a weighted repeat sales index. It measures average price changes in repeat sales or refinancings on the same properties. This information is obtained by reviewing repeat mortgage transactions on single-family properties whose mortgages have been purchased or securitized by Fannie Mae or Freddie Mac since January 1975; (1) Figures cover the Little Rock-North Little Rock-Conway, AR Metropolitan Statistical Area; (2) Rankings are based on annual percentage change for all metro areas containing at least 15,000 transactions over the last 10 years and ranges from 1 to 253; (3) figures based on a weighted average of Census Division estimates using a seasonally adjusted, purchase-only index; all figures are for the period ending December 31, 2020
Source: Federal Housing Finance Agency, Change in Metropolitan Area House Price Indexes, April 7, 2021

Median Single-Family Home Prices

Area	2018	2019	2020p	Percent Change 2019 to 2020
MSA[1]	146.4	152.5	166.9	9.4
U.S. Average	261.6	274.6	299.9	9.2

Note: Figures are median sales prices of existing single-family homes in thousands of dollars; (p) preliminary; (1) Figures cover the Little Rock-North Little Rock-Conway, AR Metropolitan Statistical Area
Source: National Association of Realtors, Median Sales Price of Existing Single-Family Homes for Metropolitan Areas, 4th Quarter 2020

Qualifying Income Based on Median Sales Price of Existing Single-Family Homes

Area	With 5% Down ($)	With 10% Down ($)	With 20% Down ($)
MSA[1]	32,835	31,107	27,651
U.S. Average	59,266	56,147	49,908

Note: Figures are preliminary; Qualifying income is based on a mortgage rate of 2.81%. Monthly principal and interest payment is limited to 25% of income; (1) Figures cover the Little Rock-North Little Rock-Conway, AR Metropolitan Statistical Area
Source: National Association of Realtors, Qualifying Income Based on Median Sales Price of Existing Single-Family Homes for Metropolitan Areas, 4th Quarter 2020

Home Value Distribution

Area	Under $50,000	$50,000 -$99,999	$100,000 -$149,999	$150,000 -$199,999	$200,000 -$299,999	$300,000 -$499,999	$500,000 -$999,999	$1,000,000 or more
City	6.5	19.3	16.8	17.5	15.9	15.4	7.0	1.6
MSA[1]	7.9	17.6	22.4	19.5	18.4	10.1	3.2	0.9
U.S.	6.9	12.0	13.3	14.0	19.6	19.3	11.4	3.4

Note: Figures are percentages and cover owner-occupied housing units; (1) Figures cover the Little Rock-North Little Rock-Conway, AR Metropolitan Statistical Area
Source: U.S. Census Bureau, 2015-2019 American Community Survey 5-Year Estimates

Year Housing Structure Built

Area	2010 or Later	2000 -2009	1990 -1999	1980 -1989	1970 -1979	1960 -1969	1950 -1959	1940 -1949	Before 1940	Median Year
City	6.2	11.2	11.2	14.3	19.6	15.2	9.9	5.2	7.1	1976
MSA[1]	9.3	18.2	16.7	13.7	17.0	10.8	7.1	3.4	3.7	1986
U.S.	5.2	14.0	13.9	13.4	15.2	10.6	10.3	4.9	12.6	1978

Note: Figures are percentages except for Median Year; Note: (1) Figures cover the Little Rock-North Little Rock-Conway, AR Metropolitan Statistical Area
Source: U.S. Census Bureau, 2015-2019 American Community Survey 5-Year Estimates

Gross Monthly Rent

Area	Under $500	$500 -$999	$1,000 -$1,499	$1,500 -$1,999	$2,000 -$2,499	$2,500 -$2,999	$3,000 and up	Median ($)
City	9.9	54.3	29.0	4.8	0.8	0.6	0.6	872
MSA[1]	10.1	58.9	25.0	4.7	0.6	0.4	0.3	845
U.S.	9.4	36.2	30.0	14.0	5.6	2.4	2.4	1,062

Note: Figures are percentages except for Median; Gross rent is the contract rent plus the estimated average monthly cost of utilities (electricity, gas, and water and sewer) and fuels (oil, coal, kerosene, wood, etc.) if these are paid by the renter (or paid for the renter by someone else); (1) Figures cover the Little Rock-North Little Rock-Conway, AR Metropolitan Statistical Area
Source: U.S. Census Bureau, 2015-2019 American Community Survey 5-Year Estimates

286 Little Rock, Arkansas

HEALTH

Health Risk Factors

Category	MSA[1] (%)	U.S. (%)
Adults aged 18–64 who have any kind of health care coverage	85.8	87.3
Adults who reported being in good or better health	76.7	82.4
Adults who have been told they have high blood cholesterol	37.3	33.0
Adults who have been told they have high blood pressure	39.8	32.3
Adults who are current smokers	24.8	17.1
Adults who currently use E-cigarettes	9.1	4.6
Adults who currently use chewing tobacco, snuff, or snus	5.2	4.0
Adults who are heavy drinkers[2]	6.1	6.3
Adults who are binge drinkers[3]	18.2	17.4
Adults who are overweight (BMI 25.0 - 29.9)	31.2	35.3
Adults who are obese (BMI 30.0 - 99.8)	35.4	31.3
Adults who participated in any physical activities in the past month	69.3	74.4
Adults who always or nearly always wears a seat belt	95.2	94.3

Note: (1) Figures cover the Little Rock-North Little Rock-Conway, AR Metropolitan Statistical Area; (2) Heavy drinkers are classified as adult men having more than 14 drinks per week and adult women having more than 7 drinks per week; (3) Binge drinkers are classified as males having five or more drinks on one occasion or females having four or more drinks on one occasion
Source: Centers for Disease Control and Prevention, Behaviorial Risk Factor Surveillance System, SMART: Selected Metropolitan Area Risk Trends, 2017

Acute and Chronic Health Conditions

Category	MSA[1] (%)	U.S. (%)
Adults who have ever been told they had a heart attack	4.9	4.2
Adults who have ever been told they have angina or coronary heart disease	5.3	3.9
Adults who have ever been told they had a stroke	3.5	3.0
Adults who have ever been told they have asthma	16.1	14.2
Adults who have ever been told they have arthritis	27.5	24.9
Adults who have ever been told they have diabetes[2]	11.1	10.5
Adults who have ever been told they had skin cancer	7.5	6.2
Adults who have ever been told they had any other types of cancer	8.3	7.1
Adults who have ever been told they have COPD	7.0	6.5
Adults who have ever been told they have kidney disease	4.0	3.0
Adults who have ever been told they have a form of depression	23.3	20.5

Note: (1) Figures cover the Little Rock-North Little Rock-Conway, AR Metropolitan Statistical Area; (2) Figures do not include pregnancy-related, borderline, or pre-diabetes
Source: Centers for Disease Control and Prevention, Behaviorial Risk Factor Surveillance System, SMART: Selected Metropolitan Area Risk Trends, 2017

Health Screening and Vaccination Rates

Category	MSA[1] (%)	U.S. (%)
Adults aged 65+ who have had flu shot within the past year	61.5	60.7
Adults aged 65+ who have ever had a pneumonia vaccination	76.1	75.4
Adults who have ever been tested for HIV	40.0	36.1
Adults who have ever had the shingles or zoster vaccine?	32.4	28.9
Adults who have had their blood cholesterol checked within the last five years	83.3	85.9

Note: n/a not available; (1) Figures cover the Little Rock-North Little Rock-Conway, AR Metropolitan Statistical Area.
Source: Centers for Disease Control and Prevention, Behaviorial Risk Factor Surveillance System, SMART: Selected Metropolitan Area Risk Trends, 2017

Disability Status

Category	MSA[1] (%)	U.S. (%)
Adults who reported being deaf	7.3	6.7
Are you blind or have serious difficulty seeing, even when wearing glasses?	5.9	4.5
Are you limited in any way in any of your usual activities due of arthritis?	16.7	12.9
Do you have difficulty doing errands alone?	9.5	6.8
Do you have difficulty dressing or bathing?	4.8	3.6
Do you have serious difficulty concentrating/remembering/making decisions?	14.0	10.7
Do you have serious difficulty walking or climbing stairs?	18.7	13.6

Note: (1) Figures cover the Little Rock-North Little Rock-Conway, AR Metropolitan Statistical Area.
Source: Centers for Disease Control and Prevention, Behaviorial Risk Factor Surveillance System, SMART: Selected Metropolitan Area Risk Trends, 2017

Mortality Rates for the Top 10 Causes of Death in the U.S.

ICD-10[a] Sub-Chapter	ICD-10[a] Code	Age-Adjusted Mortality Rate[1] per 100,000 population	
		County[2]	U.S.
Malignant neoplasms	C00-C97	154.9	149.2
Ischaemic heart diseases	I20-I25	107.1	90.5
Other forms of heart disease	I30-I51	47.8	52.2
Chronic lower respiratory diseases	J40-J47	49.3	39.6
Other degenerative diseases of the nervous system	G30-G31	75.1	37.6
Cerebrovascular diseases	I60-I69	45.7	37.2
Other external causes of accidental injury	W00-X59	32.9	36.1
Organic, including symptomatic, mental disorders	F01-F09	15.8	29.4
Hypertensive diseases	I10-I15	30.1	24.1
Diabetes mellitus	E10-E14	36.6	21.5

Note: (a) ICD-10 = International Classification of Diseases 10th Revision; (1) Mortality rates are a three-year average covering 2017-2019; (2) Figures cover Pulaski County.
Source: Centers for Disease Control and Prevention, National Center for Health Statistics. Underlying Cause of Death 1999-2019 on CDC WONDER Online Database

Mortality Rates for Selected Causes of Death

ICD-10[a] Sub-Chapter	ICD-10[a] Code	Age-Adjusted Mortality Rate[1] per 100,000 population	
		County[2]	U.S.
Assault	X85-Y09	17.4	6.0
Diseases of the liver	K70-K76	13.0	14.4
Human immunodeficiency virus (HIV) disease	B20-B24	3.3	1.5
Influenza and pneumonia	J09-J18	16.0	13.8
Intentional self-harm	X60-X84	16.5	14.1
Malnutrition	E40-E46	4.8	2.3
Obesity and other hyperalimentation	E65-E68	3.0	2.1
Renal failure	N17-N19	19.5	12.6
Transport accidents	V01-V99	16.3	12.3
Viral hepatitis	B15-B19	Unreliable	1.2

Note: (a) ICD-10 = International Classification of Diseases 10th Revision; (1) Mortality rates are a three-year average covering 2017-2019; (2) Figures cover Pulaski County; Data are suppressed when the data meet the criteria for confidentiality constraints; Mortality rates are flagged as unreliable when the rate would be calculated with a numerator of 20 or less.
Source: Centers for Disease Control and Prevention, National Center for Health Statistics. Underlying Cause of Death 1999-2019 on CDC WONDER Online Database

Health Insurance Coverage

Area	With Health Insurance	With Private Health Insurance	With Public Health Insurance	Without Health Insurance	Population Under Age 19 Without Health Insurance
City	91.6	65.6	37.6	8.4	4.8
MSA[1]	92.4	67.0	38.9	7.6	4.4
U.S.	91.2	67.9	35.1	8.8	5.1

Note: Figures are percentages that cover the civilian noninstitutionalized population; (1) Figures cover the Little Rock-North Little Rock-Conway, AR Metropolitan Statistical Area
Source: U.S. Census Bureau, 2015-2019 American Community Survey 5-Year Estimates

Number of Medical Professionals

Area	MDs[3]	DOs[3,4]	Dentists	Podiatrists	Chiropractors	Optometrists
County[1] (number)	2,890	56	304	18	88	84
County[1] (rate[2])	737.4	14.3	77.6	4.6	22.5	21.4
U.S. (rate[2])	282.9	22.7	71.2	6.2	28.1	16.9

05119
Note: Data as of 2019 unless noted; (1) Data covers Pulaski County; (2) Rate per 100,000 population; (3) Data as of 2018 and includes all active, non-federal physicians; (4) Doctor of Osteopathic Medicine
Source: U.S. Department of Health and Human Services, Health Resources and Services Administration, Bureau of Health Professions, Area Resource File (ARF) 2019-2020

Best Hospitals

According to *U.S. News,* the Little Rock-North Little Rock-Conway, AR metro area is home to one of the best hospitals in the U.S.: **UAMS Medical Center** (1 adult specialty). The hospital listed was nationally ranked in at least one of 16 adult or 10 pediatric specialties. Only 134 hospitals nationwide were nationally ranked in one or more adult or pediatric specialty; this number increases to 178 counting specialized centers within hospitals. Twenty hospitals in the U.S. made the Honor Roll. The Best Hospitals Honor Roll takes both the national rankings and the procedure and condition ratings into account. Hospitals received points if they were nationally ranked in one of the 16 adult specialties—the higher they ranked, the more points they got—and how many ratings of "high performing" they earned in the 10 procedures and conditions. *U.S. News Online, "America's Best Hospitals 2020-21"*

According to *U.S. News,* the Little Rock-North Little Rock-Conway, AR metro area is home to one of the best children's hospitals in the U.S.: **Arkansas Children's Hospital** (4 pediatric specialties). The hospital listed was highly ranked in at least one of 10 pediatric specialties. Eighty-eight children's hospitals in the U.S. were nationally ranked in at least one specialty. Hospitals received points for being ranked in a specialty, and the 10 hospitals with the most points across the 10 specialties make up the Honor Roll. *U.S. News Online, "America's Best Children's Hospitals 2020-21"*

EDUCATION

Public School District Statistics

District Name	Schls	Pupils	Pupil/ Teacher Ratio	Minority Pupils[1] (%)	Free Lunch Eligible[2] (%)	IEP[3] (%)
Arkansas Virtual Academy	3	2,361	26.7	21.5	54.1	15.6
Estem High Charter	5	3,070	17.3	73.7	38.6	9.5
Lisa Academy Charter	6	2,218	14.6	78.9	49.0	10.2
Little Rock School District	43	23,368	14.4	81.2	62.9	14.9
Pulaski Co. Spec. School Dist.	24	12,383	14.6	58.3	43.3	14.8

Note: Table includes school districts with 2,000 or more students; (1) Percentage of students that are not non-Hispanic white; (2) Percentage of students that are eligible for the free lunch program; (3) Percentage of students that have an Individualized Education Program.
Source: U.S. Department of Education, National Center for Education Statistics, Common Core of Data, Local Education Agency (School District) Universe Survey: School Year 2018-2019; U.S. Department of Education, National Center for Education Statistics, Common Core of Data, Public Elementary/Secondary School Universe Survey: School Year 2018-2019

Highest Level of Education

Area	Less than H.S.	H.S. Diploma	Some College, No Deg.	Associate Degree	Bachelor's Degree	Master's Degree	Prof. School Degree	Doctorate Degree
City	8.7	22.2	21.1	6.2	23.7	11.0	4.3	2.8
MSA[1]	9.6	29.3	23.0	7.8	18.9	8.0	2.1	1.5
U.S.	12.0	27.0	20.4	8.5	19.8	8.8	2.1	1.4

Note: Figures cover persons age 25 and over; (1) Figures cover the Little Rock-North Little Rock-Conway, AR Metropolitan Statistical Area
Source: U.S. Census Bureau, 2015-2019 American Community Survey 5-Year Estimates

Educational Attainment by Race

Area	High School Graduate or Higher (%)					Bachelor's Degree or Higher (%)				
	Total	White	Black	Asian	Hisp.[2]	Total	White	Black	Asian	Hisp.[2]
City	91.3	93.8	88.2	95.3	61.3	41.8	54.6	22.6	70.2	10.2
MSA[1]	90.4	91.8	87.4	90.5	67.5	30.4	32.7	21.8	54.3	13.8
U.S.	88.0	89.9	86.0	87.1	68.7	32.1	33.5	21.6	54.3	16.4

Note: Figures shown cover persons 25 years old and over; (1) Figures cover the Little Rock-North Little Rock-Conway, AR Metropolitan Statistical Area; (2) People of Hispanic origin can be of any race
Source: U.S. Census Bureau, 2015-2019 American Community Survey 5-Year Estimates

School Enrollment by Grade and Control

Area	Preschool (%)		Kindergarten (%)		Grades 1 - 4 (%)		Grades 5 - 8 (%)		Grades 9 - 12 (%)	
	Public	Private	Public	Private	Public	Private	Public	Private	Public	Private
City	60.3	39.7	82.3	17.7	82.7	17.3	82.0	18.0	79.8	20.2
MSA[1]	63.2	36.8	87.1	12.9	88.9	11.1	88.9	11.1	87.4	12.6
U.S.	59.1	40.9	87.6	12.4	89.5	10.5	89.4	10.6	90.1	9.9

Note: Figures shown cover persons 3 years old and over; (1) Figures cover the Little Rock-North Little Rock-Conway, AR Metropolitan Statistical Area
Source: U.S. Census Bureau, 2015-2019 American Community Survey 5-Year Estimates

Higher Education

Four-Year Colleges			Two-Year Colleges			Medical Schools[1]	Law Schools[2]	Voc/ Tech[3]
Public	Private Non-profit	Private For-profit	Public	Private Non-profit	Private For-profit			
3	2	1	0	2	0	1	1	5

Note: Figures cover institutions located within the city limits and include main campuses only; (1) includes schools accredited by the Liaison Committee on Medical Education and the American Osteopathic Association's Commission on Osteopathic College Accreditation; (2) includes ABA-accredited schools, schools with provisional ABA accreditation, and state accredited schools; (3) includes all schools with programs that are less than 2 years.
Source: National Center for Education Statistics, Integrated Postsecondary Education System (IPEDS), 2019-20; Wikipedia, List of Medical Schools in the United States, accessed April 2, 2021; Wikipedia, List of Law Schools in the United States, accessed April 2, 2021

According to *U.S. News & World Report*, the Little Rock-North Little Rock-Conway, AR metro area is home to one of the top 100 liberal arts colleges in the U.S.: **Hendrix College** (#93 tie). The indicators used to capture academic quality fall into a number of categories: assessment by administrators at peer institutions; retention of students; faculty resources; student selectivity; financial resources; alumni giving; high school counselor ratings of colleges; and graduation rate. *U.S. News & World Report, "America's Best Colleges 2021"*

According to *U.S. News & World Report*, the Little Rock-North Little Rock-Conway, AR metro area is home to one of the top 75 medical schools for research in the U.S.: **University of Arkansas for Medical Sciences** (#75). The rankings are based on a weighted average of 11 measures of quality: quality assessment; peer assessment score; assessment score by residency directors; research activity; total research activity; average research activity per faculty member; student selectivity; median MCAT total score; median undergraduate GPA; acceptance rate; and faculty resources. *U.S. News & World Report, "America's Best Graduate Schools, Medical, 2022"*

EMPLOYERS

Major Employers

Company Name	Industry
Arkansas Blue Cross and Blue Shield	Hospitals and medical service plans
Arkansas Childrens Hospital	Specialty hospitals, except psychiatric
Baptist Health Systems	General medical & surgical hospitals
Dassault Falcon Jet Corp	Aviation and or aeronautical engineering
Dept of Highway and Trans Arkansas	Regulation, administration of transportation
Dept of Finance & Admin Arkansas	Finance, taxation, and monetary policy
Fidelity Information Systems	Data processing services
Loreal USA	Toilet preparations
Mountaire Farms	Broiler, fryer and roaster chickens
Pulaski County	General practice, attorney
St. Vincent Health System	Medical services organization
United States Dept of Veteran Affairs	General medical & surgical hospitals
University of Arkansas System	Colleges & universities
Valor Telecommunications	Voice telephone communications
Veterans Health Administration	Administration of veterans affairs

Note: Companies shown are located within the Little Rock-North Little Rock-Conway, AR Metropolitan Statistical Area.
Source: Hoovers.com; Wikipedia

PUBLIC SAFETY

Crime Rate

Area	All Crimes	Violent Crimes				Property Crimes		
		Murder	Rape[3]	Robbery	Aggrav. Assault	Burglary	Larceny -Theft	Motor Vehicle Theft
City	7,638.8	19.2	105.4	197.1	1,195.2	887.2	4,696.0	538.9
Suburbs[1]	n/a	6.8	60.7	54.6	393.0	n/a	n/a	278.3
Metro[2]	n/a	10.1	72.6	92.6	607.0	n/a	n/a	347.8
U.S.	2,489.3	5.0	42.6	81.6	250.2	340.5	1,549.5	219.9

Note: Figures are crimes per 100,000 population; (1) All areas within the metro area that are located outside the city limits; (2) Figures cover the Little Rock-North Little Rock-Conway, AR Metropolitan Statistical Area; (3) All figures shown were reported using the revised Uniform Crime Reporting (UCR) definition of rape.
Source: FBI Uniform Crime Reports, 2019

Hate Crimes

Area	Number of Quarters Reported	Number of Incidents per Bias Motivation					
		Race/Ethnicity/ Ancestry	Religion	Sexual Orientation	Disability	Gender	Gender Identity
City	4	0	0	0	0	0	0
U.S.	4	3,963	1,521	1,195	157	69	198

Source: Federal Bureau of Investigation, Hate Crime Statistics 2019

Identity Theft Consumer Reports

Area	Reports	Reports per 100,000 Population	Rank[2]
MSA[1]	8,579	1,156	6
U.S.	1,387,615	423	-

Note: (1) Figures cover the Little Rock-North Little Rock-Conway, AR Metropolitan Statistical Area; (2) Rank ranges from 1 to 391 where 1 indicates greatest number of identity theft reports per 100,000 population
Source: Federal Trade Commission, Consumer Sentinel Network Data Book 2020

Fraud and Other Consumer Reports

Area	Reports	Reports per 100,000 Population	Rank[2]
MSA[1]	10,216	1,376	3
U.S.	3,385,133	1,031	-

Note: (1) Figures cover the Little Rock-North Little Rock-Conway, AR Metropolitan Statistical Area; (2) Rank ranges from 1 to 391 where 1 indicates greatest number of fraud and other consumer reports per 100,000 population
Source: Federal Trade Commission, Consumer Sentinel Network Data Book 2020

POLITICS

2020 Presidential Election Results

Area	Biden	Trump	Jorgensen	Hawkins	Other
Pulaski County	60.0	37.5	1.0	0.3	1.3
U.S.	51.3	46.8	1.2	0.3	0.5

Note: Results are percentages and may not add to 100% due to rounding
Source: Dave Leip's Atlas of U.S. Presidential Elections

SPORTS

Professional Sports Teams

Team Name	League	Year Established
No teams are located in the metro area		

Source: Wikipedia, Major Professional Sports Teams of the United States and Canada, April 6, 2021

CLIMATE

Average and Extreme Temperatures

Temperature	Jan	Feb	Mar	Apr	May	Jun	Jul	Aug	Sep	Oct	Nov	Dec	Yr.
Extreme High (°F)	83	85	91	95	98	105	112	108	103	97	86	80	112
Average High (°F)	50	54	63	73	81	89	92	91	85	75	62	53	73
Average Temp. (°F)	40	45	53	63	71	79	82	81	74	63	52	43	62
Average Low (°F)	30	34	42	51	60	68	72	70	63	51	41	34	51
Extreme Low (°F)	-4	-5	17	28	40	46	54	52	38	29	17	-1	-5

Note: Figures cover the years 1948-1990
Source: National Climatic Data Center, International Station Meteorological Climate Summary, 9/96

Average Precipitation/Snowfall/Humidity

Precip./Humidity	Jan	Feb	Mar	Apr	May	Jun	Jul	Aug	Sep	Oct	Nov	Dec	Yr.
Avg. Precip. (in.)	4.1	4.2	4.9	5.2	5.4	3.6	3.5	3.2	3.8	3.5	4.8	4.5	50.7
Avg. Snowfall (in.)	3	2	1	Tr	0	0	0	0	0	0	Tr	1	5
Avg. Rel. Hum. 6am (%)	80	80	78	81	86	86	87	88	87	86	82	80	84
Avg. Rel. Hum. 3pm (%)	57	54	50	50	53	52	54	52	52	48	52	57	53

Note: Figures cover the years 1948-1990; Tr = Trace amounts (<0.05 in. of rain; <0.5 in. of snow)
Source: National Climatic Data Center, International Station Meteorological Climate Summary, 9/96

Weather Conditions

Temperature			Daytime Sky			Precipitation		
10°F & below	32°F & below	90°F & above	Clear	Partly cloudy	Cloudy	0.01 inch or more precip.	0.1 inch or more snow/ice	Thunder-storms
1	57	73	110	142	113	104	4	57

Note: Figures are average number of days per year and cover the years 1948-1990
Source: National Climatic Data Center, International Station Meteorological Climate Summary, 9/96

HAZARDOUS WASTE

Superfund Sites

The Little Rock-North Little Rock-Conway, AR metro area is home to one site on the EPA's Superfund National Priorities List: **Vertac, Inc.** (final). There are a total of 1,375 Superfund sites with a status of proposed or final on the list in the U.S. *U.S. Environmental Protection Agency, National Priorities List, April 7, 2021*

AIR QUALITY

Air Quality Trends: Ozone

	1990	1995	2000	2005	2010	2015	2016	2017	2018	2019
MSA[1]	0.080	0.086	0.090	0.083	0.072	0.063	0.064	0.060	0.066	0.059
U.S.	0.088	0.089	0.082	0.080	0.073	0.068	0.069	0.068	0.069	0.065

Note: (1) Data covers the Little Rock-North Little Rock-Conway, AR Metropolitan Statistical Area. The values shown are the composite ozone concentration averages among trend sites based on the highest fourth daily maximum 8-hour concentration in parts per million. These trends are based on sites having an adequate record of monitoring data during the trend period. Data from exceptional events are included.
Source: U.S. Environmental Protection Agency, Air Quality Monitoring Information, "Air Quality Trends by City, 1990-2019"

Air Quality Index

Area	Percent of Days when Air Quality was...[2]					AQI Statistics[2]	
	Good	Moderate	Unhealthy for Sensitive Groups	Unhealthy	Very Unhealthy	Maximum	Median
MSA[1]	64.4	35.6	0.0	0.0	0.0	79	45

Note: (1) Data covers the Little Rock-North Little Rock-Conway, AR Metropolitan Statistical Area; (2) Based on 365 days with AQI data in 2019. Air Quality Index (AQI) is an index for reporting daily air quality. EPA calculates the AQI for five major air pollutants regulated by the Clean Air Act: ground-level ozone, particle pollution (aka particulate matter), carbon monoxide, sulfur dioxide, and nitrogen dioxide. The AQI runs from 0 to 500. The higher the AQI value, the greater the level of air pollution and the greater the health concern. There are six AQI categories: "Good" AQI is between 0 and 50. Air quality is considered satisfactory; "Moderate" AQI is between 51 and 100. Air quality is acceptable; "Unhealthy for Sensitive Groups" When AQI values are between 101 and 150, members of sensitive groups may experience health effects; "Unhealthy" When AQI values are between 151 and 200 everyone may begin to experience health effects; "Very Unhealthy" AQI values between 201 and 300 trigger a health alert; "Hazardous" AQI values over 300 trigger warnings of emergency conditions (not shown).
Source: U.S. Environmental Protection Agency, Air Quality Index Report, 2019

Air Quality Index Pollutants

Area	Percent of Days when AQI Pollutant was...[2]					
	Carbon Monoxide	Nitrogen Dioxide	Ozone	Sulfur Dioxide	Particulate Matter 2.5	Particulate Matter 10
MSA[1]	0.0	0.5	40.0	0.0	59.5	0.0

Note: (1) Data covers the Little Rock-North Little Rock-Conway, AR Metropolitan Statistical Area; (2) Based on 365 days with AQI data in 2019. The Air Quality Index (AQI) is an index for reporting daily air quality. EPA calculates the AQI for five major air pollutants regulated by the Clean Air Act: ground-level ozone, particle pollution (also known as particulate matter), carbon monoxide, sulfur dioxide, and nitrogen dioxide. The AQI runs from 0 to 500. The higher the AQI value, the greater the level of air pollution and the greater the health concern.
Source: U.S. Environmental Protection Agency, Air Quality Index Report, 2019

Maximum Air Pollutant Concentrations: Particulate Matter, Ozone, CO and Lead

	Particulate Matter 10 (ug/m^3)	Particulate Matter 2.5 Wtd AM (ug/m^3)	Particulate Matter 2.5 24-Hr (ug/m^3)	Ozone (ppm)	Carbon Monoxide (ppm)	Lead (ug/m^3)
MSA[1] Level	38	10.3	23	0.060	1	n/a
NAAQS[2]	150	15	35	0.075	9	0.15
Met NAAQS[2]	Yes	Yes	Yes	Yes	Yes	n/a

Note: (1) Data covers the Little Rock-North Little Rock-Conway, AR Metropolitan Statistical Area; Data from exceptional events are included; (2) National Ambient Air Quality Standards; ppm = parts per million; ug/m^3 = micrograms per cubic meter; n/a not available.
Concentrations: Particulate Matter 10 (coarse particulate)—highest second maximum 24-hour concentration; Particulate Matter 2.5 Wtd AM (fine particulate)—highest weighted annual mean concentration; Particulate Matter 2.5 24-Hour (fine particulate)—highest 98th percentile 24-hour concentration; Ozone—highest fourth daily maximum 8-hour concentration; Carbon Monoxide—highest second maximum non-overlapping 8-hour concentration; Lead—maximum running 3-month average
Source: U.S. Environmental Protection Agency, Air Quality Monitoring Information, "Air Quality Statistics by City, 2019"

Maximum Air Pollutant Concentrations: Nitrogen Dioxide and Sulfur Dioxide

	Nitrogen Dioxide AM (ppb)	Nitrogen Dioxide 1-Hr (ppb)	Sulfur Dioxide AM (ppb)	Sulfur Dioxide 1-Hr (ppb)	Sulfur Dioxide 24-Hr (ppb)
MSA[1] Level	8	38	n/a	13	n/a
NAAQS[2]	53	100	30	75	140
Met NAAQS[2]	Yes	Yes	n/a	Yes	n/a

Note: (1) Data covers the Little Rock-North Little Rock-Conway, AR Metropolitan Statistical Area; Data from exceptional events are included; (2) National Ambient Air Quality Standards; ppm = parts per million; ug/m^3 = micrograms per cubic meter; n/a not available.
Concentrations: Nitrogen Dioxide AM—highest arithmetic mean concentration; Nitrogen Dioxide 1-Hr—highest 98th percentile 1-hour daily maximum concentration; Sulfur Dioxide AM—highest annual mean concentration; Sulfur Dioxide 1-Hr—highest 99th percentile 1-hour daily maximum concentration; Sulfur Dioxide 24-Hr—highest second maximum 24-hour concentration
Source: U.S. Environmental Protection Agency, Air Quality Monitoring Information, "Air Quality Statistics by City, 2019"

Madison, Wisconsin

Background

Madison was selected as Wisconsin's territorial capital in 1836 before construction of the city began in 1838. Despite repeated threats to move the capital elsewhere by members of the legislature, it has maintained its status. It was named for President James Madison in 1836, and incorporated into a village in 1856. When Wisconsin attained statehood in 1848, the University of Wisconsin (one of the largest in the country) was established.

Most of the city, including its business center, is situated on an isthmus between Lake Mendota and Lake Minona in the south-central part of the state. Two other lakes, Kengonsa and Waubesa, lie to the south. By ordinance, the city's skyline is dominated by the capitol dome, which weighs 2,500 tons.

Madison serves as the trade center of a rich agricultural and dairy region. Food processing is a major industry. Batteries, dairy equipment, and machine tools are produced there as well.

Wisconsin state government and the University of Wisconsin-Madison remain the two largest Madison employers. However, Madison continues to evolve from a government-based economy to consumer services and a base for high-tech, particularly in the health, biotech, and advertising sectors. Beginning in the early 1990s, the city experienced a steady economic boom fostered by the development of high-tech companies and UW-Madison working with local businesses and entrepreneurs to transfer the results of academic research into real-world applications, especially bio-tech applications. Businesses are attracted to Madison's skill base, taking advantage of the area's high level of education.

The city has received numerous awards, beginning as early as 1948 when it was named Best Place to Live in America by *Life* magazine. Although Madison is a progressive, eclectic city, it also offers the atmosphere of a small town with many picturesque communities, four lakes, and over 200 parks. There are a total of 29,000 acres designated for recreational use, including 46 miles of hiking trails, over 150 miles of bicycle trails, 92 miles of shoreline for swimming and boating, and 20 golf courses. Bicycle tourism is an $800 million industry in Wisconsin, which has 20 percent of the nation's bicycling industry manufacturing capacity.

Madison's many restaurants boast a large variety of ethnic food, from Greek and Italian to Japanese, Mexican, and Middle Eastern, as well as many brew pubs.

> The B2 Mask, created by University of Wisconsin-Madison student Max Bock-Aronson, was selected by *Time* magazine as one of the best inventions of 2020.

Cultural life in Madison has long had a center in the downtown, at the Madison Civic Center and its associated sites. Project Overture renovated and redeveloped a variety of cultural venues, including the Madison Museum of Contemporary Art with innovative design and sculpture-garden rooftop. A 2,250-seat hall houses the Madison Symphony Orchestra, whose old home, the Oscar Meyer Theater, is used by groups such as the CTM Family Theatre and the Wisconsin Chamber group. Keeping the goal of architectural integration in mind, facades of nearby buildings have been refurbished and preserved.

In 2018, Forward Madison FC became the city's first professional soccer team.

Another major attraction in Madison is the Olbrich Botanical Gardens, with 16 acres of outdoor display gardens, including sunken, perennial, rose, rock, herb, and wildflower gardens. Over 250,000 visitors a year enjoy the gardens, which include a lush, tropical conservatory filled with exotic plants, bright flowers, a rushing waterfall, and free-flying birds.

Madison is home to many institutions of higher learning, including the University of Wisconsin-Madison, Edgewood College, Herzing College, Lakeland College, and Madison Media Institute.

The area has the typical continental climate of interior North America with a large annual temperature range and frequent short-period temperature changes. The city lies in the path of the frequent cyclones and anticyclones, which move eastward over this area during fall, winter, and spring. The most frequent air masses are of polar origin, with occasional influxes of arctic air affecting this area during the winter months. Summers are pleasant, with only occasional periods of extreme heat or high humidity.

Rankings

General Rankings

- *US News & World Report* conducted a survey of more than 3,000 people and analyzed the 150 largest metropolitan areas to determine what matters most when selecting the next place to live. Madison ranked #21 out of the top 25 as having the best combination of desirable factors. Criteria: cost of living; quality of life; net migration; job market; desirability; and other factors. *realestate.usnews.com, "The 25 Best Places to Live in the U.S. in 2020-21," October 13, 2020*

- In their seventh annual survey, Livability.com looked at data for more than 1,000 small to mid-sized U.S. cities to determine the rankings for Livability's "Top 100 Best Places to Live" in 2020. Madison ranked #3. Criteria: housing and affordable living; vibrant economy; social and civic engagement; education; demographics; health care options; transportation & infrastructure; and abundant lifestyle amenities. *Livability.com, "Top 100 Best Places to Live 2020" October 2020*

Business/Finance Rankings

- The Brookings Institution ranked the nation's largest cities based on income inequality. Madison was ranked #86 (#1 = greatest inequality). Criteria: the "95/20 ratio," a figure representing the income at which a household earns more than 95 percent of all other households, divided by the income at which a household earns more than only 20 percent of all other households. *Brookings Institution, "Household Income Inequality, Largest Cities of 97 Large U.S. Metro Areas, 2014-2016," February 5, 2018*

- The Brookings Institution ranked the 100 largest metro areas in the U.S. based on income inequality. Madison was ranked #95 (#1 = greatest inequality). Criteria: the "95/20 ratio," a figure representing the income at which a household earns more than 95 percent of all other households, divided by the income at which a household earns more than only 20 percent of all other households. *Brookings Institution, "Household Income Inequality, 100 Largest U.S. Metro Areas, 2014-2016," February 5, 2018*

- Livability.com rated Madison as #10 of ten cities where new college grads' job prospects are brightest. Criteria included: number of 22- to 29-year olds; good job opportunities; affordable housing options; public transportation users; educational attainment; variety of fun things to do. *Livability.com, "2018 Top 10 Best Cities for Recent College Grads," April 26, 2018*

- The Madison metro area appeared on the Milken Institute "2021 Best Performing Cities" list. Rank: #34 out of 200 large metro areas (population over 250,000). Criteria: job growth; wage and salary growth; high-tech output growth; housing affordability; household broadband access. *Milken Institute, "Best-Performing Cities 2021," February 16, 2021*

- *Forbes* ranked the 200 most populous metro areas to determine the nation's "Best Places for Business and Careers." The Madison metro area was ranked #57. Criteria: costs (business and living); job growth (past and projected); income growth; quality of life; educational attainment (college and high school); projected economic growth; cultural and leisure opportunities; workplace tolerance laws; net migration patterns. *Forbes, "The Best Places for Business and Careers 2019: Seattle Still On Top," October 30, 2019*

Dating/Romance Rankings

- Madison was ranked #15 out of 25 cities that stood out for inspiring romance and attracting diners on the website OpenTable.com. Criteria: percentage of people who dined out on Valentine's Day in 2018; percentage of romantic restaurants as rated by OpenTable diner reviews; and percentage of tables seated for two. *OpenTable, "25 Most Romantic Cities in America for 2019," February 7, 2019*

- Madison was selected as one of America's best cities for singles by the readers of *Travel + Leisure* in their annual "America's Favorite Cities" survey. Criteria included good-looking locals, cool shopping, an active bar scene and hipster-magnet coffee bars. *Travel + Leisure, "Best Cities in America for Singles," July 21, 2017*

Education Rankings

- Personal finance website *WalletHub* analyzed the 150 largest U.S. metropolitan statistical areas to determine where the most educated Americans are putting their degrees to work. Criteria: education levels; percentage of workers with degrees; education quality and attainment gap; public school quality rankings; quality and enrollment of each metro area's universities. Madison was ranked #6 (#1 = most educated city). *www.WalletHub.com, "Most and Least Educated Cities in America, " July 20, 2020*

- Madison was selected as one of America's most literate cities. The city ranked #10 out of the 84 largest U.S. cities. Criteria: number of booksellers; library resources; Internet resources; educational attainment; periodical publishing resources; newspaper circulation. *Central Connecticut State University, "America's Most Literate Cities, 2018," February 2019*

Health/Fitness Rankings

- For each of the 100 largest cities in the United States, the American Fitness Index®, published by the American College of Sports Medicine and the Anthem Foundation, evaluated community infrastructure and 33 health behaviors including preventive health, levels of chronic disease conditions, pedestrian safety, air quality, and community resources that support physical activity. Madison ranked #4 for "community fitness." *americanfitnessindex.org, "2020 ACSM American Fitness Index Summary Report," July 14, 2020*

- Madison was identified as a "2021 Spring Allergy Capital." The area ranked #94 out of 100. Three groups of factors were used to identify the most challenging cities for people with allergies during the spring season: annual spring pollen levels; over the counter medicine use; number of board-certified allergy specialists. *Asthma and Allergy Foundation of America, "Spring Allergy Capitals 2021," February 23, 2021*

- Madison was identified as a "2021 Fall Allergy Capital." The area ranked #85 out of 100. Three groups of factors were used to identify the most challenging cities for people with allergies during the fall season: annual fall pollen levels; over the counter medicine use; number of board-certified allergy specialists. *Asthma and Allergy Foundation of America, "Fall Allergy Capitals 2021," February 23, 2021*

- Madison was identified as a "2019 Asthma Capital." The area ranked #66 out of the nation's 100 largest metropolitan areas. Criteria: estimated asthma prevalence; crude death rate from asthma; and ER visits due to asthma. Risk factors analyzed but not factored in the rankings: annual pollen score; annual air quality; public smoking laws; number of board-certified asthma specialists; rescue medication use; controller medication use; uninsured rate; poverty rate. *Asthma and Allergy Foundation of America, "Asthma Capitals 2019: The Most Challenging Places to Live With Asthma," May 7, 2019*

Real Estate Rankings

- *WalletHub* compared the most populated U.S. cities to determine which had the best markets for real estate agents. Madison ranked #107 where demand was high and pay was the best. Criteria: sales per agent; annual median wage for real-estate agents; monthly average starting salary for real estate agents; real estate job density and competition; unemployment rate; home turnover rate; housing-market health index; and other relevant metrics. *www.WalletHub.com, "2019's Best Places to Be a Real Estate Agent," April 24, 2019*

- The Madison metro area was identified as one of the 10 worst condo markets in the U.S. in 2020. The area ranked #59 out of 63 markets. Criteria: year-over-year change of median sales price of existing apartment condo-coop homes between the 4th quarter of 2019 and the 4th quarter of 2020. *National Association of Realtors®, Median Sales Price of Existing Apartment Condo-Coops Homes for Metropolitan Areas, 4th Quarter 2020*

- Madison was ranked #93 out of 268 metro areas in terms of housing affordability in 2020 by the National Association of Home Builders (#1 = most affordable). Criteria: the share of homes sold in that area affordable to a family earning the local median income, based on standard mortgage underwriting criteria. *National Association of Home Builders®, NAHB-Wells Fargo Housing Opportunity Index, 4th Quarter 2020*

Safety Rankings

- Allstate ranked the 200 largest cities in America in terms of driver safety. Madison ranked #11. Criteria: internal property damage claims over a two-year period from January 2016 to December 2017. The report helps increase the importance of safety and awareness behind the wheel. *Allstate, "Allstate America's Best Drivers Report, 2019" June 24, 2019*

- The National Insurance Crime Bureau ranked 384 metro areas in the U.S. in terms of per capita rates of vehicle theft. The Madison metro area ranked #247 (#1 = highest rate). Criteria: number of vehicle theft offenses per 100,000 inhabitants in 2019. *National Insurance Crime Bureau, "Hot Spots 2019," July 21, 2020*

Seniors/Retirement Rankings

- From its Best Cities for Successful Aging indexes, the Milken Institute generated rankings for metropolitan areas, weighing data in nine categories—health care, wellness, living arrangements, transportation and convenience, financial characteristics, education, employment, community engagement, and overall livability. The Madison metro area was ranked #2 overall in the large metro area category. *Milken Institute, "Best Cities for Successful Aging, 2017" March 14, 2017*

Sports/Recreation Rankings

- Madison was chosen as one of America's best cities for bicycling. The city ranked #8 out of 50. Criteria: cycling infrastructure that is safe and friendly for all ages; energy and bike culture. The editors evaluated cities with populations of 100,000 or more. *Bicycling, "The 50 Best Bike Cities in America," October 10, 2018*

Women/Minorities Rankings

- Personal finance website *WalletHub* compared more than 180 U.S. cities across two key dimensions, "Hispanic Business-Friendliness" and "Hispanic Purchasing Power," to arrive at the most favorable conditions for Hispanic entrepreneurs. Madison was ranked #100 out of 182. Criteria includes: share of Hispanic-Owned Businesses; Hispanic entrepreneurship rate to median annual income of Hispanics; Small Business-Friendliness score; cost of living; and number of Hispanics with at least a bachelor's degree. *WalletHub.com, "2019's Best Cities for Hispanic Entrepreneurs," May 1, 2019*

Miscellaneous Rankings

- *MoveHub* ranked 446 hipster cities across 20 countries, using its *alternative* Hipster Index and Madison came out as #30 among the top 50. Criteria: population over 150,000; number of vintage boutiques; density of tattoo parlors; vegan places to eat; coffee shops; and density of vinyl record stores. *www.movehub.com, "The Hipster Index: Brighton Pips Portland to Global Top Spot," February 20, 2020*

- *WalletHub* compared the 150 most populated U.S. cities to determine their operating efficiency. A "Quality of City Services" score was constructed for each city and then divided by the total budget per capita to reveal which were managed the best. Madison ranked #30. Criteria: financial stability; economy; education; safety; health; infrastructure and pollution. *www.WalletHub.com, "2020's Best- & Worst-Run Cities in America," June 29, 2020*

Business Environment

DEMOGRAPHICS

Population Growth

Area	1990 Census	2000 Census	2010 Census	2019* Estimate	Population Growth (%) 1990-2019	Population Growth (%) 2010-2019
City	193,451	208,054	233,209	254,977	31.8	9.3
MSA[1]	432,323	501,774	568,593	653,725	51.2	15.0
U.S.	248,709,873	281,421,906	308,745,538	324,697,795	30.6	5.2

Note: (1) Figures cover the Madison, WI Metropolitan Statistical Area; (*) 2015-2019 5-year estimated population
Source: U.S. Census Bureau, 1990 Census, Census 2000, Census 2010, 2015-2019 American Community Survey 5-Year Estimates

Household Size

Area	Persons in Household (%) One	Two	Three	Four	Five	Six	Seven or More	Average Household Size
City	35.3	36.2	13.2	9.9	3.8	1.1	0.5	2.20
MSA[1]	30.1	36.8	14.0	12.1	4.7	1.4	0.7	2.40
U.S.	27.9	33.9	15.6	12.9	6.0	2.3	1.4	2.60

Note: (1) Figures cover the Madison, WI Metropolitan Statistical Area
Source: U.S. Census Bureau, 2015-2019 American Community Survey 5-Year Estimates

Race

Area	White Alone[2] (%)	Black Alone[2] (%)	Asian Alone[2] (%)	AIAN[3] Alone[2] (%)	NHOPI[4] Alone[2] (%)	Other Race Alone[2] (%)	Two or More Races (%)
City	78.6	7.0	9.0	0.5	0.1	1.4	3.5
MSA[1]	86.0	4.4	5.0	0.3	0.0	1.4	2.8
U.S.	72.5	12.7	5.5	0.8	0.2	4.9	3.3

Note: (1) Figures cover the Madison, WI Metropolitan Statistical Area; (2) Alone is defined as not being in combination with one or more other races; (3) American Indian and Alaska Native; (4) Native Hawaiian and Other Pacific Islander
Source: U.S. Census Bureau, 2015-2019 American Community Survey 5-Year Estimates

Hispanic or Latino Origin

Area	Total (%)	Mexican (%)	Puerto Rican (%)	Cuban (%)	Other (%)
City	7.0	4.1	0.7	0.2	2.0
MSA[1]	5.7	3.6	0.5	0.1	1.5
U.S.	18.0	11.2	1.7	0.7	4.3

Note: Persons of Hispanic or Latino origin can be of any race; (1) Figures cover the Madison, WI Metropolitan Statistical Area
Source: U.S. Census Bureau, 2015-2019 American Community Survey 5-Year Estimates

Ancestry

Area	German	Irish	English	American	Italian	Polish	French[2]	Scottish	Dutch
City	31.4	12.4	8.1	2.0	4.1	5.7	2.9	1.5	1.8
MSA[1]	37.1	13.1	8.5	2.8	3.8	5.4	2.8	1.5	1.9
U.S.	13.3	9.7	7.2	6.2	5.1	2.8	2.3	1.7	1.2

Note: Figures are the percentage of the total population reporting a particular ancestry. The nine most commonly reported ancestries in the U.S. are shown. Figures include multiple ancestries (e.g. if a person reported being Irish and Italian, they were included in both columns); (1) Figures cover the Madison, WI Metropolitan Statistical Area; (2) Excludes Basque
Source: U.S. Census Bureau, 2015-2019 American Community Survey 5-Year Estimates

Foreign-born Population

Area	Percent of Population Born in Any Foreign Country	Asia	Mexico	Europe	Caribbean	Central America[2]	South America	Africa	Canada
City	12.1	6.7	1.5	1.4	0.2	0.3	0.8	1.0	0.3
MSA[1]	7.6	3.6	1.2	1.0	0.1	0.2	0.6	0.6	0.2
U.S.	13.6	4.2	3.5	1.5	1.3	1.1	1.0	0.7	0.2

Note: (1) Figures cover the Madison, WI Metropolitan Statistical Area; (2) Excludes Mexico.
Source: U.S. Census Bureau, 2015-2019 American Community Survey 5-Year Estimates

Marital Status

Area	Never Married	Now Married[2]	Separated	Widowed	Divorced
City	50.2	37.3	0.8	3.3	8.4
MSA[1]	36.5	48.8	0.8	4.2	9.6
U.S.	33.4	48.1	1.9	5.8	10.9

Note: Figures are percentages and cover the population 15 years of age and older; (1) Figures cover the Madison, WI Metropolitan Statistical Area; (2) Excludes separated
Source: U.S. Census Bureau, 2015-2019 American Community Survey 5-Year Estimates

Disability by Age

Area	All Ages	Under 18 Years Old	18 to 64 Years Old	65 Years and Over
City	8.0	3.2	6.2	26.3
MSA[1]	8.9	3.4	6.9	26.9
U.S.	12.6	4.2	10.3	34.5

Note: Figures show percent of the civilian noninstitutionalized population that reported having a disability. Disability status is determined from six types of difficulty: vision, hearing, cognitive, ambulatory, self-care, and independent living. For children under 5 years old, hearing and vision difficulty are used to determine disability status. For children between the ages of 5 and 14, disability status is determined from hearing, vision, cognitive, ambulatory, and self-care difficulties. For people aged 15 years and older, they are considered to have a disability if they have difficulty with any one of the six difficulty types; Note: (1) Figures cover the Madison, WI Metropolitan Statistical Area
Source: U.S. Census Bureau, 2015-2019 American Community Survey 5-Year Estimates

Age

Area	Percent of Population									Median Age
	Under Age 5	Age 5–19	Age 20–34	Age 35–44	Age 45–54	Age 55–64	Age 65–74	Age 75–84	Age 85+	
City	4.9	16.4	35.5	12.2	9.7	9.7	6.9	3.2	1.5	31.0
MSA[1]	5.6	18.2	24.4	13.0	12.3	12.5	8.5	3.8	1.7	36.2
U.S.	6.1	19.1	20.7	12.6	13.0	12.9	9.1	4.6	1.9	38.1

Note: (1) Figures cover the Madison, WI Metropolitan Statistical Area
Source: U.S. Census Bureau, 2015-2019 American Community Survey 5-Year Estimates

Gender

Area	Males	Females	Males per 100 Females
City	126,190	128,787	98.0
MSA[1]	325,952	327,773	99.4
U.S.	159,886,919	164,810,876	97.0

Note: (1) Figures cover the Madison, WI Metropolitan Statistical Area
Source: U.S. Census Bureau, 2015-2019 American Community Survey 5-Year Estimates

Religious Groups by Family

Area	Catholic	Baptist	Non-Den.	Methodist[2]	Lutheran	LDS[3]	Pente-costal	Presby-terian[4]	Muslim[5]	Judaism
MSA[1]	21.8	1.1	1.6	3.7	12.8	0.5	0.4	2.2	0.5	0.5
U.S.	19.1	9.3	4.0	4.0	2.3	2.0	1.9	1.6	0.8	0.7

Note: Figures are the number of adherents as a percentage of the total population; (1) Figures cover the Madison, WI Metropolitan Statistical Area; (2) Methodist/Pietist; (3) Latter Day Saints; (4) Reformed; (5) Figures are estimates
Source: Association of Statisticians of American Religious Bodies, 2010 U.S. Religion Census: Religious Congregations & Membership Study

Religious Groups by Tradition

Area	Catholic	Evangelical Protestant	Mainline Protestant	Other Tradition	Black Protestant	Orthodox
MSA[1]	21.8	7.3	15.4	2.3	0.1	0.1
U.S.	19.1	16.2	7.3	4.3	1.6	0.3

Note: Figures are the number of adherents as a percentage of the total population; (1) Figures cover the Madison, WI Metropolitan Statistical Area
Source: Association of Statisticians of American Religious Bodies, 2010 U.S. Religion Census: Religious Congregations & Membership Study

ECONOMY

Gross Metropolitan Product

Area	2017	2018	2019	2020	Rank[2]
MSA[1]	49.5	52.1	54.5	56.5	61

Note: Figures are in billions of dollars; (1) Figures cover the Madison, WI Metropolitan Statistical Area; (2) Rank is based on 2018 data and ranges from 1 to 381
Source: U.S. Conference of Mayors, U.S. Metro Economies: GMP & Employment 2018-2020, September 2019

Economic Growth

Area	2015-17 (%)	2018 (%)	2019 (%)	2020 (%)	Rank[2]
MSA[1]	2.4	3.2	2.8	1.7	107
U.S.	1.9	2.9	2.3	2.1	–

Note: Figures are real gross metropolitan product (GMP) growth rates and represent average annual percent change; (1) Figures cover the Madison, WI Metropolitan Statistical Area; (2) Rank is based on 2017 2-year average annual percent change and ranges from 1 to 381
Source: U.S. Conference of Mayors, U.S. Metro Economies: GMP & Employment 2018-2020, September 2019

Metropolitan Area Exports

Area	2014	2015	2016	2017	2018	2019	Rank[2]
MSA[1]	2,369.5	2,280.4	2,204.8	2,187.7	2,460.2	2,337.6	93

Note: Figures are in millions of dollars; (1) Figures cover the Madison, WI Metropolitan Statistical Area; (2) Rank is based on 2019 data and ranges from 1 to 386
Source: U.S. Department of Commerce, International Trade Administration, Office of Trade and Economic Analysis, Industry and Analysis, Exports by Metropolitan Area, data extracted March 24, 2021

Building Permits

Area	Single-Family			Multi-Family			Total		
	2018	2019	Pct. Chg.	2018	2019	Pct. Chg.	2018	2019	Pct. Chg.
City	334	426	27.5	1,109	1,232	11.1	1,443	1,658	14.9
MSA[1]	1,623	1,536	-5.4	2,029	1,807	-10.9	3,652	3,343	-8.5
U.S.	855,300	862,100	0.7	473,500	523,900	10.6	1,328,800	1,386,000	4.3

Note: (1) Figures cover the Madison, WI Metropolitan Statistical Area; Figures represent new, privately-owned housing units authorized (unadjusted data); All permit data are based on estimates with imputation
Source: U.S. Census Bureau, Manufacturing, Mining, and Construction Statistics, Building Permits, 2018, 2019

Bankruptcy Filings

Area	Business Filings			Nonbusiness Filings		
	2019	2020	% Chg.	2019	2020	% Chg.
Dane County	34	28	-17.6	773	527	-31.8
U.S.	22,780	21,655	-4.9	752,160	522,808	-30.5

Note: Business filings include Chapter 7, Chapter 9, Chapter 11, Chapter 12, Chapter 13, Chapter 15, and Section 304; Nonbusiness filings include Chapter 7, Chapter 11, and Chapter 13
Source: Administrative Office of the U.S. Courts, Business and Nonbusiness Bankruptcy, County Cases Commenced by Chapter of the Bankruptcy Code, During the 12-Month Period Ending December 31, 2019 and Business and Nonbusiness Bankruptcy, County Cases Commenced by Chapter of the Bankruptcy Code, During the 12-Month Period Ending December 31, 2020

Housing Vacancy Rates

Area	Gross Vacancy Rate[2] (%)			Year-Round Vacancy Rate[3] (%)			Rental Vacancy Rate[4] (%)			Homeowner Vacancy Rate[5] (%)		
	2018	2019	2020	2018	2019	2020	2018	2019	2020	2018	2019	2020
MSA[1]	n/a	n/a	n/a	n/a	n/a	n/a	n/a	n/a	n/a	n/a	n/a	n/a
U.S.	12.3	12.0	10.6	9.7	9.5	8.2	6.9	6.7	6.3	1.5	1.4	1.0

Note: (1) Figures cover the Madison, WI Metropolitan Statistical Area; (2) The percentage of the total housing inventory that is vacant; (3) The percentage of the housing inventory (excluding seasonal units) that is year-round vacant; (4) The percentage of rental inventory that is vacant for rent; (5) The percentage of homeowner inventory that is vacant for sale; n/a not available
Source: U.S. Census Bureau, Housing Vacancies and Homeownership Annual Statistics: 2018, 2019, 2020

INCOME

Income

Area	Per Capita ($)	Median Household ($)	Average Household ($)
City	38,285	65,332	87,055
MSA[1]	39,484	72,374	93,923
U.S.	34,103	62,843	88,607

Note: (1) Figures cover the Madison, WI Metropolitan Statistical Area
Source: U.S. Census Bureau, 2015-2019 American Community Survey 5-Year Estimates

Household Income Distribution

Area	Percent of Households Earning							
	Under $15,000	$15,000 -$24,999	$25,000 -$34,999	$35,000 -$49,999	$50,000 -$74,999	$75,000 -$99,999	$100,000 -$149,999	$150,000 and up
City	10.3	7.6	8.8	12.1	17.7	13.3	16.4	13.6
MSA[1]	7.3	6.8	7.9	11.9	17.8	14.4	18.5	15.5
U.S.	10.3	8.9	8.9	12.3	17.2	12.7	15.1	14.5

Note: (1) Figures cover the Madison, WI Metropolitan Statistical Area
Source: U.S. Census Bureau, 2015-2019 American Community Survey 5-Year Estimates

300 Madison, Wisconsin

Poverty Rate

Area	All Ages	Under 18 Years Old	18 to 64 Years Old	65 Years and Over
City	16.9	11.8	19.9	5.9
MSA[1]	10.3	8.7	11.8	5.6
U.S.	13.4	18.5	12.6	9.3

Note: Figures are percentage of people whose income during the past 12 months was below the poverty level;
(1) Figures cover the Madison, WI Metropolitan Statistical Area
Source: U.S. Census Bureau, 2015-2019 American Community Survey 5-Year Estimates

CITY FINANCES

City Government Finances

Component	2017 ($000)	2017 ($ per capita)
Total Revenues	526,216	2,114
Total Expenditures	508,836	2,044
Debt Outstanding	906,358	3,641
Cash and Securities[1]	895,615	3,598

Note: (1) Cash and security holdings of a government at the close of its fiscal year,
including those of its dependent agencies, utilities, and liquor stores.
Source: U.S. Census Bureau, State & Local Government Finances 2017

City Government Revenue by Source

Source	2017 ($000)	2017 ($ per capita)	2017 (%)
General Revenue			
From Federal Government	27,724	111	5.3
From State Government	70,119	282	13.3
From Local Governments	7,180	29	1.4
Taxes			
Property	223,443	898	42.5
Sales and Gross Receipts	14,556	58	2.8
Personal Income	0	0	0.0
Corporate Income	0	0	0.0
Motor Vehicle License	0	0	0.0
Other Taxes	7,954	32	1.5
Current Charges	101,908	409	19.4
Liquor Store	0	0	0.0
Utility	44,703	180	8.5
Employee Retirement	0	0	0.0

Source: U.S. Census Bureau, State & Local Government Finances 2017

City Government Expenditures by Function

Function	2017 ($000)	2017 ($ per capita)	2017 (%)
General Direct Expenditures			
Air Transportation	0	0	0.0
Corrections	0	0	0.0
Education	0	0	0.0
Employment Security Administration	0	0	0.0
Financial Administration	6,310	25	1.2
Fire Protection	52,238	209	10.3
General Public Buildings	5,162	20	1.0
Governmental Administration, Other	8,266	33	1.6
Health	13,699	55	2.7
Highways	57,332	230	11.3
Hospitals	0	0	0.0
Housing and Community Development	43,131	173	8.5
Interest on General Debt	23,162	93	4.6
Judicial and Legal	2,737	11	0.5
Libraries	16,294	65	3.2
Parking	9,116	36	1.8
Parks and Recreation	41,309	165	8.1
Police Protection	73,348	294	14.4
Public Welfare	0	0	0.0
Sewerage	7,875	31	1.5
Solid Waste Management	15,617	62	3.1
Veterans' Services	0	0	0.0
Liquor Store	0	0	0.0
Utility	85,735	344	16.8
Employee Retirement	0	0	0.0

Source: U.S. Census Bureau, State & Local Government Finances 2017

EMPLOYMENT

Labor Force and Employment

Area	Civilian Labor Force			Workers Employed		
	Dec. 2019	Dec. 2020	% Chg.	Dec. 2019	Dec. 2020	% Chg.
City	157,534	157,457	0.0	154,347	151,326	-2.0
MSA[1]	390,192	389,396	-0.2	381,370	373,552	-2.1
U.S.	164,007,000	160,017,000	-2.4	158,504,000	149,613,000	-5.6

Note: Data is not seasonally adjusted and covers workers 16 years of age and older; (1) Figures cover the Madison, WI Metropolitan Statistical Area
Source: Bureau of Labor Statistics, Local Area Unemployment Statistics

Unemployment Rate

Area	2020											
	Jan.	Feb.	Mar.	Apr.	May	Jun.	Jul.	Aug.	Sep.	Oct.	Nov.	Dec.
City	2.7	2.3	1.9	10.4	9.7	7.8	6.2	5.4	3.9	4.3	3.7	3.9
MSA[1]	3.1	2.8	2.3	11.1	9.7	7.5	6.0	5.1	3.7	4.2	3.7	4.1
U.S.	4.0	3.8	4.5	14.4	13.0	11.2	10.5	8.5	7.7	6.6	6.4	6.5

Note: Data is not seasonally adjusted and covers workers 16 years of age and older; (1) Figures cover the Madison, WI Metropolitan Statistical Area
Source: Bureau of Labor Statistics, Local Area Unemployment Statistics

Average Wages

Occupation	$/Hr.	Occupation	$/Hr.
Accountants and Auditors	35.60	Maintenance and Repair Workers	21.20
Automotive Mechanics	23.90	Marketing Managers	64.30
Bookkeepers	21.40	Network and Computer Systems Admin.	37.60
Carpenters	27.10	Nurses, Licensed Practical	23.30
Cashiers	12.20	Nurses, Registered	39.60
Computer Programmers	52.00	Nursing Assistants	17.70
Computer Systems Analysts	44.20	Office Clerks, General	19.30
Computer User Support Specialists	28.40	Physical Therapists	41.00
Construction Laborers	20.80	Physicians	123.10
Cooks, Restaurant	13.00	Plumbers, Pipefitters and Steamfitters	32.30
Customer Service Representatives	20.70	Police and Sheriff's Patrol Officers	31.60
Dentists	117.90	Postal Service Mail Carriers	24.50
Electricians	28.10	Real Estate Sales Agents	22.40
Engineers, Electrical	46.10	Retail Salespersons	15.00
Fast Food and Counter Workers	11.00	Sales Representatives, Technical/Scientific	38.50
Financial Managers	71.60	Secretaries, Exc. Legal/Medical/Executive	20.00
First-Line Supervisors of Office Workers	31.90	Security Guards	18.10
General and Operations Managers	65.90	Surgeons	n/a
Hairdressers/Cosmetologists	13.90	Teacher Assistants, Exc. Postsecondary*	15.70
Home Health and Personal Care Aides	14.00	Teachers, Secondary School, Exc. Sp. Ed.*	27.80
Janitors and Cleaners	15.40	Telemarketers	12.00
Landscaping/Groundskeeping Workers	17.70	Truck Drivers, Heavy/Tractor-Trailer	25.50
Lawyers	57.70	Truck Drivers, Light/Delivery Services	18.10
Maids and Housekeeping Cleaners	14.10	Waiters and Waitresses	12.00

Note: Wage data covers the Madison, WI Metropolitan Statistical Area; (*) Hourly wages were calculated from annual wage data based on a 40 hour work week; n/a not available.
Source: Bureau of Labor Statistics, Metro Area Occupational Employment & Wage Estimates, May 2020

Employment by Industry

Sector	MSA[1]		U.S.
	Number of Employees	Percent of Total	Percent of Total
Construction, Mining, and Logging	18,100	4.6	5.5
Education and Health Services	49,700	12.7	16.3
Financial Activities	23,400	6.0	6.1
Government	84,300	21.5	15.2
Information	17,700	4.5	1.9
Leisure and Hospitality	25,200	6.4	9.0
Manufacturing	35,800	9.1	8.5
Other Services	20,600	5.3	3.8
Professional and Business Services	53,000	13.5	14.4
Retail Trade	40,500	10.3	10.9
Transportation, Warehousing, and Utilities	9,600	2.4	4.6
Wholesale Trade	14,100	3.6	3.9

Note: Figures are non-farm employment as of December 2020. Figures are not seasonally adjusted and include workers 16 years of age and older; (1) Figures cover the Madison, WI Metropolitan Statistical Area
Source: Bureau of Labor Statistics, Current Employment Statistics, Employment, Hours, and Earnings

Employment by Occupation

Occupation Classification	City (%)	MSA[1] (%)	U.S. (%)
Management, Business, Science, and Arts	54.3	48.5	38.5
Natural Resources, Construction, and Maintenance	3.5	6.5	8.9
Production, Transportation, and Material Moving	7.8	10.4	13.2
Sales and Office	17.5	19.2	21.6
Service	16.9	15.3	17.8

Note: Figures cover employed civilians 16 years of age and older; (1) Figures cover the Madison, WI Metropolitan Statistical Area
Source: U.S. Census Bureau, 2015-2019 American Community Survey 5-Year Estimates

Occupations with Greatest Projected Employment Growth: 2020 – 2022

Occupation[1]	2020 Employment	2022 Projected Employment	Numeric Employment Change	Percent Employment Change
Combined Food Preparation and Serving Workers, Including Fast Food	54,410	72,710	18,300	33.6
Waiters and Waitresses	29,420	41,470	12,050	41.0
Retail Salespersons	64,040	75,960	11,920	18.6
Bartenders	17,450	26,690	9,240	53.0
Cooks, Restaurant	16,530	24,010	7,480	45.3
Personal Care Aides	64,090	70,310	6,220	9.7
Cashiers	58,470	63,910	5,440	9.3
Hairdressers, Hairstylists, and Cosmetologists	9,870	15,130	5,260	53.3
First-Line Supervisors of Food Preparation and Serving Workers	12,710	17,300	4,590	36.1
Laborers and Freight, Stock, and Material Movers, Hand	51,400	55,990	4,590	8.9

Note: Projections cover Wisconsin; (1) Sorted by numeric employment change
Source: www.projectionscentral.com, State Occupational Projections, 2020–2022 Short-Term Projections

Fastest-Growing Occupations: 2020 – 2022

Occupation[1]	2020 Employment	2022 Projected Employment	Numeric Employment Change	Percent Employment Change
Film and Video Editors	70	140	70	100.0
Ushers, Lobby Attendants, and Ticket Takers	1,280	2,490	1,210	94.5
Athletes and Sports Competitors	110	190	80	72.7
Manicurists and Pedicurists	1,470	2,450	980	66.7
Hotel, Motel, and Resort Desk Clerks	2,700	4,430	1,730	64.1
Lodging Managers	250	400	150	60.0
Gaming Cage Workers	100	160	60	60.0
Amusement and Recreation Attendants	2,720	4,340	1,620	59.6
Baggage Porters and Bellhops	110	170	60	54.5
Cooks, Short Order	1,580	2,440	860	54.4

Note: Projections cover Wisconsin; (1) Sorted by percent employment change and excludes occupations with numeric employment change less than 50
Source: www.projectionscentral.com, State Occupational Projections, 2020–2022 Short-Term Projections

TAXES

State Corporate Income Tax Rates

State	Tax Rate (%)	Income Brackets ($)	Num. of Brackets	Financial Institution Tax Rate (%)[a]	Federal Income Tax Ded.
Wisconsin	7.9	Flat rate	1	7.9	No

Note: Tax rates as of January 1, 2021; (a) Rates listed are the corporate income tax rate applied to financial institutions or excise taxes based on income. Some states have other taxes based upon the value of deposits or shares.
Source: Federation of Tax Administrators, State Corporate Income Tax Rates, January 1, 2021

State Individual Income Tax Rates

State	Tax Rate (%)	Income Brackets ($)	Personal Exemptions ($)			Standard Ded. ($)	
			Single	Married	Depend.	Single	Married
Wisconsin (a)	3.54 - 7.65	12,120 - 266,930 (w)	700	1,400	700	11,200	20,730 (y)

Note: Tax rates as of January 1, 2021; Local- and county-level taxes are not included; Federal income tax is not deductible on state income tax returns; (a) 19 states have statutory provision for automatically adjusting to the rate of inflation the dollar values of the income tax brackets, standard deductions, and/or personal exemptions. Michigan indexes the personal exemption only. Oregon does not index the income brackets for $125,000 and over; (w) The Wisconsin income brackets reported are for single individuals. For married taxpayers filing jointly, the same tax rates apply income brackets ranging from $16,160, to $355,910; (y) Alabama standard deduction is phased out for incomes over $23,000. Rhode Island exemptions & standard deductions phased out for incomes over $207,700; Wisconsin standard deduciton phases out for income over $16,149.
Source: Federation of Tax Administrators, State Individual Income Tax Rates, January 1, 2021

Various State Sales and Excise Tax Rates

State	State Sales Tax (%)	Gasoline[1] (¢/gal.)	Cigarette[2] ($/pack)	Spirits[3] ($/gal.)	Wine[4] ($/gal.)	Beer[5] ($/gal.)	Recreational Marijuana (%)
Wisconsin	5	32.9	2.52	3.25	0.25	0.06	Not legal

Note: All tax rates as of January 1, 2021; (1) The American Petroleum Institute has developed a methodology for determining the average tax rate on a gallon of fuel. Rates may include any of the following: excise taxes, environmental fees, storage tank fees, other fees or taxes, general sales tax, and local taxes; (2) The federal excise tax of $1.0066 per pack and local taxes are not included; (3) Rates are those applicable to off-premise sales of 40% alcohol by volume (a.b.v.) distilled spirits in 750ml containers. Local excise taxes are excluded; (4) Rates are those applicable to off-premise sales of 11% a.b.v. non-carbonated wine in 750ml containers; (5) Rates are those applicable to off-premise sales of 4.7% a.b.v. beer in 12 ounce containers.
Source: Tax Foundation, 2021 Facts & Figures: How Does Your State Compare?

State Business Tax Climate Index Rankings

State	Overall Rank	Corporate Tax Rank	Individual Income Tax Rank	Sales Tax Rank	Property Tax Rank	Unemployment Insurance Tax Rank
Wisconsin	25	30	37	7	17	35

Note: The index is a measure of how each state's tax laws affect economic performance. The lower the rank, the more favorable a state's tax system is for business. States without a given tax are given a ranking of 1. The scores/rankings for the District of Columbia do not affect other states. The 2021 index represents the tax climate as of July 1, 2020.
Source: Tax Foundation, State Business Tax Climate Index 2021

TRANSPORTATION

Means of Transportation to Work

Area	Car/Truck/Van		Public Transportation			Bicycle	Walked	Other Means	Worked at Home
	Drove Alone	Car-pooled	Bus	Subway	Railroad				
City	64.3	7.0	9.1	0.0	0.1	4.5	9.1	1.3	4.7
MSA[1]	75.0	7.5	4.2	0.0	0.0	2.2	5.0	0.9	5.1
U.S.	76.3	9.0	2.4	1.9	0.6	0.5	2.7	1.4	5.2

Note: Figures are percentages and cover workers 16 years of age and older; (1) Figures cover the Madison, WI Metropolitan Statistical Area
Source: U.S. Census Bureau, 2015-2019 American Community Survey 5-Year Estimates

Travel Time to Work

Area	Less Than 10 Minutes	10 to 19 Minutes	20 to 29 Minutes	30 to 44 Minutes	45 to 59 Minutes	60 to 89 Minutes	90 Minutes or More
City	14.4	40.7	24.1	15.3	2.9	1.9	0.8
MSA[1]	15.6	32.6	24.3	18.6	5.2	2.5	1.1
U.S.	12.2	28.4	20.8	20.8	8.3	6.4	2.9

Note: Note: Figures are percentages and include workers 16 years old and over; (1) Figures cover the Madison, WI Metropolitan Statistical Area
Source: U.S. Census Bureau, 2015-2019 American Community Survey 5-Year Estimates

Key Congestion Measures

Measure	1982	1992	2002	2012	2017
Annual Hours of Delay, Total (000)	1,612	2,292	4,604	8,400	9,664
Annual Hours of Delay, Per Auto Commuter	15	17	26	34	38
Annual Congestion Cost, Total (million $)	12	24	63	152	179
Annual Congestion Cost, Per Auto Commuter ($)	236	231	362	518	577

Note: Covers the Madison WI urban area
Source: Texas A&M Transportation Institute, 2019 Urban Mobility Report

Freeway Travel Time Index

Measure	1982	1987	1992	1997	2002	2007	2012	2017
Urban Area Index[1]	1.07	1.08	1.08	1.10	1.13	1.15	1.15	1.15
Urban Area Rank[1,2]	35	44	76	80	75	72	71	71

Note: Freeway Travel Time Index—the ratio of travel time in the peak period to the travel time at free-flow conditions. For example, a value of 1.30 indicates a 20-minute free-flow trip takes 26 minutes in the peak (20 minutes x 1.30 = 26 minutes); (1) Covers the Madison WI urban area; (2) Rank is based on 101 larger urban areas (#1 = highest travel time index)
Source: Texas A&M Transportation Institute, 2019 Urban Mobility Report

Public Transportation

Agency Name / Mode of Transportation	Vehicles Operated in Maximum Service[1]	Annual Unlinked Passenger Trips[2] (in thous.)	Annual Passenger Miles[3] (in thous.)
Metro Transit System (Metro)			
Bus (directly operated)	183	12,856.5	50,762.5
Demand Response Taxi (purchased transportation)	51	113.3	660.8

Note: (1) Number of revenue vehicles operated by the given mode and type of service to meet the annual maximum service requirement. This is the revenue vehicle count during the peak season of the year; on the week and day that maximum service is provided. Vehicles operated in maximum service (VOMS) exclude atypical days and one-time special events; (2) Number of passengers who boarded public transportation vehicles. Passengers are counted each time they board a vehicle no matter how many vehicles they use to travel from their origin to their destination. (3) Sum of the distances ridden by all passengers during the entire fiscal year.
Source: Federal Transit Administration, National Transit Database, 2019

Air Transportation

Airport Name and Code / Type of Service	Passenger Airlines[1]	Passenger Enplanements	Freight Carriers[2]	Freight (lbs)
Dane County Regional-Truax Field (MSN)				
Domestic service (U.S. carriers - 2020)	22	413,805	8	23,737,280
International service (U.S. carriers - 2019)	1	14	1	13,306

Note: (1) Includes all U.S.-based major, minor and commuter airlines that carried at least one passenger during the year; (2) Includes all U.S.-based airlines and freight carriers that transported at least one pound of freight during the year.
Source: Bureau of Transportation Statistics, The Intermodal Transportation Database, Air Carriers: T-100 Domestic Market (U.S. Carriers), 2020; Bureau of Transportation Statistics, The Intermodal Transportation Database, Air Carriers: T-100 International Market (U.S. Carriers), 2019

BUSINESSES

Major Business Headquarters

Company Name	Industry	Rankings	
		Fortune[1]	Forbes[2]
American Family Insurance Group	Insurance, Property and Casualty (Stock)	254	-

Note: (1) Companies that produce a 10-K are ranked 1 to 500 based on 2019 revenue; (2) All private companies with at least $2 billion in annual revenue through the end of their most current fiscal year are ranked 1 to 219; companies listed are headquartered in the city; dashes indicate no ranking
Source: Fortune, "Fortune 500," June/July 2020; Forbes, "America's Largest Private Companies," 2020

Fastest-Growing Businesses

According to *Inc.*, Madison is home to three of America's 500 fastest-growing private companies: **Fetch Rewards** (#116); **SwanLeap** (#190); **GrocerKey** (#311). Criteria: must be an independent, privately-held, for-profit, U.S. corporation, proprietorship or partnership as of December 31, 2019; revenues must be at least $100,000 in 2016 and $2 million in 2019; must have four-year operating/sales history. *Inc., "America's 500 Fastest-Growing Private Companies," 2020*

According to Deloitte, Madison is home to three of North America's 500 fastest-growing high-technology companies: **SwanLeap** (#62); **Exact Sciences Corporation** (#151); **EyeKor, Inc.** (#429). Companies are ranked by percentage growth in revenue over a four-year period. Criteria for inclusion: company must be headquartered within North America; must own proprietary intellectual property or technology that is sold to customers in products that contributes to a significant portion of the company's operating revenue; must have been in business for a minumum of four years with 2016 operating revenues of at least $50,000 USD/CD and 2019 operating revenues of at least $5 million USD/CD. *Deloitte, 2020 Technology Fast 500™*

Living Environment

COST OF LIVING

Cost of Living Index

Composite Index	Groceries	Housing	Utilities	Trans-portation	Health Care	Misc. Goods/ Services
107.5	109.3	109.9	99.8	102.9	123.9	105.8

Note: The Cost of Living Index measures regional differences in the cost of consumer goods and services, excluding taxes and non-consumer expenditures, for professional and managerial households in the top income quintile. It is based on more than 50,000 prices covering almost 60 different items for which prices are collected three times a year by chambers of commerce, economic development organizations or university applied economic centers in each participating urban area. The numbers shown should be read as a percentage above or below the national average of 100. For example, a value of 115.4 in the groceries column indicates that grocery prices are 15.4% higher than the national average. Small differences in the index numbers should not be interpreted as significant; Figures cover the Madison WI urban area.
Source: The Council for Community and Economic Research, Cost of Living Index, 2020

Grocery Prices

Area[1]	T-Bone Steak ($/pound)	Frying Chicken ($/pound)	Whole Milk ($/half gal.)	Eggs ($/dozen)	Orange Juice ($/64 oz.)	Coffee ($/11.5 oz.)
City[2]	14.10	1.61	2.26	1.17	3.46	4.65
Avg.	11.78	1.39	2.05	1.47	3.57	4.34
Min.	8.03	0.94	1.03	0.74	2.94	3.02
Max.	15.86	2.65	4.31	3.77	5.44	8.69

Note: (1) Values for the local area are compared with the average, minimum and maximum values for all 284 areas in the Cost of Living Index; (2) Figures cover the Madison WI urban area; T-Bone Steak (price per pound); Frying Chicken (price per pound, whole fryer); Whole Milk (half gallon carton); Eggs (price per dozen, Grade A, large); Orange Juice (64 oz. Tropicana or Florida Natural); Coffee (11.5 oz. can, vacuum-packed, Maxwell House, Hills Bros, or Folgers).
Source: The Council for Community and Economic Research, Cost of Living Index, 2020

Housing and Utility Costs

Area[1]	New Home Price ($)	Apartment Rent ($/month)	All Electric ($/month)	Part Electric ($/month)	Other Energy ($/month)	Telephone ($/month)
City[2]	433,233	1,119	-	103.73	65.58	179.40
Avg.	368,594	1,168	170.86	100.47	65.28	184.30
Min.	190,567	502	91.58	31.42	26.08	169.60
Max.	2,227,806	4,738	470.38	280.31	280.06	206.50

Note: (1) Values for the local area are compared with the average, minimum and maximum values for all 284 areas in the Cost of Living Index; (2) Figures cover the Madison WI urban area; New Home Price (2,400 sf living area, 8,000 sf lot, in urban area with full utilities); Apartment Rent (950 sf 2 bedroom/1.5 or 2 bath, unfurnished, excluding all utilities except water); All Electric (average monthly cost for an all-electric home); Part Electric (average monthly cost for a part-electric home); Other Energy (average monthly cost for natural gas, fuel oil, coal, wood, and any other forms of energy except electricity); Telephone (price includes the base monthly rate plus taxes and fees for three lines of mobile phone service).
Source: The Council for Community and Economic Research, Cost of Living Index, 2020

Health Care, Transportation, and Other Costs

Area[1]	Doctor ($/visit)	Dentist ($/visit)	Optometrist ($/visit)	Gasoline ($/gallon)	Beauty Salon ($/visit)	Men's Shirt ($)
City[2]	201.33	113.22	57.00	2.18	48.44	33.55
Avg.	115.44	99.32	108.10	2.21	39.27	31.37
Min.	36.68	59.00	51.36	1.71	19.00	11.00
Max.	219.00	153.10	250.97	3.46	82.05	58.33

Note: (1) Values for the local area are compared with the average, minimum and maximum values for all 284 areas in the Cost of Living Index; (2) Figures cover the Madison WI urban area; Doctor (general practitioners routine exam of an established patient); Dentist (adult teeth cleaning and periodic oral examination); Optometrist (full vision eye exam for established adult patient); Gasoline (one gallon regular unleaded, national brand, including all taxes, cash price at self-service pump if available); Beauty Salon (woman's shampoo, trim, and blow-dry); Men's Shirt (cotton/polyester dress shirt, pinpoint weave, long sleeves).
Source: The Council for Community and Economic Research, Cost of Living Index, 2020

HOUSING

Homeownership Rate

Area	2012 (%)	2013 (%)	2014 (%)	2015 (%)	2016 (%)	2017 (%)	2018 (%)	2019 (%)	2020 (%)
MSA[1]	n/a	n/a	n/a	n/a	n/a	n/a	n/a	n/a	n/a
U.S.	65.4	65.1	64.5	63.7	63.4	63.9	64.4	64.6	66.6

Note: (1) Figures cover the Madison, WI Metropolitan Statistical Area; n/a not available
Source: U.S. Census Bureau, Housing Vacancies and Homeownership Annual Statistics: 2012-2020

House Price Index (HPI)

Area	National Ranking[2]	Quarterly Change (%)	One-Year Change (%)	Five-Year Change (%)	Since 1991Q1 (%)
MSA[1]	202	1.80	4.96	27.32	218.96
U.S.[3]	–	3.81	10.77	38.99	205.12

Note: The HPI is a weighted repeat sales index. It measures average price changes in repeat sales or refinancings on the same properties. This information is obtained by reviewing repeat mortgage transactions on single-family properties whose mortgages have been purchased or securitized by Fannie Mae or Freddie Mac since January 1975; (1) Figures cover the Madison, WI Metropolitan Statistical Area; (2) Rankings are based on annual percentage change for all metro areas containing at least 15,000 transactions over the last 10 years and ranges from 1 to 253; (3) figures based on a weighted average of Census Division estimates using a seasonally adjusted, purchase-only index; all figures are for the period ending December 31, 2020
Source: Federal Housing Finance Agency, Change in Metropolitan Area House Price Indexes, April 7, 2021

Median Single-Family Home Prices

Area	2018	2019	2020[p]	Percent Change 2019 to 2020
MSA[1]	283.7	299.2	326.4	9.1
U.S. Average	261.6	274.6	299.9	9.2

Note: Figures are median sales prices of existing single-family homes in thousands of dollars; (p) preliminary; (1) Figures cover the Madison, WI Metropolitan Statistical Area
Source: National Association of Realtors, Median Sales Price of Existing Single-Family Homes for Metropolitan Areas, 4th Quarter 2020

Qualifying Income Based on Median Sales Price of Existing Single-Family Homes

Area	With 5% Down ($)	With 10% Down ($)	With 20% Down ($)
MSA[1]	62,682	59,383	52,785
U.S. Average	59,266	56,147	49,908

Note: Figures are preliminary; Qualifying income is based on a mortgage rate of 2.81%. Monthly principal and interest payment is limited to 25% of income; (1) Figures cover the Madison, WI Metropolitan Statistical Area
Source: National Association of Realtors, Qualifying Income Based on Median Sales Price of Existing Single-Family Homes for Metropolitan Areas, 4th Quarter 2020

Home Value Distribution

Area	Under $50,000	$50,000 -$99,999	$100,000 -$149,999	$150,000 -$199,999	$200,000 -$299,999	$300,000 -$499,999	$500,000 -$999,999	$1,000,000 or more
City	1.6	2.6	8.5	18.5	35.6	25.7	6.7	0.8
MSA[1]	2.1	3.9	9.7	16.6	32.4	26.6	7.5	1.2
U.S.	6.9	12.0	13.3	14.0	19.6	19.3	11.4	3.4

Note: Figures are percentages and cover owner-occupied housing units; (1) Figures cover the Madison, WI Metropolitan Statistical Area
Source: U.S. Census Bureau, 2015-2019 American Community Survey 5-Year Estimates

Year Housing Structure Built

Area	2010 or Later	2000 -2009	1990 -1999	1980 -1989	1970 -1979	1960 -1969	1950 -1959	1940 -1949	Before 1940	Median Year
City	7.1	14.4	13.1	10.9	13.9	11.5	10.4	4.8	14.0	1977
MSA[1]	6.5	16.2	15.6	11.1	15.0	9.6	7.8	3.5	14.6	1980
U.S.	5.2	14.0	13.9	13.4	15.2	10.6	10.3	4.9	12.6	1978

Note: Figures are percentages except for Median Year; Note: (1) Figures cover the Madison, WI Metropolitan Statistical Area
Source: U.S. Census Bureau, 2015-2019 American Community Survey 5-Year Estimates

Gross Monthly Rent

Area	Under $500	$500 -$999	$1,000 -$1,499	$1,500 -$1,999	$2,000 -$2,499	$2,500 -$2,999	$3,000 and up	Median ($)
City	3.4	34.3	42.0	13.9	4.1	1.3	1.0	1,118
MSA[1]	5.0	40.5	38.5	11.6	2.9	0.9	0.6	1,046
U.S.	9.4	36.2	30.0	14.0	5.6	2.4	2.4	1,062

Note: Figures are percentages except for Median; Gross rent is the contract rent plus the estimated average monthly cost of utilities (electricity, gas, and water and sewer) and fuels (oil, coal, kerosene, wood, etc.) if these are paid by the renter (or paid for the renter by someone else); (1) Figures cover the Madison, WI Metropolitan Statistical Area
Source: U.S. Census Bureau, 2015-2019 American Community Survey 5-Year Estimates

HEALTH

Health Risk Factors

Category	MSA[1] (%)	U.S. (%)
Adults aged 18–64 who have any kind of health care coverage	n/a	87.3
Adults who reported being in good or better health	n/a	82.4
Adults who have been told they have high blood cholesterol	n/a	33.0
Adults who have been told they have high blood pressure	n/a	32.3
Adults who are current smokers	n/a	17.1
Adults who currently use E-cigarettes	n/a	4.6
Adults who currently use chewing tobacco, snuff, or snus	n/a	4.0
Adults who are heavy drinkers[2]	n/a	6.3
Adults who are binge drinkers[3]	n/a	17.4
Adults who are overweight (BMI 25.0 - 29.9)	n/a	35.3
Adults who are obese (BMI 30.0 - 99.8)	n/a	31.3
Adults who participated in any physical activities in the past month	n/a	74.4
Adults who always or nearly always wears a seat belt	n/a	94.3

Note: n/a not available; (1) Figures cover the Madison, WI Metropolitan Statistical Area; (2) Heavy drinkers are classified as adult men having more than 14 drinks per week and adult women having more than 7 drinks per week; (3) Binge drinkers are classified as males having five or more drinks on one occasion or females having four or more drinks on one occasion
Source: Centers for Disease Control and Prevention, Behaviorial Risk Factor Surveillance System, SMART: Selected Metropolitan Area Risk Trends, 2017

Acute and Chronic Health Conditions

Category	MSA[1] (%)	U.S. (%)
Adults who have ever been told they had a heart attack	n/a	4.2
Adults who have ever been told they have angina or coronary heart disease	n/a	3.9
Adults who have ever been told they had a stroke	n/a	3.0
Adults who have ever been told they have asthma	n/a	14.2
Adults who have ever been told they have arthritis	n/a	24.9
Adults who have ever been told they have diabetes[2]	n/a	10.5
Adults who have ever been told they had skin cancer	n/a	6.2
Adults who have ever been told they had any other types of cancer	n/a	7.1
Adults who have ever been told they have COPD	n/a	6.5
Adults who have ever been told they have kidney disease	n/a	3.0
Adults who have ever been told they have a form of depression	n/a	20.5

Note: n/a not available; (1) Figures cover the Madison, WI Metropolitan Statistical Area; (2) Figures do not include pregnancy-related, borderline, or pre-diabetes
Source: Centers for Disease Control and Prevention, Behaviorial Risk Factor Surveillance System, SMART: Selected Metropolitan Area Risk Trends, 2017

Health Screening and Vaccination Rates

Category	MSA[1] (%)	U.S. (%)
Adults aged 65+ who have had flu shot within the past year	n/a	60.7
Adults aged 65+ who have ever had a pneumonia vaccination	n/a	75.4
Adults who have ever been tested for HIV	n/a	36.1
Adults who have ever had the shingles or zoster vaccine?	n/a	28.9
Adults who have had their blood cholesterol checked within the last five years	n/a	85.9

Note: n/a not available; (1) Figures cover the Madison, WI Metropolitan Statistical Area.
Source: Centers for Disease Control and Prevention, Behaviorial Risk Factor Surveillance System, SMART: Selected Metropolitan Area Risk Trends, 2017

Disability Status

Category	MSA[1] (%)	U.S. (%)
Adults who reported being deaf	n/a	6.7
Are you blind or have serious difficulty seeing, even when wearing glasses?	n/a	4.5
Are you limited in any way in any of your usual activities due of arthritis?	n/a	12.9
Do you have difficulty doing errands alone?	n/a	6.8
Do you have difficulty dressing or bathing?	n/a	3.6
Do you have serious difficulty concentrating/remembering/making decisions?	n/a	10.7
Do you have serious difficulty walking or climbing stairs?	n/a	13.6

Note: n/a not available; (1) Figures cover the Madison, WI Metropolitan Statistical Area.
Source: Centers for Disease Control and Prevention, Behaviorial Risk Factor Surveillance System, SMART: Selected Metropolitan Area Risk Trends, 2017

Mortality Rates for the Top 10 Causes of Death in the U.S.

ICD-10[a] Sub-Chapter	ICD-10[a] Code	Age-Adjusted Mortality Rate[1] per 100,000 population	
		County[2]	U.S.
Malignant neoplasms	C00-C97	132.8	149.2
Ischaemic heart diseases	I20-I25	64.8	90.5
Other forms of heart disease	I30-I51	44.3	52.2
Chronic lower respiratory diseases	J40-J47	22.7	39.6
Other degenerative diseases of the nervous system	G30-G31	39.2	37.6
Cerebrovascular diseases	I60-I69	27.1	37.2
Other external causes of accidental injury	W00-X59	53.9	36.1
Organic, including symptomatic, mental disorders	F01-F09	39.1	29.4
Hypertensive diseases	I10-I15	13.2	24.1
Diabetes mellitus	E10-E14	13.5	21.5

Note: (a) ICD-10 = International Classification of Diseases 10th Revision; (1) Mortality rates are a three-year average covering 2017-2019; (2) Figures cover Dane County.
Source: Centers for Disease Control and Prevention, National Center for Health Statistics. Underlying Cause of Death 1999-2019 on CDC WONDER Online Database

Mortality Rates for Selected Causes of Death

ICD-10[a] Sub-Chapter	ICD-10[a] Code	Age-Adjusted Mortality Rate[1] per 100,000 population	
		County[2]	U.S.
Assault	X85-Y09	1.7	6.0
Diseases of the liver	K70-K76	8.9	14.4
Human immunodeficiency virus (HIV) disease	B20-B24	Suppressed	1.5
Influenza and pneumonia	J09-J18	9.6	13.8
Intentional self-harm	X60-X84	11.5	14.1
Malnutrition	E40-E46	Unreliable	2.3
Obesity and other hyperalimentation	E65-E68	2.0	2.1
Renal failure	N17-N19	7.8	12.6
Transport accidents	V01-V99	6.6	12.3
Viral hepatitis	B15-B19	Suppressed	1.2

Note: (a) ICD-10 = International Classification of Diseases 10th Revision; (1) Mortality rates are a three-year average covering 2017-2019; (2) Figures cover Dane County; Data are suppressed when the data meet the criteria for confidentiality constraints; Mortality rates are flagged as unreliable when the rate would be calculated with a numerator of 20 or less.
Source: Centers for Disease Control and Prevention, National Center for Health Statistics. Underlying Cause of Death 1999-2019 on CDC WONDER Online Database

Health Insurance Coverage

Area	With Health Insurance	With Private Health Insurance	With Public Health Insurance	Without Health Insurance	Population Under Age 19 Without Health Insurance
City	96.0	83.8	22.2	4.0	2.2
MSA[1]	96.1	83.5	24.7	3.9	2.1
U.S.	91.2	67.9	35.1	8.8	5.1

Note: Figures are percentages that cover the civilian noninstitutionalized population; (1) Figures cover the Madison, WI Metropolitan Statistical Area
Source: U.S. Census Bureau, 2015-2019 American Community Survey 5-Year Estimates

Number of Medical Professionals

Area	MDs[3]	DOs[3,4]	Dentists	Podiatrists	Chiropractors	Optometrists
County[1] (number)	3,307	115	404	25	241	122
County[1] (rate[2])	610.2	21.2	73.9	4.6	44.1	22.3
U.S. (rate[2])	282.9	22.7	71.2	6.2	28.1	16.9

55025
Note: Data as of 2019 unless noted; (1) Data covers Dane County; (2) Rate per 100,000 population; (3) Data as of 2018 and includes all active, non-federal physicians; (4) Doctor of Osteopathic Medicine
Source: U.S. Department of Health and Human Services, Health Resources and Services Administration, Bureau of Health Professions, Area Resource File (ARF) 2019-2020

Best Hospitals

According to *U.S. News,* the Madison, WI metro area is home to one of the best hospitals in the U.S.: **University of Wisconsin Hospitals** (6 adult specialties and 2 pediatric specialties). The hospital listed was nationally ranked in at least one of 16 adult or 10 pediatric specialties. Only 134 hospitals nationwide were nationally ranked in one or more adult or pediatric specialty; this number increases to 178 counting specialized centers within hospitals. Twenty hospitals in the U.S. made the Honor Roll. The Best Hospitals Honor Roll takes both the national rankings and the procedure and condition ratings into account. Hospitals received points if they were nationally ranked in one of the 16 adult specialties—the higher they ranked, the more points they got—and how many ratings of "high performing" they earned in the 10 procedures and conditions. *U.S. News Online, "America's Best Hospitals 2020-21"*

According to *U.S. News,* the Madison, WI metro area is home to one of the best children's hospitals in the U.S.: **American Family Children's Hospital** (2 pediatric specialties). The hospital listed was highly ranked in at least one of 10 pediatric specialties. Eighty-eight children's hospitals in the U.S. were nationally ranked in at least one specialty. Hospitals received points for being ranked in a specialty, and the 10 hospitals with the most points across the 10 specialties make up the Honor Roll. *U.S. News Online, "America's Best Children's Hospitals 2020-21"*

EDUCATION

Public School District Statistics

District Name	Schls	Pupils	Pupil/ Teacher Ratio	Minority Pupils[1] (%)	Free Lunch Eligible[2] (%)	IEP[3] (%)
Madison Metropolitan SD	54	26,917	12.0	57.8	44.0	14.6

Note: Table includes school districts with 2,000 or more students; (1) Percentage of students that are not non-Hispanic white; (2) Percentage of students that are eligible for the free lunch program; (3) Percentage of students that have an Individualized Education Program.
Source: U.S. Department of Education, National Center for Education Statistics, Common Core of Data, Local Education Agency (School District) Universe Survey: School Year 2018-2019; U.S. Department of Education, National Center for Education Statistics, Common Core of Data, Public Elementary/Secondary School Universe Survey: School Year 2018-2019

Highest Level of Education

Area	Less than H.S.	H.S. Diploma	Some College, No Deg.	Associate Degree	Bachelor's Degree	Master's Degree	Prof. School Degree	Doctorate Degree
City	4.5	14.2	15.3	8.0	32.1	16.2	4.2	5.3
MSA[1]	4.7	21.0	17.9	10.3	27.7	12.1	3.0	3.2
U.S.	12.0	27.0	20.4	8.5	19.8	8.8	2.1	1.4

Note: Figures cover persons age 25 and over; (1) Figures cover the Madison, WI Metropolitan Statistical Area
Source: U.S. Census Bureau, 2015-2019 American Community Survey 5-Year Estimates

Educational Attainment by Race

Area	High School Graduate or Higher (%)					Bachelor's Degree or Higher (%)				
	Total	White	Black	Asian	Hisp.[2]	Total	White	Black	Asian	Hisp.[2]
City	95.5	96.8	87.6	92.5	77.3	57.9	59.7	22.7	71.7	34.2
MSA[1]	95.3	96.2	88.8	90.9	76.4	46.1	46.2	23.9	68.0	26.7
U.S.	88.0	89.9	86.0	87.1	68.7	32.1	33.5	21.6	54.3	16.4

Note: Figures shown cover persons 25 years old and over; (1) Figures cover the Madison, WI Metropolitan Statistical Area; (2) People of Hispanic origin can be of any race
Source: U.S. Census Bureau, 2015-2019 American Community Survey 5-Year Estimates

School Enrollment by Grade and Control

Area	Preschool (%)		Kindergarten (%)		Grades 1 - 4 (%)		Grades 5 - 8 (%)		Grades 9 - 12 (%)	
	Public	Private	Public	Private	Public	Private	Public	Private	Public	Private
City	53.6	46.4	85.3	14.7	88.4	11.6	87.0	13.0	91.0	9.0
MSA[1]	66.3	33.7	88.6	11.4	90.0	10.0	90.0	10.0	94.2	5.8
U.S.	59.1	40.9	87.6	12.4	89.5	10.5	89.4	10.6	90.1	9.9

Note: Figures shown cover persons 3 years old and over; (1) Figures cover the Madison, WI Metropolitan Statistical Area
Source: U.S. Census Bureau, 2015-2019 American Community Survey 5-Year Estimates

Higher Education

Four-Year Colleges			Two-Year Colleges			Medical Schools[1]	Law Schools[2]	Voc/ Tech[3]
Public	Private Non-profit	Private For-profit	Public	Private Non-profit	Private For-profit			
2	2	0	1	0	1	1	1	4

Note: Figures cover institutions located within the city limits and include main campuses only; (1) includes schools accredited by the Liaison Committee on Medical Education and the American Osteopathic Association's Commission on Osteopathic College Accreditation; (2) includes ABA-accredited schools, schools with provisional ABA accreditation, and state accredited schools; (3) includes all schools with programs that are less than 2 years.
Source: National Center for Education Statistics, Integrated Postsecondary Education System (IPEDS), 2019-20; Wikipedia, List of Medical Schools in the United States, accessed April 2, 2021; Wikipedia, List of Law Schools in the United States, accessed April 2, 2021

According to *U.S. News & World Report,* the Madison, WI metro area is home to one of the top 200 national universities in the U.S.: **University of Wisconsin—Madison** (#42 tie). The indicators used to capture academic quality fall into a number of categories: assessment by administrators at peer institutions; retention of students; faculty resources; student selectivity; financial resources; alumni giving; high school counselor ratings of colleges; and graduation rate. *U.S. News & World Report, "America's Best Colleges 2021"*

According to *U.S. News & World Report,* the Madison, WI metro area is home to one of the top 100 law schools in the U.S.: **University of Wisconsin—Madison** (#29 tie). The rankings are based on a weighted average of 12 measures of quality: peer assessment score; assessment score by lawyers/judges; median LSAT scores; median undergrad GPA; acceptance rate; employment rates for graduates; placement success; bar passage rate; faculty resources; expenditures per student; student/faculty ratio; and library resources. *U.S. News & World Report, "America's Best Graduate Schools, Law, 2022"*

According to *U.S. News & World Report,* the Madison, WI metro area is home to one of the top 75 medical schools for research in the U.S.: **University of Wisconsin—Madison** (#33 tie). The rankings are based on a weighted average of 11 measures of quality: quality assessment; peer assessment score; assessment score by residency directors; research activity; total research activity; average research activity per faculty member; student selectivity; median MCAT total score; median undergraduate GPA; acceptance rate; and faculty resources. *U.S. News & World Report, "America's Best Graduate Schools, Medical, 2022"*

According to *U.S. News & World Report,* the Madison, WI metro area is home to one of the top 75 business schools in the U.S.: **University of Wisconsin—Madison** (#42 tie). The rankings are based on a weighted average of the following nine measures: quality assessment; peer assessment; recruiter assessment; placement success; mean starting salary and bonus; student selectivity; mean GMAT and GRE scores; mean undergraduate GPA; and acceptance rate. *U.S. News & World Report, "America's Best Graduate Schools, Business, 2022"*

EMPLOYERS

Major Employers

Company Name	Industry
American Family Mutual Insurance Co.	Fire, marine, & casualty insurance
Community Living Alliance	Social services for the handicapped
Covence Laboratories	Druggists preparations
CUNA Mutual Insurance Society	Telephone communication, except radio
Kraft Foods Global	Luncheon meat from purchased meat
University of Wisconsin Hospitals	General medical & surgical hospitals
Veterans Health Administration	General medical & surgical hospitals
WI Dept of Workforce Development	Administration of social & manpower programs
Wisconsin Department of Administration	Administration of general economic programs
Wisconsin Department of Health Services	Administration of public health programs
Wisconsin Department of Natural Resources	Land, mineral, & wildlife conservation
Wisconsin Department of Transportation	Regulation, administration of transportation
Wisconsin Dept of Natural Resources	Land, mineral, & wildlife conservation
Wisconsin Physicians Srvc Ins Corp	Hospital & medical services plans

Note: Companies shown are located within the Madison, WI Metropolitan Statistical Area.
Source: Hoovers.com; Wikipedia

PUBLIC SAFETY

Crime Rate

Area	All Crimes	Violent Crimes				Property Crimes		
		Murder	Rape[3]	Robbery	Aggrav. Assault	Burglary	Larceny -Theft	Motor Vehicle Theft
City	2,833.9	1.5	41.0	83.1	234.2	400.4	1,865.1	208.6
Suburbs[1]	1,351.6	1.0	24.7	18.3	82.4	169.4	971.3	84.6
Metro[2]	1,932.4	1.2	31.0	43.6	141.9	259.9	1,321.5	133.2
U.S.	2,489.3	5.0	42.6	81.6	250.2	340.5	1,549.5	219.9

Note: Figures are crimes per 100,000 population; (1) All areas within the metro area that are located outside the city limits; (2) Figures cover the Madison, WI Metropolitan Statistical Area; (3) All figures shown were reported using the revised Uniform Crime Reporting (UCR) definition of rape.
Source: FBI Uniform Crime Reports, 2019

Hate Crimes

Area	Number of Quarters Reported	Number of Incidents per Bias Motivation					
		Race/Ethnicity/ Ancestry	Religion	Sexual Orientation	Disability	Gender	Gender Identity
City	4	3	1	3	0	0	0
U.S.	4	3,963	1,521	1,195	157	69	198

Source: Federal Bureau of Investigation, Hate Crime Statistics 2019

Identity Theft Consumer Reports

Area	Reports	Reports per 100,000 Population	Rank[2]
MSA[1]	1,143	172	255
U.S.	1,387,615	423	-

Note: (1) Figures cover the Madison, WI Metropolitan Statistical Area; (2) Rank ranges from 1 to 391 where 1 indicates greatest number of identity theft reports per 100,000 population
Source: Federal Trade Commission, Consumer Sentinel Network Data Book 2020

Fraud and Other Consumer Reports

Area	Reports	Reports per 100,000 Population	Rank[2]
MSA[1]	4,659	701	186
U.S.	3,385,133	1,031	-

Note: (1) Figures cover the Madison, WI Metropolitan Statistical Area; (2) Rank ranges from 1 to 391 where 1 indicates greatest number of fraud and other consumer reports per 100,000 population
Source: Federal Trade Commission, Consumer Sentinel Network Data Book 2020

POLITICS

2020 Presidential Election Results

Area	Biden	Trump	Jorgensen	Hawkins	Other
Dane County	75.5	22.9	1.1	0.1	0.6
U.S.	51.3	46.8	1.2	0.3	0.5

Note: Results are percentages and may not add to 100% due to rounding
Source: Dave Leip's Atlas of U.S. Presidential Elections

SPORTS

Professional Sports Teams

Team Name	League	Year Established
No teams are located in the metro area		

Source: Wikipedia, Major Professional Sports Teams of the United States and Canada, April 6, 2021

CLIMATE

Average and Extreme Temperatures

Temperature	Jan	Feb	Mar	Apr	May	Jun	Jul	Aug	Sep	Oct	Nov	Dec	Yr.
Extreme High (°F)	56	61	82	94	93	101	104	102	99	90	76	62	104
Average High (°F)	26	30	42	58	70	79	84	81	72	61	44	30	57
Average Temp. (°F)	17	21	32	46	57	67	72	69	61	50	36	23	46
Average Low (°F)	8	12	22	35	45	54	59	57	49	38	27	14	35
Extreme Low (°F)	-37	-28	-29	0	19	31	36	35	25	13	-8	-25	-37

Note: Figures cover the years 1948-1990
Source: National Climatic Data Center, International Station Meteorological Climate Summary, 9/96

Average Precipitation/Snowfall/Humidity

Precip./Humidity	Jan	Feb	Mar	Apr	May	Jun	Jul	Aug	Sep	Oct	Nov	Dec	Yr.
Avg. Precip. (in.)	1.1	1.1	2.1	2.9	3.2	3.8	3.9	3.9	3.0	2.3	2.0	1.7	31.1
Avg. Snowfall (in.)	10	7	9	2	Tr	0	0	0	Tr	Tr	4	11	42
Avg. Rel. Hum. 6am (%)	78	80	81	80	79	81	85	89	90	85	84	82	83
Avg. Rel. Hum. 3pm (%)	66	63	59	50	50	51	53	55	55	54	64	69	57

Note: Figures cover the years 1948-1990; Tr = Trace amounts (<0.05 in. of rain; <0.5 in. of snow)
Source: National Climatic Data Center, International Station Meteorological Climate Summary, 9/96

Weather Conditions

Temperature			Daytime Sky			Precipitation		
5°F & below	32°F & below	90°F & above	Clear	Partly cloudy	Cloudy	0.01 inch or more precip.	0.1 inch or more snow/ice	Thunderstorms
35	161	14	88	119	158	118	38	40

Note: Figures are average number of days per year and cover the years 1948-1990
Source: National Climatic Data Center, International Station Meteorological Climate Summary, 9/96

HAZARDOUS WASTE

Superfund Sites

The Madison, WI metro area is home to five sites on the EPA's Superfund National Priorities List: **City Disposal Corp. Landfill** (final); **Hagen Farm** (final); **Madison Metropolitan Sewerage District Lagoons** (final); **Refuse Hideaway Landfill** (final); **Stoughton City Landfill** (final). There are a total of 1,375 Superfund sites with a status of proposed or final on the list in the U.S. *U.S. Environmental Protection Agency, National Priorities List, April 7, 2021*

AIR QUALITY

Air Quality Trends: Ozone

	1990	1995	2000	2005	2010	2015	2016	2017	2018	2019
MSA[1]	0.077	0.084	0.072	0.079	0.062	0.064	0.068	0.064	0.066	0.059
U.S.	0.088	0.089	0.082	0.080	0.073	0.068	0.069	0.068	0.069	0.065

Note: (1) Data covers the Madison, WI Metropolitan Statistical Area. The values shown are the composite ozone concentration averages among trend sites based on the highest fourth daily maximum 8-hour concentration in parts per million. These trends are based on sites having an adequate record of monitoring data during the trend period. Data from exceptional events are included.
Source: U.S. Environmental Protection Agency, Air Quality Monitoring Information, "Air Quality Trends by City, 1990-2019"

Air Quality Index

Area	Percent of Days when Air Quality was...[2]					AQI Statistics[2]	
	Good	Moderate	Unhealthy for Sensitive Groups	Unhealthy	Very Unhealthy	Maximum	Median
MSA[1]	78.1	21.9	0.0	0.0	0.0	93	39

Note: (1) Data covers the Madison, WI Metropolitan Statistical Area; (2) Based on 365 days with AQI data in 2019. Air Quality Index (AQI) is an index for reporting daily air quality. EPA calculates the AQI for five major air pollutants regulated by the Clean Air Act: ground-level ozone, particle pollution (aka particulate matter), carbon monoxide, sulfur dioxide, and nitrogen dioxide. The AQI runs from 0 to 500. The higher the AQI value, the greater the level of air pollution and the greater the health concern. There are six AQI categories: "Good" AQI is between 0 and 50. Air quality is considered satisfactory; "Moderate" AQI is between 51 and 100. Air quality is acceptable; "Unhealthy for Sensitive Groups" When AQI values are between 101 and 150, members of sensitive groups may experience health effects; "Unhealthy" When AQI values are between 151 and 200 everyone may begin to experience health effects; "Very Unhealthy" AQI values between 201 and 300 trigger a health alert; "Hazardous" AQI values over 300 trigger warnings of emergency conditions (not shown).
Source: U.S. Environmental Protection Agency, Air Quality Index Report, 2019

Air Quality Index Pollutants

Area	Percent of Days when AQI Pollutant was...[2]					
	Carbon Monoxide	Nitrogen Dioxide	Ozone	Sulfur Dioxide	Particulate Matter 2.5	Particulate Matter 10
MSA[1]	0.0	0.0	45.5	0.0	54.5	0.0

Note: (1) Data covers the Madison, WI Metropolitan Statistical Area; (2) Based on 365 days with AQI data in 2019. The Air Quality Index (AQI) is an index for reporting daily air quality. EPA calculates the AQI for five major air pollutants regulated by the Clean Air Act: ground-level ozone, particle pollution (also known as particulate matter), carbon monoxide, sulfur dioxide, and nitrogen dioxide. The AQI runs from 0 to 500. The higher the AQI value, the greater the level of air pollution and the greater the health concern.
Source: U.S. Environmental Protection Agency, Air Quality Index Report, 2019

Maximum Air Pollutant Concentrations: Particulate Matter, Ozone, CO and Lead

	Particulate Matter 10 (ug/m^3)	Particulate Matter 2.5 Wtd AM (ug/m^3)	Particulate Matter 2.5 24-Hr (ug/m^3)	Ozone (ppm)	Carbon Monoxide (ppm)	Lead (ug/m^3)
MSA[1] Level	35	8.0	21	0.059	n/a	n/a
NAAQS[2]	150	15	35	0.075	9	0.15
Met NAAQS[2]	Yes	Yes	Yes	Yes	n/a	n/a

Note: (1) Data covers the Madison, WI Metropolitan Statistical Area; Data from exceptional events are included; (2) National Ambient Air Quality Standards; ppm = parts per million; ug/m^3 = micrograms per cubic meter; n/a not available.
Concentrations: Particulate Matter 10 (coarse particulate)—highest second maximum 24-hour concentration; Particulate Matter 2.5 Wtd AM (fine particulate)—highest weighted annual mean concentration; Particulate Matter 2.5 24-Hour (fine particulate)—highest 98th percentile 24-hour concentration; Ozone—highest fourth daily maximum 8-hour concentration; Carbon Monoxide—highest second maximum non-overlapping 8-hour concentration; Lead—maximum running 3-month average
Source: U.S. Environmental Protection Agency, Air Quality Monitoring Information, "Air Quality Statistics by City, 2019"

Maximum Air Pollutant Concentrations: Nitrogen Dioxide and Sulfur Dioxide

	Nitrogen Dioxide AM (ppb)	Nitrogen Dioxide 1-Hr (ppb)	Sulfur Dioxide AM (ppb)	Sulfur Dioxide 1-Hr (ppb)	Sulfur Dioxide 24-Hr (ppb)
MSA[1] Level	n/a	n/a	n/a	2	n/a
NAAQS[2]	53	100	30	75	140
Met NAAQS[2]	n/a	n/a	n/a	Yes	n/a

Note: (1) Data covers the Madison, WI Metropolitan Statistical Area; Data from exceptional events are included; (2) National Ambient Air Quality Standards; ppm = parts per million; ug/m^3 = micrograms per cubic meter; n/a not available.
Concentrations: Nitrogen Dioxide AM—highest arithmetic mean concentration; Nitrogen Dioxide 1-Hr—highest 98th percentile 1-hour daily maximum concentration; Sulfur Dioxide AM—highest annual mean concentration; Sulfur Dioxide 1-Hr—highest 99th percentile 1-hour daily maximum concentration; Sulfur Dioxide 24-Hr—highest second maximum 24-hour concentration
Source: U.S. Environmental Protection Agency, Air Quality Monitoring Information, "Air Quality Statistics by City, 2019"

Milwaukee, Wisconsin

Background

Many people associate Milwaukee with beer, perhaps due to the 1970s television show *Laverne and Shirley*, where the main characters worked in a brewery, or to the large influx of German immigrants during the 1840s who left an indelible mark upon the city. However, there is a lot more Wisconsin's largest city than these superficial images suggest.

Milwaukee originally began as a trading post for French fur traders. Its favorable location on the western shore of Lake Michigan and at the confluence of the Milwaukee, Menomonee, and Kinnickinnic rivers made the site a natural meeting place. In 1818, Solomon Laurent Juneau, a son-in-law of a French fur trader, became Milwaukee's first founder and permanent white settler.

During the 1840s, Milwaukee saw a wave of German immigrants hit its shores. Many of these exiles were unsuccessful revolutionaries in the overthrow of the German monarchy. Despite their lack of success back home, these immigrants managed to impart considerable influences in the new country, including: political, with three socialist mayors; economical, with Pabst and Schlitz breweries located in Milwaukee; and cultural, with the Goethe House cultural resource center located in the central library of the Milwaukee Public Library system.

Today, Milwaukee is diverse in many ways. The city is home to many nationalities, including people of Irish, Mexican, Serbian, Scandinavian, Polish, Italian, German, and Puerto Rican descent, as well as a large and thriving African American population. And while the brewing industry does remain a major employer in the city that was once the number one producer of beer worldwide, Milwaukee's economy has widely diversified in recent years. Many Fortune 500 companies maintain their headquarters in the city. Among the most prominent industries in Milwaukee today include healthcare, financial services, education, and manufacturing.

Culture and entertainment thrive in Milwaukee. The Milwaukee Public Museum features exhibits devoted to science, technology, and natural history, and includes the first IMAX® theater in Wisconsin. The city is also home to the Florentine Opera Company, the Milwaukee Symphony Orchestra, the Milwaukee Ballet, the Milwaukee Repertory Theater, and the Milwaukee Shakespeare Company. The annual lakefront music festival Summerfest is considered the largest music festival in the world with nearly a million people attending yearly. The Milwaukee Art Museum is known worldwide; its Quadracci Pavilion, designed by Santiago Calatrava, is breathtaking. Discovery World, the city's largest science museum, is known for its high-tech, hands-on exhibits.

> One local barbershop offered its clientele more than just a haircut, when Gee's Clippers became a vaccination site on Saturdays.

Milwaukee is also home to numerous colleges and universities, including Marquette University and the University of Wisconsin-Milwaukee. The city introduced a modern street-car system in 2018, and Bublr Bikes bike-sharing system now offers nearly 100 bike stations.

Milwaukee is home to two professional sports teams, the Brewers of Major League Baseball and the Bucks of the National Basketball Association. Both have fielded highly competitive teams in recent years, each featuring a central, Most Valuable Player award-winning star, Christian Yelich and Giannis Antetokounmpo, respectively. In addition, Milwaukee is considered a home market for the popular football team, the Green Bay Packers, who play a little over an hour away. Among college sports, Marquette University's men's basketball team, the Golden Eagles, is a popular draw, playing in the competitive Big East conference.

In 2018, Fiserv Forum, a multi-purpose arena, opened in the city.

Milwaukee has a continental climate, and its weather is quite changeable. Temperatures vary widely through the year. In winter, arctic air masses from Canada bring frigid winter temperatures, while in summer high temperatures occur with brisk, hot winds from the southwest. Lake Michigan mitigates against these extremes, as do the other Great Lakes to a lesser extent: in late autumn and winter, the coldest air masses from the northwest are often warmed by the lakes before they can reach the city.

Rankings

General Rankings

- As part of its *Next Stop* series, *Insider* listed 10 places in the U.S. that were either a classic vacation destination experiencing a renaissance or a new up-and-coming hot spot. That could mean the exploding food scene, experiencing the great outdoors, where cool people are moving to, or not overrun with tourists, according to the website insider.com Milwaukee is a place to visit in 2020. *Insider, "10 Places in the U.S. You Need to Visit in 2020," December 23, 2019*

- In their seventh annual survey, Livability.com looked at data for more than 1,000 small to mid-sized U.S. cities to determine the rankings for Livability's "Top 100 Best Places to Live" in 2020. Milwaukee ranked #91. Criteria: housing and affordable living; vibrant economy; social and civic engagement; education; demographics; health care options; transportation & infrastructure; and abundant lifestyle amenities. *Livability.com, "Top 100 Best Places to Live 2020" October 2020*

Business/Finance Rankings

- Based on metro area social media reviews, the employment opinion group Glassdoor surveyed 50 of the most populous U.S. metro areas and equally weighed cost of living, hiring opportunity, and job satisfaction to compose a list of "25 Best Cities for Jobs." Median pay and home value, and number of active job openings were also factored in. The Milwaukee metro area was ranked #19 in overall job satisfaction. *www.glassdoor.com, "Best Cities for Jobs," February 25, 2020*

- The Brookings Institution ranked the nation's largest cities based on income inequality. Milwaukee was ranked #46 (#1 = greatest inequality). Criteria: the "95/20 ratio," a figure representing the income at which a household earns more than 95 percent of all other households, divided by the income at which a household earns more than only 20 percent of all other households. *Brookings Institution, "Household Income Inequality, Largest Cities of 97 Large U.S. Metro Areas, 2014-2016," February 5, 2018*

- The Brookings Institution ranked the 100 largest metro areas in the U.S. based on income inequality. Milwaukee was ranked #17 (#1 = greatest inequality). Criteria: the "95/20 ratio," a figure representing the income at which a household earns more than 95 percent of all other households, divided by the income at which a household earns more than only 20 percent of all other households. *Brookings Institution, "Household Income Inequality, 100 Largest U.S. Metro Areas, 2014-2016," February 5, 2018*

- Payscale.com ranked the 32 largest metro areas in terms of wage growth. The Milwaukee metro area ranked #8. Criteria: private-sector and education professional wage growth between the 4th quarter of 2019 and the 4th quarter of 2020. *PayScale, "Wage Trends by Metro Area-4th Quarter," January 11, 2021*

- The Milwaukee metro area appeared on the Milken Institute "2021 Best Performing Cities" list. Rank: #162 out of 200 large metro areas (population over 250,000). Criteria: job growth; wage and salary growth; high-tech output growth; housing affordability; household broadband access. *Milken Institute, "Best-Performing Cities 2021," February 16, 2021*

- *Forbes* ranked the 200 most populous metro areas to determine the nation's "Best Places for Business and Careers." The Milwaukee metro area was ranked #89. Criteria: costs (business and living); job growth (past and projected); income growth; quality of life; educational attainment (college and high school); projected economic growth; cultural and leisure opportunities; workplace tolerance laws; net migration patterns. *Forbes, "The Best Places for Business and Careers 2019: Seattle Still On Top," October 30, 2019*

Culture/Performing Arts Rankings

- Milwaukee was selected as one of the 25 best cities for moviemakers in North America. COVID-19 has spurred a quest for great film cities that offer more creative space, lower costs, and more great outdoors. NYC & LA were intentionally excluded. Criteria: longstanding reputations as film-friendly communities; efforts to deal with pandemic-specific challenges; and establish appropriate COVID-19 guidelines. The city was ranked #24. *MovieMaker Magazine, "Best Places to Live and Work as a Moviemaker, 2021," January 26, 2021*

Education Rankings

- Personal finance website *WalletHub* analyzed the 150 largest U.S. metropolitan statistical areas to determine where the most educated Americans are putting their degrees to work. Criteria: education levels; percentage of workers with degrees; education quality and attainment gap; public school quality rankings; quality and enrollment of each metro area's universities. Milwaukee was ranked #56 (#1 = most educated city). *www.WalletHub.com, "Most and Least Educated Cities in America, " July 20, 2020*

- Milwaukee was selected as one of America's most literate cities. The city ranked #40 out of the 84 largest U.S. cities. Criteria: number of booksellers; library resources; Internet resources; educational attainment; periodical publishing resources; newspaper circulation. *Central Connecticut State University, "America's Most Literate Cities, 2018," February 2019*

Environmental Rankings

- Milwaukee was highlighted as one of the 25 most ozone-polluted metro areas in the U.S. during 2016 through 2018. The area ranked #24. *American Lung Association, "State of the Air 2020," April 21, 2020*

Health/Fitness Rankings

- For each of the 100 largest cities in the United States, the American Fitness Index®, published by the American College of Sports Medicine and the Anthem Foundation, evaluated community infrastructure and 33 health behaviors including preventive health, levels of chronic disease conditions, pedestrian safety, air quality, and community resources that support physical activity. Milwaukee ranked #23 for "community fitness." *americanfitnessindex.org, "2020 ACSM American Fitness Index Summary Report," July 14, 2020*

- The Milwaukee metro area was identified as one of the worst cities for bed bugs in America by pest control company Orkin. The area ranked #32 out of 50 based on the number of bed bug treatments Orkin performed from December 2019 to November 2020. *Orkin, "New Year, New Top City on Orkin's 2021 Bed Bug Cities List: Chicago," February 1, 2021*

- Milwaukee was identified as a "2021 Spring Allergy Capital." The area ranked #97 out of 100. Three groups of factors were used to identify the most challenging cities for people with allergies during the spring season: annual spring pollen levels; over the counter medicine use; number of board-certified allergy specialists. *Asthma and Allergy Foundation of America, "Spring Allergy Capitals 2021," February 23, 2021*

- Milwaukee was identified as a "2021 Fall Allergy Capital." The area ranked #89 out of 100. Three groups of factors were used to identify the most challenging cities for people with allergies during the fall season: annual fall pollen levels; over the counter medicine use; number of board-certified allergy specialists. *Asthma and Allergy Foundation of America, "Fall Allergy Capitals 2021," February 23, 2021*

- Milwaukee was identified as a "2019 Asthma Capital." The area ranked #10 out of the nation's 100 largest metropolitan areas. Criteria: estimated asthma prevalence; crude death rate from asthma; and ER visits due to asthma. Risk factors analyzed but not factored in the rankings: annual pollen score; annual air quality; public smoking laws; number of board-certified asthma specialists; rescue medication use; controller medication use; uninsured rate; poverty rate. *Asthma and Allergy Foundation of America, "Asthma Capitals 2019: The Most Challenging Places to Live With Asthma," May 7, 2019*

Real Estate Rankings

- FitSmallBusiness looked at 50 of the largest metropolitan areas in the U.S. to determine which metro was the best to start a real estate business. Data was compiled from such sources as: Zillow, Trulia, U.S. Census Bureau, and the Bureau of Labor Statistics. Criteria: location; inventory; annual wages; median sales price of homes; days on the market; median price cut percentage; and other factors that would influence real estate professional growth. The Milwaukee metro area ranked #43. *fitsmallbusiness.com, "The Best Cities to Become a Real Estate Agent in 2018," January 30, 2018*

- *WalletHub* compared the most populated U.S. cities to determine which had the best markets for real estate agents. Milwaukee ranked #96 where demand was high and pay was the best. Criteria: sales per agent; annual median wage for real-estate agents; monthly average starting salary for real estate agents; real estate job density and competition; unemployment rate; home turnover rate; housing-market health index; and other relevant metrics. *www.WalletHub.com, "2019's Best Places to Be a Real Estate Agent," April 24, 2019*

- The Milwaukee metro area was identified as one of the 20 worst housing markets in the U.S. in 2020. The area ranked #161 out of 180 markets. Criteria: year-over-year change of median sales price of existing single-family homes between the 4th quarter of 2019 and the 4th quarter of 2020. *National Association of Realtors®, Median Sales Price of Existing Single-Family Homes for Metropolitan Areas, 4th Quarter 2020*

- The Milwaukee metro area was identified as one of the 10 worst condo markets in the U.S. in 2020. The area ranked #62 out of 63 markets. Criteria: year-over-year change of median sales price of existing apartment condo-coop homes between the 4th quarter of 2019 and the 4th quarter of 2020. *National Association of Realtors®, Median Sales Price of Existing Apartment Condo-Coops Homes for Metropolitan Areas, 4th Quarter 2020*

- Milwaukee was ranked #136 out of 268 metro areas in terms of housing affordability in 2020 by the National Association of Home Builders (#1 = most affordable). Criteria: the share of homes sold in that area affordable to a family earning the local median income, based on standard mortgage underwriting criteria. *National Association of Home Builders®, NAHB-Wells Fargo Housing Opportunity Index, 4th Quarter 2020*

Safety Rankings

- To identify the most dangerous cities in America, 24/7 Wall Street focused on violent crime categories—murder, non-negligent manslaughter, rape, robbery, and aggravated assault—and property crime as reported in the FBI's 2019 annual Uniform Crime Report. Criteria also included median income from American Community Survey and unemployment figures from Bureau of Labor Statistics. For cities with populations over 100,000, Milwaukee was ranked #11. *247wallst.com, "America's 50 Most Dangerous Cities" November 16, 2020*

- Allstate ranked the 200 largest cities in America in terms of driver safety. Milwaukee ranked #61. Criteria: internal property damage claims over a two-year period from January 2016 to December 2017. The report helps increase the importance of safety and awareness behind the wheel. *Allstate, "Allstate America's Best Drivers Report, 2019" June 24, 2019*

- Milwaukee was identified as one of the most dangerous cities in America by NeighborhoodScout. The city ranked #23 out of 100 (#1 = most dangerous). Criteria: number of violent crimes per 1,000 residents. The editors evaluated cities with 25,000 or more residents. *NeighborhoodScout.com, "2021 Top 100 Most Dangerous Cities in the U.S.," January 2, 2021*

- The National Insurance Crime Bureau ranked 384 metro areas in the U.S. in terms of per capita rates of vehicle theft. The Milwaukee metro area ranked #95 (#1 = highest rate). Criteria: number of vehicle theft offenses per 100,000 inhabitants in 2019. *National Insurance Crime Bureau, "Hot Spots 2019," July 21, 2020*

Seniors/Retirement Rankings

- From its Best Cities for Successful Aging indexes, the Milken Institute generated rankings for metropolitan areas, weighing data in nine categories—health care, wellness, living arrangements, transportation and convenience, financial characteristics, education, employment, community engagement, and overall livability. The Milwaukee metro area was ranked #33 overall in the large metro area category. *Milken Institute, "Best Cities for Successful Aging, 2017" March 14, 2017*

Sports/Recreation Rankings

- Milwaukee was chosen as one of America's best cities for bicycling. The city ranked #36 out of 50. Criteria: cycling infrastructure that is safe and friendly for all ages; energy and bike culture. The editors evaluated cities with populations of 100,000 or more. *Bicycling, "The 50 Best Bike Cities in America," October 10, 2018*

Women/Minorities Rankings

- *Women's Health*, together with the site Yelp, identified the 15 "Wellthiest" spots in the U.S. Milwaukee appeared among the top for happiest, healthiest, outdoorsiest and Zen-iest. *Women's Health, "The 15 Wellthiest Cities in the U.S." July 5, 2017*

- Personal finance website *WalletHub* compared more than 180 U.S. cities across two key dimensions, "Hispanic Business-Friendliness" and "Hispanic Purchasing Power," to arrive at the most favorable conditions for Hispanic entrepreneurs. Milwaukee was ranked #165 out of 182. Criteria includes: share of Hispanic-Owned Businesses; Hispanic entrepreneurship rate to median annual income of Hispanics; Small Business-Friendliness score; cost of living; and number of Hispanics with at least a bachelor's degree. *WalletHub.com, "2019's Best Cities for Hispanic Entrepreneurs," May 1, 2019*

Miscellaneous Rankings

- The watchdog site, Charity Navigator, conducted a study of charities in major markets both to analyze statistical differences in their financial, accountability, and transparency practices and to track year-to-year variations in individual philanthropic communities. The Milwaukee metro area was ranked #12 among the 30 metro markets in the rating category of Overall Score. *www.charitynavigator.org, "2017 Metro Market Study," May 1, 2017*

- *WalletHub* compared the 150 most populated U.S. cities to determine their operating efficiency. A "Quality of City Services" score was constructed for each city and then divided by the total budget per capita to reveal which were managed the best. Milwaukee ranked #111. Criteria: financial stability; economy; education; safety; health; infrastructure and pollution. *www.WalletHub.com, "2020's Best- & Worst-Run Cities in America," June 29, 2020*

- Milwaukee was selected as one of "America's Friendliest Cities." The city ranked #10 in the "Friendliest" category. Respondents to an online survey were asked to rate 38 top urban destinations in the United States as to general friendliness, as well as manners, politeness and warm disposition. *Travel + Leisure, "America's Friendliest Cities," October 20, 2017*

320   Milwaukee, Wisconsin

Business Environment

DEMOGRAPHICS

Population Growth

Area	1990 Census	2000 Census	2010 Census	2019* Estimate	Population Growth (%)	
					1990-2019	2010-2019
City	628,095	596,974	594,833	594,548	-5.3	0.0
MSA[1]	1,432,149	1,500,741	1,555,908	1,575,223	10.0	1.2
U.S.	248,709,873	281,421,906	308,745,538	324,697,795	30.6	5.2

Note: (1) Figures cover the Milwaukee-Waukesha-West Allis, WI Metropolitan Statistical Area; (*) 2015-2019 5-year estimated population
Source: U.S. Census Bureau, 1990 Census, Census 2000, Census 2010, 2015-2019 American Community Survey 5-Year Estimates

Household Size

Area	Persons in Household (%)							Average Household Size
	One	Two	Three	Four	Five	Six	Seven or More	
City	36.3	29.4	14.0	10.5	5.7	2.5	1.7	2.50
MSA[1]	31.5	34.4	14.0	12.0	5.3	1.9	1.0	2.50
U.S.	27.9	33.9	15.6	12.9	6.0	2.3	1.4	2.60

Note: (1) Figures cover the Milwaukee-Waukesha-West Allis, WI Metropolitan Statistical Area
Source: U.S. Census Bureau, 2015-2019 American Community Survey 5-Year Estimates

Race

Area	White Alone[2] (%)	Black Alone[2] (%)	Asian Alone[2] (%)	AIAN[3] Alone[2] (%)	NHOPI[4] Alone[2] (%)	Other Race Alone[2] (%)	Two or More Races (%)
City	44.4	38.7	4.3	0.6	0.0	8.0	4.0
MSA[1]	72.5	16.5	3.7	0.4	0.0	3.8	2.9
U.S.	72.5	12.7	5.5	0.8	0.2	4.9	3.3

Note: (1) Figures cover the Milwaukee-Waukesha-West Allis, WI Metropolitan Statistical Area; (2) Alone is defined as not being in combination with one or more other races; (3) American Indian and Alaska Native; (4) Native Hawaiian and Other Pacific Islander
Source: U.S. Census Bureau, 2015-2019 American Community Survey 5-Year Estimates

Hispanic or Latino Origin

Area	Total (%)	Mexican (%)	Puerto Rican (%)	Cuban (%)	Other (%)
City	19.0	13.4	4.4	0.2	1.1
MSA[1]	10.7	7.4	2.3	0.1	0.9
U.S.	18.0	11.2	1.7	0.7	4.3

Note: Persons of Hispanic or Latino origin can be of any race; (1) Figures cover the Milwaukee-Waukesha-West Allis, WI Metropolitan Statistical Area
Source: U.S. Census Bureau, 2015-2019 American Community Survey 5-Year Estimates

Ancestry

Area	German	Irish	English	American	Italian	Polish	French[2]	Scottish	Dutch
City	16.3	5.6	2.1	1.2	2.7	6.6	1.3	0.5	0.7
MSA[1]	33.0	9.8	4.3	2.0	4.3	10.8	2.5	0.9	1.3
U.S.	13.3	9.7	7.2	6.2	5.1	2.8	2.3	1.7	1.2

Note: Figures are the percentage of the total population reporting a particular ancestry. The nine most commonly reported ancestries in the U.S. are shown. Figures include multiple ancestries (e.g. if a person reported being Irish and Italian, they were included in both columns); (1) Figures cover the Milwaukee-Waukesha-West Allis, WI Metropolitan Statistical Area; (2) Excludes Basque
Source: U.S. Census Bureau, 2015-2019 American Community Survey 5-Year Estimates

Foreign-born Population

Area	Percent of Population Born in								
	Any Foreign Country	Asia	Mexico	Europe	Caribbean	Central America[2]	South America	Africa	Canada
City	10.0	2.9	4.8	0.8	0.4	0.2	0.2	0.7	0.1
MSA[1]	7.4	2.8	2.3	1.3	0.2	0.2	0.2	0.4	0.1
U.S.	13.6	4.2	3.5	1.5	1.3	1.1	1.0	0.7	0.2

Note: (1) Figures cover the Milwaukee-Waukesha-West Allis, WI Metropolitan Statistical Area; (2) Excludes Mexico.
Source: U.S. Census Bureau, 2015-2019 American Community Survey 5-Year Estimates

Marital Status

Area	Never Married	Now Married[2]	Separated	Widowed	Divorced
City	53.3	30.0	1.9	4.6	10.2
MSA[1]	37.0	46.4	1.1	5.5	10.1
U.S.	33.4	48.1	1.9	5.8	10.9

Note: Figures are percentages and cover the population 15 years of age and older; (1) Figures cover the Milwaukee-Waukesha-West Allis, WI Metropolitan Statistical Area; (2) Excludes separated
Source: U.S. Census Bureau, 2015-2019 American Community Survey 5-Year Estimates

Disability by Age

Area	All Ages	Under 18 Years Old	18 to 64 Years Old	65 Years and Over
City	13.0	5.7	11.8	38.8
MSA[1]	11.4	4.2	9.1	31.6
U.S.	12.6	4.2	10.3	34.5

Note: Figures show percent of the civilian noninstitutionalized population that reported having a disability. Disability status is determined from six types of difficulty: vision, hearing, cognitive, ambulatory, self-care, and independent living. For children under 5 years old, hearing and vision difficulty are used to determine disability status. For children between the ages of 5 and 14, disability status is determined from hearing, vision, cognitive, ambulatory, and self-care difficulties. For people aged 15 years and older, they are considered to have a disability if they have difficulty with any one of the six difficulty types; Note: (1) Figures cover the Milwaukee-Waukesha-West Allis, WI Metropolitan Statistical Area
Source: U.S. Census Bureau, 2015-2019 American Community Survey 5-Year Estimates

Age

Area	Percent of Population									Median Age
	Under Age 5	Age 5–19	Age 20–34	Age 35–44	Age 45–54	Age 55–64	Age 65–74	Age 75–84	Age 85+	
City	7.4	21.9	25.6	12.6	11.2	10.7	6.3	2.8	1.4	31.5
MSA[1]	6.2	19.6	20.4	12.5	12.8	13.3	8.7	4.3	2.2	37.8
U.S.	6.1	19.1	20.7	12.6	13.0	12.9	9.1	4.6	1.9	38.1

Note: (1) Figures cover the Milwaukee-Waukesha-West Allis, WI Metropolitan Statistical Area
Source: U.S. Census Bureau, 2015-2019 American Community Survey 5-Year Estimates

Gender

Area	Males	Females	Males per 100 Females
City	286,081	308,467	92.7
MSA[1]	767,950	807,273	95.1
U.S.	159,886,919	164,810,876	97.0

Note: (1) Figures cover the Milwaukee-Waukesha-West Allis, WI Metropolitan Statistical Area
Source: U.S. Census Bureau, 2015-2019 American Community Survey 5-Year Estimates

Religious Groups by Family

Area	Catholic	Baptist	Non-Den.	Methodist[2]	Lutheran	LDS[3]	Pentecostal	Presbyterian[4]	Muslim[5]	Judaism
MSA[1]	24.6	3.1	3.9	1.6	10.8	0.4	2.0	1.6	0.6	0.6
U.S.	19.1	9.3	4.0	4.0	2.3	2.0	1.9	1.6	0.8	0.7

Note: Figures are the number of adherents as a percentage of the total population; (1) Figures cover the Milwaukee-Waukesha-West Allis, WI Metropolitan Statistical Area; (2) Methodist/Pietist; (3) Latter Day Saints; (4) Reformed; (5) Figures are estimates
Source: Association of Statisticians of American Religious Bodies, 2010 U.S. Religion Census: Religious Congregations & Membership Study

Religious Groups by Tradition

Area	Catholic	Evangelical Protestant	Mainline Protestant	Other Tradition	Black Protestant	Orthodox
MSA[1]	24.6	14.6	7.2	2.3	2.5	0.6
U.S.	19.1	16.2	7.3	4.3	1.6	0.3

Note: Figures are the number of adherents as a percentage of the total population; (1) Figures cover the Milwaukee-Waukesha-West Allis, WI Metropolitan Statistical Area
Source: Association of Statisticians of American Religious Bodies, 2010 U.S. Religion Census: Religious Congregations & Membership Study

ECONOMY

Gross Metropolitan Product

Area	2017	2018	2019	2020	Rank[2]
MSA[1]	104.6	109.2	112.8	116.2	37

Note: Figures are in billions of dollars; (1) Figures cover the Milwaukee-Waukesha-West Allis, WI Metropolitan Statistical Area; (2) Rank is based on 2018 data and ranges from 1 to 381
Source: U.S. Conference of Mayors, U.S. Metro Economies: GMP & Employment 2018-2020, September 2019

Economic Growth

Area	2015-17 (%)	2018 (%)	2019 (%)	2020 (%)	Rank[2]
MSA[1]	0.9	2.1	1.5	0.9	243
U.S.	1.9	2.9	2.3	2.1	—

Note: Figures are real gross metropolitan product (GMP) growth rates and represent average annual percent change; (1) Figures cover the Milwaukee-Waukesha-West Allis, WI Metropolitan Statistical Area; (2) Rank is based on 2017 2-year average annual percent change and ranges from 1 to 381
Source: U.S. Conference of Mayors, U.S. Metro Economies: GMP & Employment 2018-2020, September 2019

Metropolitan Area Exports

Area	2014	2015	2016	2017	2018	2019	Rank[2]
MSA[1]	8,696.0	7,953.6	7,256.2	7,279.1	7,337.6	6,896.3	49

Note: Figures are in millions of dollars; (1) Figures cover the Milwaukee-Waukesha-West Allis, WI Metropolitan Statistical Area; (2) Rank is based on 2019 data and ranges from 1 to 386
Source: U.S. Department of Commerce, International Trade Administration, Office of Trade and Economic Analysis, Industry and Analysis, Exports by Metropolitan Area, data extracted March 24, 2021

Building Permits

Area	Single-Family			Multi-Family			Total		
	2018	2019	Pct. Chg.	2018	2019	Pct. Chg.	2018	2019	Pct. Chg.
City	39	15	-61.5	717	178	-75.2	756	193	-74.5
MSA[1]	1,712	1,494	-12.7	2,057	925	-55.0	3,769	2,419	-35.8
U.S.	855,300	862,100	0.7	473,500	523,900	10.6	1,328,800	1,386,000	4.3

Note: (1) Figures cover the Milwaukee-Waukesha-West Allis, WI Metropolitan Statistical Area; Figures represent new, privately-owned housing units authorized (unadjusted data); All permit data are based on estimates with imputation
Source: U.S. Census Bureau, Manufacturing, Mining, and Construction Statistics, Building Permits, 2018, 2019

Bankruptcy Filings

Area	Business Filings			Nonbusiness Filings		
	2019	2020	% Chg.	2019	2020	% Chg.
Milwaukee County	43	48	11.6	6,315	4,019	-36.4
U.S.	22,780	21,655	-4.9	752,160	522,808	-30.5

Note: Business filings include Chapter 7, Chapter 9, Chapter 11, Chapter 12, Chapter 13, Chapter 15, and Section 304; Nonbusiness filings include Chapter 7, Chapter 11, and Chapter 13
Source: Administrative Office of the U.S. Courts, Business and Nonbusiness Bankruptcy, County Cases Commenced by Chapter of the Bankruptcy Code, During the 12-Month Period Ending December 31, 2019 and Business and Nonbusiness Bankruptcy, County Cases Commenced by Chapter of the Bankruptcy Code, During the 12-Month Period Ending December 31, 2020

Housing Vacancy Rates

Area	Gross Vacancy Rate[2] (%)			Year-Round Vacancy Rate[3] (%)			Rental Vacancy Rate[4] (%)			Homeowner Vacancy Rate[5] (%)		
	2018	2019	2020	2018	2019	2020	2018	2019	2020	2018	2019	2020
MSA[1]	8.1	8.0	6.6	7.8	7.8	6.3	5.9	6.6	4.6	1.4	0.6	0.6
U.S.	12.3	12.0	10.6	9.7	9.5	8.2	6.9	6.7	6.3	1.5	1.4	1.0

Note: (1) Figures cover the Milwaukee-Waukesha-West Allis, WI Metropolitan Statistical Area; (2) The percentage of the total housing inventory that is vacant; (3) The percentage of the housing inventory (excluding seasonal units) that is year-round vacant; (4) The percentage of rental inventory that is vacant for rent; (5) The percentage of homeowner inventory that is vacant for sale
Source: U.S. Census Bureau, Housing Vacancies and Homeownership Annual Statistics: 2018, 2019, 2020

INCOME

Income

Area	Per Capita ($)	Median Household ($)	Average Household ($)
City	23,462	41,838	57,332
MSA[1]	35,491	62,389	86,290
U.S.	34,103	62,843	88,607

Note: (1) Figures cover the Milwaukee-Waukesha-West Allis, WI Metropolitan Statistical Area
Source: U.S. Census Bureau, 2015-2019 American Community Survey 5-Year Estimates

Household Income Distribution

Area	Percent of Households Earning							
	Under $15,000	$15,000 -$24,999	$25,000 -$34,999	$35,000 -$49,999	$50,000 -$74,999	$75,000 -$99,999	$100,000 -$149,999	$150,000 and up
City	17.8	13.1	11.7	15.1	17.2	10.6	9.6	4.8
MSA[1]	10.4	9.1	8.7	12.7	17.1	12.9	15.8	13.2
U.S.	10.3	8.9	8.9	12.3	17.2	12.7	15.1	14.5

Note: (1) Figures cover the Milwaukee-Waukesha-West Allis, WI Metropolitan Statistical Area
Source: U.S. Census Bureau, 2015-2019 American Community Survey 5-Year Estimates

Poverty Rate

Area	All Ages	Under 18 Years Old	18 to 64 Years Old	65 Years and Over
City	25.4	36.7	22.7	13.6
MSA[1]	13.3	19.3	12.3	8.4
U.S.	13.4	18.5	12.6	9.3

Note: Figures are percentage of people whose income during the past 12 months was below the poverty level;
(1) Figures cover the Milwaukee-Waukesha-West Allis, WI Metropolitan Statistical Area
Source: U.S. Census Bureau, 2015-2019 American Community Survey 5-Year Estimates

CITY FINANCES

City Government Finances

Component	2017 ($000)	2017 ($ per capita)
Total Revenues	1,554,524	2,590
Total Expenditures	1,541,532	2,569
Debt Outstanding	1,506,976	2,511
Cash and Securities[1]	5,325,249	8,873

Note: (1) Cash and security holdings of a government at the close of its fiscal year,
including those of its dependent agencies, utilities, and liquor stores.
Source: U.S. Census Bureau, State & Local Government Finances 2017

City Government Revenue by Source

Source	2017 ($000)	2017 ($ per capita)	2017 (%)
General Revenue			
From Federal Government	44,384	74	2.9
From State Government	288,396	481	18.6
From Local Governments	45,531	76	2.9
Taxes			
Property	269,486	449	17.3
Sales and Gross Receipts	0	0	0.0
Personal Income	0	0	0.0
Corporate Income	0	0	0.0
Motor Vehicle License	0	0	0.0
Other Taxes	16,767	28	1.1
Current Charges	233,499	389	15.0
Liquor Store	0	0	0.0
Utility	80,043	133	5.1
Employee Retirement	533,972	890	34.3

Source: U.S. Census Bureau, State & Local Government Finances 2017

City Government Expenditures by Function

Function	2017 ($000)	2017 ($ per capita)	2017 (%)
General Direct Expenditures			
Air Transportation	0	0	0.0
Corrections	6,332	10	0.4
Education	0	0	0.0
Employment Security Administration	0	0	0.0
Financial Administration	18,302	30	1.2
Fire Protection	110,894	184	7.2
General Public Buildings	36,832	61	2.4
Governmental Administration, Other	120,316	200	7.8
Health	22,926	38	1.5
Highways	152,415	254	9.9
Hospitals	0	0	0.0
Housing and Community Development	32,553	54	2.1
Interest on General Debt	48,554	80	3.1
Judicial and Legal	20,129	33	1.3
Libraries	27,976	46	1.8
Parking	24,506	40	1.6
Parks and Recreation	3,852	6	0.2
Police Protection	315,980	526	20.5
Public Welfare	0	0	0.0
Sewerage	53,002	88	3.4
Solid Waste Management	36,713	61	2.4
Veterans' Services	0	0	0.0
Liquor Store	0	0	0.0
Utility	73,447	122	4.8
Employee Retirement	351,338	585	22.8

Source: U.S. Census Bureau, State & Local Government Finances 2017

324   Milwaukee, Wisconsin

EMPLOYMENT

Labor Force and Employment

Area	Civilian Labor Force			Workers Employed		
	Dec. 2019	Dec. 2020	% Chg.	Dec. 2019	Dec. 2020	% Chg.
City	271,222	276,192	1.8	260,380	253,283	-2.7
MSA[1]	811,069	812,442	0.2	785,335	763,907	-2.7
U.S.	164,007,000	160,017,000	-2.4	158,504,000	149,613,000	-5.6

Note: Data is not seasonally adjusted and covers workers 16 years of age and older; (1) Figures cover the Milwaukee-Waukesha-West Allis, WI Metropolitan Statistical Area
Source: Bureau of Labor Statistics, Local Area Unemployment Statistics

Unemployment Rate

Area	2020											
	Jan.	Feb.	Mar.	Apr.	May	Jun.	Jul.	Aug.	Sep.	Oct.	Nov.	Dec.
City	4.9	4.7	4.1	15.8	15.7	13.1	11.4	10.1	8.2	9.2	7.9	8.3
MSA[1]	4.0	3.8	3.2	13.6	12.9	10.2	8.6	7.5	5.9	6.6	5.7	6.0
U.S.	4.0	3.8	4.5	14.4	13.0	11.2	10.5	8.5	7.7	6.6	6.4	6.5

Note: Data is not seasonally adjusted and covers workers 16 years of age and older; (1) Figures cover the Milwaukee-Waukesha-West Allis, WI Metropolitan Statistical Area
Source: Bureau of Labor Statistics, Local Area Unemployment Statistics

Average Wages

Occupation	$/Hr.	Occupation	$/Hr.
Accountants and Auditors	37.00	Maintenance and Repair Workers	22.40
Automotive Mechanics	21.70	Marketing Managers	65.20
Bookkeepers	21.40	Network and Computer Systems Admin.	36.70
Carpenters	27.70	Nurses, Licensed Practical	25.10
Cashiers	11.60	Nurses, Registered	36.90
Computer Programmers	40.30	Nursing Assistants	15.70
Computer Systems Analysts	40.50	Office Clerks, General	18.80
Computer User Support Specialists	25.90	Physical Therapists	43.10
Construction Laborers	23.30	Physicians	118.40
Cooks, Restaurant	13.10	Plumbers, Pipefitters and Steamfitters	34.10
Customer Service Representatives	20.20	Police and Sheriff's Patrol Officers	36.10
Dentists	98.30	Postal Service Mail Carriers	25.50
Electricians	34.00	Real Estate Sales Agents	24.20
Engineers, Electrical	44.40	Retail Salespersons	15.10
Fast Food and Counter Workers	10.60	Sales Representatives, Technical/Scientific	42.80
Financial Managers	72.20	Secretaries, Exc. Legal/Medical/Executive	19.70
First-Line Supervisors of Office Workers	32.60	Security Guards	15.30
General and Operations Managers	73.80	Surgeons	n/a
Hairdressers/Cosmetologists	15.70	Teacher Assistants, Exc. Postsecondary*	16.20
Home Health and Personal Care Aides	12.20	Teachers, Secondary School, Exc. Sp. Ed.*	29.90
Janitors and Cleaners	14.60	Telemarketers	16.00
Landscaping/Groundskeeping Workers	17.20	Truck Drivers, Heavy/Tractor-Trailer	25.00
Lawyers	67.20	Truck Drivers, Light/Delivery Services	17.40
Maids and Housekeeping Cleaners	13.10	Waiters and Waitresses	11.30

Note: Wage data covers the Milwaukee-Waukesha-West Allis, WI Metropolitan Statistical Area; (*) Hourly wages were calculated from annual wage data based on a 40 hour work week; n/a not available.
Source: Bureau of Labor Statistics, Metro Area Occupational Employment & Wage Estimates, May 2020

Employment by Industry

Sector	MSA[1]		U.S.
	Number of Employees	Percent of Total	Percent of Total
Construction	29,300	3.6	5.1
Education and Health Services	167,500	20.6	16.3
Financial Activities	49,200	6.0	6.1
Government	78,700	9.7	15.2
Information	12,300	1.5	1.9
Leisure and Hospitality	58,100	7.1	9.0
Manufacturing	113,300	13.9	8.5
Mining and Logging	500	0.1	0.4
Other Services	44,600	5.5	3.8
Professional and Business Services	117,000	14.4	14.4
Retail Trade	76,900	9.4	10.9
Transportation, Warehousing, and Utilities	29,700	3.6	4.6
Wholesale Trade	36,700	4.5	3.9

Note: Figures are non-farm employment as of December 2020. Figures are not seasonally adjusted and include workers 16 years of age and older; (1) Figures cover the Milwaukee-Waukesha-West Allis, WI Metropolitan Statistical Area
Source: Bureau of Labor Statistics, Current Employment Statistics, Employment, Hours, and Earnings

Employment by Occupation

Occupation Classification	City (%)	MSA[1] (%)	U.S. (%)
Management, Business, Science, and Arts	31.7	40.5	38.5
Natural Resources, Construction, and Maintenance	6.0	6.2	8.9
Production, Transportation, and Material Moving	19.3	15.1	13.2
Sales and Office	20.0	21.6	21.6
Service	23.1	16.7	17.8

Note: Figures cover employed civilians 16 years of age and older; (1) Figures cover the Milwaukee-Waukesha-West Allis, WI Metropolitan Statistical Area
Source: U.S. Census Bureau, 2015-2019 American Community Survey 5-Year Estimates

Occupations with Greatest Projected Employment Growth: 2020 – 2022

Occupation[1]	2020 Employment	2022 Projected Employment	Numeric Employment Change	Percent Employment Change
Combined Food Preparation and Serving Workers, Including Fast Food	54,410	72,710	18,300	33.6
Waiters and Waitresses	29,420	41,470	12,050	41.0
Retail Salespersons	64,040	75,960	11,920	18.6
Bartenders	17,450	26,690	9,240	53.0
Cooks, Restaurant	16,530	24,010	7,480	45.3
Personal Care Aides	64,090	70,310	6,220	9.7
Cashiers	58,470	63,910	5,440	9.3
Hairdressers, Hairstylists, and Cosmetologists	9,870	15,130	5,260	53.3
First-Line Supervisors of Food Preparation and Serving Workers	12,710	17,300	4,590	36.1
Laborers and Freight, Stock, and Material Movers, Hand	51,400	55,990	4,590	8.9

Note: Projections cover Wisconsin; (1) Sorted by numeric employment change
Source: www.projectionscentral.com, State Occupational Projections, 2020–2022 Short-Term Projections

Fastest-Growing Occupations: 2020 – 2022

Occupation[1]	2020 Employment	2022 Projected Employment	Numeric Employment Change	Percent Employment Change
Film and Video Editors	70	140	70	100.0
Ushers, Lobby Attendants, and Ticket Takers	1,280	2,490	1,210	94.5
Athletes and Sports Competitors	110	190	80	72.7
Manicurists and Pedicurists	1,470	2,450	980	66.7
Hotel, Motel, and Resort Desk Clerks	2,700	4,430	1,730	64.1
Lodging Managers	250	400	150	60.0
Gaming Cage Workers	100	160	60	60.0
Amusement and Recreation Attendants	2,720	4,340	1,620	59.6
Baggage Porters and Bellhops	110	170	60	54.5
Cooks, Short Order	1,580	2,440	860	54.4

Note: Projections cover Wisconsin; (1) Sorted by percent employment change and excludes occupations with numeric employment change less than 50
Source: www.projectionscentral.com, State Occupational Projections, 2020–2022 Short-Term Projections

TAXES

State Corporate Income Tax Rates

State	Tax Rate (%)	Income Brackets ($)	Num. of Brackets	Financial Institution Tax Rate (%)[a]	Federal Income Tax Ded.
Wisconsin	7.9	Flat rate	1	7.9	No

Note: Tax rates as of January 1, 2021; (a) Rates listed are the corporate income tax rate applied to financial institutions or excise taxes based on income. Some states have other taxes based upon the value of deposits or shares.
Source: Federation of Tax Administrators, State Corporate Income Tax Rates, January 1, 2021

State Individual Income Tax Rates

State	Tax Rate (%)	Income Brackets ($)	Personal Exemptions ($)			Standard Ded. ($)	
			Single	Married	Depend.	Single	Married
Wisconsin (a)	3.54 - 7.65	12,120 - 266,930 (w)	700	1,400	700	11,200	20,730 (y)

Note: Tax rates as of January 1, 2021; Local- and county-level taxes are not included; Federal income tax is not deductible on state income tax returns; (a) 19 states have statutory provision for automatically adjusting to the rate of inflation the dollar values of the income tax brackets, standard deductions, and/or personal exemptions. Michigan indexes the personal exemption only. Oregon does not index the income brackets for $125,000 and over; (w) The Wisconsin income brackets reported are for single individuals. For married taxpayers filing jointly, the same tax rates apply income brackets ranging from $16,160, to $355,910; (y) Alabama standard deduction is phased out for incomes over $23,000. Rhode Island exemptions & standard deductions phased out for incomes over $207,700; Wisconsin standard deduciton phases out for income over $16,149.
Source: Federation of Tax Administrators, State Individual Income Tax Rates, January 1, 2021

Various State Sales and Excise Tax Rates

State	State Sales Tax (%)	Gasoline[1] (¢/gal.)	Cigarette[2] ($/pack)	Spirits[3] ($/gal.)	Wine[4] ($/gal.)	Beer[5] ($/gal.)	Recreational Marijuana (%)
Wisconsin	5	32.9	2.52	3.25	0.25	0.06	Not legal

Note: All tax rates as of January 1, 2021; (1) The American Petroleum Institute has developed a methodology for determining the average tax rate on a gallon of fuel. Rates may include any of the following: excise taxes, environmental fees, storage tank fees, other fees or taxes, general sales tax, and local taxes; (2) The federal excise tax of $1.0066 per pack and local taxes are not included; (3) Rates are those applicable to off-premise sales of 40% alcohol by volume (a.b.v.) distilled spirits in 750ml containers. Local excise taxes are excluded; (4) Rates are those applicable to off-premise sales of 11% a.b.v. non-carbonated wine in 750ml containers; (5) Rates are those applicable to off-premise sales of 4.7% a.b.v. beer in 12 ounce containers.
Source: Tax Foundation, 2021 Facts & Figures: How Does Your State Compare?

State Business Tax Climate Index Rankings

State	Overall Rank	Corporate Tax Rank	Individual Income Tax Rank	Sales Tax Rank	Property Tax Rank	Unemployment Insurance Tax Rank
Wisconsin	25	30	37	7	17	35

Note: The index is a measure of how each state's tax laws affect economic performance. The lower the rank, the more favorable a state's tax system is for business. States without a given tax are given a ranking of 1. The scores/rankings for the District of Columbia do not affect other states. The 2021 index represents the tax climate as of July 1, 2020.
Source: Tax Foundation, State Business Tax Climate Index 2021

TRANSPORTATION

Means of Transportation to Work

Area	Car/Truck/Van		Public Transportation			Bicycle	Walked	Other Means	Worked at Home
	Drove Alone	Car-pooled	Bus	Subway	Railroad				
City	72.8	10.2	7.2	0.0	0.1	0.8	4.6	0.8	3.5
MSA[1]	80.9	7.8	3.1	0.0	0.1	0.5	2.6	0.7	4.3
U.S.	76.3	9.0	2.4	1.9	0.6	0.5	2.7	1.4	5.2

Note: Figures are percentages and cover workers 16 years of age and older; (1) Figures cover the Milwaukee-Waukesha-West Allis, WI Metropolitan Statistical Area
Source: U.S. Census Bureau, 2015-2019 American Community Survey 5-Year Estimates

Travel Time to Work

Area	Less Than 10 Minutes	10 to 19 Minutes	20 to 29 Minutes	30 to 44 Minutes	45 to 59 Minutes	60 to 89 Minutes	90 Minutes or More
City	10.1	36.6	25.8	19.3	4.0	2.7	1.5
MSA[1]	11.9	31.6	25.8	21.3	5.5	2.5	1.4
U.S.	12.2	28.4	20.8	20.8	8.3	6.4	2.9

Note: Note: Figures are percentages and include workers 16 years old and over; (1) Figures cover the Milwaukee-Waukesha-West Allis, WI Metropolitan Statistical Area
Source: U.S. Census Bureau, 2015-2019 American Community Survey 5-Year Estimates

Key Congestion Measures

Measure	1982	1992	2002	2012	2017
Annual Hours of Delay, Total (000)	8,634	20,774	30,159	37,638	42,146
Annual Hours of Delay, Per Auto Commuter	13	28	34	41	46
Annual Congestion Cost, Total (million $)	67	222	414	691	788
Annual Congestion Cost, Per Auto Commuter ($)	398	658	744	728	790

Note: Covers the Milwaukee WI urban area
Source: Texas A&M Transportation Institute, 2019 Urban Mobility Report

Milwaukee, Wisconsin 327

Freeway Travel Time Index

Measure	1982	1987	1992	1997	2002	2007	2012	2017
Urban Area Index[1]	1.06	1.10	1.13	1.15	1.15	1.16	1.17	1.17
Urban Area Rank[1,2]	43	36	37	41	61	63	50	49

Note: Freeway Travel Time Index—the ratio of travel time in the peak period to the travel time at free-flow conditions. For example, a value of 1.30 indicates a 20-minute free-flow trip takes 26 minutes in the peak (20 minutes x 1.30 = 26 minutes); (1) Covers the Milwaukee WI urban area; (2) Rank is based on 101 larger urban areas (#1 = highest travel time index)
Source: Texas A&M Transportation Institute, 2019 Urban Mobility Report

Public Transportation

Agency Name / Mode of Transportation	Vehicles Operated in Maximum Service[1]	Annual Unlinked Passenger Trips[2] (in thous.)	Annual Passenger Miles[3] (in thous.)
Milwaukee County Transit System (MCTS)			
Bus (purchased transportation)	307	28,972.7	91,779.5
Demand Response (purchased transportation)	96	451.1	3,023.6

Note: (1) Number of revenue vehicles operated by the given mode and type of service to meet the annual maximum service requirement. This is the revenue vehicle count during the peak season of the year; on the week and day that maximum service is provided. Vehicles operated in maximum service (VOMS) exclude atypical days and one-time special events; (2) Number of passengers who boarded public transportation vehicles. Passengers are counted each time they board a vehicle no matter how many vehicles they use to travel from their origin to their destination. (3) Sum of the distances ridden by all passengers during the entire fiscal year.
Source: Federal Transit Administration, National Transit Database, 2019

Air Transportation

Airport Name and Code / Type of Service	Passenger Airlines[1]	Passenger Enplanements	Freight Carriers[2]	Freight (lbs)
General Mitchell International (MKE)				
Domestic service (U.S. carriers - 2020)	26	1,258,514	14	76,437,062
International service (U.S. carriers - 2019)	5	4,748	3	3,149,552

Note: (1) Includes all U.S.-based major, minor and commuter airlines that carried at least one passenger during the year; (2) Includes all U.S.-based airlines and freight carriers that transported at least one pound of freight during the year.
Source: Bureau of Transportation Statistics, The Intermodal Transportation Database, Air Carriers: T-100 Domestic Market (U.S. Carriers), 2020; Bureau of Transportation Statistics, The Intermodal Transportation Database, Air Carriers: T-100 International Market (U.S. Carriers), 2019

BUSINESSES

Major Business Headquarters

Company Name	Industry	Rankings	
		Fortune[1]	Forbes[2]
ManpowerGroup	Temporary Help	158	-
Northwestern Mutual	Insurance, Life, Health (Mutual)	102	-
Rockwell Automation	Electronics, Electrical Equip.	452	-
WEC Energy Group	Utilities, Gas and Electric	416	-

Note: (1) Companies that produce a 10-K are ranked 1 to 500 based on 2019 revenue; (2) All private companies with at least $2 billion in annual revenue through the end of their most current fiscal year are ranked 1 to 219; companies listed are headquartered in the city; dashes indicate no ranking
Source: Fortune, "Fortune 500," June/July 2020; Forbes, "America's Largest Private Companies," 2020

Minority Business Opportunity

Milwaukee is home to one company which is on the *Black Enterprise* Industrial/Service list (100 largest companies based on gross sales): **V & J Holding Cos.** (#45). Criteria: operational in previous calendar year; at least 51% black-owned and manufactures/owns the product it sells or provides industrial or consumer services. Brokerages, real estate firms and firms that provide professional services are not eligible. *Black Enterprise, B.E. 100s, 2019*

Living Environment

COST OF LIVING

Cost of Living Index

Composite Index	Groceries	Housing	Utilities	Trans-portation	Health Care	Misc. Goods/Services
n/a	n/a	n/a	n/a	n/a	n/a	n/a

Note: The Cost of Living Index measures regional differences in the cost of consumer goods and services, excluding taxes and non-consumer expenditures, for professional and managerial households in the top income quintile. It is based on more than 50,000 prices covering almost 60 different items for which prices are collected three times a year by chambers of commerce, economic development organizations or university applied economic centers in each participating urban area. The numbers shown should be read as a percentage above or below the national average of 100. For example, a value of 115.4 in the groceries column indicates that grocery prices are 15.4% higher than the national average. Small differences in the index numbers should not be interpreted as significant; n/a not available.
Source: The Council for Community and Economic Research, Cost of Living Index, 2020

Grocery Prices

Area[1]	T-Bone Steak ($/pound)	Frying Chicken ($/pound)	Whole Milk ($/half gal.)	Eggs ($/dozen)	Orange Juice ($/64 oz.)	Coffee ($/11.5 oz.)
City[2]	279.00	279.00	279.00	279.00	279.00	279.00
Avg.	11.78	1.39	2.05	1.47	3.57	4.34
Min.	8.03	0.94	1.03	0.74	2.94	3.02
Max.	15.86	2.65	4.31	3.77	5.44	8.69

*Note: (1) Values for the local area are compared with the average, minimum and maximum values for all 284 areas in the Cost of Living Index; (2) Figures cover the urban area; **T-Bone Steak** (price per pound); **Frying Chicken** (price per pound, whole fryer); **Whole Milk** (half gallon carton); **Eggs** (price per dozen, Grade A, large); **Orange Juice** (64 oz. Tropicana or Florida Natural); **Coffee** (11.5 oz. can, vacuum-packed, Maxwell House, Hills Bros, or Folgers).*
Source: The Council for Community and Economic Research, Cost of Living Index, 2020

Housing and Utility Costs

Area[1]	New Home Price ($)	Apartment Rent ($/month)	All Electric ($/month)	Part Electric ($/month)	Other Energy ($/month)	Telephone ($/month)
City[2]	279	279	n/a	n/a	n/a	279.00
Avg.	368,594	1,168	170.86	100.47	65.28	184.30
Min.	190,567	502	91.58	31.42	26.08	169.60
Max.	2,227,806	4,738	470.38	280.31	280.06	206.50

*Note: (1) Values for the local area are compared with the average, minimum and maximum values for all 284 areas in the Cost of Living Index; (2) Figures cover the urban area; **New Home Price** (2,400 sf living area, 8,000 sf lot, in urban area with full utilities); **Apartment Rent** (950 sf 2 bedroom/1.5 or 2 bath, unfurnished, excluding all utilities except water); **All Electric** (average monthly cost for an all-electric home); **Part Electric** (average monthly cost for a part-electric home); **Other Energy** (average monthly cost for natural gas, fuel oil, coal, wood, and any other forms of energy except electricity); **Telephone** (price includes the base monthly rate plus taxes and fees for three lines of mobile phone service).*
Source: The Council for Community and Economic Research, Cost of Living Index, 2020

Health Care, Transportation, and Other Costs

Area[1]	Doctor ($/visit)	Dentist ($/visit)	Optometrist ($/visit)	Gasoline ($/gallon)	Beauty Salon ($/visit)	Men's Shirt ($)
City[2]	279.00	279.00	279.00	279.00	279.00	279.00
Avg.	115.44	99.32	108.10	2.21	39.27	31.37
Min.	36.68	59.00	51.36	1.71	19.00	11.00
Max.	219.00	153.10	250.97	3.46	82.05	58.33

*Note: (1) Values for the local area are compared with the average, minimum and maximum values for all 284 areas in the Cost of Living Index; (2) Figures cover the urban area; **Doctor** (general practitioners routine exam of an established patient); **Dentist** (adult teeth cleaning and periodic oral examination); **Optometrist** (full vision eye exam for established adult patient); **Gasoline** (one gallon regular unleaded, national brand, including all taxes, cash price at self-service pump if available); **Beauty Salon** (woman's shampoo, trim, and blow-dry); **Men's Shirt** (cotton/polyester dress shirt, pinpoint weave, long sleeves).*
Source: The Council for Community and Economic Research, Cost of Living Index, 2020

HOUSING

Homeownership Rate

Area	2012 (%)	2013 (%)	2014 (%)	2015 (%)	2016 (%)	2017 (%)	2018 (%)	2019 (%)	2020 (%)
MSA[1]	61.9	60.0	55.9	57.0	60.4	63.9	62.3	56.9	58.5
U.S.	65.4	65.1	64.5	63.7	63.4	63.9	64.4	64.6	66.6

Note: (1) Figures cover the Milwaukee-Waukesha-West Allis, WI Metropolitan Statistical Area
Source: U.S. Census Bureau, Housing Vacancies and Homeownership Annual Statistics: 2012-2020

House Price Index (HPI)

Area	National Ranking[2]	Quarterly Change (%)	One-Year Change (%)	Five-Year Change (%)	Since 1991Q1 (%)
MSA[1]	172	1.59	5.45	26.53	171.34
U.S.[3]	–	3.81	10.77	38.99	205.12

Note: The HPI is a weighted repeat sales index. It measures average price changes in repeat sales or refinancings on the same properties. This information is obtained by reviewing repeat mortgage transactions on single-family properties whose mortgages have been purchased or securitized by Fannie Mae or Freddie Mac since January 1975; (1) Figures cover the Milwaukee-Waukesha-West Allis, WI Metropolitan Statistical Area; (2) Rankings are based on annual percentage change for all metro areas containing at least 15,000 transactions over the last 10 years and ranges from 1 to 253; (3) figures based on a weighted average of Census Division estimates using a seasonally adjusted, purchase-only index; all figures are for the period ending December 31, 2020
Source: Federal Housing Finance Agency, Change in Metropolitan Area House Price Indexes, April 7, 2021

Median Single-Family Home Prices

Area	2018	2019	2020[p]	Percent Change 2019 to 2020
MSA[1]	250.3	268.4	291.3	8.5
U.S. Average	261.6	274.6	299.9	9.2

Note: Figures are median sales prices of existing single-family homes in thousands of dollars; (p) preliminary; (1) Figures cover the Milwaukee-Waukesha-West Allis, WI Metropolitan Statistical Area
Source: National Association of Realtors, Median Sales Price of Existing Single-Family Homes for Metropolitan Areas, 4th Quarter 2020

Qualifying Income Based on Median Sales Price of Existing Single-Family Homes

Area	With 5% Down ($)	With 10% Down ($)	With 20% Down ($)
MSA[1]	54,511	51,642	45,904
U.S. Average	59,266	56,147	49,908

Note: Figures are preliminary; Qualifying income is based on a mortgage rate of 2.81%. Monthly principal and interest payment is limited to 25% of income; (1) Figures cover the Milwaukee-Waukesha-West Allis, WI Metropolitan Statistical Area
Source: National Association of Realtors, Qualifying Income Based on Median Sales Price of Existing Single-Family Homes for Metropolitan Areas, 4th Quarter 2020

Home Value Distribution

Area	Under $50,000	$50,000 -$99,999	$100,000 -$149,999	$150,000 -$199,999	$200,000 -$299,999	$300,000 -$499,999	$500,000 -$999,999	$1,000,000 or more
City	9.1	27.3	29.6	17.9	10.6	3.6	1.5	0.4
MSA[1]	3.7	8.8	15.1	18.2	27.1	20.0	6.0	1.1
U.S.	6.9	12.0	13.3	14.0	19.6	19.3	11.4	3.4

Note: Figures are percentages and cover owner-occupied housing units; (1) Figures cover the Milwaukee-Waukesha-West Allis, WI Metropolitan Statistical Area
Source: U.S. Census Bureau, 2015-2019 American Community Survey 5-Year Estimates

Year Housing Structure Built

Area	2010 or Later	2000 -2009	1990 -1999	1980 -1989	1970 -1979	1960 -1969	1950 -1959	1940 -1949	Before 1940	Median Year
City	1.5	3.3	2.9	3.9	8.7	11.1	20.2	9.8	38.6	1951
MSA[1]	2.7	8.2	10.8	8.0	13.0	11.5	16.3	6.8	22.9	1964
U.S.	5.2	14.0	13.9	13.4	15.2	10.6	10.3	4.9	12.6	1978

Note: Figures are percentages except for Median Year; Note: (1) Figures cover the Milwaukee-Waukesha-West Allis, WI Metropolitan Statistical Area
Source: U.S. Census Bureau, 2015-2019 American Community Survey 5-Year Estimates

Gross Monthly Rent

Area	Under $500	$500 -$999	$1,000 -$1,499	$1,500 -$1,999	$2,000 -$2,499	$2,500 -$2,999	$3,000 and up	Median ($)
City	9.1	60.2	24.2	4.7	1.2	0.4	0.2	858
MSA[1]	7.7	54.1	28.9	6.7	1.6	0.5	0.3	903
U.S.	9.4	36.2	30.0	14.0	5.6	2.4	2.4	1,062

Note: Figures are percentages except for Median; Gross rent is the contract rent plus the estimated average monthly cost of utilities (electricity, gas, and water and sewer) and fuels (oil, coal, kerosene, wood, etc.) if these are paid by the renter (or paid for the renter by someone else); (1) Figures cover the Milwaukee-Waukesha-West Allis, WI Metropolitan Statistical Area
Source: U.S. Census Bureau, 2015-2019 American Community Survey 5-Year Estimates

HEALTH

Health Risk Factors

Category	MSA[1] (%)	U.S. (%)
Adults aged 18–64 who have any kind of health care coverage	91.4	87.3
Adults who reported being in good or better health	81.0	82.4
Adults who have been told they have high blood cholesterol	34.2	33.0
Adults who have been told they have high blood pressure	30.5	32.3
Adults who are current smokers	14.5	17.1
Adults who currently use E-cigarettes	4.5	4.6
Adults who currently use chewing tobacco, snuff, or snus	2.8	4.0
Adults who are heavy drinkers[2]	7.7	6.3
Adults who are binge drinkers[3]	21.0	17.4
Adults who are overweight (BMI 25.0 - 29.9)	38.3	35.3
Adults who are obese (BMI 30.0 - 99.8)	29.1	31.3
Adults who participated in any physical activities in the past month	75.2	74.4
Adults who always or nearly always wears a seat belt	93.3	94.3

Note: (1) Figures cover the Milwaukee-Waukesha-West Allis, WI Metropolitan Statistical Area; (2) Heavy drinkers are classified as adult men having more than 14 drinks per week and adult women having more than 7 drinks per week; (3) Binge drinkers are classified as males having five or more drinks on one occasion or females having four or more drinks on one occasion
Source: Centers for Disease Control and Prevention, Behaviorial Risk Factor Surveillance System, SMART: Selected Metropolitan Area Risk Trends, 2017

Acute and Chronic Health Conditions

Category	MSA[1] (%)	U.S. (%)
Adults who have ever been told they had a heart attack	3.2	4.2
Adults who have ever been told they have angina or coronary heart disease	3.7	3.9
Adults who have ever been told they had a stroke	2.3	3.0
Adults who have ever been told they have asthma	13.3	14.2
Adults who have ever been told they have arthritis	26.7	24.9
Adults who have ever been told they have diabetes[2]	10.3	10.5
Adults who have ever been told they had skin cancer	4.4	6.2
Adults who have ever been told they had any other types of cancer	7.0	7.1
Adults who have ever been told they have COPD	5.0	6.5
Adults who have ever been told they have kidney disease	3.5	3.0
Adults who have ever been told they have a form of depression	19.3	20.5

Note: (1) Figures cover the Milwaukee-Waukesha-West Allis, WI Metropolitan Statistical Area; (2) Figures do not include pregnancy-related, borderline, or pre-diabetes
Source: Centers for Disease Control and Prevention, Behaviorial Risk Factor Surveillance System, SMART: Selected Metropolitan Area Risk Trends, 2017

Health Screening and Vaccination Rates

Category	MSA[1] (%)	U.S. (%)
Adults aged 65+ who have had flu shot within the past year	49.8	60.7
Adults aged 65+ who have ever had a pneumonia vaccination	77.9	75.4
Adults who have ever been tested for HIV	37.6	36.1
Adults who have ever had the shingles or zoster vaccine?	29.5	28.9
Adults who have had their blood cholesterol checked within the last five years	87.5	85.9

Note: n/a not available; (1) Figures cover the Milwaukee-Waukesha-West Allis, WI Metropolitan Statistical Area.
Source: Centers for Disease Control and Prevention, Behaviorial Risk Factor Surveillance System, SMART: Selected Metropolitan Area Risk Trends, 2017

Disability Status

Category	MSA[1] (%)	U.S. (%)
Adults who reported being deaf	5.3	6.7
Are you blind or have serious difficulty seeing, even when wearing glasses?	3.3	4.5
Are you limited in any way in any of your usual activities due of arthritis?	12.8	12.9
Do you have difficulty doing errands alone?	6.8	6.8
Do you have difficulty dressing or bathing?	4.3	3.6
Do you have serious difficulty concentrating/remembering/making decisions?	10.5	10.7
Do you have serious difficulty walking or climbing stairs?	12.2	13.6

Note: (1) Figures cover the Milwaukee-Waukesha-West Allis, WI Metropolitan Statistical Area.
Source: Centers for Disease Control and Prevention, Behaviorial Risk Factor Surveillance System, SMART: Selected Metropolitan Area Risk Trends, 2017

Mortality Rates for the Top 10 Causes of Death in the U.S.

ICD-10[a] Sub-Chapter	ICD-10[a] Code	Age-Adjusted Mortality Rate[1] per 100,000 population	
		County[2]	U.S.
Malignant neoplasms	C00-C97	169.9	149.2
Ischaemic heart diseases	I20-I25	108.1	90.5
Other forms of heart disease	I30-I51	52.0	52.2
Chronic lower respiratory diseases	J40-J47	36.2	39.6
Other degenerative diseases of the nervous system	G30-G31	27.8	37.6
Cerebrovascular diseases	I60-I69	34.8	37.2
Other external causes of accidental injury	W00-X59	68.2	36.1
Organic, including symptomatic, mental disorders	F01-F09	40.2	29.4
Hypertensive diseases	I10-I15	29.6	24.1
Diabetes mellitus	E10-E14	23.7	21.5

Note: (a) ICD-10 = International Classification of Diseases 10th Revision; (1) Mortality rates are a three-year average covering 2017-2019; (2) Figures cover Milwaukee County.
Source: Centers for Disease Control and Prevention, National Center for Health Statistics. Underlying Cause of Death 1999-2019 on CDC WONDER Online Database

Mortality Rates for Selected Causes of Death

ICD-10[a] Sub-Chapter	ICD-10[a] Code	Age-Adjusted Mortality Rate[1] per 100,000 population	
		County[2]	U.S.
Assault	X85-Y09	13.4	6.0
Diseases of the liver	K70-K76	14.9	14.4
Human immunodeficiency virus (HIV) disease	B20-B24	1.1	1.5
Influenza and pneumonia	J09-J18	12.0	13.8
Intentional self-harm	X60-X84	13.3	14.1
Malnutrition	E40-E46	2.8	2.3
Obesity and other hyperalimentation	E65-E68	2.5	2.1
Renal failure	N17-N19	16.5	12.6
Transport accidents	V01-V99	10.6	12.3
Viral hepatitis	B15-B19	0.7	1.2

Note: (a) ICD-10 = International Classification of Diseases 10th Revision; (1) Mortality rates are a three-year average covering 2017-2019; (2) Figures cover Milwaukee County; Data are suppressed when the data meet the criteria for confidentiality constraints; Mortality rates are flagged as unreliable when the rate would be calculated with a numerator of 20 or less.
Source: Centers for Disease Control and Prevention, National Center for Health Statistics. Underlying Cause of Death 1999-2019 on CDC WONDER Online Database

Health Insurance Coverage

Area	With Health Insurance	With Private Health Insurance	With Public Health Insurance	Without Health Insurance	Population Under Age 19 Without Health Insurance
City	90.7	54.1	44.9	9.3	3.3
MSA[1]	94.4	71.8	34.1	5.6	2.4
U.S.	91.2	67.9	35.1	8.8	5.1

Note: Figures are percentages that cover the civilian noninstitutionalized population; (1) Figures cover the Milwaukee-Waukesha-West Allis, WI Metropolitan Statistical Area
Source: U.S. Census Bureau, 2015-2019 American Community Survey 5-Year Estimates

Number of Medical Professionals

Area	MDs[3]	DOs[3,4]	Dentists	Podiatrists	Chiropractors	Optometrists
County[1] (number)	3,547	205	793	73	193	103
County[1] (rate[2])	374.6	21.6	83.9	7.7	20.4	10.9
U.S. (rate[2])	282.9	22.7	71.2	6.2	28.1	16.9

55079
Note: Data as of 2019 unless noted; (1) Data covers Milwaukee County; (2) Rate per 100,000 population; (3) Data as of 2018 and includes all active, non-federal physicians; (4) Doctor of Osteopathic Medicine
Source: U.S. Department of Health and Human Services, Health Resources and Services Administration, Bureau of Health Professions, Area Resource File (ARF) 2019-2020

Best Hospitals

According to *U.S. News*, the Milwaukee-Waukesha-West Allis, WI metro area is home to one of the best children's hospitals in the U.S.: **Children's Hospital of Wisconsin** (6 pediatric specialties). The hospital listed was highly ranked in at least one of 10 pediatric specialties. Eighty-eight children's hospitals in the U.S. were nationally ranked in at least one specialty. Hospitals received points for being ranked in a specialty, and the 10 hospitals with the most points across the 10 specialties make up the Honor Roll. *U.S. News Online, "America's Best Children's Hospitals 2020-21"*

332 Milwaukee, Wisconsin

EDUCATION

Public School District Statistics

District Name	Schls	Pupils	Pupil/ Teacher Ratio	Minority Pupils[1] (%)	Free Lunch Eligible[2] (%)	IEP[3] (%)
Milwaukee School District	161	75,431	17.2	89.5	73.9	20.0

Note: Table includes school districts with 2,000 or more students; (1) Percentage of students that are not non-Hispanic white; (2) Percentage of students that are eligible for the free lunch program; (3) Percentage of students that have an Individualized Education Program.
Source: U.S. Department of Education, National Center for Education Statistics, Common Core of Data, Local Education Agency (School District) Universe Survey: School Year 2018-2019; U.S. Department of Education, National Center for Education Statistics, Common Core of Data, Public Elementary/Secondary School Universe Survey: School Year 2018-2019

Best High Schools

According to *U.S. News*, Milwaukee is home to two of the top 500 high schools in the U.S.: **Reagan College Preparatory High** (#223); **Carmen High School of Science and Technology** (#406). Nearly 18,000 public, magnet and charter schools were ranked based on their performance on state assessments and how well they prepare students for college. *U.S. News & World Report, "Best High Schools 2020"*

Highest Level of Education

Area	Less than H.S.	H.S. Diploma	Some College, No Deg.	Associate Degree	Bachelor's Degree	Master's Degree	Prof. School Degree	Doctorate Degree
City	16.0	30.2	21.9	7.2	15.9	6.5	1.3	0.9
MSA[1]	8.5	26.5	20.6	8.7	23.0	9.0	2.3	1.3
U.S.	12.0	27.0	20.4	8.5	19.8	8.8	2.1	1.4

Note: Figures cover persons age 25 and over; (1) Figures cover the Milwaukee-Waukesha-West Allis, WI Metropolitan Statistical Area
Source: U.S. Census Bureau, 2015-2019 American Community Survey 5-Year Estimates

Educational Attainment by Race

Area	High School Graduate or Higher (%)					Bachelor's Degree or Higher (%)				
	Total	White	Black	Asian	Hisp.[2]	Total	White	Black	Asian	Hisp.[2]
City	84.0	89.1	83.0	68.8	62.2	24.6	35.3	12.6	27.1	9.3
MSA[1]	91.5	94.4	83.8	83.5	68.7	35.6	39.9	14.3	51.0	14.5
U.S.	88.0	89.9	86.0	87.1	68.7	32.1	33.5	21.6	54.3	16.4

Note: Figures shown cover persons 25 years old and over; (1) Figures cover the Milwaukee-Waukesha-West Allis, WI Metropolitan Statistical Area; (2) People of Hispanic origin can be of any race
Source: U.S. Census Bureau, 2015-2019 American Community Survey 5-Year Estimates

School Enrollment by Grade and Control

Area	Preschool (%)		Kindergarten (%)		Grades 1 - 4 (%)		Grades 5 - 8 (%)		Grades 9 - 12 (%)	
	Public	Private	Public	Private	Public	Private	Public	Private	Public	Private
City	73.5	26.5	79.4	20.6	77.1	22.9	75.8	24.2	81.4	18.6
MSA[1]	56.6	43.4	80.0	20.0	80.5	19.5	79.7	20.3	85.2	14.8
U.S.	59.1	40.9	87.6	12.4	89.5	10.5	89.4	10.6	90.1	9.9

Note: Figures shown cover persons 3 years old and over; (1) Figures cover the Milwaukee-Waukesha-West Allis, WI Metropolitan Statistical Area
Source: U.S. Census Bureau, 2015-2019 American Community Survey 5-Year Estimates

Higher Education

Four-Year Colleges			Two-Year Colleges			Medical Schools[1]	Law Schools[2]	Voc/ Tech[3]
Public	Private Non-profit	Private For-profit	Public	Private Non-profit	Private For-profit			
3	10	0	1	0	1	1	1	2

Note: Figures cover institutions located within the city limits and include main campuses only; (1) includes schools accredited by the Liaison Committee on Medical Education and the American Osteopathic Association's Commission on Osteopathic College Accreditation; (2) includes ABA-accredited schools, schools with provisional ABA accreditation, and state accredited schools; (3) includes all schools with programs that are less than 2 years.
Source: National Center for Education Statistics, Integrated Postsecondary Education System (IPEDS), 2019-20; Wikipedia, List of Medical Schools in the United States, accessed April 2, 2021; Wikipedia, List of Law Schools in the United States, accessed April 2, 2021

According to *U.S. News & World Report*, the Milwaukee-Waukesha-West Allis, WI metro area is home to one of the top 200 national universities in the U.S.: **Marquette University** (#88 tie). The indicators used to capture academic quality fall into a number of categories: assessment by administrators at peer institutions; retention of students; faculty resources; student selectivity; financial resources; alumni giving; high school counselor ratings of colleges; and graduation rate. *U.S. News & World Report, "America's Best Colleges 2021"*

EMPLOYERS

Major Employers

Company Name	Industry
Ascension Wisconsin	Health care system
Aurora Health	Health care system
Children's Hospital of Wisconsin	Pediatric health care services
Froedtert Health	Health care services
GE Healthcare Technologies	Medical imaging & information systems
Kohl's	Department stores
Kroger Co./Roundy's	Food distributor & retailer
Medical College of Wisconsin	Medical school
Northwestern Mutual	Life insurance & investment services
ProHealth Care Inc.	Health care system
Quad/Graphics	Commercial printing and print mgmt
WEC Energy	Electric & natural gas utility

Note: Companies shown are located within the Milwaukee-Waukesha-West Allis, WI Metropolitan Statistical Area.
Source: Hoovers.com; Wikipedia

Best Companies to Work For

Baird, headquartered in Milwaukee, is among "The 100 Best Companies to Work For." To pick the best companies, *Fortune* partnered with the Great Place to Work Institute. Two-thirds of a company's score is based on the results of the Institute's Trust Index survey, which is sent to a random sample of employees from each company. The questions related to attitudes about management's credibility, job satisfaction, and camaraderie. The other third of the scoring is based on the company's responses to the Institute's Culture Audit, which includes detailed questions about pay and benefit programs, and a series of open-ended questions about hiring practices, internal communication, training, recognition programs, and diversity efforts. Any company that is at least five years old with more than 1,000 U.S. employees is eligible. *Fortune, "The 100 Best Companies to Work For," 2020*

Robert W. Baird and Co, headquartered in Milwaukee, is among the "100 Best Places to Work in IT." To qualify, companies had to be U.S.-based organizations or be non-U.S.-based employers that met the following criteria: have a minimum of 300 total employees at a U.S. headquarters and a minimum of 30 IT employees in the U.S., with at least 50% of their IT employees based in the U.S. The best places to work were selected based on compensation, benefits, work/life balance, employee morale, and satisfaction with training and development programs. In addition, *InsiderPro* and *Computerworld* looked at retention efforts, programs for recognizing and rewarding outstanding performances, and benefits such as flextime, elder care and child care, and reimbursement for college tuition and the cost of pursuing technology certifications. *InsiderPro and Computerworld, "100 Best Places to Work in IT," 2020*

PUBLIC SAFETY

Crime Rate

Area	All Crimes	Violent Crimes				Property Crimes		
		Murder	Rape[3]	Robbery	Aggrav. Assault	Burglary	Larceny -Theft	Motor Vehicle Theft
City	3,887.3	16.4	72.3	323.4	920.4	608.2	1,362.8	583.8
Suburbs[1]	1,671.2	1.4	20.7	24.3	79.0	124.4	1,348.6	72.7
Metro[2]	2,501.8	7.0	40.0	136.4	394.4	305.7	1,353.9	264.3
U.S.	2,489.3	5.0	42.6	81.6	250.2	340.5	1,549.5	219.9

Note: Figures are crimes per 100,000 population; (1) All areas within the metro area that are located outside the city limits; (2) Figures cover the Milwaukee-Waukesha-West Allis, WI Metropolitan Statistical Area; (3) All figures shown were reported using the revised Uniform Crime Reporting (UCR) definition of rape.
Source: FBI Uniform Crime Reports, 2019

Hate Crimes

Area	Number of Quarters Reported	Number of Incidents per Bias Motivation					
		Race/Ethnicity/ Ancestry	Religion	Sexual Orientation	Disability	Gender	Gender Identity
City	4	2	0	0	0	0	0
U.S.	4	3,963	1,521	1,195	157	69	198

Source: Federal Bureau of Investigation, Hate Crime Statistics 2019

Identity Theft Consumer Reports

Area	Reports	Reports per 100,000 Population	Rank[2]
MSA[1]	4,051	257	151
U.S.	1,387,615	423	-

Note: (1) Figures cover the Milwaukee-Waukesha-West Allis, WI Metropolitan Statistical Area; (2) Rank ranges from 1 to 391 where 1 indicates greatest number of identity theft reports per 100,000 population
Source: Federal Trade Commission, Consumer Sentinel Network Data Book 2020

Fraud and Other Consumer Reports

Area	Reports	Reports per 100,000 Population	Rank[2]
MSA[1]	12,470	792	105
U.S.	3,385,133	1,031	-

Note: (1) Figures cover the Milwaukee-Waukesha-West Allis, WI Metropolitan Statistical Area; (2) Rank ranges from 1 to 391 where 1 indicates greatest number of fraud and other consumer reports per 100,000 population
Source: Federal Trade Commission, Consumer Sentinel Network Data Book 2020

POLITICS

2020 Presidential Election Results

Area	Biden	Trump	Jorgensen	Hawkins	Other
Milwaukee County	69.1	29.3	0.9	0.0	0.7
U.S.	51.3	46.8	1.2	0.3	0.5

Note: Results are percentages and may not add to 100% due to rounding
Source: Dave Leip's Atlas of U.S. Presidential Elections

SPORTS

Professional Sports Teams

Team Name	League	Year Established
Milwaukee Brewers	Major League Baseball (MLB)	1970
Milwaukee Bucks	National Basketball Association (NBA)	1968

Note: Includes teams located in the Milwaukee-Waukesha-West Allis, WI Metropolitan Statistical Area.
Source: Wikipedia, Major Professional Sports Teams of the United States and Canada, April 6, 2021

CLIMATE

Average and Extreme Temperatures

Temperature	Jan	Feb	Mar	Apr	May	Jun	Jul	Aug	Sep	Oct	Nov	Dec	Yr.
Extreme High (°F)	60	65	82	91	92	101	101	103	98	89	77	63	103
Average High (°F)	27	31	40	54	65	76	80	79	71	60	45	32	55
Average Temp. (°F)	20	24	33	45	55	66	71	70	62	51	38	25	47
Average Low (°F)	12	16	26	36	45	55	62	61	53	42	30	18	38
Extreme Low (°F)	-26	-19	-10	12	21	36	40	44	28	18	-5	-20	-26

Note: Figures cover the years 1948-1990
Source: National Climatic Data Center, International Station Meteorological Climate Summary, 9/96

Average Precipitation/Snowfall/Humidity

Precip./Humidity	Jan	Feb	Mar	Apr	May	Jun	Jul	Aug	Sep	Oct	Nov	Dec	Yr.
Avg. Precip. (in.)	1.6	1.4	2.6	3.3	2.9	3.4	3.6	3.4	2.9	2.3	2.3	2.2	32.0
Avg. Snowfall (in.)	13	10	9	2	Tr	0	0	0	0	Tr	3	11	49
Avg. Rel. Hum. 6am (%)	76	77	78	78	77	79	82	86	86	82	80	80	80
Avg. Rel. Hum. 3pm (%)	68	66	64	58	58	58	59	62	61	61	66	70	63

Note: Figures cover the years 1948-1990; Tr = Trace amounts (<0.05 in. of rain; <0.5 in. of snow)
Source: National Climatic Data Center, International Station Meteorological Climate Summary, 9/96

Weather Conditions

Temperature			Daytime Sky			Precipitation		
5°F & below	32°F & below	90°F & above	Clear	Partly cloudy	Cloudy	0.01 inch or more precip.	0.1 inch or more snow/ice	Thunder-storms
22	141	10	90	118	157	126	38	35

Note: Figures are average number of days per year and cover the years 1948-1990
Source: National Climatic Data Center, International Station Meteorological Climate Summary, 9/96

HAZARDOUS WASTE

Superfund Sites

The Milwaukee-Waukesha-West Allis, WI metro area is home to six sites on the EPA's Superfund National Priorities List: **Amcast Industrial Corporation** (final); **Lauer I Sanitary Landfill** (final); **Master Disposal Service Landfill** (final); **Moss-American Co., Inc. (Kerr-Mcgee Oil Co.)** (final); **Muskego Sanitary Landfill** (final); **Waste Management of Wisconsin, Inc. (Brookfield Sanitary Landfill)** (final). There are a total of 1,375 Superfund sites with a status of proposed or final on the list in the U.S. *U.S. Environmental Protection Agency, National Priorities List, April 7, 2021*

AIR QUALITY

Air Quality Trends: Ozone

	1990	1995	2000	2005	2010	2015	2016	2017	2018	2019
MSA[1]	0.095	0.106	0.082	0.092	0.079	0.069	0.074	0.072	0.073	0.066
U.S.	0.088	0.089	0.088	0.082	0.080	0.073	0.068	0.069	0.069	0.065

Note: (1) Data covers the Milwaukee-Waukesha-West Allis, WI Metropolitan Statistical Area. The values shown are the composite ozone concentration averages among trend sites based on the highest fourth daily maximum 8-hour concentration in parts per million. These trends are based on sites having an adequate record of monitoring data during the trend period. Data from exceptional events are included.
Source: U.S. Environmental Protection Agency, Air Quality Monitoring Information, "Air Quality Trends by City, 1990-2019"

Air Quality Index

Area	Percent of Days when Air Quality was...[2]					AQI Statistics[2]	
	Good	Moderate	Unhealthy for Sensitive Groups	Unhealthy	Very Unhealthy	Maximum	Median
MSA[1]	69.6	29.6	0.8	0.0	0.0	115	44

Note: (1) Data covers the Milwaukee-Waukesha-West Allis, WI Metropolitan Statistical Area; (2) Based on 365 days with AQI data in 2019. Air Quality Index (AQI) is an index for reporting daily air quality. EPA calculates the AQI for five major air pollutants regulated by the Clean Air Act: ground-level ozone, particle pollution (aka particulate matter), carbon monoxide, sulfur dioxide, and nitrogen dioxide. The AQI runs from 0 to 500. The higher the AQI value, the greater the level of air pollution and the greater the health concern. There are six AQI categories: "Good" AQI is between 0 and 50. Air quality is considered satisfactory; "Moderate" AQI is between 51 and 100. Air quality is acceptable; "Unhealthy for Sensitive Groups" When AQI values are between 101 and 150, members of sensitive groups may experience health effects; "Unhealthy" When AQI values are between 151 and 200 everyone may begin to experience health effects; "Very Unhealthy" AQI values between 201 and 300 trigger a health alert; "Hazardous" AQI values over 300 trigger warnings of emergency conditions (not shown).
Source: U.S. Environmental Protection Agency, Air Quality Index Report, 2019

Air Quality Index Pollutants

Area	Percent of Days when AQI Pollutant was...[2]					
	Carbon Monoxide	Nitrogen Dioxide	Ozone	Sulfur Dioxide	Particulate Matter 2.5	Particulate Matter 10
MSA[1]	0.0	2.7	51.8	0.0	43.3	2.2

Note: (1) Data covers the Milwaukee-Waukesha-West Allis, WI Metropolitan Statistical Area; (2) Based on 365 days with AQI data in 2019. The Air Quality Index (AQI) is an index for reporting daily air quality. EPA calculates the AQI for five major air pollutants regulated by the Clean Air Act: ground-level ozone, particle pollution (also known as particulate matter), carbon monoxide, sulfur dioxide, and nitrogen dioxide. The AQI runs from 0 to 500. The higher the AQI value, the greater the level of air pollution and the greater the health concern.
Source: U.S. Environmental Protection Agency, Air Quality Index Report, 2019

Maximum Air Pollutant Concentrations: Particulate Matter, Ozone, CO and Lead

	Particulate Matter 10 (ug/m^3)	Particulate Matter 2.5 Wtd AM (ug/m^3)	Particulate Matter 2.5 24-Hr (ug/m^3)	Ozone (ppm)	Carbon Monoxide (ppm)	Lead (ug/m^3)
MSA[1] Level	58	9.3	24	0.068	1	n/a
NAAQS[2]	150	15	35	0.075	9	0.15
Met NAAQS[2]	Yes	Yes	Yes	Yes	Yes	n/a

Note: (1) Data covers the Milwaukee-Waukesha-West Allis, WI Metropolitan Statistical Area; Data from exceptional events are included; (2) National Ambient Air Quality Standards; ppm = parts per million; ug/m^3 = micrograms per cubic meter; n/a not available.
Concentrations: Particulate Matter 10 (coarse particulate)—highest second maximum 24-hour concentration; Particulate Matter 2.5 Wtd AM (fine particulate)—highest weighted annual mean concentration; Particulate Matter 2.5 24-Hour (fine particulate)—highest 98th percentile 24-hour concentration; Ozone—highest fourth daily maximum 8-hour concentration; Carbon Monoxide—highest second maximum non-overlapping 8-hour concentration; Lead—maximum running 3-month average
Source: U.S. Environmental Protection Agency, Air Quality Monitoring Information, "Air Quality Statistics by City, 2019"

Maximum Air Pollutant Concentrations: Nitrogen Dioxide and Sulfur Dioxide

	Nitrogen Dioxide AM (ppb)	Nitrogen Dioxide 1-Hr (ppb)	Sulfur Dioxide AM (ppb)	Sulfur Dioxide 1-Hr (ppb)	Sulfur Dioxide 24-Hr (ppb)
MSA[1] Level	13	47	n/a	4	n/a
NAAQS[2]	53	100	30	75	140
Met NAAQS[2]	Yes	Yes	n/a	Yes	n/a

Note: (1) Data covers the Milwaukee-Waukesha-West Allis, WI Metropolitan Statistical Area; Data from exceptional events are included; (2) National Ambient Air Quality Standards; ppm = parts per million; ug/m³ = micrograms per cubic meter; n/a not available.
Concentrations: Nitrogen Dioxide AM—highest arithmetic mean concentration; Nitrogen Dioxide 1-Hr—highest 98th percentile 1-hour daily maximum concentration; Sulfur Dioxide AM—highest annual mean concentration; Sulfur Dioxide 1-Hr—highest 99th percentile 1-hour daily maximum concentration; Sulfur Dioxide 24-Hr—highest second maximum 24-hour concentration
Source: U.S. Environmental Protection Agency, Air Quality Monitoring Information, "Air Quality Statistics by City, 2019"

Minneapolis, Minnesota

Background

Minneapolis is a vibrant, cosmopolitan city that boasts sunlit skyscrapers and sparkling lakes, as well as theater, museums and abundant recreation. Known for its offerings of performing arts, visual arts, education, finance, advertising, and manufacturing, Minneapolis is also a hub of trade, industry, transportation and finance for the Upper Midwest.

In 1680, a French Franciscan priest, Father Louis Hennepin, was the area's first white man to arrive. In 1819, Fort Snelling was established to protect fur traders from the Sioux and Chippewa tribes. In 1848, two towns, St. Anthony (later named St. Paul), and Minneapolis, grew simultaneously, thus forming the metropolitan area known today as the Twin Cities. A tide of Swedish, German, and Norwegian immigrants came in the late nineteenth century, giving the city a decidedly Scandinavian flavor. Its many lakes gave Minneapolis its name, which comes from the Dakota word "minne," or "of the waters," and the Greek "polis," or city.

Minneapolis's traditional industries were lumber and flour milling. Since the 1950s, technology, including electronics, computers, and other related science industries, has played a vital role in the city's economy, as has printing and advertising.

The city's economy is fueled by an influx of urban dwellers and rapid growth of rental units to house them. The Pillsbury A-Mill Apartment Complex, and the 26 Story Apartment Building are just two of the city's multi-million dollar housing projects. In 2018, the city ended single-family zoning.

In addition, the U.S. Bank Stadium was funded by its NFL tenants, the Minnesota Vikings, and the state. During construction of the stadium—built on the site of the old Metrodome—the team played its 2014 and 2015 seasons in the TCF Bank Stadium at the University of Minnesota. Called "Minnesota's biggest-ever public works project," the stadium opened in 2016 with 66,000 seats, and expanded to 70,000 for the 2018 Super Bowl.

Minneapolis has the fourth-highest percentage of gay, lesbian, or bisexual people in the adult population, behind San Francisco, Seattle, and Atlanta. In 2013, the city was among 25 U.S. cities to receive the highest possible score from the Human Rights Campaign, signifying its support for LGBTQ residents. In contrast, the city has experienced continued unrest in the wake of the 2020 death of African American George Floyd at the hands of Minneapolis police.

> Artist Piotr Szyhalski's "Daily COVID-19 posters" began life on Instagram before being exhibited in art galleries with all 225 drawings now on display at the Minneapolis Institute of Art.

Well-known for its cultural and artistic offerings, Minneapolis occupies more theater seats per capita than any U.S. city outside of New York. The Minneapolis Institute of Arts has more than 100,000 pieces of art with renovated African Art galleries. A Michael Graves-designed wing holds contemporary and modern works. Other area attractions include the Science Museum of Minnesota, the Minneapolis Zoo and the Charles A. Lindbergh Historic Site.

More than five miles of downtown Minneapolis are connected by comfortable, climate-controlled glass "skyways" one flight above ground.

Minneapolis is home to award-winning restaurants and chefs. As of 2018, six Minneapolis-based chefs have won James Beard Foundation Awards, causing the city to be named one of the ten best places to visit in the world.

Minneapolis is a major transportation hub. The Minneapolis-St. Paul International Airport is the 16th busiest in North America in terms of number of travelers served, and supports $10.1 billion in business revenue.

The city also hosts a Northstar Corridor commuter line between downtown and Big Lake on existing railroad tracks, and a Green Line linking downtown, the University of Minnesota, and downtown St. Paul. Old rail lines and bridges within the city have been converted for bicycles and pedestrians.

Minneapolis is located at the confluence of the Mississippi and Minnesota rivers. Numerous lakes mark the surrounding region, with 22 within the city park system. The climate is predominantly continental, with extreme swings in seasonal temperatures. Blizzards, freezing rain, tornadoes, wind, and hail storms do occur. Due to the spring snow melt and excessive rain, the Mississippi River sees its share of floods.

Rankings

General Rankings

- *US News & World Report* conducted a survey of more than 3,000 people and analyzed the 150 largest metropolitan areas to determine what matters most when selecting the next place to live. Minneapolis ranked #22 out of the top 25 as having the best combination of desirable factors. Criteria: cost of living; quality of life; net migration; job market; desirability; and other factors. *realestate.usnews.com, "The 25 Best Places to Live in the U.S. in 2020-21," October 13, 2020*

- In its eighth annual survey, *Travel + Leisure* readers nominated their favorite small cities and towns in America—those with 100,000 or fewer residents—voting on numerous attractive features in categories including culture, food and drink, quality of life, style, and people. After 50,000 votes, Minneapolis was ranked #12 among the proposed favorites. *www.travelandleisure.com, "America's Favorite Cities," October 20, 2017*

- Minneapolis was selected as one of the best places to live in America by *Outside Magazine*. Criteria included population, park acreage, neighborhood and resident diversity, new and upcoming things of interest, and opportunities for outdoor adventure. *Outside Magazine, "The 12 Best Places to Live in 2019," July 11, 2019*

- The human resources consulting firm Mercer ranked 231 major cities worldwide in terms of overall quality of life. Minneapolis ranked #61. Criteria: political, social, economic, and socio-cultural factors; medical and health considerations; schools and education; public services and transportation; recreation; consumer goods; housing; and natural environment. *Mercer, "Mercer 2019 Quality of Living Survey," March 13, 2019*

- Minneapolis appeared on *Travel + Leisure's* list of the 15 best cities in the United States. The city was ranked #14. Criteria: sights/landmarks; culture; food; friendliness; shopping; and overall value. *Travel + Leisure, "The World's Best Awards 2020" July 8, 2020*

Business/Finance Rankings

- Based on metro area social media reviews, the employment opinion group Glassdoor surveyed 50 of the most populous U.S. metro areas and equally weighed cost of living, hiring opportunity, and job satisfaction to compose a list of "25 Best Cities for Jobs." Median pay and home value, and number of active job openings were also factored in. The Minneapolis metro area was ranked #21 in overall job satisfaction. *www.glassdoor.com, "Best Cities for Jobs," February 25, 2020*

- The Brookings Institution ranked the nation's largest cities based on income inequality. Minneapolis was ranked #31 (#1 = greatest inequality). Criteria: the "95/20 ratio," a figure representing the income at which a household earns more than 95 percent of all other households, divided by the income at which a household earns more than only 20 percent of all other households. *Brookings Institution, "Household Income Inequality, Largest Cities of 97 Large U.S. Metro Areas, 2014-2016," February 5, 2018*

- The Brookings Institution ranked the 100 largest metro areas in the U.S. based on income inequality. Minneapolis was ranked #85 (#1 = greatest inequality). Criteria: the "95/20 ratio," a figure representing the income at which a household earns more than 95 percent of all other households, divided by the income at which a household earns more than only 20 percent of all other households. *Brookings Institution, "Household Income Inequality, 100 Largest U.S. Metro Areas, 2014-2016," February 5, 2018*

- *Forbes* ranked the 100 largest metro areas in the U.S. in terms of the "Best Cities for Young Professionals." The Minneapolis metro area ranked #13 out of 25. Criteria: median rent of a two-bedroom apartment; job growth and unemployment rate; median salary of college graduates with 5 or less years of work experience; networking opportunities; social outlook; percentage of population 25 years of age and older with college degrees. *Forbes.com, "America's 25 Best Cities for Young Professionals in 2017," May 22, 2017*

- Payscale.com ranked the 32 largest metro areas in terms of wage growth. The Minneapolis metro area ranked #21. Criteria: private-sector and education professional wage growth between the 4th quarter of 2019 and the 4th quarter of 2020. *PayScale, "Wage Trends by Metro Area-4th Quarter," January 11, 2021*

- The Minneapolis metro area was identified as one of the most debt-ridden places in America by the finance site Credit.com. The metro area was ranked #22. Criteria: residents' average credit card debt as well as median income. *Credit.com, "25 Cities With the Most Credit Card Debt," February 28, 2018*

The Minneapolis metro area appeared on the Milken Institute "2021 Best Performing Cities" list. Rank: #104 out of 200 large metro areas (population over 250,000). Criteria: job growth; wage and salary growth; high-tech output growth; housing affordability; household broadband access. *Milken Institute, "Best-Performing Cities 2021," February 16, 2021*

Forbes ranked the 200 most populous metro areas to determine the nation's "Best Places for Business and Careers." The Minneapolis metro area was ranked #32. Criteria: costs (business and living); job growth (past and projected); income growth; quality of life; educational attainment (college and high school); projected economic growth; cultural and leisure opportunities; workplace tolerance laws; net migration patterns. *Forbes, "The Best Places for Business and Careers 2019: Seattle Still On Top," October 30, 2019*

Mercer Human Resources Consulting ranked 209 cities worldwide in terms of cost-of-living. Minneapolis ranked #69 (the lower the ranking, the higher the cost-of-living). The survey measured the comparative cost of over 200 items (such as housing, food, clothing, household goods, transportation, and entertainment) in each location. *Mercer, "2020 Cost of Living Survey," June 9, 2020*

Dating/Romance Rankings

Minneapolis was selected as one of the best cities for post grads by *Rent.com*. The city ranked among the top 10. Criteria: jobs per capita; unemployment rate; mean annual income; cost of living; rental inventory. *Rent.com, "Best Cities for College Grads," December 11, 2018*

Education Rankings

Personal finance website *WalletHub* analyzed the 150 largest U.S. metropolitan statistical areas to determine where the most educated Americans are putting their degrees to work. Criteria: education levels; percentage of workers with degrees; education quality and attainment gap; public school quality rankings; quality and enrollment of each metro area's universities. Minneapolis was ranked #19 (#1 = most educated city). *www.WalletHub.com, "Most and Least Educated Cities in America," July 20, 2020*

Minneapolis was selected as one of America's most literate cities. The city ranked #4 out of the 84 largest U.S. cities. Criteria: number of booksellers; library resources; Internet resources; educational attainment; periodical publishing resources; newspaper circulation. *Central Connecticut State University, "America's Most Literate Cities, 2018," February 2019*

Environmental Rankings

Niche compiled a list of the nation's snowiest cities, based on the National Oceanic and Atmospheric Administration's 30-year average snowfall data. Among cities with a population of at least 50,000, Minneapolis ranked #24. *Niche.com, Top 25 Snowiest Cities in America, December 10, 2018*

Sperling's BestPlaces assessed the 50 largest metropolitan areas of the United States for the likelihood of dangerously extreme weather events or earthquakes. In general the Southeast and South-Central regions have the highest risk of weather extremes and earthquakes, while the Pacific Northwest enjoys the lowest risk. Of the least risky metropolitan areas, the Minneapolis metro area was ranked #7. *www.bestplaces.net, "Avoid Natural Disasters: BestPlaces Reveals The Top 10 Safest Places to Live," October 25, 2017*

The U.S. Environmental Protection Agency (EPA) released a list of U.S. metropolitan areas with the most ENERGY STAR certified buildings in 2019. The Minneapolis metro area was ranked #15 out of 25. *U.S. Environmental Protection Agency, "2020 Energy Star Top Cities," March 2020*

Food/Drink Rankings

The U.S. Chamber of Commerce Foundation conducted an in-depth study on local food truck regulations, surveyed 288 food truck owners, and ranked 20 major American cities based on how friendly they are for operating a food truck. The compiled index assessed the following: procedures for obtaining permits and licenses; complying with restrictions; and financial obligations associated with operating a food truck. Minneapolis ranked #16 overall (1 being the best). *www.foodtrucknation.us, "Food Truck Nation," March 20, 2018*

Target Field was selected as one of PETA's "Top 10 Vegan-Friendly Ballparks" for 2019. The park ranked #3. *People for the Ethical Treatment of Animals, "Top 10 Vegan-Friendly Ballparks," May 23, 2019*

Health/Fitness Rankings

- For each of the 100 largest cities in the United States, the American Fitness Index®, published by the American College of Sports Medicine and the Anthem Foundation, evaluated community infrastructure and 33 health behaviors including preventive health, levels of chronic disease conditions, pedestrian safety, air quality, and community resources that support physical activity. Minneapolis ranked #3 for "community fitness." *americanfitnessindex.org, "2020 ACSM American Fitness Index Summary Report," July 14, 2020*

- The Minneapolis metro area was identified as one of the worst cities for bed bugs in America by pest control company Orkin. The area ranked #50 out of 50 based on the number of bed bug treatments Orkin performed from December 2019 to November 2020. *Orkin, "New Year, New Top City on Orkin's 2021 Bed Bug Cities List: Chicago," February 1, 2021*

- Minneapolis was identified as a "2021 Spring Allergy Capital." The area ranked #83 out of 100. Three groups of factors were used to identify the most challenging cities for people with allergies during the spring season: annual spring pollen levels; over the counter medicine use; number of board-certified allergy specialists. *Asthma and Allergy Foundation of America, "Spring Allergy Capitals 2021," February 23, 2021*

- Minneapolis was identified as a "2021 Fall Allergy Capital." The area ranked #76 out of 100. Three groups of factors were used to identify the most challenging cities for people with allergies during the fall season: annual fall pollen levels; over the counter medicine use; number of board-certified allergy specialists. *Asthma and Allergy Foundation of America, "Fall Allergy Capitals 2021," February 23, 2021*

- Minneapolis was identified as a "2019 Asthma Capital." The area ranked #87 out of the nation's 100 largest metropolitan areas. Criteria: estimated asthma prevalence; crude death rate from asthma; and ER visits due to asthma. Risk factors analyzed but not factored in the rankings: annual pollen score; annual air quality; public smoking laws; number of board-certified asthma specialists; rescue medication use; controller medication use; uninsured rate; poverty rate. *Asthma and Allergy Foundation of America, "Asthma Capitals 2019: The Most Challenging Places to Live With Asthma," May 7, 2019*

Pet Rankings

- Minneapolis appeared on *The Dogington Post* site as one of the top cities for dog lovers, ranking #15 out of 20. The real estate brokerage, Redfin and Rover, the largest pet sitter and dog walker network, compiled a list from over 14,000 U.S. cities to come up with a "Rover Rank." Criteria: highest count of dog walks, the city's Walk Score®, for-sale home listings that mention "dog," number of dog walkers and pet sitters and the hours spent and distance logged. *www.dogingtonpost.com, "The 20 Most Dog-Friendly Cities of 2019," April 4, 2019*

Real Estate Rankings

- FitSmallBusiness looked at 50 of the largest metropolitan areas in the U.S. to determine which metro was the best to start a real estate business. Data was compiled from such sources as: Zillow, Trulia, U.S. Census Bureau, and the Bureau of Labor Statistics. Criteria: location; inventory; annual wages; median sales price of homes; days on the market; median price cut percentage; and other factors that would influence real estate professional growth. The Minneapolis metro area ranked #22. *fitsmallbusiness.com, "The Best Cities to Become a Real Estate Agent in 2018," January 30, 2018*

- *WalletHub* compared the most populated U.S. cities to determine which had the best markets for real estate agents. Minneapolis ranked #89 where demand was high and pay was the best. Criteria: sales per agent; annual median wage for real-estate agents; monthly average starting salary for real estate agents; real estate job density and competition; unemployment rate; home turnover rate; housing-market health index; and other relevant metrics. *www.WalletHub.com, "2019's Best Places to Be a Real Estate Agent," April 24, 2019*

- Minneapolis was ranked #67 out of 268 metro areas in terms of housing affordability in 2020 by the National Association of Home Builders (#1 = most affordable). Criteria: the share of homes sold in that area affordable to a family earning the local median income, based on standard mortgage underwriting criteria. *National Association of Home Builders®, NAHB-Wells Fargo Housing Opportunity Index, 4th Quarter 2020*

Safety Rankings

- To identify the most dangerous cities in America, 24/7 Wall Street focused on violent crime categories—murder, non-negligent manslaughter, rape, robbery, and aggravated assault—and property crime as reported in the FBI's 2019 annual Uniform Crime Report. Criteria also included median income from American Community Survey and unemployment figures from Bureau of Labor Statistics. For cities with populations over 100,000, Minneapolis was ranked #36. *247wallst.com, "America's 50 Most Dangerous Cities" November 16, 2020*

- Allstate ranked the 200 largest cities in America in terms of driver safety. Minneapolis ranked #137. Criteria: internal property damage claims over a two-year period from January 2016 to December 2017. The report helps increase the importance of safety and awareness behind the wheel. *Allstate, "Allstate America's Best Drivers Report, 2019" June 24, 2019*

- Minneapolis was identified as one of the most dangerous cities in America by NeighborhoodScout. The city ranked #70 out of 100 (#1 = most dangerous). Criteria: number of violent crimes per 1,000 residents. The editors evaluated cities with 25,000 or more residents. *NeighborhoodScout.com, "2021 Top 100 Most Dangerous Cities in the U.S.," January 2, 2021*

- The National Insurance Crime Bureau ranked 384 metro areas in the U.S. in terms of per capita rates of vehicle theft. The Minneapolis metro area ranked #88 (#1 = highest rate). Criteria: number of vehicle theft offenses per 100,000 inhabitants in 2019. *National Insurance Crime Bureau, "Hot Spots 2019," July 21, 2020*

Seniors/Retirement Rankings

- From its Best Cities for Successful Aging indexes, the Milken Institute generated rankings for metropolitan areas, weighing data in nine categories—health care, wellness, living arrangements, transportation and convenience, financial characteristics, education, employment, community engagement, and overall livability. The Minneapolis metro area was ranked #14 overall in the large metro area category. *Milken Institute, "Best Cities for Successful Aging, 2017" March 14, 2017*

Sports/Recreation Rankings

- Minneapolis was chosen as one of America's best cities for bicycling. The city ranked #4 out of 50. Criteria: cycling infrastructure that is safe and friendly for all ages; energy and bike culture. The editors evaluated cities with populations of 100,000 or more. *Bicycling, "The 50 Best Bike Cities in America," October 10, 2018*

Transportation Rankings

- Business Insider presented an AllTransit Performance Score ranking of public transportation in major U.S. cities and towns, with populations over 250,000, in which Minneapolis earned the #12-ranked "Transit Score," awarded for frequency of service, access to jobs, quality and number of stops, and affordability. *www.businessinsider.com, "The 17 Major U.S. Cities with the Best Public Transportation," April 17, 2018*

Women/Minorities Rankings

- NerdWallet examined data for 529 U.S. cities and ranked them based on the environment for working women. Minneapolis ranked #2. Criteria: women's earnings; labor force participation rate; cost of living; unemployment rate. *www.nerdwallet.com, "Best Cities for Women in the Workforce 2016," April 4, 2016*

- Minneapolis was selected as one of the gayest cities in America by *The Advocate*. The city ranked #22 out of 25. Criteria, among many: Trans Pride parades/festivals; gay rugby teams; lesbian bars; LGBT centers; theater screenings of "Moonlight"; LGBT-inclusive nondiscrimination ordinances; and gay bowling teams. *The Advocate, "Queerest Cities in America 2017" January 12, 2017*

- Personal finance website *WalletHub* compared more than 180 U.S. cities across two key dimensions, "Hispanic Business-Friendliness" and "Hispanic Purchasing Power," to arrive at the most favorable conditions for Hispanic entrepreneurs. Minneapolis was ranked #131 out of 182. Criteria includes: share of Hispanic-Owned Businesses; Hispanic entrepreneurship rate to median annual income of Hispanics; Small Business-Friendliness score; cost of living; and number of Hispanics with at least a bachelor's degree. *WalletHub.com, "2019's Best Cities for Hispanic Entrepreneurs," May 1, 2019*

Miscellaneous Rankings

- *MoveHub* ranked 446 hipster cities across 20 countries, using its *alternative* Hipster Index and Minneapolis came out as #13 among the top 50. Criteria: population over 150,000; number of vintage boutiques; density of tattoo parlors; vegan places to eat; coffee shops; and density of vinyl record stores. *www.movehub.com, "The Hipster Index: Brighton Pips Portland to Global Top Spot," February 20, 2020*

- The watchdog site, Charity Navigator, conducted a study of charities in major markets both to analyze statistical differences in their financial, accountability, and transparency practices and to track year-to-year variations in individual philanthropic communities. The Minneapolis metro area was ranked #8 among the 30 metro markets in the rating category of Overall Score. *www.charitynavigator.org, "2017 Metro Market Study," May 1, 2017*

- *WalletHub* compared the 150 most populated U.S. cities to determine their operating efficiency. A "Quality of City Services" score was constructed for each city and then divided by the total budget per capita to reveal which were managed the best. Minneapolis ranked #89. Criteria: financial stability; economy; education; safety; health; infrastructure and pollution. *www.WalletHub.com, "2020's Best- & Worst-Run Cities in America," June 29, 2020*

- Minneapolis was selected as one of "America's Friendliest Cities." The city ranked #18 in the "Friendliest" category. Respondents to an online survey were asked to rate 38 top urban destinations in the United States as to general friendliness, as well as manners, politeness and warm disposition. *Travel + Leisure, "America's Friendliest Cities," October 20, 2017*

- The National Alliance to End Homelessness listed the 25 most populous metro areas with the highest rate of homelessness. The Minneapolis metro area had a high rate of homelessness. Criteria: number of homeless people per 10,000 population in 2016. *National Alliance to End Homelessness, "Homelessness in the 25 Most Populous U.S. Metro Areas," September 1, 2017*

Business Environment

DEMOGRAPHICS

Population Growth

Area	1990 Census	2000 Census	2010 Census	2019* Estimate	Population Growth (%)	
					1990-2019	2010-2019
City	368,383	382,618	382,578	420,324	14.1	9.9
MSA[1]	2,538,834	2,968,806	3,279,833	3,573,609	40.8	9.0
U.S.	248,709,873	281,421,906	308,745,538	324,697,795	30.6	5.2

Note: (1) Figures cover the Minneapolis-St. Paul-Bloomington, MN-WI Metropolitan Statistical Area; (*) 2015-2019 5-year estimated population
Source: U.S. Census Bureau, 1990 Census, Census 2000, Census 2010, 2015-2019 American Community Survey 5-Year Estimates

Household Size

Area	Persons in Household (%)							Average Household Size
	One	Two	Three	Four	Five	Six	Seven or More	
City	40.4	31.3	11.9	9.6	3.6	1.7	1.6	2.30
MSA[1]	27.9	34.2	14.8	13.7	5.9	2.1	1.4	2.60
U.S.	27.9	33.9	15.6	12.9	6.0	2.3	1.4	2.60

Note: (1) Figures cover the Minneapolis-St. Paul-Bloomington, MN-WI Metropolitan Statistical Area
Source: U.S. Census Bureau, 2015-2019 American Community Survey 5-Year Estimates

Race

Area	White Alone[2] (%)	Black Alone[2] (%)	Asian Alone[2] (%)	AIAN[3] Alone[2] (%)	NHOPI[4] Alone[2] (%)	Other Race Alone[2] (%)	Two or More Races (%)
City	63.6	19.2	5.9	1.4	0.0	5.0	4.8
MSA[1]	78.7	8.5	6.6	0.6	0.0	2.2	3.4
U.S.	72.5	12.7	5.5	0.8	0.2	4.9	3.3

Note: (1) Figures cover the Minneapolis-St. Paul-Bloomington, MN-WI Metropolitan Statistical Area; (2) Alone is defined as not being in combination with one or more other races; (3) American Indian and Alaska Native; (4) Native Hawaiian and Other Pacific Islander
Source: U.S. Census Bureau, 2015-2019 American Community Survey 5-Year Estimates

Hispanic or Latino Origin

Area	Total (%)	Mexican (%)	Puerto Rican (%)	Cuban (%)	Other (%)
City	9.6	5.8	0.5	0.2	3.1
MSA[1]	5.9	3.8	0.3	0.1	1.6
U.S.	18.0	11.2	1.7	0.7	4.3

Note: Persons of Hispanic or Latino origin can be of any race; (1) Figures cover the Minneapolis-St. Paul-Bloomington, MN-WI Metropolitan Statistical Area
Source: U.S. Census Bureau, 2015-2019 American Community Survey 5-Year Estimates

Ancestry

Area	German	Irish	English	American	Italian	Polish	French[2]	Scottish	Dutch
City	20.9	10.1	5.6	1.8	2.7	4.0	2.5	1.4	1.4
MSA[1]	29.1	10.9	5.6	3.1	2.6	4.4	3.3	1.3	1.5
U.S.	13.3	9.7	7.2	6.2	5.1	2.8	2.3	1.7	1.2

Note: Figures are the percentage of the total population reporting a particular ancestry. The nine most commonly reported ancestries in the U.S. are shown. Figures include multiple ancestries (e.g. if a person reported being Irish and Italian, they were included in both columns); (1) Figures cover the Minneapolis-St. Paul-Bloomington, MN-WI Metropolitan Statistical Area; (2) Excludes Basque
Source: U.S. Census Bureau, 2015-2019 American Community Survey 5-Year Estimates

Foreign-born Population

Area	Percent of Population Born in								
	Any Foreign Country	Asia	Mexico	Europe	Caribbean	Central America[2]	South America	Africa	Canada
City	15.6	4.0	2.4	1.3	0.3	0.4	1.3	5.6	0.3
MSA[1]	10.7	4.2	1.3	1.1	0.2	0.4	0.5	2.8	0.2
U.S.	13.6	4.2	3.5	1.5	1.3	1.1	1.0	0.7	0.2

Note: (1) Figures cover the Minneapolis-St. Paul-Bloomington, MN-WI Metropolitan Statistical Area; (2) Excludes Mexico.
Source: U.S. Census Bureau, 2015-2019 American Community Survey 5-Year Estimates

344 Minneapolis, Minnesota

Marital Status

Area	Never Married	Now Married[2]	Separated	Widowed	Divorced
City	50.5	34.4	1.6	2.9	10.5
MSA[1]	33.2	51.4	1.0	4.3	10.1
U.S.	33.4	48.1	1.9	5.8	10.9

Note: Figures are percentages and cover the population 15 years of age and older; (1) Figures cover the Minneapolis-St. Paul-Bloomington, MN-WI Metropolitan Statistical Area; (2) Excludes separated
Source: U.S. Census Bureau, 2015-2019 American Community Survey 5-Year Estimates

Disability by Age

Area	All Ages	Under 18 Years Old	18 to 64 Years Old	65 Years and Over
City	11.2	4.7	10.1	32.9
MSA[1]	9.9	3.7	8.0	30.0
U.S.	12.6	4.2	10.3	34.5

Note: Figures show percent of the civilian noninstitutionalized population that reported having a disability. Disability status is determined from six types of difficulty: vision, hearing, cognitive, ambulatory, self-care, and independent living. For children under 5 years old, hearing and vision difficulty are used to determine disability status. For children between the ages of 5 and 14, disability status is determined from hearing, vision, cognitive, ambulatory, and self-care difficulties. For people aged 15 years and older, they are considered to have a disability if they have difficulty with any one of the six difficulty types; Note: (1) Figures cover the Minneapolis-St. Paul-Bloomington, MN-WI Metropolitan Statistical Area
Source: U.S. Census Bureau, 2015-2019 American Community Survey 5-Year Estimates

Age

Area	Percent of Population									Median Age
	Under Age 5	Age 5–19	Age 20–34	Age 35–44	Age 45–54	Age 55–64	Age 65–74	Age 75–84	Age 85+	
City	6.5	16.9	32.0	13.8	10.8	10.1	6.3	2.6	1.1	32.3
MSA[1]	6.5	19.7	20.7	13.3	13.3	13.0	8.0	3.8	1.7	37.1
U.S.	6.1	19.1	20.7	12.6	13.0	12.9	9.1	4.6	1.9	38.1

Note: (1) Figures cover the Minneapolis-St. Paul-Bloomington, MN-WI Metropolitan Statistical Area
Source: U.S. Census Bureau, 2015-2019 American Community Survey 5-Year Estimates

Gender

Area	Males	Females	Males per 100 Females
City	212,823	207,501	102.6
MSA[1]	1,771,443	1,802,166	98.3
U.S.	159,886,919	164,810,876	97.0

Note: (1) Figures cover the Minneapolis-St. Paul-Bloomington, MN-WI Metropolitan Statistical Area
Source: U.S. Census Bureau, 2015-2019 American Community Survey 5-Year Estimates

Religious Groups by Family

Area	Catholic	Baptist	Non-Den.	Methodist[2]	Lutheran	LDS[3]	Pente-costal	Presby-terian[4]	Muslim[5]	Judaism
MSA[1]	21.7	2.5	3.0	2.8	14.5	0.6	1.8	1.9	0.4	0.7
U.S.	19.1	9.3	4.0	4.0	2.3	2.0	1.9	1.6	0.8	0.7

Note: Figures are the number of adherents as a percentage of the total population; (1) Figures cover the Minneapolis-St. Paul-Bloomington, MN-WI Metropolitan Statistical Area; (2) Methodist/Pietist; (3) Latter Day Saints; (4) Reformed; (5) Figures are estimates
Source: Association of Statisticians of American Religious Bodies, 2010 U.S. Religion Census: Religious Congregations & Membership Study

Religious Groups by Tradition

Area	Catholic	Evangelical Protestant	Mainline Protestant	Other Tradition	Black Protestant	Orthodox
MSA[1]	21.7	12.9	14.5	2.3	0.5	0.2
U.S.	19.1	16.2	7.3	4.3	1.6	0.3

Note: Figures are the number of adherents as a percentage of the total population; (1) Figures cover the Minneapolis-St. Paul-Bloomington, MN-WI Metropolitan Statistical Area
Source: Association of Statisticians of American Religious Bodies, 2010 U.S. Religion Census: Religious Congregations & Membership Study

ECONOMY

Gross Metropolitan Product

Area	2017	2018	2019	2020	Rank[2]
MSA[1]	260.9	273.1	284.6	296.0	14

Note: Figures are in billions of dollars; (1) Figures cover the Minneapolis-St. Paul-Bloomington, MN-WI Metropolitan Statistical Area; (2) Rank is based on 2018 data and ranges from 1 to 381
Source: U.S. Conference of Mayors, U.S. Metro Economies: GMP & Employment 2018-2020, September 2019

Economic Growth

Area	2015-17 (%)	2018 (%)	2019 (%)	2020 (%)	Rank[2]
MSA[1]	1.9	2.3	2.5	1.9	144
U.S.	1.9	2.9	2.3	2.1	—

Note: Figures are real gross metropolitan product (GMP) growth rates and represent average annual percent change; (1) Figures cover the Minneapolis-St. Paul-Bloomington, MN-WI Metropolitan Statistical Area; (2) Rank is based on 2017 2-year average annual percent change and ranges from 1 to 381
Source: U.S. Conference of Mayors, U.S. Metro Economies: GMP & Employment 2018-2020, September 2019

Metropolitan Area Exports

Area	2014	2015	2016	2017	2018	2019	Rank[2]
MSA[1]	21,198.2	19,608.6	18,329.2	19,070.9	20,016.2	18,633.0	22

Note: Figures are in millions of dollars; (1) Figures cover the Minneapolis-St. Paul-Bloomington, MN-WI Metropolitan Statistical Area; (2) Rank is based on 2019 data and ranges from 1 to 386
Source: U.S. Department of Commerce, International Trade Administration, Office of Trade and Economic Analysis, Industry and Analysis, Exports by Metropolitan Area, data extracted March 24, 2021

Building Permits

Area	Single-Family			Multi-Family			Total		
	2018	2019	Pct. Chg.	2018	2019	Pct. Chg.	2018	2019	Pct. Chg.
City	162	122	-24.7	3,463	4,691	35.5	3,625	4,813	32.8
MSA[1]	8,985	9,610	7.0	9,221	12,804	38.9	18,206	22,414	23.1
U.S.	855,300	862,100	0.7	473,500	523,900	10.6	1,328,800	1,386,000	4.3

Note: (1) Figures cover the Minneapolis-St. Paul-Bloomington, MN-WI Metropolitan Statistical Area; Figures represent new, privately-owned housing units authorized (unadjusted data); All permit data are based on estimates with imputation
Source: U.S. Census Bureau, Manufacturing, Mining, and Construction Statistics, Building Permits, 2018, 2019

Bankruptcy Filings

Area	Business Filings			Nonbusiness Filings		
	2019	2020	% Chg.	2019	2020	% Chg.
Hennepin County	62	92	48.4	2,032	1,552	-23.6
U.S.	22,780	21,655	-4.9	752,160	522,808	-30.5

Note: Business filings include Chapter 7, Chapter 9, Chapter 11, Chapter 12, Chapter 13, Chapter 15, and Section 304; Nonbusiness filings include Chapter 7, Chapter 11, and Chapter 13
Source: Administrative Office of the U.S. Courts, Business and Nonbusiness Bankruptcy, County Cases Commenced by Chapter of the Bankruptcy Code, During the 12-Month Period Ending December 31, 2019 and Business and Nonbusiness Bankruptcy, County Cases Commenced by Chapter of the Bankruptcy Code, During the 12-Month Period Ending December 31, 2020

Housing Vacancy Rates

Area	Gross Vacancy Rate[2] (%)			Year-Round Vacancy Rate[3] (%)			Rental Vacancy Rate[4] (%)			Homeowner Vacancy Rate[5] (%)		
	2018	2019	2020	2018	2019	2020	2018	2019	2020	2018	2019	2020
MSA[1]	3.9	4.4	4.7	3.3	3.8	3.7	4.1	4.1	4.0	0.4	0.5	0.5
U.S.	12.3	12.0	10.6	9.7	9.5	8.2	6.9	6.7	6.3	1.5	1.4	1.0

Note: (1) Figures cover the Minneapolis-St. Paul-Bloomington, MN-WI Metropolitan Statistical Area; (2) The percentage of the total housing inventory that is vacant; (3) The percentage of the housing inventory (excluding seasonal units) that is year-round vacant; (4) The percentage of rental inventory that is vacant for rent; (5) The percentage of homeowner inventory that is vacant for sale
Source: U.S. Census Bureau, Housing Vacancies and Homeownership Annual Statistics: 2018, 2019, 2020

INCOME

Income

Area	Per Capita ($)	Median Household ($)	Average Household ($)
City	38,808	62,583	89,282
MSA[1]	41,204	80,421	104,946
U.S.	34,103	62,843	88,607

Note: (1) Figures cover the Minneapolis-St. Paul-Bloomington, MN-WI Metropolitan Statistical Area
Source: U.S. Census Bureau, 2015-2019 American Community Survey 5-Year Estimates

Household Income Distribution

Area	Percent of Households Earning							
	Under $15,000	$15,000 -$24,999	$25,000 -$34,999	$35,000 -$49,999	$50,000 -$74,999	$75,000 -$99,999	$100,000 -$149,999	$150,000 and up
City	13.0	8.7	8.2	11.6	16.0	12.3	14.6	15.5
MSA[1]	6.7	6.1	6.7	10.6	16.4	14.2	19.4	19.7
U.S.	10.3	8.9	8.9	12.3	17.2	12.7	15.1	14.5

Note: (1) Figures cover the Minneapolis-St. Paul-Bloomington, MN-WI Metropolitan Statistical Area
Source: U.S. Census Bureau, 2015-2019 American Community Survey 5-Year Estimates

Minneapolis, Minnesota

Poverty Rate

Area	All Ages	Under 18 Years Old	18 to 64 Years Old	65 Years and Over
City	19.1	25.5	18.2	13.2
MSA[1]	8.6	11.0	8.1	6.6
U.S.	13.4	18.5	12.6	9.3

Note: Figures are percentage of people whose income during the past 12 months was below the poverty level;
(1) Figures cover the Minneapolis-St. Paul-Bloomington, MN-WI Metropolitan Statistical Area
Source: U.S. Census Bureau, 2015-2019 American Community Survey 5-Year Estimates

CITY FINANCES

City Government Finances

Component	2017 ($000)	2017 ($ per capita)
Total Revenues	1,295,426	3,152
Total Expenditures	1,652,051	4,020
Debt Outstanding	2,903,428	7,065
Cash and Securities[1]	2,942,802	7,161

Note: (1) Cash and security holdings of a government at the close of its fiscal year,
including those of its dependent agencies, utilities, and liquor stores.
Source: U.S. Census Bureau, State & Local Government Finances 2017

City Government Revenue by Source

Source	2017 ($000)	2017 ($ per capita)	2017 (%)
General Revenue			
From Federal Government	26,803	65	2.1
From State Government	92,021	224	7.1
From Local Governments	104,276	254	8.0
Taxes			
Property	313,081	762	24.2
Sales and Gross Receipts	112,060	273	8.7
Personal Income	0	0	0.0
Corporate Income	0	0	0.0
Motor Vehicle License	0	0	0.0
Other Taxes	46,114	112	3.6
Current Charges	384,162	935	29.7
Liquor Store	0	0	0.0
Utility	79,840	194	6.2
Employee Retirement	0	0	0.0

Source: U.S. Census Bureau, State & Local Government Finances 2017

City Government Expenditures by Function

Function	2017 ($000)	2017 ($ per capita)	2017 (%)
General Direct Expenditures			
Air Transportation	0	0	0.0
Corrections	0	0	0.0
Education	0	0	0.0
Employment Security Administration	0	0	0.0
Financial Administration	28,578	69	1.7
Fire Protection	62,357	151	3.8
General Public Buildings	0	0	0.0
Governmental Administration, Other	17,748	43	1.1
Health	25,494	62	1.5
Highways	186,498	453	11.3
Hospitals	0	0	0.0
Housing and Community Development	187,867	457	11.4
Interest on General Debt	105,161	255	6.4
Judicial and Legal	9,396	22	0.6
Libraries	7,544	18	0.5
Parking	43,608	106	2.6
Parks and Recreation	107,109	260	6.5
Police Protection	160,137	389	9.7
Public Welfare	0	0	0.0
Sewerage	90,039	219	5.5
Solid Waste Management	33,312	81	2.0
Veterans' Services	0	0	0.0
Liquor Store	0	0	0.0
Utility	69,757	169	4.2
Employee Retirement	0	0	0.0

Source: U.S. Census Bureau, State & Local Government Finances 2017

Minneapolis, Minnesota   347

EMPLOYMENT

Labor Force and Employment

Area	Civilian Labor Force			Workers Employed		
	Dec. 2019	Dec. 2020	% Chg.	Dec. 2019	Dec. 2020	% Chg.
City	245,206	236,236	-3.7	238,869	224,977	-5.8
MSA[1]	2,037,880	1,953,111	-4.2	1,976,964	1,864,309	-5.7
U.S.	164,007,000	160,017,000	-2.4	158,504,000	149,613,000	-5.6

Note: Data is not seasonally adjusted and covers workers 16 years of age and older; (1) Figures cover the Minneapolis-St. Paul-Bloomington, MN-WI Metropolitan Statistical Area
Source: Bureau of Labor Statistics, Local Area Unemployment Statistics

Unemployment Rate

Area	2020											
	Jan.	Feb.	Mar.	Apr.	May	Jun.	Jul.	Aug.	Sep.	Oct.	Nov.	Dec.
City	2.5	2.6	2.8	10.0	11.6	11.4	10.5	10.3	7.8	5.2	4.6	4.8
MSA[1]	3.1	3.1	3.1	9.2	10.1	9.2	8.2	7.8	5.9	4.2	4.0	4.5
U.S.	4.0	3.8	4.5	14.4	13.0	11.2	10.5	8.5	7.7	6.6	6.4	6.5

Note: Data is not seasonally adjusted and covers workers 16 years of age and older; (1) Figures cover the Minneapolis-St. Paul-Bloomington, MN-WI Metropolitan Statistical Area
Source: Bureau of Labor Statistics, Local Area Unemployment Statistics

Average Wages

Occupation	$/Hr.	Occupation	$/Hr.
Accountants and Auditors	37.40	Maintenance and Repair Workers	24.90
Automotive Mechanics	23.80	Marketing Managers	74.10
Bookkeepers	22.80	Network and Computer Systems Admin.	42.80
Carpenters	28.00	Nurses, Licensed Practical	25.10
Cashiers	13.30	Nurses, Registered	41.40
Computer Programmers	43.20	Nursing Assistants	18.60
Computer Systems Analysts	49.00	Office Clerks, General	20.50
Computer User Support Specialists	28.30	Physical Therapists	41.30
Construction Laborers	28.50	Physicians	113.40
Cooks, Restaurant	16.40	Plumbers, Pipefitters and Steamfitters	39.50
Customer Service Representatives	21.30	Police and Sheriff's Patrol Officers	39.00
Dentists	105.20	Postal Service Mail Carriers	25.50
Electricians	35.80	Real Estate Sales Agents	22.40
Engineers, Electrical	50.50	Retail Salespersons	15.70
Fast Food and Counter Workers	12.90	Sales Representatives, Technical/Scientific	43.90
Financial Managers	71.90	Secretaries, Exc. Legal/Medical/Executive	21.10
First-Line Supervisors of Office Workers	31.30	Security Guards	18.80
General and Operations Managers	62.40	Surgeons	n/a
Hairdressers/Cosmetologists	16.50	Teacher Assistants, Exc. Postsecondary*	16.70
Home Health and Personal Care Aides	14.30	Teachers, Secondary School, Exc. Sp. Ed.*	32.00
Janitors and Cleaners	17.00	Telemarketers	18.30
Landscaping/Groundskeeping Workers	18.20	Truck Drivers, Heavy/Tractor-Trailer	25.50
Lawyers	65.40	Truck Drivers, Light/Delivery Services	21.50
Maids and Housekeeping Cleaners	15.40	Waiters and Waitresses	15.00

Note: Wage data covers the Minneapolis-St. Paul-Bloomington, MN-WI Metropolitan Statistical Area;
(*) Hourly wages were calculated from annual wage data based on a 40 hour work week; n/a not available.
Source: Bureau of Labor Statistics, Metro Area Occupational Employment & Wage Estimates, May 2020

Employment by Industry

Sector	MSA[1]		U.S.
	Number of Employees	Percent of Total	Percent of Total
Construction, Mining, and Logging	80,700	4.4	5.5
Education and Health Services	328,400	17.8	16.3
Financial Activities	161,500	8.7	6.1
Government	238,500	12.9	15.2
Information	30,800	1.7	1.9
Leisure and Hospitality	98,200	5.3	9.0
Manufacturing	189,600	10.3	8.5
Other Services	68,000	3.7	3.8
Professional and Business Services	307,700	16.6	14.4
Retail Trade	181,400	9.8	10.9
Transportation, Warehousing, and Utilities	74,800	4.0	4.6
Wholesale Trade	88,500	4.8	3.9

Note: Figures are non-farm employment as of December 2020. Figures are not seasonally adjusted and include workers 16 years of age and older; (1) Figures cover the Minneapolis-St. Paul-Bloomington, MN-WI Metropolitan Statistical Area
Source: Bureau of Labor Statistics, Current Employment Statistics, Employment, Hours, and Earnings

Employment by Occupation

Occupation Classification	City (%)	MSA[1] (%)	U.S. (%)
Management, Business, Science, and Arts	50.8	44.6	38.5
Natural Resources, Construction, and Maintenance	3.5	6.5	8.9
Production, Transportation, and Material Moving	9.3	12.3	13.2
Sales and Office	18.5	21.3	21.6
Service	17.8	15.3	17.8

Note: Figures cover employed civilians 16 years of age and older; (1) Figures cover the Minneapolis-St. Paul-Bloomington, MN-WI Metropolitan Statistical Area
Source: U.S. Census Bureau, 2015-2019 American Community Survey 5-Year Estimates

Occupations with Greatest Projected Employment Growth: 2020 – 2022

Occupation[1]	2020 Employment	2022 Projected Employment	Numeric Employment Change	Percent Employment Change
Combined Food Preparation and Serving Workers, Including Fast Food	50,640	65,000	14,360	28.4
Waiters and Waitresses	35,550	48,150	12,600	35.4
Cooks, Restaurant	20,300	28,020	7,720	38.0
Personal Care Aides	74,560	80,400	5,840	7.8
Bartenders	12,560	17,580	5,020	40.0
First-Line Supervisors of Food Preparation and Serving Workers	11,980	15,660	3,680	30.7
Laborers and Freight, Stock, and Material Movers, Hand	42,090	45,760	3,670	8.7
General and Operations Managers	44,920	48,210	3,290	7.3
Janitors and Cleaners, Except Maids and Housekeeping Cleaners	44,350	47,440	3,090	7.0
Maids and Housekeeping Cleaners	12,000	15,050	3,050	25.4

Note: Projections cover Minnesota; (1) Sorted by numeric employment change
Source: www.projectionscentral.com, State Occupational Projections, 2020–2022 Short-Term Projections

Fastest-Growing Occupations: 2020 – 2022

Occupation[1]	2020 Employment	2022 Projected Employment	Numeric Employment Change	Percent Employment Change
Dancers	200	330	130	65.0
Hotel, Motel, and Resort Desk Clerks	2,550	4,130	1,580	62.0
Lodging Managers	280	450	170	60.7
Gaming Cage Workers	140	220	80	57.1
Baggage Porters and Bellhops	230	360	130	56.5
Choreographers	230	340	110	47.8
Gaming Dealers	1,160	1,710	550	47.4
Cooks, Short Order	460	670	210	45.7
Gaming Change Persons and Booth Cashiers	380	550	170	44.7
First-Line Supervisors of Gaming Workers	480	680	200	41.7

Note: Projections cover Minnesota; (1) Sorted by percent employment change and excludes occupations with numeric employment change less than 50
Source: www.projectionscentral.com, State Occupational Projections, 2020–2022 Short-Term Projections

TAXES

State Corporate Income Tax Rates

State	Tax Rate (%)	Income Brackets ($)	Num. of Brackets	Financial Institution Tax Rate (%)[a]	Federal Income Tax Ded.
Minnesota	9.8 (n)	Flat rate	1	9.8 (n)	No

Note: Tax rates as of January 1, 2021; (a) Rates listed are the corporate income tax rate applied to financial institutions or excise taxes based on income. Some states have other taxes based upon the value of deposits or shares; (n) In addition, Minnesota levies a 5.8% tentative minimum tax on Alternative Minimum Taxable Income. Minnesota also imposes a surtax ranging up to $10,480.
Source: Federation of Tax Administrators, State Corporate Income Tax Rates, January 1, 2021

State Individual Income Tax Rates

State	Tax Rate (%)	Income Brackets ($)	Personal Exemptions ($)			Standard Ded. ($)	
			Single	Married	Depend.	Single	Married
Minnesota (a)	5.35 - 9.85	27,230 - 166,041 (n)	(d)	(d)	4,350	12,550	25,100 (d)

Note: Tax rates as of January 1, 2021; Local- and county-level taxes are not included; Federal income tax is not deductible on state income tax returns; (a) 19 states have statutory provision for automatically adjusting to the rate of inflation the dollar values of the income tax brackets, standard deductions, and/or personal exemptions. Michigan indexes the personal exemption only. Oregon does not index the income brackets for $125,000 and over; (d) These states use the personal exemption/standard deduction amounts provided in the federal Internal Revenue Code; (n) The income brackets reported for Minnesota are for single individuals. For married couples filing jointly, the same tax rates apply to income brackets ranging from $39,810 to $276,200.
Source: Federation of Tax Administrators, State Individual Income Tax Rates, January 1, 2021

Various State Sales and Excise Tax Rates

State	State Sales Tax (%)	Gasoline[1] (¢/gal.)	Cigarette[2] ($/pack)	Spirits[3] ($/gal.)	Wine[4] ($/gal.)	Beer[5] ($/gal.)	Recreational Marijuana (%)
Minnesota	6.875	30.6	3.65	8.61	1.22	0.46	Not legal

Note: All tax rates as of January 1, 2021; (1) The American Petroleum Institute has developed a methodology for determining the average tax rate on a gallon of fuel. Rates may include any of the following: excise taxes, environmental fees, storage tank fees, other fees or taxes, general sales tax, and local taxes; (2) The federal excise tax of $1.0066 per pack and local taxes are not included; (3) Rates are those applicable to off-premise sales of 40% alcohol by volume (a.b.v.) distilled spirits in 750ml containers. Local excise taxes are excluded; (4) Rates are those applicable to off-premise sales of 11% a.b.v. non-carbonated wine in 750ml containers; (5) Rates are those applicable to off-premise sales of 4.7% a.b.v. beer in 12 ounce containers.
Source: Tax Foundation, 2021 Facts & Figures: How Does Your State Compare?

State Business Tax Climate Index Rankings

State	Overall Rank	Corporate Tax Rank	Individual Income Tax Rank	Sales Tax Rank	Property Tax Rank	Unemployment Insurance Tax Rank
Minnesota	46	45	46	28	31	32

Note: The index is a measure of how each state's tax laws affect economic performance. The lower the rank, the more favorable a state's tax system is for business. States without a given tax are given a ranking of 1. The scores/rankings for the District of Columbia do not affect other states. The 2021 index represents the tax climate as of July 1, 2020.
Source: Tax Foundation, State Business Tax Climate Index 2021

TRANSPORTATION

Means of Transportation to Work

Area	Car/Truck/Van		Public Transportation			Bicycle	Walked	Other Means	Worked at Home
	Drove Alone	Car-pooled	Bus	Subway	Railroad				
City	60.5	7.4	11.2	1.1	0.2	4.0	7.4	2.3	5.8
MSA[1]	77.5	8.1	4.1	0.2	0.2	0.8	2.3	1.1	5.8
U.S.	76.3	9.0	2.4	1.9	0.6	0.5	2.7	1.4	5.2

Note: Figures are percentages and cover workers 16 years of age and older; (1) Figures cover the Minneapolis-St. Paul-Bloomington, MN-WI Metropolitan Statistical Area
Source: U.S. Census Bureau, 2015-2019 American Community Survey 5-Year Estimates

Travel Time to Work

Area	Less Than 10 Minutes	10 to 19 Minutes	20 to 29 Minutes	30 to 44 Minutes	45 to 59 Minutes	60 to 89 Minutes	90 Minutes or More
City	8.1	32.0	30.9	20.9	4.2	2.8	1.2
MSA[1]	10.2	27.3	25.1	23.7	8.1	4.3	1.4
U.S.	12.2	28.4	20.8	20.8	8.3	6.4	2.9

Note: Note: Figures are percentages and include workers 16 years old and over; (1) Figures cover the Minneapolis-St. Paul-Bloomington, MN-WI Metropolitan Statistical Area
Source: U.S. Census Bureau, 2015-2019 American Community Survey 5-Year Estimates

Key Congestion Measures

Measure	1982	1992	2002	2012	2017
Annual Hours of Delay, Total (000)	11,029	34,442	73,265	90,573	103,695
Annual Hours of Delay, Per Auto Commuter	12	30	48	50	56
Annual Congestion Cost, Total (million $)	82	361	981	1,601	1,896
Annual Congestion Cost, Per Auto Commuter ($)	233	501	831	805	894

Note: Covers the Minneapolis-St. Paul MN-WI urban area
Source: Texas A&M Transportation Institute, 2019 Urban Mobility Report

Minneapolis, Minnesota

Freeway Travel Time Index

Measure	1982	1987	1992	1997	2002	2007	2012	2017
Urban Area Index[1]	1.07	1.11	1.16	1.24	1.27	1.27	1.26	1.25
Urban Area Rank[1,2]	35	29	23	11	14	20	21	25

Note: Freeway Travel Time Index—the ratio of travel time in the peak period to the travel time at free-flow conditions. For example, a value of 1.30 indicates a 20-minute free-flow trip takes 26 minutes in the peak (20 minutes x 1.30 = 26 minutes); (1) Covers the Minneapolis-St. Paul MN-WI urban area; (2) Rank is based on 101 larger urban areas (#1 = highest travel time index)
Source: Texas A&M Transportation Institute, 2019 Urban Mobility Report

Public Transportation

Agency Name / Mode of Transportation	Vehicles Operated in Maximum Service[1]	Annual Unlinked Passenger Trips[2] (in thous.)	Annual Passenger Miles[3] (in thous.)
Metro Transit			
Bus (directly operated)	744	51,860.0	218,756.7
Commuter Rail (purchased transportation)	20	767.8	18,965.6
Light Rail (directly operated)	76	25,299.4	100,499.4

Note: (1) Number of revenue vehicles operated by the given mode and type of service to meet the annual maximum service requirement. This is the revenue vehicle count during the peak season of the year; on the week and day that maximum service is provided. Vehicles operated in maximum service (VOMS) exclude atypical days and one-time special events; (2) Number of passengers who boarded public transportation vehicles. Passengers are counted each time they board a vehicle no matter how many vehicles they use to travel from their origin to their destination. (3) Sum of the distances ridden by all passengers during the entire fiscal year.
Source: Federal Transit Administration, National Transit Database, 2019

Air Transportation

Airport Name and Code / Type of Service	Passenger Airlines[1]	Passenger Enplanements	Freight Carriers[2]	Freight (lbs)
Minneapolis-St. Paul International (MSP)				
Domestic service (U.S. carriers - 2020)	31	6,685,820	17	168,312,953
International service (U.S. carriers - 2019)	8	1,401,400	5	20,852,112

Note: (1) Includes all U.S.-based major, minor and commuter airlines that carried at least one passenger during the year; (2) Includes all U.S.-based airlines and freight carriers that transported at least one pound of freight during the year.
Source: Bureau of Transportation Statistics, The Intermodal Transportation Database, Air Carriers: T-100 Domestic Market (U.S. Carriers), 2020; Bureau of Transportation Statistics, The Intermodal Transportation Database, Air Carriers: T-100 International Market (U.S. Carriers), 2019

BUSINESSES

Major Business Headquarters

Company Name	Industry	Rankings	
		Fortune[1]	Forbes[2]
Ameriprise Financial	Diversified Financials	245	-
Cargill	Food, Drink & Tobacco	-	2
General Mills	Food Consumer Products	192	-
Mortenson	Construction	-	84
Target	General Merchandisers	37	-
Thrivent Financial for Lutherans	Insurance, Life, Health (Mutual)	368	-
U.S. Bancorp	Commercial Banks	113	-
Xcel Energy	Utilities, Gas and Electric	276	-

Note: (1) Companies that produce a 10-K are ranked 1 to 500 based on 2019 revenue; (2) All private companies with at least $2 billion in annual revenue through the end of their most current fiscal year are ranked 1 to 219; companies listed are headquartered in the city; dashes indicate no ranking
Source: Fortune, "Fortune 500," June/July 2020; Forbes, "America's Largest Private Companies," 2020

Fastest-Growing Businesses

According to *Inc.*, Minneapolis is home to two of America's 500 fastest-growing private companies: **Total Expert** (#288); **phData** (#484). Criteria: must be an independent, privately-held, for-profit, U.S. corporation, proprietorship or partnership as of December 31, 2019; revenues must be at least $100,000 in 2016 and $2 million in 2019; must have four-year operating/sales history. *Inc., "America's 500 Fastest-Growing Private Companies," 2020*

According to *Initiative for a Competitive Inner City (ICIC)*, Minneapolis is home to one of America's 100 fastest-growing "inner city" companies: **On-Demand Group** (#54). Criteria for inclusion: company must be headquartered in or have 51 percent or more of its physical operations in an economically distressed urban area; must be an independent, for-profit corporation, partnership or proprietorship; must have 10 or more employees and have a five-year sales history that includes sales of at least $200,000 in the base year and at least $1 million in the current year with no decrease in sales over the two most recent years. Companies were ranked overall by revenue growth over the five-year period between 2015 and 2019. *Initiative for a Competitive Inner City (ICIC), "Inner City 100 Companies," 2020*

According to Deloitte, Minneapolis is home to one of North America's 500 fastest-growing high-technology companies: **Total Expert** (#82). Companies are ranked by percentage growth in revenue over a four-year period. Criteria for inclusion: company must be headquartered within North America; must own proprietary intellectual property or technology that is sold to customers in products that contributes to a significant portion of the company's operating revenue; must have been in business for a minumum of four years with 2016 operating revenues of at least $50,000 USD/CD and 2019 operating revenues of at least $5 million USD/CD. *Deloitte, 2020 Technology Fast 500*™

352 Minneapolis, Minnesota

Living Environment

COST OF LIVING

Cost of Living Index

Composite Index	Groceries	Housing	Utilities	Trans-portation	Health Care	Misc. Goods/ Services
105.2	102.6	103.6	97.2	100.6	102.4	111.3

Note: The Cost of Living Index measures regional differences in the cost of consumer goods and services, excluding taxes and non-consumer expenditures, for professional and managerial households in the top income quintile. It is based on more than 50,000 prices covering almost 60 different items for which prices are collected three times a year by chambers of commerce, economic development organizations or university applied economic centers in each participating urban area. The numbers shown should be read as a percentage above or below the national average of 100. For example, a value of 115.4 in the groceries column indicates that grocery prices are 15.4% higher than the national average. Small differences in the index numbers should not be interpreted as significant; Figures cover the Minneapolis MN urban area.
Source: The Council for Community and Economic Research, Cost of Living Index, 2020

Grocery Prices

Area[1]	T-Bone Steak ($/pound)	Frying Chicken ($/pound)	Whole Milk ($/half gal.)	Eggs ($/dozen)	Orange Juice ($/64 oz.)	Coffee ($/11.5 oz.)
City[2]	13.63	2.10	2.60	1.81	3.71	4.67
Avg.	11.78	1.39	2.05	1.47	3.57	4.34
Min.	8.03	0.94	1.03	0.74	2.94	3.02
Max.	15.86	2.65	4.31	3.77	5.44	8.69

*Note: (1) Values for the local area are compared with the average, minimum and maximum values for all 284 areas in the Cost of Living Index; (2) Figures cover the Minneapolis MN urban area; **T-Bone Steak** (price per pound); **Frying Chicken** (price per pound, whole fryer); **Whole Milk** (half gallon carton); **Eggs** (price per dozen, Grade A, large); **Orange Juice** (64 oz. Tropicana or Florida Natural); **Coffee** (11.5 oz. can, vacuum-packed, Maxwell House, Hills Bros, or Folgers).*
Source: The Council for Community and Economic Research, Cost of Living Index, 2020

Housing and Utility Costs

Area[1]	New Home Price ($)	Apartment Rent ($/month)	All Electric ($/month)	Part Electric ($/month)	Other Energy ($/month)	Telephone ($/month)
City[2]	386,294	1,204	-	95.03	65.60	181.00
Avg.	368,594	1,168	170.86	100.47	65.28	184.30
Min.	190,567	502	91.58	31.42	26.08	169.60
Max.	2,227,806	4,738	470.38	280.31	280.06	206.50

*Note: (1) Values for the local area are compared with the average, minimum and maximum values for all 284 areas in the Cost of Living Index; (2) Figures cover the Minneapolis MN urban area; **New Home Price** (2,400 sf living area, 8,000 sf lot, in urban area with full utilities); **Apartment Rent** (950 sf 2 bedroom/1.5 or 2 bath, unfurnished, excluding all utilities except water); **All Electric** (average monthly cost for an all-electric home); **Part Electric** (average monthly cost for a part-electric home); **Other Energy** (average monthly cost for natural gas, fuel oil, coal, wood, and any other forms of energy except electricity); **Telephone** (price includes the base monthly rate plus taxes and fees for three lines of mobile phone service).*
Source: The Council for Community and Economic Research, Cost of Living Index, 2020

Health Care, Transportation, and Other Costs

Area[1]	Doctor ($/visit)	Dentist ($/visit)	Optometrist ($/visit)	Gasoline ($/gallon)	Beauty Salon ($/visit)	Men's Shirt ($)
City[2]	147.85	86.94	89.59	2.06	34.39	34.39
Avg.	115.44	99.32	108.10	2.21	39.27	31.37
Min.	36.68	59.00	51.36	1.71	19.00	11.00
Max.	219.00	153.10	250.97	3.46	82.05	58.33

*Note: (1) Values for the local area are compared with the average, minimum and maximum values for all 284 areas in the Cost of Living Index; (2) Figures cover the Minneapolis MN urban area; **Doctor** (general practitioners routine exam of an established patient); **Dentist** (adult teeth cleaning and periodic oral examination); **Optometrist** (full vision eye exam for established adult patient); **Gasoline** (one gallon regular unleaded, national brand, including all taxes, cash price at self-service pump if available); **Beauty Salon** (woman's shampoo, trim, and blow-dry); **Men's Shirt** (cotton/polyester dress shirt, pinpoint weave, long sleeves).*
Source: The Council for Community and Economic Research, Cost of Living Index, 2020

HOUSING

Homeownership Rate

Area	2012 (%)	2013 (%)	2014 (%)	2015 (%)	2016 (%)	2017 (%)	2018 (%)	2019 (%)	2020 (%)
MSA[1]	70.8	71.7	69.7	67.9	69.1	70.1	67.8	70.2	73.0
U.S.	65.4	65.1	64.5	63.7	63.4	63.9	64.4	64.6	66.6

Note: (1) Figures cover the Minneapolis-St. Paul-Bloomington, MN-WI Metropolitan Statistical Area
Source: U.S. Census Bureau, Housing Vacancies and Homeownership Annual Statistics: 2012-2020

House Price Index (HPI)

Area	National Ranking[2]	Quarterly Change (%)	One-Year Change (%)	Five-Year Change (%)	Since 1991Q1 (%)
MSA[1]	157	1.56	5.70	30.96	210.96
U.S.[3]	–	3.81	10.77	38.99	205.12

Note: The HPI is a weighted repeat sales index. It measures average price changes in repeat sales or refinancings on the same properties. This information is obtained by reviewing repeat mortgage transactions on single-family properties whose mortgages have been purchased or securitized by Fannie Mae or Freddie Mac since January 1975; (1) Figures cover the Minneapolis-St. Paul-Bloomington, MN-WI Metropolitan Statistical Area; (2) Rankings are based on annual percentage change for all metro areas containing at least 15,000 transactions over the last 10 years and ranges from 1 to 253; (3) figures based on a weighted average of Census Division estimates using a seasonally adjusted, purchase-only index; all figures are for the period ending December 31, 2020
Source: Federal Housing Finance Agency, Change in Metropolitan Area House Price Indexes, April 7, 2021

Median Single-Family Home Prices

Area	2018	2019	2020[p]	Percent Change 2019 to 2020
MSA[1]	273.4	288.6	315.2	9.2
U.S. Average	261.6	274.6	299.9	9.2

Note: Figures are median sales prices of existing single-family homes in thousands of dollars; (p) preliminary; (1) Figures cover the Minneapolis-St. Paul-Bloomington, MN-WI Metropolitan Statistical Area
Source: National Association of Realtors, Median Sales Price of Existing Single-Family Homes for Metropolitan Areas, 4th Quarter 2020

Qualifying Income Based on Median Sales Price of Existing Single-Family Homes

Area	With 5% Down ($)	With 10% Down ($)	With 20% Down ($)
MSA[1]	61,150	57,931	51,494
U.S. Average	59,266	56,147	49,908

Note: Figures are preliminary; Qualifying income is based on a mortgage rate of 2.81%. Monthly principal and interest payment is limited to 25% of income; (1) Figures cover the Minneapolis-St. Paul-Bloomington, MN-WI Metropolitan Statistical Area
Source: National Association of Realtors, Qualifying Income Based on Median Sales Price of Existing Single-Family Homes for Metropolitan Areas, 4th Quarter 2020

Home Value Distribution

Area	Under $50,000	$50,000 -$99,999	$100,000 -$149,999	$150,000 -$199,999	$200,000 -$299,999	$300,000 -$499,999	$500,000 -$999,999	$1,000,000 or more
City	1.4	4.0	10.7	16.1	31.3	24.7	10.0	1.9
MSA[1]	2.7	2.7	7.9	16.7	32.8	27.1	8.8	1.4
U.S.	6.9	12.0	13.3	14.0	19.6	19.3	11.4	3.4

Note: Figures are percentages and cover owner-occupied housing units; (1) Figures cover the Minneapolis-St. Paul-Bloomington, MN-WI Metropolitan Statistical Area
Source: U.S. Census Bureau, 2015-2019 American Community Survey 5-Year Estimates

Year Housing Structure Built

Area	2010 or Later	2000 -2009	1990 -1999	1980 -1989	1970 -1979	1960 -1969	1950 -1959	1940 -1949	Before 1940	Median Year
City	5.8	6.7	3.6	6.8	9.0	7.5	9.5	6.8	44.3	1948
MSA[1]	5.1	14.3	14.4	14.5	14.7	9.8	9.7	3.7	13.9	1979
U.S.	5.2	14.0	13.9	13.4	15.2	10.6	10.3	4.9	12.6	1978

Note: Figures are percentages except for Median Year; Note: (1) Figures cover the Minneapolis-St. Paul-Bloomington, MN-WI Metropolitan Statistical Area
Source: U.S. Census Bureau, 2015-2019 American Community Survey 5-Year Estimates

Gross Monthly Rent

Area	Under $500	$500 -$999	$1,000 -$1,499	$1,500 -$1,999	$2,000 -$2,499	$2,500 -$2,999	$3,000 and up	Median ($)
City	12.8	35.3	30.2	14.4	4.7	1.4	1.1	1,027
MSA[1]	9.2	32.4	35.9	16.1	4.2	1.2	1.1	1,102
U.S.	9.4	36.2	30.0	14.0	5.6	2.4	2.4	1,062

Note: Figures are percentages except for Median; Gross rent is the contract rent plus the estimated average monthly cost of utilities (electricity, gas, and water and sewer) and fuels (oil, coal, kerosene, wood, etc.) if these are paid by the renter (or paid for the renter by someone else); (1) Figures cover the Minneapolis-St. Paul-Bloomington, MN-WI Metropolitan Statistical Area
Source: U.S. Census Bureau, 2015-2019 American Community Survey 5-Year Estimates

HEALTH

Health Risk Factors

Category	MSA[1] (%)	U.S. (%)
Adults aged 18–64 who have any kind of health care coverage	91.0	87.3
Adults who reported being in good or better health	88.5	82.4
Adults who have been told they have high blood cholesterol	28.1	33.0
Adults who have been told they have high blood pressure	24.8	32.3
Adults who are current smokers	13.2	17.1
Adults who currently use E-cigarettes	3.4	4.6
Adults who currently use chewing tobacco, snuff, or snus	3.9	4.0
Adults who are heavy drinkers[2]	6.6	6.3
Adults who are binge drinkers[3]	20.5	17.4
Adults who are overweight (BMI 25.0 - 29.9)	35.6	35.3
Adults who are obese (BMI 30.0 - 99.8)	26.0	31.3
Adults who participated in any physical activities in the past month	78.1	74.4
Adults who always or nearly always wears a seat belt	97.3	94.3

Note: (1) Figures cover the Minneapolis-St. Paul-Bloomington, MN-WI Metropolitan Statistical Area; (2) Heavy drinkers are classified as adult men having more than 14 drinks per week and adult women having more than 7 drinks per week; (3) Binge drinkers are classified as males having five or more drinks on one occasion or females having four or more drinks on one occasion
Source: Centers for Disease Control and Prevention, Behaviorial Risk Factor Surveillance System, SMART: Selected Metropolitan Area Risk Trends, 2017

Acute and Chronic Health Conditions

Category	MSA[1] (%)	U.S. (%)
Adults who have ever been told they had a heart attack	3.0	4.2
Adults who have ever been told they have angina or coronary heart disease	3.0	3.9
Adults who have ever been told they had a stroke	2.0	3.0
Adults who have ever been told they have asthma	10.8	14.2
Adults who have ever been told they have arthritis	17.4	24.9
Adults who have ever been told they have diabetes[2]	6.7	10.5
Adults who have ever been told they had skin cancer	5.7	6.2
Adults who have ever been told they had any other types of cancer	6.3	7.1
Adults who have ever been told they have COPD	3.9	6.5
Adults who have ever been told they have kidney disease	2.5	3.0
Adults who have ever been told they have a form of depression	19.2	20.5

Note: (1) Figures cover the Minneapolis-St. Paul-Bloomington, MN-WI Metropolitan Statistical Area; (2) Figures do not include pregnancy-related, borderline, or pre-diabetes
Source: Centers for Disease Control and Prevention, Behaviorial Risk Factor Surveillance System, SMART: Selected Metropolitan Area Risk Trends, 2017

Health Screening and Vaccination Rates

Category	MSA[1] (%)	U.S. (%)
Adults aged 65+ who have had flu shot within the past year	65.7	60.7
Adults aged 65+ who have ever had a pneumonia vaccination	78.7	75.4
Adults who have ever been tested for HIV	35.8	36.1
Adults who have ever had the shingles or zoster vaccine?	33.6	28.9
Adults who have had their blood cholesterol checked within the last five years	87.9	85.9

Note: n/a not available; (1) Figures cover the Minneapolis-St. Paul-Bloomington, MN-WI Metropolitan Statistical Area.
Source: Centers for Disease Control and Prevention, Behaviorial Risk Factor Surveillance System, SMART: Selected Metropolitan Area Risk Trends, 2017

Disability Status

Category	MSA[1] (%)	U.S. (%)
Adults who reported being deaf	5.6	6.7
Are you blind or have serious difficulty seeing, even when wearing glasses?	2.6	4.5
Are you limited in any way in any of your usual activities due of arthritis?	8.1	12.9
Do you have difficulty doing errands alone?	4.8	6.8
Do you have difficulty dressing or bathing?	2.5	3.6
Do you have serious difficulty concentrating/remembering/making decisions?	9.2	10.7
Do you have serious difficulty walking or climbing stairs?	9.1	13.6

Note: (1) Figures cover the Minneapolis-St. Paul-Bloomington, MN-WI Metropolitan Statistical Area.
Source: Centers for Disease Control and Prevention, Behaviorial Risk Factor Surveillance System, SMART: Selected Metropolitan Area Risk Trends, 2017

Mortality Rates for the Top 10 Causes of Death in the U.S.

ICD-10[a] Sub-Chapter	ICD-10[a] Code	Age-Adjusted Mortality Rate[1] per 100,000 population	
		County[2]	U.S.
Malignant neoplasms	C00-C97	138.1	149.2
Ischaemic heart diseases	I20-I25	50.6	90.5
Other forms of heart disease	I30-I51	38.8	52.2
Chronic lower respiratory diseases	J40-J47	28.9	39.6
Other degenerative diseases of the nervous system	G30-G31	36.4	37.6
Cerebrovascular diseases	I60-I69	31.8	37.2
Other external causes of accidental injury	W00-X59	44.0	36.1
Organic, including symptomatic, mental disorders	F01-F09	46.1	29.4
Hypertensive diseases	I10-I15	17.5	24.1
Diabetes mellitus	E10-E14	17.2	21.5

Note: (a) ICD-10 = International Classification of Diseases 10th Revision; (1) Mortality rates are a three-year average covering 2017-2019; (2) Figures cover Hennepin County.
Source: Centers for Disease Control and Prevention, National Center for Health Statistics. Underlying Cause of Death 1999-2019 on CDC WONDER Online Database

Mortality Rates for Selected Causes of Death

ICD-10[a] Sub-Chapter	ICD-10[a] Code	Age-Adjusted Mortality Rate[1] per 100,000 population	
		County[2]	U.S.
Assault	X85-Y09	3.6	6.0
Diseases of the liver	K70-K76	13.4	14.4
Human immunodeficiency virus (HIV) disease	B20-B24	1.3	1.5
Influenza and pneumonia	J09-J18	8.7	13.8
Intentional self-harm	X60-X84	11.1	14.1
Malnutrition	E40-E46	1.4	2.3
Obesity and other hyperalimentation	E65-E68	2.2	2.1
Renal failure	N17-N19	7.7	12.6
Transport accidents	V01-V99	5.1	12.3
Viral hepatitis	B15-B19	0.9	1.2

Note: (a) ICD-10 = International Classification of Diseases 10th Revision; (1) Mortality rates are a three-year average covering 2017-2019; (2) Figures cover Hennepin County; Data are suppressed when the data meet the criteria for confidentiality constraints; Mortality rates are flagged as unreliable when the rate would be calculated with a numerator of 20 or less.
Source: Centers for Disease Control and Prevention, National Center for Health Statistics. Underlying Cause of Death 1999-2019 on CDC WONDER Online Database

Health Insurance Coverage

Area	With Health Insurance	With Private Health Insurance	With Public Health Insurance	Without Health Insurance	Population Under Age 19 Without Health Insurance
City	93.4	66.8	34.5	6.6	3.4
MSA[1]	95.7	78.0	29.6	4.3	3.0
U.S.	91.2	67.9	35.1	8.8	5.1

Note: Figures are percentages that cover the civilian noninstitutionalized population; (1) Figures cover the Minneapolis-St. Paul-Bloomington, MN-WI Metropolitan Statistical Area
Source: U.S. Census Bureau, 2015-2019 American Community Survey 5-Year Estimates

Number of Medical Professionals

Area	MDs[3]	DOs[3,4]	Dentists	Podiatrists	Chiropractors	Optometrists
County[1] (number)	6,595	280	1,263	66	927	272
County[1] (rate[2])	524.3	22.3	99.8	5.2	73.2	21.5
U.S. (rate[2])	282.9	22.7	71.2	6.2	28.1	16.9

27053
Note: Data as of 2019 unless noted; (1) Data covers Hennepin County; (2) Rate per 100,000 population; (3) Data as of 2018 and includes all active, non-federal physicians; (4) Doctor of Osteopathic Medicine
Source: U.S. Department of Health and Human Services, Health Resources and Services Administration, Bureau of Health Professions, Area Resource File (ARF) 2019-2020

Best Hospitals

According to *U.S. News,* the Minneapolis-St. Paul-Bloomington, MN-WI metro area is home to two of the best hospitals in the U.S.: **Abbott Northwestern Hospital** (2 adult specialties); **Minneapolis Heart Institute at Abbott Northwestern Hospital** (2 adult specialties). The hospitals listed were nationally ranked in at least one of 16 adult or 10 pediatric specialties. Only 134 hospitals nationwide were nationally ranked in one or more adult or pediatric specialty; this number increases to 178 counting specialized centers within hospitals. Twenty hospitals in the U.S. made the Honor Roll. The Best Hospitals Honor Roll takes both the national rankings and the procedure and condition ratings into account. Hospitals received points if they were nationally ranked in one of the 16 adult specialties—the higher they ranked, the more points they got—and how many ratings of "high performing"

Minneapolis, Minnesota

they earned in the 10 procedures and conditions. *U.S. News Online, "America's Best Hospitals 2020-21"*

According to *U.S. News,* the Minneapolis-St. Paul-Bloomington, MN-WI metro area is home to two of the best children's hospitals in the U.S.: **Children's Hospitals and Clinics of Minnesota** (1 pediatric specialty); **University of Minnesota Masonic Children's Hospital** (4 pediatric specialties). The hospitals listed were highly ranked in at least one of 10 pediatric specialties. Eighty-eight children's hospitals in the U.S. were nationally ranked in at least one specialty. Hospitals received points for being ranked in a specialty, and the 10 hospitals with the most points across the 10 specialties make up the Honor Roll. *U.S. News Online, "America's Best Children's Hospitals 2020-21"*

EDUCATION

Public School District Statistics

District Name	Schls	Pupils	Pupil/ Teacher Ratio	Minority Pupils[1] (%)	Free Lunch Eligible[2] (%)	IEP[3] (%)
Minneapolis Public School District	102	35,580	14.0	64.6	50.4	18.7
Minnesota Transitions Charter	7	3,423	19.4	38.0	48.4	17.4

Note: Table includes school districts with 2,000 or more students; (1) Percentage of students that are not non-Hispanic white; (2) Percentage of students that are eligible for the free lunch program; (3) Percentage of students that have an Individualized Education Program.
Source: U.S. Department of Education, National Center for Education Statistics, Common Core of Data, Local Education Agency (School District) Universe Survey: School Year 2018-2019; U.S. Department of Education, National Center for Education Statistics, Common Core of Data, Public Elementary/Secondary School Universe Survey: School Year 2018-2019

Highest Level of Education

Area	Less than H.S.	H.S. Diploma	Some College, No Deg.	Associate Degree	Bachelor's Degree	Master's Degree	Prof. School Degree	Doctorate Degree
City	10.0	15.1	17.1	7.3	30.4	13.6	4.0	2.5
MSA[1]	6.4	21.2	20.0	10.4	27.4	10.4	2.6	1.6
U.S.	12.0	27.0	20.4	8.5	19.8	8.8	2.1	1.4

Note: Figures cover persons age 25 and over; (1) Figures cover the Minneapolis-St. Paul-Bloomington, MN-WI Metropolitan Statistical Area
Source: U.S. Census Bureau, 2015-2019 American Community Survey 5-Year Estimates

Educational Attainment by Race

Area	High School Graduate or Higher (%)					Bachelor's Degree or Higher (%)				
	Total	White	Black	Asian	Hisp.[2]	Total	White	Black	Asian	Hisp.[2]
City	90.0	96.2	74.6	82.6	59.9	50.4	61.2	14.3	54.8	21.0
MSA[1]	93.6	96.3	82.6	81.2	68.5	42.0	44.3	22.0	45.3	20.1
U.S.	88.0	89.9	86.0	87.1	68.7	32.1	33.5	21.6	54.3	16.4

Note: Figures shown cover persons 25 years old and over; (1) Figures cover the Minneapolis-St. Paul-Bloomington, MN-WI Metropolitan Statistical Area; (2) People of Hispanic origin can be of any race
Source: U.S. Census Bureau, 2015-2019 American Community Survey 5-Year Estimates

School Enrollment by Grade and Control

Area	Preschool (%)		Kindergarten (%)		Grades 1 - 4 (%)		Grades 5 - 8 (%)		Grades 9 - 12 (%)	
	Public	Private	Public	Private	Public	Private	Public	Private	Public	Private
City	53.4	46.6	85.1	14.9	88.2	11.8	88.9	11.1	87.7	12.3
MSA[1]	59.4	40.6	88.5	11.5	89.4	10.6	90.1	9.9	91.6	8.4
U.S.	59.1	40.9	87.6	12.4	89.5	10.5	89.4	10.6	90.1	9.9

Note: Figures shown cover persons 3 years old and over; (1) Figures cover the Minneapolis-St. Paul-Bloomington, MN-WI Metropolitan Statistical Area
Source: U.S. Census Bureau, 2015-2019 American Community Survey 5-Year Estimates

Higher Education

Four-Year Colleges			Two-Year Colleges			Medical Schools[1]	Law Schools[2]	Voc/ Tech[3]
Public	Private Non-profit	Private For-profit	Public	Private Non-profit	Private For-profit			
1	5	3	1	0	0	1	2	3

Note: Figures cover institutions located within the city limits and include main campuses only; (1) includes schools accredited by the Liaison Committee on Medical Education and the American Osteopathic Association's Commission on Osteopathic College Accreditation; (2) includes ABA-accredited schools, schools with provisional ABA accreditation, and state accredited schools; (3) includes all schools with programs that are less than 2 years.
Source: National Center for Education Statistics, Integrated Postsecondary Education System (IPEDS), 2019-20; Wikipedia, List of Medical Schools in the United States, accessed April 2, 2021; Wikipedia, List of Law Schools in the United States, accessed April 2, 2021

According to *U.S. News & World Report,* the Minneapolis-St. Paul-Bloomington, MN-WI metro area is home to three of the top 200 national universities in the U.S.: **University of Minnesota—Twin**

Cities (#66 tie); **University of St. Thomas (MN)** (#133 tie); **Bethel University (MN)** (#196 tie). The indicators used to capture academic quality fall into a number of categories: assessment by administrators at peer institutions; retention of students; faculty resources; student selectivity; financial resources; alumni giving; high school counselor ratings of colleges; and graduation rate. *U.S. News & World Report, "America's Best Colleges 2021"*

According to *U.S. News & World Report,* the Minneapolis-St. Paul-Bloomington, MN-WI metro area is home to four of the top 100 liberal arts colleges in the U.S.: **Carleton College** (#9 tie); **Macalester College** (#27); **St. Olaf College** (#67 tie); **Gustavus Adolphus College** (#84 tie). The indicators used to capture academic quality fall into a number of categories: assessment by administrators at peer institutions; retention of students; faculty resources; student selectivity; financial resources; alumni giving; high school counselor ratings of colleges; and graduation rate. *U.S. News & World Report, "America's Best Colleges 2021"*

According to *U.S. News & World Report,* the Minneapolis-St. Paul-Bloomington, MN-WI metro area is home to one of the top 100 law schools in the U.S.: **University of Minnesota** (#22 tie). The rankings are based on a weighted average of 12 measures of quality: peer assessment score; assessment score by lawyers/judges; median LSAT scores; median undergrad GPA; acceptance rate; employment rates for graduates; placement success; bar passage rate; faculty resources; expenditures per student; student/faculty ratio; and library resources. *U.S. News & World Report, "America's Best Graduate Schools, Law, 2022"*

According to *U.S. News & World Report,* the Minneapolis-St. Paul-Bloomington, MN-WI metro area is home to one of the top 75 medical schools for research in the U.S.: **University of Minnesota** (#42 tie). The rankings are based on a weighted average of 11 measures of quality: quality assessment; peer assessment score; assessment score by residency directors; research activity; total research activity; average research activity per faculty member; student selectivity; median MCAT total score; median undergraduate GPA; acceptance rate; and faculty resources. *U.S. News & World Report, "America's Best Graduate Schools, Medical, 2022"*

According to *U.S. News & World Report,* the Minneapolis-St. Paul-Bloomington, MN-WI metro area is home to one of the top 75 business schools in the U.S.: **University of Minnesota—Twin Cities (Carlson)** (#28 tie). The rankings are based on a weighted average of the following nine measures: quality assessment; peer assessment; recruiter assessment; placement success; mean starting salary and bonus; student selectivity; mean GMAT and GRE scores; mean undergraduate GPA; and acceptance rate. *U.S. News & World Report, "America's Best Graduate Schools, Business, 2022"*

EMPLOYERS

Major Employers

Company Name	Industry
3M Company	Adhesives, sealants
Ameriprise Financial	Investment advice
Anderson Corporation	Millwork
Aware Integrated	Hospital & medical services plans
Bethesda Healtheast Hospital	General medical & surgical hospitals
Carlson Holdings	Hotels & motels
City of Minneapolis	Municipal government
County of Hennepin	County government
Hennepin County	County government
Honeywell International	Aircraft engines & engine parts
Lawson Software	Application computer software
Medtronic	Electromedical equipment
Minnesota Department of Human Services	Family services agency
Minnesota Department of Transportation	Regulation, administration of transportation
North Memorial Hospital	General medical & surgical hospitals
Regents of the University of Minnesota	Specialty outpatient clinics, nec
Rosemount Apple Valley and Eagan	Personal service agents, brokers, & bureaus
St. Paul Fire & Marine Insurance Company	Fire, marine, & casualty insurance
Thomson Legal Regulatory	Books, publishing & printing
United Parcel Service	Package delivery services
Wells Fargo	Mortgage bankers
West Publishing Corporation	Data base information retrieval

Note: Companies shown are located within the Minneapolis-St. Paul-Bloomington, MN-WI Metropolitan Statistical Area.
Source: Hoovers.com; Wikipedia

Best Companies to Work For

Allianz Life Insurance Co. of N. America, headquartered in Minneapolis, is among "The 100 Best Companies to Work For." To pick the best companies, *Fortune* partnered with the Great Place to Work Institute. Two-thirds of a company's score is based on the results of the Institute's Trust Index survey, which is sent to a random sample of employees from each company. The questions related to attitudes about management's credibility, job satisfaction, and camaraderie. The other third of the scoring is based on the company's responses to the Institute's Culture Audit, which includes detailed questions about pay and benefit programs, and a series of open-ended questions about hiring practices, internal communication, training, recognition programs, and diversity efforts. Any company that is at least five years old with more than 1,000 U.S. employees is eligible. *Fortune, "The 100 Best Companies to Work For," 2020*

Ceridian; General Mills; US Bank, headquartered in Minneapolis, are among the "100 Best Companies for Working Mothers." Criteria: paid time off and leaves; workforce profile; benefits; women's issues and advancement; flexible work; company culture and work life programs. *Working Mother, "100 Best Companies for Working Mothers," 2020*

General Mills; US Bank, headquartered in Minneapolis, are among the "Best Companies for Multicultural Women." *Working Mother* selected 50 companies based on a detailed application completed by public and private firms based in the United States, excluding government agencies, companies in the human resources field and non-autonomous divisions. Companies supplied data about the hiring, pay, and promotion of multicultural employees. Applications focused on representation of multicultural women, recruitment, retention and advancement programs, and company culture. *Working Mother, "Best Companies for Multicultural Women," 2020*

General Mills; US Bank, headquartered in Minneapolis, are among the "Top Companies for Executive Women." This list is determined by organizations filling out an in-depth survey that measures female demographics at every level, but with an emphasis on women in senior corporate roles, with profit & loss (P&L) responsibility, and those earning in the top 20 percent of the organization. *Working Mother* defines P&L as having responsibility that involves monitoring the net income after expenses for a department or entire organization, with direct influence on how company resources are allocated. *Working Mother, "Top Companies for Executive Women," 2020+*

Ceridian; General Mills, headquartered in Minneapolis, are among the "Best Companies for Dads." *Working Mother's* newest list recognizes the growing importance companies place on giving dads time off and support for their families. Rankings are determined by measuring gender-neutral or paternity leave offered, as well as actual time taken, phase-back policies, child- and dependent-care benefits, and corporate support groups for men and dads. *Working Mother, "Best Companies for Dads," 2020*

PUBLIC SAFETY

Crime Rate

Area	All Crimes	Violent Crimes				Property Crimes		
		Murder	Rape[3]	Robbery	Aggrav. Assault	Burglary	Larceny -Theft	Motor Vehicle Theft
City	5,442.7	10.7	106.5	299.1	509.5	788.1	3,056.0	672.8
Suburbs[1]	2,224.5	1.6	36.4	48.6	98.2	238.6	1,611.4	189.7
Metro[2]	2,605.3	2.7	44.7	78.3	146.9	303.6	1,782.3	246.9
U.S.	2,489.3	5.0	42.6	81.6	250.2	340.5	1,549.5	219.9

Note: Figures are crimes per 100,000 population; (1) All areas within the metro area that are located outside the city limits; (2) Figures cover the Minneapolis-St. Paul-Bloomington, MN-WI Metropolitan Statistical Area; (3) All figures shown were reported using the revised Uniform Crime Reporting (UCR) definition of rape.
Source: FBI Uniform Crime Reports, 2019

Hate Crimes

Area	Number of Quarters Reported	Number of Incidents per Bias Motivation					
		Race/Ethnicity/ Ancestry	Religion	Sexual Orientation	Disability	Gender	Gender Identity
City	4	17	5	6	0	1	3
U.S.	4	3,963	1,521	1,195	157	69	198

Source: Federal Bureau of Investigation, Hate Crime Statistics 2019

Identity Theft Consumer Reports

Area	Reports	Reports per 100,000 Population	Rank[2]
MSA[1]	6,219	171	258
U.S.	1,387,615	423	-

Note: (1) Figures cover the Minneapolis-St. Paul-Bloomington, MN-WI Metropolitan Statistical Area; (2) Rank ranges from 1 to 391 where 1 indicates greatest number of identity theft reports per 100,000 population
Source: Federal Trade Commission, Consumer Sentinel Network Data Book 2020

Fraud and Other Consumer Reports

Area	Reports	Reports per 100,000 Population	Rank[2]
MSA[1]	27,548	757	133
U.S.	3,385,133	1,031	-

Note: (1) Figures cover the Minneapolis-St. Paul-Bloomington, MN-WI Metropolitan Statistical Area; (2) Rank ranges from 1 to 391 where 1 indicates greatest number of fraud and other consumer reports per 100,000 population
Source: Federal Trade Commission, Consumer Sentinel Network Data Book 2020

POLITICS

2020 Presidential Election Results

Area	Biden	Trump	Jorgensen	Hawkins	Other
Hennepin County	70.5	27.2	1.0	0.3	1.0
U.S.	51.3	46.8	1.2	0.3	0.5

Note: Results are percentages and may not add to 100% due to rounding
Source: Dave Leip's Atlas of U.S. Presidential Elections

SPORTS

Professional Sports Teams

Team Name	League	Year Established
Minnesota Timberwolves	National Basketball Association (NBA)	1989
Minnesota Twins	Major League Baseball (MLB)	1961
Minnesota United FC	Major League Soccer (MLS)	2017
Minnesota Vikings	National Football League (NFL)	1961
Minnesota Wild	National Hockey League (NHL)	2000

Note: Includes teams located in the Minneapolis-St. Paul-Bloomington, MN-WI Metropolitan Statistical Area.
Source: Wikipedia, Major Professional Sports Teams of the United States and Canada, April 6, 2021

CLIMATE

Average and Extreme Temperatures

Temperature	Jan	Feb	Mar	Apr	May	Jun	Jul	Aug	Sep	Oct	Nov	Dec	Yr.
Extreme High (°F)	57	60	83	95	96	102	105	101	98	89	74	63	105
Average High (°F)	21	27	38	56	69	79	84	81	71	59	41	26	54
Average Temp. (°F)	12	18	30	46	59	69	74	71	61	50	33	19	45
Average Low (°F)	3	9	21	36	48	58	63	61	50	39	25	11	35
Extreme Low (°F)	-34	-28	-32	2	18	37	43	39	26	15	-17	-29	-34

Note: Figures cover the years 1948-1990
Source: National Climatic Data Center, International Station Meteorological Climate Summary, 9/96

Average Precipitation/Snowfall/Humidity

Precip./Humidity	Jan	Feb	Mar	Apr	May	Jun	Jul	Aug	Sep	Oct	Nov	Dec	Yr.
Avg. Precip. (in.)	0.8	0.8	1.9	2.2	3.1	4.0	3.8	3.6	2.5	1.9	1.4	1.0	27.1
Avg. Snowfall (in.)	11	9	12	3	Tr	0	0	0	Tr	Tr	7	10	52
Avg. Rel. Hum. 6am (%)	75	76	77	75	75	79	81	84	85	81	80	79	79
Avg. Rel. Hum. 3pm (%)	64	62	58	48	47	50	50	52	53	52	62	68	55

Note: Figures cover the years 1948-1990; Tr = Trace amounts (<0.05 in. of rain; <0.5 in. of snow)
Source: National Climatic Data Center, International Station Meteorological Climate Summary, 9/96

Weather Conditions

Temperature			Daytime Sky			Precipitation		
5°F & below	32°F & below	90°F & above	Clear	Partly cloudy	Cloudy	0.01 inch or more precip.	0.1 inch or more snow/ice	Thunder-storms
45	156	16	93	125	147	113	41	37

Note: Figures are average number of days per year and cover the years 1948-1990
Source: National Climatic Data Center, International Station Meteorological Climate Summary, 9/96

HAZARDOUS WASTE

Superfund Sites

The Minneapolis-St. Paul-Bloomington, MN-WI metro area is home to 16 sites on the EPA's Superfund National Priorities List: **Baytown Township Ground Water Plume** (final); **FMC Corp. (Fridley Plant)** (final); **Freeway Sanitary Landfill** (final); **General Mills/Henkel Corp.** (final); **Highway 100 and County Road 3 Groundwater Plume** (final); **Joslyn Manufacturing & Supply Co.** (final); **Koppers Coke** (final); **Kurt Manufacturing Co.** (final); **Macgillis & Gibbs Co./Bell Lumber & Pole Co.** (final); **Naval Industrial Reserve Ordnance Plant** (final); **New Brighton/Arden Hills/Tcaap (USARMY)** (final); **Oakdale Dump** (final); **Reilly Tar & Chemical Corp. (Saint Louis Park Plant)** (final); **South Andover Site** (final); **South Minneapolis Residential Soil Contamination** (final); **Spring Park Municipal Well Field** (final). There are a total of 1,375 Superfund sites with a status of proposed or final on the list in the U.S. *U.S. Environmental Protection Agency, National Priorities List, April 7, 2021*

AIR QUALITY

Air Quality Trends: Ozone

	1990	1995	2000	2005	2010	2015	2016	2017	2018	2019
MSA[1]	0.068	0.084	0.065	0.074	0.066	0.061	0.061	0.062	0.065	0.059
U.S.	0.088	0.089	0.082	0.080	0.073	0.068	0.069	0.068	0.069	0.065

Note: (1) Data covers the Minneapolis-St. Paul-Bloomington, MN-WI Metropolitan Statistical Area. The values shown are the composite ozone concentration averages among trend sites based on the highest fourth daily maximum 8-hour concentration in parts per million. These trends are based on sites having an adequate record of monitoring data during the trend period. Data from exceptional events are included.
Source: U.S. Environmental Protection Agency, Air Quality Monitoring Information, "Air Quality Trends by City, 1990-2019"

Air Quality Index

Area	Percent of Days when Air Quality was...[2]					AQI Statistics[2]	
	Good	Moderate	Unhealthy for Sensitive Groups	Unhealthy	Very Unhealthy	Maximum	Median
MSA[1]	58.6	40.5	0.5	0.3	0.0	200	46

Note: (1) Data covers the Minneapolis-St. Paul-Bloomington, MN-WI Metropolitan Statistical Area; (2) Based on 365 days with AQI data in 2019. Air Quality Index (AQI) is an index for reporting daily air quality. EPA calculates the AQI for five major air pollutants regulated by the Clean Air Act: ground-level ozone, particle pollution (aka particulate matter), carbon monoxide, sulfur dioxide, and nitrogen dioxide. The AQI runs from 0 to 500. The higher the AQI value, the greater the level of air pollution and the greater the health concern. There are six AQI categories: "Good" AQI is between 0 and 50. Air quality is considered satisfactory; "Moderate" AQI is between 51 and 100. Air quality is acceptable; "Unhealthy for Sensitive Groups" When AQI values are between 101 and 150, members of sensitive groups may experience health effects; "Unhealthy" When AQI values are between 151 and 200 everyone may begin to experience health effects; "Very Unhealthy" AQI values between 201 and 300 trigger a health alert; "Hazardous" AQI values over 300 trigger warnings of emergency conditions (not shown).
Source: U.S. Environmental Protection Agency, Air Quality Index Report, 2019

Air Quality Index Pollutants

Area	Percent of Days when AQI Pollutant was...[2]					
	Carbon Monoxide	Nitrogen Dioxide	Ozone	Sulfur Dioxide	Particulate Matter 2.5	Particulate Matter 10
MSA[1]	0.0	1.4	31.2	1.1	43.0	23.3

Note: (1) Data covers the Minneapolis-St. Paul-Bloomington, MN-WI Metropolitan Statistical Area; (2) Based on 365 days with AQI data in 2019. The Air Quality Index (AQI) is an index for reporting daily air quality. EPA calculates the AQI for five major air pollutants regulated by the Clean Air Act: ground-level ozone, particle pollution (also known as particulate matter), carbon monoxide, sulfur dioxide, and nitrogen dioxide. The AQI runs from 0 to 500. The higher the AQI value, the greater the level of air pollution and the greater the health concern.
Source: U.S. Environmental Protection Agency, Air Quality Index Report, 2019

Maximum Air Pollutant Concentrations: Particulate Matter, Ozone, CO and Lead

	Particulate Matter 10 (ug/m³)	Particulate Matter 2.5 Wtd AM (ug/m³)	Particulate Matter 2.5 24-Hr (ug/m³)	Ozone (ppm)	Carbon Monoxide (ppm)	Lead (ug/m³)
MSA[1] Level	98	8.0	23	0.062	1	0.07
NAAQS[2]	150	15	35	0.075	9	0.15
Met NAAQS[2]	Yes	Yes	Yes	Yes	Yes	Yes

Note: (1) Data covers the Minneapolis-St. Paul-Bloomington, MN-WI Metropolitan Statistical Area; Data from exceptional events are included; (2) National Ambient Air Quality Standards; ppm = parts per million; ug/m³ = micrograms per cubic meter; n/a not available.
Concentrations: Particulate Matter 10 (coarse particulate)—highest second maximum 24-hour concentration; Particulate Matter 2.5 Wtd AM (fine particulate)—highest weighted annual mean concentration; Particulate Matter 2.5 24-Hour (fine particulate)—highest 98th percentile 24-hour concentration; Ozone—highest fourth daily maximum 8-hour concentration; Carbon Monoxide—highest second maximum non-overlapping 8-hour concentration; Lead—maximum running 3-month average
Source: U.S. Environmental Protection Agency, Air Quality Monitoring Information, "Air Quality Statistics by City, 2019"

Maximum Air Pollutant Concentrations: Nitrogen Dioxide and Sulfur Dioxide

	Nitrogen Dioxide AM (ppb)	Nitrogen Dioxide 1-Hr (ppb)	Sulfur Dioxide AM (ppb)	Sulfur Dioxide 1-Hr (ppb)	Sulfur Dioxide 24-Hr (ppb)
MSA[1] Level	8	41	n/a	10	n/a
NAAQS[2]	53	100	30	75	140
Met NAAQS[2]	Yes	Yes	n/a	Yes	n/a

Note: (1) Data covers the Minneapolis-St. Paul-Bloomington, MN-WI Metropolitan Statistical Area; Data from exceptional events are included; (2) National Ambient Air Quality Standards; ppm = parts per million; ug/m³ = micrograms per cubic meter; n/a not available.
Concentrations: Nitrogen Dioxide AM—highest arithmetic mean concentration; Nitrogen Dioxide 1-Hr—highest 98th percentile 1-hour daily maximum concentration; Sulfur Dioxide AM—highest annual mean concentration; Sulfur Dioxide 1-Hr—highest 99th percentile 1-hour daily maximum concentration; Sulfur Dioxide 24-Hr—highest second maximum 24-hour concentration
Source: U.S. Environmental Protection Agency, Air Quality Monitoring Information, "Air Quality Statistics by City, 2019"

Oklahoma City, Oklahoma

Background

The 1992 film *Far and Away,* directed by Ron Howard, shows Tom Cruise charging away on his horse to claim land in the Oklahoma Territory. That dramatic scene depicted a true event from the great Oklahoma land run of 1889. A pistol was fired from the Oklahoma Station house of the Santa Fe Railroad and 10,000 homesteaders raced away to stake land claims in central Oklahoma territory. Overnight, Oklahoma City, "OKC" as the locals like to call their town, had been founded.

The town grew quickly along the tracks of the Santa Fe Railroad. Soon it became a distribution center for the territory's crops and livestock. Today, the city still functions as a major transportation center for the state's farm produce and livestock industry. By 1910 the city had become the state capital, which also furthered growth. But in 1928, growth went through the ceiling when oil was discovered within the city limits, forever changing the economic face of Oklahoma City from one of livestock and feed to one of livestock, feed, and oil.

After World War II, Oklahoma City, like many other cities, entered industry, most notably aircraft and related industries. The Tinker Air Force Base and the Federal Aviation Administration's Mike Monroney Aeronautical Center—home to the largest concentration of Dept. of Transportation personnel outside of Washington, D.C.—have made Oklahoma City a leading aviation center and, combined, employ more than 30,000 federal and civil contract workers. Major economic sectors for the Greater Oklahoma City region—the geographic center of the continent—also include energy, bioscience, and logistics.

The area caters to a Western lifestyle. The town is the home of the National Cowboy and Western Heritage Museum, with its famous 18-foot tall sculpture, "End of the Trail," by James Earle Fraser. The Oklahoma History Center, affiliated with the Smithsonian Institute, occupies a 215,000 square foot building on an 18-acre campus. The Red Earth Museum features 1,400 items of Native American art and a research center. To the north of Oklahoma City's Capitol building is the Tribal Flag Plaza, displaying the 39 native tribal flags of Oklahoma. Each September the State Fair is held in Oklahoma City, and each January the International Finals Rodeo is held at the State Fair Park. If swinging a bat is more your style than riding a bronco, there's the National Softball Hall of Fame and Museum.

> Oklahoma City rock group The Flaming Lips placed both themselves and audience members inside inflatable human-sized bubbles to defend against COVID-19 during a live show.

Oklahoma City hired famous architect I.M. Pei to redesign its downtown area. Taking inspiration from the Tivoli Gardens of Copenhagen, the downtown boasts of the Myriad Gardens, a 12-acre recreational park with gardens, an amphitheater, and the seven-story Crystal Bridge Tropical Conservatory. In 2021, a massive new central park will link the gardens near the newly renovated Crystal Bridge and the new convention center as part of the Core to Shore project.

The city is also home to the Oklahoma City Thunder, a team that's become a leading NBA contender in recent years, often making the playoffs.

A national tragedy that played out in Oklahoma City remains present in the memory of the city and the country. On April 19, 1995, Oklahoma City suffered a deadly terrorist incident when a truck bomb destroyed part of the Alfred P. Murray Federal Building in the downtown area, leaving 168 people dead and more than 500 injured. In the face of such tragedy, the world marveled at how Oklahoma City and the state of Oklahoma carried itself with dignity and generosity. The Oklahoma City National Memorial commemorates those people whose lives were ended or forever changed on that day.

Oklahoma City's weather is changeable. There are pronounced daily and seasonal temperature changes and considerable variation in seasonal and annual precipitation. Summers are long and usually hot, while winters are comparatively mild and short. The city is located in Tornado Alley, which is frequently visited in the springtime by violent thunderstorms producing damaging winds, large hail, and tornadoes.

Rankings

General Rankings

- For its "Best for Vets: Places to Live 2019" rankings, *Military Times* evaluated 599 cities (83 large, 234 medium, 282 small) and compared the locations across three broad categories: veteran and military culture/services; economic indicators; and livability factors such as health, crime, traffic, and school quality. Oklahoma City ranked #6 out of the top 25, in the large city category (population of more than 250,000). Data points more specific to veterans and the military weighed more heavily than others. *rebootcamp.militarytimes.com, "Military Times Best Places to Live 2019," September 10, 2018*

- The Oklahoma City metro area was identified as one of America's fastest-growing areas in terms of population and business growth by *MagnifyMoney*. The area ranked #31 out of 35. The 100 most populous metro areas in the U.S. were evaluated on their change from 2011-2016 in the following categories: people and housing; workforce and employment opportunities; growing industry. *www.businessinsider.com, "The 35 Cities in the US with the Biggest Influx of People, the Most Work Opportunities, and the Hottest Business Growth," August 12, 2018*

Business/Finance Rankings

- Oklahoma City was the #2-ranked city for savers, according to a study by the finance site GOBankingRates, which considered the prospects for people trying to save money. Criteria: average monthly cost of grocery items; median home listing price; median rent; median income; transportation costs; gas prices; and the cost of eating out for an inexpensive and mid-range meal in 100 U.S. cities. *www.gobankingrates.com, "The 20 Best (and Worst) Places to Live If You're Trying to Save Money," August 27, 2019*

- Oklahoma City was ranked #2 among 100 U.S. cities for most difficult conditions for savers, according to a study by the finance site GOBankingRates. Criteria: average monthly cost of grocery items; median home listing price; median rent; median income; transportation costs; gas prices; and the cost of eating out for an inexpensive and mid-range meal. *www.gobankingrates.com, "The 20 Best (and Worst) Places to Live If You're Trying to Save Money," August 27, 2019*

- Based on metro area social media reviews, the employment opinion group Glassdoor surveyed 50 of the most populous U.S. metro areas and equally weighed cost of living, hiring opportunity, and job satisfaction to compose a list of "25 Best Cities for Jobs." Median pay and home value, and number of active job openings were also factored in. The Oklahoma City metro area was ranked #12 in overall job satisfaction. *www.glassdoor.com, "Best Cities for Jobs," February 25, 2020*

- The Brookings Institution ranked the nation's largest cities based on income inequality. Oklahoma City was ranked #70 (#1 = greatest inequality). Criteria: the "95/20 ratio," a figure representing the income at which a household earns more than 95 percent of all other households, divided by the income at which a household earns more than only 20 percent of all other households. *Brookings Institution, "Household Income Inequality, Largest Cities of 97 Large U.S. Metro Areas, 2014-2016," February 5, 2018*

- The Brookings Institution ranked the 100 largest metro areas in the U.S. based on income inequality. Oklahoma City was ranked #47 (#1 = greatest inequality). Criteria: the "95/20 ratio," a figure representing the income at which a household earns more than 95 percent of all other households, divided by the income at which a household earns more than only 20 percent of all other households. *Brookings Institution, "Household Income Inequality, 100 Largest U.S. Metro Areas, 2014-2016," February 5, 2018*

- For its annual survey of the "Cheapest U.S. Cities to Live In," Kiplinger applied Cost of Living Index statistics developed by the Council for Community and Economic Research to U.S. Census Bureau population and median household income data for 270 urban areas. In the resulting ranking, Oklahoma City ranked #16. *Kiplinger.com, "The 25 Cheapest U.S. Cities to Live In," October 1, 2020*

- The Oklahoma City metro area appeared on the Milken Institute "2021 Best Performing Cities" list. Rank: #114 out of 200 large metro areas (population over 250,000). Criteria: job growth; wage and salary growth; high-tech output growth; housing affordability; household broadband access. *Milken Institute, "Best-Performing Cities 2021," February 16, 2021*

- *Forbes* ranked the 200 most populous metro areas to determine the nation's "Best Places for Business and Careers." The Oklahoma City metro area was ranked #54. Criteria: costs (business and living); job growth (past and projected); income growth; quality of life; educational attainment (college and high school); projected economic growth; cultural and leisure opportunities; workplace tolerance laws; net migration patterns. *Forbes, "The Best Places for Business and Careers 2019: Seattle Still On Top," October 30, 2019*

Culture/Performing Arts Rankings

- Oklahoma City was selected as one of the 25 best cities for moviemakers in North America. COVID-19 has spurred a quest for great film cities that offer more creative space, lower costs, and more great outdoors. NYC & LA were intentionally excluded. Criteria: longstanding reputations as film-friendly communities; efforts to deal with pandemic-specific challenges; and establish appropriate COVID-19 guidelines. The city was ranked #15. *MovieMaker Magazine, "Best Places to Live and Work as a Moviemaker, 2021," January 26, 2021*

Dating/Romance Rankings

- Oklahoma City was ranked #18 out of 25 cities that stood out for inspiring romance and attracting diners on the website OpenTable.com. Criteria: percentage of people who dined out on Valentine's Day in 2018; percentage of romantic restaurants as rated by OpenTable diner reviews; and percentage of tables seated for two. *OpenTable, "25 Most Romantic Cities in America for 2019," February 7, 2019*

Education Rankings

- Personal finance website *WalletHub* analyzed the 150 largest U.S. metropolitan statistical areas to determine where the most educated Americans are putting their degrees to work. Criteria: education levels; percentage of workers with degrees; education quality and attainment gap; public school quality rankings; quality and enrollment of each metro area's universities. Oklahoma City was ranked #81 (#1 = most educated city). *www.WalletHub.com, "Most and Least Educated Cities in America," July 20, 2020*

- Oklahoma City was selected as one of America's most literate cities. The city ranked #48 out of the 84 largest U.S. cities. Criteria: number of booksellers; library resources; Internet resources; educational attainment; periodical publishing resources; newspaper circulation. *Central Connecticut State University, "America's Most Literate Cities, 2018," February 2019*

Environmental Rankings

- Sperling's BestPlaces assessed the 50 largest metropolitan areas of the United States for the likelihood of dangerously extreme weather events or earthquakes. In general the Southeast and South-Central regions have the highest risk of weather extremes and earthquakes, while the Pacific Northwest enjoys the lowest risk. Of the most risky metropolitan areas, the Oklahoma City metro area was ranked #3. *www.bestplaces.net, "Avoid Natural Disasters: BestPlaces Reveals The Top 10 Safest Places to Live," October 25, 2017*

Health/Fitness Rankings

- For each of the 100 largest cities in the United States, the American Fitness Index®, published by the American College of Sports Medicine and the Anthem Foundation, evaluated community infrastructure and 33 health behaviors including preventive health, levels of chronic disease conditions, pedestrian safety, air quality, and community resources that support physical activity. Oklahoma City ranked #100 for "community fitness." *americanfitnessindex.org, "2020 ACSM American Fitness Index Summary Report," July 14, 2020*

- Oklahoma City was identified as a "2021 Spring Allergy Capital." The area ranked #7 out of 100. Three groups of factors were used to identify the most challenging cities for people with allergies during the spring season: annual spring pollen levels; over the counter medicine use; number of board-certified allergy specialists. *Asthma and Allergy Foundation of America, "Spring Allergy Capitals 2021," February 23, 2021*

- Oklahoma City was identified as a "2021 Fall Allergy Capital." The area ranked #13 out of 100. Three groups of factors were used to identify the most challenging cities for people with allergies during the fall season: annual fall pollen levels; over the counter medicine use; number of board-certified allergy specialists. *Asthma and Allergy Foundation of America, "Fall Allergy Capitals 2021," February 23, 2021*

- Oklahoma City was identified as a "2019 Asthma Capital." The area ranked #32 out of the nation's 100 largest metropolitan areas. Criteria: estimated asthma prevalence; crude death rate from asthma; and ER visits due to asthma. Risk factors analyzed but not factored in the rankings: annual pollen score; annual air quality; public smoking laws; number of board-certified asthma specialists; rescue medication use; controller medication use; uninsured rate; poverty rate. *Asthma and Allergy Foundation of America, "Asthma Capitals 2019: The Most Challenging Places to Live With Asthma," May 7, 2019*

Real Estate Rankings

- FitSmallBusiness looked at 50 of the largest metropolitan areas in the U.S. to determine which metro was the best to start a real estate business. Data was compiled from such sources as: Zillow, Trulia, U.S. Census Bureau, and the Bureau of Labor Statistics. Criteria: location; inventory; annual wages; median sales price of homes; days on the market; median price cut percentage; and other factors that would influence real estate professional growth. The Oklahoma City metro area ranked #35. *fitsmallbusiness.com, "The Best Cities to Become a Real Estate Agent in 2018," January 30, 2018*

- *WalletHub* compared the most populated U.S. cities to determine which had the best markets for real estate agents. Oklahoma City ranked #166 where demand was high and pay was the best. Criteria: sales per agent; annual median wage for real-estate agents; monthly average starting salary for real estate agents; real estate job density and competition; unemployment rate; home turnover rate; housing-market health index; and other relevant metrics. *www.WalletHub.com, "2019's Best Places to Be a Real Estate Agent," April 24, 2019*

- Oklahoma City was ranked #84 out of 268 metro areas in terms of housing affordability in 2020 by the National Association of Home Builders (#1 = most affordable). Criteria: the share of homes sold in that area affordable to a family earning the local median income, based on standard mortgage underwriting criteria. *National Association of Home Builders®, NAHB-Wells Fargo Housing Opportunity Index, 4th Quarter 2020*

Safety Rankings

- Allstate ranked the 200 largest cities in America in terms of driver safety. Oklahoma City ranked #45. Criteria: internal property damage claims over a two-year period from January 2016 to December 2017. The report helps increase the importance of safety and awareness behind the wheel. *Allstate, "Allstate America's Best Drivers Report, 2019" June 24, 2019*

- The National Insurance Crime Bureau ranked 384 metro areas in the U.S. in terms of per capita rates of vehicle theft. The Oklahoma City metro area ranked #47 (#1 = highest rate). Criteria: number of vehicle theft offenses per 100,000 inhabitants in 2019. *National Insurance Crime Bureau, "Hot Spots 2019," July 21, 2020*

Seniors/Retirement Rankings

- From its Best Cities for Successful Aging indexes, the Milken Institute generated rankings for metropolitan areas, weighing data in nine categories—health care, wellness, living arrangements, transportation and convenience, financial characteristics, education, employment, community engagement, and overall livability. The Oklahoma City metro area was ranked #28 overall in the large metro area category. *Milken Institute, "Best Cities for Successful Aging, 2017" March 14, 2017*

Women/Minorities Rankings

- Personal finance website *WalletHub* compared more than 180 U.S. cities across two key dimensions, "Hispanic Business-Friendliness" and "Hispanic Purchasing Power," to arrive at the most favorable conditions for Hispanic entrepreneurs. Oklahoma City was ranked #16 out of 182. Criteria includes: share of Hispanic-Owned Businesses; Hispanic entrepreneurship rate to median annual income of Hispanics; Small Business-Friendliness score; cost of living; and number of Hispanics with at least a bachelor's degree. *WalletHub.com, "2019's Best Cities for Hispanic Entrepreneurs," May 1, 2019*

Miscellaneous Rankings

- *WalletHub* compared the 150 most populated U.S. cities to determine their operating efficiency. A "Quality of City Services" score was constructed for each city and then divided by the total budget per capita to reveal which were managed the best. Oklahoma City ranked #20. Criteria: financial stability; economy; education; safety; health; infrastructure and pollution. *www.WalletHub.com, "2020's Best- & Worst-Run Cities in America," June 29, 2020*

Business Environment

DEMOGRAPHICS

Population Growth

Area	1990 Census	2000 Census	2010 Census	2019* Estimate	Population Growth (%)	
					1990-2019	2010-2019
City	445,065	506,132	579,999	643,692	44.6	11.0
MSA[1]	971,042	1,095,421	1,252,987	1,382,841	42.4	10.4
U.S.	248,709,873	281,421,906	308,745,538	324,697,795	30.6	5.2

Note: (1) Figures cover the Oklahoma City, OK Metropolitan Statistical Area; (*) 2015-2019 5-year estimated population
Source: U.S. Census Bureau, 1990 Census, Census 2000, Census 2010, 2015-2019 American Community Survey 5-Year Estimates

Household Size

Area	Persons in Household (%)							Average Household Size
	One	Two	Three	Four	Five	Six	Seven or More	
City	31.1	32.1	14.6	12.3	6.2	2.6	1.1	2.60
MSA[1]	28.3	34.1	15.4	12.6	6.1	2.4	1.1	2.60
U.S.	27.9	33.9	15.6	12.9	6.0	2.3	1.4	2.60

Note: (1) Figures cover the Oklahoma City, OK Metropolitan Statistical Area
Source: U.S. Census Bureau, 2015-2019 American Community Survey 5-Year Estimates

Race

Area	White Alone[2] (%)	Black Alone[2] (%)	Asian Alone[2] (%)	AIAN[3] Alone[2] (%)	NHOPI[4] Alone[2] (%)	Other Race Alone[2] (%)	Two or More Races (%)
City	67.7	14.3	4.5	2.9	0.1	4.1	6.3
MSA[1]	73.7	10.2	3.2	3.6	0.1	2.8	6.5
U.S.	72.5	12.7	5.5	0.8	0.2	4.9	3.3

Note: (1) Figures cover the Oklahoma City, OK Metropolitan Statistical Area; (2) Alone is defined as not being in combination with one or more other races; (3) American Indian and Alaska Native; (4) Native Hawaiian and Other Pacific Islander
Source: U.S. Census Bureau, 2015-2019 American Community Survey 5-Year Estimates

Hispanic or Latino Origin

Area	Total (%)	Mexican (%)	Puerto Rican (%)	Cuban (%)	Other (%)
City	19.7	16.6	0.3	0.1	2.8
MSA[1]	13.3	10.9	0.3	0.1	2.0
U.S.	18.0	11.2	1.7	0.7	4.3

Note: Persons of Hispanic or Latino origin can be of any race; (1) Figures cover the Oklahoma City, OK Metropolitan Statistical Area
Source: U.S. Census Bureau, 2015-2019 American Community Survey 5-Year Estimates

Ancestry

Area	German	Irish	English	American	Italian	Polish	French[2]	Scottish	Dutch
City	10.6	8.1	6.2	5.9	1.9	0.8	1.5	1.5	0.9
MSA[1]	12.0	9.1	7.2	7.6	2.0	0.9	1.7	1.7	1.2
U.S.	13.3	9.7	7.2	6.2	5.1	2.8	2.3	1.7	1.2

Note: Figures are the percentage of the total population reporting a particular ancestry. The nine most commonly reported ancestries in the U.S. are shown. Figures include multiple ancestries (e.g. if a person reported being Irish and Italian, they were included in both columns); (1) Figures cover the Oklahoma City, OK Metropolitan Statistical Area; (2) Excludes Basque
Source: U.S. Census Bureau, 2015-2019 American Community Survey 5-Year Estimates

Foreign-born Population

Area	Percent of Population Born in								
	Any Foreign Country	Asia	Mexico	Europe	Caribbean	Central America[2]	South America	Africa	Canada
City	11.8	3.3	6.0	0.4	0.2	1.0	0.3	0.6	0.1
MSA[1]	7.9	2.4	3.5	0.4	0.1	0.6	0.3	0.4	0.1
U.S.	13.6	4.2	3.5	1.5	1.3	1.1	1.0	0.7	0.2

Note: (1) Figures cover the Oklahoma City, OK Metropolitan Statistical Area; (2) Excludes Mexico.
Source: U.S. Census Bureau, 2015-2019 American Community Survey 5-Year Estimates

Marital Status

Area	Never Married	Now Married[2]	Separated	Widowed	Divorced
City	33.3	45.8	2.3	5.4	13.2
MSA[1]	31.4	48.3	2.0	5.6	12.7
U.S.	33.4	48.1	1.9	5.8	10.9

Note: Figures are percentages and cover the population 15 years of age and older; (1) Figures cover the Oklahoma City, OK Metropolitan Statistical Area; (2) Excludes separated
Source: U.S. Census Bureau, 2015-2019 American Community Survey 5-Year Estimates

Disability by Age

Area	All Ages	Under 18 Years Old	18 to 64 Years Old	65 Years and Over
City	13.2	4.2	12.0	38.6
MSA[1]	13.9	4.3	12.2	39.4
U.S.	12.6	4.2	10.3	34.5

Note: Figures show percent of the civilian noninstitutionalized population that reported having a disability. Disability status is determined from six types of difficulty: vision, hearing, cognitive, ambulatory, self-care, and independent living. For children under 5 years old, hearing and vision difficulty are used to determine disability status. For children between the ages of 5 and 14, disability status is determined from hearing, vision, cognitive, ambulatory, and self-care difficulties. For people aged 15 years and older, they are considered to have a disability if they have difficulty with any one of the six difficulty types; Note: (1) Figures cover the Oklahoma City, OK Metropolitan Statistical Area
Source: U.S. Census Bureau, 2015-2019 American Community Survey 5-Year Estimates

Age

Area	Percent of Population									Median Age
	Under Age 5	Age 5–19	Age 20–34	Age 35–44	Age 45–54	Age 55–64	Age 65–74	Age 75–84	Age 85+	
City	7.6	20.6	23.1	13.4	11.5	11.5	7.4	3.5	1.5	34.1
MSA[1]	6.8	20.6	22.2	13.0	11.8	12.0	8.1	3.9	1.6	35.2
U.S.	6.1	19.1	20.7	12.6	13.0	12.9	9.1	4.6	1.9	38.1

Note: (1) Figures cover the Oklahoma City, OK Metropolitan Statistical Area
Source: U.S. Census Bureau, 2015-2019 American Community Survey 5-Year Estimates

Gender

Area	Males	Females	Males per 100 Females
City	316,500	327,192	96.7
MSA[1]	682,133	700,708	97.3
U.S.	159,886,919	164,810,876	97.0

Note: (1) Figures cover the Oklahoma City, OK Metropolitan Statistical Area
Source: U.S. Census Bureau, 2015-2019 American Community Survey 5-Year Estimates

Religious Groups by Family

Area	Catholic	Baptist	Non-Den.	Methodist[2]	Lutheran	LDS[3]	Pentecostal	Presbyterian[4]	Muslim[5]	Judaism
MSA[1]	6.4	25.4	7.1	10.6	0.7	1.3	3.2	1.0	0.2	0.1
U.S.	19.1	9.3	4.0	4.0	2.3	2.0	1.9	1.6	0.8	0.7

Note: Figures are the number of adherents as a percentage of the total population; (1) Figures cover the Oklahoma City, OK Metropolitan Statistical Area; (2) Methodist/Pietist; (3) Latter Day Saints; (4) Reformed; (5) Figures are estimates
Source: Association of Statisticians of American Religious Bodies, 2010 U.S. Religion Census: Religious Congregations & Membership Study

Religious Groups by Tradition

Area	Catholic	Evangelical Protestant	Mainline Protestant	Other Tradition	Black Protestant	Orthodox
MSA[1]	6.4	39.1	9.9	2.8	1.9	0.2
U.S.	19.1	16.2	7.3	4.3	1.6	0.3

Note: Figures are the number of adherents as a percentage of the total population; (1) Figures cover the Oklahoma City, OK Metropolitan Statistical Area
Source: Association of Statisticians of American Religious Bodies, 2010 U.S. Religion Census: Religious Congregations & Membership Study

ECONOMY

Gross Metropolitan Product

Area	2017	2018	2019	2020	Rank[2]
MSA[1]	74.2	79.6	83.2	88.3	47

Note: Figures are in billions of dollars; (1) Figures cover the Oklahoma City, OK Metropolitan Statistical Area; (2) Rank is based on 2018 data and ranges from 1 to 381
Source: U.S. Conference of Mayors, U.S. Metro Economies: GMP & Employment 2018-2020, September 2019

Economic Growth

Area	2015-17 (%)	2018 (%)	2019 (%)	2020 (%)	Rank[2]
MSA[1]	0.7	2.8	2.9	2.2	259
U.S.	1.9	2.9	2.3	2.1	–

Note: Figures are real gross metropolitan product (GMP) growth rates and represent average annual percent change; (1) Figures cover the Oklahoma City, OK Metropolitan Statistical Area; (2) Rank is based on 2017 2-year average annual percent change and ranges from 1 to 381
Source: U.S. Conference of Mayors, U.S. Metro Economies: GMP & Employment 2018-2020, September 2019

Metropolitan Area Exports

Area	2014	2015	2016	2017	2018	2019	Rank[2]
MSA[1]	1,622.0	1,353.1	1,260.0	1,278.8	1,489.4	1,434.5	127

Note: Figures are in millions of dollars; (1) Figures cover the Oklahoma City, OK Metropolitan Statistical Area; (2) Rank is based on 2019 data and ranges from 1 to 386
Source: U.S. Department of Commerce, International Trade Administration, Office of Trade and Economic Analysis, Industry and Analysis, Exports by Metropolitan Area, data extracted March 24, 2021

Building Permits

Area	Single-Family			Multi-Family			Total		
	2018	2019	Pct. Chg.	2018	2019	Pct. Chg.	2018	2019	Pct. Chg.
City	2,955	3,243	9.7	142	128	-9.9	3,097	3,371	8.8
MSA[1]	5,430	5,924	9.1	300	633	111.0	5,730	6,557	14.4
U.S.	855,300	862,100	0.7	473,500	523,900	10.6	1,328,800	1,386,000	4.3

Note: (1) Figures cover the Oklahoma City, OK Metropolitan Statistical Area; Figures represent new, privately-owned housing units authorized (unadjusted data); All permit data are based on estimates with imputation
Source: U.S. Census Bureau, Manufacturing, Mining, and Construction Statistics, Building Permits, 2018, 2019

Bankruptcy Filings

Area	Business Filings			Nonbusiness Filings		
	2019	2020	% Chg.	2019	2020	% Chg.
Oklahoma County	89	139	56.2	2,147	1,679	-21.8
U.S.	22,780	21,655	-4.9	752,160	522,808	-30.5

Note: Business filings include Chapter 7, Chapter 9, Chapter 11, Chapter 12, Chapter 13, Chapter 15, and Section 304; Nonbusiness filings include Chapter 7, Chapter 11, and Chapter 13
Source: Administrative Office of the U.S. Courts, Business and Nonbusiness Bankruptcy, County Cases Commenced by Chapter of the Bankruptcy Code, During the 12-Month Period Ending December 31, 2019 and Business and Nonbusiness Bankruptcy, County Cases Commenced by Chapter of the Bankruptcy Code, During the 12-Month Period Ending December 31, 2020

Housing Vacancy Rates

Area	Gross Vacancy Rate[2] (%)			Year-Round Vacancy Rate[3] (%)			Rental Vacancy Rate[4] (%)			Homeowner Vacancy Rate[5] (%)		
	2018	2019	2020	2018	2019	2020	2018	2019	2020	2018	2019	2020
MSA[1]	11.5	10.8	7.5	11.2	10.4	7.3	11.8	8.6	6.4	2.7	2.7	0.9
U.S.	12.3	12.0	10.6	9.7	9.5	8.2	6.9	6.7	6.3	1.5	1.4	1.0

Note: (1) Figures cover the Oklahoma City, OK Metropolitan Statistical Area; (2) The percentage of the total housing inventory that is vacant; (3) The percentage of the housing inventory (excluding seasonal units) that is year-round vacant; (4) The percentage of rental inventory that is vacant for rent; (5) The percentage of homeowner inventory that is vacant for sale
Source: U.S. Census Bureau, Housing Vacancies and Homeownership Annual Statistics: 2018, 2019, 2020

INCOME

Income

Area	Per Capita ($)	Median Household ($)	Average Household ($)
City	30,567	55,557	77,896
MSA[1]	31,301	59,084	80,805
U.S.	34,103	62,843	88,607

Note: (1) Figures cover the Oklahoma City, OK Metropolitan Statistical Area
Source: U.S. Census Bureau, 2015-2019 American Community Survey 5-Year Estimates

Household Income Distribution

Area	Percent of Households Earning							
	Under $15,000	$15,000 -$24,999	$25,000 -$34,999	$35,000 -$49,999	$50,000 -$74,999	$75,000 -$99,999	$100,000 -$149,999	$150,000 and up
City	11.3	9.5	10.0	14.0	18.6	12.6	13.3	10.7
MSA[1]	10.1	9.2	9.6	13.6	18.8	13.3	14.1	11.2
U.S.	10.3	8.9	8.9	12.3	17.2	12.7	15.1	14.5

Note: (1) Figures cover the Oklahoma City, OK Metropolitan Statistical Area
Source: U.S. Census Bureau, 2015-2019 American Community Survey 5-Year Estimates

Oklahoma City, Oklahoma

Poverty Rate

Area	All Ages	Under 18 Years Old	18 to 64 Years Old	65 Years and Over
City	16.1	23.7	14.2	9.0
MSA[1]	13.9	19.0	13.2	7.5
U.S.	13.4	18.5	12.6	9.3

Note: Figures are percentage of people whose income during the past 12 months was below the poverty level;
(1) Figures cover the Oklahoma City, OK Metropolitan Statistical Area
Source: U.S. Census Bureau, 2015-2019 American Community Survey 5-Year Estimates

CITY FINANCES

City Government Finances

Component	2017 ($000)	2017 ($ per capita)
Total Revenues	1,516,466	2,402
Total Expenditures	1,362,700	2,158
Debt Outstanding	1,836,790	2,909
Cash and Securities[1]	2,727,642	4,320

Note: (1) Cash and security holdings of a government at the close of its fiscal year,
including those of its dependent agencies, utilities, and liquor stores.
Source: U.S. Census Bureau, State & Local Government Finances 2017

City Government Revenue by Source

Source	2017 ($000)	2017 ($ per capita)	2017 (%)
General Revenue			
From Federal Government	55,396	88	3.7
From State Government	87,648	139	5.8
From Local Governments	54,532	86	3.6
Taxes			
Property	103,227	164	6.8
Sales and Gross Receipts	472,619	749	31.2
Personal Income	0	0	0.0
Corporate Income	0	0	0.0
Motor Vehicle License	0	0	0.0
Other Taxes	66,634	106	4.4
Current Charges	273,900	434	18.1
Liquor Store	0	0	0.0
Utility	161,785	256	10.7
Employee Retirement	86,474	137	5.7

Source: U.S. Census Bureau, State & Local Government Finances 2017

City Government Expenditures by Function

Function	2017 ($000)	2017 ($ per capita)	2017 (%)
General Direct Expenditures			
Air Transportation	78,558	124	5.8
Corrections	7,188	11	0.5
Education	0	0	0.0
Employment Security Administration	0	0	0.0
Financial Administration	36,489	57	2.7
Fire Protection	129,112	204	9.5
General Public Buildings	0	0	0.0
Governmental Administration, Other	14,772	23	1.1
Health	5,580	8	0.4
Highways	77,227	122	5.7
Hospitals	0	0	0.0
Housing and Community Development	50,468	79	3.7
Interest on General Debt	36,151	57	2.7
Judicial and Legal	29,843	47	2.2
Libraries	0	0	0.0
Parking	4,242	6	0.3
Parks and Recreation	230,879	365	16.9
Police Protection	183,966	291	13.5
Public Welfare	0	0	0.0
Sewerage	31,812	50	2.3
Solid Waste Management	42,925	68	3.2
Veterans' Services	0	0	0.0
Liquor Store	0	0	0.0
Utility	301,993	478	22.2
Employee Retirement	34,727	55	2.5

Source: U.S. Census Bureau, State & Local Government Finances 2017

EMPLOYMENT

Labor Force and Employment

Area	Civilian Labor Force			Workers Employed		
	Dec. 2019	Dec. 2020	% Chg.	Dec. 2019	Dec. 2020	% Chg.
City	322,420	325,821	1.1	313,116	308,959	-1.3
MSA[1]	687,962	693,472	0.8	668,536	660,099	-1.3
U.S.	164,007,000	160,017,000	-2.4	158,504,000	149,613,000	-5.6

Note: Data is not seasonally adjusted and covers workers 16 years of age and older; (1) Figures cover the Oklahoma City, OK Metropolitan Statistical Area
Source: Bureau of Labor Statistics, Local Area Unemployment Statistics

Unemployment Rate

Area	2020											
	Jan.	Feb.	Mar.	Apr.	May	Jun.	Jul.	Aug.	Sep.	Oct.	Nov.	Dec.
City	2.9	2.7	2.7	15.8	13.7	7.2	7.6	5.9	5.5	6.3	6.0	5.2
MSA[1]	2.9	2.7	2.7	14.8	12.9	6.9	7.1	5.6	5.1	5.9	5.6	4.8
U.S.	4.0	3.8	4.5	14.4	13.0	11.2	10.5	8.5	7.7	6.6	6.4	6.5

Note: Data is not seasonally adjusted and covers workers 16 years of age and older; (1) Figures cover the Oklahoma City, OK Metropolitan Statistical Area
Source: Bureau of Labor Statistics, Local Area Unemployment Statistics

Average Wages

Occupation	$/Hr.	Occupation	$/Hr.
Accountants and Auditors	38.00	Maintenance and Repair Workers	18.60
Automotive Mechanics	23.70	Marketing Managers	66.70
Bookkeepers	19.70	Network and Computer Systems Admin.	37.70
Carpenters	20.80	Nurses, Licensed Practical	21.30
Cashiers	11.00	Nurses, Registered	32.90
Computer Programmers	38.30	Nursing Assistants	13.40
Computer Systems Analysts	38.40	Office Clerks, General	15.50
Computer User Support Specialists	24.90	Physical Therapists	43.30
Construction Laborers	16.60	Physicians	98.10
Cooks, Restaurant	13.20	Plumbers, Pipefitters and Steamfitters	27.60
Customer Service Representatives	16.50	Police and Sheriff's Patrol Officers	27.60
Dentists	80.70	Postal Service Mail Carriers	25.80
Electricians	24.20	Real Estate Sales Agents	27.10
Engineers, Electrical	47.50	Retail Salespersons	14.40
Fast Food and Counter Workers	10.50	Sales Representatives, Technical/Scientific	47.80
Financial Managers	56.40	Secretaries, Exc. Legal/Medical/Executive	16.60
First-Line Supervisors of Office Workers	26.50	Security Guards	17.60
General and Operations Managers	54.00	Surgeons	n/a
Hairdressers/Cosmetologists	13.20	Teacher Assistants, Exc. Postsecondary*	10.90
Home Health and Personal Care Aides	11.30	Teachers, Secondary School, Exc. Sp. Ed.*	23.80
Janitors and Cleaners	12.30	Telemarketers	14.00
Landscaping/Groundskeeping Workers	14.60	Truck Drivers, Heavy/Tractor-Trailer	24.40
Lawyers	60.40	Truck Drivers, Light/Delivery Services	18.00
Maids and Housekeeping Cleaners	11.40	Waiters and Waitresses	11.60

Note: Wage data covers the Oklahoma City, OK Metropolitan Statistical Area; (*) Hourly wages were calculated from annual wage data based on a 40 hour work week; n/a not available.
Source: Bureau of Labor Statistics, Metro Area Occupational Employment & Wage Estimates, May 2020

Employment by Industry

Sector	MSA[1]		U.S.
	Number of Employees	Percent of Total	Percent of Total
Construction	30,800	4.9	5.1
Education and Health Services	98,200	15.5	16.3
Financial Activities	34,700	5.5	6.1
Government	128,300	20.2	15.2
Information	5,700	0.9	1.9
Leisure and Hospitality	66,400	10.5	9.0
Manufacturing	33,000	5.2	8.5
Mining and Logging	7,800	1.2	0.4
Other Services	27,300	4.3	3.8
Professional and Business Services	81,600	12.9	14.4
Retail Trade	67,900	10.7	10.9
Transportation, Warehousing, and Utilities	30,600	4.8	4.6
Wholesale Trade	22,100	3.5	3.9

Note: Figures are non-farm employment as of December 2020. Figures are not seasonally adjusted and include workers 16 years of age and older; (1) Figures cover the Oklahoma City, OK Metropolitan Statistical Area
Source: Bureau of Labor Statistics, Current Employment Statistics, Employment, Hours, and Earnings

Oklahoma City, Oklahoma

Employment by Occupation

Occupation Classification	City (%)	MSA[1] (%)	U.S. (%)
Management, Business, Science, and Arts	36.7	37.6	38.5
Natural Resources, Construction, and Maintenance	10.6	10.5	8.9
Production, Transportation, and Material Moving	12.2	11.8	13.2
Sales and Office	23.1	23.0	21.6
Service	17.5	17.1	17.8

Note: Figures cover employed civilians 16 years of age and older; (1) Figures cover the Oklahoma City, OK Metropolitan Statistical Area
Source: U.S. Census Bureau, 2015-2019 American Community Survey 5-Year Estimates

Occupations with Greatest Projected Employment Growth: 2020 – 2022

Occupation[1]	2020 Employment	2022 Projected Employment	Numeric Employment Change	Percent Employment Change
Home Health and Personal Care Aides	20,550	21,560	1,010	4.9
Fast Food and Counter Workers	39,040	40,030	990	2.5
Registered Nurses	38,490	39,340	850	2.2
Cooks, Restaurant	17,770	18,610	840	4.7
Elementary School Teachers, Except Special Education	18,640	19,120	480	2.6
Medical and Health Services Managers	7,810	8,280	470	6.0
Laborers and Freight, Stock, and Material Movers, Hand	31,360	31,740	380	1.2
Medical Assistants	9,400	9,760	360	3.8
Secondary School Teachers, Except Special and Career/Technical Education	12,000	12,320	320	2.7
Teaching Assistants, Except Postsecondary	13,690	13,990	300	2.2

Note: Projections cover Oklahoma; (1) Sorted by numeric employment change
Source: www.projectionscentral.com, State Occupational Projections, 2020–2022 Short-Term Projections

Fastest-Growing Occupations: 2020 – 2022

Occupation[1]	2020 Employment	2022 Projected Employment	Numeric Employment Change	Percent Employment Change
Wind Turbine Service Technicians	400	460	60	15.0
Veterinary Technologists and Technicians	860	940	80	9.3
Veterinary Assistants and Laboratory Animal Caretakers	1,600	1,740	140	8.8
Nurse Practitioners	2,010	2,170	160	8.0
Veterinarians	1,360	1,460	100	7.4
Occupational Therapy Assistants	860	920	60	7.0
Physical Therapist Assistants	1,680	1,790	110	6.5
Nonfarm Animal Caretakers	2,870	3,050	180	6.3
Physician Assistants	1,640	1,740	100	6.1
Medical and Health Services Managers	7,810	8,280	470	6.0

Note: Projections cover Oklahoma; (1) Sorted by percent employment change and excludes occupations with numeric employment change less than 50
Source: www.projectionscentral.com, State Occupational Projections, 2020–2022 Short-Term Projections

TAXES

State Corporate Income Tax Rates

State	Tax Rate (%)	Income Brackets ($)	Num. of Brackets	Financial Institution Tax Rate (%)[a]	Federal Income Tax Ded.
Oklahoma	6.0	Flat rate	1	6.0	No

Note: Tax rates as of January 1, 2021; (a) Rates listed are the corporate income tax rate applied to financial institutions or excise taxes based on income. Some states have other taxes based upon the value of deposits or shares.
Source: Federation of Tax Administrators, State Corporate Income Tax Rates, January 1, 2021

State Individual Income Tax Rates

State	Tax Rate (%)	Income Brackets ($)	Personal Exemptions ($)			Standard Ded. ($)	
			Single	Married	Depend.	Single	Married
Oklahoma	0.5 - 5.0	1,000 - 7,200 (t)	1,000	2,000	1,000	6,350	12,700

Note: Tax rates as of January 1, 2021; Local- and county-level taxes are not included; Federal income tax is not deductible on state income tax returns; (t) The income brackets reported for Oklahoma are for single persons. For married persons filing jointly, the same tax rates apply to income brackets ranging from $2,000, to $12,200.
Source: Federation of Tax Administrators, State Individual Income Tax Rates, January 1, 2021

Various State Sales and Excise Tax Rates

State	State Sales Tax (%)	Gasoline[1] (¢/gal.)	Cigarette[2] ($/pack)	Spirits[3] ($/gal.)	Wine[4] ($/gal.)	Beer[5] ($/gal.)	Recreational Marijuana (%)
Oklahoma	4.5	20	2.03	5.56	0.72	0.4	Not legal

Note: All tax rates as of January 1, 2021; (1) The American Petroleum Institute has developed a methodology for determining the average tax rate on a gallon of fuel. Rates may include any of the following: excise taxes, environmental fees, storage tank fees, other fees or taxes, general sales tax, and local taxes; (2) The federal excise tax of $1.0066 per pack and local taxes are not included; (3) Rates are those applicable to off-premise sales of 40% alcohol by volume (a.b.v.) distilled spirits in 750ml containers. Local excise taxes are excluded; (4) Rates are those applicable to off-premise sales of 11% a.b.v. non-carbonated wine in 750ml containers; (5) Rates are those applicable to off-premise sales of 4.7% a.b.v. beer in 12 ounce containers.
Source: Tax Foundation, 2021 Facts & Figures: How Does Your State Compare?

State Business Tax Climate Index Rankings

State	Overall Rank	Corporate Tax Rank	Individual Income Tax Rank	Sales Tax Rank	Property Tax Rank	Unemployment Insurance Tax Rank
Oklahoma	30	11	33	39	29	1

Note: The index is a measure of how each state's tax laws affect economic performance. The lower the rank, the more favorable a state's tax system is for business. States without a given tax are given a ranking of 1. The scores/rankings for the District of Columbia do not affect other states. The 2021 index represents the tax climate as of July 1, 2020.
Source: Tax Foundation, State Business Tax Climate Index 2021

TRANSPORTATION

Means of Transportation to Work

Area	Car/Truck/Van		Public Transportation			Bicycle	Walked	Other Means	Worked at Home
	Drove Alone	Car-pooled	Bus	Subway	Railroad				
City	82.6	10.5	0.5	0.0	0.0	0.1	1.5	1.1	3.6
MSA[1]	83.2	9.4	0.4	0.0	0.0	0.3	1.6	1.0	4.1
U.S.	76.3	9.0	2.4	1.9	0.6	0.5	2.7	1.4	5.2

Note: Figures are percentages and cover workers 16 years of age and older; (1) Figures cover the Oklahoma City, OK Metropolitan Statistical Area
Source: U.S. Census Bureau, 2015-2019 American Community Survey 5-Year Estimates

Travel Time to Work

Area	Less Than 10 Minutes	10 to 19 Minutes	20 to 29 Minutes	30 to 44 Minutes	45 to 59 Minutes	60 to 89 Minutes	90 Minutes or More
City	11.2	35.5	29.5	17.7	3.3	1.5	1.3
MSA[1]	12.3	32.0	25.7	20.3	5.7	2.4	1.5
U.S.	12.2	28.4	20.8	20.8	8.3	6.4	2.9

Note: Note: Figures are percentages and include workers 16 years old and over; (1) Figures cover the Oklahoma City, OK Metropolitan Statistical Area
Source: U.S. Census Bureau, 2015-2019 American Community Survey 5-Year Estimates

Key Congestion Measures

Measure	1982	1992	2002	2012	2017
Annual Hours of Delay, Total (000)	4,550	10,361	25,336	36,587	43,448
Annual Hours of Delay, Per Auto Commuter	11	20	39	45	50
Annual Congestion Cost, Total (million $)	34	109	341	653	798
Annual Congestion Cost, Per Auto Commuter ($)	197	309	589	667	768

Note: Covers the Oklahoma City OK urban area
Source: Texas A&M Transportation Institute, 2019 Urban Mobility Report

Freeway Travel Time Index

Measure	1982	1987	1992	1997	2002	2007	2012	2017
Urban Area Index[1]	1.05	1.07	1.09	1.13	1.17	1.18	1.18	1.19
Urban Area Rank[1,2]	51	55	70	62	41	44	40	41

Note: Freeway Travel Time Index—the ratio of travel time in the peak period to the travel time at free-flow conditions. For example, a value of 1.30 indicates a 20-minute free-flow trip takes 26 minutes in the peak (20 minutes x 1.30 = 26 minutes); (1) Covers the Oklahoma City OK urban area; (2) Rank is based on 101 larger urban areas (#1 = highest travel time index)
Source: Texas A&M Transportation Institute, 2019 Urban Mobility Report

Public Transportation

Agency Name / Mode of Transportation	Vehicles Operated in Maximum Service[1]	Annual Unlinked Passenger Trips[2] (in thous.)	Annual Passenger Miles[3] (in thous.)
Central Oklahoma Transportation & Parking Authority (COTPA)			
Bus (directly operated)	49	2,921.1	14,311.2
Demand Response (directly operated)	17	56.4	493.5
Demand Response Taxi (purchased transportation)	5	3.8	23.6
Ferryboat (purchased transportation)	2	3.7	9.6
Streetcar Rail (purchased transportation)	5	133.8	373.6
Vanpool (purchased transportation)	2	4.3	130.0

Note: (1) Number of revenue vehicles operated by the given mode and type of service to meet the annual maximum service requirement. This is the revenue vehicle count during the peak season of the year; on the week and day that maximum service is provided. Vehicles operated in maximum service (VOMS) exclude atypical days and one-time special events; (2) Number of passengers who boarded public transportation vehicles. Passengers are counted each time they board a vehicle no matter how many vehicles they use to travel from their origin to their destination. (3) Sum of the distances ridden by all passengers during the entire fiscal year.
Source: Federal Transit Administration, National Transit Database, 2019

Air Transportation

Airport Name and Code / Type of Service	Passenger Airlines[1]	Passenger Enplanements	Freight Carriers[2]	Freight (lbs)
Will Rogers World Airport (OKC)				
Domestic service (U.S. carriers - 2020)	25	934,632	12	33,181,744
International service (U.S. carriers - 2019)	2	277	1	57,420

Note: (1) Includes all U.S.-based major, minor and commuter airlines that carried at least one passenger during the year; (2) Includes all U.S.-based airlines and freight carriers that transported at least one pound of freight during the year.
Source: Bureau of Transportation Statistics, The Intermodal Transportation Database, Air Carriers: T-100 Domestic Market (U.S. Carriers), 2020; Bureau of Transportation Statistics, The Intermodal Transportation Database, Air Carriers: T-100 International Market (U.S. Carriers), 2019

BUSINESSES

Major Business Headquarters

Company Name	Industry	Rankings	
		Fortune[1]	Forbes[2]
Chesapeake Energy	Mining, Crude-Oil Production	373	-
Devon Energy	Mining, Crude-Oil Production	419	-
Hobby Lobby Stores	Retailing	-	79
Love's Travel Stops & Country Stores	Convenience Stores & Gas Stations	-	16

Note: (1) Companies that produce a 10-K are ranked 1 to 500 based on 2019 revenue; (2) All private companies with at least $2 billion in annual revenue through the end of their most current fiscal year are ranked 1 to 219; companies listed are headquartered in the city; dashes indicate no ranking
Source: Fortune, "Fortune 500," June/July 2020; Forbes, "America's Largest Private Companies," 2020

Fastest-Growing Businesses

According to *Inc.*, Oklahoma City is home to one of America's 500 fastest-growing private companies: **Insights to Behavior** (#312). Criteria: must be an independent, privately-held, for-profit, U.S. corporation, proprietorship or partnership as of December 31, 2019; revenues must be at least $100,000 in 2016 and $2 million in 2019; must have four-year operating/sales history. *Inc., "America's 500 Fastest-Growing Private Companies," 2020*

According to *Fortune*, Oklahoma City is home to one of the 100 fastest-growing companies in the world: **Paycom Software** (#18). Companies were ranked by their revenue growth rate; their EPS growth rate; and their three-year annualized total return to investors for the period ending June 30, 2020. Criteria for inclusion: a company, foreign or domestic, must trade on a major U.S. stock exchange; must file quarterly reports with the SEC; must have a minimum market capitalization of $250 million; must have a stock price of at least $5 on June 30, 2020; must have been trading continuously since June 30, 2017; must have revenue and net income for the four quarters ended on or before April 30, 2020, of at least $50 million and $10 million, respectively; and must have posted a compound annual growth in revenue and earnings per share of at least 15% annually over the three years ending on or before April 30, 2020. Real estate investment trusts, limited-liability companies, limited parterships, business development companies, closed-end investment firms, companies about to be acquired, and companies that lost money in the quarter ending April 30, 2020 were excluded. *Fortune, "100 Fastest-Growing Companies," 2020*

Living Environment

COST OF LIVING

Cost of Living Index

Composite Index	Groceries	Housing	Utilities	Trans- portation	Health Care	Misc. Goods/ Services
86.3	90.8	70.7	95.6	89.7	97.9	91.9

Note: The Cost of Living Index measures regional differences in the cost of consumer goods and services, excluding taxes and non-consumer expenditures, for professional and managerial households in the top income quintile. It is based on more than 50,000 prices covering almost 60 different items for which prices are collected three times a year by chambers of commerce, economic development organizations or university applied economic centers in each participating urban area. The numbers shown should be read as a percentage above or below the national average of 100. For example, a value of 115.4 in the groceries column indicates that grocery prices are 15.4% higher than the national average. Small differences in the index numbers should not be interpreted as significant; Figures cover the Oklahoma City OK urban area.
Source: The Council for Community and Economic Research, Cost of Living Index, 2020

Grocery Prices

Area[1]	T-Bone Steak ($/pound)	Frying Chicken ($/pound)	Whole Milk ($/half gal.)	Eggs ($/dozen)	Orange Juice ($/64 oz.)	Coffee ($/11.5 oz.)
City[2]	11.70	1.34	1.87	1.23	3.23	4.07
Avg.	11.78	1.39	2.05	1.47	3.57	4.34
Min.	8.03	0.94	1.03	0.74	2.94	3.02
Max.	15.86	2.65	4.31	3.77	5.44	8.69

*Note: (1) Values for the local area are compared with the average, minimum and maximum values for all 284 areas in the Cost of Living Index; (2) Figures cover the Oklahoma City OK urban area; **T-Bone Steak** (price per pound); **Frying Chicken** (price per pound, whole fryer); **Whole Milk** (half gallon carton); **Eggs** (price per dozen, Grade A, large); **Orange Juice** (64 oz. Tropicana or Florida Natural); **Coffee** (11.5 oz. can, vacuum-packed, Maxwell House, Hills Bros, or Folgers).*
Source: The Council for Community and Economic Research, Cost of Living Index, 2020

Housing and Utility Costs

Area[1]	New Home Price ($)	Apartment Rent ($/month)	All Electric ($/month)	Part Electric ($/month)	Other Energy ($/month)	Telephone ($/month)
City[2]	258,612	873	-	92.78	58.17	188.40
Avg.	368,594	1,168	170.86	100.47	65.28	184.30
Min.	190,567	502	91.58	31.42	26.08	169.60
Max.	2,227,806	4,738	470.38	280.31	280.06	206.50

*Note: (1) Values for the local area are compared with the average, minimum and maximum values for all 284 areas in the Cost of Living Index; (2) Figures cover the Oklahoma City OK urban area; **New Home Price** (2,400 sf living area, 8,000 sf lot, in urban area with full utilities); **Apartment Rent** (950 sf 2 bedroom/1.5 or 2 bath, unfurnished, excluding all utilities except water); **All Electric** (average monthly cost for an all-electric home); **Part Electric** (average monthly cost for a part-electric home); **Other Energy** (average monthly cost for natural gas, fuel oil, coal, wood, and any other forms of energy except electricity); **Telephone** (price includes the base monthly rate plus taxes and fees for three lines of mobile phone service).*
Source: The Council for Community and Economic Research, Cost of Living Index, 2020

Health Care, Transportation, and Other Costs

Area[1]	Doctor ($/visit)	Dentist ($/visit)	Optometrist ($/visit)	Gasoline ($/gallon)	Beauty Salon ($/visit)	Men's Shirt ($)
City[2]	112.21	93.98	102.53	1.90	40.17	18.12
Avg.	115.44	99.32	108.10	2.21	39.27	31.37
Min.	36.68	59.00	51.36	1.71	19.00	11.00
Max.	219.00	153.10	250.97	3.46	82.05	58.33

*Note: (1) Values for the local area are compared with the average, minimum and maximum values for all 284 areas in the Cost of Living Index; (2) Figures cover the Oklahoma City OK urban area; **Doctor** (general practitioners routine exam of an established patient); **Dentist** (adult teeth cleaning and periodic oral examination); **Optometrist** (full vision eye exam for established adult patient); **Gasoline** (one gallon regular unleaded, national brand, including all taxes, cash price at self-service pump if available); **Beauty Salon** (woman's shampoo, trim, and blow-dry); **Men's Shirt** (cotton/polyester dress shirt, pinpoint weave, long sleeves).*
Source: The Council for Community and Economic Research, Cost of Living Index, 2020

HOUSING

Homeownership Rate

Area	2012 (%)	2013 (%)	2014 (%)	2015 (%)	2016 (%)	2017 (%)	2018 (%)	2019 (%)	2020 (%)
MSA[1]	67.3	67.6	65.7	61.4	63.1	64.7	64.6	64.3	68.3
U.S.	65.4	65.1	64.5	63.7	63.4	63.9	64.4	64.6	66.6

Note: (1) Figures cover the Oklahoma City, OK Metropolitan Statistical Area
Source: U.S. Census Bureau, Housing Vacancies and Homeownership Annual Statistics: 2012-2020

House Price Index (HPI)

Area	National Ranking[2]	Quarterly Change (%)	One-Year Change (%)	Five-Year Change (%)	Since 1991Q1 (%)
MSA[1]	182	1.07	5.23	21.46	179.09
U.S.[3]	–	3.81	10.77	38.99	205.12

Note: The HPI is a weighted repeat sales index. It measures average price changes in repeat sales or refinancings on the same properties. This information is obtained by reviewing repeat mortgage transactions on single-family properties whose mortgages have been purchased or securitized by Fannie Mae or Freddie Mac since January 1975; (1) Figures cover the Oklahoma City, OK Metropolitan Statistical Area; (2) Rankings are based on annual percentage change for all metro areas containing at least 15,000 transactions over the last 10 years and ranges from 1 to 253; (3) figures based on a weighted average of Census Division estimates using a seasonally adjusted, purchase-only index; all figures are for the period ending December 31, 2020
Source: Federal Housing Finance Agency, Change in Metropolitan Area House Price Indexes, April 7, 2021

Median Single-Family Home Prices

Area	2018	2019	2020[p]	Percent Change 2019 to 2020
MSA[1]	159.5	158.9	174.9	10.1
U.S. Average	261.6	274.6	299.9	9.2

Note: Figures are median sales prices of existing single-family homes in thousands of dollars; (p) preliminary; (1) Figures cover the Oklahoma City, OK Metropolitan Statistical Area
Source: National Association of Realtors, Median Sales Price of Existing Single-Family Homes for Metropolitan Areas, 4th Quarter 2020

Qualifying Income Based on Median Sales Price of Existing Single-Family Homes

Area	With 5% Down ($)	With 10% Down ($)	With 20% Down ($)
MSA[1]	34,254	32,451	28,845
U.S. Average	59,266	56,147	49,908

Note: Figures are preliminary; Qualifying income is based on a mortgage rate of 2.81%. Monthly principal and interest payment is limited to 25% of income; (1) Figures cover the Oklahoma City, OK Metropolitan Statistical Area
Source: National Association of Realtors, Qualifying Income Based on Median Sales Price of Existing Single-Family Homes for Metropolitan Areas, 4th Quarter 2020

Home Value Distribution

Area	Under $50,000	$50,000 -$99,999	$100,000 -$149,999	$150,000 -$199,999	$200,000 -$299,999	$300,000 -$499,999	$500,000 -$999,999	$1,000,000 or more
City	7.9	18.0	19.9	20.8	18.9	10.2	3.4	0.8
MSA[1]	7.5	17.7	21.3	19.6	18.4	10.9	3.7	1.0
U.S.	6.9	12.0	13.3	14.0	19.6	19.3	11.4	3.4

Note: Figures are percentages and cover owner-occupied housing units; (1) Figures cover the Oklahoma City, OK Metropolitan Statistical Area
Source: U.S. Census Bureau, 2015-2019 American Community Survey 5-Year Estimates

Year Housing Structure Built

Area	2010 or Later	2000 -2009	1990 -1999	1980 -1989	1970 -1979	1960 -1969	1950 -1959	1940 -1949	Before 1940	Median Year
City	9.4	13.1	9.5	14.9	16.1	12.6	10.6	5.5	8.4	1978
MSA[1]	9.3	15.0	11.1	14.8	17.2	12.0	9.6	4.8	6.2	1980
U.S.	5.2	14.0	13.9	13.4	15.2	10.6	10.3	4.9	12.6	1978

Note: Figures are percentages except for Median Year; Note: (1) Figures cover the Oklahoma City, OK Metropolitan Statistical Area
Source: U.S. Census Bureau, 2015-2019 American Community Survey 5-Year Estimates

Gross Monthly Rent

Area	Under $500	$500 -$999	$1,000 -$1,499	$1,500 -$1,999	$2,000 -$2,499	$2,500 -$2,999	$3,000 and up	Median ($)
City	8.1	57.1	27.0	6.0	1.2	0.4	0.4	871
MSA[1]	8.2	56.4	27.3	6.2	1.3	0.3	0.4	876
U.S.	9.4	36.2	30.0	14.0	5.6	2.4	2.4	1,062

Note: Figures are percentages except for Median; Gross rent is the contract rent plus the estimated average monthly cost of utilities (electricity, gas, and water and sewer) and fuels (oil, coal, kerosene, wood, etc.) if these are paid by the renter (or paid for the renter by someone else); (1) Figures cover the Oklahoma City, OK Metropolitan Statistical Area
Source: U.S. Census Bureau, 2015-2019 American Community Survey 5-Year Estimates

HEALTH

Health Risk Factors

Category	MSA[1] (%)	U.S. (%)
Adults aged 18–64 who have any kind of health care coverage	80.7	87.3
Adults who reported being in good or better health	80.8	82.4
Adults who have been told they have high blood cholesterol	35.9	33.0
Adults who have been told they have high blood pressure	34.7	32.3
Adults who are current smokers	17.1	17.1
Adults who currently use E-cigarettes	6.6	4.6
Adults who currently use chewing tobacco, snuff, or snus	5.8	4.0
Adults who are heavy drinkers[2]	4.4	6.3
Adults who are binge drinkers[3]	14.7	17.4
Adults who are overweight (BMI 25.0 - 29.9)	33.5	35.3
Adults who are obese (BMI 30.0 - 99.8)	34.6	31.3
Adults who participated in any physical activities in the past month	71.9	74.4
Adults who always or nearly always wears a seat belt	94.9	94.3

Note: (1) Figures cover the Oklahoma City, OK Metropolitan Statistical Area; (2) Heavy drinkers are classified as adult men having more than 14 drinks per week and adult women having more than 7 drinks per week; (3) Binge drinkers are classified as males having five or more drinks on one occasion or females having four or more drinks on one occasion
Source: Centers for Disease Control and Prevention, Behaviorial Risk Factor Surveillance System, SMART: Selected Metropolitan Area Risk Trends, 2017

Acute and Chronic Health Conditions

Category	MSA[1] (%)	U.S. (%)
Adults who have ever been told they had a heart attack	4.9	4.2
Adults who have ever been told they have angina or coronary heart disease	5.1	3.9
Adults who have ever been told they had a stroke	3.4	3.0
Adults who have ever been told they have asthma	14.2	14.2
Adults who have ever been told they have arthritis	26.9	24.9
Adults who have ever been told they have diabetes[2]	12.1	10.5
Adults who have ever been told they had skin cancer	5.9	6.2
Adults who have ever been told they had any other types of cancer	7.0	7.1
Adults who have ever been told they have COPD	7.2	6.5
Adults who have ever been told they have kidney disease	4.1	3.0
Adults who have ever been told they have a form of depression	23.1	20.5

Note: (1) Figures cover the Oklahoma City, OK Metropolitan Statistical Area; (2) Figures do not include pregnancy-related, borderline, or pre-diabetes
Source: Centers for Disease Control and Prevention, Behaviorial Risk Factor Surveillance System, SMART: Selected Metropolitan Area Risk Trends, 2017

Health Screening and Vaccination Rates

Category	MSA[1] (%)	U.S. (%)
Adults aged 65+ who have had flu shot within the past year	70.4	60.7
Adults aged 65+ who have ever had a pneumonia vaccination	82.0	75.4
Adults who have ever been tested for HIV	32.8	36.1
Adults who have ever had the shingles or zoster vaccine?	30.7	28.9
Adults who have had their blood cholesterol checked within the last five years	83.2	85.9

Note: n/a not available; (1) Figures cover the Oklahoma City, OK Metropolitan Statistical Area.
Source: Centers for Disease Control and Prevention, Behaviorial Risk Factor Surveillance System, SMART: Selected Metropolitan Area Risk Trends, 2017

Disability Status

Category	MSA[1] (%)	U.S. (%)
Adults who reported being deaf	7.9	6.7
Are you blind or have serious difficulty seeing, even when wearing glasses?	6.3	4.5
Are you limited in any way in any of your usual activities due of arthritis?	15.0	12.9
Do you have difficulty doing errands alone?	9.9	6.8
Do you have difficulty dressing or bathing?	5.9	3.6
Do you have serious difficulty concentrating/remembering/making decisions?	14.7	10.7
Do you have serious difficulty walking or climbing stairs?	17.4	13.6

Note: (1) Figures cover the Oklahoma City, OK Metropolitan Statistical Area.
Source: Centers for Disease Control and Prevention, Behaviorial Risk Factor Surveillance System, SMART: Selected Metropolitan Area Risk Trends, 2017

Mortality Rates for the Top 10 Causes of Death in the U.S.

ICD-10[a] Sub-Chapter	ICD-10[a] Code	Age-Adjusted Mortality Rate[1] per 100,000 population	
		County[2]	U.S.
Malignant neoplasms	C00-C97	176.3	149.2
Ischaemic heart diseases	I20-I25	116.4	90.5
Other forms of heart disease	I30-I51	47.6	52.2
Chronic lower respiratory diseases	J40-J47	59.8	39.6
Other degenerative diseases of the nervous system	G30-G31	56.6	37.6
Cerebrovascular diseases	I60-I69	41.8	37.2
Other external causes of accidental injury	W00-X59	49.7	36.1
Organic, including symptomatic, mental disorders	F01-F09	32.7	29.4
Hypertensive diseases	I10-I15	53.6	24.1
Diabetes mellitus	E10-E14	30.4	21.5

Note: (a) ICD-10 = International Classification of Diseases 10th Revision; (1) Mortality rates are a three-year average covering 2017-2019; (2) Figures cover Oklahoma County.
Source: Centers for Disease Control and Prevention, National Center for Health Statistics. Underlying Cause of Death 1999-2019 on CDC WONDER Online Database

Mortality Rates for Selected Causes of Death

ICD-10[a] Sub-Chapter	ICD-10[a] Code	Age-Adjusted Mortality Rate[1] per 100,000 population	
		County[2]	U.S.
Assault	X85-Y09	10.9	6.0
Diseases of the liver	K70-K76	19.0	14.4
Human immunodeficiency virus (HIV) disease	B20-B24	2.8	1.5
Influenza and pneumonia	J09-J18	12.8	13.8
Intentional self-harm	X60-X84	19.0	14.1
Malnutrition	E40-E46	2.6	2.3
Obesity and other hyperalimentation	E65-E68	2.0	2.1
Renal failure	N17-N19	9.8	12.6
Transport accidents	V01-V99	14.1	12.3
Viral hepatitis	B15-B19	2.4	1.2

Note: (a) ICD-10 = International Classification of Diseases 10th Revision; (1) Mortality rates are a three-year average covering 2017-2019; (2) Figures cover Oklahoma County; Data are suppressed when the data meet the criteria for confidentiality constraints; Mortality rates are flagged as unreliable when the rate would be calculated with a numerator of 20 or less.
Source: Centers for Disease Control and Prevention, National Center for Health Statistics. Underlying Cause of Death 1999-2019 on CDC WONDER Online Database

Health Insurance Coverage

Area	With Health Insurance	With Private Health Insurance	With Public Health Insurance	Without Health Insurance	Population Under Age 19 Without Health Insurance
City	85.4	64.0	32.1	14.6	7.1
MSA[1]	87.5	68.6	30.8	12.5	6.2
U.S.	91.2	67.9	35.1	8.8	5.1

Note: Figures are percentages that cover the civilian noninstitutionalized population; (1) Figures cover the Oklahoma City, OK Metropolitan Statistical Area
Source: U.S. Census Bureau, 2015-2019 American Community Survey 5-Year Estimates

Number of Medical Professionals

Area	MDs[3]	DOs[3,4]	Dentists	Podiatrists	Chiropractors	Optometrists
County[1] (number)	3,242	330	842	42	218	146
County[1] (rate[2])	410.1	41.7	105.6	5.3	27.3	18.3
U.S. (rate[2])	282.9	22.7	71.2	6.2	28.1	16.9

40109
Note: Data as of 2019 unless noted; (1) Data covers Oklahoma County; (2) Rate per 100,000 population; (3) Data as of 2018 and includes all active, non-federal physicians; (4) Doctor of Osteopathic Medicine
Source: U.S. Department of Health and Human Services, Health Resources and Services Administration, Bureau of Health Professions, Area Resource File (ARF) 2019-2020

EDUCATION

Public School District Statistics

District Name	Schls	Pupils	Pupil/ Teacher Ratio	Minority Pupils[1] (%)	Free Lunch Eligible[2] (%)	IEP[3] (%)
Epic Blended Learning Charter	6	7,773	23.6	42.2	n/a	14.6
Epic One On One Charter School	3	13,532	27.4	32.8	n/a	18.3
Oklahoma City	78	37,530	16.7	86.6	n/a	15.1
Santa Fe South (charter)	7	3,278	17.9	97.3	n/a	10.6
Western Heights	8	3,363	14.8	78.5	n/a	13.1

Note: Table includes school districts with 2,000 or more students; (1) Percentage of students that are not non-Hispanic white; (2) Percentage of students that are eligible for the free lunch program; (3) Percentage of students that have an Individualized Education Program.
Source: U.S. Department of Education, National Center for Education Statistics, Common Core of Data, Local Education Agency (School District) Universe Survey: School Year 2018-2019; U.S. Department of Education, National Center for Education Statistics, Common Core of Data, Public Elementary/Secondary School Universe Survey: School Year 2018-2019

Best High Schools

According to *U.S. News,* Oklahoma City is home to two of the top 500 high schools in the U.S.: **Classen High School of Advanced Studies** (#84); **Harding Charter Preparatory High School** (#96). Nearly 18,000 public, magnet and charter schools were ranked based on their performance on state assessments and how well they prepare students for college. *U.S. News & World Report, "Best High Schools 2020"*

Highest Level of Education

Area	Less than H.S.	H.S. Diploma	Some College, No Deg.	Associate Degree	Bachelor's Degree	Master's Degree	Prof. School Degree	Doctorate Degree
City	13.6	25.4	22.9	7.3	19.7	7.5	2.4	1.1
MSA[1]	11.0	27.3	23.6	7.5	19.6	7.6	2.0	1.3
U.S.	12.0	27.0	20.4	8.5	19.8	8.8	2.1	1.4

Note: Figures cover persons age 25 and over; (1) Figures cover the Oklahoma City, OK Metropolitan Statistical Area
Source: U.S. Census Bureau, 2015-2019 American Community Survey 5-Year Estimates

Educational Attainment by Race

Area	High School Graduate or Higher (%)					Bachelor's Degree or Higher (%)				
	Total	White	Black	Asian	Hisp.[2]	Total	White	Black	Asian	Hisp.[2]
City	86.4	87.5	89.0	81.2	54.5	30.7	33.2	20.3	41.4	10.4
MSA[1]	89.0	89.9	90.0	84.3	60.6	30.5	32.0	21.3	46.0	13.2
U.S.	88.0	89.9	86.0	87.1	68.7	32.1	33.5	21.6	54.3	16.4

Note: Figures shown cover persons 25 years old and over; (1) Figures cover the Oklahoma City, OK Metropolitan Statistical Area; (2) People of Hispanic origin can be of any race
Source: U.S. Census Bureau, 2015-2019 American Community Survey 5-Year Estimates

School Enrollment by Grade and Control

Area	Preschool (%)		Kindergarten (%)		Grades 1 - 4 (%)		Grades 5 - 8 (%)		Grades 9 - 12 (%)	
	Public	Private	Public	Private	Public	Private	Public	Private	Public	Private
City	73.4	26.6	91.7	8.3	91.8	8.2	91.0	9.0	90.2	9.8
MSA[1]	72.1	27.9	90.7	9.3	91.2	8.8	90.8	9.2	90.7	9.3
U.S.	59.1	40.9	87.6	12.4	89.5	10.5	89.4	10.6	90.1	9.9

Note: Figures shown cover persons 3 years old and over; (1) Figures cover the Oklahoma City, OK Metropolitan Statistical Area
Source: U.S. Census Bureau, 2015-2019 American Community Survey 5-Year Estimates

Higher Education

Four-Year Colleges			Two-Year Colleges			Medical Schools[1]	Law Schools[2]	Voc/ Tech[3]
Public	Private Non-profit	Private For-profit	Public	Private Non-profit	Private For-profit			
2	2	0	2	0	2	1	1	3

Note: Figures cover institutions located within the city limits and include main campuses only; (1) includes schools accredited by the Liaison Committee on Medical Education and the American Osteopathic Association's Commission on Osteopathic College Accreditation; (2) includes ABA-accredited schools, schools with provisional ABA accreditation, and state accredited schools; (3) includes all schools with programs that are less than 2 years.
Source: National Center for Education Statistics, Integrated Postsecondary Education System (IPEDS), 2019-20; Wikipedia, List of Medical Schools in the United States, accessed April 2, 2021; Wikipedia, List of Law Schools in the United States, accessed April 2, 2021

According to *U.S. News & World Report,* the Oklahoma City, OK metro area is home to one of the top 200 national universities in the U.S.: **University of Oklahoma** (#133 tie). The indicators used to capture academic quality fall into a number of categories: assessment by administrators at peer institutions; retention of students; faculty resources; student selectivity; financial resources; alumni giving; high school counselor ratings of colleges; and graduation rate. *U.S. News & World Report, "America's Best Colleges 2021"*

According to *U.S. News & World Report,* the Oklahoma City, OK metro area is home to one of the top 100 law schools in the U.S.: **University of Oklahoma** (#67 tie). The rankings are based on a weighted average of 12 measures of quality: peer assessment score; assessment score by lawyers/judges; median LSAT scores; median undergrad GPA; acceptance rate; employment rates for graduates; placement success; bar passage rate; faculty resources; expenditures per student; student/faculty ratio; and library resources. *U.S. News & World Report, "America's Best Graduate Schools, Law, 2022"*

According to *U.S. News & World Report,* the Oklahoma City, OK metro area is home to one of the top 75 medical schools for research in the U.S.: **University of Oklahoma** (#74). The rankings are based on a weighted average of 11 measures of quality: quality assessment; peer assessment score; assessment score by residency directors; research activity; total research activity; average research activity per faculty member; student selectivity; median MCAT total score; median undergraduate GPA; acceptance rate; and faculty resources. *U.S. News & World Report, "America's Best Graduate Schools, Medical, 2022"*

EMPLOYERS

Major Employers

Company Name	Industry
AT&T	Telecommunications
Chesapeake Energy Corp	Oil & gas
City of Oklahoma City	Municipal government
Devon Energy Corp	Oil & gas
FAA Mike Monroney Aeronautical Center	Aerospace
Hobby Lobby Stores	Wholesale & retail
INTEGRIS Health	Health care
Mercy Health Center	Health care
Norman Regional Hospital	Health care
OGE Energy Corp	Utility
Oklahoma City Community College	Education
OU Medical Center	Health care
Sonic Corp	Wholesale & retail
SSM Health Care of Oklahoma	Health care
State of Oklahoma	State government
The Boeing Company	Aerospace
Tinker Air Force Base	U.S. military
University of Central Oklahoma	Higher education
University of Oklahoma - Norman	Higher education
University of Oklahoma Health Sci Ctr	Higher education

Note: Companies shown are located within the Oklahoma City, OK Metropolitan Statistical Area.
Source: Hoovers.com; Wikipedia

Best Companies to Work For

American Fidelity Assurance, headquartered in Oklahoma City, is among "The 100 Best Companies to Work For." To pick the best companies, *Fortune* partnered with the Great Place to Work Institute. Two-thirds of a company's score is based on the results of the Institute's Trust Index survey, which is sent to a random sample of employees from each company. The questions related to attitudes about management's credibility, job satisfaction, and camaraderie. The other third of the scoring is based on the company's responses to the Institute's Culture Audit, which includes detailed questions about pay and benefit programs, and a series of open-ended questions about hiring practices, internal communication, training, recognition programs, and diversity efforts. Any company that is at least five years old with more than 1,000 U.S. employees is eligible. *Fortune, "The 100 Best Companies to Work For," 2020*

American Fidelity Assurance Company, headquartered in Oklahoma City, is among the "100 Best Places to Work in IT." To qualify, companies had to be U.S.-based organizations or be non-U.S.-based employers that met the following criteria: have a minimum of 300 total employees at a U.S. headquarters and a minimum of 30 IT employees in the U.S., with at least 50% of their IT employees based in the U.S. The best places to work were selected based on compensation, benefits, work/life balance, employee morale, and satisfaction with training and development programs. In addition, *InsiderPro* and *Computerworld* looked at retention efforts, programs for recognizing and rewarding outstanding performances, and benefits such as flextime, elder care and child care, and reimbursement for college tuition and the cost of pursuing technology certifications. *InsiderPro and Computerworld, "100 Best Places to Work in IT," 2020*

Oklahoma City, Oklahoma   381

PUBLIC SAFETY

Crime Rate

Area	All Crimes	Violent Crimes				Property Crimes		
		Murder	Rape[3]	Robbery	Aggrav. Assault	Burglary	Larceny -Theft	Motor Vehicle Theft
City	4,813.7	11.4	81.9	135.0	493.9	943.3	2,572.2	576.1
Suburbs[1]	2,410.6	4.4	46.1	32.5	150.0	447.5	1,495.7	234.3
Metro[2]	3,530.9	7.7	62.8	80.3	310.3	678.7	1,997.6	393.6
U.S.	2,489.3	5.0	42.6	81.6	250.2	340.5	1,549.5	219.9

Note: Figures are crimes per 100,000 population; (1) All areas within the metro area that are located outside the city limits; (2) Figures cover the Oklahoma City, OK Metropolitan Statistical Area; (3) All figures shown were reported using the revised Uniform Crime Reporting (UCR) definition of rape.
Source: FBI Uniform Crime Reports, 2019

Hate Crimes

Area	Number of Quarters Reported	Number of Incidents per Bias Motivation					
		Race/Ethnicity/ Ancestry	Religion	Sexual Orientation	Disability	Gender	Gender Identity
City	4	3	0	0	0	0	0
U.S.	4	3,963	1,521	1,195	157	69	198

Source: Federal Bureau of Investigation, Hate Crime Statistics 2019

Identity Theft Consumer Reports

Area	Reports	Reports per 100,000 Population	Rank[2]
MSA[1]	6,036	428	66
U.S.	1,387,615	423	-

Note: (1) Figures cover the Oklahoma City, OK Metropolitan Statistical Area; (2) Rank ranges from 1 to 391 where 1 indicates greatest number of identity theft reports per 100,000 population
Source: Federal Trade Commission, Consumer Sentinel Network Data Book 2020

Fraud and Other Consumer Reports

Area	Reports	Reports per 100,000 Population	Rank[2]
MSA[1]	9,277	658	228
U.S.	3,385,133	1,031	-

Note: (1) Figures cover the Oklahoma City, OK Metropolitan Statistical Area; (2) Rank ranges from 1 to 391 where 1 indicates greatest number of fraud and other consumer reports per 100,000 population
Source: Federal Trade Commission, Consumer Sentinel Network Data Book 2020

POLITICS

2020 Presidential Election Results

Area	Biden	Trump	Jorgensen	Hawkins	Other
Oklahoma County	48.1	49.2	1.8	0.0	0.9
U.S.	51.3	46.8	1.2	0.3	0.5

Note: Results are percentages and may not add to 100% due to rounding
Source: Dave Leip's Atlas of U.S. Presidential Elections

SPORTS

Professional Sports Teams

Team Name	League	Year Established
Oklahoma City Thunder	National Basketball Association (NBA)	2008

Note: Includes teams located in the Oklahoma City, OK Metropolitan Statistical Area.
Source: Wikipedia, Major Professional Sports Teams of the United States and Canada, April 6, 2021

CLIMATE

Average and Extreme Temperatures

Temperature	Jan	Feb	Mar	Apr	May	Jun	Jul	Aug	Sep	Oct	Nov	Dec	Yr.
Extreme High (°F)	80	84	93	100	104	105	109	110	104	96	87	86	110
Average High (°F)	47	52	61	72	79	87	93	92	84	74	60	50	71
Average Temp. (°F)	36	41	50	60	69	77	82	81	73	62	49	40	60
Average Low (°F)	26	30	38	49	58	66	71	70	62	51	38	29	49
Extreme Low (°F)	-4	-3	1	20	32	47	53	51	36	22	11	-8	-8

Note: Figures cover the years 1948-1990
Source: National Climatic Data Center, International Station Meteorological Climate Summary, 9/96

382 Oklahoma City, Oklahoma

Average Precipitation/Snowfall/Humidity

Precip./Humidity	Jan	Feb	Mar	Apr	May	Jun	Jul	Aug	Sep	Oct	Nov	Dec	Yr.
Avg. Precip. (in.)	1.2	1.5	2.5	2.8	5.6	4.4	2.8	2.5	3.5	3.1	1.6	1.3	32.8
Avg. Snowfall (in.)	3	3	2	Tr	0	0	0	0	0	Tr	1	2	10
Avg. Rel. Hum. 6am (%)	78	78	76	77	84	84	81	81	82	79	78	77	80
Avg. Rel. Hum. 3pm (%)	53	52	47	46	52	51	46	44	47	46	48	52	49

Note: Figures cover the years 1948-1990; Tr = Trace amounts (<0.05 in. of rain; <0.5 in. of snow)
Source: National Climatic Data Center, International Station Meteorological Climate Summary, 9/96

Weather Conditions

Temperature			Daytime Sky			Precipitation		
10°F & below	32°F & below	90°F & above	Clear	Partly cloudy	Cloudy	0.01 inch or more precip.	0.1 inch or more snow/ice	Thunder-storms
5	79	70	124	131	110	80	8	50

Note: Figures are average number of days per year and cover the years 1948-1990
Source: National Climatic Data Center, International Station Meteorological Climate Summary, 9/96

HAZARDOUS WASTE

Superfund Sites

The Oklahoma City, OK metro area is home to three sites on the EPA's Superfund National Priorities List: **Eagle Industries** (final); **Hardage/Criner** (final); **Tinker Air Force Base (Soldier Creek/Building 3001)** (final). There are a total of 1,375 Superfund sites with a status of proposed or final on the list in the U.S. *U.S. Environmental Protection Agency, National Priorities List, April 7, 2021*

AIR QUALITY

Air Quality Trends: Ozone

	1990	1995	2000	2005	2010	2015	2016	2017	2018	2019
MSA[1]	0.078	0.086	0.082	0.077	0.071	0.067	0.066	0.070	0.072	0.067
U.S.	0.088	0.089	0.082	0.080	0.073	0.068	0.069	0.068	0.069	0.065

Note: (1) Data covers the Oklahoma City, OK Metropolitan Statistical Area. The values shown are the composite ozone concentration averages among trend sites based on the highest fourth daily maximum 8-hour concentration in parts per million. These trends are based on sites having an adequate record of monitoring data during the trend period. Data from exceptional events are included.
Source: U.S. Environmental Protection Agency, Air Quality Monitoring Information, "Air Quality Trends by City, 1990-2019"

Air Quality Index

Area	Percent of Days when Air Quality was...[2]					AQI Statistics[2]	
	Good	Moderate	Unhealthy for Sensitive Groups	Unhealthy	Very Unhealthy	Maximum	Median
MSA[1]	55.9	43.6	0.5	0.0	0.0	119	48

Note: (1) Data covers the Oklahoma City, OK Metropolitan Statistical Area; (2) Based on 365 days with AQI data in 2019. Air Quality Index (AQI) is an index for reporting daily air quality. EPA calculates the AQI for five major air pollutants regulated by the Clean Air Act: ground-level ozone, particle pollution (aka particulate matter), carbon monoxide, sulfur dioxide, and nitrogen dioxide. The AQI runs from 0 to 500. The higher the AQI value, the greater the level of air pollution and the greater the health concern. There are six AQI categories: "Good" AQI is between 0 and 50. Air quality is considered satisfactory; "Moderate" AQI is between 51 and 100. Air quality is acceptable; "Unhealthy for Sensitive Groups" When AQI values are between 101 and 150, members of sensitive groups may experience health effects; "Unhealthy" When AQI values are between 151 and 200 everyone may begin to experience health effects; "Very Unhealthy" AQI values between 201 and 300 trigger a health alert; "Hazardous" AQI values over 300 trigger warnings of emergency conditions (not shown).
Source: U.S. Environmental Protection Agency, Air Quality Index Report, 2019

Air Quality Index Pollutants

Area	Percent of Days when AQI Pollutant was...[2]					
	Carbon Monoxide	Nitrogen Dioxide	Ozone	Sulfur Dioxide	Particulate Matter 2.5	Particulate Matter 10
MSA[1]	0.0	1.1	52.9	0.0	45.8	0.3

Note: (1) Data covers the Oklahoma City, OK Metropolitan Statistical Area; (2) Based on 365 days with AQI data in 2019. The Air Quality Index (AQI) is an index for reporting daily air quality. EPA calculates the AQI for five major air pollutants regulated by the Clean Air Act: ground-level ozone, particle pollution (also known as particulate matter), carbon monoxide, sulfur dioxide, and nitrogen dioxide. The AQI runs from 0 to 500. The higher the AQI value, the greater the level of air pollution and the greater the health concern.
Source: U.S. Environmental Protection Agency, Air Quality Index Report, 2019

Maximum Air Pollutant Concentrations: Particulate Matter, Ozone, CO and Lead

	Particulate Matter 10 (ug/m³)	Particulate Matter 2.5 Wtd AM (ug/m³)	Particulate Matter 2.5 24-Hr (ug/m³)	Ozone (ppm)	Carbon Monoxide (ppm)	Lead (ug/m³)
MSA[1] Level	63	10.0	21	0.066	1	n/a
NAAQS[2]	150	15	35	0.075	9	0.15
Met NAAQS[2]	Yes	Yes	Yes	Yes	Yes	n/a

Note: (1) Data covers the Oklahoma City, OK Metropolitan Statistical Area; Data from exceptional events are included; (2) National Ambient Air Quality Standards; ppm = parts per million; ug/m³ = micrograms per cubic meter; n/a not available.
Concentrations: Particulate Matter 10 (coarse particulate)—highest second maximum 24-hour concentration; Particulate Matter 2.5 Wtd AM (fine particulate)—highest weighted annual mean concentration; Particulate Matter 2.5 24-Hour (fine particulate)—highest 98th percentile 24-hour concentration; Ozone—highest fourth daily maximum 8-hour concentration; Carbon Monoxide—highest second maximum non-overlapping 8-hour concentration; Lead—maximum running 3-month average
Source: U.S. Environmental Protection Agency, Air Quality Monitoring Information, "Air Quality Statistics by City, 2019"

Maximum Air Pollutant Concentrations: Nitrogen Dioxide and Sulfur Dioxide

	Nitrogen Dioxide AM (ppb)	Nitrogen Dioxide 1-Hr (ppb)	Sulfur Dioxide AM (ppb)	Sulfur Dioxide 1-Hr (ppb)	Sulfur Dioxide 24-Hr (ppb)
MSA[1] Level	12	n/a	n/a	1	n/a
NAAQS[2]	53	100	30	75	140
Met NAAQS[2]	Yes	n/a	n/a	Yes	n/a

Note: (1) Data covers the Oklahoma City, OK Metropolitan Statistical Area; Data from exceptional events are included; (2) National Ambient Air Quality Standards; ppm = parts per million; ug/m³ = micrograms per cubic meter; n/a not available.
Concentrations: Nitrogen Dioxide AM—highest arithmetic mean concentration; Nitrogen Dioxide 1-Hr—highest 98th percentile 1-hour daily maximum concentration; Sulfur Dioxide AM—highest annual mean concentration; Sulfur Dioxide 1-Hr—highest 99th percentile 1-hour daily maximum concentration; Sulfur Dioxide 24-Hr—highest second maximum 24-hour concentration
Source: U.S. Environmental Protection Agency, Air Quality Monitoring Information, "Air Quality Statistics by City, 2019"

Omaha, Nebraska

Background

Omaha's central location in the heartland of the United States has been important to its strong economy. Located on the western banks of the Missouri River, the city has been a significant agricultural and transportation center since its establishment in 1854. In its earliest history, Omaha was a trading center and "Gateway to the West." From these roots, Omaha has seen steady growth.

There are nearly 20,000 businesses located in the metropolitan area, including Fortune 500 companies such as ConAgra Foods, Mutual of Omaha, Union Pacific Railroad, Kiewit Corporation, and Berkshire Hathaway, the last of which is headed by Omaha's most prominent businessman, Warren Buffet, famously recognized as one of the richest men in the world.

Additional Fortune 500 companies have manufacturing plants or service centers in the metropolitan area. The headquarters of insurance companies, direct response/telemarketing centers and other national and international firms call Omaha home. The city is also a regional service and trade center. Services and trade combined comprise 57 percent of metro area employment.

Omaha is large enough to offer a variety of cosmopolitan attractions, yet small enough to provide a relaxed lifestyle. Recreational activities abound, and Omaha residents enjoy a low cost of living, outstanding health care and a low crime rate.

The Omaha metropolitan area is served by several public and private school systems, and offers 11 colleges and universities, including Gallup University, offering courses that support leaders, managers, and sales professionals.

The community also has access to excellent cultural programs worthy of a much larger city, including the professional Omaha Symphony, Omaha Theater Ballet, and Opera Omaha. Performances by these groups and other touring companies are held in the magnificent Orpheum Theater, a restored 1920s vaudeville house. The Bemis Center for Contemporary Arts, the largest urban artist colony in the world, plays host to artists from all over the world.

> A waitress was fired for violating her employer's social media policy after sharing a video of Governor Ricketts without a mask inside an Omaha sports bar.

Omaha is home to world-famous Father Flanagan's Boys and Girls Town, and the award-winning Henry Doorly Zoo, which includes the world's largest indoor rainforest and a collection of rare white tigers. Other attractions include the Strategic Air & Space Museum and the birthplaces of Malcom X and former President Gerald R. Ford.

Omaha celebrated its 150th birthday in 2004, and continues to devote much effort to new projects. The acreage fronting the Missouri River, is home to a 2,700-foot bridge with a 506-foot span across the river connecting nearly 150 miles of trails in Nebraska and Iowa. The Midwestern headquarters for the National Park Service is in Omaha, the first building in Nebraska to be rated tops under the Leadership in Energy and Environmental Design system, or LEED. The nearby Riverfront Place is a six-acre urban neighborhood that includes residential units, commercial space, a public plaza, riverfront access, and connections to miles of walking trails.

Omaha's weather shows the usual contrasts of a continental climate, with cold, dry winters and warm summers. The city is situated between two climatic zones, the humid east and the dry west, and fluctuation between these zones produce for weather periods characteristic of either zone or combinations of both. Most precipitation falls between April and September in the form of sharp thunderstorms or evening lightning shows.

Rankings

General Rankings

- For its "Best for Vets: Places to Live 2019" rankings, *Military Times* evaluated 599 cities (83 large, 234 medium, 282 small) and compared the locations across three broad categories: veteran and military culture/services; economic indicators; and livability factors such as health, crime, traffic, and school quality. Omaha ranked #9 out of the top 25, in the large city category (population of more than 250,000). Data points more specific to veterans and the military weighed more heavily than others. *rebootcamp.militarytimes.com, "Military Times Best Places to Live 2019," September 10, 2018*

- The Omaha metro area was identified as one of America's fastest-growing areas in terms of population and business growth by *MagnifyMoney*. The area ranked #33 out of 35. The 100 most populous metro areas in the U.S. were evaluated on their change from 2011-2016 in the following categories: people and housing; workforce and employment opportunities; growing industry. *www.businessinsider.com, "The 35 Cities in the US with the Biggest Influx of People, the Most Work Opportunities, and the Hottest Business Growth," August 12, 2018*

Business/Finance Rankings

- Omaha was the #8-ranked city for savers, according to a study by the finance site GOBankingRates, which considered the prospects for people trying to save money. Criteria: average monthly cost of grocery items; median home listing price; median rent; median income; transportation costs; gas prices; and the cost of eating out for an inexpensive and mid-range meal in 100 U.S. cities. *www.gobankingrates.com, "The 20 Best (and Worst) Places to Live If You're Trying to Save Money," August 27, 2019*

- Omaha was ranked #8 among 100 U.S. cities for most difficult conditions for savers, according to a study by the finance site GOBankingRates. Criteria: average monthly cost of grocery items; median home listing price; median rent; median income; transportation costs; gas prices; and the cost of eating out for an inexpensive and mid-range meal. *www.gobankingrates.com, "The 20 Best (and Worst) Places to Live If You're Trying to Save Money," August 27, 2019*

- The Brookings Institution ranked the nation's largest cities based on income inequality. Omaha was ranked #67 (#1 = greatest inequality). Criteria: the "95/20 ratio," a figure representing the income at which a household earns more than 95 percent of all other households, divided by the income at which a household earns more than only 20 percent of all other households. *Brookings Institution, "Household Income Inequality, Largest Cities of 97 Large U.S. Metro Areas, 2014-2016," February 5, 2018*

- The Brookings Institution ranked the 100 largest metro areas in the U.S. based on income inequality. Omaha was ranked #90 (#1 = greatest inequality). Criteria: the "95/20 ratio," a figure representing the income at which a household earns more than 95 percent of all other households, divided by the income at which a household earns more than only 20 percent of all other households. *Brookings Institution, "Household Income Inequality, 100 Largest U.S. Metro Areas, 2014-2016," February 5, 2018*

- *Forbes* ranked the 100 largest metro areas in the U.S. in terms of the "Best Cities for Young Professionals." The Omaha metro area ranked #19 out of 25. Criteria: median rent of a two-bedroom apartment; job growth and unemployment rate; median salary of college graduates with 5 or less years of work experience; networking opportunities; social outlook; percentage of population 25 years of age and older with college degrees. *Forbes.com, "America's 25 Best Cities for Young Professionals in 2017," May 22, 2017*

- Omaha was cited as one of America's top metros for new and expanded facility projects in 2020. The area ranked #9 in the mid-sized metro area category (population 200,000 to 1 million). *Site Selection, "Top Metros of 2020," March 2021*

- The Omaha metro area appeared on the Milken Institute "2021 Best Performing Cities" list. Rank: #102 out of 200 large metro areas (population over 250,000). Criteria: job growth; wage and salary growth; high-tech output growth; housing affordability; household broadband access. *Milken Institute, "Best-Performing Cities 2021," February 16, 2021*

- *Forbes* ranked the 200 most populous metro areas to determine the nation's "Best Places for Business and Careers." The Omaha metro area was ranked #38. Criteria: costs (business and living); job growth (past and projected); income growth; quality of life; educational attainment (college and high school); projected economic growth; cultural and leisure opportunities; workplace tolerance laws; net migration patterns. *Forbes, "The Best Places for Business and Careers 2019: Seattle Still On Top," October 30, 2019*

Dating/Romance Rankings

- Omaha was ranked #19 out of 25 cities that stood out for inspiring romance and attracting diners on the website OpenTable.com. Criteria: percentage of people who dined out on Valentine's Day in 2018; percentage of romantic restaurants as rated by OpenTable diner reviews; and percentage of tables seated for two. *OpenTable, "25 Most Romantic Cities in America for 2019," February 7, 2019*

Education Rankings

- Personal finance website *WalletHub* analyzed the 150 largest U.S. metropolitan statistical areas to determine where the most educated Americans are putting their degrees to work. Criteria: education levels; percentage of workers with degrees; education quality and attainment gap; public school quality rankings; quality and enrollment of each metro area's universities. Omaha was ranked #32 (#1 = most educated city). *www.WalletHub.com, "Most and Least Educated Cities in America, " July 20, 2020*

- Omaha was selected as one of America's most literate cities. The city ranked #39 out of the 84 largest U.S. cities. Criteria: number of booksellers; library resources; Internet resources; educational attainment; periodical publishing resources; newspaper circulation. *Central Connecticut State University, "America's Most Literate Cities, 2018," February 2019*

Health/Fitness Rankings

- For each of the 100 largest cities in the United States, the American Fitness Index®, published by the American College of Sports Medicine and the Anthem Foundation, evaluated community infrastructure and 33 health behaviors including preventive health, levels of chronic disease conditions, pedestrian safety, air quality, and community resources that support physical activity. Omaha ranked #42 for "community fitness." *americanfitnessindex.org, "2020 ACSM American Fitness Index Summary Report," July 14, 2020*

- The Omaha metro area was identified as one of the worst cities for bed bugs in America by pest control company Orkin. The area ranked #30 out of 50 based on the number of bed bug treatments Orkin performed from December 2019 to November 2020. *Orkin, "New Year, New Top City on Orkin's 2021 Bed Bug Cities List: Chicago," February 1, 2021*

- Omaha was identified as a "2021 Spring Allergy Capital." The area ranked #79 out of 100. Three groups of factors were used to identify the most challenging cities for people with allergies during the spring season: annual spring pollen levels; over the counter medicine use; number of board-certified allergy specialists. *Asthma and Allergy Foundation of America, "Spring Allergy Capitals 2021," February 23, 2021*

- Omaha was identified as a "2021 Fall Allergy Capital." The area ranked #70 out of 100. Three groups of factors were used to identify the most challenging cities for people with allergies during the fall season: annual fall pollen levels; over the counter medicine use; number of board-certified allergy specialists. *Asthma and Allergy Foundation of America, "Fall Allergy Capitals 2021," February 23, 2021*

- Omaha was identified as a "2019 Asthma Capital." The area ranked #9 out of the nation's 100 largest metropolitan areas. Criteria: estimated asthma prevalence; crude death rate from asthma; and ER visits due to asthma. Risk factors analyzed but not factored in the rankings: annual pollen score; annual air quality; public smoking laws; number of board-certified asthma specialists; rescue medication use; controller medication use; uninsured rate; poverty rate. *Asthma and Allergy Foundation of America, "Asthma Capitals 2019: The Most Challenging Places to Live With Asthma," May 7, 2019*

Real Estate Rankings

- *WalletHub* compared the most populated U.S. cities to determine which had the best markets for real estate agents. Omaha ranked #86 where demand was high and pay was the best. Criteria: sales per agent; annual median wage for real-estate agents; monthly average starting salary for real estate agents; real estate job density and competition; unemployment rate; home turnover rate; housing-market health index; and other relevant metrics. *www.WalletHub.com, "2019's Best Places to Be a Real Estate Agent," April 24, 2019*

- The Omaha metro area was identified as one of the top 15 housing markets to invest in for 2021 by *Forbes*. Criteria: home price appreciation; percentage of home sales within a 2-week time frame; available inventory; number of home sales; and other factors. *Forbes.com, "Top Housing Markets To Watch In 2021," December 15, 2020*

Safety Rankings

- Allstate ranked the 200 largest cities in America in terms of driver safety. Omaha ranked #33. Criteria: internal property damage claims over a two-year period from January 2016 to December 2017. The report helps increase the importance of safety and awareness behind the wheel. *Allstate, "Allstate America's Best Drivers Report, 2019" June 24, 2019*

- The National Insurance Crime Bureau ranked 384 metro areas in the U.S. in terms of per capita rates of vehicle theft. The Omaha metro area ranked #41 (#1 = highest rate). Criteria: number of vehicle theft offenses per 100,000 inhabitants in 2019. *National Insurance Crime Bureau, "Hot Spots 2019," July 21, 2020*

Seniors/Retirement Rankings

- From its Best Cities for Successful Aging indexes, the Milken Institute generated rankings for metropolitan areas, weighing data in nine categories—health care, wellness, living arrangements, transportation and convenience, financial characteristics, education, employment, community engagement, and overall livability. The Omaha metro area was ranked #7 overall in the large metro area category. *Milken Institute, "Best Cities for Successful Aging, 2017" March 14, 2017*

Sports/Recreation Rankings

- Omaha was chosen as one of America's best cities for bicycling. The city ranked #45 out of 50. Criteria: cycling infrastructure that is safe and friendly for all ages; energy and bike culture. The editors evaluated cities with populations of 100,000 or more. *Bicycling, "The 50 Best Bike Cities in America," October 10, 2018*

Women/Minorities Rankings

- Personal finance website *WalletHub* compared more than 180 U.S. cities across two key dimensions, "Hispanic Business-Friendliness" and "Hispanic Purchasing Power," to arrive at the most favorable conditions for Hispanic entrepreneurs. Omaha was ranked #108 out of 182. Criteria includes: share of Hispanic-Owned Businesses; Hispanic entrepreneurship rate to median annual income of Hispanics; Small Business-Friendliness score; cost of living; and number of Hispanics with at least a bachelor's degree. *WalletHub.com, "2019's Best Cities for Hispanic Entrepreneurs," May 1, 2019*

Miscellaneous Rankings

- *WalletHub* compared the 150 most populated U.S. cities to determine their operating efficiency. A "Quality of City Services" score was constructed for each city and then divided by the total budget per capita to reveal which were managed the best. Omaha ranked #73. Criteria: financial stability; economy; education; safety; health; infrastructure and pollution. *www.WalletHub.com, "2020's Best- & Worst-Run Cities in America," June 29, 2020*

Business Environment

DEMOGRAPHICS

Population Growth

Area	1990 Census	2000 Census	2010 Census	2019* Estimate	Population Growth (%) 1990-2019	Population Growth (%) 2010-2019
City	371,972	390,007	408,958	475,862	27.9	16.4
MSA[1]	685,797	767,041	865,350	931,779	35.9	7.7
U.S.	248,709,873	281,421,906	308,745,538	324,697,795	30.6	5.2

Note: (1) Figures cover the Omaha-Council Bluffs, NE-IA Metropolitan Statistical Area; (*) 2015-2019 5-year estimated population
Source: U.S. Census Bureau, 1990 Census, Census 2000, Census 2010, 2015-2019 American Community Survey 5-Year Estimates

Household Size

Area	Persons in Household (%) One	Two	Three	Four	Five	Six	Seven or More	Average Household Size
City	32.6	32.0	13.6	11.2	6.1	2.8	1.6	2.50
MSA[1]	28.4	33.9	14.3	12.7	6.5	2.7	1.5	2.50
U.S.	27.9	33.9	15.6	12.9	6.0	2.3	1.4	2.60

Note: (1) Figures cover the Omaha-Council Bluffs, NE-IA Metropolitan Statistical Area
Source: U.S. Census Bureau, 2015-2019 American Community Survey 5-Year Estimates

Race

Area	White Alone[2] (%)	Black Alone[2] (%)	Asian Alone[2] (%)	AIAN[3] Alone[2] (%)	NHOPI[4] Alone[2] (%)	Other Race Alone[2] (%)	Two or More Races (%)
City	77.5	12.3	3.8	0.6	0.0	2.3	3.4
MSA[1]	84.0	7.7	2.9	0.5	0.1	1.9	2.9
U.S.	72.5	12.7	5.5	0.8	0.2	4.9	3.3

Note: (1) Figures cover the Omaha-Council Bluffs, NE-IA Metropolitan Statistical Area; (2) Alone is defined as not being in combination with one or more other races; (3) American Indian and Alaska Native; (4) Native Hawaiian and Other Pacific Islander
Source: U.S. Census Bureau, 2015-2019 American Community Survey 5-Year Estimates

Hispanic or Latino Origin

Area	Total (%)	Mexican (%)	Puerto Rican (%)	Cuban (%)	Other (%)
City	13.9	10.7	0.4	0.1	2.7
MSA[1]	10.4	7.9	0.4	0.1	2.0
U.S.	18.0	11.2	1.7	0.7	4.3

Note: Persons of Hispanic or Latino origin can be of any race; (1) Figures cover the Omaha-Council Bluffs, NE-IA Metropolitan Statistical Area
Source: U.S. Census Bureau, 2015-2019 American Community Survey 5-Year Estimates

Ancestry

Area	German	Irish	English	American	Italian	Polish	French[2]	Scottish	Dutch
City	25.2	13.1	6.9	3.0	4.1	3.6	2.0	1.3	1.4
MSA[1]	29.2	13.6	7.9	3.6	3.9	3.7	2.1	1.4	1.7
U.S.	13.3	9.7	7.2	6.2	5.1	2.8	2.3	1.7	1.2

Note: Figures are the percentage of the total population reporting a particular ancestry. The nine most commonly reported ancestries in the U.S. are shown. Figures include multiple ancestries (e.g. if a person reported being Irish and Italian, they were included in both columns); (1) Figures cover the Omaha-Council Bluffs, NE-IA Metropolitan Statistical Area; (2) Excludes Basque
Source: U.S. Census Bureau, 2015-2019 American Community Survey 5-Year Estimates

Foreign-born Population

Area	Percent of Population Born in Any Foreign Country	Asia	Mexico	Europe	Caribbean	Central America[2]	South America	Africa	Canada
City	10.7	3.4	3.8	0.6	0.1	1.0	0.3	1.3	0.1
MSA[1]	7.4	2.4	2.5	0.6	0.1	0.7	0.2	0.9	0.1
U.S.	13.6	4.2	3.5	1.5	1.3	1.1	1.0	0.7	0.2

Note: (1) Figures cover the Omaha-Council Bluffs, NE-IA Metropolitan Statistical Area; (2) Excludes Mexico.
Source: U.S. Census Bureau, 2015-2019 American Community Survey 5-Year Estimates

Marital Status

Area	Never Married	Now Married[2]	Separated	Widowed	Divorced
City	36.4	45.9	1.6	4.8	11.2
MSA[1]	31.4	51.6	1.3	4.9	10.7
U.S.	33.4	48.1	1.9	5.8	10.9

Note: Figures are percentages and cover the population 15 years of age and older; (1) Figures cover the Omaha-Council Bluffs, NE-IA Metropolitan Statistical Area; (2) Excludes separated
Source: U.S. Census Bureau, 2015-2019 American Community Survey 5-Year Estimates

Disability by Age

Area	All Ages	Under 18 Years Old	18 to 64 Years Old	65 Years and Over
City	10.9	3.3	9.7	32.3
MSA[1]	11.0	3.5	9.6	32.2
U.S.	12.6	4.2	10.3	34.5

Note: Figures show percent of the civilian noninstitutionalized population that reported having a disability. Disability status is determined from six types of difficulty: vision, hearing, cognitive, ambulatory, self-care, and independent living. For children under 5 years old, hearing and vision difficulty are used to determine disability status. For children between the ages of 5 and 14, disability status is determined from hearing, vision, cognitive, ambulatory, and self-care difficulties. For people aged 15 years and older, they are considered to have a disability if they have difficulty with any one of the six difficulty types; Note: (1) Figures cover the Omaha-Council Bluffs, NE-IA Metropolitan Statistical Area
Source: U.S. Census Bureau, 2015-2019 American Community Survey 5-Year Estimates

Age

Area	Percent of Population									Median Age
	Under Age 5	Age 5–19	Age 20–34	Age 35–44	Age 45–54	Age 55–64	Age 65–74	Age 75–84	Age 85+	
City	7.3	20.4	22.9	12.7	11.9	11.9	7.6	3.6	1.7	34.5
MSA[1]	7.2	21.0	20.8	13.2	12.3	12.2	8.0	3.8	1.6	35.7
U.S.	6.1	19.1	20.7	12.6	13.0	12.9	9.1	4.6	1.9	38.1

Note: (1) Figures cover the Omaha-Council Bluffs, NE-IA Metropolitan Statistical Area
Source: U.S. Census Bureau, 2015-2019 American Community Survey 5-Year Estimates

Gender

Area	Males	Females	Males per 100 Females
City	234,719	241,143	97.3
MSA[1]	461,556	470,223	98.2
U.S.	159,886,919	164,810,876	97.0

Note: (1) Figures cover the Omaha-Council Bluffs, NE-IA Metropolitan Statistical Area
Source: U.S. Census Bureau, 2015-2019 American Community Survey 5-Year Estimates

Religious Groups by Family

Area	Catholic	Baptist	Non-Den.	Methodist[2]	Lutheran	LDS[3]	Pente-costal	Presby-terian[4]	Muslim[5]	Judaism
MSA[1]	21.6	4.6	1.8	3.9	7.9	1.8	1.3	2.3	0.5	0.4
U.S.	19.1	9.3	4.0	4.0	2.3	2.0	1.9	1.6	0.8	0.7

Note: Figures are the number of adherents as a percentage of the total population; (1) Figures cover the Omaha-Council Bluffs, NE-IA Metropolitan Statistical Area; (2) Methodist/Pietist; (3) Latter Day Saints; (4) Reformed; (5) Figures are estimates
Source: Association of Statisticians of American Religious Bodies, 2010 U.S. Religion Census: Religious Congregations & Membership Study

Religious Groups by Tradition

Area	Catholic	Evangelical Protestant	Mainline Protestant	Other Tradition	Black Protestant	Orthodox
MSA[1]	21.6	12.1	10.8	3.3	1.5	0.1
U.S.	19.1	16.2	7.3	4.3	1.6	0.3

Note: Figures are the number of adherents as a percentage of the total population; (1) Figures cover the Omaha-Council Bluffs, NE-IA Metropolitan Statistical Area
Source: Association of Statisticians of American Religious Bodies, 2010 U.S. Religion Census: Religious Congregations & Membership Study

ECONOMY

Gross Metropolitan Product

Area	2017	2018	2019	2020	Rank[2]
MSA[1]	63.3	65.9	68.5	71.0	52

Note: Figures are in billions of dollars; (1) Figures cover the Omaha-Council Bluffs, NE-IA Metropolitan Statistical Area; (2) Rank is based on 2018 data and ranges from 1 to 381
Source: U.S. Conference of Mayors, U.S. Metro Economies: GMP & Employment 2018-2020, September 2019

Omaha, Nebraska   391

Economic Growth

Area	2015-17 (%)	2018 (%)	2019 (%)	2020 (%)	Rank[2]
MSA[1]	0.6	1.7	2.2	1.5	272
U.S.	1.9	2.9	2.3	2.1	–

Note: Figures are real gross metropolitan product (GMP) growth rates and represent average annual percent change; (1) Figures cover the Omaha-Council Bluffs, NE-IA Metropolitan Statistical Area; (2) Rank is based on 2017 2-year average annual percent change and ranges from 1 to 381
Source: U.S. Conference of Mayors, U.S. Metro Economies: GMP & Employment 2018-2020, September 2019

Metropolitan Area Exports

Area	2014	2015	2016	2017	2018	2019	Rank[2]
MSA[1]	4,528.5	3,753.4	3,509.7	3,756.2	4,371.6	3,725.7	68

Note: Figures are in millions of dollars; (1) Figures cover the Omaha-Council Bluffs, NE-IA Metropolitan Statistical Area; (2) Rank is based on 2019 data and ranges from 1 to 386
Source: U.S. Department of Commerce, International Trade Administration, Office of Trade and Economic Analysis, Industry and Analysis, Exports by Metropolitan Area, data extracted March 24, 2021

Building Permits

Area	Single-Family			Multi-Family			Total		
	2018	2019	Pct. Chg.	2018	2019	Pct. Chg.	2018	2019	Pct. Chg.
City	1,237	1,179	-4.7	1,650	965	-41.5	2,887	2,144	-25.7
MSA[1]	2,791	2,633	-5.7	1,997	1,467	-26.5	4,788	4,100	-14.4
U.S.	855,300	862,100	0.7	473,500	523,900	10.6	1,328,800	1,386,000	4.3

Note: (1) Figures cover the Omaha-Council Bluffs, NE-IA Metropolitan Statistical Area; Figures represent new, privately-owned housing units authorized (unadjusted data); All permit data are based on estimates with imputation
Source: U.S. Census Bureau, Manufacturing, Mining, and Construction Statistics, Building Permits, 2018, 2019

Bankruptcy Filings

Area	Business Filings			Nonbusiness Filings		
	2019	2020	% Chg.	2019	2020	% Chg.
Douglas County	39	16	-59.0	1,283	1,064	-17.1
U.S.	22,780	21,655	-4.9	752,160	522,808	-30.5

Note: Business filings include Chapter 7, Chapter 9, Chapter 11, Chapter 12, Chapter 13, Chapter 15, and Section 304; Nonbusiness filings include Chapter 7, Chapter 11, and Chapter 13
Source: Administrative Office of the U.S. Courts, Business and Nonbusiness Bankruptcy, County Cases Commenced by Chapter of the Bankruptcy Code, During the 12-Month Period Ending December 31, 2019 and Business and Nonbusiness Bankruptcy, County Cases Commenced by Chapter of the Bankruptcy Code, During the 12-Month Period Ending December 31, 2020

Housing Vacancy Rates

Area	Gross Vacancy Rate[2] (%)			Year-Round Vacancy Rate[3] (%)			Rental Vacancy Rate[4] (%)			Homeowner Vacancy Rate[5] (%)		
	2018	2019	2020	2018	2019	2020	2018	2019	2020	2018	2019	2020
MSA[1]	7.1	5.6	5.6	6.1	4.8	5.3	7.1	6.3	6.5	0.7	0.6	0.5
U.S.	12.3	12.0	10.6	9.7	9.5	8.2	6.9	6.7	6.3	1.5	1.4	1.0

Note: (1) Figures cover the Omaha-Council Bluffs, NE-IA Metropolitan Statistical Area; (2) The percentage of the total housing inventory that is vacant; (3) The percentage of the housing inventory (excluding seasonal units) that is year-round vacant; (4) The percentage of rental inventory that is vacant for rent; (5) The percentage of homeowner inventory that is vacant for sale
Source: U.S. Census Bureau, Housing Vacancies and Homeownership Annual Statistics: 2018, 2019, 2020

INCOME

Income

Area	Per Capita ($)	Median Household ($)	Average Household ($)
City	33,401	60,092	82,945
MSA[1]	34,825	67,885	88,578
U.S.	34,103	62,843	88,607

Note: (1) Figures cover the Omaha-Council Bluffs, NE-IA Metropolitan Statistical Area
Source: U.S. Census Bureau, 2015-2019 American Community Survey 5-Year Estimates

Household Income Distribution

Area	Percent of Households Earning							
	Under $15,000	$15,000 -$24,999	$25,000 -$34,999	$35,000 -$49,999	$50,000 -$74,999	$75,000 -$99,999	$100,000 -$149,999	$150,000 and up
City	10.5	8.8	8.8	13.5	18.5	13.4	14.4	12.1
MSA[1]	8.4	7.7	8.0	12.3	18.1	14.4	17.5	13.5
U.S.	10.3	8.9	8.9	12.3	17.2	12.7	15.1	14.5

Note: (1) Figures cover the Omaha-Council Bluffs, NE-IA Metropolitan Statistical Area
Source: U.S. Census Bureau, 2015-2019 American Community Survey 5-Year Estimates

Poverty Rate

Area	All Ages	Under 18 Years Old	18 to 64 Years Old	65 Years and Over
City	13.4	18.7	12.3	8.5
MSA[1]	10.3	13.5	9.6	7.2
U.S.	13.4	18.5	12.6	9.3

Note: Figures are percentage of people whose income during the past 12 months was below the poverty level;
(1) Figures cover the Omaha-Council Bluffs, NE-IA Metropolitan Statistical Area
Source: U.S. Census Bureau, 2015-2019 American Community Survey 5-Year Estimates

CITY FINANCES

City Government Finances

Component	2017 ($000)	2017 ($ per capita)
Total Revenues	821,214	1,850
Total Expenditures	644,976	1,453
Debt Outstanding	1,386,723	3,124
Cash and Securities[1]	908,653	2,047

Note: (1) Cash and security holdings of a government at the close of its fiscal year,
including those of its dependent agencies, utilities, and liquor stores.
Source: U.S. Census Bureau, State & Local Government Finances 2017

City Government Revenue by Source

Source	2017 ($000)	2017 ($ per capita)	2017 (%)
General Revenue			
From Federal Government	15,571	35	1.9
From State Government	46,051	104	5.6
From Local Governments	8,934	20	1.1
Taxes			
Property	155,281	350	18.9
Sales and Gross Receipts	154,989	349	18.9
Personal Income	0	0	0.0
Corporate Income	0	0	0.0
Motor Vehicle License	32,186	73	3.9
Other Taxes	85,355	192	10.4
Current Charges	216,550	488	26.4
Liquor Store	0	0	0.0
Utility	0	0	0.0
Employee Retirement	103,379	233	12.6

Source: U.S. Census Bureau, State & Local Government Finances 2017

City Government Expenditures by Function

Function	2017 ($000)	2017 ($ per capita)	2017 (%)
General Direct Expenditures			
Air Transportation	0	0	0.0
Corrections	0	0	0.0
Education	0	0	0.0
Employment Security Administration	0	0	0.0
Financial Administration	3,788	8	0.6
Fire Protection	79,033	178	12.3
General Public Buildings	14,998	33	2.3
Governmental Administration, Other	14,360	32	2.2
Health	0	0	0.0
Highways	79,362	178	12.3
Hospitals	0	0	0.0
Housing and Community Development	756	1	0.1
Interest on General Debt	52,969	119	8.2
Judicial and Legal	4,045	9	0.6
Libraries	13,875	31	2.2
Parking	1,924	4	0.3
Parks and Recreation	27,576	62	4.3
Police Protection	130,435	293	20.2
Public Welfare	0	0	0.0
Sewerage	34,707	78	5.4
Solid Waste Management	22,090	49	3.4
Veterans' Services	0	0	0.0
Liquor Store	0	0	0.0
Utility	0	0	0.0
Employee Retirement	104,783	236	16.2

Source: U.S. Census Bureau, State & Local Government Finances 2017

Omaha, Nebraska 393

EMPLOYMENT

Labor Force and Employment

Area	Civilian Labor Force			Workers Employed		
	Dec. 2019	Dec. 2020	% Chg.	Dec. 2019	Dec. 2020	% Chg.
City	243,405	245,582	0.9	236,406	237,000	0.3
MSA[1]	496,578	495,217	-0.3	483,022	480,259	-0.6
U.S.	164,007,000	160,017,000	-2.4	158,504,000	149,613,000	-5.6

Note: Data is not seasonally adjusted and covers workers 16 years of age and older; (1) Figures cover the Omaha-Council Bluffs, NE-IA Metropolitan Statistical Area
Source: Bureau of Labor Statistics, Local Area Unemployment Statistics

Unemployment Rate

Area	2020											
	Jan.	Feb.	Mar.	Apr.	May	Jun.	Jul.	Aug.	Sep.	Oct.	Nov.	Dec.
City	3.5	3.3	4.8	10.8	6.6	7.5	6.8	5.2	4.5	3.5	3.3	3.5
MSA[1]	3.2	3.1	4.3	10.0	6.4	6.9	6.0	4.6	3.9	3.0	2.9	3.0
U.S.	4.0	3.8	4.5	14.4	13.0	11.2	10.5	8.5	7.7	6.6	6.4	6.5

Note: Data is not seasonally adjusted and covers workers 16 years of age and older; (1) Figures cover the Omaha-Council Bluffs, NE-IA Metropolitan Statistical Area
Source: Bureau of Labor Statistics, Local Area Unemployment Statistics

Average Wages

Occupation	$/Hr.	Occupation	$/Hr.
Accountants and Auditors	35.80	Maintenance and Repair Workers	21.40
Automotive Mechanics	22.50	Marketing Managers	53.20
Bookkeepers	20.60	Network and Computer Systems Admin.	40.70
Carpenters	20.00	Nurses, Licensed Practical	22.70
Cashiers	12.20	Nurses, Registered	33.90
Computer Programmers	38.70	Nursing Assistants	15.60
Computer Systems Analysts	41.40	Office Clerks, General	17.70
Computer User Support Specialists	25.90	Physical Therapists	40.50
Construction Laborers	18.60	Physicians	113.20
Cooks, Restaurant	13.70	Plumbers, Pipefitters and Steamfitters	33.70
Customer Service Representatives	18.20	Police and Sheriff's Patrol Officers	32.50
Dentists	113.80	Postal Service Mail Carriers	25.60
Electricians	27.80	Real Estate Sales Agents	26.60
Engineers, Electrical	44.60	Retail Salespersons	14.50
Fast Food and Counter Workers	11.60	Sales Representatives, Technical/Scientific	27.50
Financial Managers	60.80	Secretaries, Exc. Legal/Medical/Executive	18.30
First-Line Supervisors of Office Workers	27.80	Security Guards	18.70
General and Operations Managers	51.20	Surgeons	97.60
Hairdressers/Cosmetologists	17.20	Teacher Assistants, Exc. Postsecondary*	14.40
Home Health and Personal Care Aides	12.80	Teachers, Secondary School, Exc. Sp. Ed.*	30.80
Janitors and Cleaners	14.60	Telemarketers	12.50
Landscaping/Groundskeeping Workers	16.80	Truck Drivers, Heavy/Tractor-Trailer	21.90
Lawyers	60.80	Truck Drivers, Light/Delivery Services	18.80
Maids and Housekeeping Cleaners	12.90	Waiters and Waitresses	10.80

Note: Wage data covers the Omaha-Council Bluffs, NE-IA Metropolitan Statistical Area; (*) Hourly wages were calculated from annual wage data based on a 40 hour work week; n/a not available.
Source: Bureau of Labor Statistics, Metro Area Occupational Employment & Wage Estimates, May 2020

Employment by Industry

Sector	MSA[1]		U.S.
	Number of Employees	Percent of Total	Percent of Total
Construction, Mining, and Logging	31,000	6.3	5.5
Education and Health Services	79,500	16.1	16.3
Financial Activities	45,800	9.3	6.1
Government	65,700	13.3	15.2
Information	9,500	1.9	1.9
Leisure and Hospitality	42,500	8.6	9.0
Manufacturing	33,900	6.8	8.5
Other Services	17,600	3.6	3.8
Professional and Business Services	71,100	14.4	14.4
Retail Trade	54,300	11.0	10.9
Transportation, Warehousing, and Utilities	27,300	5.5	4.6
Wholesale Trade	16,900	3.4	3.9

Note: Figures are non-farm employment as of December 2020. Figures are not seasonally adjusted and include workers 16 years of age and older; (1) Figures cover the Omaha-Council Bluffs, NE-IA Metropolitan Statistical Area
Source: Bureau of Labor Statistics, Current Employment Statistics, Employment, Hours, and Earnings

Employment by Occupation

Occupation Classification	City (%)	MSA[1] (%)	U.S. (%)
Management, Business, Science, and Arts	40.1	40.7	38.5
Natural Resources, Construction, and Maintenance	7.8	8.6	8.9
Production, Transportation, and Material Moving	12.3	12.2	13.2
Sales and Office	23.0	22.7	21.6
Service	16.7	15.9	17.8

Note: Figures cover employed civilians 16 years of age and older; (1) Figures cover the Omaha-Council Bluffs, NE-IA Metropolitan Statistical Area
Source: U.S. Census Bureau, 2015-2019 American Community Survey 5-Year Estimates

Occupations with Greatest Projected Employment Growth: 2020 – 2022

Occupation[1]	2020 Employment	2022 Projected Employment	Numeric Employment Change	Percent Employment Change
Combined Food Preparation and Serving Workers, Including Fast Food	19,330	25,690	6,360	32.9
Waiters and Waitresses	11,920	16,420	4,500	37.8
Retail Salespersons	23,300	27,380	4,080	17.5
Cashiers	22,540	24,750	2,210	9.8
Cooks, Restaurant	4,630	6,640	2,010	43.4
First-Line Supervisors of Food Preparation and Serving Workers	5,390	7,200	1,810	33.6
Childcare Workers	10,750	12,540	1,790	16.7
General and Operations Managers	16,050	17,690	1,640	10.2
Bartenders	4,140	5,770	1,630	39.4
Janitors and Cleaners, Except Maids and Housekeeping Cleaners	15,050	16,620	1,570	10.4

Note: Projections cover Nebraska; (1) Sorted by numeric employment change
Source: www.projectionscentral.com, State Occupational Projections, 2020–2022 Short-Term Projections

Fastest-Growing Occupations: 2020 – 2022

Occupation[1]	2020 Employment	2022 Projected Employment	Numeric Employment Change	Percent Employment Change
Ushers, Lobby Attendants, and Ticket Takers	290	680	390	134.5
Actors	40	90	50	125.0
Craft Artists	50	110	60	120.0
Lodging Managers	90	160	70	77.8
Baggage Porters and Bellhops	90	160	70	77.8
Hotel, Motel, and Resort Desk Clerks	1,190	2,030	840	70.6
Gaming and Sports Book Writers and Runners	270	440	170	63.0
Amusement and Recreation Attendants	650	1,030	380	58.5
Fitness Trainers and Aerobics Instructors	2,180	3,200	1,020	46.8
Concierges	110	160	50	45.5

Note: Projections cover Nebraska; (1) Sorted by percent employment change and excludes occupations with numeric employment change less than 50
Source: www.projectionscentral.com, State Occupational Projections, 2020–2022 Short-Term Projections

TAXES

State Corporate Income Tax Rates

State	Tax Rate (%)	Income Brackets ($)	Num. of Brackets	Financial Institution Tax Rate (%)[a]	Federal Income Tax Ded.
Nebraska	5.58 - 7.81	100,000	2	(a)	No

Note: Tax rates as of January 1, 2021; (a) Rates listed are the corporate income tax rate applied to financial institutions or excise taxes based on income. Some states have other taxes based upon the value of deposits or shares.
Source: Federation of Tax Administrators, State Corporate Income Tax Rates, January 1, 2021

State Individual Income Tax Rates

State	Tax Rate (%)	Income Brackets ($)	Personal Exemptions ($)			Standard Ded. ($)	
			Single	Married	Depend.	Single	Married
Nebraska (a)	2.46 - 6.84	3,340 - 32,210 (b)	142	284 (c)	142 (c)	7,100	14,200

Note: Tax rates as of January 1, 2021; Local- and county-level taxes are not included; Federal income tax is not deductible on state income tax returns; (a) 19 states have statutory provision for automatically adjusting to the rate of inflation the dollar values of the income tax brackets, standard deductions, and/or personal exemptions. Michigan indexes the personal exemption only. Oregon does not index the income brackets for $125,000 and over; (b) For joint returns, taxes are twice the tax on half the couple's income; (c) The personal exemption takes the form of a tax credit instead of a deduction
Source: Federation of Tax Administrators, State Individual Income Tax Rates, January 1, 2021

Various State Sales and Excise Tax Rates

State	State Sales Tax (%)	Gasoline[1] (¢/gal.)	Cigarette[2] ($/pack)	Spirits[3] ($/gal.)	Wine[4] ($/gal.)	Beer[5] ($/gal.)	Recreational Marijuana (%)
Nebraska	5.5	29.6	0.64	3.75	0.95	0.31	Not legal

Note: All tax rates as of January 1, 2021; (1) The American Petroleum Institute has developed a methodology for determining the average tax rate on a gallon of fuel. Rates may include any of the following: excise taxes, environmental fees, storage tank fees, other fees or taxes, general sales tax, and local taxes; (2) The federal excise tax of $1.0066 per pack and local taxes are not included; (3) Rates are those applicable to off-premise sales of 40% alcohol by volume (a.b.v.) distilled spirits in 750ml containers. Local excise taxes are excluded; (4) Rates are those applicable to off-premise sales of 11% a.b.v. non-carbonated wine in 750ml containers; (5) Rates are those applicable to off-premise sales of 4.7% a.b.v. beer in 12 ounce containers.
Source: Tax Foundation, 2021 Facts & Figures: How Does Your State Compare?

State Business Tax Climate Index Rankings

State	Overall Rank	Corporate Tax Rank	Individual Income Tax Rank	Sales Tax Rank	Property Tax Rank	Unemployment Insurance Tax Rank
Nebraska	28	32	21	15	41	11

Note: The index is a measure of how each state's tax laws affect economic performance. The lower the rank, the more favorable a state's tax system is for business. States without a given tax are given a ranking of 1. The scores/rankings for the District of Columbia do not affect other states. The 2021 index represents the tax climate as of July 1, 2020.
Source: Tax Foundation, State Business Tax Climate Index 2021

TRANSPORTATION

Means of Transportation to Work

Area	Car/Truck/Van		Public Transportation			Bicycle	Walked	Other Means	Worked at Home
	Drove Alone	Car-pooled	Bus	Subway	Railroad				
City	81.7	9.1	1.4	0.0	0.0	0.3	2.3	1.3	4.0
MSA[1]	83.8	8.2	0.8	0.0	0.0	0.2	1.7	1.0	4.2
U.S.	76.3	9.0	2.4	1.9	0.6	0.5	2.7	1.4	5.2

Note: Figures are percentages and cover workers 16 years of age and older; (1) Figures cover the Omaha-Council Bluffs, NE-IA Metropolitan Statistical Area
Source: U.S. Census Bureau, 2015-2019 American Community Survey 5-Year Estimates

Travel Time to Work

Area	Less Than 10 Minutes	10 to 19 Minutes	20 to 29 Minutes	30 to 44 Minutes	45 to 59 Minutes	60 to 89 Minutes	90 Minutes or More
City	14.0	41.0	27.8	12.4	2.3	1.5	0.9
MSA[1]	13.9	36.4	27.5	15.8	3.7	1.7	1.0
U.S.	12.2	28.4	20.8	20.8	8.3	6.4	2.9

Note: Note: Figures are percentages and include workers 16 years old and over; (1) Figures cover the Omaha-Council Bluffs, NE-IA Metropolitan Statistical Area
Source: U.S. Census Bureau, 2015-2019 American Community Survey 5-Year Estimates

Key Congestion Measures

Measure	1982	1992	2002	2012	2017
Annual Hours of Delay, Total (000)	2,280	5,374	11,017	16,444	19,117
Annual Hours of Delay, Per Auto Commuter	9	18	28	34	38
Annual Congestion Cost, Total (million $)	17	57	150	298	355
Annual Congestion Cost, Per Auto Commuter ($)	180	292	468	547	616

Note: Covers the Omaha NE-IA urban area
Source: Texas A&M Transportation Institute, 2019 Urban Mobility Report

Freeway Travel Time Index

Measure	1982	1987	1992	1997	2002	2007	2012	2017
Urban Area Index[1]	1.04	1.06	1.09	1.11	1.14	1.15	1.16	1.17
Urban Area Rank[1,2]	61	66	70	72	69	72	60	49

Note: Freeway Travel Time Index—the ratio of travel time in the peak period to the travel time at free-flow conditions. For example, a value of 1.30 indicates a 20-minute free-flow trip takes 26 minutes in the peak (20 minutes x 1.30 = 26 minutes); (1) Covers the Omaha NE-IA urban area; (2) Rank is based on 101 larger urban areas (#1 = highest travel time index)
Source: Texas A&M Transportation Institute, 2019 Urban Mobility Report

Public Transportation

Agency Name / Mode of Transportation	Vehicles Operated in Maximum Service[1]	Annual Unlinked Passenger Trips[2] (in thous.)	Annual Passenger Miles[3] (in thous.)
Transit Authority of Omaha (MAT)			
Bus (directly operated)	90	3,267.8	11,406.3
Demand Response (directly operated)	29	101.1	692.1

Note: (1) Number of revenue vehicles operated by the given mode and type of service to meet the annual maximum service requirement. This is the revenue vehicle count during the peak season of the year; on the week and day that maximum service is provided. Vehicles operated in maximum service (VOMS) exclude atypical days and one-time special events; (2) Number of passengers who boarded public transportation vehicles. Passengers are counted each time they board a vehicle no matter how many vehicles they use to travel from their origin to their destination. (3) Sum of the distances ridden by all passengers during the entire fiscal year. Source: Federal Transit Administration, National Transit Database, 2019

Air Transportation

Airport Name and Code / Type of Service	Passenger Airlines[1]	Passenger Enplanements	Freight Carriers[2]	Freight (lbs)
Eppley Airfield (OMA)				
Domestic service (U.S. carriers - 2020)	24	1,037,827	17	63,588,822
International service (U.S. carriers - 2019)	1	47	1	112,577

Note: (1) Includes all U.S.-based major, minor and commuter airlines that carried at least one passenger during the year; (2) Includes all U.S.-based airlines and freight carriers that transported at least one pound of freight during the year. Source: Bureau of Transportation Statistics, The Intermodal Transportation Database, Air Carriers: T-100 Domestic Market (U.S. Carriers), 2020; Bureau of Transportation Statistics, The Intermodal Transportation Database, Air Carriers: T-100 International Market (U.S. Carriers), 2019

BUSINESSES

Major Business Headquarters

Company Name	Industry	Rankings	
		Fortune[1]	Forbes[2]
Berkshire Hathaway	Insurance, Property and Casualty (Stock)	6	-
Kiewit	Construction	-	36
Mutual of Omaha Insurance	Insurance, Life, Health (Stock)	300	-
Peter Kiewit Sons'	Engineering, Construction	307	-
Scoular	Food, Drink & Tobacco	-	95
TD Ameritrade Holding	Securities	486	-
Tenaska	Multicompany	-	40
Union Pacific	Railroads	149	-

Note: (1) Companies that produce a 10-K are ranked 1 to 500 based on 2019 revenue; (2) All private companies with at least $2 billion in annual revenue through the end of their most current fiscal year are ranked 1 to 219; companies listed are headquartered in the city; dashes indicate no ranking Source: Fortune, "Fortune 500," June/July 2020; Forbes, "America's Largest Private Companies," 2020

Fastest-Growing Businesses

According to *Inc.*, Omaha is home to one of America's 500 fastest-growing private companies: **City Ventures** (#71). Criteria: must be an independent, privately-held, for-profit, U.S. corporation, proprietorship or partnership as of December 31, 2019; revenues must be at least $100,000 in 2016 and $2 million in 2019; must have four-year operating/sales history. *Inc., "America's 500 Fastest-Growing Private Companies," 2020*

According to Deloitte, Omaha is home to one of North America's 500 fastest-growing high-technology companies: **Buildertrend** (#437). Companies are ranked by percentage growth in revenue over a four-year period. Criteria for inclusion: company must be headquartered within North America; must own proprietary intellectual property or technology that is sold to customers in products that contributes to a significant portion of the company's operating revenue; must have been in business for a minumum of four years with 2016 operating revenues of at least $50,000 USD/CD and 2019 operating revenues of at least $5 million USD/CD. *Deloitte, 2020 Technology Fast 500*™

Minority Business Opportunity

Omaha is home to one company which is on the *Black Enterprise* Industrial/Service list (100 largest companies based on gross sales): **All American Meats** (#48). Criteria: operational in previous calendar year; at least 51% black-owned and manufactures/owns the product it sells or provides industrial or consumer services. Brokerages, real estate firms and firms that provide professional services are not eligible. *Black Enterprise, B.E. 100s, 2019*

Living Environment

COST OF LIVING

Cost of Living Index

Composite Index	Groceries	Housing	Utilities	Trans-portation	Health Care	Misc. Goods/Services
93.7	98.5	86.6	95.5	95.2	95.0	96.4

Note: The Cost of Living Index measures regional differences in the cost of consumer goods and services, excluding taxes and non-consumer expenditures, for professional and managerial households in the top income quintile. It is based on more than 50,000 prices covering almost 60 different items for which prices are collected three times a year by chambers of commerce, economic development organizations or university applied economic centers in each participating urban area. The numbers shown should be read as a percentage above or below the national average of 100. For example, a value of 115.4 in the groceries column indicates that grocery prices are 15.4% higher than the national average. Small differences in the index numbers should not be interpreted as significant; Figures cover the Omaha NE urban area.
Source: The Council for Community and Economic Research, Cost of Living Index, 2020

Grocery Prices

Area[1]	T-Bone Steak ($/pound)	Frying Chicken ($/pound)	Whole Milk ($/half gal.)	Eggs ($/dozen)	Orange Juice ($/64 oz.)	Coffee ($/11.5 oz.)
City[2]	11.27	1.24	2.00	1.87	3.47	4.87
Avg.	11.78	1.39	2.05	1.47	3.57	4.34
Min.	8.03	0.94	1.03	0.74	2.94	3.02
Max.	15.86	2.65	4.31	3.77	5.44	8.69

Note: (1) Values for the local area are compared with the average, minimum and maximum values for all 284 areas in the Cost of Living Index; (2) Figures cover the Omaha NE urban area; T-Bone Steak (price per pound); Frying Chicken (price per pound, whole fryer); Whole Milk (half gallon carton); Eggs (price per dozen, Grade A, large); Orange Juice (64 oz. Tropicana or Florida Natural); Coffee (11.5 oz. can, vacuum-packed, Maxwell House, Hills Bros, or Folgers).
Source: The Council for Community and Economic Research, Cost of Living Index, 2020

Housing and Utility Costs

Area[1]	New Home Price ($)	Apartment Rent ($/month)	All Electric ($/month)	Part Electric ($/month)	Other Energy ($/month)	Telephone ($/month)
City[2]	305,521	1,100	-	89.62	56.82	194.40
Avg.	368,594	1,168	170.86	100.47	65.28	184.30
Min.	190,567	502	91.58	31.42	26.08	169.60
Max.	2,227,806	4,738	470.38	280.31	280.06	206.50

Note: (1) Values for the local area are compared with the average, minimum and maximum values for all 284 areas in the Cost of Living Index; (2) Figures cover the Omaha NE urban area; New Home Price (2,400 sf living area, 8,000 sf lot, in urban area with full utilities); Apartment Rent (950 sf 2 bedroom/1.5 or 2 bath, unfurnished, excluding all utilities except water); All Electric (average monthly cost for an all-electric home); Part Electric (average monthly cost for a part-electric home); Other Energy (average monthly cost for natural gas, fuel oil, coal, wood, and any other forms of energy except electricity); Telephone (price includes the base monthly rate plus taxes and fees for three lines of mobile phone service).
Source: The Council for Community and Economic Research, Cost of Living Index, 2020

Health Care, Transportation, and Other Costs

Area[1]	Doctor ($/visit)	Dentist ($/visit)	Optometrist ($/visit)	Gasoline ($/gallon)	Beauty Salon ($/visit)	Men's Shirt ($)
City[2]	119.00	78.66	114.83	2.07	34.01	23.77
Avg.	115.44	99.32	108.10	2.21	39.27	31.37
Min.	36.68	59.00	51.36	1.71	19.00	11.00
Max.	219.00	153.10	250.97	3.46	82.05	58.33

Note: (1) Values for the local area are compared with the average, minimum and maximum values for all 284 areas in the Cost of Living Index; (2) Figures cover the Omaha NE urban area; Doctor (general practitioners routine exam of an established patient); Dentist (adult teeth cleaning and periodic oral examination); Optometrist (full vision eye exam for established adult patient); Gasoline (one gallon regular unleaded, national brand, including all taxes, cash price at self-service pump if available); Beauty Salon (woman's shampoo, trim, and blow-dry); Men's Shirt (cotton/polyester dress shirt, pinpoint weave, long sleeves).
Source: The Council for Community and Economic Research, Cost of Living Index, 2020

HOUSING

Homeownership Rate

Area	2012 (%)	2013 (%)	2014 (%)	2015 (%)	2016 (%)	2017 (%)	2018 (%)	2019 (%)	2020 (%)
MSA[1]	72.4	70.6	68.7	69.6	69.2	65.5	67.8	66.9	68.6
U.S.	65.4	65.1	64.5	63.7	63.4	63.9	64.4	64.6	66.6

Note: (1) Figures cover the Omaha-Council Bluffs, NE-IA Metropolitan Statistical Area
Source: U.S. Census Bureau, Housing Vacancies and Homeownership Annual Statistics: 2012-2020

House Price Index (HPI)

Area	National Ranking[2]	Quarterly Change (%)	One-Year Change (%)	Five-Year Change (%)	Since 1991Q1 (%)
MSA[1]	154	1.72	5.74	31.76	176.42
U.S.[3]	–	3.81	10.77	38.99	205.12

Note: The HPI is a weighted repeat sales index. It measures average price changes in repeat sales or refinancings on the same properties. This information is obtained by reviewing repeat mortgage transactions on single-family properties whose mortgages have been purchased or securitized by Fannie Mae or Freddie Mac since January 1975; (1) Figures cover the Omaha-Council Bluffs, NE-IA Metropolitan Statistical Area; (2) Rankings are based on annual percentage change for all metro areas containing at least 15,000 transactions over the last 10 years and ranges from 1 to 253; (3) figures based on a weighted average of Census Division estimates using a seasonally adjusted, purchase-only index; all figures are for the period ending December 31, 2020
Source: Federal Housing Finance Agency, Change in Metropolitan Area House Price Indexes, April 7, 2021

Median Single-Family Home Prices

Area	2018	2019	2020[p]	Percent Change 2019 to 2020
MSA[1]	191.7	200.7	220.6	9.9
U.S. Average	261.6	274.6	299.9	9.2

Note: Figures are median sales prices of existing single-family homes in thousands of dollars; (p) preliminary; (1) Figures cover the Omaha-Council Bluffs, NE-IA Metropolitan Statistical Area
Source: National Association of Realtors, Median Sales Price of Existing Single-Family Homes for Metropolitan Areas, 4th Quarter 2020

Qualifying Income Based on Median Sales Price of Existing Single-Family Homes

Area	With 5% Down ($)	With 10% Down ($)	With 20% Down ($)
MSA[1]	42,538	40,299	35,822
U.S. Average	59,266	56,147	49,908

Note: Figures are preliminary; Qualifying income is based on a mortgage rate of 2.81%. Monthly principal and interest payment is limited to 25% of income; (1) Figures cover the Omaha-Council Bluffs, NE-IA Metropolitan Statistical Area
Source: National Association of Realtors, Qualifying Income Based on Median Sales Price of Existing Single-Family Homes for Metropolitan Areas, 4th Quarter 2020

Home Value Distribution

Area	Under $50,000	$50,000 -$99,999	$100,000 -$149,999	$150,000 -$199,999	$200,000 -$299,999	$300,000 -$499,999	$500,000 -$999,999	$1,000,000 or more
City	4.2	14.8	25.8	21.8	19.0	10.5	3.2	0.7
MSA[1]	3.9	12.1	23.4	21.0	22.0	13.5	3.4	0.7
U.S.	6.9	12.0	13.3	14.0	19.6	19.3	11.4	3.4

Note: Figures are percentages and cover owner-occupied housing units; (1) Figures cover the Omaha-Council Bluffs, NE-IA Metropolitan Statistical Area
Source: U.S. Census Bureau, 2015-2019 American Community Survey 5-Year Estimates

Year Housing Structure Built

Area	2010 or Later	2000 -2009	1990 -1999	1980 -1989	1970 -1979	1960 -1969	1950 -1959	1940 -1949	Before 1940	Median Year
City	3.4	7.4	13.0	11.0	15.6	14.6	11.1	4.2	19.7	1970
MSA[1]	6.8	14.3	13.0	9.9	14.6	12.0	8.7	3.4	17.2	1976
U.S.	5.2	14.0	13.9	13.4	15.2	10.6	10.3	4.9	12.6	1978

Note: Figures are percentages except for Median Year; Note: (1) Figures cover the Omaha-Council Bluffs, NE-IA Metropolitan Statistical Area
Source: U.S. Census Bureau, 2015-2019 American Community Survey 5-Year Estimates

Gross Monthly Rent

Area	Under $500	$500 -$999	$1,000 -$1,499	$1,500 -$1,999	$2,000 -$2,499	$2,500 -$2,999	$3,000 and up	Median ($)
City	7.7	51.6	31.4	7.0	1.3	0.3	0.7	923
MSA[1]	8.2	50.7	31.0	7.5	1.4	0.4	0.7	927
U.S.	9.4	36.2	30.0	14.0	5.6	2.4	2.4	1,062

Note: Figures are percentages except for Median; Gross rent is the contract rent plus the estimated average monthly cost of utilities (electricity, gas, and water and sewer) and fuels (oil, coal, kerosene, wood, etc.) if these are paid by the renter (or paid for the renter by someone else); (1) Figures cover the Omaha-Council Bluffs, NE-IA Metropolitan Statistical Area
Source: U.S. Census Bureau, 2015-2019 American Community Survey 5-Year Estimates

HEALTH

Health Risk Factors

Category	MSA[1] (%)	U.S. (%)
Adults aged 18–64 who have any kind of health care coverage	86.6	87.3
Adults who reported being in good or better health	85.7	82.4
Adults who have been told they have high blood cholesterol	33.2	33.0
Adults who have been told they have high blood pressure	31.8	32.3
Adults who are current smokers	16.6	17.1
Adults who currently use E-cigarettes	4.9	4.6
Adults who currently use chewing tobacco, snuff, or snus	4.1	4.0
Adults who are heavy drinkers[2]	7.5	6.3
Adults who are binge drinkers[3]	20.6	17.4
Adults who are overweight (BMI 25.0 - 29.9)	35.2	35.3
Adults who are obese (BMI 30.0 - 99.8)	33.3	31.3
Adults who participated in any physical activities in the past month	76.9	74.4
Adults who always or nearly always wears a seat belt	91.6	94.3

Note: (1) Figures cover the Omaha-Council Bluffs, NE-IA Metropolitan Statistical Area; (2) Heavy drinkers are classified as adult men having more than 14 drinks per week and adult women having more than 7 drinks per week; (3) Binge drinkers are classified as males having five or more drinks on one occasion or females having four or more drinks on one occasion
Source: Centers for Disease Control and Prevention, Behaviorial Risk Factor Surveillance System, SMART: Selected Metropolitan Area Risk Trends, 2017

Acute and Chronic Health Conditions

Category	MSA[1] (%)	U.S. (%)
Adults who have ever been told they had a heart attack	3.7	4.2
Adults who have ever been told they have angina or coronary heart disease	3.5	3.9
Adults who have ever been told they had a stroke	2.8	3.0
Adults who have ever been told they have asthma	12.0	14.2
Adults who have ever been told they have arthritis	23.1	24.9
Adults who have ever been told they have diabetes[2]	10.3	10.5
Adults who have ever been told they had skin cancer	5.5	6.2
Adults who have ever been told they had any other types of cancer	5.7	7.1
Adults who have ever been told they have COPD	5.9	6.5
Adults who have ever been told they have kidney disease	2.5	3.0
Adults who have ever been told they have a form of depression	20.6	20.5

Note: (1) Figures cover the Omaha-Council Bluffs, NE-IA Metropolitan Statistical Area; (2) Figures do not include pregnancy-related, borderline, or pre-diabetes
Source: Centers for Disease Control and Prevention, Behaviorial Risk Factor Surveillance System, SMART: Selected Metropolitan Area Risk Trends, 2017

Health Screening and Vaccination Rates

Category	MSA[1] (%)	U.S. (%)
Adults aged 65+ who have had flu shot within the past year	67.3	60.7
Adults aged 65+ who have ever had a pneumonia vaccination	81.9	75.4
Adults who have ever been tested for HIV	31.2	36.1
Adults who have ever had the shingles or zoster vaccine?	35.0	28.9
Adults who have had their blood cholesterol checked within the last five years	86.0	85.9

Note: n/a not available; (1) Figures cover the Omaha-Council Bluffs, NE-IA Metropolitan Statistical Area.
Source: Centers for Disease Control and Prevention, Behaviorial Risk Factor Surveillance System, SMART: Selected Metropolitan Area Risk Trends, 2017

Disability Status

Category	MSA[1] (%)	U.S. (%)
Adults who reported being deaf	5.9	6.7
Are you blind or have serious difficulty seeing, even when wearing glasses?	3.5	4.5
Are you limited in any way in any of your usual activities due of arthritis?	11.2	12.9
Do you have difficulty doing errands alone?	6.1	6.8
Do you have difficulty dressing or bathing?	3.4	3.6
Do you have serious difficulty concentrating/remembering/making decisions?	10.0	10.7
Do you have serious difficulty walking or climbing stairs?	11.4	13.6

Note: (1) Figures cover the Omaha-Council Bluffs, NE-IA Metropolitan Statistical Area.
Source: Centers for Disease Control and Prevention, Behaviorial Risk Factor Surveillance System, SMART: Selected Metropolitan Area Risk Trends, 2017

Mortality Rates for the Top 10 Causes of Death in the U.S.

ICD-10[a] Sub-Chapter	ICD-10[a] Code	Age-Adjusted Mortality Rate[1] per 100,000 population	
		County[2]	U.S.
Malignant neoplasms	C00-C97	157.7	149.2
Ischaemic heart diseases	I20-I25	60.9	90.5
Other forms of heart disease	I30-I51	56.9	52.2
Chronic lower respiratory diseases	J40-J47	48.6	39.6
Other degenerative diseases of the nervous system	G30-G31	44.5	37.6
Cerebrovascular diseases	I60-I69	33.6	37.2
Other external causes of accidental injury	W00-X59	24.8	36.1
Organic, including symptomatic, mental disorders	F01-F09	38.0	29.4
Hypertensive diseases	I10-I15	24.5	24.1
Diabetes mellitus	E10-E14	29.2	21.5

Note: (a) ICD-10 = International Classification of Diseases 10th Revision; (1) Mortality rates are a three-year average covering 2017-2019; (2) Figures cover Douglas County.
Source: Centers for Disease Control and Prevention, National Center for Health Statistics. Underlying Cause of Death 1999-2019 on CDC WONDER Online Database

Mortality Rates for Selected Causes of Death

ICD-10[a] Sub-Chapter	ICD-10[a] Code	Age-Adjusted Mortality Rate[1] per 100,000 population	
		County[2]	U.S.
Assault	X85-Y09	4.4	6.0
Diseases of the liver	K70-K76	16.4	14.4
Human immunodeficiency virus (HIV) disease	B20-B24	1.1	1.5
Influenza and pneumonia	J09-J18	14.3	13.8
Intentional self-harm	X60-X84	13.9	14.1
Malnutrition	E40-E46	2.8	2.3
Obesity and other hyperalimentation	E65-E68	3.3	2.1
Renal failure	N17-N19	11.6	12.6
Transport accidents	V01-V99	9.9	12.3
Viral hepatitis	B15-B19	1.0	1.2

Note: (a) ICD-10 = International Classification of Diseases 10th Revision; (1) Mortality rates are a three-year average covering 2017-2019; (2) Figures cover Douglas County; Data are suppressed when the data meet the criteria for confidentiality constraints; Mortality rates are flagged as unreliable when the rate would be calculated with a numerator of 20 or less.
Source: Centers for Disease Control and Prevention, National Center for Health Statistics. Underlying Cause of Death 1999-2019 on CDC WONDER Online Database

Health Insurance Coverage

Area	With Health Insurance	With Private Health Insurance	With Public Health Insurance	Without Health Insurance	Population Under Age 19 Without Health Insurance
City	89.8	71.3	27.7	10.2	5.8
MSA[1]	92.3	75.9	27.0	7.7	4.3
U.S.	91.2	67.9	35.1	8.8	5.1

Note: Figures are percentages that cover the civilian noninstitutionalized population; (1) Figures cover the Omaha-Council Bluffs, NE-IA Metropolitan Statistical Area
Source: U.S. Census Bureau, 2015-2019 American Community Survey 5-Year Estimates

Number of Medical Professionals

Area	MDs[3]	DOs[3,4]	Dentists	Podiatrists	Chiropractors	Optometrists
County[1] (number)	3,062	156	554	30	235	117
County[1] (rate[2])	540.6	27.5	97.0	5.3	41.1	20.5
U.S. (rate[2])	282.9	22.7	71.2	6.2	28.1	16.9

31055
Note: Data as of 2019 unless noted; (1) Data covers Douglas County; (2) Rate per 100,000 population; (3) Data as of 2018 and includes all active, non-federal physicians; (4) Doctor of Osteopathic Medicine
Source: U.S. Department of Health and Human Services, Health Resources and Services Administration, Bureau of Health Professions, Area Resource File (ARF) 2019-2020

Best Hospitals

According to *U.S. News,* the Omaha-Council Bluffs, NE-IA metro area is home to one of the best hospitals in the U.S.: **Nebraska Medicine-Nebraska Medical Center** (2 adult specialties). The hospital listed was nationally ranked in at least one of 16 adult or 10 pediatric specialties. Only 134 hospitals nationwide were nationally ranked in one or more adult or pediatric specialty; this number increases to 178 counting specialized centers within hospitals. Twenty hospitals in the U.S. made the Honor Roll. The Best Hospitals Honor Roll takes both the national rankings and the procedure and condition ratings into account. Hospitals received points if they were nationally ranked in one of the 16 adult specialties—the higher they ranked, the more points they got—and how many ratings of "high performing" they earned in the 10 procedures and conditions. *U.S. News Online, "America's Best Hospitals 2020-21"*

According to *U.S. News,* the Omaha-Council Bluffs, NE-IA metro area is home to one of the best children's hospitals in the U.S.: **Children's Hospital and Medical Center** (4 pediatric specialties). The hospital listed was highly ranked in at least one of 10 pediatric specialties. Eighty-eight children's hospitals in the U.S. were nationally ranked in at least one specialty. Hospitals received points for being ranked in a specialty, and the 10 hospitals with the most points across the 10 specialties make up the Honor Roll. *U.S. News Online, "America's Best Children's Hospitals 2020-21"*

EDUCATION

Public School District Statistics

District Name	Schls	Pupils	Pupil/ Teacher Ratio	Minority Pupils[1] (%)	Free Lunch Eligible[2] (%)	IEP[3] (%)
Millard Public Schools	36	24,104	16.4	22.9	15.8	11.6
Omaha Public Schools	106	53,194	14.9	73.6	61.5	19.7
Westside Community Schools	14	5,942	13.6	30.2	27.2	11.0

Note: Table includes school districts with 2,000 or more students; (1) Percentage of students that are not non-Hispanic white; (2) Percentage of students that are eligible for the free lunch program; (3) Percentage of students that have an Individualized Education Program.
Source: U.S. Department of Education, National Center for Education Statistics, Common Core of Data, Local Education Agency (School District) Universe Survey: School Year 2018-2019; U.S. Department of Education, National Center for Education Statistics, Common Core of Data, Public Elementary/Secondary School Universe Survey: School Year 2018-2019

Best High Schools

According to *U.S. News,* Omaha is home to one of the top 500 high schools in the U.S.: **Elkhorn South High School** (#203). Nearly 18,000 public, magnet and charter schools were ranked based on their performance on state assessments and how well they prepare students for college. *U.S. News & World Report, "Best High Schools 2020"*

Highest Level of Education

Area	Less than H.S.	H.S. Diploma	Some College, No Deg.	Associate Degree	Bachelor's Degree	Master's Degree	Prof. School Degree	Doctorate Degree
City	10.5	22.3	21.9	7.7	24.3	8.9	2.9	1.5
MSA[1]	8.3	23.8	22.5	9.1	23.8	9.0	2.3	1.3
U.S.	12.0	27.0	20.4	8.5	19.8	8.8	2.1	1.4

Note: Figures cover persons age 25 and over; (1) Figures cover the Omaha-Council Bluffs, NE-IA Metropolitan Statistical Area
Source: U.S. Census Bureau, 2015-2019 American Community Survey 5-Year Estimates

Educational Attainment by Race

Area	High School Graduate or Higher (%)					Bachelor's Degree or Higher (%)				
	Total	White	Black	Asian	Hisp.[2]	Total	White	Black	Asian	Hisp.[2]
City	89.5	91.5	86.9	70.4	54.3	37.7	40.7	18.9	49.4	12.0
MSA[1]	91.7	93.1	88.0	76.7	61.2	36.3	37.7	21.5	49.7	14.8
U.S.	88.0	89.9	86.0	87.1	68.7	32.1	33.5	21.6	54.3	16.4

Note: Figures shown cover persons 25 years old and over; (1) Figures cover the Omaha-Council Bluffs, NE-IA Metropolitan Statistical Area; (2) People of Hispanic origin can be of any race
Source: U.S. Census Bureau, 2015-2019 American Community Survey 5-Year Estimates

School Enrollment by Grade and Control

Area	Preschool (%)		Kindergarten (%)		Grades 1 - 4 (%)		Grades 5 - 8 (%)		Grades 9 - 12 (%)	
	Public	Private	Public	Private	Public	Private	Public	Private	Public	Private
City	53.5	46.5	82.0	18.0	83.5	16.5	85.3	14.7	83.2	16.8
MSA[1]	57.3	42.7	85.4	14.6	85.7	14.3	87.2	12.8	85.9	14.1
U.S.	59.1	40.9	87.6	12.4	89.5	10.5	89.4	10.6	90.1	9.9

Note: Figures shown cover persons 3 years old and over; (1) Figures cover the Omaha-Council Bluffs, NE-IA Metropolitan Statistical Area
Source: U.S. Census Bureau, 2015-2019 American Community Survey 5-Year Estimates

Higher Education

Four-Year Colleges			Two-Year Colleges			Medical Schools[1]	Law Schools[2]	Voc/ Tech[3]
Public	Private Non-profit	Private For-profit	Public	Private Non-profit	Private For-profit			
3	4	1	1	1	3	2	1	0

Note: Figures cover institutions located within the city limits and include main campuses only; (1) includes schools accredited by the Liaison Committee on Medical Education and the American Osteopathic Association's Commission on Osteopathic College Accreditation; (2) includes ABA-accredited schools, schools with provisional ABA accreditation, and state accredited schools; (3) includes all schools with programs that are less than 2 years.
Source: National Center for Education Statistics, Integrated Postsecondary Education System (IPEDS), 2019-20; Wikipedia, List of Medical Schools in the United States, accessed April 2, 2021; Wikipedia, List of Law Schools in the United States, accessed April 2, 2021

According to *U.S. News & World Report,* the Omaha-Council Bluffs, NE-IA metro area is home to one of the top 200 national universities in the U.S.: **Creighton University** (#112 tie). The indicators used to capture academic quality fall into a number of categories: assessment by administrators at peer institutions; retention of students; faculty resources; student selectivity; financial resources; alumni giving; high school counselor ratings of colleges; and graduation rate. *U.S. News & World Report, "America's Best Colleges 2021"*

According to *U.S. News & World Report,* the Omaha-Council Bluffs, NE-IA metro area is home to one of the top 75 medical schools for research in the U.S.: **University of Nebraska Medical Center** (#54). The rankings are based on a weighted average of 11 measures of quality: quality assessment; peer assessment score; assessment score by residency directors; research activity; total research activity; average research activity per faculty member; student selectivity; median MCAT total score; median undergraduate GPA; acceptance rate; and faculty resources. *U.S. News & World Report, "America's Best Graduate Schools, Medical, 2022"*

EMPLOYERS

Major Employers

Company Name	Industry
Alegent Health	General medical & surgical hospitals
City of Omaha	Municipal government
Creighton St. Joseph Reg Healthcare Sys	General medical & surgical hospitals
Creighton University	Colleges & universities
Drivers Management	Truck driver services
First Data Resources	Data processing service
Harveys Iowa Management Company	Casino hotels
Kiewit Offshore Services	Fabricated structural metal
Metropolitan Community College	Community college
Mutual of Omaha Insurance Company	Life insurance
Nebraska Furniture Mart	Furniture stores
Omaha Public Power District	Electric services
The Archbishop Bergan Mercy Hospital	General medical & surgical hospitals
The Nebraska Medical Center	General medical & surgical hospitals
The Pacesetter Corporation	General remodeling, single-family houses
Tyson Foods	Meats & meat products
Valmont Industries	Irrigation equipment, self-propelled

Note: Companies shown are located within the Omaha-Council Bluffs, NE-IA Metropolitan Statistical Area.
Source: Hoovers.com; Wikipedia

PUBLIC SAFETY

Crime Rate

Area	All Crimes	Violent Crimes				Property Crimes		
		Murder	Rape[3]	Robbery	Aggrav. Assault	Burglary	Larceny -Theft	Motor Vehicle Theft
City	4,256.7	4.9	80.6	110.3	417.0	357.9	2,615.8	670.2
Suburbs[1]	1,880.3	2.3	43.8	23.0	147.2	232.1	1,212.2	219.7
Metro[2]	3,059.7	3.6	62.0	66.4	281.1	294.5	1,908.8	443.3
U.S.	2,489.3	5.0	42.6	81.6	250.2	340.5	1,549.5	219.9

Note: Figures are crimes per 100,000 population; (1) All areas within the metro area that are located outside the city limits; (2) Figures cover the Omaha-Council Bluffs, NE-IA Metropolitan Statistical Area; (3) All figures shown were reported using the revised Uniform Crime Reporting (UCR) definition of rape.
Source: FBI Uniform Crime Reports, 2019

Hate Crimes

Area	Number of Quarters Reported	Number of Incidents per Bias Motivation					
		Race/Ethnicity/Ancestry	Religion	Sexual Orientation	Disability	Gender	Gender Identity
City	4	0	1	0	0	0	0
U.S.	4	3,963	1,521	1,195	157	69	198

Source: Federal Bureau of Investigation, Hate Crime Statistics 2019

Identity Theft Consumer Reports

Area	Reports	Reports per 100,000 Population	Rank[2]
MSA[1]	1,364	144	303
U.S.	1,387,615	423	-

Note: (1) Figures cover the Omaha-Council Bluffs, NE-IA Metropolitan Statistical Area; (2) Rank ranges from 1 to 391 where 1 indicates greatest number of identity theft reports per 100,000 population
Source: Federal Trade Commission, Consumer Sentinel Network Data Book 2020

Fraud and Other Consumer Reports

Area	Reports	Reports per 100,000 Population	Rank[2]
MSA[1]	6,976	735	156
U.S.	3,385,133	1,031	-

Note: (1) Figures cover the Omaha-Council Bluffs, NE-IA Metropolitan Statistical Area; (2) Rank ranges from 1 to 391 where 1 indicates greatest number of fraud and other consumer reports per 100,000 population
Source: Federal Trade Commission, Consumer Sentinel Network Data Book 2020

POLITICS

2020 Presidential Election Results

Area	Biden	Trump	Jorgensen	Hawkins	Other
Douglas County	54.4	43.1	2.0	0.0	0.6
U.S.	51.3	46.8	1.2	0.3	0.5

Note: Results are percentages and may not add to 100% due to rounding
Source: Dave Leip's Atlas of U.S. Presidential Elections

SPORTS

Professional Sports Teams

Team Name	League	Year Established

No teams are located in the metro area
Source: Wikipedia, Major Professional Sports Teams of the United States and Canada, April 6, 2021

CLIMATE

Average and Extreme Temperatures

Temperature	Jan	Feb	Mar	Apr	May	Jun	Jul	Aug	Sep	Oct	Nov	Dec	Yr.
Extreme High (°F)	67	77	89	97	98	105	110	107	103	95	80	69	110
Average High (°F)	31	37	48	64	74	84	88	85	77	66	49	36	62
Average Temp. (°F)	22	27	38	52	63	73	77	75	66	54	39	27	51
Average Low (°F)	11	17	27	40	52	61	66	64	54	42	29	17	40
Extreme Low (°F)	-23	-21	-16	5	27	38	44	43	25	13	-9	-23	-23

Note: Figures cover the years 1948-1992
Source: National Climatic Data Center, International Station Meteorological Climate Summary, 9/96

Average Precipitation/Snowfall/Humidity

Precip./Humidity	Jan	Feb	Mar	Apr	May	Jun	Jul	Aug	Sep	Oct	Nov	Dec	Yr.
Avg. Precip. (in.)	0.8	0.9	2.0	2.8	4.3	4.0	3.7	3.8	3.4	2.1	1.5	0.9	30.1
Avg. Snowfall (in.)	7	6	7	1	Tr	0	0	0	Tr	Tr	3	6	29
Avg. Rel. Hum. 6am (%)	78	80	79	77	80	82	84	86	85	81	79	80	81
Avg. Rel. Hum. 3pm (%)	61	59	54	46	49	50	51	53	51	47	55	61	53

Note: Figures cover the years 1948-1992; Tr = Trace amounts (<0.05 in. of rain; <0.5 in. of snow)
Source: National Climatic Data Center, International Station Meteorological Climate Summary, 9/96

Weather Conditions

Temperature			Daytime Sky			Precipitation		
5°F & below	32°F & below	90°F & above	Clear	Partly cloudy	Cloudy	0.01 inch or more precip.	0.1 inch or more snow/ice	Thunder-storms
23	139	35	100	142	123	97	20	46

Note: Figures are average number of days per year and cover the years 1948-1992
Source: National Climatic Data Center, International Station Meteorological Climate Summary, 9/96

404 Omaha, Nebraska

HAZARDOUS WASTE

Superfund Sites

The Omaha-Council Bluffs, NE-IA metro area is home to three sites on the EPA's Superfund National Priorities List: **Nebraska Ordnance Plant (Former)** (final); **Old Hwy 275 and N 288th Street** (final); **Omaha Lead** (final). There are a total of 1,375 Superfund sites with a status of proposed or final on the list in the U.S. *U.S. Environmental Protection Agency, National Priorities List, April 7, 2021*

AIR QUALITY

Air Quality Trends: Ozone

	1990	1995	2000	2005	2010	2015	2016	2017	2018	2019
MSA[1]	0.054	0.075	0.063	0.069	0.058	0.055	0.063	0.061	0.063	0.050
U.S.	0.088	0.089	0.082	0.080	0.073	0.068	0.069	0.068	0.069	0.065

Note: (1) Data covers the Omaha-Council Bluffs, NE-IA Metropolitan Statistical Area. The values shown are the composite ozone concentration averages among trend sites based on the highest fourth daily maximum 8-hour concentration in parts per million. These trends are based on sites having an adequate record of monitoring data during the trend period. Data from exceptional events are included.
Source: U.S. Environmental Protection Agency, Air Quality Monitoring Information, "Air Quality Trends by City, 1990-2019"

Air Quality Index

Area	Percent of Days when Air Quality was...[2]					AQI Statistics[2]	
	Good	Moderate	Unhealthy for Sensitive Groups	Unhealthy	Very Unhealthy	Maximum	Median
MSA[1]	77.5	22.5	0.0	0.0	0.0	97	40

Note: (1) Data covers the Omaha-Council Bluffs, NE-IA Metropolitan Statistical Area; (2) Based on 365 days with AQI data in 2019. Air Quality Index (AQI) is an index for reporting daily air quality. EPA calculates the AQI for five major air pollutants regulated by the Clean Air Act: ground-level ozone, particle pollution (aka particulate matter), carbon monoxide, sulfur dioxide, and nitrogen dioxide. The AQI runs from 0 to 500. The higher the AQI value, the greater the level of air pollution and the greater the health concern. There are six AQI categories: "Good" AQI is between 0 and 50. Air quality is considered satisfactory; "Moderate" AQI is between 51 and 100. Air quality is acceptable; "Unhealthy for Sensitive Groups" When AQI values are between 101 and 150, members of sensitive groups may experience health effects; "Unhealthy" When AQI values are between 151 and 200 everyone may begin to experience health effects; "Very Unhealthy" AQI values between 201 and 300 trigger a health alert; "Hazardous" AQI values over 300 trigger warnings of emergency conditions (not shown).
Source: U.S. Environmental Protection Agency, Air Quality Index Report, 2019

Air Quality Index Pollutants

Area	Percent of Days when AQI Pollutant was...[2]					
	Carbon Monoxide	Nitrogen Dioxide	Ozone	Sulfur Dioxide	Particulate Matter 2.5	Particulate Matter 10
MSA[1]	0.0	0.0	52.3	3.3	40.8	3.6

Note: (1) Data covers the Omaha-Council Bluffs, NE-IA Metropolitan Statistical Area; (2) Based on 365 days with AQI data in 2019. The Air Quality Index (AQI) is an index for reporting daily air quality. EPA calculates the AQI for five major air pollutants regulated by the Clean Air Act: ground-level ozone, particle pollution (also known as particulate matter), carbon monoxide, sulfur dioxide, and nitrogen dioxide. The AQI runs from 0 to 500. The higher the AQI value, the greater the level of air pollution and the greater the health concern.
Source: U.S. Environmental Protection Agency, Air Quality Index Report, 2019

Maximum Air Pollutant Concentrations: Particulate Matter, Ozone, CO and Lead

	Particulate Matter 10 (ug/m^3)	Particulate Matter 2.5 Wtd AM (ug/m^3)	Particulate Matter 2.5 24-Hr (ug/m^3)	Ozone (ppm)	Carbon Monoxide (ppm)	Lead (ug/m^3)
MSA[1] Level	50	7.8	22	0.062	2	0.06
NAAQS[2]	150	15	35	0.075	9	0.15
Met NAAQS[2]	Yes	Yes	Yes	Yes	Yes	Yes

Note: (1) Data covers the Omaha-Council Bluffs, NE-IA Metropolitan Statistical Area; Data from exceptional events are included; (2) National Ambient Air Quality Standards; ppm = parts per million; ug/m^3 = micrograms per cubic meter; n/a not available.
Concentrations: Particulate Matter 10 (coarse particulate)—highest second maximum 24-hour concentration; Particulate Matter 2.5 Wtd AM (fine particulate)—highest weighted annual mean concentration; Particulate Matter 2.5 24-Hour (fine particulate)—highest 98th percentile 24-hour concentration; Ozone—highest fourth daily maximum 8-hour concentration; Carbon Monoxide—highest second maximum non-overlapping 8-hour concentration; Lead—maximum running 3-month average
Source: U.S. Environmental Protection Agency, Air Quality Monitoring Information, "Air Quality Statistics by City, 2019"

Maximum Air Pollutant Concentrations: Nitrogen Dioxide and Sulfur Dioxide

	Nitrogen Dioxide AM (ppb)	Nitrogen Dioxide 1-Hr (ppb)	Sulfur Dioxide AM (ppb)	Sulfur Dioxide 1-Hr (ppb)	Sulfur Dioxide 24-Hr (ppb)
MSA[1] Level	n/a	n/a	n/a	38	n/a
NAAQS[2]	53	100	30	75	140
Met NAAQS[2]	n/a	n/a	n/a	Yes	n/a

Note: (1) Data covers the Omaha-Council Bluffs, NE-IA Metropolitan Statistical Area; Data from exceptional events are included; (2) National Ambient Air Quality Standards; ppm = parts per million; ug/m³ = micrograms per cubic meter; n/a not available.
Concentrations: Nitrogen Dioxide AM—highest arithmetic mean concentration; Nitrogen Dioxide 1-Hr—highest 98th percentile 1-hour daily maximum concentration; Sulfur Dioxide AM—highest annual mean concentration; Sulfur Dioxide 1-Hr—highest 99th percentile 1-hour daily maximum concentration; Sulfur Dioxide 24-Hr—highest second maximum 24-hour concentration
Source: U.S. Environmental Protection Agency, Air Quality Monitoring Information, "Air Quality Statistics by City, 2019"

Peoria, Illinois

Background

Like most Midwestern cities at the turn of the 19th century, Peoria started out as a military fort. Originally built in 1680 by French explorers, Fort Clark burned to the ground only to be rebuilt in 1813, following the War of 1812. By 1825, Fort Clark was renamed Peoria—the name of a local tribe of Native Americans. By 1845, Peoria was incorporated as a city.

Industry came to Peoria in 1830 when John Hamlin constructed a flour mill. Other industries soon followed including foundries, carriage factories, and furniture makers. In 1837, Andrew Eitle and Almiron S. Cole founded a distillery that made Peoria a world leader in liquor production, with the greatest liquor tax revenues of any other district in the country. In fact, at the turn of the century, the federal government received 42 percent of its revenue from liquor taxes—a major factor in the prohibition debate. And nobody produced more liquor than Peoria. According to The Peoria Historical Society, between the years of 1837 and 1919, Peoria had 24 breweries and 73 distilleries. The city took a huge financial hit during prohibition, although it became a bootleg capital with the dubious distinction of being home to mobsters such as the Shelton Brothers. This economic growth due to tax revenues would draw other industries to the area, the largest being farm equipment manufacturing, which included everything from wire fencing to wheels. Today, Keystone Steel & Wire is still the nation's leader in wire manufacturing after more than 120 years.

The health care industry employs over 25 percent of Peoria's work force, and reflects some of Peoria's greatest contributions to national health. During World War II, the "Peoria Plan for Human Rehabilitation" called for the creation of the Institute of Physical Medicine and Rehabilitation, one of the first such institutions designed to rehabilitate polio victims, and to help injured veterans integrate back into civilian life and work. In 1943, a moldy cantaloupe found in Peoria would produce the world's first *Penicillium chrysogenum,* used in producing industrial penicillin at the USDA's National Center for Agricultural Utilization Research, located in Peoria.

In the 1850s, German immigrants brought the concept of the public hall to Peoria, providing theater, music and the concomitant lectures and debates. At the time it was considered great success if an act could "play in Peoria." Perhaps Peoria's reputation for theater and debate is what brought Abraham Lincoln to the city in October of 1864, a first step in his journey to the White House and the Emancipation Proclamation in his three-hour response to the Kansas-Nebraska Act.

Peoria citizenry was largely divided during the Civil War. However, a local merchant, Moses Pettengill, opened his home to the Underground Railroad, and Peoria's Camp Lyon was a Union training ground for over 7500 Union soldiers.

Other notable events include Charles Lindbergh's connection with his first airmail route. Locals debate that, had Peoria provided backing for his transatlantic flight, Lindbergh's plane might have been called the "Spirit of Peoria." Music icon, Richard Whiting was from Peoria, and wrote an extraordinary number of hits, including "Til We Meet Again," "On the Good Ship Lollipop," "Hooray for Hollywood," and "Ain't We Got Fun." He died at 46.

The Glen Oak Park is a 100-acre park featuring a zoo, conservatory and gardens. Peoria has numerous performing arts venues that include the Peoria Symphony (the 10th oldest in the nation), Peoria Ballet Company, and Opera Illinois. The Lakeview Museum of Arts and Sciences displays folk art and African art, and also features a planetarium and children's science museum. The museum square called The Block houses the Peoria Riverfront Museum, a planetarium, and the Caterpillar World Visitors Center.

The best time to visit Peoria is between May and October when the weather is usually mild and dry.

Rankings

Business/Finance Rankings

- The Peoria metro area appeared on the Milken Institute "2021 Best Performing Cities" list. Rank: #200 out of 200 large metro areas (population over 250,000). Criteria: job growth; wage and salary growth; high-tech output growth; housing affordability; household broadband access. *Milken Institute, "Best-Performing Cities 2021," February 16, 2021*

- *Forbes* ranked the 200 most populous metro areas to determine the nation's "Best Places for Business and Careers." The Peoria metro area was ranked #167. Criteria: costs (business and living); job growth (past and projected); income growth; quality of life; educational attainment (college and high school); projected economic growth; cultural and leisure opportunities; workplace tolerance laws; net migration patterns. *Forbes, "The Best Places for Business and Careers 2019: Seattle Still On Top," October 30, 2019*

Education Rankings

- Personal finance website *WalletHub* analyzed the 150 largest U.S. metropolitan statistical areas to determine where the most educated Americans are putting their degrees to work. Criteria: education levels; percentage of workers with degrees; education quality and attainment gap; public school quality rankings; quality and enrollment of each metro area's universities. Peoria was ranked #87 (#1 = most educated city). *www.WalletHub.com, "Most and Least Educated Cities in America," July 20, 2020*

Environmental Rankings

- Peoria was highlighted as one of the top 98 cleanest metro areas for short-term particle pollution (24-hour PM 2.5) in the U.S. during 2016 through 2018. Monitors in these cities reported no days with unhealthful PM 2.5 levels. *American Lung Association, "State of the Air 2020," April 21, 2020*

Health/Fitness Rankings

- The Peoria metro area was identified as one of the worst cities for bed bugs in America by pest control company Orkin. The area ranked #49 out of 50 based on the number of bed bug treatments Orkin performed from December 2019 to November 2020. *Orkin, "New Year, New Top City on Orkin's 2021 Bed Bug Cities List: Chicago," February 1, 2021*

Real Estate Rankings

- The Peoria metro area was identified as one of the 20 worst housing markets in the U.S. in 2020. The area ranked #163 out of 180 markets. Criteria: year-over-year change of median sales price of existing single-family homes between the 4th quarter of 2019 and the 4th quarter of 2020. *National Association of Realtors®, Median Sales Price of Existing Single-Family Homes for Metropolitan Areas, 4th Quarter 2020*

- The Peoria metro area was identified as one of the 20 most affordable housing markets in the U.S. in 2020. The area ranked #5 out of 183 markets. Criteria: qualification for a mortgage loan with a 10 percent down payment on a typical home. *National Association of Realtors®, Qualifying Income Based on Sales Price of Existing Single-Family Homes for Metropolitan Areas, 2020*

- Peoria was ranked #19 out of 268 metro areas in terms of housing affordability in 2020 by the National Association of Home Builders (#1 = most affordable). Criteria: the share of homes sold in that area affordable to a family earning the local median income, based on standard mortgage underwriting criteria. *National Association of Home Builders®, NAHB-Wells Fargo Housing Opportunity Index, 4th Quarter 2020*

- The nation's largest metro areas were analyzed in terms of the percentage of households entering some stage of foreclosure in 2020. The Peoria metro area ranked #1 out of 10 (#1 = highest foreclosure rate). *ATTOM Data Solutions, "2020 Year-End U.S. Foreclosure Market Report™," January 14, 2021*

Safety Rankings

- To identify the most dangerous cities in America, 24/7 Wall Street focused on violent crime categories—murder, non-negligent manslaughter, rape, robbery, and aggravated assault—and property crime as reported in the FBI's 2019 annual Uniform Crime Report. Criteria also included median income from American Community Survey and unemployment figures from Bureau of Labor Statistics. For cities with populations over 100,000, Peoria was ranked #24. *247wallst.com, "America's 50 Most Dangerous Cities" November 16, 2020*

- Peoria was identified as one of the most dangerous cities in America by NeighborhoodScout. The city ranked #53 out of 100 (#1 = most dangerous). Criteria: number of violent crimes per 1,000 residents. The editors evaluated cities with 25,000 or more residents. *NeighborhoodScout.com, "2021 Top 100 Most Dangerous Cities in the U.S.," January 2, 2021*

- The National Insurance Crime Bureau ranked 384 metro areas in the U.S. in terms of per capita rates of vehicle theft. The Peoria metro area ranked #204 (#1 = highest rate). Criteria: number of vehicle theft offenses per 100,000 inhabitants in 2019. *National Insurance Crime Bureau, "Hot Spots 2019," July 21, 2020*

Seniors/Retirement Rankings

- From its Best Cities for Successful Aging indexes, the Milken Institute generated rankings for metropolitan areas, weighing data in nine categories—health care, wellness, living arrangements, transportation and convenience, financial characteristics, education, employment, community engagement, and overall livability. The Peoria metro area was ranked #134 overall in the small metro area category. *Milken Institute, "Best Cities for Successful Aging, 2017" March 14, 2017*

Business Environment

DEMOGRAPHICS

Population Growth

Area	1990 Census	2000 Census	2010 Census	2019* Estimate	Population Growth (%)	
					1990-2019	2010-2019
City	114,341	112,936	115,007	113,532	-0.7	-1.3
MSA[1]	358,552	366,899	379,186	406,883	13.5	7.3
U.S.	248,709,873	281,421,906	308,745,538	324,697,795	30.6	5.2

Note: (1) Figures cover the Peoria, IL Metropolitan Statistical Area; (*) 2015-2019 5-year estimated population
Source: U.S. Census Bureau, 1990 Census, Census 2000, Census 2010, 2015-2019 American Community Survey 5-Year Estimates

Household Size

Area	Persons in Household (%)							Average Household Size
	One	Two	Three	Four	Five	Six	Seven or More	
City	38.2	31.4	13.3	9.1	5.2	1.7	0.9	2.40
MSA[1]	31.3	35.4	14.0	11.0	5.3	2.1	0.8	2.40
U.S.	27.9	33.9	15.6	12.9	6.0	2.3	1.4	2.60

Note: (1) Figures cover the Peoria, IL Metropolitan Statistical Area
Source: U.S. Census Bureau, 2015-2019 American Community Survey 5-Year Estimates

Race

Area	White Alone[2] (%)	Black Alone[2] (%)	Asian Alone[2] (%)	AIAN[3] Alone[2] (%)	NHOPI[4] Alone[2] (%)	Other Race Alone[2] (%)	Two or More Races (%)
City	60.1	27.1	6.1	0.3	0.0	2.1	4.3
MSA[1]	85.4	8.8	2.3	0.2	0.0	0.8	2.4
U.S.	72.5	12.7	5.5	0.8	0.2	4.9	3.3

Note: (1) Figures cover the Peoria, IL Metropolitan Statistical Area; (2) Alone is defined as not being in combination with one or more other races; (3) American Indian and Alaska Native; (4) Native Hawaiian and Other Pacific Islander
Source: U.S. Census Bureau, 2015-2019 American Community Survey 5-Year Estimates

Hispanic or Latino Origin

Area	Total (%)	Mexican (%)	Puerto Rican (%)	Cuban (%)	Other (%)
City	6.3	4.6	0.4	0.1	1.1
MSA[1]	3.5	2.5	0.3	0.0	0.6
U.S.	18.0	11.2	1.7	0.7	4.3

Note: Persons of Hispanic or Latino origin can be of any race; (1) Figures cover the Peoria, IL Metropolitan Statistical Area
Source: U.S. Census Bureau, 2015-2019 American Community Survey 5-Year Estimates

Ancestry

Area	German	Irish	English	American	Italian	Polish	French[2]	Scottish	Dutch
City	18.3	11.3	6.7	4.7	3.1	1.9	2.1	1.2	1.0
MSA[1]	27.2	12.4	9.1	6.7	3.9	2.0	2.4	1.8	1.6
U.S.	13.3	9.7	7.2	6.2	5.1	2.8	2.3	1.7	1.2

Note: Figures are the percentage of the total population reporting a particular ancestry. The nine most commonly reported ancestries in the U.S. are shown. Figures include multiple ancestries (e.g. if a person reported being Irish and Italian, they were included in both columns); (1) Figures cover the Peoria, IL Metropolitan Statistical Area; (2) Excludes Basque
Source: U.S. Census Bureau, 2015-2019 American Community Survey 5-Year Estimates

Foreign-born Population

Area	Percent of Population Born in								
	Any Foreign Country	Asia	Mexico	Europe	Caribbean	Central America[2]	South America	Africa	Canada
City	7.6	4.7	1.2	0.5	0.1	0.2	0.3	0.3	0.1
MSA[1]	3.3	1.7	0.6	0.4	0.0	0.1	0.1	0.1	0.1
U.S.	13.6	4.2	3.5	1.5	1.3	1.1	1.0	0.7	0.2

Note: (1) Figures cover the Peoria, IL Metropolitan Statistical Area; (2) Excludes Mexico.
Source: U.S. Census Bureau, 2015-2019 American Community Survey 5-Year Estimates

Marital Status

Area	Never Married	Now Married[2]	Separated	Widowed	Divorced
City	40.5	39.9	1.3	6.2	12.1
MSA[1]	29.9	50.3	1.1	7.0	11.8
U.S.	33.4	48.1	1.9	5.8	10.9

Note: Figures are percentages and cover the population 15 years of age and older; (1) Figures cover the Peoria, IL Metropolitan Statistical Area; (2) Excludes separated
Source: U.S. Census Bureau, 2015-2019 American Community Survey 5-Year Estimates

Disability by Age

Area	All Ages	Under 18 Years Old	18 to 64 Years Old	65 Years and Over
City	12.4	3.2	11.0	33.2
MSA[1]	12.0	3.4	9.5	32.2
U.S.	12.6	4.2	10.3	34.5

Note: Figures show percent of the civilian noninstitutionalized population that reported having a disability. Disability status is determined from six types of difficulty: vision, hearing, cognitive, ambulatory, self-care, and independent living. For children under 5 years old, hearing and vision difficulty are used to determine disability status. For children between the ages of 5 and 14, disability status is determined from hearing, vision, cognitive, ambulatory, and self-care difficulties. For people aged 15 years and older, they are considered to have a disability if they have difficulty with any one of the six difficulty types; Note: (1) Figures cover the Peoria, IL Metropolitan Statistical Area
Source: U.S. Census Bureau, 2015-2019 American Community Survey 5-Year Estimates

Age

Area	Percent of Population									Median Age
	Under Age 5	Age 5–19	Age 20–34	Age 35–44	Age 45–54	Age 55–64	Age 65–74	Age 75–84	Age 85+	
City	7.6	19.5	22.5	12.1	11.3	11.8	8.4	4.4	2.4	35.2
MSA[1]	6.3	19.1	18.5	12.3	12.6	13.5	9.9	5.3	2.6	39.9
U.S.	6.1	19.1	20.7	12.6	13.0	12.9	9.1	4.6	1.9	38.1

Note: (1) Figures cover the Peoria, IL Metropolitan Statistical Area
Source: U.S. Census Bureau, 2015-2019 American Community Survey 5-Year Estimates

Gender

Area	Males	Females	Males per 100 Females
City	54,542	58,990	92.5
MSA[1]	200,311	206,572	97.0
U.S.	159,886,919	164,810,876	97.0

Note: (1) Figures cover the Peoria, IL Metropolitan Statistical Area
Source: U.S. Census Bureau, 2015-2019 American Community Survey 5-Year Estimates

Religious Groups by Family

Area	Catholic	Baptist	Non-Den.	Methodist[2]	Lutheran	LDS[3]	Pentecostal	Presbyterian[4]	Muslim[5]	Judaism
MSA[1]	11.5	5.5	5.3	5.0	6.1	0.5	1.5	2.8	5.2	0.1
U.S.	19.1	9.3	4.0	4.0	2.3	2.0	1.9	1.6	0.8	0.7

Note: Figures are the number of adherents as a percentage of the total population; (1) Figures cover the Peoria, IL Metropolitan Statistical Area; (2) Methodist/Pietist; (3) Latter Day Saints; (4) Reformed; (5) Figures are estimates
Source: Association of Statisticians of American Religious Bodies, 2010 U.S. Religion Census: Religious Congregations & Membership Study

Religious Groups by Tradition

Area	Catholic	Evangelical Protestant	Mainline Protestant	Other Tradition	Black Protestant	Orthodox
MSA[1]	11.5	18.9	11.1	6.2	0.9	0.1
U.S.	19.1	16.2	7.3	4.3	1.6	0.3

Note: Figures are the number of adherents as a percentage of the total population; (1) Figures cover the Peoria, IL Metropolitan Statistical Area
Source: Association of Statisticians of American Religious Bodies, 2010 U.S. Religion Census: Religious Congregations & Membership Study

ECONOMY

Gross Metropolitan Product

Area	2017	2018	2019	2020	Rank[2]
MSA[1]	19.2	20.1	20.9	21.6	133

Note: Figures are in billions of dollars; (1) Figures cover the Peoria, IL Metropolitan Statistical Area; (2) Rank is based on 2018 data and ranges from 1 to 381
Source: U.S. Conference of Mayors, U.S. Metro Economies: GMP & Employment 2018-2020, September 2019

Economic Growth

Area	2015-17 (%)	2018 (%)	2019 (%)	2020 (%)	Rank[2]
MSA[1]	-4.0	2.5	2.0	1.3	376
U.S.	1.9	2.9	2.3	2.1	—

Note: Figures are real gross metropolitan product (GMP) growth rates and represent average annual percent change; (1) Figures cover the Peoria, IL Metropolitan Statistical Area; (2) Rank is based on 2017 2-year average annual percent change and ranges from 1 to 381
Source: U.S. Conference of Mayors, U.S. Metro Economies: GMP & Employment 2018-2020, September 2019

Metropolitan Area Exports

Area	2014	2015	2016	2017	2018	2019	Rank[2]
MSA[1]	11,234.8	9,826.9	7,260.1	9,403.6	9,683.6	8,151.9	42

Note: Figures are in millions of dollars; (1) Figures cover the Peoria, IL Metropolitan Statistical Area; (2) Rank is based on 2019 data and ranges from 1 to 386
Source: U.S. Department of Commerce, International Trade Administration, Office of Trade and Economic Analysis, Industry and Analysis, Exports by Metropolitan Area, data extracted March 24, 2021

Building Permits

Area	Single-Family			Multi-Family			Total		
	2018	2019	Pct. Chg.	2018	2019	Pct. Chg.	2018	2019	Pct. Chg.
City	32	33	3.1	0	0	0.0	32	33	3.1
MSA[1]	228	218	-4.4	106	90	-15.1	334	308	-7.8
U.S.	855,300	862,100	0.7	473,500	523,900	10.6	1,328,800	1,386,000	4.3

Note: (1) Figures cover the Peoria, IL Metropolitan Statistical Area; Figures represent new, privately-owned housing units authorized (unadjusted data); All permit data are based on estimates with imputation
Source: U.S. Census Bureau, Manufacturing, Mining, and Construction Statistics, Building Permits, 2018, 2019

Bankruptcy Filings

Area	Business Filings			Nonbusiness Filings		
	2019	2020	% Chg.	2019	2020	% Chg.
Peoria County	16	6	-62.5	548	391	-28.6
U.S.	22,780	21,655	-4.9	752,160	522,808	-30.5

Note: Business filings include Chapter 7, Chapter 9, Chapter 11, Chapter 12, Chapter 13, Chapter 15, and Section 304; Nonbusiness filings include Chapter 7, Chapter 11, and Chapter 13
Source: Administrative Office of the U.S. Courts, Business and Nonbusiness Bankruptcy, County Cases Commenced by Chapter of the Bankruptcy Code, During the 12-Month Period Ending December 31, 2019 and Business and Nonbusiness Bankruptcy, County Cases Commenced by Chapter of the Bankruptcy Code, During the 12-Month Period Ending December 31, 2020

Housing Vacancy Rates

Area	Gross Vacancy Rate[2] (%)			Year-Round Vacancy Rate[3] (%)			Rental Vacancy Rate[4] (%)			Homeowner Vacancy Rate[5] (%)		
	2018	2019	2020	2018	2019	2020	2018	2019	2020	2018	2019	2020
MSA[1]	n/a	n/a	n/a	n/a	n/a	n/a	n/a	n/a	n/a	n/a	n/a	n/a
U.S.	12.3	12.0	10.6	9.7	9.5	8.2	6.9	6.7	6.3	1.5	1.4	1.0

Note: (1) Figures cover the Peoria, IL Metropolitan Statistical Area; (2) The percentage of the total housing inventory that is vacant; (3) The percentage of the housing inventory (excluding seasonal units) that is year-round vacant; (4) The percentage of rental inventory that is vacant for rent; (5) The percentage of homeowner inventory that is vacant for sale; n/a not available
Source: U.S. Census Bureau, Housing Vacancies and Homeownership Annual Statistics: 2018, 2019, 2020

INCOME

Income

Area	Per Capita ($)	Median Household ($)	Average Household ($)
City	31,497	51,771	74,900
MSA[1]	32,575	59,397	79,057
U.S.	34,103	62,843	88,607

Note: (1) Figures cover the Peoria, IL Metropolitan Statistical Area
Source: U.S. Census Bureau, 2015-2019 American Community Survey 5-Year Estimates

Household Income Distribution

Area	Percent of Households Earning							
	Under $15,000	$15,000 -$24,999	$25,000 -$34,999	$35,000 -$49,999	$50,000 -$74,999	$75,000 -$99,999	$100,000 -$149,999	$150,000 and up
City	16.8	11.0	8.8	12.0	17.3	11.6	11.8	10.7
MSA[1]	10.4	9.1	9.0	13.2	19.5	13.5	14.8	10.5
U.S.	10.3	8.9	8.9	12.3	17.2	12.7	15.1	14.5

Note: (1) Figures cover the Peoria, IL Metropolitan Statistical Area
Source: U.S. Census Bureau, 2015-2019 American Community Survey 5-Year Estimates

Poverty Rate

Area	All Ages	Under 18 Years Old	18 to 64 Years Old	65 Years and Over
City	19.7	24.6	20.1	10.1
MSA[1]	12.2	15.5	12.4	6.9
U.S.	13.4	18.5	12.6	9.3

Note: Figures are percentage of people whose income during the past 12 months was below the poverty level;
(1) Figures cover the Peoria, IL Metropolitan Statistical Area
Source: U.S. Census Bureau, 2015-2019 American Community Survey 5-Year Estimates

CITY FINANCES

City Government Finances

Component	2017 ($000)	2017 ($ per capita)
Total Revenues	207,363	1,802
Total Expenditures	225,369	1,959
Debt Outstanding	191,860	1,667
Cash and Securities[1]	323,297	2,810

Note: (1) Cash and security holdings of a government at the close of its fiscal year,
including those of its dependent agencies, utilities, and liquor stores.
Source: U.S. Census Bureau, State & Local Government Finances 2017

City Government Revenue by Source

Source	2017 ($000)	2017 ($ per capita)	2017 (%)
General Revenue			
From Federal Government	4,379	38	2.1
From State Government	50,838	442	24.5
From Local Governments	0	0	0.0
Taxes			
Property	36,361	316	17.5
Sales and Gross Receipts	44,953	391	21.7
Personal Income	0	0	0.0
Corporate Income	0	0	0.0
Motor Vehicle License	0	0	0.0
Other Taxes	3,324	29	1.6
Current Charges	38,615	336	18.6
Liquor Store	0	0	0.0
Utility	0	0	0.0
Employee Retirement	21,476	187	10.4

Source: U.S. Census Bureau, State & Local Government Finances 2017

City Government Expenditures by Function

Function	2017 ($000)	2017 ($ per capita)	2017 (%)
General Direct Expenditures			
Air Transportation	0	0	0.0
Corrections	0	0	0.0
Education	0	0	0.0
Employment Security Administration	0	0	0.0
Financial Administration	0	0	0.0
Fire Protection	31,045	269	13.8
General Public Buildings	0	0	0.0
Governmental Administration, Other	11,631	101	5.2
Health	0	0	0.0
Highways	27,827	241	12.3
Hospitals	0	0	0.0
Housing and Community Development	243	2	0.1
Interest on General Debt	8,248	71	3.7
Judicial and Legal	0	0	0.0
Libraries	7,680	66	3.4
Parking	0	0	0.0
Parks and Recreation	0	0	0.0
Police Protection	39,593	344	17.6
Public Welfare	0	0	0.0
Sewerage	1,341	11	0.6
Solid Waste Management	8,999	78	4.0
Veterans' Services	0	0	0.0
Liquor Store	0	0	0.0
Utility	0	0	0.0
Employee Retirement	27,570	239	12.2

Source: U.S. Census Bureau, State & Local Government Finances 2017

EMPLOYMENT

Labor Force and Employment

Area	Civilian Labor Force			Workers Employed		
	Dec. 2019	Dec. 2020	% Chg.	Dec. 2019	Dec. 2020	% Chg.
City	50,615	47,156	-6.8	47,924	43,020	-10.2
MSA[1]	173,154	158,961	-8.2	165,096	148,160	-10.3
U.S.	164,007,000	160,017,000	-2.4	158,504,000	149,613,000	-5.6

Note: Data is not seasonally adjusted and covers workers 16 years of age and older; (1) Figures cover the Peoria, IL Metropolitan Statistical Area
Source: Bureau of Labor Statistics, Local Area Unemployment Statistics

Unemployment Rate

Area	2020											
	Jan.	Feb.	Mar.	Apr.	May	Jun.	Jul.	Aug.	Sep.	Oct.	Nov.	Dec.
City	5.2	4.3	4.0	19.2	18.0	16.5	13.8	13.2	11.8	8.5	8.6	8.8
MSA[1]	5.0	4.2	3.8	17.7	15.4	13.5	10.8	9.8	8.6	6.1	6.3	6.8
U.S.	4.0	3.8	4.5	14.4	13.0	11.2	10.5	8.5	7.7	6.6	6.4	6.5

Note: Data is not seasonally adjusted and covers workers 16 years of age and older; (1) Figures cover the Peoria, IL Metropolitan Statistical Area
Source: Bureau of Labor Statistics, Local Area Unemployment Statistics

Average Wages

Occupation	$/Hr.	Occupation	$/Hr.
Accountants and Auditors	38.40	Maintenance and Repair Workers	20.90
Automotive Mechanics	20.70	Marketing Managers	71.90
Bookkeepers	19.00	Network and Computer Systems Admin.	35.70
Carpenters	31.70	Nurses, Licensed Practical	22.80
Cashiers	11.40	Nurses, Registered	33.00
Computer Programmers	39.60	Nursing Assistants	14.10
Computer Systems Analysts	45.60	Office Clerks, General	18.00
Computer User Support Specialists	27.30	Physical Therapists	42.50
Construction Laborers	20.90	Physicians	108.80
Cooks, Restaurant	13.40	Plumbers, Pipefitters and Steamfitters	38.00
Customer Service Representatives	15.80	Police and Sheriff's Patrol Officers	26.30
Dentists	118.40	Postal Service Mail Carriers	25.20
Electricians	33.90	Real Estate Sales Agents	22.90
Engineers, Electrical	n/a	Retail Salespersons	13.30
Fast Food and Counter Workers	11.00	Sales Representatives, Technical/Scientific	41.10
Financial Managers	60.20	Secretaries, Exc. Legal/Medical/Executive	16.50
First-Line Supervisors of Office Workers	28.70	Security Guards	18.70
General and Operations Managers	50.70	Surgeons	n/a
Hairdressers/Cosmetologists	14.80	Teacher Assistants, Exc. Postsecondary*	12.80
Home Health and Personal Care Aides	12.90	Teachers, Secondary School, Exc. Sp. Ed.*	28.00
Janitors and Cleaners	12.80	Telemarketers	16.30
Landscaping/Groundskeeping Workers	14.90	Truck Drivers, Heavy/Tractor-Trailer	23.00
Lawyers	63.40	Truck Drivers, Light/Delivery Services	19.40
Maids and Housekeeping Cleaners	12.70	Waiters and Waitresses	10.60

Note: Wage data covers the Peoria, IL Metropolitan Statistical Area; (*) Hourly wages were calculated from annual wage data based on a 40 hour work week; n/a not available.
Source: Bureau of Labor Statistics, Metro Area Occupational Employment & Wage Estimates, May 2020

Employment by Industry

Sector	MSA[1]		U.S.
	Number of Employees	Percent of Total	Percent of Total
Construction, Mining, and Logging	7,600	4.8	5.5
Education and Health Services	31,600	19.9	16.3
Financial Activities	7,000	4.4	6.1
Government	19,000	11.9	15.2
Information	1,500	0.9	1.9
Leisure and Hospitality	11,700	7.4	9.0
Manufacturing	20,800	13.1	8.5
Other Services	7,500	4.7	3.8
Professional and Business Services	20,800	13.1	14.4
Retail Trade	18,300	11.5	10.9
Transportation, Warehousing, and Utilities	7,100	4.5	4.6
Wholesale Trade	6,100	3.8	3.9

Note: Figures are non-farm employment as of December 2020. Figures are not seasonally adjusted and include workers 16 years of age and older; (1) Figures cover the Peoria, IL Metropolitan Statistical Area
Source: Bureau of Labor Statistics, Current Employment Statistics, Employment, Hours, and Earnings

Employment by Occupation

Occupation Classification	City (%)	MSA[1] (%)	U.S. (%)
Management, Business, Science, and Arts	42.0	37.1	38.5
Natural Resources, Construction, and Maintenance	5.3	8.6	8.9
Production, Transportation, and Material Moving	11.7	14.0	13.2
Sales and Office	21.4	22.1	21.6
Service	19.6	18.1	17.8

Note: Figures cover employed civilians 16 years of age and older; (1) Figures cover the Peoria, IL Metropolitan Statistical Area
Source: U.S. Census Bureau, 2015-2019 American Community Survey 5-Year Estimates

Occupations with Greatest Projected Employment Growth: 2019 – 2021

Occupation[1]	2019 Employment	2021 Projected Employment	Numeric Employment Change	Percent Employment Change
Total,, All Occupations	6,370,620	6,449,130	78,510	1.2
Combined Food Preparation and Serving Workers,, Including Fast Food	140,460	145,280	4,820	3.4
Registered Nurses	133,320	137,300	3,980	3.0
Personal Care Aides	56,160	59,830	3,670	6.5
Laborers and Freight,, Stock,, and Material Movers,, Hand	158,620	162,170	3,550	2.2
Insurance Sales Agents	49,730	52,420	2,690	5.4
Heavy and Tractor-Trailer Truck Drivers	73,100	75,610	2,510	3.4
General and Operations Managers	120,880	123,200	2,320	1.9
Cooks,, Restaurant	47,520	49,620	2,100	4.4
Janitors and Cleaners,, Except Maids and Housekeeping Cleaners	85,160	86,710	1,550	1.8

Note: Projections cover Illinois; Projections for 2020-2022 were not available at time of publication; (1) Sorted by numeric employment change
Source: www.projectionscentral.com, State Occupational Projections, 2019–2021 Short-Term Projections

Fastest-Growing Occupations: 2019 – 2021

Occupation[1]	2019 Employment	2021 Projected Employment	Numeric Employment Change	Percent Employment Change
Actuaries	1,940	2,070	130	6.7
Personal Care Aides	56,160	59,830	3,670	6.5
Statisticians	1,910	2,030	120	6.3
Nurse Practitioners	8,130	8,610	480	5.9
Physician Assistants	3,800	4,020	220	5.8
Insurance Sales Agents	49,730	52,420	2,690	5.4
Operations Research Analysts	5,080	5,350	270	5.3
Computer Numerically Controlled Machine Tool Programmers,, Metal and Plastic	1,150	1,210	60	5.2
Veterinary Technologists and Technicians	4,010	4,210	200	5.0
Massage Therapists	6,720	7,050	330	4.9

Note: Projections cover Illinois; Projections for 2020-2022 were not available at time of publication; (1) Sorted by percent employment change and excludes occupations with numeric employment change less than 50
Source: www.projectionscentral.com, State Occupational Projections, 2019–2021 Short-Term Projections

TAXES

State Corporate Income Tax Rates

State	Tax Rate (%)	Income Brackets ($)	Num. of Brackets	Financial Institution Tax Rate (%)[a]	Federal Income Tax Ded.
Illinois	9.5 (h)	Flat rate	1	9.5 (h)	No

Note: Tax rates as of January 1, 2021; (a) Rates listed are the corporate income tax rate applied to financial institutions or excise taxes based on income. Some states have other taxes based upon the value of deposits or shares; (h) The Illinois rate of 9.5% is the sum of a corporate income tax rate of 7.0% plus a replacement tax of 2.5%.
Source: Federation of Tax Administrators, State Corporate Income Tax Rates, January 1, 2021

State Individual Income Tax Rates

State	Tax Rate (%)	Income Brackets ($)	Personal Exemptions ($)			Standard Ded. ($)	
			Single	Married	Depend.	Single	Married
Illinois (a)	4.95	Flat rate	2,325	4,650	2,325	–	–

Note: Tax rates as of January 1, 2021; Local- and county-level taxes are not included; Federal income tax is not deductible on state income tax returns; (a) 19 states have statutory provision for automatically adjusting to the rate of inflation the dollar values of the income tax brackets, standard deductions, and/or personal exemptions. Michigan indexes the personal exemption only. Oregon does not index the income brackets for $125,000 and over.
Source: Federation of Tax Administrators, State Individual Income Tax Rates, January 1, 2021

Various State Sales and Excise Tax Rates

State	State Sales Tax (%)	Gasoline[1] (¢/gal.)	Cigarette[2] ($/pack)	Spirits[3] ($/gal.)	Wine[4] ($/gal.)	Beer[5] ($/gal.)	Recreational Marijuana (%)
Illinois	6.25	52.16	2.98	8.55	1.39	0.23	(e)

Note: All tax rates as of January 1, 2021; (1) The American Petroleum Institute has developed a methodology for determining the average tax rate on a gallon of fuel. Rates may include any of the following: excise taxes, environmental fees, storage tank fees, other fees or taxes, general sales tax, and local taxes; (2) The federal excise tax of $1.0066 per pack and local taxes are not included; (3) Rates are those applicable to off-premise sales of 40% alcohol by volume (a.b.v.) distilled spirits in 750ml containers. Local excise taxes are excluded; (4) Rates are those applicable to off-premise sales of 11% a.b.v. non-carbonated wine in 750ml containers; (5) Rates are those applicable to off-premise sales of 4.7% a.b.v. beer in 12 ounce containers; (e) 7% excise tax of value at wholesale level; 10% tax on cannabis flower or products with less than 35% THC; 20% tax on products infused with cannabis, such as edible products; 25% tax on any product with a THC concentration higher than 35%
Source: Tax Foundation, 2021 Facts & Figures: How Does Your State Compare?

State Business Tax Climate Index Rankings

State	Overall Rank	Corporate Tax Rank	Individual Income Tax Rank	Sales Tax Rank	Property Tax Rank	Unemployment Insurance Tax Rank
Illinois	36	36	13	38	48	43

Note: The index is a measure of how each state's tax laws affect economic performance. The lower the rank, the more favorable a state's tax system is for business. States without a given tax are given a ranking of 1. The scores/rankings for the District of Columbia do not affect other states. The 2021 index represents the tax climate as of July 1, 2020.
Source: Tax Foundation, State Business Tax Climate Index 2021

TRANSPORTATION

Means of Transportation to Work

Area	Car/Truck/Van		Public Transportation			Bicycle	Walked	Other Means	Worked at Home
	Drove Alone	Car-pooled	Bus	Subway	Railroad				
City	80.1	9.5	2.4	0.0	0.0	0.3	2.7	1.1	3.7
MSA[1]	84.9	7.3	1.1	0.0	0.0	0.3	2.1	0.9	3.6
U.S.	76.3	9.0	2.4	1.9	0.6	0.5	2.7	1.4	5.2

Note: Figures are percentages and cover workers 16 years of age and older; (1) Figures cover the Peoria, IL Metropolitan Statistical Area
Source: U.S. Census Bureau, 2015-2019 American Community Survey 5-Year Estimates

Travel Time to Work

Area	Less Than 10 Minutes	10 to 19 Minutes	20 to 29 Minutes	30 to 44 Minutes	45 to 59 Minutes	60 to 89 Minutes	90 Minutes or More
City	18.6	49.5	19.8	7.6	1.9	1.8	0.8
MSA[1]	18.6	34.8	23.6	15.1	4.4	2.1	1.4
U.S.	12.2	28.4	20.8	20.8	8.3	6.4	2.9

Note: Note: Figures are percentages and include workers 16 years old and over; (1) Figures cover the Peoria, IL Metropolitan Statistical Area
Source: U.S. Census Bureau, 2015-2019 American Community Survey 5-Year Estimates

Key Congestion Measures

Measure	1982	1992	2002	2012	2017
Annual Hours of Delay, Total (000)	n/a	n/a	n/a	n/a	3,556
Annual Hours of Delay, Per Auto Commuter	n/a	n/a	n/a	n/a	13
Annual Congestion Cost, Total (million $)	n/a	n/a	n/a	n/a	73
Annual Congestion Cost, Per Auto Commuter ($)	n/a	n/a	n/a	n/a	258

Note: n/a not available
Source: Texas A&M Transportation Institute, 2019 Urban Mobility Report

Freeway Travel Time Index

Measure	1982	1987	1992	1997	2002	2007	2012	2017
Urban Area Index[1]	n/a	n/a	n/a	n/a	n/a	n/a	n/a	1.05
Urban Area Rank[1,2]	n/a	n/a	n/a	n/a	n/a	n/a	n/a	n/a

Note: Freeway Travel Time Index—the ratio of travel time in the peak period to the travel time at free-flow conditions. For example, a value of 1.30 indicates a 20-minute free-flow trip takes 26 minutes in the peak (20 minutes x 1.30 = 26 minutes); (1) Covers the Peoria IL urban area; (2) Rank is based on 101 larger urban areas (#1 = highest travel time index); n/a not available
Source: Texas A&M Transportation Institute, 2019 Urban Mobility Report

Public Transportation

Agency Name / Mode of Transportation	Vehicles Operated in Maximum Service[1]	Annual Unlinked Passenger Trips[2] (in thous.)	Annual Passenger Miles[3] (in thous.)
Greater Peoria Mass Transit District			
Bus (directly operated)	45	2,581.3	15,746.1
Demand Response (purchased transportation)	49	169.0	1,262.9

Note: (1) Number of revenue vehicles operated by the given mode and type of service to meet the annual maximum service requirement. This is the revenue vehicle count during the peak season of the year; on the week and day that maximum service is provided. Vehicles operated in maximum service (VOMS) exclude atypical days and one-time special events; (2) Number of passengers who boarded public transportation vehicles. Passengers are counted each time they board a vehicle no matter how many vehicles they use to travel from their origin to their destination. (3) Sum of the distances ridden by all passengers during the entire fiscal year.
Source: Federal Transit Administration, National Transit Database, 2019

Air Transportation

Airport Name and Code / Type of Service	Passenger Airlines[1]	Passenger Enplanements	Freight Carriers[2]	Freight (lbs)
General Wayne A. Downing Peoria International Airport (PIA)				
Domestic service (U.S. carriers - 2020)	12	163,350	4	18,788,596
International service (U.S. carriers - 2019)	0	0	0	0

Note: (1) Includes all U.S.-based major, minor and commuter airlines that carried at least one passenger during the year; (2) Includes all U.S.-based airlines and freight carriers that transported at least one pound of freight during the year.
Source: Bureau of Transportation Statistics, The Intermodal Transportation Database, Air Carriers: T-100 Domestic Market (U.S. Carriers), 2020; Bureau of Transportation Statistics, The Intermodal Transportation Database, Air Carriers: T-100 International Market (U.S. Carriers), 2019

BUSINESSES

Major Business Headquarters

Company Name	Industry	Rankings	
		Fortune[1]	Forbes[2]
Caterpillar	Construction and Farm Machinery	62	-

Note: (1) Companies that produce a 10-K are ranked 1 to 500 based on 2019 revenue; (2) All private companies with at least $2 billion in annual revenue through the end of their most current fiscal year are ranked 1 to 219; companies listed are headquartered in the city; dashes indicate no ranking
Source: Fortune, "Fortune 500," June/July 2020; Forbes, "America's Largest Private Companies," 2020

Fastest-Growing Businesses

According to *Inc.*, Peoria is home to one of America's 500 fastest-growing private companies: **Pop-A-Shot** (#307). Criteria: must be an independent, privately-held, for-profit, U.S. corporation, proprietorship or partnership as of December 31, 2019; revenues must be at least $100,000 in 2016 and $2 million in 2019; must have four-year operating/sales history. *Inc., "America's 500 Fastest-Growing Private Companies," 2020*

Living Environment

COST OF LIVING

Cost of Living Index

Composite Index	Groceries	Housing	Utilities	Trans-portation	Health Care	Misc. Goods/ Services
90.2	95.9	79.3	100.1	103.6	89.7	90.6

Note: The Cost of Living Index measures regional differences in the cost of consumer goods and services, excluding taxes and non-consumer expenditures, for professional and managerial households in the top income quintile. It is based on more than 50,000 prices covering almost 60 different items for which prices are collected three times a year by chambers of commerce, economic development organizations or university applied economic centers in each participating urban area. The numbers shown should be read as a percentage above or below the national average of 100. For example, a value of 115.4 in the groceries column indicates that grocery prices are 15.4% higher than the national average. Small differences in the index numbers should not be interpreted as significant; Figures cover the Peoria IL urban area.
Source: The Council for Community and Economic Research, Cost of Living Index, 2020

Grocery Prices

Area[1]	T-Bone Steak ($/pound)	Frying Chicken ($/pound)	Whole Milk ($/half gal.)	Eggs ($/dozen)	Orange Juice ($/64 oz.)	Coffee ($/11.5 oz.)
City[2]	10.98	1.03	1.32	0.93	3.45	5.99
Avg.	11.78	1.39	2.05	1.47	3.57	4.34
Min.	8.03	0.94	1.03	0.74	2.94	3.02
Max.	15.86	2.65	4.31	3.77	5.44	8.69

Note: (1) Values for the local area are compared with the average, minimum and maximum values for all 284 areas in the Cost of Living Index; (2) Figures cover the Peoria IL urban area; T-Bone Steak (price per pound); Frying Chicken (price per pound, whole fryer); Whole Milk (half gallon carton); Eggs (price per dozen, Grade A, large); Orange Juice (64 oz. Tropicana or Florida Natural); Coffee (11.5 oz. can, vacuum-packed, Maxwell House, Hills Bros, or Folgers).
Source: The Council for Community and Economic Research, Cost of Living Index, 2020

Housing and Utility Costs

Area[1]	New Home Price ($)	Apartment Rent ($/month)	All Electric ($/month)	Part Electric ($/month)	Other Energy ($/month)	Telephone ($/month)
City[2]	306,592	771	-	80.23	81.73	191.30
Avg.	368,594	1,168	170.86	100.47	65.28	184.30
Min.	190,567	502	91.58	31.42	26.08	169.60
Max.	2,227,806	4,738	470.38	280.31	280.06	206.50

Note: (1) Values for the local area are compared with the average, minimum and maximum values for all 284 areas in the Cost of Living Index; (2) Figures cover the Peoria IL urban area; New Home Price (2,400 sf living area, 8,000 sf lot, in urban area with full utilities); Apartment Rent (950 sf 2 bedroom/1.5 or 2 bath, unfurnished, excluding all utilities except water); All Electric (average monthly cost for an all-electric home); Part Electric (average monthly cost for a part-electric home); Other Energy (average monthly cost for natural gas, fuel oil, coal, wood, and any other forms of energy except electricity); Telephone (price includes the base monthly rate plus taxes and fees for three lines of mobile phone service).
Source: The Council for Community and Economic Research, Cost of Living Index, 2020

Health Care, Transportation, and Other Costs

Area[1]	Doctor ($/visit)	Dentist ($/visit)	Optometrist ($/visit)	Gasoline ($/gallon)	Beauty Salon ($/visit)	Men's Shirt ($)
City[2]	114.08	79.00	141.52	2.36	30.00	29.99
Avg.	115.44	99.32	108.10	2.21	39.27	31.37
Min.	36.68	59.00	51.36	1.71	19.00	11.00
Max.	219.00	153.10	250.97	3.46	82.05	58.33

Note: (1) Values for the local area are compared with the average, minimum and maximum values for all 284 areas in the Cost of Living Index; (2) Figures cover the Peoria IL urban area; Doctor (general practitioners routine exam of an established patient); Dentist (adult teeth cleaning and periodic oral examination); Optometrist (full vision eye exam for established adult patient); Gasoline (one gallon regular unleaded, national brand, including all taxes, cash price at self-service pump if available); Beauty Salon (woman's shampoo, trim, and blow-dry); Men's Shirt (cotton/polyester dress shirt, pinpoint weave, long sleeves).
Source: The Council for Community and Economic Research, Cost of Living Index, 2020

HOUSING

Homeownership Rate

Area	2012 (%)	2013 (%)	2014 (%)	2015 (%)	2016 (%)	2017 (%)	2018 (%)	2019 (%)	2020 (%)
MSA[1]	n/a	n/a	n/a	n/a	n/a	n/a	n/a	n/a	n/a
U.S.	65.4	65.1	64.5	63.7	63.4	63.9	64.4	64.6	66.6

Note: (1) Figures cover the Peoria, IL Metropolitan Statistical Area; n/a not available
Source: U.S. Census Bureau, Housing Vacancies and Homeownership Annual Statistics: 2012-2020

House Price Index (HPI)

Area	National Ranking[2]	Quarterly Change (%)	One-Year Change (%)	Five-Year Change (%)	Since 1991Q1 (%)
MSA[1]	238	0.87	3.00	6.40	120.92
U.S.[3]	–	3.81	10.77	38.99	205.12

Note: The HPI is a weighted repeat sales index. It measures average price changes in repeat sales or refinancings on the same properties. This information is obtained by reviewing repeat mortgage transactions on single-family properties whose mortgages have been purchased or securitized by Fannie Mae or Freddie Mac since January 1975; (1) Figures cover the Peoria, IL Metropolitan Statistical Area; (2) Rankings are based on annual percentage change for all metro areas containing at least 15,000 transactions over the last 10 years and ranges from 1 to 253; (3) figures based on a weighted average of Census Division estimates using a seasonally adjusted, purchase-only index; all figures are for the period ending December 31, 2020
Source: Federal Housing Finance Agency, Change in Metropolitan Area House Price Indexes, April 7, 2021

Median Single-Family Home Prices

Area	2018	2019	2020p	Percent Change 2019 to 2020
MSA[1]	124.3	120.7	128.1	6.1
U.S. Average	261.6	274.6	299.9	9.2

Note: Figures are median sales prices of existing single-family homes in thousands of dollars; (p) preliminary; (1) Figures cover the Peoria, IL Metropolitan Statistical Area
Source: National Association of Realtors, Median Sales Price of Existing Single-Family Homes for Metropolitan Areas, 4th Quarter 2020

Qualifying Income Based on Median Sales Price of Existing Single-Family Homes

Area	With 5% Down ($)	With 10% Down ($)	With 20% Down ($)
MSA[1]	25,024	23,706	21,072
U.S. Average	59,266	56,147	49,908

Note: Figures are preliminary; Qualifying income is based on a mortgage rate of 2.81%. Monthly principal and interest payment is limited to 25% of income; (1) Figures cover the Peoria, IL Metropolitan Statistical Area
Source: National Association of Realtors, Qualifying Income Based on Median Sales Price of Existing Single-Family Homes for Metropolitan Areas, 4th Quarter 2020

Home Value Distribution

Area	Under $50,000	$50,000 -$99,999	$100,000 -$149,999	$150,000 -$199,999	$200,000 -$299,999	$300,000 -$499,999	$500,000 -$999,999	$1,000,000 or more
City	12.6	25.4	21.8	15.6	13.8	8.1	2.4	0.4
MSA[1]	8.6	25.9	23.0	17.4	15.3	7.6	1.9	0.4
U.S.	6.9	12.0	13.3	14.0	19.6	19.3	11.4	3.4

Note: Figures are percentages and cover owner-occupied housing units; (1) Figures cover the Peoria, IL Metropolitan Statistical Area
Source: U.S. Census Bureau, 2015-2019 American Community Survey 5-Year Estimates

Year Housing Structure Built

Area	2010 or Later	2000 -2009	1990 -1999	1980 -1989	1970 -1979	1960 -1969	1950 -1959	1940 -1949	Before 1940	Median Year
City	3.3	8.7	7.4	6.8	15.2	12.5	14.0	7.9	24.3	1963
MSA[1]	3.1	9.0	8.6	6.0	17.3	12.3	14.3	8.0	21.4	1965
U.S.	5.2	14.0	13.9	13.4	15.2	10.6	10.3	4.9	12.6	1978

Note: Figures are percentages except for Median Year; Note: (1) Figures cover the Peoria, IL Metropolitan Statistical Area
Source: U.S. Census Bureau, 2015-2019 American Community Survey 5-Year Estimates

Gross Monthly Rent

Area	Under $500	$500 -$999	$1,000 -$1,499	$1,500 -$1,999	$2,000 -$2,499	$2,500 -$2,999	$3,000 and up	Median ($)
City	15.6	58.0	20.6	3.7	1.0	0.3	0.9	806
MSA[1]	16.6	60.9	17.6	2.6	1.0	0.4	1.0	764
U.S.	9.4	36.2	30.0	14.0	5.6	2.4	2.4	1,062

Note: Figures are percentages except for Median; Gross rent is the contract rent plus the estimated average monthly cost of utilities (electricity, gas, and water and sewer) and fuels (oil, coal, kerosene, wood, etc.) if these are paid by the renter (or paid for the renter by someone else); (1) Figures cover the Peoria, IL Metropolitan Statistical Area
Source: U.S. Census Bureau, 2015-2019 American Community Survey 5-Year Estimates

HEALTH

Health Risk Factors

Category	MSA[1] (%)	U.S. (%)
Adults aged 18–64 who have any kind of health care coverage	n/a	87.3
Adults who reported being in good or better health	n/a	82.4
Adults who have been told they have high blood cholesterol	n/a	33.0
Adults who have been told they have high blood pressure	n/a	32.3
Adults who are current smokers	n/a	17.1
Adults who currently use E-cigarettes	n/a	4.6
Adults who currently use chewing tobacco, snuff, or snus	n/a	4.0
Adults who are heavy drinkers[2]	n/a	6.3
Adults who are binge drinkers[3]	n/a	17.4
Adults who are overweight (BMI 25.0 - 29.9)	n/a	35.3
Adults who are obese (BMI 30.0 - 99.8)	n/a	31.3
Adults who participated in any physical activities in the past month	n/a	74.4
Adults who always or nearly always wears a seat belt	n/a	94.3

Note: n/a not available; (1) Figures cover the Peoria, IL Metropolitan Statistical Area; (2) Heavy drinkers are classified as adult men having more than 14 drinks per week and adult women having more than 7 drinks per week; (3) Binge drinkers are classified as males having five or more drinks on one occasion or females having four or more drinks on one occasion
Source: Centers for Disease Control and Prevention, Behaviorial Risk Factor Surveillance System, SMART: Selected Metropolitan Area Risk Trends, 2017

Acute and Chronic Health Conditions

Category	MSA[1] (%)	U.S. (%)
Adults who have ever been told they had a heart attack	n/a	4.2
Adults who have ever been told they have angina or coronary heart disease	n/a	3.9
Adults who have ever been told they had a stroke	n/a	3.0
Adults who have ever been told they have asthma	n/a	14.2
Adults who have ever been told they have arthritis	n/a	24.9
Adults who have ever been told they have diabetes[2]	n/a	10.5
Adults who have ever been told they had skin cancer	n/a	6.2
Adults who have ever been told they had any other types of cancer	n/a	7.1
Adults who have ever been told they have COPD	n/a	6.5
Adults who have ever been told they have kidney disease	n/a	3.0
Adults who have ever been told they have a form of depression	n/a	20.5

Note: n/a not available; (1) Figures cover the Peoria, IL Metropolitan Statistical Area; (2) Figures do not include pregnancy-related, borderline, or pre-diabetes
Source: Centers for Disease Control and Prevention, Behaviorial Risk Factor Surveillance System, SMART: Selected Metropolitan Area Risk Trends, 2017

Health Screening and Vaccination Rates

Category	MSA[1] (%)	U.S. (%)
Adults aged 65+ who have had flu shot within the past year	n/a	60.7
Adults aged 65+ who have ever had a pneumonia vaccination	n/a	75.4
Adults who have ever been tested for HIV	n/a	36.1
Adults who have ever had the shingles or zoster vaccine?	n/a	28.9
Adults who have had their blood cholesterol checked within the last five years	n/a	85.9

Note: n/a not available; (1) Figures cover the Peoria, IL Metropolitan Statistical Area.
Source: Centers for Disease Control and Prevention, Behaviorial Risk Factor Surveillance System, SMART: Selected Metropolitan Area Risk Trends, 2017

Disability Status

Category	MSA[1] (%)	U.S. (%)
Adults who reported being deaf	n/a	6.7
Are you blind or have serious difficulty seeing, even when wearing glasses?	n/a	4.5
Are you limited in any way in any of your usual activities due of arthritis?	n/a	12.9
Do you have difficulty doing errands alone?	n/a	6.8
Do you have difficulty dressing or bathing?	n/a	3.6
Do you have serious difficulty concentrating/remembering/making decisions?	n/a	10.7
Do you have serious difficulty walking or climbing stairs?	n/a	13.6

Note: n/a not available; (1) Figures cover the Peoria, IL Metropolitan Statistical Area.
Source: Centers for Disease Control and Prevention, Behaviorial Risk Factor Surveillance System, SMART: Selected Metropolitan Area Risk Trends, 2017

Mortality Rates for the Top 10 Causes of Death in the U.S.

ICD-10[a] Sub-Chapter	ICD-10[a] Code	Age-Adjusted Mortality Rate[1] per 100,000 population	
		County[2]	U.S.
Malignant neoplasms	C00-C97	167.2	149.2
Ischaemic heart diseases	I20-I25	86.0	90.5
Other forms of heart disease	I30-I51	61.7	52.2
Chronic lower respiratory diseases	J40-J47	43.7	39.6
Other degenerative diseases of the nervous system	G30-G31	30.7	37.6
Cerebrovascular diseases	I60-I69	40.0	37.2
Other external causes of accidental injury	W00-X59	47.6	36.1
Organic, including symptomatic, mental disorders	F01-F09	46.6	29.4
Hypertensive diseases	I10-I15	19.2	24.1
Diabetes mellitus	E10-E14	18.0	21.5

Note: (a) ICD-10 = International Classification of Diseases 10th Revision; (1) Mortality rates are a three-year average covering 2017-2019; (2) Figures cover Peoria County.
Source: Centers for Disease Control and Prevention, National Center for Health Statistics. Underlying Cause of Death 1999-2019 on CDC WONDER Online Database

Mortality Rates for Selected Causes of Death

ICD-10[a] Sub-Chapter	ICD-10[a] Code	Age-Adjusted Mortality Rate[1] per 100,000 population	
		County[2]	U.S.
Assault	X85-Y09	12.6	6.0
Diseases of the liver	K70-K76	13.1	14.4
Human immunodeficiency virus (HIV) disease	B20-B24	Unreliable	1.5
Influenza and pneumonia	J09-J18	20.6	13.8
Intentional self-harm	X60-X84	16.0	14.1
Malnutrition	E40-E46	Unreliable	2.3
Obesity and other hyperalimentation	E65-E68	Suppressed	2.1
Renal failure	N17-N19	14.4	12.6
Transport accidents	V01-V99	9.3	12.3
Viral hepatitis	B15-B19	Suppressed	1.2

Note: (a) ICD-10 = International Classification of Diseases 10th Revision; (1) Mortality rates are a three-year average covering 2017-2019; (2) Figures cover Peoria County; Data are suppressed when the data meet the criteria for confidentiality constraints; Mortality rates are flagged as unreliable when the rate would be calculated with a numerator of 20 or less.
Source: Centers for Disease Control and Prevention, National Center for Health Statistics. Underlying Cause of Death 1999-2019 on CDC WONDER Online Database

Health Insurance Coverage

Area	With Health Insurance	With Private Health Insurance	With Public Health Insurance	Without Health Insurance	Population Under Age 19 Without Health Insurance
City	94.2	65.7	41.1	5.8	3.0
MSA[1]	95.2	73.5	37.2	4.8	2.9
U.S.	91.2	67.9	35.1	8.8	5.1

Note: Figures are percentages that cover the civilian noninstitutionalized population; (1) Figures cover the Peoria, IL Metropolitan Statistical Area
Source: U.S. Census Bureau, 2015-2019 American Community Survey 5-Year Estimates

Number of Medical Professionals

Area	MDs[3]	DOs[3,4]	Dentists	Podiatrists	Chiropractors	Optometrists
County[1] (number)	1,009	75	155	15	91	37
County[1] (rate[2])	558.6	41.5	86.5	8.4	50.8	20.6
U.S. (rate[2])	282.9	22.7	71.2	6.2	28.1	16.9

17143
Note: Data as of 2019 unless noted; (1) Data covers Peoria County; (2) Rate per 100,000 population; (3) Data as of 2018 and includes all active, non-federal physicians; (4) Doctor of Osteopathic Medicine
Source: U.S. Department of Health and Human Services, Health Resources and Services Administration, Bureau of Health Professions, Area Resource File (ARF) 2019-2020

Best Hospitals

According to *U.S. News,* the Peoria, IL metro area is home to one of the best children's hospitals in the U.S.: **OSF HealthCare Children's Hospital of Illinois** (1 pediatric specialty). The hospital listed was highly ranked in at least one of 10 pediatric specialties. Eighty-eight children's hospitals in the U.S. were nationally ranked in at least one specialty. Hospitals received points for being ranked in a specialty, and the 10 hospitals with the most points across the 10 specialties make up the Honor Roll. *U.S. News Online, "America's Best Children's Hospitals 2020-21"*

EDUCATION

Public School District Statistics

District Name	Schls	Pupils	Pupil/ Teacher Ratio	Minority Pupils[1] (%)	Free Lunch Eligible[2] (%)	IEP[3] (%)
Dunlap CUSD 323	8	4,492	17.2	37.4	13.3	12.5
Peoria SD 150	29	12,846	14.1	79.8	70.3	17.8

Note: Table includes school districts with 2,000 or more students; (1) Percentage of students that are not non-Hispanic white; (2) Percentage of students that are eligible for the free lunch program; (3) Percentage of students that have an Individualized Education Program.
Source: U.S. Department of Education, National Center for Education Statistics, Common Core of Data, Local Education Agency (School District) Universe Survey: School Year 2018-2019; U.S. Department of Education, National Center for Education Statistics, Common Core of Data, Public Elementary/Secondary School Universe Survey: School Year 2018-2019

Highest Level of Education

Area	Less than H.S.	H.S. Diploma	Some College, No Deg.	Associate Degree	Bachelor's Degree	Master's Degree	Prof. School Degree	Doctorate Degree
City	10.6	24.3	21.5	8.6	20.7	10.2	2.7	1.3
MSA[1]	8.3	30.5	23.2	10.4	18.1	7.2	1.5	0.9
U.S.	12.0	27.0	20.4	8.5	19.8	8.8	2.1	1.4

Note: Figures cover persons age 25 and over; (1) Figures cover the Peoria, IL Metropolitan Statistical Area
Source: U.S. Census Bureau, 2015-2019 American Community Survey 5-Year Estimates

Educational Attainment by Race

Area	High School Graduate or Higher (%)					Bachelor's Degree or Higher (%)				
	Total	White	Black	Asian	Hisp.[2]	Total	White	Black	Asian	Hisp.[2]
City	89.4	92.4	81.4	94.7	71.6	34.9	39.6	13.4	75.4	21.9
MSA[1]	91.7	92.9	80.3	92.4	75.4	27.7	28.1	12.8	69.8	20.9
U.S.	88.0	89.9	86.0	87.1	68.7	32.1	33.5	21.6	54.3	16.4

Note: Figures shown cover persons 25 years old and over; (1) Figures cover the Peoria, IL Metropolitan Statistical Area; (2) People of Hispanic origin can be of any race
Source: U.S. Census Bureau, 2015-2019 American Community Survey 5-Year Estimates

School Enrollment by Grade and Control

Area	Preschool (%)		Kindergarten (%)		Grades 1 - 4 (%)		Grades 5 - 8 (%)		Grades 9 - 12 (%)	
	Public	Private	Public	Private	Public	Private	Public	Private	Public	Private
City	60.1	39.9	70.0	30.0	83.9	16.1	83.4	16.6	88.7	11.3
MSA[1]	61.4	38.6	82.9	17.1	89.1	10.9	89.1	10.9	91.0	9.0
U.S.	59.1	40.9	87.6	12.4	89.5	10.5	89.4	10.6	90.1	9.9

Note: Figures shown cover persons 3 years old and over; (1) Figures cover the Peoria, IL Metropolitan Statistical Area
Source: U.S. Census Bureau, 2015-2019 American Community Survey 5-Year Estimates

Higher Education

Four-Year Colleges			Two-Year Colleges			Medical Schools[1]	Law Schools[2]	Voc/ Tech[3]
Public	Private Non-profit	Private For-profit	Public	Private Non-profit	Private For-profit			
0	3	1	0	0	0	0	0	1

Note: Figures cover institutions located within the city limits and include main campuses only; (1) includes schools accredited by the Liaison Committee on Medical Education and the American Osteopathic Association's Commission on Osteopathic College Accreditation; (2) includes ABA-accredited schools, schools with provisional ABA accreditation, and state accredited schools; (3) includes all schools with programs that are less than 2 years.
Source: National Center for Education Statistics, Integrated Postsecondary Education System (IPEDS), 2019-20; Wikipedia, List of Medical Schools in the United States, accessed April 2, 2021; Wikipedia, List of Law Schools in the United States, accessed April 2, 2021

EMPLOYERS

Major Employers

Company Name	Industry
Advanced Technology Services	Technical job training
Ameren Illinois	Utility
Bradley University	Education
CEFCU	Banking and financial services
City of Peoria	Municipal government
G&D Integrated	Transportation, distribution
Health Professionals Ltd.	Healthcare
HGS USA	Customer support
Hostess Brands	Food manufacturing
Illinois Central College	Education
Keystone Steel and Wire Co	Steel & wire production
Kmart Corp.	Retail
Komatsu Mining Systems	Coal business
Kroger Company	Supermarkets
Matcor Metal Fabrication	Manufacturer
Methodist Medical Center	Healthcare
OSF Saint Francis Medical Center	Healthcare
Par-A-Dice Hotel/Casino	Casino resort
Pekin Hospital	Education
Pekin Insurance & Farmers Auto Insurance	Insurance
Peoria County	Government
Peoria Journal Star	Newspapers, publishing & printing
Peoria School District	Education
Proctor Hospital	Healthcare
Wal-Mart Stores	Retail

Note: Companies shown are located within the Peoria, IL Metropolitan Statistical Area.
Source: Hoovers.com; Wikipedia

PUBLIC SAFETY

Crime Rate

Area	All Crimes	Violent Crimes				Property Crimes		
		Murder	Rape[3]	Robbery	Aggrav. Assault	Burglary	Larceny -Theft	Motor Vehicle Theft
City	4,792.9	22.5	58.6	241.5	721.0	683.2	2,666.8	399.3
Suburbs[1]	1,462.2	1.7	46.0	15.2	161.7	265.2	890.0	82.4
Metro[2]	2,386.5	7.5	49.5	78.0	316.9	381.2	1,383.1	170.3
U.S.	2,489.3	5.0	42.6	81.6	250.2	340.5	1,549.5	219.9

Note: Figures are crimes per 100,000 population; (1) All areas within the metro area that are located outside the city limits; (2) Figures cover the Peoria, IL Metropolitan Statistical Area; (3) All figures shown were reported using the revised Uniform Crime Reporting (UCR) definition of rape.
Source: FBI Uniform Crime Reports, 2019

Hate Crimes

Area	Number of Quarters Reported	Number of Incidents per Bias Motivation					
		Race/Ethnicity/ Ancestry	Religion	Sexual Orientation	Disability	Gender	Gender Identity
City	4	0	0	0	0	0	0
U.S.	4	3,963	1,521	1,195	157	69	198

Source: Federal Bureau of Investigation, Hate Crime Statistics 2019

Identity Theft Consumer Reports

Area	Reports	Reports per 100,000 Population	Rank[2]
MSA[1]	3,746	935	11
U.S.	1,387,615	423	-

Note: (1) Figures cover the Peoria, IL Metropolitan Statistical Area; (2) Rank ranges from 1 to 391 where 1 indicates greatest number of identity theft reports per 100,000 population
Source: Federal Trade Commission, Consumer Sentinel Network Data Book 2020

Fraud and Other Consumer Reports

Area	Reports	Reports per 100,000 Population	Rank[2]
MSA[1]	2,554	638	247
U.S.	3,385,133	1,031	-

Note: (1) Figures cover the Peoria, IL Metropolitan Statistical Area; (2) Rank ranges from 1 to 391 where 1 indicates greatest number of fraud and other consumer reports per 100,000 population
Source: Federal Trade Commission, Consumer Sentinel Network Data Book 2020

POLITICS

2020 Presidential Election Results

Area	Biden	Trump	Jorgensen	Hawkins	Other
Peoria County	51.9	45.6	1.6	0.6	0.4
U.S.	51.3	46.8	1.2	0.3	0.5

Note: Results are percentages and may not add to 100% due to rounding
Source: Dave Leip's Atlas of U.S. Presidential Elections

SPORTS

Professional Sports Teams

Team Name	League	Year Established
No teams are located in the metro area		

Source: Wikipedia, Major Professional Sports Teams of the United States and Canada, April 6, 2021

CLIMATE

Average and Extreme Temperatures

Temperature	Jan	Feb	Mar	Apr	May	Jun	Jul	Aug	Sep	Oct	Nov	Dec	Yr.
Extreme High (°F)	71	74	87	92	104	105	113	106	102	92	81	71	113
Average High (°F)	32	36	48	62	73	82	86	84	77	65	49	36	61
Average Temp. (°F)	24	28	39	51	62	72	76	74	66	55	41	29	51
Average Low (°F)	16	19	29	41	51	60	65	63	55	43	32	21	41
Extreme Low (°F)	-25	-26	-11	14	25	39	46	41	24	13	-2	-24	-26

Note: Figures cover the years 1948-1995
Source: National Climatic Data Center, International Station Meteorological Climate Summary, 9/96

Average Precipitation/Snowfall/Humidity

Precip./Humidity	Jan	Feb	Mar	Apr	May	Jun	Jul	Aug	Sep	Oct	Nov	Dec	Yr.
Avg. Precip. (in.)	1.8	1.6	2.8	3.8	4.0	3.9	3.8	3.1	3.6	2.6	2.5	2.0	35.4
Avg. Snowfall (in.)	6	5	4	1	Tr	0	0	0	Tr	Tr	2	5	23
Avg. Rel. Hum. 6am (%)	80	81	81	78	80	82	86	89	87	84	83	83	83
Avg. Rel. Hum. 3pm (%)	67	64	58	52	52	52	55	56	52	52	61	69	57

Note: Figures cover the years 1948-1995; Tr = Trace amounts (<0.05 in. of rain; <0.5 in. of snow)
Source: National Climatic Data Center, International Station Meteorological Climate Summary, 9/96

Weather Conditions

Temperature			Daytime Sky			Precipitation		
5°F & below	32°F & below	90°F & above	Clear	Partly cloudy	Cloudy	0.01 inch or more precip.	0.1 inch or more snow/ice	Thunder-storms
16	127	27	89	127	149	115	22	49

Note: Figures are average number of days per year and cover the years 1948-1995
Source: National Climatic Data Center, International Station Meteorological Climate Summary, 9/96

HAZARDOUS WASTE

Superfund Sites

The Peoria, IL metro area has no sites on the EPA's Superfund Final National Priorities List. There are a total of 1,375 Superfund sites with a status of proposed or final on the list in the U.S. *U.S. Environmental Protection Agency, National Priorities List, April 7, 2021*

AIR QUALITY

Air Quality Trends: Ozone

	1990	1995	2000	2005	2010	2015	2016	2017	2018	2019
MSA[1]	0.071	0.082	0.072	0.075	0.064	0.062	0.067	0.066	0.070	0.063
U.S.	0.088	0.089	0.082	0.080	0.073	0.068	0.069	0.068	0.069	0.065

Note: (1) Data covers the Peoria, IL Metropolitan Statistical Area. The values shown are the composite ozone concentration averages among trend sites based on the highest fourth daily maximum 8-hour concentration in parts per million. These trends are based on sites having an adequate record of monitoring data during the trend period. Data from exceptional events are included.
Source: U.S. Environmental Protection Agency, Air Quality Monitoring Information, "Air Quality Trends by City, 1990-2019"

Air Quality Index

Area	Percent of Days when Air Quality was...[2]					AQI Statistics[2]	
	Good	Moderate	Unhealthy for Sensitive Groups	Unhealthy	Very Unhealthy	Maximum	Median
MSA[1]	78.1	21.4	0.5	0.0	0.0	101	41

Note: (1) Data covers the Peoria, IL Metropolitan Statistical Area; (2) Based on 365 days with AQI data in 2019. Air Quality Index (AQI) is an index for reporting daily air quality. EPA calculates the AQI for five major air pollutants regulated by the Clean Air Act: ground-level ozone, particle pollution (aka particulate matter), carbon monoxide, sulfur dioxide, and nitrogen dioxide. The AQI runs from 0 to 500. The higher the AQI value, the greater the level of air pollution and the greater the health concern. There are six AQI categories: "Good" AQI is between 0 and 50. Air quality is considered satisfactory; "Moderate" AQI is between 51 and 100. Air quality is acceptable; "Unhealthy for Sensitive Groups" When AQI values are between 101 and 150, members of sensitive groups may experience health effects; "Unhealthy" When AQI values are between 151 and 200 everyone may begin to experience health effects; "Very Unhealthy" AQI values between 201 and 300 trigger a health alert; "Hazardous" AQI values over 300 trigger warnings of emergency conditions (not shown).
Source: U.S. Environmental Protection Agency, Air Quality Index Report, 2019

Air Quality Index Pollutants

Area	Percent of Days when AQI Pollutant was...[2]					
	Carbon Monoxide	Nitrogen Dioxide	Ozone	Sulfur Dioxide	Particulate Matter 2.5	Particulate Matter 10
MSA[1]	0.0	0.0	55.6	0.5	43.8	0.0

Note: (1) Data covers the Peoria, IL Metropolitan Statistical Area; (2) Based on 365 days with AQI data in 2019. The Air Quality Index (AQI) is an index for reporting daily air quality. EPA calculates the AQI for five major air pollutants regulated by the Clean Air Act: ground-level ozone, particle pollution (also known as particulate matter), carbon monoxide, sulfur dioxide, and nitrogen dioxide. The AQI runs from 0 to 500. The higher the AQI value, the greater the level of air pollution and the greater the health concern.
Source: U.S. Environmental Protection Agency, Air Quality Index Report, 2019

Maximum Air Pollutant Concentrations: Particulate Matter, Ozone, CO and Lead

	Particulate Matter 10 (ug/m^3)	Particulate Matter 2.5 Wtd AM (ug/m^3)	Particulate Matter 2.5 24-Hr (ug/m^3)	Ozone (ppm)	Carbon Monoxide (ppm)	Lead (ug/m^3)
MSA[1] Level	n/a	8.0	19	0.064	n/a	n/a
NAAQS[2]	150	15	35	0.075	9	0.15
Met NAAQS[2]	n/a	Yes	Yes	Yes	n/a	n/a

Note: (1) Data covers the Peoria, IL Metropolitan Statistical Area; Data from exceptional events are included; (2) National Ambient Air Quality Standards; ppm = parts per million; ug/m^3 = micrograms per cubic meter; n/a not available.
Concentrations: Particulate Matter 10 (coarse particulate)—highest second maximum 24-hour concentration; Particulate Matter 2.5 Wtd AM (fine particulate)—highest weighted annual mean concentration; Particulate Matter 2.5 24-Hour (fine particulate)—highest 98th percentile 24-hour concentration; Ozone—highest fourth daily maximum 8-hour concentration; Carbon Monoxide—highest second maximum non-overlapping 8-hour concentration; Lead—maximum running 3-month average
Source: U.S. Environmental Protection Agency, Air Quality Monitoring Information, "Air Quality Statistics by City, 2019"

Maximum Air Pollutant Concentrations: Nitrogen Dioxide and Sulfur Dioxide

	Nitrogen Dioxide AM (ppb)	Nitrogen Dioxide 1-Hr (ppb)	Sulfur Dioxide AM (ppb)	Sulfur Dioxide 1-Hr (ppb)	Sulfur Dioxide 24-Hr (ppb)
MSA[1] Level	n/a	n/a	n/a	17	n/a
NAAQS[2]	53	100	30	75	140
Met NAAQS[2]	n/a	n/a	n/a	Yes	n/a

Note: (1) Data covers the Peoria, IL Metropolitan Statistical Area; Data from exceptional events are included; (2) National Ambient Air Quality Standards; ppm = parts per million; ug/m^3 = micrograms per cubic meter; n/a not available.
Concentrations: Nitrogen Dioxide AM—highest arithmetic mean concentration; Nitrogen Dioxide 1-Hr—highest 98th percentile 1-hour daily maximum concentration; Sulfur Dioxide AM—highest annual mean concentration; Sulfur Dioxide 1-Hr—highest 99th percentile 1-hour daily maximum concentration; Sulfur Dioxide 24-Hr—highest second maximum 24-hour concentration
Source: U.S. Environmental Protection Agency, Air Quality Monitoring Information, "Air Quality Statistics by City, 2019"

Rochester, Minnesota

Background

Rochester, Minnesota is often characterized as a medical Mecca, based on the city's history of major breakthroughs in modern medicine. Before Dr. William Mayo arrived in 1864, as an examining physician for Civil War draftees, Rochester was basically a transportation hub for the wheat markets of southeastern Minnesota. However, Rochester's destiny was set when a pioneer of medicine, a determined sister of the Order of St. Francis, and a devastating tornado converged on the evening of August 21, 1883.

Dr. William Worrall (W.W.) Mayo had been schooled in Manchester England, migrated to the U.S. and worked as many things before finishing his medical training in Indiana. In 1864, he and his young family settled in Rochester and, following the Civil War, set up a medical practice.

A deadly tornado hit Rochester on August 21, 1883, killing dozens and injuring hundreds. The Mayos (father and two sons, Will and Charlie) and other Rochester physicians called upon the Sisters of St. Francis who worked tirelessly with the Drs. Mayo, and further, established St. Mary's Hospital in 1889, in spite of the Mayos' insistence that Rochester was too small for such a hospital. In 1914, St. Mary's Hospital would become the Mayo Clinic which today is a medical model of integrated medicine consisting of teamwork, pooled knowledge, and resources among physicians, used throughout the world. Dr. Mayo personally trained his students, assuming that the best way to learn medicine is by studying large numbers of cases, and by hands-on experience, known today as residency training, a standard in medical education.

The Mayo Clinic is still a world pioneer, making Rochester a medical destination, and employing over 30,000 in Rochester alone. Additional Mayo facilities have been established in Arizona and Florida. The Mayo Clinic is the largest not-for-profit medical practice in the world. In 1973, Mayo opened its medical school, the most selective in the country.

IBM is also important to Rochester's economy, employing over 4,400 employees. IBM's nickname "Big Blue" was based on the Rochester facility, which is constructed of blue panels designed to reflect the Minnesota sky. The building is the largest IBM facility under one roof in the world. In 1990, the National Building Museum acknowledged the facility for its historic significance and innovation.

The Mayo Clinic offers history and art tours, and The History Center of Olmsted County offers an impressive variety of programs, including research facilities and rare collections. Venues include tours of the historic 38-room, Mayowood Mansion and gardens—once the home of the Mayo family. Much of the architecture was the handiwork of W. W. Mayo himself.

The oldest cultural arts institution in the community, Rochester Symphony Orchestra & Chorale was founded in 1919 as a professional performing arts organization. Its earliest ensemble—the Lawler-Dodge Orchestra—was founded in 1912 as a volunteer orchestra, driven by Daisy Plummer, wife of world-famous Mayo Clinic physician, Dr. Henry Plummer, and directed by Harold Cooke. The Orchestra performed in the former Chateau Theatre where they played background music for silent movies.

The Rochester Downtown Alliance created the Summer Market and Music Festival, and STYLE, the Runway Experience. StyleICE is a unique celebration in which local downtown bars produce an all-ice experience. Everything from glasses to couches is created out of ice, and features special lighting effects and live music. In 2019, a new, state-of-the-art movie theater opened its doors in the city.

Minnesota has one of the most extensive state park systems in the nation. Likewise, Rochester's city park system is large, with more than 100 sites covering five square miles. The city also maintains 85 miles of paved trails in addition to state trails such as the Douglas State Trail. The nearest state park is Whitewater State Park.

Rochester features a humid continental climate with four distinct seasons. Summers are very warm and winters are very cold. Rochester sees an annual average of 30 inches of rainfall and 48 inches of snowfall. Significant snow accumulation is common during the winter months. Spring and fall are transitional, with a warming trend during the spring and a cooling trend during the fall. It is not uncommon to see snowfall during early spring and late fall.

Rankings

General Rankings

- In their seventh annual survey, Livability.com looked at data for more than 1,000 small to mid-sized U.S. cities to determine the rankings for Livability's "Top 100 Best Places to Live" in 2020. Rochester ranked #5. Criteria: housing and affordable living; vibrant economy; social and civic engagement; education; demographics; health care options; transportation & infrastructure; and abundant lifestyle amenities. *Livability.com, "Top 100 Best Places to Live 2020" October 2020*

Business/Finance Rankings

- The Rochester metro area appeared on the Milken Institute "2021 Best Performing Cities" list. Rank: #56 out of 201 small metro areas (population over 60,000). Criteria: job growth; wage and salary growth; high-tech output growth; housing affordability; household broadband access. *Milken Institute, "Best-Performing Cities 2021," February 16, 2021*

- *Forbes* ranked 203 smaller metro areas (population under 268,000) to determine the nation's "Best Small Places for Business and Careers." The Rochester metro area was ranked #37. Criteria: costs (business and living); job growth (past and projected); income growth; quality of life; educational attainment (college and high school); projected economic growth; cultural and leisure opportunities; workplace tolerance laws; net migration patterns. *Forbes, "The Best Small Places for Business and Careers 2019," October 30, 2019*

Environmental Rankings

- The U.S. Conference of Mayors and Walmart Stores sponsor the Mayors' Climate Protection Awards Program which recognize mayors for outstanding and innovative practices that mayors are taking to increase energy efficiency in their cities, reduce carbon emissions and expand renewable energy. Rochester received an Honorable Mention in the large city category. *U.S. Conference of Mayors, "2020 Mayors' Climate Protection Awards," December 18, 2020*

- Rochester was highlighted as one of the cleanest metro areas for ozone air pollution in the U.S. during 2016 through 2018. The list represents cities with no monitored ozone air pollution in unhealthful ranges. *American Lung Association, "State of the Air 2020," April 21, 2020*

Real Estate Rankings

- Rochester was ranked #10 out of 268 metro areas in terms of housing affordability in 2020 by the National Association of Home Builders (#1 = most affordable). Criteria: the share of homes sold in that area affordable to a family earning the local median income, based on standard mortgage underwriting criteria. *National Association of Home Builders®, NAHB-Wells Fargo Housing Opportunity Index, 4th Quarter 2020*

Safety Rankings

- To identify the safest cities in America, 24/7 Wall Street focused on violent crime categories—murder, non-negligent manslaughter, rape, robbery, and aggravated assault—and property crime as reported in the FBI's 2018 annual Uniform Crime Report. Criteria also included median income from American Community Survey and unemployment figures from Bureau of Labor Statistics. For cities with populations over 100,000, Rochester was ranked #47. *247wallst.com, "America's Safest Cities" January 15, 2020*

- The National Insurance Crime Bureau ranked 384 metro areas in the U.S. in terms of per capita rates of vehicle theft. The Rochester metro area ranked #327 (#1 = highest rate). Criteria: number of vehicle theft offenses per 100,000 inhabitants in 2019. *National Insurance Crime Bureau, "Hot Spots 2019," July 21, 2020*

Seniors/Retirement Rankings

- From its Best Cities for Successful Aging indexes, the Milken Institute generated rankings for metropolitan areas, weighing data in nine categories—health care, wellness, living arrangements, transportation and convenience, financial characteristics, education, employment, community engagement, and overall livability. The Rochester metro area was ranked #24 overall in the small metro area category. *Milken Institute, "Best Cities for Successful Aging, 2017" March 14, 2017*

- Rochester made the 2020 *Forbes* list of "25 Best Places to Retire." Criteria, focused on high-quality retirement living at an affordable price, include: housing/living costs compared to the national average and state taxes; air quality; crime rates; good economic outlook; home price appreciation; risk associated with climate-change; availability of medical care; bikeability; walkability; healthy living. *Forbes.com, "The Best Places to Retire in 2020," August 14, 2020*

Women/Minorities Rankings

- NerdWallet examined data for 529 U.S. cities and ranked them based on the environment for working women. Rochester ranked #1. Criteria: women's earnings; labor force participation rate; cost of living; unemployment rate. *www.nerdwallet.com, "Best Cities for Women in the Workforce 2016," April 4, 2016*

430 Rochester, Minnesota

Business Environment

DEMOGRAPHICS

Population Growth

Area	1990 Census	2000 Census	2010 Census	2019* Estimate	Population Growth (%) 1990-2019	2010-2019
City	74,151	85,806	106,769	115,557	55.8	8.2
MSA[1]	141,945	163,618	186,011	217,964	53.6	17.2
U.S.	248,709,873	281,421,906	308,745,538	324,697,795	30.6	5.2

Note: (1) Figures cover the Rochester, MN Metropolitan Statistical Area; (*) 2015-2019 5-year estimated population
Source: U.S. Census Bureau, 1990 Census, Census 2000, Census 2010, 2015-2019 American Community Survey 5-Year Estimates

Household Size

Area	Persons in Household (%) One	Two	Three	Four	Five	Six	Seven or More	Average Household Size
City	31.0	33.3	14.4	13.0	4.8	1.9	1.6	2.40
MSA[1]	27.2	36.2	14.1	13.6	5.3	2.2	1.3	2.50
U.S.	27.9	33.9	15.6	12.9	6.0	2.3	1.4	2.60

Note: (1) Figures cover the Rochester, MN Metropolitan Statistical Area
Source: U.S. Census Bureau, 2015-2019 American Community Survey 5-Year Estimates

Race

Area	White Alone[2] (%)	Black Alone[2] (%)	Asian Alone[2] (%)	AIAN[3] Alone[2] (%)	NHOPI[4] Alone[2] (%)	Other Race Alone[2] (%)	Two or More Races (%)
City	79.4	8.2	7.3	0.5	0.1	1.1	3.4
MSA[1]	87.4	4.5	4.3	0.3	0.1	1.1	2.4
U.S.	72.5	12.7	5.5	0.8	0.2	4.9	3.3

Note: (1) Figures cover the Rochester, MN Metropolitan Statistical Area; (2) Alone is defined as not being in combination with one or more other races; (3) American Indian and Alaska Native; (4) Native Hawaiian and Other Pacific Islander
Source: U.S. Census Bureau, 2015-2019 American Community Survey 5-Year Estimates

Hispanic or Latino Origin

Area	Total (%)	Mexican (%)	Puerto Rican (%)	Cuban (%)	Other (%)
City	5.9	3.7	0.4	0.2	1.6
MSA[1]	4.4	2.9	0.2	0.1	1.2
U.S.	18.0	11.2	1.7	0.7	4.3

Note: Persons of Hispanic or Latino origin can be of any race; (1) Figures cover the Rochester, MN Metropolitan Statistical Area
Source: U.S. Census Bureau, 2015-2019 American Community Survey 5-Year Estimates

Ancestry

Area	German	Irish	English	American	Italian	Polish	French[2]	Scottish	Dutch
City	29.1	11.3	6.1	3.0	2.0	3.6	2.1	1.3	1.7
MSA[1]	35.4	11.7	6.2	3.2	1.7	3.3	2.2	1.3	2.0
U.S.	13.3	9.7	7.2	6.2	5.1	2.8	2.3	1.7	1.2

Note: Figures are the percentage of the total population reporting a particular ancestry. The nine most commonly reported ancestries in the U.S. are shown. Figures include multiple ancestries (e.g. if a person reported being Irish and Italian, they were included in both columns); (1) Figures cover the Rochester, MN Metropolitan Statistical Area; (2) Excludes Basque
Source: U.S. Census Bureau, 2015-2019 American Community Survey 5-Year Estimates

Foreign-born Population

Area	Percent of Population Born in Any Foreign Country	Asia	Mexico	Europe	Caribbean	Central America[2]	South America	Africa	Canada
City	14.1	5.8	1.5	1.6	0.2	0.2	0.5	3.9	0.2
MSA[1]	8.5	3.4	1.0	1.1	0.1	0.3	0.3	2.1	0.2
U.S.	13.6	4.2	3.5	1.5	1.3	1.1	1.0	0.7	0.2

Note: (1) Figures cover the Rochester, MN Metropolitan Statistical Area; (2) Excludes Mexico.
Source: U.S. Census Bureau, 2015-2019 American Community Survey 5-Year Estimates

Marital Status

Area	Never Married	Now Married[2]	Separated	Widowed	Divorced
City	32.1	52.3	1.0	5.2	9.4
MSA[1]	27.8	56.9	0.8	5.1	9.4
U.S.	33.4	48.1	1.9	5.8	10.9

Note: Figures are percentages and cover the population 15 years of age and older; (1) Figures cover the Rochester, MN Metropolitan Statistical Area; (2) Excludes separated
Source: U.S. Census Bureau, 2015-2019 American Community Survey 5-Year Estimates

Disability by Age

Area	All Ages	Under 18 Years Old	18 to 64 Years Old	65 Years and Over
City	10.5	4.7	8.2	30.1
MSA[1]	10.2	4.0	7.7	29.4
U.S.	12.6	4.2	10.3	34.5

Note: Figures show percent of the civilian noninstitutionalized population that reported having a disability. Disability status is determined from six types of difficulty: vision, hearing, cognitive, ambulatory, self-care, and independent living. For children under 5 years old, hearing and vision difficulty are used to determine disability status. For children between the ages of 5 and 14, disability status is determined from hearing, vision, cognitive, ambulatory, and self-care difficulties. For people aged 15 years and older, they are considered to have a disability if they have difficulty with any one of the six difficulty types; Note: (1) Figures cover the Rochester, MN Metropolitan Statistical Area
Source: U.S. Census Bureau, 2015-2019 American Community Survey 5-Year Estimates

Age

Area	Percent of Population									Median Age
	Under Age 5	Age 5–19	Age 20–34	Age 35–44	Age 45–54	Age 55–64	Age 65–74	Age 75–84	Age 85+	
City	7.2	18.8	22.6	13.1	11.6	11.8	8.0	4.6	2.4	35.7
MSA[1]	6.7	19.8	18.9	12.6	12.4	13.4	8.8	5.0	2.3	38.4
U.S.	6.1	19.1	20.7	12.6	13.0	12.9	9.1	4.6	1.9	38.1

Note: (1) Figures cover the Rochester, MN Metropolitan Statistical Area
Source: U.S. Census Bureau, 2015-2019 American Community Survey 5-Year Estimates

Gender

Area	Males	Females	Males per 100 Females
City	56,262	59,295	94.9
MSA[1]	107,432	110,532	97.2
U.S.	159,886,919	164,810,876	97.0

Note: (1) Figures cover the Rochester, MN Metropolitan Statistical Area
Source: U.S. Census Bureau, 2015-2019 American Community Survey 5-Year Estimates

Religious Groups by Family

Area	Catholic	Baptist	Non-Den.	Methodist[2]	Lutheran	LDS[3]	Pentecostal	Presbyterian[4]	Muslim[5]	Judaism
MSA[1]	23.4	1.7	4.7	4.9	21.1	1.1	1.3	2.9	0.3	0.2
U.S.	19.1	9.3	4.0	4.0	2.3	2.0	1.9	1.6	0.8	0.7

Note: Figures are the number of adherents as a percentage of the total population; (1) Figures cover the Rochester, MN Metropolitan Statistical Area; (2) Methodist/Pietist; (3) Latter Day Saints; (4) Reformed; (5) Figures are estimates
Source: Association of Statisticians of American Religious Bodies, 2010 U.S. Religion Census: Religious Congregations & Membership Study

Religious Groups by Tradition

Area	Catholic	Evangelical Protestant	Mainline Protestant	Other Tradition	Black Protestant	Orthodox
MSA[1]	23.4	19.0	21.1	2.1	<0.1	0.1
U.S.	19.1	16.2	7.3	4.3	1.6	0.3

Note: Figures are the number of adherents as a percentage of the total population; (1) Figures cover the Rochester, MN Metropolitan Statistical Area
Source: Association of Statisticians of American Religious Bodies, 2010 U.S. Religion Census: Religious Congregations & Membership Study

ECONOMY

Gross Metropolitan Product

Area	2017	2018	2019	2020	Rank[2]
MSA[1]	12.6	13.2	13.9	14.4	182

Note: Figures are in billions of dollars; (1) Figures cover the Rochester, MN Metropolitan Statistical Area; (2) Rank is based on 2018 data and ranges from 1 to 381
Source: U.S. Conference of Mayors, U.S. Metro Economies: GMP & Employment 2018-2020, September 2019

Economic Growth

Area	2015-17 (%)	2018 (%)	2019 (%)	2020 (%)	Rank[2]
MSA[1]	3.6	2.9	3.1	1.1	48
U.S.	1.9	2.9	2.3	2.1	—

Note: Figures are real gross metropolitan product (GMP) growth rates and represent average annual percent change; (1) Figures cover the Rochester, MN Metropolitan Statistical Area; (2) Rank is based on 2017 2-year average annual percent change and ranges from 1 to 381
Source: U.S. Conference of Mayors, U.S. Metro Economies: GMP & Employment 2018-2020, September 2019

Metropolitan Area Exports

Area	2014	2015	2016	2017	2018	2019	Rank[2]
MSA[1]	720.5	530.2	398.0	495.3	537.6	390.1	235

Note: Figures are in millions of dollars; (1) Figures cover the Rochester, MN Metropolitan Statistical Area; (2) Rank is based on 2019 data and ranges from 1 to 386
Source: U.S. Department of Commerce, International Trade Administration, Office of Trade and Economic Analysis, Industry and Analysis, Exports by Metropolitan Area, data extracted March 24, 2021

Building Permits

Area	Single-Family			Multi-Family			Total		
	2018	2019	Pct. Chg.	2018	2019	Pct. Chg.	2018	2019	Pct. Chg.
City	347	296	-14.7	1,068	478	-55.2	1,415	774	-45.3
MSA[1]	690	614	-11.0	1,126	497	-55.9	1,816	1,111	-38.8
U.S.	855,300	862,100	0.7	473,500	523,900	10.6	1,328,800	1,386,000	4.3

Note: (1) Figures cover the Rochester, MN Metropolitan Statistical Area; Figures represent new, privately-owned housing units authorized (unadjusted data); All permit data are based on estimates with imputation
Source: U.S. Census Bureau, Manufacturing, Mining, and Construction Statistics, Building Permits, 2018, 2019

Bankruptcy Filings

Area	Business Filings			Nonbusiness Filings		
	2019	2020	% Chg.	2019	2020	% Chg.
Olmsted County	9	4	-55.6	151	138	-8.6
U.S.	22,780	21,655	-4.9	752,160	522,808	-30.5

Note: Business filings include Chapter 7, Chapter 9, Chapter 11, Chapter 12, Chapter 13, Chapter 15, and Section 304; Nonbusiness filings include Chapter 7, Chapter 11, and Chapter 13
Source: Administrative Office of the U.S. Courts, Business and Nonbusiness Bankruptcy, County Cases Commenced by Chapter of the Bankruptcy Code, During the 12-Month Period Ending December 31, 2019 and Business and Nonbusiness Bankruptcy, County Cases Commenced by Chapter of the Bankruptcy Code, During the 12-Month Period Ending December 31, 2020

Housing Vacancy Rates

Area	Gross Vacancy Rate[2] (%)			Year-Round Vacancy Rate[3] (%)			Rental Vacancy Rate[4] (%)			Homeowner Vacancy Rate[5] (%)		
	2018	2019	2020	2018	2019	2020	2018	2019	2020	2018	2019	2020
MSA[1]	n/a	n/a	n/a	n/a	n/a	n/a	n/a	n/a	n/a	n/a	n/a	n/a
U.S.	12.3	12.0	10.6	9.7	9.5	8.2	6.9	6.7	6.3	1.5	1.4	1.0

Note: (1) Figures cover the Rochester, MN Metropolitan Statistical Area; (2) The percentage of the total housing inventory that is vacant; (3) The percentage of the housing inventory (excluding seasonal units) that is year-round vacant; (4) The percentage of rental inventory that is vacant for rent; (5) The percentage of homeowner inventory that is vacant for sale; n/a not available
Source: U.S. Census Bureau, Housing Vacancies and Homeownership Annual Statistics: 2018, 2019, 2020

INCOME

Income

Area	Per Capita ($)	Median Household ($)	Average Household ($)
City	39,518	73,106	96,015
MSA[1]	38,754	73,697	95,925
U.S.	34,103	62,843	88,607

Note: (1) Figures cover the Rochester, MN Metropolitan Statistical Area
Source: U.S. Census Bureau, 2015-2019 American Community Survey 5-Year Estimates

Household Income Distribution

Area	Percent of Households Earning							
	Under $15,000	$15,000 -$24,999	$25,000 -$34,999	$35,000 -$49,999	$50,000 -$74,999	$75,000 -$99,999	$100,000 -$149,999	$150,000 and up
City	8.2	7.0	7.1	11.6	17.6	14.1	17.8	16.6
MSA[1]	7.1	7.0	7.4	11.6	18.0	14.2	18.8	16.0
U.S.	10.3	8.9	8.9	12.3	17.2	12.7	15.1	14.5

Note: (1) Figures cover the Rochester, MN Metropolitan Statistical Area
Source: U.S. Census Bureau, 2015-2019 American Community Survey 5-Year Estimates

Poverty Rate

Area	All Ages	Under 18 Years Old	18 to 64 Years Old	65 Years and Over
City	10.1	12.8	10.0	5.7
MSA[1]	8.3	10.4	8.1	5.6
U.S.	13.4	18.5	12.6	9.3

Note: Figures are percentage of people whose income during the past 12 months was below the poverty level;
(1) Figures cover the Rochester, MN Metropolitan Statistical Area
Source: U.S. Census Bureau, 2015-2019 American Community Survey 5-Year Estimates

CITY FINANCES

City Government Finances

Component	2017 ($000)	2017 ($ per capita)
Total Revenues	457,950	4,081
Total Expenditures	505,289	4,502
Debt Outstanding	2,610,195	23,259
Cash and Securities[1]	2,497,662	22,256

Note: (1) Cash and security holdings of a government at the close of its fiscal year, including those of its dependent agencies, utilities, and liquor stores.
Source: U.S. Census Bureau, State & Local Government Finances 2017

City Government Revenue by Source

Source	2017 ($000)	2017 ($ per capita)	2017 (%)
General Revenue			
From Federal Government	7,670	68	1.7
From State Government	42,610	380	9.3
From Local Governments	5,760	51	1.3
Taxes			
Property	56,808	506	12.4
Sales and Gross Receipts	27,777	248	6.1
Personal Income	0	0	0.0
Corporate Income	0	0	0.0
Motor Vehicle License	0	0	0.0
Other Taxes	3,909	35	0.9
Current Charges	56,616	504	12.4
Liquor Store	0	0	0.0
Utility	168,736	1,504	36.8
Employee Retirement	0	0	0.0

Source: U.S. Census Bureau, State & Local Government Finances 2017

City Government Expenditures by Function

Function	2017 ($000)	2017 ($ per capita)	2017 (%)
General Direct Expenditures			
Air Transportation	6,597	58	1.3
Corrections	0	0	0.0
Education	0	0	0.0
Employment Security Administration	0	0	0.0
Financial Administration	2,596	23	0.5
Fire Protection	15,609	139	3.1
General Public Buildings	557	5	0.1
Governmental Administration, Other	3,918	34	0.8
Health	324	2	0.1
Highways	43,686	389	8.6
Hospitals	0	0	0.0
Housing and Community Development	1,397	12	0.3
Interest on General Debt	89,305	795	17.7
Judicial and Legal	1,966	17	0.4
Libraries	8,146	72	1.6
Parking	4,714	42	0.9
Parks and Recreation	72,335	644	14.3
Police Protection	28,341	252	5.6
Public Welfare	0	0	0.0
Sewerage	13,947	124	2.8
Solid Waste Management	0	0	0.0
Veterans' Services	0	0	0.0
Liquor Store	0	0	0.0
Utility	178,973	1,594	35.4
Employee Retirement	0	0	0.0

Source: U.S. Census Bureau, State & Local Government Finances 2017

434 Rochester, Minnesota

EMPLOYMENT

Labor Force and Employment

Area	Civilian Labor Force			Workers Employed		
	Dec. 2019	Dec. 2020	% Chg.	Dec. 2019	Dec. 2020	% Chg.
City	65,938	64,249	-2.6	64,352	61,741	-4.1
MSA[1]	125,263	121,785	-2.8	121,567	117,057	-3.7
U.S.	164,007,000	160,017,000	-2.4	158,504,000	149,613,000	-5.6

Note: Data is not seasonally adjusted and covers workers 16 years of age and older; (1) Figures cover the Rochester, MN Metropolitan Statistical Area
Source: Bureau of Labor Statistics, Local Area Unemployment Statistics

Unemployment Rate

Area	2020											
	Jan.	Feb.	Mar.	Apr.	May	Jun.	Jul.	Aug.	Sep.	Oct.	Nov.	Dec.
City	2.3	2.5	2.5	7.2	10.4	9.1	7.5	6.7	4.9	4.0	3.6	3.9
MSA[1]	3.1	3.1	3.1	6.9	9.3	8.1	6.6	5.8	4.2	3.5	3.4	3.9
U.S.	4.0	3.8	4.5	14.4	13.0	11.2	10.5	8.5	7.7	6.6	6.4	6.5

Note: Data is not seasonally adjusted and covers workers 16 years of age and older; (1) Figures cover the Rochester, MN Metropolitan Statistical Area
Source: Bureau of Labor Statistics, Local Area Unemployment Statistics

Average Wages

Occupation	$/Hr.	Occupation	$/Hr.
Accountants and Auditors	33.90	Maintenance and Repair Workers	21.00
Automotive Mechanics	21.20	Marketing Managers	55.50
Bookkeepers	21.00	Network and Computer Systems Admin.	38.80
Carpenters	26.10	Nurses, Licensed Practical	24.70
Cashiers	12.80	Nurses, Registered	34.70
Computer Programmers	29.60	Nursing Assistants	17.10
Computer Systems Analysts	41.50	Office Clerks, General	18.50
Computer User Support Specialists	27.40	Physical Therapists	41.20
Construction Laborers	23.20	Physicians	120.60
Cooks, Restaurant	14.90	Plumbers, Pipefitters and Steamfitters	36.00
Customer Service Representatives	17.50	Police and Sheriff's Patrol Officers	33.00
Dentists	93.20	Postal Service Mail Carriers	25.00
Electricians	30.40	Real Estate Sales Agents	25.70
Engineers, Electrical	48.10	Retail Salespersons	15.40
Fast Food and Counter Workers	12.90	Sales Representatives, Technical/Scientific	44.60
Financial Managers	54.00	Secretaries, Exc. Legal/Medical/Executive	18.20
First-Line Supervisors of Office Workers	27.80	Security Guards	15.80
General and Operations Managers	50.60	Surgeons	n/a
Hairdressers/Cosmetologists	14.10	Teacher Assistants, Exc. Postsecondary*	15.80
Home Health and Personal Care Aides	14.60	Teachers, Secondary School, Exc. Sp. Ed.*	30.90
Janitors and Cleaners	15.50	Telemarketers	n/a
Landscaping/Groundskeeping Workers	17.50	Truck Drivers, Heavy/Tractor-Trailer	23.50
Lawyers	56.20	Truck Drivers, Light/Delivery Services	16.40
Maids and Housekeeping Cleaners	13.60	Waiters and Waitresses	15.40

Note: Wage data covers the Rochester, MN Metropolitan Statistical Area; (*) Hourly wages were calculated from annual wage data based on a 40 hour work week; n/a not available.
Source: Bureau of Labor Statistics, Metro Area Occupational Employment & Wage Estimates, May 2020

Employment by Industry

Sector	MSA[1]		U.S.
	Number of Employees	Percent of Total	Percent of Total
Construction, Mining, and Logging	4,700	4.0	5.5
Education and Health Services	52,400	44.7	16.3
Financial Activities	2,800	2.4	6.1
Government	12,300	10.5	15.2
Information	1,300	1.1	1.9
Leisure and Hospitality	6,900	5.9	9.0
Manufacturing	9,800	8.4	8.5
Other Services	3,500	3.0	3.8
Professional and Business Services	5,600	4.8	14.4
Retail Trade	12,500	10.7	10.9
Transportation, Warehousing, and Utilities	2,600	2.2	4.6
Wholesale Trade	2,700	2.3	3.9

Note: Figures are non-farm employment as of December 2020. Figures are not seasonally adjusted and include workers 16 years of age and older; (1) Figures cover the Rochester, MN Metropolitan Statistical Area
Source: Bureau of Labor Statistics, Current Employment Statistics, Employment, Hours, and Earnings

Employment by Occupation

Occupation Classification	City (%)	MSA[1] (%)	U.S. (%)
Management, Business, Science, and Arts	52.3	46.5	38.5
Natural Resources, Construction, and Maintenance	5.2	8.2	8.9
Production, Transportation, and Material Moving	9.3	11.3	13.2
Sales and Office	16.2	17.9	21.6
Service	17.0	16.0	17.8

Note: Figures cover employed civilians 16 years of age and older; (1) Figures cover the Rochester, MN Metropolitan Statistical Area
Source: U.S. Census Bureau, 2015-2019 American Community Survey 5-Year Estimates

Occupations with Greatest Projected Employment Growth: 2020 – 2022

Occupation[1]	2020 Employment	2022 Projected Employment	Numeric Employment Change	Percent Employment Change
Combined Food Preparation and Serving Workers, Including Fast Food	50,640	65,000	14,360	28.4
Waiters and Waitresses	35,550	48,150	12,600	35.4
Cooks, Restaurant	20,300	28,020	7,720	38.0
Personal Care Aides	74,560	80,400	5,840	7.8
Bartenders	12,560	17,580	5,020	40.0
First-Line Supervisors of Food Preparation and Serving Workers	11,980	15,660	3,680	30.7
Laborers and Freight, Stock, and Material Movers, Hand	42,090	45,760	3,670	8.7
General and Operations Managers	44,920	48,210	3,290	7.3
Janitors and Cleaners, Except Maids and Housekeeping Cleaners	44,350	47,440	3,090	7.0
Maids and Housekeeping Cleaners	12,000	15,050	3,050	25.4

Note: Projections cover Minnesota; (1) Sorted by numeric employment change
Source: www.projectionscentral.com, State Occupational Projections, 2020–2022 Short-Term Projections

Fastest-Growing Occupations: 2020 – 2022

Occupation[1]	2020 Employment	2022 Projected Employment	Numeric Employment Change	Percent Employment Change
Dancers	200	330	130	65.0
Hotel, Motel, and Resort Desk Clerks	2,550	4,130	1,580	62.0
Lodging Managers	280	450	170	60.7
Gaming Cage Workers	140	220	80	57.1
Baggage Porters and Bellhops	230	360	130	56.5
Choreographers	230	340	110	47.8
Gaming Dealers	1,160	1,710	550	47.4
Cooks, Short Order	460	670	210	45.7
Gaming Change Persons and Booth Cashiers	380	550	170	44.7
First-Line Supervisors of Gaming Workers	480	680	200	41.7

Note: Projections cover Minnesota; (1) Sorted by percent employment change and excludes occupations with numeric employment change less than 50
Source: www.projectionscentral.com, State Occupational Projections, 2020–2022 Short-Term Projections

TAXES

State Corporate Income Tax Rates

State	Tax Rate (%)	Income Brackets ($)	Num. of Brackets	Financial Institution Tax Rate (%)[a]	Federal Income Tax Ded.
Minnesota	9.8 (n)	Flat rate	1	9.8 (n)	No

Note: Tax rates as of January 1, 2021; (a) Rates listed are the corporate income tax rate applied to financial institutions or excise taxes based on income. Some states have other taxes based upon the value of deposits or shares; (n) In addition, Minnesota levies a 5.8% tentative minimum tax on Alternative Minimum Taxable Income. Minnesota also imposes a surtax ranging up to $10,480.
Source: Federation of Tax Administrators, State Corporate Income Tax Rates, January 1, 2021

State Individual Income Tax Rates

State	Tax Rate (%)	Income Brackets ($)	Personal Exemptions ($)			Standard Ded. ($)	
			Single	Married	Depend.	Single	Married
Minnesota (a)	5.35 - 9.85	27,230 - 166,041 (n)	(d)	(d)	4,350	12,550	25,100 (d)

Note: Tax rates as of January 1, 2021; Local- and county-level taxes are not included; Federal income tax is not deductible on state income tax returns; (a) 19 states have statutory provision for automatically adjusting to the rate of inflation the dollar values of the income tax brackets, standard deductions, and/or personal exemptions. Michigan indexes the personal exemption only. Oregon does not index the income brackets for $125,000 and over; (d) These states use the personal exemption/standard deduction amounts provided in the federal Internal Revenue Code; (n) The income brackets reported for Minnesota are for single individuals. For married couples filing jointly, the same tax rates apply to income brackets ranging from $39,810 to $276,200.
Source: Federation of Tax Administrators, State Individual Income Tax Rates, January 1, 2021

Various State Sales and Excise Tax Rates

State	State Sales Tax (%)	Gasoline[1] (¢/gal.)	Cigarette[2] ($/pack)	Spirits[3] ($/gal.)	Wine[4] ($/gal.)	Beer[5] ($/gal.)	Recreational Marijuana (%)
Minnesota	6.875	30.6	3.65	8.61	1.22	0.46	Not legal

Note: All tax rates as of January 1, 2021; (1) The American Petroleum Institute has developed a methodology for determining the average tax rate on a gallon of fuel. Rates may include any of the following: excise taxes, environmental fees, storage tank fees, other fees or taxes, general sales tax, and local taxes; (2) The federal excise tax of $1.0066 per pack and local taxes are not included; (3) Rates are those applicable to off-premise sales of 40% alcohol by volume (a.b.v.) distilled spirits in 750ml containers. Local excise taxes are excluded; (4) Rates are those applicable to off-premise sales of 11% a.b.v. non-carbonated wine in 750ml containers; (5) Rates are those applicable to off-premise sales of 4.7% a.b.v. beer in 12 ounce containers.
Source: Tax Foundation, 2021 Facts & Figures: How Does Your State Compare?

State Business Tax Climate Index Rankings

State	Overall Rank	Corporate Tax Rank	Individual Income Tax Rank	Sales Tax Rank	Property Tax Rank	Unemployment Insurance Tax Rank
Minnesota	46	45	46	28	31	32

Note: The index is a measure of how each state's tax laws affect economic performance. The lower the rank, the more favorable a state's tax system is for business. States without a given tax are given a ranking of 1. The scores/rankings for the District of Columbia do not affect other states. The 2021 index represents the tax climate as of July 1, 2020.
Source: Tax Foundation, State Business Tax Climate Index 2021

TRANSPORTATION

Means of Transportation to Work

Area	Car/Truck/Van		Public Transportation			Bicycle	Walked	Other Means	Worked at Home
	Drove Alone	Car-pooled	Bus	Subway	Railroad				
City	70.6	12.5	6.2	0.0	0.0	1.0	4.3	0.9	4.4
MSA[1]	74.1	11.5	4.0	0.0	0.0	0.6	3.6	0.8	5.3
U.S.	76.3	9.0	2.4	1.9	0.6	0.5	2.7	1.4	5.2

Note: Figures are percentages and cover workers 16 years of age and older; (1) Figures cover the Rochester, MN Metropolitan Statistical Area
Source: U.S. Census Bureau, 2015-2019 American Community Survey 5-Year Estimates

Travel Time to Work

Area	Less Than 10 Minutes	10 to 19 Minutes	20 to 29 Minutes	30 to 44 Minutes	45 to 59 Minutes	60 to 89 Minutes	90 Minutes or More
City	19.3	55.7	13.6	6.3	2.2	1.7	1.2
MSA[1]	18.9	41.6	18.4	12.8	3.9	2.7	1.7
U.S.	12.2	28.4	20.8	20.8	8.3	6.4	2.9

Note: Note: Figures are percentages and include workers 16 years old and over; (1) Figures cover the Rochester, MN Metropolitan Statistical Area
Source: U.S. Census Bureau, 2015-2019 American Community Survey 5-Year Estimates

Key Congestion Measures

Measure	1982	1992	2002	2012	2017
Annual Hours of Delay, Total (000)	n/a	n/a	n/a	n/a	2,304
Annual Hours of Delay, Per Auto Commuter	n/a	n/a	n/a	n/a	19
Annual Congestion Cost, Total (million $)	n/a	n/a	n/a	n/a	47
Annual Congestion Cost, Per Auto Commuter ($)	n/a	n/a	n/a	n/a	390

Note: n/a not available
Source: Texas A&M Transportation Institute, 2019 Urban Mobility Report

Freeway Travel Time Index

Measure	1982	1987	1992	1997	2002	2007	2012	2017
Urban Area Index[1]	n/a	n/a	n/a	n/a	n/a	n/a	n/a	1.10
Urban Area Rank[1,2]	n/a	n/a	n/a	n/a	n/a	n/a	n/a	n/a

Note: Freeway Travel Time Index—the ratio of travel time in the peak period to the travel time at free-flow conditions. For example, a value of 1.30 indicates a 20-minute free-flow trip takes 26 minutes in the peak (20 minutes x 1.30 = 26 minutes); (1) Covers the Rochester MN urban area; (2) Rank is based on 101 larger urban areas (#1 = highest travel time index); n/a not available
Source: Texas A&M Transportation Institute, 2019 Urban Mobility Report

Public Transportation

Agency Name / Mode of Transportation	Vehicles Operated in Maximum Service[1]	Annual Unlinked Passenger Trips[2] (in thous.)	Annual Passenger Miles[3] (in thous.)
City of Rochester Public Transportation			
Bus (purchased transportation)	52	2,116.6	7,753.5
Demand Response (purchased transportation)	5	23.2	132.0
Demand Response Taxi (purchased transportation)	1	15.4	72.6

Note: (1) Number of revenue vehicles operated by the given mode and type of service to meet the annual maximum service requirement. This is the revenue vehicle count during the peak season of the year; on the week and day that maximum service is provided. Vehicles operated in maximum service (VOMS) exclude atypical days and one-time special events; (2) Number of passengers who boarded public transportation vehicles. Passengers are counted each time they board a vehicle no matter how many vehicles they use to travel from their origin to their destination. (3) Sum of the distances ridden by all passengers during the entire fiscal year.
Source: Federal Transit Administration, National Transit Database, 2019

Air Transportation

Airport Name and Code / Type of Service	Passenger Airlines[1]	Passenger Enplanements	Freight Carriers[2]	Freight (lbs)
Rochester International Airport (RST)				
Domestic service (U.S. carriers - 2020)	9	66,072	2	10,098,399
International service (U.S. carriers - 2019)	0	0	0	0

Note: (1) Includes all U.S.-based major, minor and commuter airlines that carried at least one passenger during the year; (2) Includes all U.S.-based airlines and freight carriers that transported at least one pound of freight during the year.
Source: Bureau of Transportation Statistics, The Intermodal Transportation Database, Air Carriers: T-100 Domestic Market (U.S. Carriers), 2020; Bureau of Transportation Statistics, The Intermodal Transportation Database, Air Carriers: T-100 International Market (U.S. Carriers), 2019

BUSINESSES

Major Business Headquarters

Company Name	Industry	Rankings	
		Fortune[1]	Forbes[2]
No companies listed	-	-	-

Note: (1) Companies that produce a 10-K are ranked 1 to 500 based on 2019 revenue; (2) All private companies with at least $2 billion in annual revenue through the end of their most current fiscal year are ranked 1 to 219; companies listed are headquartered in the city; dashes indicate no ranking
Source: Fortune, "Fortune 500," June/July 2020; Forbes, "America's Largest Private Companies," 2020

Living Environment

COST OF LIVING

Cost of Living Index

Composite Index	Groceries	Housing	Utilities	Trans- portation	Health Care	Misc. Goods/ Services
n/a	n/a	n/a	n/a	n/a	n/a	n/a

Note: The Cost of Living Index measures regional differences in the cost of consumer goods and services, excluding taxes and non-consumer expenditures, for professional and managerial households in the top income quintile. It is based on more than 50,000 prices covering almost 60 different items for which prices are collected three times a year by chambers of commerce, economic development organizations or university applied economic centers in each participating urban area. The numbers shown should be read as a percentage above or below the national average of 100. For example, a value of 115.4 in the groceries column indicates that grocery prices are 15.4% higher than the national average. Small differences in the index numbers should not be interpreted as significant; n/a not available.
Source: The Council for Community and Economic Research, Cost of Living Index, 2020

Grocery Prices

Area[1]	T-Bone Steak ($/pound)	Frying Chicken ($/pound)	Whole Milk ($/half gal.)	Eggs ($/dozen)	Orange Juice ($/64 oz.)	Coffee ($/11.5 oz.)
City[2]	n/a	n/a	n/a	n/a	n/a	n/a
Avg.	11.78	1.39	2.05	1.47	3.57	4.34
Min.	8.03	0.94	1.03	0.74	2.94	3.02
Max.	15.86	2.65	4.31	3.77	5.44	8.69

*Note: (1) Values for the local area are compared with the average, minimum and maximum values for all 284 areas in the Cost of Living Index; (2) Figures cover the Rochester MN urban area; n/a not available; **T-Bone Steak** (price per pound); **Frying Chicken** (price per pound, whole fryer); **Whole Milk** (half gallon carton); **Eggs** (price per dozen, Grade A, large); **Orange Juice** (64 oz. Tropicana or Florida Natural); **Coffee** (11.5 oz. can, vacuum-packed, Maxwell House, Hills Bros, or Folgers).*
Source: The Council for Community and Economic Research, Cost of Living Index, 2020

Housing and Utility Costs

Area[1]	New Home Price ($)	Apartment Rent ($/month)	All Electric ($/month)	Part Electric ($/month)	Other Energy ($/month)	Telephone ($/month)
City[2]	n/a	n/a	n/a	n/a	n/a	n/a
Avg.	368,594	1,168	170.86	100.47	65.28	184.30
Min.	190,567	502	91.58	31.42	26.08	169.60
Max.	2,227,806	4,738	470.38	280.31	280.06	206.50

*Note: (1) Values for the local area are compared with the average, minimum and maximum values for all 284 areas in the Cost of Living Index; (2) Figures cover the Rochester MN urban area; n/a not available; **New Home Price** (2,400 sf living area, 8,000 sf lot, in urban area with full utilities); **Apartment Rent** (950 sf 2 bedroom/1.5 or 2 bath, unfurnished, excluding all utilities except water); **All Electric** (average monthly cost for an all-electric home); **Part Electric** (average monthly cost for a part-electric home); **Other Energy** (average monthly cost for natural gas, fuel oil, coal, wood, and any other forms of energy except electricity); **Telephone** (price includes the base monthly rate plus taxes and fees for three lines of mobile phone service).*
Source: The Council for Community and Economic Research, Cost of Living Index, 2020

Health Care, Transportation, and Other Costs

Area[1]	Doctor ($/visit)	Dentist ($/visit)	Optometrist ($/visit)	Gasoline ($/gallon)	Beauty Salon ($/visit)	Men's Shirt ($)
City[2]	n/a	n/a	n/a	n/a	n/a	n/a
Avg.	115.44	99.32	108.10	2.21	39.27	31.37
Min.	36.68	59.00	51.36	1.71	19.00	11.00
Max.	219.00	153.10	250.97	3.46	82.05	58.33

*Note: (1) Values for the local area are compared with the average, minimum and maximum values for all 284 areas in the Cost of Living Index; (2) Figures cover the Rochester MN urban area; n/a not available; **Doctor** (general practitioners routine exam of an established patient); **Dentist** (adult teeth cleaning and periodic oral examination); **Optometrist** (full vision eye exam for established adult patient); **Gasoline** (one gallon regular unleaded, national brand, including all taxes, cash price at self-service pump if available); **Beauty Salon** (woman's shampoo, trim, and blow-dry); **Men's Shirt** (cotton/polyester dress shirt, pinpoint weave, long sleeves).*
Source: The Council for Community and Economic Research, Cost of Living Index, 2020

HOUSING

Homeownership Rate

Area	2012 (%)	2013 (%)	2014 (%)	2015 (%)	2016 (%)	2017 (%)	2018 (%)	2019 (%)	2020 (%)
MSA[1]	n/a	n/a	n/a	n/a	n/a	n/a	n/a	n/a	n/a
U.S.	65.4	65.1	64.5	63.7	63.4	63.9	64.4	64.6	66.6

Note: (1) Figures cover the Rochester, MN Metropolitan Statistical Area; n/a not available
Source: U.S. Census Bureau, Housing Vacancies and Homeownership Annual Statistics: 2012-2020

House Price Index (HPI)

Area	National Ranking[2]	Quarterly Change (%)	One-Year Change (%)	Five-Year Change (%)	Since 1991Q1 (%)
MSA[1]	116	1.70	6.45	32.58	175.69
U.S.[3]	–	3.81	10.77	38.99	205.12

Note: The HPI is a weighted repeat sales index. It measures average price changes in repeat sales or refinancings on the same properties. This information is obtained by reviewing repeat mortgage transactions on single-family properties whose mortgages have been purchased or securitized by Fannie Mae or Freddie Mac since January 1975; (1) Figures cover the Rochester, MN Metropolitan Statistical Area; (2) Rankings are based on annual percentage change for all metro areas containing at least 15,000 transactions over the last 10 years and ranges from 1 to 253; (3) figures based on a weighted average of Census Division estimates using a seasonally adjusted, purchase-only index; all figures are for the period ending December 31, 2020
Source: Federal Housing Finance Agency, Change in Metropolitan Area House Price Indexes, April 7, 2021

Median Single-Family Home Prices

Area	2018	2019	2020p	Percent Change 2019 to 2020
MSA[1]	n/a	n/a	n/a	n/a
U.S. Average	261.6	274.6	299.9	9.2

Note: Figures are median sales prices of existing single-family homes in thousands of dollars; (p) preliminary; n/a not available; (1) Figures cover the Rochester, MN Metropolitan Statistical Area
Source: National Association of Realtors, Median Sales Price of Existing Single-Family Homes for Metropolitan Areas, 4th Quarter 2020

Qualifying Income Based on Median Sales Price of Existing Single-Family Homes

Area	With 5% Down ($)	With 10% Down ($)	With 20% Down ($)
MSA[1]	n/a	n/a	n/a
U.S. Average	59,266	56,147	49,908

Note: Figures are preliminary; Qualifying income is based on a mortgage rate of 2.81%. Monthly principal and interest payment is limited to 25% of income; n/a not available; (1) Figures cover the Rochester, MN Metropolitan Statistical Area
Source: National Association of Realtors, Qualifying Income Based on Median Sales Price of Existing Single-Family Homes for Metropolitan Areas, 4th Quarter 2020

Home Value Distribution

Area	Under $50,000	$50,000 -$99,999	$100,000 -$149,999	$150,000 -$199,999	$200,000 -$299,999	$300,000 -$499,999	$500,000 -$999,999	$1,000,000 or more
City	2.9	4.5	16.5	26.0	27.6	17.9	4.2	0.4
MSA[1]	4.6	6.8	16.1	22.2	24.5	19.3	5.5	1.0
U.S.	6.9	12.0	13.3	14.0	19.6	19.3	11.4	3.4

Note: Figures are percentages and cover owner-occupied housing units; (1) Figures cover the Rochester, MN Metropolitan Statistical Area
Source: U.S. Census Bureau, 2015-2019 American Community Survey 5-Year Estimates

Year Housing Structure Built

Area	2010 or Later	2000 -2009	1990 -1999	1980 -1989	1970 -1979	1960 -1969	1950 -1959	1940 -1949	Before 1940	Median Year
City	8.9	18.3	14.3	14.6	13.0	10.1	9.6	3.3	7.9	1984
MSA[1]	7.0	18.0	14.3	12.1	13.5	9.0	8.0	3.4	14.6	1981
U.S.	5.2	14.0	13.9	13.4	15.2	10.6	10.3	4.9	12.6	1978

Note: Figures are percentages except for Median Year; Note: (1) Figures cover the Rochester, MN Metropolitan Statistical Area
Source: U.S. Census Bureau, 2015-2019 American Community Survey 5-Year Estimates

Gross Monthly Rent

Area	Under $500	$500 -$999	$1,000 -$1,499	$1,500 -$1,999	$2,000 -$2,499	$2,500 -$2,999	$3,000 and up	Median ($)
City	9.1	43.7	30.2	13.0	1.7	0.9	1.3	974
MSA[1]	11.5	47.5	27.7	10.0	1.5	0.7	0.9	908
U.S.	9.4	36.2	30.0	14.0	5.6	2.4	2.4	1,062

Note: Figures are percentages except for Median; Gross rent is the contract rent plus the estimated average monthly cost of utilities (electricity, gas, and water and sewer) and fuels (oil, coal, kerosene, wood, etc.) if these are paid by the renter (or paid for the renter by someone else); (1) Figures cover the Rochester, MN Metropolitan Statistical Area
Source: U.S. Census Bureau, 2015-2019 American Community Survey 5-Year Estimates

HEALTH

Health Risk Factors

Category	MSA[1] (%)	U.S. (%)
Adults aged 18–64 who have any kind of health care coverage	90.6	87.3
Adults who reported being in good or better health	90.8	82.4
Adults who have been told they have high blood cholesterol	30.6	33.0
Adults who have been told they have high blood pressure	26.2	32.3
Adults who are current smokers	12.4	17.1
Adults who currently use E-cigarettes	n/a	4.6
Adults who currently use chewing tobacco, snuff, or snus	3.3	4.0
Adults who are heavy drinkers[2]	5.9	6.3
Adults who are binge drinkers[3]	15.7	17.4
Adults who are overweight (BMI 25.0 - 29.9)	37.2	35.3
Adults who are obese (BMI 30.0 - 99.8)	30.5	31.3
Adults who participated in any physical activities in the past month	74.9	74.4
Adults who always or nearly always wears a seat belt	97.5	94.3

Note: n/a not available; (1) Figures cover the Rochester, MN Metropolitan Statistical Area; (2) Heavy drinkers are classified as adult men having more than 14 drinks per week and adult women having more than 7 drinks per week; (3) Binge drinkers are classified as males having five or more drinks on one occasion or females having four or more drinks on one occasion
Source: Centers for Disease Control and Prevention, Behaviorial Risk Factor Surveillance System, SMART: Selected Metropolitan Area Risk Trends, 2017

Acute and Chronic Health Conditions

Category	MSA[1] (%)	U.S. (%)
Adults who have ever been told they had a heart attack	3.3	4.2
Adults who have ever been told they have angina or coronary heart disease	3.8	3.9
Adults who have ever been told they had a stroke	2.2	3.0
Adults who have ever been told they have asthma	12.8	14.2
Adults who have ever been told they have arthritis	21.7	24.9
Adults who have ever been told they have diabetes[2]	9.2	10.5
Adults who have ever been told they had skin cancer	7.0	6.2
Adults who have ever been told they had any other types of cancer	5.8	7.1
Adults who have ever been told they have COPD	5.4	6.5
Adults who have ever been told they have kidney disease	2.6	3.0
Adults who have ever been told they have a form of depression	19.2	20.5

Note: (1) Figures cover the Rochester, MN Metropolitan Statistical Area; (2) Figures do not include pregnancy-related, borderline, or pre-diabetes
Source: Centers for Disease Control and Prevention, Behaviorial Risk Factor Surveillance System, SMART: Selected Metropolitan Area Risk Trends, 2017

Health Screening and Vaccination Rates

Category	MSA[1] (%)	U.S. (%)
Adults aged 65+ who have had flu shot within the past year	73.6	60.7
Adults aged 65+ who have ever had a pneumonia vaccination	85.4	75.4
Adults who have ever been tested for HIV	23.8	36.1
Adults who have ever had the shingles or zoster vaccine?	40.5	28.9
Adults who have had their blood cholesterol checked within the last five years	86.1	85.9

Note: n/a not available; (1) Figures cover the Rochester, MN Metropolitan Statistical Area.
Source: Centers for Disease Control and Prevention, Behaviorial Risk Factor Surveillance System, SMART: Selected Metropolitan Area Risk Trends, 2017

Disability Status

Category	MSA[1] (%)	U.S. (%)
Adults who reported being deaf	7.9	6.7
Are you blind or have serious difficulty seeing, even when wearing glasses?	3.2	4.5
Are you limited in any way in any of your usual activities due of arthritis?	10.6	12.9
Do you have difficulty doing errands alone?	3.6	6.8
Do you have difficulty dressing or bathing?	2.3	3.6
Do you have serious difficulty concentrating/remembering/making decisions?	8.5	10.7
Do you have serious difficulty walking or climbing stairs?	10.0	13.6

Note: (1) Figures cover the Rochester, MN Metropolitan Statistical Area.
Source: Centers for Disease Control and Prevention, Behaviorial Risk Factor Surveillance System, SMART: Selected Metropolitan Area Risk Trends, 2017

Mortality Rates for the Top 10 Causes of Death in the U.S.

ICD-10[a] Sub-Chapter	ICD-10[a] Code	Age-Adjusted Mortality Rate[1] per 100,000 population	
		County[2]	U.S.
Malignant neoplasms	C00-C97	125.7	149.2
Ischaemic heart diseases	I20-I25	72.8	90.5
Other forms of heart disease	I30-I51	34.3	52.2
Chronic lower respiratory diseases	J40-J47	26.8	39.6
Other degenerative diseases of the nervous system	G30-G31	49.9	37.6
Cerebrovascular diseases	I60-I69	27.6	37.2
Other external causes of accidental injury	W00-X59	29.3	36.1
Organic, including symptomatic, mental disorders	F01-F09	39.7	29.4
Hypertensive diseases	I10-I15	20.3	24.1
Diabetes mellitus	E10-E14	8.1	21.5

Note: (a) ICD-10 = International Classification of Diseases 10th Revision; (1) Mortality rates are a three-year average covering 2017-2019; (2) Figures cover Olmsted County.
Source: Centers for Disease Control and Prevention, National Center for Health Statistics. Underlying Cause of Death 1999-2019 on CDC WONDER Online Database

Mortality Rates for Selected Causes of Death

ICD-10[a] Sub-Chapter	ICD-10[a] Code	Age-Adjusted Mortality Rate[1] per 100,000 population	
		County[2]	U.S.
Assault	X85-Y09	Unreliable	6.0
Diseases of the liver	K70-K76	6.6	14.4
Human immunodeficiency virus (HIV) disease	B20-B24	Suppressed	1.5
Influenza and pneumonia	J09-J18	4.4	13.8
Intentional self-harm	X60-X84	11.8	14.1
Malnutrition	E40-E46	Suppressed	2.3
Obesity and other hyperalimentation	E65-E68	Suppressed	2.1
Renal failure	N17-N19	3.6	12.6
Transport accidents	V01-V99	6.9	12.3
Viral hepatitis	B15-B19	Suppressed	1.2

Note: (a) ICD-10 = International Classification of Diseases 10th Revision; (1) Mortality rates are a three-year average covering 2017-2019; (2) Figures cover Olmsted County; Data are suppressed when the data meet the criteria for confidentiality constraints; Mortality rates are flagged as unreliable when the rate would be calculated with a numerator of 20 or less.
Source: Centers for Disease Control and Prevention, National Center for Health Statistics. Underlying Cause of Death 1999-2019 on CDC WONDER Online Database

Health Insurance Coverage

Area	With Health Insurance	With Private Health Insurance	With Public Health Insurance	Without Health Insurance	Population Under Age 19 Without Health Insurance
City	95.7	79.4	30.4	4.3	2.4
MSA[1]	95.5	79.9	30.3	4.5	3.7
U.S.	91.2	67.9	35.1	8.8	5.1

Note: Figures are percentages that cover the civilian noninstitutionalized population; (1) Figures cover the Rochester, MN Metropolitan Statistical Area
Source: U.S. Census Bureau, 2015-2019 American Community Survey 5-Year Estimates

Number of Medical Professionals

Area	MDs[3]	DOs[3,4]	Dentists	Podiatrists	Chiropractors	Optometrists
County[1] (number)	3,897	76	200	10	65	38
County[1] (rate[2])	2,492.4	48.6	126.3	6.3	41.1	24.0
U.S. (rate[2])	282.9	22.7	71.2	6.2	28.1	16.9

27109
Note: Data as of 2019 unless noted; (1) Data covers Olmsted County; (2) Rate per 100,000 population; (3) Data as of 2018 and includes all active, non-federal physicians; (4) Doctor of Osteopathic Medicine
Source: U.S. Department of Health and Human Services, Health Resources and Services Administration, Bureau of Health Professions, Area Resource File (ARF) 2019-2020

Best Hospitals

According to *U.S. News*, the Rochester, MN metro area is home to one of the best hospitals in the U.S.: **Mayo Clinic** (Honor Roll/15 adult specialties and 8 pediatric specialties). The hospital listed was nationally ranked in at least one of 16 adult or 10 pediatric specialties. Only 134 hospitals nationwide were nationally ranked in one or more adult or pediatric specialty; this number increases to 178 counting specialized centers within hospitals. Twenty hospitals in the U.S. made the Honor Roll. The Best Hospitals Honor Roll takes both the national rankings and the procedure and condition ratings into account. Hospitals received points if they were nationally ranked in one of the 16 adult specialties—the higher they ranked, the more points they got—and how many ratings of "high performing" they earned in the 10 procedures and conditions. *U.S. News Online, "America's Best Hospitals 2020-21"*

According to *U.S. News,* the Rochester, MN metro area is home to one of the best children's hospitals in the U.S.: **Mayo Clinic Children's Center** (8 pediatric specialties). The hospital listed was highly ranked in at least one of 10 pediatric specialties. Eighty-eight children's hospitals in the U.S. were nationally ranked in at least one specialty. Hospitals received points for being ranked in a specialty, and the 10 hospitals with the most points across the 10 specialties make up the Honor Roll. *U.S. News Online, "America's Best Children's Hospitals 2020-21"*

EDUCATION

Public School District Statistics

District Name	Schls	Pupils	Pupil/ Teacher Ratio	Minority Pupils[1] (%)	Free Lunch Eligible[2] (%)	IEP[3] (%)
Rochester Public School District	45	18,015	16.1	40.8	29.9	17.6

Note: Table includes school districts with 2,000 or more students; (1) Percentage of students that are not non-Hispanic white; (2) Percentage of students that are eligible for the free lunch program; (3) Percentage of students that have an Individualized Education Program.
Source: U.S. Department of Education, National Center for Education Statistics, Common Core of Data, Local Education Agency (School District) Universe Survey: School Year 2018-2019; U.S. Department of Education, National Center for Education Statistics, Common Core of Data, Public Elementary/Secondary School Universe Survey: School Year 2018-2019

Highest Level of Education

Area	Less than H.S.	H.S. Diploma	Some College, No Deg.	Associate Degree	Bachelor's Degree	Master's Degree	Prof. School Degree	Doctorate Degree
City	6.0	18.7	17.2	11.4	25.7	12.1	5.2	3.7
MSA[1]	5.9	23.9	19.1	12.4	22.7	9.7	3.8	2.5
U.S.	12.0	27.0	20.4	8.5	19.8	8.8	2.1	1.4

Note: Figures cover persons age 25 and over; (1) Figures cover the Rochester, MN Metropolitan Statistical Area
Source: U.S. Census Bureau, 2015-2019 American Community Survey 5-Year Estimates

Educational Attainment by Race

Area	High School Graduate or Higher (%)					Bachelor's Degree or Higher (%)				
	Total	White	Black	Asian	Hisp.[2]	Total	White	Black	Asian	Hisp.[2]
City	94.0	96.3	77.2	83.8	74.1	46.7	47.8	18.0	59.9	26.2
MSA[1]	94.1	95.5	78.3	84.4	71.3	38.7	38.7	18.1	58.0	23.1
U.S.	88.0	89.9	86.0	87.1	68.7	32.1	33.5	21.6	54.3	16.4

Note: Figures shown cover persons 25 years old and over; (1) Figures cover the Rochester, MN Metropolitan Statistical Area; (2) People of Hispanic origin can be of any race
Source: U.S. Census Bureau, 2015-2019 American Community Survey 5-Year Estimates

School Enrollment by Grade and Control

Area	Preschool (%)		Kindergarten (%)		Grades 1 - 4 (%)		Grades 5 - 8 (%)		Grades 9 - 12 (%)	
	Public	Private	Public	Private	Public	Private	Public	Private	Public	Private
City	50.9	49.1	80.4	19.6	86.9	13.1	87.1	12.9	91.4	8.6
MSA[1]	62.6	37.4	85.5	14.5	87.3	12.7	89.1	10.9	92.1	7.9
U.S.	59.1	40.9	87.6	12.4	89.5	10.5	89.4	10.6	90.1	9.9

Note: Figures shown cover persons 3 years old and over; (1) Figures cover the Rochester, MN Metropolitan Statistical Area
Source: U.S. Census Bureau, 2015-2019 American Community Survey 5-Year Estimates

Higher Education

Four-Year Colleges			Two-Year Colleges			Medical Schools[1]	Law Schools[2]	Voc/ Tech[3]
Public	Private Non-profit	Private For-profit	Public	Private Non-profit	Private For-profit			
1	1	1	1	0	0	1	0	2

Note: Figures cover institutions located within the city limits and include main campuses only; (1) includes schools accredited by the Liaison Committee on Medical Education and the American Osteopathic Association's Commission on Osteopathic College Accreditation; (2) includes ABA-accredited schools, schools with provisional ABA accreditation, and state accredited schools; (3) includes all schools with programs that are less than 2 years.
Source: National Center for Education Statistics, Integrated Postsecondary Education System (IPEDS), 2019-20; Wikipedia, List of Medical Schools in the United States, accessed April 2, 2021; Wikipedia, List of Law Schools in the United States, accessed April 2, 2021

According to *U.S. News & World Report,* the Rochester, MN metro area is home to one of the top 75 medical schools for research in the U.S.: **Mayo Clinic School of Medicine (Alix)** (#11 tie). The rankings are based on a weighted average of 11 measures of quality: quality assessment; peer assessment score; assessment score by residency directors; research activity; total research activity; average research activity per faculty member; student selectivity; median MCAT total score; median undergraduate GPA; acceptance rate; and faculty resources. *U.S. News & World Report, "America's Best Graduate Schools, Medical, 2022"*

EMPLOYERS

Major Employers

Company Name	Industry
Benchmark Electronics	Contract mfg/design/engineering
Cardinal of Minnesota	Res. services/dev. disabilities
Charter Communications	Cable & other pay television services
City of Rochester	Municipal government
Crenlo	Fabricated metal
Federal Medical Center	Corrections/medical
Halcon	Furniture manufacturer
Hiawatha Homes	Res. services/dev. disabilities
IBM	Electronics
Interstate Hotels & Resorts	Hotel/restaurant services
Kemps	Food processing
Mayo Clinic	Healthcare
McNeilus Steel	Steel fabrication
McNeilus Truck	Mobile concrete mixers, garbage trucks
Olmstead County	Government
Olmstead Medical Center	Healthcare
Pace Dairy	Food processing
RCTC	Post-secondary education
Reichel Foods	Refrigerated lunch & snacks
Rochester Meat Company	Meat processor
Rochester Medical Corp	Medical device manufacturer
Rochester Public Schools	Education
Samaritan Bethany	Health care of the aging
Seneca Food	Food processing
Think Bank	Banking and financial services

Note: Companies shown are located within the Rochester, MN Metropolitan Statistical Area.
Source: Hoovers.com; Wikipedia

PUBLIC SAFETY

Crime Rate

Area	All Crimes	Violent Crimes				Property Crimes		
		Murder	Rape[3]	Robbery	Aggrav. Assault	Burglary	Larceny -Theft	Motor Vehicle Theft
City	2,096.1	0.8	52.4	28.7	132.8	238.4	1,535.5	107.4
Suburbs[1]	653.1	1.0	9.7	2.9	67.2	122.6	407.8	41.9
Metro[2]	1,425.3	0.9	32.6	16.7	102.3	184.6	1,011.3	76.9
U.S.	2,489.3	5.0	42.6	81.6	250.2	340.5	1,549.5	219.9

Note: Figures are crimes per 100,000 population; (1) All areas within the metro area that are located outside the city limits; (2) Figures cover the Rochester, MN Metropolitan Statistical Area; (3) All figures shown were reported using the revised Uniform Crime Reporting (UCR) definition of rape.
Source: FBI Uniform Crime Reports, 2019

Hate Crimes

Area	Number of Quarters Reported	Number of Incidents per Bias Motivation					
		Race/Ethnicity/ Ancestry	Religion	Sexual Orientation	Disability	Gender	Gender Identity
City	4	3	1	0	0	0	0
U.S.	4	3,963	1,521	1,195	157	69	198

Source: Federal Bureau of Investigation, Hate Crime Statistics 2019

Identity Theft Consumer Reports

Area	Reports	Reports per 100,000 Population	Rank[2]
MSA[1]	312	141	307
U.S.	1,387,615	423	-

Note: (1) Figures cover the Rochester, MN Metropolitan Statistical Area; (2) Rank ranges from 1 to 391 where 1 indicates greatest number of identity theft reports per 100,000 population
Source: Federal Trade Commission, Consumer Sentinel Network Data Book 2020

Fraud and Other Consumer Reports

Area	Reports	Reports per 100,000 Population	Rank[2]
MSA[1]	1,222	551	334
U.S.	3,385,133	1,031	-

Note: (1) Figures cover the Rochester, MN Metropolitan Statistical Area; (2) Rank ranges from 1 to 391 where 1 indicates greatest number of fraud and other consumer reports per 100,000 population
Source: Federal Trade Commission, Consumer Sentinel Network Data Book 2020

POLITICS

2020 Presidential Election Results

Area	Biden	Trump	Jorgensen	Hawkins	Other
Olmsted County	54.2	43.4	1.2	0.3	0.9
U.S.	51.3	46.8	1.2	0.3	0.5

Note: Results are percentages and may not add to 100% due to rounding
Source: Dave Leip's Atlas of U.S. Presidential Elections

SPORTS

Professional Sports Teams

Team Name	League	Year Established
No teams are located in the metro area		

Source: Wikipedia, Major Professional Sports Teams of the United States and Canada, April 6, 2021

CLIMATE

Average and Extreme Temperatures

Temperature	Jan	Feb	Mar	Apr	May	Jun	Jul	Aug	Sep	Oct	Nov	Dec	Yr.
Extreme High (°F)	55	63	79	91	92	101	102	100	97	90	74	62	102
Average High (°F)	21	26	38	55	68	78	82	79	70	59	40	26	54
Average Temp. (°F)	12	18	29	45	57	67	71	69	60	48	32	19	44
Average Low (°F)	3	8	20	34	46	56	60	58	48	38	24	10	34
Extreme Low (°F)	-40	-29	-31	5	21	35	42	35	23	11	-20	-33	-40

Note: Figures cover the years 1948-1995
Source: National Climatic Data Center, International Station Meteorological Climate Summary, 9/96

Average Precipitation/Snowfall/Humidity

Precip./Humidity	Jan	Feb	Mar	Apr	May	Jun	Jul	Aug	Sep	Oct	Nov	Dec	Yr.
Avg. Precip. (in.)	0.8	0.8	1.8	2.8	3.4	4.0	4.2	3.9	3.1	2.0	1.7	1.0	29.4
Avg. Snowfall (in.)	9	8	10	4	Tr	0	0	0	Tr	1	6	10	47
Avg. Rel. Hum. 6am (%)	80	81	82	80	80	82	86	88	87	82	83	83	83
Avg. Rel. Hum. 3pm (%)	72	68	65	54	52	53	56	57	56	54	66	74	61

Note: Figures cover the years 1948-1995; Tr = Trace amounts (<0.05 in. of rain; <0.5 in. of snow)
Source: National Climatic Data Center, International Station Meteorological Climate Summary, 9/96

Weather Conditions

Temperature			Daytime Sky			Precipitation		
5°F & below	32°F & below	90°F & above	Clear	Partly cloudy	Cloudy	0.01 inch or more precip.	0.1 inch or more snow/ice	Thunder-storms
46	165	9	87	126	152	114	40	41

Note: Figures are average number of days per year and cover the years 1948-1995
Source: National Climatic Data Center, International Station Meteorological Climate Summary, 9/96

HAZARDOUS WASTE

Superfund Sites

The Rochester, MN metro area has no sites on the EPA's Superfund Final National Priorities List. There are a total of 1,375 Superfund sites with a status of proposed or final on the list in the U.S. *U.S. Environmental Protection Agency, National Priorities List, April 7, 2021*

AIR QUALITY

Air Quality Trends: Ozone

	1990	1995	2000	2005	2010	2015	2016	2017	2018	2019
MSA[1]	n/a	n/a	n/a	n/a	n/a	n/a	n/a	n/a	n/a	n/a
U.S.	0.088	0.089	0.082	0.080	0.073	0.068	0.069	0.068	0.069	0.065

Note: (1) Data covers the Rochester, MN Metropolitan Statistical Area; n/a not available. The values shown are the composite ozone concentration averages among trend sites based on the highest fourth daily maximum 8-hour concentration in parts per million. These trends are based on sites having an adequate record of monitoring data during the trend period. Data from exceptional events are included.
Source: U.S. Environmental Protection Agency, Air Quality Monitoring Information, "Air Quality Trends by City, 1990-2019"

Rochester, Minnesota   445

Air Quality Index

Area	Percent of Days when Air Quality was...[2]					AQI Statistics[2]	
	Good	Moderate	Unhealthy for Sensitive Groups	Unhealthy	Very Unhealthy	Maximum	Median
MSA[1]	86.0	14.0	0.0	0.0	0.0	84	36

Note: (1) Data covers the Rochester, MN Metropolitan Statistical Area; (2) Based on 364 days with AQI data in 2019. Air Quality Index (AQI) is an index for reporting daily air quality. EPA calculates the AQI for five major air pollutants regulated by the Clean Air Act: ground-level ozone, particle pollution (aka particulate matter), carbon monoxide, sulfur dioxide, and nitrogen dioxide. The AQI runs from 0 to 500. The higher the AQI value, the greater the level of air pollution and the greater the health concern. There are six AQI categories: "Good" AQI is between 0 and 50. Air quality is considered satisfactory; "Moderate" AQI is between 51 and 100. Air quality is acceptable; "Unhealthy for Sensitive Groups" When AQI values are between 101 and 150, members of sensitive groups may experience health effects; "Unhealthy" When AQI values are between 151 and 200 everyone may begin to experience health effects; "Very Unhealthy" AQI values between 201 and 300 trigger a health alert; "Hazardous" AQI values over 300 trigger warnings of emergency conditions (not shown).
Source: U.S. Environmental Protection Agency, Air Quality Index Report, 2019

Air Quality Index Pollutants

Area	Percent of Days when AQI Pollutant was...[2]					
	Carbon Monoxide	Nitrogen Dioxide	Ozone	Sulfur Dioxide	Particulate Matter 2.5	Particulate Matter 10
MSA[1]	0.0	0.0	53.6	0.0	46.4	0.0

Note: (1) Data covers the Rochester, MN Metropolitan Statistical Area; (2) Based on 364 days with AQI data in 2019. The Air Quality Index (AQI) is an index for reporting daily air quality. EPA calculates the AQI for five major air pollutants regulated by the Clean Air Act: ground-level ozone, particle pollution (also known as particulate matter), carbon monoxide, sulfur dioxide, and nitrogen dioxide. The AQI runs from 0 to 500. The higher the AQI value, the greater the level of air pollution and the greater the health concern.
Source: U.S. Environmental Protection Agency, Air Quality Index Report, 2019

Maximum Air Pollutant Concentrations: Particulate Matter, Ozone, CO and Lead

	Particulate Matter 10 (ug/m^3)	Particulate Matter 2.5 Wtd AM (ug/m^3)	Particulate Matter 2.5 24-Hr (ug/m^3)	Ozone (ppm)	Carbon Monoxide (ppm)	Lead (ug/m^3)
MSA[1] Level	n/a	n/a	n/a	0.054	n/a	n/a
NAAQS[2]	150	15	35	0.075	9	0.15
Met NAAQS[2]	n/a	n/a	n/a	Yes	n/a	n/a

Note: (1) Data covers the Rochester, MN Metropolitan Statistical Area; Data from exceptional events are included; (2) National Ambient Air Quality Standards; ppm = parts per million; ug/m^3 = micrograms per cubic meter; n/a not available.
Concentrations: Particulate Matter 10 (coarse particulate)—highest second maximum 24-hour concentration; Particulate Matter 2.5 Wtd AM (fine particulate)—highest weighted annual mean concentration; Particulate Matter 2.5 24-Hour (fine particulate)—highest 98th percentile 24-hour concentration; Ozone—highest fourth daily maximum 8-hour concentration; Carbon Monoxide—highest second maximum non-overlapping 8-hour concentration; Lead—maximum running 3-month average
Source: U.S. Environmental Protection Agency, Air Quality Monitoring Information, "Air Quality Statistics by City, 2019"

Maximum Air Pollutant Concentrations: Nitrogen Dioxide and Sulfur Dioxide

	Nitrogen Dioxide AM (ppb)	Nitrogen Dioxide 1-Hr (ppb)	Sulfur Dioxide AM (ppb)	Sulfur Dioxide 1-Hr (ppb)	Sulfur Dioxide 24-Hr (ppb)
MSA[1] Level	n/a	n/a	n/a	n/a	n/a
NAAQS[2]	53	100	30	75	140
Met NAAQS[2]	n/a	n/a	n/a	n/a	n/a

Note: (1) Data covers the Rochester, MN Metropolitan Statistical Area; Data from exceptional events are included; (2) National Ambient Air Quality Standards; ppm = parts per million; ug/m^3 = micrograms per cubic meter; n/a not available.
Concentrations: Nitrogen Dioxide AM—highest arithmetic mean concentration; Nitrogen Dioxide 1-Hr—highest 98th percentile 1-hour daily maximum concentration; Sulfur Dioxide AM—highest annual mean concentration; Sulfur Dioxide 1-Hr—highest 99th percentile 1-hour daily maximum concentration; Sulfur Dioxide 24-Hr—highest second maximum 24-hour concentration
Source: U.S. Environmental Protection Agency, Air Quality Monitoring Information, "Air Quality Statistics by City, 2019"

Sioux Falls, South Dakota

Background

Sioux Falls, in southeastern South Dakota, is named for the falls on the Big Sioux River where it is located. It is the seat of Minnehaha County and overlaps Lincoln County. Sioux Falls is a Great Plains city, rich in history and scenic attractions, a dynamic economic center, and a splendid family town, offering an extensive range of outdoor activities.

The city was founded prior to the Civil War by settlers who were attracted by the nearby stone quarries and the possibility of harnessing the river for water power. Many Scottish, English, and Norwegian immigrants came to the area and used their skills as stonecutters. The community was incorporated as a village in 1877 and as a city in 1883.

At the city's popular Falls Park, the remains of a water-driven mill testify to the importance of the river. The city has preserved much of its early architectural charm, with five separate historical districts preserving buildings of considerable interest. Of particular interest are the R.F. Pettigrew home, residence of the state's first U.S. senator, and the Minnehaha County Courthouse.

Sioux Falls's restoration "Phillips to the Falls" program joined the park to the rest of downtown by extending Phillips Avenue north to Falls Park and expands the park to the south.

Sioux Falls offers one of the Midwest's most dynamic business environments, partly due to the lack of a state corporate income tax, and is home to industry leaders in agri-business, distribution and trade, financial services, high-tech manufacturing, health care, retail and tourism. City infrastructure work continues on 23,000 acres in eastern Sioux Falls, to prepare the area for growth. Two of this city's largest companies are Wells Fargo and Citigroup. Amazon has plans to open a distribution center in Sioux Falls in 2022.

The city is at the heart of a large agricultural and stock-raising area, producing corn and soybeans, and serving as a regional center for stockyards and meat-packing plants. Industries in Sioux Falls also produce computer components, electronics, and artificial flowers. Some of the nation's leading credit card operations are based in the city, employment opportunities are varied and abundant, and the city's unemployment rate is generally half that of the state as a whole. Air travel is available through the Sioux Falls Regional Airport, which connects conveniently to major air hubs.

> A Sioux Falls man who thought the novel coronavirus was fake now says he needs a double lung transplant to survive the disease.

Sioux Falls is an important center of higher education, home to the University of South Dakota, Dakota State University, South Dakota State University, Northern State University, Augustana College, National American University, Colorado Technical University at Sioux Falls, and Southeast Technical Institute. The Federal Earth Resource Observation System operates a major data collection and analysis site nearby.

The city and its environs are home to a variety of recreation, such as the Catfish Bay Water Ski & Stage Show, Empire Golf Sport Dome, Great Bear Recreation Park, Huset's Speedway, and Wild Water West, the state's largest water and amusement park. The Downtown River Greenway Project includes significant greenway reconstruction on the east bank of the Big Sioux River.

The modern Washington Pavilion of Arts and Science in the Sioux Falls historic downtown district features a performing arts space, a domed Omni theater, a science museum, and display areas for the city's Fine Arts Center. The Sioux Falls Jazz and Blues Festival celebrates its 30th anniversary in 2021.

The climate is continental with frequent daily or weekly weather changes, a result of differing, usually cold, air masses, which move in very rapidly. During the late fall and winter, cold fronts accompanied by strong, gusty winds can cause temperatures to drop significantly during a 24-hour period. Rainfall is heavier during the spring and summer, and thunderstorms are frequent. Summer daytime temperatures can be high, but the nights are usually comfortable.

Rankings

General Rankings

- In their seventh annual survey, Livability.com looked at data for more than 1,000 small to mid-sized U.S. cities to determine the rankings for Livability's "Top 100 Best Places to Live" in 2020. Sioux Falls ranked #10. Criteria: housing and affordable living; vibrant economy; social and civic engagement; education; demographics; health care options; transportation & infrastructure; and abundant lifestyle amenities. *Livability.com, "Top 100 Best Places to Live 2020" October 2020*

Business/Finance Rankings

- The Sioux Falls metro area appeared on the Milken Institute "2021 Best Performing Cities" list. Rank: #7 out of 201 small metro areas (population over 60,000). Criteria: job growth; wage and salary growth; high-tech output growth; housing affordability; household broadband access. *Milken Institute, "Best-Performing Cities 2021," February 16, 2021*

- *Forbes* ranked 203 smaller metro areas (population under 268,000) to determine the nation's "Best Small Places for Business and Careers." The Sioux Falls metro area was ranked #1. Criteria: costs (business and living); job growth (past and projected); income growth; quality of life; educational attainment (college and high school); projected economic growth; cultural and leisure opportunities; workplace tolerance laws; net migration patterns. *Forbes, "The Best Small Places for Business and Careers 2019," October 30, 2019*

Dating/Romance Rankings

- Sioux Falls was selected as one of the most romantic cities in the U.S. by video-rental kiosk company Redbox. The city ranked #7 out of 20. Criteria: number of romance-related rentals in 2016. *Redbox, "20 Most Romantic Cities," February 6, 2017*

Environmental Rankings

- Sioux Falls was highlighted as one of the top 25 cleanest metro areas for year-round particle pollution (Annual PM 2.5) in the U.S. during 2016 through 2018. The area ranked #18. *American Lung Association, "State of the Air 2020," April 21, 2020*

- Sioux Falls was highlighted as one of the top 98 cleanest metro areas for short-term particle pollution (24-hour PM 2.5) in the U.S. during 2016 through 2018. Monitors in these cities reported no days with unhealthful PM 2.5 levels. *American Lung Association, "State of the Air 2020," April 21, 2020*

Real Estate Rankings

- *WalletHub* compared the most populated U.S. cities to determine which had the best markets for real estate agents. Sioux Falls ranked #14 where demand was high and pay was the best. Criteria: sales per agent; annual median wage for real-estate agents; monthly average starting salary for real estate agents; real estate job density and competition; unemployment rate; home turnover rate; housing-market health index; and other relevant metrics. *www.WalletHub.com, "2019's Best Places to Be a Real Estate Agent," April 24, 2019*

- The Sioux Falls metro area was identified as one of the 20 worst housing markets in the U.S. in 2020. The area ranked #168 out of 180 markets. Criteria: year-over-year change of median sales price of existing single-family homes between the 4th quarter of 2019 and the 4th quarter of 2020. *National Association of Realtors®, Median Sales Price of Existing Single-Family Homes for Metropolitan Areas, 4th Quarter 2020*

Safety Rankings

- Allstate ranked the 200 largest cities in America in terms of driver safety. Sioux Falls ranked #72. Criteria: internal property damage claims over a two-year period from January 2016 to December 2017. The report helps increase the importance of safety and awareness behind the wheel. *Allstate, "Allstate America's Best Drivers Report, 2019" June 24, 2019*

- The National Insurance Crime Bureau ranked 384 metro areas in the U.S. in terms of per capita rates of vehicle theft. The Sioux Falls metro area ranked #99 (#1 = highest rate). Criteria: number of vehicle theft offenses per 100,000 inhabitants in 2019. *National Insurance Crime Bureau, "Hot Spots 2019," July 21, 2020*

Seniors/Retirement Rankings

- From its Best Cities for Successful Aging indexes, the Milken Institute generated rankings for metropolitan areas, weighing data in nine categories—health care, wellness, living arrangements, transportation and convenience, financial characteristics, education, employment, community engagement, and overall livability. The Sioux Falls metro area was ranked #5 overall in the small metro area category. *Milken Institute, "Best Cities for Successful Aging, 2017" March 14, 2017*

- Sioux Falls made the 2020 *Forbes* list of "25 Best Places to Retire." Criteria, focused on high-quality retirement living at an affordable price, include: housing/living costs compared to the national average and state taxes; air quality; crime rates; good economic outlook; home price appreciation; risk associated with climate-change; availability of medical care; bikeability; walkability; healthy living. *Forbes.com, "The Best Places to Retire in 2020," August 14, 2020*

Women/Minorities Rankings

- *Women's Health*, together with the site Yelp, identified the 15 "Wellthiest" spots in the U.S. Sioux Falls appeared among the top for happiest, healthiest, outdoorsiest and Zen-iest. *Women's Health, "The 15 Wellthiest Cities in the U.S." July 5, 2017*

- Personal finance website *WalletHub* compared more than 180 U.S. cities across two key dimensions, "Hispanic Business-Friendliness" and "Hispanic Purchasing Power," to arrive at the most favorable conditions for Hispanic entrepreneurs. Sioux Falls was ranked #19 out of 182. Criteria includes: share of Hispanic-Owned Businesses; Hispanic entrepreneurship rate to median annual income of Hispanics; Small Business-Friendliness score; cost of living; and number of Hispanics with at least a bachelor's degree. *WalletHub.com, "2019's Best Cities for Hispanic Entrepreneurs," May 1, 2019*

Miscellaneous Rankings

- *WalletHub* compared the 150 most populated U.S. cities to determine their operating efficiency. A "Quality of City Services" score was constructed for each city and then divided by the total budget per capita to reveal which were managed the best. Sioux Falls ranked #11. Criteria: financial stability; economy; education; safety; health; infrastructure and pollution. *www.WalletHub.com, "2020's Best- & Worst-Run Cities in America," June 29, 2020*

450   Sioux Falls, South Dakota

Business Environment

DEMOGRAPHICS

Population Growth

Area	1990 Census	2000 Census	2010 Census	2019* Estimate	Population Growth (%) 1990-2019	Population Growth (%) 2010-2019
City	102,262	123,975	153,888	177,117	73.2	15.1
MSA[1]	153,500	187,093	228,261	259,348	69.0	13.6
U.S.	248,709,873	281,421,906	308,745,538	324,697,795	30.6	5.2

Note: (1) Figures cover the Sioux Falls, SD Metropolitan Statistical Area; (*) 2015-2019 5-year estimated population
Source: U.S. Census Bureau, 1990 Census, Census 2000, Census 2010, 2015-2019 American Community Survey 5-Year Estimates

Household Size

Area	Persons in Household (%) One	Two	Three	Four	Five	Six	Seven or More	Average Household Size
City	32.1	34.1	13.1	12.3	5.3	2.0	1.1	2.40
MSA[1]	28.7	35.1	13.6	13.1	6.3	2.1	1.1	2.50
U.S.	27.9	33.9	15.6	12.9	6.0	2.3	1.4	2.60

Note: (1) Figures cover the Sioux Falls, SD Metropolitan Statistical Area
Source: U.S. Census Bureau, 2015-2019 American Community Survey 5-Year Estimates

Race

Area	White Alone[2] (%)	Black Alone[2] (%)	Asian Alone[2] (%)	AIAN[3] Alone[2] (%)	NHOPI[4] Alone[2] (%)	Other Race Alone[2] (%)	Two or More Races (%)
City	84.5	6.2	2.5	2.1	0.0	1.6	3.2
MSA[1]	88.3	4.5	1.8	1.6	0.0	1.1	2.7
U.S.	72.5	12.7	5.5	0.8	0.2	4.9	3.3

Note: (1) Figures cover the Sioux Falls, SD Metropolitan Statistical Area; (2) Alone is defined as not being in combination with one or more other races; (3) American Indian and Alaska Native; (4) Native Hawaiian and Other Pacific Islander
Source: U.S. Census Bureau, 2015-2019 American Community Survey 5-Year Estimates

Hispanic or Latino Origin

Area	Total (%)	Mexican (%)	Puerto Rican (%)	Cuban (%)	Other (%)
City	5.5	3.1	0.4	0.1	1.9
MSA[1]	4.3	2.5	0.3	0.1	1.5
U.S.	18.0	11.2	1.7	0.7	4.3

Note: Persons of Hispanic or Latino origin can be of any race; (1) Figures cover the Sioux Falls, SD Metropolitan Statistical Area
Source: U.S. Census Bureau, 2015-2019 American Community Survey 5-Year Estimates

Ancestry

Area	German	Irish	English	American	Italian	Polish	French[2]	Scottish	Dutch
City	35.1	11.2	5.3	3.2	1.5	1.7	2.2	1.2	5.6
MSA[1]	37.2	10.8	5.2	3.8	1.4	1.6	2.1	1.0	6.4
U.S.	13.3	9.7	7.2	6.2	5.1	2.8	2.3	1.7	1.2

Note: Figures are the percentage of the total population reporting a particular ancestry. The nine most commonly reported ancestries in the U.S. are shown. Figures include multiple ancestries (e.g. if a person reported being Irish and Italian, they were included in both columns); (1) Figures cover the Sioux Falls, SD Metropolitan Statistical Area; (2) Excludes Basque
Source: U.S. Census Bureau, 2015-2019 American Community Survey 5-Year Estimates

Foreign-born Population

Area	Percent of Population Born in Any Foreign Country	Asia	Mexico	Europe	Caribbean	Central America[2]	South America	Africa	Canada
City	8.5	2.3	0.5	0.9	0.1	0.9	0.1	3.5	0.1
MSA[1]	6.2	1.6	0.4	0.7	0.1	0.7	0.1	2.4	0.1
U.S.	13.6	4.2	3.5	1.5	1.3	1.1	1.0	0.7	0.2

Note: (1) Figures cover the Sioux Falls, SD Metropolitan Statistical Area; (2) Excludes Mexico.
Source: U.S. Census Bureau, 2015-2019 American Community Survey 5-Year Estimates

Marital Status

Area	Never Married	Now Married[2]	Separated	Widowed	Divorced
City	33.6	48.8	1.4	5.0	11.1
MSA[1]	30.2	53.1	1.2	5.0	10.5
U.S.	33.4	48.1	1.9	5.8	10.9

Note: Figures are percentages and cover the population 15 years of age and older; (1) Figures cover the Sioux Falls, SD Metropolitan Statistical Area; (2) Excludes separated
Source: U.S. Census Bureau, 2015-2019 American Community Survey 5-Year Estimates

Disability by Age

Area	All Ages	Under 18 Years Old	18 to 64 Years Old	65 Years and Over
City	10.2	3.3	9.0	30.1
MSA[1]	9.9	3.1	8.8	29.7
U.S.	12.6	4.2	10.3	34.5

Note: Figures show percent of the civilian noninstitutionalized population that reported having a disability. Disability status is determined from six types of difficulty: vision, hearing, cognitive, ambulatory, self-care, and independent living. For children under 5 years old, hearing and vision difficulty are used to determine disability status. For children between the ages of 5 and 14, disability status is determined from hearing, vision, cognitive, ambulatory, and self-care difficulties. For people aged 15 years and older, they are considered to have a disability if they have difficulty with any one of the six difficulty types; Note: (1) Figures cover the Sioux Falls, SD Metropolitan Statistical Area
Source: U.S. Census Bureau, 2015-2019 American Community Survey 5-Year Estimates

Age

Area	Percent of Population									Median Age
	Under Age 5	Age 5–19	Age 20–34	Age 35–44	Age 45–54	Age 55–64	Age 65–74	Age 75–84	Age 85+	
City	7.5	19.9	23.5	13.3	11.4	11.7	7.6	3.4	1.7	34.4
MSA[1]	7.6	20.7	21.4	13.5	11.8	12.0	7.8	3.4	1.8	35.2
U.S.	6.1	19.1	20.7	12.6	13.0	12.9	9.1	4.6	1.9	38.1

Note: (1) Figures cover the Sioux Falls, SD Metropolitan Statistical Area
Source: U.S. Census Bureau, 2015-2019 American Community Survey 5-Year Estimates

Gender

Area	Males	Females	Males per 100 Females
City	88,410	88,707	99.7
MSA[1]	130,188	129,160	100.8
U.S.	159,886,919	164,810,876	97.0

Note: (1) Figures cover the Sioux Falls, SD Metropolitan Statistical Area
Source: U.S. Census Bureau, 2015-2019 American Community Survey 5-Year Estimates

Religious Groups by Family

Area	Catholic	Baptist	Non-Den.	Methodist[2]	Lutheran	LDS[3]	Pentecostal	Presbyterian[4]	Muslim[5]	Judaism
MSA[1]	14.9	3.0	1.5	3.9	21.4	0.7	1.1	6.2	0.3	0.1
U.S.	19.1	9.3	4.0	4.0	2.3	2.0	1.9	1.6	0.8	0.7

Note: Figures are the number of adherents as a percentage of the total population; (1) Figures cover the Sioux Falls, SD Metropolitan Statistical Area; (2) Methodist/Pietist; (3) Latter Day Saints; (4) Reformed; (5) Figures are estimates
Source: Association of Statisticians of American Religious Bodies, 2010 U.S. Religion Census: Religious Congregations & Membership Study

Religious Groups by Tradition

Area	Catholic	Evangelical Protestant	Mainline Protestant	Other Tradition	Black Protestant	Orthodox
MSA[1]	14.9	12.9	28.1	1.2	0.1	0.1
U.S.	19.1	16.2	7.3	4.3	1.6	0.3

Note: Figures are the number of adherents as a percentage of the total population; (1) Figures cover the Sioux Falls, SD Metropolitan Statistical Area
Source: Association of Statisticians of American Religious Bodies, 2010 U.S. Religion Census: Religious Congregations & Membership Study

ECONOMY

Gross Metropolitan Product

Area	2017	2018	2019	2020	Rank[2]
MSA[1]	19.6	20.5	21.5	22.4	127

Note: Figures are in billions of dollars; (1) Figures cover the Sioux Falls, SD Metropolitan Statistical Area; (2) Rank is based on 2018 data and ranges from 1 to 381
Source: U.S. Conference of Mayors, U.S. Metro Economies: GMP & Employment 2018-2020, September 2019

Economic Growth

Area	2015-17 (%)	2018 (%)	2019 (%)	2020 (%)	Rank[2]
MSA[1]	1.2	1.6	3.2	2.2	206
U.S.	1.9	2.9	2.3	2.1	—

Note: Figures are real gross metropolitan product (GMP) growth rates and represent average annual percent change; (1) Figures cover the Sioux Falls, SD Metropolitan Statistical Area; (2) Rank is based on 2017 2-year average annual percent change and ranges from 1 to 381
Source: U.S. Conference of Mayors, U.S. Metro Economies: GMP & Employment 2018-2020, September 2019

Metropolitan Area Exports

Area	2014	2015	2016	2017	2018	2019	Rank[2]
MSA[1]	455.3	375.0	334.3	386.8	400.0	431.5	224

Note: Figures are in millions of dollars; (1) Figures cover the Sioux Falls, SD Metropolitan Statistical Area; (2) Rank is based on 2019 data and ranges from 1 to 386
Source: U.S. Department of Commerce, International Trade Administration, Office of Trade and Economic Analysis, Industry and Analysis, Exports by Metropolitan Area, data extracted March 24, 2021

Building Permits

Area	Single-Family			Multi-Family			Total		
	2018	2019	Pct. Chg.	2018	2019	Pct. Chg.	2018	2019	Pct. Chg.
City	1,083	1,013	-6.5	898	643	-28.4	1,981	1,656	-16.4
MSA[1]	1,380	1,376	-0.3	1,008	743	-26.3	2,388	2,119	-11.3
U.S.	855,300	862,100	0.7	473,500	523,900	10.6	1,328,800	1,386,000	4.3

Note: (1) Figures cover the Sioux Falls, SD Metropolitan Statistical Area; Figures represent new, privately-owned housing units authorized (unadjusted data); All permit data are based on estimates with imputation
Source: U.S. Census Bureau, Manufacturing, Mining, and Construction Statistics, Building Permits, 2018, 2019

Bankruptcy Filings

Area	Business Filings			Nonbusiness Filings		
	2019	2020	% Chg.	2019	2020	% Chg.
Minnehaha County	18	11	-38.9	349	268	-23.2
U.S.	22,780	21,655	-4.9	752,160	522,808	-30.5

Note: Business filings include Chapter 7, Chapter 9, Chapter 11, Chapter 12, Chapter 13, Chapter 15, and Section 304; Nonbusiness filings include Chapter 7, Chapter 11, and Chapter 13
Source: Administrative Office of the U.S. Courts, Business and Nonbusiness Bankruptcy, County Cases Commenced by Chapter of the Bankruptcy Code, During the 12-Month Period Ending December 31, 2019 and Business and Nonbusiness Bankruptcy, County Cases Commenced by Chapter of the Bankruptcy Code, During the 12-Month Period Ending December 31, 2020

Housing Vacancy Rates

Area	Gross Vacancy Rate[2] (%)			Year-Round Vacancy Rate[3] (%)			Rental Vacancy Rate[4] (%)			Homeowner Vacancy Rate[5] (%)		
	2018	2019	2020	2018	2019	2020	2018	2019	2020	2018	2019	2020
MSA[1]	n/a	n/a	n/a	n/a	n/a	n/a	n/a	n/a	n/a	n/a	n/a	n/a
U.S.	12.3	12.0	10.6	9.7	9.5	8.2	6.9	6.7	6.3	1.5	1.4	1.0

Note: (1) Figures cover the Sioux Falls, SD Metropolitan Statistical Area; (2) The percentage of the total housing inventory that is vacant; (3) The percentage of the housing inventory (excluding seasonal units) that is year-round vacant; (4) The percentage of rental inventory that is vacant for rent; (5) The percentage of homeowner inventory that is vacant for sale; n/a not available
Source: U.S. Census Bureau, Housing Vacancies and Homeownership Annual Statistics: 2018, 2019, 2020

INCOME

Income

Area	Per Capita ($)	Median Household ($)	Average Household ($)
City	33,065	59,912	79,847
MSA[1]	33,453	65,621	83,463
U.S.	34,103	62,843	88,607

Note: (1) Figures cover the Sioux Falls, SD Metropolitan Statistical Area
Source: U.S. Census Bureau, 2015-2019 American Community Survey 5-Year Estimates

Household Income Distribution

Area	Percent of Households Earning							
	Under $15,000	$15,000 -$24,999	$25,000 -$34,999	$35,000 -$49,999	$50,000 -$74,999	$75,000 -$99,999	$100,000 -$149,999	$150,000 and up
City	8.8	8.3	10.7	13.2	19.0	14.4	15.2	10.5
MSA[1]	7.6	7.5	9.7	12.5	19.2	15.6	16.9	11.0
U.S.	10.3	8.9	8.9	12.3	17.2	12.7	15.1	14.5

Note: (1) Figures cover the Sioux Falls, SD Metropolitan Statistical Area
Source: U.S. Census Bureau, 2015-2019 American Community Survey 5-Year Estimates

Poverty Rate

Area	All Ages	Under 18 Years Old	18 to 64 Years Old	65 Years and Over
City	10.4	12.9	9.9	8.0
MSA[1]	8.7	10.4	8.3	7.2
U.S.	13.4	18.5	12.6	9.3

Note: Figures are percentage of people whose income during the past 12 months was below the poverty level;
(1) Figures cover the Sioux Falls, SD Metropolitan Statistical Area
Source: U.S. Census Bureau, 2015-2019 American Community Survey 5-Year Estimates

CITY FINANCES

City Government Finances

Component	2017 ($000)	2017 ($ per capita)
Total Revenues	384,713	2,243
Total Expenditures	342,239	1,995
Debt Outstanding	380,916	2,221
Cash and Securities[1]	772,340	4,502

Note: (1) Cash and security holdings of a government at the close of its fiscal year,
including those of its dependent agencies, utilities, and liquor stores.
Source: U.S. Census Bureau, State & Local Government Finances 2017

City Government Revenue by Source

Source	2017 ($000)	2017 ($ per capita)	2017 (%)
General Revenue			
From Federal Government	8,943	52	2.3
From State Government	9,183	54	2.4
From Local Governments	0	0	0.0
Taxes			
Property	57,499	335	14.9
Sales and Gross Receipts	141,541	825	36.8
Personal Income	0	0	0.0
Corporate Income	0	0	0.0
Motor Vehicle License	0	0	0.0
Other Taxes	5,597	33	1.5
Current Charges	52,498	306	13.6
Liquor Store	0	0	0.0
Utility	44,208	258	11.5
Employee Retirement	47,974	280	12.5

Source: U.S. Census Bureau, State & Local Government Finances 2017

City Government Expenditures by Function

Function	2017 ($000)	2017 ($ per capita)	2017 (%)
General Direct Expenditures			
Air Transportation	0	0	0.0
Corrections	0	0	0.0
Education	0	0	0.0
Employment Security Administration	0	0	0.0
Financial Administration	2,378	13	0.7
Fire Protection	23,353	136	6.8
General Public Buildings	2,394	14	0.7
Governmental Administration, Other	7,714	45	2.3
Health	10,924	63	3.2
Highways	67,927	396	19.8
Hospitals	0	0	0.0
Housing and Community Development	5,606	32	1.6
Interest on General Debt	6,455	37	1.9
Judicial and Legal	1,483	8	0.4
Libraries	7,884	46	2.3
Parking	2,118	12	0.6
Parks and Recreation	40,454	235	11.8
Police Protection	29,637	172	8.7
Public Welfare	0	0	0.0
Sewerage	35,115	204	10.3
Solid Waste Management	7,497	43	2.2
Veterans' Services	0	0	0.0
Liquor Store	0	0	0.0
Utility	41,286	240	12.1
Employee Retirement	30,344	176	8.9

Source: U.S. Census Bureau, State & Local Government Finances 2017

454 Sioux Falls, South Dakota

EMPLOYMENT

Labor Force and Employment

Area	Civilian Labor Force			Workers Employed		
	Dec. 2019	Dec. 2020	% Chg.	Dec. 2019	Dec. 2020	% Chg.
City	106,508	105,414	-1.0	103,166	102,274	-0.9
MSA[1]	155,466	153,813	-1.1	150,743	149,521	-0.8
U.S.	164,007,000	160,017,000	-2.4	158,504,000	149,613,000	-5.6

Note: Data is not seasonally adjusted and covers workers 16 years of age and older; (1) Figures cover the Sioux Falls, SD Metropolitan Statistical Area
Source: Bureau of Labor Statistics, Local Area Unemployment Statistics

Unemployment Rate

Area	2020											
	Jan.	Feb.	Mar.	Apr.	May	Jun.	Jul.	Aug.	Sep.	Oct.	Nov.	Dec.
City	3.5	3.3	3.1	11.6	10.4	7.3	6.0	4.6	3.7	3.2	3.2	3.0
MSA[1]	3.4	3.2	3.0	10.5	9.4	6.7	5.6	4.3	3.4	3.0	3.0	2.8
U.S.	4.0	3.8	4.5	14.4	13.0	11.2	10.5	8.5	7.7	6.6	6.4	6.5

Note: Data is not seasonally adjusted and covers workers 16 years of age and older; (1) Figures cover the Sioux Falls, SD Metropolitan Statistical Area
Source: Bureau of Labor Statistics, Local Area Unemployment Statistics

Average Wages

Occupation	$/Hr.	Occupation	$/Hr.
Accountants and Auditors	35.00	Maintenance and Repair Workers	19.60
Automotive Mechanics	20.90	Marketing Managers	66.00
Bookkeepers	17.80	Network and Computer Systems Admin.	32.40
Carpenters	18.70	Nurses, Licensed Practical	19.40
Cashiers	12.20	Nurses, Registered	29.70
Computer Programmers	28.30	Nursing Assistants	13.80
Computer Systems Analysts	37.90	Office Clerks, General	13.70
Computer User Support Specialists	20.10	Physical Therapists	35.60
Construction Laborers	16.30	Physicians	136.20
Cooks, Restaurant	13.60	Plumbers, Pipefitters and Steamfitters	21.70
Customer Service Representatives	17.30	Police and Sheriff's Patrol Officers	30.60
Dentists	78.70	Postal Service Mail Carriers	25.70
Electricians	24.20	Real Estate Sales Agents	n/a
Engineers, Electrical	46.70	Retail Salespersons	16.20
Fast Food and Counter Workers	11.10	Sales Representatives, Technical/Scientific	59.30
Financial Managers	74.40	Secretaries, Exc. Legal/Medical/Executive	15.00
First-Line Supervisors of Office Workers	26.30	Security Guards	14.70
General and Operations Managers	71.00	Surgeons	135.60
Hairdressers/Cosmetologists	14.80	Teacher Assistants, Exc. Postsecondary*	12.30
Home Health and Personal Care Aides	13.70	Teachers, Secondary School, Exc. Sp. Ed.*	23.00
Janitors and Cleaners	14.00	Telemarketers	n/a
Landscaping/Groundskeeping Workers	16.00	Truck Drivers, Heavy/Tractor-Trailer	22.50
Lawyers	62.20	Truck Drivers, Light/Delivery Services	18.50
Maids and Housekeeping Cleaners	11.70	Waiters and Waitresses	10.60

Note: Wage data covers the Sioux Falls, SD Metropolitan Statistical Area; (*) Hourly wages were calculated from annual wage data based on a 40 hour work week; n/a not available.
Source: Bureau of Labor Statistics, Metro Area Occupational Employment & Wage Estimates, May 2020

Employment by Industry

Sector	MSA[1]		U.S.
	Number of Employees	Percent of Total	Percent of Total
Construction, Mining, and Logging	8,800	5.6	5.5
Education and Health Services	35,000	22.3	16.3
Financial Activities	15,600	9.9	6.1
Government	14,900	9.5	15.2
Information	2,400	1.5	1.9
Leisure and Hospitality	12,400	7.9	9.0
Manufacturing	14,200	9.0	8.5
Other Services	5,900	3.8	3.8
Professional and Business Services	14,900	9.5	14.4
Retail Trade	19,000	12.1	10.9
Transportation, Warehousing, and Utilities	5,700	3.6	4.6
Wholesale Trade	8,500	5.4	3.9

Note: Figures are non-farm employment as of December 2020. Figures are not seasonally adjusted and include workers 16 years of age and older; (1) Figures cover the Sioux Falls, SD Metropolitan Statistical Area
Source: Bureau of Labor Statistics, Current Employment Statistics, Employment, Hours, and Earnings

Employment by Occupation

Occupation Classification	City (%)	MSA[1] (%)	U.S. (%)
Management, Business, Science, and Arts	37.5	37.8	38.5
Natural Resources, Construction, and Maintenance	7.7	9.1	8.9
Production, Transportation, and Material Moving	14.8	14.0	13.2
Sales and Office	23.5	23.2	21.6
Service	16.5	15.9	17.8

Note: Figures cover employed civilians 16 years of age and older; (1) Figures cover the Sioux Falls, SD Metropolitan Statistical Area
Source: U.S. Census Bureau, 2015-2019 American Community Survey 5-Year Estimates

Occupations with Greatest Projected Employment Growth: 2020 – 2022

Occupation[1]	2020 Employment	2022 Projected Employment	Numeric Employment Change	Percent Employment Change
Combined Food Preparation and Serving Workers, Including Fast Food	6,610	8,870	2,260	34.2
Waiters and Waitresses	5,660	7,500	1,840	32.5
Retail Salespersons	13,300	15,060	1,760	13.2
Bartenders	2,520	3,420	900	35.7
Maids and Housekeeping Cleaners	4,230	5,080	850	20.1
Counter Attendants, Cafeteria, Food Concession, and Coffee Shop	3,150	3,860	710	22.5
Cashiers	11,290	11,960	670	5.9
Cooks, Restaurant	1,500	2,040	540	36.0
Hotel, Motel, and Resort Desk Clerks	1,260	1,800	540	42.9
Janitors and Cleaners, Except Maids and Housekeeping Cleaners	9,510	10,020	510	5.4

Note: Projections cover South Dakota; (1) Sorted by numeric employment change
Source: www.projectionscentral.com, State Occupational Projections, 2020–2022 Short-Term Projections

Fastest-Growing Occupations: 2020 – 2022

Occupation[1]	2020 Employment	2022 Projected Employment	Numeric Employment Change	Percent Employment Change
Hotel, Motel, and Resort Desk Clerks	1,260	1,800	540	42.9
Gaming Dealers	130	180	50	38.5
Cooks, Restaurant	1,500	2,040	540	36.0
Bartenders	2,520	3,420	900	35.7
Combined Food Preparation and Serving Workers, Including Fast Food	6,610	8,870	2,260	34.2
Waiters and Waitresses	5,660	7,500	1,840	32.5
Lodging Managers	230	300	70	30.4
Cooks, Fast Food	1,070	1,380	310	29.0
Cooks, Short Order	1,150	1,480	330	28.7
Dishwashers	1,540	1,970	430	27.9

Note: Projections cover South Dakota; (1) Sorted by percent employment change and excludes occupations with numeric employment change less than 50
Source: www.projectionscentral.com, State Occupational Projections, 2020–2022 Short-Term Projections

TAXES

State Corporate Income Tax Rates

State	Tax Rate (%)	Income Brackets ($)	Num. of Brackets	Financial Institution Tax Rate (%)[a]	Federal Income Tax Ded.
South Dakota	None	–	–	6.0-0.25 (b)	No

Note: Tax rates as of January 1, 2021; (a) Rates listed are the corporate income tax rate applied to financial institutions or excise taxes based on income. Some states have other taxes based upon the value of deposits or shares; (b) Minimum tax is $800 in California, $250 in District of Columbia, $50 in Arizona and North Dakota (banks), $400 ($100 banks) in Rhode Island, $200 per location in South Dakota (banks), $100 in Utah, $300 in Vermont.
Source: Federation of Tax Administrators, State Corporate Income Tax Rates, January 1, 2021

State Individual Income Tax Rates

State	Tax Rate (%)	Income Brackets ($)	Personal Exemptions ($)			Standard Ded. ($)	
			Single	Married	Depend.	Single	Married
South Dakota					– No state income tax –		

Note: Tax rates as of January 1, 2021; Local- and county-level taxes are not included
Source: Federation of Tax Administrators, State Individual Income Tax Rates, January 1, 2021

Various State Sales and Excise Tax Rates

State	State Sales Tax (%)	Gasoline[1] (¢/gal.)	Cigarette[2] ($/pack)	Spirits[3] ($/gal.)	Wine[4] ($/gal.)	Beer[5] ($/gal.)	Recreational Marijuana (%)
South Dakota	4.5	30	1.53	4.73	1.33	0.27	(m)

Note: All tax rates as of January 1, 2021; (1) The American Petroleum Institute has developed a methodology for determining the average tax rate on a gallon of fuel. Rates may include any of the following: excise taxes, environmental fees, storage tank fees, other fees or taxes, general sales tax, and local taxes; (2) The federal excise tax of $1.0066 per pack and local taxes are not included; (3) Rates are those applicable to off-premise sales of 40% alcohol by volume (a.b.v.) distilled spirits in 750ml containers. Local excise taxes are excluded; (4) Rates are those applicable to off-premise sales of 11% a.b.v. non-carbonated wine in 750ml containers; (5) Rates are those applicable to off-premise sales of 4.7% a.b.v. beer in 12 ounce containers; (m) 15% excise tax (retail price)
Source: Tax Foundation, 2021 Facts & Figures: How Does Your State Compare?

State Business Tax Climate Index Rankings

State	Overall Rank	Corporate Tax Rank	Individual Income Tax Rank	Sales Tax Rank	Property Tax Rank	Unemployment Insurance Tax Rank
South Dakota	2	1	1	33	20	42

Note: The index is a measure of how each state's tax laws affect economic performance. The lower the rank, the more favorable a state's tax system is for business. States without a given tax are given a ranking of 1. The scores/rankings for the District of Columbia do not affect other states. The 2021 index represents the tax climate as of July 1, 2020.
Source: Tax Foundation, State Business Tax Climate Index 2021

TRANSPORTATION

Means of Transportation to Work

Area	Car/Truck/Van		Public Transportation			Bicycle	Walked	Other Means	Worked at Home
	Drove Alone	Car-pooled	Bus	Subway	Railroad				
City	84.3	8.5	0.8	0.0	0.0	0.5	2.0	0.6	3.4
MSA[1]	84.3	8.1	0.5	0.0	0.0	0.4	2.1	0.6	4.1
U.S.	76.3	9.0	2.4	1.9	0.6	0.5	2.7	1.4	5.2

Note: Figures are percentages and cover workers 16 years of age and older; (1) Figures cover the Sioux Falls, SD Metropolitan Statistical Area
Source: U.S. Census Bureau, 2015-2019 American Community Survey 5-Year Estimates

Travel Time to Work

Area	Less Than 10 Minutes	10 to 19 Minutes	20 to 29 Minutes	30 to 44 Minutes	45 to 59 Minutes	60 to 89 Minutes	90 Minutes or More
City	16.1	52.3	22.4	5.4	1.4	1.3	1.1
MSA[1]	16.5	44.0	24.6	10.0	2.4	1.4	1.2
U.S.	12.2	28.4	20.8	20.8	8.3	6.4	2.9

Note: Note: Figures are percentages and include workers 16 years old and over; (1) Figures cover the Sioux Falls, SD Metropolitan Statistical Area
Source: U.S. Census Bureau, 2015-2019 American Community Survey 5-Year Estimates

Key Congestion Measures

Measure	1982	1992	2002	2012	2017
Annual Hours of Delay, Total (000)	n/a	n/a	n/a	n/a	3,274
Annual Hours of Delay, Per Auto Commuter	n/a	n/a	n/a	n/a	18
Annual Congestion Cost, Total (million $)	n/a	n/a	n/a	n/a	68
Annual Congestion Cost, Per Auto Commuter ($)	n/a	n/a	n/a	n/a	376

Note: n/a not available
Source: Texas A&M Transportation Institute, 2019 Urban Mobility Report

Freeway Travel Time Index

Measure	1982	1987	1992	1997	2002	2007	2012	2017
Urban Area Index[1]	n/a	n/a	n/a	n/a	n/a	n/a	n/a	1.06
Urban Area Rank[1,2]	n/a	n/a	n/a	n/a	n/a	n/a	n/a	n/a

Note: Freeway Travel Time Index—the ratio of travel time in the peak period to the travel time at free-flow conditions. For example, a value of 1.30 indicates a 20-minute free-flow trip takes 26 minutes in the peak (20 minutes x 1.30 = 26 minutes); (1) Covers the Sioux Falls SD urban area; (2) Rank is based on 101 larger urban areas (#1 = highest travel time index); n/a not available
Source: Texas A&M Transportation Institute, 2019 Urban Mobility Report

Public Transportation

Agency Name / Mode of Transportation	Vehicles Operated in Maximum Service[1]	Annual Unlinked Passenger Trips[2] (in thous.)	Annual Passenger Miles[3] (in thous.)
Sioux Falls Transit			
Bus (directly operated)	19	769.4	3,216.5
Demand Response (directly operated)	16	84.1	565.5

Note: (1) Number of revenue vehicles operated by the given mode and type of service to meet the annual maximum service requirement. This is the revenue vehicle count during the peak season of the year; on the week and day that maximum service is provided. Vehicles operated in maximum service (VOMS) exclude atypical days and one-time special events; (2) Number of passengers who boarded public transportation vehicles. Passengers are counted each time they board a vehicle no matter how many vehicles they use to travel from their origin to their destination. (3) Sum of the distances ridden by all passengers during the entire fiscal year.
Source: Federal Transit Administration, National Transit Database, 2019

Air Transportation

Airport Name and Code / Type of Service	Passenger Airlines[1]	Passenger Enplanements	Freight Carriers[2]	Freight (lbs)
Joe Foss Field (FSD)				
Domestic service (U.S. carriers - 2020)	18	293,271	9	38,612,504
International service (U.S. carriers - 2019)	1	28	3	14,325,639

Note: (1) Includes all U.S.-based major, minor and commuter airlines that carried at least one passenger during the year; (2) Includes all U.S.-based airlines and freight carriers that transported at least one pound of freight during the year.
Source: Bureau of Transportation Statistics, The Intermodal Transportation Database, Air Carriers: T-100 Domestic Market (U.S. Carriers), 2020; Bureau of Transportation Statistics, The Intermodal Transportation Database, Air Carriers: T-100 International Market (U.S. Carriers), 2019

BUSINESSES

Major Business Headquarters

Company Name	Industry	Rankings	
		Fortune[1]	Forbes[2]
No companies listed	-	-	-

Note: (1) Companies that produce a 10-K are ranked 1 to 500 based on 2019 revenue; (2) All private companies with at least $2 billion in annual revenue through the end of their most current fiscal year are ranked 1 to 219; companies listed are headquartered in the city; dashes indicate no ranking
Source: Fortune, "Fortune 500," June/July 2020; Forbes, "America's Largest Private Companies," 2020

458   Sioux Falls, South Dakota

Living Environment

COST OF LIVING

Cost of Living Index

Composite Index	Groceries	Housing	Utilities	Trans-portation	Health Care	Misc. Goods/ Services
n/a	n/a	n/a	n/a	n/a	n/a	n/a

Note: The Cost of Living Index measures regional differences in the cost of consumer goods and services, excluding taxes and non-consumer expenditures, for professional and managerial households in the top income quintile. It is based on more than 50,000 prices covering almost 60 different items for which prices are collected three times a year by chambers of commerce, economic development organizations or university applied economic centers in each participating urban area. The numbers shown should be read as a percentage above or below the national average of 100. For example, a value of 115.4 in the groceries column indicates that grocery prices are 15.4% higher than the national average. Small differences in the index numbers should not be interpreted as significant; n/a not available.
Source: The Council for Community and Economic Research, Cost of Living Index, 2020

Grocery Prices

Area[1]	T-Bone Steak ($/pound)	Frying Chicken ($/pound)	Whole Milk ($/half gal.)	Eggs ($/dozen)	Orange Juice ($/64 oz.)	Coffee ($/11.5 oz.)
City[2]	n/a	n/a	n/a	n/a	n/a	n/a
Avg.	11.78	1.39	2.05	1.47	3.57	4.34
Min.	8.03	0.94	1.03	0.74	2.94	3.02
Max.	15.86	2.65	4.31	3.77	5.44	8.69

*Note: (1) Values for the local area are compared with the average, minimum and maximum values for all 284 areas in the Cost of Living Index; (2) Figures cover the Sioux Falls SD urban area; n/a not available; **T-Bone Steak** (price per pound); **Frying Chicken** (price per pound, whole fryer); **Whole Milk** (half gallon carton); **Eggs** (price per dozen, Grade A, large); **Orange Juice** (64 oz. Tropicana or Florida Natural); **Coffee** (11.5 oz. can, vacuum-packed, Maxwell House, Hills Bros, or Folgers).*
Source: The Council for Community and Economic Research, Cost of Living Index, 2020

Housing and Utility Costs

Area[1]	New Home Price ($)	Apartment Rent ($/month)	All Electric ($/month)	Part Electric ($/month)	Other Energy ($/month)	Telephone ($/month)
City[2]	n/a	n/a	n/a	n/a	n/a	n/a
Avg.	368,594	1,168	170.86	100.47	65.28	184.30
Min.	190,567	502	91.58	31.42	26.08	169.60
Max.	2,227,806	4,738	470.38	280.31	280.06	206.50

*Note: (1) Values for the local area are compared with the average, minimum and maximum values for all 284 areas in the Cost of Living Index; (2) Figures cover the Sioux Falls SD urban area; n/a not available; **New Home Price** (2,400 sf living area, 8,000 sf lot, in urban area with full utilities); **Apartment Rent** (950 sf 2 bedroom/1.5 or 2 bath, unfurnished, excluding all utilities except water); **All Electric** (average monthly cost for an all-electric home); **Part Electric** (average monthly cost for a part-electric home); **Other Energy** (average monthly cost for natural gas, fuel oil, coal, wood, and any other forms of energy except electricity); **Telephone** (price includes the base monthly rate plus taxes and fees for three lines of mobile phone service).*
Source: The Council for Community and Economic Research, Cost of Living Index, 2020

Health Care, Transportation, and Other Costs

Area[1]	Doctor ($/visit)	Dentist ($/visit)	Optometrist ($/visit)	Gasoline ($/gallon)	Beauty Salon ($/visit)	Men's Shirt ($)
City[2]	n/a	n/a	n/a	n/a	n/a	n/a
Avg.	115.44	99.32	108.10	2.21	39.27	31.37
Min.	36.68	59.00	51.36	1.71	19.00	11.00
Max.	219.00	153.10	250.97	3.46	82.05	58.33

*Note: (1) Values for the local area are compared with the average, minimum and maximum values for all 284 areas in the Cost of Living Index; (2) Figures cover the Sioux Falls SD urban area; n/a not available; **Doctor** (general practitioners routine exam of an established patient); **Dentist** (adult teeth cleaning and periodic oral examination); **Optometrist** (full vision eye exam for established adult patient); **Gasoline** (one gallon regular unleaded, national brand, including all taxes, cash price at self-service pump if available); **Beauty Salon** (woman's shampoo, trim, and blow-dry); **Men's Shirt** (cotton/polyester dress shirt, pinpoint weave, long sleeves).*
Source: The Council for Community and Economic Research, Cost of Living Index, 2020

HOUSING

Homeownership Rate

Area	2012 (%)	2013 (%)	2014 (%)	2015 (%)	2016 (%)	2017 (%)	2018 (%)	2019 (%)	2020 (%)
MSA[1]	n/a	n/a	n/a	n/a	n/a	n/a	n/a	n/a	n/a
U.S.	65.4	65.1	64.5	63.7	63.4	63.9	64.4	64.6	66.6

Note: (1) Figures cover the Sioux Falls, SD Metropolitan Statistical Area; n/a not available
Source: U.S. Census Bureau, Housing Vacancies and Homeownership Annual Statistics: 2012-2020

House Price Index (HPI)

Area	National Ranking[2]	Quarterly Change (%)	One-Year Change (%)	Five-Year Change (%)	Since 1991Q1 (%)
MSA[1]	139	2.09	6.03	29.70	212.39
U.S.[3]	–	3.81	10.77	38.99	205.12

Note: The HPI is a weighted repeat sales index. It measures average price changes in repeat sales or refinancings on the same properties. This information is obtained by reviewing repeat mortgage transactions on single-family properties whose mortgages have been purchased or securitized by Fannie Mae or Freddie Mac since January 1975; (1) Figures cover the Sioux Falls, SD Metropolitan Statistical Area; (2) Rankings are based on annual percentage change for all metro areas containing at least 15,000 transactions over the last 10 years and ranges from 1 to 253; (3) figures based on a weighted average of Census Division estimates using a seasonally adjusted, purchase-only index; all figures are for the period ending December 31, 2020
Source: Federal Housing Finance Agency, Change in Metropolitan Area House Price Indexes, April 7, 2021

Median Single-Family Home Prices

Area	2018	2019	2020p	Percent Change 2019 to 2020
MSA[1]	209.3	221.4	236.3	6.7
U.S. Average	261.6	274.6	299.9	9.2

Note: Figures are median sales prices of existing single-family homes in thousands of dollars; (p) preliminary; (1) Figures cover the Sioux Falls, SD Metropolitan Statistical Area
Source: National Association of Realtors, Median Sales Price of Existing Single-Family Homes for Metropolitan Areas, 4th Quarter 2020

Qualifying Income Based on Median Sales Price of Existing Single-Family Homes

Area	With 5% Down ($)	With 10% Down ($)	With 20% Down ($)
MSA[1]	45,697	43,292	38,481
U.S. Average	59,266	56,147	49,908

Note: Figures are preliminary; Qualifying income is based on a mortgage rate of 2.81%. Monthly principal and interest payment is limited to 25% of income; (1) Figures cover the Sioux Falls, SD Metropolitan Statistical Area
Source: National Association of Realtors, Qualifying Income Based on Median Sales Price of Existing Single-Family Homes for Metropolitan Areas, 4th Quarter 2020

Home Value Distribution

Area	Under $50,000	$50,000 -$99,999	$100,000 -$149,999	$150,000 -$199,999	$200,000 -$299,999	$300,000 -$499,999	$500,000 -$999,999	$1,000,000 or more
City	5.5	6.6	17.7	24.4	27.0	14.4	3.8	0.7
MSA[1]	5.6	7.7	16.6	22.7	26.5	15.7	4.4	0.8
U.S.	6.9	12.0	13.3	14.0	19.6	19.3	11.4	3.4

Note: Figures are percentages and cover owner-occupied housing units; (1) Figures cover the Sioux Falls, SD Metropolitan Statistical Area
Source: U.S. Census Bureau, 2015-2019 American Community Survey 5-Year Estimates

Year Housing Structure Built

Area	2010 or Later	2000 -2009	1990 -1999	1980 -1989	1970 -1979	1960 -1969	1950 -1959	1940 -1949	Before 1940	Median Year
City	13.3	18.3	15.1	10.5	13.8	7.3	9.1	3.8	8.6	1987
MSA[1]	11.9	18.7	15.3	9.5	14.0	6.8	8.1	3.7	12.1	1986
U.S.	5.2	14.0	13.9	13.4	15.2	10.6	10.3	4.9	12.6	1978

Note: Figures are percentages except for Median Year; Note: (1) Figures cover the Sioux Falls, SD Metropolitan Statistical Area
Source: U.S. Census Bureau, 2015-2019 American Community Survey 5-Year Estimates

Gross Monthly Rent

Area	Under $500	$500 -$999	$1,000 -$1,499	$1,500 -$1,999	$2,000 -$2,499	$2,500 -$2,999	$3,000 and up	Median ($)
City	8.5	65.9	19.8	4.0	0.6	0.5	0.8	827
MSA[1]	9.4	64.4	20.0	4.4	0.7	0.4	0.8	829
U.S.	9.4	36.2	30.0	14.0	5.6	2.4	2.4	1,062

Note: Figures are percentages except for Median; Gross rent is the contract rent plus the estimated average monthly cost of utilities (electricity, gas, and water and sewer) and fuels (oil, coal, kerosene, wood, etc.) if these are paid by the renter (or paid for the renter by someone else); (1) Figures cover the Sioux Falls, SD Metropolitan Statistical Area
Source: U.S. Census Bureau, 2015-2019 American Community Survey 5-Year Estimates

HEALTH

Health Risk Factors

Category	MSA[1] (%)	U.S. (%)
Adults aged 18–64 who have any kind of health care coverage	83.5	87.3
Adults who reported being in good or better health	88.4	82.4
Adults who have been told they have high blood cholesterol	28.8	33.0
Adults who have been told they have high blood pressure	27.8	32.3
Adults who are current smokers	20.3	17.1
Adults who currently use E-cigarettes	n/a	4.6
Adults who currently use chewing tobacco, snuff, or snus	4.0	4.0
Adults who are heavy drinkers[2]	7.8	6.3
Adults who are binge drinkers[3]	19.4	17.4
Adults who are overweight (BMI 25.0 - 29.9)	35.5	35.3
Adults who are obese (BMI 30.0 - 99.8)	29.1	31.3
Adults who participated in any physical activities in the past month	75.1	74.4
Adults who always or nearly always wears a seat belt	88.1	94.3

Note: n/a not available; (1) Figures cover the Sioux Falls, SD Metropolitan Statistical Area; (2) Heavy drinkers are classified as adult men having more than 14 drinks per week and adult women having more than 7 drinks per week; (3) Binge drinkers are classified as males having five or more drinks on one occasion or females having four or more drinks on one occasion
Source: Centers for Disease Control and Prevention, Behaviorial Risk Factor Surveillance System, SMART: Selected Metropolitan Area Risk Trends, 2017

Acute and Chronic Health Conditions

Category	MSA[1] (%)	U.S. (%)
Adults who have ever been told they had a heart attack	5.0	4.2
Adults who have ever been told they have angina or coronary heart disease	4.7	3.9
Adults who have ever been told they had a stroke	2.0	3.0
Adults who have ever been told they have asthma	9.5	14.2
Adults who have ever been told they have arthritis	19.7	24.9
Adults who have ever been told they have diabetes[2]	8.8	10.5
Adults who have ever been told they had skin cancer	3.2	6.2
Adults who have ever been told they had any other types of cancer	6.4	7.1
Adults who have ever been told they have COPD	4.4	6.5
Adults who have ever been told they have kidney disease	1.6	3.0
Adults who have ever been told they have a form of depression	18.0	20.5

Note: (1) Figures cover the Sioux Falls, SD Metropolitan Statistical Area; (2) Figures do not include pregnancy-related, borderline, or pre-diabetes
Source: Centers for Disease Control and Prevention, Behaviorial Risk Factor Surveillance System, SMART: Selected Metropolitan Area Risk Trends, 2017

Health Screening and Vaccination Rates

Category	MSA[1] (%)	U.S. (%)
Adults aged 65+ who have had flu shot within the past year	69.1	60.7
Adults aged 65+ who have ever had a pneumonia vaccination	77.7	75.4
Adults who have ever been tested for HIV	29.3	36.1
Adults who have ever had the shingles or zoster vaccine?	41.7	28.9
Adults who have had their blood cholesterol checked within the last five years	79.3	85.9

Note: n/a not available; (1) Figures cover the Sioux Falls, SD Metropolitan Statistical Area.
Source: Centers for Disease Control and Prevention, Behaviorial Risk Factor Surveillance System, SMART: Selected Metropolitan Area Risk Trends, 2017

Disability Status

Category	MSA[1] (%)	U.S. (%)
Adults who reported being deaf	6.9	6.7
Are you blind or have serious difficulty seeing, even when wearing glasses?	n/a	4.5
Are you limited in any way in any of your usual activities due of arthritis?	8.8	12.9
Do you have difficulty doing errands alone?	6.0	6.8
Do you have difficulty dressing or bathing?	3.1	3.6
Do you have serious difficulty concentrating/remembering/making decisions?	8.5	10.7
Do you have serious difficulty walking or climbing stairs?	8.4	13.6

Note: n/a not available; (1) Figures cover the Sioux Falls, SD Metropolitan Statistical Area.
Source: Centers for Disease Control and Prevention, Behaviorial Risk Factor Surveillance System, SMART: Selected Metropolitan Area Risk Trends, 2017

Mortality Rates for the Top 10 Causes of Death in the U.S.

ICD-10[a] Sub-Chapter	ICD-10[a] Code	Age-Adjusted Mortality Rate[1] per 100,000 population	
		County[2]	U.S.
Malignant neoplasms	C00-C97	175.7	149.2
Ischaemic heart diseases	I20-I25	98.4	90.5
Other forms of heart disease	I30-I51	34.0	52.2
Chronic lower respiratory diseases	J40-J47	43.7	39.6
Other degenerative diseases of the nervous system	G30-G31	54.3	37.6
Cerebrovascular diseases	I60-I69	35.3	37.2
Other external causes of accidental injury	W00-X59	38.1	36.1
Organic, including symptomatic, mental disorders	F01-F09	18.0	29.4
Hypertensive diseases	I10-I15	39.3	24.1
Diabetes mellitus	E10-E14	17.0	21.5

Note: (a) ICD-10 = International Classification of Diseases 10th Revision; (1) Mortality rates are a three-year average covering 2017-2019; (2) Figures cover Minnehaha County.
Source: Centers for Disease Control and Prevention, National Center for Health Statistics. Underlying Cause of Death 1999-2019 on CDC WONDER Online Database

Mortality Rates for Selected Causes of Death

ICD-10[a] Sub-Chapter	ICD-10[a] Code	Age-Adjusted Mortality Rate[1] per 100,000 population	
		County[2]	U.S.
Assault	X85-Y09	Unreliable	6.0
Diseases of the liver	K70-K76	17.0	14.4
Human immunodeficiency virus (HIV) disease	B20-B24	Suppressed	1.5
Influenza and pneumonia	J09-J18	16.2	13.8
Intentional self-harm	X60-X84	20.4	14.1
Malnutrition	E40-E46	8.3	2.3
Obesity and other hyperalimentation	E65-E68	Suppressed	2.1
Renal failure	N17-N19	5.1	12.6
Transport accidents	V01-V99	10.1	12.3
Viral hepatitis	B15-B19	Suppressed	1.2

Note: (a) ICD-10 = International Classification of Diseases 10th Revision; (1) Mortality rates are a three-year average covering 2017-2019; (2) Figures cover Minnehaha County; Data are suppressed when the data meet the criteria for confidentiality constraints; Mortality rates are flagged as unreliable when the rate would be calculated with a numerator of 20 or less.
Source: Centers for Disease Control and Prevention, National Center for Health Statistics. Underlying Cause of Death 1999-2019 on CDC WONDER Online Database

Health Insurance Coverage

Area	With Health Insurance	With Private Health Insurance	With Public Health Insurance	Without Health Insurance	Population Under Age 19 Without Health Insurance
City	92.2	77.2	26.5	7.8	4.9
MSA[1]	92.8	78.9	25.1	7.2	4.5
U.S.	91.2	67.9	35.1	8.8	5.1

Note: Figures are percentages that cover the civilian noninstitutionalized population; (1) Figures cover the Sioux Falls, SD Metropolitan Statistical Area
Source: U.S. Census Bureau, 2015-2019 American Community Survey 5-Year Estimates

Number of Medical Professionals

Area	MDs[3]	DOs[3,4]	Dentists	Podiatrists	Chiropractors	Optometrists
County[1] (number)	692	49	107	12	112	37
County[1] (rate[2])	362.3	25.7	55.4	6.2	58.0	19.2
U.S. (rate[2])	282.9	22.7	71.2	6.2	28.1	16.9

46099
Note: Data as of 2019 unless noted; (1) Data covers Minnehaha County; (2) Rate per 100,000 population; (3) Data as of 2018 and includes all active, non-federal physicians; (4) Doctor of Osteopathic Medicine
Source: U.S. Department of Health and Human Services, Health Resources and Services Administration, Bureau of Health Professions, Area Resource File (ARF) 2019-2020

Best Hospitals

According to *U.S. News,* the Sioux Falls, SD metro area is home to one of the best hospitals in the U.S.: **Avera McKennan Hospital and University Health Center** (2 adult specialties). The hospital listed was nationally ranked in at least one of 16 adult or 10 pediatric specialties. Only 134 hospitals nationwide were nationally ranked in one or more adult or pediatric specialty; this number increases to 178 counting specialized centers within hospitals. Twenty hospitals in the U.S. made the Honor Roll. The Best Hospitals Honor Roll takes both the national rankings and the procedure and condition ratings into account. Hospitals received points if they were nationally ranked in one of the 16 adult specialties—the higher they ranked, the more points they got—and how many ratings of "high performing" they earned in the 10 procedures and conditions. *U.S. News Online, "America's Best Hospitals 2020-21"*

EDUCATION

Public School District Statistics

District Name	Schls	Pupils	Pupil/ Teacher Ratio	Minority Pupils[1] (%)	Free Lunch Eligible[2] (%)	IEP[3] (%)
Sioux Falls School District 49-5	43	25,018	15.8	38.5	36.9	15.9

Note: Table includes school districts with 2,000 or more students; (1) Percentage of students that are not non-Hispanic white; (2) Percentage of students that are eligible for the free lunch program; (3) Percentage of students that have an Individualized Education Program.
Source: U.S. Department of Education, National Center for Education Statistics, Common Core of Data, Local Education Agency (School District) Universe Survey: School Year 2018-2019; U.S. Department of Education, National Center for Education Statistics, Common Core of Data, Public Elementary/Secondary School Universe Survey: School Year 2018-2019

Highest Level of Education

Area	Less than H.S.	H.S. Diploma	Some College, No Deg.	Associate Degree	Bachelor's Degree	Master's Degree	Prof. School Degree	Doctorate Degree
City	7.7	24.8	20.8	11.5	23.8	8.1	2.2	1.1
MSA[1]	7.1	26.1	20.6	12.7	23.2	7.3	2.0	1.0
U.S.	12.0	27.0	20.4	8.5	19.8	8.8	2.1	1.4

Note: Figures cover persons age 25 and over; (1) Figures cover the Sioux Falls, SD Metropolitan Statistical Area
Source: U.S. Census Bureau, 2015-2019 American Community Survey 5-Year Estimates

Educational Attainment by Race

Area	High School Graduate or Higher (%)					Bachelor's Degree or Higher (%)				
	Total	White	Black	Asian	Hisp.[2]	Total	White	Black	Asian	Hisp.[2]
City	92.3	94.7	74.7	70.8	65.3	35.2	37.6	14.3	36.4	14.3
MSA[1]	92.9	94.5	75.5	72.1	66.9	33.5	35.0	14.4	37.1	15.6
U.S.	88.0	89.9	86.0	87.1	68.7	32.1	33.5	21.6	54.3	16.4

Note: Figures shown cover persons 25 years old and over; (1) Figures cover the Sioux Falls, SD Metropolitan Statistical Area; (2) People of Hispanic origin can be of any race
Source: U.S. Census Bureau, 2015-2019 American Community Survey 5-Year Estimates

School Enrollment by Grade and Control

Area	Preschool (%)		Kindergarten (%)		Grades 1 - 4 (%)		Grades 5 - 8 (%)		Grades 9 - 12 (%)	
	Public	Private	Public	Private	Public	Private	Public	Private	Public	Private
City	51.1	48.9	87.3	12.7	88.2	11.8	87.5	12.5	84.2	15.8
MSA[1]	53.6	46.4	88.3	11.7	88.4	11.6	89.2	10.8	86.8	13.2
U.S.	59.1	40.9	87.6	12.4	89.5	10.5	89.4	10.6	90.1	9.9

Note: Figures shown cover persons 3 years old and over; (1) Figures cover the Sioux Falls, SD Metropolitan Statistical Area
Source: U.S. Census Bureau, 2015-2019 American Community Survey 5-Year Estimates

Higher Education

Four-Year Colleges			Two-Year Colleges			Medical Schools[1]	Law Schools[2]	Voc/ Tech[3]
Public	Private Non-profit	Private For-profit	Public	Private Non-profit	Private For-profit			
0	3	1	1	2	0	1	0	1

Note: Figures cover institutions located within the city limits and include main campuses only; (1) includes schools accredited by the Liaison Committee on Medical Education and the American Osteopathic Association's Commission on Osteopathic College Accreditation; (2) includes ABA-accredited schools, schools with provisional ABA accreditation, and state accredited schools; (3) includes all schools with programs that are less than 2 years.
Source: National Center for Education Statistics, Integrated Postsecondary Education System (IPEDS), 2019-20; Wikipedia, List of Medical Schools in the United States, accessed April 2, 2021; Wikipedia, List of Law Schools in the United States, accessed April 2, 2021

Sioux Falls, South Dakota 463

EMPLOYERS

Major Employers

Company Name	Industry
Avera Health	Health care
Billion Automotive	Auto dealership
Capital One	Financial/credit card processing
CIGNA	Mail order pharmacy
Citi	Credit card processing
City of Sioux Falls	Municipal government
Department of Veterans Affairs	Government medical facilities
Esurance	Insurance service center
Evangelical Lutheran Good Samaritan	Health care
First Premier Bank/Premier Bankcard	Financial/credit card processing
Hy-Vee Food Stores	Retail grocery
John Morrell & Co.	Meat processing
Lewis Drug	Retail pharmacy
LifeScape	Health care
Midcontinent Communications	Telecommunications/cable services
Minnehaha County	Government
Raven Industries	Manufacturing
Sammons Financial Group/Midland National	Insurance
Sanford Health	Health care
Sioux Falls School District 49-5	Education
StarMark Cabinetry	Manufacturing
United States Postal Service	U.S. postal service
USGS EROS Data Center/SGT	Satellite info processing
Wal-Mart and Sam's Club	Retail & wholesale
Wells Fargo	Financial/credit card/student loans

Note: Companies shown are located within the Sioux Falls, SD Metropolitan Statistical Area.
Source: Hoovers.com; Wikipedia

PUBLIC SAFETY

Crime Rate

Area	All Crimes	Violent Crimes				Property Crimes		
		Murder	Rape[3]	Robbery	Aggrav. Assault	Burglary	Larceny -Theft	Motor Vehicle Theft
City	3,528.6	2.2	62.5	36.6	381.9	374.4	2,316.5	354.5
Suburbs[1]	1,221.6	1.2	42.1	3.6	128.8	358.7	568.1	119.2
Metro[2]	2,815.3	1.9	56.2	26.4	303.7	369.5	1,775.9	281.7
U.S.	2,489.3	5.0	42.6	81.6	250.2	340.5	1,549.5	219.9

Note: Figures are crimes per 100,000 population; (1) All areas within the metro area that are located outside the city limits; (2) Figures cover the Sioux Falls, SD Metropolitan Statistical Area; (3) All figures shown were reported using the revised Uniform Crime Reporting (UCR) definition of rape.
Source: FBI Uniform Crime Reports, 2019

Hate Crimes

Area	Number of Quarters Reported	Number of Incidents per Bias Motivation					
		Race/Ethnicity/ Ancestry	Religion	Sexual Orientation	Disability	Gender	Gender Identity
City	4	3	2	2	0	0	0
U.S.	4	3,963	1,521	1,195	157	69	198

Source: Federal Bureau of Investigation, Hate Crime Statistics 2019

Identity Theft Consumer Reports

Area	Reports	Reports per 100,000 Population	Rank[2]
MSA[1]	239	89	378
U.S.	1,387,615	423	-

Note: (1) Figures cover the Sioux Falls, SD Metropolitan Statistical Area; (2) Rank ranges from 1 to 391 where 1 indicates greatest number of identity theft reports per 100,000 population
Source: Federal Trade Commission, Consumer Sentinel Network Data Book 2020

Fraud and Other Consumer Reports

Area	Reports	Reports per 100,000 Population	Rank[2]
MSA[1]	1,375	513	357
U.S.	3,385,133	1,031	-

Note: (1) Figures cover the Sioux Falls, SD Metropolitan Statistical Area; (2) Rank ranges from 1 to 391 where 1 indicates greatest number of fraud and other consumer reports per 100,000 population
Source: Federal Trade Commission, Consumer Sentinel Network Data Book 2020

464   Sioux Falls, South Dakota

POLITICS

2020 Presidential Election Results

Area	Biden	Trump	Jorgensen	Hawkins	Other
Minnehaha County	43.8	53.3	2.8	0.0	0.0
U.S.	51.3	46.8	1.2	0.3	0.5

Note: Results are percentages and may not add to 100% due to rounding
Source: Dave Leip's Atlas of U.S. Presidential Elections

SPORTS

Professional Sports Teams

Team Name	League	Year Established
No teams are located in the metro area		

Source: Wikipedia, Major Professional Sports Teams of the United States and Canada, April 6, 2021

CLIMATE

Average and Extreme Temperatures

Temperature	Jan	Feb	Mar	Apr	May	Jun	Jul	Aug	Sep	Oct	Nov	Dec	Yr.
Extreme High (°F)	66	70	88	94	104	110	110	109	104	94	76	62	110
Average High (°F)	25	30	41	59	71	80	86	84	74	62	43	29	57
Average Temp. (°F)	15	20	32	47	59	69	75	72	62	50	33	20	46
Average Low (°F)	5	10	22	35	47	57	62	60	49	38	23	10	35
Extreme Low (°F)	-36	-31	-23	4	17	33	38	34	22	9	-17	-28	-36

Note: Figures cover the years 1932-1990
Source: National Climatic Data Center, International Station Meteorological Climate Summary, 9/96

Average Precipitation/Snowfall/Humidity

Precip./Humidity	Jan	Feb	Mar	Apr	May	Jun	Jul	Aug	Sep	Oct	Nov	Dec	Yr.
Avg. Precip. (in.)	0.6	0.8	1.6	2.4	3.3	3.9	2.8	3.2	2.8	1.5	1.0	0.7	24.6
Avg. Snowfall (in.)	7	8	9	2	Tr	0	0	0	Tr	Tr	5	7	38
Avg. Rel. Hum. 6am (%)	n/a	n/a	n/a	n/a	n/a	n/a	n/a	n/a	n/a	n/a	n/a	n/a	n/a
Avg. Rel. Hum. 3pm (%)	n/a	n/a	n/a	n/a	n/a	n/a	n/a	n/a	n/a	n/a	n/a	n/a	n/a

Note: Figures cover the years 1932-1990; Tr = Trace amounts (<0.05 in. of rain; <0.5 in. of snow)
Source: National Climatic Data Center, International Station Meteorological Climate Summary, 9/96

Weather Conditions

Temperature			Daytime Sky			Precipitation		
5°F & below	32°F & below	90°F & above	Clear	Partly cloudy	Cloudy	0.01 inch or more precip.	0.1 inch or more snow/ice	Thunder-storms
n/a	n/a	n/a	95	136	134	n/a	n/a	n/a

Note: Figures are average number of days per year and cover the years 1932-1990
Source: National Climatic Data Center, International Station Meteorological Climate Summary, 9/96

HAZARDOUS WASTE

Superfund Sites

The Sioux Falls, SD metro area has no sites on the EPA's Superfund Final National Priorities List. There are a total of 1,375 Superfund sites with a status of proposed or final on the list in the U.S. *U.S. Environmental Protection Agency, National Priorities List, April 7, 2021*

AIR QUALITY

Air Quality Trends: Ozone

	1990	1995	2000	2005	2010	2015	2016	2017	2018	2019
MSA[1]	n/a	n/a	n/a	n/a	n/a	n/a	n/a	n/a	n/a	n/a
U.S.	0.088	0.089	0.082	0.080	0.073	0.068	0.069	0.068	0.069	0.065

Note: (1) Data covers the Sioux Falls, SD Metropolitan Statistical Area; n/a not available. The values shown are the composite ozone concentration averages among trend sites based on the highest fourth daily maximum 8-hour concentration in parts per million. These trends are based on sites having an adequate record of monitoring data during the trend period. Data from exceptional events are included.
Source: U.S. Environmental Protection Agency, Air Quality Monitoring Information, "Air Quality Trends by City, 1990-2019"

Sioux Falls, South Dakota   465

Air Quality Index

Area	Percent of Days when Air Quality was...[2]					AQI Statistics[2]	
	Good	Moderate	Unhealthy for Sensitive Groups	Unhealthy	Very Unhealthy	Maximum	Median
MSA[1]	87.9	11.8	0.3	0.0	0.0	105	36

Note: (1) Data covers the Sioux Falls, SD Metropolitan Statistical Area; (2) Based on 365 days with AQI data in 2019. Air Quality Index (AQI) is an index for reporting daily air quality. EPA calculates the AQI for five major air pollutants regulated by the Clean Air Act: ground-level ozone, particle pollution (aka particulate matter), carbon monoxide, sulfur dioxide, and nitrogen dioxide. The AQI runs from 0 to 500. The higher the AQI value, the greater the level of air pollution and the greater the health concern. There are six AQI categories: "Good" AQI is between 0 and 50. Air quality is considered satisfactory; "Moderate" AQI is between 51 and 100. Air quality is acceptable; "Unhealthy for Sensitive Groups" When AQI values are between 101 and 150, members of sensitive groups may experience health effects; "Unhealthy" When AQI values are between 151 and 200 everyone may begin to experience health effects; "Very Unhealthy" AQI values between 201 and 300 trigger a health alert; "Hazardous" AQI values over 300 trigger warnings of emergency conditions (not shown).
Source: U.S. Environmental Protection Agency, Air Quality Index Report, 2019

Air Quality Index Pollutants

Area	Percent of Days when AQI Pollutant was...[2]					
	Carbon Monoxide	Nitrogen Dioxide	Ozone	Sulfur Dioxide	Particulate Matter 2.5	Particulate Matter 10
MSA[1]	0.0	2.5	84.1	0.0	12.9	0.5

Note: (1) Data covers the Sioux Falls, SD Metropolitan Statistical Area; (2) Based on 365 days with AQI data in 2019. The Air Quality Index (AQI) is an index for reporting daily air quality. EPA calculates the AQI for five major air pollutants regulated by the Clean Air Act: ground-level ozone, particle pollution (also known as particulate matter), carbon monoxide, sulfur dioxide, and nitrogen dioxide. The AQI runs from 0 to 500. The higher the AQI value, the greater the level of air pollution and the greater the health concern.
Source: U.S. Environmental Protection Agency, Air Quality Index Report, 2019

Maximum Air Pollutant Concentrations: Particulate Matter, Ozone, CO and Lead

	Particulate Matter 10 (ug/m^3)	Particulate Matter 2.5 Wtd AM (ug/m^3)	Particulate Matter 2.5 24-Hr (ug/m^3)	Ozone (ppm)	Carbon Monoxide (ppm)	Lead (ug/m^3)
MSA[1] Level	37	3.9	16	0.065	1	n/a
NAAQS[2]	150	15	35	0.075	9	0.15
Met NAAQS[2]	Yes	Yes	Yes	Yes	Yes	n/a

Note: (1) Data covers the Sioux Falls, SD Metropolitan Statistical Area; Data from exceptional events are included; (2) National Ambient Air Quality Standards; ppm = parts per million; ug/m^3 = micrograms per cubic meter; n/a not available.
Concentrations: Particulate Matter 10 (coarse particulate)—highest second maximum 24-hour concentration; Particulate Matter 2.5 Wtd AM (fine particulate)—highest weighted annual mean concentration; Particulate Matter 2.5 24-Hour (fine particulate)—highest 98th percentile 24-hour concentration; Ozone—highest fourth daily maximum 8-hour concentration; Carbon Monoxide—highest second maximum non-overlapping 8-hour concentration; Lead—maximum running 3-month average
Source: U.S. Environmental Protection Agency, Air Quality Monitoring Information, "Air Quality Statistics by City, 2019"

Maximum Air Pollutant Concentrations: Nitrogen Dioxide and Sulfur Dioxide

	Nitrogen Dioxide AM (ppb)	Nitrogen Dioxide 1-Hr (ppb)	Sulfur Dioxide AM (ppb)	Sulfur Dioxide 1-Hr (ppb)	Sulfur Dioxide 24-Hr (ppb)
MSA[1] Level	5	31	n/a	2	n/a
NAAQS[2]	53	100	30	75	140
Met NAAQS[2]	Yes	Yes	n/a	Yes	n/a

Note: (1) Data covers the Sioux Falls, SD Metropolitan Statistical Area; Data from exceptional events are included; (2) National Ambient Air Quality Standards; ppm = parts per million; ug/m^3 = micrograms per cubic meter; n/a not available.
Concentrations: Nitrogen Dioxide AM—highest arithmetic mean concentration; Nitrogen Dioxide 1-Hr—highest 98th percentile 1-hour daily maximum concentration; Sulfur Dioxide AM—highest annual mean concentration; Sulfur Dioxide 1-Hr—highest 99th percentile 1-hour daily maximum concentration; Sulfur Dioxide 24-Hr—highest second maximum 24-hour concentration
Source: U.S. Environmental Protection Agency, Air Quality Monitoring Information, "Air Quality Statistics by City, 2019"

Springfield, Illinois

Background

Springfield, Illinois is located the Midwest region of the United States. In the early 1800s, hunter and sugar maker Robert Pullman traveled with a small team to unexplored areas north of his home and discovered Sugar Creek, with an abundance of sugar maple trees and rich soil. He built a cabin in the area in October 1817 and became its first European settler, returning to his home in southern Illinois the following spring with the maple sugar and furs he had harvested. After Illinois entered the Union in 1818, Elisha Kelly from North Carolina discovered the Sugar Creek area and relocated his family and some friends there. They named the area Calhoun in honor of Senator John C. Calhoun of South Carolina. Another influential settler was businessman Elijah Iles who, in 1821, relocated his family there from Missouri. Iles opened the first general store. Calhoun was renamed Springfield in 1832 after Springfield, Massachusetts, a thriving town that Iles aspired to.

Abraham Lincoln, although known as Springfield, Illinois's most prominent citizen, was actually born in Hodgenville, Kentucky in 1809. He moved to the Springfield area in 1831, and into the city itself in 1837 where he practiced law and politics. Lincoln's famous farewell speech, and one of his earliest published speeches, his Lyceum address, was delivered in Springfield in January of 1838. In 1839, Springfield became the capital of Illinois due to Lincoln's efforts. In 1852, Springfield connected with the railroad system which led to its economic expansion. After Lincoln became President of the United States in 1861, Springfield became a solider training area for the Civil War, and Confederate prisoner camp. By 1900 Springfield emerged as a major player in the coal and farming industries, and a hub for the Illinois railroad.

Another celebrity resident of Springfield is architect Frank Lloyd Wright, who built the Dana Thomas House for the silver mine heiress Susan Lawrence Dana in 1902. Actually a "remodel" of Dana's Victorian mansion, this 12,000 square foot, 35-room house is the best preserved example of Lloyd's "Prairie" houses. The Dana Thomas House has the largest known collection of Wright's site-specific furniture and glass art throughout its 16 levels. It has been thoroughly renovated and is currently a museum. Other famous Springfield residents include Olympian swimmers Michael Phelps and Ryan Held, and professional athletes and authors, including Vachel Lindsay, Edgar Lee Masters, John Hay, Virginia Eiffert and Robert Fitzgerald.

> A memorial to the more than 20,000 Illinoisans who have died from COVID-19 in the past year was erected on the north lawn of the Governor's mansion in Springfield, IL.

Springfield is an American history buff's dream for all things Lincoln. The city houses Lincoln's home and law office, which are open to the public and listed as National Historic sites. The Abraham Lincoln Presidential Library and Museum, built in 2005, houses the original Gettysburg Address and the largest collection of Lincoln biographical works. The nearby Capitol Building is not only where Lincoln served in the House of Representatives, but also where mourners passed his body as it laid in state in 1865. Just a short walk from the Capitol is Oak Ridge Cemetery where Lincoln and his immediate family are buried at Lincoln's Tomb. More recently, former President Obama announced both his candidacy for the presidency and his choice for running mate Joe Biden at the State Capitol building in Springfield.

Two popular annual events hosted by the city are the Old Capitol Art Fair and the Route 66 Film Festival. Springfield is home to the Hoogland Center for the Arts, Springfield Theatre Center, Springfield Ballet Company, Illinois Symphony Orchestra and the Springfield Municipal Opera. And, the Illinois state legislature adopted a resolution proclaiming Springfield the "Chili Capital of the Civilized World."

Springfield has a humid, continental climate and was hit by two tornadoes in 2006.

Rankings

Business/Finance Rankings

- The Springfield metro area appeared on the Milken Institute "2021 Best Performing Cities" list. Rank: #107 out of 201 small metro areas (population over 60,000). Criteria: job growth; wage and salary growth; high-tech output growth; housing affordability; household broadband access. *Milken Institute, "Best-Performing Cities 2021," February 16, 2021*

- *Forbes* ranked 203 smaller metro areas (population under 268,000) to determine the nation's "Best Small Places for Business and Careers." The Springfield metro area was ranked #34. Criteria: costs (business and living); job growth (past and projected); income growth; quality of life; educational attainment (college and high school); projected economic growth; cultural and leisure opportunities; workplace tolerance laws; net migration patterns. *Forbes, "The Best Small Places for Business and Careers 2019," October 30, 2019*

Environmental Rankings

- Springfield was highlighted as one of the top 98 cleanest metro areas for short-term particle pollution (24-hour PM 2.5) in the U.S. during 2016 through 2018. Monitors in these cities reported no days with unhealthful PM 2.5 levels. *American Lung Association, "State of the Air 2020," April 21, 2020*

Real Estate Rankings

- The Springfield metro area was identified as one of the 20 worst housing markets in the U.S. in 2020. The area ranked #177 out of 180 markets. Criteria: year-over-year change of median sales price of existing single-family homes between the 4th quarter of 2019 and the 4th quarter of 2020. *National Association of Realtors®, Median Sales Price of Existing Single-Family Homes for Metropolitan Areas, 4th Quarter 2020*

- The Springfield metro area was identified as one of the 20 most affordable housing markets in the U.S. in 2020. The area ranked #9 out of 183 markets. Criteria: qualification for a mortgage loan with a 10 percent down payment on a typical home. *National Association of Realtors®, Qualifying Income Based on Sales Price of Existing Single-Family Homes for Metropolitan Areas, 2020*

- Springfield was ranked #16 out of 268 metro areas in terms of housing affordability in 2020 by the National Association of Home Builders (#1 = most affordable). Criteria: the share of homes sold in that area affordable to a family earning the local median income, based on standard mortgage underwriting criteria. *National Association of Home Builders®, NAHB-Wells Fargo Housing Opportunity Index, 4th Quarter 2020*

Safety Rankings

- The National Insurance Crime Bureau ranked 384 metro areas in the U.S. in terms of per capita rates of vehicle theft. The Springfield metro area ranked #83 (#1 = highest rate). Criteria: number of vehicle theft offenses per 100,000 inhabitants in 2019. *National Insurance Crime Bureau, "Hot Spots 2019," July 21, 2020*

Seniors/Retirement Rankings

- From its Best Cities for Successful Aging indexes, the Milken Institute generated rankings for metropolitan areas, weighing data in nine categories—health care, wellness, living arrangements, transportation and convenience, financial characteristics, education, employment, community engagement, and overall livability. The Springfield metro area was ranked #92 overall in the small metro area category. *Milken Institute, "Best Cities for Successful Aging, 2017" March 14, 2017*

Business Environment

DEMOGRAPHICS

Population Growth

Area	1990 Census	2000 Census	2010 Census	2019* Estimate	Population Growth (%)	
					1990-2019	2010-2019
City	108,997	111,454	116,250	115,888	6.3	-0.3
MSA[1]	189,550	201,437	210,170	209,167	10.3	-0.5
U.S.	248,709,873	281,421,906	308,745,538	324,697,795	30.6	5.2

Note: (1) Figures cover the Springfield, IL Metropolitan Statistical Area; (*) 2015-2019 5-year estimated population
Source: U.S. Census Bureau, 1990 Census, Census 2000, Census 2010, 2015-2019 American Community Survey 5-Year Estimates

Household Size

Area	Persons in Household (%)							Average Household Size
	One	Two	Three	Four	Five	Six	Seven or More	
City	38.0	34.1	13.3	8.8	3.2	1.5	1.1	2.20
MSA[1]	33.0	35.7	14.0	10.6	4.2	1.6	0.8	2.30
U.S.	27.9	33.9	15.6	12.9	6.0	2.3	1.4	2.60

Note: (1) Figures cover the Springfield, IL Metropolitan Statistical Area
Source: U.S. Census Bureau, 2015-2019 American Community Survey 5-Year Estimates

Race

Area	White Alone[2] (%)	Black Alone[2] (%)	Asian Alone[2] (%)	AIAN[3] Alone[2] (%)	NHOPI[4] Alone[2] (%)	Other Race Alone[2] (%)	Two or More Races (%)
City	72.9	19.9	3.1	0.1	0.0	0.5	3.5
MSA[1]	82.8	12.1	1.9	0.1	0.1	0.4	2.6
U.S.	72.5	12.7	5.5	0.8	0.2	4.9	3.3

Note: (1) Figures cover the Springfield, IL Metropolitan Statistical Area; (2) Alone is defined as not being in combination with one or more other races; (3) American Indian and Alaska Native; (4) Native Hawaiian and Other Pacific Islander
Source: U.S. Census Bureau, 2015-2019 American Community Survey 5-Year Estimates

Hispanic or Latino Origin

Area	Total (%)	Mexican (%)	Puerto Rican (%)	Cuban (%)	Other (%)
City	2.8	1.5	0.5	0.1	0.7
MSA[1]	2.3	1.3	0.4	0.1	0.5
U.S.	18.0	11.2	1.7	0.7	4.3

Note: Persons of Hispanic or Latino origin can be of any race; (1) Figures cover the Springfield, IL Metropolitan Statistical Area
Source: U.S. Census Bureau, 2015-2019 American Community Survey 5-Year Estimates

Ancestry

Area	German	Irish	English	American	Italian	Polish	French[2]	Scottish	Dutch
City	20.1	12.8	9.0	4.8	4.7	2.1	2.3	1.7	1.2
MSA[1]	23.5	13.6	10.0	5.6	5.0	2.0	2.4	1.9	1.4
U.S.	13.3	9.7	7.2	6.2	5.1	2.8	2.3	1.7	1.2

Note: Figures are the percentage of the total population reporting a particular ancestry. The nine most commonly reported ancestries in the U.S. are shown. Figures include multiple ancestries (e.g. if a person reported being Irish and Italian, they were included in both columns); (1) Figures cover the Springfield, IL Metropolitan Statistical Area; (2) Excludes Basque
Source: U.S. Census Bureau, 2015-2019 American Community Survey 5-Year Estimates

Foreign-born Population

Area	Percent of Population Born in								
	Any Foreign Country	Asia	Mexico	Europe	Caribbean	Central America[2]	South America	Africa	Canada
City	4.5	2.5	0.4	0.5	0.2	0.1	0.2	0.5	0.1
MSA[1]	3.1	1.6	0.3	0.4	0.1	0.1	0.1	0.3	0.1
U.S.	13.6	4.2	3.5	1.5	1.3	1.1	1.0	0.7	0.2

Note: (1) Figures cover the Springfield, IL Metropolitan Statistical Area; (2) Excludes Mexico.
Source: U.S. Census Bureau, 2015-2019 American Community Survey 5-Year Estimates

470   Springfield, Illinois

Marital Status

Area	Never Married	Now Married[2]	Separated	Widowed	Divorced
City	37.5	40.8	1.5	6.4	13.7
MSA[1]	32.1	47.5	1.3	6.1	13.0
U.S.	33.4	48.1	1.9	5.8	10.9

Note: Figures are percentages and cover the population 15 years of age and older; (1) Figures cover the Springfield, IL Metropolitan Statistical Area; (2) Excludes separated
Source: U.S. Census Bureau, 2015-2019 American Community Survey 5-Year Estimates

Disability by Age

Area	All Ages	Under 18 Years Old	18 to 64 Years Old	65 Years and Over
City	14.9	5.8	12.9	33.6
MSA[1]	13.7	5.4	11.4	32.9
U.S.	12.6	4.2	10.3	34.5

Note: Figures show percent of the civilian noninstitutionalized population that reported having a disability. Disability status is determined from six types of difficulty: vision, hearing, cognitive, ambulatory, self-care, and independent living. For children under 5 years old, hearing and vision difficulty are used to determine disability status. For children between the ages of 5 and 14, disability status is determined from hearing, vision, cognitive, ambulatory, and self-care difficulties. For people aged 15 years and older, they are considered to have a disability if they have difficulty with any one of the six difficulty types; Note: (1) Figures cover the Springfield, IL Metropolitan Statistical Area
Source: U.S. Census Bureau, 2015-2019 American Community Survey 5-Year Estimates

Age

Area	Under Age 5	Age 5–19	Age 20–34	Age 35–44	Age 45–54	Age 55–64	Age 65–74	Age 75–84	Age 85+	Median Age
City	6.1	18.2	20.2	11.6	12.2	14.0	10.0	5.3	2.3	39.4
MSA[1]	5.8	19.0	18.4	12.2	13.1	14.2	10.1	5.1	2.1	40.4
U.S.	6.1	19.1	20.7	12.6	13.0	12.9	9.1	4.6	1.9	38.1

Note: (1) Figures cover the Springfield, IL Metropolitan Statistical Area
Source: U.S. Census Bureau, 2015-2019 American Community Survey 5-Year Estimates

Gender

Area	Males	Females	Males per 100 Females
City	54,935	60,953	90.1
MSA[1]	100,527	108,640	92.5
U.S.	159,886,919	164,810,876	97.0

Note: (1) Figures cover the Springfield, IL Metropolitan Statistical Area
Source: U.S. Census Bureau, 2015-2019 American Community Survey 5-Year Estimates

Religious Groups by Family

Area	Catholic	Baptist	Non-Den.	Methodist[2]	Lutheran	LDS[3]	Pentecostal	Presbyterian[4]	Muslim[5]	Judaism
MSA[1]	15.6	11.7	2.7	6.8	5.6	0.8	5.0	2.0	1.6	0.2
U.S.	19.1	9.3	4.0	4.0	2.3	2.0	1.9	1.6	0.8	0.7

Note: Figures are the number of adherents as a percentage of the total population; (1) Figures cover the Springfield, IL Metropolitan Statistical Area; (2) Methodist/Pietist; (3) Latter Day Saints; (4) Reformed; (5) Figures are estimates
Source: Association of Statisticians of American Religious Bodies, 2010 U.S. Religion Census: Religious Congregations & Membership Study

Religious Groups by Tradition

Area	Catholic	Evangelical Protestant	Mainline Protestant	Other Tradition	Black Protestant	Orthodox
MSA[1]	15.6	21.5	11.7	3.2	2.1	0.1
U.S.	19.1	16.2	7.3	4.3	1.6	0.3

Note: Figures are the number of adherents as a percentage of the total population; (1) Figures cover the Springfield, IL Metropolitan Statistical Area
Source: Association of Statisticians of American Religious Bodies, 2010 U.S. Religion Census: Religious Congregations & Membership Study

ECONOMY

Gross Metropolitan Product

Area	2017	2018	2019	2020	Rank[2]
MSA[1]	10.3	10.7	11.0	11.4	202

Note: Figures are in billions of dollars; (1) Figures cover the Springfield, IL Metropolitan Statistical Area; (2) Rank is based on 2018 data and ranges from 1 to 381
Source: U.S. Conference of Mayors, U.S. Metro Economies: GMP & Employment 2018-2020, September 2019

Economic Growth

Area	2015-17 (%)	2018 (%)	2019 (%)	2020 (%)	Rank[2]
MSA[1]	-0.8	0.8	1.4	0.9	337
U.S.	1.9	2.9	2.3	2.1	—

Note: Figures are real gross metropolitan product (GMP) growth rates and represent average annual percent change; (1) Figures cover the Springfield, IL Metropolitan Statistical Area; (2) Rank is based on 2017 2-year average annual percent change and ranges from 1 to 381
Source: U.S. Conference of Mayors, U.S. Metro Economies: GMP & Employment 2018-2020, September 2019

Metropolitan Area Exports

Area	2014	2015	2016	2017	2018	2019	Rank[2]
MSA[1]	94.4	111.7	88.3	107.5	91.2	99.8	338

Note: Figures are in millions of dollars; (1) Figures cover the Springfield, IL Metropolitan Statistical Area; (2) Rank is based on 2019 data and ranges from 1 to 386
Source: U.S. Department of Commerce, International Trade Administration, Office of Trade and Economic Analysis, Industry and Analysis, Exports by Metropolitan Area, data extracted March 24, 2021

Building Permits

Area	Single-Family			Multi-Family			Total		
	2018	2019	Pct. Chg.	2018	2019	Pct. Chg.	2018	2019	Pct. Chg.
City	74	57	-23.0	219	112	-48.9	293	169	-42.3
MSA[1]	193	149	-22.8	313	180	-42.5	506	329	-35.0
U.S.	855,300	862,100	0.7	473,500	523,900	10.6	1,328,800	1,386,000	4.3

Note: (1) Figures cover the Springfield, IL Metropolitan Statistical Area; Figures represent new, privately-owned housing units authorized (unadjusted data); All permit data are based on estimates with imputation
Source: U.S. Census Bureau, Manufacturing, Mining, and Construction Statistics, Building Permits, 2018, 2019

Bankruptcy Filings

Area	Business Filings			Nonbusiness Filings		
	2019	2020	% Chg.	2019	2020	% Chg.
Sangamon County	8	8	0.0	436	311	-28.7
U.S.	22,780	21,655	-4.9	752,160	522,808	-30.5

Note: Business filings include Chapter 7, Chapter 9, Chapter 11, Chapter 12, Chapter 13, Chapter 15, and Section 304; Nonbusiness filings include Chapter 7, Chapter 11, and Chapter 13
Source: Administrative Office of the U.S. Courts, Business and Nonbusiness Bankruptcy, County Cases Commenced by Chapter of the Bankruptcy Code, During the 12-Month Period Ending December 31, 2019 and Business and Nonbusiness Bankruptcy, County Cases Commenced by Chapter of the Bankruptcy Code, During the 12-Month Period Ending December 31, 2020

Housing Vacancy Rates

Area	Gross Vacancy Rate[2] (%)			Year-Round Vacancy Rate[3] (%)			Rental Vacancy Rate[4] (%)			Homeowner Vacancy Rate[5] (%)		
	2018	2019	2020	2018	2019	2020	2018	2019	2020	2018	2019	2020
MSA[1]	n/a	n/a	n/a	n/a	n/a	n/a	n/a	n/a	n/a	n/a	n/a	n/a
U.S.	12.3	12.0	10.6	9.7	9.5	8.2	6.9	6.7	6.3	1.5	1.4	1.0

Note: (1) Figures cover the Springfield, IL Metropolitan Statistical Area; (2) The percentage of the total housing inventory that is vacant; (3) The percentage of the housing inventory (excluding seasonal units) that is year-round vacant; (4) The percentage of rental inventory that is vacant for rent; (5) The percentage of homeowner inventory that is vacant for sale; n/a not available
Source: U.S. Census Bureau, Housing Vacancies and Homeownership Annual Statistics: 2018, 2019, 2020

INCOME

Income

Area	Per Capita ($)	Median Household ($)	Average Household ($)
City	34,607	54,648	77,473
MSA[1]	35,603	62,533	82,720
U.S.	34,103	62,843	88,607

Note: (1) Figures cover the Springfield, IL Metropolitan Statistical Area
Source: U.S. Census Bureau, 2015-2019 American Community Survey 5-Year Estimates

Household Income Distribution

Area	Percent of Households Earning							
	Under $15,000	$15,000 -$24,999	$25,000 -$34,999	$35,000 -$49,999	$50,000 -$74,999	$75,000 -$99,999	$100,000 -$149,999	$150,000 and up
City	13.7	10.7	9.6	12.1	17.2	13.0	12.9	10.9
MSA[1]	10.5	9.0	8.9	11.9	17.4	14.1	16.1	12.0
U.S.	10.3	8.9	8.9	12.3	17.2	12.7	15.1	14.5

Note: (1) Figures cover the Springfield, IL Metropolitan Statistical Area
Source: U.S. Census Bureau, 2015-2019 American Community Survey 5-Year Estimates

Poverty Rate

Area	All Ages	Under 18 Years Old	18 to 64 Years Old	65 Years and Over
City	18.6	29.8	17.5	8.4
MSA[1]	14.2	22.8	13.2	6.9
U.S.	13.4	18.5	12.6	9.3

Note: Figures are percentage of people whose income during the past 12 months was below the poverty level;
(1) Figures cover the Springfield, IL Metropolitan Statistical Area
Source: U.S. Census Bureau, 2015-2019 American Community Survey 5-Year Estimates

CITY FINANCES

City Government Finances

Component	2017 ($000)	2017 ($ per capita)
Total Revenues	467,952	4,015
Total Expenditures	503,359	4,318
Debt Outstanding	1,436,900	12,327
Cash and Securities[1]	495,748	4,253

Note: (1) Cash and security holdings of a government at the close of its fiscal year,
including those of its dependent agencies, utilities, and liquor stores.
Source: U.S. Census Bureau, State & Local Government Finances 2017

City Government Revenue by Source

Source	2017 ($000)	2017 ($ per capita)	2017 (%)
General Revenue			
From Federal Government	6,789	58	1.5
From State Government	47,400	407	10.1
From Local Governments	363	3	0.1
Taxes			
Property	28,114	241	6.0
Sales and Gross Receipts	54,282	466	11.6
Personal Income	0	0	0.0
Corporate Income	0	0	0.0
Motor Vehicle License	0	0	0.0
Other Taxes	1,265	11	0.3
Current Charges	17,890	153	3.8
Liquor Store	0	0	0.0
Utility	268,121	2,300	57.3
Employee Retirement	39,276	337	8.4

Source: U.S. Census Bureau, State & Local Government Finances 2017

City Government Expenditures by Function

Function	2017 ($000)	2017 ($ per capita)	2017 (%)
General Direct Expenditures			
Air Transportation	0	0	0.0
Corrections	0	0	0.0
Education	0	0	0.0
Employment Security Administration	0	0	0.0
Financial Administration	1,981	17	0.4
Fire Protection	37,587	322	7.5
General Public Buildings	2,170	18	0.4
Governmental Administration, Other	7,583	65	1.5
Health	0	0	0.0
Highways	50,877	436	10.1
Hospitals	0	0	0.0
Housing and Community Development	7,181	61	1.4
Interest on General Debt	5,283	45	1.0
Judicial and Legal	0	0	0.0
Libraries	4,426	38	0.9
Parking	1,032	8	0.2
Parks and Recreation	2,476	21	0.5
Police Protection	45,460	390	9.0
Public Welfare	0	0	0.0
Sewerage	9,482	81	1.9
Solid Waste Management	0	0	0.0
Veterans' Services	0	0	0.0
Liquor Store	0	0	0.0
Utility	272,591	2,338	54.2
Employee Retirement	26,711	229	5.3

Source: U.S. Census Bureau, State & Local Government Finances 2017

Springfield, Illinois   **473**

EMPLOYMENT

Labor Force and Employment

Area	Civilian Labor Force			Workers Employed		
	Dec. 2019	Dec. 2020	% Chg.	Dec. 2019	Dec. 2020	% Chg.
City	56,539	55,105	-2.5	54,362	51,115	-6.0
MSA[1]	106,114	102,509	-3.4	102,129	96,019	-6.0
U.S.	164,007,000	160,017,000	-2.4	158,504,000	149,613,000	-5.6

Note: Data is not seasonally adjusted and covers workers 16 years of age and older; (1) Figures cover the Springfield, IL Metropolitan Statistical Area
Source: Bureau of Labor Statistics, Local Area Unemployment Statistics

Unemployment Rate

Area	2020											
	Jan.	Feb.	Mar.	Apr.	May	Jun.	Jul.	Aug.	Sep.	Oct.	Nov.	Dec.
City	3.8	3.2	2.9	14.9	14.2	13.2	10.5	10.0	9.2	6.5	6.9	7.2
MSA[1]	3.9	3.2	2.9	14.2	13.1	11.7	9.2	8.7	7.8	5.5	5.9	6.3
U.S.	4.0	3.8	4.5	14.4	13.0	11.2	10.5	8.5	7.7	6.6	6.4	6.5

Note: Data is not seasonally adjusted and covers workers 16 years of age and older; (1) Figures cover the Springfield, IL Metropolitan Statistical Area
Source: Bureau of Labor Statistics, Local Area Unemployment Statistics

Average Wages

Occupation	$/Hr.	Occupation	$/Hr.
Accountants and Auditors	34.50	Maintenance and Repair Workers	21.60
Automotive Mechanics	21.30	Marketing Managers	51.90
Bookkeepers	20.60	Network and Computer Systems Admin.	37.80
Carpenters	29.90	Nurses, Licensed Practical	22.00
Cashiers	11.20	Nurses, Registered	34.60
Computer Programmers	47.50	Nursing Assistants	14.70
Computer Systems Analysts	45.10	Office Clerks, General	18.70
Computer User Support Specialists	29.20	Physical Therapists	44.90
Construction Laborers	26.60	Physicians	131.60
Cooks, Restaurant	11.70	Plumbers, Pipefitters and Steamfitters	37.00
Customer Service Representatives	17.50	Police and Sheriff's Patrol Officers	33.70
Dentists	86.10	Postal Service Mail Carriers	25.80
Electricians	34.20	Real Estate Sales Agents	19.50
Engineers, Electrical	45.50	Retail Salespersons	14.60
Fast Food and Counter Workers	10.40	Sales Representatives, Technical/Scientific	42.00
Financial Managers	56.40	Secretaries, Exc. Legal/Medical/Executive	17.90
First-Line Supervisors of Office Workers	28.40	Security Guards	23.00
General and Operations Managers	47.00	Surgeons	137.30
Hairdressers/Cosmetologists	22.20	Teacher Assistants, Exc. Postsecondary*	12.00
Home Health and Personal Care Aides	12.20	Teachers, Secondary School, Exc. Sp. Ed.*	27.10
Janitors and Cleaners	14.80	Telemarketers	n/a
Landscaping/Groundskeeping Workers	16.70	Truck Drivers, Heavy/Tractor-Trailer	24.20
Lawyers	50.20	Truck Drivers, Light/Delivery Services	19.00
Maids and Housekeeping Cleaners	12.30	Waiters and Waitresses	10.10

Note: Wage data covers the Springfield, IL Metropolitan Statistical Area; (*) Hourly wages were calculated from annual wage data based on a 40 hour work week; n/a not available.
Source: Bureau of Labor Statistics, Metro Area Occupational Employment & Wage Estimates, May 2020

Employment by Industry

Sector	MSA[1]		U.S.
	Number of Employees	Percent of Total	Percent of Total
Construction, Mining, and Logging	3,400	3.4	5.5
Education and Health Services	20,600	20.4	16.3
Financial Activities	6,100	6.0	6.1
Government	26,200	26.0	15.2
Information	1,800	1.8	1.9
Leisure and Hospitality	6,700	6.6	9.0
Manufacturing	2,900	2.9	8.5
Other Services	5,800	5.7	3.8
Professional and Business Services	10,600	10.5	14.4
Retail Trade	11,900	11.8	10.9
Transportation, Warehousing, and Utilities	2,100	2.1	4.6
Wholesale Trade	2,800	2.8	3.9

Note: Figures are non-farm employment as of December 2020. Figures are not seasonally adjusted and include workers 16 years of age and older; (1) Figures cover the Springfield, IL Metropolitan Statistical Area
Source: Bureau of Labor Statistics, Current Employment Statistics, Employment, Hours, and Earnings

Employment by Occupation

Occupation Classification	City (%)	MSA[1] (%)	U.S. (%)
Management, Business, Science, and Arts	43.7	42.7	38.5
Natural Resources, Construction, and Maintenance	5.1	6.8	8.9
Production, Transportation, and Material Moving	9.1	9.7	13.2
Sales and Office	22.9	23.2	21.6
Service	19.1	17.5	17.8

Note: Figures cover employed civilians 16 years of age and older; (1) Figures cover the Springfield, IL Metropolitan Statistical Area
Source: U.S. Census Bureau, 2015-2019 American Community Survey 5-Year Estimates

Occupations with Greatest Projected Employment Growth: 2019 – 2021

Occupation[1]	2019 Employment	2021 Projected Employment	Numeric Employment Change	Percent Employment Change
Total,, All Occupations	6,370,620	6,449,130	78,510	1.2
Combined Food Preparation and Serving Workers,, Including Fast Food	140,460	145,280	4,820	3.4
Registered Nurses	133,320	137,300	3,980	3.0
Personal Care Aides	56,160	59,830	3,670	6.5
Laborers and Freight,, Stock,, and Material Movers,, Hand	158,620	162,170	3,550	2.2
Insurance Sales Agents	49,730	52,420	2,690	5.4
Heavy and Tractor-Trailer Truck Drivers	73,100	75,610	2,510	3.4
General and Operations Managers	120,880	123,200	2,320	1.9
Cooks,, Restaurant	47,520	49,620	2,100	4.4
Janitors and Cleaners,, Except Maids and Housekeeping Cleaners	85,160	86,710	1,550	1.8

Note: Projections cover Illinois; Projections for 2020-2022 were not available at time of publication; (1) Sorted by numeric employment change
Source: www.projectionscentral.com, State Occupational Projections, 2019–2021 Short-Term Projections

Fastest-Growing Occupations: 2019 – 2021

Occupation[1]	2019 Employment	2021 Projected Employment	Numeric Employment Change	Percent Employment Change
Actuaries	1,940	2,070	130	6.7
Personal Care Aides	56,160	59,830	3,670	6.5
Statisticians	1,910	2,030	120	6.3
Nurse Practitioners	8,130	8,610	480	5.9
Physician Assistants	3,800	4,020	220	5.8
Insurance Sales Agents	49,730	52,420	2,690	5.4
Operations Research Analysts	5,080	5,350	270	5.3
Computer Numerically Controlled Machine Tool Programmers,, Metal and Plastic	1,150	1,210	60	5.2
Veterinary Technologists and Technicians	4,010	4,210	200	5.0
Massage Therapists	6,720	7,050	330	4.9

Note: Projections cover Illinois; Projections for 2020-2022 were not available at time of publication; (1) Sorted by percent employment change and excludes occupations with numeric employment change less than 50
Source: www.projectionscentral.com, State Occupational Projections, 2019–2021 Short-Term Projections

TAXES

State Corporate Income Tax Rates

State	Tax Rate (%)	Income Brackets ($)	Num. of Brackets	Financial Institution Tax Rate (%)[a]	Federal Income Tax Ded.
Illinois	9.5 (h)	Flat rate	1	9.5 (h)	No

Note: Tax rates as of January 1, 2021; (a) Rates listed are the corporate income tax rate applied to financial institutions or excise taxes based on income. Some states have other taxes based upon the value of deposits or shares; (h) The Illinois rate of 9.5% is the sum of a corporate income tax rate of 7.0% plus a replacement tax of 2.5%.
Source: Federation of Tax Administrators, State Corporate Income Tax Rates, January 1, 2021

State Individual Income Tax Rates

State	Tax Rate (%)	Income Brackets ($)	Personal Exemptions ($)			Standard Ded. ($)	
			Single	Married	Depend.	Single	Married
Illinois (a)	4.95	Flat rate	2,325	4,650	2,325	–	–

Note: Tax rates as of January 1, 2021; Local- and county-level taxes are not included; Federal income tax is not deductible on state income tax returns; (a) 19 states have statutory provision for automatically adjusting to the rate of inflation the dollar values of the income tax brackets, standard deductions, and/or personal exemptions. Michigan indexes the personal exemption only. Oregon does not index the income brackets for $125,000 and over.
Source: Federation of Tax Administrators, State Individual Income Tax Rates, January 1, 2021

Various State Sales and Excise Tax Rates

State	State Sales Tax (%)	Gasoline[1] (¢/gal.)	Cigarette[2] ($/pack)	Spirits[3] ($/gal.)	Wine[4] ($/gal.)	Beer[5] ($/gal.)	Recreational Marijuana (%)
Illinois	6.25	52.16	2.98	8.55	1.39	0.23	(e)

Note: All tax rates as of January 1, 2021; (1) The American Petroleum Institute has developed a methodology for determining the average tax rate on a gallon of fuel. Rates may include any of the following: excise taxes, environmental fees, storage tank fees, other fees or taxes, general sales tax, and local taxes; (2) The federal excise tax of $1.0066 per pack and local taxes are not included; (3) Rates are those applicable to off-premise sales of 40% alcohol by volume (a.b.v.) distilled spirits in 750ml containers. Local excise taxes are excluded; (4) Rates are those applicable to off-premise sales of 11% a.b.v. non-carbonated wine in 750ml containers; (5) Rates are those applicable to off-premise sales of 4.7% a.b.v. beer in 12 ounce containers; (e) 7% excise tax of value at wholesale level; 10% tax on cannabis flower or products with less than 35% THC; 20% tax on products infused with cannabis, such as edible products; 25% tax on any product with a THC concentration higher than 35%
Source: Tax Foundation, 2021 Facts & Figures: How Does Your State Compare?

State Business Tax Climate Index Rankings

State	Overall Rank	Corporate Tax Rank	Individual Income Tax Rank	Sales Tax Rank	Property Tax Rank	Unemployment Insurance Tax Rank
Illinois	36	36	13	38	48	43

Note: The index is a measure of how each state's tax laws affect economic performance. The lower the rank, the more favorable a state's tax system is for business. States without a given tax are given a ranking of 1. The scores/rankings for the District of Columbia do not affect other states. The 2021 index represents the tax climate as of July 1, 2020.
Source: Tax Foundation, State Business Tax Climate Index 2021

TRANSPORTATION

Means of Transportation to Work

Area	Car/Truck/Van		Public Transportation			Bicycle	Walked	Other Means	Worked at Home
	Drove Alone	Car-pooled	Bus	Subway	Railroad				
City	81.8	7.9	2.2	0.1	0.0	0.7	2.1	1.3	3.9
MSA[1]	83.3	8.0	1.3	0.1	0.0	0.5	1.7	1.0	4.3
U.S.	76.3	9.0	2.4	1.9	0.6	0.5	2.7	1.4	5.2

Note: Figures are percentages and cover workers 16 years of age and older; (1) Figures cover the Springfield, IL Metropolitan Statistical Area
Source: U.S. Census Bureau, 2015-2019 American Community Survey 5-Year Estimates

Travel Time to Work

Area	Less Than 10 Minutes	10 to 19 Minutes	20 to 29 Minutes	30 to 44 Minutes	45 to 59 Minutes	60 to 89 Minutes	90 Minutes or More
City	18.2	51.5	18.5	6.1	1.8	2.3	1.6
MSA[1]	15.6	42.6	23.6	11.5	2.7	2.3	1.7
U.S.	12.2	28.4	20.8	20.8	8.3	6.4	2.9

Note: Note: Figures are percentages and include workers 16 years old and over; (1) Figures cover the Springfield, IL Metropolitan Statistical Area
Source: U.S. Census Bureau, 2015-2019 American Community Survey 5-Year Estimates

Key Congestion Measures

Measure	1982	1992	2002	2012	2017
Annual Hours of Delay, Total (000)	n/a	n/a	n/a	n/a	2,504
Annual Hours of Delay, Per Auto Commuter	n/a	n/a	n/a	n/a	14
Annual Congestion Cost, Total (million $)	n/a	n/a	n/a	n/a	53
Annual Congestion Cost, Per Auto Commuter ($)	n/a	n/a	n/a	n/a	297

Note: n/a not available
Source: Texas A&M Transportation Institute, 2019 Urban Mobility Report

Freeway Travel Time Index

Measure	1982	1987	1992	1997	2002	2007	2012	2017
Urban Area Index[1]	n/a	n/a	n/a	n/a	n/a	n/a	n/a	1.06
Urban Area Rank[1,2]	n/a	n/a	n/a	n/a	n/a	n/a	n/a	n/a

Note: Freeway Travel Time Index—the ratio of travel time in the peak period to the travel time at free-flow conditions. For example, a value of 1.30 indicates a 20-minute free-flow trip takes 26 minutes in the peak (20 minutes x 1.30 = 26 minutes); (1) Covers the Springfield IL urban area; (2) Rank is based on 101 larger urban areas (#1 = highest travel time index); n/a not available
Source: Texas A&M Transportation Institute, 2019 Urban Mobility Report

Public Transportation

Agency Name / Mode of Transportation	Vehicles Operated in Maximum Service[1]	Annual Unlinked Passenger Trips[2] (in thous.)	Annual Passenger Miles[3] (in thous.)
Springfield Mass Transit District (SMTD)			
Bus (directly operated)	52	1,487.1	5,467.4
Demand Response (directly operated)	15	86.1	538.3

Note: (1) Number of revenue vehicles operated by the given mode and type of service to meet the annual maximum service requirement. This is the revenue vehicle count during the peak season of the year; on the week and day that maximum service is provided. Vehicles operated in maximum service (VOMS) exclude atypical days and one-time special events; (2) Number of passengers who boarded public transportation vehicles. Passengers are counted each time they board a vehicle no matter how many vehicles they use to travel from their origin to their destination. (3) Sum of the distances ridden by all passengers during the entire fiscal year.
Source: Federal Transit Administration, National Transit Database, 2019

Air Transportation

Airport Name and Code / Type of Service	Passenger Airlines[1]	Passenger Enplanements	Freight Carriers[2]	Freight (lbs)
Capital Airport (SPI)				
Domestic service (U.S. carriers - 2020)	6	35,036	1	14
International service (U.S. carriers - 2019)	1	128	0	0

Note: (1) Includes all U.S.-based major, minor and commuter airlines that carried at least one passenger during the year; (2) Includes all U.S.-based airlines and freight carriers that transported at least one pound of freight during the year.
Source: Bureau of Transportation Statistics, The Intermodal Transportation Database, Air Carriers: T-100 Domestic Market (U.S. Carriers), 2020; Bureau of Transportation Statistics, The Intermodal Transportation Database, Air Carriers: T-100 International Market (U.S. Carriers), 2019

BUSINESSES

Major Business Headquarters

Company Name	Industry	Rankings	
		Fortune[1]	Forbes[2]
No companies listed	-	-	-

Note: (1) Companies that produce a 10-K are ranked 1 to 500 based on 2019 revenue; (2) All private companies with at least $2 billion in annual revenue through the end of their most current fiscal year are ranked 1 to 219; companies listed are headquartered in the city; dashes indicate no ranking
Source: Fortune, "Fortune 500," June/July 2020; Forbes, "America's Largest Private Companies," 2020

Fastest-Growing Businesses

According to *Inc.*, Springfield is home to one of America's 500 fastest-growing private companies: **bitsIO** (#498). Criteria: must be an independent, privately-held, for-profit, U.S. corporation, proprietorship or partnership as of December 31, 2019; revenues must be at least $100,000 in 2016 and $2 million in 2019; must have four-year operating/sales history. *Inc., "America's 500 Fastest-Growing Private Companies," 2020*

Living Environment

COST OF LIVING

Cost of Living Index

Composite Index	Groceries	Housing	Utilities	Trans- portation	Health Care	Misc. Goods/ Services
n/a	n/a	n/a	n/a	n/a	n/a	n/a

Note: The Cost of Living Index measures regional differences in the cost of consumer goods and services, excluding taxes and non-consumer expenditures, for professional and managerial households in the top income quintile. It is based on more than 50,000 prices covering almost 60 different items for which prices are collected three times a year by chambers of commerce, economic development organizations or university applied economic centers in each participating urban area. The numbers shown should be read as a percentage above or below the national average of 100. For example, a value of 115.4 in the groceries column indicates that grocery prices are 15.4% higher than the national average. Small differences in the index numbers should not be interpreted as significant; n/a not available.
Source: The Council for Community and Economic Research, Cost of Living Index, 2020

Grocery Prices

Area[1]	T-Bone Steak ($/pound)	Frying Chicken ($/pound)	Whole Milk ($/half gal.)	Eggs ($/dozen)	Orange Juice ($/64 oz.)	Coffee ($/11.5 oz.)
City[2]	n/a	n/a	n/a	n/a	n/a	n/a
Avg.	11.78	1.39	2.05	1.47	3.57	4.34
Min.	8.03	0.94	1.03	0.74	2.94	3.02
Max.	15.86	2.65	4.31	3.77	5.44	8.69

*Note: (1) Values for the local area are compared with the average, minimum and maximum values for all 284 areas in the Cost of Living Index; (2) Figures cover the Springfield IL urban area; n/a not available; **T-Bone Steak** (price per pound); **Frying Chicken** (price per pound, whole fryer); **Whole Milk** (half gallon carton); **Eggs** (price per dozen, Grade A, large); **Orange Juice** (64 oz. Tropicana or Florida Natural); **Coffee** (11.5 oz. can, vacuum-packed, Maxwell House, Hills Bros, or Folgers).*
Source: The Council for Community and Economic Research, Cost of Living Index, 2020

Housing and Utility Costs

Area[1]	New Home Price ($)	Apartment Rent ($/month)	All Electric ($/month)	Part Electric ($/month)	Other Energy ($/month)	Telephone ($/month)
City[2]	n/a	n/a	n/a	n/a	n/a	n/a
Avg.	368,594	1,168	170.86	100.47	65.28	184.30
Min.	190,567	502	91.58	31.42	26.08	169.60
Max.	2,227,806	4,738	470.38	280.31	280.06	206.50

*Note: (1) Values for the local area are compared with the average, minimum and maximum values for all 284 areas in the Cost of Living Index; (2) Figures cover the Springfield IL urban area; n/a not available; **New Home Price** (2,400 sf living area, 8,000 sf lot, in urban area with full utilities); **Apartment Rent** (950 sf 2 bedroom/1.5 or 2 bath, unfurnished, excluding all utilities except water); **All Electric** (average monthly cost for an all-electric home); **Part Electric** (average monthly cost for a part-electric home); **Other Energy** (average monthly cost for natural gas, fuel oil, coal, wood, and any other forms of energy except electricity); **Telephone** (price includes the base monthly rate plus taxes and fees for three lines of mobile phone service).*
Source: The Council for Community and Economic Research, Cost of Living Index, 2020

Health Care, Transportation, and Other Costs

Area[1]	Doctor ($/visit)	Dentist ($/visit)	Optometrist ($/visit)	Gasoline ($/gallon)	Beauty Salon ($/visit)	Men's Shirt ($)
City[2]	n/a	n/a	n/a	n/a	n/a	n/a
Avg.	115.44	99.32	108.10	2.21	39.27	31.37
Min.	36.68	59.00	51.36	1.71	19.00	11.00
Max.	219.00	153.10	250.97	3.46	82.05	58.33

*Note: (1) Values for the local area are compared with the average, minimum and maximum values for all 284 areas in the Cost of Living Index; (2) Figures cover the Springfield IL urban area; n/a not available; **Doctor** (general practitioners routine exam of an established patient); **Dentist** (adult teeth cleaning and periodic oral examination); **Optometrist** (full vision eye exam for established adult patient); **Gasoline** (one gallon regular unleaded, national brand, including all taxes, cash price at self-service pump if available); **Beauty Salon** (woman's shampoo, trim, and blow-dry); **Men's Shirt** (cotton/polyester dress shirt, pinpoint weave, long sleeves).*
Source: The Council for Community and Economic Research, Cost of Living Index, 2020

HOUSING

Homeownership Rate

Area	2012 (%)	2013 (%)	2014 (%)	2015 (%)	2016 (%)	2017 (%)	2018 (%)	2019 (%)	2020 (%)
MSA[1]	n/a	n/a	n/a	n/a	n/a	n/a	n/a	n/a	n/a
U.S.	65.4	65.1	64.5	63.7	63.4	63.9	64.4	64.6	66.6

Note: (1) Figures cover the Springfield, IL Metropolitan Statistical Area; n/a not available
Source: U.S. Census Bureau, Housing Vacancies and Homeownership Annual Statistics: 2012-2020

House Price Index (HPI)

Area	National Ranking[2]	Quarterly Change (%)	One-Year Change (%)	Five-Year Change (%)	Since 1991Q1 (%)
MSA[1]	248	0.83	1.79	8.16	85.25
U.S.[3]	–	3.81	10.77	38.99	205.12

Note: The HPI is a weighted repeat sales index. It measures average price changes in repeat sales or refinancings on the same properties. This information is obtained by reviewing repeat mortgage transactions on single-family properties whose mortgages have been purchased or securitized by Fannie Mae or Freddie Mac since January 1975; (1) Figures cover the Springfield, IL Metropolitan Statistical Area; (2) Rankings are based on annual percentage change for all metro areas containing at least 15,000 transactions over the last 10 years and ranges from 1 to 253; (3) figures based on a weighted average of Census Division estimates using a seasonally adjusted, purchase-only index; all figures are for the period ending December 31, 2020
Source: Federal Housing Finance Agency, Change in Metropolitan Area House Price Indexes, April 7, 2021

Median Single-Family Home Prices

Area	2018	2019	2020[p]	Percent Change 2019 to 2020
MSA[1]	133.5	141.8	148.0	4.4
U.S. Average	261.6	274.6	299.9	9.2

Note: Figures are median sales prices of existing single-family homes in thousands of dollars; (p) preliminary; (1) Figures cover the Springfield, IL Metropolitan Statistical Area
Source: National Association of Realtors, Median Sales Price of Existing Single-Family Homes for Metropolitan Areas, 4th Quarter 2020

Qualifying Income Based on Median Sales Price of Existing Single-Family Homes

Area	With 5% Down ($)	With 10% Down ($)	With 20% Down ($)
MSA[1]	27,596	26,143	23,239
U.S. Average	59,266	56,147	49,908

Note: Figures are preliminary; Qualifying income is based on a mortgage rate of 2.81%. Monthly principal and interest payment is limited to 25% of income; (1) Figures cover the Springfield, IL Metropolitan Statistical Area
Source: National Association of Realtors, Qualifying Income Based on Median Sales Price of Existing Single-Family Homes for Metropolitan Areas, 4th Quarter 2020

Home Value Distribution

Area	Under $50,000	$50,000 -$99,999	$100,000 -$149,999	$150,000 -$199,999	$200,000 -$299,999	$300,000 -$499,999	$500,000 -$999,999	$1,000,000 or more
City	10.0	24.9	23.4	15.7	15.7	7.9	2.3	0.2
MSA[1]	8.2	23.3	22.4	17.8	18.2	8.0	1.9	0.2
U.S.	6.9	12.0	13.3	14.0	19.6	19.3	11.4	3.4

Note: Figures are percentages and cover owner-occupied housing units; (1) Figures cover the Springfield, IL Metropolitan Statistical Area
Source: U.S. Census Bureau, 2015-2019 American Community Survey 5-Year Estimates

Year Housing Structure Built

Area	2010 or Later	2000 -2009	1990 -1999	1980 -1989	1970 -1979	1960 -1969	1950 -1959	1940 -1949	Before 1940	Median Year
City	2.3	8.8	12.6	9.6	16.5	12.7	11.3	7.0	19.2	1970
MSA[1]	3.1	9.9	13.2	9.1	16.9	11.9	11.6	6.7	17.5	1971
U.S.	5.2	14.0	13.9	13.4	15.2	10.6	10.3	4.9	12.6	1978

Note: Figures are percentages except for Median Year; Note: (1) Figures cover the Springfield, IL Metropolitan Statistical Area
Source: U.S. Census Bureau, 2015-2019 American Community Survey 5-Year Estimates

Gross Monthly Rent

Area	Under $500	$500 -$999	$1,000 -$1,499	$1,500 -$1,999	$2,000 -$2,499	$2,500 -$2,999	$3,000 and up	Median ($)
City	12.4	62.3	19.5	3.4	1.1	1.1	0.2	805
MSA[1]	11.4	63.1	19.9	3.6	0.9	0.9	0.2	818
U.S.	9.4	36.2	30.0	14.0	5.6	2.4	2.4	1,062

Note: Figures are percentages except for Median; Gross rent is the contract rent plus the estimated average monthly cost of utilities (electricity, gas, and water and sewer) and fuels (oil, coal, kerosene, wood, etc.) if these are paid by the renter (or paid for the renter by someone else); (1) Figures cover the Springfield, IL Metropolitan Statistical Area
Source: U.S. Census Bureau, 2015-2019 American Community Survey 5-Year Estimates

HEALTH

Health Risk Factors

Category	MSA[1] (%)	U.S. (%)
Adults aged 18–64 who have any kind of health care coverage	n/a	87.3
Adults who reported being in good or better health	n/a	82.4
Adults who have been told they have high blood cholesterol	n/a	33.0
Adults who have been told they have high blood pressure	n/a	32.3
Adults who are current smokers	n/a	17.1
Adults who currently use E-cigarettes	n/a	4.6
Adults who currently use chewing tobacco, snuff, or snus	n/a	4.0
Adults who are heavy drinkers[2]	n/a	6.3
Adults who are binge drinkers[3]	n/a	17.4
Adults who are overweight (BMI 25.0 - 29.9)	n/a	35.3
Adults who are obese (BMI 30.0 - 99.8)	n/a	31.3
Adults who participated in any physical activities in the past month	n/a	74.4
Adults who always or nearly always wears a seat belt	n/a	94.3

Note: n/a not available; (1) Figures cover the Springfield, IL Metropolitan Statistical Area; (2) Heavy drinkers are classified as adult men having more than 14 drinks per week and adult women having more than 7 drinks per week; (3) Binge drinkers are classified as males having five or more drinks on one occasion or females having four or more drinks on one occasion
Source: Centers for Disease Control and Prevention, Behaviorial Risk Factor Surveillance System, SMART: Selected Metropolitan Area Risk Trends, 2017

Acute and Chronic Health Conditions

Category	MSA[1] (%)	U.S. (%)
Adults who have ever been told they had a heart attack	n/a	4.2
Adults who have ever been told they have angina or coronary heart disease	n/a	3.9
Adults who have ever been told they had a stroke	n/a	3.0
Adults who have ever been told they have asthma	n/a	14.2
Adults who have ever been told they have arthritis	n/a	24.9
Adults who have ever been told they have diabetes[2]	n/a	10.5
Adults who have ever been told they had skin cancer	n/a	6.2
Adults who have ever been told they had any other types of cancer	n/a	7.1
Adults who have ever been told they have COPD	n/a	6.5
Adults who have ever been told they have kidney disease	n/a	3.0
Adults who have ever been told they have a form of depression	n/a	20.5

Note: n/a not available; (1) Figures cover the Springfield, IL Metropolitan Statistical Area; (2) Figures do not include pregnancy-related, borderline, or pre-diabetes
Source: Centers for Disease Control and Prevention, Behaviorial Risk Factor Surveillance System, SMART: Selected Metropolitan Area Risk Trends, 2017

Health Screening and Vaccination Rates

Category	MSA[1] (%)	U.S. (%)
Adults aged 65+ who have had flu shot within the past year	n/a	60.7
Adults aged 65+ who have ever had a pneumonia vaccination	n/a	75.4
Adults who have ever been tested for HIV	n/a	36.1
Adults who have ever had the shingles or zoster vaccine?	n/a	28.9
Adults who have had their blood cholesterol checked within the last five years	n/a	85.9

Note: n/a not available; (1) Figures cover the Springfield, IL Metropolitan Statistical Area.
Source: Centers for Disease Control and Prevention, Behaviorial Risk Factor Surveillance System, SMART: Selected Metropolitan Area Risk Trends, 2017

Disability Status

Category	MSA[1] (%)	U.S. (%)
Adults who reported being deaf	n/a	6.7
Are you blind or have serious difficulty seeing, even when wearing glasses?	n/a	4.5
Are you limited in any way in any of your usual activities due of arthritis?	n/a	12.9
Do you have difficulty doing errands alone?	n/a	6.8
Do you have difficulty dressing or bathing?	n/a	3.6
Do you have serious difficulty concentrating/remembering/making decisions?	n/a	10.7
Do you have serious difficulty walking or climbing stairs?	n/a	13.6

Note: n/a not available; (1) Figures cover the Springfield, IL Metropolitan Statistical Area.
Source: Centers for Disease Control and Prevention, Behaviorial Risk Factor Surveillance System, SMART: Selected Metropolitan Area Risk Trends, 2017

Mortality Rates for the Top 10 Causes of Death in the U.S.

ICD-10[a] Sub-Chapter	ICD-10[a] Code	Age-Adjusted Mortality Rate[1] per 100,000 population	
		County[2]	U.S.
Malignant neoplasms	C00-C97	164.2	149.2
Ischaemic heart diseases	I20-I25	87.7	90.5
Other forms of heart disease	I30-I51	60.0	52.2
Chronic lower respiratory diseases	J40-J47	37.5	39.6
Other degenerative diseases of the nervous system	G30-G31	25.2	37.6
Cerebrovascular diseases	I60-I69	34.5	37.2
Other external causes of accidental injury	W00-X59	40.8	36.1
Organic, including symptomatic, mental disorders	F01-F09	40.6	29.4
Hypertensive diseases	I10-I15	18.4	24.1
Diabetes mellitus	E10-E14	18.9	21.5

Note: (a) ICD-10 = International Classification of Diseases 10th Revision; (1) Mortality rates are a three-year average covering 2017-2019; (2) Figures cover Sangamon County.
Source: Centers for Disease Control and Prevention, National Center for Health Statistics. Underlying Cause of Death 1999-2019 on CDC WONDER Online Database

Mortality Rates for Selected Causes of Death

ICD-10[a] Sub-Chapter	ICD-10[a] Code	Age-Adjusted Mortality Rate[1] per 100,000 population	
		County[2]	U.S.
Assault	X85-Y09	6.9	6.0
Diseases of the liver	K70-K76	16.4	14.4
Human immunodeficiency virus (HIV) disease	B20-B24	Suppressed	1.5
Influenza and pneumonia	J09-J18	19.3	13.8
Intentional self-harm	X60-X84	15.4	14.1
Malnutrition	E40-E46	Unreliable	2.3
Obesity and other hyperalimentation	E65-E68	Unreliable	2.1
Renal failure	N17-N19	13.9	12.6
Transport accidents	V01-V99	11.1	12.3
Viral hepatitis	B15-B19	Suppressed	1.2

Note: (a) ICD-10 = International Classification of Diseases 10th Revision; (1) Mortality rates are a three-year average covering 2017-2019; (2) Figures cover Sangamon County; Data are suppressed when the data meet the criteria for confidentiality constraints; Mortality rates are flagged as unreliable when the rate would be calculated with a numerator of 20 or less.
Source: Centers for Disease Control and Prevention, National Center for Health Statistics. Underlying Cause of Death 1999-2019 on CDC WONDER Online Database

Health Insurance Coverage

Area	With Health Insurance	With Private Health Insurance	With Public Health Insurance	Without Health Insurance	Population Under Age 19 Without Health Insurance
City	95.7	69.1	42.2	4.3	1.7
MSA[1]	96.2	74.3	37.4	3.8	1.6
U.S.	91.2	67.9	35.1	8.8	5.1

Note: Figures are percentages that cover the civilian noninstitutionalized population; (1) Figures cover the Springfield, IL Metropolitan Statistical Area
Source: U.S. Census Bureau, 2015-2019 American Community Survey 5-Year Estimates

Number of Medical Professionals

Area	MDs[3]	DOs[3,4]	Dentists	Podiatrists	Chiropractors	Optometrists
County[1] (number)	1,236	51	166	11	78	41
County[1] (rate[2])	631.8	26.1	85.3	5.7	40.1	21.1
U.S. (rate[2])	282.9	22.7	71.2	6.2	28.1	16.9

17167
Note: Data as of 2019 unless noted; (1) Data covers Sangamon County; (2) Rate per 100,000 population; (3) Data as of 2018 and includes all active, non-federal physicians; (4) Doctor of Osteopathic Medicine
Source: U.S. Department of Health and Human Services, Health Resources and Services Administration, Bureau of Health Professions, Area Resource File (ARF) 2019-2020

EDUCATION

Public School District Statistics

District Name	Schls	Pupils	Pupil/ Teacher Ratio	Minority Pupils[1] (%)	Free Lunch Eligible[2] (%)	IEP[3] (%)
Springfield SD 186	35	14,084	13.9	58.1	55.7	22.0

Note: Table includes school districts with 2,000 or more students; (1) Percentage of students that are not non-Hispanic white; (2) Percentage of students that are eligible for the free lunch program; (3) Percentage of students that have an Individualized Education Program.
Source: U.S. Department of Education, National Center for Education Statistics, Common Core of Data, Local Education Agency (School District) Universe Survey: School Year 2018-2019; U.S. Department of Education, National Center for Education Statistics, Common Core of Data, Public Elementary/Secondary School Universe Survey: School Year 2018-2019

Highest Level of Education

Area	Less than H.S.	H.S. Diploma	Some College, No Deg.	Associate Degree	Bachelor's Degree	Master's Degree	Prof. School Degree	Doctorate Degree
City	8.7	25.9	22.1	7.6	21.5	9.8	3.3	1.2
MSA[1]	7.4	27.7	22.7	8.3	21.2	9.0	2.6	1.0
U.S.	12.0	27.0	20.4	8.5	19.8	8.8	2.1	1.4

Note: Figures cover persons age 25 and over; (1) Figures cover the Springfield, IL Metropolitan Statistical Area
Source: U.S. Census Bureau, 2015-2019 American Community Survey 5-Year Estimates

Educational Attainment by Race

Area	High School Graduate or Higher (%)					Bachelor's Degree or Higher (%)				
	Total	White	Black	Asian	Hisp.[2]	Total	White	Black	Asian	Hisp.[2]
City	91.3	93.4	81.2	91.7	87.8	35.8	38.6	17.8	64.9	33.6
MSA[1]	92.6	93.9	81.6	92.7	87.0	33.9	35.2	17.4	64.0	31.5
U.S.	88.0	89.9	86.0	87.1	68.7	32.1	33.5	21.6	54.3	16.4

Note: Figures shown cover persons 25 years old and over; (1) Figures cover the Springfield, IL Metropolitan Statistical Area; (2) People of Hispanic origin can be of any race
Source: U.S. Census Bureau, 2015-2019 American Community Survey 5-Year Estimates

School Enrollment by Grade and Control

Area	Preschool (%)		Kindergarten (%)		Grades 1 - 4 (%)		Grades 5 - 8 (%)		Grades 9 - 12 (%)	
	Public	Private	Public	Private	Public	Private	Public	Private	Public	Private
City	65.7	34.3	80.4	19.6	81.9	18.1	83.9	16.1	85.6	14.4
MSA[1]	66.2	33.8	86.4	13.6	87.2	12.8	88.6	11.4	90.1	9.9
U.S.	59.1	40.9	87.6	12.4	89.5	10.5	89.4	10.6	90.1	9.9

Note: Figures shown cover persons 3 years old and over; (1) Figures cover the Springfield, IL Metropolitan Statistical Area
Source: U.S. Census Bureau, 2015-2019 American Community Survey 5-Year Estimates

Higher Education

Four-Year Colleges			Two-Year Colleges			Medical Schools[1]	Law Schools[2]	Voc/ Tech[3]
Public	Private Non-profit	Private For-profit	Public	Private Non-profit	Private For-profit			
1	1	0	1	0	0	1	0	4

Note: Figures cover institutions located within the city limits and include main campuses only; (1) includes schools accredited by the Liaison Committee on Medical Education and the American Osteopathic Association's Commission on Osteopathic College Accreditation; (2) includes ABA-accredited schools, schools with provisional ABA accreditation, and state accredited schools; (3) includes all schools with programs that are less than 2 years.
Source: National Center for Education Statistics, Integrated Postsecondary Education System (IPEDS), 2019-20; Wikipedia, List of Medical Schools in the United States, accessed April 2, 2021; Wikipedia, List of Law Schools in the United States, accessed April 2, 2021

482 Springfield, Illinois

EMPLOYERS

Major Employers

Company Name	Industry
BlueCross BlueShield of Illinois	Insurance
Horace Mann Insurance Company	Insurance
Illinois National Guard	U.S. military
Memorial Health System	Healthcare
Southern Illinois University School of Med.	Education
Springfield Clinic	Healthcare
Springfield School District #186	Education
St. John's Medical	Healthcare
State of Illinois	State government
U.S. Postal Service	Government/postal service
University of Illinois at Springfield	Education

Note: Companies shown are located within the Springfield, IL Metropolitan Statistical Area.
Source: Hoovers.com; Wikipedia

PUBLIC SAFETY

Crime Rate

Area	All Crimes	Violent Crimes				Property Crimes		
		Murder	Rape[3]	Robbery	Aggrav. Assault	Burglary	Larceny -Theft	Motor Vehicle Theft
City	5,218.0	7.9	94.4	181.8	493.0	908.3	3,300.9	231.7
Suburbs[1]	1,395.2	1.1	40.2	32.6	269.7	340.4	605.7	105.5
Metro[2]	3,514.4	4.8	70.3	115.3	393.5	655.2	2,099.8	175.4
U.S.	2,489.3	5.0	42.6	81.6	250.2	340.5	1,549.5	219.9

Note: Figures are crimes per 100,000 population; (1) All areas within the metro area that are located outside the city limits; (2) Figures cover the Springfield, IL Metropolitan Statistical Area; (3) All figures shown were reported using the revised Uniform Crime Reporting (UCR) definition of rape.
Source: FBI Uniform Crime Reports, 2019

Hate Crimes

Area	Number of Quarters Reported	Number of Incidents per Bias Motivation					
		Race/Ethnicity/ Ancestry	Religion	Sexual Orientation	Disability	Gender	Gender Identity
City	4	1	0	0	0	0	0
U.S.	4	3,963	1,521	1,195	157	69	198

Source: Federal Bureau of Investigation, Hate Crime Statistics 2019

Identity Theft Consumer Reports

Area	Reports	Reports per 100,000 Population	Rank[2]
MSA[1]	2,056	994	9
U.S.	1,387,615	423	-

Note: (1) Figures cover the Springfield, IL Metropolitan Statistical Area; (2) Rank ranges from 1 to 391 where 1 indicates greatest number of identity theft reports per 100,000 population
Source: Federal Trade Commission, Consumer Sentinel Network Data Book 2020

Fraud and Other Consumer Reports

Area	Reports	Reports per 100,000 Population	Rank[2]
MSA[1]	1,543	746	147
U.S.	3,385,133	1,031	-

Note: (1) Figures cover the Springfield, IL Metropolitan Statistical Area; (2) Rank ranges from 1 to 391 where 1 indicates greatest number of fraud and other consumer reports per 100,000 population
Source: Federal Trade Commission, Consumer Sentinel Network Data Book 2020

POLITICS

2020 Presidential Election Results

Area	Biden	Trump	Jorgensen	Hawkins	Other
Sangamon County	46.7	51.1	1.4	0.6	0.3
U.S.	51.3	46.8	1.2	0.3	0.5

Note: Results are percentages and may not add to 100% due to rounding
Source: Dave Leip's Atlas of U.S. Presidential Elections

SPORTS

Professional Sports Teams

Team Name	League	Year Established

No teams are located in the metro area
Source: Wikipedia, Major Professional Sports Teams of the United States and Canada, April 6, 2021

Springfield, Illinois 483

CLIMATE

Average and Extreme Temperatures

Temperature	Jan	Feb	Mar	Apr	May	Jun	Jul	Aug	Sep	Oct	Nov	Dec	Yr.
Extreme High (°F)	73	78	91	90	101	104	112	108	101	93	83	74	112
Average High (°F)	35	38	50	63	74	84	88	85	79	67	51	38	63
Average Temp. (°F)	27	30	41	53	64	73	78	75	68	57	43	31	54
Average Low (°F)	19	22	32	43	53	63	67	65	57	46	34	24	44
Extreme Low (°F)	-21	-24	-12	17	28	40	48	43	32	13	-3	-21	-24

Note: Figures cover the years 1948-1995
Source: National Climatic Data Center, International Station Meteorological Climate Summary, 9/96

Average Precipitation/Snowfall/Humidity

Precip./Humidity	Jan	Feb	Mar	Apr	May	Jun	Jul	Aug	Sep	Oct	Nov	Dec	Yr.
Avg. Precip. (in.)	1.8	1.7	3.1	3.6	3.8	3.9	3.3	3.1	3.3	2.6	2.4	2.1	34.9
Avg. Snowfall (in.)	6	6	4	1	Tr	0	0	0	0	Tr	1	5	21
Avg. Rel. Hum. 6am (%)	80	81	81	79	81	82	85	89	87	83	82	82	83
Avg. Rel. Hum. 3pm (%)	67	65	59	52	51	51	54	56	50	50	60	69	57

Note: Figures cover the years 1948-1995; Tr = Trace amounts (<0.05 in. of rain; <0.5 in. of snow)
Source: National Climatic Data Center, International Station Meteorological Climate Summary, 9/96

Weather Conditions

Temperature			Daytime Sky			Precipitation		
10°F & below	32°F & below	90°F & above	Clear	Partly cloudy	Cloudy	0.01 inch or more precip.	0.1 inch or more snow/ice	Thunder-storms
19	111	34	96	126	143	111	18	49

Note: Figures are average number of days per year and cover the years 1948-1995
Source: National Climatic Data Center, International Station Meteorological Climate Summary, 9/96

HAZARDOUS WASTE

Superfund Sites

The Springfield, IL metro area has no sites on the EPA's Superfund Final National Priorities List. There are a total of 1,375 Superfund sites with a status of proposed or final on the list in the U.S. *U.S. Environmental Protection Agency, National Priorities List, April 7, 2021*

AIR QUALITY

Air Quality Trends: Ozone

	1990	1995	2000	2005	2010	2015	2016	2017	2018	2019
MSA[1]	n/a	n/a	n/a	n/a	n/a	n/a	n/a	n/a	n/a	n/a
U.S.	0.088	0.089	0.082	0.080	0.073	0.068	0.069	0.068	0.069	0.065

Note: (1) Data covers the Springfield, IL Metropolitan Statistical Area; n/a not available. The values shown are the composite ozone concentration averages among trend sites based on the highest fourth daily maximum 8-hour concentration in parts per million. These trends are based on sites having an adequate record of monitoring data during the trend period. Data from exceptional events are included.
Source: U.S. Environmental Protection Agency, Air Quality Monitoring Information, "Air Quality Trends by City, 1990-2019"

Air Quality Index

Area	Percent of Days when Air Quality was...[2]					AQI Statistics[2]	
	Good	Moderate	Unhealthy for Sensitive Groups	Unhealthy	Very Unhealthy	Maximum	Median
MSA[1]	79.7	20.3	0.0	0.0	0.0	87	40

Note: (1) Data covers the Springfield, IL Metropolitan Statistical Area; (2) Based on 360 days with AQI data in 2019. Air Quality Index (AQI) is an index for reporting daily air quality. EPA calculates the AQI for five major air pollutants regulated by the Clean Air Act: ground-level ozone, particle pollution (aka particulate matter), carbon monoxide, sulfur dioxide, and nitrogen dioxide. The AQI runs from 0 to 500. The higher the AQI value, the greater the level of air pollution and the greater the health concern. There are six AQI categories: "Good" AQI is between 0 and 50. Air quality is considered satisfactory; "Moderate" AQI is between 51 and 100. Air quality is acceptable; "Unhealthy for Sensitive Groups" When AQI values are between 101 and 150, members of sensitive groups may experience health effects; "Unhealthy" When AQI values are between 151 and 200 everyone may begin to experience health effects; "Very Unhealthy" AQI values between 201 and 300 trigger a health alert; "Hazardous" AQI values over 300 trigger warnings of emergency conditions (not shown).
Source: U.S. Environmental Protection Agency, Air Quality Index Report, 2019

Air Quality Index Pollutants

Area	Percent of Days when AQI Pollutant was...[2]					
	Carbon Monoxide	Nitrogen Dioxide	Ozone	Sulfur Dioxide	Particulate Matter 2.5	Particulate Matter 10
MSA[1]	0.0	0.0	50.8	0.0	49.2	0.0

Note: (1) Data covers the Springfield, IL Metropolitan Statistical Area; (2) Based on 360 days with AQI data in 2019. The Air Quality Index (AQI) is an index for reporting daily air quality. EPA calculates the AQI for five major air pollutants regulated by the Clean Air Act: ground-level ozone, particle pollution (also known as particulate matter), carbon monoxide, sulfur dioxide, and nitrogen dioxide. The AQI runs from 0 to 500. The higher the AQI value, the greater the level of air pollution and the greater the health concern.
Source: U.S. Environmental Protection Agency, Air Quality Index Report, 2019

Maximum Air Pollutant Concentrations: Particulate Matter, Ozone, CO and Lead

	Particulate Matter 10 (ug/m^3)	Particulate Matter 2.5 Wtd AM (ug/m^3)	Particulate Matter 2.5 24-Hr (ug/m^3)	Ozone (ppm)	Carbon Monoxide (ppm)	Lead (ug/m^3)
MSA[1] Level	n/a	8.2	18	0.062	n/a	n/a
NAAQS[2]	150	15	35	0.075	9	0.15
Met NAAQS[2]	n/a	Yes	Yes	Yes	n/a	n/a

Note: (1) Data covers the Springfield, IL Metropolitan Statistical Area; Data from exceptional events are included; (2) National Ambient Air Quality Standards; ppm = parts per million; ug/m³ = micrograms per cubic meter; n/a not available.
Concentrations: Particulate Matter 10 (coarse particulate)—highest second maximum 24-hour concentration; Particulate Matter 2.5 Wtd AM (fine particulate)—highest weighted annual mean concentration; Particulate Matter 2.5 24-Hour (fine particulate)—highest 98th percentile 24-hour concentration; Ozone—highest fourth daily maximum 8-hour concentration; Carbon Monoxide—highest second maximum non-overlapping 8-hour concentration; Lead—maximum running 3-month average
Source: U.S. Environmental Protection Agency, Air Quality Monitoring Information, "Air Quality Statistics by City, 2019"

Maximum Air Pollutant Concentrations: Nitrogen Dioxide and Sulfur Dioxide

	Nitrogen Dioxide AM (ppb)	Nitrogen Dioxide 1-Hr (ppb)	Sulfur Dioxide AM (ppb)	Sulfur Dioxide 1-Hr (ppb)	Sulfur Dioxide 24-Hr (ppb)
MSA[1] Level	n/a	n/a	n/a	n/a	n/a
NAAQS[2]	53	100	30	75	140
Met NAAQS[2]	n/a	n/a	n/a	n/a	n/a

Note: (1) Data covers the Springfield, IL Metropolitan Statistical Area; Data from exceptional events are included; (2) National Ambient Air Quality Standards; ppm = parts per million; ug/m³ = micrograms per cubic meter; n/a not available.
Concentrations: Nitrogen Dioxide AM—highest arithmetic mean concentration; Nitrogen Dioxide 1-Hr—highest 98th percentile 1-hour daily maximum concentration; Sulfur Dioxide AM—highest annual mean concentration; Sulfur Dioxide 1-Hr—highest 99th percentile 1-hour daily maximum concentration; Sulfur Dioxide 24-Hr—highest second maximum 24-hour concentration
Source: U.S. Environmental Protection Agency, Air Quality Monitoring Information, "Air Quality Statistics by City, 2019"

Tulsa, Oklahoma

Background

The city of Tulsa stands at the intersection of Tulsa, Osage, Rogers, and Wagoner counties, in the northeast part of Oklahoma. Located on the Arkansas River, Tulsa sits between the Osage Hills and the foothills of the Ozark Mountains.

Tulsa was first settled by Creek Indians in 1828. In 1848, Lewis Perryman established the first trading post at the new settlement, and his son George, in 1878, developed a regular mail station at the site, which then came to be called Tulsa, probably from the Talsi or Talasi branch of the Creek Tribe. In 2020, the U.S. Supreme Court ruled that that city was indeed Native American land.

Originally a cattle and dry goods trading center drawing attention from ranchers scattered throughout the area, Tulsa was integrated into a wider trade area in 1882, when the Frisco Railroad brought a line into the town. This facilitated a movement of new settlers into the area, and allowed "Tulsey Town" to transport cattle to the stockyards of St. Louis and Chicago and, thus, throughout the nation. The importance of the rail system can still be seen in the layout of Tulsa's downtown streets, which are aligned parallel and perpendicular to the tracks. Tulsa was incorporated as a town on January 18, 1898.

Oil was first discovered in the area in 1901 at Red Fork. In 1905, a huge strike—the world's largest at the time—was made at Glenn Pool. Since then, Tulsa's fortune has been tied to the oil industry. Oklahoma achieved statehood two years after the Glenn Pool strike, and by 1920 the city was already well-known as the "Oil Capital of the World." During this boom period, many of Tulsa's historic buildings were constructed, which explains the city's extraordinary art deco flavor in its downtown architecture. The great influx of wealthy easterners and the construction they financed left parts of the city resembling places in New York and Philadelphia.

Oil naturally fueled the growth of aviation, and Tulsa was an early center for the development of this industry. By the beginning of the Second World War, many of the nation's pilots were being trained at Spartan School of Aeronautics in the city, and Douglas Aircraft in 1942 sited a major plant there. In later years, both McDonnell-Douglas and Rockwell International based aviation and space technology operations in Tulsa.

Today, Tulsa is home to American Airlines' Maintenance & Engineering Center, one of the world's largest such commercial centers. In 2020, AA announced a $550 million renovation to its maintenance center. The city is also home to a division of Lufthansa, the headquarters of Omni Air International, the Spartan School of Aeronautics, BOK Financial Corporation, the Marshall Brewing Company, Laredo Petroleum, Samson Resources, WPX Energy, and Excel Energy. The city has more than 20,000 energy jobs in a wide range of companies and specialties.

The city's location in the center of the nation makes it a hub for logistics businesses, with its busy Tulsa International Airport and Tulsa Port of Catoosa, a 445-mile navigation system that links Tulsa to the Mississippi, making Tulsa a major inland ice-free port, with a designated foreign trade zone, and a 2,000-acre industrial park with a new Amazon distribution center. Tulsa is also part of the Oklahoma-South Kansas Unmanned Aerial Systems (drone) industry cluster, with federal funding to continue its progress as a hub in this emerging industry.

The city hosts a broad range of cultural and recreational activities, including the Gilcrease Museum, holder of the world's largest collection of art and artifacts of the American West, and the Philbrook Museum of Art. Many cultural activities are sponsored by the city's several universities, including a branch of Oklahoma State University. Discovery Land, a huge hands-on museum, educational center and amphitheater, broke ground in 2020.

The city is host to the Tulsa Rose Gardens, the Municipal Rose Gardens—built by the Works Progress Administration and opened in 1934—and the Tulsa Zoo. As a result of compacts between the state of Oklahoma and various Native American tribes, tribal gaming facilities offer table card games and slot machines.

The city's Cox Business Convention Center houses facilities ranging from an assembly hall to the state's largest ballroom to 34 meeting rooms. The BOK (Bank of Oklahoma) Center is a multi-purpose arena that plays host to the Tulsa Oilers ice hockey team. The minor league baseball team, the Tulsa Drillers, play in ONEOK Field, as do the Tulsa Roughnecks FC, a men's soccer team. The University of Tulsa's men's basketball team, the Golden Hurricane, are a highly competitive program as, to a lesser degree, is Oral Roberts University's men's basketball team, the Golden Eagles.

Tulsa's weather is continental and generally mild, with unpredictable amounts of precipitation. Winters for the region bordering on the Great Plains are comparatively short and mild.

Rankings

General Rankings

- Tulsa was selected as one of the best places in the world to "dream of now and go to later" by *National Geographic Travel* editors. The list reflects 25 of the most extraordinary and inspiring destinations that also support National Geographic's tourism goals of cultural engagement, diversity, community benefit, and value. In collaboration with its international editorial teams, the new list reports on the timeless must-see sites for 2021, framed by the five categories of Culture and History, Family, Adventure, Sustainability, and Nature. *www.nationalgeographic.com/travel, "Best of the World, Destinations on the Rise for 2021," November 17, 2020*

Business/Finance Rankings

- Tulsa was the #5-ranked city for savers, according to a study by the finance site GOBankingRates, which considered the prospects for people trying to save money. Criteria: average monthly cost of grocery items; median home listing price; median rent; median income; transportation costs; gas prices; and the cost of eating out for an inexpensive and mid-range meal in 100 U.S. cities. *www.gobankingrates.com, "The 20 Best (and Worst) Places to Live If You're Trying to Save Money," August 27, 2019*

- Tulsa was ranked #5 among 100 U.S. cities for most difficult conditions for savers, according to a study by the finance site GOBankingRates. Criteria: average monthly cost of grocery items; median home listing price; median rent; median income; transportation costs; gas prices; and the cost of eating out for an inexpensive and mid-range meal. *www.gobankingrates.com, "The 20 Best (and Worst) Places to Live If You're Trying to Save Money," August 27, 2019*

- The Brookings Institution ranked the nation's largest cities based on income inequality. Tulsa was ranked #42 (#1 = greatest inequality). Criteria: the "95/20 ratio," a figure representing the income at which a household earns more than 95 percent of all other households, divided by the income at which a household earns more than only 20 percent of all other households. *Brookings Institution, "Household Income Inequality, Largest Cities of 97 Large U.S. Metro Areas, 2014-2016," February 5, 2018*

- The Brookings Institution ranked the 100 largest metro areas in the U.S. based on income inequality. Tulsa was ranked #44 (#1 = greatest inequality). Criteria: the "95/20 ratio," a figure representing the income at which a household earns more than 95 percent of all other households, divided by the income at which a household earns more than only 20 percent of all other households. *Brookings Institution, "Household Income Inequality, 100 Largest U.S. Metro Areas, 2014-2016," February 5, 2018*

- For its annual survey of the "Cheapest U.S. Cities to Live In," Kiplinger applied Cost of Living Index statistics developed by the Council for Community and Economic Research to U.S. Census Bureau population and median household income data for 270 urban areas. In the resulting ranking, Tulsa ranked #12. *Kiplinger.com, "The 25 Cheapest U.S. Cities to Live In," October 1, 2020*

- The Tulsa metro area appeared on the Milken Institute "2021 Best Performing Cities" list. Rank: #108 out of 200 large metro areas (population over 250,000). Criteria: job growth; wage and salary growth; high-tech output growth; housing affordability; household broadband access. *Milken Institute, "Best-Performing Cities 2021," February 16, 2021*

- *Forbes* ranked the 200 most populous metro areas to determine the nation's "Best Places for Business and Careers." The Tulsa metro area was ranked #120. Criteria: costs (business and living); job growth (past and projected); income growth; quality of life; educational attainment (college and high school); projected economic growth; cultural and leisure opportunities; workplace tolerance laws; net migration patterns. *Forbes, "The Best Places for Business and Careers 2019: Seattle Still On Top," October 30, 2019*

Culture/Performing Arts Rankings

- Tulsa was selected as one of the ten best small North American cities and towns for moviemakers. Of cities with smaller populations, the area ranked #7. As with the 2021 list for bigger cities, pandemic challenges and COVID-19 guidelines were factored in. Other criteria: film community and culture; access to equipment and facilities; tax incentives; and standard of living. *MovieMaker Magazine, "Best Places to Live and Work as a Moviemaker, 2021," January 26, 2021*

Dating/Romance Rankings

- Tulsa was ranked #24 out of 25 cities that stood out for inspiring romance and attracting diners on the website OpenTable.com. Criteria: percentage of people who dined out on Valentine's Day in 2018; percentage of romantic restaurants as rated by OpenTable diner reviews; and percentage of tables seated for two. *OpenTable, "25 Most Romantic Cities in America for 2019," February 7, 2019*

Education Rankings

- Personal finance website *WalletHub* analyzed the 150 largest U.S. metropolitan statistical areas to determine where the most educated Americans are putting their degrees to work. Criteria: education levels; percentage of workers with degrees; education quality and attainment gap; public school quality rankings; quality and enrollment of each metro area's universities. Tulsa was ranked #109 (#1 = most educated city). *www.WalletHub.com, "Most and Least Educated Cities in America, " July 20, 2020*

- Tulsa was selected as one of America's most literate cities. The city ranked #24 out of the 84 largest U.S. cities. Criteria: number of booksellers; library resources; Internet resources; educational attainment; periodical publishing resources; newspaper circulation. *Central Connecticut State University, "America's Most Literate Cities, 2018," February 2019*

Health/Fitness Rankings

- For each of the 100 largest cities in the United States, the American Fitness Index®, published by the American College of Sports Medicine and the Anthem Foundation, evaluated community infrastructure and 33 health behaviors including preventive health, levels of chronic disease conditions, pedestrian safety, air quality, and community resources that support physical activity. Tulsa ranked #97 for "community fitness." *americanfitnessindex.org, "2020 ACSM American Fitness Index Summary Report," July 14, 2020*

- Tulsa was identified as a "2021 Spring Allergy Capital." The area ranked #22 out of 100. Three groups of factors were used to identify the most challenging cities for people with allergies during the spring season: annual spring pollen levels; over the counter medicine use; number of board-certified allergy specialists. *Asthma and Allergy Foundation of America, "Spring Allergy Capitals 2021," February 23, 2021*

- Tulsa was identified as a "2021 Fall Allergy Capital." The area ranked #22 out of 100. Three groups of factors were used to identify the most challenging cities for people with allergies during the fall season: annual fall pollen levels; over the counter medicine use; number of board-certified allergy specialists. *Asthma and Allergy Foundation of America, "Fall Allergy Capitals 2021," February 23, 2021*

- Tulsa was identified as a "2019 Asthma Capital." The area ranked #37 out of the nation's 100 largest metropolitan areas. Criteria: estimated asthma prevalence; crude death rate from asthma; and ER visits due to asthma. Risk factors analyzed but not factored in the rankings: annual pollen score; annual air quality; public smoking laws; number of board-certified asthma specialists; rescue medication use; controller medication use; uninsured rate; poverty rate. *Asthma and Allergy Foundation of America, "Asthma Capitals 2019: The Most Challenging Places to Live With Asthma," May 7, 2019*

Real Estate Rankings

- *WalletHub* compared the most populated U.S. cities to determine which had the best markets for real estate agents. Tulsa ranked #158 where demand was high and pay was the best. Criteria: sales per agent; annual median wage for real-estate agents; monthly average starting salary for real estate agents; real estate job density and competition; unemployment rate; home turnover rate; housing-market health index; and other relevant metrics. *www.WalletHub.com, "2019's Best Places to Be a Real Estate Agent," April 24, 2019*

- Tulsa was ranked #96 out of 268 metro areas in terms of housing affordability in 2020 by the National Association of Home Builders (#1 = most affordable). Criteria: the share of homes sold in that area affordable to a family earning the local median income, based on standard mortgage underwriting criteria. *National Association of Home Builders®, NAHB-Wells Fargo Housing Opportunity Index, 4th Quarter 2020*

Safety Rankings

- To identify the most dangerous cities in America, 24/7 Wall Street focused on violent crime categories—murder, non-negligent manslaughter, rape, robbery, and aggravated assault—and property crime as reported in the FBI's 2019 annual Uniform Crime Report. Criteria also included median income from American Community Survey and unemployment figures from Bureau of Labor Statistics. For cities with populations over 100,000, Tulsa was ranked #28. *247wallst.com, "America's 50 Most Dangerous Cities" November 16, 2020*

- Allstate ranked the 200 largest cities in America in terms of driver safety. Tulsa ranked #51. Criteria: internal property damage claims over a two-year period from January 2016 to December 2017. The report helps increase the importance of safety and awareness behind the wheel. *Allstate, "Allstate America's Best Drivers Report, 2019" June 24, 2019*

- Tulsa was identified as one of the most dangerous cities in America by NeighborhoodScout. The city ranked #60 out of 100 (#1 = most dangerous). Criteria: number of violent crimes per 1,000 residents. The editors evaluated cities with 25,000 or more residents. *NeighborhoodScout.com, "2021 Top 100 Most Dangerous Cities in the U.S.," January 2, 2021*
- The National Insurance Crime Bureau ranked 384 metro areas in the U.S. in terms of per capita rates of vehicle theft. The Tulsa metro area ranked #16 (#1 = highest rate). Criteria: number of vehicle theft offenses per 100,000 inhabitants in 2019. *National Insurance Crime Bureau, "Hot Spots 2019," July 21, 2020*

Seniors/Retirement Rankings

- From its Best Cities for Successful Aging indexes, the Milken Institute generated rankings for metropolitan areas, weighing data in nine categories—health care, wellness, living arrangements, transportation and convenience, financial characteristics, education, employment, community engagement, and overall livability. The Tulsa metro area was ranked #57 overall in the large metro area category. *Milken Institute, "Best Cities for Successful Aging, 2017" March 14, 2017*

Women/Minorities Rankings

- Personal finance website *WalletHub* compared more than 180 U.S. cities across two key dimensions, "Hispanic Business-Friendliness" and "Hispanic Purchasing Power," to arrive at the most favorable conditions for Hispanic entrepreneurs. Tulsa was ranked #33 out of 182. Criteria includes: share of Hispanic-Owned Businesses; Hispanic entrepreneurship rate to median annual income of Hispanics; Small Business-Friendliness score; cost of living; and number of Hispanics with at least a bachelor's degree. *WalletHub.com, "2019's Best Cities for Hispanic Entrepreneurs," May 1, 2019*

Miscellaneous Rankings

- Tulsa was selected as a 2020 Digital Cities Survey winner. The city ranked #10 in the large city (250,000 to 499,999 population) category. The survey examined and assessed how city governments are utilizing technology to improve transparency, enhance cybersecurity, and respond to the pandemic. Survey questions focused on ten initiatives: cybersecurity, citizen experience, disaster recovery, business intelligence, IT personnel, data governance, collaboration, infrastructure modernization, cloud computing, and mobile applications. *Center for Digital Government, "2020 Digital Cities Survey," November 10, 2020*
- *WalletHub* compared the 150 most populated U.S. cities to determine their operating efficiency. A "Quality of City Services" score was constructed for each city and then divided by the total budget per capita to reveal which were managed the best. Tulsa ranked #37. Criteria: financial stability; economy; education; safety; health; infrastructure and pollution. *www.WalletHub.com, "2020's Best- & Worst-Run Cities in America," June 29, 2020*

Business Environment

DEMOGRAPHICS

Population Growth

Area	1990 Census	2000 Census	2010 Census	2019* Estimate	Population Growth (%)	
					1990-2019	2010-2019
City	367,241	393,049	391,906	402,324	9.6	2.7
MSA[1]	761,019	859,532	937,478	990,544	30.2	5.7
U.S.	248,709,873	281,421,906	308,745,538	324,697,795	30.6	5.2

Note: (1) Figures cover the Tulsa, OK Metropolitan Statistical Area; (*) 2015-2019 5-year estimated population
Source: U.S. Census Bureau, 1990 Census, Census 2000, Census 2010, 2015-2019 American Community Survey 5-Year Estimates

Household Size

Area	Persons in Household (%)							Average Household Size
	One	Two	Three	Four	Five	Six	Seven or More	
City	35.1	32.5	13.7	10.2	5.1	2.1	1.2	2.40
MSA[1]	28.3	34.6	15.3	12.1	6.0	2.5	1.3	2.60
U.S.	27.9	33.9	15.6	12.9	6.0	2.3	1.4	2.60

Note: (1) Figures cover the Tulsa, OK Metropolitan Statistical Area
Source: U.S. Census Bureau, 2015-2019 American Community Survey 5-Year Estimates

Race

Area	White Alone[2] (%)	Black Alone[2] (%)	Asian Alone[2] (%)	AIAN[3] Alone[2] (%)	NHOPI[4] Alone[2] (%)	Other Race Alone[2] (%)	Two or More Races (%)
City	64.3	15.2	3.4	4.5	0.1	4.9	7.5
MSA[1]	71.2	8.0	2.5	7.3	0.1	2.7	8.2
U.S.	72.5	12.7	5.5	0.8	0.2	4.9	3.3

Note: (1) Figures cover the Tulsa, OK Metropolitan Statistical Area; (2) Alone is defined as not being in combination with one or more other races; (3) American Indian and Alaska Native; (4) Native Hawaiian and Other Pacific Islander
Source: U.S. Census Bureau, 2015-2019 American Community Survey 5-Year Estimates

Hispanic or Latino Origin

Area	Total (%)	Mexican (%)	Puerto Rican (%)	Cuban (%)	Other (%)
City	16.5	13.2	0.6	0.2	2.6
MSA[1]	9.9	7.8	0.4	0.1	1.6
U.S.	18.0	11.2	1.7	0.7	4.3

Note: Persons of Hispanic or Latino origin can be of any race; (1) Figures cover the Tulsa, OK Metropolitan Statistical Area
Source: U.S. Census Bureau, 2015-2019 American Community Survey 5-Year Estimates

Ancestry

Area	German	Irish	English	American	Italian	Polish	French[2]	Scottish	Dutch
City	11.0	9.1	7.5	6.2	2.0	0.9	1.9	2.0	1.0
MSA[1]	12.9	10.5	8.0	6.7	1.9	1.0	2.1	2.0	1.2
U.S.	13.3	9.7	7.2	6.2	5.1	2.8	2.3	1.7	1.2

Note: Figures are the percentage of the total population reporting a particular ancestry. The nine most commonly reported ancestries in the U.S. are shown. Figures include multiple ancestries (e.g. if a person reported being Irish and Italian, they were included in both columns); (1) Figures cover the Tulsa, OK Metropolitan Statistical Area; (2) Excludes Basque
Source: U.S. Census Bureau, 2015-2019 American Community Survey 5-Year Estimates

Foreign-born Population

Area	Percent of Population Born in								
	Any Foreign Country	Asia	Mexico	Europe	Caribbean	Central America[2]	South America	Africa	Canada
City	11.2	2.7	5.6	0.5	0.2	1.0	0.4	0.5	0.1
MSA[1]	6.6	1.9	2.9	0.5	0.1	0.5	0.3	0.3	0.1
U.S.	13.6	4.2	3.5	1.5	1.3	1.1	1.0	0.7	0.2

Note: (1) Figures cover the Tulsa, OK Metropolitan Statistical Area; (2) Excludes Mexico.
Source: U.S. Census Bureau, 2015-2019 American Community Survey 5-Year Estimates

Marital Status

Area	Never Married	Now Married[2]	Separated	Widowed	Divorced
City	34.5	42.5	2.4	5.9	14.8
MSA[1]	28.4	50.3	1.9	6.2	13.2
U.S.	33.4	48.1	1.9	5.8	10.9

Note: Figures are percentages and cover the population 15 years of age and older; (1) Figures cover the Tulsa, OK Metropolitan Statistical Area; (2) Excludes separated
Source: U.S. Census Bureau, 2015-2019 American Community Survey 5-Year Estimates

Disability by Age

Area	All Ages	Under 18 Years Old	18 to 64 Years Old	65 Years and Over
City	14.5	4.7	13.5	36.2
MSA[1]	14.5	4.6	12.9	37.9
U.S.	12.6	4.2	10.3	34.5

Note: Figures show percent of the civilian noninstitutionalized population that reported having a disability. Disability status is determined from six types of difficulty: vision, hearing, cognitive, ambulatory, self-care, and independent living. For children under 5 years old, hearing and vision difficulty are used to determine disability status. For children between the ages of 5 and 14, disability status is determined from hearing, vision, cognitive, ambulatory, and self-care difficulties. For people aged 15 years and older, they are considered to have a disability if they have difficulty with any one of the six difficulty types; Note: (1) Figures cover the Tulsa, OK Metropolitan Statistical Area
Source: U.S. Census Bureau, 2015-2019 American Community Survey 5-Year Estimates

Age

Area	Percent of Population									Median Age
	Under Age 5	Age 5–19	Age 20–34	Age 35–44	Age 45–54	Age 55–64	Age 65–74	Age 75–84	Age 85+	
City	7.1	20.0	22.8	12.4	11.4	12.3	8.1	4.0	1.9	35.1
MSA[1]	6.7	20.5	20.1	12.6	12.4	12.7	8.9	4.5	1.7	37.0
U.S.	6.1	19.1	20.7	12.6	13.0	12.9	9.1	4.6	1.9	38.1

Note: (1) Figures cover the Tulsa, OK Metropolitan Statistical Area
Source: U.S. Census Bureau, 2015-2019 American Community Survey 5-Year Estimates

Gender

Area	Males	Females	Males per 100 Females
City	195,534	206,790	94.6
MSA[1]	486,355	504,189	96.5
U.S.	159,886,919	164,810,876	97.0

Note: (1) Figures cover the Tulsa, OK Metropolitan Statistical Area
Source: U.S. Census Bureau, 2015-2019 American Community Survey 5-Year Estimates

Religious Groups by Family

Area	Catholic	Baptist	Non-Den.	Methodist[2]	Lutheran	LDS[3]	Pentecostal	Presbyterian[4]	Muslim[5]	Judaism
MSA[1]	5.8	22.9	7.6	9.2	0.8	1.2	3.3	1.3	0.3	0.3
U.S.	19.1	9.3	4.0	4.0	2.3	2.0	1.9	1.6	0.8	0.7

Note: Figures are the number of adherents as a percentage of the total population; (1) Figures cover the Tulsa, OK Metropolitan Statistical Area; (2) Methodist/Pietist; (3) Latter Day Saints; (4) Reformed; (5) Figures are estimates
Source: Association of Statisticians of American Religious Bodies, 2010 U.S. Religion Census: Religious Congregations & Membership Study

Religious Groups by Tradition

Area	Catholic	Evangelical Protestant	Mainline Protestant	Other Tradition	Black Protestant	Orthodox
MSA[1]	5.8	34.6	11.3	2.2	1.6	0.1
U.S.	19.1	16.2	7.3	4.3	1.6	0.3

Note: Figures are the number of adherents as a percentage of the total population; (1) Figures cover the Tulsa, OK Metropolitan Statistical Area
Source: Association of Statisticians of American Religious Bodies, 2010 U.S. Religion Census: Religious Congregations & Membership Study

ECONOMY

Gross Metropolitan Product

Area	2017	2018	2019	2020	Rank[2]
MSA[1]	57.2	60.9	63.7	67.4	55

Note: Figures are in billions of dollars; (1) Figures cover the Tulsa, OK Metropolitan Statistical Area; (2) Rank is based on 2018 data and ranges from 1 to 381
Source: U.S. Conference of Mayors, U.S. Metro Economies: GMP & Employment 2018-2020, September 2019

Economic Growth

Area	2015-17 (%)	2018 (%)	2019 (%)	2020 (%)	Rank[2]
MSA[1]	-3.3	1.3	3.1	1.7	373
U.S.	1.9	2.9	2.3	2.1	—

Note: Figures are real gross metropolitan product (GMP) growth rates and represent average annual percent change; (1) Figures cover the Tulsa, OK Metropolitan Statistical Area; (2) Rank is based on 2017 2-year average annual percent change and ranges from 1 to 381
Source: U.S. Conference of Mayors, U.S. Metro Economies: GMP & Employment 2018-2020, September 2019

Metropolitan Area Exports

Area	2014	2015	2016	2017	2018	2019	Rank[2]
MSA[1]	3,798.5	2,699.7	2,363.0	2,564.7	3,351.7	3,399.2	72

Note: Figures are in millions of dollars; (1) Figures cover the Tulsa, OK Metropolitan Statistical Area; (2) Rank is based on 2019 data and ranges from 1 to 386
Source: U.S. Department of Commerce, International Trade Administration, Office of Trade and Economic Analysis, Industry and Analysis, Exports by Metropolitan Area, data extracted March 24, 2021

Building Permits

Area	Single-Family			Multi-Family			Total		
	2018	2019	Pct. Chg.	2018	2019	Pct. Chg.	2018	2019	Pct. Chg.
City	471	629	33.5	343	580	69.1	814	1,209	48.5
MSA[1]	2,845	3,377	18.7	567	929	63.8	3,412	4,306	26.2
U.S.	855,300	862,100	0.7	473,500	523,900	10.6	1,328,800	1,386,000	4.3

Note: (1) Figures cover the Tulsa, OK Metropolitan Statistical Area; Figures represent new, privately-owned housing units authorized (unadjusted data); All permit data are based on estimates with imputation
Source: U.S. Census Bureau, Manufacturing, Mining, and Construction Statistics, Building Permits, 2018, 2019

Bankruptcy Filings

Area	Business Filings			Nonbusiness Filings		
	2019	2020	% Chg.	2019	2020	% Chg.
Tulsa County	44	45	2.3	1,555	1,163	-25.2
U.S.	22,780	21,655	-4.9	752,160	522,808	-30.5

Note: Business filings include Chapter 7, Chapter 9, Chapter 11, Chapter 12, Chapter 13, Chapter 15, and Section 304; Nonbusiness filings include Chapter 7, Chapter 11, and Chapter 13
Source: Administrative Office of the U.S. Courts, Business and Nonbusiness Bankruptcy, County Cases Commenced by Chapter of the Bankruptcy Code, During the 12-Month Period Ending December 31, 2019 and Business and Nonbusiness Bankruptcy, County Cases Commenced by Chapter of the Bankruptcy Code, During the 12-Month Period Ending December 31, 2020

Housing Vacancy Rates

Area	Gross Vacancy Rate[2] (%)			Year-Round Vacancy Rate[3] (%)			Rental Vacancy Rate[4] (%)			Homeowner Vacancy Rate[5] (%)		
	2018	2019	2020	2018	2019	2020	2018	2019	2020	2018	2019	2020
MSA[1]	11.7	8.4	9.4	11.6	8.0	8.8	10.1	8.5	8.6	2.6	1.6	0.8
U.S.	12.3	12.0	10.6	9.7	9.5	8.2	6.9	6.7	6.3	1.5	1.4	1.0

Note: (1) Figures cover the Tulsa, OK Metropolitan Statistical Area; (2) The percentage of the total housing inventory that is vacant; (3) The percentage of the housing inventory (excluding seasonal units) that is year-round vacant; (4) The percentage of rental inventory that is vacant for rent; (5) The percentage of homeowner inventory that is vacant for sale
Source: U.S. Census Bureau, Housing Vacancies and Homeownership Annual Statistics: 2018, 2019, 2020

INCOME

Income

Area	Per Capita ($)	Median Household ($)	Average Household ($)
City	30,970	47,650	73,816
MSA[1]	30,633	55,739	77,341
U.S.	34,103	62,843	88,607

Note: (1) Figures cover the Tulsa, OK Metropolitan Statistical Area
Source: U.S. Census Bureau, 2015-2019 American Community Survey 5-Year Estimates

Household Income Distribution

Area	Percent of Households Earning							
	Under $15,000	$15,000 -$24,999	$25,000 -$34,999	$35,000 -$49,999	$50,000 -$74,999	$75,000 -$99,999	$100,000 -$149,999	$150,000 and up
City	14.2	11.6	11.2	15.2	17.4	10.3	10.1	10.0
MSA[1]	10.9	10.0	10.1	14.0	18.4	12.6	13.4	10.4
U.S.	10.3	8.9	8.9	12.3	17.2	12.7	15.1	14.5

Note: (1) Figures cover the Tulsa, OK Metropolitan Statistical Area
Source: U.S. Census Bureau, 2015-2019 American Community Survey 5-Year Estimates

492 Tulsa, Oklahoma

Poverty Rate

Area	All Ages	Under 18 Years Old	18 to 64 Years Old	65 Years and Over
City	19.4	29.7	17.7	8.8
MSA[1]	14.3	20.9	13.3	7.7
U.S.	13.4	18.5	12.6	9.3

Note: Figures are percentage of people whose income during the past 12 months was below the poverty level;
(1) Figures cover the Tulsa, OK Metropolitan Statistical Area
Source: U.S. Census Bureau, 2015-2019 American Community Survey 5-Year Estimates

CITY FINANCES

City Government Finances

Component	2017 ($000)	2017 ($ per capita)
Total Revenues	993,265	2,462
Total Expenditures	905,909	2,245
Debt Outstanding	1,412,149	3,500
Cash and Securities[1]	1,669,350	4,137

Note: (1) Cash and security holdings of a government at the close of its fiscal year,
including those of its dependent agencies, utilities, and liquor stores.
Source: U.S. Census Bureau, State & Local Government Finances 2017

City Government Revenue by Source

Source	2017 ($000)	2017 ($ per capita)	2017 (%)
General Revenue			
From Federal Government	40,963	102	4.1
From State Government	7,495	19	0.8
From Local Governments	25,712	64	2.6
Taxes			
Property	73,800	183	7.4
Sales and Gross Receipts	306,930	761	30.9
Personal Income	0	0	0.0
Corporate Income	0	0	0.0
Motor Vehicle License	0	0	0.0
Other Taxes	8,111	20	0.8
Current Charges	278,642	691	28.1
Liquor Store	0	0	0.0
Utility	129,580	321	13.0
Employee Retirement	42,600	106	4.3

Source: U.S. Census Bureau, State & Local Government Finances 2017

City Government Expenditures by Function

Function	2017 ($000)	2017 ($ per capita)	2017 (%)
General Direct Expenditures			
Air Transportation	41,298	102	4.6
Corrections	0	0	0.0
Education	0	0	0.0
Employment Security Administration	0	0	0.0
Financial Administration	10,473	26	1.2
Fire Protection	72,064	178	8.0
General Public Buildings	0	0	0.0
Governmental Administration, Other	16,218	40	1.8
Health	76,482	189	8.4
Highways	121,060	300	13.4
Hospitals	0	0	0.0
Housing and Community Development	7,114	17	0.8
Interest on General Debt	34,077	84	3.8
Judicial and Legal	6,196	15	0.7
Libraries	20,179	50	2.2
Parking	3,811	9	0.4
Parks and Recreation	40,798	101	4.5
Police Protection	104,702	259	11.6
Public Welfare	17,689	43	2.0
Sewerage	101,124	250	11.2
Solid Waste Management	23,493	58	2.6
Veterans' Services	0	0	0.0
Liquor Store	0	0	0.0
Utility	149,817	371	16.5
Employee Retirement	35,167	87	3.9

Source: U.S. Census Bureau, State & Local Government Finances 2017

EMPLOYMENT

Labor Force and Employment

Area	Civilian Labor Force			Workers Employed		
	Dec. 2019	Dec. 2020	% Chg.	Dec. 2019	Dec. 2020	% Chg.
City	196,335	194,348	-1.0	190,196	182,480	-4.1
MSA[1]	481,673	474,408	-1.5	466,612	447,916	-4.0
U.S.	164,007,000	160,017,000	-2.4	158,504,000	149,613,000	-5.6

Note: Data is not seasonally adjusted and covers workers 16 years of age and older; (1) Figures cover the Tulsa, OK Metropolitan Statistical Area
Source: Bureau of Labor Statistics, Local Area Unemployment Statistics

Unemployment Rate

Area	2020											
	Jan.	Feb.	Mar.	Apr.	May	Jun.	Jul.	Aug.	Sep.	Oct.	Nov.	Dec.
City	3.2	3.1	3.0	16.2	14.2	7.9	8.6	6.8	6.4	7.4	7.1	6.1
MSA[1]	3.2	3.0	3.0	15.1	12.9	7.1	7.6	6.1	5.7	6.6	6.4	5.6
U.S.	4.0	3.8	4.5	14.4	13.0	11.2	10.5	8.5	7.7	6.6	6.4	6.5

Note: Data is not seasonally adjusted and covers workers 16 years of age and older; (1) Figures cover the Tulsa, OK Metropolitan Statistical Area
Source: Bureau of Labor Statistics, Local Area Unemployment Statistics

Average Wages

Occupation	$/Hr.	Occupation	$/Hr.
Accountants and Auditors	36.60	Maintenance and Repair Workers	18.90
Automotive Mechanics	19.10	Marketing Managers	66.80
Bookkeepers	21.10	Network and Computer Systems Admin.	35.70
Carpenters	24.70	Nurses, Licensed Practical	21.60
Cashiers	11.10	Nurses, Registered	32.40
Computer Programmers	40.40	Nursing Assistants	13.10
Computer Systems Analysts	45.60	Office Clerks, General	16.40
Computer User Support Specialists	24.50	Physical Therapists	42.00
Construction Laborers	16.60	Physicians	101.70
Cooks, Restaurant	12.50	Plumbers, Pipefitters and Steamfitters	26.50
Customer Service Representatives	16.10	Police and Sheriff's Patrol Officers	27.30
Dentists	n/a	Postal Service Mail Carriers	25.80
Electricians	23.70	Real Estate Sales Agents	43.70
Engineers, Electrical	49.80	Retail Salespersons	13.50
Fast Food and Counter Workers	9.60	Sales Representatives, Technical/Scientific	39.80
Financial Managers	71.10	Secretaries, Exc. Legal/Medical/Executive	17.00
First-Line Supervisors of Office Workers	28.40	Security Guards	15.20
General and Operations Managers	51.60	Surgeons	n/a
Hairdressers/Cosmetologists	13.50	Teacher Assistants, Exc. Postsecondary*	11.40
Home Health and Personal Care Aides	10.70	Teachers, Secondary School, Exc. Sp. Ed.*	26.50
Janitors and Cleaners	12.10	Telemarketers	12.50
Landscaping/Groundskeeping Workers	14.90	Truck Drivers, Heavy/Tractor-Trailer	27.50
Lawyers	68.70	Truck Drivers, Light/Delivery Services	18.90
Maids and Housekeeping Cleaners	11.10	Waiters and Waitresses	9.10

Note: Wage data covers the Tulsa, OK Metropolitan Statistical Area; (*) Hourly wages were calculated from annual wage data based on a 40 hour work week; n/a not available.
Source: Bureau of Labor Statistics, Metro Area Occupational Employment & Wage Estimates, May 2020

Employment by Industry

Sector	MSA[1]		U.S.
	Number of Employees	Percent of Total	Percent of Total
Construction	24,600	5.6	5.1
Education and Health Services	70,300	16.1	16.3
Financial Activities	22,400	5.1	6.1
Government	55,600	12.8	15.2
Information	6,000	1.4	1.9
Leisure and Hospitality	41,600	9.5	9.0
Manufacturing	48,400	11.1	8.5
Mining and Logging	4,700	1.1	0.4
Other Services	19,300	4.4	3.8
Professional and Business Services	56,800	13.0	14.4
Retail Trade	48,600	11.2	10.9
Transportation, Warehousing, and Utilities	21,700	5.0	4.6
Wholesale Trade	15,700	3.6	3.9

Note: Figures are non-farm employment as of December 2020. Figures are not seasonally adjusted and include workers 16 years of age and older; (1) Figures cover the Tulsa, OK Metropolitan Statistical Area
Source: Bureau of Labor Statistics, Current Employment Statistics, Employment, Hours, and Earnings

Employment by Occupation

Occupation Classification	City (%)	MSA[1] (%)	U.S. (%)
Management, Business, Science, and Arts	36.4	36.3	38.5
Natural Resources, Construction, and Maintenance	9.3	9.9	8.9
Production, Transportation, and Material Moving	13.6	14.3	13.2
Sales and Office	22.9	23.0	21.6
Service	17.7	16.5	17.8

Note: Figures cover employed civilians 16 years of age and older; (1) Figures cover the Tulsa, OK Metropolitan Statistical Area
Source: U.S. Census Bureau, 2015-2019 American Community Survey 5-Year Estimates

Occupations with Greatest Projected Employment Growth: 2020 – 2022

Occupation[1]	2020 Employment	2022 Projected Employment	Numeric Employment Change	Percent Employment Change
Home Health and Personal Care Aides	20,550	21,560	1,010	4.9
Fast Food and Counter Workers	39,040	40,030	990	2.5
Registered Nurses	38,490	39,340	850	2.2
Cooks, Restaurant	17,770	18,610	840	4.7
Elementary School Teachers, Except Special Education	18,640	19,120	480	2.6
Medical and Health Services Managers	7,810	8,280	470	6.0
Laborers and Freight, Stock, and Material Movers, Hand	31,360	31,740	380	1.2
Medical Assistants	9,400	9,760	360	3.8
Secondary School Teachers, Except Special and Career/Technical Education	12,000	12,320	320	2.7
Teaching Assistants, Except Postsecondary	13,690	13,990	300	2.2

Note: Projections cover Oklahoma; (1) Sorted by numeric employment change
Source: www.projectionscentral.com, State Occupational Projections, 2020–2022 Short-Term Projections

Fastest-Growing Occupations: 2020 – 2022

Occupation[1]	2020 Employment	2022 Projected Employment	Numeric Employment Change	Percent Employment Change
Wind Turbine Service Technicians	400	460	60	15.0
Veterinary Technologists and Technicians	860	940	80	9.3
Veterinary Assistants and Laboratory Animal Caretakers	1,600	1,740	140	8.8
Nurse Practitioners	2,010	2,170	160	8.0
Veterinarians	1,360	1,460	100	7.4
Occupational Therapy Assistants	860	920	60	7.0
Physical Therapist Assistants	1,680	1,790	110	6.5
Nonfarm Animal Caretakers	2,870	3,050	180	6.3
Physician Assistants	1,640	1,740	100	6.1
Medical and Health Services Managers	7,810	8,280	470	6.0

Note: Projections cover Oklahoma; (1) Sorted by percent employment change and excludes occupations with numeric employment change less than 50
Source: www.projectionscentral.com, State Occupational Projections, 2020–2022 Short-Term Projections

TAXES

State Corporate Income Tax Rates

State	Tax Rate (%)	Income Brackets ($)	Num. of Brackets	Financial Institution Tax Rate (%)[a]	Federal Income Tax Ded.
Oklahoma	6.0	Flat rate	1	6.0	No

Note: Tax rates as of January 1, 2021; (a) Rates listed are the corporate income tax rate applied to financial institutions or excise taxes based on income. Some states have other taxes based upon the value of deposits or shares.
Source: Federation of Tax Administrators, State Corporate Income Tax Rates, January 1, 2021

State Individual Income Tax Rates

State	Tax Rate (%)	Income Brackets ($)	Personal Exemptions ($)			Standard Ded. ($)	
			Single	Married	Depend.	Single	Married
Oklahoma	0.5 - 5.0	1,000 - 7,200 (t)	1,000	2,000	1,000	6,350	12,700

Note: Tax rates as of January 1, 2021; Local- and county-level taxes are not included; Federal income tax is not deductible on state income tax returns; (t) The income brackets reported for Oklahoma are for single persons. For married persons filing jointly, the same tax rates apply to income brackets ranging from $2,000, to $12,200.
Source: Federation of Tax Administrators, State Individual Income Tax Rates, January 1, 2021

Various State Sales and Excise Tax Rates

State	State Sales Tax (%)	Gasoline[1] (¢/gal.)	Cigarette[2] ($/pack)	Spirits[3] ($/gal.)	Wine[4] ($/gal.)	Beer[5] ($/gal.)	Recreational Marijuana (%)
Oklahoma	4.5	20	2.03	5.56	0.72	0.4	Not legal

Note: All tax rates as of January 1, 2021; (1) The American Petroleum Institute has developed a methodology for determining the average tax rate on a gallon of fuel. Rates may include any of the following: excise taxes, environmental fees, storage tank fees, other fees or taxes, general sales tax, and local taxes; (2) The federal excise tax of $1.0066 per pack and local taxes are not included; (3) Rates are those applicable to off-premise sales of 40% alcohol by volume (a.b.v.) distilled spirits in 750ml containers. Local excise taxes are excluded; (4) Rates are those applicable to off-premise sales of 11% a.b.v. non-carbonated wine in 750ml containers; (5) Rates are those applicable to off-premise sales of 4.7% a.b.v. beer in 12 ounce containers.
Source: Tax Foundation, 2021 Facts & Figures: How Does Your State Compare?

State Business Tax Climate Index Rankings

State	Overall Rank	Corporate Tax Rank	Individual Income Tax Rank	Sales Tax Rank	Property Tax Rank	Unemployment Insurance Tax Rank
Oklahoma	30	11	33	39	29	1

Note: The index is a measure of how each state's tax laws affect economic performance. The lower the rank, the more favorable a state's tax system is for business. States without a given tax are given a ranking of 1. The scores/rankings for the District of Columbia do not affect other states. The 2021 index represents the tax climate as of July 1, 2020.
Source: Tax Foundation, State Business Tax Climate Index 2021

TRANSPORTATION

Means of Transportation to Work

Area	Car/Truck/Van		Public Transportation			Bicycle	Walked	Other Means	Worked at Home
	Drove Alone	Car-pooled	Bus	Subway	Railroad				
City	80.2	10.7	0.9	0.0	0.0	0.3	1.8	2.1	4.0
MSA[1]	82.8	9.6	0.4	0.0	0.0	0.2	1.2	1.5	4.2
U.S.	76.3	9.0	2.4	1.9	0.6	0.5	2.7	1.4	5.2

Note: Figures are percentages and cover workers 16 years of age and older; (1) Figures cover the Tulsa, OK Metropolitan Statistical Area
Source: U.S. Census Bureau, 2015-2019 American Community Survey 5-Year Estimates

Travel Time to Work

Area	Less Than 10 Minutes	10 to 19 Minutes	20 to 29 Minutes	30 to 44 Minutes	45 to 59 Minutes	60 to 89 Minutes	90 Minutes or More
City	14.6	44.5	25.7	10.5	2.0	1.5	1.2
MSA[1]	13.3	33.9	26.5	18.1	4.5	2.2	1.4
U.S.	12.2	28.4	20.8	20.8	8.3	6.4	2.9

Note: Note: Figures are percentages and include workers 16 years old and over; (1) Figures cover the Tulsa, OK Metropolitan Statistical Area
Source: U.S. Census Bureau, 2015-2019 American Community Survey 5-Year Estimates

Key Congestion Measures

Measure	1982	1992	2002	2012	2017
Annual Hours of Delay, Total (000)	3,682	9,434	14,993	21,355	25,228
Annual Hours of Delay, Per Auto Commuter	13	25	33	37	46
Annual Congestion Cost, Total (million $)	28	99	202	382	464
Annual Congestion Cost, Per Auto Commuter ($)	240	422	523	584	669

Note: Covers the Tulsa OK urban area
Source: Texas A&M Transportation Institute, 2019 Urban Mobility Report

Freeway Travel Time Index

Measure	1982	1987	1992	1997	2002	2007	2012	2017
Urban Area Index[1]	1.05	1.07	1.10	1.12	1.14	1.17	1.16	1.15
Urban Area Rank[1,2]	51	55	59	69	69	56	60	71

Note: Freeway Travel Time Index—the ratio of travel time in the peak period to the travel time at free-flow conditions. For example, a value of 1.30 indicates a 20-minute free-flow trip takes 26 minutes in the peak (20 minutes x 1.30 = 26 minutes); (1) Covers the Tulsa OK urban area; (2) Rank is based on 101 larger urban areas (#1 = highest travel time index)
Source: Texas A&M Transportation Institute, 2019 Urban Mobility Report

Public Transportation

Agency Name / Mode of Transportation	Vehicles Operated in Maximum Service[1]	Annual Unlinked Passenger Trips[2] (in thous.)	Annual Passenger Miles[3] (in thous.)
Metropolitan Tulsa Transit Authority (MTTA)			
Bus (directly operated)	52	2,520.7	13,309.2
Bus (purchased transportation)	12	92.4	639.4
Demand Response (purchased transportation)	28	104.5	913.3

Note: (1) Number of revenue vehicles operated by the given mode and type of service to meet the annual maximum service requirement. This is the revenue vehicle count during the peak season of the year; on the week and day that maximum service is provided. Vehicles operated in maximum service (VOMS) exclude atypical days and one-time special events; (2) Number of passengers who boarded public transportation vehicles. Passengers are counted each time they board a vehicle no matter how many vehicles they use to travel from their origin to their destination. (3) Sum of the distances ridden by all passengers during the entire fiscal year.
Source: Federal Transit Administration, National Transit Database, 2019

Air Transportation

Airport Name and Code / Type of Service	Passenger Airlines[1]	Passenger Enplanements	Freight Carriers[2]	Freight (lbs)
Tulsa International (TUL)				
Domestic service (U.S. carriers - 2020)	24	665,941	19	61,959,702
International service (U.S. carriers - 2019)	1	7	1	3,630

Note: (1) Includes all U.S.-based major, minor and commuter airlines that carried at least one passenger during the year; (2) Includes all U.S.-based airlines and freight carriers that transported at least one pound of freight during the year.
Source: Bureau of Transportation Statistics, The Intermodal Transportation Database, Air Carriers: T-100 Domestic Market (U.S. Carriers), 2020; Bureau of Transportation Statistics, The Intermodal Transportation Database, Air Carriers: T-100 International Market (U.S. Carriers), 2019

BUSINESSES

Major Business Headquarters

Company Name	Industry	Rankings	
		Fortune[1]	Forbes[2]
NGL Energy Partners	Wholesalers, Diversified	127	-
Oneok	Pipelines	313	-
QuikTrip	Convenience Stores & Gas Stations	-	29
Williams	Energy	387	-

Note: (1) Companies that produce a 10-K are ranked 1 to 500 based on 2019 revenue; (2) All private companies with at least $2 billion in annual revenue through the end of their most current fiscal year are ranked 1 to 219; companies listed are headquartered in the city; dashes indicate no ranking
Source: Fortune, "Fortune 500," June/July 2020; Forbes, "America's Largest Private Companies," 2020

Living Environment

COST OF LIVING

Cost of Living Index

Composite Index	Groceries	Housing	Utilities	Transportation	Health Care	Misc. Goods/ Services
85.1	94.2	62.3	94.3	86.6	94.5	95.5

Note: The Cost of Living Index measures regional differences in the cost of consumer goods and services, excluding taxes and non-consumer expenditures, for professional and managerial households in the top income quintile. It is based on more than 50,000 prices covering almost 60 different items for which prices are collected three times a year by chambers of commerce, economic development organizations or university applied economic centers in each participating urban area. The numbers shown should be read as a percentage above or below the national average of 100. For example, a value of 115.4 in the groceries column indicates that grocery prices are 15.4% higher than the national average. Small differences in the index numbers should not be interpreted as significant; Figures cover the Tulsa OK urban area.
Source: The Council for Community and Economic Research, Cost of Living Index, 2020

Grocery Prices

Area[1]	T-Bone Steak ($/pound)	Frying Chicken ($/pound)	Whole Milk ($/half gal.)	Eggs ($/dozen)	Orange Juice ($/64 oz.)	Coffee ($/11.5 oz.)
City[2]	11.20	1.30	2.00	1.38	3.44	3.89
Avg.	11.78	1.39	2.05	1.47	3.57	4.34
Min.	8.03	0.94	1.03	0.74	2.94	3.02
Max.	15.86	2.65	4.31	3.77	5.44	8.69

Note: (1) Values for the local area are compared with the average, minimum and maximum values for all 284 areas in the Cost of Living Index; (2) Figures cover the Tulsa OK urban area; T-Bone Steak (price per pound); Frying Chicken (price per pound, whole fryer); Whole Milk (half gallon carton); Eggs (price per dozen, Grade A, large); Orange Juice (64 oz. Tropicana or Florida Natural); Coffee (11.5 oz. can, vacuum-packed, Maxwell House, Hills Bros, or Folgers).
Source: The Council for Community and Economic Research, Cost of Living Index, 2020

Housing and Utility Costs

Area[1]	New Home Price ($)	Apartment Rent ($/month)	All Electric ($/month)	Part Electric ($/month)	Other Energy ($/month)	Telephone ($/month)
City[2]	239,022	680	-	87.50	59.74	188.20
Avg.	368,594	1,168	170.86	100.47	65.28	184.30
Min.	190,567	502	91.58	31.42	26.08	169.60
Max.	2,227,806	4,738	470.38	280.31	280.06	206.50

Note: (1) Values for the local area are compared with the average, minimum and maximum values for all 284 areas in the Cost of Living Index; (2) Figures cover the Tulsa OK urban area; New Home Price (2,400 sf living area, 8,000 sf lot, in urban area with full utilities); Apartment Rent (950 sf 2 bedroom/1.5 or 2 bath, unfurnished, excluding all utilities except water); All Electric (average monthly cost for an all-electric home); Part Electric (average monthly cost for a part-electric home); Other Energy (average monthly cost for natural gas, fuel oil, coal, wood, and any other forms of energy except electricity); Telephone (price includes the base monthly rate plus taxes and fees for three lines of mobile phone service).
Source: The Council for Community and Economic Research, Cost of Living Index, 2020

Health Care, Transportation, and Other Costs

Area[1]	Doctor ($/visit)	Dentist ($/visit)	Optometrist ($/visit)	Gasoline ($/gallon)	Beauty Salon ($/visit)	Men's Shirt ($)
City[2]	109.61	90.61	99.06	1.77	35.56	23.57
Avg.	115.44	99.32	108.10	2.21	39.27	31.37
Min.	36.68	59.00	51.36	1.71	19.00	11.00
Max.	219.00	153.10	250.97	3.46	82.05	58.33

Note: (1) Values for the local area are compared with the average, minimum and maximum values for all 284 areas in the Cost of Living Index; (2) Figures cover the Tulsa OK urban area; Doctor (general practitioners routine exam of an established patient); Dentist (adult teeth cleaning and periodic oral examination); Optometrist (full vision eye exam for established adult patient); Gasoline (one gallon regular unleaded, national brand, including all taxes, cash price at self-service pump if available); Beauty Salon (woman's shampoo, trim, and blow-dry); Men's Shirt (cotton/polyester dress shirt, pinpoint weave, long sleeves).
Source: The Council for Community and Economic Research, Cost of Living Index, 2020

HOUSING

Homeownership Rate

Area	2012 (%)	2013 (%)	2014 (%)	2015 (%)	2016 (%)	2017 (%)	2018 (%)	2019 (%)	2020 (%)
MSA[1]	66.5	64.1	65.3	65.2	65.4	66.8	68.3	70.5	70.1
U.S.	65.4	65.1	64.5	63.7	63.4	63.9	64.4	64.6	66.6

Note: (1) Figures cover the Tulsa, OK Metropolitan Statistical Area
Source: U.S. Census Bureau, Housing Vacancies and Homeownership Annual Statistics: 2012-2020

House Price Index (HPI)

Area	National Ranking[2]	Quarterly Change (%)	One-Year Change (%)	Five-Year Change (%)	Since 1991Q1 (%)
MSA[1]	179	1.98	5.26	22.61	153.16
U.S.[3]	–	3.81	10.77	38.99	205.12

Note: The HPI is a weighted repeat sales index. It measures average price changes in repeat sales or refinancings on the same properties. This information is obtained by reviewing repeat mortgage transactions on single-family properties whose mortgages have been purchased or securitized by Fannie Mae or Freddie Mac since January 1975; (1) Figures cover the Tulsa, OK Metropolitan Statistical Area; (2) Rankings are based on annual percentage change for all metro areas containing at least 15,000 transactions over the last 10 years and ranges from 1 to 253; (3) figures based on a weighted average of Census Division estimates using a seasonally adjusted, purchase-only index; all figures are for the period ending December 31, 2020
Source: Federal Housing Finance Agency, Change in Metropolitan Area House Price Indexes, April 7, 2021

Median Single-Family Home Prices

Area	2018	2019	2020p	Percent Change 2019 to 2020
MSA[1]	165.3	173.2	195.9	13.1
U.S. Average	261.6	274.6	299.9	9.2

Note: Figures are median sales prices of existing single-family homes in thousands of dollars; (p) preliminary; (1) Figures cover the Tulsa, OK Metropolitan Statistical Area
Source: National Association of Realtors, Median Sales Price of Existing Single-Family Homes for Metropolitan Areas, 4th Quarter 2020

Qualifying Income Based on Median Sales Price of Existing Single-Family Homes

Area	With 5% Down ($)	With 10% Down ($)	With 20% Down ($)
MSA[1]	38,698	36,662	32,588
U.S. Average	59,266	56,147	49,908

Note: Figures are preliminary; Qualifying income is based on a mortgage rate of 2.81%. Monthly principal and interest payment is limited to 25% of income; (1) Figures cover the Tulsa, OK Metropolitan Statistical Area
Source: National Association of Realtors, Qualifying Income Based on Median Sales Price of Existing Single-Family Homes for Metropolitan Areas, 4th Quarter 2020

Home Value Distribution

Area	Under $50,000	$50,000 -$99,999	$100,000 -$149,999	$150,000 -$199,999	$200,000 -$299,999	$300,000 -$499,999	$500,000 -$999,999	$1,000,000 or more
City	9.0	22.8	22.3	15.7	13.8	10.4	4.9	1.2
MSA[1]	9.4	18.7	21.7	19.4	17.3	9.4	3.4	0.8
U.S.	6.9	12.0	13.3	14.0	19.6	19.3	11.4	3.4

Note: Figures are percentages and cover owner-occupied housing units; (1) Figures cover the Tulsa, OK Metropolitan Statistical Area
Source: U.S. Census Bureau, 2015-2019 American Community Survey 5-Year Estimates

Year Housing Structure Built

Area	2010 or Later	2000 -2009	1990 -1999	1980 -1989	1970 -1979	1960 -1969	1950 -1959	1940 -1949	Before 1940	Median Year
City	3.6	6.1	9.5	13.3	21.0	14.4	16.8	6.4	9.0	1972
MSA[1]	6.7	14.4	12.7	14.3	19.3	10.5	10.6	4.5	7.0	1979
U.S.	5.2	14.0	13.9	13.4	15.2	10.6	10.3	4.9	12.6	1978

Note: Figures are percentages except for Median Year; Note: (1) Figures cover the Tulsa, OK Metropolitan Statistical Area
Source: U.S. Census Bureau, 2015-2019 American Community Survey 5-Year Estimates

Gross Monthly Rent

Area	Under $500	$500 -$999	$1,000 -$1,499	$1,500 -$1,999	$2,000 -$2,499	$2,500 -$2,999	$3,000 and up	Median ($)
City	10.9	59.4	24.1	3.6	1.0	0.5	0.6	829
MSA[1]	10.7	56.8	26.1	4.4	1.0	0.5	0.5	852
U.S.	9.4	36.2	30.0	14.0	5.6	2.4	2.4	1,062

Note: Figures are percentages except for Median; Gross rent is the contract rent plus the estimated average monthly cost of utilities (electricity, gas, and water and sewer) and fuels (oil, coal, kerosene, wood, etc.) if these are paid by the renter (or paid for the renter by someone else); (1) Figures cover the Tulsa, OK Metropolitan Statistical Area
Source: U.S. Census Bureau, 2015-2019 American Community Survey 5-Year Estimates

HEALTH

Health Risk Factors

Category	MSA[1] (%)	U.S. (%)
Adults aged 18–64 who have any kind of health care coverage	80.4	87.3
Adults who reported being in good or better health	80.2	82.4
Adults who have been told they have high blood cholesterol	34.9	33.0
Adults who have been told they have high blood pressure	37.4	32.3
Adults who are current smokers	20.0	17.1
Adults who currently use E-cigarettes	6.9	4.6
Adults who currently use chewing tobacco, snuff, or snus	6.4	4.0
Adults who are heavy drinkers[2]	4.5	6.3
Adults who are binge drinkers[3]	14.7	17.4
Adults who are overweight (BMI 25.0 - 29.9)	34.7	35.3
Adults who are obese (BMI 30.0 - 99.8)	36.0	31.3
Adults who participated in any physical activities in the past month	68.2	74.4
Adults who always or nearly always wears a seat belt	94.4	94.3

Note: (1) Figures cover the Tulsa, OK Metropolitan Statistical Area; (2) Heavy drinkers are classified as adult men having more than 14 drinks per week and adult women having more than 7 drinks per week; (3) Binge drinkers are classified as males having five or more drinks on one occasion or females having four or more drinks on one occasion
Source: Centers for Disease Control and Prevention, Behaviorial Risk Factor Surveillance System, SMART: Selected Metropolitan Area Risk Trends, 2017

Acute and Chronic Health Conditions

Category	MSA[1] (%)	U.S. (%)
Adults who have ever been told they had a heart attack	5.1	4.2
Adults who have ever been told they have angina or coronary heart disease	4.1	3.9
Adults who have ever been told they had a stroke	4.8	3.0
Adults who have ever been told they have asthma	14.2	14.2
Adults who have ever been told they have arthritis	27.0	24.9
Adults who have ever been told they have diabetes[2]	11.7	10.5
Adults who have ever been told they had skin cancer	6.7	6.2
Adults who have ever been told they had any other types of cancer	6.8	7.1
Adults who have ever been told they have COPD	8.1	6.5
Adults who have ever been told they have kidney disease	3.5	3.0
Adults who have ever been told they have a form of depression	24.6	20.5

Note: (1) Figures cover the Tulsa, OK Metropolitan Statistical Area; (2) Figures do not include pregnancy-related, borderline, or pre-diabetes
Source: Centers for Disease Control and Prevention, Behaviorial Risk Factor Surveillance System, SMART: Selected Metropolitan Area Risk Trends, 2017

Health Screening and Vaccination Rates

Category	MSA[1] (%)	U.S. (%)
Adults aged 65+ who have had flu shot within the past year	68.8	60.7
Adults aged 65+ who have ever had a pneumonia vaccination	81.3	75.4
Adults who have ever been tested for HIV	34.2	36.1
Adults who have ever had the shingles or zoster vaccine?	27.9	28.9
Adults who have had their blood cholesterol checked within the last five years	79.0	85.9

Note: n/a not available; (1) Figures cover the Tulsa, OK Metropolitan Statistical Area.
Source: Centers for Disease Control and Prevention, Behaviorial Risk Factor Surveillance System, SMART: Selected Metropolitan Area Risk Trends, 2017

Disability Status

Category	MSA[1] (%)	U.S. (%)
Adults who reported being deaf	9.4	6.7
Are you blind or have serious difficulty seeing, even when wearing glasses?	6.2	4.5
Are you limited in any way in any of your usual activities due of arthritis?	14.2	12.9
Do you have difficulty doing errands alone?	7.7	6.8
Do you have difficulty dressing or bathing?	3.4	3.6
Do you have serious difficulty concentrating/remembering/making decisions?	13.5	10.7
Do you have serious difficulty walking or climbing stairs?	17.6	13.6

Note: (1) Figures cover the Tulsa, OK Metropolitan Statistical Area.
Source: Centers for Disease Control and Prevention, Behaviorial Risk Factor Surveillance System, SMART: Selected Metropolitan Area Risk Trends, 2017

Mortality Rates for the Top 10 Causes of Death in the U.S.

ICD-10[a] Sub-Chapter	ICD-10[a] Code	Age-Adjusted Mortality Rate[1] per 100,000 population	
		County[2]	U.S.
Malignant neoplasms	C00-C97	167.1	149.2
Ischaemic heart diseases	I20-I25	99.9	90.5
Other forms of heart disease	I30-I51	34.6	52.2
Chronic lower respiratory diseases	J40-J47	52.4	39.6
Other degenerative diseases of the nervous system	G30-G31	44.4	37.6
Cerebrovascular diseases	I60-I69	43.5	37.2
Other external causes of accidental injury	W00-X59	37.7	36.1
Organic, including symptomatic, mental disorders	F01-F09	28.9	29.4
Hypertensive diseases	I10-I15	110.7	24.1
Diabetes mellitus	E10-E14	20.3	21.5

Note: (a) ICD-10 = International Classification of Diseases 10th Revision; (1) Mortality rates are a three-year average covering 2017-2019; (2) Figures cover Tulsa County.
Source: Centers for Disease Control and Prevention, National Center for Health Statistics. Underlying Cause of Death 1999-2019 on CDC WONDER Online Database

Mortality Rates for Selected Causes of Death

ICD-10[a] Sub-Chapter	ICD-10[a] Code	Age-Adjusted Mortality Rate[1] per 100,000 population	
		County[2]	U.S.
Assault	X85-Y09	10.8	6.0
Diseases of the liver	K70-K76	17.7	14.4
Human immunodeficiency virus (HIV) disease	B20-B24	1.6	1.5
Influenza and pneumonia	J09-J18	15.9	13.8
Intentional self-harm	X60-X84	18.6	14.1
Malnutrition	E40-E46	1.7	2.3
Obesity and other hyperalimentation	E65-E68	Unreliable	2.1
Renal failure	N17-N19	7.1	12.6
Transport accidents	V01-V99	13.0	12.3
Viral hepatitis	B15-B19	2.5	1.2

Note: (a) ICD-10 = International Classification of Diseases 10th Revision; (1) Mortality rates are a three-year average covering 2017-2019; (2) Figures cover Tulsa County; Data are suppressed when the data meet the criteria for confidentiality constraints; Mortality rates are flagged as unreliable when the rate would be calculated with a numerator of 20 or less.
Source: Centers for Disease Control and Prevention, National Center for Health Statistics. Underlying Cause of Death 1999-2019 on CDC WONDER Online Database

Health Insurance Coverage

Area	With Health Insurance	With Private Health Insurance	With Public Health Insurance	Without Health Insurance	Population Under Age 19 Without Health Insurance
City	83.4	58.9	35.1	16.6	8.2
MSA[1]	86.6	65.8	32.6	13.4	7.6
U.S.	91.2	67.9	35.1	8.8	5.1

Note: Figures are percentages that cover the civilian noninstitutionalized population; (1) Figures cover the Tulsa, OK Metropolitan Statistical Area
Source: U.S. Census Bureau, 2015-2019 American Community Survey 5-Year Estimates

Number of Medical Professionals

Area	MDs[3]	DOs[3,4]	Dentists	Podiatrists	Chiropractors	Optometrists
County[1] (number)	1,744	790	454	26	253	153
County[1] (rate[2])	269.3	122.0	69.7	4.0	38.8	23.5
U.S. (rate[2])	282.9	22.7	71.2	6.2	28.1	16.9

40143
Note: Data as of 2019 unless noted; (1) Data covers Tulsa County; (2) Rate per 100,000 population; (3) Data as of 2018 and includes all active, non-federal physicians; (4) Doctor of Osteopathic Medicine
Source: U.S. Department of Health and Human Services, Health Resources and Services Administration, Bureau of Health Professions, Area Resource File (ARF) 2019-2020

EDUCATION

Public School District Statistics

District Name	Schls	Pupils	Pupil/ Teacher Ratio	Minority Pupils[1] (%)	Free Lunch Eligible[2] (%)	IEP[3] (%)
Tulsa	77	36,512	16.2	76.4	n/a	17.2
Union	17	15,773	18.4	70.6	n/a	12.2

Note: Table includes school districts with 2,000 or more students; (1) Percentage of students that are not non-Hispanic white; (2) Percentage of students that are eligible for the free lunch program; (3) Percentage of students that have an Individualized Education Program.
Source: U.S. Department of Education, National Center for Education Statistics, Common Core of Data, Local Education Agency (School District) Universe Survey: School Year 2018-2019; U.S. Department of Education, National Center for Education Statistics, Common Core of Data, Public Elementary/Secondary School Universe Survey: School Year 2018-2019

Best High Schools

According to *U.S. News*, Tulsa is home to one of the top 500 high schools in the U.S.: **Booker T. Washington High School** (#198). Nearly 18,000 public, magnet and charter schools were ranked based on their performance on state assessments and how well they prepare students for college. *U.S. News & World Report, "Best High Schools 2020"*

Highest Level of Education

Area	Less than H.S.	H.S. Diploma	Some College, No Deg.	Associate Degree	Bachelor's Degree	Master's Degree	Prof. School Degree	Doctorate Degree
City	12.7	25.3	22.6	7.9	20.7	7.2	2.5	1.1
MSA[1]	10.6	29.1	23.7	8.9	18.9	6.3	1.7	0.9
U.S.	12.0	27.0	20.4	8.5	19.8	8.8	2.1	1.4

Note: Figures cover persons age 25 and over; (1) Figures cover the Tulsa, OK Metropolitan Statistical Area
Source: U.S. Census Bureau, 2015-2019 American Community Survey 5-Year Estimates

Educational Attainment by Race

Area	High School Graduate or Higher (%)					Bachelor's Degree or Higher (%)				
	Total	White	Black	Asian	Hisp.[2]	Total	White	Black	Asian	Hisp.[2]
City	87.3	89.9	88.8	74.8	57.6	31.5	36.5	17.6	37.8	10.7
MSA[1]	89.4	90.9	89.5	77.7	63.4	27.7	29.8	19.2	37.0	12.4
U.S.	88.0	89.9	86.0	87.1	68.7	32.1	33.5	21.6	54.3	16.4

Note: Figures shown cover persons 25 years old and over; (1) Figures cover the Tulsa, OK Metropolitan Statistical Area; (2) People of Hispanic origin can be of any race
Source: U.S. Census Bureau, 2015-2019 American Community Survey 5-Year Estimates

School Enrollment by Grade and Control

Area	Preschool (%)		Kindergarten (%)		Grades 1 - 4 (%)		Grades 5 - 8 (%)		Grades 9 - 12 (%)	
	Public	Private	Public	Private	Public	Private	Public	Private	Public	Private
City	67.6	32.4	87.1	12.9	88.3	11.7	85.8	14.2	85.2	14.8
MSA[1]	69.4	30.6	88.7	11.3	88.9	11.1	88.2	11.8	87.7	12.3
U.S.	59.1	40.9	87.6	12.4	89.5	10.5	89.4	10.6	90.1	9.9

Note: Figures shown cover persons 3 years old and over; (1) Figures cover the Tulsa, OK Metropolitan Statistical Area
Source: U.S. Census Bureau, 2015-2019 American Community Survey 5-Year Estimates

Higher Education

Four-Year Colleges			Two-Year Colleges			Medical Schools[1]	Law Schools[2]	Voc/ Tech[3]
Public	Private Non-profit	Private For-profit	Public	Private Non-profit	Private For-profit			
1	3	2	2	2	3	2	1	3

Note: Figures cover institutions located within the city limits and include main campuses only; (1) includes schools accredited by the Liaison Committee on Medical Education and the American Osteopathic Association's Commission on Osteopathic College Accreditation; (2) includes ABA-accredited schools, schools with provisional ABA accreditation, and state accredited schools; (3) includes all schools with programs that are less than 2 years.
Source: National Center for Education Statistics, Integrated Postsecondary Education System (IPEDS), 2019-20; Wikipedia, List of Medical Schools in the United States, accessed April 2, 2021; Wikipedia, List of Law Schools in the United States, accessed April 2, 2021

According to *U.S. News & World Report*, the Tulsa, OK metro area is home to one of the top 200 national universities in the U.S.: **University of Tulsa** (#143 tie). The indicators used to capture academic quality fall into a number of categories: assessment by administrators at peer institutions; retention of students; faculty resources; student selectivity; financial resources; alumni giving; high school counselor ratings of colleges; and graduation rate. *U.S. News & World Report, "America's Best Colleges 2021"*

EMPLOYERS

Major Employers

Company Name	Industry
AHS Hillcrest Medical Center	General medical & surgical hospitals
American Airlines	Airports, flying fields, & services
BlueCross BlueShield of Oklahoma	Hospital & medical services plans
Caprock Pipeline Company	Pipelines, natural gas
County of Tulsa	County government
Dollar Thrifty Automotive Group	Passenger car rental
GHS Health Maintenance Organization	Health insurance carriers
IBM	Computer related consulting services
IC of Oklahoma	Truck & bus bodies
Matrix Service	Oil & gas pipeline construction
ONEOK	Natural gas transmission
Saint Francis Health System	General medical & surgical hospitals
St. John Medical Center	General medical & surgical hospitals
State Farm Fire and Casualty Company	Fire, marine, & casualty insurance
The Bama Companies	Bread, cake & related products
The Boeing Company	Missile guidance systems & equipment
The NORDAM Group	Aircraft parts & equipment, nec
The Williams Companies	Natural gas transmission

Note: Companies shown are located within the Tulsa, OK Metropolitan Statistical Area.
Source: Hoovers.com; Wikipedia

PUBLIC SAFETY

Crime Rate

Area	All Crimes	Violent Crimes				Property Crimes		
		Murder	Rape[3]	Robbery	Aggrav. Assault	Burglary	Larceny -Theft	Motor Vehicle Theft
City	6,298.2	13.7	84.9	178.7	709.5	1,206.4	3,350.0	755.0
Suburbs[1]	2,046.1	4.5	38.9	18.4	159.8	420.8	1,190.3	213.3
Metro[2]	3,757.4	8.2	57.4	83.0	381.0	737.0	2,059.5	431.3
U.S.	2,489.3	5.0	42.6	81.6	250.2	340.5	1,549.5	219.9

Note: Figures are crimes per 100,000 population; (1) All areas within the metro area that are located outside the city limits; (2) Figures cover the Tulsa, OK Metropolitan Statistical Area; (3) All figures shown were reported using the revised Uniform Crime Reporting (UCR) definition of rape.
Source: FBI Uniform Crime Reports, 2019

Hate Crimes

Area	Number of Quarters Reported	Number of Incidents per Bias Motivation					
		Race/Ethnicity/ Ancestry	Religion	Sexual Orientation	Disability	Gender	Gender Identity
City	4	1	0	2	0	0	0
U.S.	4	3,963	1,521	1,195	157	69	198

Source: Federal Bureau of Investigation, Hate Crime Statistics 2019

Identity Theft Consumer Reports

Area	Reports	Reports per 100,000 Population	Rank[2]
MSA[1]	3,858	386	80
U.S.	1,387,615	423	-

Note: (1) Figures cover the Tulsa, OK Metropolitan Statistical Area; (2) Rank ranges from 1 to 391 where 1 indicates greatest number of identity theft reports per 100,000 population
Source: Federal Trade Commission, Consumer Sentinel Network Data Book 2020

Fraud and Other Consumer Reports

Area	Reports	Reports per 100,000 Population	Rank[2]
MSA[1]	6,493	650	238
U.S.	3,385,133	1,031	-

Note: (1) Figures cover the Tulsa, OK Metropolitan Statistical Area; (2) Rank ranges from 1 to 391 where 1 indicates greatest number of fraud and other consumer reports per 100,000 population
Source: Federal Trade Commission, Consumer Sentinel Network Data Book 2020

POLITICS

2020 Presidential Election Results

Area	Biden	Trump	Jorgensen	Hawkins	Other
Tulsa County	40.9	56.5	1.8	0.0	0.8
U.S.	51.3	46.8	1.2	0.3	0.5

Note: Results are percentages and may not add to 100% due to rounding
Source: Dave Leip's Atlas of U.S. Presidential Elections

Tulsa, Oklahoma   503

SPORTS

Professional Sports Teams

Team Name	League	Year Established
No teams are located in the metro area		

Source: Wikipedia, Major Professional Sports Teams of the United States and Canada, April 6, 2021

CLIMATE

Average and Extreme Temperatures

Temperature	Jan	Feb	Mar	Apr	May	Jun	Jul	Aug	Sep	Oct	Nov	Dec	Yr.
Extreme High (°F)	79	86	96	102	96	103	112	110	105	98	85	80	112
Average High (°F)	46	52	61	72	80	88	93	93	85	74	61	50	71
Average Temp. (°F)	36	41	50	61	69	78	83	82	74	63	50	40	61
Average Low (°F)	25	30	38	50	59	68	72	70	63	51	39	29	50
Extreme Low (°F)	-6	-7	-3	22	35	49	51	52	35	26	10	-8	-8

Note: Figures cover the years 1948-1990
Source: National Climatic Data Center, International Station Meteorological Climate Summary, 9/96

Average Precipitation/Snowfall/Humidity

Precip./Humidity	Jan	Feb	Mar	Apr	May	Jun	Jul	Aug	Sep	Oct	Nov	Dec	Yr.
Avg. Precip. (in.)	1.6	1.9	3.2	3.7	5.6	4.3	3.4	3.0	4.1	3.5	2.6	1.9	38.9
Avg. Snowfall (in.)	3	2	2	Tr	0	0	0	0	0	Tr	1	2	10
Avg. Rel. Hum. 6am (%)	78	78	76	77	85	85	82	84	85	82	78	78	81
Avg. Rel. Hum. 3pm (%)	53	51	47	46	54	53	48	46	49	46	48	52	49

Note: Figures cover the years 1948-1990; Tr = Trace amounts (<0.05 in. of rain; <0.5 in. of snow)
Source: National Climatic Data Center, International Station Meteorological Climate Summary, 9/96

Weather Conditions

Temperature			Daytime Sky			Precipitation		
10°F & below	32°F & below	90°F & above	Clear	Partly cloudy	Cloudy	0.01 inch or more precip.	0.1 inch or more snow/ice	Thunder-storms
6	78	74	117	141	107	88	8	50

Note: Figures are average number of days per year and cover the years 1948-1990
Source: National Climatic Data Center, International Station Meteorological Climate Summary, 9/96

HAZARDOUS WASTE

Superfund Sites

The Tulsa, OK metro area is home to two sites on the EPA's Superfund National Priorities List: **Henryetta Iron and Metal** (final); **Wilcox Oil Company** (final). There are a total of 1,375 Superfund sites with a status of proposed or final on the list in the U.S. *U.S. Environmental Protection Agency, National Priorities List, April 7, 2021*

AIR QUALITY

Air Quality Trends: Ozone

	1990	1995	2000	2005	2010	2015	2016	2017	2018	2019
MSA[1]	0.086	0.091	0.081	0.072	0.069	0.061	0.064	0.065	0.067	0.062
U.S.	0.088	0.089	0.082	0.080	0.073	0.068	0.069	0.068	0.069	0.065

Note: (1) Data covers the Tulsa, OK Metropolitan Statistical Area. The values shown are the composite ozone concentration averages among trend sites based on the highest fourth daily maximum 8-hour concentration in parts per million. These trends are based on sites having an adequate record of monitoring data during the trend period. Data from exceptional events are included.
Source: U.S. Environmental Protection Agency, Air Quality Monitoring Information, "Air Quality Trends by City, 1990-2019"

Air Quality Index

Area	Percent of Days when Air Quality was...[2]					AQI Statistics[2]	
	Good	Moderate	Unhealthy for Sensitive Groups	Unhealthy	Very Unhealthy	Maximum	Median
MSA[1]	68.2	31.2	0.5	0.0	0.0	105	45

Note: (1) Data covers the Tulsa, OK Metropolitan Statistical Area; (2) Based on 365 days with AQI data in 2019. Air Quality Index (AQI) is an index for reporting daily air quality. EPA calculates the AQI for five major air pollutants regulated by the Clean Air Act: ground-level ozone, particle pollution (aka particulate matter), carbon monoxide, sulfur dioxide, and nitrogen dioxide. The AQI runs from 0 to 500. The higher the AQI value, the greater the level of air pollution and the greater the health concern. There are six AQI categories: "Good" AQI is between 0 and 50. Air quality is considered satisfactory; "Moderate" AQI is between 51 and 100. Air quality is acceptable; "Unhealthy for Sensitive Groups" When AQI values are between 101 and 150, members of sensitive groups may experience health effects; "Unhealthy" When AQI values are between 151 and 200 everyone may begin to experience health effects; "Very Unhealthy" AQI values between 201 and 300 trigger a health alert; "Hazardous" AQI values over 300 trigger warnings of emergency conditions (not shown).
Source: U.S. Environmental Protection Agency, Air Quality Index Report, 2019

Air Quality Index Pollutants

| Area | Percent of Days when AQI Pollutant was...[2] | | | | | |
	Carbon Monoxide	Nitrogen Dioxide	Ozone	Sulfur Dioxide	Particulate Matter 2.5	Particulate Matter 10
MSA[1]	0.0	0.0	65.2	0.0	34.8	0.0

Note: (1) Data covers the Tulsa, OK Metropolitan Statistical Area; (2) Based on 365 days with AQI data in 2019. The Air Quality Index (AQI) is an index for reporting daily air quality. EPA calculates the AQI for five major air pollutants regulated by the Clean Air Act: ground-level ozone, particle pollution (also known as particulate matter), carbon monoxide, sulfur dioxide, and nitrogen dioxide. The AQI runs from 0 to 500. The higher the AQI value, the greater the level of air pollution and the greater the health concern.
Source: U.S. Environmental Protection Agency, Air Quality Index Report, 2019

Maximum Air Pollutant Concentrations: Particulate Matter, Ozone, CO and Lead

	Particulate Matter 10 (ug/m^3)	Particulate Matter 2.5 Wtd AM (ug/m^3)	Particulate Matter 2.5 24-Hr (ug/m^3)	Ozone (ppm)	Carbon Monoxide (ppm)	Lead (ug/m^3)
MSA[1] Level	36	8.7	22	0.066	1	0.01
NAAQS[2]	150	15	35	0.075	9	0.15
Met NAAQS[2]	Yes	Yes	Yes	Yes	Yes	Yes

Note: (1) Data covers the Tulsa, OK Metropolitan Statistical Area; Data from exceptional events are included; (2) National Ambient Air Quality Standards; ppm = parts per million; ug/m^3 = micrograms per cubic meter; n/a not available.
Concentrations: Particulate Matter 10 (coarse particulate)—highest second maximum 24-hour concentration; Particulate Matter 2.5 Wtd AM (fine particulate)—highest weighted annual mean concentration; Particulate Matter 2.5 24-Hour (fine particulate)—highest 98th percentile 24-hour concentration; Ozone—highest fourth daily maximum 8-hour concentration; Carbon Monoxide—highest second maximum non-overlapping 8-hour concentration; Lead—maximum running 3-month average
Source: U.S. Environmental Protection Agency, Air Quality Monitoring Information, "Air Quality Statistics by City, 2019"

Maximum Air Pollutant Concentrations: Nitrogen Dioxide and Sulfur Dioxide

	Nitrogen Dioxide AM (ppb)	Nitrogen Dioxide 1-Hr (ppb)	Sulfur Dioxide AM (ppb)	Sulfur Dioxide 1-Hr (ppb)	Sulfur Dioxide 24-Hr (ppb)
MSA[1] Level	7	n/a	n/a	6	n/a
NAAQS[2]	53	100	30	75	140
Met NAAQS[2]	Yes	n/a	n/a	Yes	n/a

Note: (1) Data covers the Tulsa, OK Metropolitan Statistical Area; Data from exceptional events are included; (2) National Ambient Air Quality Standards; ppm = parts per million; ug/m^3 = micrograms per cubic meter; n/a not available.
Concentrations: Nitrogen Dioxide AM—highest arithmetic mean concentration; Nitrogen Dioxide 1-Hr—highest 98th percentile 1-hour daily maximum concentration; Sulfur Dioxide AM—highest annual mean concentration; Sulfur Dioxide 1-Hr—highest 99th percentile 1-hour daily maximum concentration; Sulfur Dioxide 24-Hr—highest second maximum 24-hour concentration
Source: U.S. Environmental Protection Agency, Air Quality Monitoring Information, "Air Quality Statistics by City, 2019"

Wichita, Kansas

Background

Lying in the southeastern plains of Kansas, Wichita took its name from a local Indian tribe. Starting in 1864, two white entrepreneurs, Jesse Chisholm and James R. Mead, struck up a lively trade in the area with the native people. Shortly after the tribe was relocated to Indian Territory in Oklahoma in 1867, white settlers planted roots around Chisholm's and Mead's trading post. Chisholm laid out a trail from the post to Texas, from which cowboys drove Longhorn cattle to the railhead of the Wichita and Southwestern Railroad, feeding the cows along the way.

In the 1880s, like many Plains-area cattle-shipping points, Wichita became a wide-open town, with dance halls, gambling, and saloons. Wyatt Earp served there as a lawman for a time. In 1886, the town officially became a city, having grown to over 20,000 in population, much of it due to eager speculation in prairie lands.

Other industries grew in the city. After the turn of the century, oil was discovered in the area, luring more people. The city swelled to over 100,000 by 1930. Shortly after World War I, which saw great advancements in aviation, Wichita's first airplane factory was built. The city soon became the country's leading manufacturer of aircraft. Walter H. Beech, Clyde V. Cessna, and Lloyd C. Stearman were to become famous members of the community for their early leadership in the industry.

Wichita, the largest city in the state, has long been Kansas's dominant industrial city. The oil rigs and aircraft factories kept the dire times of the Great Depression from Wichita, while much of the rest of the state was consumed by the Dust Bowl. During World War II, more airplanes rolled off the city's three assembly lines than in any other city in America. Steady aircraft industry growth continued until the 1980s, when a slump in sales occurred. By the late 1990s, however, a revival of the industry was in full swing until the early 2000s when again, major layoffs occurred. In 2013, Boeing closed its Wichita plant, but the void was filled by Spirit Aerosystems. Wichita is by now accustomed to the cyclical nature of the aircraft industry and it remains a major manufacturer of private and military aircraft, with, in addition to Spirit, Airbus Americas Engineering, Cessna, Bombardier Learjet, and Hawker Beechcraft all in operation there.

Another important Wichita company is Koch Industries, which deals in chemicals, energy, and gas liquids, among other products. The city is also heavily involved in the food industry, with large companies such as Cargill Beef headquartered here. In fact, Koch and Cargill are the two largest privately held companies in the U.S. Healthcare is also a major industry in Wichita.

Transportation to and from Wichita is easy. The Wichita Dwight D. Eisenhower Airport is the largest in the state, while the city is also serviced by the Colonel James Jabara Airport. Although Wichita does not feature passenger rail service, two railroad lines run freight service through the city. Wichita Bicycle Master Plan oversaw the city's newly-completed 149-mile Priority Bicycle Network.

Wichita State University, a public research institution, is the largest of the city's three universities and the third-largest in the state. The other two universities are Friends University, a private non-denominational Christian institution, and Newman University, a private Catholic school. All three schools feature sports teams, although Wichita State University is the only to compete at the Division I level. Wichita is also home to several minor league teams, including the Wind Surge (baseball), the Thunder (ice hockey), and the Force (indoor football).

Wichita has many acclaimed cultural institutions, including the Wichita Museum of Art, whose permanent collection features 7,000 objects, the Ulrich Museum of Art, located at Wichita State, and the Wichita Symphony Orchestra, the oldest professional symphony orchestra in Kansas. Since 1972, Wichita has hosted the River Festival, which features a host of events, and attracts nearly 400,000 people each year. The annual Wichita Black Arts Festival celebrates the cultural achievements of the city's African American community.

The climate in Wichita is continental but generally mild, punctuated occasionally by more intemperate weather conditions. Summers are usually warm and humid, but can be hot and dry. Winters are usually mild, with only brief periods of cold weather. Snowfall is light to moderate, with the ground rarely being covered for more than three days. Thunderstorms, occasionally severe, occur through the spring and summer months.

Rankings

Business/Finance Rankings

- Wichita was the #4-ranked city for savers, according to a study by the finance site GOBankingRates, which considered the prospects for people trying to save money. Criteria: average monthly cost of grocery items; median home listing price; median rent; median income; transportation costs; gas prices; and the cost of eating out for an inexpensive and mid-range meal in 100 U.S. cities. *www.gobankingrates.com, "The 20 Best (and Worst) Places to Live If You're Trying to Save Money," August 27, 2019*

- Wichita was ranked #4 among 100 U.S. cities for most difficult conditions for savers, according to a study by the finance site GOBankingRates. Criteria: average monthly cost of grocery items; median home listing price; median rent; median income; transportation costs; gas prices; and the cost of eating out for an inexpensive and mid-range meal. *www.gobankingrates.com, "The 20 Best (and Worst) Places to Live If You're Trying to Save Money," August 27, 2019*

- The Brookings Institution ranked the nation's largest cities based on income inequality. Wichita was ranked #76 (#1 = greatest inequality). Criteria: the "95/20 ratio," a figure representing the income at which a household earns more than 95 percent of all other households, divided by the income at which a household earns more than only 20 percent of all other households. *Brookings Institution, "Household Income Inequality, Largest Cities of 97 Large U.S. Metro Areas, 2014-2016," February 5, 2018*

- The Brookings Institution ranked the 100 largest metro areas in the U.S. based on income inequality. Wichita was ranked #84 (#1 = greatest inequality). Criteria: the "95/20 ratio," a figure representing the income at which a household earns more than 95 percent of all other households, divided by the income at which a household earns more than only 20 percent of all other households. *Brookings Institution, "Household Income Inequality, 100 Largest U.S. Metro Areas, 2014-2016," February 5, 2018*

- The Wichita metro area appeared on the Milken Institute "2021 Best Performing Cities" list. Rank: #64 out of 200 large metro areas (population over 250,000). Criteria: job growth; wage and salary growth; high-tech output growth; housing affordability; household broadband access. *Milken Institute, "Best-Performing Cities 2021," February 16, 2021*

- *Forbes* ranked the 200 most populous metro areas to determine the nation's "Best Places for Business and Careers." The Wichita metro area was ranked #119. Criteria: costs (business and living); job growth (past and projected); income growth; quality of life; educational attainment (college and high school); projected economic growth; cultural and leisure opportunities; workplace tolerance laws; net migration patterns. *Forbes, "The Best Places for Business and Careers 2019: Seattle Still On Top," October 30, 2019*

Education Rankings

- Personal finance website *WalletHub* analyzed the 150 largest U.S. metropolitan statistical areas to determine where the most educated Americans are putting their degrees to work. Criteria: education levels; percentage of workers with degrees; education quality and attainment gap; public school quality rankings; quality and enrollment of each metro area's universities. Wichita was ranked #90 (#1 = most educated city). *www.WalletHub.com, "Most and Least Educated Cities in America," July 20, 2020*

- Wichita was selected as one of America's most literate cities. The city ranked #63 out of the 84 largest U.S. cities. Criteria: number of booksellers; library resources; Internet resources; educational attainment; periodical publishing resources; newspaper circulation. *Central Connecticut State University, "America's Most Literate Cities, 2018," February 2019*

Environmental Rankings

- Wichita was highlighted as one of the top 98 cleanest metro areas for short-term particle pollution (24-hour PM 2.5) in the U.S. during 2016 through 2018. Monitors in these cities reported no days with unhealthful PM 2.5 levels. *American Lung Association, "State of the Air 2020," April 21, 2020*

Health/Fitness Rankings

- For each of the 100 largest cities in the United States, the American Fitness Index®, published by the American College of Sports Medicine and the Anthem Foundation, evaluated community infrastructure and 33 health behaviors including preventive health, levels of chronic disease conditions, pedestrian safety, air quality, and community resources that support physical activity. Wichita ranked #91 for "community fitness." *americanfitnessindex.org, "2020 ACSM American Fitness Index Summary Report," July 14, 2020*

- Wichita was identified as a "2021 Spring Allergy Capital." The area ranked #3 out of 100. Three groups of factors were used to identify the most challenging cities for people with allergies during the spring season: annual spring pollen levels; over the counter medicine use; number of board-certified allergy specialists. *Asthma and Allergy Foundation of America, "Spring Allergy Capitals 2021," February 23, 2021*

- Wichita was identified as a "2021 Fall Allergy Capital." The area ranked #3 out of 100. Three groups of factors were used to identify the most challenging cities for people with allergies during the fall season: annual fall pollen levels; over the counter medicine use; number of board-certified allergy specialists. *Asthma and Allergy Foundation of America, "Fall Allergy Capitals 2021," February 23, 2021*

- Wichita was identified as a "2019 Asthma Capital." The area ranked #31 out of the nation's 100 largest metropolitan areas. Criteria: estimated asthma prevalence; crude death rate from asthma; and ER visits due to asthma. Risk factors analyzed but not factored in the rankings: annual pollen score; annual air quality; public smoking laws; number of board-certified asthma specialists; rescue medication use; controller medication use; uninsured rate; poverty rate. *Asthma and Allergy Foundation of America, "Asthma Capitals 2019: The Most Challenging Places to Live With Asthma," May 7, 2019*

Real Estate Rankings

- *WalletHub* compared the most populated U.S. cities to determine which had the best markets for real estate agents. Wichita ranked #124 where demand was high and pay was the best. Criteria: sales per agent; annual median wage for real-estate agents; monthly average starting salary for real estate agents; real estate job density and competition; unemployment rate; home turnover rate; housing-market health index; and other relevant metrics. *www.WalletHub.com, "2019's Best Places to Be a Real Estate Agent," April 24, 2019*

- Wichita was ranked #77 out of 268 metro areas in terms of housing affordability in 2020 by the National Association of Home Builders (#1 = most affordable). Criteria: the share of homes sold in that area affordable to a family earning the local median income, based on standard mortgage underwriting criteria. *National Association of Home Builders®, NAHB-Wells Fargo Housing Opportunity Index, 4th Quarter 2020*

Safety Rankings

- To identify the most dangerous cities in America, 24/7 Wall Street focused on violent crime categories—murder, non-negligent manslaughter, rape, robbery, and aggravated assault—and property crime as reported in the FBI's 2019 annual Uniform Crime Report. Criteria also included median income from American Community Survey and unemployment figures from Bureau of Labor Statistics. For cities with populations over 100,000, Wichita was ranked #18. *247wallst.com, "America's 50 Most Dangerous Cities" November 16, 2020*

- Allstate ranked the 200 largest cities in America in terms of driver safety. Wichita ranked #24. Criteria: internal property damage claims over a two-year period from January 2016 to December 2017. The report helps increase the importance of safety and awareness behind the wheel. *Allstate, "Allstate America's Best Drivers Report, 2019" June 24, 2019*

- Wichita was identified as one of the most dangerous cities in America by NeighborhoodScout. The city ranked #40 out of 100 (#1 = most dangerous). Criteria: number of violent crimes per 1,000 residents. The editors evaluated cities with 25,000 or more residents. *NeighborhoodScout.com, "2021 Top 100 Most Dangerous Cities in the U.S.," January 2, 2021*

- The National Insurance Crime Bureau ranked 384 metro areas in the U.S. in terms of per capita rates of vehicle theft. The Wichita metro area ranked #22 (#1 = highest rate). Criteria: number of vehicle theft offenses per 100,000 inhabitants in 2019. *National Insurance Crime Bureau, "Hot Spots 2019," July 21, 2020*

Seniors/Retirement Rankings

- From its Best Cities for Successful Aging indexes, the Milken Institute generated rankings for metropolitan areas, weighing data in nine categories—health care, wellness, living arrangements, transportation and convenience, financial characteristics, education, employment, community engagement, and overall livability. The Wichita metro area was ranked #41 overall in the large metro area category. *Milken Institute, "Best Cities for Successful Aging, 2017" March 14, 2017*

Women/Minorities Rankings

- Personal finance website *WalletHub* compared more than 180 U.S. cities across two key dimensions, "Hispanic Business-Friendliness" and "Hispanic Purchasing Power," to arrive at the most favorable conditions for Hispanic entrepreneurs. Wichita was ranked #119 out of 182. Criteria includes: share of Hispanic-Owned Businesses; Hispanic entrepreneurship rate to median annual income of Hispanics; Small Business-Friendliness score; cost of living; and number of Hispanics with at least a bachelor's degree. *WalletHub.com, "2019's Best Cities for Hispanic Entrepreneurs," May 1, 2019*

Miscellaneous Rankings

- Wichita was selected as a 2020 Digital Cities Survey winner. The city ranked #7 in the large city (250,000 to 499,999 population) category. The survey examined and assessed how city governments are utilizing technology to improve transparency, enhance cybersecurity, and respond to the pandemic. Survey questions focused on ten initiatives: cybersecurity, citizen experience, disaster recovery, business intelligence, IT personnel, data governance, collaboration, infrastructure modernization, cloud computing, and mobile applications. *Center for Digital Government, "2020 Digital Cities Survey," November 10, 2020*

- *WalletHub* compared the 150 most populated U.S. cities to determine their operating efficiency. A "Quality of City Services" score was constructed for each city and then divided by the total budget per capita to reveal which were managed the best. Wichita ranked #52. Criteria: financial stability; economy; education; safety; health; infrastructure and pollution. *www.WalletHub.com, "2020's Best-& Worst-Run Cities in America," June 29, 2020*

Business Environment

DEMOGRAPHICS

Population Growth

Area	1990 Census	2000 Census	2010 Census	2019* Estimate	Population Growth (%)	
					1990-2019	2010-2019
City	313,693	344,284	382,368	389,877	24.3	2.0
MSA[1]	511,111	571,166	623,061	637,690	24.8	2.3
U.S.	248,709,873	281,421,906	308,745,538	324,697,795	30.6	5.2

Note: (1) Figures cover the Wichita, KS Metropolitan Statistical Area; (*) 2015-2019 5-year estimated population
Source: U.S. Census Bureau, 1990 Census, Census 2000, Census 2010, 2015-2019 American Community Survey 5-Year Estimates

Household Size

Area	Persons in Household (%)							Average Household Size
	One	Two	Three	Four	Five	Six	Seven or More	
City	33.4	31.4	13.5	11.3	6.5	2.7	1.3	2.50
MSA[1]	30.0	32.9	14.1	11.7	7.1	2.8	1.5	2.60
U.S.	27.9	33.9	15.6	12.9	6.0	2.3	1.4	2.60

Note: (1) Figures cover the Wichita, KS Metropolitan Statistical Area
Source: U.S. Census Bureau, 2015-2019 American Community Survey 5-Year Estimates

Race

Area	White Alone[2] (%)	Black Alone[2] (%)	Asian Alone[2] (%)	AIAN[3] Alone[2] (%)	NHOPI[4] Alone[2] (%)	Other Race Alone[2] (%)	Two or More Races (%)
City	74.3	10.9	5.1	1.0	0.1	4.2	4.4
MSA[1]	80.9	7.5	3.7	0.9	0.1	2.9	4.0
U.S.	72.5	12.7	5.5	0.8	0.2	4.9	3.3

Note: (1) Figures cover the Wichita, KS Metropolitan Statistical Area; (2) Alone is defined as not being in combination with one or more other races; (3) American Indian and Alaska Native; (4) Native Hawaiian and Other Pacific Islander
Source: U.S. Census Bureau, 2015-2019 American Community Survey 5-Year Estimates

Hispanic or Latino Origin

Area	Total (%)	Mexican (%)	Puerto Rican (%)	Cuban (%)	Other (%)
City	17.2	14.7	0.4	0.2	1.9
MSA[1]	13.1	11.0	0.4	0.1	1.5
U.S.	18.0	11.2	1.7	0.7	4.3

Note: Persons of Hispanic or Latino origin can be of any race; (1) Figures cover the Wichita, KS Metropolitan Statistical Area
Source: U.S. Census Bureau, 2015-2019 American Community Survey 5-Year Estimates

Ancestry

Area	German	Irish	English	American	Italian	Polish	French[2]	Scottish	Dutch
City	19.3	9.5	7.8	5.0	1.7	1.0	2.2	1.6	1.5
MSA[1]	21.8	9.9	8.1	6.7	1.7	1.0	2.3	1.9	1.6
U.S.	13.3	9.7	7.2	6.2	5.1	2.8	2.3	1.7	1.2

Note: Figures are the percentage of the total population reporting a particular ancestry. The nine most commonly reported ancestries in the U.S. are shown. Figures include multiple ancestries (e.g. if a person reported being Irish and Italian, they were included in both columns); (1) Figures cover the Wichita, KS Metropolitan Statistical Area; (2) Excludes Basque
Source: U.S. Census Bureau, 2015-2019 American Community Survey 5-Year Estimates

Foreign-born Population

Area	Percent of Population Born in								
	Any Foreign Country	Asia	Mexico	Europe	Caribbean	Central America[2]	South America	Africa	Canada
City	10.2	3.8	4.3	0.5	0.1	0.6	0.2	0.6	0.1
MSA[1]	7.4	2.7	3.0	0.4	0.1	0.4	0.2	0.4	0.1
U.S.	13.6	4.2	3.5	1.5	1.3	1.1	1.0	0.7	0.2

Note: (1) Figures cover the Wichita, KS Metropolitan Statistical Area; (2) Excludes Mexico.
Source: U.S. Census Bureau, 2015-2019 American Community Survey 5-Year Estimates

Wichita, Kansas

Marital Status

Area	Never Married	Now Married[2]	Separated	Widowed	Divorced
City	33.5	45.6	2.0	5.6	13.3
MSA[1]	30.0	50.3	1.6	5.9	12.2
U.S.	33.4	48.1	1.9	5.8	10.9

Note: Figures are percentages and cover the population 15 years of age and older; (1) Figures cover the Wichita, KS Metropolitan Statistical Area; (2) Excludes separated
Source: U.S. Census Bureau, 2015-2019 American Community Survey 5-Year Estimates

Disability by Age

Area	All Ages	Under 18 Years Old	18 to 64 Years Old	65 Years and Over
City	13.7	4.6	12.4	36.3
MSA[1]	13.4	4.9	11.7	36.1
U.S.	12.6	4.2	10.3	34.5

Note: Figures show percent of the civilian noninstitutionalized population that reported having a disability. Disability status is determined from six types of difficulty: vision, hearing, cognitive, ambulatory, self-care, and independent living. For children under 5 years old, hearing and vision difficulty are used to determine disability status. For children between the ages of 5 and 14, disability status is determined from hearing, vision, cognitive, ambulatory, and self-care difficulties. For people aged 15 years and older, they are considered to have a disability if they have difficulty with any one of the six difficulty types; Note: (1) Figures cover the Wichita, KS Metropolitan Statistical Area
Source: U.S. Census Bureau, 2015-2019 American Community Survey 5-Year Estimates

Age

Area	Percent of Population									Median Age
	Under Age 5	Age 5–19	Age 20–34	Age 35–44	Age 45–54	Age 55–64	Age 65–74	Age 75–84	Age 85+	
City	7.0	20.7	22.4	11.9	11.6	12.5	8.2	3.9	1.8	35.0
MSA[1]	6.9	21.3	20.4	12.1	11.8	12.7	8.3	4.3	1.9	36.0
U.S.	6.1	19.1	20.7	12.6	13.0	12.9	9.1	4.6	1.9	38.1

Note: (1) Figures cover the Wichita, KS Metropolitan Statistical Area
Source: U.S. Census Bureau, 2015-2019 American Community Survey 5-Year Estimates

Gender

Area	Males	Females	Males per 100 Females
City	191,730	198,147	96.8
MSA[1]	316,050	321,640	98.3
U.S.	159,886,919	164,810,876	97.0

Note: (1) Figures cover the Wichita, KS Metropolitan Statistical Area
Source: U.S. Census Bureau, 2015-2019 American Community Survey 5-Year Estimates

Religious Groups by Family

Area	Catholic	Baptist	Non-Den.	Methodist[2]	Lutheran	LDS[3]	Pentecostal	Presbyterian[4]	Muslim[5]	Judaism
MSA[1]	14.5	13.5	3.2	7.2	1.8	1.4	2.0	1.7	0.2	<0.1
U.S.	19.1	9.3	4.0	4.0	2.3	2.0	1.9	1.6	0.8	0.7

Note: Figures are the number of adherents as a percentage of the total population; (1) Figures cover the Wichita, KS Metropolitan Statistical Area; (2) Methodist/Pietist; (3) Latter Day Saints; (4) Reformed; (5) Figures are estimates
Source: Association of Statisticians of American Religious Bodies, 2010 U.S. Religion Census: Religious Congregations & Membership Study

Religious Groups by Tradition

Area	Catholic	Evangelical Protestant	Mainline Protestant	Other Tradition	Black Protestant	Orthodox
MSA[1]	14.5	20.7	11.1	2.4	1.9	0.2
U.S.	19.1	16.2	7.3	4.3	1.6	0.3

Note: Figures are the number of adherents as a percentage of the total population; (1) Figures cover the Wichita, KS Metropolitan Statistical Area
Source: Association of Statisticians of American Religious Bodies, 2010 U.S. Religion Census: Religious Congregations & Membership Study

ECONOMY

Gross Metropolitan Product

Area	2017	2018	2019	2020	Rank[2]
MSA[1]	34.3	35.7	37.0	38.0	81

Note: Figures are in billions of dollars; (1) Figures cover the Wichita, KS Metropolitan Statistical Area; (2) Rank is based on 2018 data and ranges from 1 to 381
Source: U.S. Conference of Mayors, U.S. Metro Economies: GMP & Employment 2018-2020, September 2019

Economic Growth

Area	2015-17 (%)	2018 (%)	2019 (%)	2020 (%)	Rank[2]
MSA[1]	1.9	1.5	1.8	0.5	141
U.S.	1.9	2.9	2.3	2.1	–

Note: Figures are real gross metropolitan product (GMP) growth rates and represent average annual percent change; (1) Figures cover the Wichita, KS Metropolitan Statistical Area; (2) Rank is based on 2017 2-year average annual percent change and ranges from 1 to 381
Source: U.S. Conference of Mayors, U.S. Metro Economies: GMP & Employment 2018-2020, September 2019

Metropolitan Area Exports

Area	2014	2015	2016	2017	2018	2019	Rank[2]
MSA[1]	4,011.7	3,717.6	3,054.9	3,299.2	3,817.0	3,494.7	71

Note: Figures are in millions of dollars; (1) Figures cover the Wichita, KS Metropolitan Statistical Area; (2) Rank is based on 2019 data and ranges from 1 to 386
Source: U.S. Department of Commerce, International Trade Administration, Office of Trade and Economic Analysis, Industry and Analysis, Exports by Metropolitan Area, data extracted March 24, 2021

Building Permits

Area	Single-Family			Multi-Family			Total		
	2018	2019	Pct. Chg.	2018	2019	Pct. Chg.	2018	2019	Pct. Chg.
City	532	618	16.2	326	364	11.7	858	982	14.5
MSA[1]	1,223	1,389	13.6	735	737	0.3	1,958	2,126	8.6
U.S.	855,300	862,100	0.7	473,500	523,900	10.6	1,328,800	1,386,000	4.3

Note: (1) Figures cover the Wichita, KS Metropolitan Statistical Area; Figures represent new, privately-owned housing units authorized (unadjusted data); All permit data are based on estimates with imputation
Source: U.S. Census Bureau, Manufacturing, Mining, and Construction Statistics, Building Permits, 2018, 2019

Bankruptcy Filings

Area	Business Filings			Nonbusiness Filings		
	2019	2020	% Chg.	2019	2020	% Chg.
Sedgwick County	30	15	-50.0	1,381	941	-31.9
U.S.	22,780	21,655	-4.9	752,160	522,808	-30.5

Note: Business filings include Chapter 7, Chapter 9, Chapter 11, Chapter 12, Chapter 13, Chapter 15, and Section 304; Nonbusiness filings include Chapter 7, Chapter 11, and Chapter 13
Source: Administrative Office of the U.S. Courts, Business and Nonbusiness Bankruptcy, County Cases Commenced by Chapter of the Bankruptcy Code, During the 12-Month Period Ending December 31, 2019 and Business and Nonbusiness Bankruptcy, County Cases Commenced by Chapter of the Bankruptcy Code, During the 12-Month Period Ending December 31, 2020

Housing Vacancy Rates

Area	Gross Vacancy Rate[2] (%)			Year-Round Vacancy Rate[3] (%)			Rental Vacancy Rate[4] (%)			Homeowner Vacancy Rate[5] (%)		
	2018	2019	2020	2018	2019	2020	2018	2019	2020	2018	2019	2020
MSA[1]	n/a	n/a	n/a	n/a	n/a	n/a	n/a	n/a	n/a	n/a	n/a	n/a
U.S.	12.3	12.0	10.6	9.7	9.5	8.2	6.9	6.7	6.3	1.5	1.4	1.0

Note: (1) Figures cover the Wichita, KS Metropolitan Statistical Area; (2) The percentage of the total housing inventory that is vacant; (3) The percentage of the housing inventory (excluding seasonal units) that is year-round vacant; (4) The percentage of rental inventory that is vacant for rent; (5) The percentage of homeowner inventory that is vacant for sale; n/a not available
Source: U.S. Census Bureau, Housing Vacancies and Homeownership Annual Statistics: 2018, 2019, 2020

INCOME

Income

Area	Per Capita ($)	Median Household ($)	Average Household ($)
City	28,806	52,620	71,335
MSA[1]	29,414	57,379	74,900
U.S.	34,103	62,843	88,607

Note: (1) Figures cover the Wichita, KS Metropolitan Statistical Area
Source: U.S. Census Bureau, 2015-2019 American Community Survey 5-Year Estimates

Household Income Distribution

Area	Percent of Households Earning							
	Under $15,000	$15,000 -$24,999	$25,000 -$34,999	$35,000 -$49,999	$50,000 -$74,999	$75,000 -$99,999	$100,000 -$149,999	$150,000 and up
City	12.3	10.5	10.5	14.6	18.7	12.0	12.8	8.7
MSA[1]	10.5	9.5	9.7	14.2	19.2	13.1	14.5	9.4
U.S.	10.3	8.9	8.9	12.3	17.2	12.7	15.1	14.5

Note: (1) Figures cover the Wichita, KS Metropolitan Statistical Area
Source: U.S. Census Bureau, 2015-2019 American Community Survey 5-Year Estimates

Poverty Rate

Area	All Ages	Under 18 Years Old	18 to 64 Years Old	65 Years and Over
City	15.9	22.0	15.0	8.8
MSA[1]	13.0	17.4	12.3	8.2
U.S.	13.4	18.5	12.6	9.3

Note: Figures are percentage of people whose income during the past 12 months was below the poverty level;
(1) Figures cover the Wichita, KS Metropolitan Statistical Area
Source: U.S. Census Bureau, 2015-2019 American Community Survey 5-Year Estimates

CITY FINANCES

City Government Finances

Component	2017 ($000)	2017 ($ per capita)
Total Revenues	807,298	2,070
Total Expenditures	737,913	1,892
Debt Outstanding	2,489,801	6,385
Cash and Securities[1]	2,966,314	7,607

Note: (1) Cash and security holdings of a government at the close of its fiscal year, including those of its dependent agencies, utilities, and liquor stores.
Source: U.S. Census Bureau, State & Local Government Finances 2017

City Government Revenue by Source

Source	2017 ($000)	2017 ($ per capita)	2017 (%)
General Revenue			
From Federal Government	29,227	75	3.6
From State Government	87,257	224	10.8
From Local Governments	58,660	150	7.3
Taxes			
Property	123,970	318	15.4
Sales and Gross Receipts	51,944	133	6.4
Personal Income	0	0	0.0
Corporate Income	0	0	0.0
Motor Vehicle License	0	0	0.0
Other Taxes	8,096	21	1.0
Current Charges	120,973	310	15.0
Liquor Store	0	0	0.0
Utility	79,510	204	9.8
Employee Retirement	89,816	230	11.1

Source: U.S. Census Bureau, State & Local Government Finances 2017

City Government Expenditures by Function

Function	2017 ($000)	2017 ($ per capita)	2017 (%)
General Direct Expenditures			
Air Transportation	41,863	107	5.7
Corrections	0	0	0.0
Education	0	0	0.0
Employment Security Administration	0	0	0.0
Financial Administration	4,741	12	0.6
Fire Protection	44,161	113	6.0
General Public Buildings	16,620	42	2.3
Governmental Administration, Other	7,636	19	1.0
Health	2,084	5	0.3
Highways	85,252	218	11.6
Hospitals	0	0	0.0
Housing and Community Development	562	1	0.1
Interest on General Debt	105,537	270	14.3
Judicial and Legal	9,229	23	1.3
Libraries	8,354	21	1.1
Parking	1,017	2	0.1
Parks and Recreation	33,991	87	4.6
Police Protection	82,873	212	11.2
Public Welfare	0	0	0.0
Sewerage	64,022	164	8.7
Solid Waste Management	1,863	4	0.3
Veterans' Services	0	0	0.0
Liquor Store	0	0	0.0
Utility	93,671	240	12.7
Employee Retirement	68,537	175	9.3

Source: U.S. Census Bureau, State & Local Government Finances 2017

EMPLOYMENT

Labor Force and Employment

Area	Civilian Labor Force			Workers Employed		
	Dec. 2019	Dec. 2020	% Chg.	Dec. 2019	Dec. 2020	% Chg.
City	189,743	189,451	-0.2	183,423	180,980	-1.3
MSA[1]	315,547	315,051	-0.2	305,590	301,566	-1.3
U.S.	164,007,000	160,017,000	-2.4	158,504,000	149,613,000	-5.6

Note: Data is not seasonally adjusted and covers workers 16 years of age and older; (1) Figures cover the Wichita, KS Metropolitan Statistical Area
Source: Bureau of Labor Statistics, Local Area Unemployment Statistics

Unemployment Rate

Area	2020											
	Jan.	Feb.	Mar.	Apr.	May	Jun.	Jul.	Aug.	Sep.	Oct.	Nov.	Dec.
City	4.0	4.1	3.5	19.2	15.6	12.1	12.3	11.6	9.1	7.4	7.0	4.5
MSA[1]	3.8	3.8	3.3	17.7	14.1	10.8	11.0	10.3	8.0	6.6	6.5	4.3
U.S.	4.0	3.8	4.5	14.4	13.0	11.2	10.5	8.5	7.7	6.6	6.4	6.5

Note: Data is not seasonally adjusted and covers workers 16 years of age and older; (1) Figures cover the Wichita, KS Metropolitan Statistical Area
Source: Bureau of Labor Statistics, Local Area Unemployment Statistics

Average Wages

Occupation	$/Hr.	Occupation	$/Hr.
Accountants and Auditors	33.80	Maintenance and Repair Workers	18.90
Automotive Mechanics	18.40	Marketing Managers	59.30
Bookkeepers	18.00	Network and Computer Systems Admin.	35.00
Carpenters	18.80	Nurses, Licensed Practical	21.10
Cashiers	11.20	Nurses, Registered	28.60
Computer Programmers	39.70	Nursing Assistants	13.30
Computer Systems Analysts	36.60	Office Clerks, General	14.10
Computer User Support Specialists	22.00	Physical Therapists	43.60
Construction Laborers	16.10	Physicians	72.40
Cooks, Restaurant	12.80	Plumbers, Pipefitters and Steamfitters	23.80
Customer Service Representatives	16.60	Police and Sheriff's Patrol Officers	23.60
Dentists	77.90	Postal Service Mail Carriers	25.20
Electricians	25.10	Real Estate Sales Agents	34.90
Engineers, Electrical	43.30	Retail Salespersons	16.50
Fast Food and Counter Workers	9.70	Sales Representatives, Technical/Scientific	48.40
Financial Managers	62.40	Secretaries, Exc. Legal/Medical/Executive	17.10
First-Line Supervisors of Office Workers	27.40	Security Guards	15.40
General and Operations Managers	50.90	Surgeons	n/a
Hairdressers/Cosmetologists	13.00	Teacher Assistants, Exc. Postsecondary*	13.20
Home Health and Personal Care Aides	11.20	Teachers, Secondary School, Exc. Sp. Ed.*	27.00
Janitors and Cleaners	13.90	Telemarketers	12.00
Landscaping/Groundskeeping Workers	13.60	Truck Drivers, Heavy/Tractor-Trailer	22.90
Lawyers	47.10	Truck Drivers, Light/Delivery Services	17.70
Maids and Housekeeping Cleaners	11.60	Waiters and Waitresses	9.40

Note: Wage data covers the Wichita, KS Metropolitan Statistical Area; (*) Hourly wages were calculated from annual wage data based on a 40 hour work week; n/a not available.
Source: Bureau of Labor Statistics, Metro Area Occupational Employment & Wage Estimates, May 2020

Employment by Industry

Sector	MSA[1]		U.S.
	Number of Employees	Percent of Total	Percent of Total
Construction, Mining, and Logging	16,800	5.8	5.5
Education and Health Services	47,100	16.4	16.3
Financial Activities	11,800	4.1	6.1
Government	41,300	14.4	15.2
Information	3,700	1.3	1.9
Leisure and Hospitality	29,600	10.3	9.0
Manufacturing	44,600	15.5	8.5
Other Services	10,200	3.5	3.8
Professional and Business Services	33,900	11.8	14.4
Retail Trade	30,600	10.6	10.9
Transportation, Warehousing, and Utilities	9,700	3.4	4.6
Wholesale Trade	8,100	2.8	3.9

Note: Figures are non-farm employment as of December 2020. Figures are not seasonally adjusted and include workers 16 years of age and older; (1) Figures cover the Wichita, KS Metropolitan Statistical Area
Source: Bureau of Labor Statistics, Current Employment Statistics, Employment, Hours, and Earnings

Employment by Occupation

Occupation Classification	City (%)	MSA[1] (%)	U.S. (%)
Management, Business, Science, and Arts	34.4	36.3	38.5
Natural Resources, Construction, and Maintenance	9.9	10.2	8.9
Production, Transportation, and Material Moving	15.5	15.4	13.2
Sales and Office	22.0	21.2	21.6
Service	18.3	16.9	17.8

Note: Figures cover employed civilians 16 years of age and older; (1) Figures cover the Wichita, KS Metropolitan Statistical Area
Source: U.S. Census Bureau, 2015-2019 American Community Survey 5-Year Estimates

Occupations with Greatest Projected Employment Growth: 2020 – 2022

Occupation[1]	2020 Employment	2022 Projected Employment	Numeric Employment Change	Percent Employment Change
Home Health and Personal Care Aides	25,760	26,080	320	1.2
Light Truck or Delivery Services Drivers	8,870	9,160	290	3.3
Laborers and Freight, Stock, and Material Movers, Hand	23,210	23,450	240	1.0
Software Developers and Software Quality Assurance Analysts and Testers	9,340	9,530	190	2.0
Nurse Practitioners	3,010	3,200	190	6.3
Meat, Poultry, and Fish Cutters and Trimmers	5,620	5,790	170	3.0
Farmers, Ranchers, and Other Agricultural Managers	8,170	8,320	150	1.8
Medical and Health Services Managers	4,390	4,540	150	3.4
Industrial Truck and Tractor Operators	6,920	7,050	130	1.9
Farmworkers, Farm, Ranch, and Aquacultural Animals	4,550	4,640	90	2.0

Note: Projections cover Kansas; (1) Sorted by numeric employment change
Source: www.projectionscentral.com, State Occupational Projections, 2020–2022 Short-Term Projections

Fastest-Growing Occupations: 2020 – 2022

Occupation[1]	2020 Employment	2022 Projected Employment	Numeric Employment Change	Percent Employment Change
Nurse Practitioners	3,010	3,200	190	6.3
Slaughterers and Meat Packers	1,940	2,010	70	3.6
Medical and Health Services Managers	4,390	4,540	150	3.4
Light Truck or Delivery Services Drivers	8,870	9,160	290	3.3
Meat, Poultry, and Fish Cutters and Trimmers	5,620	5,790	170	3.0
Software Developers and Software Quality Assurance Analysts and Testers	9,340	9,530	190	2.0
Farmworkers, Farm, Ranch, and Aquacultural Animals	4,550	4,640	90	2.0
Industrial Truck and Tractor Operators	6,920	7,050	130	1.9
Farmers, Ranchers, and Other Agricultural Managers	8,170	8,320	150	1.8
Pharmacy Technicians	4,120	4,190	70	1.7

Note: Projections cover Kansas; (1) Sorted by percent employment change and excludes occupations with numeric employment change less than 50
Source: www.projectionscentral.com, State Occupational Projections, 2020–2022 Short-Term Projections

TAXES

State Corporate Income Tax Rates

State	Tax Rate (%)	Income Brackets ($)	Num. of Brackets	Financial Institution Tax Rate (%)[a]	Federal Income Tax Ded.
Kansas	4.0 (k)	Flat rate	1	2.25 (k)	No

Note: Tax rates as of January 1, 2021; (a) Rates listed are the corporate income tax rate applied to financial institutions or excise taxes based on income. Some states have other taxes based upon the value of deposits or shares; (k) In addition to the flat 4% corporate income tax, Kansas levies a 3.0% surtax on taxable income over $50,000. Banks pay a privilege tax of 2.25% of net income, plus a surtax of 2.125% (2.25% for savings and loans, trust companies, and federally chartered savings banks) on net income in excess of $25,000.
Source: Federation of Tax Administrators, State Corporate Income Tax Rates, January 1, 2021

State Individual Income Tax Rates

State	Tax Rate (%)	Income Brackets ($)	Personal Exemptions ($)			Standard Ded. ($)	
			Single	Married	Depend.	Single	Married
Kansas	3.1 - 5.7	15,000 - 30,000 (b)	2,250	4,500	2,250	3,000	7,500

Note: Tax rates as of January 1, 2021; Local- and county-level taxes are not included; Federal income tax is not deductible on state income tax returns; (b) For joint returns, taxes are twice the tax on half the couple's income.
Source: Federation of Tax Administrators, State Individual Income Tax Rates, January 1, 2021

Various State Sales and Excise Tax Rates

State	State Sales Tax (%)	Gasoline[1] (¢/gal.)	Cigarette[2] ($/pack)	Spirits[3] ($/gal.)	Wine[4] ($/gal.)	Beer[5] ($/gal.)	Recreational Marijuana (%)
Kansas	6.5	24.025	1.29	2.5	0.3	0.18	Not legal

Note: All tax rates as of January 1, 2021; (1) The American Petroleum Institute has developed a methodology for determining the average tax rate on a gallon of fuel. Rates may include any of the following: excise taxes, environmental fees, storage tank fees, other fees or taxes, general sales tax, and local taxes; (2) The federal excise tax of $1.0066 per pack and local taxes are not included; (3) Rates are those applicable to off-premise sales of 40% alcohol by volume (a.b.v.) distilled spirits in 750ml containers. Local excise taxes are excluded; (4) Rates are those applicable to off-premise sales of 11% a.b.v. non-carbonated wine in 750ml containers; (5) Rates are those applicable to off-premise sales of 4.7% a.b.v. beer in 12 ounce containers.
Source: Tax Foundation, 2021 Facts & Figures: How Does Your State Compare?

State Business Tax Climate Index Rankings

State	Overall Rank	Corporate Tax Rank	Individual Income Tax Rank	Sales Tax Rank	Property Tax Rank	Unemployment Insurance Tax Rank
Kansas	35	31	24	37	30	13

Note: The index is a measure of how each state's tax laws affect economic performance. The lower the rank, the more favorable a state's tax system is for business. States without a given tax are given a ranking of 1. The scores/rankings for the District of Columbia do not affect other states. The 2021 index represents the tax climate as of July 1, 2020.
Source: Tax Foundation, State Business Tax Climate Index 2021

TRANSPORTATION

Means of Transportation to Work

Area	Car/Truck/Van		Public Transportation			Bicycle	Walked	Other Means	Worked at Home
	Drove Alone	Car-pooled	Bus	Subway	Railroad				
City	83.5	9.5	0.7	0.0	0.0	0.3	1.5	1.3	3.2
MSA[1]	84.0	8.7	0.4	0.0	0.0	0.4	1.7	1.2	3.5
U.S.	76.3	9.0	2.4	1.9	0.6	0.5	2.7	1.4	5.2

Note: Figures are percentages and cover workers 16 years of age and older; (1) Figures cover the Wichita, KS Metropolitan Statistical Area
Source: U.S. Census Bureau, 2015-2019 American Community Survey 5-Year Estimates

Travel Time to Work

Area	Less Than 10 Minutes	10 to 19 Minutes	20 to 29 Minutes	30 to 44 Minutes	45 to 59 Minutes	60 to 89 Minutes	90 Minutes or More
City	14.2	44.9	27.2	9.7	1.7	1.2	1.2
MSA[1]	16.3	37.5	26.5	14.3	2.8	1.4	1.3
U.S.	12.2	28.4	20.8	20.8	8.3	6.4	2.9

Note: Note: Figures are percentages and include workers 16 years old and over; (1) Figures cover the Wichita, KS Metropolitan Statistical Area
Source: U.S. Census Bureau, 2015-2019 American Community Survey 5-Year Estimates

Key Congestion Measures

Measure	1982	1992	2002	2012	2017
Annual Hours of Delay, Total (000)	1,912	4,651	6,974	10,495	12,081
Annual Hours of Delay, Per Auto Commuter	13	25	29	31	36
Annual Congestion Cost, Total (million $)	15	49	94	190	224
Annual Congestion Cost, Per Auto Commuter ($)	178	298	349	412	460

Note: Covers the Wichita KS urban area
Source: Texas A&M Transportation Institute, 2019 Urban Mobility Report

Freeway Travel Time Index

Measure	1982	1987	1992	1997	2002	2007	2012	2017
Urban Area Index[1]	1.06	1.08	1.12	1.14	1.15	1.15	1.15	1.14
Urban Area Rank[1,2]	43	44	40	47	61	72	71	80

Note: Freeway Travel Time Index—the ratio of travel time in the peak period to the travel time at free-flow conditions. For example, a value of 1.30 indicates a 20-minute free-flow trip takes 26 minutes in the peak (20 minutes x 1.30 = 26 minutes); (1) Covers the Wichita KS urban area; (2) Rank is based on 101 larger urban areas (#1 = highest travel time index)
Source: Texas A&M Transportation Institute, 2019 Urban Mobility Report

Public Transportation

Agency Name / Mode of Transportation	Vehicles Operated in Maximum Service[1]	Annual Unlinked Passenger Trips[2] (in thous.)	Annual Passenger Miles[3] (in thous.)
Wichita Transit (WT)			
Bus (directly operated)	42	1,286.8	6,906.0
Demand Response (directly operated)	22	80.2	772.1

Note: (1) Number of revenue vehicles operated by the given mode and type of service to meet the annual maximum service requirement. This is the revenue vehicle count during the peak season of the year; on the week and day that maximum service is provided. Vehicles operated in maximum service (VOMS) exclude atypical days and one-time special events; (2) Number of passengers who boarded public transportation vehicles. Passengers are counted each time they board a vehicle no matter how many vehicles they use to travel from their origin to their destination. (3) Sum of the distances ridden by all passengers during the entire fiscal year.
Source: Federal Transit Administration, National Transit Database, 2019

Air Transportation

Airport Name and Code / Type of Service	Passenger Airlines[1]	Passenger Enplanements	Freight Carriers[2]	Freight (lbs)
Wichita Mid-Continent Airport (ICT)				
Domestic service (U.S. carriers - 2020)	22	382,646	11	24,659,264
International service (U.S. carriers - 2019)	0	0	1	989,233

Note: (1) Includes all U.S.-based major, minor and commuter airlines that carried at least one passenger during the year; (2) Includes all U.S.-based airlines and freight carriers that transported at least one pound of freight during the year.
Source: Bureau of Transportation Statistics, The Intermodal Transportation Database, Air Carriers: T-100 Domestic Market (U.S. Carriers), 2020; Bureau of Transportation Statistics, The Intermodal Transportation Database, Air Carriers: T-100 International Market (U.S. Carriers), 2019

BUSINESSES

Major Business Headquarters

Company Name	Industry	Rankings	
		Fortune[1]	Forbes[2]
Koch Industries	Multicompany	-	1
Spirit AeroSystems Holdings	Aerospace and Defense	406	-

Note: (1) Companies that produce a 10-K are ranked 1 to 500 based on 2019 revenue; (2) All private companies with at least $2 billion in annual revenue through the end of their most current fiscal year are ranked 1 to 219; companies listed are headquartered in the city; dashes indicate no ranking
Source: Fortune, "Fortune 500," June/July 2020; Forbes, "America's Largest Private Companies," 2020

Living Environment

COST OF LIVING

Cost of Living Index

Composite Index	Groceries	Housing	Utilities	Trans-portation	Health Care	Misc. Goods/ Services
89.3	96.2	67.4	97.6	92.1	94.6	100.2

Note: The Cost of Living Index measures regional differences in the cost of consumer goods and services, excluding taxes and non-consumer expenditures, for professional and managerial households in the top income quintile. It is based on more than 50,000 prices covering almost 60 different items for which prices are collected three times a year by chambers of commerce, economic development organizations or university applied economic centers in each participating urban area. The numbers shown should be read as a percentage above or below the national average of 100. For example, a value of 115.4 in the groceries column indicates that grocery prices are 15.4% higher than the national average. Small differences in the index numbers should not be interpreted as significant; Figures cover the Wichita KS urban area.
Source: The Council for Community and Economic Research, Cost of Living Index, 2020

Grocery Prices

Area[1]	T-Bone Steak ($/pound)	Frying Chicken ($/pound)	Whole Milk ($/half gal.)	Eggs ($/dozen)	Orange Juice ($/64 oz.)	Coffee ($/11.5 oz.)
City[2]	11.94	1.23	1.75	0.94	3.70	4.17
Avg.	11.78	1.39	2.05	1.47	3.57	4.34
Min.	8.03	0.94	1.03	0.74	2.94	3.02
Max.	15.86	2.65	4.31	3.77	5.44	8.69

Note: (1) Values for the local area are compared with the average, minimum and maximum values for all 284 areas in the Cost of Living Index; (2) Figures cover the Wichita KS urban area; **T-Bone Steak** (price per pound); **Frying Chicken** (price per pound, whole fryer); **Whole Milk** (half gallon carton); **Eggs** (price per dozen, Grade A, large); **Orange Juice** (64 oz. Tropicana or Florida Natural); **Coffee** (11.5 oz. can, vacuum-packed, Maxwell House, Hills Bros, or Folgers).
Source: The Council for Community and Economic Research, Cost of Living Index, 2020

Housing and Utility Costs

Area[1]	New Home Price ($)	Apartment Rent ($/month)	All Electric ($/month)	Part Electric ($/month)	Other Energy ($/month)	Telephone ($/month)
City[2]	254,831	771	-	100.11	56.39	188.70
Avg.	368,594	1,168	170.86	100.47	65.28	184.30
Min.	190,567	502	91.58	31.42	26.08	169.60
Max.	2,227,806	4,738	470.38	280.31	280.06	206.50

Note: (1) Values for the local area are compared with the average, minimum and maximum values for all 284 areas in the Cost of Living Index; (2) Figures cover the Wichita KS urban area; **New Home Price** (2,400 sf living area, 8,000 sf lot, in urban area with full utilities); **Apartment Rent** (950 sf 2 bedroom/1.5 or 2 bath, unfurnished, excluding all utilities except water); **All Electric** (average monthly cost for an all-electric home); **Part Electric** (average monthly cost for a part-electric home); **Other Energy** (average monthly cost for natural gas, fuel oil, coal, wood, and any other forms of energy except electricity); **Telephone** (price includes the base monthly rate plus taxes and fees for three lines of mobile phone service).
Source: The Council for Community and Economic Research, Cost of Living Index, 2020

Health Care, Transportation, and Other Costs

Area[1]	Doctor ($/visit)	Dentist ($/visit)	Optometrist ($/visit)	Gasoline ($/gallon)	Beauty Salon ($/visit)	Men's Shirt ($)
City[2]	100.20	86.82	148.22	2.03	39.58	43.51
Avg.	115.44	99.32	108.10	2.21	39.27	31.37
Min.	36.68	59.00	51.36	1.71	19.00	11.00
Max.	219.00	153.10	250.97	3.46	82.05	58.33

Note: (1) Values for the local area are compared with the average, minimum and maximum values for all 284 areas in the Cost of Living Index; (2) Figures cover the Wichita KS urban area; **Doctor** (general practitioners routine exam of an established patient); **Dentist** (adult teeth cleaning and periodic oral examination); **Optometrist** (full vision eye exam for established adult patient); **Gasoline** (one gallon regular unleaded, national brand, including all taxes, cash price at self-service pump if available); **Beauty Salon** (woman's shampoo, trim, and blow-dry); **Men's Shirt** (cotton/polyester dress shirt, pinpoint weave, long sleeves).
Source: The Council for Community and Economic Research, Cost of Living Index, 2020

HOUSING

Homeownership Rate

Area	2012 (%)	2013 (%)	2014 (%)	2015 (%)	2016 (%)	2017 (%)	2018 (%)	2019 (%)	2020 (%)
MSA[1]	n/a	n/a	n/a	n/a	n/a	n/a	n/a	n/a	n/a
U.S.	65.4	65.1	64.5	63.7	63.4	63.9	64.4	64.6	66.6

Note: (1) Figures cover the Wichita, KS Metropolitan Statistical Area; n/a not available
Source: U.S. Census Bureau, Housing Vacancies and Homeownership Annual Statistics: 2012-2020

House Price Index (HPI)

Area	National Ranking[2]	Quarterly Change (%)	One-Year Change (%)	Five-Year Change (%)	Since 1991Q1 (%)
MSA[1]	49	1.50	7.67	27.26	136.03
U.S.[3]	–	3.81	10.77	38.99	205.12

Note: The HPI is a weighted repeat sales index. It measures average price changes in repeat sales or refinancings on the same properties. This information is obtained by reviewing repeat mortgage transactions on single-family properties whose mortgages have been purchased or securitized by Fannie Mae or Freddie Mac since January 1975; (1) Figures cover the Wichita, KS Metropolitan Statistical Area; (2) Rankings are based on annual percentage change for all metro areas containing at least 15,000 transactions over the last 10 years and ranges from 1 to 253; (3) figures based on a weighted average of Census Division estimates using a seasonally adjusted, purchase-only index; all figures are for the period ending December 31, 2020
Source: Federal Housing Finance Agency, Change in Metropolitan Area House Price Indexes, April 7, 2021

Median Single-Family Home Prices

Area	2018	2019	2020[p]	Percent Change 2019 to 2020
MSA[1]	142.0	158.2	175.0	10.6
U.S. Average	261.6	274.6	299.9	9.2

Note: Figures are median sales prices of existing single-family homes in thousands of dollars; (p) preliminary; (1) Figures cover the Wichita, KS Metropolitan Statistical Area
Source: National Association of Realtors, Median Sales Price of Existing Single-Family Homes for Metropolitan Areas, 4th Quarter 2020

Qualifying Income Based on Median Sales Price of Existing Single-Family Homes

Area	With 5% Down ($)	With 10% Down ($)	With 20% Down ($)
MSA[1]	34,556	32,738	29,100
U.S. Average	59,266	56,147	49,908

Note: Figures are preliminary; Qualifying income is based on a mortgage rate of 2.81%. Monthly principal and interest payment is limited to 25% of income; (1) Figures cover the Wichita, KS Metropolitan Statistical Area
Source: National Association of Realtors, Qualifying Income Based on Median Sales Price of Existing Single-Family Homes for Metropolitan Areas, 4th Quarter 2020

Home Value Distribution

Area	Under $50,000	$50,000 -$99,999	$100,000 -$149,999	$150,000 -$199,999	$200,000 -$299,999	$300,000 -$499,999	$500,000 -$999,999	$1,000,000 or more
City	8.4	26.6	22.6	18.2	14.6	7.0	2.3	0.3
MSA[1]	8.3	24.2	22.6	19.1	15.6	7.8	2.0	0.4
U.S.	6.9	12.0	13.3	14.0	19.6	19.3	11.4	3.4

Note: Figures are percentages and cover owner-occupied housing units; (1) Figures cover the Wichita, KS Metropolitan Statistical Area
Source: U.S. Census Bureau, 2015-2019 American Community Survey 5-Year Estimates

Year Housing Structure Built

Area	2010 or Later	2000 -2009	1990 -1999	1980 -1989	1970 -1979	1960 -1969	1950 -1959	1940 -1949	Before 1940	Median Year
City	4.2	10.2	12.9	12.5	12.8	9.3	20.0	7.4	10.7	1972
MSA[1]	4.7	11.9	14.1	12.2	13.3	8.5	17.9	6.0	11.3	1975
U.S.	5.2	14.0	13.9	13.4	15.2	10.6	10.3	4.9	12.6	1978

Note: Figures are percentages except for Median Year; Note: (1) Figures cover the Wichita, KS Metropolitan Statistical Area
Source: U.S. Census Bureau, 2015-2019 American Community Survey 5-Year Estimates

Gross Monthly Rent

Area	Under $500	$500 -$999	$1,000 -$1,499	$1,500 -$1,999	$2,000 -$2,499	$2,500 -$2,999	$3,000 and up	Median ($)
City	11.6	61.3	22.4	3.3	0.6	0.2	0.7	809
MSA[1]	11.4	60.3	22.5	4.0	0.9	0.3	0.7	818
U.S.	9.4	36.2	30.0	14.0	5.6	2.4	2.4	1,062

Note: Figures are percentages except for Median; Gross rent is the contract rent plus the estimated average monthly cost of utilities (electricity, gas, and water and sewer) and fuels (oil, coal, kerosene, wood, etc.) if these are paid by the renter (or paid for the renter by someone else); (1) Figures cover the Wichita, KS Metropolitan Statistical Area
Source: U.S. Census Bureau, 2015-2019 American Community Survey 5-Year Estimates

HEALTH

Health Risk Factors

Category	MSA[1] (%)	U.S. (%)
Adults aged 18–64 who have any kind of health care coverage	83.9	87.3
Adults who reported being in good or better health	81.3	82.4
Adults who have been told they have high blood cholesterol	35.0	33.0
Adults who have been told they have high blood pressure	35.0	32.3
Adults who are current smokers	18.7	17.1
Adults who currently use E-cigarettes	6.0	4.6
Adults who currently use chewing tobacco, snuff, or snus	5.2	4.0
Adults who are heavy drinkers[2]	5.5	6.3
Adults who are binge drinkers[3]	15.6	17.4
Adults who are overweight (BMI 25.0 - 29.9)	35.2	35.3
Adults who are obese (BMI 30.0 - 99.8)	33.9	31.3
Adults who participated in any physical activities in the past month	71.6	74.4
Adults who always or nearly always wears a seat belt	94.6	94.3

Note: (1) Figures cover the Wichita, KS Metropolitan Statistical Area; (2) Heavy drinkers are classified as adult men having more than 14 drinks per week and adult women having more than 7 drinks per week; (3) Binge drinkers are classified as males having five or more drinks on one occasion or females having four or more drinks on one occasion
Source: Centers for Disease Control and Prevention, Behaviorial Risk Factor Surveillance System, SMART: Selected Metropolitan Area Risk Trends, 2017

Acute and Chronic Health Conditions

Category	MSA[1] (%)	U.S. (%)
Adults who have ever been told they had a heart attack	4.2	4.2
Adults who have ever been told they have angina or coronary heart disease	4.3	3.9
Adults who have ever been told they had a stroke	2.8	3.0
Adults who have ever been told they have asthma	13.3	14.2
Adults who have ever been told they have arthritis	23.7	24.9
Adults who have ever been told they have diabetes[2]	11.3	10.5
Adults who have ever been told they had skin cancer	4.9	6.2
Adults who have ever been told they had any other types of cancer	7.4	7.1
Adults who have ever been told they have COPD	6.2	6.5
Adults who have ever been told they have kidney disease	3.0	3.0
Adults who have ever been told they have a form of depression	22.6	20.5

Note: (1) Figures cover the Wichita, KS Metropolitan Statistical Area; (2) Figures do not include pregnancy-related, borderline, or pre-diabetes
Source: Centers for Disease Control and Prevention, Behaviorial Risk Factor Surveillance System, SMART: Selected Metropolitan Area Risk Trends, 2017

Health Screening and Vaccination Rates

Category	MSA[1] (%)	U.S. (%)
Adults aged 65+ who have had flu shot within the past year	55.3	60.7
Adults aged 65+ who have ever had a pneumonia vaccination	73.7	75.4
Adults who have ever been tested for HIV	31.3	36.1
Adults who have ever had the shingles or zoster vaccine?	27.9	28.9
Adults who have had their blood cholesterol checked within the last five years	84.1	85.9

Note: n/a not available; (1) Figures cover the Wichita, KS Metropolitan Statistical Area.
Source: Centers for Disease Control and Prevention, Behaviorial Risk Factor Surveillance System, SMART: Selected Metropolitan Area Risk Trends, 2017

Disability Status

Category	MSA[1] (%)	U.S. (%)
Adults who reported being deaf	7.4	6.7
Are you blind or have serious difficulty seeing, even when wearing glasses?	3.8	4.5
Are you limited in any way in any of your usual activities due of arthritis?	11.4	12.9
Do you have difficulty doing errands alone?	6.7	6.8
Do you have difficulty dressing or bathing?	3.8	3.6
Do you have serious difficulty concentrating/remembering/making decisions?	12.0	10.7
Do you have serious difficulty walking or climbing stairs?	13.9	13.6

Note: (1) Figures cover the Wichita, KS Metropolitan Statistical Area.
Source: Centers for Disease Control and Prevention, Behaviorial Risk Factor Surveillance System, SMART: Selected Metropolitan Area Risk Trends, 2017

Mortality Rates for the Top 10 Causes of Death in the U.S.

ICD-10[a] Sub-Chapter	ICD-10[a] Code	Age-Adjusted Mortality Rate[1] per 100,000 population	
		County[2]	U.S.
Malignant neoplasms	C00-C97	158.0	149.2
Ischaemic heart diseases	I20-I25	97.3	90.5
Other forms of heart disease	I30-I51	46.0	52.2
Chronic lower respiratory diseases	J40-J47	52.1	39.6
Other degenerative diseases of the nervous system	G30-G31	42.1	37.6
Cerebrovascular diseases	I60-I69	36.2	37.2
Other external causes of accidental injury	W00-X59	39.8	36.1
Organic, including symptomatic, mental disorders	F01-F09	43.5	29.4
Hypertensive diseases	I10-I15	18.7	24.1
Diabetes mellitus	E10-E14	24.7	21.5

Note: (a) ICD-10 = International Classification of Diseases 10th Revision; (1) Mortality rates are a three-year average covering 2017-2019; (2) Figures cover Sedgwick County.
Source: Centers for Disease Control and Prevention, National Center for Health Statistics. Underlying Cause of Death 1999-2019 on CDC WONDER Online Database

Mortality Rates for Selected Causes of Death

ICD-10[a] Sub-Chapter	ICD-10[a] Code	Age-Adjusted Mortality Rate[1] per 100,000 population	
		County[2]	U.S.
Assault	X85-Y09	8.0	6.0
Diseases of the liver	K70-K76	18.7	14.4
Human immunodeficiency virus (HIV) disease	B20-B24	1.4	1.5
Influenza and pneumonia	J09-J18	15.9	13.8
Intentional self-harm	X60-X84	20.2	14.1
Malnutrition	E40-E46	1.7	2.3
Obesity and other hyperalimentation	E65-E68	1.9	2.1
Renal failure	N17-N19	17.4	12.6
Transport accidents	V01-V99	15.1	12.3
Viral hepatitis	B15-B19	1.2	1.2

Note: (a) ICD-10 = International Classification of Diseases 10th Revision; (1) Mortality rates are a three-year average covering 2017-2019; (2) Figures cover Sedgwick County; Data are suppressed when the data meet the criteria for confidentiality constraints; Mortality rates are flagged as unreliable when the rate would be calculated with a numerator of 20 or less.
Source: Centers for Disease Control and Prevention, National Center for Health Statistics. Underlying Cause of Death 1999-2019 on CDC WONDER Online Database

Health Insurance Coverage

Area	With Health Insurance	With Private Health Insurance	With Public Health Insurance	Without Health Insurance	Population Under Age 19 Without Health Insurance
City	87.9	67.3	32.3	12.1	6.6
MSA[1]	89.8	71.6	30.3	10.2	5.8
U.S.	91.2	67.9	35.1	8.8	5.1

Note: Figures are percentages that cover the civilian noninstitutionalized population; (1) Figures cover the Wichita, KS Metropolitan Statistical Area
Source: U.S. Census Bureau, 2015-2019 American Community Survey 5-Year Estimates

Number of Medical Professionals

Area	MDs[3]	DOs[3,4]	Dentists	Podiatrists	Chiropractors	Optometrists
County[1] (number)	1,325	181	340	13	220	145
County[1] (rate[2])	258.0	35.2	65.9	2.5	42.6	28.1
U.S. (rate[2])	282.9	22.7	71.2	6.2	28.1	16.9

20173
Note: Data as of 2019 unless noted; (1) Data covers Sedgwick County; (2) Rate per 100,000 population; (3) Data as of 2018 and includes all active, non-federal physicians; (4) Doctor of Osteopathic Medicine
Source: U.S. Department of Health and Human Services, Health Resources and Services Administration, Bureau of Health Professions, Area Resource File (ARF) 2019-2020

EDUCATION

Public School District Statistics

District Name	Schls	Pupils	Pupil/ Teacher Ratio	Minority Pupils[1] (%)	Free Lunch Eligible[2] (%)	IEP[3] (%)
Wichita	89	49,885	13.9	67.9	67.9	15.1

Note: Table includes school districts with 2,000 or more students; (1) Percentage of students that are not non-Hispanic white; (2) Percentage of students that are eligible for the free lunch program; (3) Percentage of students that have an Individualized Education Program.
Source: U.S. Department of Education, National Center for Education Statistics, Common Core of Data, Local Education Agency (School District) Universe Survey: School Year 2018-2019; U.S. Department of Education, National Center for Education Statistics, Common Core of Data, Public Elementary/Secondary School Universe Survey: School Year 2018-2019

Highest Level of Education

Area	Less than H.S.	H.S. Diploma	Some College, No Deg.	Associate Degree	Bachelor's Degree	Master's Degree	Prof. School Degree	Doctorate Degree
City	11.7	26.4	24.0	7.9	19.1	8.1	1.8	1.1
MSA[1]	9.9	26.5	24.4	8.6	19.6	8.3	1.7	1.0
U.S.	12.0	27.0	20.4	8.5	19.8	8.8	2.1	1.4

Note: Figures cover persons age 25 and over; (1) Figures cover the Wichita, KS Metropolitan Statistical Area
Source: U.S. Census Bureau, 2015-2019 American Community Survey 5-Year Estimates

Educational Attainment by Race

Area	High School Graduate or Higher (%)					Bachelor's Degree or Higher (%)				
	Total	White	Black	Asian	Hisp.[2]	Total	White	Black	Asian	Hisp.[2]
City	88.3	90.4	87.4	81.3	62.8	30.1	32.9	15.2	36.3	13.0
MSA[1]	90.1	91.7	87.1	81.9	65.8	30.6	32.3	17.2	36.9	15.3
U.S.	88.0	89.9	86.0	87.1	68.7	32.1	33.5	21.6	54.3	16.4

Note: Figures shown cover persons 25 years old and over; (1) Figures cover the Wichita, KS Metropolitan Statistical Area; (2) People of Hispanic origin can be of any race
Source: U.S. Census Bureau, 2015-2019 American Community Survey 5-Year Estimates

School Enrollment by Grade and Control

Area	Preschool (%)		Kindergarten (%)		Grades 1 - 4 (%)		Grades 5 - 8 (%)		Grades 9 - 12 (%)	
	Public	Private	Public	Private	Public	Private	Public	Private	Public	Private
City	62.5	37.5	83.7	16.3	85.4	14.6	84.7	15.3	84.2	15.8
MSA[1]	63.1	36.9	83.3	16.7	86.3	13.7	87.3	12.7	86.6	13.4
U.S.	59.1	40.9	87.6	12.4	89.5	10.5	89.4	10.6	90.1	9.9

Note: Figures shown cover persons 3 years old and over; (1) Figures cover the Wichita, KS Metropolitan Statistical Area
Source: U.S. Census Bureau, 2015-2019 American Community Survey 5-Year Estimates

Higher Education

Four-Year Colleges			Two-Year Colleges			Medical Schools[1]	Law Schools[2]	Voc/ Tech[3]
Public	Private Non-profit	Private For-profit	Public	Private Non-profit	Private For-profit			
1	2	1	1	0	2	1	0	4

Note: Figures cover institutions located within the city limits and include main campuses only; (1) includes schools accredited by the Liaison Committee on Medical Education and the American Osteopathic Association's Commission on Osteopathic College Accreditation; (2) includes ABA-accredited schools, schools with provisional ABA accreditation, and state accredited schools; (3) includes all schools with programs that are less than 2 years.
Source: National Center for Education Statistics, Integrated Postsecondary Education System (IPEDS), 2019-20; Wikipedia, List of Medical Schools in the United States, accessed April 2, 2021; Wikipedia, List of Law Schools in the United States, accessed April 2, 2021

522   Wichita, Kansas

EMPLOYERS

Major Employers

Company Name	Industry
AGCO Corporation	Agricultural equipment
Beechcraft Corp.	Aircraft
Boeing Defense, Space & Security	Aircraft modification
Bombardier Learjet	Aircraft
Cargill Meat Solutions	Meat products
Cessna Aircraft Company	Manufacturing
City of Wichita	Municipal government
Cox Communications	Broadband communications & entertainment company
Dillons Food Stores	Grocery stores
Koch Industries	Manufacturing, energy & commodities
McConnell Air Force Base	U.S. military
Robert J. Dole VA Medical Center	Veterans medical center
Sedgwick County	County government
Spirit AeroSystems	Manufacturing
State of Kansas	State government
U.S. Postal Service	Federal mail delivery service
Unified School District 260 Derby	Public elementary & secondary schools
Unified School District 261 Haysville	Public elementary & secondary schools
Unified School District 265 Goddard	Public elementary & secondary schools
Unified School District 490 El Dorado	Public elementary & secondary schools
United States Government	Federal government
USD 259 Wichita	Education
Via Christi Health	Healthcare
Wesley Medical Center	Health care
Wichita State University	Public higher education

Note: Companies shown are located within the Wichita, KS Metropolitan Statistical Area.
Source: Hoovers.com; Wikipedia

PUBLIC SAFETY

Crime Rate

Area	All Crimes	Violent Crimes				Property Crimes		
		Murder	Rape[3]	Robbery	Aggrav. Assault	Burglary	Larceny -Theft	Motor Vehicle Theft
City	6,462.8	9.0	94.1	118.2	919.8	686.3	4,044.6	590.9
Suburbs[1]	n/a	1.6	42.3	14.5	156.8	271.8	n/a	129.8
Metro[2]	n/a	6.1	74.0	77.9	623.3	525.2	n/a	411.7
U.S.	2,489.3	5.0	42.6	81.6	250.2	340.5	1,549.5	219.9

Note: Figures are crimes per 100,000 population; (1) All areas within the metro area that are located outside the city limits; (2) Figures cover the Wichita, KS Metropolitan Statistical Area; (3) All figures shown were reported using the revised Uniform Crime Reporting (UCR) definition of rape.
Source: FBI Uniform Crime Reports, 2019

Hate Crimes

Area	Number of Quarters Reported	Number of Incidents per Bias Motivation					
		Race/Ethnicity/ Ancestry	Religion	Sexual Orientation	Disability	Gender	Gender Identity
City	4	2	0	2	0	0	0
U.S.	4	3,963	1,521	1,195	157	69	198

Source: Federal Bureau of Investigation, Hate Crime Statistics 2019

Identity Theft Consumer Reports

Area	Reports	Reports per 100,000 Population	Rank[2]
MSA[1]	8,929	1,395	3
U.S.	1,387,615	423	-

Note: (1) Figures cover the Wichita, KS Metropolitan Statistical Area; (2) Rank ranges from 1 to 391 where 1 indicates greatest number of identity theft reports per 100,000 population
Source: Federal Trade Commission, Consumer Sentinel Network Data Book 2020

Fraud and Other Consumer Reports

Area	Reports	Reports per 100,000 Population	Rank[2]
MSA[1]	4,813	752	139
U.S.	3,385,133	1,031	-

Note: (1) Figures cover the Wichita, KS Metropolitan Statistical Area; (2) Rank ranges from 1 to 391 where 1 indicates greatest number of fraud and other consumer reports per 100,000 population
Source: Federal Trade Commission, Consumer Sentinel Network Data Book 2020

Wichita, Kansas   523

POLITICS

2020 Presidential Election Results

Area	Biden	Trump	Jorgensen	Hawkins	Other
Sedgwick County	42.6	54.4	2.4	0.0	0.5
U.S.	51.3	46.8	1.2	0.3	0.5

Note: Results are percentages and may not add to 100% due to rounding
Source: Dave Leip's Atlas of U.S. Presidential Elections

SPORTS

Professional Sports Teams

Team Name	League	Year Established
No teams are located in the metro area		

Source: Wikipedia, Major Professional Sports Teams of the United States and Canada, April 6, 2021

CLIMATE

Average and Extreme Temperatures

Temperature	Jan	Feb	Mar	Apr	May	Jun	Jul	Aug	Sep	Oct	Nov	Dec	Yr.
Extreme High (°F)	75	84	89	96	100	110	113	110	107	95	87	83	113
Average High (°F)	40	46	56	68	77	87	92	91	82	71	55	44	68
Average Temp. (°F)	30	35	45	57	66	76	81	80	71	59	45	34	57
Average Low (°F)	20	24	33	45	55	65	70	68	59	47	34	24	45
Extreme Low (°F)	-12	-21	-3	15	31	43	51	47	31	21	1	-16	-21

Note: Figures cover the years 1948-1990
Source: National Climatic Data Center, International Station Meteorological Climate Summary, 9/96

Average Precipitation/Snowfall/Humidity

Precip./Humidity	Jan	Feb	Mar	Apr	May	Jun	Jul	Aug	Sep	Oct	Nov	Dec	Yr.
Avg. Precip. (in.)	0.9	1.0	2.3	2.3	3.9	4.3	3.7	3.0	3.2	2.3	1.4	1.0	29.3
Avg. Snowfall (in.)	5	4	3	Tr	0	0	0	0	0	Tr	2	3	17
Avg. Rel. Hum. 6am (%)	78	79	77	78	83	83	78	79	82	80	79	79	80
Avg. Rel. Hum. 3pm (%)	56	54	48	46	51	47	42	43	47	47	51	56	49

Note: Figures cover the years 1948-1990; Tr = Trace amounts (<0.05 in. of rain; <0.5 in. of snow)
Source: National Climatic Data Center, International Station Meteorological Climate Summary, 9/96

Weather Conditions

Temperature			Daytime Sky			Precipitation		
10°F & below	32°F & below	90°F & above	Clear	Partly cloudy	Cloudy	0.01 inch or more precip.	0.1 inch or more snow/ice	Thunder-storms
13	110	63	117	132	116	87	13	54

Note: Figures are average number of days per year and cover the years 1948-1990
Source: National Climatic Data Center, International Station Meteorological Climate Summary, 9/96

HAZARDOUS WASTE

Superfund Sites

The Wichita, KS metro area is home to two sites on the EPA's Superfund National Priorities List: **57th and North Broadway Streets Site** (final); **Pester Refinery Co.** (final). There are a total of 1,375 Superfund sites with a status of proposed or final on the list in the U.S. *U.S. Environmental Protection Agency, National Priorities List, April 7, 2021*

AIR QUALITY

Air Quality Trends: Ozone

	1990	1995	2000	2005	2010	2015	2016	2017	2018	2019
MSA[1]	0.077	0.069	0.080	0.074	0.075	0.064	0.062	0.063	0.064	0.062
U.S.	0.088	0.089	0.082	0.080	0.073	0.068	0.069	0.068	0.069	0.065

Note: (1) Data covers the Wichita, KS Metropolitan Statistical Area. The values shown are the composite ozone concentration averages among trend sites based on the highest fourth daily maximum 8-hour concentration in parts per million. These trends are based on sites having an adequate record of monitoring data during the trend period. Data from exceptional events are included.
Source: U.S. Environmental Protection Agency, Air Quality Monitoring Information, "Air Quality Trends by City, 1990-2019"

Air Quality Index

| Area | Percent of Days when Air Quality was...[2] | | | | | AQI Statistics[2] | |
	Good	Moderate	Unhealthy for Sensitive Groups	Unhealthy	Very Unhealthy	Maximum	Median
MSA[1]	82.5	17.5	0.0	0.0	0.0	97	40

Note: (1) Data covers the Wichita, KS Metropolitan Statistical Area; (2) Based on 365 days with AQI data in 2019. Air Quality Index (AQI) is an index for reporting daily air quality. EPA calculates the AQI for five major air pollutants regulated by the Clean Air Act: ground-level ozone, particle pollution (aka particulate matter), carbon monoxide, sulfur dioxide, and nitrogen dioxide. The AQI runs from 0 to 500. The higher the AQI value, the greater the level of air pollution and the greater the health concern. There are six AQI categories: "Good" AQI is between 0 and 50. Air quality is considered satisfactory; "Moderate" AQI is between 51 and 100. Air quality is acceptable; "Unhealthy for Sensitive Groups" When AQI values are between 101 and 150, members of sensitive groups may experience health effects; "Unhealthy" When AQI values are between 151 and 200 everyone may begin to experience health effects; "Very Unhealthy" AQI values between 201 and 300 trigger a health alert; "Hazardous" AQI values over 300 trigger warnings of emergency conditions (not shown).
Source: U.S. Environmental Protection Agency, Air Quality Index Report, 2019

Air Quality Index Pollutants

| Area | Percent of Days when AQI Pollutant was...[2] | | | | | |
	Carbon Monoxide	Nitrogen Dioxide	Ozone	Sulfur Dioxide	Particulate Matter 2.5	Particulate Matter 10
MSA[1]	0.0	1.4	72.6	0.0	23.6	2.5

Note: (1) Data covers the Wichita, KS Metropolitan Statistical Area; (2) Based on 365 days with AQI data in 2019. The Air Quality Index (AQI) is an index for reporting daily air quality. EPA calculates the AQI for five major air pollutants regulated by the Clean Air Act: ground-level ozone, particle pollution (also known as particulate matter), carbon monoxide, sulfur dioxide, and nitrogen dioxide. The AQI runs from 0 to 500. The higher the AQI value, the greater the level of air pollution and the greater the health concern.
Source: U.S. Environmental Protection Agency, Air Quality Index Report, 2019

Maximum Air Pollutant Concentrations: Particulate Matter, Ozone, CO and Lead

	Particulate Matter 10 (ug/m^3)	Particulate Matter 2.5 Wtd AM (ug/m^3)	Particulate Matter 2.5 24-Hr (ug/m^3)	Ozone (ppm)	Carbon Monoxide (ppm)	Lead (ug/m^3)
MSA[1] Level	64	7.5	18	0.062	n/a	n/a
NAAQS[2]	150	15	35	0.075	9	0.15
Met NAAQS[2]	Yes	Yes	Yes	Yes	n/a	n/a

Note: (1) Data covers the Wichita, KS Metropolitan Statistical Area; Data from exceptional events are included; (2) National Ambient Air Quality Standards; ppm = parts per million; ug/m^3 = micrograms per cubic meter; n/a not available.
Concentrations: Particulate Matter 10 (coarse particulate)—highest second maximum 24-hour concentration; Particulate Matter 2.5 Wtd AM (fine particulate)—highest weighted annual mean concentration; Particulate Matter 2.5 24-Hour (fine particulate)—highest 98th percentile 24-hour concentration; Ozone—highest fourth daily maximum 8-hour concentration; Carbon Monoxide—highest second maximum non-overlapping 8-hour concentration; Lead—maximum running 3-month average
Source: U.S. Environmental Protection Agency, Air Quality Monitoring Information, "Air Quality Statistics by City, 2019"

Maximum Air Pollutant Concentrations: Nitrogen Dioxide and Sulfur Dioxide

	Nitrogen Dioxide AM (ppb)	Nitrogen Dioxide 1-Hr (ppb)	Sulfur Dioxide AM (ppb)	Sulfur Dioxide 1-Hr (ppb)	Sulfur Dioxide 24-Hr (ppb)
MSA[1] Level	6	21	n/a	3	n/a
NAAQS[2]	53	100	30	75	140
Met NAAQS[2]	Yes	Yes	n/a	Yes	n/a

Note: (1) Data covers the Wichita, KS Metropolitan Statistical Area; Data from exceptional events are included; (2) National Ambient Air Quality Standards; ppm = parts per million; ug/m^3 = micrograms per cubic meter; n/a not available.
Concentrations: Nitrogen Dioxide AM—highest arithmetic mean concentration; Nitrogen Dioxide 1-Hr—highest 98th percentile 1-hour daily maximum concentration; Sulfur Dioxide AM—highest annual mean concentration; Sulfur Dioxide 1-Hr—highest 99th percentile 1-hour daily maximum concentration; Sulfur Dioxide 24-Hr—highest second maximum 24-hour concentration
Source: U.S. Environmental Protection Agency, Air Quality Monitoring Information, "Air Quality Statistics by City, 2019"

Appendixes

Appendix A: Comparative Statistics

Table of Contents

Demographics
Population Growth: City A-4
Population Growth: Metro Area A-6
Household Size: City A-8
Household Size: Metro Area A-10
Race: City A-12
Race: Metro Area A-14
Hispanic Origin: City A-16
Hispanic Origin: Metro Area A-18
Age: City A-20
Age: Metro Area A-22
Religious Groups by Family A-24
Religious Groups by Tradition A-26
Ancestry: City A-28
Ancestry: Metro Area A-30
Foreign-born Population: City A-32
Foreign-born Population: Metro Area A-34
Marital Status: City A-36
Marital Status: Metro Area A-38
Disability by Age: City A-40
Disability by Age: Metro Area A-42
Male/Female Ratio: City A-44
Male/Female Ratio: Metro Area A-46

Economy
Gross Metropolitan Product A-48
Economic Growth A-50
Metropolitan Area Exports A-52
Building Permits: City A-54
Building Permits: Metro Area A-56
Housing Vacancy Rates A-58
Bankruptcy Filings A-60

Income and Poverty
Income: City A-62
Income: Metro Area A-64
Household Income Distribution: City A-66
Household Income Distribution: Metro Area A-68
Poverty Rate: City A-70
Poverty Rate: Metro Area A-72

Employment and Earnings
Employment by Industry A-74
Labor Force, Employment and Job Growth: City A-76
Labor Force, Employment and Job Growth: Metro Area ... A-78
Unemployment Rate: City A-80
Unemployment Rate: Metro Area A-82
Average Hourly Wages: Occupations A - C A-84
Average Hourly Wages: Occupations C - E A-86
Average Hourly Wages: Occupations F - H A-88
Average Hourly Wages: Occupations L - N A-90
Average Hourly Wages: Occupations P - S A-92
Average Hourly Wages: Occupations T - W A-94
Average Hourly Wages: Occupations T - W A-96

Means of Transportation to Work: City A-98
Means of Transportation to Work: Metro Area A-100
Travel Time to Work: City A-102
Travel Time to Work: Metro Area A-104

Election Results
2020 Presidential Election Results A-106

Housing
House Price Index (HPI) A-108
Home Value Distribution: City A-110
Home Value Distribution: Metro Area A-112
Homeownership Rate A-114
Year Housing Structure Built: City A-116
Year Housing Structure Built: Metro Area A-118
Gross Monthly Rent: City A-120
Gross Monthly Rent: Metro Area A-122

Education
Highest Level of Education: City A-124
Highest Level of Education: Metro Area A-126
School Enrollment by Grade and Control: City A-128
School Enrollment by Grade and Control: Metro Area ... A-130
Educational Attainment by Race: City A-132
Educational Attainment by Race: Metro Area A-134

Cost of Living
Cost of Living Index A-136
Grocery Prices A-138
Housing and Utility Costs A-140
Health Care, Transportation, and Other Costs A-142

Health Care
Number of Medical Professionals A-144
Health Insurance Coverage: City A-146
Health Insurance Coverage: Metro Area A-148

Public Safety
Crime Rate: City A-150
Crime Rate: Suburbs A-152
Crime Rate: Metro Area A-154

Climate
Temperature & Precipitation: Yearly Averages
   and Extremes A-156
Weather Conditions A-158

Air Quality
Air Quality Index A-160
Air Quality Index Pollutants A-162
Air Quality Trends: Ozone A-164
Maximum Air Pollutant Concentrations:
   Particulate Matter, Ozone, CO and Lead A-166
Maximum Air Pollutant Concentrations:
   Nitrogen Dioxide and Sulfur Dioxide A-168

A-4   Appendix A: Comparative Statistics

Population Growth: City

Area	1990 Census	2000 Census	2010 Census	2019* Estimate	Population Growth (%)	
					1990-2019	2010-2019
Albuquerque, NM	388,375	448,607	545,852	559,374	44.0	2.5
Allentown, PA	105,066	106,632	118,032	120,915	15.1	2.4
Anchorage, AK	226,338	260,283	291,826	293,531	29.7	0.6
Ann Arbor, MI	111,018	114,024	113,934	120,735	8.8	6.0
Athens, GA	86,561	100,266	115,452	124,719	44.1	8.0
Atlanta, GA	394,092	416,474	420,003	488,800	24.0	16.4
Austin, TX	499,053	656,562	790,390	950,807	90.5	20.3
Baton Rouge, LA	223,299	227,818	229,493	224,149	0.4	-2.3
Boise City, ID	144,317	185,787	205,671	226,115	56.7	9.9
Boston, MA	574,283	589,141	617,594	684,379	19.2	10.8
Boulder, CO	87,737	94,673	97,385	106,392	21.3	9.2
Cape Coral, FL	75,507	102,286	154,305	183,942	143.6	19.2
Cedar Rapids, IA	110,829	120,758	126,326	132,301	19.4	4.7
Charleston, SC	96,102	96,650	120,083	135,257	40.7	12.6
Charlotte, NC	428,283	540,828	731,424	857,425	100.2	17.2
Chicago, IL	2,783,726	2,896,016	2,695,598	2,709,534	-2.7	0.5
Cincinnati, OH	363,974	331,285	296,943	301,394	-17.2	1.5
Clarksville, TN	78,569	103,455	132,929	152,934	94.6	15.0
Cleveland, OH	505,333	478,403	396,815	385,282	-23.8	-2.9
College Station, TX	53,318	67,890	93,857	113,686	113.2	21.1
Colorado Springs, CO	283,798	360,890	416,427	464,871	63.8	11.6
Columbia, MO	71,069	84,531	108,500	121,230	70.6	11.7
Columbia, SC	115,475	116,278	129,272	133,273	15.4	3.1
Columbus, OH	648,656	711,470	787,033	878,553	35.4	11.6
Dallas, TX	1,006,971	1,188,580	1,197,816	1,330,612	32.1	11.1
Davenport, IA	95,705	98,359	99,685	102,169	6.8	2.5
Denver, CO	467,153	554,636	600,158	705,576	51.0	17.6
Des Moines, IA	193,569	198,682	203,433	215,636	11.4	6.0
Durham, NC	151,737	187,035	228,330	269,702	77.7	18.1
Edison, NJ	88,680	97,687	99,967	100,447	13.3	0.5
El Paso, TX	515,541	563,662	649,121	679,813	31.9	4.7
Fargo, ND	74,372	90,599	105,549	121,889	63.9	15.5
Fayetteville, NC	118,247	121,015	200,564	210,432	78.0	4.9
Fort Collins, CO	89,555	118,652	143,986	165,609	84.9	15.0
Fort Wayne, IN	205,671	205,727	253,691	265,752	29.2	4.8
Fort Worth, TX	448,311	534,694	741,206	874,401	95.0	18.0
Grand Rapids, MI	189,145	197,800	188,040	198,401	4.9	5.5
Greeley, CO	60,887	76,930	92,889	105,888	73.9	14.0
Green Bay, WI	96,466	102,313	104,057	104,777	8.6	0.7
Greensboro, NC	193,389	223,891	269,666	291,303	50.6	8.0
Honolulu, HI	376,465	371,657	337,256	348,985	-7.3	3.5
Houston, TX	1,697,610	1,953,631	2,099,451	2,310,432	36.1	10.0
Huntsville, AL	161,842	158,216	180,105	196,219	21.2	8.9
Indianapolis, IN	730,993	781,870	820,445	864,447	18.3	5.4
Jacksonville, FL	635,221	735,617	821,784	890,467	40.2	8.4
Kansas City, MO	434,967	441,545	459,787	486,404	11.8	5.8
Lafayette, LA	104,735	110,257	120,623	126,666	20.9	5.0
Lakeland, FL	73,375	78,452	97,422	107,922	47.1	10.8
Las Vegas, NV	261,374	478,434	583,756	634,773	142.9	8.7
Lexington, KY	225,366	260,512	295,803	320,601	42.3	8.4
Lincoln, NE	193,629	225,581	258,379	283,839	46.6	9.9
Little Rock, AR	177,519	183,133	193,524	197,958	11.5	2.3
Los Angeles, CA	3,487,671	3,694,820	3,792,621	3,966,936	13.7	4.6
Louisville, KY	269,160	256,231	597,337	617,790	129.5	3.4
Madison, WI	193,451	208,054	233,209	254,977	31.8	9.3

Table continued on following page.

Appendix A: Comparative Statistics   A-5

Area	1990 Census	2000 Census	2010 Census	2019* Estimate	Population Growth (%)	
					1990-2019	2010-2019
Manchester, NH	99,567	107,006	109,565	112,109	12.6	2.3
Memphis, TN	660,536	650,100	646,889	651,932	-1.3	0.8
Miami, FL	358,843	362,470	399,457	454,279	26.6	13.7
Midland, TX	89,358	94,996	111,147	138,549	55.0	24.7
Milwaukee, WI	628,095	596,974	594,833	594,548	-5.3	0.0
Minneapolis, MN	368,383	382,618	382,578	420,324	14.1	9.9
Nashville, TN	488,364	545,524	601,222	663,750	35.9	10.4
New Haven, CT	130,474	123,626	129,779	130,331	-0.1	0.4
New Orleans, LA	496,938	484,674	343,829	390,845	-21.3	13.7
New York, NY	7,322,552	8,008,278	8,175,133	8,419,316	15.0	3.0
Oklahoma City, OK	445,065	506,132	579,999	643,692	44.6	11.0
Omaha, NE	371,972	390,007	408,958	475,862	27.9	16.4
Orlando, FL	161,172	185,951	238,300	280,832	74.2	17.8
Peoria, IL	114,341	112,936	115,007	113,532	-0.7	-1.3
Philadelphia, PA	1,585,577	1,517,550	1,526,006	1,579,075	-0.4	3.5
Phoenix, AZ	989,873	1,321,045	1,445,632	1,633,017	65.0	13.0
Pittsburgh, PA	369,785	334,563	305,704	302,205	-18.3	-1.1
Portland, OR	485,833	529,121	583,776	645,291	32.8	10.5
Providence, RI	160,734	173,618	178,042	179,494	11.7	0.8
Provo, UT	87,148	105,166	112,488	116,403	33.6	3.5
Raleigh, NC	226,841	276,093	403,892	464,485	104.8	15.0
Reno, NV	139,950	180,480	225,221	246,500	76.1	9.4
Richmond, VA	202,783	197,790	204,214	226,622	11.8	11.0
Riverside, CA	226,232	255,166	303,871	326,414	44.3	7.4
Rochester, MN	74,151	85,806	106,769	115,557	55.8	8.2
Sacramento, CA	368,923	407,018	466,488	500,930	35.8	7.4
Salt Lake City, UT	159,796	181,743	186,440	197,756	23.8	6.1
San Antonio, TX	997,258	1,144,646	1,327,407	1,508,083	51.2	13.6
San Diego, CA	1,111,048	1,223,400	1,307,402	1,409,573	26.9	7.8
San Francisco, CA	723,959	776,733	805,235	874,961	20.9	8.7
San Jose, CA	784,324	894,943	945,942	1,027,690	31.0	8.6
Santa Rosa, CA	123,297	147,595	167,815	179,701	45.7	7.1
Savannah, GA	138,038	131,510	136,286	145,403	5.3	6.7
Seattle, WA	516,262	563,374	608,660	724,305	40.3	19.0
Sioux Falls, SD	102,262	123,975	153,888	177,117	73.2	15.1
Springfield, IL	108,997	111,454	116,250	115,888	6.3	-0.3
Tallahassee, FL	128,014	150,624	181,376	191,279	49.4	5.5
Tampa, FL	279,960	303,447	335,709	387,916	38.6	15.6
Tucson, AZ	417,942	486,699	520,116	541,482	29.6	4.1
Tulsa, OK	367,241	393,049	391,906	402,324	9.6	2.7
Tuscaloosa, AL	81,075	77,906	90,468	99,390	22.6	9.9
Virginia Beach, VA	393,069	425,257	437,994	450,201	14.5	2.8
Washington, DC	606,900	572,059	601,723	692,683	14.1	15.1
Wichita, KS	313,693	344,284	382,368	389,877	24.3	2.0
Winston-Salem, NC	168,139	185,776	229,617	244,115	45.2	6.3
U.S.	248,709,873	281,421,906	308,745,538	324,697,795	30.6	5.2

Note: (*) 2014-2019 5-year estimated population
Source: U.S. Census Bureau, 1990 Census, Census 2000, Census 2010, 2015-2019 American Community Survey 5-Year Estimates

A-6 Appendix A: Comparative Statistics

Population Growth: Metro Area

Area	1990 Census	2000 Census	2010 Census	2019* Estimate	Population Growth (%)	
					1990-2019	2010-2019
Albuquerque, NM	599,416	729,649	887,077	912,108	52.2	2.8
Allentown, PA	686,666	740,395	821,173	837,610	22.0	2.0
Anchorage, AK	266,021	319,605	380,821	398,900	50.0	4.7
Ann Arbor, MI	282,937	322,895	344,791	367,000	29.7	6.4
Athens, GA	136,025	166,079	192,541	208,457	53.2	8.3
Atlanta, GA	3,069,411	4,247,981	5,268,860	5,862,424	91.0	11.3
Austin, TX	846,217	1,249,763	1,716,289	2,114,441	149.9	23.2
Baton Rouge, LA	623,853	705,973	802,484	854,318	36.9	6.5
Boise City, ID	319,596	464,840	616,561	710,743	122.4	15.3
Boston, MA	4,133,895	4,391,344	4,552,402	4,832,346	16.9	6.1
Boulder, CO	208,898	269,758	294,567	322,510	54.4	9.5
Cape Coral, FL	335,113	440,888	618,754	737,468	120.1	19.2
Cedar Rapids, IA	210,640	237,230	257,940	270,056	28.2	4.7
Charleston, SC	506,875	549,033	664,607	774,508	52.8	16.5
Charlotte, NC	1,024,331	1,330,448	1,758,038	2,545,560	148.5	44.8
Chicago, IL	8,182,076	9,098,316	9,461,105	9,508,605	16.2	0.5
Cincinnati, OH	1,844,917	2,009,632	2,130,151	2,201,741	19.3	3.4
Clarksville, TN	189,277	232,000	273,949	299,470	58.2	9.3
Cleveland, OH	2,102,219	2,148,143	2,077,240	2,056,898	-2.2	-1.0
College Station, TX	150,998	184,885	228,660	258,029	70.9	12.8
Colorado Springs, CO	409,482	537,484	645,613	723,498	76.7	12.1
Columbia, MO	122,010	145,666	172,786	205,369	68.3	18.9
Columbia, SC	548,325	647,158	767,598	824,278	50.3	7.4
Columbus, OH	1,405,176	1,612,694	1,836,536	2,077,761	47.9	13.1
Dallas, TX	3,989,294	5,161,544	6,371,773	7,320,663	83.5	14.9
Davenport, IA	368,151	376,019	379,690	381,175	3.5	0.4
Denver, CO	1,666,935	2,179,296	2,543,482	2,892,066	73.5	13.7
Des Moines, IA	416,346	481,394	569,633	680,439	63.4	19.5
Durham, NC	344,646	426,493	504,357	626,695	81.8	24.3
Edison, NJ	16,845,992	18,323,002	18,897,109	19,294,236	14.5	2.1
El Paso, TX	591,610	679,622	800,647	840,477	42.1	5.0
Fargo, ND	153,296	174,367	208,777	240,421	56.8	15.2
Fayetteville, NC	297,422	336,609	366,383	519,101	74.5	41.7
Fort Collins, CO	186,136	251,494	299,630	344,786	85.2	15.1
Fort Wayne, IN	354,435	390,156	416,257	406,305	14.6	-2.4
Fort Worth, TX	3,989,294	5,161,544	6,371,773	7,320,663*	83.5	14.9
Grand Rapids, MI	645,914	740,482	774,160	1,062,392	64.5	37.2
Greeley, CO	131,816	180,926	252,825	305,345	131.6	20.8
Green Bay, WI	243,698	282,599	306,241	319,401	31.1	4.3
Greensboro, NC	540,257	643,430	723,801	762,063	41.1	5.3
Honolulu, HI	836,231	876,156	953,207	984,821	17.8	3.3
Houston, TX	3,767,335	4,715,407	5,946,800	6,884,138	82.7	15.8
Huntsville, AL	293,047	342,376	417,593	457,003	55.9	9.4
Indianapolis, IN	1,294,217	1,525,104	1,756,241	2,029,472	56.8	15.6
Jacksonville, FL	925,213	1,122,750	1,345,596	1,503,574	62.5	11.7
Kansas City, MO	1,636,528	1,836,038	2,035,334	2,124,518	29.8	4.4
Lafayette, LA	208,740	239,086	273,738	489,914	134.7	79.0
Lakeland, FL	405,382	483,924	602,095	686,218	69.3	14.0
Las Vegas, NV	741,459	1,375,765	1,951,269	2,182,004	194.3	11.8
Lexington, KY	348,428	408,326	472,099	510,647	46.6	8.2
Lincoln, NE	229,091	266,787	302,157	330,329	44.2	9.3
Little Rock, AR	535,034	610,518	699,757	737,015	37.8	5.3
Los Angeles, CA	11,273,720	12,365,627	12,828,837	13,249,614	17.5	3.3
Louisville, KY	1,055,973	1,161,975	1,283,566	1,257,088	19.0	-2.1
Madison, WI	432,323	501,774	568,593	653,725	51.2	15.0

Table continued on following page.

Appendix A: Comparative Statistics A-7

Area	1990 Census	2000 Census	2010 Census	2019* Estimate	Population Growth (%)	
					1990-2019	2010-2019
Manchester, NH	336,073	380,841	400,721	413,035	22.9	3.1
Memphis, TN	1,067,263	1,205,204	1,316,100	1,339,623	25.5	1.8
Miami, FL	4,056,100	5,007,564	5,564,635	6,090,660	50.2	9.5
Midland, TX	106,611	116,009	136,872	173,816	63.0	27.0
Milwaukee, WI	1,432,149	1,500,741	1,555,908	1,575,223	10.0	1.2
Minneapolis, MN	2,538,834	2,968,806	3,279,833	3,573,609	40.8	9.0
Nashville, TN	1,048,218	1,311,789	1,589,934	1,871,903	78.6	17.7
New Haven, CT	804,219	824,008	862,477	857,513	6.6	-0.6
New Orleans, LA	1,264,391	1,316,510	1,167,764	1,267,777	0.3	8.6
New York, NY	16,845,992	18,323,002	18,897,109	19,294,236	14.5	2.1
Oklahoma City, OK	971,042	1,095,421	1,252,987	1,382,841	42.4	10.4
Omaha, NE	685,797	767,041	865,350	931,779	35.9	7.7
Orlando, FL	1,224,852	1,644,561	2,134,411	2,508,970	104.8	17.5
Peoria, IL	358,552	366,899	379,186	406,883	13.5	7.3
Philadelphia, PA	5,435,470	5,687,147	5,965,343	6,079,130	11.8	1.9
Phoenix, AZ	2,238,480	3,251,876	4,192,887	4,761,603	112.7	13.6
Pittsburgh, PA	2,468,289	2,431,087	2,356,285	2,331,447	-5.5	-1.1
Portland, OR	1,523,741	1,927,881	2,226,009	2,445,761	60.5	9.9
Providence, RI	1,509,789	1,582,997	1,600,852	1,618,268	7.2	1.1
Provo, UT	269,407	376,774	526,810	616,791	128.9	17.1
Raleigh, NC	541,081	797,071	1,130,490	1,332,311	146.2	17.9
Reno, NV	257,193	342,885	425,417	460,924	79.2	8.3
Richmond, VA	949,244	1,096,957	1,258,251	1,269,530	33.7	0.9
Riverside, CA	2,588,793	3,254,821	4,224,851	4,560,470	76.2	7.9
Rochester, MN	141,945	163,618	186,011	217,964	53.6	17.2
Sacramento, CA	1,481,126	1,796,857	2,149,127	2,315,980	56.4	7.8
Salt Lake City, UT	768,075	968,858	1,124,197	1,201,043	56.4	6.8
San Antonio, TX	1,407,745	1,711,703	2,142,508	2,468,193	75.3	15.2
San Diego, CA	2,498,016	2,813,833	3,095,313	3,316,073	32.7	7.1
San Francisco, CA	3,686,592	4,123,740	4,335,391	4,701,332	27.5	8.4
San Jose, CA	1,534,280	1,735,819	1,836,911	1,987,846	29.6	8.2
Santa Rosa, CA	388,222	458,614	483,878	499,772	28.7	3.3
Savannah, GA	258,060	293,000	347,611	386,036	49.6	11.1
Seattle, WA	2,559,164	3,043,878	3,439,809	3,871,323	51.3	12.5
Sioux Falls, SD	153,500	187,093	228,261	259,348	69.0	13.6
Springfield, IL	189,550	201,437	210,170	209,167	10.3	-0.5
Tallahassee, FL	259,096	320,304	367,413	382,197	47.5	4.0
Tampa, FL	2,067,959	2,395,997	2,783,243	3,097,859	49.8	11.3
Tucson, AZ	666,880	843,746	980,263	1,027,207	54.0	4.8
Tulsa, OK	761,019	859,532	937,478	990,544	30.2	5.7
Tuscaloosa, AL	176,123	192,034	219,461	250,681	42.3	14.2
Virginia Beach, VA	1,449,389	1,576,370	1,671,683	1,761,729	21.5	5.4
Washington, DC	4,122,914	4,796,183	5,582,170	6,196,585	50.3	11.0
Wichita, KS	511,111	571,166	623,061	637,690	24.8	2.3
Winston-Salem, NC	361,091	421,961	477,717	666,216	84.5	39.5
U.S.	248,709,873	281,421,906	308,745,538	324,697,795	30.6	5.2

Note: (*) 2014-2019 5-year estimated population; Figures cover the Metropolitan Statistical Area (MSA)—see Appendix B for areas included
Source: U.S. Census Bureau, 1990 Census, Census 2000, Census 2010, 2015-2019 American Community Survey 5-Year Estimates

A-8   Appendix A: Comparative Statistics

Household Size: City

City	Persons in Household (%)							Average Household Size
	One	Two	Three	Four	Five	Six	Seven or More	
Albuquerque, NM	34.6	33.7	13.8	10.7	4.5	1.5	0.8	2.47
Allentown, PA	27.6	28.9	15.4	13.8	8.0	3.6	2.3	2.73
Anchorage, AK	26.3	33.0	16.9	12.5	6.6	2.4	2.0	2.69
Ann Arbor, MI	34.6	37.8	11.7	10.4	3.0	1.5	0.8	2.26
Athens, GA	33.4	35.2	14.5	11.2	3.6	1.4	0.4	2.35
Atlanta, GA	46.7	30.7	10.6	7.2	2.9	1.0	0.6	2.19
Austin, TX	34.5	32.7	14.3	11.3	4.4	1.5	0.9	2.44
Baton Rouge, LA	36.1	32.4	15.6	9.0	4.1	1.7	0.9	2.58
Boise City, ID	34.1	34.1	14.3	10.3	4.6	1.4	0.8	2.43
Boston, MA	36.2	32.4	15.4	9.4	3.9	1.6	0.8	2.36
Boulder, CO	33.8	36.8	14.5	10.9	2.7	0.7	0.3	2.27
Cape Coral, FL	23.7	43.0	14.2	12.3	4.4	1.6	0.5	2.81
Cedar Rapids, IA	34.1	33.9	14.0	10.5	4.4	2.2	0.6	2.33
Charleston, SC	35.4	37.8	14.2	9.0	2.4	0.6	0.1	2.31
Charlotte, NC	32.9	32.2	15.5	11.9	4.8	1.5	0.8	2.56
Chicago, IL	37.1	29.7	13.8	10.2	5.1	2.2	1.5	2.48
Cincinnati, OH	44.3	30.1	12.0	7.5	3.5	1.3	0.8	2.10
Clarksville, TN	24.7	30.7	19.6	15.1	5.8	2.3	1.3	2.66
Cleveland, OH	44.4	27.5	13.1	8.0	4.2	1.6	0.9	2.18
College Station, TX	29.7	33.8	16.5	14.1	3.5	1.8	0.4	2.53
Colorado Springs, CO	28.6	35.1	14.6	12.2	5.8	2.2	1.0	2.52
Columbia, MO	32.7	32.8	15.0	12.9	4.7	1.1	0.4	2.33
Columbia, SC	40.6	33.0	12.3	8.9	3.6	0.8	0.5	2.21
Columbus, OH	35.5	32.4	13.9	10.1	4.8	1.8	1.2	2.39
Dallas, TX	35.3	29.1	13.7	11.2	6.2	2.5	1.7	2.56
Davenport, IA	35.3	33.5	13.1	9.7	5.2	1.8	1.0	2.46
Denver, CO	38.2	32.9	12.0	9.5	4.3	1.6	1.2	2.29
Des Moines, IA	34.1	30.5	14.7	11.4	5.3	2.2	1.5	2.45
Durham, NC	33.9	33.5	15.4	10.1	4.4	1.6	0.8	2.36
Edison, NJ	18.9	29.0	21.1	20.3	6.4	2.5	1.5	2.86
El Paso, TX	25.5	28.5	17.7	15.9	7.5	3.2	1.3	2.97
Fargo, ND	36.4	34.0	14.4	8.9	4.2	1.3	0.5	2.14
Fayetteville, NC	35.6	31.3	15.3	10.7	4.2	1.8	0.8	2.42
Fort Collins, CO	24.7	37.9	17.8	13.8	4.3	0.9	0.4	2.44
Fort Wayne, IN	32.1	33.0	14.3	11.2	5.9	2.2	1.0	2.45
Fort Worth, TX	26.1	28.8	16.5	15.1	7.8	3.3	2.1	2.89
Grand Rapids, MI	33.1	31.4	13.8	11.1	5.9	2.5	1.9	2.53
Greeley, CO	26.0	31.4	16.1	13.3	8.2	3.2	1.3	2.72
Green Bay, WI	34.1	32.1	12.7	11.3	6.5	1.5	1.5	2.39
Greensboro, NC	34.2	33.1	15.4	10.2	4.6	1.4	0.7	2.37
Honolulu, HI	33.4	31.3	14.3	10.6	5.1	2.3	2.6	2.60
Houston, TX	32.3	28.9	15.2	12.3	6.6	2.8	1.7	2.65
Huntsville, AL	35.7	34.3	14.5	9.4	4.1	1.2	0.4	2.21
Indianapolis, IN	37.8	31.3	13.2	9.6	4.9	1.9	1.0	2.51
Jacksonville, FL	30.4	33.7	16.6	11.4	5.0	1.7	0.9	2.57
Kansas City, MO	37.0	31.9	12.9	10.0	4.9	1.8	1.1	2.35
Lafayette, LA	35.1	34.5	13.9	9.5	3.9	1.7	1.0	2.40
Lakeland, FL	33.1	37.5	14.3	8.9	3.6	1.6	0.7	2.50
Las Vegas, NV	30.6	31.6	15.3	11.5	6.2	2.7	1.7	2.70
Lexington, KY	31.5	35.0	15.1	11.2	4.6	1.6	0.6	2.37
Lincoln, NE	31.5	34.8	13.9	11.5	5.2	2.0	0.9	2.38
Little Rock, AR	36.6	32.0	14.0	10.1	4.6	1.8	0.7	2.37
Los Angeles, CA	30.2	28.8	15.3	13.0	6.8	2.9	2.5	2.80
Louisville, KY	33.3	32.9	15.3	10.5	4.8	1.8	1.0	2.43

Table continued on following page.

Appendix A: Comparative Statistics   A-9

City	Persons in Household (%)							Average Household Size
	One	Two	Three	Four	Five	Six	Seven or More	
Madison, WI	35.3	36.2	13.2	9.8	3.7	1.1	0.4	2.21
Manchester, NH	31.4	34.1	16.5	10.7	4.4	1.6	1.0	2.37
Memphis, TN	37.1	30.3	14.8	9.8	4.2	2.2	1.3	2.53
Miami, FL	37.3	31.0	16.1	8.8	3.9	1.5	0.9	2.51
Midland, TX	26.1	31.2	16.4	14.4	7.3	3.0	1.3	2.90
Milwaukee, WI	36.3	29.3	14.0	10.4	5.7	2.4	1.6	2.51
Minneapolis, MN	40.4	31.2	11.9	9.5	3.5	1.7	1.5	2.28
Nashville, TN	33.9	33.9	15.2	9.6	4.5	1.6	1.0	2.36
New Haven, CT	38.4	27.3	15.4	9.9	5.3	2.3	1.0	2.46
New Orleans, LA	45.9	29.2	12.6	7.8	2.6	1.0	0.6	2.45
New York, NY	32.2	28.4	16.2	12.5	5.9	2.5	2.0	2.60
Oklahoma City, OK	31.1	32.1	14.5	12.2	6.2	2.5	1.1	2.60
Omaha, NE	32.6	32.0	13.5	11.2	6.0	2.7	1.6	2.48
Orlando, FL	33.6	33.1	16.7	9.8	4.0	1.8	0.6	2.48
Peoria, IL	38.2	31.4	13.3	9.1	5.2	1.7	0.9	2.37
Philadelphia, PA	37.5	29.2	14.7	10.4	4.8	1.9	1.3	2.55
Phoenix, AZ	27.9	30.0	15.2	12.9	7.3	3.7	2.7	2.85
Pittsburgh, PA	43.6	32.4	12.8	6.7	2.5	1.1	0.6	2.02
Portland, OR	34.0	34.8	14.1	10.8	3.8	1.4	0.8	2.34
Providence, RI	33.2	29.0	15.6	11.7	7.0	1.7	1.5	2.67
Provo, UT	13.2	33.1	18.8	16.1	7.9	7.1	3.4	3.17
Raleigh, NC	33.0	32.4	15.2	12.4	4.7	1.3	0.6	2.42
Reno, NV	33.0	33.4	14.6	10.5	5.1	1.8	1.4	2.36
Richmond, VA	43.4	32.8	12.0	6.8	2.9	1.2	0.6	2.39
Riverside, CA	20.4	27.5	17.7	15.5	10.1	4.7	3.8	3.43
Rochester, MN	31.0	33.2	14.4	13.0	4.7	1.8	1.5	2.40
Sacramento, CA	30.9	30.7	14.7	12.1	6.0	2.9	2.3	2.66
Salt Lake City, UT	36.1	32.2	13.5	9.9	4.2	2.0	1.7	2.42
San Antonio, TX	29.9	29.5	16.2	12.9	6.7	2.8	1.7	2.96
San Diego, CA	27.5	33.4	16.1	13.1	5.7	2.3	1.5	2.70
San Francisco, CA	35.6	33.6	14.3	9.7	3.7	1.4	1.3	2.36
San Jose, CA	19.4	28.8	18.6	17.9	8.1	3.5	3.4	3.12
Santa Rosa, CA	28.2	32.6	15.3	13.2	6.2	2.3	2.0	2.66
Savannah, GA	33.5	34.0	15.6	9.8	4.3	1.4	1.0	2.55
Seattle, WA	38.5	35.6	12.5	8.8	2.9	0.8	0.6	2.11
Sioux Falls, SD	32.0	34.0	13.0	12.2	5.3	2.0	1.1	2.37
Springfield, IL	38.0	34.0	13.3	8.7	3.1	1.4	1.0	2.20
Tallahassee, FL	35.0	33.0	16.8	10.2	3.6	0.9	0.1	2.33
Tampa, FL	35.7	31.5	15.3	10.8	4.2	1.5	0.6	2.47
Tucson, AZ	34.6	31.2	14.7	10.8	5.1	2.0	1.3	2.42
Tulsa, OK	35.1	32.5	13.6	10.2	5.1	2.1	1.1	2.41
Tuscaloosa, AL	35.4	33.7	15.9	9.9	3.4	1.0	0.4	2.55
Virginia Beach, VA	24.4	34.4	17.5	14.8	5.8	1.9	0.8	2.58
Washington, DC	44.0	31.0	11.7	7.8	3.1	1.2	0.8	2.30
Wichita, KS	33.3	31.3	13.4	11.3	6.5	2.7	1.2	2.51
Winston-Salem, NC	35.7	31.5	15.0	9.4	5.2	1.8	1.1	2.46
U.S.	27.8	33.9	15.5	12.9	5.9	2.2	1.4	2.62

U.S. Census Bureau, 2015-2019 American Community Survey 5-Year Estimates

A-10 Appendix A: Comparative Statistics

Household Size: Metro Area

Metro Area	Persons in Household (%)							Average Household Size
	One	Two	Three	Four	Five	Six	Seven or More	
Albuquerque, NM	31.4	35.2	14.4	10.8	5.0	1.9	1.1	2.56
Allentown, PA	26.1	35.4	15.7	13.4	6.0	2.1	1.0	2.54
Anchorage, AK	25.5	33.6	16.4	12.7	6.8	2.6	2.1	2.83
Ann Arbor, MI	29.6	36.9	13.7	12.3	4.5	1.8	1.0	2.45
Athens, GA	28.9	35.3	15.2	13.1	4.8	1.6	0.8	2.50
Atlanta, GA	26.7	31.6	16.9	14.3	6.3	2.4	1.4	2.74
Austin, TX	27.9	33.1	15.5	13.9	6.0	2.1	1.2	2.71
Baton Rouge, LA	28.6	33.8	16.7	12.3	5.6	1.8	0.9	2.69
Boise City, ID	27.8	34.4	14.3	12.0	7.0	2.7	1.6	2.68
Boston, MA	27.7	33.0	16.6	14.3	5.4	1.7	0.9	2.55
Boulder, CO	28.7	36.3	15.5	12.9	4.6	1.2	0.4	2.44
Cape Coral, FL	28.0	44.7	11.5	9.0	4.1	1.6	0.8	2.64
Cedar Rapids, IA	29.6	36.5	13.8	11.9	5.0	2.0	0.8	2.41
Charleston, SC	29.1	35.6	16.5	11.7	4.6	1.5	0.6	2.60
Charlotte, NC	27.1	34.0	16.3	14.0	5.5	1.8	0.9	2.63
Chicago, IL	28.9	31.1	15.6	13.7	6.6	2.4	1.4	2.66
Cincinnati, OH	28.8	34.3	15.1	12.7	5.7	1.9	1.0	2.50
Clarksville, TN	24.9	32.2	18.3	14.2	6.2	2.5	1.2	2.64
Cleveland, OH	34.0	33.8	14.2	10.7	4.5	1.5	0.8	2.34
College Station, TX	28.1	33.9	15.7	13.2	5.1	2.6	1.2	2.61
Colorado Springs, CO	25.0	35.4	15.6	13.4	6.5	2.4	1.3	2.64
Columbia, MO	30.1	34.4	15.1	13.2	4.8	1.3	0.7	2.41
Columbia, SC	29.8	34.3	15.6	12.1	5.2	1.7	0.9	2.53
Columbus, OH	28.5	33.9	15.6	12.9	5.9	1.9	1.0	2.55
Dallas, TX	25.0	30.6	16.8	15.2	7.5	2.9	1.7	2.83
Davenport, IA	31.1	35.7	13.2	11.9	5.3	1.7	0.8	2.42
Denver, CO	28.2	34.3	14.9	13.2	5.7	2.1	1.3	2.57
Des Moines, IA	27.9	34.2	14.6	13.8	6.2	2.1	0.8	2.50
Durham, NC	30.5	35.7	15.4	11.2	4.8	1.3	0.7	2.42
Edison, NJ	28.0	29.4	16.9	14.5	6.5	2.4	1.9	2.70
El Paso, TX	23.8	28.1	17.8	16.5	8.3	3.5	1.6	3.06
Fargo, ND	31.1	35.0	14.5	11.6	5.0	1.5	0.8	2.31
Fayetteville, NC	30.7	31.5	16.0	12.4	5.8	2.2	1.0	2.64
Fort Collins, CO	24.2	40.2	15.7	12.3	5.1	1.5	0.5	2.45
Fort Wayne, IN	28.9	34.3	14.4	12.2	6.3	2.4	1.2	2.52
Fort Worth, TX	25.0	30.6	16.8	15.2	7.5	2.9	1.7	2.83
Grand Rapids, MI	24.8	34.6	14.9	14.3	6.9	2.7	1.4	2.65
Greeley, CO	20.5	33.4	16.7	15.7	8.3	3.2	1.8	2.85
Green Bay, WI	28.3	36.9	14.1	12.2	5.8	1.5	0.9	2.40
Greensboro, NC	29.4	35.0	16.1	11.4	5.0	1.8	1.0	2.48
Honolulu, HI	24.0	30.5	16.7	13.5	7.3	3.5	4.1	3.03
Houston, TX	24.1	29.7	17.1	15.6	8.1	3.1	1.9	2.89
Huntsville, AL	29.4	35.1	15.5	12.2	5.1	1.7	0.6	2.47
Indianapolis, IN	30.1	33.5	14.8	12.8	5.7	1.9	0.9	2.56
Jacksonville, FL	27.1	35.6	16.6	12.4	5.3	1.8	0.8	2.62
Kansas City, MO	29.0	34.1	14.8	12.9	5.8	2.0	1.1	2.52
Lafayette, LA	26.9	34.0	16.7	12.9	6.1	2.1	1.0	2.65
Lakeland, FL	25.2	37.9	15.1	11.6	5.9	2.5	1.4	2.86
Las Vegas, NV	28.5	32.8	15.3	12.3	6.5	2.6	1.7	2.76
Lexington, KY	28.4	35.6	15.9	12.3	5.0	1.7	0.7	2.44
Lincoln, NE	30.1	35.7	13.7	11.9	5.3	2.0	1.0	2.41
Little Rock, AR	29.8	34.2	15.9	11.8	5.2	1.8	0.8	2.55
Los Angeles, CA	24.5	28.6	17.0	15.4	7.9	3.4	2.8	2.99
Louisville, KY	30.3	34.1	15.7	11.7	5.1	1.8	0.9	2.51

Table continued on following page.

Appendix A: Comparative Statistics   A-11

Metro Area	Persons in Household (%)							Average Household Size
	One	Two	Three	Four	Five	Six	Seven or More	
Madison, WI	30.1	36.8	14.0	12.1	4.6	1.4	0.7	2.35
Manchester, NH	25.5	36.2	16.4	13.5	5.2	1.9	1.0	2.51
Memphis, TN	29.8	32.5	16.2	12.3	5.3	2.2	1.3	2.64
Miami, FL	28.2	32.6	16.8	13.2	5.8	2.1	1.1	2.82
Midland, TX	26.3	30.8	15.9	14.4	7.8	2.9	1.6	2.93
Milwaukee, WI	31.5	34.3	14.0	11.9	5.2	1.8	0.9	2.45
Minneapolis, MN	27.9	34.1	14.8	13.6	5.8	2.1	1.3	2.56
Nashville, TN	26.0	34.8	16.7	13.3	5.8	2.0	1.0	2.59
New Haven, CT	31.2	33.0	16.1	12.3	4.8	1.7	0.7	2.51
New Orleans, LA	33.4	32.2	15.4	11.5	4.6	1.6	0.9	2.58
New York, NY	28.0	29.4	16.9	14.5	6.5	2.4	1.9	2.70
Oklahoma City, OK	28.2	34.1	15.4	12.6	6.0	2.3	1.1	2.62
Omaha, NE	28.4	33.9	14.3	12.6	6.4	2.7	1.5	2.54
Orlando, FL	24.8	34.2	17.4	13.9	5.9	2.3	1.1	2.83
Peoria, IL	31.3	35.3	14.0	11.0	5.2	2.0	0.8	2.42
Philadelphia, PA	29.1	32.3	16.2	13.5	5.7	1.9	1.0	2.60
Phoenix, AZ	26.4	34.4	14.4	12.6	6.7	3.0	2.2	2.76
Pittsburgh, PA	33.2	35.5	14.3	10.8	4.0	1.3	0.5	2.25
Portland, OR	26.8	35.4	15.3	13.4	5.3	2.2	1.2	2.56
Providence, RI	29.8	33.3	16.6	12.8	5.0	1.5	0.7	2.48
Provo, UT	11.9	28.6	15.6	15.6	12.4	9.0	6.5	3.55
Raleigh, NC	25.0	33.1	17.6	15.3	6.1	1.8	0.8	2.64
Reno, NV	28.2	35.0	15.5	11.4	5.7	2.3	1.5	2.47
Richmond, VA	29.4	34.2	16.0	12.3	5.3	1.8	0.7	2.57
Riverside, CA	20.4	28.3	16.3	16.0	10.1	4.9	3.7	3.28
Rochester, MN	27.2	36.2	14.1	13.5	5.3	2.2	1.2	2.45
Sacramento, CA	25.3	33.2	15.9	14.4	6.6	2.7	1.7	2.74
Salt Lake City, UT	22.4	30.5	15.8	14.3	8.6	4.9	3.2	3.00
San Antonio, TX	26.3	31.2	16.5	13.8	7.1	3.0	1.7	3.00
San Diego, CA	23.8	32.6	16.9	14.7	7.0	2.8	1.9	2.87
San Francisco, CA	26.2	31.9	16.9	14.8	6.1	2.2	1.6	2.71
San Jose, CA	20.1	30.6	18.8	17.7	7.2	2.9	2.4	2.96
Santa Rosa, CA	27.4	34.8	15.4	12.9	5.9	2.0	1.3	2.59
Savannah, GA	28.0	35.9	16.1	12.2	5.0	1.5	0.9	2.62
Seattle, WA	27.1	34.5	16.0	13.5	5.2	2.0	1.3	2.54
Sioux Falls, SD	28.6	35.0	13.6	13.1	6.2	2.1	1.1	2.46
Springfield, IL	32.9	35.7	14.0	10.6	4.2	1.6	0.7	2.30
Tallahassee, FL	30.5	35.2	17.0	11.0	4.2	1.2	0.5	2.43
Tampa, FL	30.8	36.7	14.7	10.8	4.4	1.5	0.8	2.51
Tucson, AZ	30.5	35.8	13.7	11.2	5.1	2.0	1.3	2.46
Tulsa, OK	28.2	34.5	15.2	12.1	5.9	2.4	1.2	2.56
Tuscaloosa, AL	29.4	35.0	16.4	11.5	5.3	1.3	0.8	2.69
Virginia Beach, VA	27.2	34.1	17.3	13.1	5.3	1.8	0.9	2.55
Washington, DC	27.2	30.8	16.5	14.6	6.5	2.6	1.6	2.75
Wichita, KS	29.9	32.8	14.0	11.6	7.0	2.8	1.4	2.56
Winston-Salem, NC	29.5	35.9	15.4	11.3	5.0	1.6	0.9	2.46
U.S.	27.8	33.9	15.5	12.9	5.9	2.2	1.4	2.62

Note: Figures cover the Metropolitan Statistical Area (MSA)—see Appendix B for areas included
Source: U.S. Census Bureau, 2015-2019 American Community Survey 5-Year Estimates

A-12 Appendix A: Comparative Statistics

Race: City

City	White Alone[1] (%)	Black Alone[1] (%)	Asian Alone[1] (%)	AIAN[2] Alone[1] (%)	NHOPI[3] Alone[1] (%)	Other Race Alone[1] (%)	Two or More Races (%)
Albuquerque, NM	73.9	3.3	2.9	4.7	0.1	10.6	4.4
Allentown, PA	62.3	14.7	2.9	0.7	0.1	14.7	4.6
Anchorage, AK	62.6	5.6	9.6	7.9	2.4	2.4	9.5
Ann Arbor, MI	71.1	6.8	16.9	0.4	0.1	0.7	4.1
Athens, GA	63.2	28.0	3.9	0.1	0.1	2.1	2.6
Atlanta, GA	40.9	51.0	4.4	0.3	0.0	1.0	2.4
Austin, TX	72.6	7.8	7.6	0.7	0.1	7.8	3.5
Baton Rouge, LA	38.7	54.7	3.5	0.3	0.1	1.5	1.3
Boise City, ID	89.3	1.9	2.8	0.5	0.2	1.9	3.4
Boston, MA	52.8	25.2	9.7	0.3	0.1	6.7	5.3
Boulder, CO	87.4	1.2	5.8	0.2	0.1	1.5	3.8
Cape Coral, FL	89.5	5.2	1.8	0.2	0.0	1.8	1.6
Cedar Rapids, IA	83.9	7.8	2.9	0.3	0.2	1.1	3.8
Charleston, SC	74.1	21.7	1.9	0.1	0.1	0.6	1.5
Charlotte, NC	48.8	35.2	6.5	0.4	0.1	6.1	2.8
Chicago, IL	50.0	29.6	6.6	0.3	0.0	10.6	2.8
Cincinnati, OH	50.7	42.3	2.2	0.1	0.1	0.9	3.7
Clarksville, TN	65.1	24.3	2.5	0.7	0.5	1.8	5.2
Cleveland, OH	40.0	48.8	2.6	0.5	0.1	3.6	4.4
College Station, TX	77.8	7.6	10.1	0.3	0.0	1.5	2.7
Colorado Springs, CO	78.5	6.5	2.9	0.8	0.3	5.1	5.9
Columbia, MO	77.1	10.9	6.2	0.4	0.1	0.9	4.4
Columbia, SC	53.4	39.8	2.7	0.1	0.2	1.0	2.8
Columbus, OH	58.6	29.0	5.8	0.3	0.0	2.1	4.2
Dallas, TX	62.7	24.3	3.4	0.3	0.0	6.9	2.4
Davenport, IA	81.4	11.3	2.3	0.5	0.0	1.0	3.5
Denver, CO	76.1	9.2	3.7	0.9	0.2	6.1	3.8
Des Moines, IA	75.8	11.4	6.2	0.4	0.1	2.3	3.9
Durham, NC	49.2	38.7	5.4	0.3	0.0	3.4	3.2
Edison, NJ	35.3	8.2	48.7	0.3	0.1	4.0	3.5
El Paso, TX	80.1	3.6	1.4	0.6	0.2	11.4	2.7
Fargo, ND	84.6	7.0	3.5	1.2	0.0	0.5	3.1
Fayetteville, NC	44.6	42.1	2.9	1.1	0.4	2.9	6.1
Fort Collins, CO	88.3	1.6	3.5	1.0	0.1	1.5	4.0
Fort Wayne, IN	73.4	15.1	4.7	0.2	0.1	2.1	4.5
Fort Worth, TX	63.8	18.9	4.6	0.5	0.1	9.0	3.2
Grand Rapids, MI	67.2	18.6	2.4	0.4	0.0	5.7	5.6
Greeley, CO	88.3	2.4	1.4	1.2	0.2	3.7	2.8
Green Bay, WI	76.7	4.2	4.2	3.5	0.0	6.0	5.4
Greensboro, NC	47.3	41.4	5.0	0.5	0.1	2.7	3.0
Honolulu, HI	17.2	2.0	53.2	0.1	8.0	0.9	18.4
Houston, TX	57.0	22.6	6.8	0.3	0.1	11.1	2.2
Huntsville, AL	61.3	30.7	2.6	0.4	0.1	2.0	2.8
Indianapolis, IN	60.9	28.6	3.4	0.3	0.0	3.5	3.3
Jacksonville, FL	58.2	31.0	4.8	0.2	0.1	2.1	3.6
Kansas City, MO	60.9	28.2	2.7	0.4	0.2	4.0	3.6
Lafayette, LA	64.0	30.9	2.2	0.3	0.0	0.6	2.1
Lakeland, FL	72.3	20.5	2.2	0.4	0.1	2.8	1.8
Las Vegas, NV	61.9	12.2	6.9	0.9	0.8	12.1	5.2
Lexington, KY	74.9	14.6	3.8	0.2	0.0	2.8	3.8
Lincoln, NE	84.9	4.4	4.6	0.7	0.1	1.5	3.9
Little Rock, AR	50.3	42.0	3.3	0.3	0.1	1.8	2.3
Los Angeles, CA	52.1	8.9	11.6	0.7	0.2	22.8	3.8
Louisville, KY	69.9	23.6	2.7	0.2	0.1	1.0	2.6

Table continued on following page.

Appendix A: Comparative Statistics A-13

City	White Alone[1] (%)	Black Alone[1] (%)	Asian Alone[1] (%)	AIAN[2] Alone[1] (%)	NHOPI[3] Alone[1] (%)	Other Race Alone[1] (%)	Two or More Races (%)
Madison, WI	78.6	7.0	9.0	0.5	0.1	1.4	3.5
Manchester, NH	84.8	6.1	5.1	0.1	0.0	0.9	3.0
Memphis, TN	29.2	64.1	1.7	0.2	0.0	3.3	1.5
Miami, FL	76.1	16.8	1.1	0.2	0.0	4.0	1.7
Midland, TX	80.6	7.8	2.2	0.6	0.1	6.4	2.3
Milwaukee, WI	44.4	38.7	4.3	0.6	0.0	8.0	4.0
Minneapolis, MN	63.6	19.2	5.9	1.4	0.0	5.0	4.8
Nashville, TN	63.5	27.6	3.7	0.2	0.1	2.4	2.6
New Haven, CT	44.4	32.6	5.0	0.4	0.0	13.1	4.4
New Orleans, LA	33.9	59.5	2.9	0.2	0.0	1.5	1.9
New York, NY	42.7	24.3	14.1	0.4	0.1	14.7	3.6
Oklahoma City, OK	67.7	14.3	4.5	2.9	0.1	4.1	6.3
Omaha, NE	77.5	12.3	3.8	0.6	0.0	2.3	3.4
Orlando, FL	61.3	24.5	4.2	0.2	0.0	6.2	3.5
Peoria, IL	60.1	27.1	6.1	0.3	0.0	2.1	4.3
Philadelphia, PA	40.7	42.1	7.2	0.4	0.0	6.5	3.1
Phoenix, AZ	72.9	7.1	3.8	2.1	0.2	10.0	3.9
Pittsburgh, PA	66.8	23.0	5.8	0.2	0.0	0.6	3.5
Portland, OR	77.4	5.8	8.2	0.8	0.6	1.9	5.3
Providence, RI	55.1	16.8	6.0	1.0	0.1	16.3	4.7
Provo, UT	87.9	0.9	2.7	0.8	1.3	2.2	4.2
Raleigh, NC	58.3	29.0	4.6	0.4	0.0	4.8	2.9
Reno, NV	75.4	2.8	6.7	1.0	0.8	8.5	4.8
Richmond, VA	45.5	46.9	2.1	0.4	0.0	1.7	3.4
Riverside, CA	58.3	6.2	7.6	0.8	0.3	22.0	4.9
Rochester, MN	79.4	8.2	7.3	0.5	0.1	1.1	3.4
Sacramento, CA	46.3	13.2	18.9	0.7	1.7	11.7	7.4
Salt Lake City, UT	72.8	2.6	5.4	1.5	1.6	12.7	3.3
San Antonio, TX	80.3	7.0	2.8	0.8	0.1	6.0	3.0
San Diego, CA	65.1	6.4	16.7	0.5	0.4	5.6	5.3
San Francisco, CA	46.4	5.2	34.4	0.4	0.4	7.7	5.6
San Jose, CA	39.9	3.0	35.9	0.6	0.5	14.8	5.3
Santa Rosa, CA	66.8	2.6	5.5	1.3	0.6	17.1	6.0
Savannah, GA	38.9	53.9	2.6	0.3	0.1	1.4	2.8
Seattle, WA	67.3	7.3	15.4	0.5	0.3	2.3	6.9
Sioux Falls, SD	84.5	6.2	2.5	2.1	0.0	1.6	3.2
Springfield, IL	72.9	19.9	3.1	0.1	0.0	0.5	3.5
Tallahassee, FL	56.2	35.0	4.6	0.2	0.0	1.1	2.9
Tampa, FL	65.4	23.6	4.3	0.3	0.1	2.5	3.9
Tucson, AZ	72.1	5.2	3.2	3.7	0.2	10.2	5.4
Tulsa, OK	64.3	15.2	3.4	4.5	0.1	4.9	7.5
Tuscaloosa, AL	51.2	44.0	2.5	0.3	0.1	0.9	1.0
Virginia Beach, VA	66.3	19.0	6.7	0.3	0.1	2.1	5.6
Washington, DC	41.3	46.3	4.0	0.3	0.1	5.0	3.1
Wichita, KS	74.3	10.9	5.1	1.0	0.1	4.2	4.4
Winston-Salem, NC	56.6	34.9	2.5	0.3	0.1	2.8	2.8
U.S.	72.5	12.7	5.5	0.8	0.2	4.9	3.3

Note: (1) Alone is defined as not being in combination with one or more other races; (2) American Indian and Alaska Native; (3) Native Hawaiian and Other Pacific Islander
Source: U.S. Census Bureau, 2015-2019 American Community Survey 5-Year Estimates

A-14 Appendix A: Comparative Statistics

Race: Metro Area

Metro Area	White Alone[1] (%)	Black Alone[1] (%)	Asian Alone[1] (%)	AIAN[2] Alone[1] (%)	NHOPI[3] Alone[1] (%)	Other Race Alone[1] (%)	Two or More Races (%)
Albuquerque, NM	74.9	2.7	2.3	6.0	0.1	10.0	4.0
Allentown, PA	84.0	6.0	2.9	0.2	0.0	3.7	3.1
Anchorage, AK	68.0	4.4	7.5	7.5	1.9	1.8	9.0
Ann Arbor, MI	73.6	11.9	9.1	0.4	0.0	0.8	4.2
Athens, GA	72.0	20.6	3.1	0.1	0.1	1.8	2.3
Atlanta, GA	53.4	34.2	5.9	0.4	0.0	3.4	2.7
Austin, TX	76.0	7.3	5.9	0.5	0.1	6.7	3.6
Baton Rouge, LA	59.2	35.3	1.9	0.2	0.0	1.4	1.9
Boise City, ID	88.0	1.0	1.9	0.7	0.2	4.6	3.5
Boston, MA	76.0	8.3	7.9	0.2	0.0	4.2	3.3
Boulder, CO	89.0	0.9	4.7	0.4	0.1	1.8	3.0
Cape Coral, FL	84.4	8.6	1.6	0.2	0.1	3.4	1.8
Cedar Rapids, IA	89.4	4.8	2.0	0.2	0.1	0.7	2.8
Charleston, SC	67.6	25.6	1.8	0.3	0.1	1.9	2.7
Charlotte, NC	66.9	22.8	3.7	0.4	0.1	3.6	2.5
Chicago, IL	65.7	16.6	6.6	0.3	0.0	8.0	2.7
Cincinnati, OH	81.8	12.0	2.6	0.1	0.0	0.9	2.6
Clarksville, TN	72.7	19.1	1.9	0.6	0.4	1.3	4.1
Cleveland, OH	73.4	19.9	2.3	0.2	0.0	1.3	2.9
College Station, TX	77.0	11.5	5.3	0.4	0.1	3.0	2.8
Colorado Springs, CO	80.1	6.2	2.7	0.8	0.4	4.0	5.9
Columbia, MO	82.3	8.6	3.9	0.4	0.1	0.9	3.8
Columbia, SC	59.6	33.4	2.1	0.2	0.1	1.8	2.7
Columbus, OH	75.3	15.5	4.2	0.2	0.0	1.3	3.4
Dallas, TX	68.3	15.8	6.9	0.5	0.1	5.4	3.0
Davenport, IA	85.1	7.6	2.3	0.3	0.0	1.7	3.0
Denver, CO	81.0	5.7	4.2	0.8	0.1	4.4	3.7
Des Moines, IA	86.9	5.2	3.9	0.3	0.1	1.1	2.5
Durham, NC	62.5	26.6	4.5	0.4	0.0	3.0	3.1
Edison, NJ	57.5	17.3	11.2	0.3	0.0	10.5	3.1
El Paso, TX	79.6	3.3	1.2	0.6	0.1	12.4	2.7
Fargo, ND	88.0	5.1	2.5	1.2	0.1	0.6	2.7
Fayetteville, NC	53.8	32.6	2.0	2.0	0.3	4.1	5.3
Fort Collins, CO	91.3	1.0	2.2	0.8	0.1	1.5	3.2
Fort Wayne, IN	80.4	10.6	3.5	0.2	0.0	1.7	3.6
Fort Worth, TX	68.3	15.8	6.9	0.5	0.1	5.4	3.0
Grand Rapids, MI	83.9	6.7	2.6	0.3	0.0	2.9	3.5
Greeley, CO	90.3	1.2	1.6	0.8	0.1	3.0	3.0
Green Bay, WI	87.1	2.1	2.7	2.2	0.0	2.9	3.0
Greensboro, NC	63.0	26.8	3.7	0.5	0.1	3.3	2.6
Honolulu, HI	20.9	2.4	42.7	0.2	9.5	1.0	23.2
Houston, TX	65.0	17.3	7.7	0.4	0.1	7.0	2.5
Huntsville, AL	70.5	22.1	2.4	0.6	0.1	1.5	2.8
Indianapolis, IN	76.6	15.2	3.2	0.2	0.0	2.0	2.7
Jacksonville, FL	69.3	21.5	3.8	0.3	0.1	1.8	3.4
Kansas City, MO	78.3	12.3	2.9	0.4	0.2	2.7	3.3
Lafayette, LA	70.6	24.6	1.7	0.3	0.0	0.8	2.0
Lakeland, FL	77.1	15.3	1.8	0.3	0.0	3.0	2.5
Las Vegas, NV	60.2	11.7	9.7	0.9	0.8	11.5	5.4
Lexington, KY	80.7	11.0	2.7	0.2	0.0	2.3	3.1
Lincoln, NE	86.6	3.8	4.0	0.7	0.1	1.3	3.5
Little Rock, AR	70.3	23.3	1.7	0.4	0.1	1.6	2.5
Los Angeles, CA	53.6	6.6	16.0	0.7	0.3	18.8	4.0
Louisville, KY	79.4	14.8	2.1	0.2	0.0	0.9	2.5

Table continued on following page.

Appendix A: Comparative Statistics   A-15

Metro Area	White Alone[1] (%)	Black Alone[1] (%)	Asian Alone[1] (%)	AIAN[2] Alone[1] (%)	NHOPI[3] Alone[1] (%)	Other Race Alone[1] (%)	Two or More Races (%)
Madison, WI	86.0	4.4	5.0	0.3	0.0	1.4	2.8
Manchester, NH	89.4	2.9	4.0	0.1	0.1	0.9	2.5
Memphis, TN	46.3	47.1	2.1	0.2	0.0	2.3	1.9
Miami, FL	70.2	21.2	2.5	0.2	0.0	3.5	2.3
Midland, TX	82.1	6.5	1.9	0.6	0.1	6.4	2.4
Milwaukee, WI	72.5	16.5	3.7	0.4	0.0	3.8	2.9
Minneapolis, MN	78.7	8.5	6.6	0.6	0.0	2.2	3.4
Nashville, TN	77.6	15.3	2.8	0.2	0.0	1.6	2.5
New Haven, CT	73.3	13.5	4.0	0.2	0.0	5.7	3.3
New Orleans, LA	57.3	35.1	2.9	0.4	0.0	2.2	2.0
New York, NY	57.5	17.3	11.2	0.3	0.0	10.5	3.1
Oklahoma City, OK	73.7	10.2	3.2	3.6	0.1	2.8	6.5
Omaha, NE	84.0	7.7	2.9	0.5	0.1	1.9	2.9
Orlando, FL	69.7	16.6	4.3	0.3	0.1	5.7	3.3
Peoria, IL	85.4	8.8	2.3	0.2	0.0	0.8	2.4
Philadelphia, PA	66.6	21.0	5.9	0.2	0.0	3.4	2.8
Phoenix, AZ	77.8	5.5	4.0	2.3	0.2	6.5	3.7
Pittsburgh, PA	86.6	8.1	2.3	0.1	0.0	0.4	2.5
Portland, OR	81.1	2.8	6.7	0.8	0.5	3.0	5.0
Providence, RI	81.7	5.9	3.0	0.4	0.1	5.7	3.2
Provo, UT	91.7	0.6	1.5	0.5	0.9	1.8	3.1
Raleigh, NC	67.2	20.0	5.7	0.4	0.0	3.7	2.9
Reno, NV	77.6	2.3	5.3	1.6	0.6	8.1	4.4
Richmond, VA	61.1	29.7	3.8	0.3	0.1	1.8	3.1
Riverside, CA	60.5	7.4	6.8	0.8	0.3	19.5	4.7
Rochester, MN	87.4	4.5	4.3	0.3	0.1	1.1	2.4
Sacramento, CA	65.0	7.1	13.3	0.6	0.9	6.5	6.6
Salt Lake City, UT	79.7	1.8	3.9	0.8	1.4	9.0	3.4
San Antonio, TX	80.7	6.8	2.5	0.6	0.1	5.9	3.4
San Diego, CA	70.7	5.0	11.9	0.7	0.4	6.0	5.2
San Francisco, CA	49.0	7.3	26.1	0.5	0.7	10.2	6.2
San Jose, CA	45.6	2.4	35.4	0.5	0.4	10.4	5.2
Santa Rosa, CA	74.8	1.7	4.1	0.9	0.3	12.9	5.4
Savannah, GA	59.6	33.3	2.2	0.3	0.1	1.5	3.0
Seattle, WA	68.3	5.8	13.6	0.8	0.9	3.7	6.8
Sioux Falls, SD	88.3	4.5	1.8	1.6	0.0	1.1	2.7
Springfield, IL	82.8	12.1	1.9	0.1	0.1	0.4	2.6
Tallahassee, FL	60.6	32.7	2.7	0.2	0.0	1.3	2.4
Tampa, FL	77.8	12.2	3.4	0.3	0.1	2.9	3.3
Tucson, AZ	76.0	3.6	2.9	3.9	0.2	8.6	4.9
Tulsa, OK	71.2	8.0	2.5	7.3	0.1	2.7	8.2
Tuscaloosa, AL	60.6	35.8	1.4	0.2	0.0	0.8	1.1
Virginia Beach, VA	59.0	30.6	3.8	0.3	0.1	1.8	4.5
Washington, DC	53.5	25.3	10.1	0.3	0.1	6.5	4.2
Wichita, KS	80.9	7.5	3.7	0.9	0.1	2.9	4.0
Winston-Salem, NC	75.8	17.8	1.8	0.4	0.1	2.0	2.2
U.S.	72.5	12.7	5.5	0.8	0.2	4.9	3.3

Note: (1) Figures cover the Metropolitan Statistical Area (MSA)—see Appendix B for areas included; (1) Alone is defined as not being in combination with one or more other races; (2) American Indian and Alaska Native; (3) Native Hawaiian & Other Pacific Islander
Source: U.S. Census Bureau, 2015-2019 American Community Survey 5-Year Estimates

A-16 Appendix A: Comparative Statistics

Hispanic Origin: City

City	Hispanic or Latino (%)	Mexican (%)	Puerto Rican (%)	Cuban (%)	Other Hispanic or Latino (%)
Albuquerque, NM	49.2	28.0	0.6	0.5	20.2
Allentown, PA	52.5	1.9	28.8	0.9	20.9
Anchorage, AK	9.2	4.8	1.4	0.1	2.8
Ann Arbor, MI	4.8	2.2	0.4	0.3	1.9
Athens, GA	10.9	6.7	0.7	0.4	3.1
Atlanta, GA	4.3	2.0	0.6	0.3	1.4
Austin, TX	33.9	27.2	0.9	0.7	5.2
Baton Rouge, LA	3.7	1.1	0.3	0.2	2.1
Boise City, ID	9.0	7.2	0.3	0.0	1.5
Boston, MA	19.8	1.2	5.3	0.5	12.9
Boulder, CO	9.7	6.0	0.4	0.4	2.9
Cape Coral, FL	20.9	2.0	5.0	7.8	6.1
Cedar Rapids, IA	4.0	2.8	0.2	0.0	1.0
Charleston, SC	3.2	1.3	0.5	0.2	1.2
Charlotte, NC	14.3	5.3	1.2	0.5	7.3
Chicago, IL	28.8	21.3	3.6	0.3	3.5
Cincinnati, OH	3.8	1.2	0.6	0.1	2.0
Clarksville, TN	11.5	5.2	3.7	0.3	2.3
Cleveland, OH	11.9	1.3	8.5	0.2	1.9
College Station, TX	15.8	11.2	0.3	0.4	3.9
Colorado Springs, CO	17.6	11.3	1.4	0.5	4.5
Columbia, MO	3.6	2.2	0.3	0.1	1.1
Columbia, SC	5.5	2.1	1.3	0.3	1.7
Columbus, OH	6.2	3.2	0.9	0.1	1.9
Dallas, TX	41.8	35.4	0.5	0.3	5.5
Davenport, IA	8.7	7.8	0.3	0.0	0.5
Denver, CO	29.9	23.7	0.6	0.2	5.4
Des Moines, IA	13.6	10.6	0.4	0.1	2.4
Durham, NC	13.8	6.1	1.1	0.2	6.4
Edison, NJ	9.9	1.8	2.5	0.8	4.8
El Paso, TX	81.4	76.9	1.1	0.1	3.2
Fargo, ND	3.0	1.9	0.4	0.0	0.6
Fayetteville, NC	12.4	4.2	4.1	0.4	3.7
Fort Collins, CO	11.6	8.2	0.4	0.1	3.0
Fort Wayne, IN	9.2	6.8	0.5	0.1	1.7
Fort Worth, TX	35.1	30.6	1.1	0.3	3.1
Grand Rapids, MI	16.1	9.5	1.5	0.2	4.8
Greeley, CO	38.6	31.0	0.6	0.3	6.7
Green Bay, WI	15.8	12.5	1.4	0.1	1.8
Greensboro, NC	7.9	4.7	0.7	0.2	2.2
Honolulu, HI	7.3	2.0	1.8	0.2	3.4
Houston, TX	45.0	31.8	0.6	0.8	11.7
Huntsville, AL	6.2	3.8	0.9	0.2	1.4
Indianapolis, IN	10.5	7.1	0.6	0.2	2.6
Jacksonville, FL	10.0	2.0	3.0	1.2	3.7
Kansas City, MO	10.6	8.0	0.4	0.3	1.9
Lafayette, LA	3.6	1.4	0.2	0.2	1.7
Lakeland, FL	16.4	3.5	6.3	2.5	4.0
Las Vegas, NV	33.1	24.7	1.2	1.3	5.9
Lexington, KY	7.2	4.8	0.7	0.2	1.5
Lincoln, NE	7.6	5.5	0.3	0.2	1.6
Little Rock, AR	7.4	4.8	0.3	0.3	2.1
Los Angeles, CA	48.5	32.2	0.4	0.4	15.4
Louisville, KY	5.6	2.0	0.5	1.9	1.2
Madison, WI	7.0	4.1	0.7	0.2	2.0

Table continued on following page.

Appendix A: Comparative Statistics   A-17

City	Hispanic or Latino (%)	Mexican (%)	Puerto Rican (%)	Cuban (%)	Other Hispanic or Latino (%)
Manchester, NH	10.4	1.5	4.4	0.1	4.4
Memphis, TN	7.2	5.1	0.3	0.2	1.6
Miami, FL	72.7	1.9	3.4	35.0	32.4
Midland, TX	44.2	40.6	0.5	0.9	2.2
Milwaukee, WI	19.0	13.4	4.4	0.2	1.1
Minneapolis, MN	9.6	5.8	0.5	0.2	3.1
Nashville, TN	10.5	6.2	0.6	0.4	3.4
New Haven, CT	31.2	5.6	17.6	0.3	7.7
New Orleans, LA	5.5	1.3	0.3	0.4	3.5
New York, NY	29.1	4.0	8.1	0.5	16.5
Oklahoma City, OK	19.7	16.6	0.3	0.1	2.8
Omaha, NE	13.9	10.7	0.4	0.1	2.7
Orlando, FL	32.6	1.9	15.6	3.0	12.0
Peoria, IL	6.3	4.6	0.4	0.1	1.1
Philadelphia, PA	14.7	1.3	8.8	0.3	4.3
Phoenix, AZ	42.6	38.3	0.7	0.3	3.3
Pittsburgh, PA	3.2	1.0	0.7	0.2	1.3
Portland, OR	9.7	6.8	0.4	0.4	2.1
Providence, RI	43.3	1.8	9.3	0.3	31.9
Provo, UT	16.7	11.3	0.5	0.1	4.7
Raleigh, NC	11.2	5.1	1.2	0.4	4.5
Reno, NV	24.7	19.2	0.5	0.3	4.7
Richmond, VA	6.9	1.7	0.7	0.2	4.3
Riverside, CA	53.7	47.1	0.8	0.2	5.6
Rochester, MN	5.9	3.7	0.4	0.2	1.6
Sacramento, CA	28.9	24.6	0.7	0.2	3.3
Salt Lake City, UT	21.8	16.9	0.3	0.4	4.2
San Antonio, TX	64.2	56.9	1.3	0.3	5.7
San Diego, CA	30.3	26.6	0.7	0.2	2.8
San Francisco, CA	15.2	7.8	0.6	0.3	6.6
San Jose, CA	31.6	27.1	0.6	0.1	3.7
Santa Rosa, CA	32.8	28.8	0.4	0.1	3.5
Savannah, GA	5.8	2.3	1.5	0.2	1.8
Seattle, WA	6.7	3.9	0.4	0.2	2.1
Sioux Falls, SD	5.5	3.1	0.4	0.1	1.9
Springfield, IL	2.8	1.5	0.5	0.1	0.7
Tallahassee, FL	6.7	1.2	1.4	1.3	2.8
Tampa, FL	26.4	3.1	7.6	8.0	7.7
Tucson, AZ	43.6	39.5	0.8	0.2	3.1
Tulsa, OK	16.5	13.2	0.6	0.2	2.6
Tuscaloosa, AL	3.2	1.6	0.1	0.2	1.4
Virginia Beach, VA	8.2	2.5	2.4	0.3	3.0
Washington, DC	11.0	2.0	0.9	0.4	7.6
Wichita, KS	17.2	14.7	0.4	0.2	1.9
Winston-Salem, NC	15.0	9.9	1.4	0.2	3.5
U.S.	18.0	11.2	1.7	0.7	4.3

Note: Persons of Hispanic or Latino origin can be of any race
Source: U.S. Census Bureau, 2015-2019 American Community Survey 5-Year Estimates

A-18   Appendix A: Comparative Statistics

Hispanic Origin: Metro Area

Metro Area	Hispanic or Latino (%)	Mexican (%)	Puerto Rican (%)	Cuban (%)	Other Hispanic or Latino (%)
Albuquerque, NM	49.0	27.7	0.5	0.4	20.4
Allentown, PA	17.0	1.2	9.2	0.3	6.2
Anchorage, AK	8.1	4.2	1.2	0.2	2.4
Ann Arbor, MI	4.7	2.6	0.3	0.2	1.6
Athens, GA	8.6	5.0	0.7	0.3	2.6
Atlanta, GA	10.7	5.6	1.0	0.4	3.6
Austin, TX	32.4	26.8	0.9	0.5	4.3
Baton Rouge, LA	4.0	1.5	0.3	0.2	2.0
Boise City, ID	13.7	11.6	0.3	0.1	1.6
Boston, MA	11.1	0.7	2.9	0.2	7.3
Boulder, CO	13.9	10.4	0.4	0.3	2.8
Cape Coral, FL	21.4	6.0	4.3	4.9	6.2
Cedar Rapids, IA	3.0	2.1	0.1	0.0	0.8
Charleston, SC	5.6	2.7	0.8	0.1	2.0
Charlotte, NC	10.1	4.7	1.0	0.4	4.1
Chicago, IL	22.1	17.3	2.2	0.2	2.4
Cincinnati, OH	3.2	1.5	0.4	0.1	1.2
Clarksville, TN	8.8	4.2	2.7	0.2	1.7
Cleveland, OH	5.8	1.3	3.4	0.1	1.0
College Station, TX	24.9	21.4	0.2	0.2	3.0
Colorado Springs, CO	16.7	10.3	1.7	0.4	4.4
Columbia, MO	3.2	2.1	0.2	0.1	0.8
Columbia, SC	5.5	2.8	1.1	0.2	1.4
Columbus, OH	4.2	2.1	0.7	0.1	1.3
Dallas, TX	28.9	23.9	0.7	0.3	4.0
Davenport, IA	8.7	7.7	0.4	0.1	0.6
Denver, CO	23.1	17.6	0.6	0.2	4.7
Des Moines, IA	7.1	5.4	0.2	0.1	1.4
Durham, NC	11.1	5.7	0.9	0.2	4.3
Edison, NJ	24.6	3.0	6.2	0.8	14.7
El Paso, TX	82.5	78.2	1.0	0.1	3.2
Fargo, ND	3.2	2.2	0.3	0.0	0.7
Fayetteville, NC	12.1	5.3	3.5	0.3	2.9
Fort Collins, CO	11.5	8.4	0.3	0.1	2.6
Fort Wayne, IN	7.0	5.2	0.4	0.1	1.3
Fort Worth, TX	28.9	23.9	0.7	0.3	4.0
Grand Rapids, MI	9.6	6.7	0.8	0.3	1.8
Greeley, CO	29.4	24.2	0.4	0.3	4.6
Green Bay, WI	7.4	5.8	0.7	0.0	0.9
Greensboro, NC	8.4	5.5	0.7	0.2	1.9
Honolulu, HI	9.8	2.9	3.1	0.1	3.7
Houston, TX	37.3	27.8	0.7	0.6	8.3
Huntsville, AL	5.2	3.2	0.7	0.2	1.0
Indianapolis, IN	6.7	4.4	0.5	0.1	1.7
Jacksonville, FL	8.9	1.8	2.8	1.2	3.1
Kansas City, MO	9.0	6.9	0.4	0.2	1.6
Lafayette, LA	4.0	2.1	0.2	0.2	1.5
Lakeland, FL	22.5	7.5	9.3	1.6	4.0
Las Vegas, NV	31.1	23.1	1.1	1.4	5.6
Lexington, KY	6.2	4.2	0.5	0.1	1.3
Lincoln, NE	6.8	4.9	0.3	0.2	1.5
Little Rock, AR	5.3	3.7	0.2	0.1	1.3
Los Angeles, CA	45.0	35.0	0.4	0.4	9.3
Louisville, KY	4.9	2.4	0.4	1.1	1.1
Madison, WI	5.7	3.6	0.5	0.1	1.5

Table continued on following page.

Metro Area	Hispanic or Latino (%)	Mexican (%)	Puerto Rican (%)	Cuban (%)	Other Hispanic or Latino (%)
Manchester, NH	6.8	1.0	2.5	0.2	3.0
Memphis, TN	5.6	4.0	0.2	0.1	1.2
Miami, FL	45.2	2.5	3.9	19.0	19.8
Midland, TX	44.7	41.6	0.5	0.7	1.9
Milwaukee, WI	10.7	7.4	2.3	0.1	0.9
Minneapolis, MN	5.9	3.8	0.3	0.1	1.6
Nashville, TN	7.3	4.4	0.5	0.2	2.2
New Haven, CT	18.1	1.9	10.6	0.4	5.3
New Orleans, LA	8.8	1.9	0.5	0.6	5.9
New York, NY	24.6	3.0	6.2	0.8	14.7
Oklahoma City, OK	13.3	10.9	0.3	0.1	2.0
Omaha, NE	10.4	7.9	0.4	0.1	2.0
Orlando, FL	30.7	2.9	15.2	2.4	10.1
Peoria, IL	3.5	2.5	0.3	0.0	0.6
Philadelphia, PA	9.4	1.9	4.6	0.3	2.7
Phoenix, AZ	30.9	27.1	0.7	0.3	2.8
Pittsburgh, PA	1.8	0.5	0.5	0.1	0.7
Portland, OR	12.0	9.2	0.4	0.2	2.2
Providence, RI	12.9	0.9	4.3	0.2	7.4
Provo, UT	11.7	7.7	0.3	0.1	3.7
Raleigh, NC	10.6	5.5	1.3	0.4	3.4
Reno, NV	24.3	18.9	0.6	0.3	4.4
Richmond, VA	6.3	1.6	1.0	0.2	3.5
Riverside, CA	51.0	44.4	0.8	0.3	5.5
Rochester, MN	4.4	2.9	0.2	0.1	1.2
Sacramento, CA	21.6	17.7	0.7	0.2	3.1
Salt Lake City, UT	18.0	13.3	0.5	0.1	4.1
San Antonio, TX	55.4	48.8	1.3	0.2	5.0
San Diego, CA	33.7	30.0	0.7	0.2	2.8
San Francisco, CA	21.8	14.2	0.7	0.2	6.7
San Jose, CA	26.5	22.1	0.5	0.1	3.7
Santa Rosa, CA	26.7	22.6	0.4	0.1	3.6
Savannah, GA	6.2	2.9	1.2	0.4	1.6
Seattle, WA	10.0	7.1	0.6	0.2	2.2
Sioux Falls, SD	4.3	2.5	0.3	0.1	1.5
Springfield, IL	2.3	1.3	0.4	0.1	0.5
Tallahassee, FL	6.6	1.9	1.3	1.0	2.4
Tampa, FL	19.6	3.8	6.2	4.0	5.6
Tucson, AZ	37.2	33.5	0.8	0.2	2.7
Tulsa, OK	9.9	7.8	0.4	0.1	1.6
Tuscaloosa, AL	3.5	2.2	0.2	0.1	1.0
Virginia Beach, VA	6.7	2.2	2.0	0.3	2.3
Washington, DC	15.8	2.3	1.1	0.3	12.1
Wichita, KS	13.1	11.0	0.4	0.1	1.5
Winston-Salem, NC	10.2	6.7	0.9	0.2	2.5
U.S.	18.0	11.2	1.7	0.7	4.3

Note: Persons of Hispanic or Latino origin can be of any race; Figures cover the Metropolitan Statistical Area (MSA)—see Appendix B for areas included
Source: U.S. Census Bureau, 2015-2019 American Community Survey 5-Year Estimates

A-20 Appendix A: Comparative Statistics

Age: City

City	Percent of Population									Median Age
	Under Age 5	Age 5–19	Age 20–34	Age 35–44	Age 45–54	Age 55–64	Age 65–74	Age 75–84	Age 85+	
Albuquerque, NM	5.9	19.0	22.6	13.0	12.0	12.2	8.8	4.4	1.8	36.6
Allentown, PA	7.6	22.8	24.6	11.9	11.3	10.0	6.5	3.3	2.0	31.6
Anchorage, AK	7.2	19.6	25.4	12.9	12.3	12.2	7.0	2.6	0.9	33.6
Ann Arbor, MI	3.7	18.5	40.1	9.5	8.3	8.2	6.8	3.4	1.5	27.5
Athens, GA	5.3	20.8	34.5	11.2	8.8	8.8	6.3	3.2	1.0	28.0
Atlanta, GA	5.4	16.9	30.7	13.8	11.8	9.8	6.8	3.4	1.4	33.3
Austin, TX	6.4	16.7	30.2	16.0	11.9	9.8	5.6	2.3	1.0	33.3
Baton Rouge, LA	6.7	19.6	28.3	10.5	10.1	11.1	8.0	3.9	1.9	31.5
Boise City, ID	5.7	18.9	23.1	14.0	12.3	12.0	8.4	3.7	1.8	36.6
Boston, MA	5.0	15.4	34.8	12.4	10.9	10.1	6.6	3.3	1.6	32.2
Boulder, CO	2.9	18.7	37.6	10.2	10.4	8.9	6.6	3.0	1.6	28.6
Cape Coral, FL	4.4	15.9	15.7	11.4	14.2	15.7	13.2	6.7	2.8	46.7
Cedar Rapids, IA	6.5	18.9	22.8	13.0	11.6	11.9	8.4	4.4	2.4	36.3
Charleston, SC	6.0	14.5	29.8	12.4	10.7	11.9	9.0	3.7	1.9	34.8
Charlotte, NC	6.8	19.4	25.1	14.8	13.1	10.7	6.4	2.8	1.1	34.2
Chicago, IL	6.3	17.0	27.3	14.0	11.9	10.9	7.2	3.7	1.5	34.6
Cincinnati, OH	7.1	19.0	28.3	11.3	10.5	11.6	7.0	3.3	1.9	32.2
Clarksville, TN	9.0	20.6	30.7	13.0	10.0	8.5	5.2	2.1	0.9	29.6
Cleveland, OH	6.3	18.3	23.7	11.5	12.4	13.8	8.0	4.2	1.8	36.3
College Station, TX	5.1	22.9	42.6	9.9	6.8	6.0	4.3	1.9	0.6	23.0
Colorado Springs, CO	6.5	19.3	24.6	12.6	11.9	11.6	8.1	3.8	1.5	34.7
Columbia, MO	5.9	19.0	34.6	11.0	9.5	9.4	6.0	3.2	1.3	28.5
Columbia, SC	5.1	23.2	31.9	10.1	10.1	9.4	6.2	2.8	1.2	28.5
Columbus, OH	7.3	18.2	29.4	12.9	11.3	10.6	6.2	2.7	1.3	32.2
Dallas, TX	7.5	19.9	26.4	13.7	11.8	10.4	6.1	2.9	1.2	32.7
Davenport, IA	6.4	19.2	21.8	12.3	12.3	12.7	8.6	4.1	2.5	36.7
Denver, CO	6.1	15.7	29.2	15.9	11.6	10.0	7.0	3.1	1.5	34.5
Des Moines, IA	6.9	19.7	24.5	13.0	12.0	11.8	7.1	3.3	1.6	34.2
Durham, NC	6.8	18.4	26.7	14.0	11.9	10.7	7.1	3.0	1.4	33.9
Edison, NJ	6.1	18.4	17.9	15.7	14.0	13.1	8.4	4.1	2.3	39.6
El Paso, TX	7.4	22.2	23.2	12.4	11.7	10.6	7.1	3.9	1.7	32.9
Fargo, ND	6.7	17.4	32.0	12.3	9.5	10.1	6.6	3.3	2.0	31.0
Fayetteville, NC	7.7	18.9	30.9	11.0	9.8	10.1	6.7	3.5	1.4	30.0
Fort Collins, CO	5.0	19.5	33.9	11.6	9.7	9.5	6.3	3.0	1.3	29.3
Fort Wayne, IN	7.1	20.6	22.2	12.1	11.7	12.1	8.3	3.8	1.8	35.0
Fort Worth, TX	8.0	22.5	23.3	14.0	12.4	10.1	5.9	2.6	1.2	32.6
Grand Rapids, MI	6.9	18.6	30.3	11.2	10.1	10.8	6.6	3.4	2.1	31.4
Greeley, CO	6.5	23.6	24.8	12.0	10.9	10.5	6.8	3.4	1.7	31.5
Green Bay, WI	7.6	20.3	22.8	12.4	12.3	11.8	7.2	3.7	1.9	34.5
Greensboro, NC	6.0	19.9	24.0	12.5	12.4	11.5	8.0	3.9	1.8	35.1
Honolulu, HI	5.2	14.1	22.0	13.0	12.8	12.9	10.5	5.5	3.9	41.5
Houston, TX	7.6	19.9	25.9	14.0	11.7	10.4	6.3	3.0	1.2	33.0
Huntsville, AL	6.1	17.6	23.8	11.6	12.1	12.7	8.9	5.2	2.1	36.9
Indianapolis, IN	7.3	19.8	24.1	12.8	11.9	11.9	7.2	3.4	1.5	34.2
Jacksonville, FL	6.9	18.3	23.3	12.7	12.8	12.5	8.2	3.8	1.5	35.9
Kansas City, MO	6.8	18.4	24.6	13.2	12.0	12.2	7.5	3.6	1.7	35.1
Lafayette, LA	5.7	18.5	24.4	11.5	11.5	13.5	8.9	4.2	1.7	35.8
Lakeland, FL	4.9	17.8	19.9	11.9	11.4	11.9	11.8	7.2	3.2	41.1
Las Vegas, NV	6.4	19.5	20.2	13.3	13.4	12.1	9.1	4.3	1.5	37.8
Lexington, KY	6.1	18.4	26.0	13.1	11.8	11.5	7.8	3.7	1.5	34.6
Lincoln, NE	6.5	19.9	26.7	12.4	10.5	10.9	7.7	3.6	1.7	32.7
Little Rock, AR	6.7	18.8	22.1	13.5	11.9	12.8	8.4	3.6	2.2	36.7
Los Angeles, CA	5.9	17.5	25.7	14.3	13.2	11.0	7.0	3.6	1.7	35.6
Louisville, KY	6.5	18.5	21.5	12.4	12.8	13.4	8.7	4.3	1.9	37.6

Table continued on following page.

Appendix A: Comparative Statistics A-21

City	Percent of Population									Median Age
	Under Age 5	Age 5–19	Age 20–34	Age 35–44	Age 45–54	Age 55–64	Age 65–74	Age 75–84	Age 85+	
Madison, WI	4.9	16.4	35.5	12.2	9.7	9.7	6.9	3.2	1.5	31.0
Manchester, NH	6.0	15.7	26.6	12.8	13.2	12.4	7.2	3.7	2.3	36.0
Memphis, TN	7.6	19.9	23.7	12.0	11.8	12.0	7.7	3.6	1.5	34.0
Miami, FL	5.9	13.4	23.0	14.6	14.5	11.8	8.5	5.8	2.6	40.1
Midland, TX	8.8	21.0	25.5	13.0	10.8	10.5	5.7	3.1	1.6	31.7
Milwaukee, WI	7.4	21.9	25.6	12.6	11.2	10.7	6.3	2.8	1.4	31.5
Minneapolis, MN	6.5	16.9	32.0	13.8	10.8	10.1	6.3	2.6	1.1	32.3
Nashville, TN	6.8	17.0	27.6	13.8	11.8	11.4	7.1	3.3	1.3	34.2
New Haven, CT	6.3	21.2	29.6	12.6	11.1	8.9	6.4	2.7	1.2	30.8
New Orleans, LA	5.9	16.6	24.6	13.4	12.1	13.3	8.7	3.7	1.7	36.8
New York, NY	6.5	16.5	24.3	13.7	12.7	11.8	8.1	4.4	2.0	36.7
Oklahoma City, OK	7.6	20.6	23.1	13.4	11.5	11.5	7.4	3.5	1.5	34.1
Omaha, NE	7.3	20.4	22.9	12.7	11.9	11.9	7.6	3.6	1.7	34.5
Orlando, FL	6.7	15.9	29.7	15.1	12.1	10.1	6.3	2.7	1.2	33.8
Peoria, IL	7.6	19.5	22.5	12.1	11.3	11.8	8.4	4.4	2.4	35.2
Philadelphia, PA	6.7	18.0	26.2	12.4	11.7	11.6	7.7	4.0	1.8	34.4
Phoenix, AZ	7.2	21.6	23.2	13.8	12.8	10.9	6.5	2.9	1.2	33.8
Pittsburgh, PA	4.7	15.4	33.3	10.6	9.5	11.8	8.1	4.3	2.3	32.9
Portland, OR	5.3	14.6	25.9	17.1	13.1	11.3	8.0	3.3	1.5	37.1
Providence, RI	6.3	21.9	28.3	12.3	10.9	9.4	5.9	3.2	1.7	30.6
Provo, UT	7.1	20.7	47.4	8.3	5.4	5.0	3.1	2.0	0.9	23.6
Raleigh, NC	5.9	18.9	27.5	14.5	12.7	9.9	6.4	2.9	1.3	33.6
Reno, NV	6.2	17.8	24.7	12.6	11.7	12.2	9.3	4.1	1.4	35.8
Richmond, VA	5.9	15.6	30.2	11.8	11.2	12.4	7.7	3.3	1.8	34.0
Riverside, CA	6.2	22.3	26.5	12.4	12.0	10.0	6.3	3.1	1.3	31.6
Rochester, MN	7.2	18.8	22.6	13.1	11.6	11.8	8.0	4.6	2.4	35.7
Sacramento, CA	6.6	18.8	25.4	13.5	11.6	11.1	7.8	3.5	1.8	34.5
Salt Lake City, UT	6.2	17.1	31.6	13.8	10.1	10.2	6.6	3.2	1.3	32.3
San Antonio, TX	6.9	21.0	24.2	13.2	12.0	10.7	7.1	3.5	1.5	33.6
San Diego, CA	5.9	16.8	27.4	13.9	12.3	11.0	7.3	3.7	1.6	34.9
San Francisco, CA	4.5	10.5	29.0	15.8	13.2	11.6	8.5	4.5	2.5	38.2
San Jose, CA	6.1	18.4	22.7	14.4	13.9	11.8	7.3	3.7	1.5	36.7
Santa Rosa, CA	5.9	17.8	21.2	12.8	12.6	12.9	9.6	4.8	2.3	38.8
Savannah, GA	6.4	18.2	29.1	11.6	10.4	11.2	7.7	3.7	1.7	32.6
Seattle, WA	4.8	12.8	31.8	15.3	12.3	10.7	7.4	3.3	1.8	35.3
Sioux Falls, SD	7.5	19.9	23.5	13.3	11.4	11.7	7.6	3.4	1.7	34.4
Springfield, IL	6.1	18.2	20.2	11.6	12.2	14.0	10.0	5.3	2.3	39.4
Tallahassee, FL	4.9	19.2	38.0	10.0	8.8	8.7	6.3	2.8	1.2	26.9
Tampa, FL	6.4	18.5	24.2	13.5	13.4	11.8	7.3	3.5	1.5	35.7
Tucson, AZ	6.0	19.1	26.5	11.9	10.9	11.2	8.3	4.2	1.9	33.7
Tulsa, OK	7.1	20.0	22.8	12.4	11.4	12.3	8.1	4.0	1.9	35.1
Tuscaloosa, AL	5.2	22.9	29.5	10.0	9.9	10.3	6.9	3.9	1.4	29.3
Virginia Beach, VA	6.3	18.2	23.7	13.0	12.7	12.1	8.1	4.0	1.6	36.2
Washington, DC	6.5	14.5	31.0	14.8	11.0	10.1	7.0	3.5	1.6	34.0
Wichita, KS	7.0	20.7	22.4	11.9	11.6	12.5	8.2	3.9	1.8	35.0
Winston-Salem, NC	6.5	20.9	21.8	12.4	12.1	12.0	8.1	4.3	1.7	35.5
U.S.	6.1	19.1	20.7	12.6	13.0	12.9	9.1	4.6	1.9	38.1

Source: U.S. Census Bureau, 2015-2019 American Community Survey 5-Year Estimates

A-22   Appendix A: Comparative Statistics

Age: Metro Area

Metro Area	Percent of Population									Median Age
	Under Age 5	Age 5–19	Age 20–34	Age 35–44	Age 45–54	Age 55–64	Age 65–74	Age 75–84	Age 85+	
Albuquerque, NM	5.7	19.2	20.7	12.6	12.4	13.2	9.8	4.7	1.8	38.2
Allentown, PA	5.3	18.7	18.6	11.9	13.8	14.1	9.9	5.2	2.6	41.4
Anchorage, AK	7.2	20.2	24.0	13.0	12.4	12.4	7.2	2.6	0.9	34.0
Ann Arbor, MI	4.9	19.5	27.4	11.5	11.8	11.5	8.2	3.7	1.6	33.6
Athens, GA	5.4	21.1	27.1	12.0	11.0	10.7	7.8	3.8	1.2	32.2
Atlanta, GA	6.4	21.0	20.6	14.0	14.3	11.8	7.5	3.2	1.1	36.4
Austin, TX	6.4	19.7	24.3	15.5	12.9	10.6	6.7	2.7	1.1	34.7
Baton Rouge, LA	6.5	20.1	22.7	12.7	12.2	12.2	8.4	3.9	1.4	35.6
Boise City, ID	6.3	21.7	20.0	13.4	12.5	11.8	8.7	4.0	1.4	36.3
Boston, MA	5.3	17.7	22.2	12.5	13.7	13.2	8.8	4.4	2.1	38.7
Boulder, CO	4.6	19.0	24.3	12.6	13.1	12.7	8.4	3.7	1.6	36.6
Cape Coral, FL	4.7	15.2	15.8	10.3	11.9	14.1	15.5	9.3	3.3	48.5
Cedar Rapids, IA	6.2	19.5	19.6	12.7	12.9	12.9	9.0	4.8	2.3	38.4
Charleston, SC	6.1	18.5	22.1	13.2	12.7	12.8	9.3	3.9	1.5	37.2
Charlotte, NC	6.2	20.2	20.1	13.9	14.2	12.1	8.2	3.8	1.4	37.5
Chicago, IL	6.1	19.4	21.0	13.3	13.3	12.7	8.2	4.1	1.8	37.5
Cincinnati, OH	6.3	20.1	19.9	12.4	13.2	13.4	8.7	4.2	1.9	37.9
Clarksville, TN	8.4	20.8	27.0	12.4	10.8	9.8	6.6	3.2	1.2	31.1
Cleveland, OH	5.6	18.1	18.9	11.6	13.3	14.5	10.1	5.4	2.5	41.3
College Station, TX	6.1	20.9	32.9	11.0	9.5	9.2	6.1	3.0	1.2	27.8
Colorado Springs, CO	6.6	20.2	23.6	12.5	12.1	12.1	7.9	3.5	1.3	34.6
Columbia, MO	5.8	19.4	28.5	11.6	10.7	11.3	7.5	3.7	1.4	32.1
Columbia, SC	5.8	20.2	21.6	12.5	12.7	12.7	8.9	4.1	1.5	36.6
Columbus, OH	6.7	19.8	22.2	13.4	13.0	12.1	7.8	3.6	1.5	36.0
Dallas, TX	7.0	21.8	21.5	14.2	13.4	11.2	6.8	3.1	1.1	34.8
Davenport, IA	6.2	19.3	18.3	12.3	12.5	13.8	10.0	5.3	2.4	39.7
Denver, CO	6.1	18.9	22.6	14.6	13.2	12.1	7.8	3.3	1.4	36.5
Des Moines, IA	7.0	20.5	20.7	13.7	12.8	11.9	7.9	3.9	1.6	36.2
Durham, NC	5.7	18.6	22.3	13.0	13.0	12.6	9.1	4.0	1.7	37.6
Edison, NJ	6.1	17.8	21.2	13.1	13.6	12.8	8.6	4.6	2.2	38.6
El Paso, TX	7.6	22.8	23.3	12.5	11.5	10.4	6.7	3.7	1.5	32.2
Fargo, ND	7.1	19.5	27.4	12.8	10.5	10.7	6.6	3.4	1.9	32.5
Fayetteville, NC	7.7	20.7	25.7	12.5	11.4	10.6	7.0	3.4	1.1	32.3
Fort Collins, CO	5.1	18.4	25.2	12.3	11.2	12.6	9.4	4.1	1.7	36.0
Fort Wayne, IN	7.0	21.1	20.1	12.3	12.4	12.6	8.6	4.1	1.8	36.4
Fort Worth, TX	7.0	21.8	21.5	14.2	13.4	11.2	6.8	3.1	1.1	34.8
Grand Rapids, MI	6.5	20.6	21.8	12.3	12.4	12.5	8.1	4.0	1.9	35.8
Greeley, CO	7.2	22.1	21.5	13.6	12.2	11.5	7.4	3.2	1.2	34.4
Green Bay, WI	6.2	19.7	19.2	12.4	13.4	13.7	9.0	4.6	1.8	38.8
Greensboro, NC	5.8	19.7	19.8	12.1	13.7	13.0	9.3	4.7	1.9	38.8
Honolulu, HI	6.4	17.0	22.6	12.7	12.1	11.9	9.4	5.0	2.9	37.9
Houston, TX	7.3	21.9	21.7	14.2	12.8	11.2	6.8	3.0	1.0	34.3
Huntsville, AL	5.8	19.0	20.3	12.4	14.1	13.5	8.6	4.5	1.6	38.7
Indianapolis, IN	6.7	20.5	20.7	13.2	13.1	12.3	8.0	3.8	1.6	36.5
Jacksonville, FL	6.2	18.5	20.7	12.7	13.3	13.2	9.5	4.3	1.6	38.3
Kansas City, MO	6.5	20.0	20.0	13.2	12.9	12.8	8.5	4.2	1.8	37.4
Lafayette, LA	6.9	20.2	21.3	12.6	12.4	12.9	8.1	4.0	1.6	36.0
Lakeland, FL	5.8	18.8	19.0	11.8	12.1	12.3	11.4	6.7	2.1	40.2
Las Vegas, NV	6.3	19.3	21.1	13.8	13.3	11.7	8.9	4.2	1.3	37.3
Lexington, KY	6.2	19.0	23.2	13.0	12.6	12.1	8.3	4.0	1.5	36.1
Lincoln, NE	6.4	20.4	25.0	12.3	10.9	11.4	8.1	3.8	1.8	33.7
Little Rock, AR	6.4	19.6	21.3	12.9	12.4	12.5	8.9	4.2	1.8	36.9
Los Angeles, CA	6.0	18.6	22.7	13.5	13.6	12.0	7.7	4.0	1.9	36.8
Louisville, KY	6.1	18.7	19.9	12.8	13.3	13.6	9.3	4.4	1.8	39.0

Table continued on following page.

Appendix A: Comparative Statistics   A-23

| Metro Area | Percent of Population | | | | | | | | | Median Age |
	Under Age 5	Age 5–19	Age 20–34	Age 35–44	Age 45–54	Age 55–64	Age 65–74	Age 75–84	Age 85+	
Madison, WI	5.6	18.2	24.4	13.0	12.3	12.5	8.5	3.8	1.7	36.2
Manchester, NH	5.2	17.8	19.8	12.3	14.9	14.7	9.0	4.3	1.9	40.7
Memphis, TN	6.8	20.7	20.8	12.7	12.9	12.5	8.3	3.8	1.4	36.3
Miami, FL	5.7	17.0	19.4	13.1	14.2	12.8	9.4	5.8	2.7	41.0
Midland, TX	8.8	22.1	24.4	13.1	10.6	10.8	5.8	3.1	1.5	31.7
Milwaukee, WI	6.2	19.6	20.4	12.5	12.8	13.3	8.7	4.3	2.2	37.8
Minneapolis, MN	6.5	19.7	20.7	13.3	13.3	13.0	8.0	3.8	1.7	37.1
Nashville, TN	6.4	19.4	22.1	13.7	13.3	12.3	8.0	3.6	1.3	36.4
New Haven, CT	5.2	18.2	20.2	11.8	13.7	13.8	9.5	4.9	2.6	40.3
New Orleans, LA	6.2	18.3	21.0	12.8	12.8	13.7	9.3	4.3	1.7	38.3
New York, NY	6.1	17.8	21.2	13.1	13.6	12.8	8.6	4.6	2.2	38.6
Oklahoma City, OK	6.8	20.6	22.2	13.0	11.8	12.0	8.1	3.9	1.6	35.2
Omaha, NE	7.2	21.0	20.8	13.2	12.3	12.2	8.0	3.8	1.6	35.7
Orlando, FL	5.9	18.7	22.2	13.7	13.3	11.7	8.5	4.3	1.7	37.2
Peoria, IL	6.3	19.1	18.5	12.3	12.6	13.5	9.9	5.3	2.6	39.9
Philadelphia, PA	5.9	18.6	20.7	12.3	13.4	13.5	8.9	4.6	2.1	38.8
Phoenix, AZ	6.4	20.3	21.0	13.1	12.5	11.4	8.9	4.6	1.7	36.7
Pittsburgh, PA	5.1	16.5	19.2	11.5	13.1	15.2	10.8	5.8	3.0	43.1
Portland, OR	5.7	18.1	21.3	14.7	13.3	12.5	9.0	3.8	1.7	38.1
Providence, RI	5.2	17.9	20.5	11.9	13.9	13.9	9.5	4.8	2.5	40.3
Provo, UT	9.6	28.3	26.8	12.6	8.4	6.7	4.5	2.3	0.8	24.8
Raleigh, NC	6.2	20.8	20.4	14.8	14.5	11.6	7.4	3.2	1.2	36.7
Reno, NV	6.0	18.1	21.5	12.2	12.8	13.2	10.2	4.4	1.4	38.5
Richmond, VA	5.8	18.7	20.7	12.8	13.6	13.5	9.2	4.1	1.8	38.8
Riverside, CA	6.8	22.1	21.8	12.8	12.5	11.2	7.5	3.8	1.4	34.5
Rochester, MN	6.7	19.8	18.9	12.6	12.4	13.4	8.8	5.0	2.3	38.4
Sacramento, CA	6.1	19.6	21.0	12.8	12.8	12.6	8.8	4.3	1.9	37.4
Salt Lake City, UT	7.6	22.6	23.3	14.6	11.2	10.1	6.4	3.0	1.1	32.7
San Antonio, TX	6.9	21.4	22.2	13.3	12.4	11.2	7.6	3.7	1.5	34.7
San Diego, CA	6.3	18.2	24.2	13.3	12.5	11.7	7.9	4.0	1.8	35.8
San Francisco, CA	5.5	16.5	22.0	14.5	13.8	12.6	8.7	4.4	2.1	39.0
San Jose, CA	6.1	18.6	22.3	14.5	13.8	11.7	7.4	4.0	1.8	37.1
Santa Rosa, CA	5.0	17.2	18.7	12.4	13.0	14.5	11.6	5.1	2.2	42.1
Savannah, GA	6.6	19.4	23.2	12.9	12.1	11.9	8.5	4.0	1.5	35.6
Seattle, WA	6.1	17.6	23.0	14.3	13.4	12.4	7.9	3.5	1.6	37.0
Sioux Falls, SD	7.6	20.7	21.4	13.5	11.8	12.0	7.8	3.4	1.8	35.2
Springfield, IL	5.8	19.0	18.4	12.2	13.1	14.2	10.1	5.1	2.1	40.4
Tallahassee, FL	5.2	18.9	27.4	11.5	11.2	11.8	8.7	3.8	1.5	33.8
Tampa, FL	5.4	16.8	18.9	12.4	13.5	13.6	10.9	6.0	2.5	42.1
Tucson, AZ	5.7	18.6	21.5	11.4	11.2	12.6	10.9	6.0	2.2	38.5
Tulsa, OK	6.7	20.5	20.1	12.6	12.4	12.7	8.9	4.5	1.7	37.0
Tuscaloosa, AL	6.0	20.5	24.3	11.8	11.5	12.0	8.4	4.1	1.5	34.4
Virginia Beach, VA	6.3	18.6	23.4	12.3	12.4	12.7	8.5	4.2	1.7	36.3
Washington, DC	6.5	19.0	21.3	14.3	14.0	12.1	7.7	3.6	1.4	37.0
Wichita, KS	6.9	21.3	20.4	12.1	11.8	12.7	8.3	4.3	1.9	36.0
Winston-Salem, NC	5.7	19.4	18.3	11.9	14.1	13.7	9.9	5.3	1.8	40.6
U.S.	6.1	19.1	20.7	12.6	13.0	12.9	9.1	4.6	1.9	38.1

Note: Figures cover the Metropolitan Statistical Area (MSA)—see Appendix B for areas included
Source: U.S. Census Bureau, 2015-2019 American Community Survey 5-Year Estimates

A-24　Appendix A: Comparative Statistics

Religious Groups by Family

Area[1]	Catholic	Baptist	Non-Den.	Methodist[2]	Lutheran	LDS[3]	Pentecostal	Presbyterian[4]	Muslim[5]	Judaism
Albuquerque, NM	27.1	3.7	4.2	1.4	0.9	2.3	1.4	1.0	0.2	0.2
Allentown, PA	23.1	0.4	1.9	3.9	7.9	0.3	0.4	6.2	0.6	0.6
Anchorage, AK	6.9	5.0	6.4	1.3	1.9	5.1	1.8	0.6	0.2	0.1
Ann Arbor, MI	12.3	2.2	1.5	3.0	2.8	0.8	1.9	2.9	1.2	0.9
Athens, GA	4.4	16.2	2.2	8.3	0.3	0.8	2.8	2.0	0.3	0.2
Atlanta, GA	7.4	17.4	6.8	7.8	0.5	0.7	2.6	1.8	0.7	0.5
Austin, TX	16.0	10.3	4.5	3.6	1.9	1.1	0.8	1.0	1.2	0.2
Baton Rouge, LA	22.5	18.2	9.6	4.6	0.2	0.7	1.1	0.6	0.2	0.1
Boise City, ID	8.0	2.9	4.1	2.1	1.1	15.8	2.3	0.6	0.1	0.1
Boston, MA	44.3	1.1	1.0	0.9	0.3	0.4	0.6	1.6	0.4	1.4
Boulder, CO	20.1	2.3	4.7	1.7	3.0	2.9	0.4	2.0	0.1	0.7
Cape Coral, FL	16.2	4.9	3.0	2.5	1.1	0.5	4.3	1.4	0.9	0.2
Cedar Rapids, IA	18.8	2.3	3.0	7.3	11.3	0.8	1.8	3.2	0.5	0.1
Charleston, SC	6.1	12.4	7.0	10.0	1.1	0.9	2.0	2.3	0.1	0.3
Charlotte, NC	5.9	17.2	6.7	8.6	1.3	0.7	3.2	4.5	0.2	0.3
Chicago, IL	34.2	3.2	4.4	1.9	3.0	0.3	1.2	1.9	3.2	0.8
Cincinnati, OH	19.0	9.5	3.6	3.8	1.1	0.5	2.2	1.5	0.2	0.5
Clarksville, TN	4.0	30.9	2.2	6.1	0.5	1.5	1.8	1.0	0.1	<0.1
Cleveland, OH	28.8	4.3	3.3	2.8	2.5	0.3	1.1	2.0	0.1	1.4
College Station, TX	11.7	15.6	3.9	4.7	1.5	1.2	0.6	0.9	1.1	<0.1
Colorado Springs, CO	8.3	4.3	7.4	2.4	1.9	3.0	1.0	2.0	<0.1	0.1
Columbia, MO	6.6	14.6	5.4	4.3	1.7	1.3	1.0	2.3	0.3	0.2
Columbia, SC	3.1	18.0	5.2	9.3	3.4	1.0	2.6	3.3	0.1	0.2
Columbus, OH	11.7	5.3	3.5	4.7	2.4	0.7	1.9	2.0	0.8	0.5
Dallas, TX	13.3	18.7	7.7	5.2	0.7	1.1	2.1	0.9	2.4	0.3
Davenport, IA	14.9	4.9	2.7	5.3	8.6	0.8	1.4	2.9	0.9	0.1
Denver, CO	16.0	2.9	4.6	1.7	2.1	2.4	1.2	1.5	0.5	0.6
Des Moines, IA	13.6	4.7	3.3	6.9	8.2	0.9	2.3	2.9	0.3	0.3
Durham, NC	5.0	13.8	5.6	8.1	0.4	0.7	1.3	2.5	0.4	0.5
Edison, NJ	36.9	1.8	1.7	1.3	0.7	0.3	0.8	1.0	2.3	4.7
El Paso, TX	43.2	3.7	4.9	0.8	0.3	1.5	1.4	0.2	<0.1	0.2
Fargo, ND	17.4	0.4	0.4	3.3	32.5	0.6	1.5	1.8	0.1	<0.1
Fayetteville, NC	2.6	14.1	10.4	6.2	0.1	1.4	4.8	2.1	0.1	<0.1
Fort Collins, CO	11.8	2.2	6.3	4.3	3.4	2.9	4.7	1.9	0.1	<0.1
Fort Wayne, IN	14.2	6.0	6.8	5.1	8.5	0.4	1.4	1.6	0.2	0.1
Fort Worth, TX	13.3	18.7	7.7	5.2	0.7	1.1	2.1	0.9	2.4	0.3
Grand Rapids, MI	17.1	1.7	8.3	3.0	2.1	0.5	1.1	9.9	1.0	0.1
Greeley, CO	13.5	1.8	1.5	2.6	2.0	1.9	1.8	1.4	0.1	<0.1
Green Bay, WI	42.0	0.7	3.4	2.2	12.7	0.3	0.6	1.0	0.1	<0.1
Greensboro, NC	2.6	12.8	7.4	9.8	0.6	0.8	2.4	3.1	0.6	0.4
Honolulu, HI	18.2	1.9	2.2	0.8	0.3	5.1	4.1	1.4	<0.1	<0.1
Houston, TX	17.0	16.0	7.2	4.8	1.0	1.1	1.5	0.8	2.6	0.3
Huntsville, AL	3.9	27.6	3.1	7.5	0.7	1.1	1.2	1.7	0.2	0.1
Indianapolis, IN	10.5	10.2	7.1	4.9	1.6	0.7	1.6	1.6	0.2	0.3
Jacksonville, FL	9.8	18.5	7.7	4.5	0.6	1.1	1.9	1.6	0.6	0.4
Kansas City, MO	12.6	13.1	5.2	5.8	2.2	2.4	2.6	1.6	0.3	0.4
Lafayette, LA	47.0	14.7	3.9	2.5	0.2	0.4	2.9	0.1	0.1	<0.1
Lakeland, FL	7.5	13.6	5.0	3.9	0.9	0.7	4.0	1.6	0.4	<0.1
Las Vegas, NV	18.1	2.9	3.0	0.4	0.7	6.3	1.5	0.2	<0.1	0.3
Lexington, KY	6.7	24.9	2.3	5.9	0.4	1.0	2.1	1.3	0.1	0.3
Lincoln, NE	14.7	2.4	1.9	7.1	11.2	1.1	1.4	3.9	0.2	0.1
Little Rock, AR	4.5	25.9	6.0	7.3	0.5	0.9	2.8	0.8	0.1	0.1
Los Angeles, CA	33.8	2.7	3.6	1.0	0.6	1.7	1.7	0.9	0.7	0.9
Louisville, KY	13.6	25.0	1.7	3.7	0.6	0.8	0.9	1.1	0.5	0.4
Madison, WI	21.8	1.1	1.5	3.6	12.7	0.5	0.3	2.1	0.4	0.4

Table continued on following page.

Appendix A: Comparative Statistics   A-25

Area[1]	Catholic	Baptist	Non-Den.	Methodist[2]	Lutheran	LDS[3]	Pente-costal	Presby-terian[4]	Muslim[5]	Judaism
Manchester, NH	31.1	1.3	2.3	1.1	0.5	0.6	0.4	2.0	0.3	0.5
Memphis, TN	5.2	30.8	5.4	6.2	0.3	0.6	4.7	2.4	0.3	0.6
Miami, FL	18.5	5.3	4.1	1.2	0.4	0.5	1.7	0.6	0.9	1.5
Midland, TX	22.4	25.2	8.8	4.2	0.6	1.2	1.6	1.8	3.7	<0.1
Milwaukee, WI	24.6	3.1	3.8	1.5	10.7	0.4	1.9	1.5	0.5	0.5
Minneapolis, MN	21.7	2.4	2.9	2.7	14.4	0.6	1.7	1.8	0.4	0.7
Nashville, TN	4.1	25.2	5.8	6.1	0.3	0.7	2.1	2.1	0.3	0.1
New Haven, CT	35.3	1.4	1.9	1.5	0.6	0.3	1.0	2.2	0.5	1.2
New Orleans, LA	31.5	8.4	3.7	2.6	0.8	0.5	2.1	0.5	0.4	0.5
New York, NY	36.9	1.8	1.7	1.3	0.7	0.3	0.8	1.0	2.3	4.7
Oklahoma City, OK	6.3	25.3	7.0	10.6	0.7	1.2	3.1	0.9	0.2	0.1
Omaha, NE	21.6	4.5	1.8	3.9	7.8	1.7	1.2	2.2	0.5	0.4
Orlando, FL	13.2	6.9	5.6	2.9	0.9	0.9	3.2	1.3	1.3	0.2
Peoria, IL	11.4	5.5	5.2	4.9	6.1	0.5	1.5	2.8	5.2	0.1
Philadelphia, PA	33.4	3.9	2.8	2.9	1.8	0.3	0.8	2.1	1.2	1.3
Phoenix, AZ	13.3	3.4	5.1	1.0	1.6	6.1	2.9	0.6	0.1	0.3
Pittsburgh, PA	32.8	2.3	2.8	5.6	3.3	0.3	1.1	4.6	0.3	0.7
Portland, OR	10.5	2.3	4.5	1.0	1.6	3.7	2.0	0.9	0.1	0.3
Providence, RI	47.0	1.4	1.2	0.8	0.5	0.3	0.5	1.0	0.1	0.7
Provo, UT	1.3	<0.1	<0.1	0.1	<0.1	88.5	0.1	<0.1	<0.1	<0.1
Raleigh, NC	9.1	12.1	5.9	6.7	0.9	0.8	2.2	2.2	0.9	0.3
Reno, NV	14.3	1.5	3.1	0.9	0.7	4.6	1.9	0.4	<0.1	0.1
Richmond, VA	5.9	19.9	5.4	6.1	0.6	0.9	1.8	2.1	2.7	0.3
Riverside, CA	24.8	2.6	5.5	0.6	0.5	2.4	1.5	0.6	0.5	<0.1
Rochester, MN	23.3	1.6	4.6	4.8	21.0	1.1	1.2	2.9	0.2	0.2
Sacramento, CA	16.1	3.1	4.0	1.7	0.7	3.3	2.0	0.8	0.8	0.2
Salt Lake City, UT	8.9	0.8	0.5	0.5	0.5	58.9	0.6	0.3	0.4	0.1
San Antonio, TX	28.4	8.5	6.0	3.0	1.6	1.4	1.3	0.7	0.9	0.2
San Diego, CA	25.9	2.0	4.8	1.1	0.9	2.3	1.0	0.9	0.7	0.5
San Francisco, CA	20.7	2.5	2.4	1.9	0.5	1.5	1.2	1.1	1.2	0.8
San Jose, CA	26.0	1.3	4.2	1.0	0.5	1.4	1.1	0.7	1.0	0.6
Santa Rosa, CA	22.2	1.3	1.5	0.9	0.9	1.9	0.6	0.9	0.4	0.4
Savannah, GA	7.0	19.6	6.9	8.9	1.6	0.9	2.3	1.0	0.1	0.8
Seattle, WA	12.3	2.1	5.0	1.2	2.0	3.3	2.8	1.4	0.4	0.4
Sioux Falls, SD	14.9	3.0	1.5	3.8	21.4	0.7	1.0	6.2	0.3	<0.1
Springfield, IL	15.5	11.7	2.7	6.8	5.6	0.7	4.9	2.0	1.5	0.2
Tallahassee, FL	4.8	16.0	6.7	9.1	0.4	1.0	2.1	1.5	0.8	0.3
Tampa, FL	10.8	7.0	3.7	3.4	0.9	0.6	2.1	0.9	1.2	0.4
Tucson, AZ	20.7	3.3	3.7	1.3	1.5	2.9	1.5	1.0	<0.1	0.5
Tulsa, OK	5.8	22.9	7.6	9.2	0.7	1.1	3.3	1.2	0.3	0.2
Tuscaloosa, AL	1.7	32.2	4.5	8.3	<0.1	0.6	1.5	1.3	0.1	<0.1
Virginia Beach, VA	6.4	11.5	6.1	5.2	0.7	0.9	1.9	2.0	2.0	0.3
Washington, DC	14.5	7.3	4.8	4.5	1.2	1.1	1.0	1.3	2.3	1.1
Wichita, KS	14.5	13.4	3.1	7.1	1.7	1.4	1.9	1.6	0.1	<0.1
Winston-Salem, NC	3.5	17.4	9.3	12.4	0.7	0.6	2.5	2.2	0.3	0.1
U.S.	19.1	9.3	4.0	4.0	2.3	2.0	1.9	1.6	0.8	0.7

Note: Figures are the number of adherents as a percentage of the total population; (1) Figures cover the Metropolitan Statistical Area—see Appendix B for areas included; (2) Methodist/Pietist; (3) Latter Day Saints; (4) Reformed; (5) Figures are estimates
Source: Association of Statisticians of American Religious Bodies, 2010 U.S. Religion Census: Religious Congregations & Membership Study

A-26   Appendix A: Comparative Statistics

Religious Groups by Tradition

Area	Catholic	Evangelical Protestant	Mainline Protestant	Other Tradition	Black Protestant	Orthodox
Albuquerque, NM	27.1	11.2	3.2	3.9	0.2	0.1
Allentown, PA	23.1	5.3	17.7	3.0	0.1	0.6
Anchorage, AK	6.9	15.6	3.5	6.8	0.3	0.6
Ann Arbor, MI	12.3	7.3	7.5	3.7	1.5	0.2
Athens, GA	4.4	21.1	9.7	1.7	2.4	0.1
Atlanta, GA	7.4	26.0	9.8	2.9	3.1	0.2
Austin, TX	16.0	16.1	6.3	3.9	1.3	0.1
Baton Rouge, LA	22.5	24.8	5.6	1.5	5.1	<0.1
Boise City, ID	8.0	12.9	4.3	16.7	<0.1	<0.1
Boston, MA	44.3	3.2	4.5	3.4	0.1	1.0
Boulder, CO	20.1	9.7	6.4	4.8	<0.1	0.2
Cape Coral, FL	16.2	14.3	4.6	2.0	0.3	0.1
Cedar Rapids, IA	18.8	13.7	17.5	1.9	0.1	0.2
Charleston, SC	6.1	19.6	11.1	1.8	7.3	0.1
Charlotte, NC	5.9	27.5	13.3	1.6	2.7	0.4
Chicago, IL	34.2	9.7	5.1	5.0	2.0	0.9
Cincinnati, OH	19.0	15.5	7.1	1.5	1.1	0.1
Clarksville, TN	4.0	35.3	7.2	1.6	2.4	<0.1
Cleveland, OH	28.8	9.0	7.5	2.6	2.1	0.8
College Station, TX	11.7	20.6	6.6	2.5	0.9	<0.1
Colorado Springs, CO	8.3	15.2	5.3	3.7	0.4	0.1
Columbia, MO	6.6	19.9	10.4	2.3	0.4	0.1
Columbia, SC	3.1	25.5	13.4	2.1	5.4	0.1
Columbus, OH	11.7	11.8	9.5	3.1	1.1	0.2
Dallas, TX	13.3	28.3	6.9	4.7	1.7	0.1
Davenport, IA	14.9	11.3	15.1	2.3	1.5	0.1
Denver, CO	16.0	11.0	4.5	4.6	0.3	0.3
Des Moines, IA	13.6	12.3	16.8	1.8	0.9	0.1
Durham, NC	5.0	19.3	11.7	2.9	3.1	<0.1
Edison, NJ	36.9	3.9	4.1	8.3	1.2	0.9
El Paso, TX	43.2	10.8	1.2	2.0	0.2	<0.1
Fargo, ND	17.4	10.7	30.8	0.8	<0.1	<0.1
Fayetteville, NC	2.6	26.7	7.8	1.7	4.3	0.1
Fort Collins, CO	11.8	18.8	5.9	3.9	<0.1	0.1
Fort Wayne, IN	14.2	24.6	9.1	0.9	2.4	0.2
Fort Worth, TX	13.3	28.3	6.9	4.7	1.7	0.1
Grand Rapids, MI	17.1	20.7	7.5	2.1	1.0	0.2
Greeley, CO	13.5	9.2	3.8	2.1	<0.1	<0.1
Green Bay, WI	42.0	14.1	8.1	0.6	<0.1	<0.1
Greensboro, NC	2.6	23.2	14.0	2.1	2.6	<0.1
Honolulu, HI	18.2	9.6	2.9	8.4	<0.1	<0.1
Houston, TX	17.0	24.9	6.6	4.9	1.3	0.2
Huntsville, AL	3.9	33.3	9.6	1.8	1.8	<0.1
Indianapolis, IN	10.5	18.2	9.6	1.6	1.8	0.2
Jacksonville, FL	9.8	27.1	5.6	2.9	4.2	0.2
Kansas City, MO	12.6	20.5	9.9	3.6	2.6	0.1
Lafayette, LA	47.0	12.7	3.2	0.7	9.2	<0.1
Lakeland, FL	7.5	24.6	5.2	1.4	1.7	<0.1
Las Vegas, NV	18.1	7.7	1.3	7.6	0.4	0.4
Lexington, KY	6.7	28.3	10.2	1.7	2.0	0.1
Lincoln, NE	14.7	14.8	16.2	2.0	0.1	<0.1
Little Rock, AR	4.5	33.9	8.1	1.7	3.4	<0.1
Los Angeles, CA	33.8	9.0	2.3	4.6	0.8	0.6
Louisville, KY	13.6	24.5	7.1	2.0	2.9	<0.1
Madison, WI	21.8	7.2	15.3	2.2	0.1	<0.1

Table continued on following page.

Appendix A: Comparative Statistics   A-27

Area	Catholic	Evangelical Protestant	Mainline Protestant	Other Tradition	Black Protestant	Orthodox
Manchester, NH	31.1	5.1	4.4	1.8	<0.1	0.7
Memphis, TN	5.2	29.4	8.3	2.1	13.4	<0.1
Miami, FL	18.5	11.4	2.4	3.5	1.7	0.2
Midland, TX	22.4	35.4	7.2	5.3	1.0	<0.1
Milwaukee, WI	24.6	14.6	7.1	2.3	2.4	0.6
Minneapolis, MN	21.7	12.8	14.5	2.2	0.4	0.2
Nashville, TN	4.1	32.9	8.0	1.7	3.3	0.4
New Haven, CT	35.3	3.8	6.1	2.3	0.7	0.4
New Orleans, LA	31.5	12.7	4.0	2.1	2.9	0.1
New York, NY	36.9	3.9	4.1	8.3	1.2	0.9
Oklahoma City, OK	6.3	39.0	9.8	2.7	1.9	0.1
Omaha, NE	21.6	12.1	10.7	3.2	1.4	0.1
Orlando, FL	13.2	17.8	4.7	3.2	1.2	0.3
Peoria, IL	11.4	18.9	11.1	6.1	0.9	0.1
Philadelphia, PA	33.4	6.3	8.9	3.7	1.7	0.4
Phoenix, AZ	13.3	13.2	2.6	7.8	0.1	0.3
Pittsburgh, PA	32.8	7.3	13.8	2.0	0.8	0.6
Portland, OR	10.5	11.6	3.6	5.2	0.1	0.3
Providence, RI	47.0	2.8	4.7	1.6	<0.1	0.5
Provo, UT	1.3	0.4	<0.1	88.8	<0.1	<0.1
Raleigh, NC	9.1	19.9	10.1	3.2	1.7	0.2
Reno, NV	14.3	7.6	1.9	5.1	0.2	0.1
Richmond, VA	5.9	23.6	13.3	4.5	2.4	0.1
Riverside, CA	24.8	11.4	1.3	3.7	0.8	0.1
Rochester, MN	23.3	18.9	21.0	2.0	<0.1	0.1
Sacramento, CA	16.1	11.3	2.2	5.8	0.5	0.3
Salt Lake City, UT	8.9	2.6	1.2	60.0	0.1	0.4
San Antonio, TX	28.4	16.9	5.0	3.1	0.4	<0.1
San Diego, CA	25.9	9.7	2.4	5.2	0.3	0.2
San Francisco, CA	20.7	6.1	3.8	5.2	1.0	0.6
San Jose, CA	26.0	8.2	2.4	6.8	0.1	0.4
Santa Rosa, CA	22.2	5.3	2.3	4.8	<0.1	0.2
Savannah, GA	7.0	25.0	9.4	2.6	8.5	0.1
Seattle, WA	12.3	11.9	4.6	5.9	0.3	0.4
Sioux Falls, SD	14.9	12.9	28.0	1.2	0.1	0.1
Springfield, IL	15.5	21.4	11.6	3.1	2.1	0.1
Tallahassee, FL	4.8	21.9	6.3	2.9	9.1	0.1
Tampa, FL	10.8	13.6	5.1	3.1	1.1	0.8
Tucson, AZ	20.7	10.0	3.7	4.5	0.4	0.2
Tulsa, OK	5.8	34.6	11.2	2.1	1.5	<0.1
Tuscaloosa, AL	1.7	35.2	6.4	0.9	8.5	<0.1
Virginia Beach, VA	6.4	18.0	9.4	3.9	2.2	0.3
Washington, DC	14.5	12.4	8.7	5.9	2.3	0.6
Wichita, KS	14.5	20.7	11.0	2.4	1.8	0.2
Winston-Salem, NC	3.5	29.1	15.6	1.2	2.2	0.2
U.S.	19.1	16.2	7.3	4.3	1.6	0.3

Note: Figures are the number of adherents as a percentage of the total population; (1) Figures cover the Metropolitan Statistical Area—see Appendix B for areas included
Source: Association of Statisticians of American Religious Bodies, 2010 U.S. Religion Census: Religious Congregations & Membership Study

A-28   Appendix A: Comparative Statistics

Ancestry: City

City	German	Irish	English	American	Italian	Polish	French[1]	Scottish	Dutch
Albuquerque, NM	9.0	7.0	6.4	3.8	2.9	1.4	1.7	1.6	0.7
Allentown, PA	10.3	4.9	1.7	2.1	4.4	1.7	0.9	0.5	1.1
Anchorage, AK	14.4	9.7	7.8	3.6	3.0	2.1	2.4	2.6	1.4
Ann Arbor, MI	17.1	9.9	9.5	3.8	4.9	6.0	3.0	2.7	2.3
Athens, GA	8.4	8.2	8.0	4.3	3.0	1.6	1.7	2.7	1.0
Atlanta, GA	6.1	5.6	7.2	5.4	2.6	1.4	1.7	1.8	0.6
Austin, TX	10.4	7.4	7.4	3.1	3.0	1.7	2.3	2.0	0.8
Baton Rouge, LA	5.2	5.0	4.5	5.5	3.3	0.4	6.9	1.3	0.3
Boise City, ID	16.7	11.8	18.5	4.5	3.7	1.7	2.4	3.9	1.7
Boston, MA	4.6	13.4	4.3	2.5	7.7	2.2	1.9	1.2	0.5
Boulder, CO	17.4	12.1	10.5	2.5	6.0	3.5	2.6	3.2	1.3
Cape Coral, FL	14.1	11.5	7.3	15.3	10.4	3.5	2.2	1.6	1.2
Cedar Rapids, IA	30.6	13.8	7.8	4.5	1.9	1.6	2.3	1.6	1.9
Charleston, SC	10.4	9.9	9.9	23.1	4.4	1.9	2.2	2.7	0.7
Charlotte, NC	8.7	7.0	6.6	4.7	3.4	1.6	1.4	1.9	0.7
Chicago, IL	7.3	7.5	2.4	2.0	4.0	5.6	1.0	0.6	0.5
Cincinnati, OH	17.7	10.0	5.3	3.9	3.5	1.7	1.6	1.2	0.8
Clarksville, TN	10.7	8.3	5.6	7.8	3.5	1.5	1.8	1.3	1.1
Cleveland, OH	9.0	8.3	2.6	2.1	4.8	3.8	0.9	0.6	0.5
College Station, TX	16.9	8.9	7.7	3.5	3.5	2.3	3.5	2.3	0.7
Colorado Springs, CO	18.6	11.0	9.7	4.3	4.8	2.3	2.9	2.6	1.5
Columbia, MO	23.9	12.3	8.8	5.6	3.7	2.4	2.5	1.9	1.5
Columbia, SC	9.9	6.9	8.3	5.3	2.9	1.3	2.0	2.2	0.8
Columbus, OH	16.4	10.1	6.1	4.3	4.9	2.2	1.7	1.7	0.9
Dallas, TX	5.1	4.0	4.5	3.8	1.5	0.8	1.2	1.1	0.4
Davenport, IA	28.8	15.3	6.3	4.0	2.3	2.1	1.5	1.5	1.8
Denver, CO	13.8	9.7	7.8	2.9	4.6	2.7	2.3	2.1	1.4
Des Moines, IA	20.3	11.6	6.6	3.6	3.9	1.0	1.8	1.3	2.6
Durham, NC	7.4	5.8	7.0	4.3	2.8	1.7	1.6	1.5	0.6
Edison, NJ	4.9	6.8	1.6	1.7	7.8	4.6	0.8	0.6	0.3
El Paso, TX	3.6	2.3	1.7	2.4	1.2	0.5	0.8	0.4	0.2
Fargo, ND	37.1	8.8	3.9	2.2	1.1	3.1	3.6	1.2	1.1
Fayetteville, NC	8.8	6.9	6.6	3.9	2.8	1.4	1.5	1.8	0.6
Fort Collins, CO	22.5	12.7	11.4	3.7	5.3	3.0	3.3	2.9	1.8
Fort Wayne, IN	24.3	9.5	6.9	5.7	2.4	2.1	3.0	1.5	1.3
Fort Worth, TX	7.4	6.0	5.6	5.0	1.9	0.9	1.5	1.4	0.7
Grand Rapids, MI	15.0	8.7	7.0	2.3	3.0	6.8	2.2	1.6	13.9
Greeley, CO	18.4	8.5	6.8	4.2	2.5	1.4	1.6	2.1	1.0
Green Bay, WI	29.5	9.3	3.8	3.4	2.3	7.9	4.2	0.6	3.0
Greensboro, NC	7.0	5.5	7.3	4.8	2.4	1.1	1.1	1.7	0.7
Honolulu, HI	4.1	3.3	2.8	1.2	1.8	0.7	0.8	0.6	0.3
Houston, TX	4.8	3.6	3.7	4.0	1.5	0.8	1.6	0.9	0.4
Huntsville, AL	8.6	8.8	8.7	11.4	2.4	0.9	1.8	2.0	0.9
Indianapolis, IN	13.5	8.6	5.9	5.9	2.2	1.6	1.5	1.5	1.0
Jacksonville, FL	7.9	7.8	6.0	5.4	3.8	1.5	1.4	1.5	0.8
Kansas City, MO	15.4	10.5	7.0	3.9	3.5	1.4	2.0	1.6	1.1
Lafayette, LA	7.4	5.5	5.7	6.4	3.8	0.4	17.8	1.1	0.5
Lakeland, FL	10.1	8.1	8.7	8.1	4.5	1.8	2.6	1.7	1.4
Las Vegas, NV	8.9	7.7	5.6	3.4	5.3	2.1	1.8	1.3	0.8
Lexington, KY	13.7	11.8	10.8	9.2	2.9	1.7	1.9	2.9	1.1
Lincoln, NE	33.2	11.3	8.0	3.6	2.3	2.5	2.1	1.5	2.0
Little Rock, AR	7.1	6.8	7.5	5.5	1.6	0.9	1.8	1.6	0.5
Los Angeles, CA	3.9	3.5	2.8	3.6	2.6	1.4	1.1	0.7	0.4
Louisville, KY	15.1	11.5	7.8	8.7	2.5	1.0	1.9	1.6	0.9
Madison, WI	31.4	12.4	8.1	2.0	4.1	5.7	2.9	1.5	1.8
Manchester, NH	6.6	19.3	9.0	2.9	8.2	3.9	13.5	3.2	0.5

Table continued on following page.

Appendix A: Comparative Statistics   A-29

City	German	Irish	English	American	Italian	Polish	French[1]	Scottish	Dutch
Memphis, TN	3.4	4.2	3.9	3.9	1.6	0.7	1.0	1.0	0.3
Miami, FL	1.5	1.2	0.8	3.3	2.3	0.7	0.9	0.2	0.2
Midland, TX	6.8	6.0	6.7	4.4	1.4	0.6	1.6	1.6	0.7
Milwaukee, WI	16.3	5.6	2.1	1.2	2.7	6.6	1.3	0.5	0.7
Minneapolis, MN	20.9	10.1	5.6	1.8	2.7	4.0	2.5	1.4	1.4
Nashville, TN	8.4	7.9	7.3	8.2	2.4	1.3	1.7	1.9	0.8
New Haven, CT	4.1	6.5	3.2	1.1	7.7	2.1	1.3	0.6	0.5
New Orleans, LA	6.1	5.4	4.1	2.5	3.9	0.9	5.4	1.1	0.4
New York, NY	2.9	4.4	1.6	4.2	6.2	2.4	0.8	0.5	0.3
Oklahoma City, OK	10.6	8.1	6.2	5.9	1.9	0.8	1.5	1.5	0.9
Omaha, NE	25.2	13.1	6.9	3.0	4.1	3.6	2.0	1.3	1.4
Orlando, FL	6.3	5.3	4.5	5.6	4.3	1.6	1.7	1.3	0.5
Peoria, IL	18.3	11.3	6.7	4.7	3.1	1.9	2.1	1.2	1.0
Philadelphia, PA	6.4	10.4	2.6	2.3	7.4	3.3	0.7	0.5	0.3
Phoenix, AZ	9.9	7.1	5.5	3.0	3.8	2.0	1.7	1.3	0.9
Pittsburgh, PA	18.7	14.6	5.1	3.6	12.3	6.9	1.6	1.4	0.6
Portland, OR	15.9	11.1	10.5	4.6	4.3	2.3	3.0	2.9	1.9
Providence, RI	3.2	7.6	3.9	2.9	7.2	1.9	2.9	0.8	0.3
Provo, UT	10.1	4.1	23.0	3.0	2.0	0.8	1.6	4.8	1.4
Raleigh, NC	8.9	7.5	9.0	12.2	4.0	2.2	1.7	2.3	0.6
Reno, NV	12.8	10.8	9.1	3.9	6.1	1.7	2.6	2.2	1.1
Richmond, VA	6.9	6.3	7.4	4.2	3.5	1.3	1.4	2.1	0.5
Riverside, CA	5.9	4.6	4.1	3.1	2.9	0.9	1.6	1.0	0.8
Rochester, MN	29.1	11.3	6.1	3.0	2.0	3.6	2.1	1.3	1.7
Sacramento, CA	6.7	6.1	4.5	1.7	3.5	0.9	1.5	1.2	0.8
Salt Lake City, UT	10.4	6.7	14.9	3.3	3.3	1.5	2.0	3.3	1.9
San Antonio, TX	6.8	4.3	3.6	3.1	1.6	1.0	1.3	0.9	0.4
San Diego, CA	8.3	7.0	5.5	2.4	4.1	1.7	1.8	1.4	0.8
San Francisco, CA	7.1	7.7	5.1	2.8	4.5	1.8	2.3	1.4	0.8
San Jose, CA	5.0	4.0	3.5	1.8	3.3	0.9	1.2	0.8	0.5
Santa Rosa, CA	11.4	10.1	8.9	2.8	7.4	1.4	3.0	2.2	1.2
Savannah, GA	5.5	6.7	4.6	3.6	2.8	1.2	1.6	1.6	0.7
Seattle, WA	14.8	11.4	10.1	2.3	4.4	2.7	3.0	2.9	1.6
Sioux Falls, SD	35.1	11.2	5.3	3.2	1.5	1.7	2.2	1.2	5.6
Springfield, IL	20.1	12.8	9.0	4.8	4.7	2.1	2.3	1.7	1.2
Tallahassee, FL	8.5	8.1	7.8	3.8	3.7	1.8	1.9	2.1	0.7
Tampa, FL	8.7	8.0	6.0	6.2	6.0	2.0	2.0	1.5	0.8
Tucson, AZ	11.0	8.2	6.4	3.0	3.6	1.9	2.0	1.5	0.9
Tulsa, OK	11.0	9.1	7.5	6.2	2.0	0.9	1.9	2.0	1.0
Tuscaloosa, AL	5.8	6.6	5.6	7.3	2.3	0.9	1.2	2.2	0.6
Virginia Beach, VA	11.7	11.0	9.1	9.4	5.6	2.4	2.3	2.3	0.9
Washington, DC	6.9	6.7	5.2	2.3	3.9	2.2	1.5	1.4	0.7
Wichita, KS	19.3	9.5	7.8	5.0	1.7	1.0	2.2	1.6	1.5
Winston-Salem, NC	9.6	6.8	7.8	5.2	2.8	1.1	1.3	2.3	1.0
U.S.	13.3	9.7	7.2	6.2	5.1	2.8	2.3	1.7	1.2

Note: Figures are the percentage of the total population reporting a particular ancestry. The nine most commonly reported ancestries in the U.S. are shown. Figures include multiple ancestries (e.g. if a person reported being Irish and Italian, they were included in both columns);
(1) Excludes Basque
Source: U.S. Census Bureau, 2015-2019 American Community Survey 5-Year Estimates

A-30 Appendix A: Comparative Statistics

Ancestry: Metro Area

Metro Area	German	Irish	English	American	Italian	Polish	French[1]	Scottish	Dutch
Albuquerque, NM	8.7	6.8	6.4	4.3	2.8	1.3	1.7	1.6	0.7
Allentown, PA	24.3	13.5	5.8	4.5	12.8	5.2	1.6	1.1	2.3
Anchorage, AK	15.3	10.0	7.9	4.1	3.1	2.1	2.7	2.6	1.5
Ann Arbor, MI	19.0	10.7	9.9	6.6	4.7	6.4	3.1	2.6	2.1
Athens, GA	8.6	9.4	9.1	7.9	2.8	1.2	1.6	2.8	0.9
Atlanta, GA	6.6	6.6	7.2	9.2	2.5	1.2	1.4	1.7	0.6
Austin, TX	12.3	7.7	7.9	3.8	2.7	1.6	2.4	2.0	0.8
Baton Rouge, LA	6.8	6.6	5.0	7.8	4.7	0.5	12.3	1.1	0.3
Boise City, ID	16.1	9.6	17.1	5.1	3.4	1.2	2.4	3.2	2.1
Boston, MA	5.9	20.8	9.4	3.5	13.1	3.4	4.5	2.3	0.6
Boulder, CO	18.9	11.5	11.6	3.5	5.4	3.3	2.7	3.3	1.5
Cape Coral, FL	13.5	11.0	8.1	14.3	7.7	3.3	2.3	1.8	1.3
Cedar Rapids, IA	34.2	14.5	8.0	4.7	1.9	1.2	2.4	1.5	2.0
Charleston, SC	9.9	9.7	8.2	13.3	3.7	1.9	2.0	2.5	0.8
Charlotte, NC	11.0	8.4	7.8	9.1	3.9	1.7	1.6	2.3	0.9
Chicago, IL	14.3	10.8	4.2	2.6	6.6	8.8	1.4	0.9	1.2
Cincinnati, OH	27.2	13.8	8.3	7.1	4.2	1.6	1.9	1.8	1.2
Clarksville, TN	11.1	9.0	6.4	9.3	2.8	1.4	1.8	1.6	0.9
Cleveland, OH	18.8	13.4	7.0	3.8	9.8	7.7	1.5	1.5	0.9
College Station, TX	14.0	8.0	6.6	3.9	2.9	2.0	2.5	2.0	0.6
Colorado Springs, CO	18.8	10.9	9.4	4.4	4.9	2.4	2.8	2.7	1.5
Columbia, MO	25.0	11.9	9.0	6.8	3.0	1.7	2.4	2.0	1.5
Columbia, SC	10.0	7.4	7.3	8.5	2.3	1.1	1.7	2.0	0.7
Columbus, OH	21.8	12.6	8.5	6.3	5.4	2.4	1.9	2.1	1.3
Dallas, TX	8.6	6.5	6.7	6.3	2.1	1.1	1.7	1.6	0.7
Davenport, IA	27.7	14.7	7.6	4.2	2.4	2.1	1.8	1.5	2.0
Denver, CO	17.5	10.7	9.3	3.9	5.0	2.5	2.5	2.4	1.5
Des Moines, IA	27.1	13.0	8.4	4.3	3.2	1.3	1.9	1.7	3.8
Durham, NC	8.9	7.4	9.3	6.0	3.1	1.8	1.8	2.3	0.8
Edison, NJ	6.2	9.2	2.7	4.4	12.2	3.8	0.9	0.7	0.6
El Paso, TX	3.4	2.2	1.6	2.3	1.1	0.5	0.8	0.4	0.2
Fargo, ND	37.4	8.2	4.3	2.0	1.1	2.8	3.1	1.2	1.2
Fayetteville, NC	8.7	7.0	6.6	5.6	3.0	1.4	1.5	2.2	0.6
Fort Collins, CO	24.3	12.8	12.2	4.4	4.9	2.7	3.4	3.2	2.2
Fort Wayne, IN	27.0	9.3	7.2	6.9	2.6	2.1	3.3	1.6	1.4
Fort Worth, TX	8.6	6.5	6.7	6.3	2.1	1.1	1.7	1.6	0.7
Grand Rapids, MI	20.0	10.1	8.8	3.7	3.1	6.6	2.9	1.8	18.9
Greeley, CO	22.0	9.9	8.7	4.9	3.6	2.1	2.1	1.9	1.4
Green Bay, WI	36.3	9.7	4.1	3.6	2.2	9.8	4.3	0.7	4.4
Greensboro, NC	8.0	6.6	8.2	8.3	2.3	1.1	1.2	1.9	0.8
Honolulu, HI	5.1	3.8	3.3	1.3	2.0	0.9	1.1	0.9	0.4
Houston, TX	7.8	5.3	5.2	4.3	2.0	1.2	2.1	1.2	0.6
Huntsville, AL	8.9	9.5	9.3	12.2	2.2	1.1	1.8	2.1	1.0
Indianapolis, IN	17.3	10.0	8.0	9.3	2.7	1.9	1.8	1.8	1.4
Jacksonville, FL	10.0	9.6	7.9	7.9	4.6	1.9	1.9	2.0	0.9
Kansas City, MO	20.7	12.3	9.7	5.4	3.3	1.5	2.3	1.9	1.4
Lafayette, LA	6.3	4.2	3.8	9.0	2.4	0.4	18.4	0.7	0.3
Lakeland, FL	8.9	7.4	7.3	13.2	3.6	1.7	2.0	1.5	1.0
Las Vegas, NV	8.7	7.2	5.6	3.4	5.0	1.9	1.7	1.2	0.7
Lexington, KY	13.0	11.8	10.9	13.6	2.6	1.5	1.8	2.7	1.1
Lincoln, NE	34.6	11.1	8.0	3.7	2.2	2.5	2.1	1.4	2.2
Little Rock, AR	9.3	8.8	7.9	7.9	1.5	1.0	1.7	1.9	1.0
Los Angeles, CA	5.2	4.2	3.8	3.6	2.9	1.2	1.2	0.9	0.6
Louisville, KY	17.2	12.4	9.1	10.1	2.4	1.1	2.1	1.9	1.0
Madison, WI	37.1	13.1	8.5	2.8	3.8	5.4	2.8	1.5	1.9
Manchester, NH	8.4	20.8	13.0	3.5	10.0	4.4	12.4	3.4	0.8

Table continued on following page.

Appendix A: Comparative Statistics   A-31

Metro Area	German	Irish	English	American	Italian	Polish	French[1]	Scottish	Dutch
Memphis, TN	5.2	6.3	6.0	7.1	2.1	0.7	1.2	1.4	0.5
Miami, FL	4.4	4.3	2.7	6.0	5.0	1.9	1.2	0.6	0.4
Midland, TX	6.9	6.1	6.4	4.5	1.4	0.6	1.6	1.5	0.6
Milwaukee, WI	33.0	9.8	4.3	2.0	4.3	10.8	2.5	0.9	1.3
Minneapolis, MN	29.1	10.9	5.6	3.1	2.6	4.4	3.3	1.3	1.5
Nashville, TN	10.0	9.6	9.2	10.8	2.7	1.4	1.8	2.2	1.0
New Haven, CT	7.9	14.9	6.8	2.7	20.6	6.2	3.5	1.2	0.6
New Orleans, LA	9.7	7.4	4.5	5.0	7.9	0.7	11.7	1.0	0.4
New York, NY	6.2	9.2	2.7	4.4	12.2	3.8	0.9	0.7	0.6
Oklahoma City, OK	12.0	9.1	7.2	7.6	2.0	0.9	1.7	1.7	1.2
Omaha, NE	29.2	13.6	7.9	3.6	3.9	3.7	2.1	1.4	1.7
Orlando, FL	8.2	7.3	6.1	7.6	5.1	1.9	1.9	1.4	0.7
Peoria, IL	27.2	12.4	9.1	6.7	3.9	2.0	2.4	1.8	1.6
Philadelphia, PA	14.6	18.0	7.0	3.2	13.0	5.0	1.4	1.3	0.8
Phoenix, AZ	12.5	8.3	7.7	3.9	4.4	2.4	2.1	1.6	1.1
Pittsburgh, PA	26.1	17.3	8.0	3.7	15.6	8.4	1.8	1.9	1.1
Portland, OR	17.2	10.4	10.4	4.7	3.9	1.8	2.9	2.9	1.9
Providence, RI	4.5	17.6	10.6	3.4	13.6	3.7	9.4	1.6	0.4
Provo, UT	10.5	4.8	26.7	4.7	2.4	0.6	1.9	4.9	1.6
Raleigh, NC	10.3	9.0	10.1	10.3	4.8	2.2	1.9	2.5	0.9
Reno, NV	13.6	10.9	9.4	3.9	6.5	1.8	2.8	2.2	1.2
Richmond, VA	9.2	7.9	10.7	6.7	3.7	1.6	1.6	2.1	0.7
Riverside, CA	7.1	5.6	4.5	2.9	3.0	0.9	1.6	1.0	0.9
Rochester, MN	35.4	11.7	6.2	3.2	1.7	3.3	2.2	1.3	2.0
Sacramento, CA	10.6	8.1	7.5	2.8	4.8	1.3	2.1	1.7	1.1
Salt Lake City, UT	10.0	5.6	20.0	4.3	2.9	0.9	1.8	3.9	2.0
San Antonio, TX	10.1	5.5	5.1	3.5	1.9	1.5	1.7	1.2	0.5
San Diego, CA	9.3	7.6	6.2	2.7	4.1	1.7	2.0	1.5	1.0
San Francisco, CA	7.6	7.2	5.7	2.4	4.7	1.5	1.9	1.5	0.8
San Jose, CA	6.1	4.8	4.5	1.9	3.7	1.2	1.5	1.1	0.7
Santa Rosa, CA	12.9	12.2	9.8	2.7	8.6	1.8	3.3	2.6	1.4
Savannah, GA	9.1	9.7	7.4	7.9	3.3	1.3	1.8	1.8	0.7
Seattle, WA	14.6	9.7	9.3	3.2	3.7	1.9	2.8	2.6	1.5
Sioux Falls, SD	37.2	10.8	5.2	3.8	1.4	1.6	2.1	1.0	6.4
Springfield, IL	23.5	13.6	10.0	5.6	5.0	2.0	2.4	1.9	1.4
Tallahassee, FL	8.4	8.2	8.0	5.2	3.3	1.6	1.9	2.3	0.9
Tampa, FL	12.3	10.8	7.8	8.6	7.5	3.0	2.6	1.8	1.1
Tucson, AZ	13.4	9.1	8.2	3.3	4.0	2.3	2.3	1.9	1.1
Tulsa, OK	12.9	10.5	8.0	6.7	1.9	1.0	2.1	2.0	1.2
Tuscaloosa, AL	5.1	6.5	5.3	11.4	1.6	0.6	1.0	1.8	0.5
Virginia Beach, VA	9.8	8.8	8.7	9.3	4.1	1.8	1.9	1.9	0.8
Washington, DC	9.3	8.3	6.9	4.1	4.3	2.3	1.6	1.6	0.7
Wichita, KS	21.8	9.9	8.1	6.7	1.7	1.0	2.3	1.9	1.6
Winston-Salem, NC	11.7	7.8	9.0	9.8	2.5	1.0	1.3	2.4	1.1
U.S.	13.3	9.7	7.2	6.2	5.1	2.8	2.3	1.7	1.2

Note: Figures are the percentage of the total population reporting a particular ancestry. The nine most commonly reported ancestries in the U.S. are shown. Figures include multiple ancestries (e.g. if a person reported being Irish and Italian, they were included in both columns); Figures cover the Metropolitan Statistical Area—see Appendix B for areas included; (1) Excludes Basque
Source: U.S. Census Bureau, 2015-2019 American Community Survey 5-Year Estimates

A-32 Appendix A: Comparative Statistics

Foreign-Born Population: City

City	Any Foreign Country	Asia	Mexico	Europe	Caribbean	Central America[1]	South America	Africa	Canada
Albuquerque, NM	9.9	2.4	5.3	0.8	0.3	0.2	0.4	0.4	0.1
Allentown, PA	19.2	3.6	1.0	0.8	9.0	1.3	2.5	0.8	0.1
Anchorage, AK	10.9	6.2	0.9	1.1	0.5	0.1	0.5	0.6	0.4
Ann Arbor, MI	19.1	12.7	0.4	3.0	0.2	0.1	0.8	0.9	0.9
Athens, GA	10.1	2.9	3.0	0.9	0.4	1.0	1.0	0.7	0.2
Atlanta, GA	7.6	3.2	0.7	1.3	0.6	0.1	0.6	0.7	0.3
Austin, TX	18.8	6.0	7.4	1.3	0.6	1.7	0.6	0.8	0.3
Baton Rouge, LA	5.5	2.8	0.4	0.5	0.2	1.0	0.2	0.3	0.0
Boise City, ID	6.4	2.7	1.0	1.4	0.1	0.1	0.3	0.6	0.2
Boston, MA	28.3	7.6	0.4	3.4	8.2	2.6	2.4	3.1	0.4
Boulder, CO	11.0	4.4	1.2	2.8	0.2	0.3	1.0	0.3	0.4
Cape Coral, FL	15.2	1.4	0.7	2.1	6.8	0.7	2.8	0.1	0.6
Cedar Rapids, IA	6.1	2.7	0.7	0.5	0.1	0.1	0.2	1.5	0.1
Charleston, SC	4.8	1.7	0.6	1.3	0.4	0.1	0.3	0.2	0.2
Charlotte, NC	16.7	5.4	2.6	1.2	1.1	2.8	1.4	1.9	0.2
Chicago, IL	20.6	5.2	8.4	3.5	0.4	0.9	1.1	1.0	0.2
Cincinnati, OH	6.0	1.8	0.3	0.8	0.2	0.9	0.3	1.6	0.2
Clarksville, TN	5.3	1.7	1.1	0.9	0.4	0.4	0.4	0.3	0.1
Cleveland, OH	5.9	2.5	0.3	1.0	0.5	0.4	0.3	0.7	0.1
College Station, TX	13.4	7.9	1.6	1.0	0.1	0.5	1.2	0.9	0.2
Colorado Springs, CO	7.5	2.1	2.1	1.5	0.3	0.3	0.3	0.4	0.4
Columbia, MO	9.1	5.3	0.5	1.3	0.1	0.3	0.3	1.0	0.2
Columbia, SC	5.0	2.1	0.5	0.8	0.3	0.3	0.5	0.4	0.1
Columbus, OH	12.7	5.1	1.2	0.8	0.5	0.5	0.3	4.2	0.1
Dallas, TX	24.8	2.8	15.4	0.7	0.4	2.6	0.6	1.9	0.2
Davenport, IA	4.5	1.6	1.9	0.4	0.3	0.0	0.0	0.2	0.1
Denver, CO	15.0	3.0	7.3	1.4	0.3	0.8	0.5	1.4	0.3
Des Moines, IA	12.5	4.5	3.3	0.9	0.1	1.1	0.2	2.3	0.1
Durham, NC	15.0	4.6	2.8	1.1	0.6	3.2	0.7	1.5	0.4
Edison, NJ	46.9	37.6	1.0	2.8	1.5	0.3	1.7	1.8	0.2
El Paso, TX	23.1	1.1	20.7	0.5	0.1	0.3	0.2	0.2	0.0
Fargo, ND	9.0	3.5	0.1	1.0	0.2	0.1	0.2	3.7	0.2
Fayetteville, NC	7.1	2.3	0.6	1.0	0.9	0.8	0.6	0.6	0.1
Fort Collins, CO	6.8	3.0	1.2	1.4	0.1	0.2	0.4	0.3	0.2
Fort Wayne, IN	8.2	3.9	1.9	0.8	0.1	0.7	0.3	0.4	0.1
Fort Worth, TX	16.8	3.4	9.8	0.6	0.3	0.9	0.5	1.2	0.2
Grand Rapids, MI	10.9	2.3	3.3	1.2	0.6	1.8	0.2	1.3	0.3
Greeley, CO	11.5	1.0	7.4	0.4	0.2	1.2	0.2	1.1	0.1
Green Bay, WI	9.9	2.0	5.9	0.5	0.1	0.6	0.2	0.5	0.0
Greensboro, NC	11.0	3.9	2.0	1.2	0.6	0.6	0.5	2.0	0.2
Honolulu, HI	27.4	23.2	0.1	0.8	0.1	0.1	0.2	0.1	0.2
Houston, TX	29.3	6.0	11.4	1.1	1.1	6.3	1.3	1.9	0.2
Huntsville, AL	6.6	2.3	1.7	0.7	0.4	0.5	0.2	0.6	0.1
Indianapolis, IN	9.7	2.8	3.0	0.5	0.4	0.9	0.3	1.6	0.1
Jacksonville, FL	11.3	4.0	0.6	1.8	2.0	0.8	1.3	0.6	0.2
Kansas City, MO	8.2	2.5	2.3	0.6	0.5	0.6	0.3	1.2	0.1
Lafayette, LA	4.3	1.8	0.5	0.7	0.2	0.4	0.2	0.2	0.1
Lakeland, FL	10.9	1.8	1.3	0.8	4.0	0.5	1.4	0.2	0.9
Las Vegas, NV	21.0	5.3	9.2	1.6	1.1	2.3	0.8	0.4	0.4
Lexington, KY	9.7	3.7	2.4	1.0	0.2	0.5	0.3	1.2	0.2
Lincoln, NE	8.5	4.5	1.3	0.9	0.2	0.4	0.3	0.8	0.1
Little Rock, AR	7.7	2.7	2.3	0.7	0.1	1.0	0.3	0.5	0.1
Los Angeles, CA	36.9	11.0	12.5	2.4	0.3	8.4	1.1	0.7	0.4
Louisville, KY	7.7	2.5	0.7	0.9	1.6	0.4	0.3	1.2	0.1

Table continued on following page.

Appendix A: Comparative Statistics   A-33

| City | Percent of Population Born in | | | | | | | | |
	Any Foreign Country	Asia	Mexico	Europe	Caribbean	Central America[1]	South America	Africa	Canada
Madison, WI	12.1	6.7	1.5	1.4	0.2	0.3	0.8	1.0	0.3
Manchester, NH	14.5	5.1	0.5	2.5	1.6	1.2	0.8	1.9	0.8
Memphis, TN	6.2	1.5	2.2	0.3	0.2	0.9	0.2	0.8	0.1
Miami, FL	58.3	1.1	0.9	2.0	32.5	11.9	9.6	0.3	0.2
Midland, TX	14.1	1.8	8.6	0.3	1.2	0.6	0.4	0.8	0.4
Milwaukee, WI	10.0	2.9	4.8	0.8	0.4	0.2	0.2	0.7	0.1
Minneapolis, MN	15.6	4.0	2.4	1.3	0.3	0.4	1.3	5.6	0.3
Nashville, TN	13.3	4.0	3.1	0.9	0.4	1.9	0.3	2.5	0.2
New Haven, CT	17.8	4.6	3.1	1.9	2.5	1.0	2.9	1.2	0.5
New Orleans, LA	5.5	2.0	0.3	0.8	0.3	1.5	0.3	0.2	0.1
New York, NY	36.8	10.9	2.0	5.3	10.2	1.4	4.8	1.7	0.3
Oklahoma City, OK	11.8	3.3	6.0	0.4	0.2	1.0	0.3	0.6	0.1
Omaha, NE	10.7	3.4	3.8	0.6	0.1	1.0	0.3	1.3	0.1
Orlando, FL	22.0	2.9	0.5	1.5	6.9	1.2	8.0	0.6	0.3
Peoria, IL	7.6	4.7	1.2	0.5	0.1	0.2	0.3	0.3	0.1
Philadelphia, PA	14.1	5.5	0.5	2.2	2.7	0.6	0.9	1.6	0.1
Phoenix, AZ	19.4	3.4	11.9	1.3	0.3	0.9	0.4	0.8	0.4
Pittsburgh, PA	9.0	4.8	0.3	1.9	0.3	0.1	0.5	0.8	0.2
Portland, OR	13.5	5.9	2.0	2.7	0.3	0.5	0.3	1.0	0.5
Providence, RI	28.7	4.2	0.6	2.2	12.3	5.0	1.4	2.7	0.2
Provo, UT	11.0	2.0	4.4	0.5	0.1	0.6	2.3	0.3	0.4
Raleigh, NC	13.4	3.9	2.7	1.4	0.9	1.4	0.7	2.1	0.3
Reno, NV	15.9	5.3	6.2	1.3	0.2	1.6	0.4	0.3	0.3
Richmond, VA	7.0	1.5	0.8	0.7	0.4	2.5	0.4	0.6	0.2
Riverside, CA	22.6	5.1	13.2	0.9	0.2	2.0	0.6	0.3	0.2
Rochester, MN	14.1	5.8	1.5	1.6	0.2	0.2	0.5	3.9	0.2
Sacramento, CA	22.2	10.7	6.9	1.5	0.1	0.8	0.2	0.6	0.2
Salt Lake City, UT	17.1	4.6	6.4	2.0	0.3	0.6	1.3	1.0	0.4
San Antonio, TX	14.3	2.6	9.1	0.6	0.2	0.8	0.4	0.3	0.1
San Diego, CA	26.1	11.9	9.1	2.3	0.2	0.5	0.8	0.9	0.4
San Francisco, CA	34.3	22.2	2.4	4.5	0.2	2.5	1.0	0.5	0.6
San Jose, CA	39.7	25.6	9.0	2.2	0.1	1.0	0.6	0.8	0.4
Santa Rosa, CA	20.1	4.0	11.6	1.7	0.0	0.9	0.3	0.8	0.3
Savannah, GA	6.2	2.7	0.7	0.9	0.4	0.4	0.5	0.3	0.1
Seattle, WA	18.8	10.6	1.2	2.5	0.1	0.5	0.5	2.1	1.0
Sioux Falls, SD	8.5	2.3	0.5	0.9	0.1	0.9	0.1	3.5	0.1
Springfield, IL	4.5	2.5	0.4	0.5	0.2	0.1	0.2	0.5	0.1
Tallahassee, FL	8.1	3.6	0.2	0.9	1.0	0.4	0.7	0.9	0.3
Tampa, FL	17.2	3.8	1.1	1.4	6.9	1.1	2.0	0.4	0.4
Tucson, AZ	15.3	2.7	9.5	1.0	0.1	0.4	0.3	0.9	0.3
Tulsa, OK	11.2	2.7	5.6	0.5	0.2	1.0	0.4	0.5	0.1
Tuscaloosa, AL	4.6	2.2	0.5	0.4	0.1	0.9	0.1	0.3	0.1
Virginia Beach, VA	9.4	4.9	0.5	1.6	0.7	0.6	0.5	0.4	0.1
Washington, DC	13.7	3.0	0.6	2.5	1.2	2.6	1.3	2.1	0.3
Wichita, KS	10.2	3.8	4.3	0.5	0.1	0.6	0.2	0.6	0.1
Winston-Salem, NC	9.9	2.1	4.3	0.7	0.4	1.1	0.5	0.6	0.1
U.S.	13.6	4.2	3.5	1.5	1.3	1.1	1.0	0.7	0.2

Note: (1) Excludes Mexico
Source: U.S. Census Bureau, 2015-2019 American Community Survey 5-Year Estimates

A-34 Appendix A: Comparative Statistics

Foreign-Born Population: Metro Area

Metro Area	Any Foreign Country	Percent of Population Born in							
		Asia	Mexico	Europe	Caribbean	Central America[1]	South America	Africa	Canada
Albuquerque, NM	8.9	1.8	5.2	0.7	0.3	0.2	0.3	0.3	0.1
Allentown, PA	9.3	2.8	0.4	1.6	2.2	0.6	1.2	0.5	0.1
Anchorage, AK	8.9	4.9	0.7	1.1	0.4	0.1	0.4	0.5	0.3
Ann Arbor, MI	12.5	7.4	0.4	2.1	0.2	0.3	0.5	0.9	0.6
Athens, GA	7.8	2.3	2.1	0.8	0.3	0.9	0.7	0.5	0.1
Atlanta, GA	13.8	4.6	2.6	1.2	1.4	1.1	1.1	1.6	0.2
Austin, TX	15.2	4.5	6.4	1.1	0.4	1.2	0.6	0.7	0.3
Baton Rouge, LA	4.0	1.5	0.7	0.3	0.2	0.9	0.2	0.2	0.1
Boise City, ID	6.5	1.6	2.7	1.0	0.0	0.2	0.3	0.3	0.3
Boston, MA	18.9	6.1	0.2	3.3	3.4	1.6	2.1	1.6	0.5
Boulder, CO	10.7	3.5	2.8	2.3	0.1	0.3	0.7	0.3	0.5
Cape Coral, FL	16.7	1.3	2.5	2.0	5.9	1.8	2.0	0.1	1.1
Cedar Rapids, IA	3.8	1.8	0.5	0.4	0.1	0.1	0.1	0.8	0.1
Charleston, SC	5.4	1.5	1.1	1.0	0.3	0.5	0.5	0.2	0.2
Charlotte, NC	10.1	3.0	2.1	1.1	0.6	1.4	0.9	0.9	0.2
Chicago, IL	17.7	5.2	6.5	3.7	0.3	0.6	0.6	0.6	0.2
Cincinnati, OH	4.8	2.1	0.5	0.7	0.1	0.4	0.2	0.7	0.1
Clarksville, TN	4.1	1.3	0.7	0.7	0.3	0.3	0.3	0.3	0.1
Cleveland, OH	6.0	2.2	0.3	2.2	0.2	0.2	0.2	0.4	0.2
College Station, TX	12.5	4.2	5.5	0.7	0.1	0.5	0.7	0.7	0.1
Colorado Springs, CO	6.9	1.9	1.8	1.6	0.3	0.3	0.3	0.4	0.3
Columbia, MO	6.1	3.3	0.4	1.0	0.1	0.2	0.2	0.6	0.2
Columbia, SC	5.0	1.6	1.1	0.7	0.3	0.5	0.3	0.4	0.1
Columbus, OH	8.2	3.6	0.7	0.8	0.3	0.3	0.2	2.2	0.1
Dallas, TX	18.7	5.3	8.4	0.8	0.3	1.5	0.6	1.5	0.2
Davenport, IA	5.2	1.7	1.9	0.5	0.1	0.1	0.1	0.8	0.1
Denver, CO	12.1	3.3	4.9	1.4	0.2	0.5	0.5	1.0	0.3
Des Moines, IA	7.7	3.0	1.5	1.1	0.1	0.5	0.2	1.2	0.1
Durham, NC	11.7	3.6	2.6	1.4	0.4	2.0	0.5	0.9	0.4
Edison, NJ	29.5	8.7	1.5	4.4	6.9	2.0	4.4	1.4	0.2
El Paso, TX	24.2	1.0	22.0	0.4	0.1	0.3	0.2	0.2	0.0
Fargo, ND	6.7	2.7	0.2	0.8	0.1	0.1	0.2	2.4	0.3
Fayetteville, NC	6.2	1.6	1.4	0.9	0.7	0.8	0.4	0.3	0.1
Fort Collins, CO	5.6	1.9	1.3	1.3	0.1	0.2	0.4	0.2	0.2
Fort Wayne, IN	6.3	3.0	1.4	0.7	0.1	0.5	0.2	0.3	0.1
Fort Worth, TX	18.7	5.3	8.4	0.8	0.3	1.5	0.6	1.5	0.2
Grand Rapids, MI	6.8	2.1	1.8	1.0	0.4	0.6	0.1	0.5	0.2
Greeley, CO	8.7	0.9	5.9	0.4	0.2	0.6	0.2	0.5	0.1
Green Bay, WI	5.1	1.5	2.4	0.5	0.0	0.4	0.1	0.2	0.1
Greensboro, NC	8.8	2.9	2.5	0.8	0.4	0.6	0.4	1.0	0.2
Honolulu, HI	19.7	16.1	0.2	0.7	0.1	0.1	0.3	0.1	0.2
Houston, TX	23.4	6.0	8.9	1.0	0.8	3.6	1.3	1.4	0.3
Huntsville, AL	5.1	1.9	1.2	0.7	0.3	0.4	0.2	0.4	0.2
Indianapolis, IN	7.0	2.6	1.7	0.6	0.2	0.5	0.3	0.9	0.1
Jacksonville, FL	9.3	3.1	0.5	1.7	1.5	0.6	1.1	0.4	0.3
Kansas City, MO	6.9	2.3	2.0	0.6	0.2	0.6	0.3	0.7	0.1
Lafayette, LA	3.3	1.2	0.7	0.3	0.2	0.5	0.1	0.2	0.1
Lakeland, FL	10.0	1.3	2.3	0.9	2.8	0.6	1.4	0.2	0.5
Las Vegas, NV	22.2	7.2	8.2	1.6	1.1	2.0	0.9	0.8	0.4
Lexington, KY	7.5	2.6	2.1	0.9	0.2	0.5	0.2	0.8	0.1
Lincoln, NE	7.5	4.0	1.1	0.8	0.2	0.3	0.3	0.7	0.1
Little Rock, AR	4.3	1.4	1.3	0.5	0.1	0.6	0.2	0.2	0.1
Los Angeles, CA	33.1	12.8	12.1	1.7	0.3	4.3	0.9	0.6	0.3
Louisville, KY	5.9	1.9	0.9	0.7	0.9	0.3	0.2	0.7	0.1

Table continued on following page.

Appendix A: Comparative Statistics   A-35

Metro Area	Percent of Population Born in								
	Any Foreign Country	Asia	Mexico	Europe	Caribbean	Central America[1]	South America	Africa	Canada
Madison, WI	7.6	3.6	1.2	1.0	0.1	0.2	0.6	0.6	0.2
Manchester, NH	9.7	3.6	0.4	1.8	1.0	0.5	0.8	0.9	0.8
Memphis, TN	5.3	1.7	1.6	0.4	0.2	0.5	0.2	0.6	0.1
Miami, FL	40.7	2.1	1.1	2.3	21.2	4.2	8.8	0.4	0.5
Midland, TX	13.4	1.6	8.8	0.3	1.0	0.5	0.3	0.6	0.3
Milwaukee, WI	7.4	2.8	2.3	1.3	0.2	0.2	0.2	0.4	0.1
Minneapolis, MN	10.7	4.2	1.3	1.1	0.2	0.4	0.5	2.8	0.2
Nashville, TN	8.3	2.6	2.0	0.7	0.2	1.0	0.3	1.1	0.2
New Haven, CT	12.7	3.3	1.0	2.8	1.9	0.5	1.9	0.9	0.3
New Orleans, LA	7.6	2.1	0.6	0.6	0.7	2.7	0.5	0.3	0.1
New York, NY	29.5	8.7	1.5	4.4	6.9	2.0	4.4	1.4	0.2
Oklahoma City, OK	7.9	2.4	3.5	0.4	0.1	0.6	0.3	0.4	0.1
Omaha, NE	7.4	2.4	2.5	0.6	0.1	0.7	0.2	0.9	0.1
Orlando, FL	18.5	3.0	1.1	1.5	5.7	1.1	5.2	0.6	0.3
Peoria, IL	3.3	1.7	0.6	0.4	0.0	0.1	0.1	0.1	0.1
Philadelphia, PA	11.0	4.5	0.9	1.9	1.3	0.4	0.6	1.1	0.2
Phoenix, AZ	14.3	3.4	7.2	1.3	0.3	0.6	0.3	0.5	0.6
Pittsburgh, PA	3.9	2.0	0.1	1.0	0.1	0.1	0.2	0.3	0.1
Portland, OR	12.6	5.0	3.1	2.3	0.1	0.5	0.3	0.6	0.4
Providence, RI	13.3	2.3	0.2	4.2	2.3	1.4	1.0	1.6	0.2
Provo, UT	7.3	1.1	2.8	0.5	0.1	0.5	1.6	0.2	0.3
Raleigh, NC	12.3	4.4	2.6	1.4	0.6	1.1	0.6	1.2	0.4
Reno, NV	14.0	3.9	6.1	1.1	0.2	1.5	0.4	0.3	0.3
Richmond, VA	7.9	3.2	0.6	1.0	0.4	1.4	0.5	0.6	0.1
Riverside, CA	21.3	4.9	12.3	0.8	0.2	1.7	0.6	0.4	0.3
Rochester, MN	8.5	3.4	1.0	1.1	0.1	0.3	0.3	2.1	0.2
Sacramento, CA	18.6	8.8	4.7	2.7	0.1	0.6	0.3	0.5	0.3
Salt Lake City, UT	12.4	3.1	4.6	1.2	0.1	0.6	1.4	0.6	0.3
San Antonio, TX	11.8	2.2	7.3	0.6	0.2	0.7	0.4	0.3	0.1
San Diego, CA	23.4	9.0	10.1	1.8	0.2	0.5	0.6	0.6	0.4
San Francisco, CA	30.7	17.5	4.9	2.9	0.2	2.5	1.0	0.7	0.5
San Jose, CA	38.6	25.4	7.0	3.1	0.1	0.9	0.7	0.7	0.5
Santa Rosa, CA	16.4	2.9	9.0	1.9	0.1	0.9	0.5	0.4	0.4
Savannah, GA	5.7	2.0	1.1	0.8	0.5	0.4	0.4	0.3	0.2
Seattle, WA	18.7	9.9	2.4	2.6	0.2	0.5	0.5	1.5	0.7
Sioux Falls, SD	6.2	1.6	0.4	0.7	0.1	0.7	0.1	2.4	0.1
Springfield, IL	3.1	1.6	0.3	0.4	0.1	0.1	0.1	0.3	0.1
Tallahassee, FL	6.1	2.2	0.5	0.8	0.9	0.5	0.5	0.6	0.2
Tampa, FL	13.9	2.8	1.3	2.2	3.7	0.8	1.9	0.5	0.6
Tucson, AZ	13.0	2.3	7.6	1.2	0.1	0.3	0.3	0.6	0.4
Tulsa, OK	6.6	1.9	2.9	0.5	0.1	0.5	0.3	0.3	0.1
Tuscaloosa, AL	3.4	1.1	0.9	0.4	0.1	0.6	0.1	0.2	0.1
Virginia Beach, VA	6.5	2.8	0.4	1.1	0.6	0.7	0.4	0.4	0.1
Washington, DC	22.8	8.2	0.8	1.8	1.1	4.9	2.2	3.5	0.2
Wichita, KS	7.4	2.7	3.0	0.4	0.1	0.4	0.2	0.4	0.1
Winston-Salem, NC	6.8	1.4	3.0	0.6	0.2	0.9	0.4	0.3	0.1
U.S.	13.6	4.2	3.5	1.5	1.3	1.1	1.0	0.7	0.2

Note: Figures cover the Metropolitan Statistical Area—see Appendix B for areas included; (1) Excludes Mexico
Source: U.S. Census Bureau, 2015-2019 American Community Survey 5-Year Estimates

A-36 Appendix A: Comparative Statistics

Marital Status: City

City	Never Married	Now Married[1]	Separated	Widowed	Divorced
Albuquerque, NM	37.7	40.8	1.5	5.6	14.4
Allentown, PA	47.4	33.2	3.6	5.4	10.4
Anchorage, AK	34.5	48.4	1.8	3.6	11.7
Ann Arbor, MI	56.5	33.8	0.4	2.6	6.6
Athens, GA	54.4	32.2	1.6	3.5	8.2
Atlanta, GA	55.2	27.3	1.9	5.1	10.5
Austin, TX	43.2	40.9	1.7	3.1	11.0
Baton Rouge, LA	50.2	30.4	2.0	6.4	11.0
Boise City, ID	34.1	46.7	0.9	4.5	13.9
Boston, MA	56.0	30.3	2.6	3.9	7.2
Boulder, CO	55.6	32.4	0.8	2.6	8.6
Cape Coral, FL	25.5	52.0	1.5	7.3	13.7
Cedar Rapids, IA	35.2	45.7	1.0	6.0	12.1
Charleston, SC	41.9	41.6	1.5	5.2	9.7
Charlotte, NC	40.7	42.5	2.6	4.0	10.2
Chicago, IL	48.7	35.5	2.3	5.2	8.3
Cincinnati, OH	52.0	28.3	2.4	5.1	12.1
Clarksville, TN	30.2	50.9	2.2	4.0	12.6
Cleveland, OH	51.4	25.1	3.2	6.2	14.1
College Station, TX	59.7	32.4	0.8	2.1	5.0
Colorado Springs, CO	31.2	49.5	1.6	4.6	13.1
Columbia, MO	48.0	39.0	1.2	3.4	8.4
Columbia, SC	55.8	27.8	2.6	4.4	9.4
Columbus, OH	45.0	36.3	2.1	4.3	12.4
Dallas, TX	41.6	40.4	3.2	4.5	10.4
Davenport, IA	36.7	42.6	1.5	6.3	12.9
Denver, CO	42.5	39.5	1.8	4.0	12.2
Des Moines, IA	39.0	40.0	2.0	5.3	13.7
Durham, NC	43.1	39.9	2.5	4.3	10.2
Edison, NJ	25.7	61.0	1.0	6.1	6.2
El Paso, TX	35.3	44.5	3.5	5.8	10.8
Fargo, ND	42.8	42.9	1.1	4.5	8.7
Fayetteville, NC	38.4	40.7	3.6	5.5	11.8
Fort Collins, CO	46.6	40.6	0.8	3.3	8.7
Fort Wayne, IN	35.3	44.4	1.5	5.8	13.0
Fort Worth, TX	35.4	46.3	2.3	4.5	11.4
Grand Rapids, MI	46.2	36.9	1.3	5.1	10.4
Greeley, CO	35.8	46.0	1.7	5.1	11.3
Green Bay, WI	37.9	43.2	1.5	5.1	12.3
Greensboro, NC	42.2	38.4	2.6	5.7	11.0
Honolulu, HI	36.2	45.8	1.2	6.9	9.9
Houston, TX	41.0	41.3	3.2	4.6	9.9
Huntsville, AL	34.9	44.8	2.0	6.0	12.3
Indianapolis, IN	42.9	37.7	1.8	5.1	12.5
Jacksonville, FL	35.5	42.6	2.2	5.6	14.0
Kansas City, MO	39.7	39.9	2.1	5.4	12.9
Lafayette, LA	42.2	38.8	1.7	6.0	11.2
Lakeland, FL	34.9	41.7	2.1	8.2	13.1
Las Vegas, NV	34.9	43.3	2.3	5.5	14.1
Lexington, KY	38.8	43.1	1.7	4.6	11.8
Lincoln, NE	39.0	45.6	1.0	4.4	10.0
Little Rock, AR	37.7	39.9	2.5	6.2	13.7
Los Angeles, CA	45.8	38.8	2.6	4.6	8.2
Louisville, KY	36.3	42.1	2.1	6.1	13.4
Madison, WI	50.2	37.3	0.8	3.3	8.4
Manchester, NH	38.8	39.9	2.0	5.8	13.4

Table continued on following page.

Appendix A: Comparative Statistics   A-37

City	Never Married	Now Married[1]	Separated	Widowed	Divorced
Memphis, TN	47.8	31.3	3.7	5.8	11.4
Miami, FL	40.2	36.0	3.7	6.6	13.5
Midland, TX	30.1	51.1	2.1	5.1	11.6
Milwaukee, WI	53.3	30.0	1.9	4.6	10.2
Minneapolis, MN	50.5	34.4	1.6	2.9	10.5
Nashville, TN	40.7	40.8	1.8	4.7	11.9
New Haven, CT	57.8	26.1	1.9	4.3	9.9
New Orleans, LA	49.2	29.4	2.7	5.9	12.8
New York, NY	43.4	40.4	3.0	5.4	7.8
Oklahoma City, OK	33.3	45.8	2.3	5.4	13.2
Omaha, NE	36.4	45.9	1.6	4.8	11.2
Orlando, FL	43.0	36.5	3.1	4.1	13.3
Peoria, IL	40.5	39.9	1.3	6.2	12.1
Philadelphia, PA	50.7	30.6	3.3	6.2	9.3
Phoenix, AZ	39.2	42.1	2.0	4.3	12.4
Pittsburgh, PA	52.4	30.7	1.9	5.8	9.3
Portland, OR	41.3	40.9	1.5	3.8	12.5
Providence, RI	54.4	30.6	2.3	4.2	8.5
Provo, UT	47.7	44.6	1.1	2.0	4.5
Raleigh, NC	42.7	40.3	2.5	3.7	10.8
Reno, NV	35.5	42.5	2.2	4.8	14.9
Richmond, VA	52.7	27.3	3.0	5.4	11.6
Riverside, CA	43.1	40.8	2.4	4.7	9.0
Rochester, MN	32.1	52.3	1.0	5.2	9.4
Sacramento, CA	40.2	41.0	2.4	5.1	11.4
Salt Lake City, UT	42.4	41.4	1.5	3.9	10.8
San Antonio, TX	39.0	40.6	3.1	5.2	12.1
San Diego, CA	40.0	44.3	1.7	4.1	9.8
San Francisco, CA	45.8	40.3	1.3	4.6	7.9
San Jose, CA	35.4	51.0	1.6	4.2	7.8
Santa Rosa, CA	34.6	44.5	1.9	5.5	13.5
Savannah, GA	47.5	31.2	3.0	5.9	12.4
Seattle, WA	44.5	41.1	1.2	3.4	9.9
Sioux Falls, SD	33.6	48.8	1.4	5.0	11.1
Springfield, IL	37.5	40.8	1.5	6.4	13.7
Tallahassee, FL	56.3	29.3	1.3	3.3	9.8
Tampa, FL	40.4	38.4	2.7	5.0	13.6
Tucson, AZ	42.5	36.0	2.2	5.4	14.0
Tulsa, OK	34.5	42.5	2.4	5.9	14.8
Tuscaloosa, AL	53.2	30.8	1.9	4.3	9.9
Virginia Beach, VA	30.4	51.1	2.4	5.0	11.1
Washington, DC	56.4	28.9	2.1	4.1	8.5
Wichita, KS	33.5	45.6	2.0	5.6	13.3
Winston-Salem, NC	40.4	39.9	2.8	5.9	11.1
U.S.	33.4	48.1	1.9	5.8	10.9

Note: Figures are percentages and cover the population 15 years of age and older; (1) Excludes separated
Source: U.S. Census Bureau, 2015-2019 American Community Survey 5-Year Estimates

A-38 Appendix A: Comparative Statistics

Marital Status: Metro Area

Metro Area	Never Married	Now Married[1]	Separated	Widowed	Divorced
Albuquerque, NM	34.9	43.9	1.5	5.8	13.9
Allentown, PA	32.3	49.3	2.1	6.4	9.9
Anchorage, AK	33.9	48.7	1.8	3.7	11.9
Ann Arbor, MI	43.0	44.1	0.8	3.7	8.4
Athens, GA	42.7	41.9	1.6	4.7	9.1
Atlanta, GA	35.3	47.4	1.9	4.6	10.8
Austin, TX	36.4	47.4	1.7	3.7	10.8
Baton Rouge, LA	37.2	43.2	2.1	6.1	11.4
Boise City, ID	29.6	52.2	1.1	4.5	12.6
Boston, MA	37.1	47.5	1.5	5.1	8.7
Boulder, CO	38.1	46.2	1.0	3.7	11.0
Cape Coral, FL	26.2	50.8	1.6	8.2	13.2
Cedar Rapids, IA	30.0	52.0	0.9	5.8	11.2
Charleston, SC	34.5	46.9	2.4	5.5	10.7
Charlotte, NC	32.6	49.4	2.4	5.2	10.3
Chicago, IL	37.0	46.9	1.6	5.5	8.9
Cincinnati, OH	32.3	49.0	1.6	5.7	11.3
Clarksville, TN	28.3	52.5	2.0	5.1	12.0
Cleveland, OH	34.9	45.0	1.6	6.6	11.8
College Station, TX	46.3	40.1	1.9	3.8	7.9
Colorado Springs, CO	29.5	53.1	1.5	4.2	11.8
Columbia, MO	40.0	44.6	1.2	4.4	9.7
Columbia, SC	36.6	44.2	2.8	5.7	10.7
Columbus, OH	34.7	47.0	1.7	4.9	11.6
Dallas, TX	32.8	50.3	2.1	4.4	10.5
Davenport, IA	29.9	50.2	1.3	6.6	12.0
Denver, CO	33.1	49.6	1.4	4.1	11.8
Des Moines, IA	29.9	52.1	1.3	5.0	11.8
Durham, NC	36.9	45.4	2.3	5.1	10.2
Edison, NJ	37.8	46.3	2.3	5.7	7.9
El Paso, TX	35.4	45.2	3.5	5.5	10.3
Fargo, ND	36.8	49.6	0.9	4.3	8.3
Fayetteville, NC	33.8	46.1	3.2	5.8	11.2
Fort Collins, CO	34.8	50.1	0.9	4.0	10.2
Fort Wayne, IN	31.5	49.6	1.3	5.7	11.9
Fort Worth, TX	32.8	50.3	2.1	4.4	10.5
Grand Rapids, MI	32.7	51.3	1.0	4.9	10.2
Greeley, CO	28.2	55.2	1.4	4.5	10.8
Green Bay, WI	30.2	53.2	0.9	5.2	10.5
Greensboro, NC	33.6	46.1	2.7	6.3	11.3
Honolulu, HI	33.9	50.1	1.2	6.3	8.6
Houston, TX	33.7	49.8	2.5	4.5	9.6
Huntsville, AL	30.1	50.8	1.7	5.6	11.8
Indianapolis, IN	33.5	47.9	1.4	5.3	11.9
Jacksonville, FL	31.4	47.8	1.9	5.8	13.2
Kansas City, MO	30.5	50.4	1.6	5.4	12.0
Lafayette, LA	34.7	46.2	1.9	6.0	11.3
Lakeland, FL	31.8	46.9	2.1	7.2	12.1
Las Vegas, NV	34.7	43.9	2.3	5.2	13.9
Lexington, KY	34.3	46.5	1.7	5.1	12.3
Lincoln, NE	36.7	48.2	0.9	4.4	9.7
Little Rock, AR	30.7	47.4	2.1	6.3	13.6
Los Angeles, CA	39.9	44.7	2.1	4.9	8.4
Louisville, KY	31.6	47.4	1.9	6.1	13.0
Madison, WI	36.5	48.8	0.8	4.2	9.6
Manchester, NH	30.4	51.3	1.4	5.3	11.6

Table continued on following page.

Appendix A: Comparative Statistics A-39

Metro Area	Never Married	Now Married[1]	Separated	Widowed	Divorced
Memphis, TN	38.4	42.0	2.9	5.7	11.0
Miami, FL	34.6	43.3	2.8	6.4	12.8
Midland, TX	29.2	51.8	2.0	5.0	11.9
Milwaukee, WI	37.0	46.4	1.1	5.5	10.1
Minneapolis, MN	33.2	51.4	1.0	4.3	10.1
Nashville, TN	32.0	50.3	1.6	5.0	11.2
New Haven, CT	37.9	43.6	1.3	6.2	10.9
New Orleans, LA	37.8	41.3	2.3	6.3	12.2
New York, NY	37.8	46.3	2.3	5.7	7.9
Oklahoma City, OK	31.4	48.3	2.0	5.6	12.7
Omaha, NE	31.4	51.6	1.3	4.9	10.7
Orlando, FL	34.8	46.0	2.2	5.2	11.8
Peoria, IL	29.9	50.3	1.1	7.0	11.8
Philadelphia, PA	37.2	45.5	2.1	6.0	9.2
Phoenix, AZ	34.0	47.2	1.6	5.1	12.1
Pittsburgh, PA	31.7	49.4	1.7	7.3	9.9
Portland, OR	32.1	50.0	1.4	4.5	12.0
Providence, RI	36.0	45.2	1.6	6.1	11.0
Provo, UT	32.3	58.4	1.0	2.7	5.6
Raleigh, NC	32.0	51.7	2.3	4.2	9.9
Reno, NV	30.9	48.6	1.9	4.9	13.7
Richmond, VA	34.9	46.0	2.5	5.8	10.9
Riverside, CA	36.0	47.0	2.3	5.1	9.6
Rochester, MN	27.8	56.9	0.8	5.1	9.4
Sacramento, CA	33.5	48.2	2.1	5.2	10.9
Salt Lake City, UT	32.1	52.1	1.7	3.8	10.3
San Antonio, TX	35.1	45.6	2.6	5.2	11.5
San Diego, CA	35.9	47.6	1.7	4.7	10.1
San Francisco, CA	36.3	48.7	1.5	4.7	8.8
San Jose, CA	33.6	53.2	1.4	4.2	7.5
Santa Rosa, CA	32.1	47.8	1.7	5.3	13.1
Savannah, GA	34.9	44.9	2.2	5.8	12.1
Seattle, WA	32.6	50.8	1.4	4.2	11.0
Sioux Falls, SD	30.2	53.1	1.2	5.0	10.5
Springfield, IL	32.1	47.5	1.3	6.1	13.0
Tallahassee, FL	43.9	39.0	1.6	4.6	10.9
Tampa, FL	31.2	45.9	2.1	7.0	13.9
Tucson, AZ	34.4	45.0	1.8	5.9	12.9
Tulsa, OK	28.4	50.3	1.9	6.2	13.2
Tuscaloosa, AL	40.8	41.1	2.1	5.6	10.3
Virginia Beach, VA	33.5	47.3	2.7	5.6	11.0
Washington, DC	36.1	48.9	1.9	4.4	8.8
Wichita, KS	30.0	50.3	1.6	5.9	12.2
Winston-Salem, NC	29.8	49.6	2.5	6.8	11.3
U.S.	33.4	48.1	1.9	5.8	10.9

Note: Figures are percentages and cover the population 15 years of age and older; Figures cover the Metropolitan Statistical Area—see Appendix B for areas included; (1) Excludes separated
Source: U.S. Census Bureau, 2015-2019 American Community Survey 5-Year Estimates

A-40 Appendix A: Comparative Statistics

Disability by Age: City

City	All Ages	Under 18 Years Old	18 to 64 Years Old	65 Years and Over
Albuquerque, NM	13.4	4.1	11.7	34.9
Allentown, PA	17.1	9.2	16.9	37.5
Anchorage, AK	11.4	3.6	10.3	36.3
Ann Arbor, MI	7.1	3.0	4.9	25.7
Athens, GA	11.5	6.6	9.4	35.1
Atlanta, GA	11.9	4.7	9.7	36.8
Austin, TX	8.4	3.9	6.9	30.7
Baton Rouge, LA	16.8	8.5	14.6	40.3
Boise City, ID	10.9	3.3	9.0	31.7
Boston, MA	11.9	5.3	8.9	41.0
Boulder, CO	6.3	2.8	4.5	23.5
Cape Coral, FL	12.9	3.4	9.3	29.9
Cedar Rapids, IA	10.6	3.5	8.5	29.7
Charleston, SC	9.9	2.8	7.2	30.6
Charlotte, NC	7.9	2.5	6.5	29.7
Chicago, IL	10.5	2.9	8.3	35.5
Cincinnati, OH	13.3	5.5	11.9	35.8
Clarksville, TN	14.9	4.7	16.1	41.1
Cleveland, OH	20.0	8.6	18.8	44.3
College Station, TX	6.3	3.8	4.9	28.7
Colorado Springs, CO	13.0	4.6	11.7	33.8
Columbia, MO	10.1	2.9	8.0	38.2
Columbia, SC	12.6	5.4	10.8	35.7
Columbus, OH	11.7	5.0	10.5	35.3
Dallas, TX	9.6	3.3	8.1	35.0
Davenport, IA	12.4	4.8	10.3	33.5
Denver, CO	9.6	3.5	7.4	33.5
Des Moines, IA	14.0	5.8	12.7	38.2
Durham, NC	9.1	2.9	7.3	31.9
Edison, NJ	8.2	3.3	5.3	29.0
El Paso, TX	13.7	5.0	11.3	43.4
Fargo, ND	10.0	2.8	7.7	36.5
Fayetteville, NC	17.5	6.7	16.6	44.5
Fort Collins, CO	7.9	2.8	6.0	30.0
Fort Wayne, IN	13.6	5.2	12.6	34.0
Fort Worth, TX	10.2	3.8	9.1	35.9
Grand Rapids, MI	13.2	5.4	12.0	35.8
Greeley, CO	11.2	2.3	10.2	36.2
Green Bay, WI	13.0	6.6	11.6	32.5
Greensboro, NC	10.7	4.3	8.7	30.9
Honolulu, HI	11.2	2.6	7.1	31.4
Houston, TX	9.5	3.2	7.7	35.6
Huntsville, AL	13.7	4.8	11.2	34.7
Indianapolis, IN	13.3	5.1	12.0	37.5
Jacksonville, FL	13.5	5.0	11.5	37.6
Kansas City, MO	12.7	3.9	11.2	36.2
Lafayette, LA	12.4	3.7	10.7	32.7
Lakeland, FL	15.8	4.3	11.8	37.1
Las Vegas, NV	12.9	3.7	10.8	36.3
Lexington, KY	12.4	4.5	10.7	34.3
Lincoln, NE	10.8	4.4	8.6	32.7
Little Rock, AR	13.4	5.8	11.5	35.4
Los Angeles, CA	10.1	3.1	7.3	37.3
Louisville, KY	14.8	4.6	13.4	36.4
Madison, WI	8.0	3.2	6.2	26.3

Table continued on following page.

Appendix A: Comparative Statistics A-41

City	All Ages	Under 18 Years Old	18 to 64 Years Old	65 Years and Over
Manchester, NH	14.1	6.0	11.7	39.8
Memphis, TN	13.5	5.1	12.0	37.8
Miami, FL	11.8	3.9	7.7	36.3
Midland, TX	9.7	2.4	8.2	38.5
Milwaukee, WI	13.0	5.7	11.8	38.8
Minneapolis, MN	11.2	4.7	10.1	32.9
Nashville, TN	11.5	4.0	9.8	35.4
New Haven, CT	10.2	5.2	8.6	31.9
New Orleans, LA	14.2	5.0	12.3	36.4
New York, NY	10.8	3.4	7.9	35.1
Oklahoma City, OK	13.2	4.2	12.0	38.6
Omaha, NE	10.9	3.3	9.7	32.3
Orlando, FL	10.1	5.4	8.2	32.5
Peoria, IL	12.4	3.2	11.0	33.2
Philadelphia, PA	16.7	6.0	15.0	43.2
Phoenix, AZ	10.7	3.9	9.5	34.7
Pittsburgh, PA	13.9	6.9	10.7	36.8
Portland, OR	12.1	4.1	10.0	35.4
Providence, RI	13.3	5.5	12.2	38.5
Provo, UT	8.2	4.2	6.8	38.3
Raleigh, NC	9.0	4.7	6.8	31.6
Reno, NV	12.2	5.2	10.3	30.7
Richmond, VA	15.2	6.7	13.2	38.0
Riverside, CA	11.2	3.9	9.1	40.7
Rochester, MN	10.5	4.7	8.2	30.1
Sacramento, CA	11.6	3.2	9.3	38.0
Salt Lake City, UT	10.8	3.2	9.1	35.7
San Antonio, TX	14.6	5.8	13.2	41.1
San Diego, CA	9.2	3.3	6.5	32.4
San Francisco, CA	10.2	2.3	6.3	35.2
San Jose, CA	8.6	2.6	6.1	33.1
Santa Rosa, CA	12.0	4.0	9.9	30.5
Savannah, GA	15.2	6.1	12.5	43.4
Seattle, WA	9.2	2.5	6.9	30.9
Sioux Falls, SD	10.2	3.3	9.0	30.1
Springfield, IL	14.9	5.8	12.9	33.6
Tallahassee, FL	9.9	4.7	8.2	30.5
Tampa, FL	12.2	3.7	9.9	39.4
Tucson, AZ	15.3	5.5	13.2	39.5
Tulsa, OK	14.5	4.7	13.5	36.2
Tuscaloosa, AL	11.1	2.8	9.5	32.4
Virginia Beach, VA	11.2	3.5	9.4	31.6
Washington, DC	11.7	4.1	9.6	35.3
Wichita, KS	13.7	4.6	12.4	36.3
Winston-Salem, NC	9.8	2.8	8.3	28.6
U.S.	12.6	4.2	10.3	34.5

Note: Figures show percent of the civilian noninstitutionalized population that reported having a disability. Disability status is determined from from six types of difficulty: vision, hearing, cognitive, ambulatory, self-care, and independent living. For children under 5 years old, hearing and vision difficulty are used to determine disability status. For children between the ages of 5 and 14, disability status is determined from hearing, vision, cognitive, ambulatory, and self-care difficulties. For people aged 15 years and older, they are considered to have a disability if they have difficulty with any one of the six difficulty types.
Source: U.S. Census Bureau, 2015-2019 American Community Survey 5-Year Estimates

A-42   Appendix A: Comparative Statistics

Disability by Age: Metro Area

Metro Area	All Ages	Under 18 Years Old	18 to 64 Years Old	65 Years and Over
Albuquerque, NM	14.3	4.1	12.2	36.6
Allentown, PA	13.3	5.7	10.8	31.8
Anchorage, AK	11.9	3.7	11.0	36.5
Ann Arbor, MI	9.4	3.7	7.3	27.9
Athens, GA	12.5	6.0	10.1	35.8
Atlanta, GA	10.0	3.5	8.4	32.5
Austin, TX	9.2	3.7	7.6	31.4
Baton Rouge, LA	14.8	6.2	13.0	38.1
Boise City, ID	12.0	4.0	10.5	33.0
Boston, MA	10.6	4.0	7.8	31.3
Boulder, CO	8.1	3.0	6.1	25.6
Cape Coral, FL	13.9	3.8	9.9	28.2
Cedar Rapids, IA	10.4	3.6	8.1	29.8
Charleston, SC	12.2	4.0	10.0	33.9
Charlotte, NC	10.5	3.4	8.7	32.4
Chicago, IL	9.9	3.0	7.7	31.8
Cincinnati, OH	12.4	4.7	10.6	32.7
Clarksville, TN	16.5	5.7	16.6	43.2
Cleveland, OH	14.2	5.2	11.7	33.8
College Station, TX	9.5	4.1	7.3	35.2
Colorado Springs, CO	12.4	4.4	11.4	32.7
Columbia, MO	12.1	4.0	10.0	37.2
Columbia, SC	14.1	4.6	12.2	36.8
Columbus, OH	12.0	4.7	10.3	33.7
Dallas, TX	9.5	3.4	7.9	33.7
Davenport, IA	12.3	4.4	9.6	31.8
Denver, CO	9.3	3.2	7.4	30.8
Des Moines, IA	10.6	4.0	8.9	31.4
Durham, NC	11.4	3.9	9.1	32.3
Edison, NJ	10.0	3.2	7.2	31.6
El Paso, TX	13.8	5.5	11.5	44.6
Fargo, ND	9.5	3.1	7.4	33.9
Fayetteville, NC	16.4	6.0	15.7	43.7
Fort Collins, CO	9.7	3.1	7.4	28.1
Fort Wayne, IN	12.6	4.5	11.3	32.8
Fort Worth, TX	9.5	3.4	7.9	33.7
Grand Rapids, MI	11.4	4.0	9.8	31.7
Greeley, CO	10.3	3.0	8.9	34.6
Green Bay, WI	11.2	4.7	9.1	29.4
Greensboro, NC	12.7	4.5	10.7	32.5
Honolulu, HI	10.9	2.9	7.4	32.8
Houston, TX	9.4	3.3	7.8	34.0
Huntsville, AL	13.7	4.9	11.3	37.7
Indianapolis, IN	12.2	4.5	10.5	35.0
Jacksonville, FL	13.2	4.7	11.0	34.7
Kansas City, MO	12.1	3.9	10.2	34.2
Lafayette, LA	14.5	5.0	12.9	39.1
Lakeland, FL	15.4	5.7	12.4	34.7
Las Vegas, NV	12.1	3.8	9.9	34.8
Lexington, KY	13.5	5.1	11.8	35.5
Lincoln, NE	10.7	4.1	8.4	32.5
Little Rock, AR	15.7	5.9	13.8	39.5
Los Angeles, CA	9.6	3.0	6.8	33.9
Louisville, KY	14.1	4.2	12.4	35.5
Madison, WI	8.9	3.4	6.9	26.9

Table continued on following page.

Appendix A: Comparative Statistics A-43

Metro Area	All Ages	Under 18 Years Old	18 to 64 Years Old	65 Years and Over
Manchester, NH	11.8	4.7	9.5	31.8
Memphis, TN	12.9	4.5	11.2	36.4
Miami, FL	10.9	3.4	7.2	32.1
Midland, TX	9.8	2.3	8.3	39.5
Milwaukee, WI	11.4	4.2	9.1	31.6
Minneapolis, MN	9.9	3.7	8.0	30.0
Nashville, TN	12.0	4.0	10.2	35.2
New Haven, CT	11.6	4.0	8.8	31.5
New Orleans, LA	14.4	5.0	12.3	36.6
New York, NY	10.0	3.2	7.2	31.6
Oklahoma City, OK	13.9	4.3	12.2	39.4
Omaha, NE	11.0	3.5	9.6	32.2
Orlando, FL	12.2	5.1	9.6	34.5
Peoria, IL	12.0	3.4	9.5	32.2
Philadelphia, PA	12.7	4.6	10.5	33.4
Phoenix, AZ	11.5	3.7	9.3	32.6
Pittsburgh, PA	14.5	5.4	11.4	33.8
Portland, OR	11.9	3.9	9.7	34.1
Providence, RI	13.6	5.2	11.2	33.3
Provo, UT	7.8	3.3	7.1	32.8
Raleigh, NC	9.6	3.8	7.7	32.1
Reno, NV	12.1	4.7	9.9	30.7
Richmond, VA	12.6	5.0	10.4	32.6
Riverside, CA	11.3	3.6	9.1	37.5
Rochester, MN	10.2	4.0	7.7	29.4
Sacramento, CA	11.5	3.4	9.0	34.8
Salt Lake City, UT	9.4	3.5	8.3	32.4
San Antonio, TX	14.0	5.3	12.5	39.2
San Diego, CA	9.9	3.2	7.2	32.8
San Francisco, CA	9.7	2.9	6.8	31.5
San Jose, CA	8.1	2.4	5.4	31.2
Santa Rosa, CA	11.9	3.8	9.4	28.5
Savannah, GA	13.7	5.5	11.6	37.0
Seattle, WA	10.8	3.5	8.7	33.4
Sioux Falls, SD	9.9	3.1	8.8	29.7
Springfield, IL	13.7	5.4	11.4	32.9
Tallahassee, FL	12.7	5.9	10.2	33.9
Tampa, FL	14.0	4.4	10.8	34.3
Tucson, AZ	15.3	5.1	12.5	35.1
Tulsa, OK	14.5	4.6	12.9	37.9
Tuscaloosa, AL	14.4	4.0	12.4	40.2
Virginia Beach, VA	13.1	4.7	11.1	34.4
Washington, DC	8.7	3.0	6.7	29.1
Wichita, KS	13.4	4.9	11.7	36.1
Winston-Salem, NC	12.7	3.8	10.2	33.8
U.S.	12.6	4.2	10.3	34.5

Note: Figures show percent of the civilian noninstitutionalized population that reported having a disability. Disability status is determined from from six types of difficulty: vision, hearing, cognitive, ambulatory, self-care, and independent living. For children under 5 years old, hearing and vision difficulty are used to determine disability status. For children between the ages of 5 and 14, disability status is determined from hearing, vision, cognitive, ambulatory, and self-care difficulties. For people aged 15 years and older, they are considered to have a disability if they have difficulty with any one of the six difficulty types; Figures cover the Metropolitan Statistical Area—see Appendix B for areas included
Source: U.S. Census Bureau, 2015-2019 American Community Survey 5-Year Estimates

A-44   Appendix A: Comparative Statistics

Male/Female Ratio: City

City	Males	Females	Males per 100 Females
Albuquerque, NM	272,468	286,906	95.0
Allentown, PA	59,101	61,814	95.6
Anchorage, AK	149,670	143,861	104.0
Ann Arbor, MI	60,089	60,646	99.1
Athens, GA	59,357	65,362	90.8
Atlanta, GA	237,192	251,608	94.3
Austin, TX	482,605	468,202	103.1
Baton Rouge, LA	107,345	116,804	91.9
Boise City, ID	112,637	113,478	99.3
Boston, MA	328,503	355,876	92.3
Boulder, CO	55,160	51,232	107.7
Cape Coral, FL	91,158	92,784	98.2
Cedar Rapids, IA	64,863	67,438	96.2
Charleston, SC	63,863	71,394	89.5
Charlotte, NC	412,035	445,390	92.5
Chicago, IL	1,317,791	1,391,743	94.7
Cincinnati, OH	145,900	155,494	93.8
Clarksville, TN	76,399	76,535	99.8
Cleveland, OH	185,274	200,008	92.6
College Station, TX	58,117	55,569	104.6
Colorado Springs, CO	232,440	232,431	100.0
Columbia, MO	58,250	62,980	92.5
Columbia, SC	67,638	65,635	103.1
Columbus, OH	429,868	448,685	95.8
Dallas, TX	657,714	672,898	97.7
Davenport, IA	50,216	51,953	96.7
Denver, CO	353,311	352,265	100.3
Des Moines, IA	106,316	109,320	97.3
Durham, NC	126,897	142,805	88.9
Edison, NJ	50,210	50,237	99.9
El Paso, TX	332,917	346,896	96.0
Fargo, ND	61,988	59,901	103.5
Fayetteville, NC	105,869	104,563	101.2
Fort Collins, CO	83,175	82,434	100.9
Fort Wayne, IN	128,483	137,269	93.6
Fort Worth, TX	428,238	446,163	96.0
Grand Rapids, MI	97,940	100,461	97.5
Greeley, CO	52,657	53,231	98.9
Green Bay, WI	51,929	52,848	98.3
Greensboro, NC	135,572	155,731	87.1
Honolulu, HI	173,837	175,148	99.3
Houston, TX	1,153,417	1,157,015	99.7
Huntsville, AL	94,803	101,416	93.5
Indianapolis, IN	416,893	447,554	93.1
Jacksonville, FL	431,133	459,334	93.9
Kansas City, MO	235,974	250,430	94.2
Lafayette, LA	61,742	64,924	95.1
Lakeland, FL	51,105	56,817	89.9
Las Vegas, NV	316,556	318,217	99.5
Lexington, KY	157,231	163,370	96.2
Lincoln, NE	142,589	141,250	100.9
Little Rock, AR	94,939	103,019	92.2
Los Angeles, CA	1,964,984	2,001,952	98.2
Louisville, KY	299,406	318,384	94.0
Madison, WI	126,190	128,787	98.0

Table continued on following page.

Appendix A: Comparative Statistics   A-45

City	Males	Females	Males per 100 Females
Manchester, NH	56,510	55,599	101.6
Memphis, TN	308,460	343,472	89.8
Miami, FL	224,810	229,469	98.0
Midland, TX	70,558	67,991	103.8
Milwaukee, WI	286,081	308,467	92.7
Minneapolis, MN	212,823	207,501	102.6
Nashville, TN	319,844	343,906	93.0
New Haven, CT	61,926	68,405	90.5
New Orleans, LA	185,513	205,332	90.3
New York, NY	4,015,982	4,403,334	91.2
Oklahoma City, OK	316,500	327,192	96.7
Omaha, NE	234,719	241,143	97.3
Orlando, FL	134,785	146,047	92.3
Peoria, IL	54,542	58,990	92.5
Philadelphia, PA	747,479	831,596	89.9
Phoenix, AZ	813,775	819,242	99.3
Pittsburgh, PA	147,776	154,429	95.7
Portland, OR	319,869	325,422	98.3
Providence, RI	86,874	92,620	93.8
Provo, UT	57,489	58,914	97.6
Raleigh, NC	223,942	240,543	93.1
Reno, NV	124,568	121,932	102.2
Richmond, VA	107,430	119,192	90.1
Riverside, CA	162,664	163,750	99.3
Rochester, MN	56,262	59,295	94.9
Sacramento, CA	245,188	255,742	95.9
Salt Lake City, UT	100,748	97,008	103.9
San Antonio, TX	744,596	763,487	97.5
San Diego, CA	711,134	698,439	101.8
San Francisco, CA	446,286	428,675	104.1
San Jose, CA	518,708	508,982	101.9
Santa Rosa, CA	86,927	92,774	93.7
Savannah, GA	69,220	76,183	90.9
Seattle, WA	366,442	357,863	102.4
Sioux Falls, SD	88,410	88,707	99.7
Springfield, IL	54,935	60,953	90.1
Tallahassee, FL	90,053	101,226	89.0
Tampa, FL	188,134	199,782	94.2
Tucson, AZ	269,403	272,079	99.0
Tulsa, OK	195,534	206,790	94.6
Tuscaloosa, AL	47,718	51,672	92.3
Virginia Beach, VA	221,324	228,877	96.7
Washington, DC	328,644	364,039	90.3
Wichita, KS	191,730	198,147	96.8
Winston-Salem, NC	114,592	129,523	88.5
U.S.	159,886,919	164,810,876	97.0

Source: U.S. Census Bureau, 2015-2019 American Community Survey 5-Year Estimates

A-46 Appendix A: Comparative Statistics

Male/Female Ratio: Metro Area

Metro Area	Males	Females	Males per 100 Females
Albuquerque, NM	448,642	463,466	96.8
Allentown, PA	411,125	426,485	96.4
Anchorage, AK	204,508	194,392	105.2
Ann Arbor, MI	181,923	185,077	98.3
Athens, GA	100,687	107,770	93.4
Atlanta, GA	2,834,134	3,028,290	93.6
Austin, TX	1,059,553	1,054,888	100.4
Baton Rouge, LA	417,717	436,601	95.7
Boise City, ID	354,905	355,838	99.7
Boston, MA	2,347,899	2,484,447	94.5
Boulder, CO	162,211	160,299	101.2
Cape Coral, FL	361,232	376,236	96.0
Cedar Rapids, IA	133,800	136,256	98.2
Charleston, SC	378,374	396,134	95.5
Charlotte, NC	1,235,495	1,310,065	94.3
Chicago, IL	4,654,160	4,854,445	95.9
Cincinnati, OH	1,079,705	1,122,036	96.2
Clarksville, TN	151,723	147,747	102.7
Cleveland, OH	993,227	1,063,671	93.4
College Station, TX	129,895	128,134	101.4
Colorado Springs, CO	365,383	358,115	102.0
Columbia, MO	100,711	104,658	96.2
Columbia, SC	399,998	424,280	94.3
Columbus, OH	1,022,627	1,055,134	96.9
Dallas, TX	3,601,569	3,719,094	96.8
Davenport, IA	187,831	193,344	97.1
Denver, CO	1,445,090	1,446,976	99.9
Des Moines, IA	336,082	344,357	97.6
Durham, NC	301,581	325,114	92.8
Edison, NJ	9,327,459	9,966,777	93.6
El Paso, TX	413,883	426,594	97.0
Fargo, ND	120,992	119,429	101.3
Fayetteville, NC	257,939	261,162	98.8
Fort Collins, CO	172,000	172,786	99.5
Fort Wayne, IN	198,843	207,462	95.8
Fort Worth, TX	3,601,569	3,719,094	96.8
Grand Rapids, MI	527,777	534,615	98.7
Greeley, CO	154,294	151,051	102.1
Green Bay, WI	159,123	160,278	99.3
Greensboro, NC	364,321	397,742	91.6
Honolulu, HI	496,066	488,755	101.5
Houston, TX	3,417,036	3,467,102	98.6
Huntsville, AL	224,226	232,777	96.3
Indianapolis, IN	991,392	1,038,080	95.5
Jacksonville, FL	733,355	770,219	95.2
Kansas City, MO	1,042,927	1,081,591	96.4
Lafayette, LA	238,957	250,957	95.2
Lakeland, FL	336,279	349,939	96.1
Las Vegas, NV	1,089,228	1,092,776	99.7
Lexington, KY	249,429	261,218	95.5
Lincoln, NE	165,977	164,352	101.0
Little Rock, AR	356,611	380,404	93.7
Los Angeles, CA	6,533,214	6,716,400	97.3
Louisville, KY	613,822	643,266	95.4
Madison, WI	325,952	327,773	99.4

Table continued on following page.

Appendix A: Comparative Statistics   A-47

Metro Area	Males	Females	Males per 100 Females
Manchester, NH	205,394	207,641	98.9
Memphis, TN	640,257	699,366	91.5
Miami, FL	2,959,743	3,130,917	94.5
Midland, TX	87,984	85,832	102.5
Milwaukee, WI	767,950	807,273	95.1
Minneapolis, MN	1,771,443	1,802,166	98.3
Nashville, TN	913,820	958,083	95.4
New Haven, CT	413,519	443,994	93.1
New Orleans, LA	612,116	655,661	93.4
New York, NY	9,327,459	9,966,777	93.6
Oklahoma City, OK	682,133	700,708	97.3
Omaha, NE	461,556	470,223	98.2
Orlando, FL	1,226,241	1,282,729	95.6
Peoria, IL	200,311	206,572	97.0
Philadelphia, PA	2,939,397	3,139,733	93.6
Phoenix, AZ	2,366,181	2,395,422	98.8
Pittsburgh, PA	1,135,076	1,196,371	94.9
Portland, OR	1,210,509	1,235,252	98.0
Providence, RI	785,383	832,885	94.3
Provo, UT	311,659	305,132	102.1
Raleigh, NC	649,577	682,734	95.1
Reno, NV	232,199	228,725	101.5
Richmond, VA	613,475	656,055	93.5
Riverside, CA	2,270,726	2,289,744	99.2
Rochester, MN	107,432	110,532	97.2
Sacramento, CA	1,132,519	1,183,461	95.7
Salt Lake City, UT	603,034	598,009	100.8
San Antonio, TX	1,220,720	1,247,473	97.9
San Diego, CA	1,669,515	1,646,558	101.4
San Francisco, CA	2,325,587	2,375,745	97.9
San Jose, CA	1,004,573	983,273	102.2
Santa Rosa, CA	244,045	255,727	95.4
Savannah, GA	187,309	198,727	94.3
Seattle, WA	1,938,723	1,932,600	100.3
Sioux Falls, SD	130,188	129,160	100.8
Springfield, IL	100,527	108,640	92.5
Tallahassee, FL	184,249	197,948	93.1
Tampa, FL	1,502,972	1,594,887	94.2
Tucson, AZ	505,666	521,541	97.0
Tulsa, OK	486,355	504,189	96.5
Tuscaloosa, AL	120,524	130,157	92.6
Virginia Beach, VA	867,843	893,886	97.1
Washington, DC	3,028,975	3,167,610	95.6
Wichita, KS	316,050	321,640	98.3
Winston-Salem, NC	320,092	346,124	92.5
U.S.	159,886,919	164,810,876	97.0

Note: Figures cover the Metropolitan Statistical Area (MSA)—see Appendix B for areas included
Source: U.S. Census Bureau, 2015-2019 American Community Survey 5-Year Estimates

A-48   Appendix A: Comparative Statistics

Gross Metropolitan Product

MSA[1]	2017	2018	2019	2020	Rank[2]
Albuquerque, NM	42.8	44.4	46.3	48.6	68
Allentown, PA	43.9	46.2	48.1	49.9	64
Anchorage, AK	27.4	28.3	29.3	30.6	102
Ann Arbor, MI	23.5	24.6	25.5	26.4	112
Athens, GA	10.1	10.5	10.8	11.2	205
Atlanta, GA	391.0	409.9	431.6	452.0	10
Austin, TX	145.1	156.6	164.6	174.0	25
Baton Rouge, LA	53.2	56.3	58.3	61.0	59
Boise City, ID	33.9	36.5	38.7	40.8	79
Boston, MA	449.5	472.7	493.6	515.0	8
Boulder, CO	25.6	27.2	28.7	29.9	107
Cape Coral, FL	28.3	30.0	31.8	33.4	93
Cedar Rapids, IA	17.8	18.4	18.8	19.4	141
Charleston, SC	42.5	44.6	46.7	49.0	67
Charlotte, NC	174.1	185.6	195.5	205.3	20
Chicago, IL	683.3	716.3	743.3	770.7	3
Cincinnati, OH	137.2	143.5	150.7	156.1	29
Clarksville, TN	11.0	11.6	12.2	12.6	194
Cleveland, OH	138.3	145.9	152.3	157.1	28
College Station, TX	9.9	10.6	11.2	11.7	204
Colorado Springs, CO	33.1	34.9	36.6	38.5	84
Columbia, MO	9.2	9.6	9.9	10.3	220
Columbia, SC	41.4	42.3	43.9	45.8	73
Columbus, OH	135.6	142.2	148.6	154.7	32
Dallas, TX	522.3	556.9	586.7	620.6	5
Davenport, IA	19.8	20.7	21.6	22.3	124
Denver, CO	211.6	225.3	235.8	246.9	18
Des Moines, IA	55.0	57.7	60.3	62.8	58
Durham, NC	43.4	45.5	48.0	50.7	65
Edison, NJ	1,765.5	1,851.9	1,932.1	2,007.4	1
El Paso, TX	28.3	29.4	30.5	31.5	97
Fargo, ND	15.3	16.1	16.8	17.5	156
Fayetteville, NC	17.2	17.6	18.1	18.8	149
Fort Collins, CO	17.4	18.4	19.7	20.7	139
Fort Wayne, IN	21.9	22.9	23.9	24.8	117
Fort Worth, TX	522.3	556.9	586.7	620.6	5
Grand Rapids, MI	60.6	63.6	66.2	68.3	54
Greeley, CO	12.8	13.8	14.7	15.6	178
Green Bay, WI	19.4	20.4	21.3	22.1	128
Greensboro, NC	41.5	43.0	44.3	45.7	71
Honolulu, HI	68.2	70.5	73.2	75.5	50
Houston, TX	478.1	513.9	546.1	583.7	7
Huntsville, AL	25.9	27.2	28.4	29.8	106
Indianapolis, IN	140.6	147.0	152.8	159.1	27
Jacksonville, FL	77.6	82.8	86.5	90.6	45
Kansas City, MO	131.8	138.2	144.1	149.7	33
Lafayette, LA	21.4	23.0	24.0	25.4	116
Lakeland, FL	21.4	22.6	23.6	24.6	119
Las Vegas, NV	112.8	119.1	124.1	130.3	36
Lexington, KY	29.7	30.8	31.9	33.0	90
Lincoln, NE	19.7	20.6	21.2	22.0	125
Little Rock, AR	38.5	39.8	41.1	42.7	76
Los Angeles, CA	1,067.7	1,125.5	1,164.2	1,207.3	2
Louisville, KY	75.3	78.1	81.3	83.9	48
Madison, WI	49.5	52.1	54.5	56.5	61
Manchester, NH	28.7	30.0	31.2	32.5	94

Table continued on following page.

Appendix A: Comparative Statistics   A-49

MSA[1]	2017	2018	2019	2020	Rank[2]
Memphis, TN	72.9	76.2	79.4	82.2	49
Miami, FL	349.2	369.5	386.7	403.4	12
Midland, TX	27.1	35.0	38.1	44.4	83
Milwaukee, WI	104.6	109.2	112.8	116.2	37
Minneapolis, MN	260.9	273.1	284.6	296.0	14
Nashville, TN	134.3	142.5	149.8	156.5	30
New Haven, CT	46.1	47.8	49.7	51.2	62
New Orleans, LA	76.7	81.0	83.8	87.5	46
New York, NY	1,765.5	1,851.9	1,932.1	2,007.4	1
Oklahoma City, OK	74.2	79.6	83.2	88.3	47
Omaha, NE	63.3	65.9	68.5	71.0	52
Orlando, FL	134.1	142.4	150.7	158.6	31
Peoria, IL	19.2	20.1	20.9	21.6	133
Philadelphia, PA	445.1	465.5	485.8	504.6	9
Phoenix, AZ	248.0	264.9	280.3	294.0	16
Pittsburgh, PA	147.4	156.4	162.8	168.5	26
Portland, OR	165.9	175.7	183.8	191.1	21
Providence, RI	84.0	86.8	89.5	93.0	44
Provo, UT	25.7	27.9	29.5	31.2	104
Raleigh, NC	83.2	88.3	92.8	97.8	42
Reno, NV	26.8	28.8	30.8	32.3	99
Richmond, VA	83.0	87.2	91.0	94.7	43
Riverside, CA	161.6	171.0	178.3	186.9	22
Rochester, MN	12.6	13.2	13.9	14.4	182
Sacramento, CA	129.3	137.0	144.3	151.5	34
Salt Lake City, UT	87.9	93.6	97.8	102.5	41
San Antonio, TX	126.1	134.5	140.1	148.6	35
San Diego, CA	237.2	249.4	260.3	272.1	17
San Francisco, CA	512.2	547.3	578.7	605.5	6
San Jose, CA	281.6	303.1	321.2	334.7	13
Santa Rosa, CA	29.3	30.4	31.4	32.5	91
Savannah, GA	18.8	19.7	20.6	21.2	134
Seattle, WA	367.9	397.5	416.9	435.0	11
Sioux Falls, SD	19.6	20.5	21.5	22.4	127
Springfield, IL	10.3	10.7	11.0	11.4	202
Tallahassee, FL	16.4	17.1	17.9	18.7	152
Tampa, FL	148.2	156.6	164.0	172.0	24
Tucson, AZ	39.9	41.7	43.6	45.5	74
Tulsa, OK	57.2	60.9	63.7	67.4	55
Tuscaloosa, AL	11.8	12.4	13.0	13.4	190
Virginia Beach, VA	95.2	99.3	103.6	107.4	39
Washington, DC	539.6	562.6	585.8	612.1	4
Wichita, KS	34.3	35.7	37.0	38.0	81
Winston-Salem, NC	29.7	31.2	32.5	33.8	88

Note: Figures are in billions of dollars; (1) Metropolitan Statistical Area—see Appendix B for areas included; (2) Rank is based on 2018 data and ranges from 1 to 381.
Source: The U.S. Conference of Mayors, U.S. Metro Economies: GMP & Employment 2018-2020, September 2019

A-50 Appendix A: Comparative Statistics

Economic Growth

MSA[1]	2015-17 (%)	2018 (%)	2019 (%)	2020 (%)	Rank[2]
Albuquerque, NM	0.7	1.4	2.6	2.5	252
Allentown, PA	1.2	2.6	2.3	1.6	210
Anchorage, AK	-1.5	-0.9	2.4	0.6	353
Ann Arbor, MI	2.1	2.5	1.9	1.3	123
Athens, GA	6.8	1.5	1.3	1.4	6
Atlanta, GA	3.7	2.8	3.6	2.6	47
Austin, TX	6.3	4.4	3.5	2.6	9
Baton Rouge, LA	1.6	0.8	1.2	2.4	170
Boise City, ID	3.7	5.5	4.1	3.2	45
Boston, MA	2.0	3.0	2.8	2.1	134
Boulder, CO	2.5	4.1	3.9	2.1	98
Cape Coral, FL	2.7	3.7	3.7	3.0	83
Cedar Rapids, IA	-1.6	0.9	0.8	1.0	354
Charleston, SC	5.0	2.4	2.9	2.6	16
Charlotte, NC	3.4	4.2	3.7	2.8	51
Chicago, IL	0.8	2.3	2.0	1.6	247
Cincinnati, OH	2.0	1.7	3.3	1.4	132
Clarksville, TN	-0.6	3.0	3.0	1.6	331
Cleveland, OH	1.7	1.9	2.8	0.9	160
College Station, TX	1.0	3.4	3.3	1.4	224
Colorado Springs, CO	2.9	3.1	3.0	2.8	73
Columbia, MO	0.9	1.6	1.5	1.8	242
Columbia, SC	0.8	-0.1	1.9	2.3	245
Columbus, OH	2.0	2.1	2.6	1.9	130
Dallas, TX	2.7	2.8	3.7	2.7	87
Davenport, IA	-0.2	2.4	2.4	1.2	311
Denver, CO	2.6	3.7	3.0	1.9	89
Des Moines, IA	2.8	1.8	2.7	1.9	78
Durham, NC	-2.0	2.9	3.7	3.5	363
Edison, NJ	1.3	2.6	2.6	1.6	196
El Paso, TX	0.9	1.5	1.6	1.4	244
Fargo, ND	0.4	2.1	2.6	2.0	283
Fayetteville, NC	-1.0	0.0	1.2	1.5	343
Fort Collins, CO	5.3	3.7	4.7	3.1	14
Fort Wayne, IN	1.9	2.5	2.5	1.3	149
Fort Worth, TX	2.7	2.8	3.7	2.7	87
Grand Rapids, MI	1.9	3.4	2.3	1.2	139
Greeley, CO	4.1	5.3	4.5	3.9	33
Green Bay, WI	1.2	3.2	2.6	1.2	203
Greensboro, NC	-0.2	1.5	1.2	1.2	312
Honolulu, HI	1.6	1.0	1.9	0.9	165
Houston, TX	-1.7	2.9	4.6	3.1	360
Huntsville, AL	1.8	3.0	2.5	2.7	155
Indianapolis, IN	2.5	1.9	2.1	2.0	101
Jacksonville, FL	4.1	4.3	2.6	2.5	34
Kansas City, MO	0.6	2.6	2.4	1.7	263
Lafayette, LA	-4.9	2.6	3.0	2.0	380
Lakeland, FL	2.7	3.2	2.5	2.4	82
Las Vegas, NV	1.5	3.1	2.3	2.7	182
Lexington, KY	1.6	1.3	2.0	1.1	167
Lincoln, NE	0.3	2.1	1.3	1.5	287
Little Rock, AR	0.4	0.9	1.6	1.5	286
Los Angeles, CA	2.3	3.5	1.8	1.6	110
Louisville, KY	0.7	1.4	2.3	1.2	254
Madison, WI	2.4	3.2	2.8	1.7	107
Manchester, NH	2.7	2.6	2.3	1.8	84

Table continued on following page.

Appendix A: Comparative Statistics A-51

MSA[1]	2015-17 (%)	2018 (%)	2019 (%)	2020 (%)	Rank[2]
Memphis, TN	0.1	2.3	2.3	1.4	299
Miami, FL	3.2	3.5	2.9	2.1	56
Midland, TX	1.0	13.0	9.2	3.6	231
Milwaukee, WI	0.9	2.1	1.5	0.9	243
Minneapolis, MN	1.9	2.3	2.5	1.9	144
Nashville, TN	4.0	3.9	3.3	2.3	39
New Haven, CT	1.2	1.7	2.1	0.9	204
New Orleans, LA	-0.6	1.2	1.3	2.0	329
New York, NY	1.3	2.6	2.6	1.6	196
Oklahoma City, OK	0.7	2.8	2.9	2.2	259
Omaha, NE	0.6	1.7	2.2	1.5	272
Orlando, FL	2.4	3.8	4.0	3.0	109
Peoria, IL	-4.0	2.5	2.0	1.3	376
Philadelphia, PA	1.4	1.9	2.7	1.7	188
Phoenix, AZ	3.3	4.5	4.0	2.7	54
Pittsburgh, PA	2.0	2.6	2.5	1.3	137
Portland, OR	3.9	3.5	2.6	1.6	42
Providence, RI	0.7	1.0	1.3	1.7	262
Provo, UT	6.6	6.5	4.0	3.7	7
Raleigh, NC	3.1	3.9	3.4	3.3	62
Reno, NV	4.3	5.3	4.9	2.5	27
Richmond, VA	1.5	3.0	2.6	1.8	179
Riverside, CA	3.0	3.4	2.3	2.6	65
Rochester, MN	3.6	2.9	3.1	1.1	48
Sacramento, CA	2.6	3.6	3.4	2.7	90
Salt Lake City, UT	2.3	3.7	2.6	2.7	114
San Antonio, TX	4.2	2.0	2.7	1.7	30
San Diego, CA	3.1	3.0	2.6	2.3	64
San Francisco, CA	4.8	5.1	4.3	2.5	18
San Jose, CA	7.0	6.0	4.6	2.2	5
Santa Rosa, CA	2.5	1.2	1.7	1.1	100
Savannah, GA	2.3	2.7	2.4	1.2	115
Seattle, WA	4.3	6.3	3.4	2.4	29
Sioux Falls, SD	1.2	1.6	3.2	2.2	206
Springfield, IL	-0.8	0.8	1.4	0.9	337
Tallahassee, FL	3.1	2.6	2.8	1.9	61
Tampa, FL	2.7	3.5	2.9	2.6	85
Tucson, AZ	2.0	2.7	2.8	2.0	133
Tulsa, OK	-3.3	1.3	3.1	1.7	373
Tuscaloosa, AL	1.0	2.8	3.4	1.5	227
Virginia Beach, VA	-0.4	2.2	2.5	1.4	323
Washington, DC	2.0	2.3	2.4	2.1	131
Wichita, KS	1.9	1.5	1.8	0.5	141
Winston-Salem, NC	-0.2	2.6	2.6	1.6	314
U.S.	1.9	2.9	2.3	2.1	–

Note: Figures are real gross metropolitan product (GMP) growth rates and represent annual average percent change;
(1) Metropolitan Statistical Area—see Appendix B for areas included; (2) Rank is based on 2017 2-year average annual percent change and ranges from 1 to 381
Source: The U.S. Conference of Mayors, U.S. Metro Economies: GMP & Employment 2018-2020, September 2019

A-52 Appendix A: Comparative Statistics

Metropolitan Area Exports

Area	2014	2015	2016	2017	2018	2019	Rank[2]
Albuquerque, NM	1,564.0	1,761.2	999.7	624.2	771.5	1,629.7	114
Allentown, PA	3,152.5	3,439.9	3,657.2	3,639.4	3,423.2	3,796.3	66
Anchorage, AK	571.8	421.9	1,215.4	1,675.9	1,510.8	1,348.0	132
Ann Arbor, MI	1,213.6	1,053.0	1,207.9	1,447.4	1,538.7	1,432.7	128
Athens, GA	320.8	327.4	332.1	297.7	378.2	442.1	219
Atlanta, GA	19,870.3	19,163.9	20,480.1	21,748.0	24,091.6	25,800.8	14
Austin, TX	9,400.0	10,094.5	10,682.7	12,451.5	12,929.9	12,509.0	30
Baton Rouge, LA	7,528.3	6,505.4	6,580.5	8,830.3	10,506.1	8,981.2	40
Boise City, ID	3,143.4	2,668.0	3,021.7	2,483.3	2,771.7	2,062.8	101
Boston, MA	23,378.5	21,329.5	21,168.0	23,116.2	24,450.1	23,505.8	17
Boulder, CO	1,016.1	1,039.1	956.3	1,012.0	1,044.1	1,014.9	158
Cape Coral, FL	496.6	487.3	540.3	592.3	668.0	694.9	190
Cedar Rapids, IA	879.0	873.5	945.0	1,071.6	1,025.0	1,028.4	157
Charleston, SC	5,866.7	6,457.5	9,508.1	8,845.2	10,943.2	16,337.9	23
Charlotte, NC	12,885.3	13,985.8	11,944.1	13,122.5	14,083.2	13,892.4	27
Chicago, IL	47,340.1	44,820.9	43,932.7	46,140.2	47,287.8	42,438.8	4
Cincinnati, OH	22,280.7	24,127.0	26,326.2	28,581.8	27,396.3	28,778.3	11
Clarksville, TN	323.7	296.5	376.1	360.2	435.5	341.8	241
Cleveland, OH	10,706.5	9,629.7	8,752.9	8,944.9	9,382.9	8,829.9	41
College Station, TX	129.7	122.5	113.2	145.4	153.0	160.5	313
Colorado Springs, CO	856.6	832.4	786.9	819.7	850.6	864.2	172
Columbia, MO	237.7	214.0	213.7	224.0	238.6	291.4	260
Columbia, SC	2,007.9	2,011.8	2,007.7	2,123.9	2,083.8	2,184.6	97
Columbus, OH	6,245.6	6,201.6	5,675.4	5,962.2	7,529.5	7,296.6	47
Dallas, TX	28,669.4	27,372.9	27,187.8	30,269.1	36,260.9	39,474.0	7
Davenport, IA	6,563.2	5,711.8	4,497.6	5,442.7	6,761.9	6,066.3	51
Denver, CO	4,958.6	3,909.5	3,649.3	3,954.7	4,544.3	4,555.6	61
Des Moines, IA	1,361.8	1,047.8	1,052.2	1,141.2	1,293.7	1,437.8	126
Durham, NC	2,934.0	2,807.2	2,937.4	3,128.4	3,945.8	4,452.9	62
Edison, NJ	105,266.6	95,645.4	89,649.5	93,693.7	97,692.4	87,365.7	2
El Paso, TX	20,079.3	24,560.9	26,452.8	25,814.1	30,052.0	32,749.6	10
Fargo, ND	782.8	543.2	474.5	519.5	553.5	515.0	207
Fayetteville, NC	375.8	256.3	179.8	231.6	260.5	287.8	263
Fort Collins, CO	1,037.4	990.7	993.8	1,034.1	1,021.8	1,060.0	152
Fort Wayne, IN	1,581.1	1,529.0	1,322.2	1,422.8	1,593.3	1,438.5	125
Fort Worth, TX	28,669.4	27,372.9	27,187.8	30,269.1	36,260.9	39,474.0	7
Grand Rapids, MI	5,244.5	5,143.0	5,168.5	5,385.8	5,420.9	5,214.1	55
Greeley, CO	1,343.6	1,240.1	1,539.6	1,492.8	1,366.5	1,439.2	124
Green Bay, WI	988.7	968.1	1,044.0	1,054.8	1,044.3	928.2	167
Greensboro, NC	3,505.5	3,286.1	3,730.4	3,537.9	3,053.5	2,561.8	87
Honolulu, HI	765.5	446.4	330.3	393.6	438.9	308.6	250
Houston, TX	118,966.0	97,054.3	84,105.5	95,760.3	120,714.3	129,656.0	1
Huntsville, AL	1,440.4	1,344.7	1,827.3	1,889.2	1,608.7	1,534.2	122
Indianapolis, IN	9,539.4	9,809.4	9,655.4	10,544.2	11,069.9	11,148.7	33
Jacksonville, FL	2,473.7	2,564.4	2,159.0	2,141.7	2,406.7	2,975.5	79
Kansas City, MO	8,262.9	6,723.2	6,709.8	7,015.0	7,316.9	7,652.6	45
Lafayette, LA	1,532.7	1,165.2	1,335.2	954.8	1,001.7	1,086.2	148
Lakeland, FL	2,151.9	1,318.6	995.5	1,147.2	1,299.8	1,141.5	143
Las Vegas, NV	2,509.7	2,916.2	2,312.3	2,710.6	2,240.6	2,430.8	90
Lexington, KY	2,191.4	2,065.7	2,069.6	2,119.8	2,148.0	2,093.8	100
Lincoln, NE	1,173.9	1,189.3	796.9	860.9	885.6	807.0	177
Little Rock, AR	2,463.5	1,777.5	1,871.0	2,146.1	1,607.4	1,642.5	113
Los Angeles, CA	75,471.2	61,758.7	61,245.7	63,752.9	64,814.6	61,041.1	3
Louisville, KY	8,877.3	8,037.9	7,793.3	8,925.9	8,987.0	9,105.5	39
Madison, WI	2,369.5	2,280.4	2,204.8	2,187.7	2,460.2	2,337.6	93
Manchester, NH	1,575.4	1,556.6	1,465.2	1,714.7	1,651.4	1,587.1	118

Table continued on following page.

Appendix A: Comparative Statistics   A-53

Area	2014	2015	2016	2017	2018	2019	Rank[2]
Memphis, TN	11,002.0	11,819.5	11,628.7	11,233.9	12,695.4	13,751.7	28
Miami, FL	37,969.5	33,258.5	32,734.5	34,780.5	35,650.2	35,498.9	8
Midland, TX	122.7	110.1	69.6	69.4	63.6	63.7	357
Milwaukee, WI	8,696.0	7,953.6	7,256.2	7,279.1	7,337.6	6,896.3	49
Minneapolis, MN	21,198.2	19,608.6	18,329.2	19,070.9	20,016.2	18,633.0	22
Nashville, TN	9,620.9	9,353.0	9,460.1	10,164.3	8,723.7	7,940.7	44
New Haven, CT	1,834.5	1,756.3	1,819.8	1,876.3	2,082.3	2,133.8	98
New Orleans, LA	34,881.5	27,023.3	29,518.8	31,648.5	36,570.4	34,109.6	9
New York, NY	105,266.6	95,645.4	89,649.5	93,693.7	97,692.4	87,365.7	2
Oklahoma City, OK	1,622.0	1,353.1	1,260.0	1,278.8	1,489.4	1,434.5	127
Omaha, NE	4,528.5	3,753.4	3,509.7	3,756.2	4,371.6	3,725.7	68
Orlando, FL	3,134.8	3,082.7	3,363.9	3,196.7	3,131.7	3,363.9	73
Peoria, IL	11,234.8	9,826.9	7,260.1	9,403.6	9,683.6	8,151.9	42
Philadelphia, PA	26,321.3	24,236.1	21,359.9	21,689.7	23,663.2	24,721.3	15
Phoenix, AZ	12,764.4	13,821.5	12,838.2	13,223.1	13,614.9	15,136.6	24
Pittsburgh, PA	10,015.8	9,137.1	7,971.0	9,322.7	9,824.2	9,672.9	38
Portland, OR	18,667.2	18,847.8	20,256.8	20,788.8	21,442.9	23,761.9	16
Providence, RI	6,595.1	5,048.8	6,595.7	7,125.4	6,236.6	7,424.8	46
Provo, UT	2,533.4	2,216.4	1,894.8	2,065.3	1,788.1	1,783.7	107
Raleigh, NC	2,713.1	2,553.4	2,620.4	2,865.8	3,193.2	3,546.8	70
Reno, NV	2,138.9	1,943.3	2,382.1	2,517.3	2,631.7	2,598.3	86
Richmond, VA	3,307.0	3,325.9	3,525.7	3,663.7	3,535.0	3,203.2	76
Riverside, CA	9,134.8	8,970.0	10,211.6	8,782.3	9,745.7	9,737.6	37
Rochester, MN	720.5	530.2	398.0	495.3	537.6	390.1	235
Sacramento, CA	7,143.9	8,101.2	7,032.1	6,552.6	6,222.8	5,449.2	53
Salt Lake City, UT	8,361.5	10,380.5	8,653.7	7,916.9	9,748.6	13,273.9	29
San Antonio, TX	25,781.8	15,919.2	5,621.2	9,184.1	11,678.1	11,668.0	32
San Diego, CA	18,585.7	17,439.7	18,086.6	18,637.1	20,156.8	19,774.1	20
San Francisco, CA	26,863.7	25,061.1	24,506.3	29,103.8	27,417.0	28,003.8	12
San Jose, CA	21,128.8	19,827.2	21,716.8	21,464.7	22,224.2	20,909.4	19
Santa Rosa, CA	1,103.7	1,119.8	1,194.3	1,168.2	1,231.7	1,234.5	135
Savannah, GA	5,093.4	5,447.5	4,263.4	4,472.0	5,407.8	4,925.5	58
Seattle, WA	61,938.4	67,226.4	61,881.0	59,007.0	59,742.9	41,249.0	5
Sioux Falls, SD	455.3	375.0	334.3	386.8	400.0	431.5	224
Springfield, IL	94.4	111.7	88.3	107.5	91.2	99.8	338
Tallahassee, FL	174.0	191.2	223.1	241.1	270.8	219.7	291
Tampa, FL	5,817.3	5,660.4	5,702.9	6,256.0	4,966.7	6,219.7	50
Tucson, AZ	2,277.4	2,485.9	2,563.9	2,683.9	2,824.8	2,943.7	81
Tulsa, OK	3,798.5	2,699.7	2,363.0	2,564.7	3,351.7	3,399.2	72
Tuscaloosa, AL	n/a	n/a	n/a	n/a	n/a	n/a	400
Virginia Beach, VA	3,573.2	3,556.4	3,291.1	3,307.2	3,950.6	3,642.4	69
Washington, DC	13,053.6	13,900.4	13,582.4	12,736.1	13,602.7	14,563.8	25
Wichita, KS	4,011.7	3,717.6	3,054.9	3,299.2	3,817.0	3,494.7	71
Winston-Salem, NC	1,441.9	1,267.4	1,234.6	1,131.7	1,107.5	1,209.1	137

Note: Figures are in millions of dollars; (1) Metropolitan Statistical Area—see Appendix B for areas included; (2) Rank is based on 2019 data and ranges from 1 to 386
Source: U.S. Department of Commerce, International Trade Administration, Office of Trade and Economic Analysis, Industry and Analysis, Exports by Metropolitan Area, extracted March 24, 2021

A-54   Appendix A: Comparative Statistics

Building Permits: City

City	Single-Family			Multi-Family			Total		
	2018	2019	Pct. Chg.	2018	2019	Pct. Chg.	2018	2019	Pct. Chg.
Albuquerque, NM	1,115	906	-18.7	0	188	–	1,115	1,094	-1.9
Allentown, PA	0	0	0.0	0	0	0.0	0	0	0.0
Anchorage, AK	869	838	-3.6	214	221	3.3	1,083	1,059	-2.2
Ann Arbor, MI	126	96	-23.8	0	0	0.0	126	96	-23.8
Athens, GA	345	517	49.9	261	766	193.5	606	1,283	111.7
Atlanta, GA	1,184	728	-38.5	5,312	2,555	-51.9	6,496	3,283	-49.5
Austin, TX	4,433	4,568	3.0	8,850	10,141	14.6	13,283	14,709	10.7
Baton Rouge, LA	282	354	25.5	58	0	-100.0	340	354	4.1
Boise City, ID	844	698	-17.3	296	883	198.3	1,140	1,581	38.7
Boston, MA	49	37	-24.5	3,553	2,956	-16.8	3,602	2,993	-16.9
Boulder, CO	80	41	-48.8	667	286	-57.1	747	327	-56.2
Cape Coral, FL	2,245	1,878	-16.3	356	810	127.5	2,601	2,688	3.3
Cedar Rapids, IA	147	173	17.7	325	197	-39.4	472	370	-21.6
Charleston, SC	810	828	2.2	354	360	1.7	1,164	1,188	2.1
Charlotte, NC	n/a	n/a	n/a	n/a	n/a	n/a	n/a	n/a	n/a
Chicago, IL	439	410	-6.6	6,010	7,504	24.9	6,449	7,914	22.7
Cincinnati, OH	98	135	37.8	632	992	57.0	730	1,127	54.4
Clarksville, TN	669	1,428	113.5	269	160	-40.5	938	1,588	69.3
Cleveland, OH	114	78	-31.6	34	19	-44.1	148	97	-34.5
College Station, TX	459	398	-13.3	572	219	-61.7	1,031	617	-40.2
Colorado Springs, CO	n/a	n/a	n/a	n/a	n/a	n/a	n/a	n/a	n/a
Columbia, MO	261	338	29.5	2	166	8,200.0	263	504	91.6
Columbia, SC	449	464	3.3	28	10	-64.3	477	474	-0.6
Columbus, OH	555	512	-7.7	3,742	2,258	-39.7	4,297	2,770	-35.5
Dallas, TX	2,009	2,093	4.2	6,038	6,000	-0.6	8,047	8,093	0.6
Davenport, IA	68	122	79.4	0	196	–	68	318	367.6
Denver, CO	2,428	2,257	-7.0	5,450	5,073	-6.9	7,878	7,330	-7.0
Des Moines, IA	180	391	117.2	391	279	-28.6	571	670	17.3
Durham, NC	1,894	1,945	2.7	1,336	1,884	41.0	3,230	3,829	18.5
Edison, NJ	71	55	-22.5	100	175	75.0	171	230	34.5
El Paso, TX	1,588	1,873	17.9	621	413	-33.5	2,209	2,286	3.5
Fargo, ND	313	311	-0.6	897	172	-80.8	1,210	483	-60.1
Fayetteville, NC	241	240	-0.4	0	282	–	241	522	116.6
Fort Collins, CO	398	316	-20.6	673	632	-6.1	1,071	948	-11.5
Fort Wayne, IN	n/a	n/a	n/a	n/a	n/a	n/a	n/a	n/a	n/a
Fort Worth, TX	5,477	5,063	-7.6	3,833	6,276	63.7	9,310	11,339	21.8
Grand Rapids, MI	124	153	23.4	690	183	-73.5	814	336	-58.7
Greeley, CO	348	170	-51.1	190	697	266.8	538	867	61.2
Green Bay, WI	101	63	-37.6	0	0	0.0	101	63	-37.6
Greensboro, NC	597	548	-8.2	249	385	54.6	846	933	10.3
Honolulu, HI	n/a	n/a	n/a	n/a	n/a	n/a	n/a	n/a	n/a
Houston, TX	5,417	5,120	-5.5	7,820	10,343	32.3	13,237	15,463	16.8
Huntsville, AL	1,241	1,436	15.7	71	167	135.2	1,312	1,603	22.2
Indianapolis, IN	1,090	1,153	5.8	1,196	1,229	2.8	2,286	2,382	4.2
Jacksonville, FL	3,780	4,155	9.9	3,223	2,650	-17.8	7,003	6,805	-2.8
Kansas City, MO	813	619	-23.9	1,341	879	-34.5	2,154	1,498	-30.5
Lafayette, LA	n/a	n/a	n/a	n/a	n/a	n/a	n/a	n/a	n/a
Lakeland, FL	435	606	39.3	0	953	–	435	1,559	258.4
Las Vegas, NV	1,794	1,885	5.1	179	780	335.8	1,973	2,665	35.1
Lexington, KY	733	579	-21.0	1,056	804	-23.9	1,789	1,383	-22.7
Lincoln, NE	859	863	0.5	673	864	28.4	1,532	1,727	12.7
Little Rock, AR	325	480	47.7	145	539	271.7	470	1,019	116.8
Los Angeles, CA	2,636	2,647	0.4	13,663	11,740	-14.1	16,299	14,387	-11.7
Louisville, KY	1,183	1,207	2.0	2,080	2,204	6.0	3,263	3,411	4.5

Table continued on following page.

Appendix A: Comparative Statistics A-55

City	Single-Family			Multi-Family			Total		
	2018	2019	Pct. Chg.	2018	2019	Pct. Chg.	2018	2019	Pct. Chg.
Madison, WI	334	426	27.5	1,109	1,232	11.1	1,443	1,658	14.9
Manchester, NH	151	106	-29.8	59	26	-55.9	210	132	-37.1
Memphis, TN	n/a	n/a	n/a	n/a	n/a	n/a	n/a	n/a	n/a
Miami, FL	80	107	33.8	4,545	4,361	-4.0	4,625	4,468	-3.4
Midland, TX	1,222	1,290	5.6	0	0	0.0	1,222	1,290	5.6
Milwaukee, WI	39	15	-61.5	717	178	-75.2	756	193	-74.5
Minneapolis, MN	162	122	-24.7	3,463	4,691	35.5	3,625	4,813	32.8
Nashville, TN	3,560	3,830	7.6	3,268	5,935	81.6	6,828	9,765	43.0
New Haven, CT	4	4	0.0	456	695	52.4	460	699	52.0
New Orleans, LA	524	558	6.5	779	748	-4.0	1,303	1,306	0.2
New York, NY	417	332	-20.4	20,493	26,215	27.9	20,910	26,547	27.0
Oklahoma City, OK	2,955	3,243	9.7	142	128	-9.9	3,097	3,371	8.8
Omaha, NE	1,237	1,179	-4.7	1,650	965	-41.5	2,887	2,144	-25.7
Orlando, FL	790	747	-5.4	2,289	1,887	-17.6	3,079	2,634	-14.5
Peoria, IL	32	33	3.1	0	0	0.0	32	33	3.1
Philadelphia, PA	683	894	30.9	2,556	3,672	43.7	3,239	4,566	41.0
Phoenix, AZ	3,732	4,175	11.9	3,530	5,723	62.1	7,262	9,898	36.3
Pittsburgh, PA	90	78	-13.3	553	582	5.2	643	660	2.6
Portland, OR	775	703	-9.3	4,873	4,391	-9.9	5,648	5,094	-9.8
Providence, RI	1	14	1,300.0	0	183	–	1	197	19,600.0
Provo, UT	171	174	1.8	286	140	-51.0	457	314	-31.3
Raleigh, NC	1,304	380	-70.9	2,907	827	-71.6	4,211	1,207	-71.3
Reno, NV	1,351	1,176	-13.0	1,883	2,144	13.9	3,234	3,320	2.7
Richmond, VA	273	353	29.3	290	887	205.9	563	1,240	120.2
Riverside, CA	171	170	-0.6	503	509	1.2	674	679	0.7
Rochester, MN	347	296	-14.7	1,068	478	-55.2	1,415	774	-45.3
Sacramento, CA	1,610	1,538	-4.5	714	1,463	104.9	2,324	3,001	29.1
Salt Lake City, UT	109	127	16.5	793	3,359	323.6	902	3,486	286.5
San Antonio, TX	3,266	3,890	19.1	2,663	5,306	99.2	5,929	9,196	55.1
San Diego, CA	774	580	-25.1	3,678	3,361	-8.6	4,452	3,941	-11.5
San Francisco, CA	28	22	-21.4	5,150	3,178	-38.3	5,178	3,200	-38.2
San Jose, CA	238	514	116.0	2,598	1,831	-29.5	2,836	2,345	-17.3
Santa Rosa, CA	1,632	939	-42.5	69	251	263.8	1,701	1,190	-30.0
Savannah, GA	399	339	-15.0	0	0	0.0	399	339	-15.0
Seattle, WA	523	507	-3.1	7,395	10,277	39.0	7,918	10,784	36.2
Sioux Falls, SD	1,083	1,013	-6.5	898	643	-28.4	1,981	1,656	-16.4
Springfield, IL	74	57	-23.0	219	112	-48.9	293	169	-42.3
Tallahassee, FL	396	407	2.8	1,128	1,275	13.0	1,524	1,682	10.4
Tampa, FL	1,109	1,159	4.5	679	3,618	432.8	1,788	4,777	167.2
Tucson, AZ	680	999	46.9	860	817	-5.0	1,540	1,816	17.9
Tulsa, OK	471	629	33.5	343	580	69.1	814	1,209	48.5
Tuscaloosa, AL	353	321	-9.1	469	844	80.0	822	1,165	41.7
Virginia Beach, VA	534	667	24.9	245	683	178.8	779	1,350	73.3
Washington, DC	112	168	50.0	4,503	5,777	28.3	4,615	5,945	28.8
Wichita, KS	532	618	16.2	326	364	11.7	858	982	14.5
Winston-Salem, NC	1,251	1,185	-5.3	84	0	-100.0	1,335	1,185	-11.2
U.S.	855,300	862,100	0.7	473,500	523,900	10.6	1,328,800	1,386,000	4.3

Note: Figures represent new, privately-owned housing units authorized (unadjusted data); All permit data are based on estimates with imputation
Source: U.S. Census Bureau, Manufacturing, Mining, and Construction Statistics, Building Permits, 2018, 2019

A-56   Appendix A: Comparative Statistics

Building Permits: Metro Area

Metro Area	Single-Family			Multi-Family			Total		
	2018	2019	Pct. Chg.	2018	2019	Pct. Chg.	2018	2019	Pct. Chg.
Albuquerque, NM	2,086	1,872	-10.3	100	276	176.0	2,186	2,148	-1.7
Allentown, PA	1,082	1,078	-0.4	164	267	62.8	1,246	1,345	7.9
Anchorage, AK	938	878	-6.4	321	285	-11.2	1,259	1,163	-7.6
Ann Arbor, MI	652	608	-6.7	153	207	35.3	805	815	1.2
Athens, GA	729	821	12.6	340	770	126.5	1,069	1,591	48.8
Atlanta, GA	26,506	26,261	-0.9	12,935	6,575	-49.2	39,441	32,836	-16.7
Austin, TX	17,030	18,426	8.2	13,005	13,611	4.7	30,035	32,037	6.7
Baton Rouge, LA	3,509	3,612	2.9	413	10	-97.6	3,922	3,622	-7.6
Boise City, ID	6,923	7,570	9.3	1,994	3,062	53.6	8,917	10,632	19.2
Boston, MA	4,930	4,299	-12.8	9,253	10,789	16.6	14,183	15,088	6.4
Boulder, CO	899	742	-17.5	2,055	908	-55.8	2,954	1,650	-44.1
Cape Coral, FL	5,803	5,633	-2.9	3,918	3,472	-11.4	9,721	9,105	-6.3
Cedar Rapids, IA	490	509	3.9	469	305	-35.0	959	814	-15.1
Charleston, SC	4,787	4,758	-0.6	2,215	1,937	-12.6	7,002	6,695	-4.4
Charlotte, NC	16,407	16,253	-0.9	9,802	8,384	-14.5	26,209	24,637	-6.0
Chicago, IL	8,546	7,598	-11.1	9,135	10,487	14.8	17,681	18,085	2.3
Cincinnati, OH	4,282	4,488	4.8	1,794	1,535	-14.4	6,076	6,023	-0.9
Clarksville, TN	1,516	2,332	53.8	287	325	13.2	1,803	2,657	47.4
Cleveland, OH	2,733	2,584	-5.5	248	448	80.6	2,981	3,032	1.7
College Station, TX	1,023	1,091	6.6	833	389	-53.3	1,856	1,480	-20.3
Colorado Springs, CO	4,229	4,051	-4.2	1,505	1,457	-3.2	5,734	5,508	-3.9
Columbia, MO	555	633	14.1	2	166	8,200.0	557	799	43.4
Columbia, SC	4,478	4,209	-6.0	474	215	-54.6	4,952	4,424	-10.7
Columbus, OH	4,493	4,389	-2.3	4,947	3,701	-25.2	9,440	8,090	-14.3
Dallas, TX	36,832	34,939	-5.1	27,061	27,769	2.6	63,893	62,708	-1.9
Davenport, IA	490	533	8.8	69	268	288.4	559	801	43.3
Denver, CO	11,808	11,081	-6.2	9,921	8,227	-17.1	21,729	19,308	-11.1
Des Moines, IA	3,233	3,915	21.1	1,690	1,354	-19.9	4,923	5,269	7.0
Durham, NC	3,289	3,561	8.3	2,127	2,234	5.0	5,416	5,795	7.0
Edison, NJ	11,077	11,072	0.0	38,615	50,096	29.7	49,692	61,168	23.1
El Paso, TX	1,751	2,433	38.9	665	633	-4.8	2,416	3,066	26.9
Fargo, ND	1,080	939	-13.1	1,233	486	-60.6	2,313	1,425	-38.4
Fayetteville, NC	803	1,547	92.7	16	292	1,725.0	819	1,839	124.5
Fort Collins, CO	1,679	1,580	-5.9	1,265	910	-28.1	2,944	2,490	-15.4
Fort Wayne, IN	1,343	1,330	-1.0	541	626	15.7	1,884	1,956	3.8
Fort Worth, TX	36,832	34,939	-5.1	27,061	27,769	2.6	63,893	62,708	-1.9
Grand Rapids, MI	2,749	2,531	-7.9	1,105	1,624	47.0	3,854	4,155	7.8
Greeley, CO	3,194	3,335	4.4	913	1,052	15.2	4,107	4,387	6.8
Green Bay, WI	766	723	-5.6	435	407	-6.4	1,201	1,130	-5.9
Greensboro, NC	1,949	2,002	2.7	275	421	53.1	2,224	2,423	8.9
Honolulu, HI	983	912	-7.2	1,427	1,367	-4.2	2,410	2,279	-5.4
Houston, TX	40,321	39,507	-2.0	16,967	24,165	42.4	57,288	63,672	11.1
Huntsville, AL	2,870	3,399	18.4	71	167	135.2	2,941	3,566	21.3
Indianapolis, IN	7,291	7,120	-2.3	1,603	2,601	62.3	8,894	9,721	9.3
Jacksonville, FL	10,755	11,583	7.7	4,695	3,104	-33.9	15,450	14,687	-4.9
Kansas City, MO	5,608	4,811	-14.2	4,660	4,536	-2.7	10,268	9,347	-9.0
Lafayette, LA	1,657	1,632	-1.5	30	34	13.3	1,687	1,666	-1.2
Lakeland, FL	5,331	6,435	20.7	0	2,291	–	5,331	8,726	63.7
Las Vegas, NV	9,721	10,042	3.3	2,323	3,861	66.2	12,044	13,903	15.4
Lexington, KY	1,404	1,308	-6.8	1,368	938	-31.4	2,772	2,246	-19.0
Lincoln, NE	1,117	1,088	-2.6	687	1,010	47.0	1,804	2,098	16.3
Little Rock, AR	1,819	1,921	5.6	355	1,084	205.4	2,174	3,005	38.2
Los Angeles, CA	10,042	9,306	-7.3	19,482	21,248	9.1	29,524	30,554	3.5
Louisville, KY	3,104	3,122	0.6	2,409	2,644	9.8	5,513	5,766	4.6

Table continued on following page.

Appendix A: Comparative Statistics   A-57

Metro Area	Single-Family			Multi-Family			Total		
	2018	2019	Pct. Chg.	2018	2019	Pct. Chg.	2018	2019	Pct. Chg.
Madison, WI	1,623	1,536	-5.4	2,029	1,807	-10.9	3,652	3,343	-8.5
Manchester, NH	709	691	-2.5	697	561	-19.5	1,406	1,252	-11.0
Memphis, TN	3,185	3,319	4.2	1,307	355	-72.8	4,492	3,674	-18.2
Miami, FL	7,022	7,241	3.1	12,531	13,447	7.3	19,553	20,688	5.8
Midland, TX	1,227	1,306	6.4	0	0	0.0	1,227	1,306	6.4
Milwaukee, WI	1,712	1,494	-12.7	2,057	925	-55.0	3,769	2,419	-35.8
Minneapolis, MN	8,985	9,610	7.0	9,221	12,804	38.9	18,206	22,414	23.1
Nashville, TN	13,470	14,460	7.3	5,689	8,242	44.9	19,159	22,702	18.5
New Haven, CT	406	399	-1.7	760	1,054	38.7	1,166	1,453	24.6
New Orleans, LA	3,046	3,241	6.4	818	785	-4.0	3,864	4,026	4.2
New York, NY	11,077	11,072	0.0	38,615	50,096	29.7	49,692	61,168	23.1
Oklahoma City, OK	5,430	5,924	9.1	300	633	111.0	5,730	6,557	14.4
Omaha, NE	2,791	2,633	-5.7	1,997	1,467	-26.5	4,788	4,100	-14.4
Orlando, FL	16,455	14,995	-8.9	12,427	9,475	-23.8	28,882	24,470	-15.3
Peoria, IL	228	218	-4.4	106	90	-15.1	334	308	-7.8
Philadelphia, PA	6,875	6,963	1.3	6,281	8,644	37.6	13,156	15,607	18.6
Phoenix, AZ	23,526	25,026	6.4	7,817	10,847	38.8	31,343	35,873	14.5
Pittsburgh, PA	2,977	2,830	-4.9	1,060	1,154	8.9	4,037	3,984	-1.3
Portland, OR	6,869	7,688	11.9	7,311	9,127	24.8	14,180	16,815	18.6
Providence, RI	1,553	1,592	2.5	410	456	11.2	1,963	2,048	4.3
Provo, UT	5,516	5,423	-1.7	1,325	1,524	15.0	6,841	6,947	1.5
Raleigh, NC	11,160	11,142	-0.2	4,790	2,178	-54.5	15,950	13,320	-16.5
Reno, NV	2,255	2,157	-4.3	2,195	3,106	41.5	4,450	5,263	18.3
Richmond, VA	4,498	4,481	-0.4	1,563	3,859	146.9	6,061	8,340	37.6
Riverside, CA	11,591	11,147	-3.8	3,218	3,452	7.3	14,809	14,599	-1.4
Rochester, MN	690	614	-11.0	1,126	497	-55.9	1,816	1,111	-38.8
Sacramento, CA	6,393	7,184	12.4	1,480	2,247	51.8	7,873	9,431	19.8
Salt Lake City, UT	5,391	4,760	-11.7	3,359	5,920	76.2	8,750	10,680	22.1
San Antonio, TX	8,013	9,103	13.6	3,484	6,792	94.9	11,497	15,895	38.3
San Diego, CA	3,489	3,019	-13.5	6,345	5,197	-18.1	9,834	8,216	-16.5
San Francisco, CA	4,048	4,076	0.7	13,373	9,805	-26.7	17,421	13,881	-20.3
San Jose, CA	2,466	2,603	5.6	6,278	3,627	-42.2	8,744	6,230	-28.8
Santa Rosa, CA	3,169	2,079	-34.4	110	350	218.2	3,279	2,429	-25.9
Savannah, GA	2,080	2,151	3.4	1,078	440	-59.2	3,158	2,591	-18.0
Seattle, WA	9,134	8,737	-4.3	19,052	17,862	-6.2	28,186	26,599	-5.6
Sioux Falls, SD	1,380	1,376	-0.3	1,008	743	-26.3	2,388	2,119	-11.3
Springfield, IL	193	149	-22.8	313	180	-42.5	506	329	-35.0
Tallahassee, FL	2,073	1,070	-48.4	1,128	1,275	13.0	3,201	2,345	-26.7
Tampa, FL	14,228	14,670	3.1	3,224	8,870	175.1	17,452	23,540	34.9
Tucson, AZ	3,240	3,490	7.7	1,164	823	-29.3	4,404	4,313	-2.1
Tulsa, OK	2,845	3,377	18.7	567	929	63.8	3,412	4,306	26.2
Tuscaloosa, AL	578	630	9.0	469	844	80.0	1,047	1,474	40.8
Virginia Beach, VA	4,168	4,345	4.2	1,436	1,563	8.8	5,604	5,908	5.4
Washington, DC	13,588	12,977	-4.5	12,169	13,827	13.6	25,757	26,804	4.1
Wichita, KS	1,223	1,389	13.6	735	737	0.3	1,958	2,126	8.6
Winston-Salem, NC	3,123	3,160	1.2	376	174	-53.7	3,499	3,334	-4.7
U.S.	855,300	862,100	0.7	473,500	523,900	10.6	1,328,800	1,386,000	4.3

Note: Figures cover the Metropolitan Statistical Area—see Appendix B for areas included; Figures represent new, privately-owned housing units authorized (unadjusted data); All permit data are based on estimates with imputation
Source: U.S. Census Bureau, Manufacturing, Mining, and Construction Statistics, Building Permits, 2018, 2019

A-58 Appendix A: Comparative Statistics

Housing Vacancy Rates

Metro Area[1]	Gross Vacancy Rate[2] (%)			Year-Round Vacancy Rate[3] (%)			Rental Vacancy Rate[4] (%)			Homeowner Vacancy Rate[5] (%)		
	2018	2019	2020	2018	2019	2020	2018	2019	2020	2018	2019	2020
Albuquerque, NM	8.3	7.9	5.1	7.9	7.4	4.9	7.8	6.5	5.4	1.8	1.9	1.4
Allentown, PA	9.3	7.7	4.9	7.1	5.8	4.8	5.7	4.0	3.9	0.9	1.4	0.7
Anchorage, AK	n/a	n/a	n/a	n/a	n/a	n/a	n/a	n/a	n/a	n/a	n/a	n/a
Ann Arbor, MI	n/a	n/a	n/a	n/a	n/a	n/a	n/a	n/a	n/a	n/a	n/a	n/a
Athens, GA	n/a	n/a	n/a	n/a	n/a	n/a	n/a	n/a	n/a	n/a	n/a	n/a
Atlanta, GA	7.8	7.6	5.8	7.4	7.3	5.4	6.6	7.0	6.4	1.1	1.3	0.8
Austin, TX	9.7	10.7	7.0	8.7	10.3	6.8	7.0	8.2	6.6	1.2	1.8	2.0
Baton Rouge, LA	13.0	13.9	12.6	11.8	13.0	11.8	7.6	10.2	7.4	1.4	1.9	1.7
Boise City, ID	n/a	n/a	n/a	n/a	n/a	n/a	n/a	n/a	n/a	n/a	n/a	n/a
Boston, MA	7.5	7.1	6.8	6.5	6.2	5.6	3.8	3.6	4.7	1.0	0.8	0.4
Boulder, CO	n/a	n/a	n/a	n/a	n/a	n/a	n/a	n/a	n/a	n/a	n/a	n/a
Cape Coral, FL	41.5	40.0	35.1	16.6	17.9	15.8	5.8	8.5	15.5	3.0	2.3	1.9
Cedar Rapids, IA	n/a	n/a	n/a	n/a	n/a	n/a	n/a	n/a	n/a	n/a	n/a	n/a
Charleston, SC	16.0	18.4	18.1	14.5	16.6	16.5	17.0	16.7	27.7	3.4	2.2	2.3
Charlotte, NC	8.5	9.3	6.6	8.1	9.0	6.3	5.6	7.6	5.6	1.7	1.8	1.0
Chicago, IL	7.5	7.6	7.4	7.4	7.6	7.2	7.0	5.7	7.4	1.6	1.5	1.2
Cincinnati, OH	6.8	8.6	6.6	6.7	8.4	6.2	4.4	10.7	7.9	1.5	1.1	0.7
Clarksville, TN	n/a	n/a	n/a	n/a	n/a	n/a	n/a	n/a	n/a	n/a	n/a	n/a
Cleveland, OH	10.4	10.1	9.3	10.3	9.9	8.8	6.9	3.8	5.5	0.9	1.1	0.7
College Station, TX	n/a	n/a	n/a	n/a	n/a	n/a	n/a	n/a	n/a	n/a	n/a	n/a
Colorado Springs, CO	n/a	n/a	n/a	n/a	n/a	n/a	n/a	n/a	n/a	n/a	n/a	n/a
Columbia, MO	n/a	n/a	n/a	n/a	n/a	n/a	n/a	n/a	n/a	n/a	n/a	n/a
Columbia, SC	8.9	10.6	7.2	8.8	10.4	7.1	9.4	9.3	4.5	1.9	1.5	0.7
Columbus, OH	7.4	4.5	4.7	7.4	4.2	4.5	8.6	4.3	5.9	1.5	0.8	0.3
Dallas, TX	7.8	7.6	6.4	7.6	7.3	6.4	7.4	6.9	7.2	1.4	1.5	0.7
Davenport, IA	n/a	n/a	n/a	n/a	n/a	n/a	n/a	n/a	n/a	n/a	n/a	n/a
Denver, CO	8.0	7.5	5.8	7.4	7.0	5.1	3.8	4.7	4.8	0.9	1.0	0.5
Des Moines, IA	n/a	n/a	n/a	n/a	n/a	n/a	n/a	n/a	n/a	n/a	n/a	n/a
Durham, NC	n/a	n/a	n/a	n/a	n/a	n/a	n/a	n/a	n/a	n/a	n/a	n/a
Edison, NJ	10.3	9.2	9.1	9.1	7.8	7.8	4.5	4.3	4.5	1.6	1.4	1.3
El Paso, TX	n/a	n/a	n/a	n/a	n/a	n/a	n/a	n/a	n/a	n/a	n/a	n/a
Fargo, ND	n/a	n/a	n/a	n/a	n/a	n/a	n/a	n/a	n/a	n/a	n/a	n/a
Fayetteville, NC	n/a	n/a	n/a	n/a	n/a	n/a	n/a	n/a	n/a	n/a	n/a	n/a
Fort Collins, CO	n/a	n/a	n/a	n/a	n/a	n/a	n/a	n/a	n/a	n/a	n/a	n/a
Fort Wayne, IN	n/a	n/a	n/a	n/a	n/a	n/a	n/a	n/a	n/a	n/a	n/a	n/a
Fort Worth, TX	7.8	7.6	6.4	7.6	7.3	6.4	7.4	6.9	7.2	1.4	1.5	0.7
Grand Rapids, MI	8.9	7.4	7.1	6.8	5.1	4.7	6.8	4.5	4.6	0.3	0.5	1.1
Greeley, CO	n/a	n/a	n/a	n/a	n/a	n/a	n/a	n/a	n/a	n/a	n/a	n/a
Green Bay, WI	n/a	n/a	n/a	n/a	n/a	n/a	n/a	n/a	n/a	n/a	n/a	n/a
Greensboro, NC	11.6	9.9	8.3	11.5	9.5	8.2	11.4	8.1	7.2	1.0	0.7	0.7
Honolulu, HI	14.0	11.7	10.0	12.9	10.9	9.6	6.5	5.7	5.5	1.4	1.8	1.0
Houston, TX	8.8	9.8	6.8	8.2	9.1	6.3	8.8	11.4	9.7	2.0	1.9	1.1
Huntsville, AL	n/a	n/a	n/a	n/a	n/a	n/a	n/a	n/a	n/a	n/a	n/a	n/a
Indianapolis, IN	8.7	7.2	7.3	8.6	6.7	7.0	9.9	7.0	10.4	1.5	1.5	0.8
Jacksonville, FL	10.1	10.1	9.5	9.3	9.8	9.3	5.6	5.2	7.5	1.3	1.0	1.5
Kansas City, MO	7.8	8.9	9.1	7.7	8.7	9.1	7.9	10.0	9.4	1.2	1.4	0.7
Lafayette, LA	n/a	n/a	n/a	n/a	n/a	n/a	n/a	n/a	n/a	n/a	n/a	n/a
Lakeland, FL	n/a	n/a	n/a	n/a	n/a	n/a	n/a	n/a	n/a	n/a	n/a	n/a
Las Vegas, NV	11.4	10.2	7.8	10.4	9.5	7.1	6.8	5.5	5.0	0.9	2.0	1.1
Lexington, KY	n/a	n/a	n/a	n/a	n/a	n/a	n/a	n/a	n/a	n/a	n/a	n/a
Lincoln, NE	n/a	n/a	n/a	n/a	n/a	n/a	n/a	n/a	n/a	n/a	n/a	n/a
Little Rock, AR	10.5	9.9	9.4	10.2	9.6	9.1	10.9	11.4	9.1	1.8	1.7	1.3
Los Angeles, CA	6.6	6.3	5.5	6.2	5.8	4.8	4.0	4.0	3.6	1.2	1.1	0.6
Louisville, KY	7.6	7.9	6.9	7.4	7.8	6.9	7.7	10.6	6.4	1.4	0.7	1.4

Table continued on following page.

Appendix A: Comparative Statistics   A-59

Metro Area[1]	Gross Vacancy Rate[2] (%)			Year-Round Vacancy Rate[3] (%)			Rental Vacancy Rate[4] (%)			Homeowner Vacancy Rate[5] (%)		
	2018	2019	2020	2018	2019	2020	2018	2019	2020	2018	2019	2020
Madison, WI	n/a	n/a	n/a	n/a	n/a	n/a	n/a	n/a	n/a	n/a	n/a	n/a
Manchester, NH	n/a	n/a	n/a	n/a	n/a	n/a	n/a	n/a	n/a	n/a	n/a	n/a
Memphis, TN	12.6	9.9	7.3	12.5	9.9	7.0	11.7	10.6	6.6	1.6	1.4	1.0
Miami, FL	14.9	14.1	12.6	7.9	7.4	6.8	7.4	7.0	5.4	1.9	1.8	1.4
Midland, TX	n/a	n/a	n/a	n/a	n/a	n/a	n/a	n/a	n/a	n/a	n/a	n/a
Milwaukee, WI	8.1	8.0	6.6	7.8	7.8	6.3	5.9	6.6	4.6	1.4	0.6	0.6
Minneapolis, MN	3.9	4.4	4.7	3.3	3.8	3.7	4.1	4.1	4.0	0.4	0.5	0.5
Nashville, TN	5.9	7.8	6.5	5.8	7.5	6.1	7.5	8.6	7.3	0.8	1.2	0.7
New Haven, CT	10.9	11.9	9.4	10.0	11.1	8.4	5.6	8.3	7.8	1.4	1.5	0.2
New Orleans, LA	11.9	12.9	10.7	11.8	12.8	9.8	9.7	9.4	6.1	1.7	1.8	1.3
New York, NY	10.3	9.2	9.1	9.1	7.8	7.8	4.5	4.3	4.5	1.6	1.4	1.3
Oklahoma City, OK	11.5	10.8	7.5	11.2	10.4	7.3	11.8	8.6	6.4	2.7	2.7	0.9
Omaha, NE	7.1	5.6	5.6	6.1	4.8	5.3	7.1	6.3	6.5	0.7	0.6	0.5
Orlando, FL	19.4	16.0	12.9	16.2	12.7	9.8	5.8	8.3	8.6	2.6	2.5	1.2
Peoria, IL	n/a	n/a	n/a	n/a	n/a	n/a	n/a	n/a	n/a	n/a	n/a	n/a
Philadelphia, PA	9.0	8.3	6.0	8.9	8.1	5.8	6.4	7.1	5.4	1.2	1.3	0.7
Phoenix, AZ	12.6	10.3	8.9	7.8	6.2	5.3	6.2	5.0	4.9	1.4	1.0	0.7
Pittsburgh, PA	10.2	10.6	11.5	9.9	10.3	11.3	6.3	7.3	9.3	2.2	1.2	1.0
Portland, OR	6.8	6.6	5.5	6.0	5.6	4.9	3.8	4.4	4.3	1.4	0.9	0.8
Providence, RI	10.3	9.8	8.7	8.5	8.2	6.6	5.0	4.2	3.5	1.1	0.9	0.8
Provo, UT	n/a	n/a	n/a	n/a	n/a	n/a	n/a	n/a	n/a	n/a	n/a	n/a
Raleigh, NC	6.7	6.6	4.6	6.6	6.5	4.5	6.4	7.0	2.3	0.9	0.8	0.4
Reno, NV	n/a	n/a	n/a	n/a	n/a	n/a	n/a	n/a	n/a	n/a	n/a	n/a
Richmond, VA	8.0	8.5	6.0	8.0	8.5	6.0	5.4	9.5	2.7	2.1	1.3	0.9
Riverside, CA	15.1	14.9	11.8	9.1	9.6	7.5	5.1	4.5	4.4	1.6	1.7	0.8
Rochester, MN	n/a	n/a	n/a	n/a	n/a	n/a	n/a	n/a	n/a	n/a	n/a	n/a
Sacramento, CA	8.6	7.8	6.1	7.9	7.1	5.8	5.1	4.2	4.2	1.5	0.8	1.0
Salt Lake City, UT	5.0	4.8	5.7	4.7	4.8	5.6	6.1	5.0	6.2	0.5	0.8	0.3
San Antonio, TX	6.7	9.0	7.4	5.8	8.2	6.7	7.4	10.1	7.2	0.6	2.0	1.0
San Diego, CA	7.6	7.5	6.0	7.4	7.3	5.6	4.5	5.8	3.9	0.7	0.8	0.8
San Francisco, CA	7.5	7.1	6.4	7.4	6.9	6.2	5.4	3.8	5.3	0.9	0.9	0.5
San Jose, CA	5.8	5.6	4.7	5.8	5.6	4.7	4.6	3.7	4.4	0.5	0.5	n/a
Santa Rosa, CA	n/a	n/a	n/a	n/a	n/a	n/a	n/a	n/a	n/a	n/a	n/a	n/a
Savannah, GA	n/a	n/a	n/a	n/a	n/a	n/a	n/a	n/a	n/a	n/a	n/a	n/a
Seattle, WA	5.9	5.5	4.7	5.4	5.2	4.5	4.8	4.4	3.6	0.8	1.0	0.6
Sioux Falls, SD	n/a	n/a	n/a	n/a	n/a	n/a	n/a	n/a	n/a	n/a	n/a	n/a
Springfield, IL	n/a	n/a	n/a	n/a	n/a	n/a	n/a	n/a	n/a	n/a	n/a	n/a
Tallahassee, FL	n/a	n/a	n/a	n/a	n/a	n/a	n/a	n/a	n/a	n/a	n/a	n/a
Tampa, FL	16.1	16.2	13.0	11.9	12.7	10.1	9.9	10.7	8.9	2.1	1.6	1.5
Tucson, AZ	12.5	14.8	12.1	8.1	9.2	7.7	4.4	7.3	8.6	1.8	1.5	0.5
Tulsa, OK	11.7	8.4	9.4	11.6	8.0	8.8	10.1	8.5	8.6	2.6	1.6	0.8
Tuscaloosa, AL	n/a	n/a	n/a	n/a	n/a	n/a	n/a	n/a	n/a	n/a	n/a	n/a
Virginia Beach, VA	8.9	10.4	7.9	7.6	9.3	7.0	7.1	7.1	5.5	1.2	2.2	0.6
Washington, DC	7.0	7.1	6.5	6.7	6.7	6.2	6.2	5.6	5.5	1.1	1.1	0.7
Wichita, KS	n/a	n/a	n/a	n/a	n/a	n/a	n/a	n/a	n/a	n/a	n/a	n/a
Winston-Salem, NC	n/a	n/a	n/a	n/a	n/a	n/a	n/a	n/a	n/a	n/a	n/a	n/a
U.S.	12.3	12.0	10.6	9.7	9.5	8.2	6.9	6.7	6.3	1.5	1.4	1.0

Note: (1) Metropolitan Statistical Area—see Appendix B for areas included; (2) The percentage of the total housing inventory that is vacant; (3) The percentage of the housing inventory (excluding seasonal units) that is year-round vacant; (4) The percentage of rental inventory that is vacant for rent; (5) The percentage of homeowner inventory that is vacant for sale; n/a not available
Source: U.S. Census Bureau, Housing Vacancies and Homeownership Annual Statistics: 2018, 2019, 2020

A-60 Appendix A: Comparative Statistics

Bankruptcy Filings

City	Area Covered	Business Filings			Nonbusiness Filings		
		2019	2020	% Chg.	2019	2020	% Chg.
Albuquerque, NM	Bernalillo County	30	33	10.0	1,071	872	-18.6
Allentown, PA	Lehigh County	16	10	-37.5	599	433	-27.7
Anchorage, AK	Anchorage Borough	17	20	17.6	176	137	-22.2
Ann Arbor, MI	Washtenaw County	10	13	30.0	654	454	-30.6
Athens, GA	Clarke County	0	5	n/a	338	228	-32.5
Atlanta, GA	Fulton County	173	152	-12.1	4,013	2,591	-35.4
Austin, TX	Travis County	118	175	48.3	737	529	-28.2
Baton Rouge, LA	East Baton Rouge Parish	37	49	32.4	771	435	-43.6
Boise City, ID	Ada County	26	19	-26.9	878	589	-32.9
Boston, MA	Suffolk County	47	37	-21.3	530	279	-47.4
Boulder, CO	Boulder County	30	42	40.0	372	286	-23.1
Cape Coral, FL	Lee County	57	79	38.6	1,254	1,112	-11.3
Cedar Rapids, IA	Linn County	11	9	-18.2	365	285	-21.9
Charleston, SC	Charleston County	19	21	10.5	356	261	-26.7
Charlotte, NC	Mecklenburg County	64	45	-29.7	1,020	639	-37.4
Chicago, IL	Cook County	413	335	-18.9	27,789	16,384	-41.0
Cincinnati, OH	Hamilton County	48	25	-47.9	2,519	1,845	-26.8
Clarksville, TN	Montgomery County	11	6	-45.5	829	579	-30.2
Cleveland, OH	Cuyahoga County	69	96	39.1	6,013	4,189	-30.3
College Station, TX	Brazos County	7	6	-14.3	105	87	-17.1
Colorado Springs, CO	El Paso County	39	30	-23.1	1,525	1,154	-24.3
Columbia, MO	Boone County	6	8	33.3	375	263	-29.9
Columbia, SC	Richland County	11	12	9.1	837	520	-37.9
Columbus, OH	Franklin County	72	86	19.4	4,342	2,960	-31.8
Dallas, TX	Dallas County	355	568	60.0	3,572	2,452	-31.4
Davenport, IA	Scott County	10	7	-30.0	329	246	-25.2
Denver, CO	Denver County	68	91	33.8	1,338	1,029	-23.1
Des Moines, IA	Polk County	28	12	-57.1	962	782	-18.7
Durham, NC	Durham County	16	18	12.5	395	223	-43.5
Edison, NJ	Middlesex County	46	31	-32.6	1,718	1,097	-36.1
El Paso, TX	El Paso County	63	42	-33.3	2,079	1,290	-38.0
Fargo, ND	Cass County	4	5	25.0	198	183	-7.6
Fayetteville, NC	Cumberland County	8	8	0.0	795	506	-36.4
Fort Collins, CO	Larimer County	29	28	-3.4	558	404	-27.6
Fort Wayne, IN	Allen County	15	15	0.0	1,294	1,057	-18.3
Fort Worth, TX	Tarrant County	242	271	12.0	4,040	2,937	-27.3
Grand Rapids, MI	Kent County	35	47	34.3	935	613	-34.4
Greeley, CO	Weld County	20	21	5.0	691	509	-26.3
Green Bay, WI	Brown County	25	9	-64.0	599	418	-30.2
Greensboro, NC	Guilford County	25	21	-16.0	758	471	-37.9
Honolulu, HI	Honolulu County	35	46	31.4	1,225	1,106	-9.7
Houston, TX	Harris County	411	608	47.9	4,527	2,967	-34.5
Huntsville, AL	Madison County	20	42	110.0	1,463	1,024	-30.0
Indianapolis, IN	Marion County	100	39	-61.0	4,465	3,319	-25.7
Jacksonville, FL	Duval County	75	57	-24.0	2,349	1,604	-31.7
Kansas City, MO	Jackson County	36	26	-27.8	2,080	1,394	-33.0
Lafayette, LA	Lafayette Parish	44	22	-50.0	560	306	-45.4
Lakeland, FL	Polk County	31	53	71.0	1,466	1,168	-20.3
Las Vegas, NV	Clark County	228	204	-10.5	8,184	6,529	-20.2
Lexington, KY	Fayette County	56	54	-3.6	749	520	-30.6
Lincoln, NE	Lancaster County	16	11	-31.3	653	485	-25.7
Little Rock, AR	Pulaski County	233	30	-87.1	2,318	1,519	-34.5
Los Angeles, CA	Los Angeles County	882	857	-2.8	18,304	13,323	-27.2
Louisville, KY	Jefferson County	50	39	-22.0	2,893	2,174	-24.9
Madison, WI	Dane County	34	28	-17.6	773	527	-31.8

Table continued on following page.

Appendix A: Comparative Statistics   A-61

City	Area Covered	Business Filings			Nonbusiness Filings		
		2019	2020	% Chg.	2019	2020	% Chg.
Manchester, NH	Hillsborough County	25	27	8.0	519	339	-34.7
Memphis, TN	Shelby County	72	41	-43.1	9,622	5,523	-42.6
Miami, FL	Miami-Dade County	215	322	49.8	8,490	7,108	-16.3
Midland, TX	Midland County	32	11	-65.6	72	48	-33.3
Milwaukee, WI	Milwaukee County	43	48	11.6	6,315	4,019	-36.4
Minneapolis, MN	Hennepin County	62	92	48.4	2,032	1,552	-23.6
Nashville, TN	Davidson County	53	60	13.2	2,051	1,330	-35.2
New Haven, CT	New Haven County	47	33	-29.8	1,884	1,258	-33.2
New Orleans, LA	Orleans Parish	36	21	-41.7	683	391	-42.8
New York, NY	Bronx County	44	24	-45.5	2,486	1,498	-39.7
New York, NY	Kings County	327	182	-44.3	2,743	1,710	-37.7
New York, NY	New York County	244	480	96.7	1,210	854	-29.4
New York, NY	Queens County	206	127	-38.3	3,708	1,990	-46.3
New York, NY	Richmond County	22	19	-13.6	835	459	-45.0
Oklahoma City, OK	Oklahoma County	89	139	56.2	2,147	1,679	-21.8
Omaha, NE	Douglas County	39	16	-59.0	1,283	1,064	-17.1
Orlando, FL	Orange County	154	167	8.4	2,956	2,477	-16.2
Peoria, IL	Peoria County	16	6	-62.5	548	391	-28.6
Philadelphia, PA	Philadelphia County	88	116	31.8	2,222	1,162	-47.7
Phoenix, AZ	Maricopa County	344	261	-24.1	11,095	8,954	-19.3
Pittsburgh, PA	Allegheny County	140	116	-17.1	2,280	1,700	-25.4
Portland, OR	Multnomah County	62	59	-4.8	1,394	1,147	-17.7
Providence, RI	Providence County	38	29	-23.7	1,246	887	-28.8
Provo, UT	Utah County	37	31	-16.2	1,408	1,151	-18.3
Raleigh, NC	Wake County	91	75	-17.6	1,314	882	-32.9
Reno, NV	Washoe County	34	44	29.4	960	765	-20.3
Richmond, VA	Richmond city	18	21	16.7	897	695	-22.5
Riverside, CA	Riverside County	165	145	-12.1	6,195	4,455	-28.1
Rochester, MN	Olmsted County	9	4	-55.6	151	138	-8.6
Sacramento, CA	Sacramento County	95	124	30.5	3,208	2,300	-28.3
Salt Lake City, UT	Salt Lake County	56	60	7.1	4,109	3,232	-21.3
San Antonio, TX	Bexar County	191	128	-33.0	2,173	1,445	-33.5
San Diego, CA	San Diego County	308	269	-12.7	7,366	5,848	-20.6
San Francisco, CA	San Francisco County	58	67	15.5	564	384	-31.9
San Jose, CA	Santa Clara County	94	86	-8.5	1,446	1,018	-29.6
Santa Rosa, CA	Sonoma County	32	29	-9.4	531	388	-26.9
Savannah, GA	Chatham County	18	13	-27.8	1,220	729	-40.2
Seattle, WA	King County	115	96	-16.5	2,174	1,516	-30.3
Sioux Falls, SD	Minnehaha County	18	11	-38.9	349	268	-23.2
Springfield, IL	Sangamon County	8	8	0.0	436	311	-28.7
Tallahassee, FL	Leon County	35	17	-51.4	446	288	-35.4
Tampa, FL	Hillsborough County	155	110	-29.0	3,356	2,538	-24.4
Tucson, AZ	Pima County	50	32	-36.0	2,438	1,727	-29.2
Tulsa, OK	Tulsa County	44	45	2.3	1,555	1,163	-25.2
Tuscaloosa, AL	Tuscaloosa County	9	10	11.1	1,246	799	-35.9
Virginia Beach, VA	Virginia Beach city	18	14	-22.2	1,606	1,206	-24.9
Washington, DC	District of Columbia	50	50	0.0	789	449	-43.1
Wichita, KS	Sedgwick County	30	15	-50.0	1,381	941	-31.9
Winston-Salem, NC	Forsyth County	17	15	-11.8	537	363	-32.4
U.S.	U.S.	22,780	21,655	-4.9	752,160	522,808	-30.5

Note: Business filings include Chapter 7, Chapter 9, Chapter 11, Chapter 12, Chapter 13, Chapter 15, and Section 304; Nonbusiness filings include Chapter 7, Chapter 11, and Chapter 13
Source: Administrative Office of the U.S. Courts, Business and Nonbusiness Bankruptcy, County Cases Commenced by Chapter of the Bankruptcy Code, During the 12-Month Period Ending December 31, 2019 and Business and Nonbusiness Bankruptcy, County Cases Commenced by Chapter of the Bankruptcy Code, During the 12-Month Period Ending December 31, 2020

A-62 Appendix A: Comparative Statistics

Income: City

City	Per Capita ($)	Median Household ($)	Average Household ($)
Albuquerque, NM	30,403	52,911	72,265
Allentown, PA	20,792	41,167	56,842
Anchorage, AK	41,415	84,928	109,988
Ann Arbor, MI	42,674	65,745	96,906
Athens, GA	23,726	38,311	59,118
Atlanta, GA	47,424	59,948	106,300
Austin, TX	43,043	71,576	102,876
Baton Rouge, LA	28,491	44,470	70,902
Boise City, ID	34,636	60,035	82,424
Boston, MA	44,690	71,115	107,608
Boulder, CO	44,942	69,520	109,410
Cape Coral, FL	29,970	61,599	76,925
Cedar Rapids, IA	32,290	58,511	75,289
Charleston, SC	42,872	68,438	98,288
Charlotte, NC	38,000	62,817	94,516
Chicago, IL	37,103	58,247	90,713
Cincinnati, OH	30,531	40,640	65,213
Clarksville, TN	25,239	53,604	65,458
Cleveland, OH	21,223	30,907	46,137
College Station, TX	27,541	45,820	73,853
Colorado Springs, CO	34,076	64,712	84,708
Columbia, MO	30,244	51,276	74,727
Columbia, SC	30,461	47,286	76,118
Columbus, OH	29,322	53,745	69,315
Dallas, TX	34,479	52,580	86,393
Davenport, IA	28,645	51,029	68,559
Denver, CO	43,770	68,592	99,151
Des Moines, IA	28,554	53,525	69,074
Durham, NC	34,329	58,905	82,573
Edison, NJ	44,667	103,076	127,171
El Paso, TX	22,734	47,568	64,025
Fargo, ND	35,205	55,551	78,237
Fayetteville, NC	24,823	45,024	58,752
Fort Collins, CO	34,482	65,866	87,406
Fort Wayne, IN	26,970	49,411	65,377
Fort Worth, TX	29,531	62,187	82,977
Grand Rapids, MI	26,120	50,103	65,615
Greeley, CO	26,222	57,586	72,302
Green Bay, WI	26,618	49,251	64,595
Greensboro, NC	29,628	48,964	71,453
Honolulu, HI	37,834	71,465	97,456
Houston, TX	32,521	52,338	84,179
Huntsville, AL	35,634	55,305	80,877
Indianapolis, IN	28,363	47,873	68,367
Jacksonville, FL	30,064	54,701	74,873
Kansas City, MO	32,348	54,194	75,137
Lafayette, LA	32,998	51,264	78,055
Lakeland, FL	28,042	47,511	67,899
Las Vegas, NV	30,761	56,354	79,657
Lexington, KY	34,442	57,291	83,111
Lincoln, NE	31,301	57,746	76,763
Little Rock, AR	35,966	51,485	83,730
Los Angeles, CA	35,261	62,142	96,416
Louisville, KY	30,943	53,436	74,580
Madison, WI	38,285	65,332	87,055
Manchester, NH	31,951	60,711	75,665

Table continued on following page.

Appendix A: Comparative Statistics   A-63

City	Per Capita ($)	Median Household ($)	Average Household ($)
Memphis, TN	25,605	41,228	62,588
Miami, FL	28,804	39,049	68,105
Midland, TX	40,252	79,329	112,701
Milwaukee, WI	23,462	41,838	57,332
Minneapolis, MN	38,808	62,583	89,282
Nashville, TN	35,243	59,828	83,348
New Haven, CT	26,429	42,222	65,362
New Orleans, LA	31,385	41,604	71,938
New York, NY	39,828	63,998	102,946
Oklahoma City, OK	30,567	55,557	77,896
Omaha, NE	33,401	60,092	82,945
Orlando, FL	32,085	51,757	75,669
Peoria, IL	31,497	51,771	74,900
Philadelphia, PA	27,924	45,927	68,379
Phoenix, AZ	29,343	57,459	80,631
Pittsburgh, PA	34,083	48,711	72,981
Portland, OR	41,310	71,005	95,998
Providence, RI	26,560	45,610	71,136
Provo, UT	20,792	48,888	69,265
Raleigh, NC	38,494	67,266	94,359
Reno, NV	34,475	58,790	81,700
Richmond, VA	33,549	47,250	76,182
Riverside, CA	26,028	69,045	85,486
Rochester, MN	39,518	73,106	96,015
Sacramento, CA	31,956	62,335	83,189
Salt Lake City, UT	36,779	60,676	88,127
San Antonio, TX	25,894	52,455	70,778
San Diego, CA	41,112	79,673	108,864
San Francisco, CA	68,883	112,449	160,396
San Jose, CA	46,599	109,593	142,635
Santa Rosa, CA	36,935	75,630	96,786
Savannah, GA	25,664	43,307	63,984
Seattle, WA	59,835	92,263	128,184
Sioux Falls, SD	33,065	59,912	79,847
Springfield, IL	34,607	54,648	77,473
Tallahassee, FL	27,677	45,734	66,889
Tampa, FL	36,169	53,833	87,818
Tucson, AZ	23,655	43,425	58,057
Tulsa, OK	30,970	47,650	73,816
Tuscaloosa, AL	26,437	45,268	68,837
Virginia Beach, VA	37,776	76,610	96,936
Washington, DC	56,147	86,420	127,890
Wichita, KS	28,806	52,620	71,335
Winston-Salem, NC	28,821	45,750	71,423
U.S.	34,103	62,843	88,607

Source: U.S. Census Bureau, 2015-2019 American Community Survey 5-Year Estimates

A-64   Appendix A: Comparative Statistics

Income: Metro Area

Metro Area	Per Capita ($)	Median Household ($)	Average Household ($)
Albuquerque, NM	29,747	54,072	73,512
Allentown, PA	34,637	67,652	88,415
Anchorage, AK	38,725	83,048	105,968
Ann Arbor, MI	41,399	72,586	101,787
Athens, GA	27,653	47,214	70,940
Atlanta, GA	35,296	68,316	94,723
Austin, TX	39,827	76,844	104,847
Baton Rouge, LA	31,082	58,912	81,614
Boise City, ID	30,508	60,568	80,438
Boston, MA	47,604	90,333	122,399
Boulder, CO	46,826	83,019	115,966
Cape Coral, FL	33,543	57,832	82,544
Cedar Rapids, IA	34,039	64,687	82,498
Charleston, SC	35,011	63,649	88,023
Charlotte, NC	34,558	63,217	89,212
Chicago, IL	38,157	71,770	100,233
Cincinnati, OH	34,575	63,987	86,633
Clarksville, TN	25,931	53,027	67,368
Cleveland, OH	33,785	56,008	79,168
College Station, TX	27,698	50,240	73,129
Colorado Springs, CO	33,795	68,687	88,185
Columbia, MO	29,534	54,808	74,042
Columbia, SC	29,894	55,971	75,154
Columbus, OH	34,441	65,150	87,472
Dallas, TX	35,278	70,281	97,589
Davenport, IA	31,571	58,531	76,075
Denver, CO	41,988	79,664	106,322
Des Moines, IA	36,310	70,126	90,791
Durham, NC	36,322	62,289	90,054
Edison, NJ	43,409	78,773	116,604
El Paso, TX	21,644	46,795	62,663
Fargo, ND	35,812	64,666	85,794
Fayetteville, NC	24,228	48,459	61,989
Fort Collins, CO	37,363	71,881	93,301
Fort Wayne, IN	29,383	55,341	73,578
Fort Worth, TX	35,278	70,281	97,589
Grand Rapids, MI	31,388	63,302	83,235
Greeley, CO	31,793	74,150	89,427
Green Bay, WI	32,520	62,405	79,316
Greensboro, NC	28,787	50,891	71,256
Honolulu, HI	36,816	85,857	109,304
Houston, TX	34,400	67,516	97,410
Huntsville, AL	34,918	64,483	86,328
Indianapolis, IN	33,699	61,552	85,193
Jacksonville, FL	33,304	61,723	84,690
Kansas City, MO	35,761	66,632	89,308
Lafayette, LA	27,955	51,955	72,041
Lakeland, FL	24,864	50,584	66,810
Las Vegas, NV	30,704	59,340	80,762
Lexington, KY	33,153	58,685	82,094
Lincoln, NE	32,360	61,031	80,274
Little Rock, AR	30,599	54,746	76,145
Los Angeles, CA	35,916	72,998	104,698
Louisville, KY	32,630	59,158	80,682
Madison, WI	39,484	72,374	93,923
Manchester, NH	40,955	81,460	103,090

Table continued on following page.

Appendix A: Comparative Statistics   A-65

Metro Area	Per Capita ($)	Median Household ($)	Average Household ($)
Memphis, TN	29,453	53,209	76,187
Miami, FL	32,522	56,775	86,518
Midland, TX	38,966	79,140	109,861
Milwaukee, WI	35,491	62,389	86,290
Minneapolis, MN	41,204	80,421	104,946
Nashville, TN	35,479	66,347	91,202
New Haven, CT	38,009	69,905	94,740
New Orleans, LA	31,072	53,084	76,818
New York, NY	43,409	78,773	116,604
Oklahoma City, OK	31,301	59,084	80,805
Omaha, NE	34,825	67,885	88,578
Orlando, FL	29,875	58,368	80,864
Peoria, IL	32,575	59,397	79,057
Philadelphia, PA	39,091	72,343	100,889
Phoenix, AZ	32,522	63,883	87,543
Pittsburgh, PA	36,208	60,535	82,754
Portland, OR	38,544	74,792	97,930
Providence, RI	35,991	67,818	89,281
Provo, UT	26,153	74,387	93,213
Raleigh, NC	38,370	75,851	100,551
Reno, NV	36,087	64,801	89,057
Richmond, VA	36,413	68,529	92,171
Riverside, CA	27,003	65,121	85,373
Rochester, MN	38,754	73,697	95,925
Sacramento, CA	35,563	72,280	96,023
Salt Lake City, UT	32,829	74,842	96,196
San Antonio, TX	29,071	60,327	81,852
San Diego, CA	38,073	78,980	106,600
San Francisco, CA	55,252	106,025	147,703
San Jose, CA	55,547	122,478	163,355
Santa Rosa, CA	42,178	81,018	108,169
Savannah, GA	32,088	59,459	82,125
Seattle, WA	45,750	86,856	115,653
Sioux Falls, SD	33,453	65,621	83,463
Springfield, IL	35,603	62,533	82,720
Tallahassee, FL	28,766	51,874	72,487
Tampa, FL	32,276	55,285	78,248
Tucson, AZ	29,707	53,379	73,554
Tulsa, OK	30,633	55,739	77,341
Tuscaloosa, AL	25,759	50,408	67,811
Virginia Beach, VA	33,907	66,759	86,062
Washington, DC	49,881	103,751	134,513
Wichita, KS	29,414	57,379	74,900
Winston-Salem, NC	28,986	50,774	71,206
U.S.	34,103	62,843	88,607

Note: Figures cover the Metropolitan Statistical Area (MSA)—see Appendix B for areas included
Source: U.S. Census Bureau, 2015-2019 American Community Survey 5-Year Estimates

A-66 Appendix A: Comparative Statistics

Household Income Distribution: City

City	Percent of Households Earning							
	Under $15,000	$15,000 -$24,999	$25,000 -$34,999	$35,000 -$49,999	$50,000 -$74,999	$75,000 -$99,999	$100,000 -$149,999	$150,000 and up
Albuquerque, NM	13.1	10.8	10.4	13.1	17.7	12.0	13.3	9.4
Allentown, PA	15.9	13.8	13.0	15.2	19.3	10.2	8.0	4.5
Anchorage, AK	5.3	5.1	6.3	9.9	17.4	13.8	20.5	21.6
Ann Arbor, MI	14.5	7.3	7.6	9.3	15.8	11.4	14.5	19.7
Athens, GA	21.0	14.6	11.3	13.3	14.1	8.7	9.9	7.2
Atlanta, GA	15.4	9.6	8.0	10.6	14.8	10.3	12.8	18.5
Austin, TX	8.6	6.5	7.9	11.6	17.5	12.3	16.6	19.0
Baton Rouge, LA	18.2	13.1	11.0	12.0	15.5	9.1	11.4	9.7
Boise City, ID	10.2	9.7	9.3	13.2	18.2	12.3	14.8	12.3
Boston, MA	16.1	8.1	6.3	8.4	13.0	10.3	15.7	22.2
Boulder, CO	13.6	7.5	7.3	10.0	14.3	10.1	13.9	23.4
Cape Coral, FL	8.7	7.8	9.1	13.7	20.5	15.8	15.3	9.1
Cedar Rapids, IA	9.0	8.8	10.0	13.9	20.9	13.4	15.1	8.9
Charleston, SC	11.2	7.7	7.0	10.7	17.0	12.8	17.4	16.1
Charlotte, NC	8.6	7.9	9.7	13.3	17.9	12.5	14.6	15.5
Chicago, IL	14.0	10.3	8.9	11.0	15.1	11.2	13.8	15.7
Cincinnati, OH	21.1	12.6	11.2	12.3	15.6	9.1	9.4	8.7
Clarksville, TN	10.4	8.7	11.3	16.2	20.8	14.2	12.7	5.6
Cleveland, OH	27.1	15.1	12.9	13.7	14.2	7.9	5.7	3.4
College Station, TX	21.3	11.1	9.2	11.2	12.4	10.9	12.5	11.4
Colorado Springs, CO	8.8	8.3	8.5	12.5	19.0	13.8	16.2	12.8
Columbia, MO	14.8	10.6	9.8	13.8	15.2	11.2	13.6	11.0
Columbia, SC	17.9	11.5	10.8	11.7	15.6	10.9	10.4	11.2
Columbus, OH	12.1	9.7	10.2	14.4	19.5	13.3	13.4	7.3
Dallas, TX	11.8	10.4	10.7	14.7	17.9	10.6	10.8	13.1
Davenport, IA	12.5	11.4	10.6	14.6	19.1	12.3	12.1	7.4
Denver, CO	10.0	7.3	7.9	11.3	17.3	12.5	15.7	18.1
Des Moines, IA	12.0	10.6	10.2	14.2	19.9	13.7	12.4	7.1
Durham, NC	10.3	8.4	10.0	13.5	17.4	12.7	14.5	13.2
Edison, NJ	4.9	4.3	4.1	8.9	12.6	13.7	21.3	30.1
El Paso, TX	14.3	12.2	11.1	14.3	19.1	10.8	11.5	6.7
Fargo, ND	11.1	10.1	9.7	13.8	18.2	14.0	12.6	10.4
Fayetteville, NC	14.5	12.0	12.4	16.4	19.2	11.1	9.3	5.2
Fort Collins, CO	9.7	8.7	8.0	12.2	17.1	12.9	15.8	15.5
Fort Wayne, IN	11.5	11.3	11.9	15.8	19.4	12.6	10.8	6.6
Fort Worth, TX	10.2	8.3	9.5	12.0	18.8	13.4	15.5	12.3
Grand Rapids, MI	13.0	11.8	10.0	15.2	19.4	12.7	11.7	6.4
Greeley, CO	11.9	9.8	8.3	13.5	18.9	13.7	15.7	8.1
Green Bay, WI	11.9	10.9	11.8	16.2	19.6	12.6	11.4	5.5
Greensboro, NC	13.5	10.9	11.5	15.1	18.0	11.2	11.3	8.4
Honolulu, HI	10.1	6.9	6.8	11.8	16.8	12.8	17.0	17.6
Houston, TX	12.6	11.1	10.8	13.5	16.7	10.6	11.3	13.5
Huntsville, AL	13.7	10.7	10.0	11.8	15.2	10.9	13.9	13.8
Indianapolis, IN	13.5	11.1	11.8	15.3	17.9	11.3	11.0	8.0
Jacksonville, FL	11.3	9.4	10.1	14.6	19.4	13.2	12.9	9.2
Kansas City, MO	12.1	10.1	10.4	14.0	17.6	12.2	13.5	10.1
Lafayette, LA	15.8	11.1	10.1	12.0	17.1	10.2	11.1	12.7
Lakeland, FL	12.5	11.9	12.5	15.3	19.2	11.7	9.9	7.1
Las Vegas, NV	11.8	9.5	9.7	13.8	17.5	13.0	14.0	10.7
Lexington, KY	11.5	9.6	9.9	13.0	17.6	12.2	14.2	12.1
Lincoln, NE	9.6	9.2	10.5	13.9	19.3	13.0	14.7	9.9
Little Rock, AR	12.7	11.0	10.4	14.7	16.5	10.4	11.2	13.0
Los Angeles, CA	12.4	9.3	8.7	11.5	15.4	11.4	14.4	16.9
Louisville, KY	12.4	10.3	10.2	13.9	17.8	12.5	12.7	10.1

Table continued on following page.

Appendix A: Comparative Statistics A-67

City	Percent of Households Earning							
	Under $15,000	$15,000 -$24,999	$25,000 -$34,999	$35,000 -$49,999	$50,000 -$74,999	$75,000 -$99,999	$100,000 -$149,999	$150,000 and up
Madison, WI	10.3	7.6	8.8	12.1	17.7	13.3	16.4	13.6
Manchester, NH	10.1	8.6	9.9	12.5	19.8	13.3	16.3	9.3
Memphis, TN	18.3	13.5	11.8	14.6	16.5	9.4	8.8	7.0
Miami, FL	20.8	14.1	11.6	12.3	14.5	8.8	8.6	9.4
Midland, TX	6.7	6.7	6.9	9.8	17.3	13.7	18.0	20.8
Milwaukee, WI	17.8	13.1	11.7	15.1	17.2	10.6	9.6	4.8
Minneapolis, MN	13.0	8.7	8.2	11.6	16.0	12.3	14.6	15.5
Nashville, TN	9.8	8.5	9.3	14.1	18.9	13.6	14.3	11.8
New Haven, CT	20.2	11.9	11.1	12.5	15.8	9.6	9.7	9.4
New Orleans, LA	22.1	12.2	10.3	11.5	14.2	8.8	9.9	10.9
New York, NY	14.3	9.0	7.9	10.2	14.3	11.1	14.3	18.9
Oklahoma City, OK	11.3	9.5	10.0	14.0	18.6	12.6	13.3	10.7
Omaha, NE	10.5	8.8	8.8	13.5	18.5	13.4	14.4	12.1
Orlando, FL	12.5	10.4	11.1	14.2	19.8	10.9	10.8	10.3
Peoria, IL	16.8	11.0	8.8	12.0	17.3	11.6	11.8	10.7
Philadelphia, PA	19.1	11.2	10.2	12.7	15.8	10.5	11.0	9.4
Phoenix, AZ	10.4	9.3	9.5	14.3	18.5	12.6	13.6	11.9
Pittsburgh, PA	17.5	11.6	10.0	11.8	15.9	11.3	11.2	10.6
Portland, OR	10.6	7.2	7.8	10.4	16.4	13.0	16.9	17.7
Providence, RI	20.2	12.0	9.0	11.4	16.7	11.1	10.0	9.7
Provo, UT	12.2	12.9	12.3	13.5	18.9	11.8	10.6	7.8
Raleigh, NC	7.3	7.3	8.9	13.2	18.4	13.5	15.8	15.6
Reno, NV	9.2	9.5	9.5	14.5	18.6	12.7	14.5	11.5
Richmond, VA	17.6	11.0	10.1	13.3	16.2	10.2	10.5	11.0
Riverside, CA	9.0	7.6	8.3	11.4	17.8	14.8	17.6	13.6
Rochester, MN	8.2	7.0	7.1	11.6	17.6	14.1	17.8	16.6
Sacramento, CA	11.3	9.0	8.7	11.7	17.3	13.1	15.6	13.3
Salt Lake City, UT	12.0	8.5	9.1	12.4	17.6	12.5	14.3	13.7
San Antonio, TX	12.7	10.4	10.6	14.0	19.0	12.1	12.5	8.7
San Diego, CA	8.1	6.6	6.8	10.0	15.9	12.9	17.8	21.8
San Francisco, CA	9.7	5.8	4.9	6.2	9.8	9.0	15.6	38.9
San Jose, CA	6.2	4.8	4.9	7.2	12.0	10.7	18.0	36.2
Santa Rosa, CA	7.0	5.9	7.1	11.0	18.4	14.8	18.5	17.3
Savannah, GA	17.5	13.1	10.9	14.8	16.5	10.9	9.7	6.7
Seattle, WA	8.8	5.3	5.6	8.7	13.5	11.4	18.3	28.4
Sioux Falls, SD	8.8	8.3	10.7	13.2	19.0	14.4	15.2	10.5
Springfield, IL	13.7	10.7	9.6	12.1	17.2	13.0	12.9	10.9
Tallahassee, FL	16.8	10.9	11.7	13.8	17.3	10.2	10.4	8.8
Tampa, FL	14.6	10.3	9.9	12.2	15.8	10.7	12.0	14.6
Tucson, AZ	15.8	13.2	11.7	15.6	17.9	10.8	9.7	5.3
Tulsa, OK	14.2	11.6	11.2	15.2	17.4	10.3	10.1	10.0
Tuscaloosa, AL	19.4	11.0	11.0	12.3	16.5	9.4	10.2	10.2
Virginia Beach, VA	5.3	5.4	7.4	11.7	19.1	15.8	19.9	15.4
Washington, DC	12.9	6.0	5.9	7.7	12.2	10.6	16.4	28.2
Wichita, KS	12.3	10.5	10.5	14.6	18.7	12.0	12.8	8.7
Winston-Salem, NC	15.4	11.8	11.9	14.3	16.9	11.2	9.8	8.7
U.S.	10.3	8.9	8.9	12.3	17.2	12.7	15.1	14.5

Source: U.S. Census Bureau, 2015-2019 American Community Survey 5-Year Estimates

A-68 Appendix A: Comparative Statistics

Household Income Distribution: Metro Area

Metro Area	Percent of Households Earning							
	Under $15,000	$15,000 -$24,999	$25,000 -$34,999	$35,000 -$49,999	$50,000 -$74,999	$75,000 -$99,999	$100,000 -$149,999	$150,000 and up
Albuquerque, NM	12.4	10.7	10.0	13.3	18.0	12.5	13.1	9.8
Allentown, PA	7.9	8.4	8.7	12.2	17.9	13.9	16.9	14.2
Anchorage, AK	6.1	5.6	6.5	9.9	17.2	13.7	20.5	20.5
Ann Arbor, MI	10.6	7.1	7.1	10.5	16.0	12.5	16.7	19.6
Athens, GA	16.4	12.1	10.3	13.5	15.2	10.2	12.6	9.6
Atlanta, GA	8.4	7.6	8.3	12.1	17.8	13.3	16.2	16.1
Austin, TX	7.3	6.0	7.3	11.1	17.3	13.3	18.1	19.8
Baton Rouge, LA	12.6	9.8	9.4	11.5	16.4	11.9	15.5	12.9
Boise City, ID	9.5	8.6	9.4	13.5	19.8	13.6	15.2	10.5
Boston, MA	8.8	6.2	5.8	8.3	13.5	11.8	18.5	27.1
Boulder, CO	8.5	6.0	6.6	10.2	14.5	12.4	17.2	24.5
Cape Coral, FL	9.4	9.1	10.3	13.9	19.6	13.2	13.3	11.3
Cedar Rapids, IA	7.7	7.9	9.1	13.3	19.3	14.4	16.9	11.4
Charleston, SC	10.0	8.4	8.5	12.1	18.4	13.5	15.6	13.6
Charlotte, NC	8.9	8.6	9.2	12.7	18.1	13.0	15.1	14.4
Chicago, IL	9.3	7.9	7.8	10.8	16.0	12.8	17.0	18.4
Cincinnati, OH	10.2	8.7	8.6	11.8	17.6	13.2	16.0	13.8
Clarksville, TN	11.4	9.1	10.8	16.0	19.7	13.7	12.4	6.8
Cleveland, OH	12.6	9.7	9.8	13.0	17.4	12.4	13.9	11.2
College Station, TX	16.3	11.0	9.8	12.7	15.8	11.5	12.8	10.2
Colorado Springs, CO	7.8	7.4	8.1	12.0	19.0	14.3	17.4	13.9
Columbia, MO	12.0	10.0	10.1	13.9	17.4	12.8	14.2	9.5
Columbia, SC	12.2	9.1	10.1	13.4	18.4	13.4	13.6	9.8
Columbus, OH	9.2	8.1	8.6	12.4	18.2	13.5	16.5	13.5
Dallas, TX	7.7	7.1	8.3	12.0	17.8	13.2	16.7	17.2
Davenport, IA	10.2	9.4	9.5	13.4	19.0	13.8	15.4	9.3
Denver, CO	6.7	5.8	6.7	10.8	17.1	13.7	18.9	20.2
Des Moines, IA	7.2	7.5	8.1	12.0	18.8	14.4	17.6	14.3
Durham, NC	10.0	8.6	9.3	12.7	16.8	12.6	14.7	15.3
Edison, NJ	10.5	7.5	7.0	9.3	13.9	11.4	16.4	24.1
El Paso, TX	14.6	12.2	11.4	14.5	19.0	10.8	11.2	6.3
Fargo, ND	9.4	8.6	8.2	12.1	18.3	15.3	15.7	12.4
Fayetteville, NC	13.8	11.1	11.2	15.5	18.9	12.5	11.5	5.6
Fort Collins, CO	7.9	7.9	7.3	11.6	17.2	14.1	17.9	16.1
Fort Wayne, IN	9.4	9.8	10.9	14.8	19.8	13.7	13.3	8.3
Fort Worth, TX	7.7	7.1	8.3	12.0	17.8	13.2	16.7	17.2
Grand Rapids, MI	7.6	9.0	8.8	13.5	19.8	14.4	15.9	11.0
Greeley, CO	7.7	6.9	7.2	11.0	17.7	16.3	19.3	13.9
Green Bay, WI	8.2	8.5	9.5	13.5	19.2	14.6	16.4	10.0
Greensboro, NC	12.4	10.8	11.3	14.7	18.2	12.2	11.9	8.6
Honolulu, HI	7.1	5.1	5.9	9.6	15.8	13.9	20.2	22.5
Houston, TX	8.8	8.3	8.7	11.7	16.8	12.3	15.8	17.7
Huntsville, AL	10.4	9.2	8.8	11.5	16.1	12.5	16.4	15.0
Indianapolis, IN	9.6	8.7	9.4	13.2	17.9	13.3	15.1	12.8
Jacksonville, FL	9.5	8.3	9.2	13.4	18.8	13.6	14.7	12.4
Kansas City, MO	8.4	7.8	8.7	12.6	17.8	13.9	16.8	14.1
Lafayette, LA	14.4	11.5	10.3	12.4	16.1	12.4	13.4	9.6
Lakeland, FL	11.1	11.2	11.2	16.0	19.9	12.6	11.3	6.8
Las Vegas, NV	10.2	8.8	9.7	13.9	18.6	13.5	14.5	11.0
Lexington, KY	10.9	9.4	9.7	13.1	17.5	13.1	14.7	11.5
Lincoln, NE	8.9	8.8	9.9	13.4	19.0	13.3	15.9	10.8
Little Rock, AR	12.0	10.0	10.4	13.7	18.1	11.9	14.1	9.8
Los Angeles, CA	9.6	7.7	7.6	10.6	15.6	12.4	16.5	20.1
Louisville, KY	10.2	9.3	9.4	13.6	18.4	13.4	14.4	11.4

Table continued on following page.

Appendix A: Comparative Statistics   A-69

Metro Area	Percent of Households Earning							
	Under $15,000	$15,000 -$24,999	$25,000 -$34,999	$35,000 -$49,999	$50,000 -$74,999	$75,000 -$99,999	$100,000 -$149,999	$150,000 and up
Madison, WI	7.3	6.8	7.9	11.9	17.8	14.4	18.5	15.5
Manchester, NH	6.3	6.3	7.3	9.8	16.1	13.8	19.9	20.5
Memphis, TN	13.2	10.6	10.2	13.4	17.4	11.8	13.0	10.4
Miami, FL	11.8	9.9	9.8	13.0	17.2	11.7	13.3	13.4
Midland, TX	6.9	6.9	7.1	9.9	17.1	13.5	18.1	20.6
Milwaukee, WI	10.4	9.1	8.7	12.7	17.1	12.9	15.8	13.2
Minneapolis, MN	6.7	6.1	6.7	10.6	16.4	14.2	19.4	19.7
Nashville, TN	8.0	7.5	8.6	13.0	18.6	14.1	16.2	14.0
New Haven, CT	10.0	8.2	7.6	11.1	16.2	12.5	16.5	17.9
New Orleans, LA	14.8	10.9	9.6	12.2	16.4	11.6	13.0	11.5
New York, NY	10.5	7.5	7.0	9.3	13.9	11.4	16.4	24.1
Oklahoma City, OK	10.1	9.2	9.6	13.6	18.8	13.3	14.1	11.2
Omaha, NE	8.4	7.7	8.0	12.3	18.1	14.4	17.5	13.5
Orlando, FL	9.5	9.2	10.1	14.0	18.9	13.1	13.7	11.5
Peoria, IL	10.4	9.1	9.0	13.2	19.5	13.5	14.8	10.5
Philadelphia, PA	10.0	7.8	7.7	10.4	15.6	12.6	16.6	19.3
Phoenix, AZ	8.9	8.0	8.8	13.0	18.5	13.4	15.7	13.7
Pittsburgh, PA	10.6	9.7	9.3	12.3	17.4	12.9	15.5	12.3
Portland, OR	7.7	6.7	7.4	11.1	17.3	14.0	18.3	17.6
Providence, RI	11.0	8.8	7.9	10.8	15.9	13.2	17.0	15.4
Provo, UT	6.1	6.2	7.5	11.8	18.9	16.1	19.5	14.0
Raleigh, NC	6.5	6.6	7.6	11.7	17.1	13.7	18.2	18.6
Reno, NV	7.9	8.4	8.5	13.2	18.9	13.8	16.3	13.1
Richmond, VA	9.0	7.4	8.0	12.4	17.2	13.4	17.3	15.3
Riverside, CA	9.4	8.5	8.8	11.9	17.6	13.5	16.5	13.8
Rochester, MN	7.1	7.0	7.4	11.6	18.0	14.2	18.8	16.0
Sacramento, CA	9.1	7.6	7.7	10.6	16.6	13.1	17.4	17.9
Salt Lake City, UT	6.5	5.9	7.2	11.4	19.1	15.2	19.2	15.5
San Antonio, TX	10.3	8.9	9.4	12.8	18.7	13.2	14.8	11.9
San Diego, CA	7.6	6.7	7.1	10.3	16.1	13.0	18.0	21.1
San Francisco, CA	7.2	5.2	5.2	7.2	11.7	11.0	17.5	35.0
San Jose, CA	5.5	4.3	4.5	6.6	10.8	10.0	17.5	40.9
Santa Rosa, CA	6.7	6.0	6.8	10.0	16.6	14.2	18.5	21.1
Savannah, GA	10.6	9.5	9.2	13.0	17.8	13.8	14.6	11.4
Seattle, WA	6.7	5.4	5.9	9.5	15.7	13.3	19.5	23.9
Sioux Falls, SD	7.6	7.5	9.7	12.5	19.2	15.6	16.9	11.0
Springfield, IL	10.5	9.0	8.9	11.9	17.4	14.1	16.1	12.0
Tallahassee, FL	13.5	10.2	10.8	13.9	17.5	12.1	12.2	9.7
Tampa, FL	10.9	10.0	10.3	14.0	18.0	12.4	13.2	11.1
Tucson, AZ	12.0	10.6	10.2	14.3	18.2	12.3	12.7	9.6
Tulsa, OK	10.9	10.0	10.1	14.0	18.4	12.6	13.4	10.4
Tuscaloosa, AL	16.4	10.6	10.2	12.4	17.8	11.5	12.7	8.4
Virginia Beach, VA	8.7	7.7	8.2	12.3	18.8	14.4	17.1	12.7
Washington, DC	5.8	4.1	4.8	7.5	13.3	12.6	19.9	31.9
Wichita, KS	10.5	9.5	9.7	14.2	19.2	13.1	14.5	9.4
Winston-Salem, NC	12.1	11.3	11.0	14.8	18.0	12.8	11.6	8.3
U.S.	10.3	8.9	8.9	12.3	17.2	12.7	15.1	14.5

Note: Figures cover the Metropolitan Statistical Area (MSA)—see Appendix B for areas included
Source: Source: U.S. Census Bureau, 2015-2019 American Community Survey 5-Year Estimates

A-70　Appendix A: Comparative Statistics

Poverty Rate: City

City	All Ages	Under 18 Years Old	18 to 64 Years Old	65 Years and Over
Albuquerque, NM	16.9	24.0	16.1	9.5
Allentown, PA	25.7	37.4	22.4	15.8
Anchorage, AK	9.0	13.1	8.1	5.5
Ann Arbor, MI	22.3	9.8	27.3	7.7
Athens, GA	29.9	33.7	32.2	9.4
Atlanta, GA	20.8	33.5	18.1	16.1
Austin, TX	13.2	18.0	12.3	9.4
Baton Rouge, LA	24.8	35.7	23.9	11.5
Boise City, ID	13.7	16.2	13.6	10.7
Boston, MA	18.9	27.7	16.5	20.9
Boulder, CO	20.4	6.3	25.2	6.9
Cape Coral, FL	10.4	13.1	10.3	8.6
Cedar Rapids, IA	12.5	17.0	12.2	7.0
Charleston, SC	13.2	14.7	13.8	8.8
Charlotte, NC	12.8	18.6	11.4	8.6
Chicago, IL	18.4	26.8	16.2	15.5
Cincinnati, OH	26.3	39.0	24.2	13.9
Clarksville, TN	14.5	18.5	13.5	9.0
Cleveland, OH	32.7	48.2	29.8	20.5
College Station, TX	29.6	12.3	35.9	7.9
Colorado Springs, CO	11.7	15.8	11.1	7.0
Columbia, MO	21.8	15.1	26.2	5.0
Columbia, SC	21.8	26.8	21.9	13.2
Columbus, OH	19.5	29.3	17.4	11.6
Dallas, TX	18.9	29.3	15.6	14.4
Davenport, IA	16.6	24.3	15.5	9.0
Denver, CO	12.9	18.2	11.6	10.9
Des Moines, IA	16.1	23.2	14.7	9.3
Durham, NC	15.9	24.5	14.3	8.4
Edison, NJ	5.7	6.8	5.1	6.8
El Paso, TX	19.1	27.1	15.9	17.6
Fargo, ND	13.2	12.8	14.3	7.6
Fayetteville, NC	19.3	28.0	17.4	11.6
Fort Collins, CO	16.3	10.3	19.3	7.7
Fort Wayne, IN	16.0	24.1	14.5	7.5
Fort Worth, TX	14.5	20.0	12.5	11.4
Grand Rapids, MI	20.4	28.9	19.4	10.1
Greeley, CO	16.2	19.6	16.1	9.3
Green Bay, WI	14.9	19.7	13.9	9.7
Greensboro, NC	18.5	26.7	17.1	11.5
Honolulu, HI	10.6	12.2	10.1	10.9
Houston, TX	20.1	31.2	16.6	14.2
Huntsville, AL	16.8	25.5	16.2	7.9
Indianapolis, IN	18.0	26.8	16.1	10.2
Jacksonville, FL	14.9	21.9	13.0	11.3
Kansas City, MO	16.1	24.3	14.5	9.6
Lafayette, LA	19.7	27.7	18.9	11.4
Lakeland, FL	16.4	23.5	15.5	12.3
Las Vegas, NV	15.3	21.3	14.1	10.6
Lexington, KY	16.8	20.4	17.5	7.4
Lincoln, NE	13.5	14.2	14.8	6.4
Little Rock, AR	16.6	23.8	15.2	10.9
Los Angeles, CA	18.0	25.7	16.0	15.6
Louisville, KY	15.9	24.0	14.6	9.4
Madison, WI	16.9	11.8	19.9	5.9

Table continued on following page.

Appendix A: Comparative Statistics   A-71

City	All Ages	Under 18 Years Old	18 to 64 Years Old	65 Years and Over
Manchester, NH	14.1	19.8	13.2	10.1
Memphis, TN	25.1	40.8	21.1	13.6
Miami, FL	23.4	31.8	19.0	31.6
Midland, TX	9.2	11.5	7.7	11.8
Milwaukee, WI	25.4	36.7	22.7	13.6
Minneapolis, MN	19.1	25.5	18.2	13.2
Nashville, TN	15.1	24.2	13.2	9.2
New Haven, CT	26.5	36.2	24.7	16.3
New Orleans, LA	23.7	34.2	21.6	18.1
New York, NY	17.9	25.1	15.6	18.2
Oklahoma City, OK	16.1	23.7	14.2	9.0
Omaha, NE	13.4	18.7	12.3	8.5
Orlando, FL	17.2	24.4	15.4	14.8
Peoria, IL	19.7	24.6	20.1	10.1
Philadelphia, PA	24.3	34.8	22.2	17.6
Phoenix, AZ	18.0	26.6	15.6	10.8
Pittsburgh, PA	20.5	27.2	20.7	12.8
Portland, OR	13.7	15.5	13.9	10.4
Providence, RI	25.5	34.7	23.0	20.6
Provo, UT	26.3	19.6	30.2	7.9
Raleigh, NC	12.6	17.8	11.9	6.7
Reno, NV	13.5	15.8	14.0	8.2
Richmond, VA	23.2	37.0	21.5	13.2
Riverside, CA	13.9	17.9	13.0	10.5
Rochester, MN	10.1	12.8	10.0	5.7
Sacramento, CA	16.6	21.9	15.5	12.3
Salt Lake City, UT	16.6	20.4	16.4	10.9
San Antonio, TX	17.8	26.1	15.4	12.8
San Diego, CA	12.8	15.7	12.6	9.4
San Francisco, CA	10.3	10.0	9.7	13.6
San Jose, CA	8.7	9.3	8.4	9.5
Santa Rosa, CA	10.3	13.7	9.8	7.7
Savannah, GA	21.9	30.9	20.8	12.4
Seattle, WA	11.0	10.9	10.9	11.2
Sioux Falls, SD	10.4	12.9	9.9	8.0
Springfield, IL	18.6	29.8	17.5	8.4
Tallahassee, FL	26.4	24.3	29.3	9.9
Tampa, FL	18.6	26.5	16.2	17.6
Tucson, AZ	22.5	30.5	21.9	13.0
Tulsa, OK	19.4	29.7	17.7	8.8
Tuscaloosa, AL	24.0	24.2	26.6	10.3
Virginia Beach, VA	7.3	10.2	6.9	4.5
Washington, DC	16.2	24.0	14.5	14.5
Wichita, KS	15.9	22.0	15.0	8.8
Winston-Salem, NC	20.7	32.0	18.6	10.4
U.S.	13.4	18.5	12.6	9.3

Note: Figures are percentage of people whose income during the past 12 months was below the poverty level;
Source: U.S. Census Bureau, 2015-2019 American Community Survey 5-Year Estimates

A-72　Appendix A: Comparative Statistics

Poverty Rate: Metro Area

Metro Area	All Ages	Under 18 Years Old	18 to 64 Years Old	65 Years and Over
Albuquerque, NM	16.2	22.6	15.5	10.1
Allentown, PA	10.4	16.3	9.3	6.8
Anchorage, AK	9.4	12.8	8.6	6.0
Ann Arbor, MI	14.0	12.0	16.1	6.7
Athens, GA	22.0	25.1	23.8	8.1
Atlanta, GA	12.1	17.4	10.7	8.6
Austin, TX	10.8	13.3	10.5	7.2
Baton Rouge, LA	15.9	21.8	14.9	10.0
Boise City, ID	11.9	13.5	11.8	9.1
Boston, MA	9.3	11.3	8.8	9.1
Boulder, CO	11.7	8.5	13.8	6.3
Cape Coral, FL	13.1	22.1	12.8	7.9
Cedar Rapids, IA	10.0	12.8	9.8	6.6
Charleston, SC	12.9	18.9	11.7	8.7
Charlotte, NC	11.7	16.5	10.7	8.2
Chicago, IL	11.8	16.5	10.7	9.1
Cincinnati, OH	12.2	16.8	11.5	7.8
Clarksville, TN	14.7	19.0	13.7	9.7
Cleveland, OH	14.3	20.7	13.6	9.0
College Station, TX	22.7	20.1	25.8	9.1
Colorado Springs, CO	10.0	13.1	9.6	6.3
Columbia, MO	17.2	15.0	20.1	6.5
Columbia, SC	15.0	20.2	14.3	9.5
Columbus, OH	13.2	18.5	12.2	7.9
Dallas, TX	11.7	16.6	10.1	8.5
Davenport, IA	12.5	18.8	11.5	7.5
Denver, CO	8.8	11.4	8.3	6.9
Des Moines, IA	9.3	11.6	9.0	6.3
Durham, NC	14.2	20.6	13.6	7.8
Edison, NJ	12.8	17.7	11.4	12.0
El Paso, TX	20.2	28.6	16.7	18.6
Fargo, ND	11.1	11.1	11.9	6.3
Fayetteville, NC	17.9	24.8	16.3	11.4
Fort Collins, CO	11.6	9.4	13.5	6.4
Fort Wayne, IN	13.0	19.4	11.7	6.5
Fort Worth, TX	11.7	16.6	10.1	8.5
Grand Rapids, MI	11.0	13.7	10.9	6.9
Greeley, CO	10.0	12.0	9.5	8.4
Green Bay, WI	9.6	12.5	9.0	7.3
Greensboro, NC	16.0	23.2	14.9	10.0
Honolulu, HI	8.3	10.1	7.8	7.8
Houston, TX	13.7	19.8	11.7	10.0
Huntsville, AL	12.7	18.5	11.8	7.7
Indianapolis, IN	12.4	17.5	11.4	7.4
Jacksonville, FL	12.6	17.7	11.6	8.9
Kansas City, MO	10.5	15.0	9.6	6.8
Lafayette, LA	19.1	26.4	17.4	13.7
Lakeland, FL	15.8	24.7	14.5	9.9
Las Vegas, NV	13.7	19.3	12.6	9.2
Lexington, KY	15.8	20.9	15.9	7.6
Lincoln, NE	12.2	12.5	13.5	5.8
Little Rock, AR	15.1	20.5	14.2	9.7
Los Angeles, CA	13.9	19.2	12.5	12.2
Louisville, KY	12.5	18.2	11.6	7.9
Madison, WI	10.3	8.7	11.8	5.6

Table continued on following page.

Appendix A: Comparative Statistics A-73

Metro Area	All Ages	Under 18 Years Old	18 to 64 Years Old	65 Years and Over
Manchester, NH	7.8	9.4	7.6	6.1
Memphis, TN	17.6	27.8	15.0	10.1
Miami, FL	14.6	20.2	12.6	15.1
Midland, TX	9.5	13.2	7.5	11.1
Milwaukee, WI	13.3	19.3	12.3	8.4
Minneapolis, MN	8.6	11.0	8.1	6.6
Nashville, TN	11.4	15.7	10.6	7.6
New Haven, CT	11.7	17.3	11.0	7.6
New Orleans, LA	17.3	25.2	15.7	12.5
New York, NY	12.8	17.7	11.4	12.0
Oklahoma City, OK	13.9	19.0	13.2	7.5
Omaha, NE	10.3	13.5	9.6	7.2
Orlando, FL	13.7	19.6	12.5	9.9
Peoria, IL	12.2	15.5	12.4	6.9
Philadelphia, PA	12.4	16.9	11.7	8.6
Phoenix, AZ	13.7	19.6	12.8	8.2
Pittsburgh, PA	11.2	14.9	11.0	8.0
Portland, OR	10.6	13.1	10.5	7.7
Providence, RI	12.0	16.9	11.1	9.6
Provo, UT	10.7	9.5	12.0	5.5
Raleigh, NC	9.8	13.4	9.1	6.3
Reno, NV	11.2	14.0	11.2	7.7
Richmond, VA	11.2	15.8	10.5	7.6
Riverside, CA	14.8	20.5	13.2	10.7
Rochester, MN	8.3	10.4	8.1	5.6
Sacramento, CA	13.4	16.8	13.2	8.9
Salt Lake City, UT	9.0	10.7	8.6	6.7
San Antonio, TX	14.4	20.6	12.7	10.4
San Diego, CA	11.6	14.7	11.1	8.9
San Francisco, CA	9.0	10.2	8.7	8.7
San Jose, CA	7.5	7.9	7.3	8.0
Santa Rosa, CA	9.2	10.7	9.4	7.0
Savannah, GA	13.7	18.4	13.1	8.7
Seattle, WA	9.0	10.8	8.6	7.8
Sioux Falls, SD	8.7	10.4	8.3	7.2
Springfield, IL	14.2	22.8	13.2	6.9
Tallahassee, FL	20.0	22.1	21.9	8.4
Tampa, FL	13.5	18.6	12.8	10.3
Tucson, AZ	16.8	23.9	16.9	8.8
Tulsa, OK	14.3	20.9	13.3	7.7
Tuscaloosa, AL	19.2	24.7	19.2	10.6
Virginia Beach, VA	11.3	17.1	10.2	6.9
Washington, DC	7.8	9.9	7.2	7.2
Wichita, KS	13.0	17.4	12.3	8.2
Winston-Salem, NC	16.0	24.8	14.6	9.0
U.S.	13.4	18.5	12.6	9.3

Note: Figures are percentage of people whose income during the past 12 months was below the poverty level;
Figures cover the Metropolitan Statistical Area—see Appendix B for areas included
Source: U.S. Census Bureau, 2015-2019 American Community Survey 5-Year Estimates

A-74 Appendix A: Comparative Statistics

Employment by Industry

Metro Area[1]	(A)	(B)	(C)	(D)	(E)	(F)	(G)	(H)	(I)	(J)	(K)	(L)	(M)	(N)
Albuquerque, NM	6.8	n/a	17.3	4.9	20.9	1.3	8.7	3.8	n/a	2.8	16.5	10.9	2.8	2.9
Allentown, PA	3.5	n/a	20.8	3.6	10.5	1.2	7.7	10.5	n/a	3.4	12.8	10.8	10.9	3.8
Anchorage, AK	7.4	6.0	19.2	4.6	20.8	2.1	8.0	1.1	1.3	3.4	10.9	12.1	6.9	2.9
Ann Arbor, MI	2.2	n/a	13.3	3.0	38.3	2.8	4.6	6.3	n/a	2.5	14.0	7.3	2.2	3.0
Athens, GA	n/a	n/a	n/a	n/a	29.7	n/a	10.2	n/a	n/a	n/a	9.1	11.3	n/a	n/a
Atlanta, GA	4.7	4.6	13.1	6.6	12.0	3.5	8.8	6.0	<0.1	3.3	19.5	10.5	6.1	5.3
Austin, TX	6.4	n/a	11.2	6.2	16.9	3.6	9.5	5.8	n/a	3.8	18.6	10.0	2.6	4.9
Baton Rouge, LA	10.7	10.5	13.5	4.2	20.0	1.1	8.8	7.5	0.1	3.8	12.3	10.5	3.9	3.3
Boise City, ID	8.2	n/a	14.3	6.0	13.6	1.0	9.2	8.1	n/a	3.4	15.2	11.9	3.8	4.7
Boston, MA[4]	4.1	n/a	22.8	8.6	11.0	3.4	6.3	4.2	n/a	3.1	22.3	8.0	2.4	3.2
Boulder, CO	3.0	n/a	13.3	3.8	18.9	4.5	6.5	11.3	n/a	3.1	21.2	9.5	1.1	3.5
Cape Coral, FL	12.6	n/a	11.4	4.9	15.8	0.9	13.5	2.4	n/a	4.0	14.0	14.9	2.4	2.8
Cedar Rapids, IA	6.0	n/a	14.8	8.2	11.3	2.1	6.8	14.0	n/a	3.4	10.2	11.0	7.7	4.1
Charleston, SC	5.7	n/a	11.9	4.4	18.2	1.5	11.5	7.6	n/a	3.8	15.5	12.3	4.2	2.9
Charlotte, NC	5.6	n/a	10.1	9.1	12.8	1.9	9.4	8.5	n/a	3.5	17.4	10.6	6.1	4.6
Chicago, IL[2]	3.5	3.4	16.5	7.8	11.4	1.8	6.5	7.6	<0.1	4.1	19.1	9.6	6.4	5.1
Cincinnati, OH	4.2	n/a	15.8	6.9	11.8	1.2	8.9	10.5	n/a	3.4	15.7	10.1	5.7	5.2
Clarksville, TN	3.8	n/a	12.9	3.3	20.6	1.0	12.1	11.7	n/a	3.4	10.6	13.9	2.9	n/a
Cleveland, OH	3.7	n/a	19.4	6.5	12.8	1.2	8.3	11.2	n/a	3.3	15.0	9.7	3.6	4.8
College Station, TX	5.7	n/a	10.1	3.1	37.9	1.1	11.3	4.4	n/a	2.5	9.0	10.4	1.7	2.2
Colorado Springs, CO	6.3	n/a	14.7	6.5	18.4	1.8	9.5	4.0	n/a	5.9	16.6	11.6	2.2	2.0
Columbia, MO	n/a	n/a	n/a	n/a	29.2	n/a	n/a	n/a	n/a	n/a	n/a	10.9	n/a	n/a
Columbia, SC	4.4	n/a	12.2	8.1	21.7	1.2	8.9	7.9	n/a	3.8	12.4	10.8	4.4	3.6
Columbus, OH	4.1	n/a	14.5	8.0	16.4	1.3	7.6	6.7	n/a	3.6	16.4	9.3	7.9	3.7
Dallas, TX[2]	5.4	n/a	11.7	9.7	11.9	2.5	8.5	6.7	n/a	2.8	19.5	9.5	5.6	5.6
Davenport, IA	n/a	n/a	n/a	n/a	n/a	n/a	n/a	n/a	n/a	n/a	n/a	n/a	n/a	n/a
Denver, CO	7.5	n/a	12.8	7.7	13.5	3.4	7.3	4.7	n/a	3.7	18.8	9.7	5.5	5.0
Des Moines, IA	5.8	n/a	13.9	15.8	12.6	1.6	7.8	5.6	n/a	3.5	13.7	10.9	3.4	4.9
Durham, NC	2.9	n/a	22.1	5.1	19.9	1.7	6.2	10.4	n/a	3.3	15.3	7.4	2.5	2.6
Edison, NJ[2]	3.8	n/a	22.7	9.4	14.1	3.8	6.0	2.7	n/a	3.8	16.4	8.9	4.2	3.7
El Paso, TX	5.5	n/a	14.8	4.1	22.2	1.4	10.5	5.1	n/a	2.5	11.8	12.3	5.5	3.7
Fargo, ND	6.4	n/a	19.3	8.3	13.3	2.1	8.1	7.1	n/a	3.4	9.5	10.9	4.6	6.4
Fayetteville, NC	3.7	n/a	11.5	2.9	31.8	0.7	11.5	6.2	n/a	3.3	8.6	13.6	3.9	1.5
Fort Collins, CO	7.0	n/a	11.2	4.1	25.0	1.8	8.8	8.4	n/a	3.8	12.2	11.7	2.3	3.1
Fort Wayne, IN	5.3	n/a	19.1	5.5	8.8	0.9	8.4	16.5	n/a	4.7	9.9	11.3	4.6	4.6
Fort Worth, TX[2]	6.8	n/a	12.8	6.3	12.8	0.8	10.1	9.2	n/a	3.5	11.5	11.8	9.0	4.9
Grand Rapids, MI	4.7	n/a	17.6	5.0	9.0	1.0	5.8	20.4	n/a	3.7	13.6	9.2	3.5	5.9
Greeley, CO	14.9	n/a	9.8	4.2	15.9	0.4	8.1	13.1	n/a	3.4	10.7	10.5	4.6	4.0
Green Bay, WI	4.8	n/a	15.5	6.8	11.1	0.8	7.5	17.9	n/a	4.7	11.1	9.6	5.1	4.7
Greensboro, NC	4.5	n/a	14.3	5.2	12.1	1.2	8.5	14.5	n/a	3.3	13.0	11.1	6.4	5.3
Honolulu, HI	6.5	n/a	15.2	5.3	22.5	1.3	12.0	2.1	n/a	4.1	12.8	9.7	4.8	3.2
Houston, TX	8.9	6.7	13.2	5.4	14.0	0.9	9.5	6.9	2.2	3.5	16.1	10.1	5.7	5.2
Huntsville, AL	4.0	n/a	8.7	2.9	21.2	0.8	8.0	10.6	n/a	3.2	25.5	10.4	1.6	2.5
Indianapolis, IN	5.5	5.4	15.1	6.7	12.7	1.0	8.5	8.4	<0.1	3.5	15.9	9.8	7.9	4.4
Jacksonville, FL	6.6	6.5	15.4	9.6	10.8	1.2	10.4	4.4	<0.1	3.4	15.6	11.3	7.1	3.6
Kansas City, MO	4.9	n/a	14.6	7.4	13.7	1.3	8.1	7.4	n/a	3.8	17.7	10.3	5.7	4.6
Lafayette, LA	10.1	4.9	16.8	5.2	13.4	1.0	10.1	7.0	5.2	3.4	11.1	14.0	3.2	4.2
Lakeland, FL	6.3	n/a	14.6	5.8	11.7	0.7	8.7	7.2	n/a	2.5	13.9	13.5	10.0	4.5
Las Vegas, NV	7.0	6.9	11.4	5.8	11.2	1.0	21.4	2.6	<0.1	2.9	14.3	12.4	7.0	2.5
Lexington, KY	5.0	n/a	13.0	3.7	19.4	0.9	8.8	10.5	n/a	3.6	14.8	11.2	4.7	3.9
Lincoln, NE	5.1	n/a	16.6	6.8	21.9	1.7	7.6	7.0	n/a	3.6	11.4	9.8	5.9	2.3
Little Rock, AR	4.9	n/a	16.7	6.3	19.3	1.4	8.0	5.3	n/a	5.0	12.5	11.2	4.6	4.2
Los Angeles, CA[2]	3.5	3.5	20.1	5.1	13.4	4.3	8.5	7.4	<0.1	2.8	14.4	9.7	5.4	4.8
Louisville, KY	4.3	n/a	14.3	7.3	10.8	1.2	7.8	12.6	n/a	3.5	13.1	10.0	10.2	4.4
Madison, WI	4.6	n/a	12.6	5.9	21.5	4.5	6.4	9.1	n/a	5.2	13.5	10.3	2.4	3.6
Manchester, NH[3]	5.0	n/a	22.6	7.2	10.6	2.8	6.7	7.0	n/a	3.7	15.2	11.5	3.2	4.0

Table continued on following page.

Appendix A: Comparative Statistics   A-75

Metro Area[1]	(A)	(B)	(C)	(D)	(E)	(F)	(G)	(H)	(I)	(J)	(K)	(L)	(M)	(N)
Memphis, TN	3.6	n/a	14.6	4.5	12.9	0.7	8.9	6.8	n/a	4.2	15.4	10.0	12.6	5.3
Miami, FL[2]	4.5	4.4	16.5	7.2	12.1	1.6	9.2	3.7	<0.1	3.9	15.9	12.0	7.1	6.0
Midland, TX	28.0	n/a	7.3	4.8	11.2	0.7	10.1	3.3	n/a	3.7	9.4	10.5	5.2	5.2
Milwaukee, WI	3.6	3.6	20.5	6.0	9.6	1.5	7.1	13.9	<0.1	5.4	14.3	9.4	3.6	4.5
Minneapolis, MN	4.3	n/a	17.7	8.7	12.9	1.6	5.3	10.2	n/a	3.6	16.6	9.8	4.0	4.7
Nashville, TN	4.8	n/a	14.8	6.9	11.8	2.4	9.2	7.9	n/a	3.8	17.3	10.0	6.5	4.0
New Haven, CT[3]	3.5	n/a	28.4	4.0	12.7	1.3	6.5	8.2	n/a	3.5	10.9	9.6	7.1	3.8
New Orleans, LA	5.6	4.9	19.1	5.2	13.5	1.0	11.9	5.6	0.7	4.0	13.2	11.5	5.2	3.8
New York, NY[2]	3.8	n/a	22.7	9.4	14.1	3.8	6.0	2.7	n/a	3.8	16.4	8.9	4.2	3.7
Oklahoma City, OK	6.0	4.8	15.4	5.4	20.2	0.9	10.4	5.2	1.2	4.3	12.8	10.7	4.8	3.4
Omaha, NE	6.2	n/a	16.0	9.2	13.2	1.9	8.5	6.8	n/a	3.5	14.3	10.9	5.5	3.4
Orlando, FL	7.0	7.0	13.1	6.5	10.6	2.0	15.1	4.0	<0.1	3.3	18.2	12.2	3.7	3.8
Peoria, IL	4.7	n/a	19.8	4.4	11.9	0.9	7.3	13.0	n/a	4.7	13.0	11.5	4.4	3.8
Philadelphia, PA[2]	2.6	n/a	32.1	6.3	14.4	1.9	6.0	3.5	n/a	3.7	14.7	7.7	4.1	2.4
Phoenix, AZ	6.2	6.1	15.9	9.4	11.1	1.6	8.9	6.1	0.1	3.0	16.8	11.3	5.3	3.7
Pittsburgh, PA	5.8	5.1	22.8	6.8	10.2	1.6	7.5	7.2	0.6	3.7	15.5	10.6	4.4	3.4
Portland, OR	6.4	6.3	15.8	6.2	12.4	2.1	6.3	10.6	0.1	3.2	16.4	10.4	4.8	4.8
Providence, RI[3]	4.5	4.5	21.4	6.6	13.2	1.0	8.6	8.7	<0.1	4.0	13.1	11.6	3.4	3.2
Provo, UT	9.5	n/a	18.7	4.3	11.9	4.7	8.2	7.3	n/a	2.1	15.2	13.2	1.7	2.6
Raleigh, NC	6.5	n/a	12.4	5.1	14.9	3.4	9.0	4.6	n/a	3.9	20.5	11.6	3.4	4.0
Reno, NV	7.4	7.2	11.5	4.5	12.4	1.2	12.3	10.3	0.2	2.3	14.4	9.9	9.3	3.9
Richmond, VA	6.1	n/a	14.7	8.0	16.4	0.9	7.9	4.6	n/a	4.2	17.2	10.3	5.3	3.8
Riverside, CA	7.3	7.2	16.6	2.8	16.2	0.5	8.3	6.0	<0.1	2.4	10.4	11.8	12.9	4.2
Rochester, MN	4.0	n/a	44.7	2.3	10.5	1.1	5.8	8.3	n/a	2.9	4.7	10.6	2.2	2.3
Sacramento, CA	7.5	7.5	16.4	5.3	24.0	1.0	8.0	3.6	<0.1	2.8	13.8	10.5	4.0	2.7
Salt Lake City, UT	6.6	n/a	11.6	8.3	14.1	2.7	7.5	7.8	n/a	2.7	17.5	10.4	5.9	4.4
San Antonio, TX	5.8	5.2	15.1	8.9	16.6	1.7	10.8	4.8	0.5	3.2	14.7	10.6	3.8	3.4
San Diego, CA	6.3	6.3	15.2	5.3	16.9	1.5	9.3	8.1	<0.1	2.9	18.2	10.4	2.6	2.8
San Francisco, CA[2]	3.9	3.9	13.5	7.9	11.9	10.3	6.5	3.4	<0.1	2.9	26.8	6.6	3.9	1.9
San Jose, CA	4.8	4.7	15.9	3.5	8.7	10.0	5.4	15.7	<0.1	1.9	22.3	7.2	1.6	2.6
Santa Rosa, CA	8.7	8.6	17.4	3.9	14.2	1.1	8.2	11.8	0.1	3.0	11.9	12.9	2.3	4.0
Savannah, GA	4.6	n/a	14.0	3.2	13.0	0.8	12.2	9.3	n/a	3.7	14.3	11.8	9.1	3.4
Seattle, WA[2]	6.3	6.2	13.1	5.2	12.2	8.1	6.2	8.6	<0.1	3.4	16.4	12.8	3.4	3.9
Sioux Falls, SD	5.5	n/a	22.2	9.9	9.4	1.5	7.8	9.0	n/a	3.7	9.4	12.0	3.6	5.4
Springfield, IL	3.3	n/a	20.4	6.0	25.9	1.7	6.6	2.8	n/a	5.7	10.5	11.7	2.0	2.7
Tallahassee, FL	4.5	n/a	13.7	4.2	32.8	1.7	9.4	1.9	n/a	5.0	12.8	10.0	1.3	2.0
Tampa, FL	6.2	6.1	15.5	9.2	11.2	1.7	9.9	4.9	<0.1	3.3	18.7	11.7	3.2	3.9
Tucson, AZ	5.3	4.8	18.1	4.6	19.8	1.3	9.3	7.1	0.5	3.3	12.2	11.3	5.4	1.8
Tulsa, OK	6.7	5.6	16.1	5.1	12.7	1.3	9.5	11.1	1.0	4.4	13.0	11.1	4.9	3.6
Tuscaloosa, AL	6.4	n/a	8.3	3.8	26.4	0.8	9.2	16.5	n/a	3.8	9.2	10.3	2.8	1.9
Virginia Beach, VA	5.2	n/a	14.2	5.0	20.5	1.2	10.0	7.4	n/a	4.1	14.8	11.2	3.6	2.3
Washington, DC[2]	5.0	n/a	12.8	4.5	22.8	2.3	7.3	1.4	n/a	6.4	24.5	8.0	2.6	1.8
Wichita, KS	5.8	n/a	16.3	4.1	14.3	1.2	10.3	15.5	n/a	3.5	11.8	10.6	3.3	2.8
Winston-Salem, NC	4.5	n/a	20.8	4.9	11.4	0.6	9.2	12.6	n/a	3.0	13.4	11.8	4.4	2.9
U.S.	5.5	5.1	16.3	6.1	15.2	1.9	9.0	8.5	0.4	3.8	14.4	10.9	4.6	3.9

Note: All figures are percentages covering non-farm employment as of December 2020 and are not seasonally adjusted;
(1) Figures cover the Metropolitan Statistical Area (MSA) except where noted. See Appendix B for areas included; (2) Metropolitan Division; (3) New England City and Town Area; (4) New England City and Town Area Division; (A) Construction, Mining, and Logging (some areas report Construction separate from Mining and Logging); (B) Construction; (C) Education and Health Services; (D) Financial Activities; (E) Government; (F) Information; (G) Leisure and Hospitality; (H) Manufacturing; (I) Mining and Logging; (J) Other Services; (K) Professional and Business Services; (L) Retail Trade; (M) Transportation and Utilities; (N) Wholesale Trade; n/a not available
Source: Bureau of Labor Statistics, Current Employment Statistics, Employment, Hours, and Earnings, December 2020

A-76　Appendix A: Comparative Statistics

Labor Force, Employment and Job Growth: City

City	Civilian Labor Force			Workers Employed		
	Dec. 2019	Dec. 2020	% Chg.	Dec. 2019	Dec. 2020	% Chg.
Albuquerque, NM	284,609	280,764	-1.3	273,259	260,057	-4.8
Allentown, PA	56,275	55,559	-1.2	52,716	50,085	-4.9
Anchorage, AK	147,801	150,509	1.8	140,718	142,180	1.0
Ann Arbor, MI	66,802	63,917	-4.3	65,636	62,017	-5.5
Athens, GA	59,225	58,747	-0.8	57,596	55,706	-3.2
Atlanta, GA	264,779	266,767	0.7	256,964	248,040	-3.4
Austin, TX	601,055	606,519	0.9	587,607	576,501	-1.8
Baton Rouge, LA	111,969	112,989	0.9	106,514	104,304	-2.0
Boise City, ID	134,753	133,502	-0.9	131,600	127,739	-2.9
Boston, MA	399,841	382,754	-4.2	391,993	354,899	-9.4
Boulder, CO	66,229	64,864	-2.0	65,025	60,677	-6.6
Cape Coral, FL	93,172	90,468	-2.9	90,578	86,083	-4.9
Cedar Rapids, IA	73,629	67,681	-8.0	71,125	64,790	-8.9
Charleston, SC	75,308	72,571	-3.6	73,919	69,583	-5.8
Charlotte, NC	499,499	492,206	-1.4	483,932	461,278	-4.6
Chicago, IL	1,322,199	1,308,831	-1.0	1,281,869	1,177,846	-8.1
Cincinnati, OH	147,410	148,764	0.9	142,030	139,857	-1.5
Clarksville, TN	63,787	65,851	3.2	61,432	60,949	-0.7
Cleveland, OH	156,471	151,177	-3.3	149,465	137,384	-8.0
College Station, TX	62,425	62,445	0.0	60,916	59,698	-2.0
Colorado Springs, CO	238,705	245,635	2.9	232,124	223,547	-3.7
Columbia, MO	68,108	67,049	-1.5	66,459	64,199	-3.4
Columbia, SC	58,665	58,030	-1.0	57,222	55,091	-3.7
Columbus, OH	478,751	473,342	-1.1	463,416	448,688	-3.1
Dallas, TX	703,081	714,931	1.6	681,628	663,820	-2.6
Davenport, IA	51,918	47,841	-7.8	49,753	45,379	-8.7
Denver, CO	423,917	436,113	2.8	414,090	395,349	-4.5
Des Moines, IA	115,631	106,451	-7.9	111,652	101,736	-8.8
Durham, NC	150,280	147,613	-1.7	145,981	139,307	-4.5
Edison, NJ	55,345	54,084	-2.2	54,066	51,214	-5.2
El Paso, TX	305,478	303,471	-0.6	295,039	280,221	-5.0
Fargo, ND	69,702	73,397	5.3	68,423	71,067	3.8
Fayetteville, NC	76,883	75,832	-1.3	73,263	69,057	-5.7
Fort Collins, CO	103,931	102,364	-1.5	101,963	94,647	-7.1
Fort Wayne, IN	128,470	131,139	2.0	124,594	125,226	0.5
Fort Worth, TX	444,954	448,335	0.7	431,424	417,064	-3.3
Grand Rapids, MI	103,987	101,472	-2.4	100,701	95,669	-5.0
Greeley, CO	55,458	56,828	2.4	54,063	51,159	-5.3
Green Bay, WI	53,859	54,419	1.0	52,110	51,623	-0.9
Greensboro, NC	147,165	143,483	-2.5	141,957	132,895	-6.3
Honolulu, HI	452,859	447,861	-1.1	443,191	411,864	-7.0
Houston, TX	1,168,794	1,162,957	-0.5	1,128,145	1,071,532	-5.0
Huntsville, AL	99,396	97,639	-1.7	97,185	94,305	-2.9
Indianapolis, IN	446,151	467,925	4.8	433,373	443,878	2.4
Jacksonville, FL	469,934	463,646	-1.3	457,089	438,293	-4.1
Kansas City, MO	262,205	262,873	0.2	252,990	245,170	-3.0
Lafayette, LA	59,376	59,649	0.4	56,669	56,144	-0.9
Lakeland, FL	47,582	47,525	-0.1	46,092	44,428	-3.6
Las Vegas, NV	316,225	301,287	-4.7	305,003	270,332	-11.3
Lexington, KY	175,216	173,151	-1.1	170,118	164,394	-3.3
Lincoln, NE	160,552	162,129	0.9	156,783	157,418	0.4
Little Rock, AR	96,600	95,461	-1.1	93,594	90,677	-3.1
Los Angeles, CA	2,095,690	1,987,043	-5.1	2,011,531	1,777,290	-11.6
Louisville, KY	402,027	394,489	-1.8	388,284	371,824	-4.2
Madison, WI	157,534	157,457	0.0	154,347	151,326	-1.9

Table continued on following page.

Appendix A: Comparative Statistics   A-77

City	Civilian Labor Force			Workers Employed		
	Dec. 2019	Dec. 2020	% Chg.	Dec. 2019	Dec. 2020	% Chg.
Manchester, NH	66,041	64,338	-2.5	64,553	61,492	-4.7
Memphis, TN	299,167	316,351	5.7	287,040	285,384	-0.5
Miami, FL	234,913	222,511	-5.2	231,476	205,346	-11.2
Midland, TX	88,858	84,069	-5.3	87,068	77,687	-10.7
Milwaukee, WI	271,222	276,192	1.8	260,380	253,283	-2.7
Minneapolis, MN	245,206	236,236	-3.6	238,869	224,977	-5.8
Nashville, TN	413,927	420,401	1.5	404,589	396,582	-1.9
New Haven, CT	65,459	65,774	0.4	63,121	59,553	-5.6
New Orleans, LA	179,138	182,736	2.0	170,426	162,218	-4.8
New York, NY	4,055,234	3,856,031	-4.9	3,932,458	3,408,146	-13.3
Oklahoma City, OK	322,420	325,821	1.0	313,116	308,959	-1.3
Omaha, NE	243,405	245,582	0.8	236,406	237,000	0.2
Orlando, FL	170,544	162,722	-4.5	166,541	149,954	-9.9
Peoria, IL	50,615	47,156	-6.8	47,924	43,020	-10.2
Philadelphia, PA	729,738	699,455	-4.1	690,247	634,633	-8.0
Phoenix, AZ	885,177	887,360	0.2	853,111	820,050	-3.8
Pittsburgh, PA	157,702	150,397	-4.6	151,169	140,388	-7.1
Portland, OR	376,061	380,047	1.0	366,666	355,132	-3.1
Providence, RI	86,891	84,686	-2.5	83,544	77,341	-7.4
Provo, UT	68,223	69,278	1.5	66,963	67,577	0.9
Raleigh, NC	260,153	256,088	-1.5	252,404	241,439	-4.3
Reno, NV	139,960	134,597	-3.8	136,175	127,830	-6.1
Richmond, VA	119,856	116,571	-2.7	116,483	108,936	-6.4
Riverside, CA	156,209	155,456	-0.4	151,257	142,354	-5.8
Rochester, MN	65,938	64,249	-2.5	64,352	61,741	-4.0
Sacramento, CA	237,846	239,336	0.6	230,186	217,425	-5.5
Salt Lake City, UT	117,922	119,415	1.2	115,531	115,159	-0.3
San Antonio, TX	740,486	738,883	-0.2	720,097	690,895	-4.0
San Diego, CA	724,077	722,739	-0.1	704,952	665,731	-5.5
San Francisco, CA	589,286	566,193	-3.9	578,146	529,919	-8.3
San Jose, CA	558,215	552,450	-1.0	545,337	515,386	-5.4
Santa Rosa, CA	90,456	87,703	-3.0	88,298	81,635	-7.5
Savannah, GA	66,855	68,668	2.7	64,804	63,654	-1.7
Seattle, WA	475,147	468,970	-1.3	464,721	440,258	-5.2
Sioux Falls, SD	106,508	105,414	-1.0	103,166	102,274	-0.8
Springfield, IL	56,539	55,105	-2.5	54,362	51,115	-5.9
Tallahassee, FL	102,369	97,422	-4.8	99,536	91,619	-7.9
Tampa, FL	205,639	203,778	-0.9	200,162	191,493	-4.3
Tucson, AZ	271,283	268,958	-0.8	259,611	246,980	-4.8
Tulsa, OK	196,335	194,348	-1.0	190,196	182,480	-4.0
Tuscaloosa, AL	48,708	47,374	-2.7	47,449	45,126	-4.9
Virginia Beach, VA	234,164	226,000	-3.4	228,643	216,261	-5.4
Washington, DC	416,329	413,158	-0.7	397,389	376,699	-5.2
Wichita, KS	189,743	189,451	-0.1	183,423	180,980	-1.3
Winston-Salem, NC	118,986	117,479	-1.2	114,945	109,601	-4.6
U.S.	164,007,000	160,017,000	-2.4	158,504,000	149,613,000	-5.6

Note: Data is not seasonally adjusted and covers workers 16 years of age and older
Source: Bureau of Labor Statistics, Local Area Unemployment Statistics

A-78 Appendix A: Comparative Statistics

Labor Force, Employment and Job Growth: Metro Area

Metro Area[1]	Civilian Labor Force			Workers Employed		
	Dec. 2019	Dec. 2020	% Chg.	Dec. 2019	Dec. 2020	% Chg.
Albuquerque, NM	442,230	434,669	-1.7	423,884	402,897	-4.9
Allentown, PA	448,501	434,989	-3.0	428,188	408,208	-4.6
Anchorage, AK	195,036	197,957	1.5	184,796	186,758	1.0
Ann Arbor, MI	200,349	192,221	-4.0	196,082	185,271	-5.5
Athens, GA	99,032	97,723	-1.3	96,483	93,287	-3.3
Atlanta, GA	3,128,881	3,107,968	-0.6	3,045,413	2,939,513	-3.4
Austin, TX	1,255,200	1,267,150	0.9	1,224,993	1,202,103	-1.8
Baton Rouge, LA	417,880	416,461	-0.3	399,191	391,186	-2.0
Boise City, ID	381,230	377,479	-0.9	371,231	360,351	-2.9
Boston, MA[4]	1,694,809	1,609,639	-5.0	1,662,542	1,505,214	-9.4
Boulder, CO	197,746	194,238	-1.7	193,839	180,878	-6.6
Cape Coral, FL	353,248	344,421	-2.5	344,074	327,001	-4.9
Cedar Rapids, IA	148,694	136,358	-8.3	143,975	131,243	-8.8
Charleston, SC	395,683	381,666	-3.5	387,938	365,144	-5.8
Charlotte, NC	1,373,470	1,344,434	-2.1	1,331,441	1,267,112	-4.8
Chicago, IL[2]	3,687,479	3,541,085	-3.9	3,574,836	3,232,803	-9.5
Cincinnati, OH	1,128,063	1,122,791	-0.4	1,090,733	1,069,559	-1.9
Clarksville, TN	118,102	120,516	2.0	113,647	112,488	-1.0
Cleveland, OH	1,049,216	997,566	-4.9	1,009,725	921,287	-8.7
College Station, TX	137,059	137,930	0.6	133,696	130,968	-2.0
Colorado Springs, CO	356,603	365,426	2.4	346,681	333,941	-3.6
Columbia, MO	99,481	97,891	-1.6	97,069	93,768	-3.4
Columbia, SC	403,325	396,126	-1.7	394,519	379,089	-3.9
Columbus, OH	1,105,853	1,087,829	-1.6	1,070,103	1,037,232	-3.0
Dallas, TX[2]	2,719,675	2,742,810	0.8	2,640,356	2,571,653	-2.6
Davenport, IA	194,473	181,630	-6.6	185,909	172,320	-7.3
Denver, CO	1,688,220	1,720,681	1.9	1,650,053	1,575,283	-4.5
Des Moines, IA	366,728	336,296	-8.3	356,630	324,997	-8.8
Durham, NC	305,270	298,535	-2.2	296,522	283,058	-4.5
Edison, NJ[2]	7,008,087	6,694,644	-4.4	6,780,009	6,077,482	-10.3
El Paso, TX	367,648	366,204	-0.3	354,536	336,718	-5.0
Fargo, ND	138,402	143,685	3.8	135,435	139,201	2.7
Fayetteville, NC	148,437	145,648	-1.8	141,883	133,739	-5.7
Fort Collins, CO	209,156	205,612	-1.6	205,003	190,294	-7.1
Fort Wayne, IN	216,998	220,641	1.6	210,942	212,055	0.5
Fort Worth, TX[2]	1,311,941	1,316,316	0.3	1,273,454	1,230,725	-3.3
Grand Rapids, MI	575,885	557,316	-3.2	561,939	534,032	-4.9
Greeley, CO	172,545	174,099	0.9	168,655	159,598	-5.3
Green Bay, WI	172,794	173,847	0.6	167,575	165,813	-1.0
Greensboro, NC	371,920	360,292	-3.1	359,136	336,201	-6.3
Honolulu, HI	452,859	447,861	-1.1	443,191	411,864	-7.0
Houston, TX	3,462,635	3,445,575	-0.4	3,336,616	3,169,170	-5.0
Huntsville, AL	229,898	224,806	-2.2	225,028	218,441	-2.9
Indianapolis, IN	1,060,176	1,101,669	3.9	1,032,445	1,057,751	2.4
Jacksonville, FL	794,684	779,448	-1.9	774,172	742,219	-4.1
Kansas City, MO	1,145,405	1,145,812	0.0	1,109,920	1,089,310	-1.8
Lafayette, LA	210,923	212,283	0.6	200,667	199,150	-0.7
Lakeland, FL	308,057	308,560	0.1	298,597	287,817	-3.6
Las Vegas, NV	1,136,500	1,084,944	-4.5	1,096,609	971,954	-11.3
Lexington, KY	273,326	269,822	-1.2	265,044	256,418	-3.2
Lincoln, NE	186,998	188,745	0.9	182,613	183,294	0.3
Little Rock, AR	354,854	348,009	-1.9	343,794	333,024	-3.1
Los Angeles, CA[2]	5,171,306	4,867,991	-5.8	4,946,895	4,270,635	-13.6
Louisville, KY	674,729	662,325	-1.8	652,752	628,916	-3.6
Madison, WI	390,192	389,396	-0.2	381,370	373,552	-2.0

Table continued on following page.

Appendix A: Comparative Statistics   A-79

Metro Area[1]	Civilian Labor Force			Workers Employed		
	Dec. 2019	Dec. 2020	% Chg.	Dec. 2019	Dec. 2020	% Chg.
Manchester, NH[3]	123,691	119,789	-3.1	121,082	115,342	-4.7
Memphis, TN	647,507	668,382	3.2	622,648	618,793	-0.6
Miami, FL[2]	1,377,214	1,301,119	-5.5	1,353,568	1,197,859	-11.5
Midland, TX	110,792	105,257	-5.0	108,522	96,833	-10.7
Milwaukee, WI	811,069	812,442	0.1	785,335	763,907	-2.7
Minneapolis, MN	2,037,880	1,953,111	-4.1	1,976,964	1,864,309	-5.7
Nashville, TN	1,102,127	1,112,635	0.9	1,076,372	1,054,820	-2.0
New Haven, CT[3]	331,537	326,637	-1.4	321,457	303,291	-5.6
New Orleans, LA	596,687	591,186	-0.9	570,042	542,565	-4.8
New York, NY[2]	7,008,087	6,694,644	-4.4	6,780,009	6,077,482	-10.3
Oklahoma City, OK	687,962	693,472	0.8	668,536	660,099	-1.2
Omaha, NE	496,578	495,217	-0.2	483,022	480,259	-0.5
Orlando, FL	1,372,173	1,294,626	-5.6	1,337,648	1,204,999	-9.9
Peoria, IL	173,154	158,961	-8.2	165,096	148,160	-10.2
Philadelphia, PA[2]	1,031,591	989,425	-4.0	980,295	906,853	-7.4
Phoenix, AZ	2,548,680	2,536,430	-0.4	2,456,125	2,361,237	-3.8
Pittsburgh, PA	1,217,975	1,157,008	-5.0	1,162,800	1,080,640	-7.0
Portland, OR	1,332,520	1,316,280	-1.2	1,294,803	1,235,940	-4.5
Providence, RI[3]	695,900	674,373	-3.0	673,941	622,895	-7.5
Provo, UT	319,576	325,243	1.7	313,261	316,139	0.9
Raleigh, NC	731,065	715,982	-2.0	709,901	678,982	-4.3
Reno, NV	261,692	251,522	-3.8	254,486	238,896	-6.1
Richmond, VA	692,884	665,116	-4.0	675,329	631,884	-6.4
Riverside, CA	2,087,383	2,086,402	0.0	2,014,602	1,896,009	-5.8
Rochester, MN	125,263	121,785	-2.7	121,567	117,057	-3.7
Sacramento, CA	1,104,616	1,096,884	-0.7	1,069,620	1,010,465	-5.5
Salt Lake City, UT	679,607	687,168	1.1	665,544	663,455	-0.3
San Antonio, TX	1,218,568	1,213,928	-0.3	1,184,374	1,136,070	-4.0
San Diego, CA	1,597,099	1,593,875	-0.2	1,552,857	1,466,461	-5.5
San Francisco, CA[2]	1,054,065	1,010,523	-4.1	1,034,791	948,543	-8.3
San Jose, CA	1,090,183	1,071,686	-1.7	1,065,627	1,007,069	-5.5
Santa Rosa, CA	259,689	250,632	-3.4	253,575	234,440	-7.5
Savannah, GA	187,692	190,082	1.2	182,609	179,365	-1.7
Seattle, WA[2]	1,724,567	1,722,800	-0.1	1,683,121	1,619,303	-3.7
Sioux Falls, SD	155,466	153,813	-1.0	150,743	149,521	-0.8
Springfield, IL	106,114	102,509	-3.4	102,129	96,019	-5.9
Tallahassee, FL	195,372	185,262	-5.1	190,212	175,456	-7.7
Tampa, FL	1,566,692	1,540,183	-1.6	1,525,133	1,459,839	-4.2
Tucson, AZ	504,172	497,081	-1.4	483,909	460,365	-4.8
Tulsa, OK	481,673	474,408	-1.5	466,612	447,916	-4.0
Tuscaloosa, AL	120,183	116,579	-3.0	117,420	111,848	-4.7
Virginia Beach, VA	858,173	834,317	-2.7	834,872	790,145	-5.3
Washington, DC[2]	2,779,621	2,686,651	-3.3	2,705,388	2,537,166	-6.2
Wichita, KS	315,547	315,051	-0.1	305,590	301,566	-1.3
Winston-Salem, NC	329,944	323,658	-1.9	319,404	304,539	-4.6
U.S.	164,007,000	160,017,000	-2.4	158,504,000	149,613,000	-5.6

Note: Data is not seasonally adjusted and covers workers 16 years of age and older; (1) Figures cover the Metropolitan Statistical Area (MSA) except where noted. See Appendix B for areas included; (2) Metropolitan Division; (3) New England City and Town Area; (4) New England City and Town Area Division
Source: Bureau of Labor Statistics, Local Area Unemployment Statistics

A-80　Appendix A: Comparative Statistics

Unemployment Rate: City

City	2020											
	Jan.	Feb.	Mar.	Apr.	May	Jun.	Jul.	Aug.	Sep.	Oct.	Nov.	Dec.
Albuquerque, NM	4.4	4.4	5.5	12.8	9.4	9.1	13.2	11.2	9.5	7.5	6.3	7.4
Allentown, PA	6.6	6.6	8.2	20.1	18.3	19.8	19.0	16.9	12.9	12.1	10.7	9.9
Anchorage, AK	5.1	4.5	4.7	13.9	12.3	12.0	10.8	6.5	6.4	5.3	6.0	5.5
Ann Arbor, MI	2.0	1.8	1.9	12.4	11.6	8.9	6.6	5.7	5.0	3.3	2.8	3.0
Athens, GA	3.5	3.5	4.7	12.2	9.0	7.7	7.9	5.8	5.9	4.3	5.1	5.2
Atlanta, GA	3.6	3.7	5.4	13.4	11.9	11.0	10.6	8.6	8.4	6.1	7.4	7.0
Austin, TX	2.6	2.5	3.6	12.5	11.6	7.4	6.9	5.6	6.4	4.9	5.7	4.9
Baton Rouge, LA	5.7	4.1	6.2	14.7	15.0	11.6	11.3	9.1	8.8	10.1	9.2	7.7
Boise City, ID	2.8	2.4	2.3	12.6	9.6	5.9	5.2	4.0	5.8	5.3	4.8	4.3
Boston, MA	2.7	2.6	2.4	14.6	16.6	19.3	18.2	12.9	11.1	7.7	6.6	7.3
Boulder, CO	2.1	2.4	4.2	9.4	8.1	9.6	6.5	5.4	4.9	4.9	4.7	6.5
Cape Coral, FL	3.2	3.0	4.4	16.2	14.0	10.0	11.0	7.2	6.0	5.2	5.2	4.8
Cedar Rapids, IA	4.0	3.5	4.1	14.2	12.9	11.3	9.3	10.1	6.8	4.7	4.9	4.3
Charleston, SC	2.2	2.3	2.5	14.6	14.0	9.9	9.7	7.1	5.0	3.9	3.9	4.1
Charlotte, NC	3.8	3.5	4.0	13.0	13.9	8.8	10.2	8.0	8.1	6.8	6.7	6.3
Chicago, IL	3.7	3.5	5.0	18.7	17.2	18.6	15.2	15.5	14.4	10.5	8.6	10.0
Cincinnati, OH	4.7	4.3	4.7	15.1	13.7	12.7	11.1	11.2	10.0	7.5	6.4	6.0
Clarksville, TN	4.4	4.3	3.8	17.2	11.3	11.2	11.4	9.9	7.3	8.4	5.8	7.4
Cleveland, OH	5.9	6.4	9.0	26.1	21.9	19.4	17.3	15.9	15.3	10.3	9.0	9.1
College Station, TX	2.8	2.6	3.7	8.2	8.1	5.9	5.3	4.2	4.7	3.9	4.9	4.4
Colorado Springs, CO	3.3	3.4	6.1	13.0	10.0	10.7	7.1	6.4	6.1	6.1	6.2	9.0
Columbia, MO	3.1	2.4	2.5	6.6	6.7	5.8	5.2	5.2	3.0	2.7	2.9	4.3
Columbia, SC	3.1	3.1	3.1	8.9	10.2	9.1	9.1	6.9	5.1	4.4	4.6	5.1
Columbus, OH	4.1	3.7	4.1	14.6	12.4	11.3	9.8	9.8	8.8	6.5	5.7	5.2
Dallas, TX	3.4	3.3	4.8	13.0	12.8	8.9	8.4	7.1	8.4	6.9	8.0	7.1
Davenport, IA	4.9	4.2	4.7	15.4	15.0	12.1	10.3	9.6	7.0	5.2	5.3	5.1
Denver, CO	2.8	2.8	5.3	13.4	11.5	12.0	8.8	7.9	7.3	7.3	7.2	9.3
Des Moines, IA	4.6	4.0	4.4	14.6	14.0	12.2	9.5	9.1	6.6	4.6	4.5	4.4
Durham, NC	3.4	3.1	3.7	10.1	11.4	7.6	8.8	6.7	6.8	5.7	5.7	5.6
Edison, NJ	2.8	2.7	2.4	11.7	11.3	12.7	11.0	8.4	4.9	5.8	7.4	5.3
El Paso, TX	3.8	3.6	5.1	14.5	14.0	9.1	8.4	6.9	8.1	6.7	8.9	7.7
Fargo, ND	2.5	2.3	2.3	9.6	8.5	7.0	5.5	4.0	3.0	3.1	3.1	3.2
Fayetteville, NC	5.8	5.2	6.0	15.7	16.8	10.8	12.9	10.1	10.4	9.0	9.0	8.9
Fort Collins, CO	2.4	2.5	4.4	11.5	8.7	9.3	6.2	5.5	5.1	5.0	5.0	7.5
Fort Wayne, IN	3.6	3.5	3.2	20.6	14.9	12.9	9.6	7.7	6.8	6.0	5.6	4.5
Fort Worth, TX	3.5	3.3	5.0	13.5	13.1	8.9	8.3	7.1	8.1	6.7	7.9	7.0
Grand Rapids, MI	3.8	3.2	3.3	26.7	22.0	16.0	11.5	10.0	8.7	5.9	5.2	5.7
Greeley, CO	3.1	3.2	5.6	10.3	9.3	11.2	8.4	7.9	7.5	7.3	7.7	10.0
Green Bay, WI	4.2	3.8	3.2	14.6	14.4	10.2	8.1	7.0	5.1	5.7	4.9	5.1
Greensboro, NC	4.4	4.0	4.6	15.3	15.8	10.0	11.6	9.1	9.0	7.7	7.7	7.4
Honolulu, HI	2.8	2.5	2.1	20.5	20.8	12.2	11.5	11.0	13.6	12.4	9.1	8.0
Houston, TX	3.9	3.7	5.4	14.4	14.1	10.0	9.8	8.4	9.8	7.7	8.8	7.9
Huntsville, AL	2.8	2.4	2.6	11.8	8.6	7.5	7.8	5.6	6.4	5.3	3.8	3.4
Indianapolis, IN	3.4	3.2	3.1	14.0	11.3	12.6	9.9	8.4	7.7	7.0	6.4	5.1
Jacksonville, FL	3.3	3.1	4.6	11.5	11.0	8.4	9.7	6.4	5.5	5.6	5.7	5.5
Kansas City, MO	4.1	3.7	4.1	11.7	12.3	9.2	9.0	9.0	5.7	4.9	5.0	6.7
Lafayette, LA	5.4	4.0	6.1	13.5	12.8	9.3	9.1	7.2	7.0	7.9	7.0	5.9
Lakeland, FL	3.8	3.5	4.9	11.4	12.0	9.4	10.7	7.3	6.4	6.5	6.9	6.5
Las Vegas, NV	4.0	3.9	7.3	32.1	27.1	16.7	15.8	14.9	13.9	13.5	11.7	10.3
Lexington, KY	3.5	3.1	4.1	14.1	9.0	4.5	4.6	6.7	4.8	6.2	4.5	5.1
Lincoln, NE	2.8	2.7	3.7	9.6	5.3	5.9	5.2	3.9	3.3	2.7	2.7	2.9
Little Rock, AR	3.7	3.6	4.6	12.0	11.7	10.4	10.1	10.4	9.8	7.9	7.7	5.0
Los Angeles, CA	4.5	4.6	6.6	20.7	21.0	20.0	18.8	17.1	15.5	11.8	10.6	10.6
Louisville, KY	4.1	3.7	4.7	16.5	11.7	5.3	5.3	7.7	5.6	7.4	5.4	5.7
Madison, WI	2.7	2.3	1.9	10.4	9.7	7.8	6.2	5.4	3.9	4.3	3.7	3.9

Table continued on following page.

Appendix A: Comparative Statistics   A-81

City	2020											
	Jan.	Feb.	Mar.	Apr.	May	Jun.	Jul.	Aug.	Sep.	Oct.	Nov.	Dec.
Manchester, NH	3.0	3.0	2.7	20.0	18.4	10.5	9.2	7.8	6.7	4.5	4.3	4.4
Memphis, TN	4.9	4.9	4.2	14.5	12.9	15.3	17.4	16.3	12.5	13.1	8.7	9.8
Miami, FL	1.4	1.4	3.7	12.4	12.8	12.5	15.4	8.6	13.6	9.3	8.4	7.7
Midland, TX	2.3	2.3	3.3	9.9	12.3	9.2	9.1	7.8	9.2	7.7	8.8	7.6
Milwaukee, WI	4.9	4.7	4.1	15.8	15.7	13.1	11.4	10.1	8.2	9.2	7.9	8.3
Minneapolis, MN	2.5	2.6	2.8	10.0	11.6	11.4	10.5	10.3	7.8	5.2	4.6	4.8
Nashville, TN	2.7	2.7	2.4	16.1	12.3	12.0	12.3	10.6	7.7	6.9	4.7	5.7
New Haven, CT	4.9	4.8	4.0	7.0	8.8	10.6	11.8	9.7	9.1	7.5	10.0	9.5
New Orleans, LA	5.5	4.2	6.3	22.2	20.7	15.9	15.1	12.6	12.4	15.1	13.6	11.2
New York, NY	3.8	3.8	4.2	15.5	20.2	18.7	18.8	14.9	14.7	11.7	11.7	11.6
Oklahoma City, OK	2.9	2.7	2.7	15.8	13.7	7.2	7.6	5.9	5.5	6.3	6.0	5.2
Omaha, NE	3.5	3.3	4.8	10.8	6.6	7.5	6.8	5.2	4.5	3.5	3.3	3.5
Orlando, FL	2.8	2.7	4.0	18.2	21.7	16.9	17.0	12.0	10.4	9.0	8.6	7.8
Peoria, IL	5.2	4.3	4.0	19.2	18.0	16.5	13.8	13.2	11.8	8.5	8.6	8.8
Philadelphia, PA	6.0	5.9	7.0	17.0	16.4	18.2	18.1	15.8	12.0	10.8	9.7	9.3
Phoenix, AZ	4.0	3.9	5.5	12.9	8.8	10.5	11.3	6.5	6.9	8.4	8.2	7.6
Pittsburgh, PA	4.7	4.6	5.6	15.2	13.6	13.8	14.6	12.2	8.9	7.7	6.9	6.7
Portland, OR	3.2	3.2	3.4	16.2	15.9	14.3	13.1	10.7	9.0	7.5	6.4	6.6
Providence, RI	4.7	4.7	5.9	19.5	18.7	15.2	14.9	16.7	13.3	8.5	8.5	8.7
Provo, UT	2.3	2.3	3.2	6.4	5.3	4.0	3.2	3.0	3.3	2.6	2.8	2.5
Raleigh, NC	3.6	3.3	3.9	12.4	13.2	8.2	9.1	6.9	6.9	5.9	5.9	5.7
Reno, NV	3.4	3.2	5.5	20.9	16.9	9.1	8.5	7.6	7.0	6.5	5.7	5.0
Richmond, VA	3.5	3.2	3.8	14.1	12.1	11.8	12.1	9.5	9.3	7.6	6.5	6.5
Riverside, CA	3.9	3.8	4.8	13.5	13.6	13.4	12.6	9.7	9.4	8.2	7.4	8.4
Rochester, MN	2.3	2.5	2.5	7.2	10.4	9.1	7.5	6.7	4.9	4.0	3.6	3.9
Sacramento, CA	4.0	3.8	4.9	14.5	14.5	14.0	13.1	10.4	10.2	8.7	8.0	9.2
Salt Lake City, UT	2.6	2.6	4.1	12.8	10.9	7.4	6.1	5.3	5.4	4.2	4.2	3.6
San Antonio, TX	3.2	3.1	4.5	13.8	13.0	8.5	8.3	6.9	7.9	6.3	7.4	6.5
San Diego, CA	3.2	3.1	4.0	14.7	14.9	13.7	12.2	9.3	8.7	7.1	6.3	7.9
San Francisco, CA	2.3	2.3	3.1	12.6	12.7	12.5	11.1	8.5	8.3	6.7	5.7	6.4
San Jose, CA	2.8	2.7	3.6	13.8	13.1	12.4	10.9	8.4	8.1	6.5	5.7	6.7
Santa Rosa, CA	3.0	2.9	3.8	14.9	13.6	12.2	10.4	8.0	7.7	6.7	6.1	6.9
Savannah, GA	3.7	3.7	5.1	18.5	13.7	11.3	11.0	8.8	8.8	6.3	7.5	7.3
Seattle, WA	2.4	2.2	5.3	13.7	13.2	9.0	7.9	6.8	6.5	4.2	3.9	6.1
Sioux Falls, SD	3.5	3.3	3.1	11.6	10.4	7.3	6.0	4.6	3.7	3.2	3.2	3.0
Springfield, IL	3.8	3.2	2.9	14.9	14.2	13.2	10.5	10.0	9.2	6.5	6.9	7.2
Tallahassee, FL	3.4	3.0	4.4	9.2	9.1	7.8	9.5	6.2	5.3	5.7	6.0	6.0
Tampa, FL	3.1	3.0	4.3	12.6	12.2	9.7	11.6	7.8	6.6	6.4	6.4	6.0
Tucson, AZ	4.7	4.4	6.3	13.8	9.2	10.9	11.7	6.6	7.1	8.7	8.6	8.2
Tulsa, OK	3.2	3.1	3.0	16.2	14.2	7.9	8.6	6.8	6.4	7.4	7.1	6.1
Tuscaloosa, AL	3.2	2.7	3.0	17.9	11.9	10.4	10.6	7.6	8.6	7.0	5.0	4.7
Virginia Beach, VA	2.9	2.6	3.1	12.2	9.4	8.2	7.7	6.0	5.9	4.6	4.2	4.3
Washington, DC	5.0	4.9	5.5	10.6	9.0	9.2	9.5	8.9	8.8	8.2	8.4	8.8
Wichita, KS	4.0	4.1	3.5	19.2	15.6	12.1	12.3	11.6	9.1	7.4	7.0	4.5
Winston-Salem, NC	4.2	3.7	4.3	12.9	13.9	8.8	10.3	8.0	8.2	6.9	6.8	6.7
U.S.	4.0	3.8	4.5	14.4	13.0	11.2	10.5	8.5	7.7	6.6	6.4	6.5

Note: Data is not seasonally adjusted and covers workers 16 years of age and older; All figures are percentages
Source: Bureau of Labor Statistics, Local Area Unemployment Statistics

A-82 Appendix A: Comparative Statistics

Unemployment Rate: Metro Area

Metro Area[1]	2020											
	Jan.	Feb.	Mar.	Apr.	May	Jun.	Jul.	Aug.	Sep.	Oct.	Nov.	Dec.
Albuquerque, NM	4.6	4.6	5.7	12.3	9.1	9.0	13.1	11.1	9.5	7.5	6.4	7.3
Allentown, PA	5.0	5.0	5.7	16.2	13.8	14.1	12.8	10.6	7.5	6.9	6.5	6.2
Anchorage, AK	5.7	5.0	5.2	14.3	12.5	12.2	11.0	6.6	6.5	5.3	6.1	5.7
Ann Arbor, MI	2.5	2.2	2.3	14.8	13.9	10.7	8.0	6.9	6.1	4.0	3.4	3.6
Athens, GA	3.2	3.3	4.3	11.1	8.0	6.7	6.7	4.9	4.9	3.7	4.4	4.5
Atlanta, GA	3.2	3.3	4.4	12.7	9.9	8.6	8.6	6.4	6.6	4.6	5.6	5.4
Austin, TX	2.8	2.6	3.8	12.2	11.4	7.3	6.8	5.5	6.3	5.0	5.9	5.1
Baton Rouge, LA	5.1	3.8	5.6	13.0	12.6	9.6	9.2	7.2	7.0	8.0	7.2	6.1
Boise City, ID	3.2	2.7	2.6	12.3	9.2	5.8	5.2	4.1	6.0	5.4	4.9	4.5
Boston, MA[4]	2.7	2.6	2.4	14.2	15.3	16.9	15.5	10.7	9.3	6.7	5.9	6.5
Boulder, CO	2.4	2.4	4.4	9.7	8.3	9.6	6.7	5.8	5.3	5.2	5.1	6.9
Cape Coral, FL	3.1	3.0	4.3	14.6	13.0	9.6	10.7	7.1	5.9	5.4	5.4	5.1
Cedar Rapids, IA	3.8	3.4	3.9	12.5	11.1	9.6	7.9	8.3	5.6	3.8	4.1	3.8
Charleston, SC	2.4	2.5	2.6	12.1	12.2	9.0	9.2	6.9	5.0	4.0	4.0	4.3
Charlotte, NC	3.7	3.4	3.9	12.7	13.2	8.3	9.3	7.1	7.0	5.9	5.9	5.8
Chicago, IL[2]	3.8	3.7	3.9	16.4	15.8	15.7	13.3	13.0	12.2	8.8	8.9	8.7
Cincinnati, OH	4.3	4.0	4.4	14.1	11.2	9.0	7.6	7.9	6.8	5.6	4.8	4.7
Clarksville, TN	4.6	4.4	4.3	16.1	10.5	8.8	9.0	8.5	6.2	7.5	5.4	6.7
Cleveland, OH	5.0	5.4	6.2	21.8	17.3	12.7	9.2	8.1	8.8	7.2	7.1	7.6
College Station, TX	2.9	2.7	3.9	8.7	8.7	6.3	5.8	4.7	5.5	4.5	5.5	5.0
Colorado Springs, CO	3.3	3.4	6.2	12.6	9.7	10.5	6.9	6.2	5.9	6.0	6.0	8.6
Columbia, MO	3.2	2.5	2.6	6.5	6.5	5.7	5.1	5.1	2.9	2.6	2.8	4.2
Columbia, SC	2.7	2.8	2.8	8.5	9.3	7.8	7.8	6.0	4.4	3.7	3.8	4.3
Columbus, OH	4.2	3.8	4.2	13.7	11.0	9.9	8.3	8.3	7.4	5.5	4.9	4.7
Dallas, TX[2]	3.3	3.2	4.6	12.6	12.1	8.1	7.5	6.2	7.3	5.9	7.1	6.2
Davenport, IA	4.7	4.0	4.0	15.3	14.4	11.5	9.4	8.5	7.1	5.0	5.0	5.1
Denver, CO	2.7	2.8	5.2	12.3	10.5	11.1	7.9	7.0	6.5	6.5	6.4	8.5
Des Moines, IA	3.5	3.0	3.4	11.8	10.9	9.2	7.2	6.7	4.8	3.3	3.5	3.4
Durham, NC	3.5	3.1	3.7	9.6	10.6	6.9	7.9	5.9	6.0	5.2	5.2	5.2
Edison, NJ[2]	3.8	3.6	3.8	15.1	16.3	18.3	17.6	14.0	10.7	10.5	10.4	9.2
El Paso, TX	4.0	3.8	5.4	14.9	14.6	9.5	8.8	7.3	8.6	7.1	9.4	8.1
Fargo, ND	2.8	2.6	2.5	7.7	7.2	6.4	5.1	3.9	3.0	2.9	3.0	3.1
Fayetteville, NC	5.4	4.9	5.6	14.6	15.4	9.8	11.6	9.1	9.3	8.2	8.3	8.2
Fort Collins, CO	2.5	2.6	4.7	11.1	8.6	9.2	6.2	5.6	5.2	5.1	5.2	7.4
Fort Wayne, IN	3.4	3.3	3.0	19.4	13.5	11.2	8.2	6.5	5.7	5.1	4.8	3.9
Fort Worth, TX[2]	3.3	3.2	4.7	13.1	12.6	8.3	7.7	6.5	7.5	6.1	7.3	6.5
Grand Rapids, MI	2.9	2.5	2.6	21.5	17.1	12.0	8.4	7.2	6.3	4.2	3.7	4.2
Greeley, CO	2.7	2.9	5.1	9.9	8.6	10.1	7.3	6.6	6.3	6.2	6.4	8.3
Green Bay, WI	4.0	3.7	3.1	12.9	12.1	8.6	6.7	5.6	4.1	4.8	4.2	4.6
Greensboro, NC	4.3	3.9	4.5	14.8	14.5	9.0	10.2	7.8	7.9	6.9	6.9	6.7
Honolulu, HI	2.8	2.5	2.1	20.5	20.8	12.2	11.5	11.0	13.6	12.4	9.1	8.0
Houston, TX	4.1	3.9	5.5	14.3	13.9	9.7	9.5	8.1	9.6	7.7	8.9	8.0
Huntsville, AL	2.7	2.3	2.5	10.7	7.4	6.4	6.4	4.5	5.1	4.2	3.1	2.8
Indianapolis, IN	3.2	2.9	2.8	13.3	10.2	10.6	7.8	6.6	6.0	5.4	5.0	4.0
Jacksonville, FL	3.1	3.0	4.3	11.2	10.4	7.8	8.8	5.7	4.8	4.8	5.0	4.8
Kansas City, MO	3.7	3.4	3.5	11.3	10.8	7.8	7.6	7.3	5.0	4.4	4.4	4.9
Lafayette, LA	5.7	4.3	6.4	13.0	12.4	9.2	9.1	7.4	7.3	8.2	7.3	6.2
Lakeland, FL	3.7	3.5	4.9	14.0	17.6	13.6	13.2	9.2	7.9	7.1	7.0	6.7
Las Vegas, NV	3.9	3.9	7.2	34.0	28.8	17.8	16.6	15.6	14.6	13.7	11.8	10.4
Lexington, KY	3.7	3.3	4.2	15.2	9.1	4.4	4.5	6.5	4.7	6.1	4.4	5.0
Lincoln, NE	2.7	2.6	3.7	9.3	5.2	5.7	5.0	3.8	3.2	2.7	2.7	2.9
Little Rock, AR	3.7	3.6	4.6	10.9	10.2	9.0	8.3	8.4	7.8	6.4	6.4	4.3
Los Angeles, CA[2]	4.9	4.7	5.6	18.2	18.8	17.9	18.2	17.5	13.2	12.0	11.9	12.3
Louisville, KY	3.9	3.5	4.3	16.8	11.8	6.5	5.6	7.0	5.3	6.5	4.9	5.0
Madison, WI	3.1	2.8	2.3	11.1	9.7	7.5	6.0	5.1	3.7	4.2	3.7	4.1

Table continued on following page.

Appendix A: Comparative Statistics   A-83

Metro Area[1]	2020											
	Jan.	Feb.	Mar.	Apr.	May	Jun.	Jul.	Aug.	Sep.	Oct.	Nov.	Dec.
Manchester, NH[3]	2.8	2.8	2.5	17.4	15.8	9.0	7.9	6.5	5.6	3.8	3.7	3.7
Memphis, TN	4.4	4.4	3.8	12.8	10.7	11.9	13.1	11.9	9.2	9.6	6.7	7.4
Miami, FL[2]	1.8	1.6	2.2	10.3	10.3	10.1	15.2	9.1	12.6	8.5	8.2	7.9
Midland, TX	2.4	2.3	3.4	10.1	12.6	9.5	9.5	8.1	9.5	8.0	9.3	8.0
Milwaukee, WI	4.0	3.8	3.2	13.6	12.9	10.2	8.6	7.5	5.9	6.6	5.7	6.0
Minneapolis, MN	3.1	3.1	3.1	9.2	10.1	9.2	8.2	7.8	5.9	4.2	4.0	4.5
Nashville, TN	2.8	2.8	2.5	15.2	11.1	10.2	10.0	8.4	6.1	6.1	4.2	5.2
New Haven, CT[3]	4.2	4.1	3.4	7.2	8.5	9.3	9.7	7.7	7.1	5.5	7.4	7.1
New Orleans, LA	5.2	3.9	5.9	19.0	17.4	12.8	11.9	9.7	9.4	11.2	10.0	8.2
New York, NY[2]	3.8	3.6	3.8	15.1	16.3	18.3	17.6	14.0	10.7	10.5	10.4	9.2
Oklahoma City, OK	2.9	2.7	2.7	14.8	12.9	6.9	7.1	5.6	5.1	5.9	5.6	4.8
Omaha, NE	3.2	3.1	4.3	10.0	6.4	6.9	6.0	4.6	3.9	3.0	2.9	3.0
Orlando, FL	3.0	2.9	4.2	16.8	21.1	16.1	15.4	10.8	9.2	7.8	7.4	6.9
Peoria, IL	5.0	4.2	3.8	17.7	15.4	13.5	10.8	9.8	8.6	6.1	6.3	6.8
Philadelphia, PA[2]	5.5	5.4	6.4	16.3	15.5	17.0	16.7	14.5	10.9	9.8	8.8	8.3
Phoenix, AZ	4.0	3.8	5.4	12.5	8.3	9.8	10.4	5.9	6.2	7.4	7.4	6.9
Pittsburgh, PA	5.2	5.2	6.1	16.4	13.6	12.9	13.1	10.9	7.9	6.9	6.3	6.6
Portland, OR	3.4	3.5	3.6	14.2	14.0	11.8	11.2	9.1	7.9	6.6	5.8	6.1
Providence, RI[3]	4.1	4.1	4.7	18.2	16.7	13.7	12.7	12.7	10.1	6.5	6.8	7.6
Provo, UT	2.5	2.5	3.6	7.9	6.2	4.4	3.6	3.4	3.8	3.1	3.3	2.8
Raleigh, NC	3.5	3.2	3.7	11.0	11.5	7.0	7.9	6.0	6.1	5.2	5.2	5.2
Reno, NV	3.4	3.2	5.6	20.4	16.0	8.7	8.2	7.3	6.7	6.3	5.6	5.0
Richmond, VA	3.1	2.8	3.4	11.2	9.4	8.9	8.8	6.9	6.8	5.5	4.9	5.0
Riverside, CA	4.1	4.0	5.2	14.7	15.1	14.3	13.4	10.5	10.2	8.7	7.9	9.1
Rochester, MN	3.1	3.1	3.1	6.9	9.3	8.1	6.6	5.8	4.2	3.5	3.4	3.9
Sacramento, CA	3.9	3.8	4.8	14.0	13.7	12.8	11.6	9.0	8.7	7.3	6.7	7.9
Salt Lake City, UT	2.6	2.7	4.0	11.2	9.4	6.4	5.3	4.7	5.2	4.1	4.2	3.5
San Antonio, TX	3.2	3.1	4.5	13.3	12.7	8.3	8.0	6.6	7.7	6.2	7.3	6.4
San Diego, CA	3.3	3.2	4.2	15.0	15.2	13.8	12.4	9.5	8.9	7.5	6.6	8.0
San Francisco, CA[2]	2.2	2.2	3.0	12.1	12.0	11.8	10.3	7.9	7.7	6.3	5.4	6.1
San Jose, CA	2.7	2.7	3.5	12.0	11.3	10.8	9.5	7.3	7.0	5.8	5.2	6.0
Santa Rosa, CA	2.9	2.8	3.7	14.5	13.0	11.6	10.0	7.5	7.2	6.0	5.5	6.5
Savannah, GA	3.3	3.3	4.4	15.3	10.8	8.6	8.5	6.5	6.7	4.7	5.6	5.6
Seattle, WA[2]	2.7	2.6	5.3	16.2	12.6	10.7	9.5	7.9	7.4	6.5	6.1	6.0
Sioux Falls, SD	3.4	3.2	3.0	10.5	9.4	6.7	5.6	4.3	3.4	3.0	3.0	2.8
Springfield, IL	3.9	3.2	2.9	14.2	13.1	11.7	9.2	8.7	7.8	5.5	5.9	6.3
Tallahassee, FL	3.2	2.9	4.2	8.3	8.1	7.0	8.4	5.5	4.7	5.0	5.4	5.3
Tampa, FL	3.1	3.0	4.3	13.2	12.2	9.0	10.2	6.7	5.7	5.4	5.5	5.2
Tucson, AZ	4.5	4.2	6.0	12.8	8.4	9.9	10.6	5.9	6.3	7.8	7.7	7.4
Tulsa, OK	3.2	3.0	3.0	15.1	12.9	7.1	7.6	6.1	5.7	6.6	6.4	5.6
Tuscaloosa, AL	2.9	2.5	2.8	16.6	10.8	9.0	9.1	6.3	7.1	6.0	4.4	4.1
Virginia Beach, VA	3.3	3.0	3.6	12.1	10.0	9.2	9.2	7.4	7.2	5.8	5.1	5.3
Washington, DC[2]	3.1	3.0	3.4	10.0	8.9	8.4	8.1	6.9	6.9	6.4	5.7	5.6
Wichita, KS	3.8	3.8	3.3	17.7	14.1	10.8	11.0	10.3	8.0	6.6	6.5	4.3
Winston-Salem, NC	3.9	3.5	4.1	12.7	12.7	7.7	8.8	6.6	6.8	5.9	6.0	5.9
U.S.	4.0	3.8	4.5	14.4	13.0	11.2	10.5	8.5	7.7	6.6	6.4	6.5

Note: Data is not seasonally adjusted and covers workers 16 years of age and older; All figures are percentages; (1) Figures cover the Metropolitan Statistical Area (MSA) except where noted. See Appendix B for areas included; (2) Metropolitan Division; (3) New England City and Town Area; (4) New England City and Town Area Division
Source: Bureau of Labor Statistics, Local Area Unemployment Statistics

A-84 Appendix A: Comparative Statistics

Average Hourly Wages: Occupations A – C

Metro Area[1]	Accountants/ Auditors	Automotive Mechanics	Book-keepers	Carpenters	Cashiers	Computer Programmers	Computer Systems Analysts
Albuquerque, NM	33.46	21.98	20.06	20.67	11.88	38.33	39.87
Allentown, PA	36.61	21.48	20.16	23.11	11.53	40.11	42.51
Anchorage, AK	39.02	22.66	23.63	33.12	14.55	44.08	41.47
Ann Arbor, MI	36.68	30.73	21.60	27.75	12.05	38.47	40.58
Athens, GA	31.72	20.47	17.40	19.07	10.70	32.83	43.69
Atlanta, GA	42.18	23.13	21.75	20.56	11.10	44.52	45.29
Austin, TX	37.28	26.39	20.95	19.33	12.25	42.42	41.18
Baton Rouge, LA	31.10	22.33	19.99	24.74	10.14	40.35	39.72
Boise City, ID	36.48	21.60	20.17	18.39	12.59	32.61	45.73
Boston, MA[2]	43.60	24.14	25.10	31.31	14.22	49.27	50.79
Boulder, CO	40.09	24.42	22.25	25.30	14.13	39.10	48.44
Cape Coral, FL	31.26	21.32	20.50	19.97	11.99	42.99	37.54
Cedar Rapids, IA	35.32	22.27	19.62	24.33	11.59	39.02	40.35
Charleston, SC	32.87	23.69	18.26	28.28	11.63	39.15	41.06
Charlotte, NC	42.38	23.40	20.71	19.73	10.98	48.79	48.01
Chicago, IL	37.81	24.87	22.39	34.74	12.61	49.84	45.00
Cincinnati, OH	36.81	22.26	20.71	24.06	11.71	44.99	47.80
Clarksville, TN	30.21	18.81	18.23	18.80	11.06	n/a	36.97
Cleveland, OH	36.64	22.16	20.46	25.76	12.11	39.60	40.53
College Station, TX	29.37	25.23	17.40	20.32	11.70	48.32	38.11
Colorado Springs, CO	36.33	25.52	19.93	24.48	13.94	34.84	49.76
Columbia, MO	29.02	20.93	17.87	24.13	11.10	30.68	38.55
Columbia, SC	29.39	21.06	17.97	23.15	10.58	43.48	37.52
Columbus, OH	36.98	21.18	21.79	24.76	11.99	44.57	44.18
Dallas, TX	40.31	23.53	21.33	19.85	11.39	53.87	49.58
Davenport, IA	32.27	20.88	19.51	25.19	11.12	42.62	44.10
Denver, CO	42.62	24.69	22.73	25.92	14.48	43.53	51.32
Des Moines, IA	37.04	24.11	21.99	22.21	11.87	35.53	42.70
Durham, NC	39.14	22.27	21.86	19.68	10.92	47.50	45.42
Edison, NJ	50.83	24.31	24.50	34.16	14.25	46.28	55.05
El Paso, TX	31.64	16.30	16.08	16.69	10.53	40.15	37.37
Fargo, ND	32.72	24.61	20.00	23.07	12.34	36.01	42.32
Fayetteville, NC	35.70	17.98	17.77	19.91	10.55	30.98	38.38
Fort Collins, CO	35.94	24.03	21.32	23.09	14.29	35.42	42.76
Fort Wayne, IN	34.36	18.77	19.67	20.21	11.30	25.61	37.13
Fort Worth, TX	40.31	23.53	21.33	19.85	11.39	53.87	49.58
Grand Rapids, MI	33.78	21.17	19.56	23.43	11.96	34.14	37.61
Greeley, CO	39.19	25.37	20.19	22.97	13.76	n/a	58.55
Green Bay, WI	33.64	20.09	20.68	26.03	11.26	37.56	39.08
Greensboro, NC	38.57	22.14	19.86	17.69	10.55	40.70	45.51
Honolulu, HI	31.74	25.73	21.44	39.88	13.68	39.65	38.51
Houston, TX	40.30	22.98	21.66	21.53	11.62	49.83	59.65
Huntsville, AL	35.97	23.40	20.47	20.55	10.97	41.94	49.70
Indianapolis, IN	37.22	21.50	20.88	24.11	11.33	45.99	40.06
Jacksonville, FL	32.52	20.49	20.33	19.12	11.34	38.38	37.87
Kansas City, MO	35.61	23.49	20.58	28.51	12.02	42.04	36.99
Lafayette, LA	31.83	18.68	18.14	19.37	9.98	35.29	39.77
Lakeland, FL	36.15	22.44	18.64	18.81	11.96	31.46	37.47
Las Vegas, NV	33.27	21.01	20.44	29.29	12.02	41.98	43.58
Lexington, KY	34.06	20.09	19.10	22.60	11.15	37.18	39.27
Lincoln, NE	33.35	22.34	19.37	19.78	11.87	36.02	36.79
Little Rock, AR	32.28	20.29	18.68	20.70	11.78	37.05	35.10
Los Angeles, CA	40.22	25.83	24.20	32.37	14.82	47.38	53.54
Louisville, KY	36.49	20.16	19.65	25.97	11.25	36.56	41.09
Madison, WI	35.56	23.85	21.38	27.06	12.20	51.95	44.21

Table continued on following page.

Appendix A: Comparative Statistics   A-85

Metro Area[1]	Accountants/ Auditors	Automotive Mechanics	Book- keepers	Carpenters	Cashiers	Computer Program- mers	Computer Systems Analysts
Manchester, NH[2]	36.21	23.60	20.53	22.51	11.60	33.07	45.34
Memphis, TN	34.52	25.99	21.21	21.37	10.80	41.07	39.88
Miami, FL	38.52	21.77	21.28	20.93	11.76	41.74	44.55
Midland, TX	49.58	30.42	23.19	20.45	13.31	57.40	n/a
Milwaukee, WI	36.97	21.67	21.43	27.70	11.60	40.27	40.47
Minneapolis, MN	37.42	23.75	22.79	27.95	13.27	43.22	49.04
Nashville, TN	34.65	21.80	21.53	22.23	11.54	45.25	40.00
New Haven, CT[2]	40.03	23.80	23.77	29.32	12.79	47.26	46.09
New Orleans, LA	33.52	19.89	18.98	22.06	10.47	49.80	46.68
New York, NY	50.83	24.31	24.50	34.16	14.25	46.28	55.05
Oklahoma City, OK	38.02	23.73	19.72	20.80	11.03	38.30	38.44
Omaha, NE	35.78	22.47	20.56	19.96	12.22	38.65	41.38
Orlando, FL	35.16	19.62	20.04	21.12	11.70	41.55	44.36
Peoria, IL	38.38	20.73	18.98	31.69	11.40	39.55	45.55
Philadelphia, PA	41.21	22.53	22.28	30.86	11.77	48.82	50.50
Phoenix, AZ	36.29	22.21	21.58	23.50	13.39	44.18	44.56
Pittsburgh, PA	35.65	20.59	19.36	28.43	11.02	41.89	41.16
Portland, OR	38.49	24.48	22.58	29.13	14.68	45.18	48.24
Providence, RI[2]	41.50	21.85	22.70	25.77	13.17	51.83	47.51
Provo, UT	30.23	23.85	19.47	21.85	12.14	42.53	40.09
Raleigh, NC	36.22	23.93	20.23	20.64	11.17	47.69	47.56
Reno, NV	31.29	25.37	21.43	25.23	12.11	44.10	43.87
Richmond, VA	39.89	24.49	21.27	22.33	11.07	45.10	47.11
Riverside, CA	36.22	24.02	22.43	26.58	14.92	43.59	43.34
Rochester, MN	33.90	21.22	20.99	26.07	12.84	29.59	41.46
Sacramento, CA	40.32	26.48	22.61	28.08	15.49	39.13	50.27
Salt Lake City, UT	33.91	21.58	20.00	22.62	12.06	41.48	37.30
San Antonio, TX	35.76	20.68	20.96	20.42	11.81	46.43	47.72
San Diego, CA	43.00	25.61	23.56	28.60	14.50	48.42	45.56
San Francisco, CA	48.60	31.07	26.61	36.44	16.58	60.30	60.27
San Jose, CA	49.48	30.53	27.26	31.80	17.29	54.58	64.41
Santa Rosa, CA	44.34	28.46	26.79	35.33	15.89	44.87	43.31
Savannah, GA	33.08	25.13	20.20	22.91	10.51	38.06	49.67
Seattle, WA	42.21	26.17	24.43	33.25	16.50	n/a	54.00
Sioux Falls, SD	34.97	20.87	17.77	18.73	12.24	28.31	37.94
Springfield, IL	34.50	21.31	20.55	29.86	11.24	47.45	45.09
Tallahassee, FL	27.29	21.76	19.47	20.05	11.07	31.03	29.13
Tampa, FL	37.28	21.62	20.88	19.31	11.46	38.78	42.77
Tucson, AZ	34.29	21.59	18.88	20.44	13.57	42.88	41.83
Tulsa, OK	36.62	19.11	21.11	24.67	11.12	40.37	45.55
Tuscaloosa, AL	34.36	20.19	17.36	19.72	10.43	30.43	43.48
Virginia Beach, VA	36.21	25.63	20.21	20.84	11.14	n/a	47.27
Washington, DC	47.13	27.27	24.81	24.98	13.22	50.51	56.09
Wichita, KS	33.82	18.41	17.96	18.76	11.17	39.71	36.62
Winston-Salem, NC	35.91	20.17	19.63	19.79	10.16	42.82	44.65

Notes: (1) Figures cover the Metropolitan Statistical Area (MSA) except where noted. See Appendix B for areas included; (2) New England City and Town Area; n/a not available
Source: Bureau of Labor Statistics, May 2020 Metro Area Occupational Employment and Wage Estimates

A-86   Appendix A: Comparative Statistics

Average Hourly Wages: Occupations C – E

Metro Area	Comp. User Support Specialists	Construction Laborers	Cooks, Restaurant	Customer Service Reps.	Dentists	Electricians	Engineers, Electrical
Albuquerque, NM	21.74	16.94	12.77	16.16	77.97	23.25	58.20
Allentown, PA	27.07	21.92	13.74	17.59	66.64	27.36	50.31
Anchorage, AK	29.69	26.02	14.62	19.54	101.03	33.57	54.83
Ann Arbor, MI	23.79	22.53	15.59	18.78	71.19	33.74	42.05
Athens, GA	21.34	14.82	12.71	15.83	n/a	26.34	51.49
Atlanta, GA	28.15	16.51	13.35	17.73	77.08	27.77	47.62
Austin, TX	25.88	15.85	13.15	17.26	77.48	25.85	52.09
Baton Rouge, LA	24.19	17.93	12.04	16.40	91.40	26.16	53.11
Boise City, ID	24.03	16.83	12.67	16.30	105.24	24.69	48.27
Boston, MA[2]	33.22	28.35	16.99	22.68	100.75	34.07	55.65
Boulder, CO	30.99	18.47	15.58	20.26	107.71	26.35	52.75
Cape Coral, FL	23.30	16.84	15.40	16.51	83.47	21.88	53.83
Cedar Rapids, IA	20.83	19.76	11.87	19.74	55.16	29.19	51.76
Charleston, SC	26.66	16.83	13.15	18.77	70.75	22.35	47.79
Charlotte, NC	25.75	15.96	13.03	18.80	83.93	22.29	48.47
Chicago, IL	26.71	32.05	14.66	20.08	92.31	40.50	46.52
Cincinnati, OH	24.74	22.97	12.99	17.97	103.00	23.55	43.84
Clarksville, TN	20.86	15.26	10.88	16.79	n/a	23.71	42.56
Cleveland, OH	24.39	23.80	13.11	19.37	101.12	29.21	41.38
College Station, TX	21.68	15.89	11.24	14.68	n/a	24.78	19.71
Colorado Springs, CO	26.65	17.48	14.36	17.16	59.66	24.26	52.77
Columbia, MO	21.99	19.97	12.27	15.32	95.89	22.23	n/a
Columbia, SC	24.58	16.93	11.80	16.92	63.01	25.77	44.63
Columbus, OH	26.89	24.18	13.34	18.35	92.26	22.93	42.67
Dallas, TX	24.78	17.39	13.00	18.59	110.94	23.96	51.08
Davenport, IA	23.82	20.58	11.98	17.03	77.64	28.51	47.09
Denver, CO	30.27	19.27	15.39	19.75	99.20	26.85	47.84
Des Moines, IA	26.48	18.81	14.39	21.09	90.74	24.79	40.35
Durham, NC	30.19	15.67	14.28	19.11	109.88	24.99	48.84
Edison, NJ	31.34	29.45	17.33	21.93	81.29	40.48	54.54
El Paso, TX	20.29	13.74	11.29	12.83	92.58	18.18	41.46
Fargo, ND	22.59	21.54	15.48	18.69	83.78	28.94	47.67
Fayetteville, NC	23.78	15.30	11.83	16.47	92.25	21.06	41.81
Fort Collins, CO	28.31	18.20	14.74	17.04	84.69	30.01	52.44
Fort Wayne, IN	23.05	19.96	13.24	18.84	80.13	26.13	48.46
Fort Worth, TX	24.78	17.39	13.00	18.59	110.94	23.96	51.08
Grand Rapids, MI	25.00	17.99	13.49	18.78	115.44	23.51	39.99
Greeley, CO	28.57	18.27	15.14	16.42	80.53	27.27	51.35
Green Bay, WI	25.96	20.76	13.61	18.77	105.02	27.59	40.42
Greensboro, NC	24.49	15.45	12.56	18.30	72.13	23.33	49.13
Honolulu, HI	25.51	30.70	16.72	19.16	103.97	38.38	43.60
Houston, TX	24.90	17.92	12.03	17.51	69.53	25.57	54.61
Huntsville, AL	24.21	15.88	12.69	17.48	78.91	23.75	51.86
Indianapolis, IN	24.33	19.53	13.36	18.96	69.38	28.17	44.98
Jacksonville, FL	24.83	16.85	12.99	17.90	72.89	21.37	45.99
Kansas City, MO	26.35	22.20	13.89	18.68	82.22	29.28	43.98
Lafayette, LA	26.20	17.63	13.15	16.07	n/a	23.40	43.43
Lakeland, FL	26.15	16.45	12.88	15.53	97.38	19.94	43.16
Las Vegas, NV	24.94	17.98	15.83	17.00	98.54	33.90	40.75
Lexington, KY	25.92	18.55	13.47	16.56	n/a	23.98	41.54
Lincoln, NE	22.54	17.18	14.40	16.32	60.36	24.62	47.42
Little Rock, AR	23.55	14.24	11.97	17.45	95.92	19.85	44.73
Los Angeles, CA	29.62	23.18	15.95	20.32	65.87	37.25	58.88
Louisville, KY	24.98	18.87	13.45	17.72	61.30	28.14	42.60
Madison, WI	28.38	20.82	13.02	20.69	117.88	28.07	46.09

Table continued on following page.

Appendix A: Comparative Statistics   A-87

Metro Area	Comp. User Support Specialists	Construction Laborers	Cooks, Restaurant	Customer Service Reps.	Dentists	Electricians	Engineers, Electrical
Manchester, NH[2]	27.45	19.30	15.58	20.34	111.95	26.41	52.51
Memphis, TN	23.06	15.86	12.46	18.07	71.03	24.89	46.46
Miami, FL	26.17	16.41	14.96	17.41	100.72	22.68	46.88
Midland, TX	24.74	17.43	13.11	17.41	n/a	28.94	52.80
Milwaukee, WI	25.85	23.25	13.14	20.22	98.32	33.98	44.41
Minneapolis, MN	28.26	28.53	16.38	21.32	105.18	35.78	50.53
Nashville, TN	24.09	17.16	13.19	18.01	75.33	25.45	45.40
New Haven, CT[2]	28.52	22.06	15.54	20.29	120.40	34.67	50.33
New Orleans, LA	24.41	16.66	12.31	16.48	74.68	27.52	54.15
New York, NY	31.34	29.45	17.33	21.93	81.29	40.48	54.54
Oklahoma City, OK	24.90	16.58	13.18	16.47	80.68	24.21	47.52
Omaha, NE	25.85	18.60	13.66	18.15	113.83	27.78	44.63
Orlando, FL	24.93	16.61	14.06	17.02	81.37	22.29	50.42
Peoria, IL	27.32	20.86	13.39	15.80	118.44	33.87	n/a
Philadelphia, PA	29.11	24.78	14.84	20.23	81.37	36.95	53.04
Phoenix, AZ	25.78	19.60	14.46	18.18	97.79	23.86	48.56
Pittsburgh, PA	24.98	21.30	13.04	18.03	71.78	31.54	47.12
Portland, OR	29.15	23.09	16.02	20.20	107.31	37.04	46.08
Providence, RI[2]	29.98	26.78	15.08	19.39	120.18	28.88	52.32
Provo, UT	26.06	16.78	13.93	16.82	n/a	22.38	35.78
Raleigh, NC	27.29	16.83	15.74	18.53	95.72	21.78	48.22
Reno, NV	24.94	20.58	14.82	17.38	99.87	26.92	43.83
Richmond, VA	26.74	15.20	12.97	17.99	79.04	26.98	47.93
Riverside, CA	29.70	24.28	15.12	19.74	84.77	26.51	48.20
Rochester, MN	27.37	23.17	14.87	17.51	93.21	30.42	48.07
Sacramento, CA	41.51	24.49	15.22	21.08	93.37	30.07	52.08
Salt Lake City, UT	26.07	18.26	13.09	18.57	60.05	26.94	47.95
San Antonio, TX	23.60	16.05	12.33	16.77	72.46	25.37	45.10
San Diego, CA	29.34	23.87	15.90	20.38	53.63	30.22	50.09
San Francisco, CA	37.82	28.43	19.21	24.01	85.30	51.29	58.99
San Jose, CA	34.93	27.64	17.22	22.94	94.63	41.61	72.35
Santa Rosa, CA	28.84	25.31	17.33	20.34	98.37	35.19	50.52
Savannah, GA	24.02	16.07	12.17	14.71	84.25	25.83	59.47
Seattle, WA	30.88	27.11	17.85	22.61	81.64	39.81	57.72
Sioux Falls, SD	20.11	16.27	13.58	17.26	78.71	24.23	46.65
Springfield, IL	29.20	26.62	11.66	17.52	86.11	34.16	45.48
Tallahassee, FL	21.83	14.26	13.54	16.05	78.74	21.70	44.42
Tampa, FL	24.82	15.90	13.00	17.32	71.77	22.08	46.52
Tucson, AZ	24.98	17.41	13.83	16.79	102.12	25.23	44.68
Tulsa, OK	24.46	16.60	12.51	16.05	n/a	23.73	49.81
Tuscaloosa, AL	29.04	15.01	10.38	16.06	73.08	25.65	43.67
Virginia Beach, VA	26.72	16.64	13.23	15.33	88.32	23.97	46.70
Washington, DC	32.03	18.44	15.40	21.22	105.63	31.72	62.57
Wichita, KS	22.03	16.12	12.82	16.56	77.90	25.06	43.33
Winston-Salem, NC	24.73	15.83	10.93	17.29	72.88	22.44	43.40

Notes: (1) Figures cover the Metropolitan Statistical Area (MSA) except where noted. See Appendix B for areas included; (2) New England City and Town Area; n/a not available
Source: Bureau of Labor Statistics, May 2020 Metro Area Occupational Employment and Wage Estimates

A-88 Appendix A: Comparative Statistics

Average Hourly Wages: Occupations F – H

Metro Area	Fast Food and Counter Workers	Financial Managers	First-Line Supervisors/ of Office Workers	General and Operations Managers	Hair-dressers/ Cosme-tologists	Home Health and Personal Care Aides	Janitors/ Cleaners
Albuquerque, NM	10.64	55.09	27.54	56.14	10.84	11.86	12.36
Allentown, PA	11.10	75.32	28.94	57.29	15.22	12.94	15.88
Anchorage, AK	12.54	54.93	32.38	58.03	14.27	16.10	16.48
Ann Arbor, MI	11.86	65.04	29.64	68.81	13.02	12.34	16.01
Athens, GA	9.77	52.35	24.64	45.41	10.25	12.00	12.46
Atlanta, GA	9.99	72.80	28.87	59.99	18.33	12.85	12.66
Austin, TX	11.34	72.96	31.36	57.34	15.92	11.06	14.50
Baton Rouge, LA	9.49	53.55	24.60	56.42	14.04	9.70	10.97
Boise City, ID	9.99	52.76	27.07	43.73	14.95	14.05	13.26
Boston, MA[2]	14.13	79.09	34.34	73.18	21.89	16.31	18.88
Boulder, CO	13.56	90.36	31.98	76.38	20.61	16.10	17.25
Cape Coral, FL	10.94	54.85	27.05	47.49	15.61	12.65	14.35
Cedar Rapids, IA	11.05	59.04	28.10	53.31	14.88	14.05	15.15
Charleston, SC	10.81	69.92	27.74	59.94	15.78	12.19	11.86
Charlotte, NC	10.65	83.71	28.74	64.43	15.60	11.20	12.26
Chicago, IL	11.94	75.24	32.97	66.06	15.60	13.73	15.85
Cincinnati, OH	11.06	67.69	29.76	59.57	14.55	12.32	15.23
Clarksville, TN	9.43	50.27	22.51	45.76	11.69	11.14	13.50
Cleveland, OH	11.12	73.35	29.66	63.12	15.00	11.54	14.61
College Station, TX	10.09	63.69	26.16	45.76	13.83	10.56	13.33
Colorado Springs, CO	12.80	71.91	28.53	62.51	19.89	14.62	14.95
Columbia, MO	12.41	57.39	26.61	41.33	15.87	12.15	14.70
Columbia, SC	9.32	58.42	27.64	54.33	17.75	11.20	12.24
Columbus, OH	10.98	68.77	29.82	58.25	17.11	12.26	14.37
Dallas, TX	10.98	77.10	30.67	62.23	12.81	10.68	14.25
Davenport, IA	10.58	53.76	26.30	48.05	13.57	13.27	14.93
Denver, CO	13.34	85.61	32.53	74.73	20.09	14.62	14.92
Des Moines, IA	11.04	66.80	31.26	53.18	15.31	14.13	13.43
Durham, NC	11.19	79.52	30.27	68.80	15.35	11.60	14.70
Edison, NJ	14.03	103.21	36.45	82.87	18.53	15.37	18.58
El Paso, TX	9.41	51.61	24.23	45.01	11.55	9.04	10.97
Fargo, ND	12.69	70.22	27.09	55.50	16.88	15.07	14.65
Fayetteville, NC	10.16	61.97	24.74	57.51	12.44	10.47	12.75
Fort Collins, CO	13.48	72.34	28.34	58.87	16.06	15.01	15.54
Fort Wayne, IN	10.87	57.58	28.51	55.31	13.03	12.24	11.86
Fort Worth, TX	10.98	77.10	30.67	62.23	12.81	10.68	14.25
Grand Rapids, MI	11.69	58.03	27.84	58.14	16.59	12.98	14.15
Greeley, CO	13.23	81.29	30.36	63.01	16.59	15.20	15.03
Green Bay, WI	10.40	60.24	30.04	66.79	14.46	12.75	14.61
Greensboro, NC	9.88	69.84	27.42	63.64	12.88	11.02	12.65
Honolulu, HI	13.15	60.38	29.59	58.24	18.80	14.07	16.41
Houston, TX	10.42	74.03	29.80	61.00	11.85	10.15	12.52
Huntsville, AL	9.32	65.66	26.99	71.84	11.25	9.93	12.52
Indianapolis, IN	10.96	68.18	30.65	59.89	15.32	12.21	13.87
Jacksonville, FL	10.31	63.49	28.46	52.07	16.47	12.37	12.06
Kansas City, MO	11.82	72.08	30.56	53.57	15.00	12.06	14.78
Lafayette, LA	9.61	49.98	24.38	59.04	11.41	9.98	11.01
Lakeland, FL	10.43	52.81	26.80	46.19	12.89	11.86	12.29
Las Vegas, NV	10.95	57.63	25.95	62.09	10.29	12.47	15.19
Lexington, KY	9.92	57.27	28.00	48.43	11.98	12.60	13.88
Lincoln, NE	11.43	58.67	26.69	50.22	13.35	13.55	13.37
Little Rock, AR	10.81	54.43	25.88	49.18	12.59	11.53	12.24
Los Angeles, CA	14.39	76.00	30.99	67.85	18.20	14.88	17.45
Louisville, KY	10.27	58.62	27.96	50.02	15.10	14.08	13.55

Table continued on following page.

Appendix A: Comparative Statistics A-89

Metro Area	Fast Food and Counter Workers	Financial Managers	First-Line Supervisors/ of Office Workers	General and Operations Managers	Hair-dressers/ Cosme-tologists	Home Health and Personal Care Aides	Janitors/ Cleaners
Madison, WI	11.02	71.61	31.88	65.89	13.94	13.95	15.37
Manchester, NH[2]	11.88	67.78	32.11	65.40	13.19	14.37	14.07
Memphis, TN	9.95	56.29	27.64	55.82	14.51	10.93	12.43
Miami, FL	10.90	72.93	30.04	55.19	13.80	12.10	12.75
Midland, TX	11.26	68.87	32.21	66.38	12.71	11.08	12.72
Milwaukee, WI	10.56	72.24	32.60	73.76	15.73	12.15	14.55
Minneapolis, MN	12.90	71.92	31.32	62.40	16.45	14.26	16.97
Nashville, TN	10.76	59.60	28.46	59.95	15.12	11.82	14.02
New Haven, CT[2]	13.15	67.42	33.60	71.07	15.79	14.00	17.93
New Orleans, LA	10.17	61.27	24.86	60.79	9.97	9.90	11.80
New York, NY	14.03	103.21	36.45	82.87	18.53	15.37	18.58
Oklahoma City, OK	10.46	56.40	26.50	53.95	13.21	11.30	12.31
Omaha, NE	11.57	60.81	27.79	51.20	17.22	12.78	14.62
Orlando, FL	10.44	67.64	27.02	50.37	14.70	12.02	12.97
Peoria, IL	10.98	60.22	28.72	50.68	14.84	12.88	12.80
Philadelphia, PA	11.82	82.22	33.44	74.57	16.17	12.96	15.31
Phoenix, AZ	13.06	64.55	29.32	58.07	16.74	13.34	14.73
Pittsburgh, PA	10.89	70.81	29.25	62.42	13.16	12.79	14.91
Portland, OR	13.97	65.29	30.19	61.17	16.58	15.31	16.47
Providence, RI[2]	13.21	78.87	33.57	71.70	16.31	15.37	15.75
Provo, UT	10.47	59.60	25.62	41.04	16.12	13.22	12.21
Raleigh, NC	10.01	68.49	28.13	70.88	14.20	11.45	12.29
Reno, NV	10.29	63.61	28.05	58.60	14.28	11.98	14.42
Richmond, VA	10.56	75.79	29.92	63.13	17.54	10.69	11.90
Riverside, CA	14.71	62.41	29.71	57.31	15.64	14.69	18.37
Rochester, MN	12.92	53.96	27.84	50.55	14.11	14.58	15.51
Sacramento, CA	14.18	65.80	31.37	59.57	16.75	14.17	17.86
Salt Lake City, UT	10.14	56.64	27.69	44.41	16.35	14.68	12.49
San Antonio, TX	11.01	67.11	26.77	61.53	12.89	10.91	12.76
San Diego, CA	14.44	74.59	31.30	69.74	18.23	14.88	17.57
San Francisco, CA	16.35	92.01	36.43	78.04	18.55	16.57	20.31
San Jose, CA	16.36	92.45	34.48	84.61	18.18	15.80	19.37
Santa Rosa, CA	14.43	69.07	31.18	61.63	17.02	16.21	17.54
Savannah, GA	10.40	49.27	26.00	50.31	11.68	11.70	12.39
Seattle, WA	16.04	76.28	37.04	73.17	22.82	16.24	21.21
Sioux Falls, SD	11.13	74.37	26.26	71.01	14.81	13.74	13.97
Springfield, IL	10.42	56.43	28.36	47.01	22.21	12.19	14.82
Tallahassee, FL	10.45	47.46	29.66	45.46	13.94	12.80	12.76
Tampa, FL	10.81	67.64	29.24	54.46	14.14	11.61	16.79
Tucson, AZ	12.90	53.26	25.41	46.52	16.70	13.18	14.72
Tulsa, OK	9.55	71.06	28.40	51.58	13.46	10.71	12.05
Tuscaloosa, AL	9.61	66.99	25.70	56.16	13.19	9.91	13.78
Virginia Beach, VA	10.94	66.75	28.75	53.58	12.55	10.52	12.31
Washington, DC	13.58	85.16	34.55	74.88	19.24	14.06	16.30
Wichita, KS	9.74	62.41	27.44	50.93	12.99	11.16	13.86
Winston-Salem, NC	10.40	73.56	26.29	59.21	12.93	11.42	11.67

Notes: (1) Figures cover the Metropolitan Statistical Area (MSA) except where noted. See Appendix B for areas included;
(2) New England City and Town Area; n/a not available
Source: Bureau of Labor Statistics, May 2020 Metro Area Occupational Employment and Wage Estimates

A-90   Appendix A: Comparative Statistics

Average Hourly Wages: Occupations L – N

Metro Area	Landscapers	Lawyers	Maids/ House-keepers	Main-tenance/ Repairers	Marketing Managers	Network Admin.	Nurses, Licensed Practical
Albuquerque, NM	14.47	55.30	10.78	19.40	47.06	39.32	24.25
Allentown, PA	16.36	68.66	12.98	22.76	63.74	37.86	24.54
Anchorage, AK	17.23	55.18	15.11	24.45	49.02	39.64	33.65
Ann Arbor, MI	16.81	55.39	13.25	22.11	61.92	39.05	25.79
Athens, GA	16.07	37.80	10.10	17.26	61.63	32.23	21.52
Atlanta, GA	15.33	71.75	10.69	20.23	70.03	43.84	23.16
Austin, TX	15.64	69.36	11.26	18.11	74.00	41.06	23.83
Baton Rouge, LA	15.13	54.49	10.56	21.06	50.44	37.90	20.42
Boise City, ID	15.86	54.48	11.86	19.32	63.98	39.11	23.88
Boston, MA[2]	20.13	84.41	16.40	25.61	74.50	48.82	29.40
Boulder, CO	19.74	n/a	14.29	23.36	85.29	44.95	26.24
Cape Coral, FL	14.77	n/a	11.54	19.02	54.42	35.40	21.43
Cedar Rapids, IA	16.24	55.33	12.33	22.65	68.01	40.48	21.30
Charleston, SC	15.16	52.10	11.57	19.55	60.30	41.69	23.22
Charlotte, NC	15.09	69.55	11.69	21.36	72.17	40.33	22.77
Chicago, IL	16.89	76.45	14.09	23.38	68.69	43.67	28.45
Cincinnati, OH	14.62	67.43	12.24	21.32	66.12	38.88	23.84
Clarksville, TN	14.10	38.91	11.38	21.41	n/a	33.32	20.91
Cleveland, OH	17.07	71.56	12.07	21.06	66.16	42.80	23.78
College Station, TX	14.63	61.53	11.96	17.32	77.65	33.45	23.37
Colorado Springs, CO	15.28	57.73	13.68	20.63	80.71	39.94	27.45
Columbia, MO	14.70	43.61	11.43	15.89	54.36	34.22	21.46
Columbia, SC	13.75	57.84	11.26	19.16	57.61	38.25	21.20
Columbus, OH	15.69	54.42	12.55	21.51	73.13	41.93	22.50
Dallas, TX	16.49	72.23	12.05	21.14	74.99	43.23	25.11
Davenport, IA	16.09	70.60	11.68	20.79	61.19	37.00	21.77
Denver, CO	18.07	73.11	13.60	21.58	83.15	46.05	27.16
Des Moines, IA	17.08	63.08	12.53	21.27	64.28	41.04	23.35
Durham, NC	15.20	59.34	13.46	22.26	74.28	46.08	24.21
Edison, NJ	18.58	86.62	18.17	24.50	93.77	50.99	27.54
El Paso, TX	11.21	60.78	9.75	15.17	54.66	32.96	23.69
Fargo, ND	18.32	54.07	13.61	21.03	61.56	36.75	22.24
Fayetteville, NC	12.88	59.59	10.39	19.76	54.51	41.86	22.65
Fort Collins, CO	16.84	69.74	14.18	21.34	88.50	36.89	25.42
Fort Wayne, IN	14.26	59.12	11.29	21.47	60.08	32.57	22.79
Fort Worth, TX	16.49	72.23	12.05	21.14	74.99	43.23	25.11
Grand Rapids, MI	16.69	57.05	13.11	19.48	60.07	34.56	23.52
Greeley, CO	18.15	51.46	13.31	22.36	72.61	35.49	28.99
Green Bay, WI	16.03	51.55	12.13	22.68	60.63	33.41	20.81
Greensboro, NC	13.66	59.43	10.64	20.20	69.84	41.07	22.20
Honolulu, HI	19.34	56.12	19.89	24.13	52.09	40.41	26.08
Houston, TX	14.69	70.00	11.44	20.96	78.48	46.20	23.54
Huntsville, AL	15.69	56.43	10.54	17.99	72.22	40.01	19.99
Indianapolis, IN	16.30	60.41	12.05	20.39	61.76	40.98	23.39
Jacksonville, FL	14.63	61.24	12.55	19.96	68.66	37.71	22.65
Kansas City, MO	19.56	62.18	12.00	21.06	69.34	41.35	23.04
Lafayette, LA	15.41	45.40	9.86	17.55	43.77	34.54	19.08
Lakeland, FL	14.43	44.81	11.52	20.58	62.00	36.25	20.98
Las Vegas, NV	15.39	63.43	15.89	22.82	65.55	42.05	28.50
Lexington, KY	15.36	51.94	11.20	20.46	50.14	30.83	21.39
Lincoln, NE	14.29	56.03	13.51	21.24	43.46	35.90	22.16
Little Rock, AR	13.87	42.89	11.04	16.67	55.06	35.22	21.72
Los Angeles, CA	19.04	86.64	16.19	22.77	77.25	46.74	29.91
Louisville, KY	15.83	57.01	12.16	22.04	68.47	37.55	21.89
Madison, WI	17.69	57.68	14.08	21.18	64.29	37.64	23.27

Table continued on following page.

Appendix A: Comparative Statistics   A-91

Metro Area	Landscapers	Lawyers	Maids/House-keepers	Main-tenance/Repairers	Marketing Managers	Network Admin.	Nurses, Licensed Practical
Manchester, NH[2]	16.72	66.91	12.82	23.16	75.31	41.64	27.45
Memphis, TN	13.86	51.22	11.39	19.63	47.56	36.25	21.46
Miami, FL	14.82	81.48	11.96	18.62	65.38	41.99	23.34
Midland, TX	16.68	79.48	12.97	19.94	81.11	44.09	25.03
Milwaukee, WI	17.16	67.17	13.05	22.36	65.22	36.67	25.10
Minneapolis, MN	18.17	65.42	15.37	24.86	74.13	42.76	25.10
Nashville, TN	14.16	62.16	12.20	20.31	59.03	37.49	21.95
New Haven, CT[2]	21.07	72.97	14.36	24.76	62.79	46.03	27.76
New Orleans, LA	13.11	59.17	11.03	19.02	48.62	34.09	21.91
New York, NY	18.58	86.62	18.17	24.50	93.77	50.99	27.54
Oklahoma City, OK	14.58	60.36	11.38	18.60	66.70	37.72	21.30
Omaha, NE	16.84	60.84	12.85	21.39	53.21	40.66	22.70
Orlando, FL	14.06	58.70	11.93	18.05	58.36	40.84	22.30
Peoria, IL	14.85	63.40	12.71	20.89	71.93	35.66	22.80
Philadelphia, PA	16.87	73.14	14.54	22.62	75.68	41.45	27.69
Phoenix, AZ	14.91	68.90	13.30	20.64	64.49	42.05	27.24
Pittsburgh, PA	15.16	60.20	12.74	21.02	67.26	38.22	21.99
Portland, OR	18.52	68.32	15.17	22.37	65.90	43.03	27.81
Providence, RI[2]	17.76	61.76	15.61	24.03	78.17	44.50	28.42
Provo, UT	16.13	73.52	12.41	20.26	54.83	39.72	22.86
Raleigh, NC	15.42	66.00	12.05	21.71	71.46	43.77	23.23
Reno, NV	15.83	59.64	13.96	23.28	55.19	41.53	30.36
Richmond, VA	15.83	67.92	12.10	21.90	74.21	43.79	23.80
Riverside, CA	16.79	79.37	15.65	22.90	62.78	43.26	29.90
Rochester, MN	17.47	56.23	13.55	20.95	55.51	38.82	24.74
Sacramento, CA	19.87	73.57	18.56	22.64	73.63	45.57	31.24
Salt Lake City, UT	16.86	72.69	12.37	20.90	62.53	39.60	25.62
San Antonio, TX	14.36	61.79	11.83	18.51	71.37	38.99	22.64
San Diego, CA	16.37	70.82	15.49	22.57	71.15	47.47	31.68
San Francisco, CA	21.71	97.08	21.46	27.95	94.36	51.30	35.83
San Jose, CA	22.59	111.35	19.47	26.36	101.54	64.55	36.51
Santa Rosa, CA	19.15	84.04	16.93	25.05	77.45	43.90	35.97
Savannah, GA	14.12	60.11	10.61	17.68	53.92	36.94	21.45
Seattle, WA	20.08	66.70	16.36	24.21	81.40	48.50	29.46
Sioux Falls, SD	16.01	62.19	11.67	19.64	66.03	32.40	19.44
Springfield, IL	16.70	50.23	12.27	21.57	51.93	37.76	21.99
Tallahassee, FL	13.54	48.96	10.81	17.35	47.03	31.12	20.87
Tampa, FL	14.01	57.69	11.21	18.38	70.07	40.32	22.60
Tucson, AZ	14.30	70.81	14.77	18.16	54.39	37.56	26.53
Tulsa, OK	14.93	68.67	11.08	18.93	66.79	35.66	21.60
Tuscaloosa, AL	14.92	54.99	10.48	16.55	46.18	36.95	19.30
Virginia Beach, VA	14.23	62.89	12.23	19.55	70.12	36.79	21.44
Washington, DC	17.19	89.46	15.44	24.33	84.55	49.25	26.79
Wichita, KS	13.64	47.07	11.59	18.91	59.34	35.01	21.14
Winston-Salem, NC	14.43	60.44	11.31	19.93	64.53	39.48	22.11

Notes: (1) Figures cover the Metropolitan Statistical Area (MSA) except where noted. See Appendix B for areas included; (2) New England City and Town Area; n/a not available
Source: Bureau of Labor Statistics, May 2020 Metro Area Occupational Employment and Wage Estimates

A-92 Appendix A: Comparative Statistics

Average Hourly Wages: Occupations N – P

Metro Area	Nurses, Registered	Nursing Assistants	Office Clerks	Physical Therapists	Physicians	Plumbers	Police Officers
Albuquerque, NM	36.89	14.68	13.26	42.37	93.46	22.34	27.77
Allentown, PA	34.19	16.29	18.15	42.47	n/a	33.01	34.49
Anchorage, AK	45.34	19.45	21.95	50.03	131.18	42.17	46.36
Ann Arbor, MI	39.09	17.55	16.78	42.90	92.84	35.65	33.41
Athens, GA	34.14	13.24	15.96	38.70	95.71	n/a	21.06
Atlanta, GA	36.53	16.57	17.83	42.77	127.01	26.53	24.70
Austin, TX	35.23	14.69	19.62	41.53	107.02	25.23	36.91
Baton Rouge, LA	31.33	12.25	13.85	43.09	104.38	29.38	21.21
Boise City, ID	35.63	14.84	17.45	39.54	115.74	24.22	30.14
Boston, MA[2]	47.79	18.34	21.18	41.62	86.54	40.46	37.76
Boulder, CO	39.80	17.23	22.67	44.97	132.80	25.79	40.27
Cape Coral, FL	34.06	15.25	17.14	41.34	125.98	21.62	26.01
Cedar Rapids, IA	29.59	14.88	18.09	37.39	120.60	29.06	31.16
Charleston, SC	33.46	14.93	15.18	37.56	134.84	26.03	24.33
Charlotte, NC	33.86	14.08	17.52	41.50	100.25	21.86	25.91
Chicago, IL	37.48	15.55	19.15	47.77	108.91	44.20	39.61
Cincinnati, OH	34.60	15.17	18.74	43.02	116.48	26.11	33.14
Clarksville, TN	31.25	13.32	15.39	43.19	113.83	24.00	22.17
Cleveland, OH	35.16	14.82	19.54	42.93	n/a	32.16	31.03
College Station, TX	33.67	12.92	15.42	40.64	n/a	20.44	31.50
Colorado Springs, CO	36.85	15.90	20.41	41.34	106.98	24.78	35.01
Columbia, MO	31.38	14.29	16.36	37.16	123.11	31.70	24.57
Columbia, SC	31.88	13.61	13.78	42.64	92.46	20.01	21.56
Columbus, OH	33.37	13.95	19.08	42.28	108.46	28.16	39.05
Dallas, TX	37.50	14.89	18.25	46.10	98.81	24.37	35.24
Davenport, IA	28.77	14.33	15.96	38.74	125.45	28.20	29.69
Denver, CO	38.12	17.19	22.26	42.29	119.46	29.30	41.15
Des Moines, IA	30.83	15.70	19.88	41.96	118.88	25.94	33.62
Durham, NC	34.04	14.98	18.39	37.70	60.22	23.42	25.52
Edison, NJ	45.63	19.48	19.03	47.81	99.88	35.78	41.48
El Paso, TX	35.14	13.03	15.07	46.19	113.76	18.19	30.62
Fargo, ND	35.67	16.56	20.46	39.52	n/a	26.34	32.53
Fayetteville, NC	36.31	12.73	15.84	41.85	125.79	21.51	22.19
Fort Collins, CO	37.00	16.20	20.49	38.37	114.80	26.03	40.60
Fort Wayne, IN	30.07	14.32	16.90	42.52	122.85	27.79	29.01
Fort Worth, TX	37.50	14.89	18.25	46.10	98.81	24.37	35.24
Grand Rapids, MI	33.54	14.54	18.46	40.21	103.72	25.17	30.97
Greeley, CO	34.49	15.51	21.15	43.71	117.71	25.41	36.09
Green Bay, WI	33.10	15.41	17.63	43.41	134.65	32.94	34.68
Greensboro, NC	33.75	13.32	16.51	43.44	133.51	24.87	24.42
Honolulu, HI	51.33	18.53	18.01	46.01	129.46	32.64	39.30
Houston, TX	40.85	14.11	20.18	40.55	97.14	26.71	32.55
Huntsville, AL	28.17	13.37	12.64	41.60	126.02	26.09	25.95
Indianapolis, IN	33.96	14.71	18.04	42.89	125.04	25.96	31.19
Jacksonville, FL	32.50	13.39	16.95	39.98	120.42	22.43	28.73
Kansas City, MO	33.77	14.40	17.65	42.64	77.69	32.53	27.86
Lafayette, LA	n/a	10.90	13.13	41.06	97.24	26.72	20.08
Lakeland, FL	31.77	13.41	16.98	45.93	111.82	21.29	28.08
Las Vegas, NV	44.58	16.81	18.26	54.41	112.43	29.48	38.04
Lexington, KY	30.92	14.26	16.76	41.60	117.61	30.48	23.72
Lincoln, NE	32.83	14.76	15.31	41.91	114.19	26.77	31.80
Little Rock, AR	33.20	13.43	17.00	37.99	90.23	22.80	24.32
Los Angeles, CA	54.38	18.28	19.87	50.77	111.66	29.04	53.23
Louisville, KY	31.94	14.54	17.26	41.20	119.15	28.33	25.33
Madison, WI	39.58	17.70	19.30	41.01	123.11	32.30	31.59

Table continued on following page.

Appendix A: Comparative Statistics   A-93

Metro Area	Nurses, Registered	Nursing Assistants	Office Clerks	Physical Therapists	Physicians	Plumbers	Police Officers
Manchester, NH[2]	36.90	16.63	19.87	40.56	145.31	27.62	30.42
Memphis, TN	32.84	13.99	16.64	44.13	60.99	25.56	24.96
Miami, FL	34.76	13.66	17.51	39.20	103.07	22.66	35.19
Midland, TX	32.87	15.50	19.18	51.29	n/a	22.43	32.02
Milwaukee, WI	36.90	15.65	18.75	43.06	118.39	34.14	36.14
Minneapolis, MN	41.41	18.64	20.45	41.29	113.38	39.45	38.98
Nashville, TN	32.75	13.98	17.06	37.77	98.61	27.20	25.18
New Haven, CT[2]	41.58	17.50	19.49	48.99	109.62	37.97	36.22
New Orleans, LA	34.10	12.28	13.40	43.01	105.80	27.86	24.02
New York, NY	45.63	19.48	19.03	47.81	99.88	35.78	41.48
Oklahoma City, OK	32.94	13.44	15.49	43.27	98.08	27.58	27.64
Omaha, NE	33.90	15.61	17.67	40.54	113.21	33.69	32.51
Orlando, FL	32.37	13.57	17.28	41.78	87.69	21.20	28.75
Peoria, IL	32.97	14.10	18.03	42.48	108.82	38.03	26.30
Philadelphia, PA	38.45	15.82	19.59	45.60	110.75	33.19	36.66
Phoenix, AZ	39.13	16.56	20.25	44.20	117.44	25.87	34.93
Pittsburgh, PA	33.74	15.25	17.82	41.00	61.88	31.40	32.43
Portland, OR	47.45	18.03	19.73	44.08	84.07	37.75	39.52
Providence, RI[2]	39.75	16.41	19.47	41.73	101.63	29.94	31.88
Provo, UT	32.54	14.31	17.04	43.98	101.67	26.23	26.67
Raleigh, NC	33.71	14.25	17.60	40.47	131.23	21.78	25.39
Reno, NV	38.61	15.69	19.47	43.31	n/a	32.93	n/a
Richmond, VA	38.19	14.34	17.47	48.16	100.13	24.50	28.11
Riverside, CA	52.80	17.66	18.80	49.86	101.93	28.90	50.52
Rochester, MN	34.67	17.06	18.54	41.15	120.62	35.99	33.04
Sacramento, CA	64.59	20.17	19.88	53.64	125.17	30.79	48.23
Salt Lake City, UT	34.93	15.33	17.52	39.40	120.03	26.94	30.14
San Antonio, TX	36.11	13.97	17.09	41.28	104.54	21.49	29.60
San Diego, CA	53.66	19.08	19.89	47.32	115.36	30.73	44.39
San Francisco, CA	71.73	23.28	23.83	49.69	90.09	51.01	58.93
San Jose, CA	70.61	20.18	21.97	51.92	106.37	40.79	63.02
Santa Rosa, CA	60.02	18.91	21.01	52.11	110.94	36.11	55.62
Savannah, GA	31.19	12.86	17.14	42.25	79.65	25.97	22.03
Seattle, WA	45.73	18.20	21.98	44.19	121.55	39.45	41.70
Sioux Falls, SD	29.70	13.76	13.70	35.64	136.24	21.69	30.58
Springfield, IL	34.64	14.66	18.74	44.92	131.59	36.97	33.66
Tallahassee, FL	31.79	12.60	14.97	40.99	100.02	21.64	27.13
Tampa, FL	34.28	14.08	17.66	39.93	104.01	22.02	30.94
Tucson, AZ	36.86	15.70	19.72	42.86	96.12	24.44	31.18
Tulsa, OK	32.44	13.14	16.37	41.95	101.73	26.45	27.25
Tuscaloosa, AL	28.76	12.79	12.79	47.83	104.43	22.88	26.12
Virginia Beach, VA	35.27	14.43	15.93	43.59	103.50	23.91	27.28
Washington, DC	40.14	16.19	20.88	46.02	98.67	27.93	37.03
Wichita, KS	28.59	13.31	14.06	43.59	72.44	23.76	23.57
Winston-Salem, NC	33.96	13.84	16.40	47.63	59.26	21.42	21.49

Notes: (1) Figures cover the Metropolitan Statistical Area (MSA) except where noted. See Appendix B for areas included;
(2) New England City and Town Area; n/a not available
Source: Bureau of Labor Statistics, May 2020 Metro Area Occupational Employment and Wage Estimates

A-94 Appendix A: Comparative Statistics

Average Hourly Wages: Occupations P – S

Metro Area	Postal Mail Carriers	R.E. Sales Agents	Retail Sales-persons	Sales Reps., Technical/ Scientific	Secretaries, Exc. Leg./ Med./Exec.	Security Guards	Surgeons
Albuquerque, NM	25.35	27.94	13.71	53.85	17.98	14.03	117.34
Allentown, PA	25.45	20.93	13.51	35.66	18.99	14.13	n/a
Anchorage, AK	25.19	35.74	16.71	41.68	21.33	21.46	n/a
Ann Arbor, MI	25.59	23.92	15.17	50.25	21.85	18.21	n/a
Athens, GA	24.88	27.22	12.23	22.13	15.66	15.56	121.05
Atlanta, GA	25.44	35.07	13.86	41.84	17.67	13.91	120.75
Austin, TX	25.90	32.45	13.91	51.09	18.80	16.12	123.62
Baton Rouge, LA	25.30	20.08	12.82	38.42	17.00	15.22	140.15
Boise City, ID	25.46	19.41	14.97	29.05	17.35	13.31	97.30
Boston, MA[2]	26.35	43.81	16.09	51.61	23.99	18.44	130.15
Boulder, CO	25.69	29.36	16.67	52.42	20.24	16.82	138.32
Cape Coral, FL	25.50	25.90	13.39	35.11	18.26	13.12	117.59
Cedar Rapids, IA	25.60	20.45	13.27	55.20	19.13	17.64	n/a
Charleston, SC	25.11	24.16	14.34	31.33	17.96	15.38	n/a
Charlotte, NC	25.80	26.82	14.40	45.84	19.39	15.19	n/a
Chicago, IL	25.88	21.35	14.74	43.30	20.83	16.67	126.47
Cincinnati, OH	26.01	22.97	14.27	54.66	18.99	17.36	136.71
Clarksville, TN	25.31	13.84	13.05	28.37	16.54	17.01	n/a
Cleveland, OH	25.57	25.39	13.80	44.45	18.72	15.88	n/a
College Station, TX	25.72	26.12	12.40	38.39	16.65	12.99	n/a
Colorado Springs, CO	25.33	36.06	15.75	51.66	17.72	16.33	138.49
Columbia, MO	24.78	15.74	16.35	37.54	17.90	15.12	n/a
Columbia, SC	25.03	21.37	13.33	35.54	19.69	15.89	n/a
Columbus, OH	25.57	24.24	14.13	43.53	19.06	17.50	130.76
Dallas, TX	25.84	32.44	14.22	42.11	19.17	15.96	96.15
Davenport, IA	25.05	35.10	16.04	41.15	17.40	16.63	n/a
Denver, CO	25.33	43.38	16.33	53.97	20.86	17.65	122.99
Des Moines, IA	25.38	24.89	13.93	48.46	21.68	16.81	n/a
Durham, NC	26.10	23.48	12.83	64.20	20.51	24.93	n/a
Edison, NJ	25.82	47.39	17.06	53.94	21.58	18.33	103.27
El Paso, TX	25.52	28.82	11.77	n/a	15.48	12.85	n/a
Fargo, ND	25.35	30.08	15.57	41.70	19.41	14.99	n/a
Fayetteville, NC	25.38	31.75	12.89	n/a	17.36	19.85	n/a
Fort Collins, CO	25.02	28.43	15.06	44.49	18.64	14.53	n/a
Fort Wayne, IN	25.01	23.92	13.59	39.15	18.02	17.34	102.77
Fort Worth, TX	25.84	32.44	14.22	42.11	19.17	15.96	96.15
Grand Rapids, MI	25.56	26.79	14.74	36.78	18.94	14.23	n/a
Greeley, CO	24.67	n/a	17.48	42.69	18.73	16.81	n/a
Green Bay, WI	25.05	27.21	15.84	45.73	18.17	14.03	n/a
Greensboro, NC	26.02	21.07	13.99	47.50	18.17	14.07	n/a
Honolulu, HI	26.27	34.78	16.86	41.95	22.13	16.81	125.38
Houston, TX	25.54	30.11	13.06	45.56	19.08	14.70	109.57
Huntsville, AL	25.08	n/a	14.19	40.45	17.89	15.08	n/a
Indianapolis, IN	25.51	24.10	15.14	58.59	18.14	15.06	83.72
Jacksonville, FL	26.36	32.81	12.90	55.76	18.29	12.98	n/a
Kansas City, MO	25.56	25.16	14.32	42.28	18.80	19.75	134.82
Lafayette, LA	25.61	20.02	13.19	41.34	15.02	11.63	n/a
Lakeland, FL	25.73	24.66	13.99	50.71	16.80	13.69	125.71
Las Vegas, NV	25.67	33.49	14.32	55.81	19.28	15.70	n/a
Lexington, KY	25.61	21.40	13.53	40.76	18.81	13.31	n/a
Lincoln, NE	25.26	26.16	13.66	39.84	18.52	17.86	142.38
Little Rock, AR	25.59	n/a	13.77	31.84	16.05	14.70	n/a
Los Angeles, CA	26.77	29.45	17.09	49.22	22.28	16.50	89.22
Louisville, KY	25.74	31.08	13.26	42.65	18.47	13.24	134.53
Madison, WI	24.45	22.36	15.01	38.52	20.01	18.11	n/a

Table continued on following page.

Appendix A: Comparative Statistics   A-95

Metro Area	Postal Mail Carriers	R.E. Sales Agents	Retail Sales-persons	Sales Reps., Technical/ Scientific	Secretaries, Exc. Leg./ Med./Exec.	Security Guards	Surgeons
Manchester, NH[2]	25.30	23.78	14.27	48.55	18.80	17.13	n/a
Memphis, TN	25.90	28.54	14.05	42.81	18.28	13.18	n/a
Miami, FL	25.74	33.05	14.10	43.52	17.95	14.33	102.70
Midland, TX	24.14	43.87	15.66	47.47	18.67	17.54	n/a
Milwaukee, WI	25.52	24.22	15.05	42.81	19.69	15.28	n/a
Minneapolis, MN	25.48	22.43	15.67	43.88	21.10	18.83	n/a
Nashville, TN	25.66	22.88	14.62	38.86	20.08	14.59	87.98
New Haven, CT[2]	25.57	n/a	15.78	51.87	23.42	16.82	n/a
New Orleans, LA	25.18	n/a	12.85	32.30	17.67	14.16	n/a
New York, NY	25.82	47.39	17.06	53.94	21.58	18.33	103.27
Oklahoma City, OK	25.83	27.06	14.42	47.84	16.56	17.63	n/a
Omaha, NE	25.62	26.55	14.47	27.54	18.29	18.67	97.62
Orlando, FL	25.63	21.86	13.90	45.86	17.38	13.36	107.64
Peoria, IL	25.20	22.91	13.31	41.09	16.53	18.73	n/a
Philadelphia, PA	25.80	23.80	15.36	39.35	20.84	15.80	127.73
Phoenix, AZ	26.14	25.87	15.31	45.74	18.93	15.32	n/a
Pittsburgh, PA	25.28	35.64	14.07	41.12	18.26	14.45	n/a
Portland, OR	25.16	27.75	16.66	51.50	22.16	16.55	137.03
Providence, RI[2]	25.36	34.42	16.55	43.31	22.02	15.82	135.97
Provo, UT	25.17	19.82	14.08	35.28	17.09	18.95	n/a
Raleigh, NC	25.99	25.85	13.72	53.76	18.82	16.13	n/a
Reno, NV	25.58	18.91	16.30	50.40	20.94	18.12	n/a
Richmond, VA	25.32	31.14	14.11	52.19	19.17	13.71	129.69
Riverside, CA	26.10	n/a	16.16	47.48	21.05	16.42	116.37
Rochester, MN	24.97	25.68	15.36	44.55	18.15	15.79	n/a
Sacramento, CA	26.14	40.54	16.20	49.21	21.10	17.05	n/a
Salt Lake City, UT	25.55	n/a	15.78	45.08	19.50	17.37	120.78
San Antonio, TX	25.93	30.87	13.97	43.36	17.05	16.35	n/a
San Diego, CA	26.30	n/a	16.36	49.07	21.27	16.24	n/a
San Francisco, CA	26.61	35.07	18.15	57.04	25.23	20.24	120.47
San Jose, CA	26.28	48.70	20.75	69.16	24.97	21.24	124.63
Santa Rosa, CA	25.08	n/a	18.83	58.81	22.47	17.86	n/a
Savannah, GA	25.33	26.46	13.07	42.67	16.91	15.61	135.03
Seattle, WA	25.94	34.15	18.51	53.25	23.36	19.56	110.96
Sioux Falls, SD	25.69	n/a	16.24	59.28	14.98	14.66	135.63
Springfield, IL	25.77	19.54	14.55	41.97	17.85	23.01	137.30
Tallahassee, FL	25.24	26.87	14.02	38.03	17.26	13.85	n/a
Tampa, FL	25.84	27.84	14.16	38.88	17.85	16.60	99.80
Tucson, AZ	26.13	28.26	14.92	41.86	17.67	14.50	n/a
Tulsa, OK	25.76	43.74	13.54	39.78	16.99	15.16	n/a
Tuscaloosa, AL	24.94	29.55	14.23	n/a	17.36	13.60	n/a
Virginia Beach, VA	25.12	31.60	12.74	47.42	19.12	16.77	n/a
Washington, DC	25.68	32.62	15.08	60.70	23.83	22.34	128.61
Wichita, KS	25.19	34.94	16.50	48.42	17.11	15.40	n/a
Winston-Salem, NC	26.12	29.77	12.78	46.13	18.63	19.14	n/a

Notes: (1) Figures cover the Metropolitan Statistical Area (MSA) except where noted. See Appendix B for areas included;
(2) New England City and Town Area; n/a not available
Source: Bureau of Labor Statistics, May 2020 Metro Area Occupational Employment and Wage Estimates

A-96   Appendix A: Comparative Statistics

Average Hourly Wages: Occupations T – W

Metro Area	Teacher Assistants[3]	Teachers, Secondary School[3]	Telemarketers	Truck Drivers, Heavy	Truck Drivers, Light	Waiters/ Waitresses
Albuquerque, NM	10.86	25.68	n/a	20.15	18.42	10.00
Allentown, PA	14.41	34.29	13.77	23.61	17.65	13.50
Anchorage, AK	19.53	40.19	n/a	28.67	24.80	12.41
Ann Arbor, MI	14.25	30.94	n/a	23.07	20.97	12.42
Athens, GA	9.86	28.26	n/a	24.12	22.33	11.05
Atlanta, GA	11.99	30.58	13.88	24.03	19.17	11.09
Austin, TX	12.63	28.51	16.75	21.42	23.43	11.41
Baton Rouge, LA	10.61	25.88	13.65	20.24	16.72	9.75
Boise City, ID	13.33	24.81	13.26	22.95	18.28	12.34
Boston, MA[2]	18.17	39.93	18.30	25.04	22.25	16.02
Boulder, CO	16.60	33.44	n/a	21.44	21.14	15.29
Cape Coral, FL	14.99	31.83	13.57	21.06	18.21	12.55
Cedar Rapids, IA	12.78	25.85	12.92	18.16	16.81	10.61
Charleston, SC	12.41	28.34	9.27	20.05	17.41	9.82
Charlotte, NC	12.78	25.96	16.80	23.25	17.99	11.80
Chicago, IL	14.87	39.72	15.22	26.10	23.89	11.30
Cincinnati, OH	14.28	30.87	15.21	24.06	19.05	11.05
Clarksville, TN	13.56	33.45	n/a	19.83	19.57	10.91
Cleveland, OH	14.60	34.51	11.42	23.90	19.82	10.71
College Station, TX	9.90	23.45	n/a	18.16	17.70	9.94
Colorado Springs, CO	14.25	25.06	16.71	23.30	19.39	15.23
Columbia, MO	13.47	25.88	n/a	21.47	19.86	11.41
Columbia, SC	12.27	28.01	16.21	21.90	17.53	9.40
Columbus, OH	14.60	33.80	14.44	22.67	19.28	11.77
Dallas, TX	11.50	28.25	17.10	24.27	20.71	9.50
Davenport, IA	13.57	27.87	14.32	23.94	17.03	11.62
Denver, CO	15.53	29.76	18.67	26.50	20.37	15.26
Des Moines, IA	13.66	29.67	14.89	24.12	16.86	10.63
Durham, NC	12.80	26.34	12.24	19.82	20.75	12.65
Edison, NJ	17.07	43.94	18.00	27.38	21.27	18.12
El Paso, TX	13.05	30.31	10.36	23.37	17.27	9.93
Fargo, ND	16.34	31.20	n/a	24.48	20.00	12.90
Fayetteville, NC	11.91	22.89	n/a	17.95	17.42	9.29
Fort Collins, CO	14.31	n/a	n/a	22.10	18.76	16.23
Fort Wayne, IN	12.40	26.62	n/a	21.76	19.38	13.50
Fort Worth, TX	11.50	28.25	17.10	24.27	20.71	9.50
Grand Rapids, MI	14.25	29.14	12.06	22.41	20.39	14.47
Greeley, CO	14.61	25.80	n/a	25.81	20.06	12.56
Green Bay, WI	16.03	28.94	n/a	22.82	19.81	9.89
Greensboro, NC	12.38	24.19	n/a	24.63	17.87	10.40
Honolulu, HI	15.68	n/a	12.79	25.82	18.43	30.11
Houston, TX	10.92	29.18	14.80	23.21	20.42	11.44
Huntsville, AL	10.13	26.12	n/a	19.59	17.60	9.19
Indianapolis, IN	13.05	27.37	16.60	23.26	20.81	12.55
Jacksonville, FL	12.80	30.73	12.86	21.69	18.78	12.21
Kansas City, MO	13.33	26.10	15.91	24.16	18.51	11.20
Lafayette, LA	11.30	25.17	n/a	20.88	14.72	9.79
Lakeland, FL	11.20	24.22	12.40	22.02	22.47	11.43
Las Vegas, NV	15.75	28.05	12.82	23.35	17.59	13.15
Lexington, KY	15.32	28.71	n/a	25.24	22.54	10.77
Lincoln, NE	14.87	30.70	11.05	26.01	19.74	10.59
Little Rock, AR	11.35	26.77	12.43	24.40	14.91	10.92
Los Angeles, CA	18.25	41.94	15.89	24.13	21.40	16.07
Louisville, KY	15.06	27.29	n/a	25.60	20.42	11.01
Madison, WI	15.69	27.83	12.02	25.51	18.09	12.03

Table continued on following page.

Appendix A: Comparative Statistics   A-97

Metro Area	Teacher Assistants[3]	Teachers, Secondary School[3]	Telemarketers	Truck Drivers, Heavy	Truck Drivers, Light	Waiters/ Waitresses
Manchester, NH[2]	15.12	28.80	n/a	24.56	18.27	13.46
Memphis, TN	12.21	26.97	15.50	22.93	19.09	9.84
Miami, FL	13.47	31.76	14.05	19.63	17.20	12.57
Midland, TX	10.43	28.63	n/a	24.50	21.89	9.28
Milwaukee, WI	16.15	29.89	16.04	24.97	17.36	11.33
Minneapolis, MN	16.69	31.99	18.31	25.51	21.47	15.04
Nashville, TN	13.09	25.02	18.69	25.40	17.83	9.89
New Haven, CT[2]	15.38	37.68	17.96	24.73	19.11	13.86
New Orleans, LA	12.38	26.55	17.07	22.70	18.90	9.90
New York, NY	17.07	43.94	18.00	27.38	21.27	18.12
Oklahoma City, OK	10.86	23.79	14.03	24.44	18.01	11.61
Omaha, NE	14.35	30.82	12.49	21.91	18.84	10.79
Orlando, FL	13.12	27.96	12.95	22.29	19.05	12.53
Peoria, IL	12.78	28.02	16.30	23.04	19.39	10.60
Philadelphia, PA	14.25	34.95	17.40	25.10	20.12	13.00
Phoenix, AZ	13.68	27.18	16.21	23.93	19.25	19.03
Pittsburgh, PA	14.11	34.46	12.75	26.03	17.58	13.55
Portland, OR	17.44	39.42	18.26	25.23	20.13	15.65
Providence, RI[2]	17.30	37.01	16.66	24.14	20.19	14.06
Provo, UT	13.67	38.46	14.13	20.44	18.31	12.13
Raleigh, NC	11.87	27.24	n/a	22.00	16.96	11.79
Reno, NV	10.42	25.59	14.61	25.19	21.37	11.35
Richmond, VA	12.74	n/a	14.96	23.73	21.33	12.03
Riverside, CA	17.96	41.62	15.27	25.57	22.32	14.16
Rochester, MN	15.75	30.87	n/a	23.53	16.41	15.44
Sacramento, CA	17.41	39.16	15.61	25.88	19.96	16.21
Salt Lake City, UT	13.35	29.93	12.47	24.57	20.04	10.55
San Antonio, TX	11.97	28.34	19.63	20.54	21.17	10.02
San Diego, CA	16.96	41.03	15.07	24.67	23.99	15.63
San Francisco, CA	19.29	44.41	n/a	27.78	25.20	19.64
San Jose, CA	19.75	44.47	16.69	27.47	24.95	17.28
Santa Rosa, CA	17.76	42.66	n/a	26.90	23.21	17.56
Savannah, GA	12.45	26.54	n/a	22.16	17.24	9.30
Seattle, WA	19.79	38.01	21.37	26.88	22.88	20.75
Sioux Falls, SD	12.32	23.01	n/a	22.48	18.48	10.59
Springfield, IL	12.03	27.07	n/a	24.22	18.96	10.05
Tallahassee, FL	13.00	24.52	14.79	20.09	17.87	12.10
Tampa, FL	14.49	30.07	13.79	20.31	17.75	14.24
Tucson, AZ	13.63	21.17	14.70	23.53	18.79	17.12
Tulsa, OK	11.41	26.46	12.45	27.46	18.88	9.11
Tuscaloosa, AL	9.49	24.81	n/a	20.28	18.27	9.02
Virginia Beach, VA	13.86	32.96	13.91	19.71	19.40	11.59
Washington, DC	17.52	41.57	14.54	24.43	22.49	15.99
Wichita, KS	13.20	27.00	12.02	22.85	17.72	9.40
Winston-Salem, NC	11.38	24.47	n/a	23.68	17.90	10.37

Notes: (1) Figures cover the Metropolitan Statistical Area (MSA) except where noted. See Appendix B for areas included;
(2) New England City and Town Area; (3) Hourly wages were calculated from annual wage data assuming a 40 hour work week;
n/a not available
Source: Bureau of Labor Statistics, May 2020 Metro Area Occupational Employment and Wage Estimates

A-98   Appendix A: Comparative Statistics

Means of Transportation to Work: City

City	Car/Truck/Van		Public Transportation			Bicycle	Walked	Other Means	Worked at Home
	Drove Alone	Car-pooled	Bus	Subway	Railroad				
Albuquerque, NM	80.6	9.0	1.8	0.0	0.1	1.1	1.9	1.0	4.4
Allentown, PA	67.4	17.2	4.9	0.0	0.0	0.1	5.4	1.2	3.9
Anchorage, AK	76.3	11.8	1.5	0.0	0.0	1.3	2.9	2.3	4.0
Ann Arbor, MI	54.0	6.4	10.3	0.2	0.0	3.9	16.5	0.7	8.0
Athens, GA	72.5	10.0	4.6	0.0	0.0	1.4	4.4	1.5	5.6
Atlanta, GA	67.1	6.3	6.6	3.4	0.2	1.1	5.0	2.2	8.1
Austin, TX	73.7	9.1	3.2	0.1	0.1	1.3	2.4	1.3	8.7
Baton Rouge, LA	80.3	9.8	2.4	0.0	0.0	0.6	3.4	0.6	2.9
Boise City, ID	79.6	7.3	0.6	0.0	0.0	2.8	2.5	1.1	6.0
Boston, MA	38.3	5.9	13.5	17.8	1.1	2.3	15.1	2.6	3.4
Boulder, CO	50.8	5.5	7.3	0.0	0.0	9.9	11.1	1.1	14.5
Cape Coral, FL	81.7	9.0	0.1	0.0	0.0	0.2	0.8	1.2	7.0
Cedar Rapids, IA	84.0	8.2	0.8	0.0	0.0	0.5	1.7	1.1	3.6
Charleston, SC	76.4	7.0	0.8	0.0	0.0	2.4	5.0	1.7	6.8
Charlotte, NC	76.3	9.3	2.4	0.4	0.2	0.1	2.1	1.5	7.7
Chicago, IL	48.8	7.7	13.3	13.0	1.8	1.7	6.5	2.0	5.2
Cincinnati, OH	72.3	8.8	7.0	0.0	0.0	0.4	5.7	1.1	4.7
Clarksville, TN	85.9	7.8	0.9	0.0	0.0	0.0	1.3	1.3	2.7
Cleveland, OH	69.3	10.8	8.9	0.5	0.1	0.6	5.1	1.5	3.2
College Station, TX	78.2	9.3	2.8	0.0	0.0	2.1	2.7	1.0	3.8
Colorado Springs, CO	77.8	10.9	0.9	0.0	0.0	0.6	1.9	0.9	6.9
Columbia, MO	77.1	10.5	1.3	0.0	0.0	1.3	4.8	0.9	4.2
Columbia, SC	64.1	6.1	1.8	0.0	0.0	0.5	21.9	2.2	3.4
Columbus, OH	79.4	8.3	3.1	0.0	0.0	0.6	3.1	1.1	4.4
Dallas, TX	76.7	11.0	2.9	0.4	0.3	0.2	2.1	1.5	4.9
Davenport, IA	85.6	6.6	0.9	0.0	0.0	0.4	2.3	0.5	3.7
Denver, CO	69.1	7.7	4.4	0.9	0.5	2.2	4.7	1.9	8.5
Des Moines, IA	80.1	9.7	2.2	0.1	0.0	0.4	2.9	1.2	3.5
Durham, NC	76.9	9.3	3.6	0.0	0.0	0.6	2.4	1.3	5.8
Edison, NJ	69.4	9.0	0.5	0.5	12.6	0.3	1.7	1.2	4.8
El Paso, TX	81.1	10.6	1.6	0.0	0.0	0.2	1.4	1.9	3.2
Fargo, ND	82.8	8.3	0.9	0.0	0.0	0.6	3.7	0.8	2.9
Fayetteville, NC	77.2	9.4	0.6	0.0	0.0	0.2	7.8	1.7	3.1
Fort Collins, CO	71.9	7.2	2.2	0.0	0.0	5.4	4.2	1.0	8.0
Fort Wayne, IN	83.4	9.6	0.8	0.0	0.0	0.3	1.6	0.7	3.7
Fort Worth, TX	81.5	11.4	0.6	0.0	0.2	0.2	1.2	0.8	4.1
Grand Rapids, MI	75.3	11.1	3.6	0.1	0.0	1.1	4.1	1.0	3.8
Greeley, CO	79.5	11.3	0.6	0.0	0.0	0.7	2.8	1.2	3.9
Green Bay, WI	79.7	10.2	1.4	0.0	0.0	0.5	2.3	1.9	3.9
Greensboro, NC	81.9	7.6	1.9	0.0	0.0	0.2	1.9	0.9	5.6
Honolulu, HI	57.2	13.0	11.6	0.0	0.0	1.6	8.5	4.0	3.9
Houston, TX	77.7	10.4	3.5	0.1	0.0	0.4	2.0	2.0	4.0
Huntsville, AL	86.1	7.0	0.4	0.0	0.0	0.2	1.3	1.1	4.0
Indianapolis, IN	82.0	9.2	1.8	0.0	0.0	0.5	1.9	1.1	3.5
Jacksonville, FL	80.3	9.2	1.8	0.0	0.0	0.5	1.7	1.6	4.8
Kansas City, MO	81.5	7.8	2.5	0.0	0.0	0.2	2.0	1.2	4.9
Lafayette, LA	84.3	6.7	1.2	0.0	0.0	1.2	2.3	0.9	3.5
Lakeland, FL	80.5	10.5	0.8	0.0	0.0	0.3	1.6	1.8	4.6
Las Vegas, NV	78.0	9.8	3.4	0.0	0.0	0.2	1.5	2.8	4.2
Lexington, KY	78.5	9.3	1.9	0.0	0.0	0.6	3.7	1.5	4.4
Lincoln, NE	81.0	9.0	1.3	0.0	0.0	1.2	3.4	0.6	3.4
Little Rock, AR	81.6	9.8	0.9	0.0	0.0	0.1	1.8	1.5	4.2
Los Angeles, CA	69.6	8.8	7.8	0.9	0.2	1.0	3.4	2.0	6.3
Louisville, KY	79.6	8.9	3.1	0.0	0.0	0.4	2.0	1.8	4.3

Table continued on following page.

Appendix A: Comparative Statistics   A-99

City	Car/Truck/Van		Public Transportation			Bicycle	Walked	Other Means	Worked at Home
	Drove Alone	Car-pooled	Bus	Subway	Railroad				
Madison, WI	64.3	7.0	9.1	0.0	0.1	4.5	9.1	1.3	4.7
Manchester, NH	79.1	11.0	0.7	0.0	0.1	0.3	3.2	1.3	4.2
Memphis, TN	82.0	10.5	1.4	0.0	0.0	0.2	1.6	1.3	2.9
Miami, FL	69.4	8.3	7.9	1.0	0.2	0.9	4.0	3.2	5.2
Midland, TX	85.1	10.1	0.2	0.0	0.0	0.1	0.6	1.0	2.8
Milwaukee, WI	72.8	10.2	7.2	0.0	0.1	0.8	4.6	0.8	3.5
Minneapolis, MN	60.5	7.4	11.2	1.1	0.2	4.0	7.4	2.3	5.8
Nashville, TN	77.7	10.0	2.0	0.0	0.1	0.2	2.4	1.2	6.4
New Haven, CT	58.7	9.1	10.5	0.1	1.1	3.1	11.4	1.2	4.7
New Orleans, LA	68.0	9.1	5.9	0.0	0.0	3.1	5.4	2.7	5.7
New York, NY	22.3	4.5	10.1	43.9	1.5	1.3	10.0	2.2	4.3
Oklahoma City, OK	82.6	10.5	0.5	0.0	0.0	0.1	1.5	1.1	3.6
Omaha, NE	81.7	9.1	1.4	0.0	0.0	0.3	2.3	1.3	4.0
Orlando, FL	79.0	8.0	3.4	0.1	0.0	0.6	1.8	1.9	5.3
Peoria, IL	80.1	9.5	2.4	0.0	0.0	0.3	2.7	1.1	3.7
Philadelphia, PA	50.3	8.2	16.0	5.6	2.8	2.1	8.5	2.3	4.2
Phoenix, AZ	74.6	12.6	2.7	0.1	0.1	0.6	1.6	1.9	5.9
Pittsburgh, PA	55.3	8.1	16.9	0.4	0.0	1.8	10.7	1.2	5.6
Portland, OR	57.3	8.3	9.9	0.9	0.3	6.0	5.8	3.0	8.5
Providence, RI	64.5	12.0	5.2	0.1	1.2	0.7	9.5	1.3	5.5
Provo, UT	62.0	11.8	2.6	0.2	1.1	2.4	13.0	1.6	5.3
Raleigh, NC	78.2	8.0	1.9	0.1	0.0	0.4	1.6	1.3	8.5
Reno, NV	75.2	12.6	2.3	0.0	0.0	0.8	3.6	1.1	4.4
Richmond, VA	71.1	9.5	5.5	0.1	0.1	2.1	5.2	1.8	4.6
Riverside, CA	76.4	12.6	1.7	0.0	0.7	0.7	2.6	1.1	4.2
Rochester, MN	70.6	12.5	6.2	0.0	0.0	1.0	4.3	0.9	4.4
Sacramento, CA	74.4	10.4	2.0	0.2	0.4	1.9	2.8	2.2	5.6
Salt Lake City, UT	67.8	10.5	4.8	0.4	0.8	2.5	5.1	2.7	5.5
San Antonio, TX	78.7	11.3	2.9	0.0	0.0	0.2	1.7	1.5	3.8
San Diego, CA	74.7	8.6	3.6	0.0	0.1	0.8	3.1	1.8	7.2
San Francisco, CA	32.1	6.9	22.0	8.8	1.7	4.0	11.8	6.1	6.6
San Jose, CA	75.8	11.7	2.6	0.3	1.2	0.8	1.8	1.6	4.2
Santa Rosa, CA	77.9	11.5	1.6	0.0	0.1	1.2	1.7	1.1	4.8
Savannah, GA	72.0	11.0	4.4	0.1	0.0	1.7	4.7	1.9	4.2
Seattle, WA	46.5	7.2	20.1	1.3	0.1	3.5	11.3	2.5	7.4
Sioux Falls, SD	84.3	8.5	0.8	0.0	0.0	0.5	2.0	0.6	3.4
Springfield, IL	81.8	7.9	2.2	0.1	0.0	0.7	2.1	1.3	3.9
Tallahassee, FL	78.5	8.7	2.4	0.0	0.0	0.8	3.3	1.5	4.8
Tampa, FL	77.1	8.8	2.1	0.0	0.0	1.0	2.4	1.5	6.9
Tucson, AZ	74.5	10.6	3.3	0.0	0.0	2.4	3.1	1.7	4.5
Tulsa, OK	80.2	10.7	0.9	0.0	0.0	0.3	1.8	2.1	4.0
Tuscaloosa, AL	84.2	8.1	0.8	0.1	0.0	0.5	1.8	0.6	3.9
Virginia Beach, VA	82.1	8.6	0.7	0.0	0.0	0.5	2.4	1.6	3.9
Washington, DC	33.5	5.2	13.2	21.1	0.3	4.5	13.4	2.3	6.6
Wichita, KS	83.5	9.5	0.7	0.0	0.0	0.3	1.5	1.3	3.2
Winston-Salem, NC	81.9	8.3	1.7	0.0	0.0	0.2	2.1	1.1	4.7
U.S.	76.3	9.0	2.4	1.9	0.6	0.5	2.7	1.4	5.2

Note: Figures are percentages and cover workers 16 years of age and older
Source: U.S. Census Bureau, 2015-2019 American Community Survey 5-Year Estimates

A-100 Appendix A: Comparative Statistics

Means of Transportation to Work: Metro Area

Metro Area	Car/Truck/Van		Public Transportation			Bicycle	Walked	Other Means	Worked at Home
	Drove Alone	Car-pooled	Bus	Subway	Railroad				
Albuquerque, NM	80.6	9.6	1.3	0.0	0.2	0.8	1.7	1.1	4.8
Allentown, PA	81.7	8.4	1.5	0.1	0.1	0.2	2.4	1.1	4.6
Anchorage, AK	75.7	11.5	1.3	0.0	0.0	1.0	2.7	3.2	4.5
Ann Arbor, MI	71.8	7.9	5.1	0.1	0.0	1.6	7.0	0.6	5.9
Athens, GA	76.3	10.3	2.8	0.0	0.0	0.9	2.9	1.2	5.6
Atlanta, GA	77.3	9.2	2.0	0.8	0.1	0.2	1.3	1.6	7.4
Austin, TX	76.3	9.2	1.8	0.1	0.1	0.8	1.8	1.2	8.8
Baton Rouge, LA	84.8	8.7	0.8	0.0	0.0	0.3	1.5	0.9	3.1
Boise City, ID	79.9	8.9	0.3	0.0	0.0	1.2	1.7	1.1	6.8
Boston, MA	66.4	7.2	4.1	6.7	2.2	1.1	5.4	1.7	5.3
Boulder, CO	65.0	7.2	4.7	0.0	0.0	4.2	5.0	1.0	12.8
Cape Coral, FL	79.0	10.2	0.6	0.0	0.0	0.6	1.2	2.0	6.3
Cedar Rapids, IA	84.7	7.5	0.5	0.0	0.0	0.3	2.0	0.7	4.2
Charleston, SC	81.1	8.2	0.7	0.0	0.0	0.7	2.3	1.2	5.8
Charlotte, NC	80.4	8.9	1.1	0.2	0.1	0.1	1.4	1.2	6.6
Chicago, IL	70.0	7.7	4.4	4.4	3.3	0.7	3.0	1.4	5.2
Cincinnati, OH	82.3	8.0	1.7	0.0	0.0	0.2	2.0	0.8	5.0
Clarksville, TN	84.0	8.1	0.7	0.0	0.0	0.1	3.1	1.3	2.7
Cleveland, OH	81.4	7.7	2.7	0.2	0.1	0.3	2.2	1.1	4.4
College Station, TX	79.8	10.7	1.7	0.0	0.0	1.3	1.9	1.1	3.5
Colorado Springs, CO	77.0	10.4	0.6	0.0	0.0	0.4	3.4	1.0	7.0
Columbia, MO	78.9	10.7	0.8	0.0	0.0	0.8	3.3	0.9	4.5
Columbia, SC	80.7	8.6	0.6	0.0	0.0	0.1	4.4	1.9	3.6
Columbus, OH	82.2	7.6	1.6	0.0	0.0	0.4	2.2	1.0	5.0
Dallas, TX	80.6	9.7	0.9	0.2	0.2	0.1	1.2	1.2	5.8
Davenport, IA	85.6	6.8	0.9	0.0	0.0	0.2	2.0	0.9	3.6
Denver, CO	75.3	8.1	2.8	0.6	0.3	0.8	2.2	1.5	8.4
Des Moines, IA	83.6	7.8	1.1	0.0	0.0	0.2	1.8	0.8	4.6
Durham, NC	76.5	8.7	3.4	0.0	0.0	0.7	2.8	1.3	6.7
Edison, NJ	49.2	6.3	7.5	20.0	3.9	0.7	5.9	2.0	4.5
El Paso, TX	80.7	10.6	1.3	0.0	0.0	0.1	1.6	2.1	3.5
Fargo, ND	82.2	8.6	0.7	0.0	0.0	0.5	2.8	0.8	4.4
Fayetteville, NC	81.3	9.2	0.3	0.0	0.0	0.1	4.2	1.4	3.4
Fort Collins, CO	74.9	8.0	1.5	0.0	0.0	3.1	2.7	1.2	8.6
Fort Wayne, IN	83.9	9.0	0.6	0.0	0.0	0.3	1.4	0.7	4.2
Fort Worth, TX	80.6	9.7	0.9	0.2	0.2	0.1	1.2	1.2	5.8
Grand Rapids, MI	81.9	9.1	1.4	0.0	0.0	0.5	2.2	0.8	4.2
Greeley, CO	80.4	9.6	0.5	0.0	0.0	0.3	1.9	1.0	6.2
Green Bay, WI	83.8	7.9	0.7	0.0	0.0	0.2	1.8	0.9	4.7
Greensboro, NC	82.7	9.0	0.9	0.0	0.0	0.1	1.4	0.9	4.9
Honolulu, HI	64.7	14.2	8.0	0.0	0.0	0.9	5.5	2.7	4.0
Houston, TX	80.8	9.8	1.9	0.0	0.0	0.2	1.3	1.4	4.5
Huntsville, AL	88.0	6.2	0.2	0.0	0.0	0.1	0.8	1.0	3.7
Indianapolis, IN	83.2	8.3	0.8	0.0	0.0	0.3	1.5	0.9	4.9
Jacksonville, FL	80.9	8.2	1.2	0.0	0.0	0.5	1.5	1.7	6.0
Kansas City, MO	83.7	7.8	0.8	0.0	0.0	0.1	1.2	0.9	5.4
Lafayette, LA	84.8	8.2	0.5	0.0	0.0	0.4	1.9	1.1	3.0
Lakeland, FL	83.4	9.4	0.5	0.0	0.0	0.4	1.0	1.4	4.0
Las Vegas, NV	78.8	9.8	3.3	0.0	0.0	0.3	1.5	2.2	4.2
Lexington, KY	79.9	9.3	1.3	0.0	0.0	0.4	3.1	1.3	4.6
Lincoln, NE	81.3	8.9	1.1	0.0	0.0	1.1	3.3	0.6	3.7
Little Rock, AR	83.9	9.5	0.5	0.0	0.0	0.2	1.3	1.1	3.5
Los Angeles, CA	75.1	9.5	4.1	0.4	0.3	0.7	2.5	1.6	5.8
Louisville, KY	82.0	8.5	1.8	0.0	0.0	0.2	1.6	1.3	4.6

Table continued on following page.

Appendix A: Comparative Statistics   A-101

Metro Area	Car/Truck/Van		Public Transportation			Bicycle	Walked	Other Means	Worked at Home
	Drove Alone	Car-pooled	Bus	Subway	Railroad				
Madison, WI	75.0	7.5	4.2	0.0	0.0	2.2	5.0	0.9	5.1
Manchester, NH	81.4	8.1	0.8	0.0	0.1	0.1	2.1	0.9	6.4
Memphis, TN	84.6	9.2	0.7	0.0	0.0	0.1	1.0	1.1	3.3
Miami, FL	77.9	9.1	2.8	0.3	0.2	0.6	1.6	1.8	5.7
Midland, TX	84.8	9.7	0.2	0.0	0.0	0.1	1.1	0.8	3.3
Milwaukee, WI	80.9	7.8	3.1	0.0	0.1	0.5	2.6	0.7	4.3
Minneapolis, MN	77.5	8.1	4.1	0.2	0.2	0.8	2.3	1.1	5.8
Nashville, TN	80.8	9.4	0.9	0.0	0.1	0.1	1.3	1.1	6.3
New Haven, CT	78.3	8.4	2.8	0.1	0.9	0.5	3.3	1.0	4.7
New Orleans, LA	78.1	9.8	2.3	0.0	0.0	1.1	2.5	1.7	4.5
New York, NY	49.2	6.3	7.5	20.0	3.9	0.7	5.9	2.0	4.5
Oklahoma City, OK	83.2	9.4	0.4	0.0	0.0	0.3	1.6	1.0	4.1
Omaha, NE	83.8	8.2	0.8	0.0	0.0	0.2	1.7	1.0	4.2
Orlando, FL	79.7	9.8	1.5	0.0	0.1	0.4	1.1	1.6	5.9
Peoria, IL	84.9	7.3	1.1	0.0	0.0	0.3	2.1	0.9	3.6
Philadelphia, PA	72.5	7.6	5.0	1.9	2.3	0.6	3.6	1.3	5.2
Phoenix, AZ	76.1	11.1	1.7	0.1	0.0	0.8	1.5	1.8	7.0
Pittsburgh, PA	76.6	8.3	5.1	0.2	0.0	0.3	3.4	1.1	5.0
Portland, OR	70.3	9.1	4.8	0.7	0.2	2.2	3.4	2.0	7.4
Providence, RI	80.7	8.6	1.5	0.2	1.0	0.2	3.1	0.8	3.9
Provo, UT	73.1	11.4	1.1	0.2	0.9	0.9	4.1	1.2	7.2
Raleigh, NC	79.7	8.3	0.8	0.0	0.0	0.2	1.1	0.9	8.9
Reno, NV	77.2	12.0	1.8	0.0	0.0	0.6	2.6	1.1	4.7
Richmond, VA	81.1	8.6	1.4	0.0	0.1	0.5	1.7	1.3	5.3
Riverside, CA	78.9	11.5	0.9	0.1	0.4	0.3	1.5	1.3	5.3
Rochester, MN	74.1	11.5	4.0	0.0	0.0	0.6	3.6	0.8	5.3
Sacramento, CA	76.8	9.4	1.6	0.2	0.2	1.4	1.8	1.5	7.1
Salt Lake City, UT	75.4	11.1	2.1	0.3	0.5	0.8	2.1	1.5	6.2
San Antonio, TX	79.5	10.7	1.9	0.0	0.0	0.2	1.7	1.3	4.7
San Diego, CA	76.2	8.6	2.5	0.0	0.2	0.6	2.9	1.9	7.0
San Francisco, CA	57.6	9.5	7.6	7.6	1.5	1.9	4.7	3.0	6.6
San Jose, CA	74.9	10.6	2.4	0.3	1.5	1.7	2.1	1.6	5.0
Santa Rosa, CA	74.6	11.3	1.6	0.0	0.2	1.0	2.7	1.3	7.4
Savannah, GA	79.5	9.7	1.8	0.1	0.0	0.8	2.4	1.6	4.2
Seattle, WA	67.5	10.0	8.7	0.4	0.5	1.1	4.0	1.5	6.2
Sioux Falls, SD	84.3	8.1	0.5	0.0	0.0	0.4	2.1	0.6	4.1
Springfield, IL	83.3	8.0	1.3	0.1	0.0	0.5	1.7	1.0	4.3
Tallahassee, FL	81.1	9.2	1.4	0.0	0.0	0.6	2.0	1.3	4.3
Tampa, FL	78.9	8.8	1.3	0.0	0.0	0.6	1.4	1.6	7.4
Tucson, AZ	76.8	10.0	2.2	0.0	0.0	1.5	2.3	1.8	5.4
Tulsa, OK	82.8	9.6	0.4	0.0	0.0	0.2	1.2	1.5	4.2
Tuscaloosa, AL	85.3	9.0	0.5	0.0	0.0	0.2	1.1	0.5	3.4
Virginia Beach, VA	81.3	8.3	1.4	0.0	0.0	0.4	3.3	1.4	3.8
Washington, DC	65.8	9.3	4.8	7.8	0.8	0.9	3.3	1.5	5.9
Wichita, KS	84.0	8.7	0.4	0.0	0.0	0.4	1.7	1.2	3.5
Winston-Salem, NC	83.6	8.9	0.7	0.0	0.0	0.1	1.3	0.9	4.5
U.S.	76.3	9.0	2.4	1.9	0.6	0.5	2.7	1.4	5.2

Note: Figures are percentages and cover workers 16 years of age and older; (1) Figures cover the Metropolitan Statistical Area—see Appendix B for areas included
Source: U.S. Census Bureau, 2015-2019 American Community Survey 5-Year Estimates

A-102 Appendix A: Comparative Statistics

Travel Time to Work: City

City	Less Than 10 Minutes	10 to 19 Minutes	20 to 29 Minutes	30 to 44 Minutes	45 to 59 Minutes	60 to 89 Minutes	90 Minutes or More
Albuquerque, NM	11.1	35.8	28.1	17.7	3.1	2.8	1.4
Allentown, PA	11.5	34.8	28.6	14.6	4.2	4.1	2.2
Anchorage, AK	16.3	44.7	23.7	10.4	2.3	1.1	1.5
Ann Arbor, MI	12.9	45.5	19.9	13.3	5.3	2.4	0.7
Athens, GA	17.4	48.3	16.9	8.8	3.6	3.0	2.0
Atlanta, GA	6.8	28.7	26.4	22.2	7.6	5.2	3.1
Austin, TX	9.5	31.8	24.3	22.1	7.1	3.8	1.4
Baton Rouge, LA	11.9	39.3	25.5	15.1	3.6	2.8	1.9
Boise City, ID	13.7	46.2	25.8	10.4	1.5	1.3	1.1
Boston, MA	7.1	19.1	19.6	30.3	12.1	9.6	2.2
Boulder, CO	17.6	45.9	16.3	10.3	5.6	3.3	1.0
Cape Coral, FL	7.9	23.9	23.5	26.5	10.4	5.8	2.0
Cedar Rapids, IA	18.0	49.5	18.0	9.7	2.2	1.5	1.1
Charleston, SC	11.4	31.9	26.3	21.1	6.5	1.5	1.3
Charlotte, NC	8.2	28.3	26.6	24.4	7.1	3.5	2.0
Chicago, IL	4.5	16.0	17.4	30.6	15.3	12.8	3.5
Cincinnati, OH	11.0	33.2	27.0	19.2	4.5	3.2	1.9
Clarksville, TN	10.8	34.3	24.5	15.6	5.7	7.4	1.7
Cleveland, OH	9.4	33.3	27.0	19.5	5.0	3.7	2.0
College Station, TX	16.5	56.7	17.6	5.9	0.5	1.8	1.2
Colorado Springs, CO	11.6	35.9	28.5	15.2	3.5	3.0	2.3
Columbia, MO	20.2	55.0	11.8	8.2	2.8	0.8	1.2
Columbia, SC	31.3	36.6	17.6	9.7	1.8	1.8	1.2
Columbus, OH	10.0	34.5	29.8	18.8	3.7	2.1	1.1
Dallas, TX	7.9	26.6	23.0	26.5	8.0	5.9	2.0
Davenport, IA	17.0	47.8	20.8	9.0	3.1	1.2	1.0
Denver, CO	7.5	28.5	24.6	26.0	8.0	3.9	1.5
Des Moines, IA	13.0	43.8	27.2	11.9	1.9	1.1	1.0
Durham, NC	9.4	37.4	26.3	18.0	4.5	3.0	1.6
Edison, NJ	6.4	23.1	17.4	18.1	11.2	14.0	9.7
El Paso, TX	9.8	34.4	27.7	19.6	4.4	2.2	1.9
Fargo, ND	20.9	54.9	17.6	3.3	1.0	1.4	0.8
Fayetteville, NC	20.6	37.5	22.3	12.5	3.3	2.1	1.6
Fort Collins, CO	16.5	42.6	19.9	11.0	5.1	3.5	1.4
Fort Wayne, IN	12.2	40.5	27.4	12.5	3.1	2.4	1.9
Fort Worth, TX	8.4	28.3	22.5	23.9	8.7	6.2	2.0
Grand Rapids, MI	15.0	42.9	24.4	11.6	3.3	2.0	0.9
Greeley, CO	16.1	37.4	16.2	14.7	5.9	7.4	2.3
Green Bay, WI	18.1	48.8	19.4	7.7	3.1	1.8	1.1
Greensboro, NC	12.1	41.4	24.1	14.7	3.5	2.6	1.6
Honolulu, HI	7.9	35.3	23.7	22.0	5.5	4.3	1.4
Houston, TX	7.3	25.5	22.2	27.8	8.9	6.4	1.9
Huntsville, AL	12.8	41.7	26.3	15.2	2.3	0.7	0.9
Indianapolis, IN	9.7	30.0	29.9	22.1	4.3	2.5	1.5
Jacksonville, FL	8.3	27.7	27.5	25.6	6.5	2.9	1.6
Kansas City, MO	11.4	33.4	28.1	20.0	4.5	1.6	1.1
Lafayette, LA	16.4	42.1	20.4	12.5	2.5	2.8	3.3
Lakeland, FL	10.8	43.4	20.1	14.4	5.8	3.5	2.0
Las Vegas, NV	6.9	23.9	29.3	28.7	6.4	2.7	2.0
Lexington, KY	12.4	38.0	27.6	14.9	3.2	2.5	1.4
Lincoln, NE	17.2	44.8	23.1	9.3	2.5	2.1	1.1
Little Rock, AR	14.0	44.4	26.5	10.8	2.0	1.3	1.1
Los Angeles, CA	5.9	21.8	19.0	28.3	10.8	10.5	3.8
Louisville, KY	9.3	32.4	30.1	20.3	4.4	2.2	1.4
Madison, WI	14.4	40.7	24.1	15.3	2.9	1.9	0.8

Table continued on following page.

Appendix A: Comparative Statistics   A-103

City	Less Than 10 Minutes	10 to 19 Minutes	20 to 29 Minutes	30 to 44 Minutes	45 to 59 Minutes	60 to 89 Minutes	90 Minutes or More
Manchester, NH	14.1	38.3	19.2	14.5	5.9	4.8	3.2
Memphis, TN	10.2	32.9	30.2	20.5	3.6	1.6	1.0
Miami, FL	4.9	21.3	22.7	31.7	10.2	7.4	1.8
Midland, TX	16.1	49.1	17.2	11.1	2.6	2.0	1.9
Milwaukee, WI	10.1	36.6	25.8	19.3	4.0	2.7	1.5
Minneapolis, MN	8.1	32.0	30.9	20.9	4.2	2.8	1.2
Nashville, TN	8.7	29.1	26.2	23.8	7.2	3.5	1.5
New Haven, CT	13.6	40.4	20.1	13.1	4.7	4.7	3.4
New Orleans, LA	9.9	33.9	25.4	19.7	4.5	4.2	2.3
New York, NY	3.8	12.1	13.4	27.1	16.4	19.5	7.7
Oklahoma City, OK	11.2	35.5	29.5	17.7	3.3	1.5	1.3
Omaha, NE	14.0	41.0	27.8	12.4	2.3	1.5	0.9
Orlando, FL	7.8	27.2	25.9	26.7	6.8	3.4	2.2
Peoria, IL	18.6	49.5	19.8	7.6	1.9	1.8	0.8
Philadelphia, PA	6.1	18.7	19.7	28.0	12.6	10.6	4.4
Phoenix, AZ	8.8	26.7	25.5	24.9	7.5	4.7	1.9
Pittsburgh, PA	9.4	31.5	25.8	22.9	5.1	3.7	1.6
Portland, OR	7.8	26.3	27.0	24.5	7.7	4.9	1.8
Providence, RI	12.2	39.9	20.8	14.3	5.6	4.1	3.1
Provo, UT	21.3	45.3	17.3	9.0	2.7	2.9	1.4
Raleigh, NC	9.8	33.0	25.8	21.0	5.7	3.1	1.7
Reno, NV	14.4	43.5	22.1	12.1	3.7	2.7	1.5
Richmond, VA	9.8	37.9	28.5	16.4	3.2	2.6	1.5
Riverside, CA	8.9	26.2	19.9	21.7	7.6	9.4	6.4
Rochester, MN	19.3	55.7	13.6	6.3	2.2	1.7	1.2
Sacramento, CA	8.0	31.2	25.1	22.5	5.9	4.0	3.3
Salt Lake City, UT	12.3	45.3	22.8	13.0	3.6	1.9	1.0
San Antonio, TX	8.5	30.8	27.2	22.1	6.1	3.3	2.0
San Diego, CA	7.6	32.1	27.6	21.7	5.7	3.4	1.8
San Francisco, CA	3.8	18.0	20.5	30.3	12.3	11.2	3.9
San Jose, CA	5.1	22.4	22.1	27.7	10.8	8.7	3.1
Santa Rosa, CA	13.8	39.2	21.7	13.6	3.9	4.6	3.2
Savannah, GA	16.0	40.0	22.3	12.8	4.4	3.2	1.4
Seattle, WA	6.7	23.4	24.4	28.6	10.5	5.0	1.5
Sioux Falls, SD	16.1	52.3	22.4	5.4	1.4	1.3	1.1
Springfield, IL	18.2	51.5	18.5	6.1	1.8	2.3	1.6
Tallahassee, FL	14.6	44.7	23.9	12.3	2.1	1.3	1.0
Tampa, FL	11.1	30.5	23.6	21.8	6.7	4.3	1.9
Tucson, AZ	11.9	34.4	25.0	19.7	4.8	2.5	1.6
Tulsa, OK	14.6	44.5	25.7	10.5	2.0	1.5	1.2
Tuscaloosa, AL	14.6	44.8	25.9	7.4	3.5	2.8	1.0
Virginia Beach, VA	10.7	29.8	28.1	22.3	5.1	2.7	1.4
Washington, DC	4.9	18.5	22.5	32.4	12.6	7.1	2.0
Wichita, KS	14.2	44.9	27.2	9.7	1.7	1.2	1.2
Winston-Salem, NC	13.6	40.8	23.8	13.7	4.2	2.1	1.8
U.S.	12.2	28.4	20.8	20.8	8.3	6.4	2.9

Note: Figures are percentages and include workers 16 years old and over
Source: U.S. Census Bureau, 2015-2019 American Community Survey 5-Year Estimates

A-104   Appendix A: Comparative Statistics

Travel Time to Work: Metro Area

Metro Area	Less Than 10 Minutes	10 to 19 Minutes	20 to 29 Minutes	30 to 44 Minutes	45 to 59 Minutes	60 to 89 Minutes	90 Minutes or More
Albuquerque, NM	10.8	31.6	26.2	20.5	5.7	3.6	1.6
Allentown, PA	12.4	27.6	23.1	18.1	7.4	7.3	4.1
Anchorage, AK	15.7	41.0	21.8	10.8	4.3	4.0	2.5
Ann Arbor, MI	10.6	32.7	24.5	19.3	7.6	4.1	1.3
Athens, GA	14.1	41.1	21.4	12.9	4.7	3.5	2.2
Atlanta, GA	7.0	22.1	19.6	24.9	12.3	10.4	3.8
Austin, TX	9.6	27.1	22.3	23.1	10.0	6.1	1.8
Baton Rouge, LA	9.8	27.7	22.0	22.5	9.2	6.5	2.3
Boise City, ID	12.7	34.6	25.6	18.4	5.1	2.2	1.3
Boston, MA	9.0	22.0	17.9	24.4	12.1	11.0	3.7
Boulder, CO	13.7	34.4	21.4	17.6	7.0	4.6	1.3
Cape Coral, FL	8.7	25.3	23.1	25.6	10.2	5.1	2.0
Cedar Rapids, IA	17.4	40.6	21.6	13.1	3.9	2.0	1.3
Charleston, SC	8.7	25.6	24.3	26.0	9.3	4.4	1.7
Charlotte, NC	9.3	27.1	22.7	24.0	9.6	5.2	2.1
Chicago, IL	8.2	21.5	18.4	25.2	12.4	10.8	3.5
Cincinnati, OH	10.9	27.5	25.3	23.4	7.8	3.6	1.5
Clarksville, TN	15.2	32.1	21.1	17.4	6.1	6.0	2.1
Cleveland, OH	11.2	28.3	25.5	23.1	7.3	3.3	1.4
College Station, TX	15.6	49.4	19.1	10.1	2.3	2.1	1.5
Colorado Springs, CO	11.6	32.8	27.2	17.4	5.0	3.7	2.3
Columbia, MO	17.5	45.5	17.3	12.4	4.3	1.5	1.4
Columbia, SC	12.5	29.6	23.5	22.3	6.8	3.4	1.9
Columbus, OH	11.0	29.7	26.3	21.8	6.6	3.2	1.4
Dallas, TX	8.6	25.0	21.3	25.6	10.5	7.0	2.1
Davenport, IA	17.9	37.4	24.3	13.6	3.7	1.9	1.3
Denver, CO	8.0	24.9	23.0	26.3	10.2	5.8	1.8
Des Moines, IA	15.2	35.2	27.3	16.3	3.4	1.5	1.1
Durham, NC	9.8	31.6	24.8	21.2	6.8	4.2	1.5
Edison, NJ	6.7	18.2	16.1	23.9	12.7	15.3	7.1
El Paso, TX	10.7	32.6	26.8	20.6	4.9	2.4	2.0
Fargo, ND	18.5	50.6	19.3	7.0	2.0	1.6	1.1
Fayetteville, NC	14.4	29.4	23.3	20.1	6.6	4.1	2.1
Fort Collins, CO	14.5	34.6	22.0	15.6	6.4	5.1	1.9
Fort Wayne, IN	12.7	36.5	28.2	15.0	3.5	2.3	1.8
Fort Worth, TX	8.6	25.0	21.3	25.6	10.5	7.0	2.1
Grand Rapids, MI	14.8	35.3	24.9	16.1	5.0	2.5	1.5
Greeley, CO	11.9	27.1	19.2	22.3	9.5	7.5	2.5
Green Bay, WI	18.1	40.0	21.7	12.9	3.8	2.0	1.5
Greensboro, NC	12.2	34.8	25.3	18.4	5.0	2.6	1.7
Honolulu, HI	9.0	24.9	19.6	25.3	9.8	8.5	3.0
Houston, TX	7.7	23.3	19.4	26.5	11.8	8.9	2.5
Huntsville, AL	10.3	32.1	27.8	21.7	5.6	1.6	1.0
Indianapolis, IN	11.4	27.5	24.4	24.1	7.6	3.5	1.5
Jacksonville, FL	8.8	25.4	24.4	26.0	9.0	4.5	1.8
Kansas City, MO	12.2	30.7	25.2	21.7	6.6	2.6	1.1
Lafayette, LA	15.1	32.4	21.0	18.4	5.2	3.7	4.3
Lakeland, FL	8.4	30.0	21.7	21.0	9.9	6.3	2.7
Las Vegas, NV	7.4	27.5	29.0	26.1	5.4	2.7	1.9
Lexington, KY	14.3	34.6	25.1	17.7	4.5	2.5	1.3
Lincoln, NE	17.1	41.8	23.8	11.2	2.9	2.0	1.2
Little Rock, AR	12.6	33.0	23.4	19.9	7.0	2.8	1.3
Los Angeles, CA	6.9	24.4	19.5	25.4	10.2	9.8	3.7
Louisville, KY	9.7	29.9	27.3	22.6	6.4	2.6	1.5
Madison, WI	15.6	32.6	24.3	18.6	5.2	2.5	1.1

Table continued on following page.

Appendix A: Comparative Statistics   A-105

Metro Area	Less Than 10 Minutes	10 to 19 Minutes	20 to 29 Minutes	30 to 44 Minutes	45 to 59 Minutes	60 to 89 Minutes	90 Minutes or More
Manchester, NH	11.1	29.7	19.7	19.8	8.6	7.2	3.9
Memphis, TN	10.2	28.3	26.7	24.1	6.8	2.7	1.2
Miami, FL	6.4	22.6	22.0	27.9	10.3	8.1	2.7
Midland, TX	15.8	46.2	17.9	12.5	3.1	2.6	1.8
Milwaukee, WI	11.9	31.6	25.8	21.3	5.5	2.5	1.4
Minneapolis, MN	10.2	27.3	25.1	23.7	8.1	4.3	1.4
Nashville, TN	9.2	26.5	21.7	23.4	10.6	6.6	2.0
New Haven, CT	11.5	31.8	22.9	19.5	6.6	4.8	2.9
New Orleans, LA	10.5	30.6	22.2	20.9	7.6	5.6	2.5
New York, NY	6.7	18.2	16.1	23.9	12.7	15.3	7.1
Oklahoma City, OK	12.3	32.0	25.7	20.3	5.7	2.4	1.5
Omaha, NE	13.9	36.4	27.5	15.8	3.7	1.7	1.0
Orlando, FL	7.1	22.9	22.9	28.1	11.1	5.6	2.3
Peoria, IL	18.6	34.8	23.6	15.1	4.4	2.1	1.4
Philadelphia, PA	9.2	23.6	20.3	24.0	11.1	8.5	3.3
Phoenix, AZ	9.9	26.2	23.7	23.7	9.0	5.7	1.9
Pittsburgh, PA	11.8	26.6	21.0	22.8	9.5	6.2	2.1
Portland, OR	10.2	26.9	22.6	23.1	9.3	5.8	2.1
Providence, RI	11.9	29.9	21.9	19.6	7.6	5.9	3.2
Provo, UT	18.0	35.3	20.1	15.5	5.6	3.9	1.6
Raleigh, NC	8.9	27.5	24.4	23.9	8.7	4.8	1.9
Reno, NV	12.1	37.7	25.0	16.6	4.2	2.7	1.7
Richmond, VA	8.7	29.1	27.4	23.2	6.3	3.1	2.0
Riverside, CA	9.4	26.2	18.6	19.7	8.5	10.4	7.2
Rochester, MN	18.9	41.6	18.4	12.8	3.9	2.7	1.7
Sacramento, CA	9.9	28.2	22.3	23.0	8.1	4.9	3.5
Salt Lake City, UT	10.5	33.4	27.0	19.6	5.6	2.8	1.1
San Antonio, TX	9.0	28.1	24.3	23.2	8.5	4.7	2.2
San Diego, CA	8.2	28.9	24.3	23.5	7.7	5.1	2.2
San Francisco, CA	6.4	22.0	17.4	23.7	12.5	12.9	5.1
San Jose, CA	6.6	25.0	22.6	25.1	9.6	7.8	3.2
Santa Rosa, CA	15.1	32.2	20.4	16.8	5.8	5.9	3.9
Savannah, GA	11.0	30.6	24.1	21.2	7.7	4.1	1.3
Seattle, WA	7.7	22.2	20.8	25.5	11.4	9.0	3.4
Sioux Falls, SD	16.5	44.0	24.6	10.0	2.4	1.4	1.2
Springfield, IL	15.6	42.6	23.6	11.5	2.7	2.3	1.7
Tallahassee, FL	11.0	34.3	24.8	20.4	5.6	2.4	1.5
Tampa, FL	9.6	26.9	21.6	23.0	10.1	6.5	2.3
Tucson, AZ	10.7	28.9	24.6	23.6	7.4	3.0	1.9
Tulsa, OK	13.3	33.9	26.5	18.1	4.5	2.2	1.4
Tuscaloosa, AL	11.3	32.4	26.5	16.5	6.6	5.0	1.7
Virginia Beach, VA	11.3	30.6	23.9	21.4	7.1	4.0	1.7
Washington, DC	5.9	18.9	17.7	25.7	14.2	13.1	4.6
Wichita, KS	16.3	37.5	26.5	14.3	2.8	1.4	1.3
Winston-Salem, NC	12.0	33.3	24.5	19.1	6.1	2.8	2.1
U.S.	12.2	28.4	20.8	20.8	8.3	6.4	2.9

Note: Figures are percentages and include workers 16 years old and over; Figures cover the Metropolitan Statistical Area—see Appendix B for areas included
Source: U.S. Census Bureau, 2015-2019 American Community Survey 5-Year Estimates

A-106 Appendix A: Comparative Statistics

2020 Presidential Election Results

City	Area Covered	Biden	Trump	Jorgensen	Hawkins	Other
Albuquerque, NM	Bernalillo County	61.0	36.6	1.5	0.5	0.4
Allentown, PA	Lehigh County	53.1	45.5	1.2	0.1	0.2
Anchorage, AK	State of Alaska	42.8	52.8	2.5	0.0	1.9
Ann Arbor, MI	Washtenaw County	72.4	25.9	0.9	0.3	0.4
Athens, GA	Clarke County	70.1	28.1	1.6	0.1	0.1
Atlanta, GA	Fulton County	72.6	26.2	1.2	0.0	0.0
Austin, TX	Travis County	71.4	26.4	1.5	0.3	0.4
Baton Rouge, LA	East Baton Rouge Parish	55.5	42.5	1.2	0.0	0.8
Boise City, ID	Ada County	46.1	50.0	2.0	0.1	1.8
Boston, MA	Suffolk County	80.6	17.5	0.9	0.5	0.5
Boulder, CO	Boulder County	77.2	20.6	1.2	0.3	0.6
Cape Coral, FL	Lee County	39.9	59.1	0.5	0.1	0.3
Cedar Rapids, IA	Linn County	55.6	41.9	1.6	0.3	0.7
Charleston, SC	Charleston County	55.5	42.6	1.5	0.3	0.1
Charlotte, NC	Mecklenburg County	66.7	31.6	1.0	0.3	0.5
Chicago, IL	Cook County	74.2	24.0	0.8	0.5	0.5
Cincinnati, OH	Hamilton County	57.1	41.3	1.2	0.3	0.0
Clarksville, TN	Montgomery County	42.3	55.0	1.9	0.2	0.7
Cleveland, OH	Cuyahoga County	66.4	32.3	0.7	0.3	0.3
College Station, TX	Brazos County	41.6	55.9	2.1	0.3	0.1
Colorado Springs, CO	El Paso County	42.7	53.5	2.4	0.3	1.0
Columbia, MO	Boone County	54.8	42.3	2.2	0.3	0.4
Columbia, SC	Richland County	68.4	30.1	1.0	0.4	0.1
Columbus, OH	Franklin County	64.7	33.4	1.2	0.3	0.4
Dallas, TX	Dallas County	64.9	33.3	1.0	0.4	0.4
Davenport, IA	Scott County	50.7	47.2	1.2	0.2	0.7
Denver, CO	Denver County	79.6	18.2	1.2	0.3	0.7
Des Moines, IA	Polk County	56.5	41.3	1.3	0.2	0.7
Durham, NC	Durham County	80.4	18.0	0.8	0.3	0.4
Edison, NJ	Middlesex County	60.2	38.2	0.7	0.3	0.6
El Paso, TX	El Paso County	66.7	31.6	1.0	0.5	0.2
Fargo, ND	Cass County	46.8	49.5	2.9	0.0	0.7
Fayetteville, NC	Cumberland County	57.4	40.8	1.1	0.3	0.4
Fort Collins, CO	Larimer County	56.2	40.8	1.8	0.3	0.9
Fort Wayne, IN	Allen County	43.2	54.3	2.2	0.0	0.3
Fort Worth, TX	Tarrant County	49.3	49.1	1.2	0.3	0.0
Grand Rapids, MI	Kent County	51.9	45.8	1.5	0.3	0.5
Greeley, CO	Weld County	39.6	57.6	1.7	0.2	0.9
Green Bay, WI	Brown County	45.5	52.7	1.3	0.0	0.5
Greensboro, NC	Guilford County	60.8	37.7	0.8	0.2	0.4
Honolulu, HI	Honolulu County	62.5	35.7	0.9	0.6	0.4
Houston, TX	Harris County	56.0	42.7	1.0	0.3	0.0
Huntsville, AL	Madison County	44.8	52.8	1.9	0.0	0.5
Indianapolis, IN	Marion County	63.3	34.3	1.8	0.1	0.4
Jacksonville, FL	Duval County	51.1	47.3	1.0	0.2	0.5
Kansas City, MO	Jackson County	59.8	37.9	1.4	0.4	0.5
Lafayette, LA	Lafayette Parish	34.7	63.3	1.3	0.0	0.7
Lakeland, FL	Polk County	42.2	56.6	0.8	0.1	0.4
Las Vegas, NV	Clark County	53.7	44.3	0.9	0.0	1.1
Lexington, KY	Fayette County	59.2	38.5	1.6	0.1	0.6
Lincoln, NE	Lancaster County	52.3	44.6	2.4	0.0	0.7
Little Rock, AR	Pulaski County	60.0	37.5	1.0	0.3	1.3
Los Angeles, CA	Los Angeles County	71.0	26.9	0.8	0.5	0.8
Louisville, KY	Jefferson County	59.1	39.0	1.2	0.1	0.7
Madison, WI	Dane County	75.5	22.9	1.1	0.1	0.6
Manchester, NH	Hillsborough County	52.8	45.2	1.7	0.0	0.3

Table continued on following page.

Appendix A: Comparative Statistics   A-107

City	Area Covered	Biden	Trump	Jorgensen	Hawkins	Other
Memphis, TN	Shelby County	64.4	34.0	0.6	0.2	0.8
Miami, FL	Miami-Dade County	53.3	46.0	0.3	0.1	0.3
Midland, TX	Midland County	20.9	77.3	1.3	0.2	0.2
Milwaukee, WI	Milwaukee County	69.1	29.3	0.9	0.0	0.7
Minneapolis, MN	Hennepin County	70.5	27.2	1.0	0.3	1.0
Nashville, TN	Davidson County	64.5	32.4	1.1	0.2	1.8
New Haven, CT	New Haven County	58.0	40.6	0.9	0.4	0.0
New Orleans, LA	Orleans Parish	83.1	15.0	0.9	0.0	1.0
New York, NY	Bronx County	83.3	15.9	0.2	0.3	0.3
New York, NY	Kings County	76.8	22.1	0.3	0.4	0.4
New York, NY	New York County	86.4	12.2	0.5	0.4	0.5
New York, NY	Queens County	72.0	26.9	0.3	0.4	0.4
New York, NY	Richmond County	42.0	56.9	0.4	0.3	0.4
Oklahoma City, OK	Oklahoma County	48.1	49.2	1.8	0.0	0.9
Omaha, NE	Douglas County	54.4	43.1	2.0	0.0	0.6
Orlando, FL	Orange County	60.9	37.8	0.7	0.2	0.4
Peoria, IL	Peoria County	51.9	45.6	1.6	0.6	0.4
Philadelphia, PA	Philadelphia County	81.2	17.9	0.7	0.1	0.2
Phoenix, AZ	Maricopa County	50.1	48.0	1.5	0.0	0.3
Pittsburgh, PA	Allegheny County	59.4	39.0	1.2	0.0	0.4
Portland, OR	Multnomah County	79.2	17.9	1.2	0.6	1.0
Providence, RI	Providence County	60.5	37.6	0.8	0.0	1.0
Provo, UT	Utah County	26.3	66.7	3.6	0.3	3.1
Raleigh, NC	Wake County	62.3	35.8	1.2	0.3	0.5
Reno, NV	Washoe County	50.8	46.3	1.4	0.0	1.5
Richmond, VA	Richmond City	82.9	14.9	1.5	0.0	0.6
Riverside, CA	Riverside County	53.0	45.0	1.0	0.3	0.6
Rochester, MN	Olmsted County	54.2	43.4	1.2	0.3	0.9
Sacramento, CA	Sacramento County	61.4	36.1	1.4	0.5	0.7
Salt Lake City, UT	Salt Lake County	53.0	42.1	2.2	0.4	2.2
San Antonio, TX	Bexar County	58.2	40.1	1.1	0.4	0.2
San Diego, CA	San Diego County	60.2	37.5	1.3	0.5	0.5
San Francisco, CA	San Francisco County	85.3	12.7	0.7	0.6	0.7
San Jose, CA	Santa Clara County	72.6	25.2	1.1	0.5	0.6
Santa Rosa, CA	Sonoma County	74.5	23.0	1.3	0.6	0.6
Savannah, GA	Chatham County	58.6	39.9	1.4	0.0	0.0
Seattle, WA	King County	75.0	22.2	1.5	0.5	0.8
Sioux Falls, SD	Minnehaha County	43.8	53.3	2.8	0.0	0.0
Springfield, IL	Sangamon County	46.7	51.1	1.4	0.6	0.3
Tallahassee, FL	Leon County	63.3	35.1	0.8	0.2	0.5
Tampa, FL	Hillsborough County	52.7	45.8	0.8	0.2	0.5
Tucson, AZ	Pima County	58.4	39.8	1.5	0.0	0.3
Tulsa, OK	Tulsa County	40.9	56.5	1.8	0.0	0.8
Tuscaloosa, AL	Tuscaloosa County	41.9	56.7	1.0	0.0	0.4
Virginia Beach, VA	Virginia Beach City	51.6	46.2	1.8	0.0	0.4
Washington, DC	District of Columbia	92.1	5.4	0.6	0.5	1.4
Wichita, KS	Sedgwick County	42.6	54.4	2.4	0.0	0.5
Winston-Salem, NC	Forsyth County	56.2	42.3	0.9	0.2	0.4
U.S.	U.S.	51.3	46.8	1.2	0.3	0.5

Note: Results are percentages and may not add to 100% due to rounding
Source: Dave Leip's Atlas of U.S. Presidential Elections

A-108 Appendix A: Comparative Statistics

House Price Index (HPI)

Metro Area[1]	National Ranking[3]	Quarterly Change (%)	One-Year Change (%)	Five-Year Change (%)	Since 1991Q1 (%)
Albuquerque, NM	42	2.20	7.86	27.05	163.46
Allentown, PA	59	2.10	7.47	23.78	102.86
Anchorage, AK	205	1.39	4.88	9.73	184.56
Ann Arbor, MI	224	0.98	3.78	29.65	164.45
Athens, GA	66	1.41	7.40	43.79	181.78
Atlanta, GA	110	1.95	6.57	40.75	164.55
Austin, TX	30	3.27	8.26	41.08	401.86
Baton Rouge, LA	230	1.37	3.54	17.61	188.52
Boise City, ID	1	4.90	13.83	78.91	350.41
Boston, MA[2]	167	1.93	5.51	29.37	228.40
Boulder, CO	227	1.79	3.59	36.23	436.16
Cape Coral, FL	84	3.11	7.07	33.53	188.18
Cedar Rapids, IA	218	1.99	4.00	17.00	130.16
Charleston, SC	130	1.32	6.11	36.39	284.93
Charlotte, NC	60	2.55	7.46	41.48	183.15
Chicago, IL[2]	239	1.11	2.98	16.74	122.65
Cincinnati, OH	98	1.97	6.79	31.23	131.06
Clarksville, TN	n/a	n/a	n/a	n/a	n/a
Cleveland, OH	50	2.24	7.63	30.38	104.70
College Station, TX	n/a	n/a	n/a	n/a	n/a
Colorado Springs, CO	19	3.08	8.89	51.30	301.84
Columbia, MO	212	1.63	4.42	20.40	150.92
Columbia, SC	181	1.37	5.23	24.67	125.47
Columbus, OH	65	2.05	7.40	37.73	163.06
Dallas, TX[2]	206	2.07	4.81	38.75	203.48
Davenport, IA	225	0.97	3.73	15.46	153.27
Denver, CO	164	1.71	5.57	42.32	404.42
Des Moines, IA	237	1.39	3.15	20.11	154.39
Durham, NC	161	1.51	5.61	34.97	182.89
Edison, NJ[2]	220	1.50	3.91	23.15	199.59
El Paso, TX	158	1.05	5.68	18.03	118.41
Fargo, ND	240	0.70	2.82	16.07	201.82
Fayetteville, NC	n/a	n/a	n/a	n/a	n/a
Fort Collins, CO	217	1.38	4.19	38.15	365.72
Fort Wayne, IN	53	1.29	7.55	35.84	111.44
Fort Worth, TX[2]	191	2.39	5.13	42.54	191.04
Grand Rapids, MI	71	2.11	7.32	44.57	175.35
Greeley, CO	177	1.80	5.33	46.65	333.63
Green Bay, WI	169	2.46	5.48	28.92	157.42
Greensboro, NC	128	1.99	6.14	27.91	106.32
Honolulu, HI	250	1.23	0.53	16.08	154.83
Houston, TX	211	1.45	4.53	23.50	211.24
Huntsville, AL	9	3.60	9.98	30.56	124.28
Indianapolis, IN	46	2.17	7.74	36.43	135.15
Jacksonville, FL	136	2.34	6.06	43.85	224.14
Kansas City, MO	75	2.00	7.29	37.81	175.77
Lafayette, LA	221	0.62	3.89	8.70	180.99
Lakeland, FL	8	4.29	10.11	53.44	194.73
Las Vegas, NV	171	1.70	5.46	50.47	163.25
Lexington, KY	200	1.46	5.04	28.47	155.18
Lincoln, NE	198	2.22	5.09	30.00	177.71
Little Rock, AR	196	1.79	5.10	16.24	131.58
Los Angeles, CA[2]	193	1.98	5.13	31.04	214.04
Louisville, KY	111	2.46	6.56	29.08	178.89
Madison, WI	202	1.80	4.96	27.32	218.96

Table continued on following page.

Appendix A: Comparative Statistics   A-109

Metro Area[1]	National Ranking[3]	Quarterly Change (%)	One-Year Change (%)	Five-Year Change (%)	Since 1991Q1 (%)
Manchester, NH	17	3.48	9.02	33.95	167.53
Memphis, TN	90	1.82	6.94	33.17	120.34
Miami, FL[2]	124	1.83	6.32	38.91	334.89
Midland, TX	n/a	n/a	n/a	n/a	n/a
Milwaukee, WI	172	1.59	5.45	26.53	171.34
Minneapolis, MN	157	1.56	5.70	30.96	210.96
Nashville, TN	88	1.88	6.96	45.40	266.19
New Haven, CT	99	2.80	6.78	15.33	80.58
New Orleans, LA	174	2.09	5.37	22.52	226.15
New York, NY[2]	220	1.50	3.91	23.15	199.59
Oklahoma City, OK	182	1.07	5.23	21.46	179.09
Omaha, NE	154	1.72	5.74	31.76	176.42
Orlando, FL	119	1.83	6.36	44.80	198.33
Peoria, IL	238	0.87	3.00	6.40	120.92
Philadelphia, PA[2]	145	1.50	5.90	33.20	191.57
Phoenix, AZ	7	3.44	10.26	47.39	283.82
Pittsburgh, PA	123	1.67	6.33	26.47	167.39
Portland, OR	127	2.22	6.27	37.96	381.42
Providence, RI	89	2.66	6.95	31.83	154.93
Provo, UT	23	3.08	8.61	46.91	339.23
Raleigh, NC	159	1.84	5.67	34.46	180.65
Reno, NV	96	2.61	6.81	48.07	229.64
Richmond, VA	134	2.05	6.10	28.56	172.25
Riverside, CA	86	2.74	7.03	34.65	169.25
Rochester, MN	116	1.70	6.45	32.58	175.69
Sacramento, CA	93	2.73	6.92	37.42	166.72
Salt Lake City, UT	15	3.24	9.07	50.25	408.84
San Antonio, TX	149	2.10	5.83	34.99	224.63
San Diego, CA	141	1.97	6.01	30.38	235.91
San Francisco, CA[2]	253	-3.20	-6.72	10.12	283.50
San Jose, CA	251	0.55	0.10	18.04	296.60
Santa Rosa, CA	246	1.59	2.15	26.52	225.13
Savannah, GA	214	0.50	4.40	33.56	221.18
Seattle, WA[2]	97	2.16	6.81	48.46	324.48
Sioux Falls, SD	139	2.09	6.03	29.70	212.39
Springfield, IL	248	0.83	1.79	8.16	85.25
Tallahassee, FL	186	1.55	5.20	30.45	154.52
Tampa, FL	33	2.36	8.17	52.43	254.29
Tucson, AZ	29	2.33	8.30	39.73	202.45
Tulsa, OK	179	1.98	5.26	22.61	153.16
Tuscaloosa, AL	n/a	n/a	n/a	n/a	n/a
Virginia Beach, VA	144	1.54	5.90	17.40	170.16
Washington, DC[2]	189	1.67	5.16	21.40	197.71
Wichita, KS	49	1.50	7.67	27.26	136.03
Winston-Salem, NC	94	2.58	6.92	28.40	118.04
U.S.[4]	–	3.81	10.77	38.99	205.12

Note: The HPI is a weighted repeat sales index. It measures average price changes in repeat sales or refinancings on the same properties. This information is obtained by reviewing repeat mortgage transactions on single-family properties whose mortgages have been purchased or securitized by Fannie Mae or Freddie Mac since January 1975; (1) figures cover the Metropolitan Statistical Area (MSA) unless noted otherwise—see Appendix B for areas included; (2) Metropolitan Division—see Appendix B for areas included; (3) Rankings are based on annual percentage change, for all MSAs containing at least 15,000 transactions over the last 10 years and ranges from 1 to 253; (4) figures based on a weighted division average; all figures are for the period ended December 31, 2020; n/a not available
Source: Federal Housing Finance Agency, Change in Metropolitan Area House Price Indexes, April 7, 2021

A-110   Appendix A: Comparative Statistics

Home Value Distribution: City

Area	Under $50,000	$50,000 -$99,999	$100,000 -$149,999	$150,000 -$199,999	$200,000 -$299,999	$300,000 -$499,999	$500,000 -$999,999	$1,000,000 or more
Albuquerque, NM	4.5	4.4	16.9	25.1	29.5	15.9	3.3	0.5
Allentown, PA	4.5	22.0	35.2	24.0	8.7	4.1	1.1	0.4
Anchorage, AK	5.3	1.9	4.8	7.0	26.9	40.9	12.2	1.0
Ann Arbor, MI	1.3	3.6	6.0	8.2	25.2	37.6	15.7	2.4
Athens, GA	6.3	12.9	19.9	21.9	20.3	12.7	5.4	0.7
Atlanta, GA	4.5	10.1	9.6	10.6	16.6	19.7	20.2	8.8
Austin, TX	2.2	2.2	4.8	9.1	24.3	33.0	20.1	4.3
Baton Rouge, LA	5.6	17.7	15.6	19.4	21.4	12.9	5.8	1.6
Boise City, ID	3.9	1.9	8.6	17.4	31.6	26.6	9.0	1.0
Boston, MA	1.6	0.3	0.4	1.4	8.2	34.1	40.4	13.5
Boulder, CO	3.8	1.7	1.8	3.3	4.1	13.3	48.9	23.1
Cape Coral, FL	1.6	3.1	11.1	22.6	34.1	20.2	6.5	0.9
Cedar Rapids, IA	5.5	16.3	34.2	20.9	16.3	5.1	1.4	0.2
Charleston, SC	1.5	2.6	4.6	8.2	26.4	31.1	19.0	6.6
Charlotte, NC	2.1	8.2	17.3	17.6	21.0	19.5	10.9	3.4
Chicago, IL	2.7	7.0	11.1	15.0	23.8	24.1	12.5	3.9
Cincinnati, OH	6.9	25.4	22.2	11.9	14.7	11.5	6.2	1.3
Clarksville, TN	4.3	14.1	28.9	26.6	19.0	5.6	0.9	0.5
Cleveland, OH	28.8	44.0	14.0	5.9	3.6	2.1	1.2	0.4
College Station, TX	2.1	1.3	7.4	21.9	35.6	24.9	6.1	0.9
Colorado Springs, CO	3.0	2.1	6.5	14.5	33.6	30.4	8.6	1.2
Columbia, MO	3.4	7.4	19.0	22.8	25.7	17.2	4.2	0.3
Columbia, SC	4.5	15.3	19.7	16.0	15.6	16.5	10.9	1.6
Columbus, OH	5.9	19.5	23.8	20.7	19.8	7.9	2.0	0.3
Dallas, TX	6.7	19.2	15.4	10.7	12.6	17.6	13.2	4.6
Davenport, IA	6.3	24.6	28.4	16.1	15.6	7.4	1.1	0.4
Denver, CO	1.3	1.6	3.3	6.8	19.5	34.6	27.3	5.6
Des Moines, IA	5.9	21.6	33.1	20.5	12.1	4.8	1.8	0.2
Durham, NC	1.8	5.3	14.5	20.5	30.8	20.3	5.9	1.0
Edison, NJ	2.1	1.8	1.9	2.7	17.0	47.4	25.4	1.6
El Paso, TX	5.1	25.0	32.7	18.5	12.5	4.8	1.2	0.3
Fargo, ND	4.0	4.3	12.6	25.0	30.8	18.6	4.0	0.6
Fayetteville, NC	5.0	26.2	28.2	19.3	13.7	5.5	1.7	0.3
Fort Collins, CO	3.2	1.1	1.5	3.6	19.8	52.8	16.7	1.3
Fort Wayne, IN	10.6	30.1	28.9	16.1	9.6	3.7	0.9	0.1
Fort Worth, TX	6.2	17.3	17.6	19.3	22.9	11.9	4.0	0.8
Grand Rapids, MI	4.7	19.6	30.0	24.3	15.0	5.0	1.3	0.2
Greeley, CO	7.1	2.5	7.2	15.2	36.3	27.2	4.3	0.2
Green Bay, WI	3.3	20.8	35.3	20.4	12.8	5.7	1.5	0.3
Greensboro, NC	3.5	19.2	24.5	18.3	18.2	11.4	3.7	1.2
Honolulu, HI	0.8	0.8	0.8	1.4	7.2	22.6	42.5	24.0
Houston, TX	5.4	19.6	18.1	13.0	14.5	15.8	10.0	3.6
Huntsville, AL	5.3	17.9	15.0	16.6	22.8	16.6	4.6	1.1
Indianapolis, IN	7.1	22.9	27.0	18.8	12.5	8.0	3.1	0.7
Jacksonville, FL	7.4	15.2	17.4	19.0	24.0	11.9	3.9	1.2
Kansas City, MO	11.2	17.4	19.4	18.4	18.5	10.8	3.6	0.7
Lafayette, LA	5.5	8.2	14.9	23.2	23.8	16.0	6.5	1.9
Lakeland, FL	18.2	15.4	16.7	19.4	18.7	8.6	2.6	0.5
Las Vegas, NV	2.4	4.3	8.7	15.4	31.4	27.3	8.6	1.9
Lexington, KY	2.6	8.8	21.0	21.1	22.4	16.6	6.0	1.4
Lincoln, NE	3.5	9.8	25.5	23.9	23.3	11.2	2.4	0.5
Little Rock, AR	6.5	19.3	16.8	17.5	15.9	15.4	7.0	1.6
Los Angeles, CA	1.2	0.8	0.7	0.8	4.8	25.2	44.5	22.1
Louisville, KY	5.5	15.7	24.8	18.2	17.6	13.0	4.4	0.8
Madison, WI	1.6	2.6	8.5	18.5	35.6	25.7	6.7	0.8

Table continued on following page.

Appendix A: Comparative Statistics   A-111

Area	Under $50,000	$50,000 -$99,999	$100,000 -$149,999	$150,000 -$199,999	$200,000 -$299,999	$300,000 -$499,999	$500,000 -$999,999	$1,000,000 or more
Manchester, NH	1.9	3.0	8.3	21.6	47.9	15.7	1.4	0.2
Memphis, TN	14.5	34.7	17.4	12.4	9.9	6.8	3.3	1.0
Miami, FL	2.2	4.6	6.0	9.8	24.1	29.6	16.1	7.5
Midland, TX	4.9	9.0	12.7	17.4	28.4	18.3	7.8	1.4
Milwaukee, WI	9.1	27.3	29.6	17.9	10.6	3.6	1.5	0.4
Minneapolis, MN	1.4	4.0	10.7	16.1	31.3	24.7	10.0	1.9
Nashville, TN	2.1	5.0	13.5	17.4	27.0	23.1	10.0	1.9
New Haven, CT	2.7	7.9	14.1	25.8	28.0	14.9	6.0	0.7
New Orleans, LA	2.8	7.9	13.8	18.6	19.9	20.5	13.0	3.7
New York, NY	2.9	1.3	1.9	2.4	6.6	23.7	41.4	19.9
Oklahoma City, OK	7.9	18.0	19.9	20.8	18.9	10.2	3.4	0.8
Omaha, NE	4.2	14.8	25.8	21.8	19.0	10.5	3.2	0.7
Orlando, FL	2.9	10.7	13.4	13.0	24.6	24.6	8.8	2.1
Peoria, IL	12.6	25.4	21.8	15.6	13.8	8.1	2.4	0.4
Philadelphia, PA	6.7	19.4	18.6	18.0	19.6	11.3	5.1	1.3
Phoenix, AZ	4.3	6.3	11.0	17.7	26.4	23.0	9.6	1.7
Pittsburgh, PA	11.8	27.6	18.0	12.8	12.4	10.6	5.7	1.0
Portland, OR	1.9	0.8	1.5	3.8	16.7	41.6	30.5	3.2
Providence, RI	2.1	5.3	16.9	25.7	23.9	15.6	8.6	1.9
Provo, UT	3.5	1.2	6.4	13.5	34.5	29.0	9.8	2.2
Raleigh, NC	2.0	2.7	11.4	19.4	27.1	24.8	10.8	1.8
Reno, NV	4.1	2.9	3.7	7.5	22.3	43.2	13.7	2.5
Richmond, VA	2.0	11.4	13.9	15.4	20.8	21.7	11.5	3.3
Riverside, CA	2.9	1.6	1.7	3.4	17.5	55.6	15.4	1.9
Rochester, MN	2.9	4.5	16.5	26.0	27.6	17.9	4.2	0.4
Sacramento, CA	2.5	2.0	3.5	7.2	26.0	39.6	17.2	2.0
Salt Lake City, UT	2.9	1.4	6.7	13.0	23.6	29.7	19.5	3.3
San Antonio, TX	6.8	24.5	20.0	18.4	17.9	9.4	2.5	0.6
San Diego, CA	1.6	1.0	0.8	1.1	5.3	27.4	47.6	15.3
San Francisco, CA	1.1	0.5	0.4	0.3	1.2	3.9	34.9	57.8
San Jose, CA	1.5	1.4	1.4	0.9	1.9	7.2	50.0	35.6
Santa Rosa, CA	2.7	2.0	1.7	1.5	5.2	30.6	50.0	6.2
Savannah, GA	6.1	20.2	20.4	19.5	18.7	9.4	4.6	1.1
Seattle, WA	0.6	0.4	0.4	1.0	5.0	22.3	52.5	17.8
Sioux Falls, SD	5.5	6.6	17.7	24.4	27.0	14.4	3.8	0.7
Springfield, IL	10.0	24.9	23.4	15.7	15.7	7.9	2.3	0.2
Tallahassee, FL	2.9	9.9	16.8	19.3	26.8	19.3	4.0	1.0
Tampa, FL	3.8	10.8	11.7	14.7	20.7	20.1	13.6	4.5
Tucson, AZ	10.6	13.5	22.6	24.6	19.6	6.8	1.9	0.3
Tulsa, OK	9.0	22.8	22.3	15.7	13.8	10.4	4.9	1.2
Tuscaloosa, AL	4.4	11.2	21.2	19.0	19.4	15.1	8.2	1.4
Virginia Beach, VA	2.2	1.5	6.1	12.6	33.7	30.5	11.1	2.3
Washington, DC	1.2	0.8	1.1	1.9	9.5	25.7	41.0	18.8
Wichita, KS	8.4	26.6	22.6	18.2	14.6	7.0	2.3	0.3
Winston-Salem, NC	6.6	19.7	24.8	20.8	13.4	8.8	5.2	0.8
U.S.	6.9	12.0	13.3	14.0	19.6	19.3	11.4	3.4

Note: Figures are percentages and cover owner-occupied housing units.
Source: U.S. Census Bureau, 2015-2019 American Community Survey 5-Year Estimates

A-112 Appendix A: Comparative Statistics

Home Value Distribution: Metro Area

MSA[1]	Under $50,000	$50,000 -$99,999	$100,000 -$149,999	$150,000 -$199,999	$200,000 -$299,999	$300,000 -$499,999	$500,000 -$999,999	$1,000,000 or more
Albuquerque, NM	5.8	7.6	16.8	22.7	25.8	15.5	4.8	1.0
Allentown, PA	3.8	7.3	14.4	20.0	28.2	21.4	4.3	0.6
Anchorage, AK	4.9	2.6	5.2	9.3	29.6	37.3	10.3	0.9
Ann Arbor, MI	5.5	6.1	8.0	13.7	24.9	28.8	11.3	1.7
Athens, GA	8.8	12.2	17.4	17.3	21.0	16.1	6.2	1.0
Atlanta, GA	3.7	9.2	14.8	18.0	22.5	20.7	9.3	1.8
Austin, TX	3.3	3.9	6.9	12.7	27.8	28.3	13.9	3.2
Baton Rouge, LA	8.7	12.3	15.0	20.4	24.0	14.3	4.3	1.0
Boise City, ID	4.4	4.2	11.1	17.9	28.9	25.3	7.3	1.0
Boston, MA	1.6	1.0	1.6	3.6	14.5	38.5	31.8	7.4
Boulder, CO	2.9	1.1	1.3	2.9	10.6	31.6	38.3	11.3
Cape Coral, FL	6.2	8.9	11.8	16.4	24.5	20.2	9.2	2.8
Cedar Rapids, IA	6.5	13.7	27.1	19.7	20.8	9.2	2.4	0.6
Charleston, SC	6.0	7.5	11.6	15.3	23.1	21.1	11.7	3.7
Charlotte, NC	4.8	11.4	16.7	17.1	21.5	18.7	7.8	1.9
Chicago, IL	3.2	7.2	12.4	16.4	25.5	23.1	9.9	2.4
Cincinnati, OH	4.8	15.3	21.4	18.8	21.0	13.6	4.3	0.7
Clarksville, TN	6.6	17.3	23.7	21.4	19.5	9.0	1.8	0.7
Cleveland, OH	7.6	20.0	21.6	17.9	18.4	10.7	3.0	0.7
College Station, TX	10.0	13.0	13.2	18.1	23.3	16.1	5.3	1.0
Colorado Springs, CO	3.1	2.0	6.1	14.3	31.7	31.1	10.4	1.2
Columbia, MO	5.4	11.2	19.9	20.9	22.9	14.8	4.3	0.7
Columbia, SC	8.6	16.9	22.6	18.7	17.1	11.2	4.2	0.8
Columbus, OH	4.8	13.1	18.2	18.8	23.1	16.5	4.9	0.7
Dallas, TX	4.5	11.1	14.5	15.9	23.1	20.9	7.9	1.9
Davenport, IA	7.3	23.5	24.9	17.5	15.3	9.1	2.0	0.4
Denver, CO	2.2	1.3	2.3	5.3	19.2	42.7	23.3	3.5
Des Moines, IA	4.5	11.9	19.7	19.9	24.4	14.9	4.2	0.5
Durham, NC	5.0	7.8	14.2	16.4	23.6	22.0	9.7	1.4
Edison, NJ	2.0	1.4	2.4	3.9	13.2	35.1	32.1	9.9
El Paso, TX	7.7	26.8	31.4	17.2	11.2	4.3	1.1	0.2
Fargo, ND	3.7	5.3	13.1	23.0	30.1	19.4	4.8	0.7
Fayetteville, NC	8.8	21.8	23.2	20.1	18.1	6.2	1.5	0.4
Fort Collins, CO	3.9	1.4	1.6	4.7	20.7	46.4	19.1	2.2
Fort Wayne, IN	8.4	24.8	26.3	17.2	13.7	7.2	2.0	0.4
Fort Worth, TX	4.5	11.1	14.5	15.9	23.1	20.9	7.9	1.9
Grand Rapids, MI	6.7	11.6	20.2	21.8	22.4	13.0	3.6	0.7
Greeley, CO	4.6	2.7	4.6	9.7	28.6	36.6	12.0	1.1
Green Bay, WI	4.0	11.9	22.8	22.2	24.5	11.3	2.6	0.6
Greensboro, NC	7.0	19.7	23.7	17.7	17.2	10.7	3.4	0.7
Honolulu, HI	0.7	0.6	0.8	1.0	5.0	19.6	54.6	17.7
Houston, TX	5.3	12.1	16.7	17.8	22.0	16.9	6.9	2.3
Huntsville, AL	6.4	13.8	17.3	19.0	23.7	15.1	3.9	0.8
Indianapolis, IN	5.6	16.1	22.3	19.0	18.5	13.4	4.4	0.8
Jacksonville, FL	5.8	12.0	14.1	16.8	24.6	18.1	6.7	1.8
Kansas City, MO	6.2	12.8	17.6	18.7	22.7	16.1	5.0	0.9
Lafayette, LA	14.7	16.0	16.1	19.5	19.3	10.1	3.5	0.8
Lakeland, FL	14.7	18.2	16.8	18.6	20.6	8.3	2.2	0.6
Las Vegas, NV	3.5	4.3	8.0	14.1	31.6	28.6	8.2	1.7
Lexington, KY	3.5	9.9	22.0	20.7	21.4	15.4	5.9	1.3
Lincoln, NE	3.2	9.4	23.4	22.6	23.4	13.8	3.7	0.5
Little Rock, AR	7.9	17.6	22.4	19.5	18.4	10.1	3.2	0.9
Los Angeles, CA	1.9	1.4	0.9	1.2	4.9	25.2	47.5	17.0
Louisville, KY	4.8	13.7	22.6	18.9	20.8	13.6	4.5	0.9
Madison, WI	2.1	3.9	9.7	16.6	32.4	26.6	7.5	1.2

Table continued on following page.

Appendix A: Comparative Statistics   A-113

MSA[1]	Under $50,000	$50,000 -$99,999	$100,000 -$149,999	$150,000 -$199,999	$200,000 -$299,999	$300,000 -$499,999	$500,000 -$999,999	$1,000,000 or more
Manchester, NH	1.9	2.5	5.9	12.0	37.5	32.8	6.7	0.7
Memphis, TN	9.1	21.8	18.2	16.5	18.6	11.2	3.6	0.9
Miami, FL	4.0	7.1	8.7	11.9	22.9	28.5	12.5	4.5
Midland, TX	8.7	10.4	11.9	15.9	26.2	17.9	7.5	1.3
Milwaukee, WI	3.7	8.8	15.1	18.2	27.1	20.0	6.0	1.1
Minneapolis, MN	2.7	2.7	7.9	16.7	32.8	27.1	8.8	1.4
Nashville, TN	2.9	6.1	13.1	16.5	25.6	23.0	10.5	2.3
New Haven, CT	2.0	4.9	10.6	17.0	29.8	26.8	7.6	1.2
New Orleans, LA	4.2	9.0	16.8	20.8	24.8	16.4	6.4	1.6
New York, NY	2.0	1.4	2.4	3.9	13.2	35.1	32.1	9.9
Oklahoma City, OK	7.5	17.7	21.3	19.6	18.4	10.9	3.7	1.0
Omaha, NE	3.9	12.1	23.4	21.0	22.0	13.5	3.4	0.7
Orlando, FL	6.1	8.5	11.7	17.0	28.6	20.3	6.2	1.7
Peoria, IL	8.6	25.9	23.0	17.4	15.3	7.6	1.9	0.4
Philadelphia, PA	3.4	7.3	10.2	14.8	26.3	26.2	10.1	1.7
Phoenix, AZ	5.5	5.2	8.7	15.2	28.2	25.2	9.8	2.2
Pittsburgh, PA	8.8	20.3	19.2	17.8	17.5	12.0	3.6	0.7
Portland, OR	3.2	1.3	2.1	4.9	21.0	42.8	22.1	2.6
Providence, RI	2.1	2.0	5.7	14.1	33.3	31.2	10.0	1.7
Provo, UT	2.4	0.9	3.6	10.1	32.2	37.0	12.1	1.7
Raleigh, NC	3.5	5.0	11.9	15.5	25.7	27.6	9.6	1.3
Reno, NV	4.0	2.8	4.2	7.5	23.6	38.4	15.4	4.1
Richmond, VA	2.4	5.3	11.7	18.2	29.4	23.7	8.2	1.2
Riverside, CA	4.9	3.4	4.1	6.8	21.0	40.8	17.0	2.0
Rochester, MN	4.6	6.8	16.1	22.2	24.5	19.3	5.5	1.0
Sacramento, CA	2.8	1.7	2.2	4.5	17.7	42.3	25.8	3.0
Salt Lake City, UT	2.9	1.2	5.2	11.5	29.6	34.2	13.7	1.7
San Antonio, TX	6.8	18.2	16.6	17.7	20.5	14.2	4.9	1.2
San Diego, CA	2.5	1.9	1.4	1.4	5.2	29.3	46.1	12.2
San Francisco, CA	1.2	0.9	0.8	0.8	2.8	13.2	43.9	36.2
San Jose, CA	1.3	1.0	1.2	0.9	1.8	6.4	40.1	47.3
Santa Rosa, CA	2.6	2.6	1.6	1.2	4.2	22.2	51.9	13.7
Savannah, GA	5.7	11.2	17.1	19.2	23.1	14.9	7.1	1.6
Seattle, WA	2.5	1.2	2.0	4.2	15.3	34.2	32.0	8.5
Sioux Falls, SD	5.6	7.7	16.6	22.7	26.5	15.7	4.4	0.8
Springfield, IL	8.2	23.3	22.4	17.8	18.2	8.0	1.9	0.2
Tallahassee, FL	8.3	15.3	16.5	16.9	22.4	15.2	4.6	0.8
Tampa, FL	8.8	13.0	13.5	16.7	23.7	16.4	6.4	1.6
Tucson, AZ	8.4	10.7	16.2	19.9	22.5	15.4	5.8	1.0
Tulsa, OK	9.4	18.7	21.7	19.4	17.3	9.4	3.4	0.8
Tuscaloosa, AL	13.0	14.9	17.5	20.5	19.7	9.8	3.9	0.7
Virginia Beach, VA	3.3	3.8	10.2	17.0	31.5	25.1	7.7	1.2
Washington, DC	1.5	1.0	2.1	4.7	17.1	35.8	31.2	6.7
Wichita, KS	8.3	24.2	22.6	19.1	15.6	7.8	2.0	0.4
Winston-Salem, NC	7.4	16.9	24.5	20.0	17.2	9.9	3.5	0.6
U.S.	6.9	12.0	13.3	14.0	19.6	19.3	11.4	3.4

Note: (1) Figures cover the Metropolitan Statistical Area (MSA)—see Appendix B for areas included; Figures are percentages and cover owner-occupied housing units.
Source: U.S. Census Bureau, 2015-2019 American Community Survey 5-Year Estimates

A-114 Appendix A: Comparative Statistics

Homeownership Rate

Metro Area	2012	2013	2014	2015	2016	2017	2018	2019	2020
Albuquerque, NM	62.8	65.9	64.4	64.3	66.9	67.0	67.9	70.0	69.5
Allentown, PA	75.5	71.5	68.2	69.2	68.9	73.1	72.1	67.8	68.8
Anchorage, AK	n/a	n/a	n/a	n/a	n/a	n/a	n/a	n/a	n/a
Ann Arbor, MI	n/a	n/a	n/a	n/a	n/a	n/a	n/a	n/a	n/a
Athens, GA	n/a	n/a	n/a	n/a	n/a	n/a	n/a	n/a	n/a
Atlanta, GA	62.1	61.6	61.6	61.7	61.5	62.4	64.0	64.2	66.4
Austin, TX	60.1	59.6	61.1	57.5	56.5	55.6	56.1	59.0	65.4
Baton Rouge, LA	71.4	66.6	64.8	64.2	64.8	66.9	66.6	66.2	72.1
Boise City, ID	n/a	n/a	n/a	n/a	n/a	n/a	n/a	n/a	n/a
Boston, MA	66.0	66.3	62.8	59.3	58.9	58.8	61.0	60.9	61.2
Boulder, CO	n/a	n/a	n/a	n/a	n/a	n/a	n/a	n/a	n/a
Cape Coral, FL	n/a	n/a	n/a	62.9	66.5	65.5	75.1	72.0	77.4
Cedar Rapids, IA	n/a	n/a	n/a	n/a	n/a	n/a	n/a	n/a	n/a
Charleston, SC	n/a	n/a	n/a	65.8	62.1	67.7	68.8	70.7	75.5
Charlotte, NC	58.3	58.9	58.1	62.3	66.2	64.6	67.9	72.3	73.3
Chicago, IL	67.1	68.2	66.3	64.3	64.5	64.1	64.6	63.4	66.0
Cincinnati, OH	63.4	63.3	65.5	65.9	64.9	65.7	67.3	67.4	71.1
Clarksville, TN	n/a	n/a	n/a	n/a	n/a	n/a	n/a	n/a	n/a
Cleveland, OH	64.2	65.8	69.2	68.4	64.8	66.6	66.7	64.4	66.3
College Station, TX	n/a	n/a	n/a	n/a	n/a	n/a	n/a	n/a	n/a
Colorado Springs, CO	n/a	n/a	n/a	n/a	n/a	n/a	n/a	n/a	n/a
Columbia, MO	n/a	n/a	n/a	n/a	n/a	n/a	n/a	n/a	n/a
Columbia, SC	65.6	68.9	69.5	66.1	63.9	70.7	69.3	65.9	69.7
Columbus, OH	60.7	60.5	60.0	59.0	57.5	57.9	64.8	65.7	65.6
Dallas, TX	61.8	59.9	57.7	57.8	59.7	61.8	62.0	60.6	64.7
Davenport, IA	n/a	n/a	n/a	n/a	n/a	n/a	n/a	n/a	n/a
Denver, CO	61.8	61.0	61.9	61.6	61.6	59.3	60.1	63.5	62.9
Des Moines, IA	n/a	n/a	n/a	n/a	n/a	n/a	n/a	n/a	n/a
Durham, NC	n/a	n/a	n/a	n/a	n/a	n/a	n/a	n/a	n/a
Edison, NJ	51.5	50.6	50.7	49.9	50.4	49.9	49.7	50.4	50.9
El Paso, TX	n/a	n/a	n/a	n/a	n/a	n/a	n/a	n/a	n/a
Fargo, ND	n/a	n/a	n/a	n/a	n/a	n/a	n/a	n/a	n/a
Fayetteville, NC	n/a	n/a	n/a	n/a	n/a	n/a	n/a	n/a	n/a
Fort Collins, CO	n/a	n/a	n/a	n/a	n/a	n/a	n/a	n/a	n/a
Fort Wayne, IN	n/a	n/a	n/a	n/a	n/a	n/a	n/a	n/a	n/a
Fort Worth, TX	61.8	59.9	57.7	57.8	59.7	61.8	62.0	60.6	64.7
Grand Rapids, MI	76.9	73.7	71.6	75.8	76.2	71.7	73.0	75.2	71.8
Greeley, CO	n/a	n/a	n/a	n/a	n/a	n/a	n/a	n/a	n/a
Green Bay, WI	n/a	n/a	n/a	n/a	n/a	n/a	n/a	n/a	n/a
Greensboro, NC	64.9	67.9	68.1	65.4	62.9	61.9	63.2	61.7	65.8
Honolulu, HI	56.1	57.9	58.2	59.6	57.9	53.8	57.7	59.0	56.9
Houston, TX	62.1	60.5	60.4	60.3	59.0	58.9	60.1	61.3	65.3
Huntsville, AL	n/a	n/a	n/a	n/a	n/a	n/a	n/a	n/a	n/a
Indianapolis, IN	67.1	67.5	66.9	64.6	63.9	63.9	64.3	66.2	70.0
Jacksonville, FL	66.6	69.9	65.3	62.5	61.8	65.2	61.4	63.1	64.8
Kansas City, MO	65.1	65.6	66.1	65.0	62.4	62.4	64.3	65.0	66.7
Lafayette, LA	n/a	n/a	n/a	n/a	n/a	n/a	n/a	n/a	n/a
Lakeland, FL	n/a	n/a	n/a	n/a	n/a	n/a	n/a	n/a	n/a
Las Vegas, NV	52.6	52.8	53.2	52.1	51.3	54.4	58.1	56.0	57.3
Lexington, KY	n/a	n/a	n/a	n/a	n/a	n/a	n/a	n/a	n/a
Lincoln, NE	n/a	n/a	n/a	n/a	n/a	n/a	n/a	n/a	n/a
Little Rock, AR	n/a	n/a	n/a	65.8	64.9	61.0	62.2	65.0	67.7
Los Angeles, CA	49.9	48.7	49.0	49.1	47.1	49.1	49.5	48.2	48.5
Louisville, KY	63.3	64.5	68.9	67.7	67.6	71.7	67.9	64.9	69.3
Madison, WI	n/a	n/a	n/a	n/a	n/a	n/a	n/a	n/a	n/a
Manchester, NH	n/a	n/a	n/a	n/a	n/a	n/a	n/a	n/a	n/a

Table continued on following page.

Metro Area	2012	2013	2014	2015	2016	2017	2018	2019	2020
Memphis, TN	60.5	56.2	57.2	59.6	61.8	62.4	63.5	63.7	62.5
Miami, FL	61.8	60.1	58.8	58.6	58.4	57.9	59.9	60.4	60.6
Midland, TX	n/a	n/a	n/a	n/a	n/a	n/a	n/a	n/a	n/a
Milwaukee, WI	61.9	60.0	55.9	57.0	60.4	63.9	62.3	56.9	58.5
Minneapolis, MN	70.8	71.7	69.7	67.9	69.1	70.1	67.8	70.2	73.0
Nashville, TN	64.9	63.9	67.1	67.4	65.0	69.4	68.3	69.8	69.8
New Haven, CT	62.2	62.0	62.4	64.6	59.4	58.7	65.0	65.1	63.4
New Orleans, LA	62.4	61.4	60.6	62.8	59.3	61.7	62.6	61.1	66.3
New York, NY	51.5	50.6	50.7	49.9	50.4	49.9	49.7	50.4	50.9
Oklahoma City, OK	67.3	67.6	65.7	61.4	63.1	64.7	64.6	64.3	68.3
Omaha, NE	72.4	70.6	68.7	69.6	69.2	65.5	67.8	66.9	68.6
Orlando, FL	68.0	65.5	62.3	58.4	58.5	59.5	58.5	56.1	64.2
Peoria, IL	n/a	n/a	n/a	n/a	n/a	n/a	n/a	n/a	n/a
Philadelphia, PA	69.5	69.1	67.0	67.0	64.7	65.6	67.4	67.4	69.2
Phoenix, AZ	63.1	62.2	61.9	61.0	62.6	64.0	65.3	65.9	67.9
Pittsburgh, PA	67.9	68.3	69.1	71.0	72.2	72.7	71.7	71.5	69.8
Portland, OR	63.9	60.9	59.8	58.9	61.8	61.1	59.2	60.0	62.5
Providence, RI	61.7	60.1	61.6	60.0	57.5	58.6	61.3	63.5	64.8
Provo, UT	n/a	n/a	n/a	n/a	n/a	n/a	n/a	n/a	n/a
Raleigh, NC	67.7	65.5	65.5	67.4	65.9	68.2	64.9	63.0	68.2
Reno, NV	n/a	n/a	n/a	n/a	n/a	n/a	n/a	n/a	n/a
Richmond, VA	67.0	65.4	72.6	67.4	61.7	63.1	62.9	66.4	66.5
Riverside, CA	58.2	56.3	56.8	61.1	62.9	59.9	62.3	64.4	65.8
Rochester, MN	n/a	n/a	n/a	n/a	n/a	n/a	n/a	n/a	n/a
Sacramento, CA	58.6	60.4	60.1	60.8	60.5	60.1	64.1	61.6	63.4
Salt Lake City, UT	66.9	66.8	68.2	69.1	69.2	68.1	69.5	69.2	68.0
San Antonio, TX	67.5	70.1	70.2	66.0	61.6	62.5	64.4	62.6	64.2
San Diego, CA	55.4	55.0	57.4	51.8	53.3	56.0	56.1	56.7	57.8
San Francisco, CA	53.2	55.2	54.6	56.3	55.8	55.7	55.6	52.8	53.0
San Jose, CA	58.6	56.4	56.4	50.7	49.9	50.4	50.4	52.4	52.6
Santa Rosa, CA	n/a	n/a	n/a	n/a	n/a	n/a	n/a	n/a	n/a
Savannah, GA	n/a	n/a	n/a	n/a	n/a	n/a	n/a	n/a	n/a
Seattle, WA	60.4	61.0	61.3	59.5	57.7	59.5	62.5	61.5	59.4
Sioux Falls, SD	n/a	n/a	n/a	n/a	n/a	n/a	n/a	n/a	n/a
Springfield, IL	n/a	n/a	n/a	n/a	n/a	n/a	n/a	n/a	n/a
Tallahassee, FL	n/a	n/a	n/a	n/a	n/a	n/a	n/a	n/a	n/a
Tampa, FL	67.0	65.3	64.9	64.9	62.9	60.4	64.9	68.0	72.2
Tucson, AZ	64.9	66.1	66.7	61.4	56.0	60.1	63.8	60.1	67.1
Tulsa, OK	66.5	64.1	65.3	65.2	65.4	66.8	68.3	70.5	70.1
Tuscaloosa, AL	n/a	n/a	n/a	n/a	n/a	n/a	n/a	n/a	n/a
Virginia Beach, VA	62.0	63.3	64.1	59.4	59.6	65.3	62.8	63.0	65.8
Washington, DC	66.9	66.0	65.0	64.6	63.1	63.3	62.9	64.7	67.9
Wichita, KS	n/a	n/a	n/a	n/a	n/a	n/a	n/a	n/a	n/a
Winston-Salem, NC	n/a	n/a	n/a	n/a	n/a	n/a	n/a	n/a	n/a
U.S.	65.4	65.1	64.5	63.7	63.4	63.9	64.4	64.6	66.6

Note: Figures are percentages and cover the Metropolitan Statistical Area—see Appendix B for areas included; n/a not available
Source: U.S. Census Bureau, Housing Vacancies and Homeownership Annual Statistics: 2012-2020

A-116 Appendix A: Comparative Statistics

Year Housing Structure Built: City

City	2010 or Later	2000 -2009	1990 -1999	1980 -1989	1970 -1979	1960 -1969	1950 -1959	1940 -1949	Before 1940	Median Year
Albuquerque, NM	4.3	16.3	15.3	15.5	19.6	10.3	11.5	4.4	2.8	1981
Allentown, PA	2.1	5.0	3.8	5.5	10.6	12.1	16.1	7.2	37.6	1953
Anchorage, AK	3.5	12.2	11.6	26.4	28.2	10.8	6.0	1.0	0.3	1981
Ann Arbor, MI	3.7	6.3	10.8	10.8	17.2	18.2	12.6	5.0	15.6	1969
Athens, GA	3.8	17.7	20.3	15.6	16.5	12.2	6.6	2.4	4.8	1985
Atlanta, GA	8.1	22.3	10.6	7.9	8.4	12.6	11.7	6.1	12.3	1979
Austin, TX	12.8	18.1	15.7	19.6	15.9	7.6	4.9	2.6	2.8	1988
Baton Rouge, LA	5.9	9.9	8.7	12.9	22.4	17.3	11.7	5.9	5.3	1974
Boise City, ID	6.5	11.9	22.5	15.0	19.2	7.1	7.1	4.4	6.2	1984
Boston, MA	5.0	6.5	4.2	5.9	7.9	7.8	7.3	5.8	49.6	1941
Boulder, CO	6.2	7.7	11.2	17.3	21.5	18.3	8.1	2.0	7.6	1976
Cape Coral, FL	3.8	37.8	17.8	22.9	11.9	4.7	0.8	0.2	0.1	1995
Cedar Rapids, IA	6.9	11.1	13.0	8.2	14.4	13.9	12.3	4.2	16.0	1972
Charleston, SC	12.3	20.3	12.8	13.8	10.2	8.3	6.1	4.1	12.2	1987
Charlotte, NC	8.9	23.1	19.4	15.1	12.0	9.5	6.6	2.6	2.8	1991
Chicago, IL	2.6	8.0	4.9	4.3	7.5	9.7	11.9	9.3	41.8	1949
Cincinnati, OH	2.3	3.7	4.2	5.3	9.9	13.0	12.2	8.1	41.2	1951
Clarksville, TN	13.0	22.8	20.9	13.2	12.4	8.6	4.7	2.5	2.0	1993
Cleveland, OH	1.7	3.8	3.2	2.4	5.4	7.1	12.5	11.3	52.6	<1940
College Station, TX	16.2	24.0	19.8	16.0	16.5	4.0	2.2	0.7	0.6	1995
Colorado Springs, CO	6.5	15.7	15.9	18.6	18.3	10.2	7.1	1.9	5.8	1984
Columbia, MO	12.6	21.5	17.9	12.0	12.5	10.7	5.1	2.2	5.5	1991
Columbia, SC	6.1	15.8	11.6	8.9	10.1	11.9	13.6	11.2	10.8	1972
Columbus, OH	5.9	11.4	15.4	13.0	15.0	12.0	10.8	5.0	11.6	1977
Dallas, TX	7.1	10.6	10.3	17.2	17.3	13.4	13.7	5.2	5.2	1977
Davenport, IA	3.4	8.6	7.9	5.9	15.7	13.3	11.2	5.6	28.5	1964
Denver, CO	9.0	11.3	6.6	7.4	14.2	10.9	15.0	6.6	18.9	1969
Des Moines, IA	3.2	7.3	6.5	6.4	13.4	10.5	15.2	8.2	29.3	1958
Durham, NC	11.6	21.0	16.3	15.4	10.5	8.8	6.6	3.8	6.1	1989
Edison, NJ	1.7	4.7	9.3	23.3	13.6	20.3	17.4	4.5	5.1	1972
El Paso, TX	9.8	15.2	13.4	14.0	16.5	10.8	11.5	4.1	4.6	1982
Fargo, ND	16.1	15.8	16.5	13.8	14.0	6.0	6.9	2.6	8.2	1989
Fayetteville, NC	6.9	11.9	18.1	16.9	21.6	13.2	6.6	2.9	1.8	1982
Fort Collins, CO	10.2	17.5	21.3	15.2	18.8	7.1	3.2	1.6	5.2	1989
Fort Wayne, IN	1.5	6.6	14.3	11.7	16.7	15.0	12.2	6.6	15.3	1970
Fort Worth, TX	9.9	24.5	11.5	13.2	9.8	8.2	11.3	5.3	6.3	1987
Grand Rapids, MI	2.5	4.2	6.1	7.0	8.5	10.3	15.7	8.9	36.8	1953
Greeley, CO	6.3	19.3	15.7	10.1	21.2	10.3	6.7	2.6	7.8	1982
Green Bay, WI	1.6	7.6	10.3	12.9	17.8	13.1	15.0	5.7	16.0	1970
Greensboro, NC	5.2	15.0	17.9	16.6	14.4	11.2	10.2	3.8	5.5	1983
Honolulu, HI	4.2	6.9	7.9	9.5	25.3	22.8	12.8	5.5	5.1	1971
Houston, TX	8.6	13.4	9.9	14.6	21.1	13.4	10.3	4.5	4.3	1978
Huntsville, AL	11.8	12.9	10.8	15.6	13.2	21.0	9.5	2.4	2.8	1981
Indianapolis, IN	3.4	9.2	13.2	12.1	13.5	13.1	12.7	6.1	16.8	1971
Jacksonville, FL	6.2	19.3	15.3	15.5	12.7	10.0	11.1	4.8	5.1	1984
Kansas City, MO	4.6	9.9	9.3	8.6	12.0	12.7	14.3	6.3	22.1	1966
Lafayette, LA	7.2	13.3	10.4	18.0	21.7	13.4	9.0	3.9	3.1	1979
Lakeland, FL	3.4	15.1	13.2	19.6	20.2	10.4	8.8	3.3	6.0	1981
Las Vegas, NV	5.2	23.0	32.0	16.6	9.9	7.4	4.2	1.3	0.5	1993
Lexington, KY	6.1	15.5	15.8	14.0	15.0	13.5	9.7	3.1	7.3	1981
Lincoln, NE	7.3	13.7	15.0	10.4	15.3	10.0	11.2	3.0	14.0	1978
Little Rock, AR	6.2	11.2	11.2	14.3	19.6	15.2	9.9	5.2	7.1	1976
Los Angeles, CA	3.2	5.6	5.7	10.2	13.7	14.1	17.4	9.8	20.3	1962
Louisville, KY	4.3	11.0	11.7	6.9	12.7	13.8	14.8	7.4	17.4	1968
Madison, WI	7.1	14.4	13.1	10.9	13.9	11.5	10.4	4.8	14.0	1977

Table continued on following page.

Appendix A: Comparative Statistics   A-117

City	2010 or Later	2000 -2009	1990 -1999	1980 -1989	1970 -1979	1960 -1969	1950 -1959	1940 -1949	Before 1940	Median Year
Manchester, NH	1.9	6.7	8.1	15.9	10.4	7.9	10.3	6.1	32.6	1961
Memphis, TN	2.0	7.0	10.0	12.4	18.2	14.9	19.1	8.7	7.7	1970
Miami, FL	7.6	19.0	6.4	8.3	13.3	9.8	14.7	11.7	9.2	1973
Midland, TX	12.9	8.5	13.8	18.4	11.7	11.6	18.5	3.0	1.5	1982
Milwaukee, WI	1.5	3.3	2.9	3.9	8.7	11.1	20.2	9.8	38.6	1951
Minneapolis, MN	5.8	6.7	3.6	6.8	9.0	7.5	9.5	6.8	44.3	1948
Nashville, TN	9.3	14.6	12.4	15.3	14.8	12.2	10.6	4.5	6.2	1981
New Haven, CT	3.1	4.8	2.6	7.1	8.0	9.7	9.4	7.5	47.7	1943
New Orleans, LA	3.4	7.1	3.5	7.3	13.7	11.1	12.1	7.7	34.0	1957
New York, NY	2.8	5.6	3.7	4.8	7.1	12.5	13.0	9.9	40.6	1949
Oklahoma City, OK	9.4	13.1	9.5	14.9	16.1	12.6	10.6	5.5	8.4	1978
Omaha, NE	3.4	7.4	13.0	11.0	15.6	14.6	11.1	4.2	19.7	1970
Orlando, FL	9.6	21.6	16.3	16.9	13.9	7.2	8.6	2.9	3.0	1989
Peoria, IL	3.3	8.7	7.4	6.8	15.2	12.5	14.0	7.9	24.3	1963
Philadelphia, PA	2.7	3.0	3.2	3.7	7.1	10.7	16.3	11.6	41.7	1947
Phoenix, AZ	4.3	16.7	16.3	17.1	19.6	11.7	10.1	2.5	1.8	1983
Pittsburgh, PA	2.3	3.0	3.5	4.4	6.7	8.7	12.6	8.9	49.8	1940
Portland, OR	5.8	10.5	8.8	6.4	10.7	9.2	12.0	8.2	28.3	1962
Providence, RI	0.6	4.5	3.7	5.5	9.2	5.9	7.6	6.8	56.2	<1940
Provo, UT	4.6	11.8	21.1	14.3	17.7	10.4	7.6	5.1	7.3	1981
Raleigh, NC	10.7	25.0	19.0	17.3	10.6	7.7	4.5	2.1	3.1	1992
Reno, NV	6.2	19.7	19.2	13.9	18.3	9.5	7.2	3.0	3.0	1987
Richmond, VA	4.0	5.4	4.9	6.3	11.3	12.4	15.0	9.1	31.7	1956
Riverside, CA	2.8	11.5	10.6	16.4	18.4	12.1	16.0	5.0	7.2	1975
Rochester, MN	8.9	18.3	14.3	14.6	13.0	10.1	9.6	3.3	7.9	1984
Sacramento, CA	2.3	15.7	8.9	15.7	14.6	11.7	12.4	7.9	10.9	1975
Salt Lake City, UT	5.3	6.6	7.4	7.7	12.1	10.0	13.2	8.7	29.1	1959
San Antonio, TX	7.3	15.9	13.7	16.6	15.0	10.2	10.1	5.7	5.6	1982
San Diego, CA	3.9	10.3	11.4	17.7	21.2	12.5	12.1	4.3	6.7	1977
San Francisco, CA	3.7	6.6	4.3	5.3	7.6	8.2	8.4	9.1	46.8	1944
San Jose, CA	5.2	9.3	10.6	12.9	24.2	18.6	11.0	3.0	5.2	1975
Santa Rosa, CA	2.9	12.4	13.0	19.4	21.8	11.8	8.2	4.9	5.6	1979
Savannah, GA	6.3	11.3	7.4	9.8	12.7	12.6	15.0	8.1	16.7	1968
Seattle, WA	10.4	13.2	8.3	7.9	8.2	8.7	9.8	8.3	25.2	1968
Sioux Falls, SD	13.3	18.3	15.1	10.5	13.8	7.3	9.1	3.8	8.6	1987
Springfield, IL	2.3	8.8	12.6	9.6	16.5	12.7	11.3	7.0	19.2	1970
Tallahassee, FL	3.9	18.2	20.8	17.7	18.0	9.2	7.5	3.2	1.5	1986
Tampa, FL	7.8	17.9	12.4	11.8	11.9	10.0	14.4	5.2	8.7	1980
Tucson, AZ	2.6	12.6	13.4	16.2	21.4	11.5	14.8	3.9	3.7	1978
Tulsa, OK	3.6	6.1	9.5	13.3	21.0	14.4	16.8	6.4	9.0	1972
Tuscaloosa, AL	12.9	17.6	15.5	11.5	13.7	10.4	8.8	5.2	4.3	1987
Virginia Beach, VA	4.9	10.8	13.7	27.9	21.4	12.8	6.1	1.3	1.1	1983
Washington, DC	7.3	8.1	3.3	4.4	7.1	11.4	12.6	11.7	34.1	1953
Wichita, KS	4.2	10.2	12.9	12.5	12.8	9.3	20.0	7.4	10.7	1972
Winston-Salem, NC	4.7	14.0	12.1	14.3	16.7	13.6	11.8	5.4	7.4	1977
U.S.	5.2	14.0	13.9	13.4	15.2	10.6	10.3	4.9	12.6	1978

Note: Figures are percentages except for Median Year
Source: U.S. Census Bureau, 2015-2019 American Community Survey 5-Year Estimates

A-118   Appendix A: Comparative Statistics

Year Housing Structure Built: Metro Area

Metro Area	2010 or Later	2000 -2009	1990 -1999	1980 -1989	1970 -1979	1960 -1969	1950 -1959	1940 -1949	Before 1940	Median Year
Albuquerque, NM	4.2	17.6	18.2	17.0	18.0	9.2	9.1	3.7	3.0	1984
Allentown, PA	3.0	11.5	10.6	11.1	12.0	9.7	11.2	5.3	25.5	1968
Anchorage, AK	4.5	17.2	13.0	25.7	24.4	9.0	5.0	0.9	0.4	1984
Ann Arbor, MI	3.7	13.2	17.0	11.5	16.1	12.6	10.1	4.2	11.8	1977
Athens, GA	5.0	18.1	21.7	17.4	15.3	10.1	5.5	2.0	5.0	1987
Atlanta, GA	6.2	24.3	21.5	17.7	13.0	7.6	4.8	1.9	2.9	1991
Austin, TX	16.4	25.1	18.1	16.4	11.6	4.9	3.3	1.8	2.3	1995
Baton Rouge, LA	9.4	19.8	14.6	15.0	17.4	10.2	6.9	2.9	3.9	1986
Boise City, ID	10.5	24.6	21.4	10.3	16.2	4.7	4.4	3.0	4.9	1993
Boston, MA	4.0	7.6	7.4	10.4	11.2	10.2	10.8	5.3	33.2	1961
Boulder, CO	6.5	12.1	19.3	17.2	20.8	11.6	4.6	1.5	6.4	1983
Cape Coral, FL	5.6	31.3	17.7	21.4	14.8	5.5	2.5	0.5	0.7	1993
Cedar Rapids, IA	6.8	14.2	14.6	7.5	13.4	12.3	9.9	3.6	17.7	1975
Charleston, SC	11.9	21.4	16.6	16.4	14.2	8.2	5.2	2.4	3.6	1990
Charlotte, NC	9.2	24.1	19.5	13.5	11.5	8.4	6.5	3.1	4.2	1991
Chicago, IL	2.4	11.5	11.1	9.0	14.2	11.6	13.0	6.1	21.0	1968
Cincinnati, OH	3.7	12.4	14.4	10.7	13.8	10.7	11.9	4.9	17.6	1974
Clarksville, TN	10.7	20.0	20.9	12.1	15.2	9.2	6.2	2.5	3.1	1991
Cleveland, OH	2.3	7.1	8.7	6.8	12.4	13.4	18.1	7.6	23.7	1960
College Station, TX	12.7	21.0	17.7	17.0	15.8	6.1	5.2	2.0	2.4	1991
Colorado Springs, CO	7.6	18.8	16.9	17.5	17.0	8.9	6.5	1.6	5.2	1986
Columbia, MO	9.5	19.4	18.0	12.8	15.4	10.1	5.3	2.5	7.2	1988
Columbia, SC	8.0	19.5	18.5	14.3	15.9	9.7	7.0	3.3	3.8	1987
Columbus, OH	5.8	14.2	16.5	11.7	14.4	11.1	10.2	4.1	12.2	1979
Dallas, TX	10.0	20.0	16.1	18.1	14.2	8.7	7.5	2.7	2.7	1988
Davenport, IA	3.6	7.5	8.3	6.4	16.6	13.4	11.9	7.1	25.2	1964
Denver, CO	7.4	16.4	15.2	14.2	18.6	9.3	9.2	2.8	6.8	1982
Des Moines, IA	10.4	16.7	12.6	8.7	13.6	8.6	9.1	4.2	16.1	1979
Durham, NC	9.3	19.7	18.7	15.8	12.4	9.2	6.4	3.0	5.6	1989
Edison, NJ	2.8	6.7	6.1	7.7	9.8	13.7	15.9	8.8	28.6	1958
El Paso, TX	11.0	16.5	14.6	14.5	15.7	9.7	10.1	3.6	4.2	1985
Fargo, ND	15.1	18.4	14.2	11.2	14.9	6.9	7.4	2.7	9.1	1988
Fayetteville, NC	9.3	17.9	21.7	14.5	16.4	9.6	5.6	2.4	2.5	1989
Fort Collins, CO	10.3	18.8	20.1	13.5	19.1	7.1	3.6	1.7	5.8	1989
Fort Wayne, IN	3.8	11.0	15.2	10.9	15.2	13.0	10.8	5.4	14.7	1974
Fort Worth, TX	10.0	20.0	16.1	18.1	14.2	8.7	7.5	2.7	2.7	1988
Grand Rapids, MI	4.7	12.4	16.3	12.1	14.0	9.5	10.4	5.0	15.7	1977
Greeley, CO	10.9	28.6	16.3	7.4	15.2	6.2	4.4	2.4	8.6	1994
Green Bay, WI	5.2	15.0	16.4	12.4	15.4	9.6	9.3	4.2	12.4	1979
Greensboro, NC	5.0	15.9	18.9	14.5	14.7	10.9	9.5	4.5	6.1	1983
Honolulu, HI	5.1	10.2	11.5	12.2	24.1	18.9	10.7	4.0	3.3	1975
Houston, TX	11.9	21.5	14.4	15.5	16.9	8.4	6.2	2.6	2.4	1989
Huntsville, AL	10.8	19.7	17.8	16.1	11.3	13.7	6.4	1.9	2.2	1989
Indianapolis, IN	6.5	15.5	16.7	10.6	12.5	10.6	10.3	4.4	12.8	1979
Jacksonville, FL	8.6	22.7	16.6	16.6	12.4	8.0	8.0	3.4	3.9	1989
Kansas City, MO	4.8	13.7	14.5	12.3	15.4	11.6	11.4	4.4	11.8	1977
Lafayette, LA	9.5	16.6	12.9	15.5	16.4	10.4	9.3	4.1	5.2	1983
Lakeland, FL	5.8	23.8	17.7	18.2	15.1	7.7	6.5	2.1	3.2	1989
Las Vegas, NV	7.2	30.1	29.1	14.6	10.6	5.1	2.2	0.7	0.4	1996
Lexington, KY	6.4	17.2	17.0	13.9	14.8	11.5	8.0	3.3	7.9	1983
Lincoln, NE	7.3	14.1	15.1	10.1	15.6	10.0	10.3	2.8	14.7	1978
Little Rock, AR	9.3	18.2	16.7	13.7	17.0	10.8	7.1	3.4	3.7	1986
Los Angeles, CA	2.9	6.1	7.6	12.3	16.1	15.9	18.7	8.4	11.9	1967
Louisville, KY	4.4	13.1	14.2	9.2	15.2	12.4	12.6	6.2	12.8	1974
Madison, WI	6.5	16.2	15.6	11.1	15.0	9.6	7.8	3.5	14.6	1980

Table continued on following page.

Appendix A: Comparative Statistics   A-119

Metro Area	2010 or Later	2000 -2009	1990 -1999	1980 -1989	1970 -1979	1960 -1969	1950 -1959	1940 -1949	Before 1940	Median Year
Manchester, NH	3.0	10.1	10.3	20.9	15.3	9.6	7.1	3.7	19.9	1976
Memphis, TN	4.2	15.7	17.1	13.7	16.2	10.8	11.9	5.3	5.1	1980
Miami, FL	4.1	13.0	15.1	19.4	21.4	12.3	9.8	2.8	2.1	1981
Midland, TX	14.0	11.4	14.5	18.0	11.2	10.5	15.9	2.8	1.7	1984
Milwaukee, WI	2.7	8.2	10.8	8.0	13.0	11.5	16.3	6.8	22.9	1964
Minneapolis, MN	5.1	14.3	14.4	14.5	14.7	9.8	9.7	3.7	13.9	1979
Nashville, TN	10.7	19.7	17.8	14.3	13.6	9.2	6.9	3.1	4.7	1989
New Haven, CT	1.8	5.6	7.1	12.3	13.3	12.3	15.2	7.1	25.2	1962
New Orleans, LA	3.8	11.9	9.8	13.3	19.3	13.6	10.1	4.8	13.5	1974
New York, NY	2.8	6.7	6.1	7.7	9.8	13.7	15.9	8.8	28.6	1958
Oklahoma City, OK	9.3	15.0	11.1	14.8	17.2	12.0	9.6	4.8	6.2	1980
Omaha, NE	6.8	14.3	13.0	9.9	14.6	12.0	8.7	3.4	17.2	1976
Orlando, FL	8.8	23.8	20.6	20.2	12.8	5.9	5.2	1.2	1.5	1992
Peoria, IL	3.1	9.0	8.6	6.0	17.3	12.3	14.3	8.0	21.4	1965
Philadelphia, PA	3.1	7.8	9.6	10.0	12.1	11.9	15.7	7.5	22.2	1964
Phoenix, AZ	6.6	25.4	20.3	17.2	16.1	7.3	5.1	1.2	0.9	1991
Pittsburgh, PA	2.8	6.5	7.7	7.5	11.9	11.5	16.7	8.9	26.4	1959
Portland, OR	6.3	14.5	18.6	11.3	17.2	8.4	7.1	4.6	11.9	1981
Providence, RI	1.9	6.3	8.1	11.1	12.2	11.0	11.6	6.6	31.4	1960
Provo, UT	14.0	25.9	19.2	9.3	13.6	5.0	5.4	3.1	4.6	1995
Raleigh, NC	12.7	25.9	23.0	15.2	9.3	5.9	3.7	1.6	2.8	1995
Reno, NV	5.5	21.1	20.6	15.2	18.9	8.9	5.3	2.2	2.3	1988
Richmond, VA	5.9	14.9	15.3	16.1	15.1	9.7	9.4	4.3	9.2	1981
Riverside, CA	4.2	20.5	14.6	21.9	15.7	8.9	8.5	2.8	2.8	1985
Rochester, MN	7.0	18.0	14.3	12.1	13.5	9.0	8.0	3.4	14.6	1981
Sacramento, CA	3.5	17.6	15.1	16.6	18.3	10.9	10.0	3.7	4.2	1982
Salt Lake City, UT	8.9	15.5	15.5	12.6	18.4	8.8	8.7	3.6	8.0	1982
San Antonio, TX	11.4	20.2	14.5	15.4	13.5	8.4	7.7	4.2	4.6	1988
San Diego, CA	3.7	12.0	12.5	18.6	22.6	12.2	10.7	3.5	4.2	1979
San Francisco, CA	3.2	7.7	8.2	11.1	14.9	13.4	13.7	7.8	19.9	1966
San Jose, CA	5.6	9.0	10.6	12.6	21.6	18.0	13.9	3.6	5.1	1974
Santa Rosa, CA	2.5	10.6	13.6	18.6	21.0	11.6	8.5	5.0	8.4	1978
Savannah, GA	9.0	20.7	16.3	13.8	12.0	7.8	8.1	4.3	8.0	1987
Seattle, WA	7.7	15.2	15.5	14.4	14.2	11.0	7.4	4.4	10.1	1982
Sioux Falls, SD	11.9	18.7	15.3	9.5	14.0	6.8	8.1	3.7	12.1	1986
Springfield, IL	3.1	9.9	13.2	9.1	16.9	11.9	11.6	6.7	17.5	1971
Tallahassee, FL	4.0	18.7	22.6	19.2	16.2	8.3	6.6	2.6	1.7	1988
Tampa, FL	5.6	16.4	14.1	20.1	21.0	9.5	8.5	2.0	2.7	1983
Tucson, AZ	4.5	18.6	17.5	17.8	19.6	8.5	8.9	2.5	2.2	1985
Tulsa, OK	6.7	14.4	12.7	14.3	19.3	10.5	10.6	4.5	7.0	1979
Tuscaloosa, AL	9.2	18.7	18.7	14.2	14.6	9.7	7.1	4.0	3.9	1988
Virginia Beach, VA	6.0	12.7	15.2	18.9	15.8	11.8	9.7	4.2	5.7	1981
Washington, DC	6.7	14.5	14.4	15.8	14.0	12.0	9.4	4.9	8.3	1981
Wichita, KS	4.7	11.9	14.1	12.2	13.3	8.5	17.9	6.0	11.3	1975
Winston-Salem, NC	4.5	15.6	17.2	15.7	16.7	10.9	8.9	4.3	6.3	1982
U.S.	5.2	14.0	13.9	13.4	15.2	10.6	10.3	4.9	12.6	1978

Note: Figures are percentages except for Median Year; Figures cover the Metropolitan Statistical Area—see Appendix B for areas included
Source: U.S. Census Bureau, 2015-2019 American Community Survey 5-Year Estimates

A-120 Appendix A: Comparative Statistics

Gross Monthly Rent: City

City	Under $500	$500 -$999	$1,000 -$1,499	$1,500 -$1,999	$2,000 -$2,499	$2,500 -$2,999	$3,000 and up	Median ($)
Albuquerque, NM	8.1	54.4	29.1	6.5	1.1	0.3	0.4	873
Allentown, PA	10.0	39.6	38.7	10.0	1.4	0.3	0.0	1,004
Anchorage, AK	4.0	21.8	36.9	19.9	11.7	4.1	1.4	1,320
Ann Arbor, MI	4.6	23.6	39.5	19.8	7.3	2.4	2.8	1,237
Athens, GA	7.9	59.5	24.2	6.6	1.4	0.2	0.1	856
Atlanta, GA	11.3	27.5	33.6	18.8	5.6	1.7	1.5	1,153
Austin, TX	3.1	18.1	45.2	22.4	7.1	2.3	1.8	1,280
Baton Rouge, LA	10.1	54.4	25.7	5.9	3.2	0.5	0.3	879
Boise City, ID	5.6	50.5	34.7	6.9	1.4	0.3	0.7	957
Boston, MA	16.5	11.4	16.6	22.7	15.3	8.2	9.3	1,620
Boulder, CO	2.8	9.4	35.1	25.4	14.8	5.5	6.9	1,554
Cape Coral, FL	0.9	22.4	46.8	22.5	5.0	1.0	1.4	1,244
Cedar Rapids, IA	15.8	61.0	20.2	1.5	0.6	0.3	0.7	767
Charleston, SC	6.4	20.8	40.8	22.1	5.9	1.8	2.2	1,257
Charlotte, NC	3.8	30.9	46.3	14.5	2.9	0.8	0.7	1,135
Chicago, IL	9.6	31.9	31.5	15.2	6.7	3.0	2.1	1,112
Cincinnati, OH	19.1	56.0	18.0	4.5	1.3	0.4	0.7	738
Clarksville, TN	5.8	48.7	35.6	7.8	1.8	0.1	0.1	961
Cleveland, OH	21.9	58.1	15.8	2.7	0.9	0.3	0.2	719
College Station, TX	3.2	48.7	27.6	14.1	5.0	1.0	0.5	983
Colorado Springs, CO	3.9	34.3	38.3	17.5	3.5	1.8	0.7	1,131
Columbia, MO	6.1	58.0	26.4	5.7	3.3	0.3	0.2	887
Columbia, SC	10.1	48.2	31.9	7.6	1.6	0.1	0.5	933
Columbus, OH	6.4	48.7	35.7	7.1	1.5	0.4	0.3	961
Dallas, TX	4.3	41.0	36.7	11.7	3.6	1.4	1.1	1,052
Davenport, IA	9.2	68.6	16.4	3.2	0.8	0.7	1.1	771
Denver, CO	8.2	18.4	35.8	23.2	9.6	3.2	1.6	1,311
Des Moines, IA	8.6	61.1	25.1	4.1	0.9	0.2	0.1	855
Durham, NC	7.4	36.4	42.6	10.3	2.0	0.5	0.8	1,058
Edison, NJ	2.8	5.8	39.4	35.3	13.2	2.6	0.9	1,528
El Paso, TX	15.2	53.4	25.4	4.9	0.5	0.3	0.2	837
Fargo, ND	7.0	65.6	20.7	5.3	1.1	0.2	0.1	823
Fayetteville, NC	5.6	51.7	36.6	5.2	0.7	0.2	0.1	947
Fort Collins, CO	2.9	20.0	39.7	26.3	9.1	1.4	0.7	1,346
Fort Wayne, IN	11.5	71.0	15.0	1.5	0.7	0.2	0.1	764
Fort Worth, TX	4.9	39.7	35.0	15.5	3.1	0.9	0.9	1,060
Grand Rapids, MI	10.2	48.9	31.0	6.5	2.8	0.5	0.1	925
Greeley, CO	9.2	40.3	32.2	14.0	3.2	0.6	0.5	1,007
Green Bay, WI	12.0	71.3	15.4	1.0	0.1	0.1	0.2	730
Greensboro, NC	6.8	61.7	26.0	3.4	1.2	0.4	0.5	877
Honolulu, HI	6.9	13.3	30.4	22.3	11.3	6.7	9.2	1,491
Houston, TX	3.8	42.7	34.6	12.8	3.3	1.4	1.4	1,041
Huntsville, AL	11.3	59.9	24.2	3.2	0.5	0.6	0.4	827
Indianapolis, IN	6.2	58.7	28.2	5.3	1.0	0.2	0.3	892
Jacksonville, FL	6.6	36.6	42.2	11.8	2.2	0.3	0.4	1,065
Kansas City, MO	8.7	48.0	33.8	7.2	1.5	0.5	0.4	941
Lafayette, LA	9.9	54.6	27.8	6.1	1.3	0.3	0.1	890
Lakeland, FL	5.6	44.6	39.6	7.9	1.4	0.6	0.3	999
Las Vegas, NV	4.7	35.4	41.8	13.8	2.9	0.8	0.6	1,102
Lexington, KY	8.1	52.5	30.6	5.8	2.2	0.4	0.3	896
Lincoln, NE	9.5	58.4	25.0	4.9	0.8	0.3	1.0	852
Little Rock, AR	9.9	54.3	29.0	4.8	0.8	0.6	0.6	872
Los Angeles, CA	5.3	15.7	32.0	22.6	12.4	6.1	5.9	1,450
Louisville, KY	13.7	54.1	25.9	4.9	0.7	0.4	0.3	846
Madison, WI	3.4	34.3	42.0	13.9	4.1	1.3	1.0	1,118

Table continued on following page.

Appendix A: Comparative Statistics   A-121

City	Under $500	$500 -$999	$1,000 -$1,499	$1,500 -$1,999	$2,000 -$2,499	$2,500 -$2,999	$3,000 and up	Median ($)
Manchester, NH	7.4	28.2	45.1	15.4	2.5	0.7	0.6	1,135
Memphis, TN	8.1	54.6	31.2	4.7	0.9	0.2	0.2	901
Miami, FL	10.7	26.3	30.0	17.0	9.3	3.8	2.9	1,183
Midland, TX	1.7	26.0	41.3	19.5	7.5	2.9	1.2	1,262
Milwaukee, WI	9.1	60.2	24.2	4.7	1.2	0.4	0.2	858
Minneapolis, MN	12.8	35.3	30.2	14.4	4.7	1.4	1.1	1,027
Nashville, TN	8.7	31.5	39.8	14.1	4.0	1.1	0.8	1,100
New Haven, CT	13.3	18.7	41.2	19.5	5.1	1.5	0.8	1,196
New Orleans, LA	12.8	37.4	33.7	11.5	3.0	0.9	0.6	998
New York, NY	10.6	14.6	28.1	22.1	11.0	5.6	8.0	1,443
Oklahoma City, OK	8.1	57.1	27.0	6.0	1.2	0.4	0.4	871
Omaha, NE	7.7	51.6	31.4	7.0	1.3	0.3	0.7	923
Orlando, FL	3.7	24.7	48.8	17.6	4.0	0.8	0.4	1,196
Peoria, IL	15.6	58.0	20.6	3.7	1.0	0.3	0.9	806
Philadelphia, PA	11.0	35.4	34.7	11.6	4.4	1.5	1.3	1,042
Phoenix, AZ	4.5	40.2	40.2	11.5	2.4	0.6	0.5	1,053
Pittsburgh, PA	13.6	40.7	28.8	11.2	4.0	1.0	0.7	958
Portland, OR	6.5	22.1	38.1	20.9	8.1	2.7	1.6	1,248
Providence, RI	19.5	31.1	35.2	9.8	2.6	0.7	1.1	994
Provo, UT	12.8	49.7	24.3	10.2	2.3	0.5	0.2	877
Raleigh, NC	3.9	31.6	47.0	13.2	3.0	0.5	0.8	1,121
Reno, NV	5.6	42.2	33.7	14.3	3.2	0.5	0.6	1,029
Richmond, VA	12.6	35.0	37.0	11.7	2.7	0.3	0.6	1,025
Riverside, CA	3.4	16.0	39.3	28.9	9.9	1.8	0.7	1,378
Rochester, MN	9.1	43.7	30.2	13.0	1.7	0.9	1.3	974
Sacramento, CA	5.9	24.1	38.5	23.4	6.1	1.4	0.6	1,263
Salt Lake City, UT	8.9	42.8	31.8	12.5	3.1	0.6	0.4	985
San Antonio, TX	7.6	43.3	36.4	10.0	1.7	0.4	0.6	992
San Diego, CA	3.4	10.2	25.9	26.9	18.7	8.9	6.0	1,695
San Francisco, CA	9.3	13.0	15.6	15.3	13.6	11.7	21.4	1,895
San Jose, CA	4.5	6.9	13.6	20.9	19.2	16.2	18.7	2,107
Santa Rosa, CA	5.4	8.4	30.1	27.8	18.2	6.9	3.2	1,609
Savannah, GA	10.0	38.1	39.8	8.9	1.8	0.5	1.0	1,019
Seattle, WA	6.5	10.0	27.1	28.0	14.9	7.0	6.4	1,614
Sioux Falls, SD	8.5	65.9	19.8	4.0	0.6	0.5	0.8	827
Springfield, IL	12.4	62.3	19.5	3.4	1.1	1.1	0.2	805
Tallahassee, FL	5.3	42.2	39.8	8.5	3.2	0.6	0.3	1,023
Tampa, FL	8.1	30.2	37.6	16.0	4.8	1.9	1.5	1,131
Tucson, AZ	7.9	57.2	27.6	5.4	1.1	0.4	0.5	846
Tulsa, OK	10.9	59.4	24.1	3.6	1.0	0.5	0.6	829
Tuscaloosa, AL	13.1	57.0	22.2	4.6	1.9	0.3	1.0	844
Virginia Beach, VA	3.2	12.0	47.9	26.8	6.9	1.7	1.6	1,367
Washington, DC	10.4	13.2	24.7	21.1	13.6	8.2	8.9	1,541
Wichita, KS	11.6	61.3	22.4	3.3	0.6	0.2	0.7	809
Winston-Salem, NC	10.9	62.6	21.5	3.5	0.9	0.2	0.4	806
U.S.	9.4	36.2	30.0	14.0	5.6	2.4	2.4	1,062

Note: Figures are percentages except for Median; Gross rent is the contract rent plus the estimated average monthly cost of utilities (electricity, gas, and water and sewer) and fuels (oil, coal, kerosene, wood, etc.) if these are paid by the renter (or paid for the renter by someone else).

Source: U.S. Census Bureau, 2015-2019 American Community Survey 5-Year Estimates

A-122 Appendix A: Comparative Statistics

Gross Monthly Rent: Metro Area

MSA[1]	Under $500	$500 -$999	$1,000 -$1,499	$1,500 -$1,999	$2,000 -$2,499	$2,500 -2,999	$3,000 and up	Median ($)
Albuquerque, NM	8.0	52.5	30.1	7.5	1.1	0.3	0.4	892
Allentown, PA	9.5	34.3	38.5	13.6	2.6	0.7	0.8	1,066
Anchorage, AK	4.2	23.2	37.1	19.7	10.8	3.7	1.3	1,288
Ann Arbor, MI	5.5	33.9	37.6	14.7	4.5	1.6	2.2	1,114
Athens, GA	8.4	59.5	23.6	6.2	1.5	0.5	0.2	853
Atlanta, GA	4.8	28.9	45.0	16.1	3.4	0.9	0.8	1,156
Austin, TX	3.1	19.4	44.5	22.7	6.7	2.1	1.6	1,273
Baton Rouge, LA	8.9	50.9	29.0	7.6	2.9	0.4	0.3	922
Boise City, ID	8.2	47.3	34.8	7.4	1.6	0.4	0.5	958
Boston, MA	12.4	13.4	25.6	23.5	13.2	6.1	5.8	1,475
Boulder, CO	4.0	11.7	34.6	27.2	13.3	5.0	4.2	1,495
Cape Coral, FL	4.2	29.8	43.3	14.3	4.8	1.6	2.0	1,154
Cedar Rapids, IA	16.9	60.9	18.9	1.9	0.5	0.3	0.7	753
Charleston, SC	6.1	29.6	40.2	17.0	4.2	1.5	1.4	1,156
Charlotte, NC	6.1	41.0	37.9	11.2	2.4	0.8	0.6	1,030
Chicago, IL	7.7	32.0	34.9	15.8	5.8	2.2	1.7	1,122
Cincinnati, OH	12.3	54.7	24.8	5.7	1.5	0.4	0.7	842
Clarksville, TN	8.7	49.9	32.7	7.3	1.3	0.2	0.0	919
Cleveland, OH	13.0	57.6	23.2	4.3	1.1	0.3	0.5	817
College Station, TX	6.3	51.7	26.5	10.6	3.6	0.8	0.5	935
Colorado Springs, CO	3.8	31.8	36.9	21.1	4.0	1.8	0.6	1,173
Columbia, MO	7.9	59.1	25.3	4.5	2.8	0.3	0.2	862
Columbia, SC	7.6	50.4	32.4	7.2	1.5	0.5	0.4	933
Columbus, OH	7.6	48.3	34.3	7.3	1.6	0.5	0.4	953
Dallas, TX	3.4	33.2	40.0	16.3	4.7	1.4	1.0	1,139
Davenport, IA	15.1	61.8	17.1	3.9	0.9	0.4	0.8	765
Denver, CO	5.1	16.7	37.2	26.2	10.2	2.9	1.7	1,380
Des Moines, IA	7.3	54.0	30.1	6.2	1.3	0.2	0.7	904
Durham, NC	7.9	38.7	39.1	10.0	2.5	0.6	1.1	1,033
Edison, NJ	9.4	13.9	30.7	23.1	11.0	5.3	6.7	1,439
El Paso, TX	15.0	53.4	25.4	5.2	0.5	0.3	0.2	837
Fargo, ND	8.0	62.0	21.3	6.7	1.4	0.4	0.3	837
Fayetteville, NC	7.3	50.9	33.4	7.2	1.1	0.1	0.1	932
Fort Collins, CO	4.1	23.2	37.4	25.2	7.7	1.7	0.7	1,297
Fort Wayne, IN	11.5	69.3	16.1	2.0	0.8	0.2	0.1	771
Fort Worth, TX	3.4	33.2	40.0	16.3	4.7	1.4	1.0	1,139
Grand Rapids, MI	8.8	56.1	26.7	5.7	1.9	0.3	0.3	884
Greeley, CO	7.7	36.4	33.4	16.3	4.0	1.0	1.2	1,085
Green Bay, WI	9.9	69.3	18.6	1.4	0.3	0.2	0.3	784
Greensboro, NC	9.6	63.4	22.4	2.9	1.0	0.3	0.5	834
Honolulu, HI	5.6	10.4	24.1	20.3	14.1	10.0	15.5	1,745
Houston, TX	3.8	37.0	37.0	15.6	4.0	1.4	1.2	1,101
Huntsville, AL	10.9	59.8	24.0	3.9	0.6	0.5	0.3	836
Indianapolis, IN	6.3	54.7	30.5	6.4	1.4	0.3	0.5	916
Jacksonville, FL	5.9	34.8	41.3	13.6	3.2	0.7	0.6	1,093
Kansas City, MO	8.2	46.4	34.4	8.0	2.0	0.5	0.6	961
Lafayette, LA	15.3	57.0	21.5	4.8	1.2	0.1	0.1	811
Lakeland, FL	6.7	45.8	33.6	11.3	1.8	0.5	0.3	978
Las Vegas, NV	2.8	34.4	42.1	15.9	3.5	0.8	0.6	1,132
Lexington, KY	9.6	55.1	28.1	4.9	1.7	0.3	0.3	867
Lincoln, NE	9.9	58.2	24.9	4.8	0.8	0.4	1.0	848
Little Rock, AR	10.1	58.9	25.0	4.7	0.6	0.4	0.3	845
Los Angeles, CA	4.2	12.7	30.8	25.7	14.0	6.7	5.9	1,545
Louisville, KY	13.1	54.3	26.6	4.6	0.8	0.4	0.3	854
Madison, WI	5.0	40.5	38.5	11.6	2.9	0.9	0.6	1,046

Table continued on following page.

Appendix A: Comparative Statistics   A-123

MSA[1]	Under $500	$500 -$999	$1,000 -$1,499	$1,500 -$1,999	$2,000 -$2,499	$2,500 -2,999	$3,000 and up	Median ($)
Manchester, NH	6.9	24.7	42.8	19.9	4.2	0.9	0.5	1,191
Memphis, TN	7.8	50.9	32.8	6.4	1.5	0.3	0.3	930
Miami, FL	5.2	17.0	37.9	24.5	9.5	3.4	2.4	1,363
Midland, TX	2.0	25.1	41.0	20.1	7.5	3.2	1.1	1,269
Milwaukee, WI	7.7	54.1	28.9	6.7	1.6	0.5	0.3	903
Minneapolis, MN	9.2	32.4	35.9	16.1	4.2	1.2	1.1	1,102
Nashville, TN	8.0	35.2	38.0	13.3	3.6	1.1	0.8	1,073
New Haven, CT	10.4	24.6	41.3	17.0	4.6	1.2	1.0	1,153
New Orleans, LA	9.3	41.9	35.6	10.0	2.2	0.6	0.5	991
New York, NY	9.4	13.9	30.7	23.1	11.0	5.3	6.7	1,439
Oklahoma City, OK	8.2	56.4	27.3	6.2	1.3	0.3	0.4	876
Omaha, NE	8.2	50.7	31.0	7.5	1.4	0.4	0.7	927
Orlando, FL	2.9	25.1	46.3	19.7	4.2	1.1	0.7	1,210
Peoria, IL	16.6	60.9	17.6	2.6	1.0	0.4	1.0	764
Philadelphia, PA	8.1	29.1	38.4	15.9	5.4	1.7	1.4	1,143
Phoenix, AZ	3.6	34.4	40.9	15.4	3.6	1.1	1.1	1,124
Pittsburgh, PA	15.6	51.9	23.2	6.0	1.9	0.6	0.8	831
Portland, OR	4.8	20.9	42.1	21.8	7.1	1.8	1.4	1,271
Providence, RI	16.0	37.6	31.8	10.3	2.8	0.6	0.7	968
Provo, UT	6.6	39.1	33.3	15.8	3.7	0.9	0.6	1,054
Raleigh, NC	4.9	32.8	43.7	13.4	3.4	0.8	1.0	1,113
Reno, NV	4.9	39.3	34.7	15.9	3.7	0.8	0.8	1,074
Richmond, VA	7.3	30.2	44.1	13.9	2.9	0.8	0.8	1,117
Riverside, CA	4.2	22.6	34.7	23.5	9.9	3.7	1.5	1,326
Rochester, MN	11.5	47.5	27.7	10.0	1.5	0.7	0.9	908
Sacramento, CA	4.6	22.7	37.5	23.2	8.1	2.4	1.4	1,290
Salt Lake City, UT	5.4	33.3	41.2	15.4	3.3	0.8	0.7	1,114
San Antonio, TX	7.0	40.8	36.6	11.8	2.3	0.7	0.8	1,024
San Diego, CA	3.5	9.9	28.1	27.2	17.0	8.2	6.2	1,658
San Francisco, CA	6.0	9.4	17.2	21.4	18.2	11.9	15.8	1,905
San Jose, CA	3.5	5.8	11.6	18.8	20.7	17.2	22.4	2,249
Santa Rosa, CA	5.2	10.6	27.7	27.0	17.3	7.6	4.5	1,621
Savannah, GA	7.3	33.4	43.3	12.0	2.8	0.4	0.8	1,086
Seattle, WA	5.1	14.0	31.4	27.7	12.8	5.0	4.0	1,492
Sioux Falls, SD	9.4	64.4	20.0	4.4	0.7	0.4	0.8	829
Springfield, IL	11.4	63.1	19.9	3.6	0.9	0.9	0.2	818
Tallahassee, FL	6.9	44.2	36.9	8.4	2.9	0.5	0.2	991
Tampa, FL	4.9	33.9	40.4	14.9	3.6	1.4	1.0	1,115
Tucson, AZ	7.2	51.4	30.9	7.5	1.6	0.7	0.8	907
Tulsa, OK	10.7	56.8	26.1	4.4	1.0	0.5	0.5	852
Tuscaloosa, AL	17.1	54.6	21.8	4.2	1.5	0.2	0.6	819
Virginia Beach, VA	7.0	26.2	41.2	18.4	4.9	1.3	1.0	1,180
Washington, DC	4.6	7.8	25.4	32.2	16.6	7.3	6.1	1,690
Wichita, KS	11.4	60.3	22.5	4.0	0.9	0.3	0.7	818
Winston-Salem, NC	12.9	63.9	18.9	3.1	0.7	0.2	0.2	773
U.S.	9.4	36.2	30.0	14.0	5.6	2.4	2.4	1,062

Note: (1) Figures cover the Metropolitan Statistical Area (MSA)—see Appendix B for areas included; Figures are percentages except for Median; Gross rent is the contract rent plus the estimated average monthly cost of utilities (electricity, gas, and water and sewer) and fuels (oil, coal, kerosene, wood, etc.) if these are paid by the renter (or paid for the renter by someone else).
Source: U.S. Census Bureau, 2015-2019 American Community Survey 5-Year Estimates

A-124   Appendix A: Comparative Statistics

Highest Level of Education: City

City	Less than H.S.	H.S. Diploma	Some College, No Deg.	Associate Degree	Bachelors Degree	Masters Degree	Profess. School Degree	Doctorate Degree
Albuquerque, NM	10.3	22.5	23.4	8.5	19.4	10.6	2.7	2.5
Allentown, PA	21.0	38.0	18.3	7.4	9.6	3.9	1.0	0.8
Anchorage, AK	6.1	23.4	25.4	9.0	22.2	9.5	3.1	1.3
Ann Arbor, MI	2.7	7.1	10.0	4.2	30.2	26.9	7.1	11.7
Athens, GA	12.1	19.8	17.1	6.9	22.1	13.4	3.0	5.6
Atlanta, GA	9.1	18.9	15.3	4.9	28.9	15.1	5.3	2.5
Austin, TX	10.6	15.6	16.7	5.4	32.3	13.6	3.3	2.5
Baton Rouge, LA	12.0	27.8	22.5	4.5	19.3	8.8	2.6	2.5
Boise City, ID	4.9	21.4	23.1	9.1	26.8	10.1	2.7	1.9
Boston, MA	12.8	19.7	13.1	4.6	27.0	14.5	4.8	3.4
Boulder, CO	3.1	6.2	11.1	3.6	36.2	24.7	6.4	8.7
Cape Coral, FL	8.2	37.3	21.0	10.1	15.8	5.3	1.3	0.9
Cedar Rapids, IA	6.7	26.6	22.2	12.4	22.9	6.6	1.5	1.0
Charleston, SC	5.1	17.6	16.3	7.9	33.8	12.6	4.5	2.2
Charlotte, NC	10.9	17.1	20.0	7.7	28.9	11.7	2.6	1.1
Chicago, IL	14.9	22.5	17.3	5.8	23.3	11.3	3.3	1.6
Cincinnati, OH	11.9	24.4	19.1	7.4	21.4	10.4	3.1	2.1
Clarksville, TN	7.1	27.9	26.9	10.5	18.7	6.9	0.8	1.2
Cleveland, OH	19.2	32.7	23.2	7.4	10.9	4.5	1.4	0.7
College Station, TX	5.6	11.4	17.0	7.4	29.3	15.7	3.3	10.3
Colorado Springs, CO	6.1	20.0	23.4	10.6	24.3	12.0	2.0	1.5
Columbia, MO	4.8	18.1	18.7	6.2	27.4	14.9	4.6	5.3
Columbia, SC	10.6	20.1	18.6	6.9	24.4	12.8	3.9	2.7
Columbus, OH	10.2	25.5	20.6	7.2	23.8	9.4	1.9	1.5
Dallas, TX	22.5	21.7	17.8	4.6	21.0	8.3	2.9	1.1
Davenport, IA	9.5	32.5	21.8	10.7	17.0	6.3	1.5	0.8
Denver, CO	12.0	16.8	16.5	5.3	30.2	13.1	4.2	2.0
Des Moines, IA	13.7	29.5	21.2	8.9	18.6	5.5	1.7	0.9
Durham, NC	11.9	16.4	15.5	6.5	25.8	14.7	4.2	4.8
Edison, NJ	7.9	19.5	11.7	5.4	30.0	20.3	2.8	2.5
El Paso, TX	19.7	23.0	24.0	8.2	16.7	6.4	1.2	0.8
Fargo, ND	5.7	20.9	19.6	13.8	28.0	8.0	2.1	1.8
Fayetteville, NC	8.3	24.4	29.4	10.6	18.0	6.7	1.5	1.0
Fort Collins, CO	3.5	15.1	17.7	8.3	32.3	16.8	2.4	4.0
Fort Wayne, IN	11.5	28.2	22.1	10.3	18.3	7.1	1.4	1.0
Fort Worth, TX	17.8	24.9	20.8	6.9	20.0	7.1	1.5	1.1
Grand Rapids, MI	13.3	21.9	20.5	7.9	24.4	8.7	2.0	1.4
Greeley, CO	15.5	27.2	23.4	9.1	15.4	7.2	1.2	1.0
Green Bay, WI	12.5	31.4	20.1	11.2	17.9	5.1	1.1	0.7
Greensboro, NC	10.2	21.5	21.7	8.4	24.1	10.0	2.3	1.8
Honolulu, HI	11.0	23.5	18.3	10.1	23.7	8.3	3.2	2.0
Houston, TX	21.1	22.8	17.8	5.5	20.0	8.6	2.6	1.6
Huntsville, AL	9.0	18.7	20.3	7.9	26.4	13.8	1.8	2.2
Indianapolis, IN	14.2	27.9	19.4	7.6	20.0	7.6	2.1	1.1
Jacksonville, FL	10.5	28.4	22.3	10.1	19.1	7.0	1.7	0.8
Kansas City, MO	10.0	25.3	22.0	7.4	22.2	9.3	2.5	1.2
Lafayette, LA	10.5	27.0	20.0	4.3	25.6	8.5	2.7	1.4
Lakeland, FL	12.0	33.0	19.5	9.6	16.8	6.7	1.6	0.9
Las Vegas, NV	15.2	27.6	24.6	8.0	16.0	5.9	1.9	0.8
Lexington, KY	8.8	19.6	20.5	7.5	24.4	12.0	4.1	3.2
Lincoln, NE	6.7	21.3	21.2	11.2	24.8	9.8	2.2	2.8
Little Rock, AR	8.7	22.2	21.1	6.2	23.7	11.0	4.3	2.8
Los Angeles, CA	22.5	19.2	17.6	6.2	22.6	7.6	2.8	1.4
Louisville, KY	10.4	28.6	22.9	8.1	17.9	8.5	2.3	1.2
Madison, WI	4.5	14.2	15.3	8.0	32.1	16.2	4.2	5.3

Table continued on following page.

Appendix A: Comparative Statistics   A-125

City	Less than H.S.	H.S. Diploma	Some College, No Deg.	Associate Degree	Bachelors Degree	Masters Degree	Profess. School Degree	Doctorate Degree
Manchester, NH	12.7	29.1	18.9	9.3	20.3	7.3	1.7	0.9
Memphis, TN	14.3	30.6	23.3	5.6	15.7	7.1	2.0	1.3
Miami, FL	22.0	28.4	12.5	7.4	17.9	7.1	3.6	1.1
Midland, TX	14.9	25.2	23.2	7.7	20.7	5.9	1.7	0.7
Milwaukee, WI	16.0	30.2	21.9	7.2	15.9	6.5	1.3	0.9
Minneapolis, MN	10.0	15.1	17.1	7.3	30.4	13.6	4.0	2.5
Nashville, TN	11.2	22.3	18.9	6.4	25.8	10.3	2.9	2.1
New Haven, CT	14.4	32.2	14.0	4.5	15.7	10.7	4.2	4.3
New Orleans, LA	13.5	22.8	21.5	4.7	21.2	9.9	4.4	2.0
New York, NY	17.8	24.0	13.7	6.3	22.2	11.2	3.2	1.5
Oklahoma City, OK	13.6	25.4	22.9	7.3	19.7	7.5	2.4	1.1
Omaha, NE	10.5	22.3	21.9	7.7	24.3	8.9	2.9	1.5
Orlando, FL	9.6	23.2	18.4	10.8	25.4	8.3	3.0	1.3
Peoria, IL	10.6	24.3	21.5	8.6	20.7	10.2	2.7	1.3
Philadelphia, PA	15.3	32.6	16.7	5.7	17.3	8.1	2.6	1.6
Phoenix, AZ	18.1	23.6	22.0	7.7	18.3	7.3	2.0	1.0
Pittsburgh, PA	7.1	25.5	15.1	7.9	23.2	13.1	4.3	3.9
Portland, OR	7.6	15.1	20.3	6.6	30.1	13.8	4.1	2.4
Providence, RI	18.4	31.4	15.2	5.0	16.1	8.6	2.9	2.5
Provo, UT	7.1	14.3	26.5	8.9	29.7	8.9	1.6	2.8
Raleigh, NC	8.2	15.6	17.8	7.5	32.4	13.1	3.1	2.3
Reno, NV	11.0	22.2	25.0	8.2	20.6	8.4	2.3	2.3
Richmond, VA	14.6	21.8	18.4	5.6	23.5	11.0	3.1	2.0
Riverside, CA	19.4	26.3	23.7	7.7	13.5	6.4	1.4	1.7
Rochester, MN	6.0	18.7	17.2	11.4	25.7	12.1	5.2	3.7
Sacramento, CA	14.7	21.3	22.4	8.5	21.2	7.7	2.9	1.3
Salt Lake City, UT	11.2	17.5	17.7	7.0	25.7	12.5	4.6	3.7
San Antonio, TX	17.6	26.3	22.4	7.7	16.6	6.7	1.7	1.0
San Diego, CA	11.9	15.1	19.7	7.4	27.0	12.2	3.7	3.0
San Francisco, CA	11.5	12.1	13.3	5.0	34.8	15.4	5.0	2.8
San Jose, CA	15.4	16.6	16.8	7.5	25.7	13.6	2.0	2.5
Santa Rosa, CA	13.8	19.3	24.5	9.8	20.1	8.0	2.9	1.5
Savannah, GA	12.4	26.8	25.9	6.7	17.8	7.6	1.6	1.2
Seattle, WA	5.2	9.6	15.0	6.2	36.7	18.1	5.3	3.9
Sioux Falls, SD	7.7	24.8	20.8	11.5	23.8	8.1	2.2	1.1
Springfield, IL	8.7	25.9	22.1	7.6	21.5	9.8	3.3	1.2
Tallahassee, FL	6.5	17.0	19.0	9.3	26.2	13.8	3.9	4.3
Tampa, FL	12.1	25.6	16.0	7.7	23.3	9.6	3.9	1.7
Tucson, AZ	15.0	23.6	25.6	8.4	16.5	7.8	1.4	1.6
Tulsa, OK	12.7	25.3	22.6	7.9	20.7	7.2	2.5	1.1
Tuscaloosa, AL	10.9	27.3	19.9	5.0	21.0	10.3	2.5	3.1
Virginia Beach, VA	6.5	21.0	25.7	10.9	22.6	10.2	2.1	1.1
Washington, DC	9.1	16.8	12.6	3.0	24.8	21.2	8.4	4.2
Wichita, KS	11.7	26.4	24.0	7.9	19.1	8.1	1.8	1.1
Winston-Salem, NC	11.8	24.9	21.5	7.4	20.8	8.9	3.0	1.9
U.S.	12.0	27.0	20.4	8.5	19.8	8.8	2.1	1.4

Note: Figures cover persons age 25 and over
Source: U.S. Census Bureau, 2015-2019 American Community Survey 5-Year Estimates

A-126   Appendix A: Comparative Statistics

Highest Level of Education: Metro Area

Metro Area	Less than H.S.	H.S. Diploma	Some College, No Deg.	Associate Degree	Bachelors Degree	Masters Degree	Profess. School Degree	Doctorate Degree
Albuquerque, NM	11.4	24.6	23.3	8.5	17.9	9.8	2.3	2.2
Allentown, PA	10.0	34.2	17.1	9.3	18.3	8.4	1.6	1.2
Anchorage, AK	6.3	26.0	26.2	9.1	20.1	8.5	2.6	1.2
Ann Arbor, MI	4.7	14.6	17.6	7.1	26.3	18.8	4.7	6.0
Athens, GA	12.2	24.5	16.8	7.1	19.9	11.8	3.1	4.5
Atlanta, GA	10.4	23.9	19.5	7.6	24.0	10.6	2.5	1.5
Austin, TX	10.1	19.1	19.6	6.5	28.8	11.6	2.5	1.9
Baton Rouge, LA	12.6	32.2	21.4	6.2	18.0	6.6	1.7	1.3
Boise City, ID	8.2	25.8	24.8	9.4	21.3	7.4	1.7	1.3
Boston, MA	8.3	22.1	14.5	7.0	26.0	15.2	3.5	3.3
Boulder, CO	5.0	11.7	15.1	6.1	34.0	18.8	4.1	5.2
Cape Coral, FL	11.6	31.0	20.3	8.9	17.6	7.2	2.2	1.2
Cedar Rapids, IA	5.7	29.0	21.5	12.8	21.9	6.9	1.4	0.8
Charleston, SC	9.3	25.4	20.1	9.5	23.0	8.9	2.4	1.2
Charlotte, NC	11.0	23.5	21.1	9.2	23.5	9.0	1.8	0.9
Chicago, IL	11.3	23.9	19.5	7.2	23.0	10.9	2.6	1.4
Cincinnati, OH	9.0	29.7	19.2	8.4	21.0	9.3	2.0	1.4
Clarksville, TN	9.3	30.2	25.4	10.3	16.1	6.8	1.1	0.9
Cleveland, OH	9.4	28.9	21.8	8.7	18.9	8.7	2.4	1.2
College Station, TX	13.4	22.2	20.4	6.5	20.6	9.6	2.2	5.1
Colorado Springs, CO	5.6	20.5	24.0	11.3	23.5	11.8	1.8	1.4
Columbia, MO	6.4	23.7	19.8	7.4	24.5	11.3	3.2	3.7
Columbia, SC	10.1	26.9	21.2	9.0	20.1	9.2	1.8	1.5
Columbus, OH	8.5	27.7	19.6	7.5	23.4	9.7	2.2	1.4
Dallas, TX	14.4	22.3	21.1	7.0	23.0	9.2	1.9	1.1
Davenport, IA	9.0	30.5	23.0	10.5	17.2	7.3	1.5	0.8
Denver, CO	8.8	19.9	19.8	7.7	27.7	11.8	2.7	1.6
Des Moines, IA	7.5	25.6	20.2	10.3	25.4	7.7	2.2	1.1
Durham, NC	11.2	19.8	16.1	7.6	23.2	13.2	4.0	4.9
Edison, NJ	13.5	24.7	14.8	6.7	23.4	12.1	3.3	1.6
El Paso, TX	21.7	23.7	23.1	8.2	15.7	5.7	1.1	0.7
Fargo, ND	5.2	21.0	21.0	14.2	27.4	7.9	1.8	1.5
Fayetteville, NC	10.4	27.3	27.5	11.1	15.7	6.2	1.0	0.8
Fort Collins, CO	4.1	19.0	20.4	9.2	28.0	13.9	2.1	3.2
Fort Wayne, IN	10.4	29.2	21.7	10.9	18.4	6.9	1.5	0.9
Fort Worth, TX	14.4	22.3	21.1	7.0	23.0	9.2	1.9	1.1
Grand Rapids, MI	8.8	27.2	22.0	9.3	21.8	8.1	1.7	1.1
Greeley, CO	11.9	27.3	24.1	9.1	18.6	7.0	1.1	0.9
Green Bay, WI	8.0	32.1	19.7	12.4	19.6	6.0	1.5	0.7
Greensboro, NC	13.2	26.7	21.7	8.9	19.2	7.5	1.5	1.3
Honolulu, HI	8.1	25.9	20.3	10.7	22.9	8.1	2.5	1.5
Houston, TX	16.3	23.2	20.6	7.1	21.0	8.4	2.0	1.5
Huntsville, AL	9.8	22.7	20.2	8.1	24.2	11.9	1.4	1.7
Indianapolis, IN	10.3	27.9	19.3	7.9	22.4	8.8	2.2	1.3
Jacksonville, FL	9.1	27.7	21.8	10.0	20.6	7.9	1.9	1.1
Kansas City, MO	8.0	25.5	21.6	7.7	23.5	10.2	2.3	1.2
Lafayette, LA	15.9	36.4	18.6	5.7	16.4	5.0	1.3	0.7
Lakeland, FL	15.0	34.7	20.9	9.2	13.2	5.2	1.1	0.7
Las Vegas, NV	13.9	28.5	25.1	8.1	16.2	5.8	1.6	0.8
Lexington, KY	9.9	24.2	20.8	7.9	21.3	10.3	3.2	2.4
Lincoln, NE	6.3	21.9	21.2	11.7	24.5	9.7	2.2	2.6
Little Rock, AR	9.6	29.3	23.0	7.8	18.9	8.0	2.1	1.5
Los Angeles, CA	19.3	19.8	19.2	7.2	22.4	8.2	2.5	1.4
Louisville, KY	9.9	29.6	22.3	8.6	17.9	8.4	2.2	1.1
Madison, WI	4.7	21.0	17.9	10.3	27.7	12.1	3.0	3.2

Table continued on following page.

Appendix A: Comparative Statistics   A-127

Metro Area	Less than H.S.	H.S. Diploma	Some College, No Deg.	Associate Degree	Bachelors Degree	Masters Degree	Profess. School Degree	Doctorate Degree
Manchester, NH	7.9	25.8	18.2	10.0	24.3	10.9	1.6	1.3
Memphis, TN	12.0	29.2	23.5	7.1	17.4	7.9	1.9	1.2
Miami, FL	14.5	26.5	17.4	9.3	20.2	7.9	2.9	1.2
Midland, TX	15.7	25.9	23.5	7.8	19.3	5.8	1.4	0.6
Milwaukee, WI	8.5	26.5	20.6	8.7	23.0	9.0	2.3	1.3
Minneapolis, MN	6.4	21.2	20.0	10.4	27.4	10.4	2.6	1.6
Nashville, TN	10.0	26.4	20.2	7.3	23.5	9.0	2.2	1.6
New Haven, CT	9.9	30.7	17.1	7.3	18.6	11.2	3.1	2.1
New Orleans, LA	13.1	28.2	22.5	5.8	19.0	7.3	2.8	1.2
New York, NY	13.5	24.7	14.8	6.7	23.4	12.1	3.3	1.6
Oklahoma City, OK	11.0	27.3	23.6	7.5	19.6	7.6	2.0	1.3
Omaha, NE	8.3	23.8	22.5	9.1	23.8	9.0	2.3	1.3
Orlando, FL	10.5	25.8	19.9	11.5	21.3	7.8	2.0	1.0
Peoria, IL	8.3	30.5	23.2	10.4	18.1	7.2	1.5	0.9
Philadelphia, PA	9.3	29.0	16.7	7.1	22.4	10.8	2.7	1.9
Phoenix, AZ	12.5	23.0	24.4	8.6	20.0	8.3	1.9	1.2
Pittsburgh, PA	6.1	32.4	16.4	10.2	21.3	9.8	2.3	1.7
Portland, OR	7.9	19.9	23.6	8.8	24.7	10.5	2.6	1.9
Providence, RI	12.3	28.8	18.0	8.6	19.6	9.2	1.9	1.5
Provo, UT	5.5	16.8	26.7	10.7	27.7	9.2	1.6	1.7
Raleigh, NC	8.3	17.7	18.2	9.0	29.6	12.6	2.4	2.2
Reno, NV	11.3	23.6	25.7	8.6	19.2	7.8	2.1	1.8
Richmond, VA	10.1	25.1	20.0	7.4	23.1	10.5	2.3	1.6
Riverside, CA	18.9	26.6	24.6	8.2	13.9	5.6	1.3	0.9
Rochester, MN	5.9	23.9	19.1	12.4	22.7	9.7	3.8	2.5
Sacramento, CA	10.7	21.2	24.7	9.9	21.8	7.8	2.6	1.4
Salt Lake City, UT	9.2	23.0	23.9	9.0	22.5	8.7	2.3	1.5
San Antonio, TX	14.9	26.3	22.6	8.0	18.0	7.5	1.7	1.0
San Diego, CA	12.6	18.2	22.3	8.1	23.8	10.0	2.9	2.1
San Francisco, CA	10.9	15.5	17.3	6.6	29.3	13.7	3.8	2.9
San Jose, CA	11.9	14.4	15.4	6.9	27.3	17.5	2.7	3.9
Santa Rosa, CA	11.2	18.7	25.0	9.6	22.2	8.6	3.1	1.6
Savannah, GA	10.2	26.3	24.2	7.9	19.5	8.4	2.2	1.3
Seattle, WA	7.4	19.4	21.0	9.3	26.6	11.7	2.7	2.0
Sioux Falls, SD	7.1	26.1	20.6	12.7	23.2	7.3	2.0	1.0
Springfield, IL	7.4	27.7	22.7	8.3	21.2	9.0	2.6	1.0
Tallahassee, FL	9.4	23.7	19.8	8.7	22.0	10.4	2.9	3.1
Tampa, FL	10.4	28.9	20.5	9.8	19.6	7.6	2.0	1.2
Tucson, AZ	11.6	22.2	25.1	8.7	18.7	9.4	2.3	2.0
Tulsa, OK	10.6	29.1	23.7	8.9	18.9	6.3	1.7	0.9
Tuscaloosa, AL	12.9	31.7	21.1	6.9	16.6	7.5	1.4	1.9
Virginia Beach, VA	8.6	24.9	24.7	9.9	19.5	9.3	1.8	1.2
Washington, DC	9.1	18.2	16.0	5.9	25.8	17.6	4.3	3.2
Wichita, KS	9.9	26.5	24.4	8.6	19.6	8.3	1.7	1.0
Winston-Salem, NC	13.0	29.4	21.6	9.3	17.4	6.5	1.6	1.2
U.S.	12.0	27.0	20.4	8.5	19.8	8.8	2.1	1.4

Note: Figures cover persons age 25 and over; Figures cover the Metropolitan Statistical Area—see Appendix B for areas included
Source: U.S. Census Bureau, 2015-2019 American Community Survey 5-Year Estimates

A-128   Appendix A: Comparative Statistics

School Enrollment by Grade and Control: City

City	Preschool (%)		Kindergarten (%)		Grades 1 - 4 (%)		Grades 5 - 8 (%)		Grades 9 - 12 (%)	
	Public	Private	Public	Private	Public	Private	Public	Private	Public	Private
Albuquerque, NM	59.3	40.7	87.2	12.8	91.8	8.2	90.0	10.0	92.0	8.0
Allentown, PA	73.8	26.2	82.8	17.2	87.8	12.2	88.3	11.7	89.0	11.0
Anchorage, AK	56.6	43.4	94.0	6.0	92.3	7.7	92.5	7.5	95.1	4.9
Ann Arbor, MI	25.7	74.3	94.1	5.9	91.8	8.2	87.6	12.4	94.2	5.8
Athens, GA	67.9	32.1	92.6	7.4	91.9	8.1	88.8	11.2	88.5	11.5
Atlanta, GA	54.3	45.7	84.5	15.5	87.8	12.2	79.5	20.5	80.1	19.9
Austin, TX	51.0	49.0	86.9	13.1	89.3	10.7	88.9	11.1	91.0	9.0
Baton Rouge, LA	66.8	33.2	75.3	24.7	80.3	19.7	79.5	20.5	80.8	19.2
Boise City, ID	30.6	69.4	84.8	15.2	90.0	10.0	91.7	8.3	89.1	10.9
Boston, MA	50.7	49.3	84.9	15.1	85.7	14.3	86.8	13.2	87.8	12.2
Boulder, CO	44.0	56.0	84.5	15.5	92.5	7.5	93.4	6.6	92.2	7.8
Cape Coral, FL	84.8	15.2	94.8	5.2	92.0	8.0	93.0	7.0	91.8	8.2
Cedar Rapids, IA	67.5	32.5	86.4	13.6	88.9	11.1	93.0	7.0	90.0	10.0
Charleston, SC	41.2	58.9	78.8	21.2	83.4	16.6	78.9	21.1	78.9	21.1
Charlotte, NC	47.5	52.5	90.5	9.5	90.7	9.3	87.6	12.4	89.8	10.2
Chicago, IL	58.4	41.6	79.9	20.1	85.9	14.1	85.4	14.6	87.4	12.6
Cincinnati, OH	64.7	35.3	73.1	26.9	77.6	22.4	80.1	19.9	80.8	19.2
Clarksville, TN	57.3	42.7	90.6	9.4	93.7	6.3	92.5	7.5	92.4	7.6
Cleveland, OH	74.3	25.7	79.3	20.7	79.6	20.4	77.9	22.1	79.8	20.2
College Station, TX	46.9	53.1	85.1	14.9	86.5	13.5	93.5	6.5	92.7	7.3
Colorado Springs, CO	57.1	42.9	89.3	10.7	92.5	7.5	92.5	7.5	92.0	8.0
Columbia, MO	36.1	63.9	76.7	23.3	87.5	12.5	88.1	11.9	88.8	11.2
Columbia, SC	57.2	42.8	74.3	25.7	88.1	11.9	87.7	12.3	86.7	13.3
Columbus, OH	60.3	39.7	85.3	14.7	87.7	12.3	87.2	12.8	87.3	12.7
Dallas, TX	69.2	30.8	91.0	9.0	92.0	8.0	91.7	8.3	91.6	8.4
Davenport, IA	57.0	43.0	86.1	13.9	89.3	10.7	84.3	15.7	92.8	7.2
Denver, CO	64.4	35.6	86.3	13.7	91.4	8.6	91.0	9.0	91.4	8.6
Des Moines, IA	73.0	27.0	90.0	10.0	89.0	11.0	91.7	8.3	92.3	7.7
Durham, NC	52.1	47.9	91.9	8.1	88.8	11.2	87.3	12.7	89.7	10.3
Edison, NJ	30.2	69.8	67.7	32.3	90.1	9.9	90.0	10.0	91.6	8.4
El Paso, TX	78.5	21.5	93.3	6.7	95.0	5.0	94.6	5.4	96.2	3.8
Fargo, ND	53.4	46.6	94.7	5.3	90.4	9.6	89.3	10.7	93.7	6.3
Fayetteville, NC	63.5	36.5	88.7	11.3	87.2	12.8	87.4	12.6	89.7	10.3
Fort Collins, CO	41.9	58.1	91.7	8.3	94.5	5.5	95.1	4.9	94.6	5.4
Fort Wayne, IN	45.5	54.5	83.5	16.5	79.5	20.5	82.2	17.8	81.3	18.7
Fort Worth, TX	62.0	38.0	87.1	12.9	92.6	7.4	90.7	9.3	92.8	7.2
Grand Rapids, MI	60.4	39.6	74.5	25.5	83.4	16.6	83.4	16.6	84.9	15.1
Greeley, CO	69.6	30.4	83.6	16.4	91.5	8.5	92.6	7.4	95.3	4.7
Green Bay, WI	71.8	28.2	85.7	14.3	90.6	9.4	84.6	15.4	91.1	8.9
Greensboro, NC	53.2	46.8	89.5	10.5	93.4	6.6	90.2	9.8	91.6	8.4
Honolulu, HI	34.7	65.3	79.6	20.4	83.3	16.7	73.0	27.0	74.8	25.2
Houston, TX	66.9	33.1	90.8	9.2	94.2	5.8	92.7	7.3	93.5	6.5
Huntsville, AL	59.4	40.6	87.2	12.8	80.1	19.9	82.9	17.1	84.8	15.2
Indianapolis, IN	61.8	38.2	85.6	14.4	88.5	11.5	87.1	12.9	89.2	10.8
Jacksonville, FL	57.5	42.5	84.3	15.7	84.3	15.7	81.7	18.3	83.5	16.5
Kansas City, MO	57.7	42.3	85.3	14.7	90.1	9.9	88.3	11.7	85.4	14.6
Lafayette, LA	60.7	39.3	64.2	35.8	74.4	25.6	73.3	26.7	80.6	19.4
Lakeland, FL	61.7	38.3	85.0	15.0	83.6	16.4	83.7	16.3	88.0	12.0
Las Vegas, NV	65.7	34.3	88.6	11.4	91.3	8.7	91.7	8.3	93.0	7.0
Lexington, KY	44.2	55.8	86.4	13.6	87.2	12.8	86.6	13.4	86.1	13.9
Lincoln, NE	44.8	55.2	73.8	26.2	84.9	15.1	86.5	13.5	86.4	13.6
Little Rock, AR	60.3	39.7	82.3	17.7	82.7	17.3	82.0	18.0	79.8	20.2
Los Angeles, CA	60.2	39.8	88.1	11.9	89.0	11.0	88.6	11.4	88.8	11.2
Louisville, KY	51.1	48.9	80.2	19.8	83.4	16.6	79.9	20.1	79.3	20.7
Madison, WI	53.6	46.4	85.3	14.7	88.4	11.6	87.0	13.0	91.0	9.0

Table continued on following page.

Appendix A: Comparative Statistics   A-129

City	Preschool (%)		Kindergarten (%)		Grades 1 - 4 (%)		Grades 5 - 8 (%)		Grades 9 - 12 (%)	
	Public	Private	Public	Private	Public	Private	Public	Private	Public	Private
Manchester, NH	52.6	47.4	86.1	13.9	89.9	10.1	93.1	6.9	89.5	10.5
Memphis, TN	67.2	32.8	87.3	12.7	87.9	12.1	87.2	12.8	85.5	14.5
Miami, FL	56.0	44.0	86.7	13.3	88.1	11.9	85.6	14.4	90.8	9.2
Midland, TX	64.4	35.6	89.1	10.9	86.0	14.0	88.3	11.7	89.9	10.1
Milwaukee, WI	73.5	26.5	79.4	20.6	77.1	22.9	75.8	24.2	81.4	18.6
Minneapolis, MN	53.4	46.6	85.1	14.9	88.2	11.8	88.9	11.1	87.7	12.3
Nashville, TN	50.7	49.3	87.4	12.6	85.6	14.4	83.4	16.6	82.0	18.0
New Haven, CT	83.6	16.4	94.0	6.0	94.8	5.2	93.8	6.2	92.2	7.8
New Orleans, LA	50.3	49.7	77.0	23.0	80.1	19.9	80.0	20.0	78.9	21.1
New York, NY	60.9	39.1	79.2	20.8	82.7	17.3	82.2	17.8	82.3	17.7
Oklahoma City, OK	73.4	26.6	91.7	8.3	91.8	8.2	91.0	9.0	90.2	9.8
Omaha, NE	53.5	46.5	82.0	18.0	83.5	16.5	85.3	14.7	83.2	16.8
Orlando, FL	62.2	37.8	86.4	13.6	91.2	8.8	85.0	15.0	93.3	6.7
Peoria, IL	60.1	39.9	70.0	30.0	83.9	16.1	83.4	16.6	88.7	11.3
Philadelphia, PA	56.8	43.2	79.1	20.9	79.1	20.9	80.6	19.4	80.1	19.9
Phoenix, AZ	62.7	37.3	90.0	10.0	92.9	7.1	92.4	7.6	93.1	6.9
Pittsburgh, PA	48.0	52.0	77.1	22.9	73.1	26.9	75.8	24.2	81.5	18.5
Portland, OR	39.4	60.6	84.8	15.2	88.0	12.0	87.1	12.9	85.1	14.9
Providence, RI	51.6	48.4	87.8	12.2	86.0	14.0	85.4	14.6	88.6	11.4
Provo, UT	53.8	46.2	95.7	4.3	93.9	6.1	95.8	4.2	88.5	11.5
Raleigh, NC	43.5	56.5	89.3	10.7	90.6	9.4	89.2	10.8	90.6	9.4
Reno, NV	60.7	39.3	86.1	13.9	94.1	5.9	93.2	6.8	94.0	6.0
Richmond, VA	58.6	41.4	91.1	8.9	87.8	12.2	80.8	19.2	87.1	12.9
Riverside, CA	66.0	34.0	90.5	9.5	94.0	6.0	93.6	6.4	95.0	5.0
Rochester, MN	50.9	49.1	80.4	19.6	86.9	13.1	87.1	12.9	91.4	8.6
Sacramento, CA	68.9	31.1	92.8	7.2	93.2	6.8	92.9	7.1	92.6	7.4
Salt Lake City, UT	47.7	52.3	88.2	11.8	91.2	8.8	91.0	9.0	92.8	7.2
San Antonio, TX	70.1	29.9	90.3	9.7	93.1	6.9	92.9	7.1	92.6	7.4
San Diego, CA	52.5	47.5	92.9	7.1	90.9	9.1	91.2	8.8	91.5	8.5
San Francisco, CA	37.5	62.5	73.1	26.9	72.2	27.8	68.1	31.9	75.0	25.0
San Jose, CA	41.9	58.1	81.2	18.8	87.0	13.0	87.0	13.0	86.8	13.2
Santa Rosa, CA	53.6	46.4	94.6	5.4	95.9	4.1	92.5	7.5	92.0	8.0
Savannah, GA	67.6	32.4	93.0	7.0	90.1	9.9	91.0	9.0	89.6	10.4
Seattle, WA	32.6	67.4	79.7	20.3	81.6	18.4	75.9	24.1	79.8	20.2
Sioux Falls, SD	51.1	48.9	87.3	12.7	88.2	11.8	87.5	12.5	84.2	15.8
Springfield, IL	65.7	34.3	80.4	19.6	81.9	18.1	83.9	16.1	85.6	14.4
Tallahassee, FL	48.6	51.4	86.3	13.7	85.9	14.1	83.3	16.7	87.4	12.6
Tampa, FL	49.9	50.1	83.4	16.6	89.5	10.5	85.7	14.3	84.5	15.5
Tucson, AZ	74.0	26.0	85.8	14.2	89.6	10.4	91.3	8.7	92.8	7.2
Tulsa, OK	67.6	32.4	87.1	12.9	88.3	11.7	85.8	14.2	85.2	14.8
Tuscaloosa, AL	62.5	37.5	91.8	8.2	86.2	13.8	92.2	7.8	85.1	14.9
Virginia Beach, VA	37.7	62.3	77.3	22.7	90.2	9.8	88.7	11.3	92.7	7.3
Washington, DC	77.1	22.9	92.3	7.7	87.6	12.4	82.7	17.3	82.6	17.4
Wichita, KS	62.5	37.5	83.7	16.3	85.4	14.6	84.7	15.3	84.2	15.8
Winston-Salem, NC	55.3	44.7	94.1	5.9	93.3	6.7	90.8	9.2	93.2	6.8
U.S.	59.1	40.9	87.6	12.4	89.5	10.5	89.4	10.6	90.1	9.9

Note: Figures shown cover persons 3 years old and over
Source: U.S. Census Bureau, 2015-2019 American Community Survey 5-Year Estimates

A-130 Appendix A: Comparative Statistics

School Enrollment by Grade and Control: Metro Area

Metro Area	Preschool (%)		Kindergarten (%)		Grades 1 - 4 (%)		Grades 5 - 8 (%)		Grades 9 - 12 (%)	
	Public	Private	Public	Private	Public	Private	Public	Private	Public	Private
Albuquerque, NM	64.5	35.5	85.6	14.4	90.1	9.9	89.4	10.6	91.7	8.3
Allentown, PA	49.0	51.0	85.5	14.5	89.4	10.6	90.5	9.5	91.0	9.0
Anchorage, AK	58.3	41.7	92.4	7.6	90.7	9.3	90.5	9.5	92.8	7.2
Ann Arbor, MI	49.6	50.4	89.6	10.4	87.3	12.7	87.7	12.3	91.8	8.2
Athens, GA	67.9	32.1	90.9	9.1	90.1	9.9	86.0	14.0	86.7	13.3
Atlanta, GA	56.0	44.0	86.9	13.1	91.0	9.0	89.2	10.8	89.9	10.1
Austin, TX	51.5	48.5	88.1	11.9	90.7	9.3	90.7	9.3	92.4	7.6
Baton Rouge, LA	57.1	42.9	76.9	23.1	81.4	18.6	81.7	18.3	81.4	18.6
Boise City, ID	37.7	62.3	86.1	13.9	91.1	8.9	92.8	7.2	90.5	9.5
Boston, MA	45.7	54.3	87.7	12.3	91.2	8.8	89.8	10.2	86.9	13.1
Boulder, CO	50.7	49.3	84.7	15.3	90.8	9.2	90.8	9.2	93.9	6.1
Cape Coral, FL	65.5	34.5	89.7	10.3	92.6	7.4	91.5	8.5	90.8	9.2
Cedar Rapids, IA	69.1	30.9	87.8	12.2	89.0	11.0	92.3	7.7	92.3	7.7
Charleston, SC	51.2	48.8	86.2	13.8	89.8	10.2	89.3	10.7	90.4	9.6
Charlotte, NC	50.2	49.8	90.0	10.0	90.5	9.5	88.9	11.1	90.4	9.6
Chicago, IL	58.0	42.0	84.8	15.2	89.3	10.7	89.0	11.0	90.6	9.4
Cincinnati, OH	53.4	46.6	78.8	21.2	83.1	16.9	83.9	16.1	82.5	17.5
Clarksville, TN	62.9	37.1	92.1	7.9	88.8	11.2	89.5	10.5	89.0	11.0
Cleveland, OH	54.9	45.1	81.2	18.8	81.4	18.6	82.0	18.0	84.1	15.9
College Station, TX	60.1	39.9	86.1	13.9	88.9	11.1	92.4	7.6	93.3	6.7
Colorado Springs, CO	62.1	37.9	89.5	10.5	92.5	7.5	92.6	7.4	92.2	7.8
Columbia, MO	47.1	52.9	84.2	15.8	88.0	12.0	89.0	11.0	90.3	9.7
Columbia, SC	57.9	42.1	88.4	11.6	91.0	9.0	92.1	7.9	92.9	7.1
Columbus, OH	55.0	45.0	85.2	14.8	88.8	11.2	88.9	11.1	89.3	10.7
Dallas, TX	58.9	41.1	90.2	9.8	92.6	7.4	92.3	7.7	92.4	7.6
Davenport, IA	69.0	31.0	89.9	10.1	91.6	8.4	91.6	8.4	93.2	6.8
Denver, CO	59.6	40.4	90.1	9.9	92.5	7.5	92.0	8.0	91.9	8.1
Des Moines, IA	65.6	34.4	87.6	12.4	91.6	8.4	91.3	8.7	92.1	7.9
Durham, NC	49.5	50.5	88.6	11.4	89.6	10.4	88.8	11.2	90.8	9.2
Edison, NJ	54.8	45.2	82.3	17.7	85.6	14.4	85.7	14.3	85.1	14.9
El Paso, TX	81.0	19.0	93.9	6.1	95.1	4.9	94.8	5.2	96.4	3.6
Fargo, ND	58.8	41.2	93.6	6.4	89.5	10.5	89.3	10.7	93.8	6.2
Fayetteville, NC	63.5	36.5	88.7	11.3	87.7	12.3	88.9	11.1	89.4	10.6
Fort Collins, CO	52.2	47.8	91.0	9.0	92.3	7.7	91.9	8.1	91.4	8.6
Fort Wayne, IN	42.6	57.4	78.5	21.5	77.9	22.1	79.3	20.7	81.7	18.3
Fort Worth, TX	58.9	41.1	90.2	9.8	92.6	7.4	92.3	7.7	92.4	7.6
Grand Rapids, MI	62.5	37.5	82.2	17.8	84.8	15.2	86.2	13.8	86.1	13.9
Greeley, CO	69.7	30.3	89.1	10.9	91.9	8.1	94.0	6.0	93.9	6.1
Green Bay, WI	69.2	30.8	85.4	14.6	88.9	11.1	88.4	11.6	93.2	6.8
Greensboro, NC	50.5	49.5	89.4	10.6	90.3	9.7	89.1	10.9	90.3	9.7
Honolulu, HI	36.3	63.7	80.0	20.0	85.3	14.7	78.3	21.7	76.8	23.2
Houston, TX	58.1	41.9	90.2	9.8	93.1	6.9	93.0	7.0	93.3	6.7
Huntsville, AL	54.3	45.7	85.8	14.2	82.9	17.1	82.7	17.3	86.0	14.0
Indianapolis, IN	53.8	46.2	87.2	12.8	89.5	10.5	89.2	10.8	89.2	10.8
Jacksonville, FL	55.1	44.9	86.2	13.8	86.3	13.7	84.3	15.7	86.7	13.3
Kansas City, MO	58.1	41.9	88.5	11.5	89.6	10.4	89.2	10.8	89.4	10.6
Lafayette, LA	66.9	33.1	79.2	20.8	81.0	19.0	79.8	20.2	81.3	18.7
Lakeland, FL	69.5	30.5	85.9	14.1	89.0	11.0	86.1	13.9	90.5	9.5
Las Vegas, NV	61.7	38.3	89.8	10.2	92.5	7.5	92.9	7.1	93.4	6.6
Lexington, KY	47.1	52.9	83.9	16.1	88.1	11.9	86.9	13.1	86.8	13.2
Lincoln, NE	44.3	55.7	75.3	24.7	84.3	15.7	86.7	13.3	86.9	13.1
Little Rock, AR	63.2	36.8	87.1	12.9	88.9	11.1	88.9	11.1	87.4	12.6
Los Angeles, CA	58.5	41.5	88.4	11.6	90.8	9.2	91.0	9.0	91.4	8.6
Louisville, KY	49.2	50.8	82.9	17.1	84.2	15.8	81.4	18.6	81.3	18.7
Madison, WI	66.3	33.7	88.6	11.4	90.0	10.0	90.0	10.0	94.2	5.8

Table continued on following page.

Appendix A: Comparative Statistics   A-131

Metro Area	Preschool (%)		Kindergarten (%)		Grades 1 - 4 (%)		Grades 5 - 8 (%)		Grades 9 - 12 (%)	
	Public	Private	Public	Private	Public	Private	Public	Private	Public	Private
Manchester, NH	42.4	57.6	83.7	16.3	87.1	12.9	89.9	10.1	88.9	11.1
Memphis, TN	61.4	38.6	86.2	13.8	86.6	13.4	86.3	13.7	84.7	15.3
Miami, FL	50.3	49.7	83.3	16.7	86.2	13.8	86.7	13.3	87.2	12.8
Midland, TX	64.3	35.7	89.1	10.9	86.9	13.1	90.0	10.0	90.3	9.7
Milwaukee, WI	56.6	43.4	80.0	20.0	80.5	19.5	79.7	20.3	85.2	14.8
Minneapolis, MN	59.4	40.6	88.5	11.5	89.4	10.6	90.1	9.9	91.6	8.4
Nashville, TN	47.3	52.7	86.2	13.8	87.1	12.9	86.3	13.7	84.4	15.6
New Haven, CT	65.1	34.9	90.7	9.3	92.2	7.8	90.5	9.5	89.3	10.7
New Orleans, LA	53.6	46.4	77.3	22.7	78.1	21.9	77.7	22.3	76.0	24.0
New York, NY	54.8	45.2	82.3	17.7	85.6	14.4	85.7	14.3	85.1	14.9
Oklahoma City, OK	72.1	27.9	90.7	9.3	91.2	8.8	90.8	9.2	90.7	9.3
Omaha, NE	57.3	42.7	85.4	14.6	85.7	14.3	87.2	12.8	85.9	14.1
Orlando, FL	55.2	44.8	81.0	19.0	86.3	13.7	85.6	14.4	89.6	10.4
Peoria, IL	61.4	38.6	82.9	17.1	89.1	10.9	89.1	10.9	91.0	9.0
Philadelphia, PA	46.0	54.0	81.8	18.2	84.9	15.1	84.9	15.1	83.3	16.7
Phoenix, AZ	60.3	39.7	89.4	10.6	92.0	8.0	92.5	7.5	92.9	7.1
Pittsburgh, PA	49.3	50.7	85.0	15.0	88.0	12.0	88.3	11.7	89.8	10.2
Portland, OR	42.8	57.2	86.2	13.8	89.0	11.0	89.5	10.5	90.3	9.7
Providence, RI	53.8	46.2	89.9	10.1	90.4	9.6	89.6	10.4	88.5	11.5
Provo, UT	53.3	46.7	91.6	8.4	92.9	7.1	94.4	5.6	94.4	5.6
Raleigh, NC	38.9	61.1	88.2	11.8	89.0	11.0	87.8	12.2	89.9	10.1
Reno, NV	58.2	41.8	85.6	14.4	92.7	7.3	92.9	7.1	93.2	6.8
Richmond, VA	41.9	58.1	89.0	11.0	89.8	10.2	88.6	11.4	90.3	9.7
Riverside, CA	68.6	31.4	91.8	8.2	94.4	5.6	94.2	5.8	94.9	5.1
Rochester, MN	62.6	37.4	85.5	14.5	87.3	12.7	89.1	10.9	92.1	7.9
Sacramento, CA	62.3	37.7	90.7	9.3	92.4	7.6	92.5	7.5	93.1	6.9
Salt Lake City, UT	54.5	45.5	88.8	11.2	92.6	7.4	93.4	6.6	93.7	6.3
San Antonio, TX	65.9	34.1	90.4	9.6	92.9	7.1	92.1	7.9	92.5	7.5
San Diego, CA	54.0	46.0	90.5	9.5	92.1	7.9	92.1	7.9	92.4	7.6
San Francisco, CA	41.3	58.7	84.2	15.8	86.3	13.7	85.8	14.2	87.2	12.8
San Jose, CA	36.2	63.8	81.2	18.8	85.7	14.3	85.4	14.6	86.2	13.8
Santa Rosa, CA	48.6	51.4	93.0	7.0	92.8	7.2	90.3	9.7	90.9	9.1
Savannah, GA	58.3	41.7	92.2	7.8	86.1	13.9	87.8	12.2	85.9	14.1
Seattle, WA	41.4	58.6	83.9	16.1	88.3	11.7	88.3	11.7	90.5	9.5
Sioux Falls, SD	53.6	46.4	88.3	11.7	88.4	11.6	89.2	10.8	86.8	13.2
Springfield, IL	66.2	33.8	86.4	13.6	87.2	12.8	88.6	11.4	90.1	9.9
Tallahassee, FL	49.6	50.4	86.3	13.7	86.0	14.0	81.7	18.3	86.2	13.8
Tampa, FL	57.1	42.9	84.8	15.2	86.9	13.1	87.1	12.9	88.3	11.7
Tucson, AZ	65.7	34.3	87.8	12.2	90.4	9.6	90.1	9.9	92.1	7.9
Tulsa, OK	69.4	30.6	88.7	11.3	88.9	11.1	88.2	11.8	87.7	12.3
Tuscaloosa, AL	66.5	33.5	89.8	10.2	87.4	12.6	90.3	9.7	86.1	13.9
Virginia Beach, VA	53.4	46.6	83.0	17.0	89.4	10.6	89.3	10.7	91.4	8.6
Washington, DC	44.9	55.1	86.1	13.9	88.7	11.3	87.9	12.1	88.3	11.7
Wichita, KS	63.1	36.9	83.3	16.7	86.3	13.7	87.3	12.7	86.6	13.4
Winston-Salem, NC	56.2	43.8	91.8	8.2	93.0	7.0	90.3	9.7	90.8	9.2
U.S.	59.1	40.9	87.6	12.4	89.5	10.5	89.4	10.6	90.1	9.9

Note: Figures shown cover persons 3 years old and over; Figures cover the Metropolitan Statistical Area—see Appendix B for areas included
Source: U.S. Census Bureau, 2015-2019 American Community Survey 5-Year Estimates

A-132　Appendix A: Comparative Statistics

Educational Attainment by Race: City

City	High School Graduate or Higher (%)					Bachelor's Degree or Higher (%)				
	Total	White	Black	Asian	Hisp.[1]	Total	White	Black	Asian	Hisp.[1]
Albuquerque, NM	89.7	91.1	92.0	85.5	82.5	35.2	38.1	31.2	48.3	21.5
Allentown, PA	79.0	81.5	83.0	81.3	68.2	15.3	17.9	7.3	37.1	6.0
Anchorage, AK	93.9	96.5	93.6	84.0	85.3	36.1	43.2	19.6	25.2	22.3
Ann Arbor, MI	97.3	98.1	90.6	97.8	92.0	76.0	78.4	38.2	86.4	68.6
Athens, GA	87.9	90.9	81.5	94.5	57.0	44.0	54.8	18.6	73.2	19.8
Atlanta, GA	90.9	97.7	84.4	96.1	82.5	51.8	78.0	25.7	84.6	46.0
Austin, TX	89.4	91.2	89.6	93.9	72.3	51.7	55.1	28.8	77.0	25.8
Baton Rouge, LA	88.0	96.2	82.2	84.1	73.9	33.2	53.4	15.9	54.7	21.7
Boise City, ID	95.1	95.7	86.2	89.1	84.2	41.6	41.8	29.9	51.2	22.0
Boston, MA	87.2	93.0	83.8	78.9	70.0	49.7	65.7	21.8	53.2	23.7
Boulder, CO	96.9	97.5	92.2	96.1	76.4	76.0	76.9	39.9	80.4	42.1
Cape Coral, FL	91.8	92.3	89.3	88.5	86.9	23.3	23.7	19.8	24.7	18.7
Cedar Rapids, IA	93.3	94.7	83.4	83.8	75.8	32.1	32.7	15.0	51.2	21.0
Charleston, SC	94.9	97.4	86.9	93.5	91.4	53.1	61.0	22.3	67.3	45.6
Charlotte, NC	89.1	92.7	90.4	81.4	60.0	44.3	55.4	29.4	58.3	17.0
Chicago, IL	85.1	88.7	85.2	87.1	68.4	39.5	50.9	21.4	60.5	16.5
Cincinnati, OH	88.1	92.1	83.0	93.1	73.2	37.1	52.6	14.5	80.7	31.0
Clarksville, TN	92.9	93.5	92.6	85.2	87.2	27.6	28.1	24.7	41.9	18.2
Cleveland, OH	80.8	83.3	80.0	71.5	67.4	17.5	24.9	9.7	39.5	9.0
College Station, TX	94.4	95.1	87.8	95.2	85.6	58.6	58.8	29.4	80.9	45.8
Colorado Springs, CO	93.9	95.3	94.2	86.3	80.6	39.9	42.7	25.7	48.4	20.9
Columbia, MO	95.2	96.3	90.0	94.6	91.4	52.2	54.8	21.2	73.9	36.0
Columbia, SC	89.4	95.4	81.8	96.8	86.4	43.8	62.6	19.6	78.1	35.2
Columbus, OH	89.8	92.0	86.8	85.3	75.6	36.6	42.3	19.7	57.7	23.2
Dallas, TX	77.5	75.2	86.8	85.5	51.1	33.4	38.9	19.4	65.8	11.0
Davenport, IA	90.5	92.2	83.6	69.2	72.8	25.6	27.4	10.5	28.0	15.5
Denver, CO	88.0	90.3	86.9	83.4	64.7	49.4	54.5	24.7	53.9	15.9
Des Moines, IA	86.3	89.7	81.3	60.8	57.2	26.7	29.2	13.6	20.3	9.0
Durham, NC	88.1	90.1	87.6	90.5	49.4	49.6	60.1	34.2	73.9	13.6
Edison, NJ	92.1	92.8	94.7	93.0	82.0	55.5	37.2	35.0	77.0	24.1
El Paso, TX	80.3	81.1	95.7	90.1	76.4	25.1	25.7	30.5	54.0	20.7
Fargo, ND	94.3	96.1	81.9	71.8	92.0	40.0	41.7	20.2	46.6	21.2
Fayetteville, NC	91.7	93.7	90.6	86.3	88.5	27.2	31.3	22.9	43.0	21.7
Fort Collins, CO	96.5	96.9	97.0	93.4	84.3	55.5	55.8	40.2	72.3	34.2
Fort Wayne, IN	88.5	91.9	84.4	52.6	61.8	27.8	30.7	15.6	28.3	9.8
Fort Worth, TX	82.2	84.4	88.6	80.8	59.2	29.7	33.8	21.5	42.8	12.2
Grand Rapids, MI	86.7	90.8	83.2	72.3	50.3	36.4	43.1	17.4	43.9	11.9
Greeley, CO	84.5	86.2	79.2	80.0	65.6	24.8	25.9	16.6	43.4	8.4
Green Bay, WI	87.5	90.4	83.1	74.3	53.5	24.8	27.0	15.3	20.0	6.5
Greensboro, NC	89.8	93.4	88.5	75.2	64.2	38.2	49.1	24.5	41.9	18.2
Honolulu, HI	89.0	97.6	97.5	85.5	91.9	37.2	53.0	24.5	36.6	27.9
Houston, TX	78.9	78.0	88.8	86.9	58.5	32.9	37.4	22.6	58.9	13.6
Huntsville, AL	91.0	94.0	85.4	91.1	63.8	44.1	50.3	28.4	59.3	22.8
Indianapolis, IN	85.8	88.0	84.6	76.2	57.3	30.9	36.0	18.2	47.1	12.5
Jacksonville, FL	89.5	91.0	86.7	88.7	82.3	28.6	31.5	19.1	49.5	24.6
Kansas City, MO	90.0	93.2	86.5	80.3	70.2	35.2	43.5	16.6	47.2	18.6
Lafayette, LA	89.5	93.6	79.4	94.8	57.4	38.2	47.0	15.1	56.8	21.2
Lakeland, FL	88.0	89.3	83.3	81.6	78.8	25.9	27.5	15.7	51.0	19.5
Las Vegas, NV	84.8	87.5	89.2	91.1	63.5	24.6	26.9	18.2	40.7	9.9
Lexington, KY	91.2	93.4	85.4	91.1	61.0	43.6	47.7	19.5	68.5	19.2
Lincoln, NE	93.3	95.0	86.1	79.2	70.1	39.6	40.7	23.8	46.7	19.3
Little Rock, AR	91.3	93.8	88.2	95.3	61.3	41.8	54.6	22.6	70.2	10.2
Los Angeles, CA	77.5	80.9	88.7	90.3	56.3	34.4	39.8	26.5	54.9	12.3
Louisville, KY	89.6	90.7	86.9	81.4	80.2	29.9	32.9	17.8	49.0	25.8
Madison, WI	95.5	96.8	87.6	92.5	77.3	57.9	59.7	22.7	71.7	34.2

Table continued on following page.

Appendix A: Comparative Statistics   A-133

City	High School Graduate or Higher (%)					Bachelor's Degree or Higher (%)				
	Total	White	Black	Asian	Hisp.[1]	Total	White	Black	Asian	Hisp.[1]
Manchester, NH	87.3	88.4	79.2	76.4	67.0	30.1	29.7	22.1	44.6	14.9
Memphis, TN	85.7	91.7	84.1	87.0	49.5	26.2	44.5	15.9	57.0	11.2
Miami, FL	78.0	78.7	74.2	90.4	75.3	29.6	32.2	14.8	63.5	25.9
Midland, TX	85.1	85.8	85.6	81.7	71.3	28.9	30.3	18.1	51.7	11.9
Milwaukee, WI	84.0	89.1	83.0	68.8	62.2	24.6	35.3	12.6	27.1	9.3
Minneapolis, MN	90.0	96.2	74.6	82.6	59.9	50.4	61.2	14.3	54.8	21.0
Nashville, TN	88.8	90.4	88.2	77.9	57.0	41.1	46.5	27.6	49.2	15.4
New Haven, CT	85.6	87.5	87.2	96.8	70.9	34.9	46.6	19.9	78.7	13.6
New Orleans, LA	86.5	95.7	81.0	75.8	80.9	37.6	63.9	19.7	40.4	35.9
New York, NY	82.2	88.7	83.5	76.1	68.9	38.1	51.0	24.4	42.4	18.6
Oklahoma City, OK	86.4	87.5	89.0	81.2	54.5	30.7	33.2	20.3	41.4	10.4
Omaha, NE	89.5	91.5	86.9	70.4	54.3	37.7	40.7	18.9	49.4	12.0
Orlando, FL	90.4	92.8	84.6	92.6	86.8	38.1	43.3	21.8	60.3	28.8
Peoria, IL	89.4	92.4	81.4	94.7	71.6	34.9	39.6	13.4	75.4	21.9
Philadelphia, PA	84.7	89.2	84.6	73.0	67.2	29.7	41.6	17.3	40.3	14.6
Phoenix, AZ	81.9	84.0	87.5	84.9	62.1	28.6	30.2	21.8	57.4	10.3
Pittsburgh, PA	92.9	94.5	88.6	90.9	87.1	44.6	50.2	18.4	78.3	48.4
Portland, OR	92.4	94.8	85.9	76.9	76.1	50.4	54.3	23.9	41.2	31.0
Providence, RI	81.6	86.4	84.4	79.3	71.9	30.1	38.0	19.1	48.1	10.4
Provo, UT	92.9	93.1	98.0	93.2	75.2	43.1	43.4	27.2	52.9	18.6
Raleigh, NC	91.8	95.9	89.7	86.8	61.2	50.9	61.8	31.0	60.0	21.9
Reno, NV	89.0	91.4	91.3	91.6	64.6	33.5	35.3	21.2	48.1	12.5
Richmond, VA	85.4	92.3	78.8	81.7	50.8	39.6	61.8	15.5	62.5	14.3
Riverside, CA	80.6	83.5	92.0	87.2	68.5	23.0	23.8	26.5	47.8	11.8
Rochester, MN	94.0	96.3	77.2	83.8	74.1	46.7	47.8	18.0	59.9	26.2
Sacramento, CA	85.3	89.2	90.1	79.7	73.0	33.1	39.6	21.0	37.4	17.7
Salt Lake City, UT	88.8	94.2	82.2	83.8	62.2	46.5	51.8	26.7	61.5	16.5
San Antonio, TX	82.4	82.4	91.1	87.2	74.8	26.0	26.0	23.9	53.1	16.4
San Diego, CA	88.1	89.2	91.3	88.7	69.1	45.9	48.1	25.8	53.8	20.4
San Francisco, CA	88.5	96.7	88.4	79.3	78.9	58.1	73.8	30.5	46.7	34.2
San Jose, CA	84.6	88.6	91.8	87.0	67.5	43.7	44.2	35.5	55.9	15.9
Santa Rosa, CA	86.2	91.3	87.6	87.1	62.8	32.6	37.4	30.2	40.2	12.1
Savannah, GA	87.6	93.0	83.3	85.8	79.4	28.2	42.9	15.5	46.7	27.1
Seattle, WA	94.8	97.8	86.8	88.4	83.5	64.0	69.8	29.5	61.5	43.0
Sioux Falls, SD	92.3	94.7	74.7	70.8	65.3	35.2	37.6	14.3	36.4	14.3
Springfield, IL	91.3	93.4	81.2	91.7	87.8	35.8	38.6	17.8	64.9	33.6
Tallahassee, FL	93.5	96.4	88.2	96.0	88.5	48.2	56.9	28.1	80.7	39.6
Tampa, FL	87.9	90.1	82.9	86.7	78.3	38.6	44.4	16.8	63.0	23.5
Tucson, AZ	85.0	88.0	84.3	86.7	72.7	27.4	30.1	21.3	48.0	14.0
Tulsa, OK	87.3	89.9	88.8	74.8	57.6	31.5	36.5	17.6	37.8	10.7
Tuscaloosa, AL	89.1	94.4	84.1	84.5	73.8	36.9	54.1	17.6	53.0	11.5
Virginia Beach, VA	93.5	95.3	91.1	88.2	84.5	36.0	38.8	26.4	40.6	25.5
Washington, DC	90.9	98.1	86.3	94.9	73.1	58.5	89.5	27.3	81.9	47.3
Wichita, KS	88.3	90.4	87.4	81.3	62.8	30.1	32.9	15.2	36.3	13.0
Winston-Salem, NC	88.2	89.9	87.8	87.7	58.1	34.5	41.8	21.0	65.7	13.5
U.S.	88.0	89.9	86.0	87.1	68.7	32.1	33.5	21.6	54.3	16.4

Note: Figures shown cover persons 25 years old and over; (1) People of Hispanic origin can be of any race
Source: U.S. Census Bureau, 2015-2019 American Community Survey 5-Year Estimates

A-134   Appendix A: Comparative Statistics

Educational Attainment by Race: Metro Area

Metro Area	High School Graduate or Higher (%)					Bachelor's Degree or Higher (%)				
	Total	White	Black	Asian	Hisp.[1]	Total	White	Black	Asian	Hisp.[1]
Albuquerque, NM	88.6	90.4	91.0	87.3	81.1	32.2	35.0	30.4	47.8	19.1
Allentown, PA	90.0	91.1	88.0	87.5	74.9	29.5	30.1	19.5	54.6	13.2
Anchorage, AK	93.7	95.6	93.5	83.9	86.3	32.3	37.0	19.5	25.0	21.3
Ann Arbor, MI	95.3	96.3	89.2	96.6	85.5	55.9	57.7	27.4	83.0	42.9
Athens, GA	87.8	90.1	80.3	91.0	60.0	39.4	44.5	17.6	69.9	22.2
Atlanta, GA	89.6	91.0	90.5	87.5	64.9	38.6	42.6	30.2	58.1	20.6
Austin, TX	89.9	91.4	91.0	92.5	74.0	44.8	46.7	29.1	71.8	23.0
Baton Rouge, LA	87.4	90.5	82.8	86.1	67.5	27.6	31.9	18.5	53.2	16.4
Boise City, ID	91.8	93.4	88.7	86.6	67.8	31.7	32.5	27.9	46.7	11.4
Boston, MA	91.7	94.3	85.2	86.0	72.0	48.1	50.6	26.3	62.3	22.8
Boulder, CO	95.0	95.8	87.8	93.8	71.6	62.1	62.8	30.5	72.5	26.5
Cape Coral, FL	88.4	90.0	79.5	88.6	71.0	28.2	29.4	15.9	45.3	14.8
Cedar Rapids, IA	94.3	95.2	84.0	81.4	77.6	31.0	31.3	15.4	51.7	22.0
Charleston, SC	90.7	93.7	84.4	86.3	71.1	35.6	42.6	16.5	49.0	20.5
Charlotte, NC	89.0	90.8	88.4	84.9	63.1	35.1	37.7	25.9	58.1	17.7
Chicago, IL	88.7	91.4	87.8	90.7	68.0	38.0	41.6	22.7	64.7	14.8
Cincinnati, OH	91.0	91.9	86.6	88.9	74.1	33.6	34.8	19.2	65.9	24.6
Clarksville, TN	90.7	91.2	89.6	85.6	86.2	24.8	24.9	22.2	43.3	19.1
Cleveland, OH	90.6	92.3	85.2	86.8	74.6	31.2	34.5	15.1	61.5	15.8
College Station, TX	86.6	87.3	85.3	94.0	63.3	37.5	39.3	16.5	78.4	15.9
Colorado Springs, CO	94.4	95.5	94.5	87.4	82.7	38.5	40.5	27.2	44.8	20.9
Columbia, MO	93.6	94.3	89.3	93.9	86.8	42.7	43.8	18.8	71.2	34.4
Columbia, SC	89.9	91.7	87.9	90.5	65.1	32.7	37.3	23.2	58.9	20.0
Columbus, OH	91.5	92.7	87.4	88.5	76.6	36.7	38.3	21.5	63.7	25.6
Dallas, TX	85.6	85.9	91.0	88.8	60.3	35.2	35.8	27.4	62.0	14.0
Davenport, IA	91.0	92.6	79.5	80.4	72.9	26.9	27.6	13.8	46.8	15.6
Denver, CO	91.2	92.8	89.8	86.0	71.0	43.8	46.2	27.0	52.1	16.7
Des Moines, IA	92.5	94.2	84.6	74.1	62.8	36.5	37.6	19.8	38.7	13.6
Durham, NC	88.8	91.0	86.3	91.3	52.7	45.3	51.4	28.8	72.3	16.9
Edison, NJ	86.5	90.8	85.4	83.5	71.4	40.4	46.0	25.6	54.5	19.6
El Paso, TX	78.3	79.5	95.3	90.1	74.4	23.2	24.0	29.9	52.6	19.2
Fargo, ND	94.8	96.1	81.7	78.4	83.4	38.6	39.8	22.2	46.8	19.5
Fayetteville, NC	89.6	91.5	89.7	84.8	80.2	23.7	25.6	21.5	39.3	19.3
Fort Collins, CO	95.9	96.2	95.7	92.2	83.8	47.3	47.5	37.8	62.7	25.1
Fort Wayne, IN	89.6	91.9	85.2	57.5	63.5	27.8	29.4	15.8	33.7	10.4
Fort Worth, TX	85.6	85.9	91.0	88.8	60.3	35.2	35.8	27.4	62.0	14.0
Grand Rapids, MI	91.2	93.1	85.7	75.2	63.7	32.7	34.3	18.3	37.3	14.2
Greeley, CO	88.1	89.1	84.2	87.9	66.6	27.5	28.0	27.2	42.4	9.1
Green Bay, WI	92.0	93.5	83.2	83.1	57.0	27.8	28.5	17.3	44.2	9.2
Greensboro, NC	86.8	88.9	86.1	76.4	57.6	29.5	32.0	23.0	42.6	13.7
Honolulu, HI	91.9	97.3	97.0	88.8	93.4	35.0	48.3	29.9	36.1	25.2
Houston, TX	83.7	83.6	91.0	87.8	64.1	32.8	33.3	27.5	56.6	15.0
Huntsville, AL	90.2	91.6	86.8	92.7	66.6	39.2	40.9	31.4	61.9	24.3
Indianapolis, IN	89.7	91.3	85.9	82.6	63.7	34.7	36.7	20.7	56.2	17.6
Jacksonville, FL	90.9	92.2	87.2	89.4	84.3	31.4	33.8	19.7	49.7	27.0
Kansas City, MO	92.0	93.6	88.5	85.5	69.0	37.1	39.7	20.7	54.8	17.8
Lafayette, LA	84.1	87.0	76.3	73.1	63.9	23.4	26.4	13.0	34.9	12.3
Lakeland, FL	85.0	86.1	82.2	80.4	73.1	20.2	20.6	15.0	41.5	14.6
Las Vegas, NV	86.1	88.3	89.7	90.4	66.8	24.5	25.9	17.8	38.8	10.5
Lexington, KY	90.1	91.6	85.1	91.1	60.8	37.3	39.2	19.0	64.5	16.9
Lincoln, NE	93.7	95.2	86.1	78.9	70.4	39.0	39.8	23.9	46.3	19.7
Little Rock, AR	90.4	91.8	87.4	90.5	67.5	30.4	32.7	21.8	54.3	13.8
Los Angeles, CA	80.7	83.2	89.9	88.2	62.2	34.5	36.6	27.3	53.4	13.3
Louisville, KY	90.1	90.9	87.2	86.3	74.0	29.6	31.0	18.3	54.2	22.7
Madison, WI	95.3	96.2	88.8	90.9	76.4	46.1	46.2	23.9	68.0	26.7

Table continued on following page.

Appendix A: Comparative Statistics   A-135

Metro Area	High School Graduate or Higher (%)					Bachelor's Degree or Higher (%)				
	Total	White	Black	Asian	Hisp.[1]	Total	White	Black	Asian	Hisp.[1]
Manchester, NH	92.1	92.6	83.7	88.3	71.7	38.1	37.4	24.0	64.8	19.4
Memphis, TN	88.0	91.9	85.2	87.9	57.7	28.3	35.7	19.1	58.2	14.8
Miami, FL	85.5	86.9	81.4	87.5	80.0	32.3	35.4	19.8	51.6	27.7
Midland, TX	84.3	84.9	85.7	83.4	69.6	27.1	28.3	18.3	54.5	10.6
Milwaukee, WI	91.5	94.4	83.8	83.5	68.7	35.6	39.9	14.3	51.0	14.5
Minneapolis, MN	93.6	96.3	82.6	81.2	68.5	42.0	44.3	22.0	45.3	20.1
Nashville, TN	90.0	90.9	88.5	84.0	62.9	36.2	37.5	28.2	51.5	17.3
New Haven, CT	90.1	91.8	87.6	90.1	74.4	35.0	37.4	20.2	65.3	15.6
New Orleans, LA	86.9	90.6	82.0	77.4	75.1	30.3	36.8	18.7	38.7	19.2
New York, NY	86.5	90.8	85.4	83.5	71.4	40.4	46.0	25.6	54.5	19.6
Oklahoma City, OK	89.0	89.9	90.0	84.3	60.6	30.5	32.0	21.3	46.0	13.2
Omaha, NE	91.7	93.1	88.0	76.7	61.2	36.3	37.7	21.5	49.7	14.8
Orlando, FL	89.5	91.1	85.8	88.8	83.6	32.2	33.9	22.8	52.3	23.2
Peoria, IL	91.7	92.9	80.3	92.4	75.4	27.7	28.1	12.8	69.8	20.9
Philadelphia, PA	90.7	93.2	87.5	84.6	70.1	37.9	42.1	21.4	57.1	17.8
Phoenix, AZ	87.5	89.1	90.1	88.6	68.5	31.5	32.3	25.7	58.9	13.1
Pittsburgh, PA	93.9	94.4	89.7	88.2	88.0	34.9	35.3	20.2	70.7	36.8
Portland, OR	92.1	93.5	88.2	86.7	68.7	39.8	40.3	28.0	52.1	19.5
Providence, RI	87.7	89.2	85.5	85.5	73.3	32.3	33.7	22.3	51.6	14.0
Provo, UT	94.5	94.9	97.4	94.6	75.3	40.3	40.6	35.4	58.9	20.2
Raleigh, NC	91.7	94.1	89.0	92.4	62.5	46.8	50.5	30.8	73.2	20.1
Reno, NV	88.7	91.0	90.3	91.8	63.3	30.8	32.5	21.7	45.4	11.0
Richmond, VA	89.9	92.8	85.0	88.8	67.3	37.4	43.4	21.8	64.0	21.3
Riverside, CA	81.1	83.7	89.6	90.4	67.4	21.7	22.0	23.8	48.6	10.7
Rochester, MN	94.1	95.5	78.3	84.4	71.3	38.7	38.7	18.1	58.0	23.1
Sacramento, CA	89.3	92.0	90.4	84.3	74.1	33.5	34.8	23.0	44.1	17.9
Salt Lake City, UT	90.8	94.0	85.4	86.8	69.0	35.0	37.2	25.1	51.4	14.3
San Antonio, TX	85.1	85.3	92.2	87.5	76.1	28.2	28.4	28.8	51.7	17.2
San Diego, CA	87.4	88.2	91.8	89.2	69.8	38.8	39.5	25.9	51.3	17.8
San Francisco, CA	89.1	93.6	90.7	87.3	71.5	49.7	56.1	28.8	55.4	21.7
San Jose, CA	88.1	90.4	92.0	90.8	69.3	51.5	49.4	38.2	65.5	17.6
Santa Rosa, CA	88.8	92.9	89.3	88.9	64.6	35.5	39.3	29.8	44.4	14.1
Savannah, GA	89.8	92.0	86.2	84.2	81.2	31.5	36.7	19.8	45.2	26.2
Seattle, WA	92.6	95.0	89.6	88.8	73.3	43.0	43.8	25.8	56.1	22.4
Sioux Falls, SD	92.9	94.5	75.5	72.1	66.9	33.5	35.0	14.4	37.1	15.6
Springfield, IL	92.6	93.9	81.6	92.7	87.0	33.9	35.2	17.4	64.0	31.5
Tallahassee, FL	90.6	93.9	83.5	96.3	82.1	38.4	44.1	23.0	79.3	30.2
Tampa, FL	89.6	90.8	87.0	85.4	80.2	30.4	30.9	22.4	51.7	22.6
Tucson, AZ	88.4	90.9	87.6	88.0	75.8	32.4	35.1	25.6	53.1	16.3
Tulsa, OK	89.4	90.9	89.5	77.7	63.4	27.7	29.8	19.2	37.0	12.4
Tuscaloosa, AL	87.1	89.9	82.8	81.1	70.1	27.4	33.4	16.2	51.8	11.5
Virginia Beach, VA	91.4	93.9	87.2	87.3	84.0	31.9	36.2	22.1	43.3	24.8
Washington, DC	90.9	94.1	91.5	91.1	68.0	50.9	59.2	34.8	65.1	25.7
Wichita, KS	90.1	91.7	87.1	81.9	65.8	30.6	32.3	17.2	36.9	15.3
Winston-Salem, NC	87.0	87.9	86.9	87.2	56.7	26.6	27.7	20.6	54.6	12.2
U.S.	88.0	89.9	86.0	87.1	68.7	32.1	33.5	21.6	54.3	16.4

Note: Figures shown cover persons 25 years old and over; Figures cover the Metropolitan Statistical Area—see Appendix B for areas included; (1) People of Hispanic origin can be of any race
Source: U.S. Census Bureau, 2015-2019 American Community Survey 5-Year Estimates

A-136 Appendix A: Comparative Statistics

Cost of Living Index

Urban Area	Composite	Groceries	Housing	Utilities	Transp.	Health	Misc.
Albuquerque, NM	93.8	104.8	84.5	87.7	97.2	99.8	96.6
Allentown, PA	104.4	98.4	114.0	103.4	104.8	94.6	100.6
Anchorage, AK	124.5	132.6	140.0	124.0	114.8	144.2	109.7
Ann Arbor, MI	n/a	n/a	n/a	n/a	n/a	n/a	n/a
Athens, GA	n/a	n/a	n/a	n/a	n/a	n/a	n/a
Atlanta, GA	102.8	103.4	103.5	85.1	103.6	107.1	106.0
Austin, TX	99.7	91.2	105.5	95.2	90.7	105.8	101.4
Baton Rouge	99.4	102.6	92.3	85.4	100.5	104.5	106.5
Boise City, ID	98.7	94.5	97.5	81.9	108.5	103.0	102.8
Boston, MA	151.0	109.3	228.6	120.5	112.0	118.3	129.3
Boulder, CO	n/a	n/a	n/a	n/a	n/a	n/a	n/a
Cape Coral, FL	100.6	107.8	89.6	98.8	98.7	108.5	106.3
Cedar Rapids, IA	96.2	94.8	83.0	102.1	96.6	107.0	103.9
Charleston, SC	97.2	99.7	93.2	120.4	86.6	97.5	95.9
Charlotte, NC	98.2	101.7	88.8	95.6	90.7	105.1	106.0
Chicago, IL	120.6	101.9	155.7	92.4	125.9	100.0	109.4
Cincinnati, OH	99.7	91.2	105.5	95.2	90.7	105.8	101.4
Clarksville, TN	n/a	n/a	n/a	n/a	n/a	n/a	n/a
Cleveland, OH	96.9	106.0	83.3	96.1	99.4	104.4	102.6
College Station, TX	n/a	n/a	n/a	n/a	n/a	n/a	n/a
Colorado Springs, CO	101.1	95.9	101.3	97.2	97.7	108.6	104.1
Columbia, MO	91.8	95.5	75.0	100.0	92.0	102.6	99.8
Columbia, SC	93.5	103.1	72.7	126.2	87.1	79.9	100.5
Columbus, OH	92.6	98.6	81.2	89.1	95.5	88.5	99.7
Dallas, TX	108.2	100.2	118.8	106.8	96.7	105.4	106.7
Davenport, IA	92.0	99.7	76.9	98.9	105.8	105.3	93.7
Denver, CO	111.3	98.3	139.3	80.5	100.9	103.6	106.6
Des Moines, IA	89.9	95.2	80.2	90.1	99.1	95.4	92.3
Durham, NC	n/a	n/a	n/a	n/a	n/a	n/a	n/a
Edison, NJ[1]	120.6	108.7	149.3	105.8	107.8	102.5	112.4
El Paso, TX	87.7	102.3	73.7	85.7	99.0	99.3	89.0
Fargo, ND	98.6	111.5	77.6	90.5	100.4	120.1	108.9
Fayetteville, NC	n/a	n/a	n/a	n/a	n/a	n/a	n/a
Fort Collins, CO	n/a	n/a	n/a	n/a	n/a	n/a	n/a
Fort Wayne, IN	86.9	86.7	62.3	95.7	99.5	101.5	98.6
Fort Worth, TX	94.9	92.4	88.4	107.2	96.9	101.5	96.2
Grand Rapids, MI	94.1	92.8	87.4	98.5	104.1	92.3	96.3
Greeley, CO	n/a	n/a	n/a	n/a	n/a	n/a	n/a
Green Bay, WI	91.1	91.0	77.9	97.4	97.7	101.8	96.6
Greensboro, NC[2]	90.8	101.4	66.7	94.6	92.0	119.5	100.5
Honolulu, HI	192.9	165.0	332.6	172.3	138.2	118.8	124.2
Houston, TX	95.8	88.4	91.2	105.8	95.2	92.0	100.3
Huntsville, AL	91.3	95.1	66.6	99.0	97.3	96.4	104.7
Indianapolis, IN	92.4	94.1	78.4	105.4	97.9	90.6	98.0
Jacksonville, FL	91.7	98.4	88.0	97.7	86.0	83.7	92.7
Kansas City, MO	95.8	102.4	82.6	100.6	92.6	105.9	101.7
Lafayette, LA	88.9	101.8	72.0	88.0	104.7	88.0	93.3
Lakeland, FL	n/a	n/a	n/a	n/a	n/a	n/a	n/a
Las Vegas, NV	103.6	95.8	118.3	98.6	114.0	100.2	94.2
Lexington, KY	92.7	89.9	83.7	95.6	96.7	78.9	100.7
Lincoln, NE	93.0	95.6	78.7	90.2	93.4	105.8	102.2
Little Rock, AR	96.0	95.1	88.1	97.4	94.7	89.6	103.2
Los Angeles, CA	146.7	116.3	230.6	106.2	134.8	110.8	112.0
Louisville, KY	94.1	91.8	79.8	94.6	98.1	105.2	103.7
Madison, WI	107.0	107.6	108.6	99.8	104.4	124.0	106.0
Manchester, NH	108.9	102.2	109.6	117.9	104.1	116.0	108.9

Table continued on following page.

Appendix A: Comparative Statistics   A-137

Urban Area	Composite	Groceries	Housing	Utilities	Transp.	Health	Misc.
Memphis, TN	99.7	91.2	105.5	95.2	90.7	105.8	101.4
Miami, FL	115.0	110.5	144.3	102.0	101.5	100.6	102.7
Midland, TX	102.1	93.6	91.5	106.6	104.1	96.5	112.6
Milwaukee, WI	96.7	93.4	100.5	94.8	99.8	115.9	92.4
Minneapolis, MN	106.6	103.6	102.9	97.5	104.4	105.6	113.9
Nashville, TN	98.9	99.5	98.5	97.0	97.9	92.4	100.4
New Haven, CT	122.3	111.0	128.5	136.7	110.6	115.8	121.9
New Orleans, LA	105.0	102.6	125.5	81.5	101.3	115.1	96.1
New York, NY[3]	181.6	128.4	339.0	121.4	113.7	107.1	123.1
Oklahoma City, OK	86.0	93.3	69.6	95.3	86.2	95.0	92.1
Omaha, NE	92.3	96.8	83.6	99.4	98.3	96.4	93.3
Orlando, FL	92.1	100.7	85.1	97.2	89.3	88.3	94.1
Peoria, IL	92.9	89.7	76.5	93.7	106.3	96.8	102.7
Philadelphia, PA	110.9	118.7	116.5	105.6	116.1	101.8	104.8
Phoenix, AZ	99.3	99.7	103.8	109.5	107.2	90.1	91.9
Pittsburgh, PA	103.1	111.9	105.7	116.1	114.0	93.1	92.6
Portland, OR	134.7	112.4	186.4	87.1	131.0	115.6	119.4
Providence, RI	119.2	106.7	132.8	126.4	112.1	109.3	114.6
Provo, UT	98.2	93.0	96.1	84.7	100.7	94.5	105.4
Raleigh, NC	95.4	92.7	89.0	98.3	90.9	103.8	100.9
Reno, NV	114.1	118.7	125.8	85.9	126.3	113.9	107.6
Richmond, VA	94.2	89.0	86.0	97.6	86.9	106.7	102.1
Riverside, CA	99.7	91.2	105.5	95.2	90.7	105.8	101.4
Rochester, MN	n/a	n/a	n/a	n/a	n/a	n/a	n/a
Sacramento, CA	118.4	120.2	134.2	102.9	139.0	113.6	104.8
Salt Lake City, UT	103.6	108.0	106.7	87.8	103.6	105.7	103.6
San Antonio, TX	89.5	88.0	82.2	87.6	89.1	87.2	96.5
San Diego, CA	142.1	116.1	216.3	123.2	129.2	107.3	107.3
San Francisco, CA	197.9	131.3	368.9	123.0	145.3	129.6	133.4
San Jose, CA	n/a	n/a	n/a	n/a	n/a	n/a	n/a
Santa Rosa, CA	n/a	n/a	n/a	n/a	n/a	n/a	n/a
Savannah, GA	89.5	95.7	66.2	96.0	94.9	106.1	100.0
Seattle, WA	157.5	129.1	227.6	108.0	137.8	128.6	136.2
Sioux Falls, SD	92.5	96.3	86.3	84.7	91.9	107.7	96.3
Springfield, IL	n/a	n/a	n/a	n/a	n/a	n/a	n/a
Tallahassee, FL	97.5	107.4	93.3	86.5	96.2	99.6	99.9
Tampa, FL	91.2	104.8	79.2	85.9	99.4	98.3	93.7
Tucson, AZ	97.5	100.5	87.9	99.9	101.1	98.7	102.0
Tulsa, OK	86.0	96.2	62.7	99.5	84.4	91.6	96.1
Tuscaloosa, AL	n/a	n/a	n/a	n/a	n/a	n/a	n/a
Virginia Beach, VA[4]	94.1	92.7	89.1	97.4	92.2	90.4	98.7
Washington, DC	159.9	116.0	277.1	117.9	110.6	95.8	118.1
Wichita, KS	91.1	94.3	69.6	99.3	95.3	96.1	102.5
Winston-Salem, NC	90.8	101.4	66.7	94.6	92.0	119.5	100.5
U.S.	100.0	100.0	100.0	100.0	100.0	100.0	100.0

Note: The Cost of Living Index measures regional differences in the cost of consumer goods and services, excluding taxes and non-consumer expenditures, for professional and managerial households in the top income quintile. It is based on more than 50,000 prices covering almost 60 different items for which prices are collected three times a year by chambers of commerce, economic development organizations or university applied economic centers in each participating urban area. The numbers shown should be read as a percentage above or below the national average of 100. For example, a value of 115.4 in the groceries column indicates that grocery prices are 15.4% higher than the national average. Small differences in the index numbers should not be interpreted as significant. In cases where data is not available for the city, data for the metro area or for a neighboring city has been provided and noted as follows: (1) Middlesex-Monmouth NJ; (2) Winston-Salem, NC; (3) Brooklyn, NY; (4) Hampton Roads-SE Virginia
Source: The Council for Community and Economic Research (formerly ACCRA), Cost of Living Index, 2020

A-138 Appendix A: Comparative Statistics

Grocery Prices

Urban Area	T-Bone Steak ($/pound)	Frying Chicken ($/pound)	Whole Milk ($/half gal.)	Eggs ($/dozen)	Orange Juice ($/64 oz.)	Coffee ($/11.5 oz.)
Albuquerque, NM	11.18	1.16	2.10	1.41	3.96	4.63
Allentown, PA	13.52	1.36	2.09	1.36	3.47	3.73
Anchorage, AK	13.95	1.71	2.73	2.19	4.39	5.84
Ann Arbor, MI	n/a	n/a	n/a	n/a	n/a	n/a
Athens, GA	n/a	n/a	n/a	n/a	n/a	n/a
Atlanta, GA	14.32	1.30	1.99	1.25	3.76	4.92
Austin, TX	9.67	1.02	1.84	1.39	3.22	4.23
Baton Rouge	11.70	1.42	2.65	1.53	3.69	4.26
Boise City, ID	11.77	1.13	1.37	1.18	3.69	4.46
Boston, MA	13.53	1.64	2.27	2.00	3.73	4.41
Boulder, CO	n/a	n/a	n/a	n/a	n/a	n/a
Cape Coral, FL	11.21	1.92	2.40	1.51	3.36	3.34
Cedar Rapids, IA	10.99	1.68	2.49	1.24	3.31	4.86
Charleston, SC	12.80	1.27	2.25	1.26	3.53	4.42
Charlotte, NC	12.19	1.46	1.69	1.34	3.54	4.02
Chicago, IL	12.67	1.99	2.42	1.47	3.96	4.48
Cincinnati, OH	13.16	1.25	1.42	1.09	3.61	4.28
Clarksville, TN	n/a	n/a	n/a	n/a	n/a	n/a
Cleveland, OH	14.49	1.83	1.55	1.32	3.72	4.57
College Station, TX	n/a	n/a	n/a	n/a	n/a	n/a
Colorado Springs, CO	13.95	1.39	1.76	1.27	3.39	4.55
Columbia, MO	11.89	1.53	2.18	1.08	3.56	4.44
Columbia, SC	12.24	1.40	2.19	1.31	3.54	4.28
Columbus, OH	12.68	1.16	1.58	1.17	3.53	7.19
Dallas, TX	10.44	1.48	1.97	1.15	3.45	4.51
Davenport, IA	11.56	1.53	2.60	1.32	3.44	4.60
Denver, CO	12.57	1.48	1.76	1.46	3.36	4.17
Des Moines, IA	12.05	1.51	2.18	1.34	3.05	4.24
Durham, NC	n/a	n/a	n/a	n/a	n/a	n/a
Edison, NJ[1]	13.96	1.67	2.41	1.60	3.51	4.06
El Paso, TX	10.83	2.02	2.67	1.85	3.93	5.38
Fargo, ND	n/a	n/a	n/a	n/a	n/a	n/a
Fayetteville, NC	n/a	n/a	n/a	n/a	n/a	n/a
Fort Collins, CO	n/a	n/a	n/a	n/a	n/a	n/a
Fort Wayne, IN	11.87	1.07	1.31	0.74	3.13	3.47
Fort Worth, TX	9.35	1.87	1.92	1.26	3.55	4.49
Grand Rapids, MI	12.68	1.12	1.59	1.25	3.34	3.25
Greeley, CO	n/a	n/a	n/a	n/a	n/a	n/a
Green Bay, WI	11.37	1.10	1.93	1.51	3.64	4.47
Greensboro, NC[2]	11.86	1.27	1.55	1.45	3.94	4.03
Honolulu, HI	13.84	2.45	4.31	3.77	5.44	8.69
Houston, TX	11.29	1.13	1.58	1.42	3.50	3.84
Huntsville, AL	13.10	1.45	1.62	0.95	3.75	4.36
Indianapolis, IN	11.98	1.37	1.68	1.13	3.34	4.17
Jacksonville, FL	12.36	1.49	2.21	1.46	3.30	3.86
Kansas City, MO	11.83	1.92	1.87	1.17	3.22	3.44
Lafayette, LA	11.14	1.16	2.19	1.69	3.82	4.26
Lakeland, FL	n/a	n/a	n/a	n/a	n/a	n/a
Las Vegas, NV	10.89	1.35	2.46	2.07	3.99	4.69
Lexington, KY	10.82	1.11	1.64	1.16	3.18	3.69
Lincoln, NE	11.88	1.46	2.21	1.42	3.03	4.13
Little Rock, AR	10.99	1.16	1.78	1.43	3.23	3.89
Los Angeles, CA	12.32	1.72	2.19	2.88	4.09	4.90
Louisville, KY	12.70	1.09	1.15	1.02	3.13	4.01
Madison, WI	14.10	1.61	2.26	1.17	3.46	4.65

Table continued on following page.

Appendix A: Comparative Statistics   A-139

Urban Area	T-Bone Steak ($/pound)	Frying Chicken ($/pound)	Whole Milk ($/half gal.)	Eggs ($/dozen)	Orange Juice ($/64 oz.)	Coffee ($/11.5 oz.)
Manchester, NH	13.66	1.19	2.79	1.52	3.41	3.66
Memphis, TN	9.64	0.98	1.79	1.27	3.09	4.05
Miami, FL	12.55	1.73	3.16	1.71	3.67	4.00
Midland, TX	10.05	1.16	1.51	1.47	3.37	4.14
Milwaukee, WI	12.91	1.22	1.98	1.11	3.38	4.14
Minneapolis, MN	13.63	2.10	2.60	1.81	3.71	4.67
Nashville, TN	13.20	1.42	1.96	1.05	3.65	4.37
New Haven, CT	10.42	1.51	2.52	1.73	3.32	4.03
New Orleans, LA	10.51	1.21	2.30	1.63	3.63	3.83
New York, NY[3]	15.20	2.36	2.82	2.78	4.36	4.74
Oklahoma City, OK	11.70	1.34	1.87	1.23	3.23	4.07
Omaha, NE	11.27	1.24	2.00	1.87	3.47	4.87
Orlando, FL	11.14	1.27	2.39	1.31	3.60	3.91
Peoria, IL	10.98	1.03	1.32	0.93	3.45	5.99
Philadelphia, PA	13.82	1.60	2.18	1.99	4.08	4.54
Phoenix, AZ	13.58	1.68	1.63	1.80	3.71	4.84
Pittsburgh, PA	13.64	1.61	2.03	1.35	3.36	4.62
Portland, OR	11.98	1.58	2.12	2.36	4.10	5.30
Providence, RI	12.73	1.75	2.52	2.17	3.57	4.42
Provo, UT	11.04	1.66	1.50	1.46	3.65	4.66
Raleigh, NC	10.15	0.97	1.61	1.19	3.79	3.83
Reno, NV	12.84	1.58	2.93	2.07	3.36	5.86
Richmond, VA	11.36	1.05	1.58	0.86	3.20	3.78
Riverside, CA	n/a	n/a	n/a	n/a	n/a	n/a
Rochester, MN	n/a	n/a	n/a	n/a	n/a	n/a
Sacramento, CA	10.84	1.31	2.66	2.50	4.16	5.46
Salt Lake City, UT	11.44	1.81	1.73	1.32	3.44	4.51
San Antonio, TX	9.89	1.01	1.63	1.66	3.14	3.93
San Diego, CA	12.27	1.72	2.19	2.88	4.09	5.21
San Francisco, CA	14.94	1.80	2.83	3.16	4.26	6.63
San Jose, CA	n/a	n/a	n/a	n/a	n/a	n/a
Santa Rosa, CA	n/a	n/a	n/a	n/a	n/a	n/a
Savannah, GA	11.65	1.51	1.76	1.50	3.22	3.92
Seattle, WA	12.88	2.15	2.50	2.13	4.05	6.00
Sioux Falls, SD	n/a	n/a	n/a	n/a	n/a	n/a
Springfield, IL	n/a	n/a	n/a	n/a	n/a	n/a
Tallahassee, FL	11.54	1.56	2.71	1.70	3.95	3.85
Tampa, FL	11.11	1.74	2.66	1.68	3.43	4.28
Tucson, AZ	13.61	1.65	1.59	1.89	3.70	5.03
Tulsa, OK	11.20	1.30	2.00	1.38	3.44	3.89
Tuscaloosa, AL	n/a	n/a	n/a	n/a	n/a	n/a
Virginia Beach, VA[4]	11.03	1.20	1.75	1.35	3.88	3.85
Washington, DC	13.57	1.80	2.46	1.80	3.91	4.77
Wichita, KS	11.94	1.23	1.75	0.94	3.70	4.17
Winston-Salem, NC	11.86	1.27	1.55	1.45	3.94	4.03
Average*	11.78	1.39	2.05	1.47	3.57	4.34
Minimum*	8.03	0.94	1.03	0.74	2.94	3.02
Maximum*	15.86	2.65	4.31	3.77	5.44	8.69

Note: ***T-Bone Steak*** *(price per pound);* ***Frying Chicken*** *(price per pound, whole fryer);* ***Whole Milk*** *(half gallon carton);* ***Eggs*** *(price per dozen, Grade A, large);* ***Orange Juice*** *(64 oz. Tropicana or Florida Natural);* ***Coffee*** *(11.5 oz. can, vacuum-packed, Maxwell House, Hills Bros, or Folgers); (*) Average, minimum, and maximum values for all 284 areas in the Cost of Living Index report; n/a not available; In cases where data is not available for the city, data for the metro area or for a neighboring city has been provided and noted as follows: (1) Middlesex-Monmouth NJ; (2) Winston-Salem, NC; (3) Brooklyn, NY; (4) Hampton Roads-SE Virginia Source: The Council for Community and Economic Research (formerly ACCRA), Cost of Living Index, 2020*

A-140 Appendix A: Comparative Statistics

Housing and Utility Costs

Urban Area	New Home Price ($)	Apartment Rent ($/month)	All Electric ($/month)	Part Electric ($/month)	Other Energy ($/month)	Telephone ($/month)
Albuquerque, NM	329,645	874	-	114.55	40.75	183.90
Allentown, PA	397,306	1,488	-	100.14	86.52	189.10
Anchorage, AK	535,483	1,257	-	111.07	136.23	184.30
Ann Arbor, MI	n/a	n/a	n/a	n/a	n/a	n/a
Athens, GA	n/a	n/a	n/a	n/a	n/a	n/a
Atlanta, GA	380,418	1,245	-	87.42	33.41	185.10
Austin, TX	370,234	1,530	-	105.65	45.12	185.50
Baton Rouge	333,881	1,144	101.95	-	-	179.00
Boise City, ID	366,858	1,252	-	63.83	62.43	170.20
Boston, MA	744,522	3,157	-	72.47	161.39	181.10
Boulder, CO	n/a	n/a	n/a	n/a	n/a	n/a
Cape Coral, FL	328,513	1,061	158.56	-	-	187.80
Cedar Rapids, IA	322,911	831	-	139.90	48.93	180.80
Charleston, SC	325,960	1,372	228.13	-	-	187.30
Charlotte, NC	269,325	1,257	158.05	-	-	179.90
Chicago, IL	537,912	2,334	-	80.80	51.09	203.20
Cincinnati, OH	293,448	944	-	76.98	57.83	179.10
Clarksville, TN	n/a	n/a	n/a	n/a	n/a	n/a
Cleveland, OH	291,327	1,120	-	84.52	69.85	180.60
College Station, TX	n/a	n/a	n/a	n/a	n/a	n/a
Colorado Springs, CO	377,643	1,386	-	89.03	76.10	182.20
Columbia, MO	313,945	808	-	96.59	60.50	190.50
Columbia, SC	258,420	885	-	116.56	131.89	185.80
Columbus, OH	281,476	1,136	-	68.54	59.10	179.90
Dallas, TX	371,745	1,705	-	133.58	55.19	185.50
Davenport, IA	248,085	880	-	85.19	52.80	191.30
Denver, CO	530,852	1,545	-	59.31	46.19	186.50
Des Moines, IA	300,464	712	-	79.70	55.44	180.80
Durham, NC	n/a	n/a	n/a	n/a	n/a	n/a
Edison, NJ[1]	532,983	1,597	-	102.88	71.38	179.90
El Paso, TX	242,558	908	-	93.81	45.21	185.50
Fargo, ND	n/a	n/a	n/a	n/a	n/a	n/a
Fayetteville, NC	n/a	n/a	n/a	n/a	n/a	n/a
Fort Collins, CO	n/a	n/a	n/a	n/a	n/a	n/a
Fort Wayne, IN	204,729	859	-	93.81	50.38	184.30
Fort Worth, TX	258,331	1,164	-	133.52	54.42	184.70
Grand Rapids, MI	299,711	1,144	-	102.23	68.00	181.00
Greeley, CO	n/a	n/a	n/a	n/a	n/a	n/a
Green Bay, WI	304,129	813	-	82.41	78.05	179.40
Greensboro, NC[2]	248,204	1,242	158.18	-	-	169.60
Honolulu, HI	1,386,483	3,315	470.38	-	-	178.30
Houston, TX	297,296	1,119	-	161.68	38.31	184.00
Huntsville, AL	256,311	792	156.41	-	-	181.80
Indianapolis, IN	278,798	1,039	-	104.81	67.00	184.30
Jacksonville, FL	275,940	1,277	158.65	-	-	188.30
Kansas City, MO	299,164	1,207	-	96.98	60.15	189.70
Lafayette, LA	244,456	952	-	88.34	52.94	180.20
Lakeland, FL	n/a	n/a	n/a	n/a	n/a	n/a
Las Vegas, NV	412,949	1,205	-	120.44	50.07	175.30
Lexington, KY	309,955	976	-	79.97	77.60	206.50
Lincoln, NE	296,778	867	-	70.14	53.85	194.40
Little Rock, AR	371,333	740	-	85.47	57.54	197.30
Los Angeles, CA	841,834	2,775	-	122.73	62.94	189.50
Louisville, KY	273,187	1,038	-	80.02	77.60	180.80
Madison, WI	433,233	1,119	-	103.73	65.58	179.40

Table continued on following page.

Appendix A: Comparative Statistics   A-141

Urban Area	New Home Price ($)	Apartment Rent ($/month)	All Electric ($/month)	Part Electric ($/month)	Other Energy ($/month)	Telephone ($/month)
Manchester, NH	362,551	1,625	-	117.62	88.11	180.00
Memphis, TN	273,404	903	-	90.75	43.22	185.00
Miami, FL	447,771	2,208	162.18	-	-	188.20
Midland, TX	301,432	1,078	-	125.29	39.71	184.40
Milwaukee, WI	358,549	1,315	-	102.30	56.96	178.70
Minneapolis, MN	386,294	1,204	-	95.03	65.60	181.00
Nashville, TN	339,380	1,130	-	88.87	55.47	185.00
New Haven, CT	393,588	1,995	-	170.80	131.69	178.60
New Orleans, LA	520,536	1,618	-	58.74	38.53	180.20
New York, NY[3]	1,278,996	3,486	-	95.03	78.96	189.50
Oklahoma City, OK	258,612	873	-	92.78	58.17	188.40
Omaha, NE	305,521	1,100	-	89.62	56.82	194.40
Orlando, FL	294,196	1,148	164.06	-	-	187.90
Peoria, IL	306,592	771	-	80.23	81.73	191.30
Philadelphia, PA	426,075	1,517	-	100.69	93.28	192.10
Phoenix, AZ	362,970	1,639	189.67	-	-	178.50
Pittsburgh, PA	378,703	1,232	-	108.94	101.72	190.60
Portland, OR	623,494	2,459	-	81.22	62.64	170.50
Providence, RI	430,197	1,800	-	125.74	114.83	189.00
Provo, UT	382,813	1,129	-	68.02	58.46	187.20
Raleigh, NC	308,897	1,309	-	103.82	58.98	179.90
Reno, NV	489,573	1,330	-	82.05	42.67	177.90
Richmond, VA	318,880	1,135	-	94.98	81.43	178.00
Riverside, CA	n/a	n/a	n/a	n/a	n/a	n/a
Rochester, MN	n/a	n/a	n/a	n/a	n/a	n/a
Sacramento, CA	484,470	1,948	-	145.58	46.79	186.50
Salt Lake City, UT	401,866	1,164	-	74.91	60.06	187.80
San Antonio, TX	271,143	1,396	-	96.33	37.17	184.30
San Diego, CA	797,634	2,351	-	183.35	64.21	176.00
San Francisco, CA	1,362,163	4,098	-	183.22	84.62	198.20
San Jose, CA	n/a	n/a	n/a	n/a	n/a	n/a
Santa Rosa, CA	n/a	n/a	n/a	n/a	n/a	n/a
Savannah, GA	218,111	905	155.12	-	-	182.20
Seattle, WA	854,748	2,680	186.95	-	-	194.20
Sioux Falls, SD	n/a	n/a	n/a	n/a	n/a	n/a
Springfield, IL	n/a	n/a	n/a	n/a	n/a	n/a
Tallahassee, FL	344,867	1,132	124.57	-	-	189.90
Tampa, FL	278,508	1,296	165.98	-	-	189.50
Tucson, AZ	372,120	955	-	121.08	48.38	185.50
Tulsa, OK	239,022	680	-	87.50	59.74	188.20
Tuscaloosa, AL	n/a	n/a	n/a	n/a	n/a	n/a
Virginia Beach, VA[4]	317,054	1,200	-	97.52	76.48	185.90
Washington, DC	1,020,885	3,033	-	135.39	69.36	184.50
Wichita, KS	254,831	771	-	100.11	56.39	188.70
Winston-Salem, NC	248,204	1,242	158.18	-	-	169.60
Average*	368,594	1,168	170.86	100.47	65.28	184.30
Minimum*	190,567	502	91.58	31.42	26.08	169.60
Maximum*	2,227,806	4,738	470.38	280.31	280.06	206.50

Note: **New Home Price** *(2,400 sf living area, 8,000 sf lot, in urban area with full utilities);* **Apartment Rent** *(950 sf 2 bedroom/1.5 or 2 bath, unfurnished, excluding all utilities except water);* **All Electric** *(average monthly cost for an all-electric home);* **Part Electric** *(average monthly cost for a part-electric home);* **Other Energy** *(average monthly cost for natural gas, fuel oil, coal, wood, and any other forms of energy except electricity);* **Telephone** *(price includes the base monthly rate plus taxes and fees for three lines of mobile phone service); (*) Average, minimum, and maximum values for all 284 areas in the Cost of Living Index report; n/a not available; In cases where data is not available for the city, data for the metro area or for a neighboring city has been provided and noted as follows: (1) Middlesex-Monmouth NJ; (2) Winston-Salem, NC; (3) Brooklyn, NY; (4) Hampton Roads-SE Virginia*
Source: The Council for Community and Economic Research (formerly ACCRA), Cost of Living Index, 2020

A-142 Appendix A: Comparative Statistics

Health Care, Transportation, and Other Costs

Urban Area	Doctor ($/visit)	Dentist ($/visit)	Optometrist ($/visit)	Gasoline ($/gallon)	Beauty Salon ($/visit)	Men's Shirt ($)
Albuquerque, NM	106.93	98.97	108.12	1.85	39.81	30.50
Allentown, PA	75.54	110.86	106.13	2.54	43.55	25.80
Anchorage, AK	206.08	147.12	219.89	2.59	54.87	16.85
Ann Arbor, MI	n/a	n/a	n/a	n/a	n/a	n/a
Athens, GA	n/a	n/a	n/a	n/a	n/a	n/a
Atlanta, GA	119.80	105.78	110.27	2.23	47.13	27.27
Austin, TX	117.55	121.27	114.00	2.00	50.41	32.54
Baton Rouge	114.78	104.33	127.76	1.89	50.62	40.67
Boise City, ID	124.87	83.97	133.84	2.37	36.81	42.44
Boston, MA	194.00	108.27	102.75	2.19	64.17	44.46
Boulder, CO	n/a	n/a	n/a	n/a	n/a	n/a
Cape Coral, FL	123.46	110.14	85.53	2.45	33.41	25.30
Cedar Rapids, IA	122.25	115.00	102.58	2.15	37.59	28.78
Charleston, SC	131.23	102.76	81.87	2.06	57.83	27.44
Charlotte, NC	121.12	112.88	119.06	2.35	39.10	31.86
Chicago, IL	104.96	101.82	96.76	2.51	65.57	32.92
Cincinnati, OH	109.23	105.08	96.61	2.29	34.80	33.72
Clarksville, TN	n/a	n/a	n/a	n/a	n/a	n/a
Cleveland, OH	121.47	119.67	86.00	2.25	31.40	37.72
College Station, TX	n/a	n/a	n/a	n/a	n/a	n/a
Colorado Springs, CO	126.71	105.77	114.08	2.41	42.90	28.17
Columbia, MO	126.58	89.08	104.24	1.99	39.17	33.37
Columbia, SC	102.00	59.00	51.67	2.00	41.63	20.62
Columbus, OH	130.99	84.54	59.28	2.38	39.83	34.09
Dallas, TX	121.08	133.84	97.86	1.92	44.45	38.73
Davenport, IA	142.33	96.83	93.08	2.16	34.50	43.03
Denver, CO	111.77	105.51	104.86	2.49	44.29	30.30
Des Moines, IA	110.85	82.19	108.45	2.17	32.13	15.16
Durham, NC	n/a	n/a	n/a	n/a	n/a	n/a
Edison, NJ[1]	94.50	113.15	101.33	2.26	36.40	41.77
El Paso, TX	133.61	82.94	87.16	2.15	30.42	28.66
Fargo, ND	n/a	n/a	n/a	n/a	n/a	n/a
Fayetteville, NC	n/a	n/a	n/a	n/a	n/a	n/a
Fort Collins, CO	n/a	n/a	n/a	n/a	n/a	n/a
Fort Wayne, IN	129.50	94.17	89.56	2.30	33.00	33.48
Fort Worth, TX	91.05	108.33	92.25	1.83	53.57	39.58
Grand Rapids, MI	98.00	94.78	105.11	2.23	32.55	17.24
Greeley, CO	n/a	n/a	n/a	n/a	n/a	n/a
Green Bay, WI	176.50	81.33	74.00	1.71	22.70	30.51
Greensboro, NC[2]	124.74	139.81	109.70	2.12	35.48	39.18
Honolulu, HI	145.88	86.68	195.37	3.30	70.00	58.06
Houston, TX	88.11	111.03	119.84	1.92	61.37	33.46
Huntsville, AL	112.22	100.06	109.44	2.06	33.33	31.87
Indianapolis, IN	88.25	92.92	65.90	2.12	37.63	42.14
Jacksonville, FL	77.42	94.87	70.67	2.20	56.67	23.45
Kansas City, MO	108.18	107.03	106.75	2.02	38.27	33.28
Lafayette, LA	113.42	79.60	103.22	1.92	40.73	32.66
Lakeland, FL	n/a	n/a	n/a	n/a	n/a	n/a
Las Vegas, NV	106.13	96.98	105.92	2.36	46.67	29.07
Lexington, KY	82.39	76.80	74.07	2.08	37.90	38.67
Lincoln, NE	148.06	94.73	104.48	2.20	40.62	43.69
Little Rock, AR	125.22	69.23	101.50	1.89	42.83	35.86
Los Angeles, CA	125.00	110.78	125.58	3.31	76.50	32.87
Louisville, KY	133.98	82.89	71.56	2.28	49.58	32.27
Madison, WI	201.33	113.22	57.00	2.18	48.44	33.55

Table continued on following page.

Appendix A: Comparative Statistics   A-143

Urban Area	Doctor ($/visit)	Dentist ($/visit)	Optometrist ($/visit)	Gasoline ($/gallon)	Beauty Salon ($/visit)	Men's Shirt ($)
Manchester, NH	152.49	121.64	101.89	2.00	41.18	34.23
Memphis, TN	84.25	77.68	74.47	1.94	36.63	25.89
Miami, FL	111.06	107.78	105.63	2.24	70.00	23.08
Midland, TX	98.67	109.17	103.22	2.03	33.61	25.58
Milwaukee, WI	175.40	101.10	60.00	2.01	41.93	22.41
Minneapolis, MN	147.85	86.94	89.59	2.06	34.39	34.39
Nashville, TN	94.18	107.94	91.08	2.05	35.67	32.97
New Haven, CT	130.27	107.76	112.13	2.30	47.72	35.60
New Orleans, LA	156.11	111.89	94.77	2.02	48.89	27.54
New York, NY[3]	116.89	116.47	100.16	2.32	70.14	49.22
Oklahoma City, OK	112.21	93.98	102.53	1.90	40.17	18.12
Omaha, NE	119.00	78.66	114.83	2.07	34.01	23.77
Orlando, FL	83.46	97.71	100.39	2.10	54.17	17.78
Peoria, IL	114.08	79.00	141.52	2.36	30.00	29.99
Philadelphia, PA	133.89	96.86	108.61	2.43	60.55	31.89
Phoenix, AZ	96.33	89.83	96.17	2.49	41.67	27.57
Pittsburgh, PA	93.55	102.37	90.39	2.55	34.18	22.73
Portland, OR	168.67	101.75	146.25	2.78	56.44	41.23
Providence, RI	157.87	92.75	131.39	2.15	48.53	38.26
Provo, UT	99.81	84.76	97.49	2.39	36.53	24.62
Raleigh, NC	145.22	99.00	98.89	2.27	48.42	30.33
Reno, NV	155.00	114.56	117.17	2.98	40.13	21.17
Richmond, VA	139.74	99.40	116.20	2.01	44.43	29.26
Riverside, CA	n/a	n/a	n/a	n/a	n/a	n/a
Rochester, MN	n/a	n/a	n/a	n/a	n/a	n/a
Sacramento, CA	194.75	94.80	148.50	3.24	62.28	24.56
Salt Lake City, UT	107.49	101.65	89.78	2.44	34.97	23.53
San Antonio, TX	86.07	87.61	97.83	1.90	45.96	31.37
San Diego, CA	125.00	107.18	117.65	3.24	64.57	32.48
San Francisco, CA	149.63	132.68	144.57	3.46	82.05	42.08
San Jose, CA	n/a	n/a	n/a	n/a	n/a	n/a
Santa Rosa, CA	n/a	n/a	n/a	n/a	n/a	n/a
Savannah, GA	109.21	127.37	93.79	2.10	35.80	25.61
Seattle, WA	136.39	143.77	158.73	3.19	50.33	36.89
Sioux Falls, SD	n/a	n/a	n/a	n/a	n/a	n/a
Springfield, IL	n/a	n/a	n/a	n/a	n/a	n/a
Tallahassee, FL	126.07	111.09	69.75	2.25	36.64	33.99
Tampa, FL	99.22	105.57	99.12	2.11	37.26	23.11
Tucson, AZ	138.05	91.20	96.00	2.14	51.51	49.50
Tulsa, OK	109.61	90.61	99.06	1.77	35.56	23.57
Tuscaloosa, AL	n/a	n/a	n/a	n/a	n/a	n/a
Virginia Beach, VA[4]	83.17	103.67	98.57	2.00	38.97	36.02
Washington, DC	109.41	94.31	79.25	2.31	66.76	37.74
Wichita, KS	100.20	86.82	148.22	2.03	39.58	43.51
Winston-Salem, NC	124.74	139.81	109.70	2.12	35.48	39.18
Average*	115.44	99.32	108.10	2.21	39.27	31.37
Minimum*	36.68	59.00	51.36	1.71	19.00	11.00
Maximum*	219.00	153.10	250.97	3.46	82.05	58.33

Note: **Doctor** *(general practitioners routine exam of an established patient);* **Dentist** *(adult teeth cleaning and periodic oral examination);* **Optometrist** *(full vision eye exam for established adult patient);* **Gasoline** *(one gallon regular unleaded, national brand, including all taxes, cash price at self-service pump if available);* **Beauty Salon** *(woman's shampoo, trim, and blow-dry);* **Men's Shirt** *(cotton/polyester dress shirt, pinpoint weave, long sleeves); (*) Average, minimum, and maximum values for all 284 areas in the Cost of Living Index report; n/a not available; In cases where data is not available for the city, data for the metro area or for a neighboring city has been provided and noted as follows: (1) Middlesex-Monmouth NJ; (2) Winston-Salem, NC; (3) Brooklyn, NY; (4) Hampton Roads-SE Virginia*
Source: The Council for Community and Economic Research (formerly ACCRA), Cost of Living Index, 2020

A-144 Appendix A: Comparative Statistics

Number of Medical Professionals

City	Area Covered	MDs[1]	DOs[1,2]	Dentists	Podiatrists	Chiropractors	Optometrists
Albuquerque, NM	Bernalillo County	457.1	20.1	87.2	9.9	24.4	16.9
Allentown, PA	Lehigh County	347.8	83.3	88.3	12.2	29.5	20.0
Anchorage, AK	Anchorage Borough	360.0	46.1	128.5	4.9	63.2	31.3
Ann Arbor, MI	Washtenaw County	1,272.3	41.4	183.4	7.3	26.7	17.1
Athens, GA	Clarke County	313.5	14.9	53.8	4.7	21.0	16.4
Atlanta, GA	Fulton County	510.9	12.8	71.1	5.3	55.1	17.2
Austin, TX	Travis County	320.3	19.2	72.2	4.2	34.0	16.3
Baton Rouge, LA	East Baton Rouge Parish	388.4	7.2	75.9	4.5	12.5	13.9
Boise City, ID	Ada County	290.3	33.1	81.0	3.5	55.4	19.5
Boston, MA	Suffolk County	1,479.8	15.2	222.3	10.0	14.1	34.1
Boulder, CO	Boulder County	351.8	32.7	106.1	6.1	80.9	26.4
Cape Coral, FL	Lee County	190.7	29.8	49.8	8.3	27.4	12.6
Cedar Rapids, IA	Linn County	185.1	22.1	73.7	8.4	59.5	18.1
Charleston, SC	Charleston County	796.9	31.0	109.6	4.9	50.8	21.9
Charlotte, NC	Mecklenburg County	329.6	14.2	69.9	3.4	32.8	14.0
Chicago, IL	Cook County	432.8	23.4	94.5	12.4	28.7	20.8
Cincinnati, OH	Hamilton County	612.8	25.1	75.7	10.0	20.3	21.8
Clarksville, TN	Montgomery County	95.5	14.6	46.9	2.4	13.4	12.9
Cleveland, OH	Cuyahoga County	714.3	51.5	109.6	18.1	18.4	17.2
College Station, TX	Brazos County	258.7	19.0	52.4	3.1	17.5	15.7
Colorado Springs, CO	El Paso County	196.9	31.0	104.5	4.4	43.6	24.6
Columbia, MO	Boone County	815.9	59.8	69.8	5.5	35.5	27.2
Columbia, SC	Richland County	356.3	15.9	91.6	7.2	23.8	19.7
Columbus, OH	Franklin County	424.6	61.9	93.1	7.1	24.8	27.1
Dallas, TX	Dallas County	335.5	20.5	86.8	4.0	36.5	13.5
Davenport, IA	Scott County	233.2	52.1	79.2	4.6	182.7	16.8
Denver, CO	Denver County	595.6	32.7	76.3	6.6	36.2	16.9
Des Moines, IA	Polk County	213.2	96.7	73.9	10.8	55.3	21.0
Durham, NC	Durham County	1,131.3	15.8	75.0	4.0	19.3	14.6
Edison, NJ	Middlesex County	375.0	19.5	90.9	9.9	25.5	20.0
El Paso, TX	El Paso County	195.0	12.9	46.5	3.9	8.7	10.1
Fargo, ND	Cass County	392.7	19.4	79.7	4.4	73.1	31.3
Fayetteville, NC	Cumberland County	200.3	23.1	104.9	6.0	9.8	18.2
Fort Collins, CO	Larimer County	239.5	29.9	79.6	5.9	55.5	21.0
Fort Wayne, IN	Allen County	264.5	27.5	66.4	5.5	21.9	25.8
Fort Worth, TX	Tarrant County	183.1	34.4	60.4	4.4	27.0	15.9
Grand Rapids, MI	Kent County	343.8	69.5	74.6	4.7	37.0	25.1
Greeley, CO	Weld County	129.9	16.5	45.9	2.8	22.8	12.3
Green Bay, WI	Brown County	244.7	24.3	80.5	3.4	46.9	18.1
Greensboro, NC	Guilford County	252.9	14.1	57.0	5.0	14.1	10.2
Honolulu, HI	Honolulu County	351.0	17.3	101.1	3.4	19.6	24.3
Houston, TX	Harris County	333.5	11.5	70.7	4.7	22.3	20.4
Huntsville, AL	Madison County	275.5	12.0	56.6	3.8	23.3	19.0
Indianapolis, IN	Marion County	438.4	21.4	90.3	6.1	15.8	19.8
Jacksonville, FL	Duval County	351.1	22.9	83.3	8.4	25.0	16.2
Kansas City, MO	Jackson County	307.2	59.9	90.2	6.4	45.2	20.2
Lafayette, LA	Lafayette Parish	367.7	9.9	68.7	3.7	32.7	13.1
Lakeland, FL	Polk County	124.5	10.0	34.1	4.3	18.1	9.7
Las Vegas, NV	Clark County	177.4	34.8	63.7	4.3	19.6	13.1
Lexington, KY	Fayette County	728.8	36.6	148.5	7.4	22.6	23.2
Lincoln, NE	Lancaster County	218.3	12.6	101.5	5.3	45.1	21.6
Little Rock, AR	Pulaski County	737.4	14.3	77.6	4.6	22.5	21.4
Los Angeles, CA	Los Angeles County	302.4	13.5	89.6	6.4	30.1	18.7
Louisville, KY	Jefferson County	476.6	13.3	109.6	7.8	28.8	15.5
Madison, WI	Dane County	610.2	21.2	73.9	4.6	44.1	22.3
Manchester, NH	Hillsborough County	237.8	25.3	82.7	5.5	25.9	20.1

Table continued on following page.

Appendix A: Comparative Statistics   A-145

City	Area Covered	MDs[1]	DOs[1,2]	Dentists	Podiatrists	Chiropractors	Optometrists
Memphis, TN	Shelby County	403.7	10.3	73.6	3.6	13.2	31.6
Miami, FL	Miami-Dade County	344.1	16.5	69.8	10.3	18.3	14.4
Midland, TX	Midland County	150.1	9.3	54.9	2.3	13.6	11.9
Milwaukee, WI	Milwaukee County	374.6	21.6	83.9	7.7	20.4	10.9
Minneapolis, MN	Hennepin County	524.3	22.3	99.8	5.2	73.2	21.5
Nashville, TN	Davidson County	647.2	12.2	81.1	4.3	25.6	16.9
New Haven, CT	New Haven County	556.7	10.7	79.9	10.1	26.9	17.3
New Orleans, LA	Orleans Parish	808.2	18.2	74.3	3.8	9.5	6.2
New York, NY	New York City	483.9	16.6	91.0	13.6	16.5	17.6
Oklahoma City, OK	Oklahoma County	410.1	41.7	105.6	5.3	27.3	18.3
Omaha, NE	Douglas County	540.6	27.5	97.0	5.3	41.1	20.5
Orlando, FL	Orange County	311.3	22.1	50.7	3.7	26.6	12.8
Peoria, IL	Peoria County	558.6	41.5	86.5	8.4	50.8	20.6
Philadelphia, PA	Philadelphia County	571.9	44.8	81.1	17.2	15.6	17.7
Phoenix, AZ	Maricopa County	245.6	31.3	68.2	6.6	33.2	15.5
Pittsburgh, PA	Allegheny County	642.7	43.9	98.1	10.9	44.7	20.9
Portland, OR	Multnomah County	634.2	31.0	99.8	5.3	74.7	22.4
Providence, RI	Providence County	496.3	18.1	60.6	9.9	20.3	20.7
Provo, UT	Utah County	116.3	19.0	61.0	4.6	25.5	11.0
Raleigh, NC	Wake County	276.9	11.4	71.6	3.5	26.5	16.6
Reno, NV	Washoe County	294.4	20.9	70.0	4.0	28.0	24.0
Richmond, VA	Richmond City	740.3	28.4	143.2	10.8	7.4	16.5
Riverside, CA	Riverside County	127.8	15.3	52.4	2.6	16.3	12.8
Rochester, MN	Olmsted County	2,492.4	48.6	126.3	6.3	41.1	24.0
Sacramento, CA	Sacramento County	315.5	15.7	78.3	4.6	22.0	18.1
Salt Lake City, UT	Salt Lake County	376.7	17.1	78.4	6.5	27.1	13.5
San Antonio, TX	Bexar County	324.7	18.6	89.2	5.3	16.3	18.1
San Diego, CA	San Diego County	325.9	18.3	90.9	4.3	34.4	19.1
San Francisco, CA	San Francisco County	814.1	13.6	156.7	10.4	39.6	29.4
San Jose, CA	Santa Clara County	421.9	10.9	118.4	6.8	42.7	27.5
Santa Rosa, CA	Sonoma County	279.6	18.2	93.7	6.7	40.9	18.2
Savannah, GA	Chatham County	352.0	18.0	69.8	6.9	19.0	13.5
Seattle, WA	King County	489.5	15.6	109.7	6.4	46.7	21.8
Sioux Falls, SD	Minnehaha County	362.3	25.7	55.4	6.2	58.0	19.2
Springfield, IL	Sangamon County	631.8	26.1	85.3	5.7	40.1	21.1
Tallahassee, FL	Leon County	304.5	14.1	49.0	3.4	23.8	18.7
Tampa, FL	Hillsborough County	344.9	26.1	58.9	5.6	26.4	14.2
Tucson, AZ	Pima County	361.9	24.6	65.1	5.4	19.1	15.9
Tulsa, OK	Tulsa County	269.3	122.0	69.7	4.0	38.8	23.5
Tuscaloosa, AL	Tuscaloosa County	228.0	9.1	49.7	5.3	20.5	15.8
Virginia Beach, VA	Virginia Beach City	252.3	13.3	77.3	7.6	27.3	16.9
Washington, DC	District of Columbia	779.6	16.7	123.0	8.9	9.4	14.5
Wichita, KS	Sedgwick County	258.0	35.2	65.9	2.5	42.6	28.1
Winston-Salem, NC	Forsyth County	660.3	29.3	62.3	5.8	16.5	17.8
U.S.	U.S.	282.9	22.7	71.2	6.2	28.1	16.9

Note: All figures are rates per 100,000 population; Data as of 2019 unless noted; (1) Data as of 2018 and includes all active, non-federal physicians; (2) Doctor of Osteopathic Medicine
Source: U.S. Department of Health and Human Services, Health Resources and Services Administration, Bureau of Health Professions, Area Resource File (ARF) 2019-2020

A-146   Appendix A: Comparative Statistics

Health Insurance Coverage: City

City	With Health Insurance	With Private Health Insurance	With Public Health Insurance	Without Health Insurance	Population Under Age 19 Without Health Insurance
Albuquerque, NM	92.1	60.9	43.0	7.9	3.4
Allentown, PA	88.8	47.3	49.7	11.2	5.0
Anchorage, AK	88.8	70.3	30.4	11.2	8.2
Ann Arbor, MI	97.3	87.7	19.7	2.7	1.1
Athens, GA	86.5	68.5	26.9	13.5	7.3
Atlanta, GA	89.7	69.2	28.3	10.3	4.9
Austin, TX	86.4	73.3	20.2	13.6	8.9
Baton Rouge, LA	90.3	59.2	41.1	9.7	3.5
Boise City, ID	91.1	75.8	26.8	8.9	4.4
Boston, MA	96.5	67.2	36.7	3.5	1.3
Boulder, CO	95.9	84.0	20.1	4.1	1.2
Cape Coral, FL	87.4	65.9	36.8	12.6	8.6
Cedar Rapids, IA	95.5	74.3	34.3	4.5	2.7
Charleston, SC	91.9	78.0	25.5	8.1	3.3
Charlotte, NC	87.5	68.5	26.3	12.5	6.4
Chicago, IL	90.4	60.3	36.9	9.6	3.4
Cincinnati, OH	92.7	59.1	41.6	7.3	4.5
Clarksville, TN	91.6	71.5	33.7	8.4	3.4
Cleveland, OH	92.3	44.0	57.3	7.7	3.1
College Station, TX	92.0	85.0	13.7	8.0	4.9
Colorado Springs, CO	92.2	68.7	36.6	7.8	4.2
Columbia, MO	93.2	81.9	20.6	6.8	3.6
Columbia, SC	91.2	72.0	29.7	8.8	2.7
Columbus, OH	91.0	64.0	34.8	9.0	5.4
Dallas, TX	76.4	51.8	30.3	23.6	14.8
Davenport, IA	94.4	66.2	40.2	5.6	3.3
Denver, CO	90.7	65.5	33.0	9.3	4.2
Des Moines, IA	93.1	64.7	41.0	6.9	3.5
Durham, NC	87.5	68.8	28.3	12.5	7.3
Edison, NJ	94.6	81.1	22.8	5.4	1.3
El Paso, TX	80.9	54.7	33.8	19.1	9.1
Fargo, ND	93.5	80.6	24.3	6.5	4.1
Fayetteville, NC	90.0	65.3	40.4	10.0	3.3
Fort Collins, CO	94.0	78.7	24.3	6.0	5.0
Fort Wayne, IN	91.0	65.0	36.5	9.0	5.6
Fort Worth, TX	81.7	60.6	27.5	18.3	11.7
Grand Rapids, MI	91.4	62.1	39.6	8.6	3.9
Greeley, CO	91.5	63.7	38.4	8.5	4.3
Green Bay, WI	92.1	66.1	35.9	7.9	3.7
Greensboro, NC	89.7	65.9	34.1	10.3	4.5
Honolulu, HI	96.1	77.7	34.5	3.9	2.4
Houston, TX	76.9	51.9	30.8	23.1	13.1
Huntsville, AL	90.2	72.8	32.9	9.8	4.2
Indianapolis, IN	89.5	62.3	36.7	10.5	6.0
Jacksonville, FL	88.0	64.7	33.9	12.0	6.8
Kansas City, MO	88.2	68.6	29.1	11.8	6.6
Lafayette, LA	91.3	67.0	35.3	8.7	3.1
Lakeland, FL	90.0	62.2	41.4	10.0	5.2
Las Vegas, NV	87.7	61.6	36.0	12.3	7.2
Lexington, KY	93.2	71.6	32.5	6.8	4.3
Lincoln, NE	92.3	78.5	25.2	7.7	5.2
Little Rock, AR	91.6	65.6	37.6	8.4	4.8
Los Angeles, CA	88.6	54.4	40.5	11.4	4.2
Louisville, KY	94.6	67.1	40.3	5.4	2.7
Madison, WI	96.0	83.8	22.2	4.0	2.2

Table continued on following page.

Appendix A: Comparative Statistics

City	With Health Insurance	With Private Health Insurance	With Public Health Insurance	Without Health Insurance	Population Under Age 19 Without Health Insurance
Manchester, NH	90.1	64.0	36.3	9.9	3.7
Memphis, TN	86.3	55.7	41.0	13.7	6.3
Miami, FL	80.2	46.7	36.7	19.8	8.6
Midland, TX	83.3	71.1	19.7	16.7	14.7
Milwaukee, WI	90.7	54.1	44.9	9.3	3.3
Minneapolis, MN	93.4	66.8	34.5	6.6	3.4
Nashville, TN	87.9	67.1	29.8	12.1	6.9
New Haven, CT	91.1	50.8	46.7	8.9	2.8
New Orleans, LA	90.8	56.3	42.9	9.2	3.4
New York, NY	92.5	58.3	43.0	7.5	2.4
Oklahoma City, OK	85.4	64.0	32.1	14.6	7.1
Omaha, NE	89.8	71.3	27.7	10.2	5.8
Orlando, FL	84.8	62.3	29.4	15.2	7.5
Peoria, IL	94.2	65.7	41.1	5.8	3.0
Philadelphia, PA	91.9	56.9	45.2	8.1	3.5
Phoenix, AZ	85.9	57.2	36.0	14.1	9.5
Pittsburgh, PA	94.7	73.5	33.4	5.3	3.3
Portland, OR	93.6	71.5	32.0	6.4	2.8
Providence, RI	92.5	53.2	46.4	7.5	3.1
Provo, UT	88.8	77.8	17.3	11.2	10.7
Raleigh, NC	89.8	74.2	24.5	10.2	5.4
Reno, NV	90.2	68.4	32.1	9.8	8.1
Richmond, VA	88.0	62.6	34.9	12.0	6.5
Riverside, CA	90.6	58.9	38.2	9.4	3.6
Rochester, MN	95.7	79.4	30.4	4.3	2.4
Sacramento, CA	94.2	62.2	42.1	5.8	2.2
Salt Lake City, UT	87.4	72.5	22.1	12.6	11.7
San Antonio, TX	83.3	60.1	32.7	16.7	8.6
San Diego, CA	92.2	69.7	31.6	7.8	3.6
San Francisco, CA	96.3	75.7	29.4	3.7	1.5
San Jose, CA	94.8	72.3	30.4	5.2	2.1
Santa Rosa, CA	92.4	67.6	37.9	7.6	4.9
Savannah, GA	83.0	57.3	34.5	17.0	7.7
Seattle, WA	95.8	80.6	24.0	4.2	1.4
Sioux Falls, SD	92.2	77.2	26.5	7.8	4.9
Springfield, IL	95.7	69.1	42.2	4.3	1.7
Tallahassee, FL	91.6	76.3	25.1	8.4	4.2
Tampa, FL	88.3	62.5	32.9	11.7	5.4
Tucson, AZ	88.5	56.5	42.8	11.5	8.1
Tulsa, OK	83.4	58.9	35.1	16.6	8.2
Tuscaloosa, AL	92.6	72.0	31.2	7.4	2.5
Virginia Beach, VA	92.4	80.7	25.8	7.6	3.8
Washington, DC	96.3	70.4	35.6	3.7	2.0
Wichita, KS	87.9	67.3	32.3	12.1	6.6
Winston-Salem, NC	87.6	62.4	36.3	12.4	4.9
U.S.	91.2	67.9	35.1	8.8	5.1

Note: Figures are percentages that cover the civilian noninstitutionalized population
Source: U.S. Census Bureau, 2015-2019 American Community Survey 5-Year Estimates

A-148 Appendix A: Comparative Statistics

Health Insurance Coverage: Metro Area

Metro Area	With Health Insurance	With Private Health Insurance	With Public Health Insurance	Without Health Insurance	Population Under Age 19 Without Health Insurance
Albuquerque, NM	91.7	60.2	44.2	8.3	4.1
Allentown, PA	94.5	73.3	35.4	5.5	3.0
Anchorage, AK	87.8	68.3	31.3	12.2	9.4
Ann Arbor, MI	96.5	83.3	25.9	3.5	1.8
Athens, GA	87.6	69.5	28.5	12.4	6.7
Atlanta, GA	87.2	69.3	26.8	12.8	7.5
Austin, TX	87.5	74.5	21.7	12.5	8.1
Baton Rouge, LA	91.7	66.4	35.5	8.3	3.3
Boise City, ID	89.6	71.7	30.2	10.4	4.8
Boston, MA	97.1	76.7	32.7	2.9	1.3
Boulder, CO	95.4	79.5	25.6	4.6	2.1
Cape Coral, FL	86.7	62.4	43.6	13.3	9.3
Cedar Rapids, IA	96.5	77.1	33.1	3.5	2.0
Charleston, SC	89.5	71.1	31.4	10.5	5.7
Charlotte, NC	89.8	70.7	29.3	10.2	4.8
Chicago, IL	92.4	70.2	31.7	7.6	3.2
Cincinnati, OH	94.8	73.1	32.8	5.2	3.1
Clarksville, TN	91.8	69.1	37.2	8.2	5.3
Cleveland, OH	94.7	69.2	38.4	5.3	3.4
College Station, TX	87.4	73.5	23.1	12.6	8.4
Colorado Springs, CO	92.8	71.1	35.3	7.2	4.1
Columbia, MO	92.8	79.5	24.1	7.2	4.6
Columbia, SC	90.5	70.4	33.6	9.5	3.7
Columbus, OH	93.3	71.2	32.1	6.7	4.2
Dallas, TX	83.6	66.0	24.9	16.4	11.0
Davenport, IA	95.3	72.9	37.3	4.7	2.7
Denver, CO	92.6	72.6	29.2	7.4	4.0
Des Moines, IA	95.6	77.4	31.2	4.4	2.2
Durham, NC	89.7	71.7	29.7	10.3	6.1
Edison, NJ	92.8	67.2	36.0	7.2	2.9
El Paso, TX	79.7	52.6	33.9	20.3	9.8
Fargo, ND	94.6	82.1	24.4	5.4	4.2
Fayetteville, NC	89.3	64.6	38.7	10.7	3.6
Fort Collins, CO	94.1	76.0	29.1	5.9	4.7
Fort Wayne, IN	91.5	69.2	33.1	8.5	6.4
Fort Worth, TX	83.6	66.0	24.9	16.4	11.0
Grand Rapids, MI	94.6	75.5	31.5	5.4	3.1
Greeley, CO	92.1	70.1	32.2	7.9	4.6
Green Bay, WI	94.8	75.7	30.4	5.2	3.6
Greensboro, NC	89.6	65.5	35.2	10.4	4.7
Honolulu, HI	96.7	80.4	32.2	3.3	2.0
Houston, TX	81.9	62.1	26.6	18.1	11.1
Huntsville, AL	91.4	76.2	29.9	8.6	3.3
Indianapolis, IN	91.9	71.6	31.0	8.1	5.3
Jacksonville, FL	89.1	68.7	32.7	10.9	6.6
Kansas City, MO	91.1	75.3	27.2	8.9	5.2
Lafayette, LA	90.1	62.1	38.5	9.9	3.6
Lakeland, FL	87.3	59.0	41.4	12.7	7.2
Las Vegas, NV	88.3	64.2	33.7	11.7	7.4
Lexington, KY	93.7	70.8	34.5	6.3	4.0
Lincoln, NE	92.9	79.5	24.9	7.1	4.8
Little Rock, AR	92.4	67.0	38.9	7.6	4.4
Los Angeles, CA	90.9	60.6	37.4	9.1	3.8
Louisville, KY	94.6	71.4	36.4	5.4	3.3
Madison, WI	96.1	83.5	24.7	3.9	2.1

Table continued on following page.

Appendix A: Comparative Statistics   A-149

Metro Area	With Health Insurance	With Private Health Insurance	With Public Health Insurance	Without Health Insurance	Population Under Age 19 Without Health Insurance
Manchester, NH	93.8	76.9	28.9	6.2	2.6
Memphis, TN	89.2	64.7	35.4	10.8	5.0
Miami, FL	84.9	58.9	33.6	15.1	7.8
Midland, TX	83.6	71.1	20.2	16.4	14.0
Milwaukee, WI	94.4	71.8	34.1	5.6	2.4
Minneapolis, MN	95.7	78.0	29.6	4.3	3.0
Nashville, TN	90.7	72.1	28.7	9.3	5.1
New Haven, CT	95.0	68.2	38.7	5.0	2.2
New Orleans, LA	90.3	60.4	40.1	9.7	3.7
New York, NY	92.8	67.2	36.0	7.2	2.9
Oklahoma City, OK	87.5	68.6	30.8	12.5	6.2
Omaha, NE	92.3	75.9	27.0	7.7	4.3
Orlando, FL	87.6	65.5	31.5	12.4	6.9
Peoria, IL	95.2	73.5	37.2	4.8	2.9
Philadelphia, PA	94.4	73.2	34.0	5.6	2.9
Phoenix, AZ	89.5	65.4	34.9	10.5	8.2
Pittsburgh, PA	96.2	77.0	35.8	3.8	1.7
Portland, OR	94.0	73.3	32.6	6.0	2.8
Providence, RI	96.1	70.9	38.8	3.9	2.1
Provo, UT	91.9	81.7	17.4	8.1	6.0
Raleigh, NC	91.0	75.9	24.8	9.0	4.6
Reno, NV	90.6	69.8	32.2	9.4	7.7
Richmond, VA	91.8	75.2	29.4	8.2	4.6
Riverside, CA	91.4	57.5	42.0	8.6	3.9
Rochester, MN	95.5	79.9	30.3	4.5	3.7
Sacramento, CA	94.9	69.3	38.2	5.1	2.5
Salt Lake City, UT	89.7	77.5	20.1	10.3	8.2
San Antonio, TX	85.3	65.1	31.0	14.7	8.1
San Diego, CA	92.2	68.4	33.8	7.8	3.8
San Francisco, CA	95.7	75.5	30.5	4.3	2.1
San Jose, CA	95.6	76.7	27.4	4.4	1.9
Santa Rosa, CA	93.9	71.6	36.7	6.1	3.2
Savannah, GA	87.0	67.6	30.1	13.0	6.2
Seattle, WA	94.4	75.9	29.2	5.6	2.5
Sioux Falls, SD	92.8	78.9	25.1	7.2	4.5
Springfield, IL	96.2	74.3	37.4	3.8	1.6
Tallahassee, FL	91.2	73.4	30.0	8.8	4.6
Tampa, FL	88.1	63.3	36.8	11.9	6.3
Tucson, AZ	90.8	62.2	42.6	9.2	7.1
Tulsa, OK	86.6	65.8	32.6	13.4	7.6
Tuscaloosa, AL	92.3	70.5	33.7	7.7	2.5
Virginia Beach, VA	91.6	75.2	30.5	8.4	4.6
Washington, DC	92.4	78.2	25.2	7.6	4.5
Wichita, KS	89.8	71.6	30.3	10.2	5.8
Winston-Salem, NC	89.1	66.0	35.7	10.9	4.9
U.S.	91.2	67.9	35.1	8.8	5.1

Note: Figures are percentages that cover the civilian noninstitutionalized population; Figures cover the Metropolitan Statistical Area (MSA)—see Appendix B for areas included
Source: U.S. Census Bureau, 2015-2019 American Community Survey 5-Year Estimates

A-150   Appendix A: Comparative Statistics

Crime Rate: City

City	All Crimes	Violent Crimes				Property Crimes		
		Murder	Rape	Robbery	Aggrav. Assault	Burglary	Larceny -Theft	Motor Vehicle Theft
Albuquerque, NM	n/a	14.9	86.5	302.4	948.0	n/a	3,672.1	965.4
Allentown, PA	2,669.6	5.7	52.5	139.5	188.7	427.6	1,656.1	199.4
Anchorage, AK	5,505.8	11.1	187.7	215.8	829.9	588.0	3,141.1	532.1
Ann Arbor, MI	1,979.8	1.6	62.7	37.4	149.7	160.3	1,455.7	112.3
Athens, GA[2]	3,562.0	4.8	45.6	98.5	266.6	546.8	2,415.5	184.1
Atlanta, GA[1]	5,423.2	17.7	49.4	221.5	480.1	621.2	3,366.4	666.8
Austin, TX	4,111.4	3.2	54.2	98.5	245.0	440.5	2,962.9	307.1
Baton Rouge, LA	6,226.7	31.7	23.6	292.3	588.7	1,023.3	3,904.9	362.1
Boise City, ID	1,859.8	1.7	70.9	19.0	188.9	203.2	1,276.2	99.9
Boston, MA	n/a	6.0	33.1	148.7	419.5	243.7	1,515.1	n/a
Boulder, CO	3,282.4	0.9	37.8	34.1	183.4	373.2	2,421.7	231.3
Cape Coral, FL	1,237.0	2.6	8.2	18.5	87.0	141.1	895.5	83.9
Cedar Rapids, IA	3,593.1	1.5	20.1	61.9	173.9	624.6	2,438.7	272.4
Charleston, SC	2,632.8	5.8	36.9	68.7	261.8	211.2	1,688.9	359.5
Charlotte, NC	4,665.2	10.9	33.6	209.2	485.8	574.6	2,997.5	353.7
Chicago, IL	3,925.8	18.2	65.1	294.9	565.0	353.8	2,293.4	335.5
Cincinnati, OH	5,147.1	21.1	92.3	287.5	443.7	911.5	2,945.6	445.4
Clarksville, TN	3,370.7	8.8	64.4	72.5	433.1	339.4	2,160.7	291.9
Cleveland, OH	5,983.8	24.1	125.4	496.3	870.8	1,129.0	2,610.6	727.6
College Station, TX	1,948.1	0.8	40.3	36.1	111.5	327.9	1,282.2	149.3
Colorado Springs, CO	4,251.7	4.8	89.9	101.1	389.2	500.4	2,521.6	644.6
Columbia, MO	2,914.8	8.8	55.2	59.2	197.6	399.1	1,944.5	250.4
Columbia, SC	6,027.4	21.7	65.8	164.4	523.2	684.7	3,898.6	669.0
Columbus, OH	3,811.3	8.9	97.3	199.8	197.3	641.1	2,274.1	392.8
Dallas, TX	4,184.2	14.5	58.5	322.7	467.2	675.6	1,893.4	752.4
Davenport, IA	4,421.2	2.0	82.0	121.1	389.7	727.6	2,763.9	335.0
Denver, CO	4,492.4	9.2	97.8	165.3	476.6	544.2	2,473.0	726.3
Des Moines, IA	4,802.5	6.4	53.6	129.6	522.5	1,045.9	2,443.4	601.2
Durham, NC	4,537.6	13.2	43.2	223.3	450.3	703.6	2,833.6	270.4
Edison, NJ	1,450.9	1.0	9.0	18.9	54.8	137.6	1,139.8	89.7
El Paso, TX	1,863.7	5.8	45.1	49.2	252.5	152.6	1,234.6	123.9
Fargo, ND	3,572.4	3.9	87.1	61.2	298.2	651.4	2,163.7	306.9
Fayetteville, NC	4,401.4	11.4	55.8	134.1	674.1	651.2	2,691.1	183.7
Fort Collins, CO	2,389.9	0.6	24.0	21.1	171.5	204.8	1,834.5	133.4
Fort Wayne, IN	3,122.5	9.7	53.8	132.5	165.6	367.5	2,182.5	210.9
Fort Worth, TX	3,132.8	7.5	51.4	106.2	279.4	433.7	1,890.3	364.4
Grand Rapids, MI	2,545.1	4.0	71.4	135.8	426.2	294.8	1,364.7	248.3
Greeley, CO	2,680.0	1.8	65.0	61.3	225.2	309.4	1,737.2	280.1
Green Bay, WI	2,145.9	2.9	74.3	46.7	380.0	233.4	1,290.6	118.1
Greensboro, NC	4,507.7	14.4	37.9	208.4	558.0	743.2	2,614.5	331.2
Honolulu, HI	n/a	n/a	n/a	n/a	n/a	n/a	n/a	n/a
Houston, TX	5,391.7	11.7	53.0	388.3	619.2	723.3	3,040.2	556.0
Huntsville, AL[2]	5,635.0	11.3	88.1	184.5	621.0	731.7	3,462.6	535.9
Indianapolis, IN[1]	5,402.0	18.5	77.1	351.1	826.1	893.6	2,671.9	563.7
Jacksonville, FL	3,956.9	14.2	60.9	142.3	430.0	539.6	2,460.9	309.0
Kansas City, MO	5,287.3	30.2	70.0	290.9	1,040.2	619.0	2,470.5	766.4
Lafayette, LA	4,829.0	11.1	12.6	116.8	383.6	814.6	3,236.9	253.4
Lakeland, FL	3,189.7	6.2	56.1	86.4	163.0	390.2	2,306.7	180.9
Las Vegas, NV	3,302.8	5.0	86.3	127.1	312.8	638.7	1,694.3	438.6
Lexington, KY	3,294.7	8.0	53.7	111.0	123.9	471.4	2,248.9	277.9
Lincoln, NE	3,133.7	1.7	110.9	57.0	213.3	339.4	2,255.4	155.9
Little Rock, AR	7,638.8	19.2	105.4	197.1	1,195.2	887.2	4,696.0	538.9
Los Angeles, CA	3,115.5	6.4	56.6	240.4	428.7	343.9	1,649.9	389.5
Louisville, KY	4,578.4	13.9	29.8	149.2	494.0	638.9	2,670.2	582.4

Table continued on following page.

Appendix A: Comparative Statistics   A-151

City	All Crimes	Violent Crimes				Property Crimes		
		Murder	Rape	Robbery	Aggrav. Assault	Burglary	Larceny -Theft	Motor Vehicle Theft
Madison, WI	2,833.9	1.5	41.0	83.1	234.2	400.4	1,865.1	208.6
Manchester, NH	2,972.7	5.3	54.9	117.8	422.5	264.8	1,970.9	136.4
Memphis, TN	8,029.9	29.2	72.0	373.9	1,426.3	1,204.3	4,302.1	622.1
Miami, FL	4,260.9	8.9	31.6	160.0	392.5	368.6	2,959.2	340.1
Midland, TX[1]	2,261.0	3.6	42.8	42.1	199.2	269.9	1,504.9	198.5
Milwaukee, WI	3,887.3	16.4	72.3	323.4	920.4	608.2	1,362.8	583.8
Minneapolis, MN	5,442.7	10.7	106.5	299.1	509.5	788.1	3,056.0	672.8
Nashville, TN	5,114.2	12.1	63.7	287.8	709.5	490.9	3,150.5	399.8
New Haven, CT	4,694.5	10.0	34.5	246.0	604.6	505.0	2,743.4	551.0
New Orleans, LA	6,437.3	30.7	196.2	256.8	661.1	543.2	4,001.3	748.0
New York, NY	2,030.3	3.8	33.1	159.9	374.0	117.5	1,276.2	65.9
Oklahoma City, OK	4,813.7	11.4	81.9	135.0	493.9	943.3	2,572.2	576.1
Omaha, NE	4,256.7	4.9	80.6	110.3	417.0	357.9	2,615.8	670.2
Orlando, FL	5,565.2	8.6	69.8	183.5	476.5	501.2	3,889.5	436.1
Peoria, IL	4,792.9	22.5	58.6	241.5	721.0	683.2	2,666.8	399.3
Philadelphia, PA[1]	4,005.6	22.1	69.0	331.6	486.0	409.4	2,329.5	357.9
Phoenix, AZ	4,013.5	7.8	67.4	189.3	434.4	560.8	2,334.7	419.0
Pittsburgh, PA[1]	3,594.8	18.8	40.0	230.0	289.9	443.2	2,331.9	241.0
Portland, OR	5,748.0	4.4	55.6	147.9	336.8	634.3	3,597.6	971.4
Providence, RI	3,507.4	7.2	59.0	134.1	295.9	397.7	2,349.8	263.7
Provo, UT	1,623.0	0.9	37.5	11.1	65.7	139.1	1,259.5	109.2
Raleigh, NC	2,038.8	1.0	34.3	67.4	153.0	251.1	1,375.4	156.5
Reno, NV	2,658.9	4.7	70.0	121.1	362.1	323.2	1,314.3	463.5
Richmond, VA	3,962.4	23.8	19.5	166.9	252.7	427.4	2,702.0	370.1
Riverside, CA	3,443.6	5.1	41.7	142.8	316.3	390.7	2,099.6	447.4
Rochester, MN	2,096.1	0.8	52.4	28.7	132.8	238.4	1,535.5	107.4
Sacramento, CA	3,809.2	6.6	24.7	202.2	393.6	582.4	2,071.1	528.7
Salt Lake City, UT	6,369.7	6.4	115.6	199.1	391.3	637.3	4,397.7	622.4
San Antonio, TX	5,032.7	6.7	104.5	126.0	471.1	524.1	3,301.1	499.0
San Diego, CA	2,244.2	3.5	38.9	93.4	226.0	245.7	1,278.0	358.7
San Francisco, CA	6,175.2	4.5	36.6	344.8	283.7	524.1	4,501.9	479.6
San Jose, CA	2,858.0	3.1	64.5	128.7	242.0	395.6	1,435.0	589.0
Santa Rosa, CA	2,097.4	1.7	82.1	70.8	327.2	273.2	1,167.6	174.8
Savannah, GA[1]	2,865.5	11.6	35.1	110.2	248.5	364.9	1,824.4	270.8
Seattle, WA	5,081.0	3.7	46.9	175.3	359.6	944.1	3,074.2	477.3
Sioux Falls, SD	3,528.6	2.2	62.5	36.6	381.9	374.4	2,316.5	354.5
Springfield, IL	5,218.0	7.9	94.4	181.8	493.0	908.3	3,300.9	231.7
Tallahassee, FL	4,675.5	10.3	101.0	129.2	456.2	608.4	3,022.5	348.0
Tampa, FL	2,033.7	7.7	30.0	71.2	296.1	255.2	1,242.9	130.6
Tucson, AZ	3,960.4	7.3	96.1	201.5	383.5	455.3	2,406.4	410.3
Tulsa, OK	6,298.2	13.7	84.9	178.7	709.5	1,206.4	3,350.0	755.0
Tuscaloosa, AL[1]	4,843.6	4.9	46.2	137.6	316.4	739.9	3,289.0	309.5
Virginia Beach, VA	1,890.0	6.7	17.6	43.6	61.5	118.0	1,513.7	128.9
Washington, DC	5,223.0	23.5	48.5	334.3	570.9	260.7	3,659.5	325.6
Wichita, KS	6,462.8	9.0	94.1	118.2	919.8	686.3	4,044.6	590.9
Winston-Salem, NC	n/a	n/a	n/a	n/a	n/a	n/a	n/a	n/a
U.S.	2,489.3	5.0	42.6	81.6	250.2	340.5	1,549.5	219.9

Note: Figures are crimes per 100,000 population in 2019 except where noted; n/a not available; (1) 2018 data; (2) 2017 data
Source: FBI Uniform Crime Reports, 2017, 2018, 2019

A-152 Appendix A: Comparative Statistics

Crime Rate: Suburbs

Suburbs[1]	All Crimes	Violent Crimes				Property Crimes		
		Murder	Rape	Robbery	Aggrav. Assault	Burglary	Larceny-Theft	Motor Vehicle Theft
Albuquerque, NM	n/a	2.5	28.6	23.0	502.8	n/a	995.5	214.2
Allentown, PA	n/a	n/a	n/a	n/a	n/a	n/a	n/a	n/a
Anchorage, AK	5,634.3	10.9	32.6	92.4	277.1	787.8	3,955.4	478.1
Ann Arbor, MI	2,017.9	2.4	69.1	38.7	296.3	218.0	1,258.3	135.0
Athens, GA[3]	1,855.9	1.2	18.1	14.5	111.2	289.0	1,349.3	72.5
Atlanta, GA[2]	2,666.3	4.6	24.0	82.5	168.8	373.2	1,770.4	242.7
Austin, TX	1,564.4	1.9	43.6	23.6	126.5	212.3	1,059.4	97.1
Baton Rouge, LA	3,048.0	7.9	29.9	42.8	339.8	380.5	2,107.7	139.3
Boise City, ID	1,329.9	1.2	52.7	7.5	176.3	201.4	798.8	92.1
Boston, MA	n/a	1.4	30.1	41.9	212.4	126.0	804.5	n/a
Boulder, CO	2,439.7	0.9	83.1	20.9	175.3	269.8	1,686.5	203.0
Cape Coral, FL	1,476.1	3.1	40.1	61.0	201.4	186.4	880.9	103.2
Cedar Rapids, IA	911.9	0.0	21.6	5.0	95.2	183.1	523.4	83.6
Charleston, SC	3,168.8	9.6	42.3	61.1	290.1	419.0	2,025.9	320.8
Charlotte, NC	n/a	n/a	n/a	n/a	n/a	n/a	n/a	n/a
Chicago, IL	n/a	n/a	n/a	n/a	n/a	n/a	n/a	n/a
Cincinnati, OH	1,749.6	1.5	34.0	32.1	73.6	224.7	1,269.6	114.0
Clarksville, TN	1,876.6	4.7	31.4	23.3	124.1	401.6	1,146.8	144.8
Cleveland, OH	1,401.7	1.8	21.7	34.6	90.5	189.4	985.7	77.9
College Station, TX	2,466.8	2.7	79.5	46.6	193.9	419.9	1,565.3	158.9
Colorado Springs, CO	1,634.0	3.7	56.3	25.7	166.4	213.4	951.5	216.8
Columbia, MO	1,774.1	3.5	37.8	13.0	145.2	253.8	1,150.8	170.0
Columbia, SC	3,564.0	5.9	45.8	67.3	428.2	503.6	2,152.4	360.8
Columbus, OH	1,836.3	2.6	36.4	25.9	60.9	251.9	1,366.9	91.7
Dallas, TX	n/a	n/a	n/a	n/a	n/a	n/a	n/a	n/a
Davenport, IA	1,880.3	2.2	46.1	31.4	202.5	306.7	1,169.0	122.5
Denver, CO	n/a	n/a	n/a	n/a	n/a	n/a	n/a	n/a
Des Moines, IA	n/a	n/a	n/a	n/a	n/a	n/a	n/a	n/a
Durham, NC	1,853.6	2.7	22.5	32.4	157.6	332.5	1,221.8	84.0
Edison, NJ	n/a	n/a	n/a	n/a	n/a	n/a	n/a	n/a
El Paso, TX	1,251.9	0.6	37.2	15.8	195.1	156.6	746.2	100.4
Fargo, ND	1,642.9	0.0	34.9	22.4	76.5	277.5	1,087.8	143.8
Fayetteville, NC	n/a	n/a	n/a	n/a	n/a	n/a	n/a	n/a
Fort Collins, CO	1,855.9	1.1	44.9	14.6	189.3	184.4	1,296.7	124.9
Fort Wayne, IN	1,097.2	2.8	35.5	32.1	128.3	146.4	649.7	102.5
Fort Worth, TX	n/a	n/a	n/a	n/a	n/a	n/a	n/a	n/a
Grand Rapids, MI	n/a	1.8	81.2	19.6	146.3	n/a	933.5	85.2
Greeley, CO	1,419.9	1.4	41.0	12.3	90.5	171.1	940.9	162.6
Green Bay, WI	928.9	0.9	26.1	3.2	61.9	81.6	725.8	29.3
Greensboro, NC	2,421.7	6.7	29.9	53.7	258.8	475.5	1,421.1	175.9
Honolulu, HI	n/a	n/a	n/a	n/a	n/a	n/a	n/a	n/a
Houston, TX	n/a	n/a	n/a	n/a	n/a	n/a	n/a	n/a
Huntsville, AL[3]	2,220.1	4.2	32.4	31.2	227.3	432.2	1,337.1	155.6
Indianapolis, IN[2]	1,699.1	2.5	23.1	28.7	114.1	199.2	1,200.7	130.7
Jacksonville, FL	1,592.3	2.2	35.2	25.3	166.6	235.0	1,031.9	96.1
Kansas City, MO	n/a	n/a	n/a	n/a	n/a	n/a	n/a	n/a
Lafayette, LA	2,832.6	6.6	29.8	51.6	358.4	551.2	1,694.4	140.6
Lakeland, FL	1,687.2	2.6	17.0	33.6	217.9	249.4	1,045.5	121.2
Las Vegas, NV	2,501.4	4.6	36.8	114.4	354.9	390.7	1,310.3	289.7
Lexington, KY	2,369.2	0.5	30.9	28.3	60.2	318.5	1,748.7	182.1
Lincoln, NE	1,017.1	0.0	77.9	0.0	41.1	119.0	705.4	73.6
Little Rock, AR	n/a	6.8	60.7	54.6	393.0	n/a	n/a	278.3
Los Angeles, CA	2,574.0	4.1	31.4	148.3	263.3	400.2	1,366.0	360.7
Louisville, KY	1,847.8	1.9	21.7	30.8	98.0	230.7	1,263.0	201.7

Table continued on following page.

Appendix A: Comparative Statistics   A-153

Suburbs[1]	All Crimes	Violent Crimes				Property Crimes		
		Murder	Rape	Robbery	Aggrav. Assault	Burglary	Larceny -Theft	Motor Vehicle Theft
Madison, WI	1,351.6	1.0	24.7	18.3	82.4	169.4	971.3	84.6
Manchester, NH	1,000.0	1.6	42.2	12.2	35.9	81.4	789.2	37.5
Memphis, TN	2,498.8	6.8	34.3	50.8	297.1	361.2	1,515.0	233.6
Miami, FL	3,417.0	6.9	35.0	125.5	289.7	268.7	2,428.8	262.4
Midland, TX[2]	2,400.0	11.5	25.9	31.7	368.8	299.6	1,293.6	368.8
Milwaukee, WI	1,671.2	1.4	20.7	24.3	79.0	124.4	1,348.6	72.7
Minneapolis, MN	2,224.5	1.6	36.4	48.6	98.2	238.6	1,611.4	189.7
Nashville, TN	1,872.5	2.8	29.2	26.7	236.4	201.0	1,238.9	137.5
New Haven, CT	1,934.6	2.2	24.3	47.9	77.5	206.4	1,361.4	214.9
New Orleans, LA	2,472.9	9.3	22.9	43.8	209.1	290.9	1,767.8	129.1
New York, NY	n/a	n/a	n/a	n/a	n/a	n/a	n/a	n/a
Oklahoma City, OK	2,410.6	4.4	46.1	32.5	150.0	447.5	1,495.7	234.3
Omaha, NE	1,880.3	2.3	43.8	23.0	147.2	232.1	1,212.2	219.7
Orlando, FL	2,485.9	4.1	42.0	75.9	269.2	341.2	1,573.1	180.5
Peoria, IL	1,462.2	1.7	46.0	15.2	161.7	265.2	890.0	82.4
Philadelphia, PA[2]	1,935.5	7.6	16.3	96.8	235.8	202.8	1,235.3	140.9
Phoenix, AZ	n/a	2.9	40.6	49.3	192.6	n/a	1,530.6	165.3
Pittsburgh, PA[2]	1,402.7	3.5	23.7	33.2	168.7	159.1	958.5	55.9
Portland, OR	2,077.6	1.6	48.3	37.5	128.0	233.0	1,381.8	247.4
Providence, RI	1,466.1	1.7	43.0	37.4	173.7	203.4	912.5	94.2
Provo, UT	1,312.0	1.1	30.2	7.2	46.1	131.5	1,018.1	77.8
Raleigh, NC	1,325.7	2.1	14.8	21.7	90.6	209.5	912.4	74.6
Reno, NV	1,965.3	1.4	55.1	47.4	262.9	331.5	1,041.2	225.8
Richmond, VA	2,045.4	4.9	28.3	37.0	106.2	170.5	1,580.8	117.6
Riverside, CA	2,643.4	5.8	29.0	111.1	273.8	441.1	1,367.7	414.9
Rochester, MN	653.1	1.0	9.7	2.9	67.2	122.6	407.8	41.9
Sacramento, CA	2,195.0	3.4	28.3	73.9	172.0	335.6	1,366.4	215.3
Salt Lake City, UT	3,178.0	2.3	62.6	48.1	186.0	349.3	2,211.9	317.8
San Antonio, TX	1,855.5	2.5	37.7	25.0	148.4	294.5	1,199.2	148.3
San Diego, CA	1,801.2	1.9	28.6	81.2	214.0	218.1	1,020.7	236.8
San Francisco, CA	2,534.2	1.3	42.6	87.1	128.4	294.1	1,778.4	202.3
San Jose, CA	2,582.6	1.5	27.9	54.6	118.4	291.8	1,875.3	213.0
Santa Rosa, CA	1,577.8	1.9	41.0	36.6	283.0	232.0	903.5	79.7
Savannah, GA[2]	3,497.3	5.3	37.2	67.1	245.2	497.1	2,366.1	279.1
Seattle, WA	n/a	n/a	n/a	n/a	n/a	n/a	n/a	n/a
Sioux Falls, SD	1,221.6	1.2	42.1	3.6	128.8	358.7	568.1	119.2
Springfield, IL	1,395.2	1.1	40.2	32.6	269.7	340.4	605.7	105.5
Tallahassee, FL	2,203.5	2.6	40.1	31.7	278.9	510.7	1,198.9	140.5
Tampa, FL	1,969.7	3.4	37.9	46.7	187.8	210.4	1,356.1	127.3
Tucson, AZ	2,634.2	3.2	25.3	38.5	115.5	349.9	1,905.9	195.9
Tulsa, OK	2,046.1	4.5	38.9	18.4	159.8	420.8	1,190.3	213.3
Tuscaloosa, AL[2]	2,503.0	3.3	28.5	41.7	249.6	518.3	1,449.1	212.5
Virginia Beach, VA	3,057.1	8.5	39.5	83.1	293.8	282.1	2,149.5	200.6
Washington, DC	n/a	n/a	26.7	61.2	96.5	98.4	1,055.9	126.4
Wichita, KS	n/a	1.6	42.3	14.5	156.8	271.8	n/a	129.8
Winston-Salem, NC	n/a	n/a	n/a	n/a	n/a	n/a	n/a	n/a
U.S.	2,489.3	5.0	42.6	81.6	250.2	340.5	1,549.5	219.9

Note: Figures are crimes per 100,000 population in 2019 except where noted; n/a not available; (1) All areas within the metro area that are located outside the city limits; (2) 2018 data; (3) 2017 data
Source: FBI Uniform Crime Reports, 2017, 2018, 2019

A-154 Appendix A: Comparative Statistics

Crime Rate: Metro Area

Metro Area[1]	All Crimes	Violent Crimes				Property Crimes		
		Murder	Rape	Robbery	Aggrav. Assault	Burglary	Larceny -Theft	Motor Vehicle Theft
Albuquerque, NM	n/a	10.1	64.0	194.0	775.3	n/a	2,633.7	674.0
Allentown, PA	n/a	n/a	n/a	n/a	n/a	n/a	n/a	n/a
Anchorage, AK	5,513.6	11.1	178.4	208.4	796.7	600.1	3,190.1	528.8
Ann Arbor, MI	2,005.3	2.1	67.0	38.3	248.1	199.0	1,323.3	127.5
Athens, GA[4]	2,882.3	3.4	34.7	65.0	204.7	444.1	1,990.8	139.7
Atlanta, GA[3]	2,895.7	5.7	26.1	94.1	194.7	393.9	1,903.2	278.0
Austin, TX	2,697.1	2.5	48.3	56.9	179.2	313.8	1,905.9	190.5
Baton Rouge, LA	3,871.0	14.1	28.3	107.4	404.3	547.0	2,573.0	197.0
Boise City, ID	1,493.5	1.3	58.3	11.1	180.2	201.9	946.2	94.5
Boston, MA[2]	n/a	3.0	31.1	78.6	283.6	166.5	1,048.9	n/a
Boulder, CO	2,717.9	0.9	68.2	25.3	178.0	303.9	1,929.3	212.4
Cape Coral, FL	1,415.7	3.0	32.0	50.3	172.4	174.9	884.6	98.3
Cedar Rapids, IA	2,229.3	0.7	20.9	33.0	133.8	400.0	1,464.5	176.4
Charleston, SC	3,076.7	8.9	41.4	62.4	285.2	383.3	1,968.0	327.5
Charlotte, NC	n/a	n/a	n/a	n/a	n/a	n/a	n/a	n/a
Chicago, IL[2]	n/a	n/a	n/a	n/a	n/a	n/a	n/a	n/a
Cincinnati, OH	2,214.3	4.1	42.0	67.0	124.2	318.7	1,498.9	159.4
Clarksville, TN	2,648.0	6.8	48.4	48.7	283.6	369.5	1,670.2	220.7
Cleveland, OH	2,254.7	5.9	41.0	120.5	235.8	364.4	1,288.2	198.9
College Station, TX	2,233.6	1.9	61.8	41.9	156.8	378.5	1,438.0	154.6
Colorado Springs, CO	3,313.4	4.4	77.8	74.1	309.4	397.5	1,958.8	491.3
Columbia, MO	2,454.0	6.7	48.2	40.5	176.4	340.4	1,623.9	217.9
Columbia, SC	3,955.7	8.4	49.0	82.7	443.3	532.4	2,430.1	409.8
Columbus, OH	2,676.7	5.3	62.3	99.9	119.0	417.5	1,752.9	219.8
Dallas, TX[2]	n/a	n/a	n/a	n/a	n/a	n/a	n/a	n/a
Davenport, IA	2,565.2	2.1	55.8	55.5	253.0	420.1	1,598.8	179.8
Denver, CO	n/a	n/a	n/a	n/a	n/a	n/a	n/a	n/a
Des Moines, IA	n/a	n/a	n/a	n/a	n/a	n/a	n/a	n/a
Durham, NC	3,020.8	7.3	31.5	115.4	284.9	493.9	1,922.7	165.1
Edison, NJ[2]	n/a	n/a	n/a	n/a	n/a	n/a	n/a	n/a
El Paso, TX	1,749.1	4.9	43.7	42.9	241.7	153.3	1,143.1	119.5
Fargo, ND	2,635.2	2.0	61.8	42.4	190.5	469.8	1,641.1	227.6
Fayetteville, NC	n/a	n/a	n/a	n/a	n/a	n/a	n/a	n/a
Fort Collins, CO	2,112.3	0.8	34.8	17.7	180.7	194.2	1,555.0	129.0
Fort Wayne, IN	2,418.7	7.3	47.5	97.6	152.6	290.7	1,649.8	173.2
Fort Worth, TX[2]	n/a	n/a	n/a	n/a	n/a	n/a	n/a	n/a
Grand Rapids, MI	n/a	2.2	79.4	41.3	198.6	n/a	1,014.1	115.7
Greeley, CO	1,848.3	1.6	49.2	28.9	136.3	218.1	1,211.6	202.6
Green Bay, WI	1,324.3	1.5	41.8	17.3	165.3	130.9	909.3	58.2
Greensboro, NC	3,226.1	9.7	33.0	113.3	374.2	578.8	1,881.3	235.7
Honolulu, HI	n/a	n/a	n/a	n/a	n/a	n/a	n/a	n/a
Houston, TX	n/a	n/a	n/a	n/a	n/a	n/a	n/a	n/a
Huntsville, AL[4]	3,685.7	7.3	56.3	97.0	396.3	560.7	2,249.3	318.9
Indianapolis, IN[3]	3,285.3	9.3	46.3	166.8	419.1	496.7	1,830.9	316.2
Jacksonville, FL	2,980.1	9.2	50.3	94.0	321.2	413.8	1,870.6	221.0
Kansas City, MO	n/a	n/a	n/a	n/a	n/a	n/a	n/a	n/a
Lafayette, LA	3,349.4	7.8	25.3	68.5	365.0	619.4	2,093.7	169.8
Lakeland, FL	1,922.4	3.2	23.1	41.8	209.3	271.5	1,242.9	130.5
Las Vegas, NV	3,089.8	4.9	73.2	123.7	324.0	572.8	1,592.2	399.1
Lexington, KY	2,949.0	5.2	45.2	80.1	100.1	414.3	2,062.1	242.1
Lincoln, NE	2,843.7	1.5	106.4	49.2	189.7	309.2	2,043.0	144.7
Little Rock, AR	n/a	10.1	72.6	92.6	607.0	n/a	n/a	347.8
Los Angeles, CA[2]	2,790.2	5.1	41.5	185.0	329.4	377.7	1,479.4	372.2
Louisville, KY	3,300.8	8.3	26.0	93.8	308.7	447.9	2,011.8	404.3

Table continued on following page.

Appendix A: Comparative Statistics   A-155

Metro Area[1]	All Crimes	Violent Crimes				Property Crimes		
		Murder	Rape	Robbery	Aggrav. Assault	Burglary	Larceny -Theft	Motor Vehicle Theft
Madison, WI	1,932.4	1.2	31.0	43.6	141.9	259.9	1,321.5	133.2
Manchester, NH	1,534.7	2.6	45.6	40.8	140.7	131.1	1,109.5	64.3
Memphis, TN	5,173.9	17.6	52.5	207.1	843.3	769.0	2,863.0	421.5
Miami, FL[2]	3,563.1	7.3	34.4	131.5	307.5	286.0	2,520.6	275.9
Midland, TX[3]	2,288.6	5.1	39.5	40.1	232.9	275.8	1,463.0	232.3
Milwaukee, WI	2,501.8	7.0	40.0	136.4	394.4	305.7	1,353.9	264.3
Minneapolis, MN	2,605.3	2.7	44.7	78.3	146.9	303.6	1,782.3	246.9
Nashville, TN	3,020.0	6.1	41.4	119.1	403.9	303.6	1,915.5	230.4
New Haven, CT	2,383.4	3.5	25.9	80.1	163.2	255.0	1,586.2	269.5
New Orleans, LA	3,701.4	15.9	76.6	109.8	349.1	369.1	2,459.9	320.9
New York, NY[2]	n/a	n/a	n/a	n/a	n/a	n/a	n/a	n/a
Oklahoma City, OK	3,530.9	7.7	62.8	80.3	310.3	678.7	1,997.6	393.6
Omaha, NE	3,059.7	3.6	62.0	66.4	281.1	294.5	1,908.8	443.3
Orlando, FL	2,829.9	4.6	45.1	87.9	292.4	359.1	1,831.9	209.0
Peoria, IL	2,386.5	7.5	49.5	78.0	316.9	381.2	1,383.1	170.3
Philadelphia, PA[2,3]	3,462.1	18.3	55.2	270.0	420.3	355.2	2,042.3	300.9
Phoenix, AZ	n/a	4.6	49.8	97.1	275.1	n/a	1,804.9	251.9
Pittsburgh, PA[3]	1,687.7	5.5	25.8	58.8	184.5	196.1	1,137.0	80.0
Portland, OR	3,049.5	2.4	50.2	66.7	183.3	339.3	1,968.5	439.1
Providence, RI	1,692.5	2.3	44.8	48.1	187.3	225.0	1,071.9	113.0
Provo, UT	1,368.4	1.1	31.6	7.9	49.6	132.9	1,061.8	83.5
Raleigh, NC	1,570.3	1.7	21.5	37.4	112.0	223.8	1,071.2	102.7
Reno, NV	2,336.2	3.2	63.1	86.8	315.9	327.1	1,187.2	352.9
Richmond, VA	2,388.9	8.3	26.7	60.3	132.4	216.6	1,781.7	162.9
Riverside, CA	2,700.9	5.7	29.9	113.4	276.9	437.5	1,420.4	417.2
Rochester, MN	1,425.3	0.9	32.6	16.7	102.3	184.6	1,011.3	76.9
Sacramento, CA	2,548.0	4.1	27.5	102.0	220.5	389.6	1,520.5	283.8
Salt Lake City, UT	3,700.3	3.0	71.3	72.8	219.5	396.4	2,569.6	367.6
San Antonio, TX	3,796.6	5.1	78.5	86.7	345.6	434.8	2,483.3	362.6
San Diego, CA	1,992.1	2.6	33.1	86.4	219.1	230.0	1,131.6	289.3
San Francisco, CA[2]	4,482.9	3.0	39.4	225.0	211.5	417.2	3,236.0	350.7
San Jose, CA	2,725.6	2.3	46.9	93.1	182.6	345.7	1,646.7	408.3
Santa Rosa, CA	1,763.5	1.8	55.7	48.8	298.8	246.8	997.9	113.7
Savannah, GA[3]	3,107.5	9.2	35.9	93.7	247.2	415.6	2,032.0	274.0
Seattle, WA[2]	n/a	n/a	n/a	n/a	n/a	n/a	n/a	n/a
Sioux Falls, SD	2,815.3	1.9	56.2	26.4	303.7	369.5	1,775.9	281.7
Springfield, IL	3,514.4	4.8	70.3	115.3	393.5	655.2	2,099.8	175.4
Tallahassee, FL	3,458.0	6.5	71.0	81.2	368.9	560.3	2,124.4	245.8
Tampa, FL	1,977.8	4.0	36.9	49.8	201.5	216.1	1,341.8	127.7
Tucson, AZ	3,328.8	5.3	62.4	123.9	255.9	405.1	2,168.0	308.2
Tulsa, OK	3,757.4	8.2	57.4	83.0	381.0	737.0	2,059.5	431.3
Tuscaloosa, AL[3]	3,445.1	4.0	35.6	80.3	276.5	607.5	2,189.7	251.6
Virginia Beach, VA	2,759.6	8.0	33.9	73.0	234.6	240.3	1,987.4	182.3
Washington, DC[2]	n/a	n/a	29.8	99.9	163.6	121.4	1,424.4	154.6
Wichita, KS	n/a	6.1	74.0	77.9	623.3	525.2	n/a	411.7
Winston-Salem, NC[3]	n/a	n/a	n/a	n/a	n/a	n/a	n/a	n/a
U.S.	2,489.3	5.0	42.6	81.6	250.2	340.5	1,549.5	219.9

Note: Figures are crimes per 100,000 population in 2019 except where noted; n/a not available; (1) Figures cover the Metropolitan Statistical Area except where noted; (2) Metropolitan Division (MD); (3) 2018 data; (4) 2017 data
Source: FBI Uniform Crime Reports, 2017, 2018, 2019

A-156 Appendix A: Comparative Statistics

Temperature & Precipitation: Yearly Averages and Extremes

City	Extreme Low (°F)	Average Low (°F)	Average Temp. (°F)	Average High (°F)	Extreme High (°F)	Average Precip. (in.)	Average Snow (in.)
Albuquerque, NM	-17	43	57	70	105	8.5	11
Allentown, PA	-12	42	52	61	105	44.2	32
Anchorage, AK	-34	29	36	43	85	15.7	71
Ann Arbor, MI	-21	39	49	58	104	32.4	41
Athens, GA	-8	52	62	72	105	49.8	2
Atlanta, GA	-8	52	62	72	105	49.8	2
Austin, TX	-2	58	69	79	109	31.1	1
Baton Rouge, LA	8	57	68	78	103	58.5	Trace
Boise City, ID	-25	39	51	63	111	11.8	22
Boston, MA	-12	44	52	59	102	42.9	41
Boulder, CO	-25	37	51	64	103	15.5	63
Cape Coral, FL	26	65	75	84	103	53.9	0
Cedar Rapids, IA	-34	36	47	57	105	34.4	33
Charleston, SC	6	55	66	76	104	52.1	1
Charlotte, NC	-5	50	61	71	104	42.8	6
Chicago, IL	-27	40	49	59	104	35.4	39
Cincinnati, OH	-25	44	54	64	103	40.9	23
Clarksville, TN	-17	49	60	70	107	47.4	11
Cleveland, OH	-19	41	50	59	104	37.1	55
College Station, TX	-2	58	69	79	109	31.1	1
Colorado Springs, CO	-24	36	49	62	99	17.0	48
Columbia, MO	-20	44	54	64	111	40.6	25
Columbia, SC	-1	51	64	75	107	48.3	2
Columbus, OH	-19	42	52	62	104	37.9	28
Dallas, TX	-2	56	67	77	112	33.9	3
Davenport, IA	-24	40	50	60	108	31.8	33
Denver, CO	-25	37	51	64	103	15.5	63
Des Moines, IA	-24	40	50	60	108	31.8	33
Durham, NC	-9	48	60	71	105	42.0	8
Edison, NJ	-8	46	55	63	105	43.5	27
El Paso, TX	-8	50	64	78	114	8.6	6
Fargo, ND	-36	31	41	52	106	19.6	40
Fayetteville, NC	-9	48	60	71	105	42.0	8
Fort Collins, CO	-25	37	51	64	103	15.5	63
Fort Wayne, IN	-22	40	50	60	106	35.9	33
Fort Worth, TX	-1	55	66	76	113	32.3	3
Grand Rapids, MI	-22	38	48	57	102	34.7	73
Greeley, CO	-25	37	51	64	103	15.5	63
Green Bay, WI	-31	34	44	54	99	28.3	46
Greensboro, NC	-8	47	58	69	103	42.5	10
Honolulu, HI	52	70	77	84	94	22.4	0
Houston, TX	7	58	69	79	107	46.9	Trace
Huntsville, AL	-11	50	61	71	104	56.8	4
Indianapolis, IN	-23	42	53	62	104	40.2	25
Jacksonville, FL	7	58	69	79	103	52.0	0
Kansas City, MO	-23	44	54	64	109	38.1	21
Lafayette, LA	8	57	68	78	103	58.5	Trace
Lakeland, FL	18	63	73	82	99	46.7	Trace
Las Vegas, NV	8	53	67	80	116	4.0	1
Lexington, KY	-21	45	55	65	103	45.1	17
Lincoln, NE	-33	39	51	62	108	29.1	27
Little Rock, AR	-5	51	62	73	112	50.7	5
Los Angeles, CA	27	55	63	70	110	11.3	Trace
Louisville, KY	-20	46	57	67	105	43.9	17
Madison, WI	-37	35	46	57	104	31.1	42

Table continued on following page.

Appendix A: Comparative Statistics   A-157

City	Extreme Low (°F)	Average Low (°F)	Average Temp. (°F)	Average High (°F)	Extreme High (°F)	Average Precip. (in.)	Average Snow (in.)
Manchester, NH	-33	34	46	57	102	36.9	63
Memphis, TN	0	52	65	77	107	54.8	1
Miami, FL	30	69	76	83	98	57.1	0
Midland, TX	-11	50	64	77	116	14.6	4
Milwaukee, WI	-26	38	47	55	103	32.0	49
Minneapolis, MN	-34	35	45	54	105	27.1	52
Nashville, TN	-17	49	60	70	107	47.4	11
New Haven, CT	-7	44	52	60	103	41.4	25
New Orleans, LA	11	59	69	78	102	60.6	Trace
New York, NY	-2	47	55	62	104	47.0	23
Oklahoma City, OK	-8	49	60	71	110	32.8	10
Omaha, NE	-23	40	51	62	110	30.1	29
Orlando, FL	19	62	72	82	100	47.7	Trace
Peoria, IL	-26	41	51	61	113	35.4	23
Philadelphia, PA	-7	45	55	64	104	41.4	22
Phoenix, AZ	17	59	72	86	122	7.3	Trace
Pittsburgh, PA	-18	41	51	60	103	37.1	43
Portland, OR	-3	45	54	62	107	37.5	7
Providence, RI	-13	42	51	60	104	45.3	35
Provo, UT	-22	40	52	64	107	15.6	63
Raleigh, NC	-9	48	60	71	105	42.0	8
Reno, NV	-16	33	50	67	105	7.2	24
Richmond, VA	-8	48	58	69	105	43.0	13
Riverside, CA	24	53	66	78	114	n/a	n/a
Rochester, MN	-40	34	44	54	102	29.4	47
Sacramento, CA	18	48	61	73	115	17.3	Trace
Salt Lake City, UT	-22	40	52	64	107	15.6	63
San Antonio, TX	0	58	69	80	108	29.6	1
San Diego, CA	29	57	64	71	111	9.5	Trace
San Francisco, CA	24	49	57	65	106	19.3	Trace
San Jose, CA	21	50	59	68	105	13.5	Trace
Santa Rosa, CA	23	42	57	71	109	29.0	n/a
Savannah, GA	3	56	67	77	105	50.3	Trace
Seattle, WA	0	44	52	59	99	38.4	13
Sioux Falls, SD	-36	35	46	57	110	24.6	38
Springfield, IL	-24	44	54	63	112	34.9	21
Tallahassee, FL	6	56	68	79	103	63.3	Trace
Tampa, FL	18	63	73	82	99	46.7	Trace
Tucson, AZ	16	55	69	82	117	11.6	2
Tulsa, OK	-8	50	61	71	112	38.9	10
Tuscaloosa, AL	-6	51	63	74	106	53.5	2
Virginia Beach, VA	-3	51	60	69	104	44.8	8
Washington, DC	-5	49	58	67	104	39.5	18
Wichita, KS	-21	45	57	68	113	29.3	17
Winston-Salem, NC	-8	47	58	69	103	42.5	10

Source: National Climatic Data Center, International Station Meteorological Climate Summary, 9/96

A-158 Appendix A: Comparative Statistics

Weather Conditions

City	Temperature			Daytime Sky			Precipitation		
	10°F & below	32°F & below	90°F & above	Clear	Partly cloudy	Cloudy	0.01 inch or more precip.	1.0 inch or more snow/ice	Thunder-storms
Albuquerque, NM	4	114	65	140	161	64	60	9	38
Allentown, PA	n/a	123	15	77	148	140	123	20	31
Anchorage, AK	n/a	194	n/a	50	115	200	113	49	2
Ann Arbor, MI	n/a	136	12	74	134	157	135	38	32
Athens, GA	1	49	38	98	147	120	116	3	48
Atlanta, GA	1	49	38	98	147	120	116	3	48
Austin, TX	< 1	20	111	105	148	112	83	1	41
Baton Rouge, LA	< 1	21	86	99	150	116	113	< 1	73
Boise City, ID	n/a	124	45	106	133	126	91	22	14
Boston, MA	n/a	97	12	88	127	150	253	48	18
Boulder, CO	24	155	33	99	177	89	90	38	39
Cape Coral, FL	n/a	n/a	115	93	220	52	110	0	92
Cedar Rapids, IA	n/a	156	16	89	132	144	109	28	42
Charleston, SC	< 1	33	53	89	162	114	114	1	59
Charlotte, NC	1	65	44	98	142	125	113	3	41
Chicago, IL	n/a	132	17	83	136	146	125	31	38
Cincinnati, OH	14	107	23	80	126	159	127	25	39
Clarksville, TN	5	76	51	98	135	132	119	8	54
Cleveland, OH	n/a	123	12	63	127	175	157	48	34
College Station, TX	< 1	20	111	105	148	112	83	1	41
Colorado Springs, CO	21	161	18	108	157	100	98	33	49
Columbia, MO	17	108	36	99	127	139	110	17	52
Columbia, SC	< 1	58	77	97	149	119	110	1	53
Columbus, OH	n/a	118	19	72	137	156	136	29	40
Dallas, TX	1	34	102	108	160	97	78	2	49
Davenport, IA	n/a	137	26	99	129	137	106	25	46
Denver, CO	24	155	33	99	177	89	90	38	39
Des Moines, IA	n/a	137	26	99	129	137	106	25	46
Durham, NC	n/a	n/a	39	98	143	124	110	3	42
Edison, NJ	n/a	90	24	80	146	139	122	16	46
El Paso, TX	1	59	106	147	164	54	49	3	35
Fargo, ND	n/a	180	15	81	145	139	100	38	31
Fayetteville, NC	n/a	n/a	39	98	143	124	110	3	42
Fort Collins, CO	24	155	33	99	177	89	90	38	39
Fort Wayne, IN	n/a	131	16	75	140	150	131	31	39
Fort Worth, TX	1	40	100	123	136	106	79	3	47
Grand Rapids, MI	n/a	146	11	67	119	179	142	57	34
Greeley, CO	24	155	33	99	177	89	90	38	39
Green Bay, WI	n/a	163	7	86	125	154	120	40	33
Greensboro, NC	3	85	32	94	143	128	113	5	43
Honolulu, HI	n/a	n/a	23	25	286	54	98	0	7
Houston, TX	n/a	n/a	96	83	168	114	101	1	62
Huntsville, AL	2	66	49	70	118	177	116	2	54
Indianapolis, IN	19	119	19	83	128	154	127	24	43
Jacksonville, FL	< 1	16	83	86	181	98	114	1	65
Kansas City, MO	22	110	39	112	134	119	103	17	51
Lafayette, LA	< 1	21	86	99	150	116	113	< 1	73
Lakeland, FL	n/a	n/a	85	81	204	80	107	< 1	87
Las Vegas, NV	< 1	37	134	185	132	48	27	2	13
Lexington, KY	11	96	22	86	136	143	129	17	44
Lincoln, NE	n/a	145	40	108	135	122	94	19	46
Little Rock, AR	1	57	73	110	142	113	104	4	57
Los Angeles, CA	0	< 1	5	131	125	109	34	0	1
Louisville, KY	8	90	35	82	143	140	125	15	45

Table continued on following page.

Appendix A: Comparative Statistics   A-159

City	Temperature			Daytime Sky			Precipitation		
	10°F & below	32°F & below	90°F & above	Clear	Partly cloudy	Cloudy	0.01 inch or more precip.	1.0 inch or more snow/ice	Thunder-storms
Madison, WI	n/a	161	14	88	119	158	118	38	40
Manchester, NH	n/a	171	12	87	131	147	125	32	19
Memphis, TN	1	53	86	101	152	112	104	2	59
Miami, FL	n/a	n/a	55	48	263	54	128	0	74
Midland, TX	1	62	102	144	138	83	52	3	38
Milwaukee, WI	n/a	141	10	90	118	157	126	38	35
Minneapolis, MN	n/a	156	16	93	125	147	113	41	37
Nashville, TN	5	76	51	98	135	132	119	8	54
New Haven, CT	n/a	n/a	7	80	146	139	118	17	22
New Orleans, LA	0	13	70	90	169	106	114	1	69
New York, NY	n/a	n/a	18	85	166	114	120	11	20
Oklahoma City, OK	5	79	70	124	131	110	80	8	50
Omaha, NE	n/a	139	35	100	142	123	97	20	46
Orlando, FL	n/a	n/a	90	76	208	81	115	0	80
Peoria, IL	n/a	127	27	89	127	149	115	22	49
Philadelphia, PA	5	94	23	81	146	138	117	14	27
Phoenix, AZ	0	10	167	186	125	54	37	< 1	23
Pittsburgh, PA	n/a	121	8	62	137	166	154	42	35
Portland, OR	n/a	37	11	67	116	182	152	4	7
Providence, RI	n/a	117	9	85	134	146	123	21	21
Provo, UT	n/a	128	56	94	152	119	92	38	38
Raleigh, NC	n/a	n/a	39	98	143	124	110	3	42
Reno, NV	14	178	50	143	139	83	50	17	14
Richmond, VA	3	79	41	90	147	128	115	7	43
Riverside, CA	0	4	82	124	178	63	n/a	n/a	5
Rochester, MN	n/a	165	9	87	126	152	114	40	41
Sacramento, CA	0	21	73	175	111	79	58	< 1	2
Salt Lake City, UT	n/a	128	56	94	152	119	92	38	38
San Antonio, TX	n/a	n/a	112	97	153	115	81	1	36
San Diego, CA	0	< 1	4	115	126	124	40	0	5
San Francisco, CA	0	6	4	136	130	99	63	< 1	5
San Jose, CA	0	5	5	106	180	79	57	< 1	6
Santa Rosa, CA	n/a	43	30	n/a	365	n/a	n/a	n/a	2
Savannah, GA	< 1	29	70	97	155	113	111	< 1	63
Seattle, WA	n/a	38	3	57	121	187	157	8	8
Sioux Falls, SD	n/a	n/a	n/a	95	136	134	n/a	n/a	n/a
Springfield, IL	19	111	34	96	126	143	111	18	49
Tallahassee, FL	< 1	31	86	93	175	97	114	1	83
Tampa, FL	n/a	n/a	85	81	204	80	107	< 1	87
Tucson, AZ	0	18	140	177	119	69	54	2	42
Tulsa, OK	6	78	74	117	141	107	88	8	50
Tuscaloosa, AL	1	57	59	91	161	113	119	1	57
Virginia Beach, VA	< 1	53	33	89	149	127	115	5	38
Washington, DC	2	71	34	84	144	137	112	9	30
Wichita, KS	13	110	63	117	132	116	87	13	54
Winston-Salem, NC	3	85	32	94	143	128	113	5	43

Note: Figures are average number of days per year
Source: National Climatic Data Center, International Station Meteorological Climate Summary, 9/96

A-160 Appendix A: Comparative Statistics

Air Quality Index

MSA[1] (Days[2])	Percent of Days when Air Quality was...					AQI Statistics	
	Good	Moderate	Unhealthy for Sensitive Groups	Unhealthy	Very Unhealthy	Maximum	Median
Albuquerque, NM (365)	44.1	54.8	1.1	0.0	0.0	108	53
Allentown, PA (365)	75.3	23.6	1.1	0.0	0.0	119	42
Anchorage, AK (365)	71.8	24.9	2.2	1.1	0.0	160	31
Ann Arbor, MI (365)	80.5	19.5	0.0	0.0	0.0	88	39
Athens, GA (365)	67.1	32.9	0.0	0.0	0.0	87	44
Atlanta, GA (365)	44.4	50.4	4.9	0.3	0.0	172	52
Austin, TX (365)	68.2	31.2	0.5	0.0	0.0	115	44
Baton Rouge, LA (365)	61.4	36.2	2.5	0.0	0.0	119	45
Boise City, ID (365)	67.9	31.2	0.5	0.3	0.0	165	44
Boston, MA (365)	79.7	20.0	0.3	0.0	0.0	122	43
Boulder, CO (365)	62.2	36.4	1.4	0.0	0.0	119	47
Cape Coral, FL (365)	89.9	9.9	0.3	0.0	0.0	108	36
Cedar Rapids, IA (365)	78.6	21.4	0.0	0.0	0.0	84	39
Charleston, SC (357)	84.3	15.4	0.3	0.0	0.0	140	38
Charlotte, NC (365)	54.8	40.3	4.9	0.0	0.0	136	49
Chicago, IL (365)	33.2	62.2	4.4	0.3	0.0	174	55
Cincinnati, OH (365)	38.1	56.4	5.5	0.0	0.0	147	54
Clarksville, TN (365)	84.1	15.9	0.0	0.0	0.0	87	40
Cleveland, OH (365)	50.7	47.4	1.9	0.0	0.0	119	50
College Station, TX (352)	100.0	0.0	0.0	0.0	0.0	17	0
Colorado Springs, CO (365)	71.0	29.0	0.0	0.0	0.0	100	45
Columbia, MO (245)	97.6	2.4	0.0	0.0	0.0	71	38
Columbia, SC (365)	72.3	27.1	0.5	0.0	0.0	136	43
Columbus, OH (365)	64.9	34.8	0.3	0.0	0.0	101	46
Dallas, TX (365)	49.6	42.5	7.7	0.3	0.0	156	51
Davenport, IA (365)	59.5	39.7	0.8	0.0	0.0	115	46
Denver, CO (365)	24.9	69.0	5.5	0.5	0.0	154	58
Des Moines, IA (365)	83.8	16.2	0.0	0.0	0.0	100	39
Durham, NC (365)	75.3	24.7	0.0	0.0	0.0	92	44
Edison, NJ (365)	46.3	49.3	4.4	0.0	0.0	150	51
El Paso, TX (365)	40.3	56.2	3.0	0.5	0.0	157	53
Fargo, ND (363)	90.1	9.4	0.3	0.3	0.0	156	33
Fayetteville, NC (363)	77.7	22.3	0.0	0.0	0.0	84	41
Fort Collins, CO (365)	57.0	41.4	1.6	0.0	0.0	129	48
Fort Wayne, IN (365)	64.7	35.1	0.3	0.0	0.0	101	45
Fort Worth, TX (365)	49.6	42.5	7.7	0.3	0.0	156	51
Grand Rapids, MI (365)	81.6	18.4	0.0	0.0	0.0	100	38
Greeley, CO (365)	69.0	30.1	0.8	0.0	0.0	125	45
Green Bay, WI (365)	85.2	14.8	0.0	0.0	0.0	97	36
Greensboro, NC (365)	79.7	20.3	0.0	0.0	0.0	90	43
Honolulu, HI (365)	92.9	7.1	0.0	0.0	0.0	94	29
Houston, TX (365)	46.8	44.7	7.1	1.1	0.3	202	52
Huntsville, AL (361)	70.6	29.4	0.0	0.0	0.0	93	44
Indianapolis, IN (365)	40.5	58.1	1.4	0.0	0.0	119	54
Jacksonville, FL (365)	67.1	32.6	0.3	0.0	0.0	114	43
Kansas City, MO (365)	57.5	42.2	0.3	0.0	0.0	137	47
Lafayette, LA (365)	76.7	23.3	0.0	0.0	0.0	84	41
Lakeland, FL (365)	86.0	14.0	0.0	0.0	0.0	100	36
Las Vegas, NV (365)	42.2	56.4	1.4	0.0	0.0	122	54
Lexington, KY (365)	83.0	17.0	0.0	0.0	0.0	80	42
Lincoln, NE (360)	93.9	6.1	0.0	0.0	0.0	66	31
Little Rock, AR (365)	64.4	35.6	0.0	0.0	0.0	79	45
Los Angeles, CA (365)	18.1	57.0	17.0	7.7	0.3	201	72
Louisville, KY (365)	53.4	45.5	1.1	0.0	0.0	136	49

Table continued on following page.

Appendix A: Comparative Statistics   A-161

MSA[1] (Days[2])	Percent of Days when Air Quality was...					AQI Statistics	
	Good	Moderate	Unhealthy for Sensitive Groups	Unhealthy	Very Unhealthy	Maximum	Median
Madison, WI (365)	78.1	21.9	0.0	0.0	0.0	93	39
Manchester, NH (365)	96.7	3.3	0.0	0.0	0.0	80	37
Memphis, TN (365)	60.5	38.1	1.4	0.0	0.0	148	45
Miami, FL (364)	78.3	21.2	0.5	0.0	0.0	146	41
Midland, TX (n/a)	n/a	n/a	n/a	n/a	n/a	n/a	n/a
Milwaukee, WI (365)	69.6	29.6	0.8	0.0	0.0	115	44
Minneapolis, MN (365)	58.6	40.5	0.5	0.3	0.0	200	46
Nashville, TN (365)	62.7	37.0	0.3	0.0	0.0	101	45
New Haven, CT (365)	76.7	19.5	3.3	0.5	0.0	159	41
New Orleans, LA (365)	62.7	36.7	0.5	0.0	0.0	112	45
New York, NY (365)	46.3	49.3	4.4	0.0	0.0	150	51
Oklahoma City, OK (365)	55.9	43.6	0.5	0.0	0.0	119	48
Omaha, NE (365)	77.5	22.5	0.0	0.0	0.0	97	40
Orlando, FL (365)	81.1	17.3	1.6	0.0	0.0	122	39
Peoria, IL (365)	78.1	21.4	0.5	0.0	0.0	101	41
Philadelphia, PA (365)	49.3	46.3	4.4	0.0	0.0	150	51
Phoenix, AZ (365)	13.7	71.5	11.5	0.5	0.8	886	74
Pittsburgh, PA (365)	35.3	60.3	3.3	1.1	0.0	161	56
Portland, OR (365)	78.1	21.1	0.8	0.0	0.0	128	38
Providence, RI (365)	79.2	20.3	0.5	0.0	0.0	126	44
Provo, UT (365)	69.3	30.4	0.3	0.0	0.0	107	46
Raleigh, NC (365)	65.5	34.5	0.0	0.0	0.0	93	46
Reno, NV (365)	66.8	33.2	0.0	0.0	0.0	97	46
Richmond, VA (365)	74.5	25.5	0.0	0.0	0.0	100	44
Riverside, CA (365)	11.5	48.8	21.6	15.9	2.2	213	89
Rochester, MN (364)	86.0	14.0	0.0	0.0	0.0	84	36
Sacramento, CA (365)	47.1	47.1	5.8	0.0	0.0	140	52
Salt Lake City, UT (365)	46.3	49.0	4.7	0.0	0.0	136	51
San Antonio, TX (365)	53.7	44.7	1.4	0.3	0.0	169	49
San Diego, CA (365)	23.8	69.3	6.3	0.5	0.0	169	64
San Francisco, CA (365)	69.6	27.9	2.5	0.0	0.0	150	43
San Jose, CA (365)	72.1	26.8	1.1	0.0	0.0	136	43
Santa Rosa, CA (365)	95.3	4.7	0.0	0.0	0.0	87	33
Savannah, GA (365)	80.8	19.2	0.0	0.0	0.0	87	39
Seattle, WA (365)	64.7	34.8	0.5	0.0	0.0	142	45
Sioux Falls, SD (365)	87.9	11.8	0.3	0.0	0.0	105	36
Springfield, IL (360)	79.7	20.3	0.0	0.0	0.0	87	40
Tallahassee, FL (365)	74.5	25.2	0.3	0.0	0.0	119	40
Tampa, FL (365)	73.2	25.2	1.6	0.0	0.0	132	43
Tucson, AZ (365)	61.6	37.8	0.5	0.0	0.0	103	47
Tulsa, OK (365)	68.2	31.2	0.5	0.0	0.0	105	45
Tuscaloosa, AL (264)	90.9	9.1	0.0	0.0	0.0	87	35
Virginia Beach, VA (365)	86.8	13.2	0.0	0.0	0.0	97	40
Washington, DC (365)	57.3	39.7	2.7	0.3	0.0	157	47
Wichita, KS (365)	82.5	17.5	0.0	0.0	0.0	97	40
Winston-Salem, NC (365)	61.6	38.4	0.0	0.0	0.0	97	45

Note: The Air Quality Index (AQI) is an index for reporting daily air quality. EPA calculates the AQI for five major air pollutants regulated by the Clean Air Act: ground-level ozone, particle pollution (also known as particulate matter), carbon monoxide, sulfur dioxide, and nitrogen dioxide. The AQI runs from 0 to 500. The higher the AQI value, the greater the level of air pollution and the greater the health concern. There are six AQI categories: "Good" The AQI is between 0 and 50. Air quality is considered satisfactory; "Moderate" The AQI is between 51 and 100. Air quality is acceptable; "Unhealthy for Sensitive Groups" When AQI values are between 101 and 150, members of sensitive groups may experience health effects; "Unhealthy" When AQI values are between 151 and 200 everyone may begin to experience health effects; "Very Unhealthy" AQI values between 201 and 300 trigger a health alert; "Hazardous" AQI values over 300 trigger health warnings of emergency conditions; Data covers the entire county unless noted otherwise; (1) Data covers the Metropolitan Statistical Area—see Appendix B for areas included; (2) Number of days with AQI data in 2019
Source: U.S. Environmental Protection Agency, Air Quality Index Report, 2019

A-162   Appendix A: Comparative Statistics

Air Quality Index Pollutants

MSA[1] (Days[2])	Percent of Days when AQI Pollutant was...					
	Carbon Monoxide	Nitrogen Dioxide	Ozone	Sulfur Dioxide	Particulate Matter 2.5	Particulate Matter 10
Albuquerque, NM (365)	0.0	0.0	69.0	0.0	18.1	12.9
Allentown, PA (365)	0.0	3.6	61.4	0.0	35.1	0.0
Anchorage, AK (365)	1.4	0.0	0.0	0.0	69.9	28.8
Ann Arbor, MI (365)	0.0	0.0	66.6	0.0	33.4	0.0
Athens, GA (365)	0.0	0.0	37.3	0.0	62.7	0.0
Atlanta, GA (365)	0.0	2.5	46.8	0.0	50.7	0.0
Austin, TX (365)	0.0	1.9	48.8	0.0	49.3	0.0
Baton Rouge, LA (365)	0.0	1.6	47.9	0.3	50.1	0.0
Boise City, ID (365)	0.0	1.1	44.4	0.0	51.0	3.6
Boston, MA (365)	0.0	4.1	57.5	0.0	38.4	0.0
Boulder, CO (365)	0.0	0.0	73.7	0.0	26.3	0.0
Cape Coral, FL (365)	0.0	0.0	68.8	0.0	30.1	1.1
Cedar Rapids, IA (365)	0.0	0.0	47.9	1.1	51.0	0.0
Charleston, SC (357)	0.0	0.0	67.2	0.0	32.5	0.3
Charlotte, NC (365)	0.0	0.0	66.6	0.0	33.4	0.0
Chicago, IL (365)	0.0	5.5	24.1	4.9	62.5	3.0
Cincinnati, OH (365)	0.0	1.6	41.4	6.0	50.1	0.8
Clarksville, TN (365)	0.0	0.0	72.9	0.0	27.1	0.0
Cleveland, OH (365)	0.0	0.3	40.5	0.5	55.1	3.6
College Station, TX (352)	0.0	0.0	0.0	100.0	0.0	0.0
Colorado Springs, CO (365)	0.0	0.0	94.5	0.0	4.9	0.5
Columbia, MO (245)	0.0	0.0	100.0	0.0	0.0	0.0
Columbia, SC (365)	0.0	0.0	71.8	0.0	28.2	0.0
Columbus, OH (365)	0.0	1.4	49.0	0.0	49.3	0.3
Dallas, TX (365)	0.0	3.0	56.2	0.0	40.8	0.0
Davenport, IA (365)	0.0	0.0	37.8	0.0	41.9	20.3
Denver, CO (365)	0.0	16.4	57.8	0.3	17.3	8.2
Des Moines, IA (365)	0.0	0.8	67.4	0.0	31.8	0.0
Durham, NC (365)	0.0	0.0	56.7	1.6	41.6	0.0
Edison, NJ (365)	0.0	17.5	39.2	0.0	43.3	0.0
El Paso, TX (365)	0.0	5.8	55.9	0.0	37.5	0.8
Fargo, ND (363)	0.0	2.5	72.7	0.0	24.2	0.6
Fayetteville, NC (363)	0.0	0.0	56.7	0.0	42.1	1.1
Fort Collins, CO (365)	0.0	0.0	92.3	0.0	7.7	0.0
Fort Wayne, IN (365)	0.0	0.0	48.5	0.0	51.5	0.0
Fort Worth, TX (365)	0.0	3.0	56.2	0.0	40.8	0.0
Grand Rapids, MI (365)	0.0	2.5	69.9	0.0	26.3	1.4
Greeley, CO (365)	0.0	0.0	64.7	0.0	35.3	0.0
Green Bay, WI (365)	0.0	0.0	51.0	1.1	47.9	0.0
Greensboro, NC (365)	0.0	0.0	63.6	0.0	29.3	7.1
Honolulu, HI (365)	0.3	0.8	71.8	17.8	9.0	0.3
Houston, TX (365)	0.0	4.4	47.1	0.5	47.1	0.8
Huntsville, AL (361)	0.0	0.0	42.9	0.0	55.1	1.9
Indianapolis, IN (365)	0.0	0.0	34.2	1.1	64.7	0.0
Jacksonville, FL (365)	0.0	0.0	48.2	2.7	49.0	0.0
Kansas City, MO (365)	0.0	2.5	48.2	0.0	45.5	3.8
Lafayette, LA (365)	0.0	0.0	58.4	0.0	41.6	0.0
Lakeland, FL (365)	0.0	0.0	67.9	0.5	31.5	0.0
Las Vegas, NV (365)	0.3	5.5	69.0	0.0	23.0	2.2
Lexington, KY (365)	0.0	2.7	52.9	0.0	44.4	0.0
Lincoln, NE (360)	0.0	0.0	63.6	21.1	15.3	0.0
Little Rock, AR (365)	0.0	0.5	40.0	0.0	59.5	0.0
Los Angeles, CA (365)	0.0	9.0	56.2	0.0	32.3	2.5
Louisville, KY (365)	0.0	2.7	45.8	0.0	51.5	0.0

Table continued on following page.

Appendix A: Comparative Statistics   A-163

MSA[1] (Days[2])	Percent of Days when AQI Pollutant was...					
	Carbon Monoxide	Nitrogen Dioxide	Ozone	Sulfur Dioxide	Particulate Matter 2.5	Particulate Matter 10
Madison, WI (365)	0.0	0.0	45.5	0.0	54.5	0.0
Manchester, NH (365)	0.0	0.0	97.5	0.0	2.5	0.0
Memphis, TN (365)	0.0	2.5	51.0	0.0	46.6	0.0
Miami, FL (364)	0.3	3.6	37.4	0.0	58.5	0.3
Midland, TX (n/a)	n/a	n/a	n/a	n/a	n/a	n/a
Milwaukee, WI (365)	0.0	2.7	51.8	0.0	43.3	2.2
Minneapolis, MN (365)	0.0	1.4	31.2	1.1	43.0	23.3
Nashville, TN (365)	0.0	6.8	40.5	0.0	52.6	0.0
New Haven, CT (365)	0.0	4.1	67.7	0.0	27.1	1.1
New Orleans, LA (365)	0.0	0.8	45.8	8.8	44.4	0.3
New York, NY (365)	0.0	17.5	39.2	0.0	43.3	0.0
Oklahoma City, OK (365)	0.0	1.1	52.9	0.0	45.8	0.3
Omaha, NE (365)	0.0	0.0	52.3	3.3	40.8	3.6
Orlando, FL (365)	0.0	0.0	80.5	0.0	19.5	0.0
Peoria, IL (365)	0.0	0.0	55.6	0.5	43.8	0.0
Philadelphia, PA (365)	0.0	3.6	50.1	0.0	46.3	0.0
Phoenix, AZ (365)	0.0	0.8	46.3	0.0	19.7	33.2
Pittsburgh, PA (365)	0.0	0.0	29.3	6.3	64.4	0.0
Portland, OR (365)	0.0	2.2	56.4	0.0	41.4	0.0
Providence, RI (365)	0.0	2.2	70.7	0.0	26.8	0.3
Provo, UT (365)	0.0	1.9	81.4	0.0	16.2	0.5
Raleigh, NC (365)	0.3	0.3	46.8	0.0	52.6	0.0
Reno, NV (365)	0.0	1.1	80.5	0.0	17.0	1.4
Richmond, VA (365)	0.0	4.4	67.4	0.0	28.2	0.0
Riverside, CA (365)	0.0	3.0	62.5	0.0	24.4	10.1
Rochester, MN (364)	0.0	0.0	53.6	0.0	46.4	0.0
Sacramento, CA (365)	0.0	0.3	71.0	0.0	27.1	1.6
Salt Lake City, UT (365)	0.0	8.8	67.1	0.0	22.7	1.4
San Antonio, TX (365)	0.0	0.8	44.1	0.0	54.8	0.3
San Diego, CA (365)	0.0	0.5	48.2	0.0	50.4	0.8
San Francisco, CA (365)	0.0	6.3	52.1	0.0	41.6	0.0
San Jose, CA (365)	0.0	0.5	64.7	0.0	33.7	1.1
Santa Rosa, CA (365)	0.0	0.8	70.7	0.0	25.8	2.7
Savannah, GA (365)	0.0	0.0	40.0	15.9	44.1	0.0
Seattle, WA (365)	0.0	8.5	43.3	0.0	48.2	0.0
Sioux Falls, SD (365)	0.0	2.5	84.1	0.0	12.9	0.5
Springfield, IL (360)	0.0	0.0	50.8	0.0	49.2	0.0
Tallahassee, FL (365)	0.0	0.0	47.7	0.0	52.3	0.0
Tampa, FL (365)	0.0	0.0	58.4	1.1	39.5	1.1
Tucson, AZ (365)	0.0	0.3	71.5	0.0	5.5	22.7
Tulsa, OK (365)	0.0	0.0	65.2	0.0	34.8	0.0
Tuscaloosa, AL (264)	0.0	0.0	71.2	0.0	28.8	0.0
Virginia Beach, VA (365)	0.0	12.1	61.9	0.0	26.0	0.0
Washington, DC (365)	0.0	6.8	61.9	0.0	31.2	0.0
Wichita, KS (365)	0.0	1.4	72.6	0.0	23.6	2.5
Winston-Salem, NC (365)	0.0	2.7	47.1	0.0	50.1	0.0

Note: The Air Quality Index (AQI) is an index for reporting daily air quality. EPA calculates the AQI for five major air pollutants regulated by the Clean Air Act: ground-level ozone, particle pollution (also known as particulate matter), carbon monoxide, sulfur dioxide, and nitrogen dioxide. The AQI runs from 0 to 500. The higher the AQI value, the greater the level of air pollution and the greater the health concern; (1) Data covers the Metropolitan Statistical Area—see Appendix B for areas included; (2) Number of days with AQI data in 2019
Source: U.S. Environmental Protection Agency, Air Quality Index Report, 2019

A-164　Appendix A: Comparative Statistics

Air Quality Trends: Ozone

MSA[1]	1990	1995	2000	2005	2010	2015	2016	2017	2018	2019
Albuquerque, NM	0.072	0.070	0.072	0.073	0.066	0.066	0.065	0.069	0.074	0.067
Allentown, PA	0.093	0.091	0.091	0.086	0.080	0.070	0.073	0.067	0.067	0.064
Anchorage, AK	n/a	n/a	n/a	n/a	n/a	n/a	n/a	n/a	n/a	n/a
Ann Arbor, MI	n/a	n/a	n/a	n/a	n/a	n/a	n/a	n/a	n/a	n/a
Athens, GA	n/a	n/a	n/a	n/a	n/a	n/a	n/a	n/a	n/a	n/a
Atlanta, GA	0.104	0.103	0.101	0.087	0.076	0.070	0.073	0.068	0.068	0.071
Austin, TX	0.088	0.089	0.088	0.082	0.074	0.073	0.064	0.070	0.072	0.065
Baton Rouge, LA	0.105	0.091	0.090	0.090	0.075	0.069	0.066	0.069	0.069	0.066
Boise City, ID	n/a	n/a	n/a	n/a	n/a	n/a	n/a	n/a	n/a	n/a
Boston, MA	n/a	n/a	n/a	n/a	n/a	n/a	n/a	n/a	n/a	n/a
Boulder, CO	n/a	n/a	n/a	n/a	n/a	n/a	n/a	n/a	n/a	n/a
Cape Coral, FL	n/a	n/a	n/a	n/a	n/a	n/a	n/a	n/a	n/a	n/a
Cedar Rapids, IA	n/a	n/a	n/a	n/a	n/a	n/a	n/a	n/a	n/a	n/a
Charleston, SC	0.068	0.071	0.078	0.073	0.067	0.054	0.059	0.062	0.058	0.064
Charlotte, NC	n/a	n/a	n/a	n/a	n/a	n/a	n/a	n/a	n/a	n/a
Chicago, IL	0.074	0.094	0.073	0.084	0.070	0.066	0.074	0.071	0.073	0.069
Cincinnati, OH	0.091	0.091	0.081	0.085	0.075	0.068	0.071	0.067	0.074	0.067
Clarksville, TN	n/a	n/a	n/a	n/a	n/a	n/a	n/a	n/a	n/a	n/a
Cleveland, OH	0.085	0.092	0.076	0.083	0.077	0.071	0.072	0.070	0.074	0.070
College Station, TX	n/a	n/a	n/a	n/a	n/a	n/a	n/a	n/a	n/a	n/a
Colorado Springs, CO	n/a	n/a	n/a	n/a	n/a	n/a	n/a	n/a	n/a	n/a
Columbia, MO	n/a	n/a	n/a	n/a	n/a	n/a	n/a	n/a	n/a	n/a
Columbia, SC	0.093	0.079	0.096	0.082	0.070	0.056	0.065	0.059	0.060	0.066
Columbus, OH	0.090	0.091	0.085	0.084	0.073	0.066	0.069	0.065	0.062	0.060
Dallas, TX	0.095	0.105	0.096	0.097	0.080	0.077	0.070	0.073	0.078	0.071
Davenport, IA	n/a	n/a	n/a	n/a	n/a	n/a	n/a	n/a	n/a	n/a
Denver, CO	0.077	0.070	0.069	0.072	0.070	0.073	0.071	0.072	0.071	0.068
Des Moines, IA	n/a	n/a	n/a	n/a	n/a	n/a	n/a	n/a	n/a	n/a
Durham, NC	n/a	n/a	n/a	n/a	n/a	n/a	n/a	n/a	n/a	n/a
Edison, NJ	0.101	0.106	0.090	0.091	0.081	0.075	0.073	0.070	0.073	0.067
El Paso, TX	0.080	0.078	0.082	0.074	0.072	0.071	0.068	0.073	0.077	0.074
Fargo, ND	n/a	n/a	n/a	n/a	n/a	n/a	n/a	n/a	n/a	n/a
Fayetteville, NC	0.087	0.081	0.086	0.084	0.071	0.060	0.064	0.063	0.064	0.061
Fort Collins, CO	0.066	0.072	0.074	0.076	0.072	0.069	0.070	0.067	0.073	0.065
Fort Wayne, IN	0.086	0.094	0.086	0.081	0.067	0.061	0.068	0.063	0.071	0.063
Fort Worth, TX	0.095	0.105	0.096	0.097	0.080	0.077	0.070	0.073	0.078	0.071
Grand Rapids, MI	0.102	0.089	0.073	0.085	0.071	0.066	0.075	0.065	0.072	0.065
Greeley, CO	n/a	n/a	n/a	n/a	n/a	n/a	n/a	n/a	n/a	n/a
Green Bay, WI	n/a	n/a	n/a	n/a	n/a	n/a	n/a	n/a	n/a	n/a
Greensboro, NC	n/a	n/a	n/a	n/a	n/a	n/a	n/a	n/a	n/a	n/a
Honolulu, HI	0.034	0.049	0.044	0.042	0.046	0.048	0.047	0.046	0.046	0.053
Houston, TX	0.119	0.114	0.102	0.087	0.079	0.083	0.066	0.070	0.073	0.074
Huntsville, AL	0.079	0.080	0.088	0.075	0.071	0.063	0.066	0.063	0.065	0.063
Indianapolis, IN	0.084	0.094	0.081	0.080	0.069	0.064	0.070	0.067	0.073	0.067
Jacksonville, FL	0.080	0.068	0.072	0.076	0.068	0.060	0.057	0.059	0.060	0.062
Kansas City, MO	0.075	0.098	0.088	0.084	0.072	0.063	0.066	0.069	0.073	0.063
Lafayette, LA	n/a	n/a	n/a	n/a	n/a	n/a	n/a	n/a	n/a	n/a
Lakeland, FL	0.066	0.071	0.079	0.074	0.064	0.062	0.064	0.072	0.065	0.066
Las Vegas, NV	n/a	n/a	n/a	n/a	n/a	n/a	n/a	n/a	n/a	n/a
Lexington, KY	0.078	0.088	0.077	0.078	0.070	0.069	0.066	0.063	0.063	0.059
Lincoln, NE	0.057	0.060	0.057	0.056	0.050	0.061	0.058	0.062	0.062	0.056
Little Rock, AR	0.080	0.086	0.090	0.083	0.072	0.063	0.064	0.060	0.066	0.059
Los Angeles, CA	0.134	0.114	0.091	0.085	0.076	0.083	0.083	0.093	0.084	0.080
Louisville, KY	0.075	0.087	0.088	0.083	0.076	0.070	0.070	0.064	0.067	0.064
Madison, WI	0.077	0.084	0.072	0.079	0.062	0.064	0.068	0.064	0.066	0.059
Manchester, NH	n/a	n/a	n/a	n/a	n/a	n/a	n/a	n/a	n/a	n/a

Table continued on following page.

Appendix A: Comparative Statistics   A-165

MSA[1]	1990	1995	2000	2005	2010	2015	2016	2017	2018	2019
Memphis, TN	0.088	0.095	0.092	0.086	0.076	0.065	0.069	0.063	0.069	0.065
Miami, FL	0.068	0.072	0.075	0.065	0.064	0.061	0.061	0.064	0.064	0.058
Midland, TX	n/a	n/a	n/a	n/a	n/a	n/a	n/a	n/a	n/a	n/a
Milwaukee, WI	0.095	0.106	0.082	0.092	0.079	0.069	0.074	0.072	0.073	0.066
Minneapolis, MN	0.068	0.084	0.065	0.074	0.066	0.061	0.061	0.062	0.065	0.059
Nashville, TN	0.089	0.092	0.084	0.078	0.073	0.065	0.067	0.063	0.068	0.064
New Haven, CT	n/a	n/a	n/a	n/a	n/a	n/a	n/a	n/a	n/a	n/a
New Orleans, LA	0.082	0.088	0.091	0.079	0.074	0.067	0.065	0.063	0.065	0.062
New York, NY	0.101	0.106	0.090	0.091	0.081	0.075	0.073	0.070	0.073	0.067
Oklahoma City, OK	0.078	0.086	0.082	0.077	0.071	0.067	0.066	0.070	0.072	0.067
Omaha, NE	0.054	0.075	0.063	0.069	0.058	0.055	0.063	0.061	0.063	0.050
Orlando, FL	0.081	0.075	0.080	0.083	0.069	0.060	0.064	0.067	0.062	0.062
Peoria, IL	0.071	0.082	0.072	0.075	0.064	0.062	0.067	0.066	0.070	0.063
Philadelphia, PA	0.102	0.109	0.099	0.091	0.083	0.074	0.075	0.073	0.075	0.067
Phoenix, AZ	0.080	0.087	0.082	0.077	0.076	0.072	0.071	0.075	0.074	0.071
Pittsburgh, PA	0.080	0.095	0.082	0.082	0.075	0.069	0.068	0.066	0.068	0.062
Portland, OR	0.081	0.065	0.059	0.059	0.056	0.064	0.057	0.073	0.062	0.058
Providence, RI	0.106	0.107	0.087	0.090	0.072	0.070	0.075	0.076	0.074	0.064
Provo, UT	0.070	0.068	0.083	0.078	0.070	0.073	0.072	0.073	0.073	0.073
Raleigh, NC	0.093	0.081	0.087	0.082	0.071	0.065	0.069	0.066	0.063	0.064
Reno, NV	0.074	0.069	0.067	0.069	0.068	0.071	0.070	0.068	0.077	0.063
Richmond, VA	0.083	0.089	0.080	0.082	0.079	0.062	0.065	0.063	0.062	0.061
Riverside, CA	0.146	0.129	0.104	0.102	0.093	0.094	0.096	0.099	0.097	0.091
Rochester, MN	n/a	n/a	n/a	n/a	n/a	n/a	n/a	n/a	n/a	n/a
Sacramento, CA	0.088	0.093	0.087	0.087	0.074	0.074	0.077	0.073	0.079	0.068
Salt Lake City, UT	n/a	n/a	n/a	n/a	n/a	n/a	n/a	n/a	n/a	n/a
San Antonio, TX	0.090	0.095	0.078	0.084	0.072	0.079	0.071	0.073	0.072	0.075
San Diego, CA	0.112	0.093	0.084	0.079	0.075	0.070	0.073	0.077	0.069	0.071
San Francisco, CA	0.058	0.074	0.057	0.057	0.061	0.062	0.059	0.060	0.053	0.060
San Jose, CA	0.079	0.085	0.070	0.065	0.073	0.067	0.063	0.065	0.061	0.062
Santa Rosa, CA	0.063	0.071	0.061	0.050	0.053	0.059	0.055	0.062	0.055	0.056
Savannah, GA	n/a	n/a	n/a	n/a	n/a	n/a	n/a	n/a	n/a	n/a
Seattle, WA	0.082	0.062	0.056	0.053	0.053	0.059	0.054	0.076	0.067	0.052
Sioux Falls, SD	n/a	n/a	n/a	n/a	n/a	n/a	n/a	n/a	n/a	n/a
Springfield, IL	n/a	n/a	n/a	n/a	n/a	n/a	n/a	n/a	n/a	n/a
Tallahassee, FL	n/a	n/a	n/a	n/a	n/a	n/a	n/a	n/a	n/a	n/a
Tampa, FL	0.080	0.075	0.081	0.075	0.067	0.062	0.064	0.064	0.065	0.065
Tucson, AZ	0.073	0.078	0.074	0.075	0.068	0.065	0.065	0.070	0.069	0.065
Tulsa, OK	0.086	0.091	0.081	0.072	0.069	0.061	0.064	0.065	0.067	0.062
Tuscaloosa, AL	n/a	n/a	n/a	n/a	n/a	n/a	n/a	n/a	n/a	n/a
Virginia Beach, VA	0.085	0.084	0.083	0.078	0.074	0.061	0.062	0.059	0.061	0.059
Washington, DC	0.088	0.093	0.082	0.081	0.077	0.067	0.069	0.065	0.066	0.061
Wichita, KS	0.077	0.069	0.080	0.074	0.075	0.064	0.062	0.063	0.064	0.062
Winston-Salem, NC	0.084	0.086	0.089	0.080	0.078	0.065	0.069	0.066	0.064	0.062
U.S.	0.088	0.089	0.082	0.080	0.073	0.068	0.069	0.068	0.069	0.065

Note: (1) Data covers the Metropolitan Statistical Area—see Appendix B for areas included; n/a not available. The values shown are the composite ozone concentration averages among trend sites based on the highest fourth daily maximum 8-hour concentration in parts per million. These trends are based on sites having an adequate record of monitoring data during the trend period. Data from exceptional events are included.

Source: U.S. Environmental Protection Agency, Air Quality Monitoring Information, "Air Quality Trends by City, 1990-2019"

A-166 Appendix A: Comparative Statistics

Maximum Air Pollutant Concentrations: Particulate Matter, Ozone, CO and Lead

Metro Aea	PM 10 (ug/m³)	PM 2.5 Wtd AM (ug/m³)	PM 2.5 24-Hr (ug/m³)	Ozone (ppm)	Carbon Monoxide (ppm)	Lead (ug/m³)
Albuquerque, NM	141	7.7	20	0.069	1	n/a
Allentown, PA	31	8.5	26	0.065	n/a	0.04
Anchorage, AK	148	8.2	42	n/a	2	n/a
Ann Arbor, MI	n/a	8.5	22	0.060	n/a	n/a
Athens, GA	n/a	9.8	21	0.063	n/a	n/a
Atlanta, GA	40	10.8	24	0.075	2	n/a
Austin, TX	38	9.5	21	0.065	2	n/a
Baton Rouge, LA	51	9.2	23	0.070	1	0
Boise City, ID	83	6.9	25	0.057	1	n/a
Boston, MA	34	7.5	17	0.065	1	n/a
Boulder, CO	52	7.4	36	0.069	n/a	n/a
Cape Coral, FL	51	7.4	14	0.062	n/a	n/a
Cedar Rapids, IA	38	7.9	20	0.060	n/a	n/a
Charleston, SC	54	6.9	14	0.064	n/a	n/a
Charlotte, NC	36	9.5	18	0.074	1	n/a
Chicago, IL	73	10.8	26	0.071	2	0.19
Cincinnati, OH	108	11.9	26	0.072	2	n/a
Clarksville, TN	n/a	n/a	n/a	0.061	n/a	n/a
Cleveland, OH	79	10.8	26	0.071	2	0.01
College Station, TX	n/a	n/a	n/a	n/a	n/a	n/a
Colorado Springs, CO	32	5.0	13	0.065	2	n/a
Columbia, MO	n/a	n/a	n/a	0.058	n/a	n/a
Columbia, SC	35	7.2	15	0.067	1	n/a
Columbus, OH	39	9.7	22	0.068	1	n/a
Dallas, TX	40	9.0	19	0.076	1	0.23
Davenport, IA	129	8.6	22	0.066	1	n/a
Denver, CO	111	10.0	29	0.078	2	n/a
Des Moines, IA	39	7.0	19	0.064	1	n/a
Durham, NC	27	7.7	15	0.063	n/a	n/a
Edison, NJ	34	11.0	24	0.073	2	n/a
El Paso, TX	79	8.5	25	0.075	2	0.01
Fargo, ND	78	6.5	18	0.062	n/a	n/a
Fayetteville, NC	30	7.4	16	0.061	n/a	n/a
Fort Collins, CO	n/a	6.0	20	0.071	1	n/a
Fort Wayne, IN	n/a	9.0	22	0.063	n/a	n/a
Fort Worth, TX	40	9.0	19	0.076	1	0.23
Grand Rapids, MI	104	8.3	24	0.065	1	0.01
Greeley, CO	n/a	9.0	26	0.065	1	n/a
Green Bay, WI	n/a	7.3	19	0.061	n/a	n/a
Greensboro, NC	33	6.8	15	0.064	n/a	n/a
Honolulu, HI	32	3.9	8	0.053	1	n/a
Houston, TX	63	10.7	27	0.081	2	n/a
Huntsville, AL	34	7.4	14	0.063	n/a	n/a
Indianapolis, IN	57	12.6	27	0.067	2	n/a
Jacksonville, FL	57	8.6	20	0.065	1	n/a
Kansas City, MO	71	7.6	17	0.064	1	n/a
Lafayette, LA	52	7.9	17	0.063	n/a	n/a
Lakeland, FL	57	7.7	19	0.067	n/a	n/a
Las Vegas, NV	104	8.0	26	0.070	2	n/a
Lexington, KY	28	8.0	17	0.059	n/a	n/a
Lincoln, NE	n/a	6.5	17	0.056	n/a	n/a
Little Rock, AR	38	10.3	23	0.060	1	n/a
Los Angeles, CA	159	11.0	28	0.101	3	0.02
Louisville, KY	40	10.5	23	0.068	2	n/a
Madison, WI	35	8.0	21	0.059	n/a	n/a

Table continued on following page.

Appendix A: Comparative Statistics   A-167

Metro Aea	PM 10 (ug/m^3)	PM 2.5 Wtd AM (ug/m^3)	PM 2.5 24-Hr (ug/m^3)	Ozone (ppm)	Carbon Monoxide (ppm)	Lead (ug/m^3)
Manchester, NH	n/a	3.0	10	0.057	0	n/a
Memphis, TN	54	8.8	19	0.070	1	n/a
Miami, FL	54	8.9	19	0.060	2	n/a
Midland, TX	n/a	n/a	n/a	n/a	n/a	n/a
Milwaukee, WI	58	9.3	24	0.068	1	n/a
Minneapolis, MN	98	8.0	23	0.062	1	0.07
Nashville, TN	32	9.2	18	0.066	1	n/a
New Haven, CT	67	7.7	18	0.084	1	n/a
New Orleans, LA	79	7.8	17	0.063	2	0.09
New York, NY	34	11.0	24	0.073	2	n/a
Oklahoma City, OK	63	10.0	21	0.066	1	n/a
Omaha, NE	50	7.8	22	0.062	2	0.06
Orlando, FL	49	6.9	16	0.072	1	n/a
Peoria, IL	n/a	8.0	19	0.064	n/a	n/a
Philadelphia, PA	49	9.8	26	0.072	2	0
Phoenix, AZ	990	10.9	30	0.076	2	0.05
Pittsburgh, PA	86	12.2	39	0.064	3	0
Portland, OR	32	7.0	25	0.065	1	n/a
Providence, RI	37	8.3	18	0.066	2	n/a
Provo, UT	53	6.1	21	0.066	1	n/a
Raleigh, NC	30	8.9	17	0.064	1	n/a
Reno, NV	78	6.0	16	0.066	2	n/a
Richmond, VA	27	8.4	20	0.064	1	n/a
Riverside, CA	243	12.8	36	0.106	1	0.01
Rochester, MN	n/a	n/a	n/a	0.054	n/a	n/a
Sacramento, CA	90	8.4	30	0.079	1	n/a
Salt Lake City, UT	67	9.0	31	0.073	1	n/a
San Antonio, TX	42	8.9	21	0.075	1	n/a
San Diego, CA	153	13.7	27	0.076	2	0.02
San Francisco, CA	34	9.4	19	0.072	2	n/a
San Jose, CA	75	9.1	21	0.064	2	0.07
Santa Rosa, CA	73	5.7	14	0.056	1	n/a
Savannah, GA	n/a	n/a	n/a	0.060	n/a	n/a
Seattle, WA	22	8.5	28	0.056	1	n/a
Sioux Falls, SD	37	3.9	16	0.065	1	n/a
Springfield, IL	n/a	8.2	18	0.062	n/a	n/a
Tallahassee, FL	n/a	7.7	20	0.063	1	n/a
Tampa, FL	64	7.7	17	0.070	1	0.09
Tucson, AZ	139	3.8	9	0.065	1	n/a
Tulsa, OK	36	8.7	22	0.066	1	0.01
Tuscaloosa, AL	n/a	7.9	15	0.060	n/a	n/a
Virginia Beach, VA	20	7.1	18	0.061	1	n/a
Washington, DC	46	9.1	25	0.075	2	n/a
Wichita, KS	64	7.5	18	0.062	n/a	n/a
Winston-Salem, NC	33	9.5	24	0.065	n/a	n/a
NAAQS[1]	150	15.0	35	0.075	9	0.15

*Note: Data from exceptional events are included; Data covers the Metropolitan Statistical Area—see Appendix B for areas included;
(1) National Ambient Air Quality Standards; ppm = parts per million; ug/m^3 = micrograms per cubic meter; n/a not available
Concentrations: Particulate Matter 10 (coarse particulate)—highest second maximum 24-hour concentration; Particulate Matter 2.5 Wtd
AM (fine particulate)—highest weighted annual mean concentration; Particulate Matter 2.5 24-Hour (fine particulate)—highest 98th
percentile 24-hour concentration; Ozone—highest fourth daily maximum 8-hour concentration; Carbon Monoxide—highest second
maximum non-overlapping 8-hour concentration; Lead—maximum running 3-month average
Source: U.S. Environmental Protection Agency, Air Quality Monitoring Information, "Air Quality Statistics by City, 2019"*

A-168   Appendix A: Comparative Statistics

Maximum Air Pollutant Concentrations: Nitrogen Dioxide and Sulfur Dioxide

Metro Area	Nitrogen Dioxide AM (ppb)	Nitrogen Dioxide 1-Hr (ppb)	Sulfur Dioxide AM (ppb)	Sulfur Dioxide 1-Hr (ppb)	Sulfur Dioxide 24-Hr (ppb)
Albuquerque, NM	9	44	n/a	4	n/a
Allentown, PA	11	43	n/a	6	n/a
Anchorage, AK	n/a	n/a	n/a	n/a	n/a
Ann Arbor, MI	n/a	n/a	n/a	n/a	n/a
Athens, GA	n/a	n/a	n/a	n/a	n/a
Atlanta, GA	16	50	n/a	5	n/a
Austin, TX	12	32	n/a	2	n/a
Baton Rouge, LA	10	45	n/a	16	n/a
Boise City, ID	n/a	n/a	n/a	3	n/a
Boston, MA	14	49	n/a	10	n/a
Boulder, CO	n/a	n/a	n/a	n/a	n/a
Cape Coral, FL	n/a	n/a	n/a	n/a	n/a
Cedar Rapids, IA	n/a	n/a	n/a	25	n/a
Charleston, SC	n/a	n/a	n/a	14	n/a
Charlotte, NC	11	37	n/a	3	n/a
Chicago, IL	17	56	n/a	79	n/a
Cincinnati, OH	18	49	n/a	134	n/a
Clarksville, TN	n/a	n/a	n/a	n/a	n/a
Cleveland, OH	10	45	n/a	23	n/a
College Station, TX	n/a	n/a	n/a	8	n/a
Colorado Springs, CO	n/a	n/a	n/a	10	n/a
Columbia, MO	n/a	n/a	n/a	n/a	n/a
Columbia, SC	3	31	n/a	3	n/a
Columbus, OH	10	42	n/a	n/a	n/a
Dallas, TX	12	46	n/a	7	n/a
Davenport, IA	n/a	n/a	n/a	5	n/a
Denver, CO	27	69	n/a	7	n/a
Des Moines, IA	6	37	n/a	n/a	n/a
Durham, NC	n/a	n/a	n/a	41	n/a
Edison, NJ	21	66	n/a	11	n/a
El Paso, TX	14	n/a	n/a	n/a	n/a
Fargo, ND	4	39	n/a	3	n/a
Fayetteville, NC	n/a	n/a	n/a	n/a	n/a
Fort Collins, CO	n/a	n/a	n/a	n/a	n/a
Fort Wayne, IN	n/a	n/a	n/a	n/a	n/a
Fort Worth, TX	12	46	n/a	7	n/a
Grand Rapids, MI	6	36	n/a	14	n/a
Greeley, CO	n/a	n/a	n/a	n/a	n/a
Green Bay, WI	n/a	n/a	n/a	5	n/a
Greensboro, NC	n/a	n/a	n/a	n/a	n/a
Honolulu, HI	4	28	n/a	62	n/a
Houston, TX	17	56	n/a	14	n/a
Huntsville, AL	n/a	n/a	n/a	n/a	n/a
Indianapolis, IN	9	37	n/a	n/a	n/a
Jacksonville, FL	11	39	n/a	41	n/a
Kansas City, MO	11	47	n/a	7	n/a
Lafayette, LA	n/a	n/a	n/a	n/a	n/a
Lakeland, FL	n/a	n/a	n/a	26	n/a
Las Vegas, NV	24	58	n/a	5	n/a
Lexington, KY	6	42	n/a	4	n/a
Lincoln, NE	n/a	n/a	n/a	33	n/a
Little Rock, AR	8	38	n/a	13	n/a
Los Angeles, CA	23	78	n/a	8	n/a
Louisville, KY	15	49	n/a	15	n/a
Madison, WI	n/a	n/a	n/a	2	n/a

Table continued on following page.

Appendix A: Comparative Statistics   A-169

Metro Area	Nitrogen Dioxide AM (ppb)	Nitrogen Dioxide 1-Hr (ppb)	Sulfur Dioxide AM (ppb)	Sulfur Dioxide 1-Hr (ppb)	Sulfur Dioxide 24-Hr (ppb)
Manchester, NH	n/a	n/a	n/a	1	n/a
Memphis, TN	10	40	n/a	2	n/a
Miami, FL	15	48	n/a	1	n/a
Midland, TX	n/a	n/a	n/a	n/a	n/a
Milwaukee, WI	13	47	n/a	4	n/a
Minneapolis, MN	8	41	n/a	10	n/a
Nashville, TN	14	51	n/a	n/a	n/a
New Haven, CT	12	46	n/a	2	n/a
New Orleans, LA	10	43	n/a	53	n/a
New York, NY	21	66	n/a	11	n/a
Oklahoma City, OK	12	n/a	n/a	1	n/a
Omaha, NE	n/a	n/a	n/a	38	n/a
Orlando, FL	4	30	n/a	3	n/a
Peoria, IL	n/a	n/a	n/a	17	n/a
Philadelphia, PA	13	52	n/a	17	n/a
Phoenix, AZ	25	52	n/a	5	n/a
Pittsburgh, PA	10	37	n/a	80	n/a
Portland, OR	11	33	n/a	3	n/a
Providence, RI	17	52	n/a	2	n/a
Provo, UT	9	42	n/a	n/a	n/a
Raleigh, NC	9	34	n/a	2	n/a
Reno, NV	11	46	n/a	3	n/a
Richmond, VA	12	43	n/a	14	n/a
Riverside, CA	29	74	n/a	7	n/a
Rochester, MN	n/a	n/a	n/a	n/a	n/a
Sacramento, CA	12	55	n/a	3	n/a
Salt Lake City, UT	18	55	n/a	13	n/a
San Antonio, TX	7	40	n/a	4	n/a
San Diego, CA	14	47	n/a	1	n/a
San Francisco, CA	15	48	n/a	15	n/a
San Jose, CA	14	52	n/a	2	n/a
Santa Rosa, CA	4	28	n/a	n/a	n/a
Savannah, GA	n/a	n/a	n/a	50	n/a
Seattle, WA	18	57	n/a	6	n/a
Sioux Falls, SD	5	31	n/a	2	n/a
Springfield, IL	n/a	n/a	n/a	n/a	n/a
Tallahassee, FL	n/a	n/a	n/a	n/a	n/a
Tampa, FL	10	37	n/a	11	n/a
Tucson, AZ	7	30	n/a	1	n/a
Tulsa, OK	7	n/a	n/a	6	n/a
Tuscaloosa, AL	n/a	n/a	n/a	n/a	n/a
Virginia Beach, VA	8	40	n/a	3	n/a
Washington, DC	16	49	n/a	5	n/a
Wichita, KS	6	21	n/a	3	n/a
Winston-Salem, NC	7	34	n/a	5	n/a
NAAQS[1]	53	100	30	75	140

Note: Data from exceptional events are included; Data covers the Metropolitan Statistical Area—see Appendix B for areas included;
(1) National Ambient Air Quality Standards; ppb = parts per billion; n/a not available
Concentrations: Nitrogen Dioxide AM—highest arithmetic mean concentration; Nitrogen Dioxide 1-Hr—highest 98th percentile 1-hour daily maximum concentration; Sulfur Dioxide AM—highest annual mean concentration; Sulfur Dioxide 1-Hr—highest 99th percentile 1-hour daily maximum concentration; Sulfur Dioxide 24-Hr—highest second maximum 24-hour concentration
Source: U.S. Environmental Protection Agency, Air Quality Monitoring Information, "Air Quality Statistics by City, 2019"

Appendix B: Metropolitan Area Definitions

Metropolitan Statistical Areas (MSA), Metropolitan Divisions (MD), New England City and Town Areas (NECTA), and New England City and Town Area Divisions (NECTAD)

Note: In March 2020, the Office of Management and Budget (OMB) announced changes to metropolitan and micropolitan statistical area definitions. Both current and historical definitions (December 2009) are shown below. If the change only affected the name of the metro area, the counties included were not repeated.

Albuquerque, NM MSA
Bernalillo, Sandoval, Torrance, and Valencia Counties

Allentown-Bethlehem-Easton, PA-NJ MSA
Carbon, Lehigh, and Northampton Counties, PA; Warren County, NJ

Anchorage, AK MSA
Anchorage Municipality and Matanuska-Susitna Borough

Ann Arbor, MI MSA
Washtenaw County

Athens-Clarke County, GA MSA
Clarke, Madison, Oconee, and Oglethorpe Counties

Atlanta-Sandy Springs-Roswell, GA MSA
Barrow, Bartow, Butts, Carroll, Cherokee, Clayton, Cobb, Coweta, Dawson, DeKalb, Douglas, Fayette, Forsyth, Fulton, Gwinnett, Haralson, Heard, Henry, Jasper, Lamar, Meriwether, Morgan, Newton, Paulding, Pickens, Pike, Rockdale, Spalding, and Walton Counties
Previously Atlanta-Sandy Springs-Marietta, GA MSA
Barrow, Bartow, Butts, Carroll, Cherokee, Clayton, Cobb, Coweta, Dawson, DeKalb, Douglas, Fayette, Forsyth, Fulton, Gwinnett, Haralson, Heard, Henry, Jasper, Lamar, Meriwether, Newton, Paulding, Pickens, Pike, Rockdale, Spalding, and Walton Counties

Austin-Round Rock, TX MSA
Previously Austin-Round Rock-San Marcos, TX MSA
Bastrop, Caldwell, Hays, Travis, and Williamson Counties

Baton Rouge, LA MSA
Ascension, East Baton Rouge, East Feliciana, Iberville, Livingston, Pointe Coupee, St. Helena, West Baton Rouge, and West Feliciana Parishes
Previously Baton Rouge, LA MSA
Ascension, East Baton Rouge, Livingston, and West Baton Rouge Parishes

Boise City, ID MSA
Previously Boise City-Nampa, ID MSA
Ada, Boise, Canyon, Gem, and Owyhee Counties

Boston, MA

Boston-Cambridge-Newton, MA-NH MSA
Previously Boston-Cambridge-Quincy, MA-NH MSA
Essex, Middlesex, Norfolk, Plymouth, and Suffolk Counties, MA; Rockingham and Strafford Counties, NH

Boston, MA MD
Previously Boston-Quincy, MA MD
Norfolk, Plymouth, and Suffolk Counties

Boston-Cambridge-Nashua, MA-NH NECTA
Includes 157 cities and towns in Massachusetts and 34 cities and towns in New Hampshire
Previously Boston-Cambridge-Quincy, MA-NH NECTA
Includes 155 cities and towns in Massachusetts and 38 cities and towns in New Hampshire

Boston-Cambridge-Newton, MA NECTA Division
Includes 92 cities and towns in Massachusetts
Previously Boston-Cambridge-Quincy, MA NECTA Division
Includes 97 cities and towns in Massachusetts

Boulder, CO MSA
Boulder County

Cape Coral-Fort Myers, FL MSA
Lee County

Cedar Rapids, IA, MSA
Benton, Jones, and Linn Counties

Charleston-North Charleston, SC MSA
Previously Charleston-North Charleston- Summerville, SC MSA
Berkeley, Charleston, and Dorchester Counties

Charlotte-Concord-Gastonia, NC-SC MSA
Cabarrus, Gaston, Iredell, Lincoln, Mecklenburg, Rowan, and Union Counties, NC; Chester, Lancaster, and York Counties, SC
Previously Charlotte-Gastonia-Rock Hill, NC-SC MSA
Anson, Cabarrus, Gaston, Mecklenburg, and Union Counties, NC; York County, SC

Chicago, IL

Chicago-Naperville-Elgin, IL-IN-WI MSA
Previous name: Chicago-Joliet-Naperville, IL-IN-WI MSA
Cook, DeKalb, DuPage, Grundy, Kane, Kendall, Lake, McHenry, and Will Counties, IL; Jasper, Lake, Newton, and Porter Counties, IN; Kenosha County, WI

Chicago-Naperville-Arlington Heights, IL MD
Cook, DuPage, Grundy, Kendall, McHenry, and Will Counties
Previous name: Chicago-Joliet-Naperville, IL MD
Cook, DeKalb, DuPage, Grundy, Kane, Kendall, McHenry, and Will Counties

Elgin, IL MD
DeKalb and Kane Counties
Previously part of the Chicago-Joliet-Naperville, IL MD

Gary, IN MD
Jasper, Lake, Newton, and Porter Counties

Lake County-Kenosha County, IL-WI MD
Lake County, IL; Kenosha County, WI

Cincinnati, OH-KY-IN MSA
Brown, Butler, Clermont, Hamilton, and Warren Counties, OH; Boone, Bracken, Campbell, Gallatin, Grant, Kenton, and Pendleton County, KY; Dearborn, Franklin, Ohio, and Union Counties, IN
Previously Cincinnati-Middletown, OH-KY-IN MSA
Brown, Butler, Clermont, Hamilton, and Warren Counties, OH; Boone, Bracken, Campbell, Gallatin, Grant, Kenton, and Pendleton County, KY; Dearborn, Franklin, and Ohio Counties, IN

Clarksville, TN-KY MSA
Montgomery and Stewart Counties, TN; Christian and Trigg Counties, KY

A-172 Appendix B: Metropolitan Area Definitions

Cleveland-Elyria-Mentor, OH MSA
Cuyahoga, Geauga, Lake, Lorain, and Medina Counties

College Station-Bryan, TX MSA
Brazos, Burleson and Robertson Counties

Colorado Springs, CO MSA
El Paso and Teller Counties

Columbia, MO MSA
Boone and Howard Counties

Columbia, SC MSA
Calhoun, Fairfield, Kershaw, Lexington, Richland and Saluda Counties

Columbus, OH MSA
Delaware, Fairfield, Franklin, Licking, Madison, Morrow, Pickaway, and Union Counties

Dallas, TX

Dallas-Fort Worth-Arlington, TX MSA
Collin, Dallas, Denton, Ellis, Hunt, Johnson, Kaufman, Parker, Rockwall, Tarrant, and Wise Counties

Dallas-Plano-Irving, TX MD
Collin, Dallas, Denton, Ellis, Hunt, Kaufman, and Rockwall Counties

Davenport-Moline-Rock Island, IA-IL MSA
Henry, Mercer, and Rock Island Counties, IA; Scott County

Denver-Aurora-Lakewood, CO MSA
Previously Denver-Aurora-Broomfield, CO MSA
Adams, Arapahoe, Broomfield, Clear Creek, Denver, Douglas, Elbert, Gilpin, Jefferson, and Park Counties

Des Moines-West Des Moines, IA MSA
Dallas, Guthrie, Madison, Polk, and Warren Counties

Durham-Chapel Hill, NC MSA
Chatham, Durham, Orange, and Person Counties

Edison, NJ
See New York, NY (New York-Jersey City-White Plains, NY-NJ MD)

El Paso, TX MSA
El Paso County

Fargo, ND-MN MSA
Cass County, ND; Clay County, MN

Fayetteville, NC MSA
Cumberland, and Hoke Counties

Fort Collins, CO MSA
Previously Fort Collins-Loveland, CO MSA
Larimer County

Fort Wayne, IN MSA
Allen, Wells, and Whitley Counties

Fort Worth, TX

Dallas-Fort Worth-Arlington, TX MSA
Collin, Dallas, Denton, Ellis, Hunt, Johnson, Kaufman, Parker, Rockwall, Tarrant, and Wise Counties

Fort Worth-Arlington, TX MD
Hood, Johnson, Parker, Somervell, Tarrant, and Wise Counties

Grand Rapids-Wyoming, MI MSA
Barry, Kent, Montcalm, and Ottawa Counties
Previously Grand Rapids-Wyoming, MI MSA
Barry, Ionia, Kent, and Newaygo Counties

Greeley, CO MSA
Weld County

Green Bay, WI MSA
Brown, Kewaunee, and Oconto Counties

Greensboro-High Point, NC MSA
Guilford, Randolph, and Rockingham Counties

Honolulu, HI MSA
Honolulu County

Houston-The Woodlands-Sugar Land-Baytown, TX MSA
Austin, Brazoria, Chambers, Fort Bend, Galveston, Harris, Liberty, Montgomery, and Waller Counties
Previously Houston-Sugar Land-Baytown, TX MSA
Austin, Brazoria, Chambers, Fort Bend, Galveston, Harris, Liberty, Montgomery, San Jacinto, and Waller Counties

Huntsville, AL MSA
Limestone and Madison Counties

Indianapolis-Carmel, IN MSA
Boone, Brown, Hamilton, Hancock, Hendricks, Johnson, Marion, Morgan, Putnam, and Shelby Counties

Jacksonville, FL MSA
Baker, Clay, Duval, Nassau, and St. Johns Counties

Kansas City, MO-KS MSA
Franklin, Johnson, Leavenworth, Linn, Miami, and Wyandotte Counties, KS; Bates, Caldwell, Cass, Clay, Clinton, Jackson, Lafayette, Platte, and Ray Counties, MO

Lafayette, LA MSA
Acadia, Iberia, Lafayette, St. Martin, and Vermilion Parishes

Lakeland-Winter Haven, FL MSA
Polk County

Las Vegas-Henderson-Paradise, NV MSA
Previously Las Vegas-Paradise, NV MSA
Clark County

Lexington-Fayette, KY MSA
Bourbon, Clark, Fayette, Jessamine, Scott, and Woodford Counties

Lincoln, NE MSA
Lancaster and Seward Counties

Little Rock-North Little Rock-Conway, AR MSA
Faulkner, Grant, Lonoke, Perry, Pulaski, and Saline Counties

Los Angeles, CA

Los Angeles-Long Beach-Anaheim, CA MSA
Previously Los Angeles-Long Beach-Santa Ana, CA MSA
Los Angeles and Orange Counties

Los Angeles-Long Beach-Glendale, CA MD
Los Angeles County

Anaheim-Santa Ana-Irvine, CA MD
Previously Santa Ana-Anaheim-Irvine, CA MD
Orange County

Appendix B: Metropolitan Area Definitions   A-173

Louisville/Jefferson, KY-IN MSA
Clark, Floyd, Harrison, Scott, and Washington Counties, IN; Bullitt, Henry, Jefferson, Oldham, Shelby, Spencer, and Trimble Counties, KY

Madison, WI MSA
Columbia, Dane, and Iowa Counties

Manchester, NH

Manchester-Nashua, NH MSA
Hillsborough County

Manchester, NH NECTA
Includes 11 cities and towns in New Hampshire
Previously Manchester, NH NECTA
Includes 9 cities and towns in New Hampshire

Memphis, TN-AR-MS MSA
Fayette, Shelby and Tipton Counties, TN; Crittenden County, AR; DeSoto, Marshall, Tate and Tunica Counties, MS

Miami, FL

Miami-Fort Lauderdale-West Palm Beach, FL MSA
Previously Miami-Fort Lauderdale-Pompano Beach, FL MSA
Broward, Miami-Dade, and Palm Beach Counties

Miami-Miami Beach-Kendall, FL MD
Miami-Dade County

Midland, TX MSA
Martin, and Midland Counties

Milwaukee-Waukesha-West Allis, WI MSA
Milwaukee, Ozaukee, Washington, and Waukesha Counties

Minneapolis-St. Paul-Bloomington, MN-WI MSA
Anoka, Carver, Chisago, Dakota, Hennepin, Isanti, Le Sueur, Mille Lacs, Ramsey, Scott, Sherburne, Sibley, Washington, and Wright Counties, MN; Pierce and St. Croix Counties, WI

Nashville-Davidson-Murfreesboro-Franklin, TN MSA
Cannon, Cheatham, Davidson, Dickson, Hickman, Macon, Robertson, Rutherford, Smith, Sumner, Trousdale, Williamson, and Wilson Counties

New Haven-Milford, CT MSA
New Haven County

New Orleans-Metarie-Kenner, LA MSA
Jefferson, Orleans, Plaquemines, St. Bernard, St. Charles, St. James, St. John the Baptist, and St. Tammany Parish
Previously New Orleans-Metarie-Kenner, LA MSA
Jefferson, Orleans, Plaquemines, St. Bernard, St. Charles, St. John the Baptist, and St. Tammany Parish

New York, NY

New York-Newark-Jersey City, NY-NJ-PA MSA
Bergen, Essex, Hudson, Hunterdon, Middlesex, Monmouth, Morris, Ocean, Passaic, Somerset, Sussex, and Union Counties, NJ; Bronx, Dutchess, Kings, Nassau, New York, Orange, Putnam, Queens, Richmond, Rockland, Suffolk, and Westchester Counties, NY; Pike County, PA
Previous name: New York-Northern New Jersey-Long Island, NY-NJ-PA MSA
Bergen, Essex, Hudson, Hunterdon, Middlesex, Monmouth, Morris, Ocean, Passaic, Somerset, Sussex, and Union Counties, NJ; Bronx, Kings, Nassau, New York, Putnam, Queens, Richmond, Rockland, Suffolk, and Westchester Counties, NY; Pike County, PA

Dutchess County-Putnam County, NY MD
Dutchess and Putnam Counties
Dutchess County was previously part of the Poughkeepsie-Newburgh-Middletown, NY MSA. Putnam County was previously part of the New York-Wayne-White Plains, NY-NJ MD

Nassau-Suffolk, NY MD
Nassau and Suffolk Counties

New York-Jersey City-White Plains, NY-NJ MD
Bergen, Hudson, Middlesex, Monmouth, Ocean, and Passaic Counties, NJ; Bronx, Kings, New York, Orange, Queens, Richmond, Rockland, and Westchester Counties, NY
Previous name: New York-Wayne-White Plains, NY-NJ MD
Bergen, Hudson, and Passaic Counties, NJ; Bronx, Kings, New York, Putnam, Queens, Richmond, Rockland, and Westchester Counties, NY

Newark, NJ-PA MD
Essex, Hunterdon, Morris, Somerset, Sussex, and Union Counties, NJ; Pike County, PA
Previous name: Newark-Union, NJ-PA MD
Essex, Hunterdon, Morris, Sussex, and Union Counties, NJ; Pike County, PA

Oklahoma City, OK MSA
Canadian, Cleveland, Grady, Lincoln, Logan, McClain, and Oklahoma Counties

Omaha-Council Bluffs, NE-IA MSA
Harrison, Mills, and Pottawattamie Counties, IA; Cass, Douglas, Sarpy, Saunders, and Washington Counties, NE

Orlando-Kissimmee-Sanford, FL MSA
Lake, Orange, Osceola, and Seminole Counties

Peoria, IL MSA
Marshall, Peoria, Stark, Tazewell, and Woodford Counties

Philadelphia, PA

Philadelphia-Camden-Wilmington, PA-NJ-DE-MD MSA
New Castle County, DE; Cecil County, MD; Burlington, Camden, Gloucester, and Salem Counties, NJ; Bucks, Chester, Delaware, Montgomery, and Philadelphia Counties, PA

Camden, NJ MD
Burlington, Camden, and Gloucester Counties

Montgomery County-Bucks County-Chester County, PA MD
Bucks, Chester, and Montgomery Counties
Previously part of the Philadelphia, PA MD

Philadelphia, PA MD
Delaware and Philadelphia Counties
Previous name: Philadelphia, PA MD
Bucks, Chester, Delaware, Montgomery, and Philadelphia Counties

Wilmington, DE-MD-NJ MD
New Castle County, DE; Cecil County, MD; Salem County, NJ

Phoenix-Mesa-Scottsdale, AZ MSA
Previously Phoenix-Mesa-Glendale, AZ MSA
Maricopa and Pinal Counties

Pittsburgh, PA MSA
Allegheny, Armstrong, Beaver, Butler, Fayette, Washington, and Westmoreland Counties

Portland-Vancouver-Hillsboro, OR-WA MSA
Clackamas, Columbia, Multnomah, Washington, and Yamhill Counties, OR; Clark and Skamania Counties, WA

A-174 Appendix B: Metropolitan Area Definitions

Providence, RI

Providence-New Bedford-Fall River, RI-MA MSA
Previously Providence-New Bedford-Fall River, RI-MA MSA
Bristol County, MA; Bristol, Kent, Newport, Providence, and
Washington Counties, RI

Providence-Warwick, RI-MA NECTA
Includes 12 cities and towns in Massachusetts and 36 cities and towns
in Rhode Island
Previously Providence-Fall River-Warwick, RI-MA NECTA
Includes 12 cities and towns in Massachusetts and 37 cities and towns
in Rhode Island

Provo-Orem, UT MSA
Juab and Utah Counties

Raleigh, NC MSA
Previously Raleigh-Cary, NC MSA
Franklin, Johnston, and Wake Counties

Reno, NV MSA
Previously Reno-Sparks, NV MSA
Storey and Washoe Counties

Richmond, VA MSA
Amelia, Caroline, Charles City, Chesterfield, Dinwiddie, Goochland,
Hanover, Henrico, King William, New Kent, Powhatan, Prince
George, and Sussex Counties; Colonial Heights, Hopewell,
Petersburg, and Richmond Cities

Riverside-San Bernardino-Ontario, CA MSA
Riverside and San Bernardino Counties

Rochester, MN MSA
Dodge, Fillmore, Olmsted, and Wabasha Counties

Sacramento—Roseville—Arden-Arcade, CA MSA
El Dorado, Placer, Sacramento, and Yolo Counties

Salt Lake City, UT MSA
Salt Lake and Tooele Counties

San Antonio-New Braunfels, TX MSA
Atascosa, Bandera, Bexar, Comal, Guadalupe, Kendall, Medina, and
Wilson Counties

San Diego-Carlsbad, CA MSA
Previously San Diego-Carlsbad-San Marcos, CA MSA
San Diego County

San Francisco, CA

San Francisco-Oakland-Hayward, CA MSA
Previously San Francisco-Oakland- Fremont, CA MSA
Alameda, Contra Costa, Marin, San Francisco, and San Mateo Counties

San Francisco-Redwood City-South San Francisco, CA MD
San Francisco and San Mateo Counties

Previously San Francisco-San Mateo-Redwood City, CA MD
Marin, San Francisco, and San Mateo Counties

San Jose-Sunnyvale-Santa Clara, CA MSA
San Benito and Santa Clara Counties

Santa Rosa, CA MSA
Previously Santa Rosa-Petaluma, CA MSA
Sonoma County

Savannah, GA MSA
Bryan, Chatham, and Effingham Counties

Seattle, WA

Seattle-Tacoma-Bellevue, WA MSA
King, Pierce, and Snohomish Counties

Seattle-Bellevue-Everett, WA MD
King and Snohomish Counties

Sioux Falls, SD MSA
Lincoln, McCook, Minnehaha, and Turner Counties

Springfield, IL MSA
Menard and Sangamon Counties

Tallahassee, FL MSA
Gadsden, Jefferson, Leon, and Wakulla Counties

Tampa-St. Petersburg-Clearwater, FL MSA
Hernando, Hillsborough, Pasco, and Pinellas Counties

Tucson, AZ MSA
Pima County

Tulsa, OK MSA
Creek, Okmulgee, Osage, Pawnee, Rogers, Tulsa, and Wagoner
Counties

Tuscaloosa, AL MSA
Hale, Pickens, and Tuscaloosa Counties

Virginia Beach-Norfolk-Newport News, VA-NC MSA
Currituck County, NC; Chesapeake, Hampton, Newport News,
Norfolk, Poquoson, Portsmouth, Suffolk, Virginia Beach and
Williamsburg cities, VA; Gloucester, Isle of Wight, James City,
Mathews, Surry, and York Counties, VA

Washington, DC

Washington-Arlington-Alexandria, DC-VA-MD-WV MSA
District of Columbia; Calvert, Charles, Frederick, Montgomery, and
Prince George's Counties, MD; Alexandria, Fairfax, Falls Church,
Fredericksburg, Manassas Park, and Manassas cities, VA; Arlington,
Clarke, Culpepper, Fairfax, Fauquier, Loudoun, Prince William,
Rappahannock, Spotsylvania, Stafford, and Warren Counties, VA;
Jefferson County, WV
Previously Washington-Arlington-Alexandria, DC-VA-MD-WV MSA
District of Columbia; Calvert, Charles, Frederick, Montgomery, and
Prince George's Counties, MD; Alexandria, Fairfax, Falls Church,
Fredericksburg, Manassas Park, and Manassas cities, VA; Arlington,
Clarke, Fairfax, Fauquier, Loudoun, Prince William, Spotsylvania,
Stafford, and Warren Counties, VA; Jefferson County, WV

Washington-Arlington-Alexandria, DC-VA-MD-WV MD
District of Columbia; Calvert, Charles, and Prince George's Counties,
MD; Alexandria, Fairfax, Falls Church, Fredericksburg, Manassas
Park, and Manassas cities, VA; Arlington, Clarke, Culpepper, Fairfax,
Fauquier, Loudoun, Prince William, Rappahannock, Spotsylvania,
Stafford, and Warren Counties, VA; Jefferson County, WV
Previously Washington-Arlington-Alexandria, DC-VA-MD-WV MD
District of Columbia; Calvert, Charles, and Prince George's Counties,
MD; Alexandria, Fairfax, Falls Church, Fredericksburg, Manassas
Park, and Manassas cities, VA; Arlington, Clarke, Fairfax, Fauquier,
Loudoun, Prince William, Spotsylvania, Stafford, and Warren
Counties, VA; Jefferson County, WV

Wichita, KS MSA
Butler, Harvey, Kingman, Sedgwick, and Sumner Counties

Winston-Salem, NC MSA
Davidson, Davie, Forsyth, Stokes, and Yadkin Counties

Appendix C: Government Type and Primary County

This appendix includes the government structure of each place included in this book. It also includes the county or county equivalent in which each place is located. If a place spans more than one county, the county in which the majority of the population resides is shown.

Albuquerque, NM
Government Type: City
County: Bernalillo

Allentown, PA
Government Type: City
County: Lehigh

Anchorage, AK
Government Type: Municipality
Borough: Anchorage

Ann Arbor, MI
Government Type: City
County: Washtenaw

Athens, GA
Government Type: Consolidated
  city-county
County: Clarke

Atlanta, GA
Government Type: City
County: Fulton

Austin, TX
Government Type: City
County: Travis

Baton Rouge, LA
Government Type: Consolidated city-parish
Parish: East Baton Rouge

Boise City, ID
Government Type: City
County: Ada

Boston, MA
Government Type: City
County: Suffolk

Boulder, CO
Government Type: City
County: Boulder

Cape Coral, FL
Government Type: City
County: Lee

Cedar Rapids, IA
Government Type: City
County: Linn

Charleston, SC
Government Type: City
County: Charleston

Charlotte, NC
Government Type: City
County: Mecklenburg

Chicago, IL
Government Type: City
County: Cook

Cincinnati, OH
Government Type: City
County: Hamilton

Clarksville, TN
Government Type: City
County: Montgomery

Cleveland, OH
Government Type: City
County: Cuyahoga

College Station, TX
Government Type: City
County: Brazos

Colorado Springs, CO
Government Type: City
County: El Paso

Columbia, MO
Government Type: City
County: Boone

Columbia, SC
Government Type: City
County: Richland

Columbus, OH
Government Type: City
County: Franklin

Dallas, TX
Government Type: City
County: Dallas

Davenport, IA
Government Type: City
County: Scott

Denver, CO
Government Type: City
County: Denver

Des Moines, IA
Government Type: City
County: Polk

Durham, NC
Government Type: City
County: Durham

Edison, NJ
Government Type: Township
County: Middlesex

El Paso, TX
Government Type: City
County: El Paso

Fargo, ND
Government Type: City
County: Cass

Fayetteville, NC
Government Type: City
County: Cumberland

Fort Collins, CO
Government Type: City
County: Larimer

Fort Wayne, IN
Government Type: City
County: Allen

Fort Worth, TX
Government Type: City
County: Tarrant

Grand Rapids, MI
Government Type: City
County: Kent

Greeley, CO
Government Type: City
County: Weld

Green Bay, WI
Government Type: City
County: Brown

Greensboro, NC
Government Type: City
County: Guilford

Honolulu, HI
Government Type: Census Designated Place
  (CDP)
County: Honolulu

Houston, TX
Government Type: City
County: Harris

Huntsville, AL
Government Type: City
County: Madison

Indianapolis, IN
Government Type: City
County: Marion

Jacksonville, FL
Government Type: City
County: Duval

Kansas City, MO
Government Type: City
County: Jackson

Lafayette, LA
Government Type: City
Parish: Lafayette

Lakeland, FL
Government Type: City
County: Polk

A-176 Appendix C: Government Type and Primary County

Las Vegas, NV
Government Type: City
County: Clark

Lexington, KY
Government Type: Consolidated city-county
County: Fayette

Lincoln, NE
Government Type: City
County: Lancaster

Little Rock, AR
Government Type: City
County: Pulaski

Los Angeles, CA
Government Type: City
County: Los Angeles

Louisville, KY
Government Type: Consolidated city-county
County: Jefferson

Madison, WI
Government Type: City
County: Dane

Manchester, NH
Government Type: City
County: Hillsborough

Memphis, TN
Government Type: City
County: Shelby

Miami, FL
Government Type: City
County: Miami-Dade

Midland, TX
Government Type: City
County: Midland

Milwaukee, WI
Government Type: City
County: Milwaukee

Minneapolis, MN
Government Type: City
County: Hennepin

Nashville, TN
Government Type: Consolidated city-county
County: Davidson

New Haven, CT
Government Type: City
County: New Haven

New Orleans, LA
Government Type: City
Parish: Orleans

New York, NY
Government Type: City
Counties: Bronx; Kings; New York; Queens;
Staten Island

Oklahoma City, OK
Government Type: City
County: Oklahoma

Omaha, NE
Government Type: City
County: Douglas

Orlando, FL
Government Type: City
County: Orange

Peoria, IL
Government Type: City
County: Peoria

Philadelphia, PA
Government Type: City
County: Philadelphia

Phoenix, AZ
Government Type: City
County: Maricopa

Pittsburgh, PA
Government Type: City
County: Allegheny

Portland, OR
Government Type: City
County: Multnomah

Providence, RI
Government Type: City
County: Providence

Provo, UT
Government Type: City
County: Utah

Raleigh, NC
Government Type: City
County: Wake

Reno, NV
Government Type: City
County: Washoe

Richmond, VA
Government Type: Independent city
County: Richmond city

Riverside, CA
Government Type: City
County: Riverside

Rochester, MN
Government Type: City
County: Olmsted

Sacramento, CA
Government Type: City
County: Sacramento

Salt Lake City, UT
Government Type: City
County: Salt Lake

San Antonio, TX
Government Type: City
County: Bexar

San Diego, CA
Government Type: City
County: San Diego

San Francisco, CA
Government Type: City
County: San Francisco

San Jose, CA
Government Type: City
County: Santa Clara

Santa Rosa, CA
Government Type: City
County: Sonoma

Savannah, GA
Government Type: City
County: Chatham

Seattle, WA
Government Type: City
County: King

Sioux Falls, SD
Government Type: City
County: Minnehaha

Springfield, IL
Government Type: City
County: Sangamon

Tallahassee, FL
Government Type: City
County: Leon

Tampa, FL
Government Type: City
County: Hillsborough

Tucson, AZ
Government Type: City
County: Pima

Tulsa, OK
Government Type: City
County: Tulsa

Tuscaloosa, AL
Government Type: City
County: Tuscaloosa

Virginia Beach, VA
Government Type: Independent city
County: Virginia Beach city

Washington, DC
Government Type: City
County: District of Columbia

Wichita, KS
Government Type: City
County: Sedgwick

Winston-Salem, NC
Government Type: City
County: Forsyth

Appendix D: Chambers of Commerce

Albuquerque, NM
Albuquerque Chamber of Commerce
P.O. Box 25100
Albuquerque, NM 87125
Phone: (505) 764-3700
Fax: (505) 764-3714
http://www.abqchamber.com

Albuquerque Economic Development Dept
851 University Blvd SE, Suite 203
Albuquerque, NM 87106
Phone: (505) 246-6200
Fax: (505) 246-6219
http://www.cabq.gov/econdev

Allentown, PA
Greater Lehigh Valley Chamber of
Commerce
Allentown Office
840 Hamilton Street, Suite 205
Allentown, PA 18101
Phone: (610) 751-4929
Fax: (610) 437-4907
http://www.lehighvalleychamber.org

Anchorage, AK
Anchorage Chamber of Commerce
1016 W Sixth Avenue
Suite 303
Anchorage, AK 99501
Phone: (907) 272-2401
Fax: (907) 272-4117
http://www.anchoragechamber.org

Anchorage Economic Development
Department
900 W 5th Avenue
Suite 300
Anchorage, AK 99501
Phone: (907) 258-3700
Fax: (907) 258-6646
http://aedcweb.com

Ann Arbor, MI
Ann Arbor Area Chamber of Commerce
115 West Huron
3rd Floor
Ann Arbor, MI 48104
Phone: (734) 665-4433
Fax: (734) 665-4191
http://www.annarborchamber.org

Ann Arbor Economic Development
Department
201 S Division
Suite 430
Ann Arbor, MI 48104
Phone: (734) 761-9317
http://www.annarborspark.org

Athens, GA
Athens Area Chamber of Commerce
246 W Hancock Avenue
Athens, GA 30601
Phone: (706) 549-6800
Fax: (706) 549-5636
http://www.aacoc.org

Athens-Clarke County Economic
Development Department
246 W. Hancock Avenue
Athens, GA 30601
Phone: (706) 613-3233
Fax: (706) 613-3812
http://www.athensbusiness.org

Atlanta, GA
Metro Atlanta Chamber of Commerce
235 Andrew Young International Blvd NW
Atlanta, GA 30303
Phone: (404) 880-9000
Fax: (404) 586-8464
http://www.metroatlantachamber.com

Austin, TX
Greater Austin Chamber of Commerce
210 Barton Springs Road
Suite 400
Austin, TX 78704
Phone: (512) 478-9383
Fax: (512) 478-6389
http://www.austin-chamber.org

Baton Rouge, LA
Baton Rouge Area Chamber
451 Florida Street
Suite 1050
Baton Rouge, LA 70801
Phone (225) 381-7125
http://www.brac.org

Boise City, ID
Boise Metro Chamber of Commerce
250 S 5th Street
Suite 800
Boise City, ID 83701
Phone: (208) 472-5200
Fax: (208) 472-5201
http://www.boisechamber.org

Boston, MA
Greater Boston Chamber of Commerce
265 Franklin Street
12th Floor
Boston, MA 02110
Phone: (617) 227-4500
Fax: (617) 227-7505
http://www.bostonchamber.com

Boulder, CO
Boulder Chamber of Commerce
2440 Pearl Street
Boulder, CO 80302
Phone: (303) 442-1044
Fax: (303) 938-8837
http://www.boulderchamber.com

City of Boulder Economic Vitality Program
P.O. Box 791
Boulder, CO 80306
Phone: (303) 441-3090
http://www.bouldercolorado.gov

Cape Coral, FL
Chamber of Commerce of Cape Coral
2051 Cape Coral Parkway East
Cape Coral, FL 33904
Phone: (239) 549-6900
Fax: (239) 549-9609
http://www.capecoralchamber.com

Cedar Rapids, IA
Cedar Rapids Chamber of Commerce
424 First Avenue NE
Cedar Rapids, IA 52401
Phone: (319) 398-5317
Fax: (319) 398-5228
http://www.cedarrapids.org

Cedar Rapids Economic Development
50 Second Avenue Bridge
Sixth Floor
Cedar Rapids, IA 52401-1256
Phone: (319) 286-5041
Fax: (319) 286-5141
http://www.cedar-rapids.org

Charleston, SC
Charleston Metro Chamber of Commerce
P.O. Box 975
Charleston, SC 29402
Phone: (843) 577-2510
http://www.charlestonchamber.net

Charlotte, NC
Charlotte Chamber of Commerce
330 S Tryon Street
P.O. Box 32785
Charlotte, NC 28232
Phone: (704) 378-1300
Fax: (704) 374-1903
http://www.charlottechamber.com

Charlotte Regional Partnership
1001 Morehead Square Drive
Suite 200
Charlotte, NC 28203
Phone: (704) 347-8942
Fax: (704) 347-8981
http://www.charlotteusa.com

Chicago, IL
Chicagoland Chamber of Commerce
200 E Randolph Street
Suite 2200
Chicago, IL 60601-6436
Phone: (312) 494-6700
Fax: (312) 861-0660
http://www.chicagolandchamber.org

City of Chicago Department of Planning
and Development
City Hall, Room 1000
121 North La Salle Street
Chicago, IL 60602
Phone: (312) 744-4190
Fax: (312) 744-2271
https://www.cityofchicago.org/city/en/
depts/dcd.html

A-178   Appendix D: Chambers of Commerce

Cincinnati, OH
Cincinnati USA Regional Chamber
3 East 4th Street
Suite 200
Cincinnati, Ohio 45202
Phone: (513) 579-3111
https://www.cincinnatichamber.com

Clarksville, TN
Clarksville Area Chamber of Commerce
25 Jefferson Street
Suite 300
Clarksville, TN 37040
Phone: (931) 647-2331
http://www.clarksvillechamber.com

Cleveland, OH
Greater Cleveland Partnership
1240 Huron Rd. E
Suite 300
Cleveland, OH 44115
Phone: (216) 621-3300
https://www.gcpartnership.com

College Station, TX
Bryan-College Station Chamber of
Commerce
4001 East 29th St, Suite 175
Bryan, TX 77802
Phone: (979) 260-5200
http://www.bcschamber.org

Colorado Springs, CO
Colorado Springs Chamber and EDC
102 South Tejon Street
Suite 430
Colorado Springs, CO 80903
Phone: (719) 471-8183
https://coloradospringschamberedc.com

Columbia, MO
Columbia Chamber of Commerce
300 South Providence Rd.
P.O. Box 1016
Columbia, MO 65205-1016
Phone: (573) 874-1132
Fax: (573) 443-3986
http://www.columbiamochamber.com

Columbia, SC
The Columbia Chamber
930 Richland Street
Columbia, SC 29201
Phone: (803) 733-1110
Fax: (803) 733-1113
http://www.columbiachamber.com

Columbus, OH
Greater Columbus Chamber
37 North High Street
Columbus, OH 43215
Phone: (614) 221-1321
Fax: (614) 221-1408
http://www.columbus.org

Dallas, TX
City of Dallas Economic Development
Department
1500 Marilla Street
5C South
Dallas, TX 75201
Phone: (214) 670-1685
Fax: (214) 670-0158
http://www.dallas-edd.org

Greater Dallas Chamber of Commerce
700 North Pearl Street
Suite1200
Dallas, TX 75201
Phone: (214) 746-6600
Fax: (214) 746-6799
http://www.dallaschamber.org

Davenport, IA
Quad Cities Chamber
331 W. 3rd Street
Suite 100
Davenport, IA 52801
Phone: (563) 322-1706
https://quadcitieschamber.com

Denver, CO
Denver Metro Chamber of Commerce
1445 Market Street
Denver, CO 80202
Phone: (303) 534-8500
Fax: (303) 534-3200
http://www.denverchamber.org

Downtown Denver Partnership
511 16th Street
Suite 200
Denver, CO 80202
Phone: (303) 534-6161
Fax: (303) 534-2803
http://www.downtowndenver.com

Des Moines, IA
Des Moines Downtown Chamber
301 Grand Ave
Des Moines, IA 50309
Phone: (515) 309-3229
http://desmoinesdowntownchamber.com

Greater Des Moines Partnership
700 Locust Street
Suite 100
Des Moines, IA 50309
Phone: (515) 286-4950
Fax: (515) 286-4974
http://www.desmoinesmetro.com

Durham, NC
Durham Chamber of Commerce
P.O. Box 3829
Durham, NC 27702
Phone: (919) 682-2133
Fax: (919) 688-8351
http://www.durhamchamber.org

North Carolina Institute of Minority
Economic Development
114 W Parish Street
Durham, NC 27701
Phone: (919) 956-8889
Fax: (919) 688-7668
http://www.ncimed.com

Edison, NJ
Edison Chamber of Commerce
939 Amboy Avenue
Edison, NJ 08837
Phone: (732) 738-9482
http://www.edisonchamber.com

El Paso, TX
City of El Paso Department of Economic
Development
2 Civic Center Plaza
El Paso, TX 79901
Phone: (915) 541-4000
Fax: (915) 541-1316
http://www.elpasotexas.gov

Greater El Paso Chamber of Commerce
10 Civic Center Plaza
El Paso, TX 79901
Phone: (915) 534-0500
Fax: (915) 534-0510
http://www.elpaso.org

Southwest Indiana Chamber
318 Main Street
Suite 401
Evansville, IN 47708
Phone: (812) 425-8147
Fax: (812) 421-5883
https://swinchamber.com

Fargo, ND
Chamber of Commerce of Fargo Moorhead
202 First Avenue North
Fargo, ND 56560
Phone: (218) 233-1100
Fax: (218) 233-1200
http://www.fmchamber.com

Greater Fargo-Moorhead Economic
Development Corporation
51 Broadway, Suite 500
Fargo, ND 58102
Phone: (701) 364-1900
Fax: (701) 293-7819
http://www.gfmedc.com

Fayetteville, NC
Fayetteville Regional Chamber
1019 Hay Street
Fayetteville, NC 28305
Phone: (910) 483-8133
Fax: (910) 483-0263
http://www.fayettevillencchamber.org

Fort Collins, CO
Fort Collins Chamber of Commerce
225 South Meldrum
Fort Collins, CO 80521
Phone: (970) 482-3746
Fax: (970) 482-3774
https://fortcollinschamber.com

Fort Wayne, IN
City of Fort Wayne Economic Development
1 Main St
1 Main Street
Fort Wayne, IN 46802
Phone: (260) 427-1111
Fax: (260) 427-1375
http://www.cityoffortwayne.org

Appendix D: Chambers of Commerce   A-179

Greater Fort Wayne Chamber of Commerce
826 Ewing Street
Fort Wayne, IN 46802
Phone: (260) 424-1435
Fax: (260) 426-7232
http://www.fwchamber.org

Fort Worth, TX
City of Fort Worth Economic Development
City Hall
900 Monroe Street
Suite 301
Fort Worth, TX 76102
Phone: (817) 392-6103
Fax: (817) 392-2431
http://www.fortworthgov.org

Fort Worth Chamber of Commerce
777 Taylor Street
Suite 900
Fort Worth, TX 76102-4997
Phone: (817) 336-2491
Fax: (817) 877-4034
http://www.fortworthchamber.com

Grand Rapids, MI
Grands Rapids Area Chamber of Commerce
111 Pearl Street N.W.
Grand Rapids, MI 49503
Phone: (616) 771-0300
Fax: (616) 771-0318
http://www.grandrapids.org

Greeley, CO
Greeley Chamber of Commerce
902 7th Avenue
Greeley, CO 80631
Phone: (970) 352-3566
https://greeleychamber.com

Green Bay, WI
Economic Development
100 N Jefferson St
Room 202
Green Bay, WI 54301
Phone: (920) 448-3397
Fax: (920) 448-3063
http://www.ci.green-bay.wi.us

Green Bay Area Chamber of Commerce
300 N. Broadway
Suite 3A
Green Bay, WI 54305-1660
Phone: (920) 437-8704
Fax: (920) 593-3468
http://www.titletown.org

Greensboro, NC
Greensboro Area Chamber of Commerce
342 N. Elm Street
Greensboro, NC 27401
Phone: (336) 387-8301
Fax: (336) 275-9299
http://www.greensboro.org

Honolulu, HI
The Chamber of Commerce of Hawaii
1132 Bishop Street
Suite 402
Honolulu, HI 96813
Phone: (808) 545-4300
Fax: (808) 545-4369
http://www.cochawaii.com

Houston, TX
Greater Houston Partnership
1200 Smith Street
Suite 700
Houston, TX 77002-4400
Phone: (713) 844-3600
Fax: (713) 844-0200
http://www.houston.org

Huntsville, AL
Chamber of Commerce of
Huntsville/Madison County
225 Church Street
Huntsville, AL 35801
Phone: (256) 535-2000
Fax: (256) 535-2015
http://www.huntsvillealabamausa.com

Indianapolis, IN
Greater Indianapolis Chamber of Commerce
111 Monument Circle
Suite 1950
Indianapolis, IN 46204
Phone: (317) 464-2222
Fax: (317) 464-2217
http://www.indychamber.com

The Indy Partnership
111 Monument Circle
Suite 1800
Indianapolis, IN 46204
Phone: (317) 236-6262
Fax: (317) 236-6275
http://indypartnership.com

Jacksonville, FL
Jacksonville Chamber of Commerce
3 Independent Drive
Jacksonville, FL 32202
Phone: (904) 366-6600
Fax: (904) 632-0617
http://www.myjaxchamber.com

Kansas City, MO
Greater Kansas City Chamber of Commerce
2600 Commerce Tower
911 Main Street
Kansas City, MO 64105
Phone: (816) 221-2424
Fax: (816) 221-7440
http://www.kcchamber.com

Kansas City Area Development Council
2600 Commerce Tower
911 Main Street
Kansas City, MO 64105
Phone: (816) 221-2121
Fax: (816) 842-2865
http://www.thinkkc.com

Lafayette, LA
Greater Lafayette Chamber of Commerce
804 East Saint Mary Blvd.
Lafayette, LA 70503
Phone: (337) 233-2705
Fax: (337) 234-8671
http://www.lafchamber.org

Lakeland, FL
Lakeland Chamber of Commerce
35 Lake Morton Dr.
Lakeland, FL 33801
Phone: (863) 688-8551
https://www.lakelandchamber.com

Las Vegas, NV
Las Vegas Chamber of Commerce
6671 Las Vegas Blvd South
Suite 300
Las Vegas, NV 89119
Phone: (702) 735-1616
Fax: (702) 735-0406
http://www.lvchamber.org

Las Vegas Office of Business Development
400 Stewart Avenue
City Hall
Las Vegas, NV 89101
Phone: (702) 229-6011
Fax: (702) 385-3128
http://www.lasvegasnevada.gov

Lexington, KY
Greater Lexington Chamber of Commerce
330 East Main Street
Suite 100
Lexington, KY 40507
Phone: (859) 254-4447
Fax: (859) 233-3304
http://www.commercelexington.com

Lexington Downtown Development
Authority
101 East Vine Street
Suite 500
Lexington, KY 40507
Phone: (859) 425-2296
Fax: (859) 425-2292
http://www.lexingtondda.com

Lincoln, NE
Lincoln Chamber of Commerce
1135 M Street
Suite 200
Lincoln, NE 68508
Phone: (402) 436-2350
Fax: (402) 436-2360
http://www.lcoc.com

Little Rock, AR
Little Rock Regional Chamber
One Chamber Plaza
Little Rock, AR 72201
Phone: (501) 374-2001
Fax: (501) 374-6018
http://www.littlerockchamber.com

A-180   Appendix D: Chambers of Commerce

Los Angeles, CA
Los Angeles Area Chamber of Commerce
350 South Bixel Street
Los Angeles, CA 90017
Phone: (213) 580-7500
Fax: (213) 580-7511
http://www.lachamber.org

Los Angeles County Economic
Development Corporation
444 South Flower Street
34th Floor
Los Angeles, CA 90071
Phone: (213) 622-4300
Fax: (213) 622-7100
http://www.laedc.org

Louisville, KY
The Greater Louisville Chamber of
Commerce
614 West Main Street
Suite 6000
Louisville, KY 40202
Phone: (502) 625-0000
Fax: (502) 625-0010
http://www.greaterlouisville.com

Madison, WI
Greater Madison Chamber of Commerce
615 East Washington Avenue
P.O. Box 71
Madison, WI 53701-0071
Phone: (608) 256-8348
Fax: (608) 256-0333
http://www.greatermadisonchamber.com

Manchester, NH
Greater Manchester Chamber of Commerce
889 Elm Street
Manchester, NH 03101
Phone: (603) 666-6600
Fax: (603) 626-0910
http://www.manchester-chamber.org

Manchester Economic Development Office
One City Hall Plaza
Manchester, NH 03101
Phone: (603) 624-6505
Fax: (603) 624-6308
http://www.yourmanchesternh.com

Memphis, TN
Greater Memphis Chamber
22 North Front Street, Suite 200
Memphis, TN 38103-2100
Phone: (901) 543-3500
https://memphischamber.com

Miami, FL
Greater Miami Chamber of Commerce
1601 Biscayne Boulevard
Ballroom Level
Miami, FL 33132-1260
Phone: (305) 350-7700
Fax: (305) 374-6902
http://www.miamichamber.com

The Beacon Council
80 Southwest 8th Street
Suite 2400
Miami, FL 33130
Phone: (305) 579-1300
Fax: (305) 375-0271
http://www.beaconcouncil.com

Midland, TX
Midland Chamber of Commerce
109 N. Main
Midland, TX 79701
Phone: (432) 683-3381
Fax: (432) 686-3556
http://www.midlandtxchamber.com

Milwaukee, WI
Greater Milwaukee Chamber of Commerce
6815 W. Capitol Drive
Suite 300
Milwaukee, WI 53216
Phone: (414) 465-2422
http://www.gmcofc.org

Metropolitan Milwaukee Association of
Commerce
756 N. Milwaukee Street
Suite 400
Milwaukee, WI 53202
Phone: (414) 287-4100
Fax: (414) 271-7753
https://www.mmac.org

Minneapolis, MN
Minneapolis Community Development
Agency
Crown Roller Mill
105 5th Avenue South
Suite 200
Minneapolis, MN 55401
Phone: (612) 673-5095
Fax: (612) 673-5100
http://www.ci.minneapolis.mn.us

Minneapolis Regional Chamber
81 South Ninth Street
Suite 200
Minneapolis, MN 55402
Phone: (612) 370-9100
Fax: (612) 370-9195
http://www.minneapolischamber.org

Nashville, TN
Nashville Area Chamber of Commerce
211 Commerce Street
Suite 100
Nashville, TN 37201
Phone: (615) 743-3000
Fax: (615) 256-3074
http://www.nashvillechamber.com

Tennessee Valley Authority Economic
Development
400 West Summit Hill Drive
Knoxville TN 37902
Phone: (865) 632-2101
http://www.tvaed.com

New Haven, CT
Greater New Haven Chamber of Commerce
900 Chapel Street
10th Floor
New Haven, CT 06510
Phone: (203) 787-6735
https://www.gnhcc.com

New Orleans, LA
New Orleans Chamber of Commerce
1515 Poydras Street
Suite 1010
New Orleans, LA 70112
Phone: (504) 799-4260
Fax: (504) 799-4259
http://www.neworleanschamber.org

New York, NY
New York City Economic Development
Corporation
110 William Street
New York, NY 10038
Phone: (212) 619-5000
http://www.nycedc.com

The Partnership for New York City
One Battery Park Plaza
5th Floor
New York, NY 10004
Phone: (212) 493-7400
Fax: (212) 344-3344
http://www.pfnyc.org

Oklahoma City, OK
Greater Oklahoma City Chamber of
Commerce
123 Park Avenue
Oklahoma City, OK 73102
Phone: (405) 297-8900
Fax: (405) 297-8916
http://www.okcchamber.com

Omaha, NE
Omaha Chamber of Commerce
1301 Harney Street
Omaha, NE 68102
Phone: (402) 346-5000
Fax: (402) 346-7050
http://www.omahachamber.org

Orlando, FL
Metro Orlando Economic Development
Commission of Mid-Florida
301 East Pine Street
Suite 900
Orlando, FL 32801
Phone: (407) 422-7159
Fax: (407) 425.6428
http://www.orlandoedc.com

Orlando Regional Chamber of Commerce
75 South Ivanhoe Boulevard
P.O. Box 1234
Orlando, FL 32802
Phone: (407) 425-1234
Fax: (407) 839-5020
http://www.orlando.org

Appendix D: Chambers of Commerce   A-181

Peoria, IL
Peoria Area Chamber
100 SW Water Street
Peoria, IL 61602
Phone: (309) 495-5900
http://www.peoriachamber.org

Philadelphia, PA
Greater Philadelphia Chamber of
Commerce
200 South Broad Street
Suite 700
Philadelphia, PA 19102
Phone: (215) 545-1234
Fax: (215) 790-3600
http://www.greaterphilachamber.com

Phoenix, AZ
Greater Phoenix Chamber of Commerce
201 North Central Avenue
27th Floor
Phoenix, AZ 85073
Phone: (602) 495-2195
Fax: (602) 495-8913
http://www.phoenixchamber.com

Greater Phoenix Economic Council
2 North Central Avenue
Suite 2500
Phoenix, AZ 85004
Phone: (602) 256-7700
Fax: (602) 256-7744
http://www.gpec.org

Pittsburgh, PA
Allegheny County Industrial Development
Authority
425 6th Avenue
Suite 800
Pittsburgh, PA 15219
Phone: (412) 350-1067
Fax: (412) 642-2217
http://www.alleghenycounty.us

Greater Pittsburgh Chamber of Commerce
425 6th Avenue
12th Floor
Pittsburgh, PA 15219
Phone: (412) 392-4500
Fax: (412) 392-4520
http://www.alleghenyconference.org

Portland, OR
Portland Business Alliance
200 SW Market Street
Suite 1770
Portland, OR 97201
Phone: (503) 224-8684
Fax: (503) 323-9186
http://www.portlandalliance.com

Providence, RI
Greater Providence Chamber of Commerce
30 Exchange Terrace
Fourth Floor
Providence, RI 02903
Phone: (401) 521-5000
Fax: (401) 351-2090
http://www.provchamber.com

Rhode Island Economic Development
Corporation
Providence City Hall
25 Dorrance Street
Providence, RI 02903
Phone: (401) 421-7740
Fax: (401) 751-0203
http://www.providenceri.com

Provo, UT
Provo-Orem Chamber of Commerce
51 South University Avenue
Suite 215
Provo, UT 84601
Phone: (801) 851-2555
Fax: (801) 851-2557
http://www.thechamber.org

Raleigh, NC
Greater Raleigh Chamber of Commerce
800 South Salisbury Street
Raleigh, NC 27601-2978
Phone: (919) 664-7000
Fax: (919) 664-7099
http://www.raleighchamber.org

Reno, NV
Greater Reno-Sparks Chamber of
Commerce
1 East First Street
16th Floor
Reno, NV 89505
Phone: (775) 337-3030
Fax: (775) 337-3038
http://www.reno-sparkschamber.org

The Chamber Reno-Sparks-Northern
Nevada
449 S. Virginia St.
2nd Floor
Reno, NV 89501
Phone: (775) 636-9550
http://www.thechambernv.org

Richmond, VA
Greater Richmond Chamber
600 East Main Street
Suite 700
Richmond, VA 23219
Phone: (804) 648-1234
http://www.grcc.com

Greater Richmond Partnership
901 East Byrd Street
Suite 801
Richmond, VA 23219-4070
Phone: (804) 643-3227
Fax: (804) 343-7167
http://www.grpva.com

Riverside, CA
Greater Riverside Chambers of Commerce
3985 University Avenue
Riverside, CA 92501
Phone: (951) 683-7100
https://www.riverside-chamber.com

Rochester, MN
Rochester Area Chamber of Commerce
220 South Broadway
Suite 100
Rochester, MN 55904
Phone: (507) 288-1122
Fax: (507) 282-8960
http://www.rochestermnchamber.com

Sacramento, CA
Sacramento Metro Chamber
One Capitol Mall
Suite 700
Sacramento, CA 95814
Phone: (916) 552-6800
https://metrochamber.org

Salt Lake City, UT
Department of Economic Development
451 South State Street
Room 425
Salt Lake City, UT 84111
Phone: (801) 535-7240
Fax: (801) 535-6331
http://www.slcgov.com/economic-developm
ent

Salt Lake Chamber
175 E. University Blvd. (400 S)
Suite 600
Salt Lake City, UT 84111
Phone: (801) 364-3631
http://www.slchamber.com

San Antonio, TX
The Greater San Antonio Chamber of
Commerce
602 E. Commerce Street
San Antonio, TX 78205
Phone: (210) 229-2100
Fax: (210) 229-1600
http://www.sachamber.org

San Antonio Economic Development
Department
P.O. Box 839966
San Antonio, TX 78283-3966
Phone: (210) 207-8080
Fax: (210) 207-8151
http://www.sanantonio.gov/edd

San Diego, CA
San Diego Economic Development Corp.
401 B Street
Suite 1100
San Diego, CA 92101
Phone: (619) 234-8484
Fax: (619) 234-1935
http://www.sandiegobusiness.org

San Diego Regional Chamber of Commerce
402 West Broadway
Suite 1000
San Diego, CA 92101-3585
Phone: (619) 544-1300
Fax: (619) 744-7481
http://www.sdchamber.org

A-182   Appendix D: Chambers of Commerce

San Francisco, CA
San Francisco Chamber of Commerce
235 Montgomery Street
12th Floor
San Francisco, CA 94104
Phone: (415) 392-4520
Fax: (415) 392-0485
http://www.sfchamber.com

San Jose, CA
Office of Economic Development
60 South Market Street
Suite 470
San Jose, CA 95113
Phone: (408) 277-5880
Fax: (408) 277-3615
http://www.sba.gov

The Silicon Valley Organization
101 W Santa Clara Street
San Jose, CA 95113
Phone: (408) 291-5250
https://www.thesvo.com

Santa Rosa, CA
Santa Rosa Chamber of Commerce
1260 North Dutton Avenue
Suite 272
Santa Rosa, CA 95401
Phone: (707) 545-1414
http://www.santarosachamber.com

Savannah, GA
Economic Development Authority
131 Hutchinson Island Road
4th Floor
Savannah, GA 31421
Phone: (912) 447-8450
Fax: (912) 447-8455
http://www.seda.org

Savannah Chamber of Commerce
101 E. Bay Street
Savannah, GA 31402
Phone: (912) 644-6400
Fax: (912) 644-6499
http://www.savannahchamber.com

Seattle, WA
Greater Seattle Chamber of Commerce
1301 Fifth Avenue
Suite 2500
Seattle, WA 98101
Phone: (206) 389-7200
Fax: (206) 389-7288
http://www.seattlechamber.com

Sioux Falls, SD
Sioux Falls Area Chamber of Commerce
200 N. Phillips Avenue
Suite 102
Sioux Falls, SD 57104
Phone: (605) 336-1620
Fax: (605) 336-6499
http://www.siouxfallschamber.com

Springfield, IL
The Greater Springfield Chamber of
Commerce
1011 S. Second Street
Springfield, IL 62704
Phone: (217) 525-1173
Fax: (217) 525-8768
http://www.gscc.org

Tallahassee, FL
Greater Tallahassee Chamber of Commerce
300 E. Park Avenue
P.O. Box 1638
Tallahassee, FL 32301
Phone: (850) 224-8116
Fax: (850) 561-3860
http://www.talchamber.com

Tampa, FL
Greater Tampa Chamber of Commerce
P.O. Box 420
Tampa, FL 33601-0420
Phone: (813) 276-9401
Fax: (813) 229-7855
http://www.tampachamber.com

Tucson, AZ
Tucson Metro Chamber
212 E. Broadway Blvd
Tucson, AZ 85701
Phone: (520) 792-1212
https://tucsonchamber.org

Tulsa, OK
Tulsa Regional Chamber
One West Third Street
Suite 100
Tulsa, OK 74103
Phone: (918) 585-1201
https://www.tulsachamber.com

Tuscaloosa, AL
The Chamber of Commerce of West
Alabama
2201 Jack Warner Parkway
Building C
Tuscaloosa, AL 35401
Phone: (205) 758-7588
https://tuscaloosachamber.com

Virginia Beach, VA
Hampton Roads Chamber of Commerce
500 East Main Street
Suite 700
Virginia Beach, VA 23510
Phone: (757) 664-2531
http://www.hamptonroadschamber.com

Washington, DC
District of Columbia Chamber of
Commerce
1213 K Street NW
Washington, DC 20005
Phone: (202) 347-7201
Fax: (202) 638-6762
http://www.dcchamber.org

District of Columbia Office of Planning and
Economic Development
J.A. Wilson Building
1350 Pennsylvania Ave NW
Suite 317
Washington, DC 20004
Phone: (202) 727-6365
Fax: (202) 727-6703
http://www.dcbiz.dc.gov

Wichita, KS
Wichita Regional Chamber of Commerce
350 W Douglas Avennue
Wichita, KS 67202
Phone: (316) 265-7771
https://www.wichitachamber.org

Winston-Salem, NC
Winston-Salem Chamber of Commerce
411 West Fourth Street
Suite 211
Winston-Salem, NC 27101
Phone: (336) 728-9200
http://www.winstonsalem.com

Appendix E: State Departments of Labor

Alabama
Alabama Department of Labor
P.O. Box 303500
Montgomery, AL 36130-3500
Phone: (334) 242-3072
https://www.labor.alabama.gov

Alaska
Dept of Labor and Workforce Devel.
P.O. Box 11149
Juneau, AK 99822-2249
Phone: (907) 465-2700
http://www.labor.state.ak.us

Arizona
Industrial Commission or Arizona
800 West Washington Street
Phoenix, AZ 85007
Phone: (602) 542-4411
https://www.azica.gov

Arkansas
Department of Labor
10421 West Markham
Little Rock, AR 72205
Phone: (501) 682-4500
http://www.labor.ar.gov

California
Labor and Workforce Development
445 Golden Gate Ave., 10th Floor
San Francisco, CA 94102
Phone: (916) 263-1811
http://www.labor.ca.gov

Colorado
Dept of Labor and Employment
633 17th St., 2nd Floor
Denver, CO 80202-3660
Phone: (888) 390-7936
https://www.colorado.gov/CDLE

Connecticut
Department of Labor
200 Folly Brook Blvd.
Wethersfield, CT 06109-1114
Phone: (860) 263-6000
http://www.ctdol.state.ct.us

Delaware
Department of Labor
4425 N. Market St., 4th Floor
Wilmington, DE 19802
Phone: (302) 451-3423
http://dol.delaware.gov

District of Columbia
Department of Employment Services
614 New York Ave., NE, Suite 300
Washington, DC 20002
Phone: (202) 671-1900
http://does.dc.gov

Florida
Florida Department of Economic
Opportunity
The Caldwell Building
107 East Madison St. Suite 100
Tallahassee, FL 32399-4120
Phone: (800) 342-3450
http://www.floridajobs.org

Georgia
Department of Labor
Sussex Place, Room 600
148 Andrew Young Intl Blvd., NE
Atlanta, GA 30303
Phone: (404) 656-3011
http://dol.georgia.gov

Hawaii
Dept of Labor & Industrial Relations
830 Punchbowl Street
Honolulu, HI 96813
Phone: (808) 586-8842
http://labor.hawaii.gov

Idaho
Department of Labor
317 W. Main St.
Boise, ID 83735-0001
Phone: (208) 332-3579
http://www.labor.idaho.gov

Illinois
Department of Labor
160 N. LaSalle Street, 13th Floor
Suite C-1300
Chicago, IL 60601
Phone: (312) 793-2800
https://www.illinois.gov/idol

Indiana
Indiana Department of Labor
402 West Washington Street, Room W195
Indianapolis, IN 46204
Phone: (317) 232-2655
http://www.in.gov/dol

Iowa
Iowa Workforce Development
1000 East Grand Avenue
Des Moines, IA 50319-0209
Phone: (515) 242-5870
http://www.iowadivisionoflabor.gov

Kansas
Department of Labor
401 S.W. Topeka Blvd.
Topeka, KS 66603-3182
Phone: (785) 296-5000
http://www.dol.ks.gov

Kentucky
Department of Labor
1047 U.S. Hwy 127 South, Suite 4
Frankfort, KY 40601-4381
Phone: (502) 564-3070
http://www.labor.ky.gov

Louisiana
Louisiana Workforce Commission
1001 N. 23rd Street
Baton Rouge, LA 70804-9094
Phone: (225) 342-3111
http://www.laworks.net

Maine
Department of Labor
45 Commerce Street
Augusta, ME 04330
Phone: (207) 623-7900
http://www.state.me.us/labor

Maryland
Department of Labor, Licensing &
Regulation
500 N. Calvert Street
Suite 401
Baltimore, MD 21202
Phone: (410) 767-2357
http://www.dllr.state.md.us

Massachusetts
Dept of Labor & Workforce Development
One Ashburton Place
Room 2112
Boston, MA 02108
Phone: (617) 626-7100
http://www.mass.gov/lwd

Michigan
Department of Licensing and Regulatory
Affairs
611 W. Ottawa
P.O. Box 30004
Lansing, MI 48909
Phone: (517) 373-1820
http://www.michigan.gov/lara

Minnesota
Dept of Labor and Industry
443 Lafayette Road North
Saint Paul, MN 55155
Phone: (651) 284-5070
http://www.doli.state.mn.us

Mississippi
Dept of Employment Security
P.O. Box 1699
Jackson, MS 39215-1699
Phone: (601) 321-6000
http://www.mdes.ms.gov

Missouri
Labor and Industrial Relations
P.O. Box 599
3315 W. Truman Boulevard
Jefferson City, MO 65102-0599
Phone: (573) 751-7500
https://labor.mo.gov

A-184   Appendix E: State Departments of Labor

Montana
Dept of Labor and Industry
P.O. Box 1728
Helena, MT 59624-1728
Phone: (406) 444-9091
http://www.dli.mt.gov

Nebraska
Department of Labor
550 S 16th Street
Lincoln, NE 68508
Phone: (402) 471-9000
https://dol.nebraska.gov

Nevada
Dept of Business and Industry
3300 W. Sahara Ave
Suite 425
Las Vegas, NV 89102
Phone: (702) 486-2750
http://business.nv.gov

New Hampshire
Department of Labor
State Office Park South
95 Pleasant Street
Concord, NH 03301
Phone: (603) 271-3176
https://www.nh.gov/labor

New Jersey
Department of Labor & Workforce
Development
John Fitch Plaza, 13th Floor
Suite D
Trenton, NJ 08625-0110
Phone: (609) 777-3200
http://lwd.dol.state.nj.us/labor

New Mexico
Department of Workforce Solutions
401 Broadway, NE
Albuquerque, NM 87103-1928
Phone: (505) 841-8450
https://www.dws.state.nm.us

New York
Department of Labor
State Office Bldg. # 12
W.A. Harriman Campus
Albany, NY 12240
Phone: (518) 457-9000
https://www.labor.ny.gov

North Carolina
Department of Labor
4 West Edenton Street
Raleigh, NC 27601-1092
Phone: (919) 733-7166
https://www.labor.nc.gov

North Dakota
North Dakota Department of Labor and
Human Rights
State Capitol Building
600 East Boulevard, Dept 406
Bismark, ND 58505-0340
Phone: (701) 328-2660
http://www.nd.gov/labor

Ohio
Department of Commerce
77 South High Street, 22nd Floor
Columbus, OH 43215
Phone: (614) 644-2239
http://www.com.state.oh.us

Oklahoma
Department of Labor
4001 N. Lincoln Blvd.
Oklahoma City, OK 73105-5212
Phone: (405) 528-1500
https://www.ok.gov/odol

Oregon
Bureau of Labor and Industries
800 NE Oregon St., #32
Portland, OR 97232
Phone: (971) 673-0761
http://www.oregon.gov/boli

Pennsylvania
Dept of Labor and Industry
1700 Labor and Industry Bldg
7th and Forster Streets
Harrisburg, PA 17120
Phone: (717) 787-5279
http://www.dli.pa.gov

Rhode Island
Department of Labor and Training
1511 Pontiac Avenue
Cranston, RI 02920
Phone: (401) 462-8000
http://www.dlt.state.ri.us

South Carolina
Dept of Labor, Licensing & Regulations
P.O. Box 11329
Columbia, SC 29211-1329
Phone: (803) 896-4300
http://www.llr.state.sc.us

South Dakota
Department of Labor & Regulation
700 Governors Drive
Pierre, SD 57501-2291
Phone: (605) 773-3682
http://dlr.sd.gov

Tennessee
Dept of Labor & Workforce Development
Andrew Johnson Tower
710 James Robertson Pkwy
Nashville, TN 37243-0655
Phone: (615) 741-6642
http://www.tn.gov/workforce

Texas
Texas Workforce Commission
101 East 15th St.
Austin, TX 78778
Phone: (512) 475-2670
http://www.twc.state.tx.us

Utah
Utah Labor Commission
160 East 300 South, 3rd Floor
Salt Lake City, UT 84114-6600
Phone: (801) 530-6800
https://laborcommission.utah.gov

Vermont
Department of Labor
5 Green Mountain Drive
P.O. Box 488
Montpelier, VT 05601-0488
Phone: (802) 828-4000
http://labor.vermont.gov

Virginia
Dept of Labor and Industry
Powers-Taylor Building
13 S. 13th Street
Richmond, VA 23219
Phone: (804) 371-2327
http://www.doli.virginia.gov

Washington
Dept of Labor and Industries
P.O. Box 44001
Olympia, WA 98504-4001
Phone: (360) 902-4200
http://www.lni.wa.gov

West Virginia
Division of Labor
749 B Building 6
Capitol Complex
Charleston, WV 25305
Phone: (304) 558-7890
https://labor.wv.gov

Wisconsin
Dept of Workforce Development
201 E. Washington Ave., #A400
P.O. Box 7946
Madison, WI 53707-7946
Phone: (608) 266-6861
http://dwd.wisconsin.gov

Wyoming
Department of Workforce Services
1510 East Pershing Blvd.
Cheyenne, WY 82002
Phone: (307) 777-7261
http://www.wyomingworkforce.org

2021 Title List

Visit www.GreyHouse.com for Product Information, Table of Contents, and Sample Pages.

Opinions Throughout History
Opinions Throughout History: The Death Penalty
Opinions Throughout History: Diseases & Epidemics
Opinions Throughout History: Drug Use & Abuse
Opinions Throughout History: The Environment
Opinions Throughout History: Gender: Roles & Rights
Opinions Throughout History: Globalization
Opinions Throughout History: Guns in America
Opinions Throughout History: Immigration
Opinions Throughout History: Law Enforcement in America
Opinions Throughout History: National Security vs. Civil & Privacy Rights
Opinions Throughout History: Presidential Authority
Opinions Throughout History: Robotics & Artificial Intelligence
Opinions Throughout History: Social Media Issues
Opinions Throughout History: Sports & Games
Opinions Throughout History: Voters' Rights

This is Who We Were
This is Who We Were: Colonial America (1492-1775)
This is Who We Were: 1880-1899
This is Who We Were: In the 1900s
This is Who We Were: In the 1910s
This is Who We Were: In the 1920s
This is Who We Were: A Companion to the 1940 Census
This is Who We Were: In the 1940s (1940-1949)
This is Who We Were: In the 1950s
This is Who We Were: In the 1960s
This is Who We Were: In the 1970s
This is Who We Were: In the 1980s
This is Who We Were: In the 1990s
This is Who We Were: In the 2000s
This is Who We Were: In the 2010s

Working Americans
Working Americans—Vol. 1: The Working Class
Working Americans—Vol. 2: The Middle Class
Working Americans—Vol. 3: The Upper Class
Working Americans—Vol. 4: Children
Working Americans—Vol. 5: At War
Working Americans—Vol. 6: Working Women
Working Americans—Vol. 7: Social Movements
Working Americans—Vol. 8: Immigrants
Working Americans—Vol. 9: Revolutionary War to the Civil War
Working Americans—Vol. 10: Sports & Recreation
Working Americans—Vol. 11: Inventors & Entrepreneurs
Working Americans—Vol. 12: Our History through Music
Working Americans—Vol. 13: Education & Educators
Working Americans—Vol. 14: African Americans
Working Americans—Vol. 15: Politics & Politicians
Working Americans—Vol. 16: Farming & Ranching
Working Americans—Vol. 17: Teens in America

Education
Complete Learning Disabilities Resource Guide
Educators Resource Guide
The Comparative Guide to Elem. & Secondary Schools
Charter School Movement
Special Education: A Reference Book for Policy & Curriculum Development

Grey House Health & Wellness Guides
Autoimmune Disorders Handbook & Resource Guide
Cancer Handbook & Resource Guide
Cardiovascular Disease Handbook & Resource Guide
Dementia Handbook & Resource Guide

Consumer Health
Autoimmune Disorders Handbook & Resource Guide
Cancer Handbook & Resource Guide
Cardiovascular Disease Handbook & Resource Guide
Comparative Guide to American Hospitals
Complete Mental Health Resource Guide
Complete Resource Guide for Pediatric Disorders
Complete Resource Guide for People with Chronic Illness
Complete Resource Guide for People with Disabilities
Older Americans Information Resource

General Reference
African Biographical Dictionary
American Environmental Leaders
America's College Museums
Constitutional Amendments
Encyclopedia of African-American Writing
Encyclopedia of Invasions & Conquests
Encyclopedia of Prisoners of War & Internment
Encyclopedia of Rural America
Encyclopedia of the Continental Congresses
Encyclopedia of the United States Cabinet
Encyclopedia of War Journalism
The Environmental Debate
The Evolution Wars: A Guide to the Debates
Financial Literacy Starter Kit
From Suffrage to the Senate
The Gun Debate: Gun Rights & Gun Control in the U.S.
History of Canada
Historical Warrior Peoples & Modern Fighting Groups
Human Rights and the United States
Political Corruption in America
Privacy Rights in the Digital Age
The Religious Right and American Politics
Speakers of the House of Representatives, 1789-2021
US Land & Natural Resources Policy
The Value of a Dollar 1600-1865 Colonial to Civil War
The Value of a Dollar 1860-2019
World Cultural Leaders of the 20th Century

Business Information
Business Information Resources
The Complete Broadcasting Industry Guide: Television, Radio, Cable & Streaming
Directory of Mail Order Catalogs
Environmental Resource Handbook
Food & Beverage Market Place
The Grey House Guide to Homeland Security Resources
The Grey House Performing Arts Industry Guide
Guide to Healthcare Group Purchasing Organizations
Guide to U.S. HMOs and PPOs
Guide to Venture Capital & Private Equity Firms
Hudson's Washington News Media Contacts Guide
New York State Directory
Sports Market Place

Grey House Publishing | Salem Press | H.W. Wilson | 4919 Route, 22 PO Box 56, Amenia NY 12501-0056

2021 Title List

Visit www.GreyHouse.com for Product Information, Table of Contents, and Sample Pages.

Statistics & Demographics
America's Top-Rated Cities
America's Top-Rated Smaller Cities
The Comparative Guide to American Suburbs
Profiles of America
Profiles of California
Profiles of Florida
Profiles of Illinois
Profiles of Indiana
Profiles of Massachusetts
Profiles of Michigan
Profiles of New Jersey
Profiles of New York
Profiles of North Carolina & South Carolina
Profiles of Ohio
Profiles of Pennsylvania
Profiles of Texas
Profiles of Virginia
Profiles of Wisconsin

Weiss Financial Ratings
Financial Literacy Basics
Financial Literacy: How to Become an Investor
Financial Literacy: Planning for the Future
Weiss Ratings Consumer Guides
Weiss Ratings Guide to Banks
Weiss Ratings Guide to Credit Unions
Weiss Ratings Guide to Health Insurers
Weiss Ratings Guide to Life & Annuity Insurers
Weiss Ratings Guide to Property & Casualty Insurers
Weiss Ratings Investment Research Guide to Bond & Money Market Mutual Funds
Weiss Ratings Investment Research Guide to Exchange-Traded Funds
Weiss Ratings Investment Research Guide to Stock Mutual Funds
Weiss Ratings Investment Research Guide to Stocks

Canadian Resources
Associations Canada
Canadian Almanac & Directory
Canadian Environmental Resource Guide
Canadian Parliamentary Guide
Canadian Venture Capital & Private Equity Firms
Canadian Who's Who
Cannabis Canada
Careers & Employment Canada
Financial Post: Directory of Directors
Financial Services Canada
FP Bonds: Corporate
FP Bonds: Government
FP Equities: Preferreds & Derivatives
FP Survey: Industrials
FP Survey: Mines & Energy
FP Survey: Predecessor & Defunct
Health Guide Canada
Libraries Canada
Major Canadian Cities: Compared & Ranked, First Edition

Books in Print Series
American Book Publishing Record® Annual
American Book Publishing Record® Monthly
Books In Print®
Books In Print® Supplement
Books Out Loud™
Bowker's Complete Video Directory™
Children's Books In Print®
El-Hi Textbooks & Serials In Print®
Forthcoming Books®
Law Books & Serials In Print™
Medical & Health Care Books In Print™
Publishers, Distributors & Wholesalers of the US™
Subject Guide to Books In Print®
Subject Guide to Children's Books In Print®

Grey House Publishing | Salem Press | H.W. Wilson | 4919 Route, 22 PO Box 56, Amenia NY 12501-0056

2021 Title List

Visit www.SalemPress.com for Product Information, Table of Contents, and Sample Pages.

LITERATURE

Critical Insights: Authors
Louisa May Alcott
Sherman Alexie
Isabel Allende
Maya Angelou
Isaac Asimov
Margaret Atwood
Jane Austen
James Baldwin
Saul Bellow
Roberto Bolano
Ray Bradbury
Gwendolyn Brooks
Albert Camus
Raymond Carver
Willa Cather
Geoffrey Chaucer
John Cheever
Joseph Conrad
Charles Dickens
Emily Dickinson
Frederick Douglass
T. S. Eliot
George Eliot
Harlan Ellison
Louise Erdrich
William Faulkner
F. Scott Fitzgerald
Gustave Flaubert
Horton Foote
Benjamin Franklin
Robert Frost
Neil Gaiman
Gabriel Garcia Marquez
Thomas Hardy
Nathaniel Hawthorne
Robert A. Heinlein
Lillian Hellman
Ernest Hemingway
Langston Hughes
Zora Neale Hurston
Henry James
Thomas Jefferson
James Joyce
Jamaica Kincaid
Stephen King
Martin Luther King, Jr.
Barbara Kingsolver
Abraham Lincoln
Mario Vargas Llosa
Jack London
James McBride
Cormac McCarthy
Herman Melville
Arthur Miller
Toni Morrison
Alice Munro
Tim O'Brien
Flannery O'Connor
Eugene O'Neill
George Orwell
Sylvia Plath
Philip Roth
Salman Rushdie
Mary Shelley
John Steinbeck
Amy Tan
Leo Tolstoy
Mark Twain
John Updike
Kurt Vonnegut
Alice Walker
David Foster Wallace
Edith Wharton
Walt Whitman
Oscar Wilde
Tennessee Williams
Richard Wright
Malcolm X

Critical Insights: Works
Absalom, Absalom!
Adventures of Huckleberry Finn
Aeneid
All Quiet on the Western Front
Animal Farm
Anna Karenina
The Awakening
The Bell Jar
Beloved
Billy Budd, Sailor
The Book Thief
Brave New World
The Canterbury Tales
Catch-22
The Catcher in the Rye
The Crucible
Death of a Salesman
The Diary of a Young Girl
Dracula
Fahrenheit 451
The Grapes of Wrath
Great Expectations
The Great Gatsby
Hamlet
The Handmaid's Tale
Harry Potter Series
Heart of Darkness
The Hobbit
The House on Mango Street
How the Garcia Girls Lost Their Accents
The Hunger Games Trilogy
I Know Why the Caged Bird Sings
In Cold Blood
The Inferno
Invisible Man
Jane Eyre
The Joy Luck Club
King Lear
The Kite Runner
Life of Pi
Little Women
Lolita
Lord of the Flies
Macbeth
The Metamorphosis
Midnight's Children
A Midsummer Night's Dream
Moby-Dick
Mrs. Dalloway
Nineteen Eighty-Four
The Odyssey
Of Mice and Men
One Flew Over the Cuckoo's Nest
One Hundred Years of Solitude
Othello
The Outsiders
Paradise Lost
The Pearl
The Poetry of Baudelaire
The Poetry of Edgar Allan Poe
A Portrait of the Artist as a Young Man
Pride and Prejudice
The Red Badge of Courage
Romeo and Juliet
The Scarlet Letter
Short Fiction of Flannery O'Connor
Slaughterhouse-Five
The Sound and the Fury
A Streetcar Named Desire
The Sun Also Rises
A Tale of Two Cities
The Tales of Edgar Allan Poe
Their Eyes Were Watching God
Things Fall Apart
To Kill a Mockingbird
War and Peace
The Woman Warrior

Critical Insights: Themes
The American Comic Book
American Creative Non-Fiction
The American Dream
American Multicultural Identity
American Road Literature
American Short Story
American Sports Fiction
The American Thriller
American Writers in Exile
Censored & Banned Literature
Civil Rights Literature, Past & Present
Coming of Age
Conspiracies
Contemporary Canadian Fiction
Contemporary Immigrant Short Fiction
Contemporary Latin American Fiction
Contemporary Speculative Fiction
Crime and Detective Fiction
Crisis of Faith
Cultural Encounters
Dystopia
Family
The Fantastic
Feminism

Grey House Publishing | Salem Press | H.W. Wilson | 4919 Route, 22 PO Box 56, Amenia NY 12501-0056

2021 Title List

Visit www.SalemPress.com for Product Information, Table of Contents, and Sample Pages.

Flash Fiction
Gender, Sex and Sexuality
Good & Evil
The Graphic Novel
Greed
Harlem Renaissance
The Hero's Quest
Historical Fiction
Holocaust Literature
The Immigrant Experience
Inequality
LGBTQ Literature
Literature in Times of Crisis
Literature of Protest
Magical Realism
Midwestern Literature
Modern Japanese Literature
Nature & the Environment
Paranoia, Fear & Alienation
Patriotism
Political Fiction
Postcolonial Literature
Pulp Fiction of the '20s and '30s
Rebellion
Russia's Golden Age
Satire
The Slave Narrative
Social Justice and American Literature
Southern Gothic Literature
Southwestern Literature
Survival
Technology & Humanity
Violence in Literature
Virginia Woolf & 20th Century Women Writers
War

Critical Insights: Film
Bonnie & Clyde
Casablanca
Alfred Hitchcock
Stanley Kubrick

Critical Approaches to Literature
Critical Approaches to Literature: Feminist
Critical Approaches to Literature: Moral
Critical Approaches to Literature: Multicultural
Critical Approaches to Literature: Psychological

Critical Surveys of Literature
Critical Survey of American Literature
Critical Survey of Drama
Critical Survey of Graphic Novels: Heroes & Superheroes
Critical Survey of Graphic Novels: History, Theme, and Technique
Critical Survey of Graphic Novels: Independents and Underground Classics
Critical Survey of Graphic Novels: Manga
Critical Survey of Long Fiction
Critical Survey of Mystery and Detective Fiction
Critical Survey of Mythology & Folklore: Gods & Goddesses
Critical Survey of Mythology & Folklore: Heroes and Heroines
Critical Survey of Mythology & Folklore: Love, Sexuality, and Desire
Critical Survey of Mythology & Folklore: World Mythology
Critical Survey of Poetry
Critical Survey of Poetry: Contemporary Poets
Critical Survey of Science Fiction & Fantasy Literature
Critical Survey of Shakespeare's Plays
Critical Survey of Shakespeare's Sonnets
Critical Survey of Short Fiction
Critical Survey of World Literature
Critical Survey of Young Adult Literature

Cyclopedia of Literary Characters & Places
Cyclopedia of Literary Characters
Cyclopedia of Literary Places

Introduction to Literary Context
American Poetry of the 20th Century
American Post-Modernist Novels
American Short Fiction
English Literature
Plays
World Literature

Magill's Literary Annual
Magill's Literary Annual, 2021
Magill's Literary Annual, 2020
Magill's Literary Annual, 2019

Masterplots
Masterplots, Fourth Edition
Masterplots, 2010-2018 Supplement

Notable Writers
Notable African American Writers
Notable American Women Writers
Notable Mystery & Detective Fiction Writers
Notable Native American Writers & Writers of the American West
Novels into Film: Adaptations & Interpretation
Recommended Reading: 600 Classics Reviewed

Grey House Publishing | Salem Press | H.W. Wilson | 4919 Route, 22 PO Box 56, Amenia NY 12501-0056

2021 Title List

Visit www.SalemPress.com for Product Information, Table of Contents, and Sample Pages.

HISTORY

The Decades
The 1910s in America
The Twenties in America
The Thirties in America
The Forties in America
The Fifties in America
The Sixties in America
The Seventies in America
The Eighties in America
The Nineties in America
The 2000s in America
The 2010s in America

Defining Documents in American History
Defining Documents: The 1900s
Defining Documents: The 1910s
Defining Documents: The 1920s
Defining Documents: The 1930s
Defining Documents: The 1950s
Defining Documents: The 1960s
Defining Documents: The 1970s
Defining Documents: American Citizenship
Defining Documents: The American Economy
Defining Documents: The American Revolution
Defining Documents: The American West
Defining Documents: Business Ethics
Defining Documents: Capital Punishment
Defining Documents: Civil Rights
Defining Documents: Civil War
Defining Documents: The Cold War
Defining Documents: Dissent & Protest
Defining Documents: Drug Policy
Defining Documents: The Emergence of Modern America
Defining Documents: Environment & Conservation
Defining Documents: Espionage & Intrigue
Defining Documents: Exploration and Colonial America
Defining Documents: The Formation of the States
Defining Documents: The Free Press
Defining Documents: The Gun Debate
Defining Documents: Immigration & Immigrant Communities
Defining Documents: The Legacy of 9/11
Defining Documents: LGBTQ+
Defining Documents: Manifest Destiny and the New Nation
Defining Documents: Native Americans
Defining Documents: Political Campaigns, Candidates & Discourse
Defining Documents: Postwar 1940s
Defining Documents: Prison Reform
Defining Documents: Secrets, Leaks & Scandals
Defining Documents: Slavery
Defining Documents: Supreme Court Decisions
Defining Documents: Reconstruction Era
Defining Documents: The Vietnam War
Defining Documents: U.S. Involvement in the Middle East
Defining Documents: World War I
Defining Documents: World War II

Defining Documents in World History
Defining Documents: The 17th Century
Defining Documents: The 18th Century
Defining Documents: The 19th Century
Defining Documents: The 20th Century (1900-1950)
Defining Documents: The Ancient World
Defining Documents: Asia
Defining Documents: Genocide & the Holocaust
Defining Documents: Nationalism & Populism
Defining Documents: Pandemics, Plagues & Public Health
Defining Documents: Renaissance & Early Modern Era
Defining Documents: The Middle Ages
Defining Documents: The Middle East
Defining Documents: Women's Rights

Great Events from History
Great Events from History: The Ancient World
Great Events from History: The Middle Ages
Great Events from History: The Renaissance & Early Modern Era
Great Events from History: The 17th Century
Great Events from History: The 18th Century
Great Events from History: The 19th Century
Great Events from History: The 20th Century, 1901-1940
Great Events from History: The 20th Century, 1941-1970
Great Events from History: The 20th Century, 1971-2000
Great Events from History: Modern Scandals
Great Events from History: African American History
Great Events from History: The 21st Century, 2000-2016
Great Events from History: LGBTQ Events
Great Events from History: Human Rights

Great Lives from History
Computer Technology Innovators
Fashion Innovators
Great Athletes
Great Athletes of the Twenty-First Century
Great Lives from History: African Americans
Great Lives from History: American Heroes
Great Lives from History: American Women
Great Lives from History: Asian and Pacific Islander Americans
Great Lives from History: Inventors & Inventions
Great Lives from History: Jewish Americans
Great Lives from History: Latinos
Great Lives from History: Scientists and Science
Great Lives from History: The 17th Century
Great Lives from History: The 18th Century
Great Lives from History: The 19th Century
Great Lives from History: The 20th Century
Great Lives from History: The 21st Century, 2000-2017
Great Lives from History: The Ancient World
Great Lives from History: The Incredibly Wealthy
Great Lives from History: The Middle Ages
Great Lives from History: The Renaissance & Early Modern Era
Human Rights Innovators
Internet Innovators
Music Innovators
Musicians and Composers of the 20th Century
World Political Innovators

Grey House Publishing | Salem Press | H.W. Wilson | 4919 Route, 22 PO Box 56, Amenia NY 12501-0056

2021 Title List

Visit www.SalemPress.com for Product Information, Table of Contents, and Sample Pages.

History & Government
American First Ladies
American Presidents
The 50 States
The Ancient World: Extraordinary People in Extraordinary Societies
The Bill of Rights
The Criminal Justice System
The U.S. Supreme Court

SOCIAL SCIENCES
Civil Rights Movements: Past & Present
Countries, Peoples and Cultures
Countries: Their Wars & Conflicts: A World Survey
Education Today: Issues, Policies & Practices
Encyclopedia of American Immigration
Ethics: Questions & Morality of Human Actions
Issues in U.S. Immigration
Principles of Sociology: Group Relationships & Behavior
Principles of Sociology: Personal Relationships & Behavior
Principles of Sociology: Societal Issues & Behavior
Racial & Ethnic Relations in America
World Geography

SCIENCE
Ancient Creatures
Applied Science
Applied Science: Engineering & Mathematics
Applied Science: Science & Medicine
Applied Science: Technology
Biomes and Ecosystems
Earth Science: Earth Materials and Resources
Earth Science: Earth's Surface and History
Earth Science: Earth's Weather, Water and Atmosphere
Earth Science: Physics and Chemistry of the Earth
Encyclopedia of Climate Change
Encyclopedia of Energy
Encyclopedia of Environmental Issues
Encyclopedia of Global Resources
Encyclopedia of Mathematics and Society
Forensic Science
Notable Natural Disasters
The Solar System
USA in Space

Principles of Science
Principles of Anatomy
Principles of Astronomy
Principles of Behavioral Science
Principles of Biology
Principles of Biotechnology
Principles of Botany
Principles of Chemistry
Principles of Climatology
Principles of Information Technology
Principles of Computer Science
Principles of Ecology
Principles of Energy
Principles of Geology

Principles of Marine Science
Principles of Mathematics
Principles of Modern Agriculture
Principles of Pharmacology
Principles of Physical Science
Principles of Physics
Principles of Programming & Coding
Principles of Robotics & Artificial Intelligence
Principles of Scientific Research
Principles of Sustainability
Principles of Zoology

HEALTH
Addictions, Substance Abuse & Alcoholism
Adolescent Health & Wellness
Aging
Cancer
Community & Family Health Issues
Integrative, Alternative & Complementary Medicine
Genetics and Inherited Conditions
Infectious Diseases and Conditions
Magill's Medical Guide
Nutrition
Psychology & Behavioral Health
Women's Health

Principles of Health
Principles of Health: Allergies & Immune Disorders
Principles of Health: Anxiety & Stress
Principles of Health: Depression
Principles of Health: Diabetes
Principles of Health: Nursing
Principles of Health: Obesity
Principles of Health: Pain Management
Principles of Health: Prescription Drug Abuse

Grey House Publishing | Salem Press | H.W. Wilson | 4919 Route, 22 PO Box 56, Amenia NY 12501-0056

2021 Title List

Visit www.SalemPress.com for Product Information, Table of Contents, and Sample Pages.

CAREERS

Careers: Paths to Entrepreneurship
Careers in the Arts: Fine, Performing & Visual
Careers in Building Construction
Careers in Business
Careers in Chemistry
Careers in Communications & Media
Careers in Education & Training
Careers in Environment & Conservation
Careers in Financial Services
Careers in Forensic Science
Careers in Gaming
Careers in Green Energy
Careers in Healthcare
Careers in Hospitality & Tourism
Careers in Human Services
Careers in Information Technology
Careers in Law, Criminal Justice & Emergency Services
Careers in the Music Industry
Careers in Manufacturing & Production
Careers in Nursing
Careers in Physics
Careers in Protective Services
Careers in Psychology & Behavioral Health
Careers in Public Administration
Careers in Sales, Insurance & Real Estate
Careers in Science & Engineering
Careers in Social Media
Careers in Sports & Fitness
Careers in Sports Medicine & Training
Careers in Technical Services & Equipment Repair
Careers in Transportation
Careers in Writing & Editing
Careers Outdoors
Careers Overseas
Careers Working with Infants & Children
Careers Working with Animals

BUSINESS

Principles of Business: Accounting
Principles of Business: Economics
Principles of Business: Entrepreneurship
Principles of Business: Finance
Principles of Business: Globalization
Principles of Business: Leadership
Principles of Business: Management
Principles of Business: Marketing

Grey House Publishing | Salem Press | H.W. Wilson | 4919 Route, 22 PO Box 56, Amenia NY 12501-0056

2021 Title List

Visit www.HWWilsonInPrint.com for Product Information, Table of Contents, and Sample Pages.

The Reference Shelf

Affordable Housing
Aging in America
Alternative Facts, Post-Truth and the Information War
The American Dream
American Military Presence Overseas
Arab Spring
Artificial Intelligence
The Business of Food
Campaign Trends & Election Law
College Sports
Conspiracy Theories
Democracy Evolving
The Digital Age
Dinosaurs
Embracing New Paradigms in Education
Faith & Science
Families - Traditional & New Structures
Food Insecurity & Hunger in the United States
Future of U.S. Economic Relations: Mexico, Cuba, & Venezuela
Global Climate Change
Graphic Novels and Comic Books
Guns in America
Hate Crimes
Immigration
Internet Abuses & Privacy Rights
Internet Law
LGBTQ in the 21st Century
Marijuana Reform
National Debate Topic 2014/2015: The Ocean
National Debate Topic 2015/2016: Surveillance
National Debate Topic 2016/2017: US/China Relations
National Debate Topic 2017/2018: Education Reform
National Debate Topic 2018/2019: Immigration
National Debate Topic 2019/2021: Arms Sales
National Debate Topic 2020/2021: Criminal Justice Reform
National Debate Topic 2021/2022
New Frontiers in Space
The News and its Future
Policing in 2020
Politics of the Oceans
Pollution
Prescription Drug Abuse
Propaganda and Misinformation
Racial Tension in a Postracial Age
Reality Television
Representative American Speeches, Annual Edition
Rethinking Work
Revisiting Gender
Robotics
Russia
Social Networking
The South China Sea Conflict
Space Exploration and Development
Sports in America
The Supreme Court
The Transformation of American Cities
The Two Koreas
U.S. Infrastructure
Vaccinations
Whistleblowers

Core Collections

Children's Core Collection
Fiction Core Collection
Graphic Novels Core Collection
Middle & Junior High School Core
Public Library Core Collection: Nonfiction
Senior High Core Collection
Young Adult Fiction Core Collection

Current Biography

Current Biography Cumulative Index 1946-2021
Current Biography Monthly Magazine
Current Biography Yearbook

Readers' Guide to Periodical Literature

Abridged Readers' Guide to Periodical Literature
Readers' Guide to Periodical Literature

Indexes

Index to Legal Periodicals & Books
Short Story Index
Book Review Digest

Sears List

Sears List of Subject Headings
Sears: Lista de Encabezamientos de Materia

History

American Game Changers: Invention, Innovation & Transformation
American Reformers
Speeches of the American Presidents

Facts About Series

Facts About the 20th Century
Facts About American Immigration
Facts About China
Facts About the Presidents
Facts About the World's Languages

Nobel Prize Winners

Nobel Prize Winners: 1901-1986
Nobel Prize Winners: 1987-1991
Nobel Prize Winners: 1992-1996
Nobel Prize Winners: 1997-2001
Nobel Prize Winners: 2002-2018

Famous First Facts

Famous First Facts
Famous First Facts About American Politics
Famous First Facts About Sports
Famous First Facts About the Environment
Famous First Facts: International Edition

American Book of Days

The American Book of Days
The International Book of Days

Grey House Publishing | Salem Press | H.W. Wilson | 4919 Route, 22 PO Box 56, Amenia NY 12501-0056